Western Canada & Alaska

SO-AUN-857

Published by AAA Publishing
1000 AAA Drive, Heathrow, FL 32746-5063
Copyright AAA 2019, All rights reserved

The publisher has made every effort to provide accurate, up-to-date information but accepts no responsibility for loss or injury sustained by any person using this book. TourBook® guides are published for the exclusive use of AAA members. Not for sale.

Advertising Rate and Circulation Information: (407) 444-8280

Printed in the USA by Quad/Graphics

This book is printed on paper certified by third-party standards for sustainably managed forestry and production.

Printed on recyclable paper.
Please recycle whenever possible.

Stock #4601

CONTENTS

Get more travel information
at AAA.com/travelguides
and AAA.com/traveltips

Attractions, hotels, restaurants and other travel experience information are all grouped under the alphabetical listing of the city in which those experiences are physically located—or the nearest recognized city.

free to
rock the boat

TripAssist travel insurance allows you to go with the flow. It can free you up to make the most of your vacation. Nothing will hold you back knowing that you and your travel plans are safe.

Talk to your AAA Travel Agent today for more information.

Terms, conditions and exclusions apply. Insurance products are underwritten by BCS Insurance Company or Jefferson Insurance Company. AGA Service Company is the licensed producer and administrator of these plans.   400003588_053018

ESCAPE

SHOP

ENJOY

EARN[1]

3x ✈

points on eligible travel and AAA purchases

2x 🛒

points on gas, grocery store, wholesale club and drugstore purchases

1x 🥤

1 point per $1 on all other purchases

AAA Member Rewards   AAA

4000 1234 5678 9123

VALID THRU 00/00

CHRIS L HARTIN

VISA
Signature

FROM **EVERYDAY** TO **EXTRAORDINARY**

APPLY TODAY!
Visit your local AAA office or AAA.com/CreditCard

For information about rates, fees, other costs and benefits associated with the use of this card or to apply, visit the web site listed above or your local AAA office. [1]*How You Earn Points:* You earn points when you use your card to make purchases, minus returns, credits and adjustments ("Net Purchases"). The following transactions are not considered purchases and will not earn points: Balance Transfers and Cash Advances (each as defined in your Credit Card Agreement), fees, interest charges, fraudulent transactions and certain other charges. *1 Point:* Earn 1 point (base point) for every $1 of Net Purchases charged to the credit card each billing cycle. *2 Points:* Earn 2 points (consisting of 1 bonus point and 1 base point) per $1 for Net Purchases made with the card at any eligible gas, grocery store, wholesale club and drugstore merchant categories as designated by Bank of America. *3 Points:* Earn 3 points (consisting of 2 bonus points and 1 base point) per $1 for Net Purchases made with the card through any participating AAA Club when AAA is the merchant of record, or at eligible retail travel merchant categories as designated by Bank of America. *Points Expiration:* Points expire 5 years after the month they were earned. *Points Forfeiture:* If the owner(s) of the card account voluntarily closes the card account, or if for any reason we close the card account, any unredeemed points associated with the account are subject to immediate forfeiture, unless specifically authorized by us. *Rewards Program Rules:* Program Rules containing additional details will be sent to you with your new account materials. Other significant terms apply. Program subject to change. This credit card program is issued and administered by Bank of America, N.A. Visa and Visa Signature are registered trademarks of Visa International Service Association and are used by the issuer pursuant to license from Visa U.S.A. Inc. AAA is a registered trademark of American Automobile Association, Inc. ©2019 Bank of America Corporation ©2019 AAA.   ARWYJ769

Using Your Guide

AAA TourBook guides are packed with travel insights, maps and listings of places to stay, play, eat and save. For more listings, more details and online booking, visit AAA.com/travelguides.

Helping You Make the Connection

Look for this symbol ⊘ throughout the guides for direct links to related content.

A to Z City Listings

Cities and places are listed alphabetically within each state or province. Attractions, hotels and restaurants are listed once — under the city in which they are physically located.

Cities that are considered part of a larger destination city or area have an expanded city header. The header identifies the larger region and cross-references pages that contain shared trip-planning resources:

- Destination map – outline map of the cities that comprise a destination city or area
- Attraction spotting map – regional street map marked with attraction locations
- Hotel/restaurant spotting map and index – regional street map numbered with hotel and restaurant locations identified in an accompanying index

Cities that are not considered part of a larger destination city or area but have a significant number of listings may have these resources within the individual city section:

- Attraction spotting map
- Hotel/restaurant spotting map and index

Location Abbreviations

Directions are from the center of town unless otherwise specified, using these highway abbreviations:

Bus. Rte.=business route
CR=county road
FM=farm to market
FR=forest road
Hwy.=Canadian highway
I=interstate highway
LR=legislative route
R.R.=rural route
SR/PR=state or provincial route
US=federal highway

About Listed Establishments

Hotels and restaurants are listed on the basis of merit alone after careful evaluation by full-time, professionally trained AAA inspectors. An establishment's decision to advertise in the TourBook guide has no bearing on its evaluation or designation; nor does inclusion of advertising imply AAA endorsement of products and services.

Information in this guide was believed accurate at the time of publication. However, since changes inevitably occur between annual editions, please contact your AAA travel professional, visit AAA.com/travelguides or download the free AAA Mobile app to confirm prices and schedules.

Attraction Listing Icons

[SAVE] AAA Discounts & Rewards® member discount

⊡ Electric vehicle charging station on premises. Domestic station information provided by the U.S. Department of Energy. Canadian station information provided by Plug'n Drive Ontario.

[GT] Guided Tours available

[▲] Camping facilities

[¶¶] Food on premises

[✕] Recreational activities

[🐾] Pet friendly (Call for restrictions/fees.)

[☂] Picnicking allowed

In select cities only:

[🚍] Mass transit station within 1 mile. Icon is followed by station name and AAA/CAA designated station number within listing.

[GEM] AAA/CAA travel experts may designate an attraction of exceptional interest and quality as a AAA GEM — a *Great Experience for Members®*. See GEM Attraction Index (listed on CONTENTS page) for a complete list of locations.

Consult the online travel guides at AAA.com/travelguides or visit AAA Mobile for additional things to do if you have time.

Hotel Listing Icons

May be preceded by CALL and/or SOME UNITS.

Member Information:

[SAVE] Member rates: discounted standard room rate or lowest public rate available at time of booking for dates of stay.

ECO Eco-certified by government or private organization.

⊞ Electric vehicle charging station on premises. Domestic station information provided by the U.S. Department of Energy. Canadian station information provided by Plug'n Drive Ontario.

⊠ Smoke-free premises

In select cities only:

⊞ Mass transit station within 1 mile. Icon is followed by station name and AAA/CAA designated station number within listing.

Services:

✈ Airport transportation

🐾 Pet friendly (Call for restrictions/fees.)

🍴 Restaurant on premises

🍴• Restaurant off premises

🍽 Room service for 2 or more meals

🍸 Full bar

👶 Child care

BIZ Business center

♿ Accessible features (Call property for available services and amenities.)

Activities:

♣ Full-service casino

🏊 Pool

🏋 Health club or exercise room on premises

In-Room Amenities:

HS High-speed Internet service

$HS High-speed Internet service (Call property for fees.)

📶 Wireless Internet service

$📶 Wireless Internet service (Call property for fees.)

📶 No wireless Internet service

📺 Pay movies

🔲 Refrigerator

📟 Microwave

☕ Coffeemaker

❄ No air conditioning

📺 No TV

☎ No telephones

Restaurant Listing Icons

SAVE AAA Discounts & Rewards® member discount

ECO Eco-certified by government or private organization.

⊞ Electric vehicle charging station on premises. Domestic station information provided by the U.S. Department of Energy. Canadian station information provided by Plug'n Drive Ontario.

❄ No air conditioning

♿ Accessible features (Call property for available services and amenities.)

⊠ Designated smoking section

B Breakfast

L Lunch

D Dinner

24 Open 24 hours

LATE Open after 11 p.m.

🐾 Pet friendly (Call for restrictions/fees.)

In select cities only:

⊞ Mass transit station within 1 mile. Icon is followed by station name and AAA/CAA designated station number within listing.

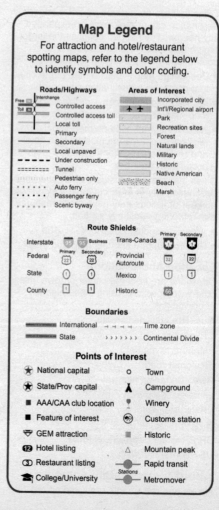

Map Legend

For attraction and hotel/restaurant spotting maps, refer to the legend below to identify symbols and color coding.

Roads/Highways
- Controlled access
- Controlled access toll
- Local toll
- Primary
- Secondary
- Local unpaved
- Under construction
- Tunnel
- Pedestrian only
- Auto ferry
- Passenger ferry
- Scenic byway

Areas of Interest
- Incorporated city
- Int'l/Regional airport
- Park
- Recreation sites
- Forest
- Natural lands
- Military
- Historic
- Native American
- Beach
- Marsh

Route Shields
- Interstate
- Federal
- State
- County
- Trans-Canada
- Provincial Autoroute
- Mexico
- Historic

Boundaries
- International
- State
- Time zone
- Continental Divide

Points of Interest
- ⭐ National capital
- ★ State/Prov capital
- ■ AAA/CAA club location
- ■ Feature of interest
- ⬥ GEM attraction
- 12 Hotel listing
- 3 Restaurant listing
- 🎓 College/University
- ○ Town
- ⛏ Campground
- ⚲ Winery
- ⊗ Customs station
- ■ Historic
- △ Mountain peak
- Rapid transit (Stations)
- Metromover

Understanding the Diamond Designations

Hotel and restaurant inspections are unscheduled to ensure our trained professionals encounter the same unbiased experience members do.

- The first step for every hotel and restaurant is to demonstrate they meet expected standards of cleanliness, comfort and hospitality.

- Only hotels and restaurants that pass AAA's rigorous on-site inspection receive a AAA Diamond designation.

Learn more at **AAA.com/Diamonds**.

Hotels	Restaurants
APPROVED	**APPROVED**
Noteworthy by meeting the industry-leading standards of AAA inspections.	Noteworthy by meeting the industry-leading standards of AAA inspections.
THREE DIAMOND	**THREE DIAMOND**
Comprehensive amenities, style and comfort level.	Trendy food skillfully presented in a remarkable setting.
FOUR DIAMOND	**FOUR DIAMOND**
Upscale style and amenities enhanced with the right touch of service.	Distinctive fine dining, well-served amid upscale ambience.
FIVE DIAMOND	**FIVE DIAMOND**
World-class luxury, amenities and indulgence for a once-in-a-lifetime experience.	Leading-edge cuisine, ingredients and preparation with extraordinary service and surroundings.

Guest Safety

Inspectors view a sampling of rooms during hotel evaluations and, therefore, AAA/CAA cannot guarantee working locks and operational fire safety equipment in every guest unit.

Contacting AAA/CAA About the TourBook Guide

Tell us what you think about the TourBook guides or your experience at a listed hotel, restaurant or attraction. If your visit doesn't meet your expectations, please contact us **during your visit or within 30 days**. Be sure to save your receipts. We also welcome your recommendations on places to inspect.

Use the easy online form at **AAA.com/MemberFeedback**, email memberrelations@national.aaa.com or mail your feedback to: AAA Member Comments, 1000 AAA Dr., Box 61, Heathrow, FL 32746.

Calgary

Alberta

Alberta is the great outdoors personified. Mirror images of mountain peaks are reflected on the surface of glacially fed, brilliantly blue lakes. The twinkling, shimmering dance of lights known as aurora borealis provides a surreal sky show. Golden wheat and the bright yellow flowers of the canola plant create blankets of color across endlessly rolling countryside. Is this your typical version of the Wild West? Hardly—but Alberta urges you to stretch the definition of what the Canadian West is all about.

Plenty in Canada's fourth-largest province does fit neatly into the Western mold. Take Calgary, for instance. This former cow town's earliest roots were in ranching and meat-packing. Even the roof of the Scotiabank Saddledome is in the shape of you know what. The home of the National Hockey League's Calgary Flames, the Western Hockey League's Calgary Hitmen and the

Banff National Park

National Lacrosse League's Calgary Roughnecks also is the venue of choice for everyone from country superstar Kenny Chesney to the Dalai Lama of Tibet, who visited the city in 2009.

Thousands of folks decked out in cowboy boots and ten-gallon hats gather at Stampede Park every July to watch bull ridin', barrel racin' and other rough-and-tumble rodeo events at the Calgary Stampede, which celebrated its centennial in 2012. The city wears its Western heritage proudly, but Calgary also prides itself on being remarkably well-rounded.

Take the XV Olympic Winter Games in 1988, for instance. Besides showcasing the world's best athletes—including the memorable "Battle of the Brians" between Brian Boitano of the United States and Brian Orser of Canada—the city was in the glare of the world spotlight. Not to worry; five world-class facilities were built, and a concerted grassroots effort enlisted more than 10,000 resident volunteers to help stage the games.

From grizzly bears to wood bison, the Calgary Zoo, Botanical Garden & Prehistoric Park offers outstanding opportunities to view native wildlife. It also is home to more than 4,000 plants and a collection of life-size replicas of dinosaurs in a simulated Mesozoic landscape. In futuristic contrast are the elevated "pedways" that link many downtown buildings.

Such dichotomies are commonplace in this vast province. Hikers in Cypress Hills Interprovincial Park might catch the scent of pine and the subtle fragrance of wild orchids. But just to the northwest, Medicine Hat harnesses an extensive reserve of natural gas that once prompted Rudyard Kipling to describe the city, in an olfactory sense, as having "all hell for a basement."

Rafters steel themselves against the raging rapids of the Elbow, Highwood and Kananaskis rivers in Kananaskis Country. Turbulent rushes of water sweeping over rock at Athabasca and Sunwapta falls become imposing frozen challenges for ice climbers who chink away at them in winter. In serene contrast, canoeists play the placid, emerald waters of Banff National Park's Moraine Lake on still summer mornings, gazing at a backdrop of unspoiled wilderness.

A Canadian Melting Pot

Alberta's ethnic diversity is on display at places like the Ukrainian Cultural Heritage Village east of Edmonton, where costumed interpreters demonstrate what life was like for settlers from the 1890s to 1930. In Vegreville, the design of a famed bronze, gold and silver pysanka, or Ukrainian Easter egg, depicts the people's faith and commemorates the protection provided to them by the Royal Canadian Mounted Police. The Basilian Fathers Museum in Mundare chronicles the order's work in eastern Alberta and holds a collection of Canadian and Ukrainian religious and folk artifacts.

The history of native cultures comes alive at the Head-Smashed-In Buffalo Jump Interpretive Centre near Fort Macleod and in the petroglyphs and pictographs at Writing-on-Stone Provincial Park/Áísínai'pi National Historic Site, near Milk River. Indian Battle Park in Lethbridge details a dust-up between the Cree and Blackfoot, the last intertribal conflict in North America.

And let's not forget dinosaurs. They left their mark on the Red Deer Valley by way of fossils buried in walls of sediment. Drumheller pays tribute to that bygone age along the Dinosaur Trail (hwys. 838 and 837). To the southeast, a fertile fossil bed at Dinosaur Provincial Park, near Patricia, contains the remains of 39 species of extinct reptiles.

Recreation

Nature and outdoor lovers need only look to Alberta's five national parks. In fact Banff is Canada's first national park. Elk Island is an oasis for rare and endangered species. Jasper is a feast of glaciers. The Rockies and the prairie meet at Waterton Lakes. And Wood Buffalo reaches north into neighboring Northwest Territories.

But they're not the only popular outdoor destinations in untamed Alberta. Experienced guides lead trail riding expeditions through the Elbow and Sheep valleys in the Kananaskis high country, west of Calgary. Hiking, mountain climbing and mountain biking are ways to experience the challenging peaks of the Rockies.

White-water rafting fans gravitate to the Athabasca, Elbow, Highwood, Kananaskis, Kicking Horse, Red Deer and Sunwapta rivers. The Blackstone River, a hot spot for kayaking in inflatable boats, cuts through the foothills of the Rockies.

Or take advantage of one of North America's longest ski seasons. Some of the best downhill skiing and snowboarding Alberta has to offer is at Marmot Basin, south of Jasper; Lake Louise, northwest of Banff; Sunshine Village and Banff Mount Norquay, both within 15 minutes of Banff; Fortress Mountain, in Kananaskis Country; and Nakiska, west of Calgary.

Plus, there are opportunities galore for fishing. The Bow River offers exceptional trout fly-fishing, while notable fly-in trophy lakes are Gardiner and Namur, northwest of Fort McMurray, and Winefred, northeast of Lac La Biche.

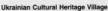
Ukrainian Cultural Heritage Village

Historic Timeline

1670	The Hudson's Bay Co. obtains fur-trading rights to a portion of what is now Alberta.
1795	Fort Edmonton is founded as a Hudson's Bay trading post.
1875	Calgary is designated a North West Mounted Police fort.
1883	The Canadian Pacific Railway reaches Calgary.
1905	The province of Alberta is created.
1930	Jasper National Park is established.
1967	The Great Canadian Oil Sands Co. in Fort McMurray begins producing synthetic crude oil from large deposits of oil sands.
1981	West Edmonton Mall—now one of the world's largest shopping centers following three expansions—opens.
1988	Calgary hosts the XV Olympic Winter Games.
2005	Alberta celebrates its centennial.
2016	Vast forest fires around Fort McMurray cause mass evacuation from the city and surroundings.

What To Pack

Temperature Averages Maximum/Minimum (Celsius)	JANUARY	FEBRUARY	MARCH	APRIL	MAY	JUNE	JULY	AUGUST	SEPTEMBER	OCTOBER	NOVEMBER	DECEMBER
Banff NP	-5/-15	0/-11	4/-8	9/-3	14/2	19/6	22/7	22/7	16/3	10/-1	1/-8	-5/-14
Calgary	-3/-16	-1/-12	3/-8	11/-2	17/3	21/7	23/9	23/9	17/4	13/-1	3/-9	-2/-14
Edmonton	-8/-17	-4/-14	1/-9	10/-1	17/6	21/9	23/12	22/11	16/6	11/1	-1/-9	-7/-15
Fort McMurray	-15/-25	-9/-21	-1/-15	9/-4	17/3	21/7	23/10	22/8	15/3	8/-2	-5/-14	-13/-22
Grande Prairie	-10/-21	-6/-18	-1/-12	9/-3	16/3	20/8	22/9	21/8	16/3	10/-2	-2/-12	-8/-19
Jasper NP	-6/-16	-1/-12	4/-8	10/-3	15/2	19/6	22/8	22/7	16/3	10/-1	0/-9	-6/-14

From the records of The Weather Channel Interactive, Inc.

Good Facts To Know

ABOUT THE PROVINCE

POPULATION: 3,645,257.

AREA: 640,045 sq km (247,123 sq mi.); ranks 6th.

CAPITAL: Edmonton.

HIGHEST POINT: 3,747 m (12,293 ft.), Mount Columbia.

LOWEST POINT: 152 m (499 ft.), Salt River at border with the Northwest Territories.

TIME ZONE(S): Mountain. DST.

GAMBLING

MINIMUM AGE FOR GAMBLING: 18.

REGULATIONS

TEEN DRIVING LAWS: For probationary licensees, driving is not permitted daily midnight-5 a.m. The minimum age for an unrestricted driver's license is 18. Phone (780) 427-8901 in Edmonton or (403) 297-6679 in Calgary for more information about Alberta driver's license regulations.

SEAT BELT/CHILD RESTRAINT LAWS: Seat belts are required for driver and all passengers ages 16 and over. Children ages 6-15 and 18 kilograms (40 lbs.) and over are required to be in a child restraint or seat belt. Appropriate child restraints are required for children under age 6 and under 18 kilograms (40 lbs.). AAA recommends the use of seat belts and appropriate child restraints for the driver and all passengers.

CELLPHONE RESTRICTIONS: The use of handheld cellphones and text messaging while driving are prohibited.

HELMETS FOR MOTORCYCLISTS: Required for all riders.

RADAR DETECTORS: Permitted.

MOVE OVER LAW: A motorist may not drive more than 60 kph (37 mph) or the maximum speed limit, whichever is lower, if traveling in the same direction in the lane immediately adjacent and passing a stopped emergency vehicle or tow truck using flashing signals.

FIREARMS LAWS: By federal law, all nonresidents entering Canada with a firearm must declare their weapon in writing and pay a fee of $25 (Canadian). Contact the Canadian Firearms Centre at (800) 731-4000 to receive a declaration form or for additional information.

ALCOHOL CONSUMPTION: Legal age 18.

HOLIDAYS

HOLIDAYS: Jan. 1 ▪ Family Day, Feb. (3rd Mon.) ▪ Good Friday ▪ Victoria Day, May 24 (if a Mon.) or the closest prior Mon. ▪ Canada Day, July 1 ▪ Heritage Day, Aug. (1st Mon.) ▪ Labour Day, Sept. (1st Mon.) ▪ Thanksgiving, Oct. (2nd Mon.) ▪ Remembrance Day, Nov. 11 ▪ Christmas, Dec. 25.

MONEY

TAXES: Alberta has no provincial sales tax. However, there is a 4 percent hotel tax, plus a 1-2 percent tourism levy in some areas. In addition there is a 5 percent national Goods and Service Tax (GST).

VISITOR INFORMATION

INFORMATION CENTERS: Travel Alberta Visitor Centres provide information about accommodations and campgrounds as well as maps. They are located at Canmore on Hwy. 1 ▪ Crowsnest Pass on Hwy. 3 ▪ Field, British Columbia, on Hwy. 1 ▪ Grande Prairie on 106th St. ▪ Hinton on Hwy. 16 ▪ Lloydminster on Hwy. 16 ▪ Milk River on Hwy. 4 ▪ Oyen at the junction of hwys. 9 and 41 ▪ Walsh on Hwy. 1 ▪ and West Glacier, Mont., at the junction of Hwy. 2 and Going-to-the-Sun Road. Most centers are open daily 9-6, mid-May through Labour Day. A tourism office is open year-round in Canmore.

FURTHER INFORMATION FOR VISITORS:
Travel Alberta
400, 1601 9th Ave. S.E.
Calgary, AB T2G 0H4
Canada
(403) 648-1000

FISHING AND HUNTING REGULATIONS:
Alberta Environment and Parks (AEP)
9920 108th St., Main Floor
Edmonton, AB T5K 2M4
Canada
(780) 944-0313
(877) 310-3773 (in Alberta)

RECREATION INFORMATION:
Alberta Tourism, Parks and Recreation
Parks & Protected Areas
9820 106th St., 2nd Floor
Edmonton, AB T5K 2J6
Canada
(780) 427-3582
(866) 427-3582

Alberta Annual Events

Please call ahead to confirm event details.

 Visit **AAA.com/travelguides/events** to find AAA-listed events for every day of the year

WINTER

Dec. - Christmas Concerts / Calgary 403-571-0849
- Airdrie Festival of Lights / Airdrie 403-948-3249
- Once Upon a Christmas at Heritage Park / Calgary / 403-268-8500

Jan. - Jasper in January / Jasper 780-852-3858
- Ice Magic Festival International Ice Sculpture Competition / Lake Louise / 403-762-0270
- Ice on Whyte Festival / Edmonton 780-439-9166

Feb. - Canadian Birkebeiner Ski Festival Edmonton / 780-430-7153
- Calgary Midwinter Bluesfest / Calgary 403-668-7144
- Silver Skate Festival / Edmonton 780-496-4000

SPRING

Mar. - Edmonton Home and Garden Show Edmonton / 780-459-2008
- Edmonton Boat and Sportsmen's Show / Edmonton / 888-800-7275
- Outdoor Adventure & Travel Show Calgary / 403-261-0101

Apr. - Red Deer Festival of the Performing Arts / Red Deer / 403-342-3526
- Edmonton Kiwanis Music Festival Edmonton / 780-488-3498
- Aggie Days Family Fun Days Calgary / 403-261-0162

May - Grande Prairie Stompede / Grande Prairie / 780-532-4646
- Lilac Festival at 4th Street / Calgary 403-229-0902

SUMMER

June - Grande Prairie Highland Games Grande Prairie / 780-513-2492
- Medicine Hat JazzFest / Medicine Hat / 403-527-5214
- Edmonton International Jazz Festival Edmonton / 780-990-0222

July - Medicine Hat Exhibition & Stampede Medicine Hat / 403-527-1234
- Edmonton's K-Days / Edmonton 780-471-7210
- Calgary Stampede / Calgary 403-261-0172

Aug. - Edmonton Folk Music Festival Edmonton / 780-429-1899
- Canmore Highland Games Canmore / 403-678-9454
- Taste of Calgary / Calgary 403-293-2888
- Edmonton International Fringe Theatre Festival / Edmonton 780-448-9000

FALL

Sept. - BBQ on the Bow / Calgary 403-264-6450
- Masters Tournament / Calgary 403-974-4200

Oct. - Rocky Mountain Wine and Food Festival / Calgary / 403-261-0101

Nov. - Spruce Meadows International Christmas Market / Calgary 403-974-4200
- Banff Mountain Film and Book Festival / Banff / 800-413-8368
- Canadian Finals Rodeo / Red Deer / 403-343-7800

 Love the great outdoors? Find places to camp

at AAA.com/campgrounds

Banff Gondola

Aurora borealis

Moraine Lake, Banff National Park

Lake Minnewanka, Banff National Park

Bighorn sheep

Index: Great Experience for Members

AAA editor's picks of exceptional note

Royal Alberta
Museum

Ukrainian Cultural
Heritage Village

Lake Louise

West Edmonton Mall

See Orientation map on p. 20 for corresponding grid coordinates, if applicable.
*Indicates the GEM is temporarily closed.

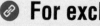 **For exclusive AAA member savings**

and benefits: AAA.com/hertz

Alberta
Atlas Section

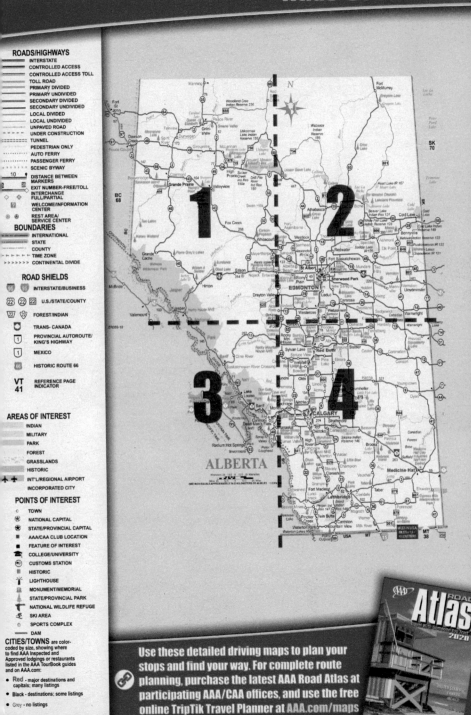

ROADS/HIGHWAYS
- INTERSTATE
- CONTROLLED ACCESS
- CONTROLLED ACCESS TOLL
- TOLL ROAD
- PRIMARY DIVIDED
- PRIMARY UNDIVIDED
- SECONDARY DIVIDED
- SECONDARY UNDIVIDED
- LOCAL DIVIDED
- LOCAL UNDIVIDED
- UNPAVED ROAD
- UNDER CONSTRUCTION
- TUNNEL
- PEDESTRIAN ONLY
- AUTO FERRY
- PASSENGER FERRY
- SCENIC BYWAY
- DISTANCE BETWEEN MARKERS
- EXIT NUMBER-FREE/TOLL
- INTERCHANGE FULL/PARTIAL
- WELCOME/INFORMATION CENTER
- REST AREA/ SERVICE CENTER

BOUNDARIES
- INTERNATIONAL
- STATE
- COUNTY
- TIME ZONE
- CONTINENTAL DIVIDE

ROAD SHIELDS
- INTERSTATE/BUSINESS
- U.S./STATE/COUNTY
- FOREST/INDIAN
- TRANS- CANADA
- PROVINCIAL AUTOROUTE/ KING'S HIGHWAY
- MEXICO
- HISTORIC ROUTE 66
- VT 41 REFERENCE PAGE INDICATOR

AREAS OF INTEREST
- INDIAN
- MILITARY
- PARK
- FOREST
- GRASSLANDS
- HISTORIC
- INTL/REGIONAL AIRPORT
- INCORPORATED CITY

POINTS OF INTEREST
- TOWN
- NATIONAL CAPITAL
- STATE/PROVINCIAL CAPITAL
- AAA/CAA CLUB LOCATION
- FEATURE OF INTEREST
- COLLEGE/UNIVERSITY
- CUSTOMS STATION
- HISTORIC
- LIGHTHOUSE
- MONUMENT/MEMORIAL
- STATE/PROVINCIAL PARK
- NATIONAL WILDLIFE REFUGE
- SKI AREA
- SPORTS COMPLEX
- DAM

CITIES/TOWNS are color-coded by size, showing where to find AAA Inspected and Approved lodgings or restaurants listed in the AAA TourBook guides and on AAA.com:
- **Red** - major destinations and capitals; many listings
- Black - destinations; some listings
- Grey - no listings

Use these detailed driving maps to plan your stops and find your way. For complete route planning, purchase the latest AAA Road Atlas at participating AAA/CAA offices, and use the free online TripTik Travel Planner at AAA.com/maps

AAA Road Atlas 2020

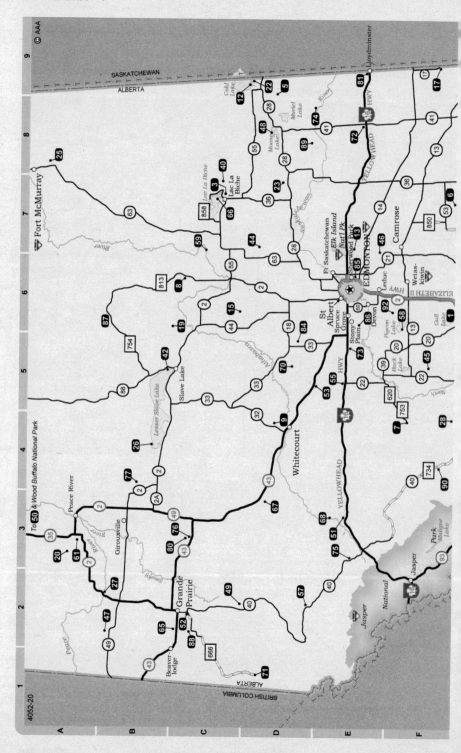

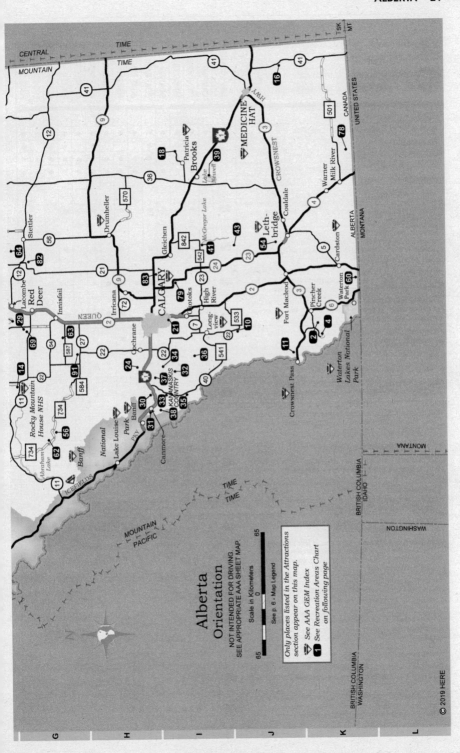

Recreation Areas Chart

The map location numerals in column 2 show an area's location on the preceding map.

Find thousands of places to camp at AAA.com/campgrounds

	MAP LOCATION	CAMPING	PICNICKING	HIKING TRAILS	BOATING	BOAT RAMP	BOAT RENTAL	FISHING	SWIMMING	PET FRIENDLY	BICYCLE TRAILS	WINTER SPORTS	VISITOR CENTER	LODGE/CABINS	FOOD SERVICE
NATIONAL PARKS *(See place listings.)*															
Banff (G-5) 6,641 square kilometres. Horse rental.		•	•	•	•	•	•	•	•	•	•	•	•	•	•
Elk Island (E-7) 194 square kilometres.		•	•	•	•	•		•	•	•	•	•	•	•	•
Jasper (E-2) 11,228 square kilometres. Horse rental.		•	•	•	•	•	•	•	•	•	•	•	•	•	•
Waterton Lakes (K-5) 505 square kilometres. Golf; horse rental.		•	•	•	•	•	•	•	•	•	•	•	•	•	•
PROVINCIAL															
Aspen Beach (F-6) 214 hectares on Gull Lake, 17 km w. of Lacombe on Hwy. 12. Baseball, canoeing, cross-country skiing, ice fishing, kayaking, powerboating, water skiing, windsurfing; swimming beach.	**1**	•	•		•	•		•	•	•		•			
Beauvais Lake (K-5) 1,160 hectares 11 km w. of Pincher Creek on Hwy. 507, then 8 km s. on Hwy. 775. Backcountry camping, bird-watching, canoeing, cross-country skiing, ice fishing, kayaking, snowshoeing, windsurfing, winter camping.	**2**	•	•	•	•	•		•	•	•		•			
Beaver Lake (C-7) 96 hectares 6 km s.e. of Lac La Biche off Hwy. 36, on the n.e. shore of Beaver Lake. Bird-watching, canoeing, kayaking, water skiing, windsurfing; swimming beach.	**3**	•			•	•	•	•	•	•					
Beaver Mines Lake (K-6) 118 hectares 20 km w. of Pincher Creek on Hwy. 507, 10 km s.w. on Hwy. 774, then 5 km s. on access road. Canoeing, horseback riding, ice fishing, kayaking.	**4**	•		•	•			•	•						
Beaverdam (D-9) 110 hectares 5 km e. of Nordegg on Hwy. 11. Canoeing, kayaking.	**5**	•	•	•	•			•	•	•					
Big Knife (F-7) 295 hectares 8 km w. and 13 km s. of Forestburg on Hwy. 855. Canoeing, cross-country skiing, kayaking, snowshoeing; horseshoe pitch, playground.	**6**	•	•	•	•	•		•		•		•			
Brazeau Reservoir (F-4) 130 hectares 60 km s.w. of Drayton Valley along Hwy. 620. Bird-watching, canoeing, kayaking, sailing, water skiing, windsurfing.	**7**	•			•	•		•		•		•			
Calling Lake (C-6) 738 hectares 55 km n. of Athabasca on Hwy. 813. Bird-watching, canoeing, kayaking, powerboating, sailing, water skiing, windsurfing; playground.	**8**	•	•		•	•		•	•	•					
Carson-Pegasus (D-4) 1,209 hectares 6 km w. of Whitecourt on Hwy. 43, 11 km n. on Hwy. 32, then 5 km e. on access road. Bird-watching, canoeing, kayaking, cross-country skiing, ice fishing, kayaking, snowmobiling, wildlife observation; amphitheater, swimming beach.	**9**	•	•	•	•	•	•	•	•	•		•			•
Chain Lakes (J-6) 409 hectares 38 km s.w. of Nanton on Hwy. 533. Canoeing, ice fishing, kayaking, powerboating, sailing, windsurfing; horseshoe pitch, swimming beach.	**10**	•	•		•	•		•	•	•		•			
Chinook (J-5) 48 hectares 8 km w. of Crowsnest Pass off Hwy. 3. Canoeing, cross-country skiing, kayaking.	**11**	•	•		•				•			•			
Cold Lake (C-8) 5,849 hectares 3 km n.e. of Cold Lake off Hwy. 28. Interpretive programs. Bird-watching, canoeing, cross-country skiing, ice fishing, kayaking, sailing, water skiing, windsurfing; amphitheater.	**12**	•	•	•	•	•		•	•	•		•			
Cooking Lake-Blackfoot (E-7) 9,700 hectares 24 km e. of Sherwood Park s. of Hwy. 16. Bird-watching, canoeing, cross-country skiing, dog sledding, horseback riding, hunting, ice-skating, kayaking, snowmobiling.	**13**		•	•						•	•	•	•		
Crimson Lake (G-5) 3,209 hectares 14 km w. of Rocky Mountain House on Hwy. 11, then 6 km n. on Hwy. 756. Interpretive programs. Bird-watching, canoeing, cross-country skiing, ice fishing, kayaking, sailing, volleyball, water skiing, windsurfing; horseshoe pitch.	**14**	•		•	•	•		•	•	•	•	•		•	
Cross Lake (C-6) 2,076 hectares 8 km n. and 19 km n.e. of Jarvie off Hwy. 663. Bird-watching, canoeing, cross-country skiing, ice fishing, kayaking, water skiing, windsurfing; horseshoe pitch.	**15**	•		•	•	•		•	•	•		•			
Cypress Hills (J-9) 20,451 hectares 1.5 km s. of Elkwater on Hwy. 41. Historic. Interpretive programs. Canoeing, cross-country skiing, golf, kayaking, sailing, windsurfing; amphitheater.	**16**	•	•	•	•	•	•	•	•	•	•	•	•	•	•

Recreation Areas Chart

The map location numerals in column 2 show an area's location on the preceding map.

Find thousands of places to camp at AAA.com/campgrounds

	MAP LOCATION	CAMPING	PICNICKING	HIKING TRAILS	BOATING	BOAT RAMP	BOAT RENTAL	FISHING	SWIMMING	PET FRIENDLY	BICYCLE TRAILS	WINTER SPORTS	VISITOR CENTER	LODGE/CABINS	FOOD SERVICE
Dillberry Lake (F-9) 1,205 hectares 15 km s.e. of Chauvin on Hwy. 17 at Alberta/Saskatchewan border. Bird-watching, canoeing, cross-country skiing, ice fishing, kayaking, powerboating, sailing, snowshoeing, windsurfing; playground, swimming beach.	17	•	•	•	•	•		•	•	•		•			
Dinosaur (I-8) 8,085 hectares 13 km n.e. of Patricia via Hwy. 210. Historic. Interpretive programs. Bird-watching, canoeing, kayaking, winter camping; amphitheater.	18	•	•	•	•					•		•	•	•	•
Fawcett Lake (West) (C-6) 48 hectares 55 km s.e. of Slave Lake on Hwy. 2, 20 km n. on Hwy. 2A, then 18 km n. on access road. Canoeing, kayaking, snowmobiling; swimming beach.	19	•	•	•	•			•	•	•		•			
Figure Eight Lake (A-3) 90 hectares 25 km w. of Peace River off Hwy. 35. Canoeing, cross-country skiing, dog sledding, ice fishing, kayaking, snowmobiling, windsurfing.	20	•	•	•	•			•	•	•	•	•			
Fish Creek (I-6) 1,355 hectares in Calgary between 37th St. S.W. and the Bow River. Interpretive programs. Bird-watching, golf; amphitheater, beach, playground.	21		•	•	•	•	•	•	•	•	•	•	•		•
French Bay (D-9) 449 hectares 11 km e. and 3 km n. of Cold Lake off Hwy. 55. Canoeing, kayaking, powerboating, sailing, skiing, water skiing, windsurfing; swimming beach.	22	•						•	•	•		•			
Garner Lake (D-7) 74 hectares 5 km n. of Spedden off Hwy. 28. Canoeing, cross-country skiing, ice fishing, kayaking, powerboating, sailing, volleyball, water skiing, windsurfing; swimming beach.	23	•	•	•	•	•		•	•	•		•			
Ghost Reservoir (H-5) 24 hectares 18 km w. of Cochrane on Hwy. 1A. Canoeing, ice fishing, kayaking, sailing, water skiing, windsurfing.	24	•	•		•	•		•		•					
Gregoire Lake (A-8) 696 hectares 19 km s. of Fort McMurray on Hwy. 63, then 10 km e. on Hwy. 881. Canoeing, cross-country skiing, ice fishing, sailing, snowmobiling, water skiing, windsurfing; horseshoe pitch, playground.	25	•	•	•	•			•	•	•		•			
Hilliard's Bay (B-4) 2,323 hectares 10 km e. of Grouard off Hwy. 750. Canoeing, ice fishing, kayaking, powerboating, sailing, water skiing, windsurfing; horseshoe pitch, playground, swimming beach.	26	•	•	•	•	•		•	•	•					
Historic Dunvegan (B-2) 9 hectares off Queen Elizabeth II Hwy. on the n. side of the Peace River beside Dunvegan Suspension Bridge. Historic. Canoeing, kayaking, wildlife viewing; playground.	27	•	•		•			•		•			•		
Jackfish Lake (F-4) 203 hectares 50 km w. of Rocky Mountain House on Hwy. 11, then 2 km n. on access road. Canoeing, ice fishing, kayaking, powerboating, snowmobiling.	28	•			•	•		•	•	•		•	•		
Jarvis Bay (G-6) 86 hectares 4 km n. of Sylvan Lake townsite on Hwy. 20. Cross-country skiing, snowshoeing; pier, playground.	29	•		•				•	•	•		•			
Kananaskis Country (G-4)															
Bow Valley (H-5) 3,129 hectares 25 km e. of Canmore on Hwy. 1 and .5 km n. on Hwy. 1X. Backcountry camping, canoeing, horseback riding, hunting, kayaking, rock climbing, snowshoeing.	30	•		•				•		•		•	•		•
Canmore Nordic Centre (H-4) 804 hectares 3 km s. of Canmore on Spray Lakes Rd. Cross-country skiing, disc golf, ice-skating, roller skating.	31		•	•						•	•	•	•	•	•
Elbow River (I-5) 245 hectares 20 km w. of Bragg Creek on Hwy. 66. Interpretive programs. Horseback riding; playground.	32	•	•	•				•		•	•				
Evan-Thomas (I-5) 2,571 hectares 30 km e. of Canmore on Spray Lakes Rd. Cross-country and down-hill skiing, horseback riding, hunting.	33	•	•	•						•					
McLean Creek (I-5) 238 hectares 12 km w. of Bragg Creek on Hwy. 66, then 1.3 km s. on McLean Creek Trail. Snowmobiling.	34	•		•				•		•		•			

Recreation Areas Chart

The map location numerals in column 2 show an area's location on the preceding map.

Find thousands of places to camp at AAA.com/campgrounds

	MAP LOCATION	CAMPING	PICNICKING	HIKING TRAILS	BOATING	BOAT RAMP	BOAT RENTAL	FISHING	SWIMMING	PET FRIENDLY	BICYCLE TRAILS	WINTER SPORTS	VISITOR CENTER	LODGE/CABINS	FOOD SERVICE
Peter Lougheed (I-5) 50,142 hectares 43 km s.e. of Canmore on Hwy. 40. Interpretive programs. Canoeing, cross-country skiing, ice fishing, kayaking, powerboating, sailing, snowshoeing, windsurfing; playground.	35	•	•	•	•	•		•		•	•	•	•		
Sheep River (I-5) 6,191 hectares 25 km w. of Turner Valley on Hwy. 546. Cross-country skiing, horseback riding, ice-skating.	36	•		•				•		•	•	•			
Sibbald Lake (I-5) 79 hectares 30 km e. of Canmore on Hwy. 1, 6 km s. on Hwy. 40, then 12 km e. on Hwy. 68. Canoeing, kayaking.	37	•	•	•	•			•		•		•			
Spray Valley (I-5) 27,471 hectares s.w. of Canmore, surrounding the Spray Lakes Reservoir. Interpretive programs. Backcountry camping, canoeing, cross-country skiing, ice fishing, kayaking, powerboating, sailing, windsurfing.	38	•	•	•	•			•		•	•	•			
Kinbrook Island (I-8) 540 hectares 13 km s. of Brooks off Hwy. 873. Bird-watching, canoeing, cross-country skiing, ice fishing, ice-skating, kayaking, powerboating, sailing, snowmobiling, volleyball, water skiing, windsurfing; playground.	39	•		•	•	•		•		•		•			
Lakeland (C-8) 59,030 hectares 13 km e. of Lac La Biche off Hwy. 663. Bird-watching, canoeing, dog sledding, ice fishing, kayaking, sailing, snowmobiling, snowshoeing, water skiing, windsurfing, winter camping; swimming beach.	40	•	•	•	•			•	•	•	•	•	•		
Lake McGregor (I-7) 140 hectares 20 km n. of Vulcan on Hwy. 23, then 25 km e. on Hwy. 542. Bird-watching, canoeing, ice fishing, kayaking, powerboating, sailing, water skiing, windsurfing.	41	•				•		•		•					
Lesser Slave Lake (B-5) 7,566 hectares 6 km n. of Slave Lake on Hwy. 88. Interpretive programs. Bird-watching, cross-country skiing, ice fishing, sailing, snowshoeing, water skiing, windsurfing; horseshoe pitch.	42	•	•	•	•	•		•	•	•	•	•			
Little Bow (J-7) 110 hectares 20 km s. of Vulcan on Hwy. 23, 16 km e. on Hwy. 529, then 1 km s. on access road. Bird-watching, canoeing, hunting, ice fishing, kayaking, powerboating, sailing, water skiing, windsurfing; horseshoe pitch, swimming beach.	43	•	•	•	•	•	•	•	•	•		•			•
Long Lake (D-7) 769 hectares 20 km s. of Boyle on Hwy. 831, then 2 km n.e. on access road. Canoeing, cross-country and downhill skiing, golf (adjacent to park), ice fishing, kayaking, powerboating, sailing, snowmobiling, water skiing, windsurfing; horseshoe pitch.	44	•	•	•	•	•		•	•	•	•	•			•
Medicine Lake (F-5) 24 hectares 47 km n. of Rocky Mountain House on Hwy. 22, then 8 km s.e. on access road. Canoeing, kayaking, powerboating; horseshoe pitch, playground.	45	•	•	•				•	•	•	•				
Miquelon Lake (E-7) 1,299 hectares 3 km s. of New Sarepta on Hwy. 21, then 20 km e. on Hwy. 623. Interpretive programs. Baseball, bird-watching, canoeing, cross-country skiing, golf (adjacent to park), ice-skating, kayaking, sailing, snowshoeing, windsurfing, winter camping; horseshoe pitch, swimming beach.	46	•		•					•	•		•	•	•	
Moonshine Lake (B-2) 1,103 hectares 27 km w. of Spirit River on Hwy. 49, then 7 km n. on Hwy. 725. Interpretive programs. Baseball, bird-watching, canoeing, cross-country skiing, ice fishing, ice-skating, powerboating, sailing, snowshoeing, windsurfing; horseshoe pitch, playground, swimming beach.	47	•		•	•	•		•	•	•	•	•	•		
Moose Lake (D-8) 736 hectares 5 km n. of Bonnyville on Hwy. 41, 10 km w. on Hwy. 660, then 2 km s. on access road. Canoeing, kayaking, sailing, water skiing, windsurfing; swimming beach.	48	•	•	•	•	•		•	•	•	•				
Musreau Lake (C-2) 1,803 hectares 80 km s. of Grande Prairie on Hwy. 40, then 2 km e. on access road. Canoeing, kayaking, powerboating; swimming beach.	49	•	•	•	•	•	•	•							
Notikewin (A-3) 9,697 hectares 37 km n. of Manning via Hwy. 35, then 30 km e. on Hwy. 692. Bird-watching, canoeing, cross-country skiing, golf, kayaking, powerboating; swimming beach.	50	•				•		•	•	•	•	•			
Obed Lake (E-3) 3,402 hectares 55 km w. of Edson off Hwy. 16. Canoeing, ice fishing, kayaking, powerboating.	51	•			•	•		•		•		•			

Recreation Areas Chart

The map location numerals in column 2 show an area's location on the preceding map.

Find thousands of places to camp at AAA.com/campgrounds

	MAP LOCATION	CAMPING	PICNICKING	HIKING TRAILS	BOATING	BOAT RAMP	BOAT RENTAL	FISHING	SWIMMING	PET FRIENDLY	BICYCLE TRAILS	WINTER SPORTS	VISITOR CENTER	LODGE/CABINS	FOOD SERVICE
O'Brien (C-2) 65 hectares 10 km s. of Grande Prairie on Hwy. 40. Canoeing, kayaking, powerboating; swimming beach.	52		•		•	•		•	•	•	•				
Paddle River Dam (E-5) 70 hectares 10 km n.w. of Sangudo on Hwy. 43. Canoeing, ice fishing, kayaking, powerboating, sailing, snowmobiling, tobogganing, water skiing, windsurfing.	53		•		•	•		•	•	•		•			
Park Lake (J-7) 224 hectares 17 km n.w. of Lethbridge on Hwy. 25, then 5 km n.w. on Hwy. 101. Canoeing, ice fishing, kayaking, sailing; playground, swimming beach.	54	•	•		•	•		•	•	•		•			
Pembina River (E-5) 167 hectares 2 km n.e. of Entwistle on Hwy. 16A. Canoeing, kayaking, volleyball.	55	•	•	•				•	•	•					
Peppers Lake (G-4) 18 hectares 84 km s.e. of Nordegg on Forestry Trunk Rd. (Hwy. 734). Canoeing, horseback riding, kayaking, powerboating.	56	•			•			•		•					
Pierre Grey's Lakes (D-2) 633 hectares 37 km s. of Grande Cache off Hwy. 40 on access road. Historic. Canoeing, ice fishing, kayaking, powerboating, snowmobiling, water skiing; swimming beach.	57	•	•	•	•	•		•	•	•		•	•		
Pigeon Lake (F-6) 443 hectares 5 km w. and 10 km n. of Westerose off Hwy. 771. Canoeing, cross-country skiing, ice fishing, kayaking, powerboating, sailing, snowmobiling, water skiing, windsurfing; horseshoe pitch, playground, swimming beach.	58	•	•	•	•	•		•	•	•		•			•
Poacher's Landing (C-7) 1,518 hectares 35 km n.e. of Athabasca on Hwy. 55, then 25 km n. on access road. Horseback riding; horse corrals, playground.	59	•	•	•		•		•		•					
Police Outpost (K-6) 223 hectares 10 km s. and 23 km w. of Cardston on Queen Elizabeth II Hwy. Bird-watching, canoeing, cross-country skiing, kayaking, powerboating; playground.	60	•	•	•	•	•		•		•		•			
Queen Elizabeth (A-3) 86 hectares 3 km n. and 5 km w. of Grimshaw off Hwy. 35. Bird-watching, canoeing, cross-country skiing, kayaking, powerboating, sailing, snowmobiling, snowshoeing, volleyball, water skiing, windsurfing, winter camping; horseshoe pitch, swimming beach.	61	•	•					•	•	•		•			
Ram Falls (G-4) 409 hectares 64 km s. of Nordegg on Forestry Trunk Rd. (Hwy. 734). Cross-country skiing, snowmobiling.	62	•	•					•		•					
Red Lodge (G-6) 129 hectares 15 km w. of Bowden on Hwy. 587. Canoeing, kayaking; horseshoe pitch.	63	•	•	•				•		•					
Rochon Sands (G-7) 119 hectares 12 km w. of Stettler on Hwy. 12, then 16 km n. on Hwy. 835. Bird-watching, canoeing, kayaking, powerboating, sailing, water skiing, windsurfing; swimming beach.	64	•	•		•	•		•	•	•					
Saskatoon Island (B-2) 101 hectares 21 km w. of Grande Prairie on Hwy. 43, then 4 km n. on an access road. Interpretive programs. Baseball, bird-watching, canoeing, cross-country skiing, kayaking, snowshoeing, volleyball; horseshoe pitch.	65	•	•	•	•	•				•	•	•	•		
Sir Winston Churchill (C-7) 662 hectares 11 km n.e. of Lac La Biche off Hwy. 881. Interpretive programs. Bird-watching, canoeing, cross-country skiing, kayaking, powerboating, sailing, snowshoeing, water skiing, windsurfing; swimming beach.	66	•	•	•	•	•		•	•	•		•			
Smoke Lake (D-3) 102 hectares 9 km s.w. of Fox Creek off Hwy. 43. Canoeing, ice fishing, kayaking, snowmobiling, water skiing; swimming beach.	67			•	•	•		•	•	•		•			
Sundance (E-3) 151 hectares 56 km n.e. of Hinton on Emerson Creek Rd. Canoeing, ice fishing, kayaking, powerboating (electric motors only), snowmobiling.	68	•			•	•		•		•		•			
Sylvan Lake (G-5) 67 hectares 18 km n.w. of Red Deer on Hwy. 11 in the town of Sylvan Lake. Canoeing, golf, ice fishing, iceskating, kayaking, powerboating, sailing, water skiing, windsurfing; swimming beach.	69		•		•	•		•	•			•			•
Thunder Lake (D-5) 208 hectares 21 km w. of Barrhead on Hwy. 18. Baseball, canoeing, ice fishing, kayaking, sailing, volleyball, water skiing, windsurfing; beach, playground.	70	•	•		•	•		•	•	•		•			•

Recreation Areas Chart

The map location numerals in column 2 show an area's location on the preceding map.

Find thousands of places to camp at AAA.com/campgrounds

	MAP LOCATION	CAMPING	PICNICKING	HIKING TRAILS	BOATING	BOAT RAMP	BOAT RENTAL	FISHING	SWIMMING	PET FRIENDLY	BICYCLE TRAILS	WINTER SPORTS	VISITOR CENTER	LODGE/CABINS	FOOD SERVICE
Two Lakes (D-1) 1,566 hectares 130 km s.w. of Grande Prairie on Two Lakes Rd. Canoeing, ice fishing, kayaking, powerboating.	71	•		•	•	•		•		•	•	•			
Vermilion (E-8) 759 hectares 1.5 km n. of Vermilion on Hwy. 41 from jct. Hwy. 16, then w. on 50th Ave. following signs. Baseball, canoeing, cross-country skiing, ice fishing, kayaking, sailing, tobogganing, winter camping.	72	•	•	•				•		•		•			
Wabamun Lake (E-5) 231 hectares 3 km e. and 1 km s. of Wabamun off Hwy. 16A. Baseball, bird-watching, canoeing, kayaking, sailing, water skiing, windsurfing.	73	•	•	•	•	•	•	•		•	•	•			
Whitney Lakes (D-8) 1,489 hectares 24 km e. of Elk Point off Hwy. 646. Historic. Bird-watching, canoeing, cross-country skiing, ice fishing, kayaking, powerboating, sailing, volleyball, water skiing, windsurfing; beach, horseshoe pitch, playground.	74	•		•	•	•		•	•	•					
William A. Switzer (E-3) 6,268 hectares 3 km w. of Hinton on Hwy. 16, then 19 km n. on Hwy. 40. Historic. Interpretive programs. Bird-watching, canoeing, cross-country skiing, ice fishing, kayaking, powerboating, winter camping; swimming beach.	75	•	•	•	•	•		•	•	•	•	•	•	•	•
Williamson (C-3) 17 hectares 17 km w. of Valleyview on Hwy. 43, then 2 km n. on an access road. Canoeing, ice fishing, kayaking, sailing, snowmobiling, water skiing, windsurfing; horseshoe pitch, swimming beach.	76	•		•	•	•		•	•	•		•			
Winagami Lake (B-4) 6,542 hectares 20 km n. of High Prairie on Hwy. 749, 10 km w. on Hwy. 679, then 7 km n. on access road. Bird-watching, canoeing, cross-country skiing, ice fishing, kayaking, powerboating, sailing, snowshoeing, water skiing, windsurfing; playground, swimming beach.	77	•	•	•	•	•		•	•	•		•			
Writing-on-Stone (K-8) 1,718 hectares 35 km e. of Milk River off Hwy. 501. Historic. Interpretive programs. Bird-watching, canoeing, kayaking.	78	•	•	•				•	•	•			•		
Wyndham-Carseland (I-6) 178 hectares 2 km e. and 2 km s. of Carseland on Hwy. 24. Canoeing, cross-country skiing, kayaking; horseshoe pitch, playground.	79	•	•	•	•			•		•		•			
Young's Point (B-3) 3,072 hectares 26 km w. of Valleyview on Hwy. 43, then 10 km n.e. on an access road. Canoeing, cross-country skiing, ice fishing, kayaking, sailing, snowshoeing, water skiing, windsurfing; beach, horseshoe pitch.	80	•	•	•	•	•		•	•	•		•			
OTHER															
Bud Miller All Seasons Park (E-9) 81 hectares at 2902 59th Ave. in Lloydminster. Bird-watching, cross-country skiing, disc golf, ice-skating, lawn bowling, miniature golf, soccer, tennis, volleyball; aquatic complex, horseshoe pitch, indoor pool, interpretive trails, playgrounds, skateboard park.	81		•	•					•	•		•	•		
Content Bridge (G-6) 12 hectares 6 km s. of Nevis on Hwy. 21. Baseball, canoeing, kayaking.	82	•	•					•	•	•					
Eagle Lake Park (H-6) 7 km e. and 6 km s. of Strathmore via Hwy. 1. Horseshoe pitch, playground.	83	•	•	•	•	•	•	•	•	•					•
Elks Beach (D-6) 14 km s. of Barrhead on Hwy. 33, then e. on Hwy. 651. Cross-country skiing, ice fishing; playground.	84	•	•					•				•			
Half Moon Lake (E-6) 4 hectares 3 km e. of Sherwood Park on Hwy. 630. Canoeing, kayaking; beach, horseshoe pitch, paddleboats.	85	•	•	•	•			•	•	•					•
Hasse Lake (E-6) 81 hectares 5 km w. and 10 km s. of Stony Plain on Hwy. 16. Basketball, cross-country skiing, golf, volleyball; beach, playground.	86		•	•				•	•	•		•			
North Wabasca (B-6) 77 hectares 38 km n. of Slave Lake on Hwy. 88, 100 km n.e. on Hwy. 754, then 7 km n. on access road.	87	•	•		•	•		•	•	•					
Pipestone Creek (C-2) 15 km s. of Wembley. Disc golf; dinosaur museum, interpretive trails, horseshoe pitch, playground.	88	•	•					•		•					
Stoney Lake (D-8) 174 hectares on Stony Lake, 16 km s.w. of Elk Point off Hwy. 646. Playground.	89	•	•		•	•		•		•					

Recreation Areas Chart

The map location numerals in column 2 show an area's location on the preceding map.

Find thousands of places to camp at AAA.com/campgrounds

	MAP LOCATION	CAMPING	PICNICKING	HIKING TRAILS	BOATING	BOAT RAMP	BOAT RENTAL	FISHING	SWIMMING	PET FRIENDLY	BICYCLE TRAILS	WINTER SPORTS	VISITOR CENTER	LODGE/CABINS	FOOD SERVICE
Upper Shunda Creek (F-4) 47 hectares 3 km w. of Nordegg off Hwy. 11.	90	•		•				•		•	•				
Westward Ho (G-5) 8 km e. of Sundre on Hwy. 27. Baseball, canoeing, kayaking, volleyball; beach, horseshoe pitch, playgrounds.	91	•	•		•			•	•	•			•		
Wizard Lake (E-6) 33 hectares 19 km s. of Calmar on Hwy. 795. Canoeing; playground, swimming beach.	92	•	•		•	•		•	•	•					•

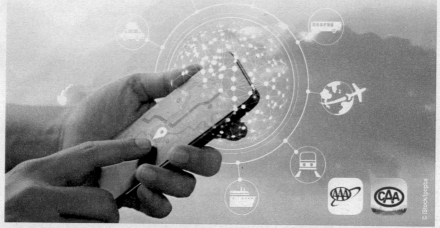

STAY CONNECTED

to all the things membership can do for you

- **Member discounts around you**
- **Cheapest gas nearby**
- **Diamond hotels and restaurants**
- **Travel information and reservations**
- **Roadside assistance**

Download today. Connect every day.
AAA.com/mobile | CAA.ca/mobile

AAA
Life Insurance
Company

Have you ever stopped to think about the countless reasons why you need life insurance?

Your why isn't just about who you're protecting, it's about what you're doing to protect them.

Whether it's a new house, a new grandchild or a new life with the one we love, life insurance can cover you for the now and whatever's next.

What's your why?

Get a free quote at AAALife.com

Products and their features may not be available in all states. Life insurance underwritten by AAA Life Insurance Company, Livonia, MI. AAA Life (CA Certificate of Authority #07861) is licensed in all states except NY. Automobile Club of Southern California CA License #0003259. CSAA Life Insurance Agency of California, Inc. CA License #0D12130. Insurance products in Northern California offered through AAA Northern California Insurance Agency, License #0175868, in Nevada by AAA Nevada and in Utah by AAA Utah. Your local AAA club and/or its affiliates act as agents for AAA Life.

ALAN-25514-519-XX

AIRDRIE pop. 42,564, elev. 1,077m/3,533'
• Part of Calgary area — see map p. 43

AIRDRIE RAMADA INN & SUITES   403/945-1288
THREE DIAMOND Hotel. **Address:** 191 E Lake Crescent T4A 2H7

BEST WESTERN AIRDRIE   403/948-3838
APPROVED
Hotel

BW **Best Western.** **AAA Benefit:** Members save up to 15% and earn bonus points!

Address: 121 Edmonton Tr SE T4B 1S2 **Location:** Hwy 2 exit Airdrie/Irricana, just w, then 0.5 mi (0.9 km) s. **Facility:** 60 units. 3 stories, interior/exterior corridors. **Parking:** winter plug-ins. **Activities:** hot tub, exercise room. **Guest Services:** coin laundry.

DAYS INN & SUITES AIRDRIE   403/945-7000
THREE DIAMOND Hotel. **Address:** 911 Highland Park Cove NE T4A 0R2

HAMPTON INN & SUITES BY HILTON AIRDRIE   403/980-4477
THREE DIAMOND Hotel. **Address:** 52 E Lake Ave NE T4A 2G8
AAA Benefit: Members save up to 15%!

HOLIDAY INN EXPRESS & SUITES AIRDRIE-CALGARY NORTH   403/912-1952
THREE DIAMOND Hotel. **Address:** 64 E Lake Ave NE T4A 2G8

SUPER 8 AIRDRIE   403/948-4188
APPROVED Hotel. **Address:** 815 E Lake Blvd T4A 2G4

WINGATE BY WYNDHAM AIRDRIE   587/775-6171
THREE DIAMOND Hotel. **Address:** 513 Gateway Rd NE T4B 0J6

WHERE TO EAT

HAYLOFT RESTAURANT   403/980-8123
THREE DIAMOND Regional Canadian. Casual Dining. **Address:** 403 MacKenzie Way SW T4B 3V7

MR MIKES STEAKHOUSECASUAL   403/948-3701
APPROVED American. Casual Dining. **Address:** 130 Sierra Springs Dr T4B 3G6

SMITTY'S   403/945-1225
APPROVED American. Casual Dining. **Address:** 191 E Lake Crescent T4A 2H7

Exciting Itineraries | Engaging Experiences | Exclusive Values

DESIGNED FOR AAA MEMBERS

AAA® Vacations offers vacation options and experiences all over the world. In addition to our 24/7 Member Care and Best Price Guarantee*, we deliver value with every itinerary.

These exclusive values may include:

- Savings or spending credits
- Pre-night hotel stay
- Priority check-in
- *And more!*
- Complimentary excursions
- Complimentary specialty dining
- Pre-paid gratuities

Call your AAA Travel Agent or visit AAA.com/AAAVacations

* If you book a qualifying *AAA Vacations®* cruise or tour package and find a valid better rate for the exact itinerary within 24 hours of your booking, AAA will match the lower rate and send you a $50 *AAA Vacations®* future travel credit certificate. Certain restrictions apply. Visit AAA.com/AAAVacations for full details.

BANFF NATIONAL PARK (G-5)
• Attractions map p. 32

Elevations in the park range from 1,326 metres (4,350 ft.) around the Bow River to 3,612 metres (11,851 ft.) at Mount Forbes. Refer to CAA/AAA maps for additional elevation information.

Banff National Park sprawls across the jagged backs of the Rocky Mountains, offering some of the most beautiful alpine scenery in the world. It is a land of breathtaking vistas no photo can do justice to—no matter how gifted the photographer. Craggy, snow-capped peaks encircle forested valleys and glacier-fed lakes. Sheltered meadows wear a glorious mantle of wildflowers, vibrant with fireweed, Indian paintbrush, columbine and anemone. Rushing streams sparkle in the crisp mountain air, flowing through forests of lodgepole pine and Douglas fir.

Banff was established in 1885, 2 years after railway workers discovered a misty cave containing thermal springs, a find that led to a legal battle over who would develop the springs as a bathing resort. The conflict was resolved when the Canadian government set aside the rugged land for the benefit of all its citizens, creating what would become the country's first national park. Although bathing in these mineral springs is no longer permitted, you can still see the natural grotto where it all began at Cave and Basin Historic Site (see attraction listing p. 34).

To attract wealthy tourists, the Canadian Pacific Railway built the luxurious Banff Springs Hotel in 1888. The castle-like stone-and-concrete building you see today replaced the original wooden hotel after it burned in 1926, but the idea of providing guests with opulent accommodations while they enjoy the area's scenic beauty remains unchanged. The image of the hotel's stately, high-peaked roofline rising above the surrounding evergreens is a fixture on postcards.

Known today as The Fairmont Banff Springs, the hotel stands on the outskirts of the charming resort

This map shows cities in Banff National Park where you will find attractions, hotels and restaurants. Cities are listed alphabetically in this book on the following pages.

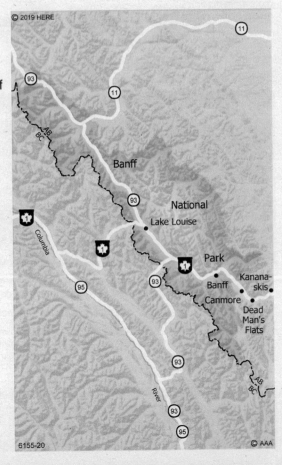

town of Banff *(see place listing p. 33)*, where most development within the park is focused and where you'll find the largest number of hotels. Rustic mountain lodge-style buildings house boutiques, sporting goods stores, gift shops and restaurants. In spring and summer the sidewalks—radiant with colorful annuals planted in window boxes and hanging baskets—are crowded with visitors; in winter the streets in the town center can be just as packed as in warm-weather months with the difference being roof racks now carry skis and winter gear instead of canoes and kayaks.

The village of Lake Louise *(see place listing p. 126)* is the park's second most developed area, where you'll find a small shopping center, cafes, hotels and a ski resort. The community takes its name from the beautiful lake nearby, which is fed by meltwater from Victoria Glacier. The runoff carries finely ground rock flour that gives the lake a striking milky turquoise color you'll see in the area's other glacially fed lakes. Facing the glacier on the opposite shore is The Fairmont Chateau Lake Louise, a grand hotel with more than 500 rooms. The hotel, lake and glacier together create one of the most photographed settings in the park.

Another highlight of Banff National Park is Bow Valley Parkway *(see attraction listing)*, a scenic roadway that parallels Trans-Canada Highway (Hwy. 1), connecting the towns of Banff and Lake Louise. Nestled in Valley of the Ten Peaks, Moraine Lake *(see attraction listing p. 33)* dazzles visitors with its sparkling blue waters, earning it the nickname, "Jewel of the Rockies."

Other sights for which the park is famous: Johnston Canyon *(see attraction listing p. 33)*, Crow Foot Glacier, the sawtooth profile of Mount Rundle reflected in the clear waters of Vermilion Lakes and, in winter, the frozen waterfall known as Weeping Wall. And while you make your way among these scenic points, you'll likely encounter Banff's abundant wildlife. Elk, deer and bighorn sheep are most common, and if you have binoculars you may catch sight of mountain goats and moose in the distance. If you should spot them, you may want to steer clear of the area's predators: bears, wolves, coyotes and lynx, but odds are they'll want to keep their distance from you, too.

General Information and Activities

The park, which is open all year, has about 354 kilometres (219 mi.) of scenic roads. Hwy. 1 to Vancouver and Calgary and Hwy. 93S (Banff-Windermere Hwy.) are open year-round, as is the northern end of Hwy. 93N (Icefields Parkway) from Lake Louise to Jasper; check locally for road conditions. One- or multiple-day bus tours of the park's major points of interest and things to do also are available.

More than 1,500 kilometres (932 mi.) of trails traverse the park. All activities involving an overnight stay in the backcountry require a wilderness permit that is available for purchase at visitor centers in the Banff and Lake Louise townsites. Most public campgrounds in the park are available by reservation; book your campsite online or phone (877) 737-3783.

Lake Louise's waters, about 4 C (39 F), are too cold for swimming but are ideal for canoeing or kayaking. Motorboats may be used only on Lake Minnewanka. Cruises on Lake Minnewanka are offered during the summer. Skating, skiing, curling and hockey are available in the park in winter.

Park naturalists conduct interpretive programs at major campgrounds most evenings and at key attractions daily throughout the summer. Bankhead, a once-booming mining town 4.8 kilometres (3 mi.) northeast of Banff, has a self-guiding trail with explanatory signs and a mining exhibit.

Special events include the Banff Mountain Film and Book Festival, held late October through early November. From May through August, The Banff Centre, a performing arts venue off Tunnel Mountain Drive in the town of Banff, hosts the 🐟 Banff Summer Arts Festival.

Throughout the summer guides and outfitters offer fishing, hiking, float trips and other adventurous things to do in Banff. Saddle horses are available for treks through the mountains to glacier-fed lakes. White-water rafting trips and helicopter tours can be arranged outside the park boundaries in Canmore and in Golden, British Columbia *(see place listings p. 76 and p. 187)*.

Information, interpretive program schedules and backcountry trail tips are available at the Banff Visitor Information Centre, (403) 762-1550, 224 Banff Ave., and the Lake Louise Visitor Information Centre, (403) 522-3833, 201 Village Rd.; topographical maps and trail guides are sold at both locations. Visitor center hours vary throughout the year; phone ahead for current schedules.

A public shuttle runs to the viewpoint at Lake Louise and to Moraine Lake mid-May through mid-October. Both shuttles run from the Lake Louise Park and Ride lot, 10 km (6.2 mi.) east of Lake Louise. The Lake Louise shuttle fare is $4; $2 (ages 7-17 and 65+). The Moraine Lake shuttle fare is $6; $3 (7-17 and 65+). Fares are paid in debit/credit only.

Fishing is permitted; national park fishing permits are sold at park visitor centers as well as at some boat concessionaires and tackle shops. Check at the visitor centers in Banff or Lake Louise for a summary of park fishing regulations.

Note: Hunting is strictly prohibited; visitors entering the area must have firearms dismantled. Motorists driving at dusk, dawn and during the nighttime should be attentive to wildlife on roadways. It is not only dangerous but also against national park regulations to feed, approach or harass any wildlife in a national park. *See Recreation Areas Chart.*

ADMISSION to the park is $9.80; $8.30 (ages 65+); free (ages 0-16); $19.60 (up to seven people arriving in a single vehicle). An annual pass, valid at most Canadian national parks, marine areas and historic sites, is available.

PETS are allowed in the park but must be leashed or physically contained at all times. Pets are restricted in some areas during winter months; phone ahead for more information.

ADDRESS inquiries to the Banff Visitor Centre, 224 Banff Ave., Town of Banff, AB, Canada T1L 1K2; phone (403) 762-1550.

BOW VALLEY PARKWAY (HWY. 1A) is 5 km (3 mi.) w. of the town of Banff off Hwy. 1. The parkway, the original road between the town of Banff and the village of Lake Louise, runs along the Bow River parallel to the Trans-Canada Hwy. The parkway's speed limit of 60 kph (37 mph) provides a slower, more scenic alternative to Hwy. 1. Each curve in the road brings postcardlike images of snow-capped mountains.

There are frequent pull-offs with viewpoints, interpretive panels, picnic sites and trailheads. Wildlife such as bears, bighorn sheep, elk and deer frequent the area. If wildlife is present, slow down and stay in your vehicle. Consider not stopping and moving on quickly to give the animals some space. **Note:** In order to help protect wildlife, there is a seasonal travel restriction on driving a 17-kilometre (10.5 mi.) section of the parkway between Banff and Johnston Canyon daily 8 p.m.-8 a.m., Mar. 1-June 25. Use Hwy. 1 instead.

ICEFIELDS PARKWAY (HWY. 93) crosses Banff and Jasper national parks. The scenic highway parallels the Continental Divide for 232 kilometres (144 mi.) between Lake Louise and the town of Jasper, passing through a breathtaking landscape of snowcapped mountains, waterfalls, lakes and rivers. The park's most visited sights are either along the parkway or just a short distance from it. Driving this spectacular route—roughly a 3-hour trip one way—is an experience you shouldn't miss.

The parkway gets its chilly name from the vast bodies of ice you can see along its length, the most impressive being the massive Columbia Icefield (see attraction listing p. 119), source of eight glaciers including the Athabasca Glacier, which is within walking distance of the parkway just inside Jasper National Park (see place listing p. 118). For

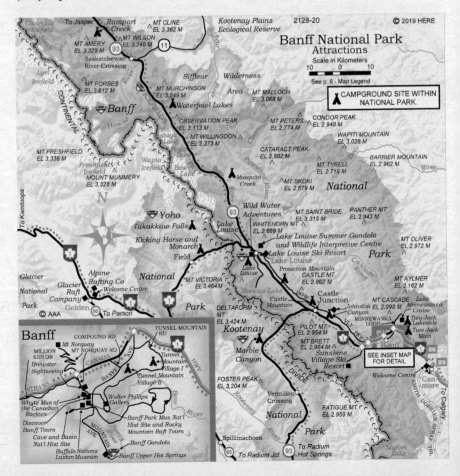

an up-close look at the glacier, climb aboard a specially designed Ice Explorer snowcoach departing from the Columbia Icefield Glacier Discovery Centre *(see attraction listing p. 121)* for a narrated excursion and walk out onto the glacier's frozen surface.

There are too many scenic overlooks and turnouts along the parkway to name, but some of the most outstanding include Bow Glacier, Peyto Lake from Bow Summit and Saskatchewan River Crossing, where several display panels explain the history of the Howse Pass and the fur trade. Farther north are viewpoints taking in the Weeping Wall, Bridal Veil Falls and Cirrus Mountain.

Many turnouts also serve as trailheads for day hikes to even more panoramas. One of the best: Parker Ridge just south of Banff's northern boundary. The trail leads up to a fantastic vista encompassing a narrow river valley with the Saskatchewan Glacier at one end. In Jasper National Park, you can enjoy amazing views at Wilcox Pass or Tangle Falls right from the parkway, and both Sunwapta and Athabasca falls are just a short drive off the main road. Popular viewpoints are Stutfield Glacier and Athabasca Pass, where interpretive panels explain the national importance of this remote location.

Note: Drivers should be alert for slow or stopped vehicles and animals. Snow tires or chains are mandatory in winter; check 511 Alberta for weather and road conditions. **Cost:** Parkway free; drivers must pay the national park entrance fee regardless of whether they stop inside the park. **Phone:** (780) 852-6176.

JOHNSTON CANYON is 22 km (14 mi.) w. of the town of Banff on the Bow Valley Pkwy. (Hwy. 1A). A gentle uphill hike to one or both of the two waterfalls at this canyon follows a partially-paved pathway through a wooded area along Johnston Creek. Observation points along the way allow for scenic views of the rushing water in the canyon below. At points along the trail, the pathway becomes more of a catwalk that is literally attached to the canyon wall.

The Lower Falls are reached after a hike of about 1.2 kilometres (.75 mi.); the trail continues another 1.2 kilometres (.75 mi.) to the Upper Falls. **Note:** This is a popular trail and the parking lot can become crowded (frequently filling up by 10 a.m.). A Roam shuttle provides transportation between the Banff High School Transit Hub (on Banff Avenue between Elk and Moose streets) and Johnston Canyon late June to mid-Sept. One-way fare (cash only) is $4; $2 (ages 13-18 and 65+).

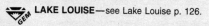 **LAKE LOUISE**—see Lake Louise p. 126.

LAKE MINNEWANKA CRUISE is on Lake Minnewanka, 8 km (5 mi.) n.e. of the town of Banff on Hwy. 1, then n. 4.7 km (2.9 mi.) from the beginning of Lake Minnewanka Scenic Drive. The interpretive sightseeing cruises, in glass-enclosed, heated boats, last 1 hour. Rental motorboats, paddleboats and charter fishing tours also are available. Visitors should arrive

at least 30 minutes prior to departure time. **Hours:** Sightseeing cruises depart daily on the hour 10-6, early June to mid-Sept.; Mon.-Thurs. at 11, 1, 3, and 5, Fri.-Sun. on the hour 10-5, mid-May to early June; daily on the hour noon-5, mid-Sept. to early Oct. **Cost:** Sightseeing cruise $64; $32 (ages 6-15). **Phone:** (403) 762-6700 or (866) 606-6700. GT

MORAINE LAKE is about 14 km (8.7 mi.) s. of the Lake Louise townsite and about 71 km (44 mi.) n.w. of the town of Banff. Though roughly half the size of better-known nearby Lake Louise, many believe blue-green Moraine Lake is equally as beautiful. Known as "the jewel of the Rockies," the lake is in the Valley of the Ten Peaks, which provides the ten saw-toothed ridges that rise dramatically from the lakeshore. A number of hikes begin at the lake. A short trek to the top of a rockslide leads to panoramic views of the lake and valley. Canoe rentals are available in summer, and cross-country skiing can be enjoyed in winter.

Note: Due to the risk of avalanches, the road to Moraine Lake is closed from early fall to late spring. The precise dates vary depending on weather conditions. Some trails may not be available in summer; phone ahead for current trail information. **Phone:** (403) 522-3833 for the Lake Louise Visitor Information Centre.

RECREATIONAL ACTIVITIES
Skiing
- **Sunshine Village Ski Resort** is just off Sunshine Road, 20 km (12.4 mi.) w. of the town of Banff via Hwy. 1. Other activities are offered. **Hours:** Daily 8-5:30, early Nov.-late May. **Phone:** (403) 705-4000 or (877) 542-2633.

BANFF (H-4) pop. 7,584
- Hotels p. 37 • Restaurants p. 39
- Hotels & Restaurants map & index p. 35
- Part of Banff National Park area — see map p. 30

BANFF GONDOLA is at 1 Mountain Ave. An enclosed gondola journeys along the eastern slope of Sulphur Mountain. The lift rises 698 metres (2,290 ft.) from the 1,583-metre (5,194 ft.) level to the 2,281-metre (7,484 ft.) summit ridge in 8 minutes. The Summit Complex includes observation decks offering stunning panoramic views, an interpretive center with natural and cultural history exhibits and a multisensory theater that treats audiences to a thrilling flight over the surrounding mountains by simulating an eagle's point of view. A boardwalk affords more 360-degree vistas and leads to a historic cosmic ray station and weather observatory.

Time: Allow 1 hour, 30 minutes minimum. **Hours:** Daily 8 a.m.-10:30 p.m., mid-May through Sept. 2; 8 a.m.-9:30 p.m., Sept. 3 to mid-Oct.; Wed.-Sun. 10 a.m.-8:30 p.m., Mon.-Tues. 10-4:30, mid-Oct. to mid-Dec.; daily 10 a.m.-8:30, mid-Dec. through Dec. 31. Last ride up 30 minutes prior to closing, and last ride down at closing. **Cost:** Round-trip fare $43-$69;

(See map & index p. 35.)

$21.50-$34.50 (ages 6-15). **Phone:** (403) 762-2523.
⊺⊺

SAVE **BANFF UPPER HOT SPRINGS** is 4 km (2.5 mi.) s. via Mountain Ave. Natural hot springs feed this bathing pool with temperatures ranging between 34 C (93 F) and 42 C (108 F). A day spa is on the premises. Swimsuit, towel and locker rentals are available. **Time:** Allow 1 hour minimum. **Hours:** Daily 9 a.m.-11 p.m., mid-May to mid-Oct.; Sun.-Thurs. 10-10 (also Fri.-Sat. 10-11 p.m.), rest of year. Phone ahead to confirm schedule. **Cost:** $8.30; $7.30 (ages 65+); $6.30 (ages 3-17); $24.50 (family, two adults and two children, $3.40 for each additional child). **Phone:** (403) 762-1515 or (800) 767-1611. ⊺⊺

BREWSTER SIGHTSEEING departs from several area hotels. Guides discuss local history during the 4.5-hour Explore Banff tour, which offers views of wildlife and such points of interest as the Banff Gondola and the Lake Minnewanka Cruise. A variety of full- and half-day narrated excursions of and from Banff to Lake Louise, the Columbia Icefield and Jasper also are offered. **Hours:** Tours are offered daily, early May to mid-Oct. Departure times vary; phone ahead. **Cost:** Explore Banff tour from $135; $68 (ages 6-15). **Phone:** (403) 762-6700 or (866) 606-6700. GT

BUFFALO NATIONS LUXTON MUSEUM is just w. of Banff Ave. at 1 Birch Ave. This log-fort museum re-creates the era when Europeans first arrived on the Plains to find a culture rich in ceremonies, songs and legends. Arts, crafts, dioramas and displays showcase the historical journey of the Northern Plains people, their culture and the flora and fauna of the surrounding area.

Time: Allow 30 minutes minimum. **Hours:** Daily 10-7, May-Sept.; 11-5, rest of year. Closed Christmas. Phone ahead to confirm schedule. **Cost:** $10; $9 (ages 65+); $5 (ages 7-17). **Phone:** (403) 762-2388. GT

CAVE AND BASIN NATIONAL HISTORIC SITE is at 311 Cave Ave. The beginnings of Canada's national park system are founded on a cave and hot springs discovered in 1883 by three Canadian Pacific Railway workers. Disputes over the ownership of the area prompted the Canadian government to declare the area a national reserve 2 years later. The site consists of naturally occurring warm mineral springs inside the cave and an emerald-colored basin outside. A four-screen high-definition film presents the history of the springs and the development of Banff National Park and the Canadian national park system. Exhibits and interpretive trails also are offered.

Time: Allow 1 hour minimum. **Hours:** Daily 9-5, May 15-Oct. 15; Wed.-Sun. 11-5, rest of year. Guided tours are given daily at 11 and 2:30, mid-May to early Sept. Closed Jan. 1, Christmas and day after Christmas. **Cost:** $3.90; $3.40 (ages 65+); free (ages 0-17). **Phone:** (403) 762-1566. GT

DISCOVER BANFF TOURS is at 215 Banff Ave. in the Sundance Mall. Passengers also are picked up at area hotels. Various year-round guided tours are offered, including ice walks, snowshoe treks, dog sled trips, sleigh rides, mountain hikes, wildlife safaris, horseback riding and white-water rafting. Some tours include lunch. Self-guiding tours also are available.

Inquire about cancellation policies. Allow 2-9 hours minimum, depending on tour. **Hours:** Tours depart daily (weather permitting) 8:30-6:30. Tour times vary; phone ahead. **Cost:** Fees vary, depending on activity. **Phone:** (403) 760-5007 or (877) 565-9372. GT

ROCKY MOUNTAIN RAFT TOURS has a launch point meeting area below Bow Falls on Golf Course Loop Rd. Tickets are available at a kiosk at the launch point. Scenic 1-hour Hoodoo Tours and 2.5-hour Bow River Safari guided raft tours travel the Bow Valley below Tunnel and Rundle mountains. Both tours end with a bus ride back to base. The River Safari also includes a 20-minute forest hike. **Hours:** Hoodoo Tours depart daily at 9:20, 11:20, 1:20, 3:20 and 5:20, mid-May to late Sept. Bow River Safaris depart daily at 3:30, June 1-late Aug. (weather permitting). Phone ahead to confirm schedule. **Cost:** Hoodoo Tour $60; $20 (ages 2-15). Bow River Safari $90.48; $38.10 (ages 4-15). Reservations are required. **Phone:** (403) 762-3632. GT

SAVE **WHYTE MUSEUM OF THE CANADIAN ROCKIES**, 111 Bear St., presents the heritage of the region through galleries exhibiting cultural and natural history displays and historic and contemporary artwork. Museum interpreters also guide visitors through two historic houses on-site, including the former residence of the museum's founders, Peter and Catharine Whyte.

Time: Allow 30 minutes minimum. **Hours:** Museum daily 10-5. Archives and library Tues.-Fri. 1-5; otherwise by appointment. Heritage Homes Tours at 11:30, June-Aug.; by appointment, rest of year. Closed Jan. 1, Christmas Eve, Christmas and day after Christmas. Phone ahead to confirm schedule. **Cost:** $10; $9 (ages 65+); $5 (students with ID); free (ages 0-12). **Phone:** (403) 762-2291. GT

🔗 **AAA.com/campgrounds**—For overnights under the stars

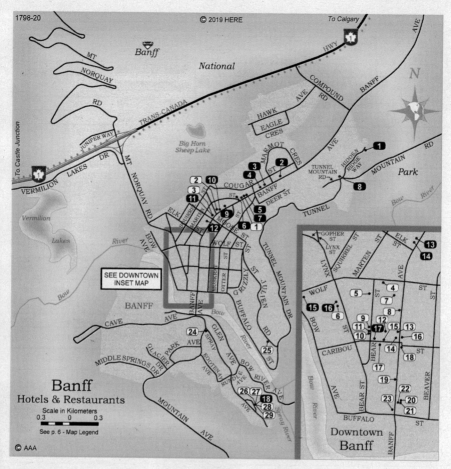

Banff
Hotels & Restaurants

Scale in Kilometers
0.3   0   0.3
See p. 6 - Map Legend

Banff

This index helps you "spot" where hotels and restaurants are located on the corresponding detailed maps. Restaurant price range is a combination of lunch and/or dinner. Turn to the listing page for more information and consult display ads for special promotions.

For more details, rates and reservations: AAA.com/travelguides/hotels

BANFF

Map Page	Hotels	Designation	Member Savings	Page
1 this page	Hidden Ridge Resort	THREE DIAMOND		38
2 this page	Rundlestone Lodge	APPROVED		39
3 this page	Banff Caribou Lodge	THREE DIAMOND		37
4 this page	Charlton's Banff (See ad p. 37.)	THREE DIAMOND		37
5 this page	Royal Canadian Lodge Banff (See ad p. 38.)	THREE DIAMOND		39
6 this page	**Best Western Plus Siding 29 Lodge**	THREE DIAMOND	✔	37
7 this page	The Fox Hotel & Suites	THREE DIAMOND		38
8 this page	Tunnel Mountain Resort	APPROVED		39
9 this page	Red Carpet Inn	APPROVED		38
10 this page	High Country Inn	THREE DIAMOND		38
11 this page	**Banff Aspen Lodge**	THREE DIAMOND	✔	37
12 this page	Moose Hotel & Suites	THREE DIAMOND		38

BANFF (cont'd)

Map Page	Hotels (cont'd)	Designation	Member Savings	Page
13 p. 35	Banff Ptarmigan Inn	THREE DIAMOND		37
14 p. 35	Elk + Avenue	THREE DIAMOND		38
15 p. 35	Bow View Lodge	APPROVED		37
16 p. 35	Banff Park Lodge Resort Hotel & Conference Centre	THREE DIAMOND		37
17 p. 35	**Brewster's Mountain Lodge**	APPROVED	✔	37
18 p. 35	**Fairmont Banff Springs**	FOUR DIAMOND	✔	38

Map Page	Restaurants	Designation	Cuisine	Price Range	Page
1 p. 35	The Evergreen (See ad p. 38.)	THREE DIAMOND	International	$15-$39	39
2 p. 35	Ticino Swiss-Italian Restaurant	APPROVED	Continental	$17-$32	40
3 p. 35	Whitebark Cafe	APPROVED	Coffee/Tea	$6-$7	40
4 p. 35	St. James's Gate Olde Irish Pub	APPROVED	Irish	$11-$28	40
5 p. 35	The Bear Street Tavern	APPROVED	Pizza	$15-$23	39
6 p. 35	La Terrazza	THREE DIAMOND	Italian	$28-$48	39
7 p. 35	Indian Curry House	APPROVED	Indian	$15-$19	39
8 p. 35	Park Distillery Restaurant + Bar	THREE DIAMOND	New Canadian	$17-$48	40
9 p. 35	Saltlik A Rare Steakhouse	THREE DIAMOND	Steak	$14-$35	40
10 p. 35	Wild Flour Bakery Cafe	APPROVED	Natural/Organic Breads/Pastries	$6-$12	40
11 p. 35	The Bison Restaurant & Terrace	THREE DIAMOND	Regional Canadian	$16-$66	39
12 p. 35	Tooloulou's	APPROVED	Cajun	$10-$42	40
13 p. 35	Nourish Bistro	APPROVED	Vegetarian	$15-$26	40
14 p. 35	Block Kitchen + Bar	APPROVED	Mediterranean Small Plates	$14-$26	39
15 p. 35	Coyotes Southwestern Grill	APPROVED	New Southwestern	$14-$34	39
16 p. 35	Grizzly House	APPROVED	Fondue	$20-$64	39
17 p. 35	The Eddie Burger + Bar	APPROVED	Burgers	$13-$22	39
18 p. 35	The Maple Leaf Grille & Spirits	THREE DIAMOND	Canadian	$16-$32	39
19 p. 35	Elk & Oarsman	APPROVED	Canadian	$18-$30	39
20 p. 35	Tommy's Neighbourhood Pub	APPROVED	American	$7-$13	40
21 p. 35	Banff Ave Brewing Co	APPROVED	American	$16-$36	39
22 p. 35	Balkan The Greek Restaurant	APPROVED	Greek	$11-$38	39
23 p. 35	Chuck's Steakhouse	THREE DIAMOND	Steak	$15-$89	39
24 p. 35	**Silver Dragon Restaurant Banff**	APPROVED	Chinese	$17-$39	40
25 p. 35	Three Ravens Restaurant & Wine Bar	THREE DIAMOND	New Canadian	$30-$56	40
26 p. 35	Rundle Lounge	THREE DIAMOND	International	$17-$35	40
27 p. 35	Waldhaus Restaurant	THREE DIAMOND	German	$35-$50	40
28 p. 35	1888 Chop House	THREE DIAMOND	Steak	$45-$76	39
29 p. 35	**Grapes Wine Bar**	THREE DIAMOND	Small Plates	$30-$47	39

AAA DISCOUNTS»REWARDS

DISCOUNTS WITHOUT LIMITS

AAA.com/discounts

(See map & index p. 35.)

BANFF ASPEN LODGE 403/762-4401 **11**

THREE DIAMOND

Hotel

Address: 401 Banff Ave T1L 1A9 **Location:** Between Moose and Rabbit sts. **Facility:** 89 units. 3 stories, interior/exterior corridors. **Parking:** winter plug-ins. **Amenities:** safes. **Activities:** sauna, hot tub, steamroom. **Guest Services:** valet and coin laundry, area transportation. **Featured Amenity:** breakfast buffet.

[icons]

BANFF CARIBOU LODGE 403/762-5887 **3**
THREE DIAMOND Hotel. **Address:** 521 Banff Ave T1L 1A4

BANFF PARK LODGE RESORT HOTEL & CONFERENCE CENTRE 403/762-4433 **16**
THREE DIAMOND Hotel. **Address:** 222 Lynx St T1L 1K5

BANFF PTARMIGAN INN 403/762-2207 **13**
THREE DIAMOND Hotel. **Address:** 337 Banff Ave T1L 1B1

BANFF ROCKY MOUNTAIN RESORT 403/762-5531
THREE DIAMOND Resort Hotel. **Address:** 1029 Banff Ave T1L 1A2

BEST WESTERN PLUS SIDING 29 LODGE
403/762-5575 **6**

THREE DIAMOND

Hotel

BW Best Western PLUS.

AAA Benefit: Members save up to 15% and earn bonus points!

Address: 453 Marten St T1L 1B3 **Location:** 0.6 mi (1 km) ne, just off Banff Ave. Located in a residential area. **Facility:** 57 units, some kitchens. 3 stories, interior corridors. **Pool:** heated indoor. **Activities:** hot tub. **Guest Services:** valet laundry. **Featured Amenity:** breakfast buffet.

[icons]

BOW VIEW LODGE 403/762-2261 **15**
APPROVED Motel. **Address:** 228 Bow Ave T1L 1A5

BREWSTER'S MOUNTAIN LODGE 403/762-2900 **17**

APPROVED

Boutique Hotel

Address: 208 Caribou St T1L 1C1 **Location:** Just w off Banff Ave; downtown. **Facility:** Perfect to access shopping, dining and the mountains, this hotel has rooms ranging from standard units to spacious lofts all with historic black and white photos and vivid red design blankets. 77 units. 3 stories, interior corridors. **Parking:** on-site (fee). **Terms:** check-in 4 pm. **Amenities:** safes. **Activities:** sauna, exercise room. **Guest Services:** valet and coin laundry. **Featured Amenity: continental breakfast.**

[icons]

CASTLE MOUNTAIN CHALETS 403/762-3868

APPROVED

Cabin

Address: Bow Valley Pkwy (Hwy 1A) & Hwy 93 S T1L 1B5 **Location:** 20 mi (32 km) w on Trans-Canada Hwy 1 to jct Castle Mountain, 0.6 mi (1 km) ne on Hwy 1A (Bow Valley Pkwy). **Facility:** 21 cabins. 2 stories (no elevator), exterior corridors. **Parking:** winter plug-ins. **Terms:** check-in 4 pm. **Activities:** cross country skiing, bicycles, game room, picnic facilities, trails, limited exercise equipment. **Guest Services:** coin laundry.

[icons]

CHARLTON'S BANFF 403/762-4485 **4**

THREE DIAMOND Motel. **Address:** 513 Banff Ave T1L 1B4 *(See ad this page.)*

▼ *See AAA listing this page* ▼

Start a new tradition.

Banff's Alpine Style Boutique property located at the quiet end of Banff Avenue, just a 10 minute walk to downtown.

Deluxe, Loft Suites, Kitchenette & Deluxe Mountain View Guestrooms
Indoor Pool & Hot Tub
Daily Continental Breakfast
Free Parking & Wi-Fi

513 Banff Avenue, Banff, Alberta | charltonresorts.com | 1-800-661-1225

CHARLTONS
banff

(See map & index p. 35.)

ELK + AVENUE   403/762-5666 **14**
THREE DIAMOND Hotel. **Address:** 333 Banff Ave T1L 1B1

FAIRMONT BANFF SPRINGS   403/762-2211 **18**
FOUR DIAMOND

Classic Historic
Resort Hotel

Address: 405 Spray Ave T1L 1J4 **Location:** Just s on Banff Ave over the bridge, 0.3 mi (0.5 km) e. **Facility:** There are many impressive public areas to explore at this iconic jewel, which brings to mind a magnificent castle. Guest rooms range from upscale, compact units to extravagant suites. 757 units. 3-9 stories, interior corridors. **Parking:** on-site (fee) and valet, winter plug-ins. **Terms:** check-in 4 pm. **Amenities:** safes. **Dining:** 6 restaurants, also, 1888 Chop House, Grapes Wine Bar, Rundle Lounge, Waldhaus Restaurant, see separate listings. **Pool:** heated outdoor, heated indoor. **Activities:** sauna, hot tub, steamroom, regulation golf, tennis, cross country skiing, sledding, ice skating, recreation programs, kids club, bicycles, playground, game room, lawn sports, trails, health club, spa. **Guest Services:** valet laundry, rental car service.

THE FOX HOTEL & SUITES   403/760-8500 **7**
THREE DIAMOND Hotel. **Address:** 461 Banff Ave T1L 1B1

HIDDEN RIDGE RESORT   403/762-3544 **1**
THREE DIAMOND Condominium. **Address:** 901 Hidden Ridge Way T1L 1B7

HIGH COUNTRY INN   403/762-2236 **10**
THREE DIAMOND Hotel. **Address:** 419 Banff Ave T1L 1A7

JOHNSTON CANYON RESORT   403/762-2971
APPROVED

Historic Cabin

Address: Hwy 1A T1L 1A9 **Location:** 15 mi (24 km) nw on Hwy 1A (Bow Valley Pkwy). Located at Johnston Canyon. **Facility:** This 1927 property is at the base of the trail to the iconic Johnston Canyon waterfalls and Ink Pots. The rustic yet charming wood cabins have a variety of décors and comfort levels. 42 cabins, some efficiencies. 1 story, exterior corridors. **Terms:** check-in 4 pm. **Dining:** 2 restaurants. **Activities:** tennis, picnic facilities, trails. **Featured Amenity:** continental breakfast.

7 spectacular waterfalls.
Scenic & wildlife photo opportunities.
All located at your doorstep.

MOOSE HOTEL & SUITES   403/760-8570 **12**
THREE DIAMOND Contemporary Hotel. **Address:** 345 Banff Ave T1L 1H8

RED CARPET INN   403/762-4184 **9**
APPROVED Hotel. **Address:** 425 Banff Ave T1L 1B6

▼ See AAA listing p. 39 ▼

ROYAL CANADIAN LODGE BANFF

- A modern mountain lodge located a short walk from Banff's vibrant downtown.
- 99 Guestrooms, featuring Premier Fireplace rooms and Deluxe Junior suites.
- Amenities in all guestrooms include bathrobes, large TVs, free WIFI, coffee makers, kettles and in-room safety deposit boxes.
- Relax in the Grotto Pool and Spa featuring a pool and hot tub and fitness area.
- Massage therapy and body treatments available by appointment.
- Our Evergreen Restaurant and Lounge is on-site and open daily for breakfast, lunch and dinner.

ROYAL CANADIAN LODGE
Banff

459 Banff Avenue, Banff, Alberta • www.royalcanadianlodge.com • 1-800-661-1379

Save on travel, shopping and more:
AAA.com/discounts

(See map & index p. 35.)

THE RIMROCK RESORT HOTEL   403/762-3356

WW FOUR DIAMOND   **Address:** 300 Mountain Ave T1L 1J2
Resort Hotel   **Location:** 2.4 mi (4 km) s via Sulphur Mountain Rd; adjacent to Upper Hot Springs Pool. Located in a quiet secluded area. **Facility:** This luxury hotel is literally built on the slope of a mountain. Upscale rooms have two comfy armchairs and you'll find the best views on the highest floors. 343 units. 9 stories, interior corridors. **Parking:** on-site (fee) and valet, winter plug-ins. **Terms:** check-in 4 pm. **Amenities:** safes. **Dining:** 2 restaurants, also, Eden, see separate listing. **Pool:** heated indoor. **Activities:** sauna, hot tub, steamroom, cross country skiing, ice skating, bicycles, trails, health club, spa. **Guest Services:** valet laundry, area transportation. **Featured Amenity:** full hot breakfast.

ROYAL CANADIAN LODGE BANFF   403/762-3307 **5**

WW THREE DIAMOND Boutique Hotel. **Address:** 459 Banff Ave T1L 1B4 *(See ad p. 38.)*

RUNDLESTONE LODGE   403/762-2201 **2**

WW APPROVED Hotel. **Address:** 537 Banff Ave T1L 1A6

SUNSHINE MOUNTAIN LODGE   403/762-6500

WW THREE DIAMOND   **Address:** 1 Sunshine Access Rd T1L
Resort Hotel   1J5 **Location:** 4.2 mi (7 km) w on Trans-Canada Hwy 1 exit Sunshine Village, 4.2 mi (7 km) s. **Facility:** Leave the stress behind in the car and ride the gondola to this first-class hotel while the staff takes care of your luggage. Some of these attractive, cozy rooms have jetted tubs, balconies or lofts. 84 units. 2-5 stories, interior corridors. **Terms:** check-in 4 pm. **Dining:** 4 restaurants. **Activities:** sauna, hot tub, downhill & cross country skiing, snowboarding, sledding, recreation programs in season, trails, exercise room, spa. **Guest Services:** valet laundry, area transportation.

TUNNEL MOUNTAIN RESORT   403/762-4515 **8**

WW APPROVED Condominium. **Address:** 502 Tunnel Mountain Rd T1L 1B1

WHERE TO EAT

1888 CHOP HOUSE   403/762-6860 **28**
WW THREE DIAMOND Steak. Fine Dining. **Address:** 405 Spray Ave T1L 1J4

BALKAN THE GREEK RESTAURANT   403/762-3454 **22**
WW APPROVED Greek. Casual Dining. **Address:** 120 Banff Ave T1L 1A4

BANFF AVE BREWING CO   403/762-1003 **21**
WW APPROVED American. Gastropub. **Address:** 110 Banff Ave T1L 1C9

THE BEAR STREET TAVERN   403/762-2021 **5**
WW APPROVED Pizza. Gastropub. **Address:** 211 Bear St T1L 1E4

THE BISON RESTAURANT & TERRACE   403/762-5550 **11**
WW THREE DIAMOND Regional Canadian. Casual Dining. **Address:** 211 Bear St T1L 1E4

BLOCK KITCHEN + BAR   403/985-2887 **14**
WW APPROVED Mediterranean Small Plates. Casual Dining. **Address:** 201 Banff Ave T1L 1C6

CHUCK'S STEAKHOUSE   403/762-4825 **23**
WW THREE DIAMOND Steak. Casual Dining. **Address:** 101 Banff Ave T1L 1B3

COYOTES SOUTHWESTERN GRILL   403/762-3963 **15**
WW APPROVED New Southwestern. Casual Dining. **Address:** 206 Caribou St T1L 1A2

THE EDDIE BURGER + BAR   403/762-2230 **17**
WW APPROVED Burgers. Casual Dining. **Address:** 137 Banff Ave, #6 T1L 1B7

EDEN   403/762-3356

WW FIVE DIAMOND   **AAA Inspector Notes:** A touch of something magical is in the air here
New French Fine Dining $85-$215   where tastes, textures, creativity and imagination mingle to produce an exquisite meal. Hours will pass unnoticed as you unwind in comfy chairs, gazing out at the spectacular Rocky Mountains. Professional and engaging servers provide knowledgeable service with an impressive food delivery where entrées arrive in a perfectly synchronized fashion. An à la carte menu (minimum three courses) and tasting menus, including a vegetarian option, are offered. **Features:** full bar. **Reservations:** suggested. **Address:** 300 Mountain Ave T1L 1J2 **Location:** 2.4 mi (4 km) s via Sulphur Mountain Rd; adjacent to Upper Hot Springs Pool; in The Rimrock Resort Hotel. **Parking:** on-site and valet.

ELK & OARSMAN   403/762-4616 **19**
WW APPROVED Canadian. Gastropub. **Address:** 119 Banff Ave T1L 1B6

THE EVERGREEN   403/762-3307 **1**
WW THREE DIAMOND International. Fine Dining. **Address:** 459 Banff Ave T1L 1B4 *(See ad p. 38.)*

GRAPES WINE BAR   403/762-6860 **29**

WW THREE DIAMOND   **AAA Inspector Notes:** A carved grape ceiling trim dating from 1926 was uncov-
Small Plates Casual Dining $30-$47   ered in the 1980s and thus this intimate, upscale wine bar was born. It features dark wood, stonework, stained glass and mountain views. Delicious housemade charcuterie, pâté and an array of candied nuts, pickles and chutneys along with artisan bread and cheese form the backbone of the menu. The cheese fondue is a crowd favorite. **Features:** full bar. **Address:** 405 Spray Ave T1L 1J4 **Location:** Just s on Banff Ave over the bridge, 0.3 mi (0.5 km) e; in Fairmont Banff Springs. **Parking:** on-site and valet.

GRIZZLY HOUSE   403/762-4055 **16**
WW APPROVED Fondue. Casual Dining. **Address:** 207 Banff Ave T1L 1B4

INDIAN CURRY HOUSE   587/222-8779 **7**
WW APPROVED Indian. Casual Dining. **Address:** 225 Banff Ave T1L 1A2

LA TERRAZZA   403/760-3271 **6**
WW THREE DIAMOND Italian. Fine Dining. **Address:** 222 Lynx St T1L 1K5

THE MAPLE LEAF GRILLE & SPIRITS   403/760-7680 **18**
WW THREE DIAMOND Canadian. Casual Dining. **Address:** 137 Banff Ave T1L 1C8

(See map & index p. 35.)

NOURISH BISTRO   403/760-3933   (13)
APPROVED   Vegetarian. Casual Dining. **Address:** 211 Banff Ave T1L 1B4

PARK DISTILLERY RESTAURANT + BAR   403/762-5114   (8)
THREE DIAMOND   New Canadian. Casual Dining. **Address:** 219 Banff Ave T1L 1A7

RUNDLE LOUNGE   403/762-6860   (26)
THREE DIAMOND   International. Casual Dining. **Address:** 405 Spray Ave T1L 1J4

ST. JAMES'S GATE OLDE IRISH PUB   403/762-9355   (4)
APPROVED   Irish. Casual Dining. **Address:** 207 Wolf St T1L 1C2

SALTLIK A RARE STEAKHOUSE   403/762-2467   (9)
THREE DIAMOND   Steak. Casual Dining. **Address:** 221 Bear St T1L 1B3

SILVER DRAGON RESTAURANT BANFF
       403/762-3939   (24)

APPROVED
Chinese
Casual Dining
$17-$39

AAA Inspector Notes: For those who crave Chinese food, there is an extensive variety of classic dishes including ginger beef and Peking duck. It is freshly prepared and served piping hot. Mountain views from the wide expanse of windows is an added bonus of the spacious, open dining room, which sports giant red hanging paper lanterns. **Features:** full bar. **Reservations:** suggested. **Address:** 109 Spray Ave T1L 1C4 **Location:** Just se of Banff Ave bridge.

L   D   CALL

THREE RAVENS RESTAURANT & WINE BAR
       403/762-6300   (25)
THREE DIAMOND   New Canadian. Casual Dining. **Address:** 107 Tunnel Mountain Dr T1L 1G7

TICINO SWISS-ITALIAN RESTAURANT   403/762-3848   (2)
APPROVED   Continental. Casual Dining. **Address:** 415 Banff Ave T1L 1B5

TOMMY'S NEIGHBOURHOOD PUB   403/762-8888   (20)
APPROVED   American. Casual Dining. **Address:** 120 Banff Ave T1L 1A4

TOOLOULOU'S   403/762-2633   (12)
APPROVED   Cajun. Casual Dining. **Address:** 204 Caribou St T1L 1A6

WALDHAUS RESTAURANT   403/762-6860   (27)
THREE DIAMOND   German. Casual Dining. **Address:** 405 Spray Ave T1L 1J4

WHITEBARK CAFE   403/760-7298   (3)
APPROVED   Coffee/Tea. Quick Serve. **Address:** 401 Banff Ave T1L 1A9

WILD FLOUR BAKERY CAFE   403/760-5074   (10)
APPROVED   Natural/Organic Breads/Pastries. Quick Serve. **Address:** 211 Bear St, #101 T1L 1E8

🔗 **For complete hotel, dining and attraction listings:**

AAA.com/travelguides

BEAVERLODGE (C-1) pop. 2,365

First settled in 1908, Beaverlodge derives its name from the Beaver First Nation who made their temporary home, or lodge, in the area. With the arrival of the railway in 1928, a new townsite was created about 1.6 kilometres (1 mi.) northwest of the original hamlet; many original buildings were moved. In the Beaverlodge Valley, the town serves as a gateway to Monkman Pass and is a large agricultural center.

Beaverlodge & District Chamber of Commerce: 508 5th Ave., P.O. Box 303, Beaverlodge, AB, Canada T0H 0C0. **Phone:** (780) 354-8785.

SOUTH PEACE CENTENNIAL MUSEUM AND INTERPRETIVE CENTER is 3 km (1.9 mi.) n.w. on Hwy. 43. With an emphasis on fully restored antique tractors, cars and trucks, the 16-hectare (40-acre) site displays pioneer items, equipment and furnishings used in the early 1900s. A 1928 pioneer house is furnished in period. Other exhibits include a trading post, a general store, a flour mill, a schoolhouse, an Anglican church and a railway caboose. Antique steam engines are fired up for the Pioneer Days festival in mid-July. **Hours:** Daily 10-6, mid-May to late Sept. **Cost:** $5; free (ages 0-6). Cash only. **Phone:** (780) 354-8869.

BONNYVILLE pop. 6,216

BEST WESTERN BONNYVILLE INN & SUITES
       780/826-6226
THREE DIAMOND
Hotel

Best Western   **AAA Benefit:** Members save up to 15% and earn bonus points!

Address: 5401 43rd St T9N 0H3 **Location:** Hwy 28, just n at 44th St. **Facility:** 94 units. 4 stories, interior corridors. **Parking:** winter plug-ins. **Terms:** check-in 4 pm. **Activities:** game room, picnic facilities, exercise room. **Guest Services:** valet and coin laundry.

SAVE   🚭   🍴   CALL   👔   BIZ
📶   ✉   🔲   🖥   📄
/ SOME UNITS   🐾

COMFORT INN & SUITES BONNYVILLE   780/826-2020
THREE DIAMOND   Hotel. **Address:** 5404 Lakeland Rd T9N 0B2

MICROTEL INN & SUITES BY WYNDHAM BONNYVILLE
       780/687-2120
APPROVED   Hotel. **Address:** 5409 Lakeland Rd T9N 0E7

WHERE TO EAT

JENNIE'S DINER & BAKERY   780/826-1956
APPROVED   American Comfort Food. Casual Dining. **Address:** 5101 51st St T9N 2B1

MR MIKES STEAKHOUSECASUAL   780/826-3393
APPROVED   American. Casual Dining. **Address:** 5306 50 Ave T9N 1Y4

BROOKS pop. 13,676

Brooks is surrounded by 105,222 hectares (260,000 acres) of irrigated farmland and more than 404,700 hectares (1 million acres) of rangeland used for cattle grazing. This semiarid shortgrass section of the province is the setting for wildlife and horticultural research centers.

Brooks Visitor Information Centre: 568 Sutherland Dr. E., Brooks, AB, Canada T1R 1C7. **Phone:** (403) 362-5073.

DINOSAUR PROVINCIAL PARK—see Patricia p. 134.

HERITAGE INN & SUITES BROOKS   403/362-8688
THREE DIAMOND Hotel. **Address:** 1239 2nd St W T1R 1P7

HERITAGE INN HOTEL & CONVENTION CENTRE BROOKS
                                        403/362-6666
APPROVED   Hotel. **Address:** 1217 2nd St W T1R 1P7

RAMADA BROOKS   403/362-6440
THREE DIAMOND Hotel. **Address:** 1319 2nd St W T1R 1P7

WHERE TO EAT

INDIAN PAN FLAME   403/501-0045
APPROVED   Indian. Casual Dining. **Address:** 1131 2nd St T1R 0N9

iStockphoto.com_LeoPatrizi

Expert Travel Insight

Make a good trip great with insight from AAA's travel experts. Use their recommended picks and itineraries to find best places to go, stay, dine and play.

Photo source iStockphoto.com

 Get AAA travel information at club offices and on AAA.com for experiences you'll remember for a lifetime.

Calgary

Then & Now

Calgary, once considered a cow town, now is one of Canada's fastest-growing cities, with skyscrapers, light-rail transit, shopping complexes, restaurants and a $245-million library said to be one of the world's most futuristic. The city's economy began with—and still includes—ranching and the subsequent meatpacking industry, but the discovery of oil just south of the city in 1914 and just north in 1947 fueled a spurt of growth that turned an agricultural community into a metropolis.

Calgary today boasts a high concentration of corporate head offices, the highest in Canada. Energy, technology, agriculture, manufacturing and tourism comprise Calgary's industrial base.

The city's modern skyline, jagged with skyscrapers, makes a dramatic appearance on the vast expanse of Alberta prairie. To the west, almost mirroring Calgary's silhouette, are the Canadian Rockies, jutting into the sky just over an hour's drive away and a popular place for those in search of adventure travel. The Trans-Canada Highway, a major national east-west roadway, runs through the heart of the city; in Calgary the highway also is known as 16th Avenue N.W.

AAA.com/travelguides—
more ways to look, book and save

The region's history of human habitation began almost 10,000 years before the first 19th-century fur and whiskey traders arrived. First Nations tribes chose the confluence of the Bow and Elbow rivers as a campsite; emerging as the dominant tribe was the Blackfoot. Their acquisition of horses allowed them to hunt buffalo and fight almost every other prairie tribe with great success. As European settlement increased, so did friction between natives and newcomers.

An 1877 treaty calmed the rough waters, and relative peace among all factions has existed since. Several reservations, including the Tsuu T'ina Reserve south of the city, are near Calgary. Native North Americans have sought to assimilate themselves into Canadian culture while retaining their native heritage.

Chinese were recruited abroad in the late 1800s to build railroads; once the trains were running, however, immigration was restricted. Oil and money lured Americans who brought technology and investment funds needed to get Calgary's petroleum industry started. But many of those who came for the money enjoyed the area and stayed, becoming Canadian citizens.

Calgary's modern sophistication is offset by a romantic perception of the past—a past in which the city was established as a North West Mounted Police

Calgary skyline

(Continued on p. 44.)

Destination Calgary

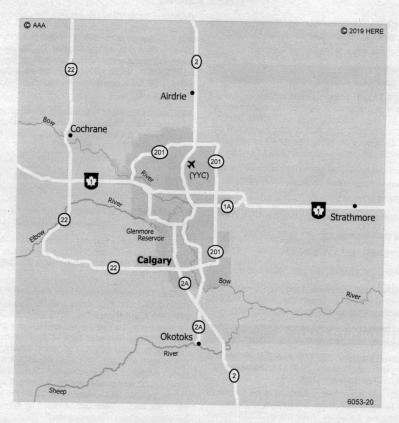

This map shows cities in the Calgary vicinity where you will find attractions, hotels and restaurants. Cities are listed alphabetically in this book on the following pages.

Fast Facts

ABOUT THE CITY

POP: 1,096,833 ▪ **ELEV:** 1,048 m/3,440 ft.

MONEY

SALES TAX: The federal Goods and Service Tax is 5 percent and applies to most goods, food/beverages and services, including lodgings. Alberta does not have a provincial sales tax but does impose a 3 percent Destination Marketing Fee (DMF) as well as a 4 percent Municipal and Regional District Tax (MRDT).

WHOM TO CALL

EMERGENCY: 911

POLICE (non-emergency): (403) 266-1234

FIRE (non-emergency): 311

TEMPERATURE: (403) 299-7878

ROAD CONDITIONS: (877) 262-4997 or 511

HOSPITALS: Foothills Medical Centre, (403) 944-1110 ▪ Peter Lougheed Centre, (403) 943-4555 ▪ Rockyview General Hospital, (403) 943-3000.

VISITOR INFORMATION

Tourism Calgary: 238 11th Ave. S.E., Room 200, Calgary, AB, Canada T2G 0X8. **Phone:** (403) 263-8510 or (800) 661-1678.

Visitor information also is available at the Calgary International Airport on the arrivals level and downtown at the base of Calgary Tower and at TELUS Convention Centre.

TRANSPORTATION

AIR TRAVEL: Calgary International Airport (YYC) is northeast of downtown off Hwy. 2 exit 266. Cheap airline flights are available from many airline carriers and travel sites. Check with your local AAA office to book flights and vacation packages.

Public bus transportation to and from the airport is offered by Calgary Transit via Route 300, with service to and from downtown for $10.75; airport fare includes all-day access to buses and CTrains. Taxi service between the airport and downtown destinations typically costs $40-$45. Sedan service to or from the airport is $48-$54.75. Some hotels also offer free shuttle service for their guests.

RENTAL CARS: Hertz, with multiple downtown locations and one at Calgary International Airport, offers discounts to CAA and AAA members; phone (403) 221-1676 or (800) 654-3131.

 Book and save at **AAA.com/hertz**

RAIL SERVICE: The nearest VIA Rail stations are in Jasper and Edmonton; phone (888) 842-7245.

BUSES: Red Arrow Express operates luxury motor coaches between Calgary, Red Deer, Edmonton, Fort McMurray and Lethbridge; phone (403) 531-0350 or (800) 232-1958.

TAXIS: Taxi companies include Associated Cab, (403) 299-1111 ▪ Checker Yellow Cab, (403) 299-9999 ▪ and Mayfair Taxi, (403) 255-6555. Allied Limousine provides town car and limo service ▪ phone (403) 299-9555. Taxi rates begin at $3.80 for the first 120 metres (about .074 mi.) or portion thereof, plus 20c for each additional 120 metres (about .074 mi.) or portion thereof (unless departing from Calgary International Airport, where rates are $8.30 for the first 120 metres, then 20c for each additional 120 metres with a $4.50 surcharge). Cabs can be hailed on the street, but phoning ahead is recommended.

PUBLIC TRANSPORTATION: Calgary has both bus and light-rail transit (LRT) service; the latter, known as the CTrain, is free in the downtown core between 3rd Street S.E. and 11th Street S.W. Calgary Transit's office, 125 7th Ave. S.E., has schedules and maps and sells transit passes. Fare is $3.40; $2.35 (ages 6-17). A 1-day pass is $10.75; $7.75 (ages 6-17). Phone (403) 262-1000.

(Continued from p. 42.)

fort in 1875. The Calgary Stampede, a 10-day Western wingding, is attended by more than a million residents and visitors every July who relive the days of chuck wagons and lassos. Those days existed more than a century ago, after the North West Mounted Police—the forerunner of today's Royal Canadian Mounted Police—and the railroad brought law, order and homesteaders to a region previously settled by trappers, buffalo hunters and whiskey traders.

Although Calgary's growth has been rapid, it has been practical. The downtown district was designed to accommodate a large amount of activity, even

during winter. A system of enclosed walkways called the "Plus 15" (since the walkways are 15 feet above street level) connects almost half the downtown buildings, making it possible to eat, work and shop without ever having to put on a coat.

The Stephen Avenue Walk, a pedestrian mall in the city center lined with late 19th- and early 20th-century buildings, is an urban refuge from traffic as well as a nice place to people watch in warm weather. It's pedestrian only from 6 a.m. to 6 p.m.

Nearby is Olympic Plaza, the site of the awards ceremonies during the 15th Olympic Winter Games, held in Calgary in 1988, and now a popular venue for events and festivals.

Must Do: AAA Editor's Picks

- Zip to the top of the **Calgary Tower** (101 9th Ave. S.W.) via high-speed elevator to take in a fantastic 360-degree view of the city, a great way to get your bearings. Built to commemorate Canada's centennial, the tower has been a distinctive city landmark since 1968.

- Pull on a pair of cowboy boots and celebrate all things wild and western during the **Calgary Stampede,** a rodeo-centered event attended by more than a million people. For 10 days each July, the Stampede puts on a tremendous show that not only includes barrel racing, bull riding and chuck wagon races, but also fireworks, parades, a carnival midway and a huge outdoor music festival.

- Walk in the footsteps of Olympic greats from the 1988 Winter Games at **Canada Olympic Park** (88 Canada Olympic Rd. S.W.), a year-round destination for sports offering a zipline and bobsleigh runs in summer and skiing, snowboarding and tubing in winter.

- Hop aboard a steam train or ride in a horse-drawn wagon as you explore nearly a century's worth of local history at **Heritage Park Historical Village** (1900 Heritage Dr. S.W.). You'll get a feel for life in the isolated prairie settlement that Calgary once was when you tour the historic buildings relocated to the park, chat with the costumed "townspeople" and find other fun things to do.

- Listen to birdsong as you wander through the **Inglewood Bird Sanctuary** (2425 9th Ave. S.E.), a lovely bit of wooded parkland just minutes from downtown Calgary. And once your inner peace has been restored, explore nearby Inglewood, one of the city's oldest neighborhoods. It's a place known for boutiques, art galleries, antique stores and local restaurants, especially along 9th Avenue S.E.

- At **TELUS Spark** (220 St. George's Dr. N.E.), get answers to such weighty questions as: What does it mean to be human? What natural forces have shaped our world? How can we harness energy for our use? The state-of-the-art science center is filled with high-tech displays that engage both children and adults. The two-level building houses exhibit galleries, the HD Dome Theatre, learning labs, an interactive kids museum and more. The outdoor Brainasium, a .4-hectare (1-acre) park, teaches young visitors about gravity and acoustics.

- Discover the bravery of Canada's heroes at **The Military Museums** (4520 Crowchild Tr. S.W.), showcasing the nation's army, navy and air force as well as four army regiments. Tanks and a fighter jet seem poised for battle outside the museum, while inside dramatic dioramas and displays of weaponry, medals and photographs bring Canada's military history to life.

- Flip, fly and fall courtesy of thrill rides at **Calaway Park** (245033 Range Rd. 33), where the amusements range from tame to terrifying. The Adrenaline Test Zone, Chaos and the Vortex roller coaster are in the latter group, but there are plenty of rides designed for smaller children as well. Plus, with various carnival games on-site, the whole family can compete for plush prizes—and glory. The park also offers a miniature golf course, live shows and a 3-D theater.

- Take a trip back through time to the age of the dinosaurs at the **Calgary Zoo, Botanical Garden & Prehistoric Park** (1300 Zoo Rd. N.E.), home to a collection of fierce-looking dinosaur replicas, to say nothing of the even more impressive collection of living, breathing animals from all over the world. Such creatures as gentoo penguins, grizzly bears, cougars, bison, mountain goats and wolves thrive within re-created habitats.

- Imagine rubbing elbows with one of 19th-century Calgary's wealthiest and most influential families when you enter **Lougheed House** (707 13th Ave. S.W.), their imposing sandstone mansion. Stroll through the formal gardens and you'll understand why the estate was named Beaulieu, French for "beautiful place."

Inglewood Bird Sanctuary

Calgary 1-day Itinerary

AAA editors suggest these activities for a great short vacation experience.

Morning

- Start your day out and about in Calgary with breakfast at **Diner Deluxe** (804 Edmonton Tr. N.E.). This fun, 1950s retro-cool eatery serves classic eggs-and-toast breakfasts along with French toast stuffed with Gouda and Canadian bacon and a French-Canadian twist on hash browns involving cheese curds and hollandaise sauce.

- Diner Deluxe makes a good starting point not just for the hearty food or the mid-century modern ambience but also because it's just a few minutes from the 🐾 **Calgary Zoo, Botanical Garden & Prehistoric Park** (1300 Zoo Rd. N.E.).

- You'll want to spend a few hours exploring the zoo's carefully designed animal enclosures and exhibits. Learn about grizzly bears and wolves in the zoo's Canadian Wilds section, check out the life-size dinosaur models in Prehistoric Park and witness four species of penguins waddling and shaking their tail feathers in an indoor-outdoor exhibit called Penguin Plunge.

- Daily zoo activities offer plenty to keep you busy, with zookeeper talks, animal training sessions, nature walks and daily meet and greets with zoo residents. If you're traveling with kids in Calgary, don't miss the storytime presentations and the game-filled activity center.

Afternoon

- Cross the river into Inglewood for an afternoon exploring one of Calgary's oldest neighborhoods. Independent shops line both sides of Inglewood's main street (9th Avenue S.E.), with women's clothing boutiques, spice and tea shops, a surplus store, a vinyl record shop and other unique places that are fun to browse. If you like art, pop into **Esker Foundation** (1011 9th Ave. S.E.) and check out their latest collection of thought-provoking contemporary art (admission is free).

- For lunch, find the unassuming entrance to **Without Papers Pizza** (1216 9th Ave. S.E.), a local favorite for thin-crust pizzas and house-made ice cream. If you need to walk off your meal, consider taking the scenic route along the Bow River. The RiverWalk, a pedestrian- and bike-friendly urban trail, connects Inglewood with downtown and is protected from vehicle traffic.

- Make your way toward the Calgary Tower (it's hard to miss) and spend some time exploring the **Stephen Avenue Walk,** a portion of 8th Avenue S.W. that is closed to car traffic from 6 a.m. to 6 p.m. Towering steel tree sculptures serve both to beautify and reduce gusting winds, and bars, restaurants, boutiques and historic buildings line the pedestrian mall. On weekdays

Lougheed House

during warm weather months, street performers entertain the crowds.

- As you stroll along Stephen Avenue, you'll notice pedestrian bridges spanning the street. These are part of the Plus 15 pedestrian system, so-called because the walkways are generally 15 feet (4.6 metres) above street level. The network of enclosed walkways allows people to reach office buildings and shopping malls throughout a 50-block area in climate-controlled comfort, something Calgarians appreciate in the freezing cold of winter.

Evening

- After a long day of sightseeing, head to Prince's Island Park for dinner with a fantastic view of the city skyline. Park at the **Eau Claire Market** (200 Barclay Parade S.W.) and take the pedestrian bridge at 2nd Street S.W. across to the island. The **River Café** (25 Prince's Island Park) occupies a rustic wood-and-stone building that evokes a cabin deep in the woods, yet looking out over the river from its patio, you see downtown's office towers. Make reservations because the café's lovely setting and Canadian Rocky Mountain cuisine make it a popular dinner spot highly sought after by both locals and visitors.

- There are plenty more dining options just north of the river in Kensington Village. The walkable district includes top spots like **Vero Bistro Moderne** (209 10th St. N.W.), serving contemporary Italian dishes; **Modern Steak** (107 10A St. N.W.), with beef from local Alberta ranchers; and **Hayden Block Smoke & Whiskey** (1136 Kensington Rd.), a lively barbecue joint with TVs and picnic-style seating.

Top Picks for Kids

Under 13

- Kids can learn how to fish at **Bow Habitat Station** (1440 17A St. S.E.), where a stocked trout pond and rental rods are available mid-May to late Oct. After learning the art of catch and release, take a trip through the wetland trails, a discovery center and a fish hatchery that raises more than 1 million trout every year.

- Any horse lovers in your group? If so, you can't beat a day spent at **Spruce Meadows** (18011 Spruce Meadows Way S.W.), an equestrian center just south of the city. On days when there are no show jumping events, guests may wander the well-kept grounds for free and pet the horses in their stables.

- If you're anywhere near downtown's CORE Shopping Centre, plan to pop in and head to the fourth level to see the indoor **Devonian Gardens**. Fish ponds, waterfalls, fountains and hundreds of trees and plants will help keep kids entertained on a rainy or chilly day. There's a fun indoor playground with seating for adults, too.

Teens

- Get your adrenaline flowing at WinSport's ⌇ **Canada Olympic Park** (88 Canada Olympic Rd. S.W.). Originally built for the 1988 Winter Olympics, the sprawling facility now offers a variety of high-speed thrills year-round. The Skyline Luge is a must-try in summer; you'll take a chairlift up to the start of the track and then race downhill on a wheeled luge through more than 50 twists and turns. This destination is not for the faint of heart.

- Teens in pursuit of the perfect Instagram shot on their vacation will find one at the top of the **Calgary Tower** (101 9th Ave. S.W.). A 1-minute elevator ride whisks you to the observation deck level, where you're treated to snap-worthy views from 161 metres in the air (about 626 feet). If you're brave enough, stand on the glass viewing floor to look straight down on the city streets below.

- Those who speak the language of music will appreciate a visit to **Studio Bell, Home of the National Music Centre** (850 4 St. S.E.). The architecturally striking building—opened in 2016 with a $191 million price tag—features interactive exhibits and memorabilia covering Canada's music history, lots of musical instruments for you to play and even vocal booths where you can test your singing abilities.

All Ages

- Try traditional Dutch pancakes ("pannenkoek") at **Pfanntastic Pannenkoek Haus** (2439 54th Ave. S.W.), a local favorite that has appeared on the Food Network's "You Gotta Eat Here." Not your typical fluffy pancake, the Dutch variety is rolled thin like a crepe. Diners choose from savory and sweet ingredients including pineapple, smoked sausage and even ice cream.

- Lemurs and tigers and dinosaurs—oh my! One of the most popular Calgary attractions and fun places to go is the ⌇ **Calgary Zoo, Botanical Garden & Prehistoric Park** (1300 Zoo Rd. N.E.), which just so happens to be as fun for adults as it is for children. Don't miss the Prehistoric Park where dozens of life-size dinosaur models occupy the grounds.

- Pack some sunscreen and join throngs of Calgarians at the ⌇ **Calgary Folk Music Festival** (698 Eau Claire Ave. S.W.), held in bucolic Prince's Island Park in July. Dozens of stage performances showcase all sorts of music genres, from folk and blues to country and indie rock. The festival is not only eco-friendly but family-friendly, too, with plenty of fun things to do with kids in the Family Zone.

- Welcoming families since 1979, **Nick's Steakhouse & Pizza** (2430 Crowchild Tr. N.W.) is a great place to gather after a day of sightseeing. A kids' menu offers the chance to try some of the house specialties like grade AAA Alberta beef and pizza with homemade dough.

- See what all the fuss is about at **Village Ice Cream**, the dessert spot that consistently tops the lists of the "Best Ice Cream in Calgary." Hand-crafted and locally sourced flavors are anything but boring; maple pecan, huckleberry, Earl Grey and dairy-free varieties are among the selections. Find three locations around the city.

Studio Bell, Home of the National Music Centre

Arriving
By Car

Two major highways pass through Calgary. Queen Elizabeth II Hwy. runs north and south through the city; Trans-Canada Hwy. provides access from the east and west. Hwy. 1A, which connects Calgary and Cochrane, also serves as an alternate travel route between Calgary and the towns of Canmore and Banff. Hwy. 8 connects Calgary with Bragg Creek.

Getting Around
Street System

Calgary is divided into quadrants, with Centre Street separating the east and west sectors and the Bow River and Memorial Drive delineating north and south. Streets run north and south, avenues east and west. All are numbered from the intersection of Centre Street and Centre Avenue, just north of downtown. Roads in suburban areas are numbered where they form grids and named where they do not.

The speed limit is 50 kilometres per hour (30 mph) or as posted. A right turn on red after stopping is permitted unless otherwise posted; U-turns are not. Other restrictions apply during rush hours in certain areas; be aware of signs, especially in school and playground zones. Pedestrian crosswalks are designated by "X" signs, and motorists must yield to pedestrians.

Parking

Parking is not permitted on major roads in the downtown core during rush hours, between 6:30 and 9 a.m. and 3:30 and 6 p.m. Downtown metered street parking usually is limited to 2 hours at a

The CORE Shopping Centre

maximum cost of $5 per hour. Pay parking for extended periods is available at numerous locations. Rates for downtown parking lots range from $2-$4 per half-hour during the day.

Shopping

Stephen Avenue Walk, a downtown pedestrian mall and shopping destination, extends from Bankers Hall to the city municipal buildings. This popular spot for people watching features shops, galleries and restaurants housed within historic buildings. Also downtown, a five-block shopping complex linked by indoor walkways includes the more than 200 boutiques, department stores and retail chains of **The CORE Shopping Centre** (333 7th Ave. S.W.), **Bankers Hall** (315 8th Ave. S.W.) and **Scotia Centre** (225 7th Ave. S.W.).

Unique specialty shops, kiosks and local restaurants are the draw at **Eau Claire Market,** adjacent to the Bow River and Prince's Island Park at 2nd Avenue and 2nd Street S.W.

Trendy **17th Avenue,** a retail and entertainment district, features stylish fashion shops, restaurants and eclectic craft boutiques. **Kensington Village** features smaller stores in new and old buildings. Inglewood's **Ninth Avenue S.E.** is lined with antique stores, clothing boutiques, gift shops and places to eat.

Major department stores and a wide variety of chain and specialty stores occupy the city's shopping centers. If your vacation isn't complete without a trip to a mall, check out **CF Chinook Centre** (6455 Macleod Tr. S.W.), **CF Market Mall** (3625 Shaganappi Tr. N.W.), **North Hill Centre** (1384-1414 19th Ave. N.W.), **Northland Village** (5111 Northland Dr. N.W.), **Southcentre Mall** (100 Anderson Rd. S.E.), **Sunridge Mall** (2525 36th St. N.E.) and **Willow Park Village** (10816 Macleod Tr. S.E.).

Nightlife

Whether you're in town for a business trip, a family vacation or the 10-day Calgary Stampede held in July, there's no shortage of fun things to do in Calgary after dark.

Just south of the downtown core (between 11th and 17th avenues S.W.) is the Beltline district, home to a handful of trendy restaurants, bars and cocktail lounges and one of the best areas for nightlife in Calgary.

If it's cold brews you're after, head to **CRAFT Beer Market** (345 10th Ave. S.W.), a casual bar and restaurant that claims to have Canada's largest selection of draft beer. You're bound to find something you like among the more than 100 local and international beers on tap. After 9 p.m. admittance is 18 years and up; phone (403) 514-2337.

National on 8th (225 8th Ave. S.W.; (403) 237-5556) draws crowds for its selection of beer, cocktails, boozy slushies and rooftop patio games like ping pong and foosball. This beer-hall-turned-neighborhood-hangout has two other downtown locations that offer fun things to do with friends; check out the eight-lane bowling alley inside National on 10th (341 10th Ave. S.W.; (403) 474-2739) and the large communal tables at National on 17th (550 17th Ave. S.W.; (403) 229-0026), the chain's original location.

Handcrafted cocktails earn rave reviews at **Milk Tiger Lounge** (1410 4th St. S.W.), an unassuming spot with a full range of classic drinks. Skilled mixologists will whip you up something from the extensive menu—a Pimm's Cup or a Manhattan, anyone?—with a side of friendly conversation. To find the lounge, just look for the small logo of a white tiger above the door; phone (403) 261-5009.

Another bar that draws a decidedly hipster clientele is **Proof** (1302 1st St. S.W.), where inventive cocktails and old-fashioned service reign supreme. Comfy leather seats and a menu of 40+ alcoholic and non-alcoholic cocktails plus beer, wine, espresso drinks and small plates means you can sit and stay here a while. Admittance is 18 years and up; phone (403) 246-2414.

The **Ship & Anchor Pub** (534 17th Ave. S.W.) has been a long-standing favorite on 17th Avenue for more than two decades; its outdoor patio draws a crowd on sunny afternoons. Minors welcome until 7 p.m.

For a wild night out in Calgary, you'll want to hit a nightclub or dance hall. **The Hifi Club** (219 10th Ave. S.W.) is one of the most popular places to go for electronic music, rap, hip-hop, soul and funk. The club books big-name DJs and live music acts like Calvin Harris, Diplo and Jamie XX. A cover is charged after 10 p.m.; phone (403) 263-5222.

If you're visiting Calgary during Stampede week, show off your line-dancing skills (or learn how to two-step) at **Ranchman's Cookhouse & Dancehall** (9615 Macleod Trail S.), where many pro rodeo contestants go after Stampede competitions. The country nightclub has been a Calgary destination since 1972 and offers live country music daily plus top 40, rock and other genres; phone (403) 253-1100.

Stampede-goers dance until the wee hours of the morning at parties held in venues near the Stampede grounds. **Wildhorse Saloon** (500 6th Ave. S.W.) has a non-stop dance floor and daily concerts in a massive outdoor tent; phone (403) 244-6773. Admission tickets are required, and the venue is open only during Stampede. **Cowboys Dance Hall** (421 12th Ave. S.E.) draws a younger crowd and is open for music and dancing Wed.-Sat. year-round and for special events. A cover is charged; phone (403) 265-0699.

If you're looking for something a little more relaxed to do after dinner, a stroll on the RiverWalk makes for a pleasant evening. The promenade follows the Bow River's south shore from the Centre Street Bridge in Chinatown to 9th Avenue S.E. near Fort Calgary, with benches and observation decks along the way. In the East Village, pop into **The Simmons Building** (618 Confluence Way S.E.), a restored 1912 mattress factory that now houses **Phil & Sebastian Coffee Roasters** (open until 9 p.m.) and the adults-only **Rooftop Bar @ Simmons**;

RiverWalk

phone (587) 353-2268 for Phil & Sebastian and (403) 452-3115 for the rooftop bar.

Big Events

The **Calgary Midwinter BluesFest** takes place over 6 days in late February in venues throughout Calgary. The event features concerts by national blues performers; dance parties; and the Singing the Blues Vocal Camp, a workshop for aspiring singers.

In early June, the **Lilac Festival at 4th Street** features a parade and concerts—along with tons of vendors hawking artisan crafts.

Despite a focus on the modern oil and gas industry, Calgary citizens recall their past with the **Calgary Stampede**, held in July. This 10-day Wild West exhibition features a rodeo, chuck wagon races, livestock shows, beach-themed attractions, educational displays, shopping, extreme sporting events and a midway. Parades, fireworks, street dancing, pancake breakfasts and other activities create a carnival-like atmosphere. Contact a travel advisor at your local AAA travel agency to book vacation packages that include the Calgary Stampede. Families enjoy the cultural and musical events that take place during the **Calgary Folk Music Festival**, held over 4 days in late July.

GlobalFest takes place in August and features such events as an international fireworks competition and a multicultural celebration. Visitors can sample fine foods and beverages from local restaurants at the **Eau Claire Market** during **Taste of Calgary** in mid-August.

During Labour Day weekend **BBQ on the Bow** offers a barbecue competition, live performances by local bands, a children's craft tent, and vendors selling food samples and take-home goods. The **Masters Tournament** takes place in September at the **Spruce Meadows** outdoor equestrian center, off Hwy. 22X (Spruce Meadows Trail) and Macleod Trail. Other racing and dressage events are held at the center throughout the year.

Sports & Rec

Calgary was an appropriate choice as host of the 1988 Winter Olympic Games—opportunities for adventurous things to do indoors and outdoors abound. For information about recreational activities, programs and facilities visitors can phone the city's recreation department by dialing 311 in Calgary or (403) 268-2489.

In winter public **skiing** facilities at **Canada Olympic Park** (see attraction listing p. 53) and in numerous areas nearby are available. Canada Olympic Park also is where to go for other **winter sports,** such as bobsledding, luge, ski jumping and snowboarding.

At **Repsol Sport Centre,** 2225 Macleod Tr. S., **swimming, track events** and **weight lifting** are among the popular activities; phone (403) 233-8393. Similar facilities are offered at the following leisure centers: **Gray Family Eau Claire YMCA,** 101 3rd St. S.W.; phone (403) 269-6701; **Southland Leisure Center,** 2000 Southland Dr. S.W.; phone (403) 648-6555; and **Village Square Leisure Center,** 2623 56th St. N.E.; phone (403) 366-3900. The latter two offer wave pools.

Ice-skating is featured during the winter at Olympic Plaza as well as year-round at more than

Prince's Island Park

two dozen other locations. The **Olympic Oval,** at 288 Collegiate Boulevard N.W., is the site of the 1988 Olympic speed-skating events; skate rentals are available.

Several parks are in the city, particularly along the **Bow River. Fish Creek Provincial Park** (see Recreation Areas Chart) has a visitor center and a small lake providing swimming in summer and ice-skating in winter. Joggers and bicyclists use the park's extensive trail system. Other recreation sites include **Bowness, Edworthy** and **Riley** parks in northwest Calgary and **Prince's Island Park** in the city center, which is easily accessed from the **Bow River Pathway** system. The 145-hectare (360-acre) **Glenmore Reservoir** provides ample space for **sailing** and **canoeing;** the Dragon Boat races are held in late August.

With spectacular natural areas nearby, many visitors to Calgary will be lured to the wilds to enjoy canoeing, **camping, rafting, hiking** and other outdoor pursuits. **Walking** and **bicycling** trails meander through these regions, as do **cross-country skiing** routes. **Tennis** and swimming enthusiasts will find courts and pools throughout Calgary.

Golf lovers can play at more than 40 local courses, including 18 holes at **Maple Ridge,** 1240 Mapleglade Dr. S.E.; **McCall Lake,** 1600 32nd Ave. N.E.; **McKenzie Meadows,** 17215 McKenzie Meadows Dr.; and **Shaganappi Point,** 1200 26th St. S.W. Nine-hole courses are at **Confederation Park,** 3204 Collingwood Dr. N.W.; and **Lakeview,** 5840 19th St. S.W. Some private courses accept visiting golfers; check locally for greens fees and restrictions.

The **Calgary Flames** play **ice hockey** at **Scotiabank Saddledome,** 555 Saddledome Rise S.E. in Stampede Park; phone (403) 777-4646.

The local Canadian **Football** League team, the **Calgary Stampeders,** pounds the turf at **McMahon Stadium,** off 16th Avenue at 1817 Crowchild Tr. N.W. Tickets can be obtained by phoning the box office at (403) 289-0258 or (800) 667-3267. Ticket prices are $36.50-$123.50.

Spruce Meadows, an outdoor equestrian center and show jumping venue 3 kilometres (2 mi.) west on Hwy. 22X (Spruce Meadows Trail) from Macleod Trail at 18011 Spruce Meadows Way S.W., has world-class programs, including international show jumping events. On days when no shows are scheduled the grounds are open free to the public, daily 9-6. Visitors are invited to wander the grounds, picnic and view horses as they are exercised by the trainers; phone (403) 974-4200 for a schedule of Spruce Meadows events.

Spruce Meadows is also home to the **Cavalry Football Club;** soccer matches are held from early May to mid-Oct. Phone (403) 974-4567 for the ticket office.

Performing Arts

Whether you're in Calgary on vacation or just looking for things to do this weekend, you'll find

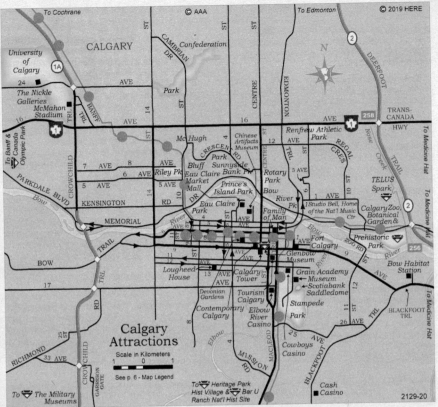

Calgary Attractions

Scale in Kilometers

See p. 6 - Map Legend

© 2019 HERE

2129-20

plenty of options in Calgary. The city's most popular theater and music companies perform in the **Arts Commons** at 205 8th Ave. S.E. The center is shared by **Alberta Theatre Projects, Theatre Calgary, One Yellow Rabbit Performance Theatre,** Downstage and the **Calgary Philharmonic Orchestra.** In addition to four theaters and a concert hall, it contains shops, a restaurant and a coffee bar. For information about performance schedules and ticket sales phone the Arts Commons box office at (403) 294-9494.

Southern Alberta Jubilee Auditorium, 1415 14th Ave. N.W., stages a variety of performing arts, including touring companies of Broadway musicals and presentations by **Calgary Opera;** for details phone the opera company at (403) 262-7286 or the auditorium at (403) 297-8000.

Loose Moose Theatre Company, 1235 26th Ave. S.E., is a destination for adult comedy and drama as well as children's theater; phone (403) 265-5682. **Pumphouse Theatre,** 2140 Pumphouse Ave. S.W., gets its name from the 1913 former pump house that the city converted into two theaters; phone (403) 263-0079, for schedule and ticket information. Midday performances take place in the aptly named **Lunchbox Theatre,** at the base of Calgary Tower at 160 9th Ave. S.E.; phone (403) 265-4292, ext. 0.

A popular dinner theater that often showcases well-known performers in its productions is **Stage West,** 727 42nd Ave. S.E.; phone (403) 243-6642. Other theater, dance and music companies operate locally; check newspapers for performance schedules. Check with your local AAA travel office for information about vacation packages and additional things to do in Calgary to add to your trip.

ATTRACTIONS

For a complete list of attractions, visit AAA.com/travelguides/attractions

BOW HABITAT STATION is at 1440 17A St. S.E. in Pearce Estate City Park. Located along the Bow River, the site features a fish hatchery where six species of trout are raised, 8.5 hectares (21 acres) of interpretive wetland, a discovery center and a trout pond. The Discovery Centre educates visitors about fish management, aquatic ecosystems and Alberta's wetlands through both interactive exhibits and aquariums that shelter a variety of local fish species. Highlights include a large model outlining the anatomy of a fish, an exhibit that explores the cycle of water and the 40-minute film "Wet Alberta."

A stocked fish pond is available for children to experience catch-and-release fishing. Interpretive trails allow for exploration of Pearce Estate Park Wetland. Guided tours of the Sam Livingston Fish Hatchery, one of the largest fish hatcheries in North America, are available.

Time: Allow 2 hours minimum. **Hours:** Discovery Centre Tues.-Sun. 10-4, mid-May through Aug. 31; Tues.-Sat. 10-4, rest of year. Fish hatchery tours vary; phone ahead. Trout pond and interpretive wetland daily 5 a.m.-11 p.m. (fishing season May 15-Oct. 31). **Cost:** Discovery Centre $10; $8 (ages 65+ and students with ID); $6 (ages 4-17); $30 (family, two adults and up to four children). Fishing rod rental $5. **Phone:** (403) 297-6561. GT AT

BUTTERFIELD ACRES CHILDREN'S FARM is at 254077 Rocky Ridge Rd. At this whimsical, educational farm, visitors can meet and interact with many animals such as chicks and chickens, ducks, turkeys, horses, piglets, ponies, goats, lambs, rabbits, sheep, emus and yaks. In addition to interactive displays and pony and wagon rides, children also can try their hands at milking.

Note: Closed footwear with socks is required. Pets are not permitted. **Time:** Allow 2 hours minimum. **Hours:** Daily 10-4, July-Aug.; Mon.-Fri. 10-2, Sat.-Sun. 10-4, Apr.-June and in Sept. **Cost:** $15.49; $14.49 (ages 65+); $13.49 (ages 1-17). Pony ride $2, or four rides for $7. **Phone:** (403) 239-0638. TI AT

CALAWAY PARK, 10 km (6 mi.) w. off Trans-Canada Hwy. Springbank Rd. exit at 245033 Range Rd. 33, is said to be western Canada's largest outdoor amusement park. It features 32 rides, including a roller coaster, a log ride and bumper boats. Live stage shows are presented daily. The landscaped grounds also include an interactive maze and a miniature golf course.

Kennel, stroller and wheelchair rentals are available. **Time:** Allow 4 hours minimum. **Hours:** Daily 10-7, July 1-Labour Day; Sat.-Sun. and Mon. holidays 10-7, Victoria Day weekend-June 30; Sat.-Sun. and Mon. holidays 11-6, day after Labour Day-Thanksgiving Day. **Cost:** $41.95; $33 (ages 50+); free (ages 0-2); $129.95 (family of four); $28 for each additional family member). After 2 p.m. $24.95; free (ages 0-2). Admission includes unlimited rides, attractions, stage shows and parking; prices for individual games, the maze and miniature golf vary. Phone ahead to confirm schedule and prices. **Phone:** (403) 240-3822. *(See ad this page.)* A TI AT

CALGARY TOWER is in Tower Centre at 101 9th Ave. S.W. at Centre St. S. The tower rises 191 metres (626 ft.) above the city. An observation deck and revolving restaurant provide a panorama of the city and the nearby Rocky Mountains. The observation deck features a glass floor and glass walls, which create the sensation of floating high above the city. A torch atop the tower burned nonstop during the 1988 Olympic Games; it is illuminated on special occasions.

Using multimedia, a self-guiding tour presents the history of Calgary as well as information about some of the landmarks visible from the tower. **Hours:** Daily 9 a.m.-10 p.m., June-Aug.; 9-9, rest of year. Hours may vary Oct.-May; phone ahead. **Cost:** $18; $16 (ages 65+); $9 (ages 4-12). **Phone:** (403) 266-7171.

GEM **CALGARY ZOO, BOTANICAL GARDEN & PREHISTORIC PARK** is at 1000 Zoo Rd. N.E. at Memorial Dr. and 12th St. E. In themed areas like Destination Africa and Eurasia, visitors observe nearly 900 animals, including big cats, river hippos and such rare and endangered species as

▼ See AAA listing this page ▼

CALAWAY PARK

JUST 4 FUN CALAWAY PARK IT'S ABOUT FAMILY FUN!

FOR DISCOUNT TICKETS AND CAMPGROUND RESERVATIONS, VISIT CALAWAYPARK.COM

the Amur tiger and red panda. The Land of Lemurs is an immersive habit home to three species of lemurs. Giant pandas arrived in the spring of 2018 for a 5-year-stay in the Panda Passage habitat.

Basking in an icy, state-of-the-art habitat, four penguin species pretend not to notice the crowds of chilly onlookers drawn to the Penguin Plunge exhibit. In the TransAlta Rainforest, bold guests can thump their chests along with the resident western lowland gorilla troop and enjoy the antics of colobus monkeys.

Black and grizzly bears, cougars and bison are among the creatures children and parents can learn about in the Canadian Wilds. The 2.6-hectare (6.5-acre) Prehistoric Park, dotted by life-size dinosaur replicas, transports you to western Canada's bygone Mesozoic landscape. **Time:** Allow 3 hours minimum. **Hours:** Daily 9-6. Last admission 1 hour before closing. Phone ahead to confirm schedule. **Cost:** $34.95; $32.95 (ages 60+); $24.95 (ages 3-15). Prices may vary; phone ahead. **Parking:** $12. **Phone:** (403) 232-9300 or (800) 588-9993. *(See ad this page.)* 🍴

CANADA OLYMPIC PARK is at 88 Canada Olympic Rd. S.W. The park, the host area for ski jumping, freestyle skiing, bobsled and luge events at the 1988 Winter Olympic Games, remains a site for year-round sports activities. In winter visitors can learn to ski and snowboard or ride down the trails at one of Western Canada's largest tube parks. In warmer weather, a mountain bike park with more than 20 kilometres (12.4 mi.) of trails can be enjoyed along with one of North America's fastest ziplines, a scenic chairlift and an 18-hole miniature golf course. The Markin MacPhail Centre, home to several national sports organizations including Hockey Canada, has one international-sized rink and three North American-sized rinks.

Time: Allow 2 hours minimum. **Hours:** Park main gate open daily 5 a.m.-1 a.m. Schedule for facilities and activities vary. **Cost:** Prices for activities and rides vary; phone ahead. **Phone:** (403) 247-5452. 🍴 ⛷

Canada's Sports Hall of Fame is at 169 Canada Olympic Rd. S.W., at Canada Olympic Park. The facility highlights the inspiring achievements of more than 650 Hall of Famers. Twelve interactive galleries—including the Motion, Bounce and Olympic & Paralympic galleries—house exhibits relating to 67 different sports, such as hockey, baseball, figure skating, horse racing, downhill and cross-country skiing, curling and football.

Visitors to the hall of fame are greeted by a sculpture of hockey legend Wayne Gretzky. In the 120-seat Riddell Family Theatre, an 11-minute film featuring rare Olympic footage about Canadian athletes over the years is shown every half-hour. There are more than 2,000 items on display including the #1 1988 Olympic Winter Games Calgary relay torch and over 30 Olympic and Paralympic Games torches dating

▼ See AAA listing p. 52 ▼

VISIT
THE
PANDAS

The Calgary Zoo
is more irresistible
than ever!

CALGARYZOO.COM

calgaryzoo

PANDA
PASSAGE

back to the 1930s. The Women in Sport Gallery showcases the amazing contributions of many of Canada's elite female athletes and builders, including Cassie Campbell-Pascall, Chandra Crawford and Senator Chantal Petitclerc.

Interactive displays include ski jumping, shadowboxing, rowing and wheelchair racing. Videos of awe-inspiring moments in sports history are sure to get visitors' hearts pounding as well. **Time:** Allow 2 hours minimum. **Hours:** Daily 10-5, July-Aug.; Wed.-Sun. 10-5 (also Mon. holidays), rest of year. Closed Jan. 1 and Christmas. **Cost:** $12; $10 (ages 65+); $8 (ages 4-18); $35 (family, two adults and two children). **Phone:** (403) 776-1040.

FORT CALGARY is at 750 9th Ave. S.E. The 16-hectare (40-acre) riverside park marks the location of the 1875 North West Mounted Police fort and the Deane House Historic Site, the last remaining building from the site's days as a garrison. Interactive exhibits, hands-on activities and audiovisual presentations tell the story of the site, the settlement and the people of Calgary.

Hours: Daily 9-5. Closed Jan. 1, Good Friday, July 2, Christmas Eve, Christmas, day after Christmas and Dec. 31. **Cost:** $12; $11 (ages 65+ and college students with ID); $7 (ages 7-17); $5 (ages 3-6). Prices may vary; phone ahead. **Parking:** Parking $6-$10 (before 4 p.m.); $1-$4 (after 4 p.m.). **Phone:** (403) 290-1875. 🍽

GLENBOW MUSEUM is at 130 9th Ave. S.E., across from the Calgary Tower. The complex includes a museum and art gallery. Fascinating men and women who contributed to the development of the province are highlighted in Mavericks: An Incorrigible History of Alberta. Niitsitapiisinni: Our Way of Life features artifacts and interactive displays illustrating Blackfoot traditions and values.

Other galleries feature contemporary art exhibitions, exhibits about warriors, gemstones and West Africa. An Asian sculpture gallery and a hands-on art studio also are on site. **Time:** Allow 2 hours minimum. **Hours:** Mon.-Sat. 9-5 (also 5-9 first Thurs. of the month), Sun. noon-5, July-Aug.; Tues.-Sat. 9-5 (also 5-9 first Thurs. of the month), Sun. noon-5, rest of year. Closed Christmas. **Cost:** $18; $12 (ages 65+ and college students with ID); $11 (ages 7-17); $45 (family, two adults and four children); free (to all first Thurs. of the month 5-9 p.m.). **Phone:** (403) 268-4110. 🍽

THE HANGAR FLIGHT MUSEUM is at 4629 McCall Way N.E. In a former Royal Air Force drill hall, the museum contains exhibits about western Canada's aviation history. Twenty-seven aircraft are displayed, including an F86 Sabre jet, a Bell 47G helicopter and one of the few remaining World War II Avro Lancasters. Also featured are piston and jet aircraft engines and a Martin Baker ejection seat.

Time: Allow 30 minutes minimum. **Hours:** Daily 10-4. Holiday hours in Dec. vary; phone ahead. Closed Jan. 1, Jan. 31 and Christmas. **Cost:** $15;

$11 (ages 65+); $10 (students 12-17 with ID); $8 (ages 3-11); $35 (family, two adults and up to four children ages 0-17). **Phone:** (403) 250-3752.

HERITAGE PARK HISTORICAL VILLAGE is 2.5 km (1.5 mi.) w. off Queen Elizabeth II Hwy. to 1900 Heritage Dr. S.W. This living-history museum resembles a pre-1914 village and reflects the fur trade of the 1860s, the pre-railway settlements of the 1880s and businesses and residences 1900-14. Among the park's more than 200 exhibits and attractions are a ranch house, a saloon, pioneer farm machinery and a Hudson's Bay Co. trading post. Most of the buildings are originals that have been moved to the 51-hectare (127-acre) site.

An antique steam train circles the park, and a paddlewheel boat cruises Glenmore Reservoir. The Gasoline Alley Museum features interactive displays and a collection of vintage vehicles. Representing the 1930s, '40s and '50s, Heritage Town Square depicts the prairie's urban enclaves.

Hours: Historical village daily 10-5, late May-Labour Day; Sat.-Sun. 10-5, day after Labour Day to mid-Oct. Heritage Town Square daily 10-4, year-round. Gasoline Alley daily 10-5, early May to mid-Oct.; Tues.-Sun. 10-4, rest of year. **Cost:** (includes unlimited rides) late May to mid-Oct. $26.50; $20.70 (ages 65+); $18.95 (ages 7-15); $13.65 (ages 3-6). Rest of year $11; $8.85 (ages 65+); $7 (ages 7-15); $5.70 (ages 3-6). Prices may vary; phone ahead. **Parking:** $6 for 7 hours. **Phone:** (403) 268-8500.

INGLEWOOD BIRD SANCTUARY is at 2425 9th Ave. S.E. on the Bow River. Self-guiding trails wind throughout the forest, where some 270 species of birds and 21 species of mammals have been sighted among the 347 species of plants. **Note:** The nature center is closed for renovations until late 2020, but temporary bathroom facilities are available and walking paths remain open. A new outdoor learning center is under construction; phone ahead for updates. **Time:** Allow 1 hour minimum. **Hours:** Trails daily dawn-dusk. **Cost:** Free. **Phone:** (403) 268-2489. 🏞

LOUGHEED HOUSE is at 707 13th Ave. S.W. Built in 1891, this 14,000 square-foot sandstone prairie mansion was built by cabinet minister and Senator James Alexander Lougheed and his wife Isabella Clarke Hardisty Lougheed. They raised their family here, made the opulent Victorian mansion one of the finest residences in Alberta, and provided the political and social hub of fast-growing Calgary until 1936. Today the house offers interpretive exhibits detailing the history of the house, the family and the connection to Calgary's history.

The lovely 1.1-hectare (2.8-acre) estate includes the formal Beaulieu Gardens featuring flower and vegetable gardens. Guided tours by historical interpreters as well as self-guiding audio tours are available. Special programs and exhibits are offered throughout the year. **Time:** Allow 30 minutes minimum. **Hours:** House Wed.-Fri. 11-4, Sat.-Sun.

10-4. Gardens daily 7 a.m.-dusk. **Cost:** House $8.50; $6.50 (students with ID and ages 65+); $5 (ages 6-12); $25 (family, two adults and three children); free (Canadian military with ID). Gardens free. **Phone:** (403) 244-6333. GT 🕊

THE MILITARY MUSEUMS, 4520 Crowchild Tr. S.W., off Flanders Ave. exit, is home to seven museums detailing the history of the Canadian Armed Forces. On-site are the Naval Museum of Alberta, the Army Museum of Alberta and the Air Force Museum of Alberta as well as museums highlighting Lord Strathcona's Horse Regiment (the Royal Canadians), Princess Patricia's Canadian Light Infantry, The King's Own Calgary Regiment and the Calgary Highlanders.

Galleries re-create battle scenes and specific acts of heroism with audio and artifacts. Featured are an impressive collection of weapons, including small arms, navel deck guns and torpedoes; Naval fighter aircraft such as a Banshee jet fighter, Supermarine Seafire and a Hawker Sea Fury; a submarine exhibit; and other equipment relating to life in all branches of Canada's military. The Cold War exhibit focuses on the contribution of the RCAF with three fighter jets on display—an F-86 Sabre, a CF-104 Starfighter and a CF-18 Hornet.

Visitors also can view a huge mural in the Queen Elizabeth II Atrium entry hall; interactive touchscreen monitors explain what each mosaic piece represents. Outside, vintage tanks and carriers dot the landscaped grounds.

Time: Allow 3 hours minimum. **Hours:** Daily 9-5. **Cost:** $15; $5 (ages 7-17 and 65+ and students with ID); free (veterans and active military with ID); $30 family (six people). **Phone:** (403) 410-2340. 🅰

THE NICKLE GALLERIES is on the University of Calgary campus on the main floor of the Taylor Family Digital Library at 410 University Ct. N.W. The galleries were first established with an initial donation by Sam Nickle. In addition to its vast array of ancient coins, the museum also possesses Asian carpets and textiles as well as an important collection of art from Western Canada. Lectures, gallery talks and other events are offered during the school year.

Time: Allow 1 hour minimum. **Hours:** Mon.-Fri. 10-5 (also Thurs. 5-8), Sat. 11-4, Sept.-Apr.; Mon.-Fri. 10-5, rest of year. Closed major holidays. Phone ahead to confirm schedule. **Cost:** Free. **Phone:** (403) 210-6201.

TELUS SPARK is at 220 St. George's Dr. N.E. S.T.E.A.M. (science, technology, engineering, art and math) are at the core of this educational feast for the senses with more than 100 interactive displays. In Energy & Innovation, you can inspect a wind turbine and see how much energy your household electronics use. Create snowflakes or view distant galaxies in the Earth & Sky gallery. Check your mood on a special camera or monitor your reaction

time in the Being Human exhibit area. In the Open Studio, you can build an invention using toothpicks, take apart a machine or digitally animate a story.

High-definition films and live planetarium shows are the highlight of the HD Digital Dome Theatre; "Pandas: The Journey Home" is the feature film. The Creative Kids Museum offers hands-on activities geared toward children under age 8. Daily educational programs and performances connecting science and the arts take place in the 164-seat Presentation Theatre. Brainasium, an outdoor park, offers a 19-metre (63 ft.) slide and other activities for children.

Time: Allow 3 hours minimum. **Hours:** Daily 10-5, July-Aug.; Sun.-Fri. 10-4, Sat. 10-5, rest of year. Closed Aug. 31-Sept. 4 and Christmas. **Cost:** $26; $24 (ages 65+); $22 (ages 13-17); $19 (ages 3-12). **Parking:** $10 (before 5 p.m.), $5 (after 5 p.m.). **Phone:** (403) 817-6800. 🕊

Sightseeing
Bus, Train and Van Tours

Brewster Sightseeing offers trips around Banff, Lake Louise, Jasper and the Columbia Icefield; phone (403) 762-6700 or (866) 606-6700 for schedules and fares.

Rocky Mountaineer Vacations offers scenic vacation packages, including the Rocky Mountaineer, a 2-day, all-daylight, narrated rail tour between Canada's west and the Canadian Rockies. The Rocky Mountaineer tour departs mid-April to mid-October; phone (604) 606-7245 or (877) 460-3200. Contact your local AAA travel agency for information about vacation packages and group travel options.

Walking Tours

Free pamphlets detailing a self-guiding tour of the Stephen Avenue Walk, a heavily trafficked commercial area, are available from the Calgary Downtown Association, 304 8th Ave. S.W., (403) 215-1570. A showcase for historical buildings, the pedestrian mall extends along 8th Avenue S.W. between 1st Street S.E. and 4th Street S.W. and is open to pedestrians only from 6 a.m. to 6 p.m. Fun places to go along Stephen Avenue include shops, pubs and restaurants with outdoor patios.

CALGARYWALKS & BUS TOURS departs from various locations. The Downtown Intro Walking Tour departs from Calgary Municipal Plaza, 800 Macleod Trail S.E., and takes guests on a 2-hour guided tour of the downtown core, with stops at the Stephen Avenue Walk, the Calgary Public Library, Olympic Plaza, the Plus 15 Pedway system and other architecturally and historically significant landmarks. Additional walking tours cover the Calgary Stampede grounds, and bus tours include destinations outside the downtown core.

Hours: Downtown Intro Walking Tour departs daily at 10:45, first full week in Jan. through Dec. 23. Check online calendar for schedule of additional walking tours and bus tours. Phone ahead to confirm schedule. **Cost:** $28; $20 (ages 65+); $18 (ages 3-15). Reservations are required. **Phone:** (587) 435-5433 or (855) 620-6520.

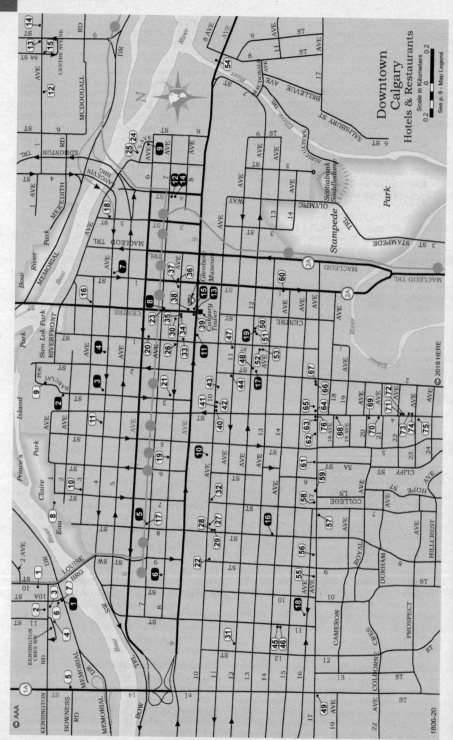

Downtown
Calgary
Hotels & Restaurants

Scale in Kilometers
0.2   0   0.2

See p. 6 - Map Legend

© 2019 HERE

© AAA

1806-20

Downtown Calgary

This index helps you "spot" where hotels and restaurants are located on the corresponding detailed maps. Restaurant price range is a combination of lunch and/or dinner. Turn to the listing page for more information and consult display ads for special promotions.

 For more details, rates and reservations: AAA.com/travelguides/hotels

DOWNTOWN CALGARY

Map Page	Hotels	Designation	Member Savings	Page
1 p. 56	Hotel Arts Kensington	THREE DIAMOND		66
2 p. 56	**Sheraton Suites Calgary Eau Claire**	FOUR DIAMOND	✔	66
3 p. 56	**The Westin Calgary Downtown**	THREE DIAMOND	✔	67
4 p. 56	International Hotel of Calgary	THREE DIAMOND		66
5 p. 56	Sandman Hotel Downtown Calgary	APPROVED		66
6 p. 56	Holiday Inn Express Hotel & Suites Calgary Downtown	THREE DIAMOND		66
7 p. 56	**Delta Hotels by Marriott Calgary Downtown**	THREE DIAMOND	✔	65
8 p. 56	**Hyatt Regency Calgary**	FOUR DIAMOND	✔	66
9 p. 56	Alt Hotel Calgary East Village	THREE DIAMOND		65
10 p. 56	Residence Inn by Marriott Calgary Downtown Beltline District	THREE DIAMOND	✔	66
11 p. 56	**Fairmont Palliser**	FOUR DIAMOND	✔	66
12 p. 56	**Homewood Suites by Hilton Calgary Downtown**	THREE DIAMOND	✔	66
13 p. 56	Hotel Le Germain Calgary	FOUR DIAMOND		66
14 p. 56	**Hilton Garden Inn Calgary Downtown**	THREE DIAMOND	✔	66
15 p. 56	**Calgary Marriott Downtown**	THREE DIAMOND	✔	65
16 p. 56	**Best Western Plus Suites Downtown** *(See ad p. 65.)*	THREE DIAMOND	✔	65
17 p. 56	**Fairfield Inn & Suites by Marriott Calgary Downtown**	THREE DIAMOND	✔	65
18 p. 56	Hotel Elan	THREE DIAMOND		66
19 p. 56	Hotel Arts	THREE DIAMOND		66

Map Page	Restaurants	Designation	Cuisine	Price Range	Page
① p. 56	Vero Bistro Moderne	THREE DIAMOND	New Italian	$16-$39	69
② p. 56	Hayden Block Smoke & Whiskey	APPROVED	Barbecue	$12-$35	68
③ p. 56	Winebar Kensington	THREE DIAMOND	New World Small Plates	$14-$29	69
④ p. 56	Pulcinella	APPROVED	Pizza	$10-$25	68
⑤ p. 56	Sultan's Tent	APPROVED	Traditional Moroccan	$20-$29	69
⑥ p. 56	Modern Steak	THREE DIAMOND	Steak	$15-$79	68
⑦ p. 56	Oxbow	THREE DIAMOND	Canadian	$18-$40	68
⑧ p. 56	Q Haute Cuisine	FOUR DIAMOND	New World	$20-$125	68
⑨ p. 56	Prego Cucina Italiana	APPROVED	Italian	$19-$35	68
⑩ p. 56	Buchanan's Chop House & Whisky Bar	THREE DIAMOND	Steak	$19-$110	67
⑪ p. 56	**Caesar's Steakhouse**	THREE DIAMOND	Steak	$15-$52	67
⑫ p. 56	Blue Star Diner	APPROVED	New Canadian Comfort Food	$15-$27	67
⑬ p. 56	La Brezza	APPROVED	Italian	$16-$47	68
⑭ p. 56	Sushi Bar Zipang	APPROVED	Japanese	$15-$25	69
⑮ p. 56	The Main Dish	APPROVED	Deli	$12-$25	68
⑯ p. 56	**Silver Dragon Restaurant**	APPROVED	Chinese	$12-$45	69
⑰ p. 56	Moxie's Classic Grill	APPROVED	American	$14-$45	68
⑱ p. 56	Bookers BBQ Grill & Crab Shack	APPROVED	Barbecue	$14-$30	67
⑲ p. 56	Escoba Bistro & Wine Bar	THREE DIAMOND	Mediterranean	$20-$36	67
⑳ p. 56	WORKSHOP kitchen + culture	THREE DIAMOND	New World	$15-$29	69

Map Page	Restaurants (cont'd)	Designation	Cuisine	Price Range	Page
㉑ p. 56	Cactus Club Cafe	THREE DIAMOND	New American	$15-$49	67
㉒ p. 56	Donna Mac	THREE DIAMOND	New Canadian	$14-$36	67
㉓ p. 56	Thomson's Restaurant	THREE DIAMOND	New American	$14-$34	69
㉔ p. 56	Sidewalk Citizen Bakery	APPROVED	Breads/Pastries Sandwiches	$10-$16	69
㉕ p. 56	charbar	THREE DIAMOND	New World	$9-$26	67
㉖ p. 56	The Guild	THREE DIAMOND	Regional Canadian	$19-$39	68
㉗ p. 56	The Holy Grill	APPROVED	American	$7-$16	68
㉘ p. 56	Posto Pizzeria and Bar	APPROVED	Pizza	$19-$24	68
㉙ p. 56	Bonterra Trattoria	THREE DIAMOND	New Italian	$19-$32	67
㉚ p. 56	Klein / Harris	THREE DIAMOND	New Canadian	$12-$21	68
㉛ p. 56	Pizzeria Gaga	APPROVED	Pizza	$8-$22	68
㉜ p. 56	Bridgette Bar	THREE DIAMOND	New Canadian	$18-$40	67
㉝ p. 56	Murrieta's Bar & Grill	THREE DIAMOND	Pacific Northwest	$20-$40	68
㉞ p. 56	blink Restaurant & Bar	THREE DIAMOND	Regional Canadian	$25-$39	67
㉟ p. 56	Saltlik A Rare Steakhouse	THREE DIAMOND	Steak	$17-$46	68
㊱ p. 56	Teatro	THREE DIAMOND	New Italian	$18-$55	69
㊲ p. 56	Centini Restaurant and Lounge	THREE DIAMOND	Italian	$19-$58	67
㊳ p. 56	One18 Empire	THREE DIAMOND	New World	$15-$38	68
㊴ p. 56	CHARCUT Roast House	THREE DIAMOND	New Canadian	$16-$50	67
㊵ p. 56	Rodney's Oyster House	APPROVED	Seafood	$14-$30	68
㊶ p. 56	Thai Sa-On Restaurant	APPROVED	Thai	$11-$25	69
㊷ p. 56	Craft Beer Market	APPROVED	American	$15-$28	67
㊸ p. 56	Briggs Kitchen + Bar	THREE DIAMOND	New International	$16-$29	67
㊹ p. 56	Vintage Chophouse & Tavern	THREE DIAMOND	Steak	$12-$54	69
㊺ p. 56	Myhre's Deli	APPROVED	Sandwiches	$7-$16	68
㊻ p. 56	Galaxie Diner	APPROVED	Breakfast	$9-$16	68
㊼ p. 56	Foreign Concept	THREE DIAMOND	New Vietnamese	$16-$59	67
㊽ p. 56	Native Tongues Taqueria	APPROVED	New Mexican Small Plates	$25-$53	68
㊾ p. 56	Moti Mahal	APPROVED	Northern Indian	$5-$12	68
㊿ p. 56	Yellow Door Bistro	THREE DIAMOND	New Mediterranean	$16-$37	69
(51) p. 56	Raw Bar	THREE DIAMOND	New Vietnamese	$22-$35	68
(52) p. 56	Ten Foot Henry	THREE DIAMOND	Canadian	$7-$14	69
(53) p. 56	Two Penny	THREE DIAMOND	New Chinese	$16-$40	69
(54) p. 56	Deane House	THREE DIAMOND	Regional Canadian	$18-$44	67
(55) p. 56	Cibo	THREE DIAMOND	New Italian	$14-$27	67
(56) p. 56	The Coup	THREE DIAMOND	Vegetarian	$7-$24	67
(57) p. 56	Manies Pizzaria and Greek Cuisine	APPROVED	Greek Pizza	$17-$28	68
(58) p. 56	Royale	THREE DIAMOND	New French	$19-$35	68
(59) p. 56	MARKET	THREE DIAMOND	New Canadian	$17-$37	68
(60) p. 56	Manuel Latruwe Belgian Patisserie & Bread Shop	APPROVED	Breads/Pastries Sandwiches	$9-$17	68
(61) p. 56	Una Pizza + Wine	THREE DIAMOND	Mediterranean Pizza	$16-$24	69
(62) p. 56	Ox Bar de Tapas	THREE DIAMOND	Spanish	$11-$22	68
(63) p. 56	The Living Room	THREE DIAMOND	New International	$22-$36	68

Map Page	Restaurants (cont'd)	Designation	Cuisine	Price Range	Page
⑥④ p. 56	Anju	💎💎 THREE DIAMOND	New Korean Small Plates	$18-$95	67
⑥⑤ p. 56	Calcutta Cricket Club	💎💎 THREE DIAMOND	New Indian Small Plates	$11-$37	67
⑥⑥ p. 56	Pigeonhole	💎💎 THREE DIAMOND	New World Small Plates	$10-$55	68
⑥⑦ p. 56	Model Milk	💎💎 THREE DIAMOND	New World	$16-$38	68
⑥⑧ p. 56	Hana Sushi	💎💎 APPROVED	Japanese	$8-$15	68
⑥⑨ p. 56	Shokunin Izakaya	💎💎 APPROVED	New Japanese	$20-$40	69
⑦⓪ p. 56	Fleur de Sel	💎💎 APPROVED	New French	$15-$45	67
⑦① p. 56	Carino Riserva	💎💎 THREE DIAMOND	Italian Fusion	$24-$33	67
⑦② p. 56	Aida's Bistro	💎💎 APPROVED	Lebanese	$10-$30	67
⑦③ p. 56	Purple Perk	💎💎 APPROVED	Coffee/Tea Comfort Food	$9-$15	68
⑦④ p. 56	Mercato	💎💎 THREE DIAMOND	Italian	$16-$57	68
⑦⑤ p. 56	Famoso Neapolitan Pizzeria	💎💎 APPROVED	Pizza	$14-$18	67
⑦⑥ p. 56	Lulu Bar	💎💎 THREE DIAMOND	New Pacific Rim	$25-$34	68

Let the IDP Speak for You.

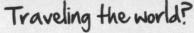

INTERNATIONAL DRIVING PERMIT
— DRIVE THE WORLD! —

Traveling the world?

Before you go, purchase an International Driving Permit for a recognizable form of identification, even if you're not driving.

Translated into 10 languages, the IDP is valid in more than 150 countries — mandatory in some and highly recommended in others.

**U.S. residents apply at AAA offices. Canadian residents apply at CAA offices.
Or visit us online at: AAA.com/IDP   or   CAA.ca/travelling/idp**

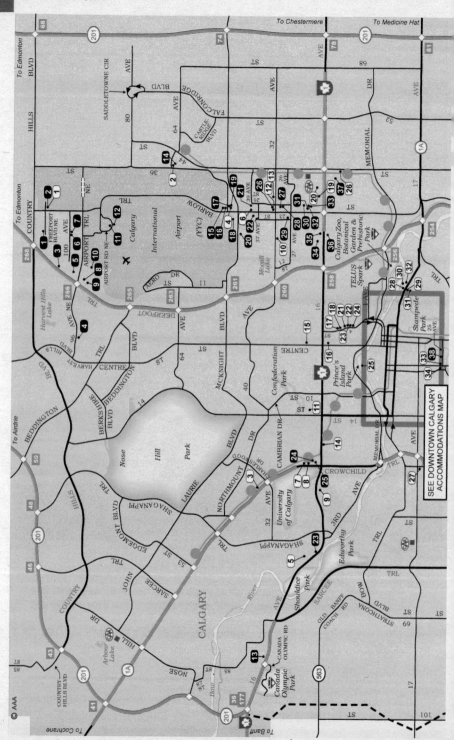

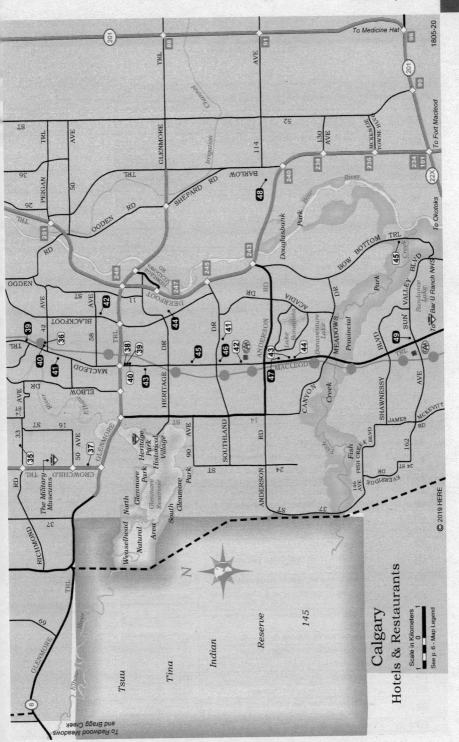

Calgary
Hotels & Restaurants

Scale in Kilometers
0   1
See p. 6 - Map Legend

© 2019 HERE

1805-20

✈ Airport Hotels

Map Page	CALGARY INTERNATIONAL AIRPORT (Maximum driving distance from airport: 2.8 mi (4.5 km))	Designation	Member Savings	Page
2 p. 60	Acclaim Hotel, 1.9 mi (3.0 km)	THREE DIAMOND		69
9 p. 60	Applause Hotel, 2.8 mi (4.5 km)	THREE DIAMOND		69
1 p. 60	**Best Western Premier Freeport Inn & Suites, 2.2 mi (3.5 km)**	THREE DIAMOND	✔	70
12 p. 60	**Calgary Airport Marriott In-Terminal Hotel, on airport property**	THREE DIAMOND	✔	71
3 p. 60	**Comfort Inn & Suites, 2.7 mi (4.4 km)**	THREE DIAMOND	✔	71
11 p. 60	**Delta Hotels by Marriott Calgary Airport In-Terminal, on airport property**	THREE DIAMOND	✔	72
7 p. 60	**Hampton Inn by Hilton Calgary Airport North, 1.8 mi (2.9 km)**	THREE DIAMOND	✔	72
6 p. 60	Homewood Suites by Hilton Calgary Airport, 1.7 mi (2.8 km)	THREE DIAMOND	✔	73
8 p. 60	Hotel Clique, 2.7 mi (4.3 km)	THREE DIAMOND		73
10 p. 60	**The Westin Calgary Airport, 2.3 mi (3.8km)**	THREE DIAMOND	✔	74
5 p. 60	Wingate by Wyndham Calgary Airport, 2.3 mi (3.8 km)	THREE DIAMOND		74

Calgary

This index helps you "spot" where hotels and restaurants are located on the corresponding detailed maps. Restaurant price range is a combination of lunch and/or dinner. Turn to the listing page for more information and consult display ads for special promotions.

 For more details, rates and reservations: AAA.com/travelguides/hotels

CALGARY

Map Page	Hotels	Designation	Member Savings	Page
1 p. 60	**Best Western Premier Freeport Inn & Suites**	THREE DIAMOND	✔	70
2 p. 60	Acclaim Hotel	THREE DIAMOND		69
3 p. 60	**Comfort Inn & Suites**	THREE DIAMOND	✔	71
4 p. 60	**Executive Residency by Best Western Calgary City View North**	THREE DIAMOND	✔	72
5 p. 60	Wingate by Wyndham Calgary Airport	THREE DIAMOND		74
6 p. 60	Homewood Suites by Hilton Calgary Airport	THREE DIAMOND	✔	73
7 p. 60	**Hampton Inn by Hilton Calgary Airport North**	THREE DIAMOND	✔	72
8 p. 60	Hotel Clique	THREE DIAMOND		73
9 p. 60	Applause Hotel	THREE DIAMOND		69
10 p. 60	**The Westin Calgary Airport**	THREE DIAMOND	✔	74
11 p. 60	**Delta Hotels by Marriott Calgary Airport In-Terminal**	THREE DIAMOND	✔	72
12 p. 60	**Calgary Airport Marriott In-Terminal Hotel**	THREE DIAMOND	✔	71
13 p. 60	Four Points by Sheraton Hotel & Suites, Calgary West	THREE DIAMOND	✔	72
14 p. 60	**Radisson Hotel & Conference Centre Calgary Airport**	THREE DIAMOND	✔	73
15 p. 60	**Residence Inn by Marriott Calgary Airport**	THREE DIAMOND	✔	73
16 p. 60	**Courtyard by Marriott Calgary Airport**	THREE DIAMOND	✔	71
17 p. 60	Sandman Hotel Suites & Spa Calgary Airport	THREE DIAMOND		74
18 p. 60	**Hilton Garden Inn-Calgary Airport**	THREE DIAMOND	✔	72
19 p. 60	Holiday Inn Express Airport Calgary	THREE DIAMOND		73
20 p. 60	**Best Western Plus Port O'Call Hotel** *(See ad p. 70.)*	THREE DIAMOND	✔	70
21 p. 60	Lakeview Signature Inn	THREE DIAMOND		73

CALGARY (cont'd)

Map Page	Hotels (cont'd)	Designation	Member Savings	Page
22 p. 60	Country Inn & Suites by Radisson, Calgary-Airport	◈ THREE DIAMOND	✔	71
23 p. 60	Days Inn Calgary Northwest	◈ APPROVED		72
24 p. 60	Aloft Calgary University	◈ THREE DIAMOND	✔	69
25 p. 60	Best Western Plus Village Park Inn	◈ THREE DIAMOND	✔	70
26 p. 60	Sheraton Cavalier Hotel	◈ THREE DIAMOND	✔	74
27 p. 60	Comfort Inn & Suites-Airport South	◈ APPROVED	✔	71
28 p. 60	Super 8 Calgary Airport	◈ APPROVED	✔	74
29 p. 60	Executive Royal Hotel North Calgary	◈ THREE DIAMOND		72
30 p. 60	Days Inn Calgary Airport	◈ APPROVED		71
31 p. 60	Staybridge Suites Calgary Airport	◈ THREE DIAMOND	✔	74
32 p. 60	Element by Westin Calgary Airport	◈ THREE DIAMOND	✔	72
33 p. 60	Four Points by Sheraton Calgary Airport	◈ THREE DIAMOND	✔	72
34 p. 60	Best Western Airport Inn	◈ APPROVED	✔	69
35 p. 60	Clarion Hotel & Conference Centre Calgary Airport	◈ APPROVED		71
36 p. 60	Holiday Inn Calgary-Airport	◈ APPROVED		72
37 p. 60	Best Western Premier Calgary Plaza Hotel & Conference Centre	◈ THREE DIAMOND	✔	70
38 p. 60	Calgary Westways Guest House	◈ THREE DIAMOND		71
39 p. 60	Best Western Plus Calgary Centre Inn	◈ APPROVED	✔	69
40 p. 60	Holiday Inn Calgary-Macleod Trail South	◈ THREE DIAMOND	✔	72
41 p. 60	Comfort Inn & Suites-South	◈ THREE DIAMOND	✔	71
42 p. 60	Hotel Blackfoot (See ad p. 73.)	◈ THREE DIAMOND	✔	73
43 p. 60	Econo Lodge South	◈ APPROVED	✔	72
44 p. 60	Holiday Inn & Suites Calgary South Conference Centre	◈ THREE DIAMOND		72
45 p. 60	Carriage House Inn	◈ THREE DIAMOND	✔	71
46 p. 60	Delta Hotels by Marriott Calgary South	◈ THREE DIAMOND	✔	72
47 p. 60	Holiday Inn Express Hotel & Suites Calgary-South	◈ THREE DIAMOND		73
48 p. 60	Service Plus Inn & Suites Calgary	◈ THREE DIAMOND		74
49 p. 60	Wingate by Wyndham Calgary	◈ THREE DIAMOND		74

Map Page	Restaurants	Designation	Cuisine	Price Range	Page
1 p. 60	Pacini Pasta & Grill Ristorante	◈ APPROVED	Italian	$10-$32	75
2 p. 60	XS Lounge and Grill	◈ APPROVED	International	$13-$36	76
3 p. 60	Jamesons Irish Pub	◈ APPROVED	American	$15-$20	75
4 p. 60	Moxie's Classic Grill	◈ APPROVED	American	$11-$45	75
5 p. 60	NOtaBLE - The Restaurant	◈ THREE DIAMOND	New Canadian Comfort Food	$17-$42	75
6 p. 60	Cactus Club Cafe	◈ THREE DIAMOND	New American	$15-$49	74
7 p. 60	Nick's Steakhouse & Pizza	◈ APPROVED	Steak Pizza	$14-$60	75
8 p. 60	Big T's BBQ	◈ APPROVED	Barbecue	$12-$32	74
9 p. 60	Gus's Pizza	◈ APPROVED	Pizza	$8-$24	75
10 p. 60	Misai Japanese Restaurant	◈ APPROVED	Japanese	$10-$20	75
11 p. 60	Jimmy's A & A Deli	◈ APPROVED	Mediterranean Deli	$7-$12	75
12 p. 60	Carver's Steakhouse	◈ THREE DIAMOND	Steak	$29-$54	74
13 p. 60	Basil	◈ APPROVED	Vietnamese	$6-$16	74
14 p. 60	Juree's Thai Place Restaurant	◈ APPROVED	Thai	$14-$22	75
15 p. 60	Lina's Italian Market	◈ APPROVED	Italian Deli	$4-$10	75
16 p. 60	Santorini Greek Taverna	◈ APPROVED	Greek	$25-$39	76
17 p. 60	Open Range Steaks & Chops	◈ THREE DIAMOND	New American	$22-$49	75
18 p. 60	Big Fish	◈ THREE DIAMOND	Seafood	$15-$32	74
19 p. 60	Pio Peruvian Rotisserie Chicken	◈ APPROVED	Peruvian	$11-$22	75

Map Page	Restaurants (cont'd)	Designation	Cuisine	Price Range	Page
⑳ p. 60	Pita Basket	◈ APPROVED	Lebanese	$6-$13	75
㉑ p. 60	Boogie's Burgers	◈ APPROVED	Burgers	$6-$20	74
㉒ p. 60	OEB Breakfast Co.	◈ APPROVED	Breakfast	$8-$22	75
㉓ p. 60	SS106 Aperitivo Bar	◈ APPROVED	Italian	$13-$26	76
㉔ p. 60	Diner Deluxe	◈ APPROVED	American	$11-$23	75
㉕ p. 60	River Cafe	◈ THREE DIAMOND	Regional Canadian	$21-$46	76
㉖ p. 60	Forbidden City Seafood & Dim Sum Restaurant	◈ APPROVED	Chinese Dim Sum	$15-$39	75
㉗ p. 60	Cassis Bistro	◈ THREE DIAMOND	French	$17-$37	75
㉘ p. 60	Without Papers Pizza	◈ APPROVED	Pizza	$17-$22	76
㉙ p. 60	Kane's Harley Diner	◈ APPROVED	Comfort Food	$8-$18	75
㉚ p. 60	Rouge Restaurant	◈ FOUR DIAMOND	New French	$16-$46	76
㉛ p. 60	The Nash	◈ THREE DIAMOND	New World	$15-$51	75
㉜ p. 60	Spolumbo's Deli	◈ APPROVED	Deli Sandwiches	$9-$12	76
㉝ p. 60	Rajdoot	◈ APPROVED	Indian	$13-$17	75
㉞ p. 60	La Boulangerie	◈ APPROVED	Breads/Pastries	$8-$14	75
㉟ p. 60	Belmont Diner	◈ APPROVED	American	$10-$16	74
㊱ p. 60	Alloy	◈ THREE DIAMOND	New International	$17-$49	74
㊲ p. 60	**Pfanntastic Pannenkoek Haus**	◈ APPROVED	Dutch Specialty	$11-$21	75
㊳ p. 60	Open Sesame	◈ APPROVED	Asian	$13-$24	75
㊴ p. 60	Smuggler's Inn	◈ APPROVED	Steak	$15-$48	76
㊵ p. 60	Cactus Club Cafe	◈ THREE DIAMOND	New American	$15-$49	74
㊶ p. 60	Italian Centre Shop	◈ APPROVED	Italian Sandwiches Pizza	$8-$15	75
㊷ p. 60	Broken Plate Kitchen & Bar	◈ APPROVED	Greek	$13-$30	74
㊸ p. 60	La Piccola Napoli Ristorante	◈ APPROVED	Italian	$18-$39	75
㊹ p. 60	Pies Plus Café	◈ APPROVED	Specialty	$9-$13	75
㊺ p. 60	Bow Valley Ranche Restaurant	◈ THREE DIAMOND	Regional Canadian	$16-$65	74

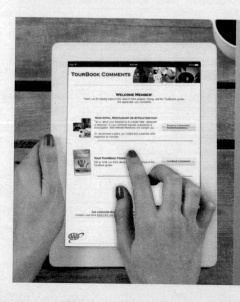

Let Your Voice Be Heard

- Tell us if a listed establishment doesn't meet your expectations.

- Recommend a favorite hotel or restaurant for inspection.

AAA.com/MemberFeedback

DOWNTOWN CALGARY

ALT HOTEL CALGARY EAST VILLAGE 587/441-6635 **9**
THREE DIAMOND Boutique Contemporary Hotel. **Address:** 635 Confluence Way SE T2G 0G1

BEST WESTERN PLUS SUITES DOWNTOWN
403/228-6900 **16**

THREE DIAMOND
Hotel

Best Western PLUS

AAA Benefit: Members save up to 15% and earn bonus points!

Address: 1330 8th St SW T2R 1B6 **Location:** Corner of 8th St and 13th Ave SW. **Facility:** 124 units, some two bedrooms, efficiencies and kitchens. 16 stories, interior corridors. **Amenities:** safes. **Activities:** sauna, exercise room. **Guest Services:** valet and coin laundry. *(See ad this page.)*

CALGARY MARRIOTT DOWNTOWN 403/266-7331 **15**

THREE DIAMOND
Contemporary Hotel

MARRIOTT

AAA Benefit: Members save 5% or more!

Address: 110 9th Ave SE T2G 5A6 **Location:** Jct 9th Ave and Centre St; adjacent to TELUS Convention Centre. Across from Calgary Tower. **Facility:** 388 units. 22 stories, interior corridors. **Parking:** valet only. **Amenities:** safes. **Dining:** One18 Empire, see separate listing. **Pool:** heated indoor. **Activities:** hot tub, exercise room. **Guest Services:** valet laundry.

DELTA HOTELS BY MARRIOTT CALGARY DOWNTOWN
403/266-1980 **7**

THREE DIAMOND
Hotel

DELTA HOTELS

AAA Benefit: Members save 5% or more!

Address: 209 4th Ave SE T2G 0C6 **Location:** Jct 1st St SE and 4th Ave SE. **Facility:** 395 units. 25 stories, interior corridors. **Parking:** on-site (fee) and valet. **Pool:** heated indoor. **Activities:** sauna, hot tub, exercise room. **Guest Services:** valet laundry.

FAIRFIELD INN & SUITES BY MARRIOTT CALGARY DOWNTOWN
403/351-6500 **17**

THREE DIAMOND
Hotel

Fairfield

AAA Benefit: Members save 5% or more!

Address: 239 12th Ave SW T2R 1H7 **Location:** Corner of 2nd St SW. **Facility:** 124 units. 11 stories, interior corridors. *Bath:* shower only. **Parking:** valet only. **Dining:** Native Tongues Taqueria, see separate listing. **Activities:** exercise room. **Guest Services:** valet and coin laundry. **Featured Amenity: breakfast buffet.**

AAA.com/hertz—

When your ideal road trip

includes a comfortable ride

▼ See AAA listing this page ▼

BW **Best Western PLUS**

Best Western Plus Suites Downtown Calgary

Whether you are visiting Calgary for business or pleasure, Best Western Plus Suites Downtown is your home away from home! Enjoy complimentary hot buffet breakfast and high speed Internet. Free Parking available for all Best Western and Hotel direct bookings.

1330 8th St SW, Calgary, AB T2R 1B6
403-228-6900 | 1-800-981-2555
bestwesternsuitescalgary.com

THREE DIAMOND

(See map & index p. 56.)

FAIRMONT PALLISER
403/262-1234 **11**

FOUR DIAMOND

Historic Hotel

Address: 133 9th Ave SW T2P 2M3 **Location:** Jct 9th Ave SW and 1st St SW. **Facility:** The spacious lobby at this grand hotel has a stunning imperial theme with a stylish open lounge. Rooms combine modern décor with distinctive historical elements to create an elegant upscale ambience. 407 units, some kitchens. 12 stories, interior corridors. **Parking:** on-site (fee) and valet, winter plug-ins. **Amenities:** safes. **Pool:** heated indoor. **Activities:** hot tub, steamroom, bicycles, health club, in-room exercise equipment, spa. **Guest Services:** valet laundry.

SAVE ECO [icons] BIZ SHS [icons]

HILTON GARDEN INN CALGARY DOWNTOWN
587/352-2020 **14**

THREE DIAMOND

Contemporary Hotel

Hilton Garden Inn

AAA Benefit: Members save up to 15%!

Address: 711 4th St T2R 1L6 **Location:** Between 7th and 8th aves SE; in East Village. **Facility:** 198 units. 13 stories, interior corridors. **Parking:** on-site. **Pool:** heated indoor. **Activities:** hot tub, picnic facilities, exercise room. **Guest Services:** valet and coin laundry, area transportation.

SAVE [icons] BIZ

HS [icons] / SOME UNITS

HOLIDAY INN EXPRESS HOTEL & SUITES CALGARY DOWNTOWN
403/269-8262 **6**

THREE DIAMOND Hotel. **Address:** 1020 8th Ave SW T2P 1J2

HOMEWOOD SUITES BY HILTON CALGARY DOWNTOWN
587/352-5500 **12**

THREE DIAMOND

Extended Stay Contemporary Hotel

HOMEWOOD SUITES BY HILTON

AAA Benefit: Members save up to 15%!

Address: 711 4th St E T2G 1N3 **Location:** Between 7th and 8th aves SE; in East Village. **Facility:** 119 units. 15 stories, interior corridors. **Parking:** valet only. **Pool:** heated indoor. **Activities:** hot tub, picnic facilities, exercise room. **Guest Services:** valet and coin laundry, area transportation.

SAVE [icons] CALL [icons]

[icons] BIZ HS [icons] / SOME UNITS

HOTEL ARTS
403/266-4611 **19**

THREE DIAMOND Boutique Contemporary Hotel. **Address:** 119 12th Ave SW T2R 0G8

HOTEL ARTS KENSINGTON
403/228-4442 **1**

THREE DIAMOND Boutique Hotel. **Address:** 1126 Memorial Dr NW T2N 3E3

HOTEL ELAN
403/229-2040 **18**

THREE DIAMOND Boutique Contemporary Hotel. **Address:** 1122 16th Ave SW T2R 0T6

HOTEL LE GERMAIN CALGARY
403/264-8990 **13**

FOUR DIAMOND Boutique Contemporary Hotel. **Address:** 899 Centre St SW T2G 1B8

HYATT REGENCY CALGARY
403/717-1234 **8**

FOUR DIAMOND

Contemporary Hotel

HYATT REGENCY

AAA Benefit: Members save up to 10%!

Address: 700 Centre St SE T2G 5P6 **Location:** Corner of Centre St and 7th Ave SW. Adjacent to TELUS Convention Centre. **Facility:** These upscale rooms feature gorgeous African wood furnishings and oversize TVs. The same wood features are in the striking bathrooms, along with marble counters and tub surrounds. 355 units. 22 stories, interior corridors. **Parking:** on-site (fee) and valet. **Amenities:** safes. **Dining:** Thomson's Restaurant, see separate listing. **Pool:** heated indoor. **Activities:** hot tub, steamroom, bicycles, exercise room, in-room exercise equipment, spa. **Guest Services:** valet laundry, boarding pass kiosk.

SAVE [icons] CALL [icons] BIZ HS [icons]

[icons] / SOME UNITS

INTERNATIONAL HOTEL OF CALGARY
403/265-9600 **4**

THREE DIAMOND Hotel. **Address:** 220 4th Ave SW T2P 0H5

RESIDENCE INN BY MARRIOTT CALGARY DOWNTOWN BELTLINE DISTRICT
587/885-2288 **10**

THREE DIAMOND SAVE Extended Stay Contemporary Hotel. **Address:** 610 10th Ave SW T2R 1M3

AAA Benefit: Members save 5% or more!

SANDMAN HOTEL DOWNTOWN CALGARY
403/237-8626 **5**

APPROVED Hotel. **Address:** 888 7th Ave SW T2P 3J3

SHERATON SUITES CALGARY EAU CLAIRE
403/266-7200 **2**

FOUR DIAMOND

Hotel

SHERATON

AAA Benefit: Members save 5% or more!

Address: 255 Barclay Parade SW T2P 5C2 **Location:** At 3rd St SW and 2nd Ave SW. **Facility:** This downtown location is prime being next to Eau Claire Market and Prince's Island Park. All of the upscale suites include separate living areas with plenty of seating and large two-sided desks. 323 units, some two bedrooms. 15 stories, interior corridors. **Parking:** valet only. **Amenities:** safes. **Dining:** 2 restaurants. **Pool:** heated indoor. **Activities:** hot tub, trails, exercise room. **Guest Services:** valet and coin laundry.

SAVE ECO [icons] CALL [icons] BIZ SHS

[icons] / SOME UNITS

What's for dinner?

AAA.com/travelguides/restaurants

(See map & index p. 56.)

THE WESTIN CALGARY DOWNTOWN

403/266-1611 **3**

THREE DIAMOND
Hotel

WESTIN HOTELS & RESORTS

AAA Benefit: Members save 5% or more!

Address: 320 4th Ave SW T2P 2S6 **Location:** Corner of 4th Ave SW and 3rd St. **Facility:** 525 units. 20 stories, interior corridors. **Parking:** on-site (fee) and valet. **Amenities:** safes. **Dining:** 2 restaurants. **Pool:** heated indoor. **Activities:** sauna, exercise room, in-room exercise equipment. **Guest Services:** valet laundry.

WHERE TO EAT

AIDA'S BISTRO 403/541-1189 **72**
APPROVED Lebanese. Casual Dining. **Address:** 2208 4th St SW T2S 1W9

ANJU 403/460-3341 **64**
THREE DIAMOND New Korean Small Plates. Casual Dining. **Address:** 344 17th Ave SW T2S 0A5

BLINK RESTAURANT & BAR 403/263-5330 **34**
THREE DIAMOND Regional Canadian. Casual Dining. **Address:** 111 8th Ave SW T2B 1B4

BLUE STAR DINER 403/261-9998 **12**
APPROVED New Canadian Comfort Food. Casual Dining. **Address:** 809 1st Ave NE T2E 0C2

BONTERRA TRATTORIA 403/262-8480 **29**
THREE DIAMOND New Italian. Casual Dining. **Address:** 1016 8th St SW T2R 1K2

BOOKERS BBQ GRILL & CRAB SHACK 403/264-6419 **18**
APPROVED Barbecue. Casual Dining. **Address:** 316 3rd St SE T2G 2S4

BRIDGETTE BAR 587/319-6827 **32**
THREE DIAMOND New Canadian. Casual Dining. **Address:** 739 10th Ave SW T2R 0B3

BRIGGS KITCHEN + BAR 587/350-5015 **43**
THREE DIAMOND New International. Casual Dining. **Address:** 317 10 Ave SW, #100 T2R 0A5

BUCHANAN'S CHOP HOUSE & WHISKY BAR 403/261-4646 **10**
THREE DIAMOND Steak. Casual Dining. **Address:** 738 3rd Ave SW T2P 0G7

CACTUS CLUB CAFE 403/454-9399 **21**
THREE DIAMOND New American. Casual Dining. **Address:** 178-317 7th Ave SW T2P 2Y9

🔗 **Love the great outdoors?**

Find places to camp

at **AAA.com/campgrounds**

CAESAR'S STEAKHOUSE 403/264-1222 **11**
THREE DIAMOND
Steak
Fine Dining
$15-$52

AAA Inspector Notes: A trip to the West is not complete without a stop at this great steakhouse, one of the city's first and finest. Serving wonderful Alberta AAA beef, grilled and seasoned to perfection, along with other classic menu choices. The upscale room has intimate lighting, beautiful wood paneling, interesting Roman themed artwork and buzzes with downtown energy. Service flows smoothly with a team of professional dressed servers. **Features:** full bar. **Reservations:** suggested. **Address:** 512 4th Ave SW T2P 0J6 **Location:** Just e of 5th St SW. **Parking:** valet and street only. L D

CALCUTTA CRICKET CLUB 403/719-1555 **65**
THREE DIAMOND New Indian Small Plates. Casual Dining. **Address:** 340 17th Ave SW T2S 0A8

CARINO RISERVA 403/454-7668 **71**
THREE DIAMOND Italian Fusion. Casual Dining. **Address:** 2206 4th St SW T2S 1W9

CENTINI RESTAURANT AND LOUNGE 403/269-1600 **37**
THREE DIAMOND Italian. Fine Dining. **Address:** 160 8th Ave SE T2G 0K6

CHARBAR 403/452-3115 **25**
THREE DIAMOND New World. Casual Dining. **Address:** 618 Confluence Way SE T2G 0G1

CHARCUT ROAST HOUSE 403/984-2180 **39**
THREE DIAMOND New Canadian. Casual Dining. **Address:** 899 Centre St SW T2G 1B8

CIBO 403/984-4755 **55**
THREE DIAMOND New Italian. Casual Dining. **Address:** 1012 17th Ave SW T2T 0A5

THE COUP 403/541-1041 **56**
THREE DIAMOND Vegetarian. Casual Dining. **Address:** 924 B 17th Ave SW T2T 0A2

CRAFT BEER MARKET 403/514-2337 **42**
APPROVED American. Gastropub. **Address:** 345 10th Ave SW T2R 0A5

DEANE HOUSE 403/264-0595 **54**
THREE DIAMOND Regional Canadian. Casual Dining. **Address:** 806 9th Ave SE T2P 2M5

DONNA MAC 403/719-3622 **22**
THREE DIAMOND New Canadian. Casual Dining. **Address:** 1002 9th St SW T2R 1B3

EARLS KITCHEN + BAR
APPROVED American. Casual Dining.
LOCATIONS:
Address: 2401 4th St SW T2S 1X5 **Phone:** 403/228-4141
Address: 315 8th Ave SW T2P 1C4 **Phone:** 403/265-3275

ESCOBA BISTRO & WINE BAR 403/543-8911 **19**
THREE DIAMOND Mediterranean. Casual Dining. **Address:** 624 8th Ave SW T2P 1G4

FAMOSO NEAPOLITAN PIZZERIA 403/455-3839 **75**
APPROVED Pizza. Casual Dining. **Address:** 2303 4th St SW, #105 T2S 2S7

FLEUR DE SEL 403/228-9764 **70**
APPROVED New French. Casual Dining. **Address:** 2015 4th St SW, #2 T2S 1W6

FOREIGN CONCEPT 403/719-7288 **47**
THREE DIAMOND New Vietnamese. Casual Dining. **Address:** 1011 1st St T2R 1J2

(See map & index p. 56.)

GALAXIE DINER   403/228-0001 46
APPROVED Breakfast. Casual Dining. **Address:** 1413 11th St SW T2R 1G7

THE GUILD   403/770-2213 26
THREE DIAMOND Regional Canadian. Fine Dining. **Address:** 200 8th Ave SW T2P 1B5

HANA SUSHI   403/229-1499 68
APPROVED Japanese. Casual Dining. **Address:** 1807 4th St SW T2S 1W2

HAYDEN BLOCK SMOKE & WHISKEY   403/283-3021 2
APPROVED Barbecue. Casual Dining. **Address:** 1136 Kensington Rd T2N 3P3

THE HOLY GRILL   403/261-9759 27
APPROVED American. Quick Serve. **Address:** 827 10th Ave SW T2R 0B4

JOEY RESTAURANTS   403-263-6336
APPROVED American. Casual Dining. **Address:** 200 Barclay Parade SW T2P 4R5

KLEIN / HARRIS   403/262-8100 30
THREE DIAMOND New Canadian. Casual Dining. **Address:** 110 8th Ave SW T2P 1B3

LA BREZZA   403/262-6230 13
APPROVED Italian. Casual Dining. **Address:** 990 1st Ave NE T2E 8J3

THE LIVING ROOM   403/228-9830 63
THREE DIAMOND New International. Casual Dining. **Address:** 514 17th Ave SW T5W 4X6

LULU BAR   403/930-5707 76
THREE DIAMOND New Pacific Rim. Casual Dining. **Address:** 510 17th Ave T2S 0B1

THE MAIN DISH   403/265-3474 15
APPROVED Deli. Casual Dining. **Address:** 903 General Ave NE T2E 0P4

MANIES PIZZARIA AND GREEK CUISINE   403/228-9207 57
APPROVED Greek Pizza. Casual Dining. **Address:** 819 17th Ave SW T2T 0A1

MANUEL LATRUWE BELGIAN PATISSERIE & BREAD SHOP
                                       403/261-1092 60
APPROVED Breads/Pastries Sandwiches. Quick Serve. **Address:** 1333 1st St SE T2G 5L1

MARKET   403/474-4414 59
THREE DIAMOND New Canadian. Casual Dining. **Address:** 718 17th Ave SW T2S 0B7

MERCATO   403/263-5535 74
THREE DIAMOND Italian. Casual Dining. **Address:** 2224 4th Rd SW T2S 1W9

MODEL MILK   403/265-7343 67
THREE DIAMOND New World. Casual Dining. **Address:** 308 17th Ave SW T2S 0A8

MODERN STEAK   403/670-6873 6
THREE DIAMOND Steak. Fine Dining. **Address:** 107 10A St NW T2N 4M7

MOTI MAHAL   403/228-9990 49
APPROVED Northern Indian. Casual Dining. **Address:** 1805 14th St SW T2T 3P1

MOXIE'S CLASSIC GRILL   403/234-7507 17
APPROVED American. Casual Dining. **Address:** 888 7th Ave SW T2P 3J3

MURRIETA'S BAR & GRILL   403/269-7707 33
THREE DIAMOND Pacific Northwest. Casual Dining. **Address:** 200-808 1st St SW T2P 1M9

MYHRE'S DELI   403/244-6602 45
APPROVED Sandwiches. Quick Serve. **Address:** 1411 11th St SW T2R 1G7

NATIVE TONGUES TAQUERIA   403/263-9444 48
APPROVED New Mexican Small Plates. Casual Dining. **Address:** 235 12th Ave SW T2R 1H7

ONE18 EMPIRE   403/269-0299 38
THREE DIAMOND New World. Casual Dining. **Address:** 820 Centre St SE T2G 5J2

OX BAR DE TAPAS   403/457-1432 62
THREE DIAMOND Spanish. Casual Dining. **Address:** 528 17th Ave SW T2S 0A9

OXBOW   403/670-7387 7
THREE DIAMOND Canadian. Casual Dining. **Address:** 1126 Memorial Dr NW T2N 3E3

PIGEONHOLE   403/452-4694 66
THREE DIAMOND New World Small Plates. Casual Dining. **Address:** 306 17 Ave SW T2S 1V5

PIZZERIA GAGA   403/264-2421 31
APPROVED Pizza. Quick Serve. **Address:** 1236 12 Ave SW T3C 1A7

POSTO PIZZERIA AND BAR   403/262-4876 28
APPROVED Pizza. Casual Dining. **Address:** 1014 8th St SW T2R 1K2

PREGO CUCINA ITALIANA   403/233-7885 9
APPROVED Italian. Casual Dining. **Address:** 200 Barclay Parade S, #218 T2P 4R5

PULCINELLA   403/283-1166 4
APPROVED Pizza. Casual Dining. **Address:** 1147 Kensington Cres NW T2N 1X7

PURPLE PERK   403/244-1300 73
APPROVED Coffee/Tea Comfort Food. Quick Serve. **Address:** 2212 4th St SW T2S 1W9

Q HAUTE CUISINE   403/262-5554 8
FOUR DIAMOND New World. Fine Dining. **Address:** 100 La Caille Pl SW T2P 5E2

RAW BAR   403/206-9565 51
THREE DIAMOND New Vietnamese. Casual Dining. **Address:** 119 12th Ave SW T2R 0G8

RODNEY'S OYSTER HOUSE   403/460-0026 40
APPROVED Seafood. Casual Dining. **Address:** 355 10th Ave SW T2R 0A5

ROYALE   403/475-9457 58
THREE DIAMOND New French. Casual Dining. **Address:** 730 17th Ave SW T2S 0B7

SALTLIK A RARE STEAKHOUSE   403/537-1160 35
THREE DIAMOND Steak. Fine Dining. **Address:** 101 8th Ave SW T2P 1B4

(See map & index p. 56.)

SHOKUNIN IZAKAYA   403/229-3444 (69)
♦ APPROVED New Japanese. Casual Dining. **Address:**
2016 4th St T2S 1W3

SIDEWALK CITIZEN BAKERY   403/457-2245 (24)
♦ APPROVED Breads/Pastries Sandwiches. Quick
Serve. **Address:** 618 Confluence Way SE T2G 0G1

SILVER DRAGON RESTAURANT   403/264-5326 (16)
♦ APPROVED **AAA Inspector Notes:** This restaurant
Chinese specializes in Cantonese and Szechuan
Casual Dining cuisine, including excellent ginger beef.
$12-$45 A delicious dim sum selection is served
each day. The contemporary decor comprises nouveau Oriental artwork.
Servers are cordial. **Features:** full bar. **Reservations:** suggested. **Address:** 106 3rd Ave SE T2G 0B6 **Location:** In Chinatown. **Parking:** street only. [L] [D]

SULTAN'S TENT   403/244-2333 (5)
♦ APPROVED Traditional Moroccan. Casual Dining.
Address: 4 14th St NW T2N 1Z4

SUSHI BAR ZIPANG   403/262-1888 (14)
♦ APPROVED Japanese. Casual Dining. **Address:** 1010
1st Ave NE T2E 7W7

TEATRO   403/290-1012 (36)
♦ THREE DIAMOND New Italian. Fine Dining. **Address:** 200
8th Ave SE T2G 0K7

TEN FOOT HENRY   403/475-5537 (52)
♦ THREE DIAMOND Canadian. Casual Dining. **Address:** 1209
1st St SW T2R 0V3

THAI SA-ON RESTAURANT   403/264-3526 (41)
♦ APPROVED Thai. Casual Dining. **Address:** 351 10th
Ave SW T2R 0A5

THOMSON'S RESTAURANT   403/537-4449 (23)
♦ THREE DIAMOND New American. Casual Dining. **Address:**
700 Centre St SE T2G 5P6

TWO PENNY   403/474-7766 (53)
♦ THREE DIAMOND New Chinese. Casual Dining. **Address:**
1213 1st St SW T2R 0V3

UNA PIZZA + WINE   403/453-1183 (61)
♦ THREE DIAMOND Mediterranean Pizza. Casual Dining.
Address: 618 17th Ave SW T2S 0B4

VERO BISTRO MODERNE   403/283-8988 (1)
♦ THREE DIAMOND New Italian. Casual Dining. **Address:**
209 10th St NW T2N 1V5

VINTAGE CHOPHOUSE & TAVERN   403/262-7262 (44)
♦ THREE DIAMOND Steak. Fine Dining. **Address:** 322 11th
Ave SW T2R 0C5

WINEBAR KENSINGTON   403/457-1144 (3)
♦ THREE DIAMOND New World Small Plates. Casual Dining.
Address: 1131 Kensington Rd NW T2N 3P4

WORKSHOP KITCHEN + CULTURE   403/266-7062 (20)
♦ THREE DIAMOND New World. Casual Dining. **Address:** 608
1st St SW T2P 1M6

YELLOW DOOR BISTRO   403/206-9585 (50)
♦ THREE DIAMOND New Mediterranean. Casual Dining.
Address: 119 12 Ave SW T2R 0G8

CALGARY
• Restaurants p. 74
• Hotels & Restaurants map & index p. 60

ACCLAIM HOTEL   403/291-8000 (2)
♦ THREE DIAMOND Hotel. **Address:** 123 Freeport Blvd NE T3N 0A3

ALOFT CALGARY UNIVERSITY   403/289-1973 (24)
♦ THREE DIAMOND
Contemporary Hotel   **AAA Benefit:** Members save 5% or more!

Address: 2359 Banff Tr NW T2M 4L2 **Location:** Just n of jct Trans-Canada Hwy 1 and Crowchild Tr. Located in Motel Village. **Facility:** 143 units. 3 stories, interior corridors. *Bath:* shower only. **Amenities:** safes. **Pool:** heated indoor. **Activities:** exercise room, spa. **Guest Services:** valet and coin laundry.

[SAVE][TI+][Y][🏊][✦][BIZ][HS]
[📶][✕][🎥][🔌][💻]/SOME UNITS[🐾]

APPLAUSE HOTEL   403/460-9589 (9)
♦ THREE DIAMOND Contemporary Hotel. **Address:** 22 Aero Cres NE T2E 7Y5

BEST WESTERN AIRPORT INN   403/250-5015 (34)
♦ APPROVED
Hotel Best Western. **AAA Benefit:** Members save up to 15% and earn bonus points!

Address: 1947 18th Ave NE T2E 7T8 **Location:** 0.6 mi (1 km) e of jct Hwy 2 (Deerfoot Tr) and 16th Ave NE (Trans-Canada Hwy 1), just n on 19th St NE, then just w. **Facility:** 76 units. 3 stories, interior corridors. **Parking:** winter plug-ins. **Amenities:** safes. **Pool:** heated indoor. **Activities:** hot tub, exercise room. **Guest Services:** valet and coin laundry. **Featured Amenity:** continental breakfast.

[SAVE][ECO][✈][TI+][🏊][✦][BIZ][📶][✕][🎥][🔌]
[💻]/SOME UNITS[HS]

BEST WESTERN PLUS CALGARY CENTRE INN
403/287-3900 (39)
♦ APPROVED
Hotel Best Western PLUS. **AAA Benefit:** Members save up to 15% and earn bonus points!

Address: 3630 Macleod Tr S T2G 2P9 **Location:** East side of Hwy 2A (Macleod Tr) at 36th Ave SE. **Facility:** 71 units. 4 stories, interior corridors. **Parking:** winter plug-ins. **Pool:** heated indoor. **Activities:** hot tub, exercise room. **Guest Services:** valet and coin laundry. **Featured Amenity:** full hot breakfast.

[SAVE][TI+][🏊][✦][BIZ][HS][📶]
[🔌][💻]/SOME UNITS[📺]

🔗 **For exclusive AAA member savings and benefits: AAA.com/hertz**

(See map & index p. 60.)

BEST WESTERN PLUS PORT O'CALL HOTEL
403/291-4600   **20**

 THREE DIAMOND
Hotel

 Best Western PLUS

AAA Benefit: Members save up to 15% and earn bonus points!

Address: 1935 McKnight Blvd NE T2E 6V4 **Location:** 1.6 mi (2.5 km) ne of jct Hwy 2 (Deerfoot Tr); at 19th St NE. **Facility:** 201 units. 6-7 stories, interior corridors. **Dining:** 2 restaurants. **Pool:** heated indoor. **Activities:** hot tub, steamroom, exercise room. **Guest Services:** valet laundry. *(See ad this page.)*

BEST WESTERN PLUS VILLAGE PARK INN
403/289-0241   **25**

THREE DIAMOND
Contemporary Hotel

Best Western PLUS

AAA Benefit: Members save up to 15% and earn bonus points!

Address: 1804 Crowchild Tr NW T2M 3Y7 **Location:** Just ne of jct Trans-Canada Hwy 1 and Crowchild Tr. Located in Motel Village. **Facility:** 160 units. 5 stories, interior corridors. **Amenities:** safes. **Pool:** heated indoor. **Activities:** hot tub, exercise room. **Guest Services:** valet and coin laundry. **Featured Amenity:** full hot breakfast.

BEST WESTERN PREMIER CALGARY PLAZA HOTEL & CONFERENCE CENTRE
403/248-8888   **37**

 THREE DIAMOND
Contemporary Hotel

 PREMIER BEST WESTERN.

AAA Benefit: Members save up to 15% and earn bonus points!

Address: 1316 33rd St NE T2A 6B6 **Location:** Just s of jct 16th Ave (Trans-Canada Hwy 1) and 36th St NE, just w on 12th Ave NE. Adjacent to Pacific Place Mall. **Facility:** 248 units. 6-11 stories, interior corridors. **Parking:** winter plug-ins. **Amenities:** safes. **Pool:** heated indoor. **Activities:** sauna, hot tub, picnic facilities, exercise room. **Guest Services:** valet laundry, area transportation.

BEST WESTERN PREMIER FREEPORT INN & SUITES
403/264-9650   **1**

THREE DIAMOND
Hotel

PREMIER BEST WESTERN.

AAA Benefit: Members save up to 15% and earn bonus points!

Address: 86 Freeport Blvd NE T3J 5J9 **Location:** 1 mi (1.6 km) n of Calgary International Airport on Barlow Tr, just w. **Facility:** 97 units. 4 stories, interior corridors. **Parking:** winter plug-ins. **Amenities:** safes. **Pool:** heated indoor. **Activities:** hot tub, exercise room. **Guest Services:** valet and coin laundry, area transportation. **Featured Amenity:** breakfast buffet.

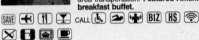

Where Diamonds make the difference:
AAA.com/travelguides/hotels

▼ See AAA listing this page ▼

THREE DIAMOND

BW Best Western PLUS.

Heated Indoor Parking
24 Hour Airport Shuttle Service
Skyharbour Grill, Jetz Bar and Lounge
Easy Access to all Major Driving Routes
Within Minutes to Downtown and Calgary International Airport

Port O'Call Hotel
1935 McKnight Blvd NE | Calgary, Alberta T2E 6V4
Toll Free: 1.800.661.1161 | www.bwportocallhotel.com

 CAA Rewards

(See map & index p. 60.)

CALGARY AIRPORT MARRIOTT IN-TERMINAL HOTEL
403/717-0522

THREE DIAMOND

Contemporary Hotel

AAA Benefit: Members save 5% or more!

Address: 2008 Airport Rd NE T2E 3B9 **Location:** At Calgary International Airport. **Facility:** 318 units. 7 stories, interior corridors. **Parking:** on-site (fee) and valet. **Amenities:** safes. **Pool:** heated indoor. **Activities:** hot tub, exercise room, in-room exercise equipment, spa. **Guest Services:** valet laundry, boarding pass kiosk, rental car service.

[SAVE] [▮▮] [👶] [⟐] CALL [&] [🛏] [👤▾] [BIZ] [SHS] [S🛜]
[✕] [🍴] [💻] / SOME UNITS [🐾]

CALGARY WESTWAYS GUEST HOUSE
403/229-1758 38

THREE DIAMOND Historic Bed & Breakfast. **Address:** 216 25th Ave SW T2S 0L1

CARRIAGE HOUSE INN
403/253-1101 45

THREE DIAMOND

Hotel

Address: 9030 Macleod Tr S T2H 0M4 **Location:** On Hwy 2A (Macleod Tr); corner of 90th Ave SW. **Facility:** 157 units. 4-10 stories, interior corridors. **Parking:** winter plug-ins. **Amenities:** *Some:* safes. **Dining:** 2 restaurants. **Pool:** heated outdoor. **Activities:** hot tub, steamroom, exercise room, massage. **Guest Services:** valet laundry. **Featured Amenity: full hot breakfast.**

[SAVE] [ECO] [▮▮] [👶] [⟐] [🛏] [👤▾]
[BIZ] [HS] [🛜] [✕] [🍴] [💻]
/ SOME UNITS [🐾] [🖨]

CLARION HOTEL & CONFERENCE CENTRE CALGARY AIRPORT
403/291-4666 35

APPROVED Hotel. **Address:** 2120 16th Ave NE T2E 1L4

COMFORT INN & SUITES
587/349-7289 3

THREE DIAMOND

Hotel

Address: 147 Freeport Cres NE T3J 0T3 **Location:** Hwy 2 (Deerfoot Tr) exit 266, just ne. Located in an industrial area. **Facility:** 100 units. 4 stories, interior corridors. **Parking:** winter plug-ins. **Pool:** heated indoor. **Activities:** hot tub, exercise room. **Guest Services:** valet and coin laundry. **Featured Amenity: breakfast buffet.**

[SAVE] [🛏] [🛜] [👤▾] [BIZ] [HS] [🛜]
[✕] [🍴] [💻]

COMFORT INN & SUITES-AIRPORT SOUTH
403/735-1966 27

APPROVED

Hotel

Address: 3111 26th St NE T1Y 7E4 **Location:** Just se of jct 32nd Ave NE and Barlow Tr NE. **Facility:** 74 units. 4 stories, interior corridors. **Parking:** winter plug-ins. **Amenities:** safes. **Pool:** heated indoor. **Activities:** hot tub, exercise room. **Guest Services:** valet and coin laundry. **Featured Amenity: full hot breakfast.**

[SAVE] [🛏] [▮▮] [🛜] [👤▾] [BIZ] [HS]
[🛜] [✕] [💻] / SOME UNITS [🍴] [🖨]

COMFORT INN & SUITES-SOUTH
403/287-7070 41

THREE DIAMOND

Hotel

Address: 4611 Macleod Tr SW T2G 0A6 **Location:** Hwy 2A (Macleod Tr), w on 45th Ave. **Facility:** 93 units. 4 stories, interior corridors. **Parking:** winter plug-ins. **Amenities:** safes. **Pool:** heated indoor. **Activities:** hot tub, exercise room. **Guest Services:** valet and coin laundry, rental car service. **Featured Amenity: full hot breakfast.**

[SAVE] [▮▮] [🛏] [👤▾] [BIZ] [HS] [🛜]
[📺] [✕] [🍴] [💻]

COUNTRY INN & SUITES BY RADISSON, CALGARY-AIRPORT
403/250-1800 22

THREE DIAMOND

Hotel

Address: 2481 39th Ave NE T2E 8V8 **Location:** Jct Barlow Tr and 39th Ave NE; access via 37th Ave. **Facility:** 106 units. 3 stories, interior corridors. **Parking:** winter plug-ins. **Pool:** heated indoor. **Activities:** hot tub, exercise room. **Guest Services:** valet and coin laundry. **Featured Amenity: breakfast buffet.**

[SAVE] [ECO] [🛏] [▮▮] CALL [&] [🛏]
[👤▾] [BIZ] [HS] [🛜] [✕] [🍴] [💻]
[💻]

COURTYARD BY MARRIOTT CALGARY AIRPORT
403/238-1000 16

THREE DIAMOND

Hotel

COURTYARD' **AAA Benefit:** Members save 5% or more!

Address: 2500 48th Ave NE T3J 4V8 **Location:** Just n of jct Barlow Tr NE and McKnight Blvd NE. **Facility:** 171 units. 6 stories, interior corridors. **Parking:** winter plug-ins. **Terms:** check-in 4 pm. **Amenities:** safes. **Pool:** heated indoor. **Activities:** picnic facilities, exercise room. **Guest Services:** valet and coin laundry, boarding pass kiosk.

[SAVE] [🛏] [▮▮] [🍴] CALL [&] [🛏]
[👤▾] [BIZ] [HS] [🛜] [✕] [🍴] [💻] / SOME UNITS [🖨]

COURTYARD BY MARRIOTT CALGARY SOUTH
587/349-7599

THREE DIAMOND

Contemporary Hotel

COURTYARD' **AAA Benefit:** Members save 5% or more!

Address: 3750 Market St SE T3M 2P2 **Location:** Hwy 2 (Deerfoot Tr) exit Seton Blvd SE, just e. Across from South Health Campus. **Facility:** 128 units. 7 stories, interior corridors. *Bath:* shower only. **Terms:** check-in 4 pm. **Pool:** heated indoor. **Activities:** hot tub, exercise room, spa. **Guest Services:** valet and coin laundry.

[SAVE] [▮▮] [🍴] CALL [&] [🛏] [👤▾]
[BIZ] [🛜] [✕] [🍴] [💻] / SOME UNITS [🖨]

DAYS INN CALGARY AIRPORT
403/250-3297 30

APPROVED Hotel. **Address:** 2799 Sunridge Way NE T1Y 7K7

🔗 **Get member rates and reservations at AAA.com/hertz**

(See map & index p. 60.)

DAYS INN CALGARY NORTHWEST   403-288-7115 **23**
◆◆ **APPROVED** Hotel. **Address:** 4420 16th Ave NW T3B 0M4

DELTA HOTELS BY MARRIOTT CALGARY AIRPORT IN-TERMINAL   403-291-2600 **11**

◆◆◆ **THREE DIAMOND**
Hotel

D DELTA HOTELS **AAA Benefit:** Members save 5% or more!

Address: 2001 Airport Rd NE T2E 6Z8 **Location:** At Calgary International Airport. **Facility:** 296 units. 3-8 stories, interior corridors, valet. **Pool:** heated indoor. **Activities:** hot tub, exercise room, in-room exercise equipment. **Guest Services:** valet laundry.

[icons] SAVE ECO [icons] CALL [icons] BIZ HS [icons] / SOME UNITS

DELTA HOTELS BY MARRIOTT CALGARY SOUTH   403-278-5050 **46**

◆◆◆ **THREE DIAMOND** SAVE Hotel. **Address:** 135 Southland Dr SE T2J 5X5

AAA Benefit: Members save 5% or more!

ECONO LODGE SOUTH   403-252-4401 **43**

◆◆ **APPROVED**
Motel

Address: 7505 Macleod Tr SW T2H 0L8 **Location:** Corner of Hwy 2A (Macleod Tr) and 75th Ave SW. **Facility:** 73 units, some efficiencies and kitchens. 2-3 stories (no elevator), interior/exterior corridors. **Parking:** winter plug-ins. **Pool:** heated indoor. **Activities:** hot tub, limited exercise equipment. **Guest Services:** coin laundry. **Featured Amenity: continental breakfast.**

[icons] SAVE ECO [icons] BIZ [icons] / SOME UNITS

ELEMENT BY WESTIN CALGARY AIRPORT   403/984-5515 **32**

◆◆◆ **THREE DIAMOND** SAVE Extended Stay Contemporary Hotel. **Address:** 2855 Sunridge Way NE T1Y 7K7

AAA Benefit: Members save 5% or more!

EXECUTIVE RESIDENCY BY BEST WESTERN CALGARY CITY VIEW NORTH   403/984-6999 **4**

◆◆◆ **THREE DIAMOND**
Extended Stay Contemporary Hotel

Executive **Residency** **AAA Benefit:** Members save up to 15% and earn bonus points!

Address: 9665 Aurora Park Link NE T3K 0S2 **Location:** Hwy 2 (Deerfoot Tr) exit 266, 1.2 mi (2 km) w. Located in a residential area. **Facility:** 117 units, some efficiencies. 4 stories, interior corridors. **Parking:** winter plug-ins. **Amenities:** safes. **Pool:** heated indoor. **Activities:** hot tub, exercise room. **Guest Services:** valet and coin laundry.

EXECUTIVE ROYAL HOTEL NORTH CALGARY   403/291-2003 **29**
◆◆◆ **THREE DIAMOND** Hotel. **Address:** 2828 23rd St NE T2E 8T4

FOUR POINTS BY SHERATON CALGARY AIRPORT   403/648-3180 **33**
◆◆◆ **THREE DIAMOND** SAVE Hotel. **Address:** 2875 Sunridge Way NE T1Y 7K7

AAA Benefit: Members save 5% or more!

FOUR POINTS BY SHERATON HOTEL & SUITES, CALGARY WEST   403/288-4441 **13**
◆◆◆ **THREE DIAMOND** SAVE Hotel. **Address:** 8220 Bowridge Cres NW T3B 2V1

AAA Benefit: Members save 5% or more!

HAMPTON INN BY HILTON CALGARY AIRPORT NORTH   403/452-9888 **7**

◆◆◆ **THREE DIAMOND**
Hotel

Hampton by Hilton **AAA Benefit:** Members save up to 15%!

Address: 2000 2021 100th Ave NE T3J 0R3 **Location:** Hwy 2 (Deerfoot Tr) exit 266, 1.1 mi (1.8 km) e on Airport Tr NE, then just n on 19th St NE. **Facility:** 135 units. 10 stories, interior corridors. **Amenities:** safes. **Pool:** heated indoor. **Activities:** hot tub, picnic facilities, exercise room. **Guest Services:** coin laundry, rental car service. **Featured Amenity: full hot breakfast.**

[icons] SAVE [icons] CALL [icons] BIZ HS [icons] / SOME UNITS

HILTON GARDEN INN-CALGARY AIRPORT   403/717-1999 **18**

◆◆◆ **THREE DIAMOND**
Hotel

Hilton **Garden Inn** **AAA Benefit:** Members save up to 15%!

Address: 2335 Pegasus Rd NE T2E 8C3 **Location:** Jct Barlow Tr and McKnight Blvd, just w, n on 19th St NE, then just e. **Facility:** 135 units. 5 stories, interior corridors. **Pool:** heated indoor. **Activities:** hot tub, exercise room, in-room exercise equipment. **Guest Services:** valet and coin laundry, area transportation. **Featured Amenity: breakfast buffet.**

[icons] SAVE [icons] HS [icons]

HOLIDAY INN & SUITES CALGARY SOUTH CONFERENCE CENTRE   403/475-8561 **44**
◆◆◆ **THREE DIAMOND** Hotel. **Address:** 8360 Blackfoot Tr SE T2J 7E1

HOLIDAY INN CALGARY-AIRPORT   403/230-1999 **36**
◆◆ **APPROVED** Hotel. **Address:** 1250 McKinnon Dr NE T2E 7T7

HOLIDAY INN CALGARY-MACLEOD TRAIL SOUTH   403/287-2700 **40**

◆◆◆ **THREE DIAMOND**
Hotel

Address: 4206 Macleod Tr S T2G 2R7 **Location:** Corner of 42nd Ave SW and Macleod Tr S. **Facility:** 151 units. 4 stories, interior corridors. **Parking:** winter plug-ins. **Pool:** heated indoor. **Activities:** exercise room. **Guest Services:** valet and coin laundry.

(See map & index p. 60.)

HOLIDAY INN EXPRESS AIRPORT CALGARY
403/769-1888 **19**
THREE DIAMOND Hotel. **Address:** 45 Hopewell Way NE T3J 4V7

HOLIDAY INN EXPRESS HOTEL & SUITES CALGARY-SOUTH
403/225-3000 **47**
THREE DIAMOND Hotel. **Address:** 12025 Lake Fraser Dr SE (Macleod Tr S) T2J 7G5

HOMEWOOD SUITES BY HILTON CALGARY AIRPORT
403/453-7888 **6**
THREE DIAMOND SAVE Extended Stay Hotel. **Address:** 1000 2021 100th Ave NE T3J 0R3

AAA Benefit: Members save up to 15%!

HOTEL BLACKFOOT   403/252-2253 **42**
THREE DIAMOND
Contemporary Hotel

Address: 5940 Blackfoot Tr SE T2H 2B5 **Location:** At 58th Ave SE. Access to property from 58th Ave only. **Facility:** 193 units. 7 stories, interior corridors. *Bath:* shower only. **Amenities:** safes. **Dining:** 3 restaurants, nightclub. **Pool:** heated outdoor. **Activities:** hot tub, steamroom, exercise room. **Guest Services:** valet laundry. **Featured Amenity: full hot breakfast.** *(See ad this page.)*

HOTEL CLIQUE   403/460-9588 **8**
THREE DIAMOND Contemporary Hotel. **Address:** 24 Aero Cres NE T2E 7Y5

LAKEVIEW SIGNATURE INN   403/735-3336 **21**
THREE DIAMOND Hotel. **Address:** 2622 39th Ave NE T1Y 7J9

RADISSON HOTEL & CONFERENCE CENTRE CALGARY AIRPORT   403/475-1111 **14**
THREE DIAMOND
Contemporary Hotel

Address: 6620 36th St NE T3J 4C8 **Location:** Jct McKnight Blvd NE and Barlow Tr NE, just n, then 1.6 mi (2.6 km) ne on 48th Ave NE. **Facility:** 120 units. 4 stories, interior corridors. **Parking:** *Some:* safes. **Dining:** XS Lounge and Grill, see separate listing. **Pool:** heated indoor. **Activities:** sauna, hot tub, exercise room, spa. **Guest Services:** valet laundry, area transportation. **Featured Amenity: breakfast buffet.**

RESIDENCE INN BY MARRIOTT CALGARY AIRPORT
403/278-1000 **15**
THREE DIAMOND
Extended Stay Hotel

Residence INN. **AAA Benefit:** Members save 5% or more!

Address: 2530 48th Ave NE T3J 4V8 **Location:** Just n of jct Barlow Tr NE and McKnight Blvd NE. **Facility:** 158 units, some two bedrooms, efficiencies and kitchens. 6 stories, interior corridors. **Parking:** winter plug-ins. **Terms:** check-in 4 pm. **Amenities:** safes. **Pool:** heated indoor. **Activities:** picnic facilities, exercise room. **Guest Services:** valet and coin laundry, boarding pass kiosk.

▼ *See AAA listing this page* ▼

hotel blackfoot always here for you

Boutique hotel minutes from downtown Calgary.

Inviting Social Spaces. High end amenities. Service you Expect. Prices you won't!

5940 Blackfoot Trail SE Calgary, AB T2H 2B5 +1 403-252-2253 (800) 661-1151 hotelblackfoot.com

THREE DIAMOND

🔗 **For complete hotel, dining and attraction listings: AAA.com/travelguides**

(See map & index p. 60.)

RESIDENCE INN BY MARRIOTT CALGARY SOUTH
587/349-8633

◈ THREE DIAMOND

Extended Stay
Contemporary
Hotel

Residence INN. **AAA Benefit:** Members save 5% or more!

Address: 3710 Market St SE T3M 2P2 **Location:** Hwy 2 (Deerfoot Tr) exit Seton Blvd SE, just e. Across from South Health Campus. **Facility:** 97 units, some two bedrooms, efficiencies and kitchens. 6 stories, interior corridors. **Pool:** heated indoor. **Activities:** hot tub, exercise room, spa. **Guest Services:** valet and coin laundry. **Featured Amenity:** breakfast buffet.

SAVE ⬥⬥ CALL ⬥⬥ ⬥ BIZ ⬥ ⬥ ⬥ ⬥ ⬥ / SOME UNITS ⬥

SANDMAN HOTEL SUITES & SPA CALGARY AIRPORT
403/219-2475 **17**

◈ THREE DIAMOND Hotel. **Address:** 25 Hopewell Way NE T3J 4V7

SERVICE PLUS INN & SUITES CALGARY 403/256-5352 **48**

◈ THREE DIAMOND Hotel. **Address:** 3503 114th Ave SE T2Z 3X2

SHERATON CAVALIER HOTEL 403/291-0107 **26**

◈ THREE DIAMOND

Hotel

SHERATON **AAA Benefit:** Members save 5% or more!

Address: 2620 32nd Ave NE T1Y 6B8 **Location:** Barlow Tr at 32nd Ave NE. **Facility:** 305 units. 7 stories, interior corridors. **Parking:** on-site and valet, winter plug-ins. **Amenities:** safes. **Dining:** 2 restaurants, also, Carver's Steakhouse, see separate listing. **Pool:** heated indoor. **Activities:** sauna, hot tub, exercise room. **Guest Services:** valet laundry.

SAVE ECO ⬥⬥ ⬥ ⬥ ⬥ ⬥⬥
⬥ BIZ HS ⬥ ⬥ ⬥ ⬥ ⬥ / SOME UNITS

STAYBRIDGE SUITES CALGARY AIRPORT
403/204-7829 **31**

◈ THREE DIAMOND

Extended Stay
Hotel

Address: 2825 Sunridge Way NE T1Y 7K7 **Location:** Trans-Canada Hwy 1 exit Barlow Tr NE, just n, then just e. **Facility:** 96 efficiencies, some two bedrooms. 4 stories, interior corridors. **Parking:** winter plug-ins. **Pool:** heated indoor. **Activities:** hot tub, picnic facilities, exercise room. **Guest Services:** complimentary and valet laundry. **Featured Amenity:** breakfast buffet.

SAVE ⬥⬥ ⬥ CALL ⬥ ⬥ ⬥⬥
BIZ HS ⬥ ⬥ ⬥ ⬥ ⬥ / SOME UNITS ⬥

SUPER 8 CALGARY AIRPORT 403/291-9888 **28**

◈ APPROVED

Hotel

Address: 3030 Barlow Tr NE T1Y 1A2 **Location:** Corner of 32nd Ave NE and Barlow Tr NE. **Facility:** 61 units. 4 stories, interior corridors. **Parking:** winter plug-ins. **Amenities:** safes. **Guest Services:** valet and coin laundry.

SAVE ⬥⬥ ⬥⬥ BIZ ⬥ ⬥ ⬥
⬥ / SOME UNITS ⬥

THE WESTIN CALGARY AIRPORT 403/452-4506 **10**

◈ THREE DIAMOND

Contemporary
Hotel

WESTIN HOTELS & RESORTS **AAA Benefit:** Members save 5% or more!

Address: 671 Aero Dr NE T2E 7Y5 **Location:** Hwy 2 (Deerfoot Tr) exit 266, just se. **Facility:** 247 units. 5 stories, interior corridors. **Parking:** winter plug-ins. **Amenities:** safes. **Pool:** heated indoor. **Activities:** hot tub, exercise room. **Guest Services:** valet laundry.

SAVE ⬥⬥ ⬥⬥ ⬥ CALL ⬥
⬥ ⬥⬥ HS ⬥ ⬥ ⬥ ⬥ / SOME UNITS ⬥

WINGATE BY WYNDHAM CALGARY 403/514-0099 **49**

◈ THREE DIAMOND Hotel. **Address:** 400 Midpark Way SE T2X 3S4

WINGATE BY WYNDHAM CALGARY AIRPORT
587/393-0700 **5**

◈ THREE DIAMOND Hotel. **Address:** 57 Freeport Crescent NE T3J 0T4

WHERE TO EAT

ALLOY 403/287-9255 **36**
◈ THREE DIAMOND New International. Fine Dining. **Address:** 220 42 Ave SE T2G 1Y4

BASIL 403/457-0808 **13**
◈ APPROVED Vietnamese. Casual Dining. **Address:** 2770 32nd Ave NE, #10 T1Y 5S5

BELMONT DINER 403/242-6782 **35**
◈ APPROVED American. Casual Dining. **Address:** 2008 33rd Ave SW T2T 1Z6

BIG FISH 403/277-3403 **18**
◈ THREE DIAMOND Seafood. Casual Dining. **Address:** 1112 Edmonton Tr NE T2E 3K4

BIG T'S BBQ 403/284-5959 **8**
◈ APPROVED Barbecue. Casual Dining. **Address:** 2138 Crowchild Tr NW T2M 3Y7

BOOGIE'S BURGERS 403/230-7070 **21**
◈ APPROVED Burgers. Quick Serve. **Address:** 908 Edmonton Tr NE T2E 3K1

BOW VALLEY RANCHE RESTAURANT 403/476-1310 **45**
◈ THREE DIAMOND Regional Canadian. Fine Dining. **Address:** 15979 Bow Bottom Tr SE T2J 6T5

BROKEN PLATE KITCHEN & BAR 403/225-9650 **42**
◈ APPROVED Greek. Casual Dining. **Address:** 590-10816 Macleod Tr SE T2J 5N8

CACTUS CLUB CAFE
◈ THREE DIAMOND New American. Casual Dining.
LOCATIONS:
Address: 2612 39th Ave NE T1Y 7S9 **Phone:** 403/250-1120 **6**
Address: 7010 Macleod Tr SE T2H 0L3
Phone: 403/255-1088 **40**

CARVER'S STEAKHOUSE 403/250-6327 **12**
◈ THREE DIAMOND Steak. Fine Dining. **Address:** 2620 32nd Ave NE T1Y 6B8

(See map & index p. 60.)

CASSIS BISTRO 403/262-0036 (27)
THREE DIAMOND French. Casual Dining. **Address:** 2505 17th Ave SW T3C 1J7

THE CHEESECAKE CAFE 403/255-7443
APPROVED American. Casual Dining. **Address:** 7600 Macleod Tr SE T2H 0L9

CHEZ CORA 403/457-2672
APPROVED Breakfast Sandwiches. Casual Dining. **Address:** 2525 36th St T1Y 5T4

DINER DELUXE 403/276-5499 (24)
APPROVED American. Casual Dining. **Address:** 804 Edmonton Tr NE T2E 3J6

EARLS KITCHEN + BAR
APPROVED American. Casual Dining.
LOCATIONS:
Address: 3030 23rd St NE T2E 8R7 **Phone:** 403/291-6700
Address: 1110 16th Ave NW T2M 0K8 **Phone:** 403/289-2566
Address: 5155 130th Ave SE, #200 SE T2Z 0N3 **Phone:** 403/255-3275

FORBIDDEN CITY SEAFOOD & DIM SUM RESTAURANT
403/250-1848 (26)
APPROVED Chinese Dim Sum. Casual Dining. **Address:** 999 36th St NE, #220 T2A 7X6

GUS'S PIZZA 403/282-4005 (9)
APPROVED Pizza. Casual Dining. **Address:** 1620 29th St NW, #180 T2W 4L7

ITALIAN CENTRE SHOP 403/238-4869 (41)
APPROVED Italian Sandwiches Pizza. Quick Serve. **Address:** 9919 Fairmount Dr SE T2J 0S3

JAMESONS IRISH PUB 403/220-9888 (3)
APPROVED American. Gastropub. **Address:** 3790 Brentwood Rd NW T2L 1K8

JIMMY'S A & A DELI 403/289-1400 (11)
APPROVED Mediterranean Deli. Quick Serve. **Address:** 1401 20th Ave NW T2M 1G6

JOEY RESTAURANTS
APPROVED American. Casual Dining.
LOCATIONS:
Address: 3026 23rd St NE T2E 8R7 **Phone:** 403/219-8465
Address: 50 Crowfoot Way NW T3G 4C8 **Phone:** 403/547-5639
Address: 6455 Macleod Tr SW, #100A T2H 0K8 **Phone:** 403/692-6626

JUREE'S THAI PLACE RESTAURANT 403/264-6477 (14)
APPROVED Thai. Casual Dining. **Address:** 2055 16th Ave NW T2M 0M3

KANE'S HARLEY DINER 403/269-7311 (29)
APPROVED Comfort Food. Casual Dining. **Address:** 1209 9th Ave SE T2G 3E8

LA BOULANGERIE 403/984-9294 (34)
APPROVED Breads/Pastries. Quick Serve. **Address:** 2435 4th St SW T2S 2T4

LA PICCOLA NAPOLI RISTORANTE 403/278-2282 (43)
APPROVED Italian. Casual Dining. **Address:** 12445 Lake Fraser Dr SE, #105 T2J 7A4

LINA'S ITALIAN MARKET 403/277-9166 (15)
APPROVED Italian Deli. Quick Serve. **Address:** 2202 Centre St NE T2E 2T4

MISAI JAPANESE RESTAURANT 403/250-1688 (10)
APPROVED Japanese. Casual Dining. **Address:** 1915 32nd Ave NE T2E 7C8

MOXIE'S CLASSIC GRILL 403/291-4636 (4)
APPROVED American. Casual Dining. **Address:** 29 Hopewell Way NE T3J 4V7

THE NASH 403/984-3365 (31)
THREE DIAMOND New World. Casual Dining. **Address:** 925 11 St SE T2G 0R4

NICK'S STEAKHOUSE & PIZZA 403/282-9278 (7)
APPROVED Steak Pizza. Casual Dining. **Address:** 2430 Crowchild Tr NW T2M 3N5

NOTABLE - THE RESTAURANT 403/288-4372 (5)
THREE DIAMOND New Canadian Comfort Food. Casual Dining. **Address:** 4611 Bowness Rd NW T3B 0B2

OEB BREAKFAST CO. 403/278-3447 (22)
APPROVED Breakfast. Casual Dining. **Address:** 824 Edmonton Tr NE T2E 3J6

OPEN RANGE STEAKS & CHOPS 403/277-3408 (17)
THREE DIAMOND New American. Casual Dining. **Address:** 1114 Edmonton Tr NE T2E 3K4

OPEN SESAME 403/259-0123 (38)
APPROVED Asian. Casual Dining. **Address:** 6920 Macleod Tr S T2H 0L3

ORIENTAL PHOENIX 403/253-8189
APPROVED Vietnamese. Casual Dining. **Address:** 104 58th Ave SW, #80 T2H 0N7

ORIGINAL JOE'S RESTAURANT & BAR 403/452-6449
APPROVED American. Gastropub. **Address:** 12100 Macleod Tr SE T2J 7G9

PACINI PASTA & GRILL RISTORANTE 403/930-8080 (1)
APPROVED Italian. Casual Dining. **Address:** 123 Freeport Blvd NE T3N 0A3

PFANNTASTIC PANNENKOEK HAUS
403/243-7757 (37)
APPROVED
Dutch Specialty Casual Dining
$11-$21
AAA Inspector Notes: There is a pleasing décor at this eatery with lovely displays of Delft Blue pottery, which is available for sale along with treats and snacks from the Netherlands. Traditional "pannenkoeken" with all kinds of yummy savory and sweet combinations are offered and you can also build your own concoction. Dutch-inspired soups, salads, omelets and open-face sandwiches round out the menu. You can rely on super friendly, efficient servers to recommend their favorites and help you to pronounce them. **Features:** full bar. **Address:** 2439 54th Ave SW T3E 1M4 **Location:** Just ne of jct Hwy 8 (Glenmore Tr) and Crowchild Tr; in small strip mall. [B] [L] [D]

PIES PLUS CAFÉ 403/271-6616 (44)
APPROVED Specialty. Quick Serve. **Address:** 12445 Lake Fraser Dr T2J 7A4

PIO PERUVIAN ROTISSERIE CHICKEN 403/681-7378 (19)
APPROVED Peruvian. Casual Dining. **Address:** 2929 Sunridge Way NE T1Y 7K7

PITA BASKET 403/219-2747 (20)
APPROVED Lebanese. Quick Serve. **Address:** 3221 Sunridge Way NE, #140 T1Y 7M4

RAJDOOT 403/245-0181 (33)
APPROVED Indian. Casual Dining. **Address:** 2424 4th St SW T2S 2T4

(See map & index p. 60.)

RICKY'S ALL DAY GRILL   403/571-3220
▼▼ APPROVED   American. Casual Dining. **Address:** 3321 20th Ave NE T1Y 7A8

RIVER CAFE   403/261-7670 (25)
▼▼ THREE DIAMOND Regional Canadian. Fine Dining. **Address:** 25 Prince's Island Park T2P 0R1

ROUGE RESTAURANT   403/531-2767 (30)
▼▼ FOUR DIAMOND New French. Fine Dining. **Address:** 1240 8th Ave SE T2G 0M7

SANTORINI GREEK TAVERNA   403/276-8363 (16)
▼▼ APPROVED   Greek. Casual Dining. **Address:** 1502 Centre St N T2E 2R9

SMUGGLER'S INN   403/253-5355 (39)
▼▼ APPROVED   Steak. Casual Dining. **Address:** 6920 Macleod Tr S T2H 0L3

SPOLUMBO'S DELI   403/264-6452 (32)
▼▼ APPROVED   Deli Sandwiches. Quick Serve. **Address:** 1308 9th Ave SE T2G 0T3

SS106 APERITIVO BAR   403/219-0949 (23)
▼▼ APPROVED   Italian. Casual Dining. **Address:** 824D Edmonton Tr T2E 3J6

STARBELLY OPEN KITCHEN & LOUNGE   403/570-0133
▼▼ THREE DIAMOND Regional Canadian. Casual Dining. **Address:** 19489 Seton Cres SE T3M 1T4

WHITE SPOT   403/278-8212
▼▼ APPROVED   American. Casual Dining. **Address:** 10440 Macleod Tr SE T2J 0P8

WITHOUT PAPERS PIZZA   403/457-1154 (28)
▼▼ APPROVED   Pizza. Casual Dining. **Address:** 1216 9th Ave SE T2G 0T1

XS LOUNGE AND GRILL   403/475-1010 (2)
▼▼ APPROVED   International. Casual Dining. **Address:** 6625 36th St NE T3J 4C8

CAMROSE (F-7) pop. 17,286

Camrose, first settled around 1900 as a trading post, has a strong sense of its Scandinavian heritage. Known originally as the Hamlet of Sparling, its name was changed to Camrose in 1906. Camrose salutes country music during the ▼▼ Big Valley Jamboree, a 4-day festival that typically begins in late July or early August.

Tourism Camrose: 4522 53rd St., Camrose, AB, Canada T4V 4E3. **Phone:** (780) 672-4255.

CAMROSE AND DISTRICT CENTENNIAL MU-SEUM is 2 blks. s. of Hwy. 13 at 4522 53rd St. at jct. 46th Ave. The museum houses items from Camrose's pioneer days. Buildings include a country school; a fire hall; and a restored log pioneer house and church, both furnished in period. A steam engine, a replica of the first newspaper building and a working model of an early threshing machine are displayed. **Hours:** Wed.-Sun. 10-5, mid-May to early Sept.; by appointment rest of year. **Cost:** Donations. **Phone:** (780) 672-3298.

CANALTA HOTEL CAMROSE   780/672-7303
▼▼ APPROVED   Hotel. **Address:** 4710 73rd St T4V 0E5

HOTEL CAMROSE RESORT CASINO-BW PREMIER
COLLECTION   780/679-2376
▼▼ THREE DIAMOND [SAVE] Hotel. **Ad-dress:** 3201 48th Ave T4V 0K9

AAA Benefit:
Members save up to 15% and earn bonus points!

NORSEMEN INN   780/672-9171
▼▼ APPROVED   Hotel. **Address:** 6505 48th Ave T4V 3K3

RAMADA INN CAMROSE   780/672-5220
▼▼ APPROVED   Hotel. **Address:** 4702 73rd St T4V 0E5

WHERE TO EAT

THE CANADIAN BREWHOUSE   780/672-8880
▼▼ APPROVED   International. Sports Bar. **Address:** 6608 48th Ave T4V 4R1

THE LEFSE HOUSE SCANDINAVIAN BAKERY   780/672-7555
▼▼ APPROVED   Scandinavian. Casual Dining. **Address:** 5210 51st Ave T4V 4N5

MR MIKES STEAKHOUSECASUAL   780/608-1886
▼▼ APPROVED   American. Casual Dining. **Address:** 4706 73rd St T4V 0E5

SKYWAY RESTAURANT   780/672-8363
▼▼ APPROVED   Asian. Casual Dining. **Address:** 4941 50th St T4V 0S5

CANMORE (H-5) pop. 12,288,
elev. 1,341m/4,400'
• Restaurants p. 78
• Part of Banff National Park area — see map p. 30

Established in 1883 as a coal-mining center, Canmore was the first Canadian Pacific Railroad divisional point west of Calgary. The town also was the site of the biathlon and cross-country ski events of the 1988 Winter Olympics. Year-round recreational activities are abundant; fly-fishing, rock climbing, snowshoeing and dog sledding are just a few activities visitors can enjoy. Hiking, mountain biking and cross-country skiing are popular along the area's numerous trails. The Canmore Highland Games on Labour Day weekend also keeps sports enthusiasts entertained with a variety of athletic competitions. Scottish and Celtic dance and musical performances and sheep dog demonstrations take place during the daylong festival as well.

Tourism Canmore Kananaskis: 2801 Bow Valley Tr., P.O. Box 8608, Canmore, AB, Canada T1W 3K1. **Phone:** (855) 678-1295.

ALPINE HELICOPTERS LTD. is off Hwy. 1 Canmore exit, following signs to Canmore Municipal Heliport at 91 Bow Valley Tr. Scenic flights over the Canadian Rockies are offered. Passengers can view alpine valleys, glaciers, the Continental Divide, Banff National Park and towering Mount Assiniboine—"the Matterhorn of the Canadian Rockies." Helicopters carry two to six passengers.

Hours: Departures require a minimum of two passengers. Sightseeing flights are offered daily (weather permitting) except Three Sisters Peaks, Mon.-Fri., May 1-Oct. 1, daily, rest of year. Departure times vary. Closed Christmas. Phone ahead to confirm schedule. **Cost:** Marvel Pass 45-minute tour with a 15-minute stop in the mountains, $1,199 (per two passengers minimum). Mt. Assiniboine & Glaciers 30-minute tour $330 (per passenger). Royal Canadian 25-minute tour $275 (per passenger). Three Sisters Peaks 12-minute tour $150 (per passenger). Reservations are required. **Phone:** (403) 678-4802. [GT]

BEST WESTERN POCATERRA INN   403/678-4334

THREE DIAMOND

Hotel

AAA Benefit: Members save up to 15% and earn bonus points!

Address: 1725 Mountain Ave T1W 2W1 **Location:** Trans-Canada Hwy 1 exit 86, 1.3 mi (2.1 km) e. **Facility:** 83 units. 4 stories, interior corridors. **Parking:** winter plug-ins. **Terms:** check-in 4 pm. **Pool:** heated indoor. **Activities:** sauna, hot tub, exercise room. **Guest Services:** valet and coin laundry.

BLACKSTONE MOUNTAIN LODGE   403/609-8098
THREE DIAMOND Hotel. **Address:** 170 Kananaskis Way T1W 0A8

CANADIAN ROCKIES CHALETS   403/678-3799
APPROVED Condominium. **Address:** 1206 Bow Valley Tr T1W 1N6

CANMORE INN & SUITES BY SUNRISE   403/609-4656
APPROVED Hotel. **Address:** 1402 Bow Valley Tr T1W 1N5

COAST CANMORE HOTEL & CONFERENCE CENTRE   403/678-3625
THREE DIAMOND Hotel. **Address:** 511 Bow Valley Tr T1W 1N7

DAYS INN CANMORE   403/678-5488
APPROVED Hotel. **Address:** 1602 2nd Ave T1W 1M8

FALCON CREST LODGE   403/678-6150
THREE DIAMOND Condominium. **Address:** 190 Kananaskis Way T1W 3K5

FIRE MOUNTAIN LODGE   403/609-9949
APPROVED Condominium. **Address:** 121 Kananaskis Way T1W 2X2

THE GRANDE ROCKIES RESORT   403/678-8880
THREE DIAMOND Hotel. **Address:** 901 Mountain St T1W 0C9

HOLIDAY INN CANMORE   403/609-4422

THREE DIAMOND

Hotel

Address: 1 Silver Tip Tr T1W 2Z7 **Location:** Trans-Canada Hwy 1 exit 89, just s. **Facility:** 99 units. 3 stories, interior corridors. **Parking:** winter plug-ins. **Activities:** hot tub, trails, exercise room. **Guest Services:** valet and coin laundry.

MYSTIC SPRINGS CHALETS & HOT POOLS   403/609-0333
APPROVED Condominium. **Address:** 140 Kananaskis Way T1W 2X2

QUALITY RESORT-CHATEAU CANMORE   403/678-6699
APPROVED Hotel. **Address:** 1720 Bow Valley Tr T1W 2X3

ROCKY MOUNTAIN SKI LODGE   403/678-5445

APPROVED

Motel

Address: 1711 Bow Valley Tr T1W 2T8 **Location:** Trans-Canada Hwy 1 exit 86, 0.5 mi (0.8 km) s. Located in a commercial area. **Facility:** 87 units, some two bedrooms, kitchens and cottages. 1-2 stories, exterior corridors. **Terms:** check-in 4 pm. **Activities:** sauna, hot tub, playground, picnic facilities, trails. **Guest Services:** coin laundry.

RUNDLE CLIFFS LODGE   403/678-5108

THREE DIAMOND

Condominium

Address: 375 Spring Creek Dr T1W 0G9 **Location:** Trans-Canada Hwy 1 exit 89, 1.2 mi (2 km) s; in Spring Creek Village. **Facility:** Marvelous, modern one- to three-bedroom suites feature designer kitchens, balconies or decks with a grill and great bathrooms. In-floor heating throughout the units will be welcomed in the ski season. 14 condominiums. 4 stories, interior corridors. **Terms:** check-in 4 pm. **Activities:** hot tub, ice skating, bicycles, playground, game room, trails, exercise room. **Guest Services:** complimentary laundry.

SILVER CREEK LODGE   403/678-4242
THREE DIAMOND Extended Stay Hotel. **Address:** 1818 Mountain Ave T1W 3M3

SOLARA RESORT & SPA   403/609-3600
THREE DIAMOND Condominium. **Address:** 187 Kananaskis Way T1W 0A3

STONERIDGE MOUNTAIN RESORT CANMORE   403/675-5000
THREE DIAMOND Condominium. **Address:** 30 Lincoln Park T1W 3E9

SUPER 8 BY WYNDHAM CANMORE   403/609-9999
APPROVED Hotel. **Address:** 1506 Bow Valley Tr T1W 1N5

Booth or table? AAA.com/travelguides/restaurants

WHERE TO EAT

BLAKE   403/675-3663
APPROVED Asian Fusion. Casual Dining. **Address:** 810 Bow Valley Tr T1W 1N6

COMMUNITEA CAFE   403/678-6818
APPROVED Vegetarian. Quick Serve. **Address:** 1001 6th Ave, #117 T1W 3L8

CRAZYWEED KITCHEN   403/609-2530
THREE DIAMOND New American. Casual Dining. **Address:** 1600 Railway Ave T1W 1P6

GAUCHO BRAZILIAN BARBECUE   403/678-9886
APPROVED Brazilian. Casual Dining. **Address:** 629 Main St T1W 2B1

THE GRIZZLY PAW PUB & BREWING COMPANY
     403/678-9983
APPROVED Canadian. Gastropub. **Address:** 622 8th St T1W 2B5

THE IRON GOAT PUB & GRILL   403/609-0222
APPROVED American. Casual Dining. **Address:** 703 Benchlands Tr T1W 3G9

LE FOURNIL BAKERY   403/675-5005
APPROVED French Breads/Pastries. Quick Serve. **Address:** 1205 Bow Valley Tr T1W 1P5

MOUNTAIN MERCATO   403/609-6631
APPROVED Deli. Quick Serve. **Address:** 817 Main St, #102 T1W 2B3

MURRIETA'S BAR & GRILL   403/609-9500
THREE DIAMOND Western Pacific Rim. Casual Dining. **Address:** 200-737 Main St T1W 2B2

PATRINOS STEAKHOUSE & PUB   403/678-4060
APPROVED International. Casual Dining. **Address:** 1602 Bow Valley Tr T1W 1N5

RED ROCK PIZZA   403/675-4443
APPROVED Pizza. Casual Dining. **Address:** 1005 Cougar Creek Dr T1W 1E1

ROCKY MOUNTAIN FLATBREAD COMPANY   403/609-5508
APPROVED Pizza. Casual Dining. **Address:** 838 10th St, Unit 101 T1W 2A8

RUSTICA STEAKHOUSE   403/678-1600
THREE DIAMOND Steak. Fine Dining. **Address:** 2000 Silvertip Tr T1W 3J4

SAGE BISTRO   403/678-4878
THREE DIAMOND New Canadian. Casual Dining. **Address:** 1712 Bow Valley Tr T1W 1P2

SANTA LUCIA TRATTORIA   403/678-3414
APPROVED Italian. Casual Dining. **Address:** 714 8th St T1W 2B6

THE SUMMIT CAFE   403/609-2120
APPROVED Breakfast Sandwiches. Quick Serve. **Address:** 1001 Cougar Creek Dr T1W 1E1

TABLE FOOD + DRINK   403/609-5441
THREE DIAMOND New Canadian. Casual Dining. **Address:** 511 Bow Valley Tr T1W 1N7

TAPAS RESTAURANT   403/609-0583
THREE DIAMOND Mediterranean Small Plates. Casual Dining. **Address:** 633 10th St T1W 2A2

THE TROUGH DINING CO.   403/678-2820
THREE DIAMOND New Canadian. Fine Dining. **Address:** 725 9th St T1W 2V7

VALBELLA GOURMET FOODS   403/678-9989
APPROVED Deli. Quick Serve. **Address:** 104 Elk Run Blvd T1W 2W8

WHERE THE BUFFALO ROAM SALOON   403/675-2222
APPROVED Regional Canadian Small Plates. Casual Dining. **Address:** 626 8th St T1W 2V7

WILD ORCHID BISTRO & SUSHI LOUNGE   403/675-0755
APPROVED Asian. Casual Dining. **Address:** 1818 Mountain Ave T1W 3M3

CARDSTON (K-6) pop. 3,580, elev. 1,185m/3,888'

A son-in-law of Brigham Young, Charles Ora Card, led 10 Mormon families from Utah into Canada in 1887, hoping to find freedom from American anti-polygamy laws. Settling in Cardston, the immigrants founded the country's first Mormon settlement and named the town after their leader, who became its first mayor.

Today, a considerable percentage of Cardston residents are Mormon. Completed and dedicated in 1923, Cardston Alberta Temple of the Church of Jesus Christ of Latter-day Saints, 348 3rd St. W., was the first temple to be built in Canada. Non-Mormons are not permitted to enter the structure but can tour the grounds, where a visitor center offers information; phone (403) 653-3552.

Cardston & District Chamber of Commerce: 490 Main St., P.O. Box 1212, Cardston, AB, Canada T0K 0K0. **Phone:** (403) 795-1032.

REMINGTON CARRIAGE MUSEUM is at 623 Main St. More than 250 19th- and early 20th-century horse-drawn vehicles are showcased. Interactive displays and exhibit galleries provide the feeling of riding in the horse-drawn transportation of that era, and an introductory multimedia presentation provides an overview of that time.

The exhibit galleries, which include a blacksmith shop and livery stable, carriage factory, carriage dealership, working restoration shop, frontier settlement and racetrack, depict 19th-century society and its dependence on this mode of transportation. Sound effects, lighting and audiovisual presentations enhance many of the presentations. In summer visitors may schedule 15-minute rides on vintage and reproduction carriages.

Time: Allow 1 hour, 30 minutes minimum. **Hours:** Daily 9-5, July-Aug.; 9-4, rest of year. Carriage rides are offered daily 11-noon and 1-5, July-Aug.; 11-noon and 1-4, in June. Closed Jan. 1, Easter, Christmas Eve and Christmas. **Cost:** $13; $11 (ages 65+); $9 (ages 7-17); $35 (family, two adults and four children). Carriage ride $6.67; $4.76 (ages 4-17); $19.05 (family). **Phone:** (403) 653-5139.
GT

CHESTERMERE pop. 14,824

BEST WESTERN PLUS CHESTERMERE   587/349-7444

 THREE DIAMOND
Hotel

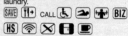 Best Western PLUS

AAA Benefit: Members save up to 15% and earn bonus points!

Address: 200 Marina Dr T1X 1N2 **Location:** Trans-Canada Hwy 1 exit Hwy 1A/Chestermere, 0.8 mi (1.4 km) sw, then just n. **Facility:** 80 units. 3 stories, interior corridors. **Pool:** heated indoor. **Activities:** hot tub, exercise room. **Guest Services:** valet and coin laundry.

[SAVE] [†↑] CALL [&] [≈] [🐾] [BIZ] [HS] [📶] [✕] [🛁] [▢] / SOME UNITS [🐾]

WHERE TO EAT

VAN SON VIETNAMESE CUISINE   403/248-8311
 APPROVED   Vietnamese. Casual Dining. **Address:** 100 Marina Dr T1X 0R9

COALDALE (J-7) pop. 7,493

THE ALBERTA BIRDS OF PREY CENTRE is at 2124 16th Ave. The facility, a working conservation center, rehabilitates injured and orphaned birds of prey and prepares them for release back into the wild. A self-guiding nature walk provides a close-up view of captive hawks, falcons, owls, eagles and vultures; visitors also can pose for photos with owls. Birds fly freely during daily demonstrations at this 28-hectare (70-acre) prairie wetland site.

Time: Allow 1 hour, 30 minutes minimum. **Hours:** Daily 9:30-5, May 10-Sept. 10. **Cost:** $12; $10 (ages 60+); $8 (ages 6-18); $6 (ages 3-5). Reservations are required for guided tours. **Phone:** (403) 345-4262. [GT] [🎫]

COCHRANE (H-5) pop. 17,580
• Part of Calgary area — see map p. 43

Cochrane—named for Sen. Matthew Henry Cochrane, who began the first large-scale cattle ranch in the area in the 1880s—is known locally for its homemade ice cream, made by the same family since 1948; hang gliding; horseback riding; and canoe trips down the Bow River. Stoney First Nations Reserve, 16 kilometres (10 mi.) west on Hwy. 1A, was the filming site of several movies, including Arthur Penn's "Legends of the Fall" and "Little Big Man," and of the television series "Lonesome Dove."

Downtown Cochrane's Western-style architecture provides a backdrop for local arts and crafts and specialty shops. Of particular interest is Studio West, a foundry and art gallery where visitors can view the 3,000-year-old sculpting technique known as the "lost wax" process.

Also noteworthy is the town's "Trust" mural, on display at The Cochrane RancheHouse at 101 RancheHouse Rd. A montage of small paintings, the collective work of nearly 200 artists, forms a large Western image of a cowboy and his horse. The mural is accessible Mon.-Fri. 8:30-4:30. Closed holidays.

Cochrane Visitor Information Centre: 521 First St. W., Cochrane, AB, Canada T4C 0A4. **Phone:** (403) 851-2960.

DAYS INN & SUITES BY WYNDHAM COCHRANE   403/932-5588
 APPROVED   Hotel. **Address:** 5 West Side Dr T4C 1M1

RAMADA BY WYNDHAM COCHRANE   403/932-6355
 THREE DIAMOND   Hotel. **Address:** 10 Westside Dr T4C 1M1

SUPER 8 BY WYNDHAM COCHRANE   403/932-1410
 APPROVED   Hotel. **Address:** 11 West Side Dr T4C 1M1

WHERE TO EAT

JAIPUR INDIA CUISINE   403/981-9988
 APPROVED   Indian. Casual Dining. **Address:** 114 3rd Ave W T4C 1Z6

MR MIKES STEAKHOUSECASUAL   403/851-7447
 APPROVED   American. Casual Dining. **Address:** 50 Quarry St W T4C 0W5

MY GREEK PLATE   587/362-3332
 APPROVED   Greek. Casual Dining. **Address:** 110 3rd Ave T4C 1A6

PORTOFINO ITALIAN RISTORANTE   403/932-1777
 APPROVED   Italian. Casual Dining. **Address:** 205 1st St E, Bay 18 T4C 1X6

COLD LAKE pop. 13,839, elev. 555m/1,820'
• Restaurants p. 80

BEST WESTERN COLD LAKE INN   780/594-4888

 THREE DIAMOND
Hotel

Best Western

AAA Benefit: Members save up to 15% and earn bonus points!

Address: 4815 52nd St T9M 1P1 **Location:** Corner of 55th Ave (Hwy 26 and 55) and 52nd St; south end of city. **Facility:** 131 units, some efficiencies. 2-4 stories, interior/exterior corridors. **Parking:** winter plug-ins. **Dining:** Sawmill Prime Rib & Steak House, see separate listing. **Pool:** heated indoor. **Activities:** hot tub, picnic facilities, exercise room. **Guest Services:** valet laundry.

[SAVE] [†↑] [♨] CALL [&] [≈] [🐾] [BIZ] [HS] [📶] [✕] [🛁] [▢] [▢] / SOME UNITS [🐾]

COURTYARD BY MARRIOTT COLD LAKE   780/594-0989
 THREE DIAMOND [SAVE] Hotel. **Address:** Rt 28 & Hwy 897 T9M 1P4

AAA Benefit: Members save 5% or more!

HOLIDAY INN EXPRESS & SUITES COLD LAKE   780/654-3688
 THREE DIAMOND   Hotel. **Address:** 5315 48 Ave T9M 1P1

RAMADA INN & SUITES COLD LAKE   780/594-7747
▽ APPROVED   Hotel. **Address:** 4005 50th St T9M 1K6

WHERE TO EAT

BEANTREES CAFÉ   780/594-4177
▽ APPROVED   Coffee/Tea Sandwiches. Quick Serve.
Address: 5112 50th Ave T9M 1Y2

CLARKS GENERAL STORE & EATERY   780/639-4782
▽ APPROVED   American. Casual Dining. **Address:** 701
Lakeshore Dr T9M 1N1

ORIGINAL JOE'S RESTAURANT & BAR   780/594-1215
▽ APPROVED   American. Gastropub. **Address:** 5302 50
Ave T9M 1P2

SAWMILL PRIME RIB & STEAK HOUSE   780/594-5985
▽ APPROVED   Steak. Casual Dining. **Address:** 4815
52nd St T9M 1P1

COLUMBIA ICEFIELD—See Jasper National
Park p. 118.

CROWSNEST PASS (J-5) pop. 5,565

An area of wild beauty and haunting legends, the
municipality of Crowsnest Pass is an amalgamation
of the former coal-mining towns of Bellevue, Blair-
more, Coleman, Frank and Hillcrest. Scenic Hwy. 3
through Crowsnest Pass connects Burmis to Fernie,
British Columbia, via the Rocky Mountain Range
and the Continental Divide.

The area provides visitors with recreational opportunities and stimulates the imagination with such
stories as the curse of the Lost Lemon Gold Mine,
rum-running and the shoot-out at Bellevue Cafe.

The town of Frank made national headlines April
29, 1903, when close to 70 residents were killed in
the dramatic slide of Turtle Mountain on the east
side of the pass. Ninety million tons of limestone
swept over 1.5 kilometres (.9 mi.) of the valley before dawn, destroying part of the town and burying a
mine plant and railway. The old town was at the
western edge of the slide; many cellars still are
visible.

BELLEVUE UNDERGROUND MINE TOUR is n. off
Hwy. 3 Bellevue exit, following signs to the Bellevue
Underground Mine access road at 2531-213 St. Participants don a miner's helmet with a lamp and a
battery pack and follow guides along the same path
taken by coal miners 1903-61 when the coal mine
was operational. The 1-hour tour provides insights
into the lives of coal miners and the work they did in
the mine.

Note: The temperature in the mine is around 1 C
(35 F); dress in warm clothing and wear sturdy footwear, even in summer months. **Time:** Allow 1 hour
minimum. **Hours:** Daily 10-6 July-Aug.; daily 9-5,
May-June; Mon.-Fri. 9-4, Sept.-Oct. Last tour departs 30 minutes before closing. **Cost:** $16; $13
(ages 65+); $10 (ages 6-17); $40 (family, two adults
and two children ages 6-17; additional children $5).
Phone: (403) 564-4700. GT

▽ GEM SAVE **FRANK SLIDE INTERPRETIVE
CENTRE** is 1.5 km (.9 mi.) n. off Hwy.
3 at w. edge of Frank Slide. The center overlooks
the site of the 1903 rockslide. Visitors experience
the impact of Canada's deadliest rockslide through
interactive exhibits and high-definition presentations. Walkways outside the center provide spectacular views of the surrounding Canadian Rockies.
A 1.5-kilometre (.9 mi.) self-guiding trail through the
slide provides a close-up look at the debris. Interpretive programs are offered in summer.

Time: Allow 1 hour, 30 minutes minimum. **Hours:**
Daily 9-6, July 1-Labour Day; 10-5, rest of year.
Closed Jan. 1, Easter, Christmas Eve and
Christmas. **Cost:** $13; $11 (ages 65+); $9 (ages
7-17); free (Canadian military and family with ID);
$35 (family, two adults and children). **Phone:** (403)
562-7388.

DEAD MAN'S FLATS pop. 121
• Part of Banff National Park area — see map
p. 30

COPPERSTONE RESORT HOTEL   403/678-0303
▽ THREE DIAMOND   Condominium. **Address:** 250 2nd Ave T1W
2W4

WHERE TO EAT

MAD DOG CAFE & MARKET   403/609-3671
▽ APPROVED   Indian. Quick Serve. **Address:** 120 1st
Ave T1W 2W4

DEVON (E-6) pop. 6,510, elev. 680m/2,230'
• Part of Edmonton area — see map p. 84

Canada's first planned community, Devon was
created by Imperial Oil Resources Ltd. in 1948 to
provide accommodations for the workers employed
in the company's oilfields. Imperial Leduc No. 1, the
area's first well, had just put the town of Devon on
the map. The town's name was derived from the Devonian formation, the oil's source, a stratum 1,524
metres (5,000 ft.) underground.

Devon is on the banks of the North Saskatchewan River, where fishing often yields northern pike,
walleye and goldeye. Year-round recreational activities include canoeing, cross-country skiing, golf,
hiking, ice-skating and swimming.

Town of Devon: 1 Columbia Ave. W., Devon, AB,
Canada T9G 1A1. **Phone:** (780) 987-8300.

LEDUC #1 ENERGY DISCOVERY CENTRE is 2
km (1.2 mi.) s. on Hwy. 60 at 50339 Hwy. 60 S. The
center not only provides insight into the workings of
the oil industry but also looks at area history, the
story behind Leduc No. 1 and how Canada became
self-sufficient in oil production. A 15-minute video
presentation, interactive energy displays, geological
exhibits, equipment, artifacts, photographs, scale
models, murals and an outdoor interpretive trail help
explain how oil is produced and refined.

A 53-metre (174 ft.) replica of the original derrick has been erected on the discovery site. **Note:** The Living Energy Project, launched in 2016, will demonstrate renewable resources—including geothermal, solar and wind power—when it is completed. **Time:** Allow 1 hour minimum. **Hours:** Daily 9-5, mid-May through Aug. 31; Mon.-Fri. 9-5, mid-May and Sept.-Nov. **Cost:** $10; $8 (ages 65+); $6 (ages 6-17); $25 (family, two adults and all children). **Phone:** (780) 987-4323 or (866) 987-4323.

DRAYTON VALLEY pop. 7,049

BEST WESTERN PLUS DRAYTON VALLEY ALL SUITES
780/621-2378

THREE DIAMOND

Extended Stay Contemporary Hotel

Best Western PLUS

AAA Benefit: Members save up to 15% and earn bonus points!

Address: 2252 50th St T7A 1R5 **Location:** Just n on Hwy 39; south end of town. **Facility:** 90 efficiencies, some two bedrooms. 4 stories, interior corridors. **Parking:** winter plug-ins. **Amenities:** safes. **Activities:** game room, picnic facilities, exercise room. **Guest Services:** coin laundry. **Featured Amenity: full hot breakfast.**

SAVE [T+] CALL [&] [img] BIZ HS
[wifi] [X] [pet] [fridge] [micro] [iron] / SOME UNITS [coffee]

HOLIDAY INN EXPRESS HOTEL & SUITES   780/515-9888
APPROVED Hotel. **Address:** 5001 Brougham Dr T7A 0A1

RAMADA DRAYTON VALLEY   780/514-7861
THREE DIAMOND Hotel. **Address:** 2051 50th St T7A 1S5

SUPER 8 BY WYNDHAM DRAYTON VALLEY   780/542-9122
APPROVED Hotel. **Address:** 3727 50th St T7A 1S4

WHERE TO EAT

COBBLESTONE CAFE   780/621-0203
APPROVED Coffee/Tea Sandwiches. Quick Serve. **Address:** 5147 50th Ave T7A 1J7

MR MIKES STEAKHOUSECASUAL   780/515-8433
APPROVED American. Casual Dining. **Address:** 2248 50th St T7A 0A1

THREE KNIGHTS STEAK HOUSE & PIZZA   780/542-5222
APPROVED American. Casual Dining. **Address:** 5211 50th St T7A 1R5

THE WHITE BULL CAFE   780/542-5695
APPROVED Comfort Food. Casual Dining. **Address:** 5105 51st St T7A 1K9

DRUMHELLER (H-7) pop. 8,029
• Hotels p. 82 • Restaurants p. 82

About 65 million years before Sam Drumheller began promoting the 1910 townsite later named for him, the surrounding Red Deer Valley was the home of immense dinosaurs. Plant-eating hadrosaurs, flesh-eating tyrannosaurs and their formidable cousins stomped through the swampy lowlands and forests bordering the Mowry Sea, which once covered the North American plains. Fossils of prehistoric creatures often are discovered in the multi-layered sedimentary walls of the valley; several life-size dinosaur replicas can be seen in town.

A larger-than-life version of one of these prehistoric beings, a 25-metre-tall (84-ft.) facsimile of a tyrannosaurus rex, has been built over the top of the Drumheller & District Chamber of Commerce at 60 1st Ave. W. Visitors can climb up to a viewing platform in the dinosaur's mouth.

Although the local coal industry founded in 1911 by American Jesse Gouge has declined, remnants of old mines still exist. Six kilometres (3.7 mi.) w. on N. Dinosaur Trail (Hwy. 838), Midland Provincial Park features Badlands Trail, a self-guiding walking trail that leads to the former site of Midland Mine. Gas and oil wells sporadically dot the nearby rolling prairies, but the shortgrass country is occupied mostly by geese and antelope.

Hoodoos—mushroom-shaped pillars of rock that have been carved into unusual formations by centuries of wind and rain—can be seen 18 kilometres (11 mi.) southeast on Hwy. 10. Because of their fragile nature, climbing these formations is not permitted.

Another nearby remarkable natural site is Horseshoe Canyon, 17 kilometres (11 mi.) southwest on Hwy. 9. Deriving its name from its horseshoe shape, the canyon is in an area of badlands in the Alberta prairies. Viewpoints provide opportunities to survey multicolored canyon walls and unusual rock formations.

A natural amphitheater is the site in early July for 9 days of performances of The Canadian Badlands Passion Play. In a setting closely resembling the Holy Land, a cast of 150 and a 100-voice choir relate the life of Christ; phone (403) 823-2001 or (888) 823-2001.

Stretching over the Red Deer River, the Rosedale Suspension Bridge on Hwy. 10 originally was used to carry miners across the river to the now-abandoned Star Mine. In 1931 the swinging bridge replaced the original cable car system and was used until the mine closed in 1957. A park with picnic facilities is available.

Drumheller Visitor Information Centre: 60 1st Ave. W., P.O. Box 999, Drumheller, AB, Canada T0J 0Y0. **Phone:** (403) 823-1331 or (866) 823-8100.

ROYAL TYRRELL MUSEUM is 6 km (4 mi.) n.w. at 1500 N. Dinosaur Tr. (Hwy. 838) in Midland Provincial Park. The museum is in the badlands of the Red Deer River Valley, surrounded by one of the richest fossil deposits in the world. Dinosaurs that once roamed Alberta are now showcased in the museum's Dinosaur Hall, where more than 45 skeletons are displayed.

Fossils, a preparation laboratory, hands-on exhibits and an indoor garden illustrate millions of years of geological and biological development; educational programs also are offered. Fossils in

Focus, a rotating exhibit, highlights some of the most scientifically significant fossils in the museum collection. In addition the museum houses a research center and operates a field station near Patricia *(see attraction listing p. 134)*.

Time: Allow 3 hours minimum. **Hours:** Daily 9-9, May 15-Aug. 31; daily 10-5, in Sept.; Tues.-Sat. 10-5 (also Mon. holidays), rest of year. Closed Jan. 1 and Christmas. **Cost:** $19; $14 (ages 65+); $10 (ages 7-17); $48 (family, two adults and all children). Two-day tickets $27; $21 (ages 65+); $15 (ages 7-17); $69 (family, two adults and all children). **Phone:** (403) 823-7707, or (888) 440-4240 out of Alberta.

CANALTA JURASSIC HOTEL   403/823-7700
♦ APPROVED   Hotel. **Address:** 1103 Hwy 9 S T0J 0Y0

RAMADA BY WYNDHAM INN & SUITES   403/823-2028
♦ APPROVED   Hotel. **Address:** 680 2nd St SE T0J 0Y0

SUPER 8 DRUMHELLER   403/823-8887
♦ APPROVED   Hotel. **Address:** 600-680 2nd St SE T0J 0Y0

WHERE TO EAT

ATHENS GREEK RESTAURANT   403/823-3225
♦ APPROVED   Greek. Casual Dining. **Address:** 71 Bridge St T0J 0Y6

BERNIE & THE BOYS BISTRO   403/823-3318
♦ APPROVED   American. Quick Serve. **Address:** 305 4th St W T0J 0Y3

O'SHEA'S EATERY & ALE HOUSE   403/823-2460
♦ APPROVED   American. Casual Dining. **Address:** 2nd St SE, #600B T0J 0Y0

SUBLIME FOOD AND WINE   403/823-2344
♦ THREE DIAMOND   New American. Casual Dining. **Address:** 109 Centre St T0J 0Y0

Hit the Road with Financial Services

Providing peace-of-mind benefits exclusively for members—at home or abroad.

- Credit Cards
- Prepaid Cards
- Gift Cards
- Deposit Accounts
- Foreign Currency
- Loans
- Identity Theft Protection

Visit your local AAA office or online at **AAA.com/Financial**

All products not available at all locations.

Edmonton

Then & Now

Few first-time visitors to Edmonton are prepared for what they discover when they arrive. From trading post to metropolis within some 200 years, Edmonton continues to surprise visitors by its size, quality of life, sophistication and beautiful river valley location.

Edmonton owes its existence to an abundant and varied supply of natural resources, which prompted each of its three major booms. In 1795 the Hudson's Bay Co. founded Fort Edmonton on the banks of the North Saskatchewan River. Traders bartered with Cree and Blackfoot First Nations people for sought-after pelts of otters, beavers, muskrats, minks and foxes. A trading settlement developed and became the main stopover on routes to the north and to the Pacific.

This stopping point became a starting point for gold seekers rushing to the Klondike; they gathered supplies in Edmonton for the harsh trip north. When gold failed to materialize and many prospectors realized they weren't going to get rich, let alone get rich quick, they returned to Edmonton to settle for a slower but surer way of life.

AAA.com/travelguides—
more ways to look, book and save

A bust for prospectors was a boom for Edmonton. The city grew to six times its previous size, making it a prime choice for the provincial capital when Alberta was formed in 1905.

In the years that followed, the capital city earned its nickname, "Gateway to the North," because of its status as a transportation hub and gateway to the regions beyond. In 1915 Edmonton became a major link in the Canadian Pacific Transcontinental Railroad, emerging as an important crossroads stop between east and west as well as north and south.

In February 1947, the Leduc No. 1 Well gushed crude oil 40 kilometres (25 mi.) southwest of Edmonton. Since then more than 2,250 wells within a 40-kilometre radius of Edmonton have coaxed the precious natural resource to the surface. Enormous industrial growth resulted; the city's population quadrupled in the 25 years following the Leduc gusher. Today more than 450,000 barrels of crude oil are refined daily in greater Edmonton.

With nearly 1 million residents in the greater metropolitan area, Edmonton has been careful not to sacrifice the natural resource that makes it livable—its green space. Edmonton's river valley parkland is reputed to be the largest stretch of urban parkland in North America, encompassing 7,340

Edmonton skyline

(Continued on p. 85.)

Destination Edmonton

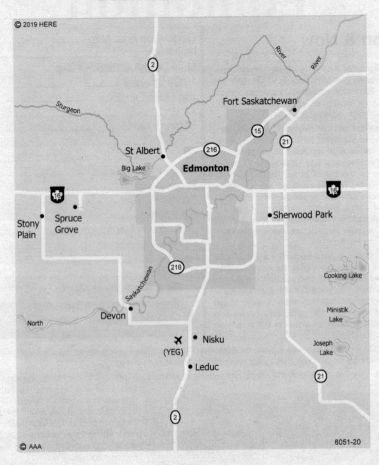

This map shows cities in the Edmonton vicinity where you will find attractions, hotels and restaurants. Cities are listed alphabetically in this book on the following pages.

Fast Facts

ABOUT THE CITY

POP: 812,201 ▪ **ELEV:** 670 m/2,198 ft.

MONEY

SALES TAX: The federal Goods and Service Tax is 5 percent and applies to most goods, food/beverages and services, including lodgings. Alberta does not have a provincial sales tax but does impose a 3 percent Destination Marketing Fee (DMF) as well as a 4 percent Municipal and Regional District Tax (MRDT).

WHOM TO CALL

EMERGENCY: 911

POLICE (non-emergency): (780) 423-4567

FIRE (non-emergency): 311

TEMPERATURE: (780) 468-4940

HOSPITALS: Grey Nuns Community Hospital, (780) 735-7000 ▪ Misericordia Community Hospital, (780) 735-2000 ▪ Royal Alexandra Hospital, (780) 735-4111 ▪ University of Alberta Hospital, (780) 407-8822.

VISITOR INFORMATION

Edmonton Welcome Centre: 9990 Jasper Ave., World Trade Centre building, Edmonton, AB, Canada T5J 1P7. **Phone:** (780) 401-7696.
The office is open Mon.-Fri. 8-4.
Visitor information also is available at the Edmonton International Airport.

TRANSPORTATION

AIR TRAVEL: Edmonton International Airport (YEG) is 29 kilometres (18 mi.) south of the city center; for information phone (780) 890-8382 or (800) 268-7134. Cheap plane tickets and international flights are available from many airline carriers and travel sites. Check with your local AAA office for flights and vacation packages.

The Skyshuttle provides transportation to and from the airport for $18 one way or $30 round-trip. Return trips must be pre-booked; phone (780) 465-8515 or (888) 438-2342 for Skyshuttle information and booking. Taxi service between the airport and a downtown destination typically costs $55; a limousine costs $66.

RENTAL CARS: Hertz, with offices at the airport and downtown (inside Edmonton House, 10205 100 Ave. N.W.), offers discounts to CAA and AAA members; phone (780) 890-4435 at the airport, (780) 423-3431 downtown, (800) 654-3131 in North America or (800) 654-3001 outside of North America. Contact a travel advisor at your local AAA club office to add rental cars to your travel packages.

 Book and save at **AAA.com/hertz**

RAIL SERVICE: The VIA Rail station is at 12360 121 St. N.W.; phone (888) 842-7245.

BUSES: Red Arrow Express offers luxury motor coach service between Edmonton, Calgary, Fort McMurray and Red Deer; phone (403) 531-0350 or (800) 232-1958.

TAXIS: Taxi companies include Co-Op Taxi Line, (780) 425-2525 ▪ Barrel Taxi (780) 489-7777 ▪ and Yellow Cab, (780) 462-3456. Taxi rates start at $3.60, plus $0.20 is charged for each additional 135 metres (about 1/12 mile) or a portion thereof. Taxis can be hailed, but phoning is recommended.

PUBLIC TRANSPORTATION: Edmonton has both bus and light-rail transit (LRT) service. Edmonton Transit System's Customer Service Centre, on the second floor of Edmonton Tower at 10111 104 Ave., sells ETS passes and is open Mon.-Fri. 8-4:30; phone 331 within Edmonton or (780) 442-5311. Buses operate Mon.-Fri. 5:20 a.m.-1:30 a.m., Sat.-Sun. 6:30 a.m.-1:30 a.m. On holidays hours may be extended for special events. Light-rail transit operates on a similar schedule; check the website for full schedule. Fare is $3.50; free (ages 0-12). A 1-day pass is $9.75.

(Continued from p. 83.)
hectares (18,348 acres), which is about 22 times the size of New York's City's Central Park. The city contains more than 11,000 hectares (27,181 acres) of parkland, playgrounds and green space.

Stretches of parks along the North Saskatchewan River Valley let residents and visitors spend long summer days enjoying such warm-weather activities as golfing, hiking, biking, canoeing and even panning for gold. When the winter chill arrives, the park system provides a playground for cross-country skiing, ice-skating and snowshoeing.

An extensive system of underground and overhead "pedways" in the downtown area makes it possible to travel in climate-controlled comfort regardless of the weather. Those who'd rather play indoors head to West Edmonton Mall, which combines 800-plus retail stores with restaurants and fun places to go like an amusement park, a water park with a giant wave pool, an ice-skating rink and two miniature golf courses. The largest of its kind in North America, this shopping and entertainment center has undergone three major expansions since its 1981 opening and draws an estimated 30.8 million people each year.

Must Do: AAA Editor's Picks

- Travel back in time at ⇌ **Fort Edmonton Park** (7000 143 St. N.W.), dubbed Canada's largest living-history park and one of the top things to do with kids. Staffed by costumed interpreters, the site features both original and re-created historical structures—everything from a replicated Hudson's Bay Co. fort to a 1920s-style midway.

- Spend a few hours exploring the ⇌ **West Edmonton Mall** (8882 170 St. N.W.), the largest shopping and entertainment destination in North America. The gargantuan complex boasts an amusement park, a water park with an indoor wave pool, an aquarium, miniature golf courses, an ice rink, dozens of restaurants and more than 800 stores.

- Attend a show at the **Francis Winspear Centre for Music** (4 Sir Winston Churchill Sq.). Built in 1997, the main performance space is a modern interpretation of such shoebox-style concert halls as the Tonhalle in Zurich and the Musikverein in Vienna. The downtown Edmonton facility is renowned for its acoustics (there isn't a bad seat in the house) as well as a stunning 6,551-pipe concert organ fashioned by Orgues Létourneau Limitée of Québec.

- Wrap your head around architect Randall Stout's **Art Gallery of Alberta** (2 Sir Winston Churchill Sq.), a curvy blend of steel and glass inspired by the aurora borealis and the North Saskatchewan River. When you're done ogling the ultra-modern exterior, take a trip inside and admire the handiwork of such Canadian painters as Maxwell Bates, Emily Carr and David Milne.

- Tour the four futuristic pyramid-shaped greenhouses and changing exhibitions at the **Muttart Conservatory** (9626 96a St. N.W.), either on your own or with the help of a guide. Located in the North Saskatchewan River Valley, the botanical garden is one of the city's most iconic landmarks and is one of the top things to do in Edmonton. (Note: The conservatory is closed for major renovations until early 2021.)

- Cheer on the National Hockey League's Edmonton Oilers at **Rogers Place** (10220 104 Ave. N.W.), which became the team's new, state-of-the-art home in 2016. Outside the arena is a 9-foot-tall bronze statue of legendary player Wayne Gretzky. The monument honoring "The Great One," who led his team to four Stanley Cup victories, has become a beloved city landmark and also a favorite photo spot.

- Find places to eat, drink and be merry in **Old Strathcona**, a five-block historic district now dominated by bohemian coffee shops, funky stores, live performance venues, local restaurants and bars. Whether the agenda calls for a bit of window-shopping or some late-night carousing, your best bet is to stick to the section of Whyte Avenue between 99 and 109 streets where there are plenty of fun places to go.

- Explore Edmonton's "Ribbon of Green," a 48-kilometre (30-mi.) stretch of the **North Saskatchewan River Valley** with bragging rights to more than 20 major parks and public facilities. In winter, strap on your cross-country skis and traverse William Hawrelak Park (9930 Groat Rd. N.W.). Or, if the weather's warm, play a round at Victoria Golf Course (12130 River Valley Rd.), said to be the oldest municipal golf course in Canada.

- Party like an Edmontonian. A jam-packed calendar filled with more than 50 annual events—including July's **Edmonton International Street Performers Festival** and August's ⇌ **Edmonton Folk Music Festival**—at one time earned the provincial capital the nickname "Festival City." You're sure to find fun things to do with friends or family.

- Visit the 1912 Beaux Arts **Alberta Legislature Building** (10800 97 Ave. N.W.) and take the guided tour to learn about Alberta's history and the building's impressive architecture. The grounds around the building are easy on the eyes, too, with monuments, wading pools and shooting water fountains that draw crowds of kids in summer. In wintertime, holiday light and ice sculpture displays dazzle visitors of all ages.

Whyte Avenue

Edmonton 1-day Itinerary

AAA editors suggest these activities for a great short vacation experience.

Morning

- Operating from late May to mid-October, the **High Level Bridge Streetcar** *(see Sightseeing p. 95)* is a fun way to travel between downtown Edmonton and the Old Strathcona historic district. As your vintage vehicle crosses the High Level Bridge, you'll catch a glimpse—and likely a shaky snapshot or two—of the idyllic North Saskatchewan River Valley.

- Along the streetcar line are three intermediary stops, including one in the Garneau neighborhood. Disembark here and try a specialty brew from **Transcend Coffee** (8708 109 St. N.W.), a local chain that hawks gourmet blends and ethically sourced beans.

- Hankering for a hearty breakfast? Look no further than **Highlevel Diner** (10922 88 Ave. N.W.), an eclectic space known far and wide for its comfort food and weekend brunches.

- At the High Level Bridge Streetcar's southern terminus is the Strathcona Streetcar Barn Museum, where rail buffs can peruse antique model trains and ticket punches. The museum is at the north end of the **Old Strathcona Farmers' Market** (10310 83 Ave. N.W.), an indoor market open every Saturday from 8 a.m. to 3 p.m., year-round.

- On rainy days or during the streetcar's off-season, spend the morning at the ▽ **Royal Alberta Museum** (9810 103a Ave. N.W.). Fresh from a $375.5 million renovation, the museum is home to a Natural History hall, with displays about the Ice Age, dinosaurs and Alberta's plants and animals; a Human History hall that explores the people of Alberta; an interactive Children's Gallery; and a Bug Gallery. The impressive facility, the largest in Western Canada, was known as the Provincial Museum and Archives of Alberta until Queen Elizabeth II rechristened it in 2005.

Afternoon

- First-time visitors to Edmonton will no doubt want to check the ▽ **West Edmonton Mall** (8882 170 St. N.W.) off their to-do lists. The mega mall is home to more than 800 stores in addition to an amusement park, an ice rink, miniature golf courses and an indoor water park. After raiding the sales racks, strike a few cover model poses in the shopping center's three "theme streets": Bourbon Street, Chinatown and Europa Boulevard.

- There are plenty of places to grab a bite inside WEM. Two good options for casual fare are **Famoso Neapolitan Pizzeria** and **Moxie's Classic Grill.** Or, skip the mall food court and head about 5 kilometres (3 mi.) north to family-owned **Fifendekel Pie Shop Cafe** (10646 170 St. N.W.) for delectable deli meats sandwiched between slices of freshly baked

High Level Bridge Streetcar

sunflower bread. More importantly, for dessert, there's pie!

Evening

- A cluster of restaurants near downtown's 4th Street Promenade (104 Street N.W. near Jasper Avenue) will entice serious foodies at dinnertime. Get a reservation at **Tzin Wine and Tapas** (10115 104 St.) for New World small plates served in a romantic, intimate space, or try nearby **Bar Bricco** (10347 Jasper Ave.) or **Uccellino** (10349 Jasper Ave.) for out-of-this-world pastas. (The two sister restaurants are located right next to each other and joined by a third, more exclusive spot also known for its Italian cuisine: **Corso 32,** 10345 Jasper Ave.).

- Walk off your meal with a leisurely stroll down the 4th Street Promenade (104 Street N.W.) to the outdoor **Neon Sign Museum,** a collection of 20 restored neon signs displayed on the exteriors of two brick buildings. The collection is especially photogenic at dusk when the neon begins to glow.

- Before turning in for the night, cab it back to Old Strathcona in south-central Edmonton. The entertainment district is centered on Whyte Avenue. An abundance of watering holes and live music venues makes this area a popular late-night destination. If you're a serious lover of jazz, **Yardbird Suite** (11 Tommy Banks Way), founded in the 1950s, is without equal. Meanwhile, laid-back **Funky Buddha** (10341 Whyte Ave.) offers a jammed activities calendar with fun events like karaoke and Latin dance lessons.

Top Picks for Kids

Under 13

- Budding young scientists can spend hours at ◆TELUS World of Science—Edmonton (11211 142 St. N.W.), where interactive exhibits encourage both learning and fun. The Body Fantastic gallery is a kid-friendly favorite; carnival games, 3-D models and a "Gallery of the Gross" explore the human body and all sorts of bodily functions. Water tables and creative play areas spark the imagination in the Discoveryland Gallery, designed for children ages 8 and under.

- On hot summer days, join throngs of Edmontonians for a splash in the public fountains and wading pools outside the Alberta Legislature Building (10800 97 Ave. N.W.). The building and its grounds are an entertainment destination in winter, too, with ice-skating, holiday light displays and other fun things to do with kids offered from mid- to late December.

- Ride the rails on an authentic steam train or streetcar at ◆Fort Edmonton Park (7000 143 St. N.W.), one of the top things to do in Edmonton with kids. You can easily spend a whole day at this living-history park, where re-created buildings and old-time demonstrations transport visitors back to various periods in Edmonton's history. Midway games, a petting zoo and pony rides guarantee a memorable day.

- Next to Fort Edmonton Park is another attraction packed with fun activities for kids—the John Janzen Nature Centre (7000 143 St. N.W.), where hands-on displays encourage an appreciation of nature. Search for nature items on an outdoor scavenger hunt, get face-to-face with salamanders and frogs, or crawl around from the perspective of an animal at the Tegler Discovery Zone's indoor playground.

Teens

- Aviation enthusiasts in search of a cool Instagram shot will find one at the Alberta Aviation Museum (11410 Kingsway Ave. N.W.). Housed in one of the last remaining World War II-era airplane hangars, the museum showcases more than 30 restored aircraft including all-season bush planes, Cold War-era fighter jets and a replica of the plane that delivered the first airmail in Western Canada. A restoration area allows visitors to watch as volunteers work on various aircraft.

- Boutiques, music stores and funky shops line the streets of Old Strathcona, a historic district centered on Whyte Avenue (82 Avenue N.W.) between 99 and 109 streets. There are more opportunities to browse local goods at the Old Strathcona Farmers' Market held each Saturday.

All Ages

- A fun way to travel between downtown and the Old Strathcona district is via the High Level Bridge Streetcar (10340 84 Ave. N.W.), a historic 1900s trolley system that runs late May to mid-October. Have your camera ready as you cross the North Saskatchewan River on what is reputedly the world's highest streetcar bridge.

- Have a laid-back brunch or lunch at Highlevel Diner (10912 88 Ave. N.W.), at the top of the hill just off the High Level Bridge. Sample local favorites like classic eggs Benedict, chicken and cheddar sandwiches and cinnamon buns so big they're served with a steak knife.

- Make a game plan before tackling the massive ◆West Edmonton Mall (8882 170 St. N.W.). Opportunities for family-friendly activities are seemingly endless, with an amusement park, water park, IMAX theater, glow-in-the-dark mini golf, escape room and more than 800 stores under one gigantic roof.

- Family events in Edmonton are plentiful, and one of most popular summer celebrations is the Edmonton International Street Performers Festival (8331 104 St. N.W.). Magicians, jugglers, clowns and acrobats from around the world host outdoor performances during this multiday festival.

- Reward well-behaved travelers with a sweet treat from Duchess Bake Shop (10718 124 St.), a small French-inspired bakery that serves up made-from-scratch macarons, meringues, croissants and other delicacies. The popular shop draws crowds from far and wide; among its most renowned patrons is Canadian Prime Minister Justin Trudeau.

Alberta Aviation Museum

Arriving
By Car

Two major highways run through Edmonton. The Trans-Canada Yellowhead Hwy. (Hwy. 16) provides access from the east and west; Queen Elizabeth II Hwy. runs north and south between Edmonton and Calgary.

Getting Around
Street System

Edmonton's street system is a grid with streets running north and south and avenues running east and west. Most streets and avenues are numbered starting from the southeast corner of the city; a few are named.

Edmonton's streetscape includes several traffic circles. When approaching a traffic circle, make sure you are in the correct lane. Use the right lane if you plan to exit, the left lane if you are traveling around the circle. When in the circle, the vehicle on the outside must yield to the vehicle on the inside.

The city speed limit is 50 kilometres per hour (30 mph) or as posted. A right turn on red after stopping is permitted; U-turns are not. A sign that reads "Bus and Taxi Lane Only" means it is illegal to drive, park or stop any vehicle other than the above in that lane.

Parking

Street parking restrictions vary throughout the city; watch for and heed the signs. Parking is not permitted in the residential areas surrounding RE/MAX Field and Commonwealth Stadium during major events; cars parked there will be towed.

Rates for city-operated parking meters are $2.50-$3.50 per hour. Most meters are free after 6 p.m. and on Sundays and holidays; however, there are some 24-hour meters. Rates for downtown parking lots range $2.50-$4 per half-hour during the day.

Shopping

For the intrepid shopper, there is nothing like a trip to the ⚓ **West Edmonton Mall** (*see attraction listing p. 95*), housed in a 44-hectare (110-acre) building at 8882 170 St. N.W. Inside are more than 800 retail stores and dozens of fun things to do under one gigantic roof, including a waterpark, underground aquarium, ice rink and blacklight miniature golf course.

South Edmonton Common (1978 99 St. N.W.) offers about 130 hectares (320 acres) of retail space. The massive outdoor shopping complex at 23rd Avenue and Calgary Trail is home to more than 150 businesses, including IKEA, Tommy Hilfiger, Nike, Roots and Saks Fifth Avenue Off 5th. With more than 150 retailers, **Southgate Centre** (5015 111 St. N.W.) is South Edmonton's largest shopping center and includes Edmonton's largest Hudson's Bay department store.

Find deals near the airport at **Premium Outlet Collection Edmonton International Airport** (1 Outlet Collection Way). The complex, opened in summer 2018, counts Nike Factory Store, H&M, Old Navy Outlet and Designer Shoe Warehouse among

High Level Bridge

its more than 100 stores. Luggage storage, flight status screens and boarding pass printing services are available for travelers en route to the airport or just arriving.

For those who want shopping on a less imposing scale, other popular malls include **Kingsway Mall** (109 Street and Kingsway N.W.) and **Londonderry Mall** (258 137 Ave. N.W. at 66 Street N.W.).

Downtown Edmonton offers boutiques and local restaurants as well as covered shopping areas joined by enclosed walkways or pedways. The **Edmonton City Centre** complex between 100 and 103 streets on 102 Avenue N.W. contains Hudson's Bay, a nine-screen theater and 110 other shops and places to eat among its four glittering floors.

Manulife Place (10180 101 St. N.W.) is a destination for designer boutiques. **Rice Howard Way,** an attractive outdoor pedestrian area lined with sidewalk seating and eateries, is downtown near 100 Street N.W. and 101a Avenue N.W.

At 102 Avenue and 97 Street N.W., the Chinatown Gate symbolizes friendship and welcomes visitors to **Chinatown,** which features several ethnic restaurants, shops and outdoor vendors selling fresh produce.

The **124 Street & Area** commercial district, which extends from Jasper Avenue north to 111 Avenue N.W., is home to a wide variety of businesses, including the handful of art galleries and boutique shops comprising the 12-block **Gallery Walk** area.

Old Strathcona at Whyte Avenue (82 Avenue N.W. from 99 to 109 streets), the main outdoor shopping street on the south side of the city, has the look of historic Edmonton and offers boutiques, specialty shops, nearby restaurants, bistros and coffee bars.

Don't forget that the major museums have interesting shops with items and vacation souvenirs sometimes impossible to find elsewhere. Of particular interest is the Alberta-branded shop in the visitor center at the **Alberta Legislature Building** *(see attraction listing p. 92)*, the gift shop inside the **Royal Alberta Museum** *(see attraction listing p. 94)* and the six period shops in **Fort Edmonton Park** *(see attraction listing p. 93)*.

Nightlife

Edmonton offers plenty of things to do after dark, whether you're interested in having a low-key night out or listening to live music at a pub. Here are a few of the best bars and late-night hangouts in Edmonton. (Note: The legal drinking age in Edmonton, Alberta, is 18 years of age. If you need a safe ride, consider using Uber or a local taxi company.)

Dozens of restaurants and bars in downtown Edmonton cater to the after-work crowd. Less than a block from the Shaw Conference Centre is **The Confederation Lounge.** Located inside the **Fairmont Hotel Macdonald** (10065 100 St.), the lounge is a good destination for business or solo travelers, with comfy leather seating around a large fireplace and floor-to-ceiling windows overlooking a large patio and the North Saskatchewan River Valley. Skilled bartenders will mix you up a cocktail or mocktail made with honey sourced from the hotel's beehives.

River Valley Parks

If beer is more your style, two popular Edmonton bars are nearby. **CRAFT Beer Market** (10013 101a Ave. N.W.) claims to have the largest selection of draft beer in Canada, with more than 100 local and international beers on tap, plus cocktails, wine and spirits. Sip your selection inside—where soaring ceilings and exposed pipes create an industrial vibe—or out on the rooftop patio where there are fireplaces and space heaters for year-round comfort. Across the street is the downtown location of **The Sherlock Holmes Pub** (10012 101a Ave.), a cozy English-style pub that draws a crowd for live music performances Thursday through Saturday.

Downtown's Jasper Avenue has many options for Edmonton nightlife. **Red Star Pub** (10534 Jasper Ave.) is an off-the-beaten-path gastropub offering great food and a wide selection of beers and liquor. Visit on Thursday nights for DJs and drink specials. (Note: Red Star Pub is closed on Sunday and Monday.)

Where do the locals go before or after an Edmonton Oilers game? Just across from Rogers Place arena is Mercer Warehouse, a century-old brick building that now houses two fun destinations on 104 Street: **Mercer Tavern** (10363 104 St. N.W.), a fun spot for craft beer and sports, and **Baijiu** (10359 104 St. N.W.), a hip, Asian-inspired restaurant with a sophisticated cocktail menu and a clubby late-night vibe. (Be sure to ask about the hidden speakeasy inside Baijiu.)

A bit farther down 104 Street (also known as the 4th Street Promenade) is **Drunken Ox/Sober Cat** (10190 104 St. N.W.). Merging three concepts in one, the restaurant includes a front-of-house café ("Sober Cat") that stays open late and a steakhouse and cocktail bar ("Drunken Ox") in the back that serves locally sourced food and handmade drinks. The interior is chic and romantic; leather couches, cozy chairs, crystal chandeliers and exposed wood beams add to the ambiance.

For a happening nightlife scene—and one popular with college students and the younger crowd—make your way to Whyte Avenue and the Old Strathcona district just south of downtown. Whyte Ave. bars and lounges cater to just about every taste. For blues music every night of the week, check out **Blues on Whyte** (inside the Commercial Hotel at 10329 82 Ave.), a long-standing favorite for live music in Edmonton. Fans of jazz enjoy a night out at **Yardbird Suite** (11 Tommy Banks Way). The volunteer-run venue hosts jazz concerts and Tuesday night jam sessions from mid-September to late June. **Cook County Saloon** (8010 Gateway Blvd. N.W.) is where you go for country music (both live and DJ-spun) on Friday and Saturday nights.

Big Events

Edmonton offers a smorgasbord of events. Concerts, workshops, jam sessions and outdoor events characterize the **Edmonton International Jazz Festival,** held late June to early July. Also occurring late June to early July, **The Works Art and Design**

Festival brings together artists and artisans at some 30 venues offering demonstrations, entertainment, exhibits and tours.

In June and July the **Freewill Shakespeare Festival** presents evening performances during the week and two shows on weekends at the **Heritage Amphitheatre in Hawrelak Park**. The **Edmonton International Street Performers Festival** in early July offers 6 days of free performances by street acts including magicians, clowns, jugglers, mime artists, musicians and comics at Dr. Wilbert Mcintyre Park. Attending the festival is one of the many family-friendly things to do in Edmonton.

Two music venues, several parades and midway entertainment keep the city alive with activities during 🞂 **Edmonton's K-Days**, a 10-day celebration held in July. Kids can pan for gold and learn about the history and cultures of First Nations peoples in gold rush–themed Klondike Park. The fun comes to a close with a large fireworks display. Contact a travel advisor at your local AAA club to add this event to your vacation packages.

The 🞂 **Edmonton Heritage Festival** in early August offers more than 70 outdoor ethnic pavilions showcasing 100 countries and cultures. Also in August is the 🞂 **Edmonton Folk Music Festival; Cariwest**, a Caribbean arts festival; the **Edmonton Blues Festival**; the **Edmonton Dragon Boat Festival**; and the 🞂 **Edmonton International Fringe Theatre Festival,** an 11-day extravaganza of plays, dance, music, mime and street performances. The Edmonton Symphony Orchestra's 3-day **Symphony Under the Sky** festival takes place at **William Hawrelak Park** from late August to early September.

Post-summer events include the **Edmonton International Film Festival**, featuring independent short and feature-length movies from late September to early October, as well as **New Year's Eve special events** that are among the memorable things for couples to do.

Sports & Rec

Whatever the season, there are opportunities for both indoor and outdoor recreation. The **North Saskatchewan River Valley** is an oasis of parkland, with 160 kilometres (99.4 mi.) of trails, four lake systems and more than 20 major parks. Depending on the time of year, you can **golf, hike, jog, cycle, ride horseback, fish, ski (cross-country and downhill), skate** or even pan for gold in Edmonton's river valley parks.

William Hawrelak Park, home to many of Edmonton's festivals and events, is located next to the North Saskatchewan River and is one of the many fun places to go for walking, jogging and paddleboating as well as ice-skating and cross-country skiing in winter.

Playing host to three major sporting events—the Commonwealth Games in 1978, the World University Games in 1983 and the World Championships in Athletics in 2001—has provided Edmonton with a legacy of world-class sporting facilities. Several multiple-purpose centers—including **Kinsmen Sports Centre**, 9100 Walterdale Hill, and **Mill Woods Recreation Centre**, 7207 28 Ave. N.W.— offer such activities as **swimming, diving, racquetball, squash** and **track** events.

For information about activities and facilities at Edmonton parks and things to do this weekend, phone the information line at (780) 442-5311 Monday through Friday.

Bring your set of clubs on vacation and try out one of more than 70 **golf** courses scattered around the Edmonton area. Three courses in the city's river valley are **Riverside Golf Course**, 8630 Rowland Rd.; **Rundle Park Golf Course**, 2902 118 Ave. N.W.; and **Victoria Golf Course & Driving Range**, said to be the oldest municipal golf course in Canada, at 12130 River Valley Rd. For information on all city-run golf courses, phone (780) 496-4710.

Spectator sports can be enjoyed throughout the year. **Castrol Raceway**, 2 kilometres (1.2 mi.) west of Queen Elizabeth II Hwy. on Hwy. 19, offers **motorsport racing** May through October; phone (780) 461-5801 or (877) 331-7223.

Home to several professional sports teams, Edmonton is referred to fondly as the City of Champions and offers many options for group travel and sports fans. The **Edmonton Oilers**, several-time Stanley Cup champions of the National **Hockey** League, play from September to April in **Rogers Place**, 10220 104 Ave. N.W.; phone (780) 414-5483 for stadium or (780) 414-4625 for ticket office. The **Edmonton Eskimos football** team, many times the Grey Cup champions of the Canadian Football League, play at **Commonwealth Stadium**, 11000 Stadium Rd., from June to November; phone 311 within Edmonton or (780) 442-5311 for stadium or (780) 448-3757 for ticket office.

Performing Arts

Whether you're in Edmonton on vacation or just looking for cultural things to do this weekend, you'll find plenty of options and fun places to go around the city.

Theater season runs from September through May. For live theater visit the **Citadel Theatre** complex, 99 Street and 101a Avenue N.W., which consists of four theaters, an amphitheater and a beautiful atrium; phone (780) 425-1820 or (888) 425-1820. Family-themed theater, produced by **Fringe Theatre Adventures,** can be enjoyed by all ages from October through May at the ATB Financial Arts Barns in Old Strathcona at 10330 84 Ave. N.W.; phone (780) 409-1910.

Prominent Canadian and American performers take to the stage at **Mayfield Dinner Theatre** at 16615 109 Ave. N.W.; phone (780) 483-4051 or (877) 529-7829. **Jubilations Dinner Theatre,** in the West Edmonton Mall at the intersection of 87 Avenue N.W. and 170 Street N.W., features musical comedy and is one of the fun things for couples to do; phone (780) 484-2424.

Francis Winspear Centre for Music

The **Alberta Ballet,** (780) 428-6839, and the **Edmonton Opera,** (780) 429-1000, perform in **Northern Alberta Jubilee Auditorium** on the University of Alberta campus at 87 Avenue N.W. and 114 Street N.W.; phone (780) 427-2760 for auditorium information. The **Edmonton Symphony Orchestra** performs at the **Francis Winspear Centre for Music,** 4 Sir Winston Churchill Sq.; phone (780) 428-1414 or (800) 563-5081 for concert information. The Winspear Centre also hosts a variety of concerts ranging from classical music to rock, as does the **Shaw Conference Centre,** phone (780) 421-9797; and **Rogers Place,** phone (780) 414-5483.

The free publication *Where Edmonton* gives detailed, up-to-date information about arts and entertainment and things to do in Edmonton. Ticketmaster outlets handle ticket sales for most sports, recreation, theater and concert events; phone (855) 985-5000. Contact your local AAA club office for help with your Edmonton vacation packages and reservations.

ATTRACTIONS

 For a complete list of attractions, visit AAA.com/travelguides/attractions

ALBERTA AVIATION MUSEUM is at 11410 Kingsway Ave., N.W. This hangar was part of a training facility for air crews during World War II. The museum displays more than 30 historic aircraft including a carefully restored Fairchild 71, a fighter-bomber version of the de Havilland Mosquito, as well as 1920s biplanes and jet fighters from the Cold War era. Other displays detail the history of aviation in Edmonton and Alberta and include "story islands" featuring videos, dioramas, artifacts and the museum's most iconic aircraft.

Time: Allow 1 hour minimum. **Hours:** Daily 10-5, June-Aug.; Tues.-Fri. 10-4, Sat.-Sun. and holidays 10-5, rest of year. Closed Jan. 1, Christmas and day after Christmas. **Cost:** $12; $9.50 (ages 60+ and students with ID); $8.50 (ages 13-17); $7.50 (ages 6-12); $30 (family, two adults and up to four children ages 6-18). **Phone:** (780) 451-1175.

ALBERTA LEGISLATURE BUILDING is at 10800 97 Ave. N.W. Constructed of sandstone and marble in the Beaux Arts style, the 1912 building (affectionately called "The Ledge" by Edmontonians) houses the Legislative Assembly of Alberta as well as the offices of government officials. The interior can be explored via guided 45-minute tours, which depart from the lower rotunda. Tours cover the history of Alberta and allow visitors to see the Legislative Chamber and portraits of Alberta's former premiers and lieutenant governors.

Also on the grounds is the Legislative Assembly Visitor Centre (see attraction listing p. #) with exhibits and a 4-D movie about the history and governance of the province. **Time:** Allow 1 hour minimum. **Hours:** Daily 10-5, June-Aug.; Mon.-Fri. 10-5, Sat.-Sun. noon-5, rest of year. Guided tours are offered on the hour year-round. Last tour is given at 4. Closed Jan. 1, Good Friday and Christmas. Phone ahead to confirm schedule. **Cost:** Free. **Phone:** (780) 427-7362. [GT]

Legislative Assembly Visitor Centre is on the main floor of the Edmonton Federal Building at 9820 107 St. N.W. Interactive exhibits about Alberta's history, culture and identity are housed in the Agora Interpretive Centre, while The Borealis Gallery features temporary exhibits. The Pehonan Theatre presents the 11-minute film *Our People Our Province,* which celebrates the province's history on a 360-degree screen complete with 4-D special effects. **Hours:** Daily 10-5 (also Thurs. 5-8 p.m.), June-Aug.; Mon.-Fri. 10-5 (also Thurs. 5-8 p.m.), Sat.-Sun. noon-5, rest of year. Theater shows offered every half-hour during open hours; last show is 30 minutes before closing. Closed Jan. 1, Good Friday and Christmas. **Cost:** Free. **Phone:** (780) 427-7362.

ART GALLERY OF ALBERTA, 2 Sir Winston Churchill Sq., is dedicated to the development and presentation of contemporary and historical art from Canada and around the world. The gallery features three levels of exhibition space in a stunning four-level building—a work of art in and of itself—designed by Los Angeles architect Randall Stout. The AGA is the oldest cultural institution in the province and offers a full range of cultural programming, educational classes and art exhibitions.

Time: Allow 2 hours minimum. **Hours:** Tues.-Sun. 11-5 (also Thurs. 5-8 p.m.). Guided tours are offered Tues.-Sun. at 1:30, 2:30 and 3:30 (also Thurs. at 5:30, 6:30 and 7:30). **Cost:** $12.50; $8.50 (ages 65+ and out of province students with ID); free (ages 0-17, Alberta students and to all Thurs. 5-8 p.m.). **Phone:** (780) 422-6223. GT 🍴

EDMONTON PUBLIC SCHOOLS ARCHIVES AND MUSEUM is at 10425 99 Ave. in the historic 1904 McKay Avenue School, site of the first two sessions of the Alberta Legislature. The building has been carefully restored and features the 1906 legislative chamber, period classrooms and displays tracing the history of Edmonton Public Schools.

Also on the grounds is the restored Edmonton 1881 Schoolhouse, the first free public school in Alberta. **Time:** Allow 1 hour minimum. **Hours:** Mon.-Fri. 8:30-4, Sept.-June; 9-3:30, rest of year. Closed major holidays. **Cost:** Free. **Phone:** (780) 422-1970.

FORT EDMONTON PARK is at jct. Fox and Whitemud drs. at 7000 143 St. N.W. Reputed to be Canada's largest living-history park, it depicts Edmonton in four eras: as an 1846 Hudson's Bay Co. fur-trading fort and Cree encampment, as an 1885 settlement, as a developing capital in 1905 and as a 1929 business community and midway.

Streets named for historical eras from the 1840s to the 1920s feature historically appropriate old-time activities. Visitors can visit a wheelwright shop, pump water for tea and play in a penny arcade. Costumed interpreters give demonstrations of pioneer activities such as beading, bannock making and fur pressing. A short 4-D film about the history and development of Edmonton is screened in a reconstructed 1929 cinema. Mini golf, a shooting gallery, wagon and pony rides and streetcar rides also are available. A 1920s-style midway—complete with Ferris wheel, fun house and other attractions—is included.

Pets are not permitted. **CLOSURE INFORMATION:** The park is currently closed for major renovations and is expected to reopen in May 2021; phone for updates. **Phone:** (780) 496-7381.

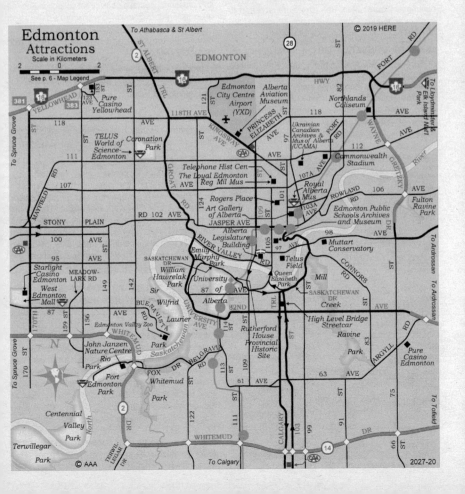

Edmonton Attractions

JOHN JANZEN NATURE CENTRE is at jct. Fox and Whitemud drs., adjacent to Fort Edmonton Park. The center has exhibits, self-guiding nature trails through the river valley, small animals, hands-on exhibits for children, and interpretive programs and events designed to promote awareness and appreciation of wildlife and the environment.

Time: Allow 1 hour minimum. **Hours:** Daily 9-4; 11-4, on holidays. Closed Jan. 1 and Christmas. **Cost:** $8 (one parent and child ages 2+); $3 (one parent and child ages 0-23 months); $17 (family, maximum seven people of same household; $3 per additional parent or child). **Phone:** (780) 442-5311.

THE LOYAL EDMONTON REGIMENT MILITARY MUSEUM is at 10440 108 Ave. N.W. in the Prince of Wales Armouries Heritage Centre. The museum's two galleries examine the history of The Loyal Edmonton Regiment, Alberta's oldest infantry unit, and explore military life. Displays include weapons, military equipment, uniforms, medals and badges, photographs and documents. **Time:** Allow 1 hour minimum. **Hours:** Mon.-Fri. 10-4. Phone ahead to confirm schedule. **Cost:** Donations. **Phone:** (780) 421-9943.

MUTTART CONSERVATORY is at 9626 96a St. N.W., at the e. end of the James MacDonald Bridge. Four pyramid-shaped glass greenhouses showcase a variety of flora. Plants that thrive in warm, moist climates—including palm trees, orchids, hibiscus and a corpse flower—thrive in the rain forest atmosphere of the Tropical Pyramid, while the Arid Pyramid displays vegetation indigenous to parts of

North America and Africa. The Temperate Pyramid exhibits plant life from temperate climates around the world, and the Feature Pyramid has seasonal floral displays. The conservatory's outdoor grounds can be enjoyed on a stroll.

Guided and self-guiding tours are available. **CLOSURE INFORMATION:** The conservatory is closed for major renovations until early 2021; phone for updates. Schedule and admission prices may vary. **Time:** Allow 1 hour minimum. **Hours:** Daily 10-5 (also Thurs. 5-9). Guided tours of the Tropical, Arid and Temperate Pyramids are given Sat.-Sun. and Wed. Closed Christmas. Phone ahead to confirm schedule. **Cost:** (includes guided tours) $12.50; $10.50 (ages 13-17 and 65+); $6.50 (ages 2-12); $37 (family). Prices may vary. Reservations are required. **Phone:** (780) 442-5311. GT ⑪

⛋ᴳᴱᴹ **ROYAL ALBERTA MUSEUM** is at 9810 103a Ave. N.W. Fresh from a $375.5-million renovation in 2018, Alberta's natural and human history museum houses a permanent collection in three main galleries, in addition to a children's gallery with hands-on play areas, a bug gallery with spiders and other invertebrates, and a feature gallery with changing exhibits.

The Human History hall on the first floor tells the story of Alberta's people through artifacts, displays and multimedia about early Indigenous inhabitants, European settlers, cowboys, pioneers and revolutionary figures in the province's history. The second floor Natural History hall showcases animals and plants from the Ice Age and beyond with dioramas, fossils and life-size skeletons of mastodons, mammoths and rare prehistoric beasts.

Time: Allow 2 hours minimum. **Hours:** Daily 10-6 (also Thurs.-Fri. 6-8 p.m.), mid-May through Sept. 2; 10-5 (also Thurs. 5-8 p.m.), rest of year. Closed last Mon. of the month, Christmas Eve and Christmas. Hours may vary during special exhibits. Phone ahead to confirm schedule. **Cost:** $19; $14 (ages 65+); $10 (ages 7-17); $48 (family, two adults and children). **Phone:** (825) 468-6000. ⑪

⛋ᴳᴱᴹ SAVE **TELUS WORLD OF SCIENCE—EDMONTON** is at 11211 142 St. N.W. Five galleries house interactive exhibits that explain and explore science and technology with a fun, hands-on approach. The S.P.A.C.E. Gallery allows guests of all ages to launch rockets, command a lunar lander and see the Aurora Borealis. Guests also can experience the *Destination: Moon Object Theatre* to learn how the science center acquired a real Moon rock. Inside the *Syncrude Environment Gallery* guests can get hands-on with Touch Tank explorations, meet Doc the yellowfin surgeon fish and create lighting and tornados as they learn about weather systems. Staff scientists in *Science on a Sphere*, use the 1.8-metre (6 ft.) diameter globe to enhance presentations about the earth's environment.

Royal Alberta Museum

CuriousCITY, a tactile adventure for children 8-years-old and younger, offers fun and learning through activity and role play as youngsters crawl through the River Valley to discover fossils and get to know local animals, or climb the Fort Edmonton Park tree house to examine pelts and pretend to prepare a meal. Children can even pilot the EIA Airplane or command the YEG Control Tower and will be delighted as they splash around at a Water Exploration Zone or explore several iconic Edmonton landmarks such as the Muttart Conservatory, the Queen Elizabeth Planetarium and the High Level Bridge.

At the *Science Garage* guests can flex their creative muscles as they design, build and create. *The Body Fantastic* teaches visitors about the inner-workings of the human body as they explore the *Gallery of the Gross* to identify different smells, and test their knowledge of anatomy when they put together a life-size X-ray puzzle.

In addition guests can enjoy live science demonstrations on the *Science Stage,* or explore the day and night sky at the RASC Observatory, equipped with high-powered telescopes. Guests can see the latest IMAX film or enjoy an out-of-this-world planetarium show in the Zeidler Dome, a digital visualization theater featuring 10k resolution capabilities.

Hours: Building and galleries daily 9-6, in summer; Sun.-Thurs. 9-5, Fri.-Sat. 9-6, rest of year. Holidays 9-6. Observatory Fri. 7-10, Sat.-Sun. 1-4 and 7-10 (weather permitting). IMAX and Zeidler Dome hours vary. Closed Christmas. Phone ahead to confirm schedule.

Cost: Science center (includes dome shows and science demonstrations) $25.95; $20.95 (ages 13-17 and 65+); $17.95 (ages 3-12); $99 (family, two adults and four children). IMAX film $13.95; $11.95 (ages 13-17 and 65+); $9.50 (ages 3-12); $54.95 (family, two adults and four children). Combination ticket (science center and IMAX film) $35.95; $29.95 (ages 13-17 and 65+); $24.95 (ages 3-12); $138.95 (family, two adults and four children). **Phone:** (780) 451-3344. [Ⅱ]

UKRAINIAN CULTURAL HERITAGE VILLAGE is 52 km (32 mi.) e. on Hwy. 16, 3 km e. of the entrance to Elk Island National Park. The open-air living history museum re-creates the lifestyle of Ukrainian immigrants who settled in east central Alberta 1892-1930. Costumed interpreters demonstrate settlers' daily routines and talk about their struggles, and the grounds include more than 35 restored buildings, houses, churches and stores that can be toured.

Special events are held throughout the summer. Horse-drawn wagon rides are available Mon.-Fri. in May and June and Thurs.-Mon. in July and Aug.

Time: Allow 3 hours minimum. **Hours:** Daily 10-5, Victoria Day weekend-Labour Day. Guided tours offered Wed.-Mon. on the hour 11-2 in July; Thurs.-Tues. on the hour 11-2 in Aug.; Sat.-Sun. on the hour 11-2 in May-June. **Cost:** $15; $13 (ages 65+); $10 (ages 7-17); $40 (family, two adults and children). **Phone:** (780) 662-3640. [GT] [Ⅱ] [🛬]

WEST EDMONTON MALL is at 8882 170 St. N.W. The huge, two-level complex is North America's largest shopping and entertainment center. It contains more than 800 stores, more than 70 eateries and 11 themed attractions. Galaxyland features 27 rides and attractions. World Waterpark offers more than 2 hectares (5 acres) of indoor fun, including a giant wave pool with surfing and an overhead zipline. Sea Life Caverns contains about 100 species of marine life, including South African penguins and California sea lions. Other attractions include the Ice Palace, an NHL-size ice rink; two miniature golf courses; an escape room; and a family-friendly recreation center with bowling, billiards and an arcade.

Time: Allow a full day. **Hours:** Shops open Mon.-Sat. 10-9, Sun. 11-6, most holidays 10-6. Hours for attractions, theaters and restaurants vary; phone ahead. **Cost:** Prices for individual attractions vary. **Phone:** (780) 444-5321 for general mall information, (780) 444-5300, or (800) 661-8890 for more information about attractions, including hours of operation and prices. [Ⅱ] [✗]

Sightseeing

Driving Tours

The most scenic areas in Edmonton are along the North Saskatchewan River Valley. On the south side, the drive north along Saskatchewan Drive from 76 Avenue N.W. and 120 Street N.W. to 99 Street N.W. offers a picturesque trip around the University of Alberta campus.

Streetcar Tours

If you're looking for things to do with a historical bent, consider a ride on the High Level Bridge Streetcar from downtown to Old Strathcona.

HIGH LEVEL BRIDGE STREETCAR departs from the Old Strathcona stop at Gateway Blvd. N.W. and 84 Ave. N.W. and from downtown s. of Jasper Ave. and w. of 109 St. N.W. A vintage streetcar takes passengers along the old Canadian Pacific Railway (CPR) line across the 48-metre (157 ft.) High Level Bridge, built 1910-13 to link Old Strathcona and downtown Edmonton. The narrated, 6-kilometre (3.7 mi.) trip offers excellent views of the city and the North Saskatchewan River Valley.

The Strathcona Streetcar Barn Museum features exhibits relating the history of the Edmonton Streetcar System; included are conductor uniforms, photographs and antique ticket punches. **Time:** Allow 45 minutes minimum. **Hours:** Streetcars operate Sun.-Fri. 11-4:20, Sat. 9-4:20, Victoria Day-Labour Day; Fri. and Sun. 11-4:20, Sat. 9-4:20, day after Labour Day-Thanksgiving. Hours extended to 10 p.m. during the Fringe Festival in Aug. Museum open Sat. 10-2, late May-early Oct. Phone ahead to confirm schedule. **Cost:** Round-trip streetcar fare $7; free (ages 0-5); $25 (family, two adults and three children). One-way fare $4; free (ages 0-5). Museum free. Cash only. **Phone:** (780) 437-7721. GT

Walking Tours

Heritage Trail leads from the Shaw Conference Centre to the Alberta Legislature Building, a route that links government and industry by way of Edmonton's past. Old Strathcona, a destination south of the North Saskatchewan River, offers a view of many original buildings and street scenes characteristic of an early 20th-century prairie town. The Downtown Business Association hosts free guided walking tours by reservation from late June through mid-August; phone (780) 424-4085 for information.

Make the Conn⚭ction

AAA guidebooks are just the beginning. Open the door to a whole lot more on AAA.com. Get extra travel insight, more information and online booking.

 Find this symbol for places to look, book and save on AAA.com.

iStockphoto.com_shapecharge

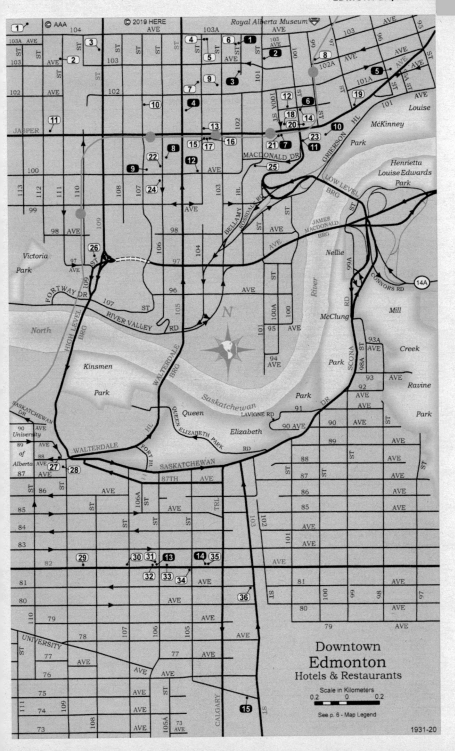

Downtown
Edmonton
Hotels & Restaurants

Scale in Kilometers

See p. 6 - Map Legend

1931-20

Downtown Edmonton

This index helps you "spot" where hotels and restaurants are located on the corresponding detailed maps. Restaurant price range is a combination of lunch and/or dinner. Turn to the listing page for more information and consult display ads for special promotions.

 For more details, rates and reservations: AAA.com/travelguides/hotels

DOWNTOWN EDMONTON

Map Page	Hotels	Designation	Member Savings	Page
1 p. 97	JW Marriott Edmonton ICE District	FOUR DIAMOND	✔	105
2 p. 97	The Sutton Place Hotel Edmonton	THREE DIAMOND		105
3 p. 97	**Delta Hotels by Marriott Edmonton Centre Suite Hotel**	THREE DIAMOND	✔	104
4 p. 97	Coast Edmonton Plaza Hotel by APA	THREE DIAMOND		104
5 p. 97	DoubleTree by Hilton Edmonton Downtown	[fyi]	✔	104
6 p. 97	**The Westin Edmonton**	THREE DIAMOND	✔	105
7 p. 97	**Union Bank Inn**	THREE DIAMOND	✔	105
8 p. 97	Days Inn Downtown Edmonton	APPROVED		104
9 p. 97	Matrix Hotel	THREE DIAMOND		105
10 p. 97	**Courtyard by Marriott Edmonton Downtown**	THREE DIAMOND	✔	104
11 p. 97	**Fairmont Hotel Macdonald** (See ad p. 104.)	FOUR DIAMOND	✔	104
12 p. 97	Holiday Inn Express Edmonton Downtown	THREE DIAMOND		105
13 p. 97	**Varscona Hotel on Whyte**	THREE DIAMOND	✔	105
14 p. 97	**Metterra Hotel on Whyte**	THREE DIAMOND	✔	105
15 p. 97	Days Inn Edmonton South	APPROVED		104

Map Page	Restaurants	Designation	Cuisine	Price Range	Page
1 p. 97	Cibo Bistro	THREE DIAMOND	New Italian	$26-$45	105
2 p. 97	Louisiana Purchase	APPROVED	Cajun	$18-$38	106
3 p. 97	Mikado Sushi & Robata	APPROVED	Japanese Sushi	$12-$25	106
4 p. 97	Baijiu	THREE DIAMOND	Asian Small Plates	$17-$30	105
5 p. 97	Rostizado	THREE DIAMOND	New Mexican	$19-$31	106
6 p. 97	Braven	THREE DIAMOND	Steak	$19-$62	105
7 p. 97	Bündok	THREE DIAMOND	New Canadian Small Plates	$20-$40	105
8 p. 97	Zinc Restaurant	THREE DIAMOND	New American	$14-$41	106
9 p. 97	SABOR Restaurant	THREE DIAMOND	Mediterranean	$14-$48	106
10 p. 97	Khazana	APPROVED	Indian	$13-$72	106
11 p. 97	Cactus Club Cafe	THREE DIAMOND	New American	$15-$40	105
12 p. 97	The Sherlock Holmes Pub	APPROVED	American	$14-$19	106
13 p. 97	Tzin Wine and Tapas	THREE DIAMOND	New World Small Plates	$15-$36	106
14 p. 97	Share	THREE DIAMOND	American	$17-$38	106
15 p. 97	Uccellino	THREE DIAMOND	New Italian	$25-$43	106
16 p. 97	Bar Bricco	APPROVED	Italian Small Plates	$20-$35	105
17 p. 97	Corso 32	THREE DIAMOND	Italian	$26-$37	105
18 p. 97	Tres Carnales Taqueria	APPROVED	New Mexican	$14-$17	106
19 p. 97	Hardware Grill	THREE DIAMOND	Regional Canadian	$17-$50	106
20 p. 97	Ruth's Chris Steak House	THREE DIAMOND	Steak	$30-$79	106
21 p. 97	Madison's Grill	THREE DIAMOND	New Canadian	$16-$48	106
22 p. 97	Select	THREE DIAMOND	Continental	$15-$55	106
23 p. 97	**The Harvest Room**	THREE DIAMOND	New Canadian	$39-$48	106
24 p. 97	The Marc Restaurant	THREE DIAMOND	French	$14-$41	106
25 p. 97	La Ronde Revolving Restaurant	THREE DIAMOND	Continental	$30-$54	106
26 p. 97	The Butternut Tree	FOUR DIAMOND	New Canadian	$33-$52	105

Map Page	Restaurants (cont'd)	Designation	Cuisine	Price Range	Page
㉗ p. 97	Highlevel Diner	APPROVED	American	$10-$23	106
㉘ p. 97	Rosso Pizzeria	APPROVED	Italian Pizza	$12-$21	106
㉙ p. 97	Cafe Mosaics	APPROVED	Vegetarian	$12-$18	105
㉚ p. 97	The King & I	APPROVED	Thai	$9-$25	106
㉛ p. 97	Ampersand 27	THREE DIAMOND	American	$17-$45	105
㉜ p. 97	O'Byrne's Irish Pub	APPROVED	Irish	$13-$23	106
㉝ p. 97	Continental Treat Fine Bistro	APPROVED	European	$20-$45	105
㉞ p. 97	Chianti Cafe & Restaurant	APPROVED	Italian	$13-$28	105
㉟ p. 97	Yiannis Taverna	APPROVED	Greek	$12-$44	106
㊱ p. 97	Von's Steak House & Oyster Bar	THREE DIAMOND	Steak	$18-$58	106

iStockphoto.com_pixelfit

Love the Great Outdoors?

When getting away means getting off the beaten path,
visit AAA.com/campgrounds or AAA.com/maps for:

⌃ Thousands of places to camp across the
U.S. and Canada

⌃ Complete mapping and travel information to
plan your adventure

Look for locations with the
trusted mark of approval. .

Inspected & Approved

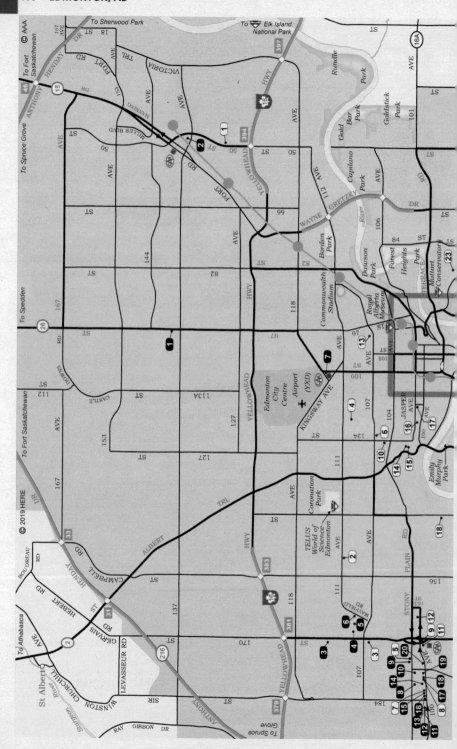

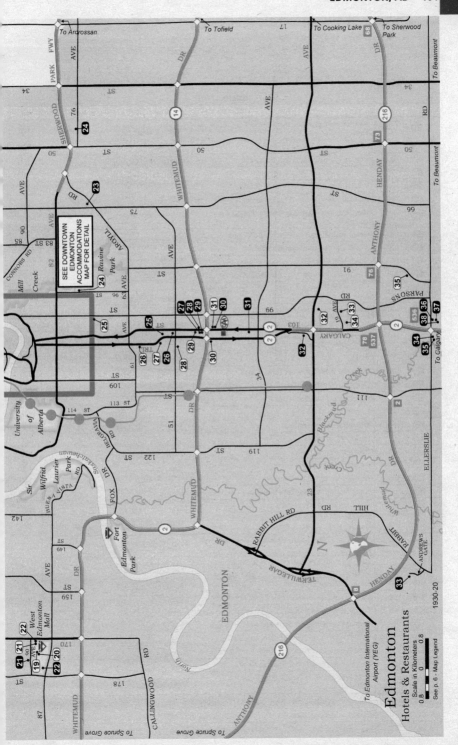

To Ardrossan

To Tofield

To Cooking Lake

To Sherwood Park

To Beaumont

To Beaumont

To Calgary

To Spruce Grove

To Spruce Grove

To Edmonton International Airport (YEG)

SEE DOWNTOWN EDMONTON ACCOMMODATIONS MAP FOR DETAIL

University of Alberta

Sir Wilfrid Laurier Park

West Edmonton Mall

Fort Edmonton Park

Mill Creek

Ravine Park

Edmonton
Hotels & Restaurants

Scale in Kilometers
0   0.8

See p. 6 - Map Legend

1930-20

Edmonton

This index helps you "spot" where hotels and restaurants are located on the corresponding detailed maps. Restaurant price range is a combination of lunch and/or dinner. Turn to the listing page for more information and consult display ads for special promotions.

 For more details, rates and reservations: AAA.com/travelguides/hotels

EDMONTON

Map Page	Hotels	Designation	Member Savings	Page
1 p. 100	**Fairfield Inn & Suites by Marriott Edmonton North**	THREE DIAMOND	✔	108
2 p. 100	Holiday Inn Express & Suites Edmonton North	THREE DIAMOND		109
3 p. 100	Holiday Inn & Suites, West Edmonton	THREE DIAMOND		109
4 p. 100	Staybridge Suites West Edmonton	THREE DIAMOND		110
5 p. 100	Home2 Suites by Hilton West Edmonton	THREE DIAMOND	✔	109
6 p. 100	DoubleTree by Hilton West Edmonton	THREE DIAMOND	✔	108
7 p. 100	**Best Western Plus City Centre Inn** *(See ad p. 107.)*	THREE DIAMOND	✔	107
8 p. 100	Coast West Edmonton Hotel & Conference Centre	THREE DIAMOND		108
9 p. 100	**Hilton Garden Inn-West Edmonton**	THREE DIAMOND	✔	109
10 p. 100	Quality Inn West Edmonton	APPROVED		109
11 p. 100	Candlewood Suites West Edmonton-Mall Area	THREE DIAMOND		108
12 p. 100	Holiday Inn Express & Suites West Edmonton-Mall Area	THREE DIAMOND		109
13 p. 100	**Courtyard by Marriott Edmonton West**	THREE DIAMOND	✔	108
14 p. 100	**Hyatt Place Edmonton-West**	THREE DIAMOND	✔	109
15 p. 100	Wingate Inn Edmonton West	THREE DIAMOND		110
16 p. 100	**Hampton Inn & Suites by Hilton - Edmonton West**	THREE DIAMOND		109
17 p. 100	**Days Inn & Suites West Edmonton**	APPROVED	✔	108
18 p. 100	Ramada West Edmonton	APPROVED		110
19 p. 100	Royal Hotel, Trademark Collection by Wyndham	THREE DIAMOND		110
20 p. 100	**Comfort Inn West**	APPROVED		108
21 p. 100	**West Edmonton Mall Inn**	APPROVED	✔	110
22 p. 100	**Fantasyland Hotel**	THREE DIAMOND	✔	108
23 p. 100	Four Points by Sheraton Edmonton South	THREE DIAMOND	✔	109
24 p. 100	Radisson Hotel and Convention Centre Edmonton	THREE DIAMOND		109
25 p. 100	Ramada by Wyndham Edmonton South	APPROVED		110
26 p. 100	**Best Western Cedar Park Inn** *(See ad p. 107.)*	THREE DIAMOND	✔	107
27 p. 100	Radisson Hotel Edmonton South	THREE DIAMOND		109
28 p. 100	**Holiday Inn Conference Centre Edmonton South**	THREE DIAMOND	✔	109
29 p. 100	**Delta Edmonton South Hotel and Conference Centre**	THREE DIAMOND	✔	108
30 p. 100	**Sawridge Inn Edmonton South & Conference Cent**	THREE DIAMOND	✔	110
31 p. 100	Super 8 Edmonton South	APPROVED		110
32 p. 100	Holiday Inn Express & Suites Edmonton South	THREE DIAMOND		109
33 p. 100	Tru by Hilton Windermere	APPROVED	✔	110
34 p. 100	TownePlace Suites by Marriott Edmonton South	THREE DIAMOND	✔	110
35 p. 100	**Home2 Suites by Hilton Edmonton South**	THREE DIAMOND	✔	109
36 p. 100	**Four Points by Sheraton Edmonton Gateway**	THREE DIAMOND	✔	108
37 p. 100	Hampton Inn by Hilton Edmonton South	THREE DIAMOND	✔	109
38 p. 100	**Best Western Plus South Edmonton Inn & Suites**	THREE DIAMOND	✔	108

Map Page	Restaurants	Designation	Cuisine	Price Range	Page
1 p. 100	Franco's Steak & Pizza	APPROVED	Italian	$12-$48	110
2 p. 100	Haus Falkenstein	APPROVED	German	$15-$31	111

Map Page	Restaurants (cont'd)	Designation	Cuisine	Price Range	Page
③ p. 100	Fifendekel Pie Shop Cafe	APPROVED	Sandwiches	$6-$10	110
④ p. 100	café LINNEA	THREE DIAMOND	French	$19-$45	110
⑤ p. 100	Cha For Tea Palace	APPROVED	Chinese Dim Sum Seafood	$8-$22	110
⑥ p. 100	RGE RD	THREE DIAMOND	Regional Canadian	$15-$39	111
⑦ p. 100	Homefire Grill	APPROVED	International	$16-$35	111
⑧ p. 100	ConYac's Bar & Grill	APPROVED	American	$12-$30	110
⑨ p. 100	Guru Fine Indian Cuisine	THREE DIAMOND	Indian	$15-$32	111
⑩ p. 100	Canteen	THREE DIAMOND	New Canadian	$22-$30	110
⑪ p. 100	Moxie's Classic Grill	APPROVED	American	$11-$45	111
⑫ p. 100	Bucas & Pastas	APPROVED	Italian	$7-$14	110
⑬ p. 100	Padmanadi	APPROVED	Asian Vegetarian	$14-$16	111
⑭ p. 100	Urban Diner	APPROVED	American	$11-$20	111
⑮ p. 100	Violino Ristorante	THREE DIAMOND	Italian	$15-$39	111
⑯ p. 100	Clementine	THREE DIAMOND	Small Plates	$20-$40	110
⑰ p. 100	Normand's	THREE DIAMOND	French	$20-$40	111
⑱ p. 100	Delux Burger Bar	APPROVED	American	$10-$19	110
⑲ p. 100	Cactus Club Cafe	THREE DIAMOND	American	$16-$37	110
⑳ p. 100	ATLAS Steak + Fish	THREE DIAMOND	Steak Seafood	$32-$42	110
㉑ p. 100	Famoso Neapolitan Pizzeria	APPROVED	Pizza	$14-$18	110
㉒ p. 100	Moxie's Classic Grill	APPROVED	American	$10-$30	111
㉓ p. 100	Red Ox Inn	THREE DIAMOND	New American	$29-$38	111
㉔ p. 100	Biera	THREE DIAMOND	New International	$16-$29	110
㉕ p. 100	Old Country Inn	APPROVED	German	$9-$26	111
㉖ p. 100	Tropika	APPROVED	Thai	$14-$27	111
㉗ p. 100	The Bothy Wine & Whisky Bar	APPROVED	New American	$16-$26	110
㉘ p. 100	Lemongrass Cafe	APPROVED	Vietnamese	$10-$19	111
㉙ p. 100	Vaticano Cucina	APPROVED	Italian	$13-$27	111
㉚ p. 100	Sawmill Prime Rib & Steak House	APPROVED	Steak	$16-$40	111
㉛ p. 100	Creations Dining Room & Lounge	THREE DIAMOND	Canadian	$17-$34	110
㉜ p. 100	The Burger's Priest	APPROVED	Burgers	$7-$25	110
㉝ p. 100	Local Public Eatery	APPROVED	American	$10-$20	111
㉞ p. 100	Moxie's Classic Grill	APPROVED	American	$11-$45	111
㉟ p. 100	Zaika Indian Bistro	APPROVED	Indian	$14-$19	111

AAA/CAA Members Save on Hotels - For Any Occasion

ASSURED STAY

BW | Best Western Hotels & Resorts

Hilton

HYATT

Marriott INTERNATIONAL

MGM RESORTS INTERNATIONAL

VISIT over 1,100 AAA/CAA Offices | **CLICK** AAA.com/greatrates | **CALL** 1-866-222-7283

DOWNTOWN EDMONTON
• Hotels & Restaurants map & index p. 97

COAST EDMONTON PLAZA HOTEL BY APA
780/423-4811 **4**

⬥ THREE DIAMOND Contemporary Hotel. **Address:** 10155 105th St NW T5J 1E2

COURTYARD BY MARRIOTT EDMONTON DOWNTOWN
780/423-9999 **10**

⬥ THREE DIAMOND

Contemporary Hotel

COURTYARD **AAA Benefit:** Members save 5% or more!

Address: 1 Thornton Ct T5J 2E7 **Location:** Just off Jasper Ave; between 99th and 97th sts. **Facility:** 188 units. 11 stories, interior corridors. **Parking:** on-site (fee) and valet. **Activities:** exercise room. **Guest Services:** valet and coin laundry.

[SAVE] [🍴] [icon] [Y] [CALL] [♿] [icon]
[BIZ] [HS] [📶] [✕] [icon] [icon]
/ SOME UNITS [icon]

DAYS INN DOWNTOWN EDMONTON   780/423-1925 **8**
⬥ APPROVED   Hotel. **Address:** 10041 106th St T5J 1G3

DAYS INN EDMONTON SOUTH   780/430-0011 **15**
⬥ APPROVED   Hotel. **Address:** 10333 University Ave T6E 6N3

🔗 **Get the scoop**

from AAA inspectors:

AAA.com/travelguides/restaurants

DELTA HOTELS BY MARRIOTT EDMONTON CENTRE SUITE HOTEL   780/429-3900 **3**

⬥ THREE DIAMOND

Contemporary Hotel

Ⅾ DELTA HOTELS **AAA Benefit:** Members save 5% or more!

Address: 10222 102nd St NW T5J 4C5 **Location:** At 102nd St NW and 103rd Ave NW. Attached to a shopping centre. **Facility:** 169 units. 7 stories, interior corridors. **Parking:** on-site (fee) and valet, winter plug-ins. **Activities:** exercise room. **Guest Services:** complimentary and valet laundry.

[SAVE] [ECO] [🍴] [icon] [Y] [CALL] [♿]
[icon] [BIZ] [HS] [📶] [✕] [icon] [icon]
/ SOME UNITS [icon] [icon]

DOUBLETREE BY HILTON EDMONTON DOWNTOWN
587/525-1234 **5**

[fyi] [SAVE] Hotel. Under major renovation, call for details. **Last Designation:** Three Diamond. **Address:** 9576 Jasper Ave NW T5H 4H7

AAA Benefit: Members save up to 15%!

FAIRMONT HOTEL MACDONALD   780/424-5181 **11**

⬥ FOUR DIAMOND

Historic Hotel

Address: 10065 100th St T5J 0N6 **Location:** Just s of Jasper Ave. **Facility:** Since this landmark hotel with its majestic ambience is perched above the river valley, the elegant lobby lounge has a beautiful view. Upscale rooms range from a more cozy size to spectacular suites. 198 units. 9 stories, interior corridors. **Parking:** on-site (fee) and valet, winter plug-ins. **Amenities:** safes. **Dining:** The Harvest Room, see separate listing. **Pool:** heated indoor. **Activities:** sauna, hot tub, steamroom, bicycles, health club, in-room exercise equipment, massage. **Guest Services:** valet laundry, area transportation. *(See ad this page.)*

[SAVE] [ECO] [🍴] [icon] [Y] [icon] [CALL] [♿] [icon] [icon] [BIZ]
[$HS] [$] [✕] [icon] [icon] [icon] / SOME UNITS [icon]

▼ See AAA listing this page ▼

For more than a century, Fairmont Hotel Macdonald has effortlessly delivered timeless luxury in the heart of downtown Edmonton. Nestled upon the North Saskatchewan River Valley, the hotel's charm and ever-evolving elegance has earned it the spotlight as one of the city's most sought after locations. The four-diamond Chateau on the River offers unparalleled views of North America's largest expanse of urban parkland. We invite you to celebrate our longstanding history in Alberta's capital, and make Fairmont Hotel Macdonald your home away from home.

BOOK NOW   FROM **$215** PER NIGHT*

FOR DETAILS CALL 1 866-540-4468 OR EMAIL MAC.RESERVATIONS@FAIRMONT.COM VISIT FAIRMONT.COM/MACDONALD-EDMONTON

Fairmont HOTEL MACDONALD

2:59PM
The moment you discovered Alberta's hidden gem.

f 🐦 📷 FOLLOW @FAIRMONTMAC AND SHARE YOUR #MACMEMORIES.

*Rates are CAD, based on single and double occupancy. Taxes and Gratuities not included. Based on availability. Rates are based on 10% off Best Available Rate at time of booking.

(See map & index p. 97.)

HOLIDAY INN EXPRESS EDMONTON DOWNTOWN
780/423-2450   **12**
THREE DIAMOND Hotel. **Address:** 10010 104th St T5J 0Z1

JW MARRIOTT EDMONTON ICE DISTRICT
780/784-7950   **1**
FOUR DIAMOND [SAVE]
Contemporary Hotel. **Address:** 10344
102 St NW T5J 0K9
AAA Benefit: Members save 5% or more!

MATRIX HOTEL   780/429-2861   **9**
THREE DIAMOND Boutique Hotel. **Address:** 10640 100th Ave T5J 3N8

METTERRA HOTEL ON WHYTE   780/465-8150   **14**
THREE DIAMOND
Boutique Contemporary Hotel
Address: 10454 82nd Ave (Whyte Ave) T6E 4Z7 **Location:** Just e of 105th St. **Facility:** Trendy and chic, this hotel has beautiful art and wonderful areas to relax. Handsome rooms, many with private balconies, feature stocked mini-bars and upscale bath amenities. 98 units. 8 stories, interior corridors. **Parking:** valet only. **Amenities:** *Some:* safes. **Activities:** exercise room. **Guest Services:** valet laundry. **Featured Amenity:** breakfast buffet.

[SAVE] [T+] [Y] CALL [&] [T+] [BIZ]
[HS] [wifi] [X] [日] [🖥]
/ SOME UNITS [🛏] [📷]

THE SUTTON PLACE HOTEL EDMONTON
780/428-7111   **2**
THREE DIAMOND Hotel. **Address:** 10235 101st St T5J 3E9

UNION BANK INN   780/423-3600   **7**
THREE DIAMOND
Boutique Hotel
Address: 10053 Jasper Ave T5J 1S5 **Location:** Corner of 101st St. **Facility:** Originally built in 1911, this former bank is now a beautiful hotel with designer heritage or contemporary rooms and suites. All have fireplaces, luxurious bedding, and daily wine and cheese delivery. 40 units. 3-5 stories, interior corridors. **Parking:** on-site (fee), winter plug-ins. **Amenities:** safes. **Dining:** Madison's Grill, see separate listing. **Activities:** limited exercise equipment. **Guest Services:** valet laundry. **Featured Amenity:** full hot breakfast.

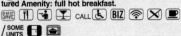

[SAVE] [T|] [T+] [Y] CALL [&] [BIZ] [wifi] [X] [🖥]
/ SOME UNITS [日] [📷]

VARSCONA HOTEL ON WHYTE   780/434-6111   **13**
THREE DIAMOND
Hotel
Address: 8208 106th St T6E 6R9 **Location:** Corner of 82nd Ave (Whyte Ave) and 106th St. **Facility:** 89 units. 6 stories, interior corridors. **Parking:** on-site (fee) and valet. **Dining:** Ampersand 27, O'Byrne's Irish Pub, see separate listings. **Activities:** bicycles, exercise room. **Guest Services:** valet laundry. **Featured Amenity:** breakfast buffet.

[SAVE] [ECO] [T|] [T+] CALL [&] [T+]
[BIZ] [HS] [wifi] [X] [日] [🖥]
/ SOME UNITS [🛏] [📷]

THE WESTIN EDMONTON   780/426-3636   **6**
THREE DIAMOND
Hotel
WESTIN HOTELS & RESORTS
AAA Benefit: Members save 5% or more!

Address: 10135 100th St T5J 0N7 **Location:** Jct 101st Ave. **Facility:** 416 units, some two bedrooms. 20 stories, interior corridors. **Parking:** on-site (fee) and valet. **Amenities:** safes. **Dining:** Share, see separate listing. **Pool:** heated indoor. **Activities:** sauna, exercise room, spa. **Guest Services:** valet laundry.

[SAVE] [ECO] [T|] [T+] [Y] CALL [&]
[swim] [T+] [BIZ] [wifi] [X] [📹] [日] [🖥]
/ SOME UNITS [🛏] [HS]

WHERE TO EAT

AMPERSAND 27   780/757-2727   **31**
THREE DIAMOND American. Casual Dining. **Address:** 10612 82 Ave NW T6E 2A7

BAIJIU   780/421-7060   **4**
THREE DIAMOND Asian Small Plates. Casual Dining. **Address:** 10359 104th St T5J 1B9

BAR BRICCO   780/424-5588   **16**
APPROVED Italian Small Plates. Casual Dining. **Address:** 10347 Jasper Ave T5J 1Y7

BRAVEN   780/784-8580   **6**
THREE DIAMOND Steak. Fine Dining. **Address:** 10344 102nd St NW T5J 0K9

BÜNDOK   780/420-0192   **7**
THREE DIAMOND New Canadian Small Plates. Casual Dining. **Address:** 10228 104th St NW T5J 1B8

THE BUTTERNUT TREE   780/760-2271   **26**
FOUR DIAMOND New Canadian. Casual Dining. **Address:** 9707 110th St NW T5K 2L9

CACTUS CLUB CAFE   587/523-8030   **11**
THREE DIAMOND New American. Casual Dining. **Address:** 11130 Jasper Ave T5K 0L1

CAFE MOSAICS   780/433-9702   **29**
APPROVED Vegetarian. Casual Dining. **Address:** 10844 82nd Ave T6E 2B3

CHEZ CORA   780/429-7903
APPROVED Breakfast. Casual Dining. **Address:** 10041 106th St T5J 1G3

CHIANTI CAFE & RESTAURANT   780/439-9829   **34**
APPROVED Italian. Casual Dining. **Address:** 10501 82nd Ave NW T6E 2A3

CIBO BISTRO   780/757-2426   **1**
THREE DIAMOND New Italian. Casual Dining. **Address:** 11244 104th Ave NW T5K 2X4

CONTINENTAL TREAT FINE BISTRO   780/433-7432   **33**
APPROVED European. Fine Dining. **Address:** 10560 82nd Ave NW T6E 2A4

CORSO 32   780/421-4622   **17**
THREE DIAMOND Italian. Fine Dining. **Address:** 10345 Jasper Ave T5J 1Y7

(See map & index p. 97.)

HARDWARE GRILL   780/423-0969 (19)
THREE DIAMOND Regional Canadian. Fine Dining.
Address: 9698 Jasper Ave T5H 3V5

THE HARVEST ROOM   780/424-5181 (23)
THREE DIAMOND

**New
Canadian
Fine Dining
$39-$48**

AAA Inspector Notes: The atmosphere is warm and vibrant in the elegant surroundings of this restaurant that offers beautiful views of the North Saskatchewan River. Creative prairie cuisine is prepared in the open-concept kitchen utilizing local farmer products and sustainable ingredients. Examples could include tempting preparations of bison rib-eye, organic hay-smoked chicken or salmon. There is a set-price choose-your-own dinner offered, which is a great deal. Check for seasonal lunch openings. **Features:** full bar, patio dining, Sunday brunch. **Reservations:** suggested. **Address:** 10065 100th St T5J 0N6 **Location:** Just s of Jasper Ave; in The Fairmont Hotel Macdonald. **Parking:** on-site (fee) and valet. (B) (D) CALL (&)

HIGHLEVEL DINER   780/433-0993 (27)
APPROVED American. Casual Dining. **Address:** 10912 88th Ave NW T6G 0Z1

KHAZANA   780/702-0330 (10)
APPROVED Indian. Casual Dining. **Address:** 10177 107 St T5J 1J5

THE KING & I   780/433-2222 (30)
APPROVED Thai. Casual Dining. **Address:** 8208 107th St T6E 6P4

LA RONDE REVOLVING RESTAURANT   780/420-8366 (25)
THREE DIAMOND Continental. Fine Dining. **Address:** 10111 Bellamy Hill T5J 1N7

LOUISIANA PURCHASE   780/420-6779 (2)
APPROVED Cajun. Casual Dining. **Address:** 10320 111th St T5K 1L2

MADISON'S GRILL   780/401-2222 (21)
THREE DIAMOND New Canadian. Fine Dining. **Address:** 10053 Jasper Ave T5J 1S5

THE MARC RESTAURANT   780/429-2828 (24)
THREE DIAMOND French. Casual Dining. **Address:** 9940 106th St, 100 Sterling Pl T5K 2N2

MIKADO SUSHI & ROBATA   780/425-8096 (3)
APPROVED Japanese Sushi. Casual Dining.
Address: 10350 109th St T5J 4X9

O'BYRNE'S IRISH PUB   780/414-6766 (32)
APPROVED Irish. Casual Dining. **Address:** 10616 82nd Ave NW (Whyte Ave) T6E 2A7

ROSSO PIZZERIA   780/433-5382 (28)
APPROVED Italian Pizza. Casual Dining. **Address:** 8738 109th St NW T6G 1E9

ROSTIZADO   780/761-0911 (5)
THREE DIAMOND New Mexican. Casual Dining. **Address:** 10359 104th St, #102 T5J 1B9

RUTH'S CHRIS STEAK HOUSE   780/990-0123 (20)
THREE DIAMOND Steak. Fine Dining. **Address:** 9990 Jasper Ave T6G 1Y5

SABOR RESTAURANT   780/757-1114 (9)
THREE DIAMOND Mediterranean. Fine Dining. **Address:** 10220 103rd St NW T5J 4C9

SELECT   780/428-1629 (22)
THREE DIAMOND Continental. Casual Dining. **Address:** 10018 106th St T5J 1G1

SHARE   780/493-8994 (14)
THREE DIAMOND American. Fine Dining. **Address:** 10135 100th St T5J 0N7

THE SHERLOCK HOLMES PUB   780/426-7784 (12)
APPROVED American. Casual Dining. **Address:** 10012 101A Ave T5J 3Z1

TRES CARNALES TAQUERIA   780/429-0911 (18)
APPROVED New Mexican. Quick Serve. **Address:** 10119 100A St T5J 0R5

TZIN WINE AND TAPAS   780/428-8946 (13)
THREE DIAMOND New World Small Plates. Casual Dining. **Address:** 10115 104th St T5J 0Z9

UCCELLINO   780/426-0346 (15)
THREE DIAMOND New Italian. Casual Dining. **Address:** 10349 Jasper Ave T5J 1Y7

VON'S STEAK HOUSE & OYSTER BAR   780/439-0041 (36)
THREE DIAMOND Steak. Casual Dining. **Address:** 10309 81st Ave T6E 1X3

YIANNIS TAVERNA   780/433-6768 (35)
APPROVED Greek. Casual Dining. **Address:** 10444 82nd Ave NW (Whyte Ave) T6E 2A2

ZINC RESTAURANT   780/392-2501 (8)
THREE DIAMOND New American. Casual Dining. **Address:** 2 Sir Winston Churchill Sq T5J 2C1

Be Vacation Ready

Before you travel, get your car checked out by a service facility trusted by AAA/CAA repair experts.

AAA.com/autorepair

EDMONTON
• Restaurants p. 110
• Hotels & Restaurants map & index p. 100

BEST WESTERN CEDAR PARK INN
780/434-7411

 THREE DIAMOND
Hotel

 Best Western

AAA Benefit: Members save up to 15% and earn bonus points!

Address: 5116 Gateway Blvd T6H 2H4 **Location:** Hwy 2 (Gateway Blvd) at 51st Ave. **Facility:** 190 units. 4-5 stories (no elevator), interior corridors. **Parking:** winter plug-ins. **Terms:** check-in 4 pm. **Amenities:** Some: safes. **Pool:** heated indoor. **Activities:** exercise room. **Guest Services:** valet laundry. *(See ad this page.)*

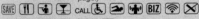

BEST WESTERN PLUS CITY CENTRE INN
780/479-2042

 THREE DIAMOND
Hotel

 Best Western PLUS

AAA Benefit: Members save up to 15% and earn bonus points!

Address: 11310 109th St T5G 2T7 **Location:** From Kingsway Ave NW, just n. **Facility:** 109 units. 2 stories, interior corridors. **Parking:** winter plug-ins. **Pool:** heated indoor. **Activities:** hot tub, exercise room. **Guest Services:** valet and coin laundry. *(See ad this page.)*

🔗 **Rest assured:**

AAA.com/travelguides/hotels

▼ See AAA listing this page ▼

BW Best Western

Cedar Park Inn

Convenient South Edmonton location
Indoor Saltwater Pool | Free Wi-Fi & Parking | Restaurant & Lounge | Free Hot Breakfast Buffet

5116 Gateway Blvd., Edmonton, AB T6H 2H4
1-800-661-9461 | 780-434-7411 | bestwestern.com
 CAA Rewards

▼ See AAA listing this page ▼

BW Best Western PLUS
City Centre Inn

• Tim Hortons on-site
• Indoor Pool with Waterslide & Jacuzzi
• Next to Kingsway Mall

 THREE DIAMOND

CAA Rewards
Members Receive
10% discount
Off Published Rates

1-800-666-5026 | bestwestern.com/aaa

(See map & index p. 100.)

BEST WESTERN PLUS SOUTH EDMONTON INN & SUITES
780/801-3580

 THREE DIAMOND
Hotel

Best Western PLUS **AAA Benefit:** Members save up to 15% and earn bonus points!

Address: 1204 101st St T6X 0P1 **Location:** Hwy 2 (Gateway Blvd) exit Ellerslie Rd. **Facility:** 105 units. 4 stories, interior corridors. **Parking:** winter plug-ins. **Terms:** check-in 4 pm. **Pool:** heated indoor. **Activities:** hot tub, exercise room. **Guest Services:** valet and coin laundry. **Featured Amenity: full hot breakfast.**

SAVE ECO ¶† CALL ⌕ ⛱ ⊞
BIZ HS 🛜 ✕ ⊟ ⊡

CANDLEWOOD SUITES WEST EDMONTON-MALL AREA
780/756-6944 **11**

THREE DIAMOND Extended Stay Contemporary Hotel. **Address:** 18520 100th Ave T5S 0K6

COAST WEST EDMONTON HOTEL & CONFERENCE CENTRE
780/483-7770 **8**

THREE DIAMOND Hotel. **Address:** 18035 Stony Plain Rd T5S 1B2

COMFORT INN WEST
780/484-4415 **20**

 ◆ **APPROVED**
Hotel

Address: 17610 100th Ave T5S 1S9 **Location:** At 176th St. **Facility:** 100 units. 2 stories (no elevator), interior corridors. **Guest Services:** valet and coin laundry.

SAVE ECO ¶† BIZ 🛜 ✕ ⊟
⊞ ⊡ / SOME UNITS 🐾

COURTYARD BY MARRIOTT EDMONTON WEST
780/638-6070 **13**

THREE DIAMOND
Hotel

COURTYARD **AAA Benefit:** Members save 5% or more!

Address: 10011 184th St T5S 0C7 **Location:** From Anthony Henday Dr, 0.8 mi (1.3 km) e. **Facility:** 136 units. 5 stories, interior corridors. **Parking:** winter plug-ins. **Pool:** heated indoor. **Activities:** hot tub, exercise room. **Guest Services:** valet and coin laundry.

SAVE ¶† ⛖ ⅄ CALL ⌕ ⛱
⛖ BIZ HS 🛜 ✕ ⊟ ⊡
/ SOME UNITS ⊞

DAYS INN & SUITES WEST EDMONTON
780/444-4440 **17**

 ◆ **APPROVED**
Hotel

Address: 10010 179A St T5S 2T1 **Location:** From Anthony Henday Dr, 1.2 mi (2 km) e. **Facility:** 108 units, some efficiencies. 4 stories, interior corridors. **Parking:** winter plug-ins. **Terms:** check-in 4 pm. **Dining:** ConYac's Bar & Grill, see separate listing. **Pool:** heated indoor. **Activities:** hot tub, exercise room. **Guest Services:** valet and coin laundry. **Featured Amenity:** breakfast buffet.

SAVE ¶† ⛖ ⅄ ⛱ ⛖ BIZ
HS 🛜 ✕ ⅌ ⊟ ⊞ ⊡

DELTA EDMONTON SOUTH HOTEL AND CONFERENCE CENTRE
780/434-6415 **29**

 THREE DIAMOND
Hotel

D DELTA HOTELS **AAA Benefit:** Members save 5% or more!

Address: 4404 Gateway Blvd NW T6H 5C2 **Location:** Jct Hwy 2 (Gateway Blvd) and Whitemud Dr. **Facility:** 237 units. 11 stories, interior corridors. **Parking:** on-site and valet, winter plug-ins. **Pool:** heated indoor. **Activities:** hot tub, exercise room. **Guest Services:** valet laundry.

SAVE ECO ¶† ⛖ ⅄ CALL ⌕
⛱ ⛖ BIZ HS 🛜 ✕ ⊟ ⊡ / SOME UNITS ⊞ ⊡

DOUBLETREE BY HILTON WEST EDMONTON
780/484-0821 **6**

THREE DIAMOND SAVE Hotel. **Address:** 16615 109th Ave T5P 4K8

AAA Benefit: Members save up to 15%!

FAIRFIELD INN & SUITES BY MARRIOTT EDMONTON NORTH
780/540-5100 **1**

THREE DIAMOND
Contemporary Hotel

Fairfield **AAA Benefit:** Members save 5% or more!

Address: 581 Griesbach Parade NW T5E 6W1 **Location:** Jct Hwy 16 (Yellowhead Hwy) and 97th St NW, 1.5 mi (2.5 km) n. **Facility:** 102 units. 4 stories, interior corridors. **Parking:** winter plug-ins. **Terms:** check-in 4 pm. **Pool:** heated indoor. **Activities:** exercise room. **Guest Services:** valet and coin laundry, boarding pass kiosk. **Featured Amenity:** breakfast buffet.

SAVE ¶† CALL ⌕ ⛱ ⛖ BIZ HS 🛜 ✕ ⊟
⊞ ⊡

FANTASYLAND HOTEL
780/444-3000 **22**

 THREE DIAMOND
Hotel

Address: 17700 87th Ave T5T 4V4 **Location:** At 178th St; in West Edmonton Mall, at southwest end. Adjacent to amusement park. **Facility:** 355 units. 12 stories, interior corridors. **Parking:** on-site and valet. **Terms:** check-in 4 pm. **Amenities:** safes. **Dining:** 3 restaurants. **Guest Services:** valet laundry. **Featured Amenity:** breakfast buffet.

SAVE ECO ¶† ⛖ ⅄ CALL ⌕
BIZ 🛜 ✕ ⛖ ⊟ ⊡
/ SOME UNITS ⊞

FOUR POINTS BY SHERATON EDMONTON GATEWAY
780/801-4000 **36**

 THREE DIAMOND
Hotel

FOUR POINTS BY SHERATON **AAA Benefit:** Members save 5% or more!

Address: 10010 12th Ave SW T6X 0P9 **Location:** Hwy 2 (Gateway Blvd) exit Ellerslie Rd. **Facility:** 154 units. 8 stories, interior corridors. **Parking:** winter plug-ins. **Amenities:** safes. **Pool:** heated indoor. **Activities:** hot tub, exercise room, spa. **Guest Services:** valet and coin laundry.

SAVE ¶† ⛖ ⅄ CALL ⌕ ⛱
⛖ BIZ HS 🛜 ✕ ⊟ ⊡
⊡

(See map & index p. 100.)

FOUR POINTS BY SHERATON EDMONTON SOUTH
780/465-7931   **23**

THREE DIAMOND SAVE Hotel. **Address:** 7230 Argyll Rd T6C 4A6

AAA Benefit: Members save 5% or more!

HAMPTON INN & SUITES BY HILTON - EDMONTON WEST
780/484-7280   **16**

THREE DIAMOND
Hotel

AAA Benefit: Members save up to 15%!

Address: 18304 100th Ave T5S 2V2 **Location:** From Anthony Henday Dr, 0.8 mi (1.3 km) e. **Facility:** 103 units. 5 stories, interior corridors. **Parking:** winter plug-ins. **Amenities:** safes. **Pool:** heated indoor. **Activities:** hot tub, exercise room. **Guest Services:** valet and coin laundry. **Featured Amenity:** breakfast buffet.

SAVE ⬚ CALL ⬚ ⬚ ⬚ BIZ

HS ⬚ ⬚ ⬚ ⬚ / SOME UNITS ⬚ ⬚

HAMPTON INN BY HILTON EDMONTON SOUTH
780/801-2600   **37**

THREE DIAMOND SAVE Hotel. **Address:** 10020 12th Ave T6X 0P6

AAA Benefit: Members save up to 15%!

HILTON GARDEN INN-WEST EDMONTON
780/443-2233   **9**

THREE DIAMOND
Hotel

  Hilton Garden Inn

AAA Benefit: Members save up to 15%!

Address: 17610 Stony Plain Rd T5S 1A2 **Location:** From 176th St, just w. **Facility:** 160 units. 6 stories, interior corridors. **Parking:** winter plug-ins. **Amenities:** safes. **Pool:** heated indoor. **Activities:** hot tub, exercise room. **Guest Services:** valet and coin laundry.

SAVE ECO ⬚ ⬚ CALL ⬚ ⬚

⬚ BIZ HS ⬚ ⬚ ⬚ ⬚

⬚ ⬚

HOLIDAY INN & SUITES, WEST EDMONTON
780/444-3110   **3**

THREE DIAMOND Hotel. **Address:** 11330 170th St T5S 2X1

HOLIDAY INN CONFERENCE CENTRE EDMONTON SOUTH
780/431-1100   **28**

THREE DIAMOND
Hotel

Address: 4485 Gateway Blvd T6H 5C3 **Location:** Hwy 2 (Gateway Blvd), just n of Whitemud Dr. **Facility:** 224 units. 6 stories, interior corridors. **Parking:** winter plug-ins. **Amenities:** video games. **Dining:** 2 restaurants. **Pool:** heated indoor. **Activities:** hot tub, exercise room. **Guest Services:** complimentary and valet laundry.

SAVE ECO ⬚ ⬚ ⬚ CALL ⬚

⬚ ⬚ BIZ ⬚ ⬚ ⬚ ⬚
/ SOME UNITS ⬚ HS ⬚

HOLIDAY INN EXPRESS & SUITES EDMONTON NORTH
780/476-9898   **2**

THREE DIAMOND Hotel. **Address:** 13742 50th St NW T5A 4Y3

HOLIDAY INN EXPRESS & SUITES EDMONTON SOUTH
780/440-5000   **32**

THREE DIAMOND Hotel. **Address:** 2440 Calgary Tr NW T6J 5J6

HOLIDAY INN EXPRESS & SUITES WEST EDMONTON-MALL AREA
780/756-2134   **12**

THREE DIAMOND Contemporary Hotel. **Address:** 18520 100th Ave T5S 0K6

HOME2 SUITES BY HILTON EDMONTON SOUTH
780/250-3000   **35**

THREE DIAMOND
Extended Stay Contemporary Hotel

 HOME2 SUITES BY HILTON

AAA Benefit: Members save up to 15%!

Address: 1140 103A St SW T5J 2Z2 **Location:** Hwy 2 exit Ellerslie Rd SW, just w. **Facility:** 120 units. 6 stories, interior corridors. **Parking:** winter plug-ins. **Pool:** heated indoor. **Activities:** hot tub, picnic facilities, exercise room. **Guest Services:** valet and coin laundry.

SAVE ⬚ CALL ⬚ ⬚ ⬚ BIZ

⬚ ⬚ ⬚ ⬚ ⬚
// SOME UNITS ⬚

HOME2 SUITES BY HILTON WEST EDMONTON
780/509-1230   **5**

THREE DIAMOND SAVE Extended Stay Contemporary Hotel. **Address:** 16675 109th Ave NW T5P 4K8

AAA Benefit: Members save up to 15%!

HYATT PLACE EDMONTON-WEST   780/244-4900   **14**

THREE DIAMOND
Contemporary Hotel

 HYATT PLACE

AAA Benefit: Members save up to 10%!

Address: 18004 100th Ave NW T5S 2T6 **Location:** Hwy 216 exit 100 Ave NW, 1 mi (1.6 km) e. **Facility:** 161 units. 7 stories, interior corridors. **Parking:** winter plug-ins. **Pool:** heated indoor. **Activities:** hot tub, exercise room. **Guest Services:** valet and coin laundry. **Featured Amenity:** breakfast buffet.

SAVE ⬚ ⬚ CALL ⬚ ⬚ ⬚

BIZ HS ⬚ ⬚ ⬚ ⬚

/ SOME UNITS ⬚ ⬚

QUALITY INN WEST EDMONTON   780/484-8000   **10**

APPROVED Hotel. **Address:** 17803 Stony Plain Rd NW T5S 1B4

RADISSON HOTEL AND CONVENTION CENTRE EDMONTON
780/468-5400   **24**

THREE DIAMOND Hotel. **Address:** 4520 76th Ave T6B 0A5

RADISSON HOTEL EDMONTON SOUTH   780/437-6010   **27**

THREE DIAMOND Hotel. **Address:** 4440 Gateway Blvd NW T6H 5C2

🔗 **Use the free travel planning tools**

at AAA.com/maps

(See map & index p. 100.)

RAMADA BY WYNDHAM EDMONTON SOUTH
780/434-3431 **25**
◆ APPROVED Hotel. **Address:** 5359 Calgary Tr NW T6H 4J9

RAMADA WEST EDMONTON   780/483-4000 **18**
◆ APPROVED Hotel. **Address:** 10017 179A St T5S 2L4

RIVER CREE RESORT AND CASINO   780/484-2121
◆ THREE DIAMOND Hotel. **Address:** 300 E Lapotac Blvd T7X 3Y3

ROYAL HOTEL, TRADEMARK COLLECTION BY WYNDHAM
780/484-6000 **19**
◆ THREE DIAMOND Hotel. **Address:** 10010 178th St T5S 1T3

SAWRIDGE INN EDMONTON SOUTH & CONFERENCE CENT   780/438-1222 **30**

◆ THREE DIAMOND
Hotel

Address: 4235 Gateway Blvd T6J 5H2 **Location:** Just s of Whitemud Dr. **Facility:** 135 units. 5 stories, interior corridors. **Parking:** winter plug-ins. **Dining:** Creations Dining Room & Lounge, see separate listing. **Activities:** exercise room. **Guest Services:** complimentary and valet laundry. **Featured Amenity:** breakfast buffet.

SAVE ECO 🔌 🍴 🖥 🍸
CALL ♿ 🏋 BIZ 📶 ✖ 🎦
🛏 🖨 /SOME UNITS 🐾 📷

STAYBRIDGE SUITES WEST EDMONTON 780/484-6223 **4**
◆ THREE DIAMOND Extended Stay Hotel. **Address:** 16929 109 Ave NW T5P 4P6

SUPER 8 EDMONTON SOUTH   780/433-8688 **31**
◆ APPROVED Hotel. **Address:** 3610 Gateway Blvd T6J 7H8

TOWNEPLACE SUITES BY MARRIOTT EDMONTON SOUTH
780/540-5110 **34**
◆ THREE DIAMOND SAVE Extended Stay Hotel. **Address:** 1115 103A St SW T6W 1A1

AAA Benefit: Members save 5% or more!

TRU BY HILTON WINDERMERE   780/752-8781 **33**
◆ APPROVED SAVE
Contemporary Hotel. **Address:** 6025 Andrews Way SW T6W 1A4

Members save up to 15%!

WEST EDMONTON MALL INN   780/444-9378 **21**
◆ APPROVED
Hotel

Address: 17504 90th Ave T5T 6L6 **Location:** From Whitemud Dr exit 170th St N, just w. Next to West Edmonton Mall. **Facility:** 88 units. 3 stories, interior corridors. **Parking:** winter plug-ins. **Terms:** check-in 4 pm. **Guest Services:** valet laundry. **Featured Amenity:** continental breakfast.

SAVE 🍴 CALL ♿ 📶 ✖ 🎦
🛏 🖨 /SOME UNITS 🐾

WINGATE INN EDMONTON WEST   780/443-1000 **15**
◆ THREE DIAMOND Hotel. **Address:** 18220 100th Ave T5S 2V2

ATLAS STEAK + FISH   587/460-2423 **20**
◆ THREE DIAMOND Steak Seafood. Fine Dining. **Address:** 8882 170th St NW T5T 4J2

BIERA   587/525-8589 **24**
◆ THREE DIAMOND New International. Brewpub. **Address:** 9570 NW 76th St T6C 0K2

THE BOTHY WINE & WHISKY BAR   780/761-1761 **27**
◆ APPROVED New American. Gastropub. **Address:** 5482 Calgary Tr T6H 4J8

BUCAS & PASTAS   780/496-2461 **12**
◆ APPROVED Italian. Quick Serve. **Address:** 16516 100th Ave NW T5P 4Y2

THE BURGER'S PRIEST   780/652-0529 **32**
◆ APPROVED Burgers. Quick Serve. **Address:** 2125 98 St NW T6N 1K7

CACTUS CLUB CAFE   780/489-1002 **19**
◆ THREE DIAMOND American. Casual Dining. **Address:** 8882 170th St T5T 3J7

CAFÉ LINNEA   780/721-8443 **4**
◆ THREE DIAMOND French. Casual Dining. **Address:** 10932 119th St T5H 3P5

CANTEEN   780/485-6125 **10**
◆ THREE DIAMOND New Canadian. Casual Dining. **Address:** 10522 124th St T5N 1R9

CHA FOR TEA PALACE   780/443-2832 **5**
◆ APPROVED Chinese Dim Sum Seafood. Casual Dining. **Address:** 17512 Stony Plain Rd T5S 1L1

CLEMENTINE   780/756-4570 **16**
◆ THREE DIAMOND Small Plates. Casual Dining. **Address:** 11957 Jasper Ave T5K 0P1

CONYAC'S BAR & GRILL   780/483-2255 **8**
◆ APPROVED American. Casual Dining. **Address:** 10010 179A St T5S 2T1

CREATIONS DINING ROOM & LOUNGE   780/989-4439 **31**
◆ THREE DIAMOND Canadian. Casual Dining. **Address:** 4235 Gateway Blvd T6J 5H2

DELUX BURGER BAR   780/420-0101 **18**
◆ APPROVED American. Casual Dining. **Address:** 9682 142nd St T5N 4B2

EARLS KITCHEN + BAR
◆ APPROVED American. Casual Dining.
LOCATIONS:
Address: 13330 50th St T5A 4Z8 **Phone:** 780/473-9008
Address: 4250 Calgary Tr NW T6J 6Y8 **Phone:** 780/439-5888

FAMOSO NEAPOLITAN PIZZERIA   780/487-0046 **21**
◆ APPROVED Pizza. Casual Dining. **Address:** 8882 170th St, Unit 1951 St T5T 4M2

FIFENDEKEL PIE SHOP CAFE   780/489-6436 **3**
◆ APPROVED Sandwiches. Quick Serve. **Address:** 10646 170th St T5S 1P3

FRANCO'S STEAK & PIZZA   780/476-4333 **1**
◆ APPROVED Italian. Casual Dining. **Address:** 12981 50th St NE T5A 3P3

(See map & index p. 100.)

GURU FINE INDIAN CUISINE 780/484-4300 (9)
THREE DIAMOND Indian. Casual Dining. **Address:** 17021 100th Ave NW T5S 1T9

HAUS FALKENSTEIN 780/483-5904 (2)
APPROVED German. Casual Dining. **Address:** 15215 111 Ave NW T5M 2R1

HOMEFIRE GRILL 780/489-8086 (7)
APPROVED International. Casual Dining. **Address:** 18210 100th Ave T5S 2V2

JOEY RESTAURANTS 780/465-1880
APPROVED American. Casual Dining. **Address:** 9911 19th Ave NW T6N 1M4

LEMONGRASS CAFE 780/413-0088 (28)
APPROVED Vietnamese. Casual Dining. **Address:** 10417 51st Ave NW T6H 0K4

LOCAL PUBLIC EATERY 780/989-5898 (33)
APPROVED American. Gastropub. **Address:** 1820 99th St T6N 1M5

MOXIE'S CLASSIC GRILL 780/484-6669 (22)
APPROVED American. Casual Dining. **Address:** 1670 8882-170th St T5T 4M2

MOXIE'S CLASSIC GRILL 780/484-2040 (11)
APPROVED American. Casual Dining. **Address:** 17109 100th Ave NW T5S 2GS

MOXIE'S CLASSIC GRILL 780/468-3098 (34)
APPROVED American. Casual Dining. **Address:** 1739 102 St NW T6N 0B1

NORMAND'S 780/482-2600 (17)
THREE DIAMOND French. Casual Dining. **Address:** 11639A Jasper Ave NW T5K 0M9

OLD COUNTRY INN 780/433-3242 (25)
APPROVED German. Casual Dining. **Address:** 9906 72nd Ave NW T6E 0Z3

ORIGINAL JOE'S RESTAURANT & BAR 780/486-0909
APPROVED American. Gastropub. **Address:** 2512 Guardian Rd NW T5T 1K8

PADMANADI 780/428-8899 (13)
APPROVED Asian Vegetarian. Casual Dining. **Address:** 10740 101st St NW T5H 2S3

RED OX INN 780/465-5727 (23)
THREE DIAMOND New American. Casual Dining. **Address:** 9429 91st St T6C 3P4

RGE RD 780/447-4577 (6)
THREE DIAMOND Regional Canadian. Casual Dining. **Address:** 10643 123rd St T5N 1P3

RICKY'S ALL DAY GRILL
APPROVED American. Casual Dining.
LOCATIONS:
Address: 9917 170th St T5P 4S2 **Phone:** 780/486-7109
Address: 11330 170th St T5S 2X1 **Phone:** 780/444-3110

SAWMILL PRIME RIB & STEAK HOUSE 780/437-5616 (30)
APPROVED Steak. Casual Dining. **Address:** 4810 Calgary Tr S T6H 5H5

SC DAMN GOOD FOOD 780/930-2636
THREE DIAMOND New Canadian Comfort Food. Casual Dining. **Address:** 300 E Lapotac Blvd T7X 3Y3

THAI FLAVOURS 780/484-7911
APPROVED Thai. Casual Dining. **Address:** 2570 Guardian Rd NW T5T 1K8

TROPIKA 780/439-6699 (26)
APPROVED Thai. Casual Dining. **Address:** 6004 104th St T6H 2K3

URBAN DINER 780/488-7274 (14)
APPROVED American. Casual Dining. **Address:** 12427 102nd Ave T5N 0M2

VATICANO CUCINA 780/250-1110 (29)
APPROVED Italian. Casual Dining. **Address:** 10310 45th Ave NW T6H 5K3

VIOLINO RISTORANTE 780/757-8701 (15)
THREE DIAMOND Italian. Fine Dining. **Address:** 10133 125th St T5N 1S7

WHITE SPOT 780/485-3534
APPROVED American. Casual Dining. **Address:** 10010 12th Ave T6X 0P9

ZAIKA INDIAN BISTRO 780/462-8722 (35)
APPROVED Indian. Casual Dining. **Address:** 2303 Ellwood Dr SW T6X 0A9

EDSON pop. 8,475
• Restaurants p. 112

BEST WESTERN HIGH ROAD INN 780/712-2378
THREE DIAMOND
Hotel

AAA Benefit: Members save up to 15% and earn bonus points!

Address: 300 52nd St T7E 1V8 **Location:** Between 52nd and 53rd sts; center. **Facility:** 115 units, some two bedrooms. 4 stories, interior corridors. **Parking:** winter plug-ins. **Pool:** heated indoor. **Activities:** hot tub, exercise room. **Guest Services:** valet laundry.

SAVE 🍴 🛁 🍸 CALL 🛗 ➰
🛗 BIZ HS 🛜 ✕ 🔌 🖥
🖥 / SOME UNITS 🐾

COMFORT INN & SUITES EDSON 780/723-7303
APPROVED
Hotel

Address: 5517 4th Ave T7E 1L6 **Location:** Hwy 16; west end of town. **Facility:** 40 units, some kitchens. 4 stories, interior corridors. **Parking:** winter plug-ins. **Activities:** exercise room. **Guest Services:** valet and coin laundry. **Featured Amenity:** full hot breakfast.

SAVE 🍴 CALL 🛗 🛗 BIZ HS
🛜 ✕ 🔌 🖥 🖥

HOLIDAY INN EXPRESS HOTEL & SUITES EDSON
780/723-4011
THREE DIAMOND Hotel. **Address:** 4520 2nd Ave T7E 1C3

RAMADA BY WYNDHAM EDSON 780/723-9797
APPROVED Hotel. **Address:** 4536 2nd Ave T7E 1C3

SUPER 8 BY WYNDHAM EDSON   780/723-7373
⬥ APPROVED   Hotel. **Address:** 5220 2nd Ave T7E 1X5

WHERE TO EAT

MOUNTAIN PIZZA & STEAK HOUSE   780/723-3900
⬥ APPROVED   Steak Pizza. Casual Dining. **Address:**
5102 4th Ave T7E 1T8

ORIGINAL JOE'S RESTAURANT & BAR   780/723-6445
⬥ APPROVED   American. Gastropub. **Address:** 330 45th
St T7E 1C3

🔻 ELK ISLAND NATIONAL PARK
(E-7)

Elevations in the park range from 709 metres
(2,326 ft.) at Goose Lake to 754 metres
(2,475 ft.) at Tawayik Lake. Refer to CAA/
AAA maps for additional elevation
information.

About 35 kilometres (22 mi.) east of Edmonton,
Elk Island National Park is reached by Hwy. 15 from
the north and Hwy. 16 from the south. The lakes,
ponds, forests and meadows of this 194-square-
kilometre (75-sq.-mi.) park provide a haven for many
species of plants and animals, including bison, deer,
moose, coyotes, beavers and elk. Drive the Bison
Loop Road at dawn or dusk for the best chance to
see free-roaming plains bison.

Many small lakes dot the landscape, but the
major bodies are Tawayik and Astotin, the latter
being the larger. The lakes and marshes support
more than 250 bird species, including ducks,
grebes, gulls, loons, pelicans, rare trumpeter swans
and terns.

Marsh marigolds and several types of lilies are
among several plants rarely seen outside the park.
Song birds occupy the many aspen, spruce and
birch forests, but few fish inhabit the waters due to
low oxygen levels. The herd of elk for which the park
was established flourish among the meadows and
forests, as do reintroduced colonies of beavers.

The park occupies the Beaver Hills region, which
first was settled by Sarcee and Plains Cree First Nations. They trapped beavers and hunted bison and
elk, as did the European fur traders who arrived between the late 18th and the mid-19th centuries.
Soon the animals became nearly extinct, and the
natives were forced to seek sustenance elsewhere.

In 1906 five local men asked that the government
establish a wildlife refuge to preserve the remaining
elk. A year later 400 plains bison were added, while
another preserve near Wainwright was being established. Most of these animals later were transferred,
but about 50 stayed and produced the plains bison
herd of more than 300 that remains today north of
Hwy. 16, and now provides bison to conservation
projects in Canada and elsewhere. A herd of several
hundred wood bison, a threatened subspecies, is
kept separate from this herd south of Hwy. 16.

General Information and Activities

The park is open daily all year. More than 80 kilometres (50 mi.) of trails crisscross the park; stop at
the Visitor Information Centre near the park's south
entrance gate for information and maps. Staff members and displays describe Elk Island and other national parks. The center is open daily 9:30-4:30,
mid-May through Labour Day; phone (780)
922-5790 to confirm schedule.

Most recreation facilities center on Astotin Lake,
which offers non-motorized boating, wildlife obser-
vations, picnic facilities, a nine-hole golf course,
camping, hiking and walking trails. Canoe, kayak
and paddleboard rentals are available June through
August. Sandy Beach campground is on the east
side of the lake.

Guided interpretive experiences are offered on
weekends in July and August and include behind-
the-scenes tours of the bison handling facility (Sat.-
Sun. on the hour noon-5). Hunting and fishing are
prohibited. *See Recreation Areas Chart.*

ADMISSION $7.80; $6.80 (ages 65+); free (ages
0-16); $15.70 (up to seven people arriving in a
single vehicle). An annual pass, valid at all Canadian national parks, is available.

PETS must be kept on a leash at all times.

ADDRESS inquiries for additional information to Elk
Island National Park, Site 4, R.R. 1, Fort Saskatchewan, AB, Canada T8L 2N7; phone (780) 922-5790.

🔻 UKRAINIAN CULTURAL HERITAGE
VILLAGE—see Edmonton p. 95.

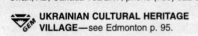

FORT MACLEOD (J-6) pop. 3,117,
elev. 955m/3,133'

In 1874 at the end of their 1,126-kilometre (700-
mi.) march through the prairie wilderness to rid
western Canada of whiskey traders, the North West
Mounted Police, now the Royal Canadian Mounted
Police, chose the site of what is now Fort Macleod
as their first headquarters.

A commanding view of the countryside and the
natural protection afforded by the Oldman River
made Fort Macleod an important outpost; a cairn at
2nd Avenue and 25th Street commemorates the
fort's founding. Guided walking tours of the historic
district, ranging from 30 minutes to 1 hour, can be
arranged in advance during the summer by con-
tacting The Fort Museum; phone (403) 553-4703.

The highland physical geography that made the
Fort Macleod outpost successful also helped the
Plains people survive long before the first traders
appeared in the area. In order to kill the buffalo for
food, the Plains hunters stampeded them over the
high cliffs.

Self-guiding tours: A brochure describing a self-
guiding tour of the Fort Macleod historic district is
available at The Fort Museum, 219 25th St.

HEAD-SMASHED-IN BUFFALO JUMP IN-TERPRETIVE CENTRE is 3 km (1.9 mi.) n. on Queen Elizabeth II Hwy., then 16 km (10 mi.) w. on Hwy. 785. For at least 6,000 years people of the Plains First Nations stampeded herds of buffalo over sandstone cliffs to their deaths. The hunters then butchered the kill at their campsite below the cliffs. This is one of the oldest, best-preserved buffalo jump sites. A theater screens a 12-minute film that re-creates the buffalo hunts. The hunting grounds are preserved, and short trails lead to the main areas.

The site's name is derived from a young brave who stood under a ledge of the cliff to watch the buffalo as they fell past him. As the number of carcasses multiplied, his skull was crushed as he became trapped between the animals and the cliff. Built into that cliff today is a seven-story interpretive center with displays. Exhibits focus on the geographical and climatic factors affecting these tribes as well as their lifestyle and history.

Time: Allow 2 hours minimum. **Hours:** Daily 9-5, May 15-Labour Day; 10-5, rest of year. Closed Jan. 1, Easter, Christmas Eve and Christmas. **Cost:** $15; $13 (ages 65+); $10 (ages 7-17); $40 (family, two adults and up to six children); free (Canadian military and family with ID). **Phone:** (403) 553-2731.

FORT MCMURRAY (A-8) pop. 61,374
• Restaurants p. 114

At the confluence of the Clearwater and Athabasca rivers in the fur country of northern Alberta, Fort McMurray began as the home of the Woodland Cree and Chipewyan First Nations. In 1778 explorers and fur traders led by Peter Pond opened the vast fur trade region of the Mackenzie River basin. In 1870 Henry John Moberly built a post and named it Fort McMurray after his chief factor, William McMurray of Hudson's Bay Co.

Soon after a steamboat terminus was established near Fort McMurray in 1884, the region's vast resources began to attract attention. Oil sands containing some 1.7 trillion barrels of oil were found around Lake Athabasca. The first commercially successful extractions, however, did not take place until the late 1960s. Since then Fort McMurray has boomed, serving oil recovery plants that now extract from the sands more than 600,000 barrels of synthetic crude oil per day.

The city is the southern terminus of the vast water transportation system that navigates Great Slave Lake and the Mackenzie River en route to the Arctic. Logging and tourism further bolster the economy. Fort McMurray is a service center for surrounding areas and the oil sands plants.

Note: In 2016, a devastating wildfire swept through Fort McMurray and the surrounding area prompting mass evacuations and destroying thousands of homes. Most attractions have returned to their normal schedules as of press time, but it's a good idea to phone ahead to confirm hours of operation.

Fort McMurray Tourism: 515 MacKenzie Blvd., Fort McMurray, AB, Canada T9H 4X3. **Phone:** (780) 791-4336 or (800) 565-3947.

OIL SANDS DISCOVERY CENTRE is at 515 MacKenzie Blvd. Exhibits relate the geology, history and technology of Alberta's Athabasca oil sands, said to be the world's single largest oil deposit. Oil sands extraction methods, history, science and technology, and new methods of exploration are explained through interpretive displays and films and interactive demonstrations. Outdoor exhibits include retired mining machines, research equipment and one of the largest land-based artifacts in Canada, a seven-story bucket-wheel excavator.

Time: Allow 1 hour minimum. **Hours:** Daily 9-5, mid-May through Labour Day; Tues.-Sun. 10-4, rest of year. Phone ahead to confirm schedule. **Cost:** $11; $8 (ages 65+); $7 (ages 7-17); $29 (family, two adults and up to six children); free (Canadian military and family with ID). Prices are subject to change; phone ahead. **Phone:** (780) 743-7167.

BEST WESTERN PLUS SAWRIDGE SUITES
780/799-4552

▼ THREE DIAMOND
Extended Stay Contemporary Hotel

AAA Benefit: Members save up to 15% and earn bonus points!

Address: 410 Taiganova Cres T9H 4W1 **Location:** Hwy 63 exit Taiganova Cres, then 0.6 mi (1 km) e. **Facility:** 151 efficiencies. 4 stories, interior corridors. *Bath:* shower only. **Parking:** winter plug-ins. **Amenities:** video games, safes. **Activities:** steamroom, trails, exercise room. **Guest Services:** valet and coin laundry. **Featured Amenity:** full hot breakfast.

CLEARWATER SUITE HOTEL   780/799-7676
▼ THREE DIAMOND Extended Stay Hotel. **Address:** 4 Haineault St T9H 1L6

FRANKLIN SUITE HOTEL   780/788-2199
▼ THREE DIAMOND Extended Stay Hotel. **Address:** 10300 Franklin Ave T9H 0A5

MERIT HOTEL & SUITES   780/714-9444
▼ APPROVED Hotel. **Address:** 8200 Franklin Ave T9H 2H9

🔗 **For complete hotel, dining and attraction listings:**
AAA.com/travelguides

MICROTEL INN & SUITES BY WYNDHAM FORT MCMURRAY
587/452-0533
◇ APPROVED   Hotel. **Address:** 317 Sakitaway Tr T9H 5E7

SUPER 8 BY WYNDHAM FORT MCMURRAY   780/743-8000
◇ APPROVED   Motel. **Address:** 230 Parent Way T9H 5E6

TOWNEPLACE SUITES BY MARRIOTT FORT MCMURRAY
780/750-8530
◇ THREE DIAMOND [SAVE] Extended
Stay Contemporary Hotel. **Address:**
321 Sakitaway Tr T9H 5E7

AAA Benefit:
Members save 5%
or more!

VANTAGE INN & SUITES   780/713-4111
◇ APPROVED   Hotel. **Address:** 200 Parent Way T9H 5E6

WHERE TO EAT

ASTI TRATTORIA ITALIANA   780/750-3330
◇ APPROVED   Italian. Casual Dining. **Address:** 10020
Franklin Ave, #200 T9H 2K6

EARLS KITCHEN + BAR   780/791-3275
◇ APPROVED   American. Casual Dining. **Address:** 9802
Morrison St T9H 5B8

FUJI JAPANESE RESTAURANT   780/788-2128
◇ APPROVED   Japanese. Casual Dining. **Address:** 8706
Franklin Ave T9H 2J6

MOXIE'S CLASSIC GRILL   780/791-1996
◇ APPROVED   American. Casual Dining. **Address:** 9521
Franklin Ave T9H 3Z7

MR MIKES STEAKHOUSECASUAL   780/215-6453
◇ APPROVED   American. Casual Dining. **Address:** 8520
Manning Ave T9H 5G2

ORIGINAL JOE'S RESTAURANT & BAR   780/750-6544
◇ APPROVED   American. Casual Dining. **Address:**
8406B Franklin Ave T9H 2J3

TOWNHALL PUBLIC HOUSE FORT MCMURRAY
587/275-0240
◇ APPROVED   International. Gastropub. **Address:** 8104
Fraser Ave T9H 1W5

FORT SASKATCHEWAN (E-6) pop. 19,051, elev. 622m/2,043'
• Part of Edmonton area — see map p. 84

Fort Saskatchewan is located along the North
Saskatchewan River, about 25 kilometres (15.5 mi.)
northeast of Edmonton. The city has more than 30
kilometres (18.6 mi.) of multiuse pathways and sidewalks and numerous parks and recreation areas. It
is known for the flock of sheep that graze in Peter T.
Ream Historic Park during the summer months. The
historic park, at 101st Street and 101st Avenue, is
home to the Fort Saskatchewan Museum, which encompasses such historical structures as the
1875-85 North West Mounted Police Fort and the
1937 Warden's House; phone (780) 998-1783.

BEST WESTERN PLUS FORT SASKATCHEWAN INN &
SUITES   587/285-8033
◇ THREE DIAMOND
Hotel

AAA Benefit:
Members save up to
15% and earn bonus
points!

Address: 50 Westpark Blvd T8L 0B2
Location: Just e of Hwy 15/21. **Facility:**
100 units, some two bedrooms and
kitchens. 4 stories, interior corridors.
Parking: winter plug-ins. **Pool:** indoor.
Activities: sauna, hot tub, exercise
room. **Guest Services:** valet and coin
laundry. **Featured Amenity:** continental breakfast.

COMFORT INN & SUITES   780/998-4000
◇ THREE DIAMOND Hotel. **Address:** 120 Town Crest Rd T8L 0G7

HAMPTON INN BY HILTON FORT SASKATCHEWAN
780/997-1001
◇ THREE DIAMOND [SAVE] Hotel. **Address:** 8709 101st St T8L 0H9

AAA Benefit:
Members save up to
15%!

HOLIDAY INN EXPRESS & SUITES   780/997-9700
◇ THREE DIAMOND Hotel. **Address:** 10120 86th Ave T8L 0N6

THE KANATA   780/998-2770
◇ THREE DIAMOND Hotel. **Address:** 9820 86th Ave T8L 4P4

SUPER 8 HOTEL-FORT SASKATCHEWAN   780/998-2898
◇ APPROVED   Hotel. **Address:** 8750 84th St T8L 4P5

WHERE TO EAT

THE ATLANTIC KITCHEN   780/992-1501
◇ APPROVED   Comfort Food Seafood. Casual Dining.
Address: 9904 102nd St T8L 2C3

THE CANADIAN BREWHOUSE   780/912-0453
◇ APPROVED   American. Sports Bar. **Address:** 60
Westpark Blvd T8L 0B2

HANABI JAPANESE CUISINE   780/589-1755
◇ APPROVED   Japanese. Casual Dining. **Address:**
10404 99th Ave T8L 3W2

ORIGINAL JOE'S RESTAURANT & BAR   780/998-0520
◇ APPROVED   American. Gastropub. **Address:** 9372
Southfort Dr, #103 T8L 0C5

RICKY'S ALL DAY GRILL   780/997-0606
◇ APPROVED   American. Casual Dining. **Address:** 8770
84th St T8L 4R5

SAWMILL PRIME RIB & STEAK HOUSE   780/992-2255
◇ THREE DIAMOND Steak. Casual Dining. **Address:** 21
Westpark Blvd T8L 4M5

TUMMY FULL FUSION RESTAURANT   587/285-3855
◇ APPROVED   International. Quick Serve. **Address:** 121
Town Crest Rd T8L 0G7

FOX CREEK pop. 1,969

BEST WESTERN PLUS FOX CREEK   780/548-3338

 THREE DIAMOND

Hotel

 **AAA Benefit:** Members save up to 15% and earn bonus points!

 Address: 313 1st Ave T0H 1P0 **Location:** Hwy 43, just n. **Facility:** 95 units, some efficiencies. 4 stories, interior corridors. **Parking:** winter plug-ins. **Pool:** heated indoor. **Activities:** steamroom, picnic facilities, exercise room. **Guest Services:** coin laundry. **Featured Amenity: continental breakfast.**

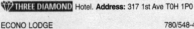

COMFORT INN & SUITES   780/622-3311

THREE DIAMOND Hotel. **Address:** 317 1st Ave T0H 1P0

ECONO LODGE   780/548-4000

APPROVED Hotel. **Address:** 104 Highway Ave T0H 1P0

WHERE TO EAT

PIZZA JOINT   780/622-2699

APPROVED Pizza Comfort Food. Quick Serve. **Address:** 2 Commercial Ct T0H 1P0

GIROUXVILLE (B-3) pop. 266

GIROUXVILLE MUSEUM is on Main St. (Hwy. 49). More than 6,000 artifacts tell the story of the indigenous people, devout missionaries and rugged pioneers who lived here. The museum also displays mounted birds and fur-bearing animals (the most famous being a five-legged squirrel) and the works of local artists Leon Tremblay and Alfred Gaboury.

Transportation Means of Yesterday includes sleighs, an antique snowmobile, a birch bark canoe, a 1927 Chevrolet truck and various other historic vehicles and machinery. **Time:** Allow 1 hour minimum. **Hours:** Mon.-Fri. 10-4:30, May-Aug.; by appointment rest of year. **Cost:** $2.86; $1.43 (ages 4-17). **Phone:** (780) 323-4252.

GLEICHEN (I-7) pop. 336, elev. 899m/2,952'

BLACKFOOT CROSSING HISTORICAL PARK is 11 km (7 mi.) e. on Hwy. 1, then 9.7 km (6 mi.) s. on Hwy. 842. Used by the Siksika (Blackfoot) First Nation as a wintering grounds, Blackfoot Crossing was the site of the signing of Treaty No. 7 by representatives of the Blackfoot Confederacy and the Canadian and British governments in 1877. An on-site cultural center offers several galleries describing the culture and history of the Siksika people, along with an introductory video in the Vision Quest Theatre.

Housed in a striking, eco-friendly edifice are exhibits about hunting, early life, societies, storytelling and warriors. The collection features such artifacts as tools, weapons, clothing and utensils as well as multimedia displays. The building's architectural features also document First Nations heritage, with tepee-shaped skylights and stained glass eagle feather fans incorporated into the structure's design.

Time: Allow 1 hour, 30 minutes minimum. **Hours:** Mon.-Fri. 9-5. Phone ahead to confirm schedule. **Cost:** $12; $8 (ages 8-17 and 65+). **Phone:** (403) 734-5171.

GRANDE PRAIRIE (C-2) pop. 55,032
• Restaurants p. 116

Surrounded by a colorful checkerboard of rich farmland along the gateway to the Alaska Hwy., Grande Prairie serves as the business and transportation center of Alberta's Peace River country.

Glimpses into the Peace River region's past are evident in the Kleskun Hills, just east via Hwy. 43. Erosion of the glacial drift of clay, sand, gravel and boulders has uncovered dinosaur tracks and aquatic fossils embedded in a prehistoric river delta formed more than 70 million years ago.

Muskoseepi Park has hiking and bicycling trails, picnicking areas and recreation facilities. Other area recreational pursuits include swimming, boating, bird-watching and fishing. A pioneer-oriented event is the Grande Prairie Stompede the last 5 days in May. Other festivals celebrated throughout the summer highlight the region's diversity.

Grande Prairie Regional Tourism Association: 11330 106th St., Suite 114, Grande Prairie, AB, Canada T8V 7X9. **Phone:** (780) 539-7688 or (866) 202-2202.

HERITAGE DISCOVERY CENTRE is at 11330-106 St. on the lower level of Centre 2000, Grand Prairie's Tourism Information Centre. The hands-on interpretive center depicts regional history through pioneer artifacts, a geology timeline, an animatronic dinosaur named Piper, a tepee, photographs, films, a caboose and interactive games. Changing exhibits also are featured.

Hours: Mon.-Fri. 8:30-6:30, Sat.-Sun. 10-6, late May-Labour Day; Mon.-Fri. 8:30-4:30, Sat.-Sun. 10-4:30, rest of year. Closed Jan. 1, third Mon. in Feb., Good Friday, Christmas and day after Christmas. **Cost:** Free. **Phone:** (780) 532-5790.

BEST WESTERN GRANDE PRAIRIE HOTEL & SUITES   780/402-2378

 APPROVED

Hotel

Best Western. **AAA Benefit:** Members save up to 15% and earn bonus points!

 Address: 10745 117th Ave T8V 7N6 **Location:** Corner of Hwy 43 (100th Ave) and 117th Ave. **Facility:** 99 units. 4 stories, interior corridors. **Parking:** winter plug-ins. **Dining:** Padrino's Italian Ristorante, see separate listing. **Pool:** heated indoor. **Activities:** exercise room. **Guest Services:** valet and coin laundry.

ENCORE SUITES BY SERVICE PLUS INNS 587/259-0425
THREE DIAMOND Hotel. **Address:** 10639 110 St T8V 7P9

FOUR POINTS BY SHERATON GRANDE PRAIRIE
587/771-1300
THREE DIAMOND **SAVE** Hotel. **Ad-dress:** 6702 106th St T8W 0K8

AAA Benefit:
Members save 5%
or more!

HAMPTON INN & SUITES BY HILTON GRANDE PRAIRIE
780/538-0722
THREE DIAMOND **SAVE** Hotel. **Ad-dress:** 10405 117th St T8V 6M8

AAA Benefit:
Members save up to
15%!

HOLIDAY INN HOTEL & SUITEN 780/402-6886
THREE DIAMOND Hotel. **Address:** 9816 107th St T8V 8E7

MOTEL 6 GRANDE PRAIRIE 780/830-7744
APPROVED Hotel. **Address:** 15402 101st St T8V 0P7

PODOLLAN INN & SPA 780/830-2000
THREE DIAMOND Hotel. **Address:** 10612 99th Ave T8V 8E8

POMEROY HOTEL & CONFERENCE CENTRE 780/532-5221
THREE DIAMOND Hotel. **Address:** 11633 100th St T8V 3Y4

QUALITY INN & SUITES 780/831-2999
APPROVED Hotel. **Address:** 11710 102nd St T8V 7S7

SERVICE PLUS INNS AND SUITES 780/538-3900
APPROVED Hotel. **Address:** 10810 107A Ave T8V 7A9

STONEBRIDGE HOTEL 780/539-5561
APPROVED Hotel. **Address:** 12102 100th St T8V 5P1

SUPER 8 BY WYNDHAM GRANDE PRAIRIE 780/532-8288
APPROVED Hotel. **Address:** 10050 116th Ave T8V 4K5

WHERE TO EAT

ACROPOLIS GREEK RESTAURANT & PUB 780/538-4424
APPROVED Greek. Casual Dining. **Address:** 10011 101st Ave T8V 0X9

BURGER HEAVEN 780/814-7015
APPROVED Burgers. Casual Dining. **Address:** 9805 116th St, #103 T8V 2N1

HONG FAH THAI RESTAURANT 780/357-9988
APPROVED Thai. Casual Dining. **Address:** 11735 105th St T8V 8L1

JAX GRILL & LOUNGE 780/830-2000
APPROVED International. Casual Dining. **Address:** 10612 99th Ave T8V 8E8

JEFFERY'S CAFE COMPANY 780/830-0140
APPROVED American. Casual Dining. **Address:** 10605 West Side Dr, Suite 106 T8V 8E6

MOXIE'S CLASSIC GRILL 780/532-4401
APPROVED American. Casual Dining. **Address:** 11801 100th St, #212 T8V 3Y2

MR MIKES STEAKHOUSECASUAL 780/538-9378
APPROVED American. Casual Dining. **Address:** 10214 116th Ave T8V 4K5

THE OFFICE 780/832-2441
THREE DIAMOND American. Casual Dining. **Address:** 11633 100th St T8V 3Y4

PADRINO'S ITALIAN RISTORANTE 780/814-7171
APPROVED Italian. Casual Dining. **Address:** 10745 117th Ave T8V 7N6

RED ROCK URBAN BBQ 780/402-7431
APPROVED Barbecue. Gastropub. **Address:** 10408 67th Ave T8W 0K8

SOTO TEPPANYAKI AND FUSION SUSHI 780/533-3323
APPROVED Japanese. Casual Dining. **Address:** 10210 111th St, Suite 106 St T8V 7L3

TITO'S BISTRO & CAFE 780/539-4881
APPROVED Lebanese. Quick Serve. **Address:** 10006 101st Ave T8V 0Y1

HIGH LEVEL pop. 3,641

BEST WESTERN PLUS MIRAGE HOTEL & RESORT
780/821-1000

THREE DIAMOND
Hotel

AAA Benefit: Members save up to 15% and earn bonus points!

Address: 9616 Hwy 58 T0H 1Z0 **Location:** Jct Hwy 35 and 58; north end of town. **Facility:** 92 units, some two bedrooms and kitchens. 2 stories, interior/exterior corridors. **Parking:** winter plug-ins. **Terms:** check-in 4 pm. **Dining:** Mirage Taste House, see separate listing. **Pool:** heated indoor. **Activities:** hot tub, exercise room. **Guest Services:** valet and coin laundry.

SUPER 8 HIGH LEVEL 780/841-3448
APPROVED Hotel. **Address:** 9502 114th Ave T0H 1Z0

WHERE TO EAT

MIRAGE TASTE HOUSE 780/821-1000
APPROVED Canadian. Casual Dining. **Address:** 9616 Hwy 58 T0H 1Z0

HIGH RIVER (I-6) pop. 12,920

A ranching and farming town, High River hosts Guy Weadick Days, which encompasses a rodeo and WPCA chuckwagon races, in June. The Little Britches Rodeo and Parade is held in July. The winter holiday season is ushered in the first weekend in December with the evening Santa Claus Parade.

High River Visitor Information Centre: 228 12th Ave. S.E., Bob Snodgrass Recreation Complex, High River, AB, Canada T1V 1Z5. **Phone:** (403) 603-3101.

HIGH RIVER HISTORICAL MURALS are at various locations throughout town. Many colorful paintings illustrate area history. The murals present a variety of subjects, ranging from cattle ranching and polo to well-known residents, including author W.O. Mitchell and former Prime Minister Joe Clark. **Hours:** Murals visible daily 24 hours. Closed Jan. 1 and Christmas. **Cost:** Free. **Phone:** (403) 603-3101.

HERITAGE INN HOTEL & CONVENTION CENTRE
403/652-3834
APPROVED Hotel. **Address:** 1104 11th Ave SE T1V 1M4

RAMADA INN & SUITES HIGH RIVER   403/603-3183
THREE DIAMOND Hotel. **Address:** 1512 13th Ave SE T1V 2B1

SUPER 8 HIGH RIVER   403/652-4448
APPROVED Hotel. **Address:** 1601 13th Ave SE T1V 2B1

WHERE TO EAT

EVELYN'S MEMORY LANE CAFE   403/336-1925
APPROVED Sandwiches Desserts. Casual Dining. **Address:** 118 4th Ave SW T1V 1P7

THE WHISTLE STOP DINER   403/652-7026
APPROVED American. Casual Dining. **Address:** 406 1st St SW T1V 1S2

HINTON pop. 9,640, elev. 1,049m/3,444'
• **Part of Jasper National Park area — see map p. 118**

BEST WESTERN PLUS HINTON INN & SUITES
780/817-7000
THREE DIAMOND
Hotel

Best Western PLUS. **AAA Benefit:** Members save up to 15% and earn bonus points!

Address: 340 Smith St T7V 2A1 **Location:** 1.2 mi (2 km) e on Hwy 16. **Facility:** 100 units, some efficiencies and kitchens. 5 stories, interior corridors. **Parking:** winter plug-ins. **Pool:** heated indoor. **Activities:** hot tub, exercise room. **Guest Services:** valet and coin laundry.

[SAVE] [❯❮] CALL [♿] [▦] [♥] [BIZ]
[HS] [📶] [✕] [🎦] [🗄] [🛒] [🖵]

HOLIDAY INN EXPRESS & SUITES   780/865-2048
THREE DIAMOND Hotel. **Address:** 462 Smith St T7V 2A1

HOLIDAY INN HINTON   780/865-3321
APPROVED Hotel. **Address:** 393 Gregg Ave T7V 1N1

WHERE TO EAT

L & W PIZZA & SPAGHETTI HOUSE   780/865-4892
APPROVED American. Casual Dining. **Address:** 414 Carmichael Ln T7V 1X7

MR MIKES STEAKHOUSECASUAL   587/467-8580
APPROVED American. Casual Dining. **Address:** 600-900 Carmichael Lane T7V 1Y6

RANCHER'S SPORTS BAR & GRILL   780/865-9785
APPROVED American. Casual Dining. **Address:** 438 Smith St T7V 2A1

SMITTY'S   780/865-6151
APPROVED American. Casual Dining. **Address:** 445 Gregg Ave T7V 1N1

INNISFAIL (G-6) pop. 7,876, elev. 945m/3,100'

DISCOVERY WILDLIFE PARK is off Queen Elizabeth II Hwy. N. Innisfail exit; take Hwy. 2A 2 blks. n.e., then just n.w. on 42nd Ave., following signs. The 36-hectare (90-acre) park is home to a variety of rescued exotic and native animals, including jaguars, bears, monkeys, tigers and wolves. Some of the creatures are trained to work in show business and have been featured in major film and television productions. Educational shows and interactive programs are offered daily.

   Time: Allow 1 hour, 30 minutes minimum. **Hours:** Daily 10-7, May 1 to mid-Oct. Last admission 1 hour before closing. **Cost:** $17.50; $15.50 (ages 13-17 and 60+); $11.50 (ages 3-12); $1 (ages 0-2). **Phone:** (403) 227-3211. [❯❮] [🖼]

DAYS INN INNISFAIL   403/227-4405
THREE DIAMOND Hotel. **Address:** 5010 40th Ave T4G 1Z1

IRRICANA (H-6) pop. 1,162

PIONEER ACRES OF ALBERTA MUSEUM is off Hwy. 9, 1 km n., then 1 km w. The museum features one of the largest collections of antique farm equipment in western Canada. It also displays furniture, tools, memorabilia, clothing and vehicles. A collection of early buildings includes a school, a steam-engine shop and a blacksmith shop. **Time:** Allow 1 hour, 30 minutes minimum. **Hours:** Thurs.-Mon. 9-5, May 16-Sept. 30. **Cost:** $10; $5 (ages 6-12). Cash only. **Phone:** (403) 935-4357. [GT]

 **Save on travel, shopping, dining and more: AAA.com/discounts**

JASPER NATIONAL PARK (E-2)
• Attractions map p. 120

Elevations in the park range from 1,067
metres (3,500 ft.) in the town of Jasper to
3,747 metres (12,293 ft.) at Mount Columbia.
Refer to CAA/AAA maps for additional
elevation information.

The largest national park in the Canadian Rocky
Mountains, Jasper preserves a spectacular wilderness of forested glacial valleys, dazzling snowcapped peaks, roaring waterfalls and sparkling blue-
green lakes. Jasper is less developed and less
crowded than Banff National Park to the south, so it
tends to attract those seeking the solitude and tran-
quility that are among the park's greatest assets.
Nearly a thousand kilometres (600 mi.) of maintained trails help visitors escape into the virtually
pristine countryside.

The park's wildlife is as diverse as its peaks and
valleys. Mountain goats and bighorn sheep inhabit
the crags and highlands, although the sheep frequently wander down from the heights and into the
camera viewfinders of tourists. The lower slopes
and meadows are home to deer, elk and moose.
Bears, coyotes, wolves, lynx and other predators
usually avoid humans.

Whistlers Mountain, whose peak looms above the
town of Jasper *(see place listing p. 122)*, is named
for the whistling call of the hoary marmot, which
looks like something between a squirrel and a
beaver. You might encounter marmots along Jasper
National Park's trails, along with Columbian ground
squirrels and tiny pikas, which look like mice but are
actually related to rabbits, as you might guess from
their other name: rock rabbits.

Jasper National Park was named for Jasper
Hawes who operated Jasper's House, an early 19th-
century fur-trading post in the area. The town, originally called Fitzhugh, adopted the name of the
surrounding park in 1913. It's a laid-back place with

This map shows cities in
Jasper National Park where
you will find attractions, hotels
and restaurants. Cities are
listed alphabetically in this
book on the following pages.

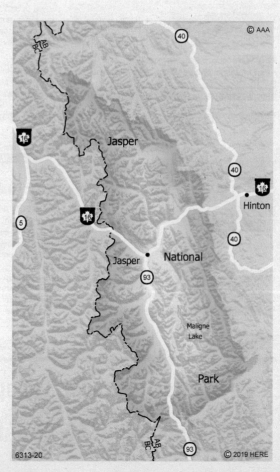

a surprisingly small-town feel despite catering to the millions who visit the park annually. You will find one of the park's two tourist information centers in a rustic cobblestone building on the town's main street. Completed in 1914, it once housed the park's headquarters; its design established the style now common for national park buildings.

Looked at from above, the town's curved layout appropriately enough resembles the letter J. Take a look for yourself by making the 7.5-minute journey via the Jasper SkyTram *(see attraction listing p. 122)* to the upper station on Whistlers Mountain, 2,263 metres (7,425 ft.) above sea level. The view of the town, the Athabasca River Valley and surrounding mountains is unforgettable, and you'll see why the Jasper SkyTram is one of the most popular things to do in Jasper National Park.

Strolling the streets of Jasper, you can't help but notice the distinctive profile of Mount Edith Cavell, a prominent local peak with contrasting parallel bands of rock and snow. A half-hour drive will take you to the mountain, called "the White Ghost" by the indigenous Stoney people. Trails there lead to the wildflower-strewn Cavell Meadows and offer fantastic views of Angel Glacier, named for its outstretched "wings." Below the glacier, little icebergs bob in Cavell Pond, even in summer. **Note:** In 2012, the left wing of the Angel Glacier broke off and caused a major flood which damaged the trails and parking lot on Cavell Road. During construction of the trails and parking lot, a vehicle permit is required to access the road. First-come-first-served permits can be picked up at the Jasper National Park Information Centre, 500 Connaught Dr., daily 8 a.m.-10 a.m.

Other places that would make the Jasper National Park Top 10: the scenic Maligne Lake Road connecting Maligne Canyon and lovely Medicine and Maligne lakes; thundering Athabasca and Sunwapta falls; Pyramid and Patricia lakes; Marmot Basin ski resort; and the breathtaking Icefields Parkway running south to the Columbia Icefield and the Athabasca Glacier, where a short trail leads from the parkway right up to the glacier.

General Information and Activities

The park is open all year, though weather conditions in winter make some portions inaccessible except to cross-country skiers and those on snowshoes. Some facilities are open only from May to June or September to October. A Parks Canada information center is in the townsite of Jasper at 500 Connaught Dr. It's open daily late March to late October, and Wednesday through Sunday the rest of the year.

Many hiking trails, including the 11.2-kilometre (7-mi.) trip to Valley of the Five Lakes and the loop to Lac Beauvert, depart from Old Fort Point, 1.6 kilometres (1 mi.) east of Jasper on Hwy. 93. The Valley of the Five Lakes also can be accessed from the trailhead on the Icefields Parkway, 9 km (6 mi.) south of the townsite.

Hikers and skiers interested in Jasper National Park camping backcountry must have a valid backcountry use permit. These permits are available at the Parks Canada information center in Jasper and at the Columbia Icefield Glacier Discovery Centre from early June to mid-September.

Campgrounds are open varying durations, and limited camping facilities are available in winter. For more information, phone (780) 852-6176.

There are many ways to explore the park's features, either alone or with a guide. One- or multiple-day bus tours to tourist attractions within the park depart from Jasper. Several stables in the Jasper area offer 1-hour and half- and full-day trail rides from mid-May to mid-September and sleigh rides in winter.

Winter sports include curling, skating, skiing, tobogganing, ice climbing, snowshoeing and hockey. Cross-country skiing tours operate out of Jasper. Downhill skiing is available at Marmot Basin. Approximately 75 kilometres of cross-country trails traverse the park; trails are groomed from early December to March. Interpretive guides share their insights in theatrical productions. Wildlife and stand-up paddleboarding tours also are available. Self-guiding tour brochures are available at the Jasper National Park Information Centre, 500 Connaught Dr.; phone (780) 852-6176.

Note: Since hunting is illegal, some wildlife may have lost their natural fear of human contact. Be alert for animals on the highways both day and night, and never feed them. Fishing permits can be obtained at information centers, campgrounds and local sport fishing shops. Boats with electric motors (without onboard generators) are allowed on most road-accessible lakes unless signs indicate otherwise. Gas-powered motors are prohibited in the park. Boat launches are available at lakes Annette, Patricia, Pyramid, Maligne and Medicine. *See Recreation Areas Chart.*

ADMISSION to the park is $9.80; $8.30 (ages 65+); $4.90 (ages 6-16); $19.60 (up to seven people arriving in a single vehicle). An annual pass, valid at Jasper and more than 100 other Canadian national parks and historic sites, is available.

PETS are allowed in some areas of the park but must be leashed, crated or physically restrained at all times. A fenced area for leashed pets is located on Sleepy Hollow Road adjacent to the industrial park.

ADDRESS inquiries to the Jasper National Park Information Centre, Jasper National Park, P.O. Box 10, Jasper, AB, Canada T0E 1E0; phone (780) 852-6176. For other area information contact Jasper Park Chamber of Commerce, P.O. Box 98, Jasper, AB, Canada T0E 1E0; phone (780) 852-3858.

COLUMBIA ICEFIELD, just inside the Jasper National Park boundary next to Banff National Park, is

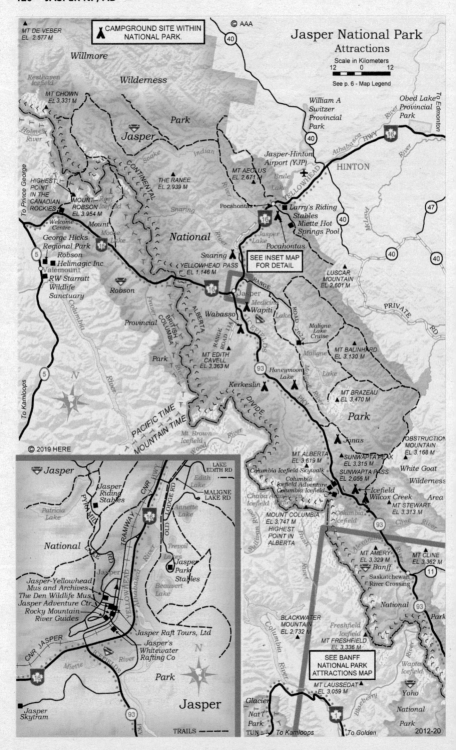

the largest ice mass in the Rocky Mountains. Its main bulk, about 16 by 24 kilometres (10 by 15 mi.), straddles the Great Divide, part of the British Columbia border and portions of Banff and Jasper national parks. The ice covers about 325 square kilometres (130 sq. mi.) to an estimated depth of 300 metres (984 ft.). Three glaciers—Stutfield, Athabasca and Dome—can be seen from Icefields Parkway.

Columbia Icefield Glacier Discovery Centre is 105 km (64 mi.) s. of the town of Jasper on Hwy. 93. The center overlooks Athabasca and Dome glaciers and offers views of major mountain peaks surrounding the Columbia Icefield. An interpretive center contains exhibits about the ice field and local wildlife as well as a theater that screens the film "Through Ice and Time." Also inside the center is a Parks Canada information desk, which offers maps, information and details about interpretive programs. **Time:** Allow 30 minutes minimum. **Hours:** Daily 9-5. **Cost:** Free. **Phone:** (780) 852-5288 or (877) 423-7433. 🍴

COLUMBIA ICEFIELD ADVENTURE departs from Columbia Icefield Glacier Discovery Centre, 105 km (64 mi.) s. of the town of Jasper on Hwy. 93. Tours provide an opportunity to see and walk on a field of moving glacier ice formed by snow falling as long ago as 400 years. The bus driver provides anecdotes and information during this 80-minute excursion.

   Time: Allow 1 hour, 30 minutes minimum. **Hours:** Tours depart every 15-30 minutes daily 9-6 (weather permitting), late May-early Sept.; 10-5, late Apr.-late May and early Sept.-early Oct.; 10-4, mid-Apr. to late Apr. and early Oct. to mid-Oct. **Cost:** (includes admission to Columbia Icefield Skywalk) $114; $57 (ages 6-15); free (ages 0-5 in lap). **Phone:** (403) 762-6700 or (877) 423-7433. 🅶🆃

COLUMBIA ICEFIELD SKYWALK is accessible via free shuttles departing from the Columbia Icefield Glacier Discovery Centre, 105 km (64 mi.) s. of the town of Jasper on Hwy. 93. Interpretive signs along the walkway running along the edge of the Sunwapta Valley educate visitors about the Canadian Rockies' ecology and geological and evolutionary history. The walkway leads to the site's showpiece, a glass-floored observation platform 280 metres (918 ft.) over spectacular glacier-formed valleys and rushing waterfalls.

   Hours: Daily 10-6, late May to mid-July; 10-7, mid-July to early Sept.; 10-5:30, early Sept.-early Oct.; 10-4, early Oct. to mid-Oct. Shuttles depart daily every 15 minutes from the Columbia Icefield Glacier Discovery Centre (weather permitting). Phone ahead to confirm schedule. **Cost:** $37; $19 (ages 6-15). Combination tickets are available. **Phone:** (403) 762-6701 or (866) 816-2758.

ICEFIELDS PARKWAY (HWY. 93)—see Banff National Park p. 32.

MALIGNE CANYON is 10 km (6.2 mi.) n.e. of Jasper via Maligne Lake Rd. A steep-walled ravine more than 50 metres (164 ft.) deep, this spectacular gorge carved by the rushing Maligne River is spanned by six footbridges. Evergreen-shaded trails hug the edge of the chasm, providing excellent views into its depths, and interpretive signs line the way. Nourished by cool mist from the river, bright green moss clings to the nearly vertical limestone walls. A parking lot at the Upper Canyon affords easy access to Maligne's most impressive waterfalls. **Time:** Allow 1 hour minimum. **Cost:** Free. **Phone:** (780) 852-6176 or (780) 852-6162. 🍴

MALIGNE LAKE CRUISE is 48 km (30 mi.) s.e. of the Jasper townsite via Maligne Lake Rd.; tickets can be purchased from the office at 616 Patricia St. in Jasper and at some area hotels. The 90-minute tours, which offer a brief stop at Spirit Island, provide exceptional views of Maligne Narrows as well as insight into area geology and wildlife. Hiking and trout-fishing trips along with boat, canoe and sea kayak rentals are available June to September. A 2.5-hour photography tour, accompanied by a professional photographer, runs July through mid-September.

   Time: Allow 1 hour, 30 minutes minimum. **Hours:** Boat tours depart daily on the hour (weather permitting) 10-5, July 1-early Sept.; 10-4, early June-June 30 and early Sept.-early Oct.; 10-3, early May-early June. **Cost:** $79; $40 (ages 6-15). **Phone:** (780) 852-3370 for general information. 🅶🆃

SAVE **MIETTE HOT SPRINGS POOL** is e. on Hwy. 16 from the town of Jasper for 44 km (27.3 mi.) to the Pocahontas Bungalows and jct. Miette Rd., then s. 17 km (11 mi.) to the end of Miette Rd. Natural sulfur hot springs feed two man-made pools, with the water temperature ranging between 37 C (98 F) and 40 C (104 F). Pool depth ranges from .5 metres (18 in.) to 1.5 metres (5 ft.) deep. Visitors also can cool off in two plunge pools.

   Wildlife viewing, hiking trails and picnic sites are available in the area. Changing rooms as well as swimsuit, towel and locker rentals are available. **Time:** Allow 45 minutes minimum. **Hours:** Daily 9 a.m.-11 p.m., mid-June through Labour Day; 10:30-9, early May to mid-June and day after Labour Day to mid-Oct. **Cost:** $6.05; $5.15 (ages 3-17 and 65+); $18.35 (family, two adults and two children, $3.40 for each additional child). Prices may vary; phone ahead. **Phone:** (780) 866-3939 or (800) 767-1611. 🍴 🧖

RECREATIONAL ACTIVITIES
White-water Rafting
- **Jasper's Whitewater Rafting Co.** departs from the parking lot .3 km (.19 mi.) s. of Sunwapta Falls Resort off Hwy. 93. Other trips are available. **Hours:** Trips are offered May 1-early Oct. Schedule varies; phone ahead. **Phone:** (780) 852-7238. 🅶🆃

JASPER (F-2) pop. 4,051

• Part of Jasper National Park area — see map p. 118

JASPER ADVENTURE CENTRE is at 611 Patricia St. May through October and at 414 Connaught Dr. in winter. The company offers guided interpretive van tours, wildlife tours and walking tours. Summer adventures include exploration of the Columbia Icefield, Maligne Valley and Morro Peak. Winter activities include ice walks, train tours, dog sledding and cross-country skiing. Horseback riding trips, canoe and rafting tours, and wildlife tours also are offered seasonally. **Hours:** Daily 8-6, May-Oct.; 8-5, rest of year. Closed Christmas. **Cost:** Fares $65-$114. **Phone:** (780) 852-5595 May-Oct., (780) 852-4056 Nov.-Apr., or (800) 565-7547 year-round. GT

JASPER SKYTRAM is 3 km (1.8 mi.) s. on Hwy. 93, then 4 km (2.5 mi.) w. at Whistlers Mountain Rd. Take a 7.5-minute narrated ride in an enclosed tram car 1,005 metres (3,297 ft.) up into the alpine zone on Whistlers Mountain, where stunning scenic views await. From the aerial tram's upper station at 2,263 metres (7,425 ft.) you can see six surrounding mountain ranges, several turquoise lakes, the Athabasca River and the town of Jasper. On a clear day you may even see Mount Robson in British Columbia, the highest mountain in the Canadian Rockies.

Once at the upper station, you can stroll along the wooden boardwalk and read the interpretive panels posted along the way, or if you're feeling energetic, hike the remaining 1.4 km (.87 mi.) up to the summit and gain 200 metres (656 ft.) for a breathtaking 360-degree view.

Step carefully here; the plants that cling to life in this harsh alpine climate are delicate, small and easily damaged. Several have tiny but beautiful flowers. Ptarmigans are the most common birds in this rugged environment, and other frequently seen inhabitants include the diminutive pika and the hoary marmot, although you may hear these creatures before you ever see them. Pikas make a recognizable "eep" sound while the hoary marmot's call resembles a whistle, which is how Whistlers Mountain got its name.

Time: Allow 1 hour minimum. **Hours:** Daily 8 a.m.-9 p.m., late June-early Sept.; 9-8, mid-May to late June; 10-5, late Mar. to mid-May and early Sept.-late Oct. **Cost:** $46.95; $24.95 (ages 6-15); $118.85 (family, two adults and two children). **Phone:** (780) 852-3093. *(See ad this page.)*

▼ *See AAA listing this page* ▼

JASPER SKYTRAM
Canadian Rockies

EXPLORE
the HIGH ALPINE in JASPER

EARLY SEASON   SUMMER   LATE SEASON

LEARN MORE AT:
JASPER.SKYTRAM.COM

OPEN LATE MARCH to END OF OCTOBER
FOLLOW US @ JASPERSKYTRAM

ALPINE VILLAGE
780/852-3285

THREE DIAMOND

Cabin

Address: Hwy 93A T0E 1E0 **Location:** Jct Hwy 16 and 93, 0.9 mi (1.4 km) s on Hwy 93, just e. **Facility:** Stay outside town amid towering spruce trees along the river in one of the really lovely, smaller cabins or one of the larger upscale units. A large outdoor hot tub is great for easing muscle pains. 50 cabins, some kitchens. 1 story, exterior corridors. **Terms:** check-in 4 pm. **Activities:** hot tub, playground, trails. **Guest Services:** valet laundry.

[SAVE] [icons] / SOME UNITS

BECKER'S CHALETS
780/852-3779

APPROVED

Cabin

Address: Hwy 93 S T0E 1E0 **Location:** Waterfront. 4.3 mi (6.8 km) s. Located in a quiet rustic area. **Facility:** 118 units, some two bedrooms. 2 stories (no elevator), exterior corridors. **Terms:** check-in 4 pm. **Activities:** playground, trails. **Guest Services:** coin laundry. **Featured Amenity:** breakfast buffet.

[SAVE] [ECO] [icons]

CHATEAU JASPER
780/852-5644

THREE DIAMOND Hotel. **Address:** 96 Geikie St T0E 1E0

THE CRIMSON JASPER
780/852-3394

THREE DIAMOND Hotel. **Address:** 200 Connaught Dr T0E 1E0

FAIRMONT JASPER PARK LODGE
780/852-3301

THREE DIAMOND

Resort Hotel

Address: 1 Old Lodge Rd T0E 1E0 **Location:** 3 mi (4.8 km) ne via Hwy 16, 2 mi (3.2 km) se off highway via Maligne Rd, follow signs. **Facility:** It's said that at one time Marilyn Monroe frequented this resort set along the shore of gorgeous Lac Beauvert in its spectacular mountain setting. Rooms range from upscale rustic to fabulous décors. 442 units, some kitchens. 1-2 stories (no elevator), exterior corridors. **Parking:** on-site and valet, winter plug-ins. **Terms:** check-in 4 pm. **Amenities:** safes. **Dining:** 2 restaurants, also, The Moose's Nook Chophouse, Orso Trattoria, see separate listings, entertainment. **Pool:** heated outdoor. **Activities:** sauna, hot tub, steamroom, self-propelled boats, boat dock, fishing, regulation golf, miniature golf, tennis, cross country skiing, sledding, ice skating, recreation programs, kids club, bicycles, playground, game room, lawn sports, trails, health club, in-room exercise equipment, spa. **Guest Services:** valet laundry, area transportation.

[SAVE] [ECO] [icons] CALL [icons] BIZ [icons] / SOME UNITS

JASPER INN AND SUITES
780/852-4461

APPROVED

Hotel

Address: 98 Geikie St T0E 1E0 **Location:** Corner of Geikie and Bonhomme sts. Located in a residential area. **Facility:** 143 units, some kitchens. 2-3 stories (no elevator), interior/exterior corridors. **Parking:** winter plug-ins. **Terms:** check-in 4 pm. **Amenities:** safes. **Pool:** heated indoor. **Activities:** sauna, hot tub, steamroom. **Guest Services:** coin laundry, area transportation.

[SAVE] [icons] BIZ [icons] / SOME UNITS

LOBSTICK LODGE
780/852-4431

APPROVED Hotel. **Address:** 94 Geikie St T0E 1E0

MARMOT LODGE
780/852-4471

APPROVED Motel. **Address:** 86 Connaught Dr T0E 1E0

MOUNT ROBSON INN
780/852-3327

APPROVED Motel. **Address:** 902 Connaught Dr T0E 1E0

PARK PLACE INN
780/852-9770

THREE DIAMOND Boutique Hotel. **Address:** 623 Patricia St T0E 1E0

PATRICIA LAKE BUNGALOWS
780/852-3560

APPROVED Cabin. **Address:** Pyramid Lake Rd T0E 1E0

PYRAMID LAKE RESORT
780/852-4900

THREE DIAMOND Hotel. **Address:** Pyramid Lake Rd T0E 1E0

SAWRIDGE INN & CONFERENCE CENTRE JASPER
780/852-5111

THREE DIAMOND Hotel. **Address:** 76 Connaught Dr T0E 1E0

SUNWAPTA FALLS ROCKY MOUNTAIN LODGE
780/852-4852

APPROVED Cabin. **Address:** Hwy 93 T0E 1E0

TONQUIN INN
780/852-4987

APPROVED Motel. **Address:** 100 Juniper St T0E 1E0

WHERE TO EAT

AGNI BISTRO
780/852-2724

APPROVED Asian. Casual Dining. **Address:** 620 Connaught Dr T0E 1E0

BECKER'S GOURMET RESTAURANT
780/852-3535

THREE DIAMOND Canadian. Fine Dining. **Address:** Hwy 93 T0E 1E0

CASSIO'S ITALIAN RESTAURANT
780/852-4070

APPROVED Italian. Casual Dining. **Address:** 602 Connaught Dr T0E 1E0

DOWNSTREAM RESTAURANT & LOUNGE
780/852-9449

APPROVED International. Gastropub. **Address:** 620 Connaught Dr T0E 1E0

EARLS KITCHEN + BAR
780/852-2393

APPROVED American. Casual Dining. **Address:** 600 Patricia St, 2nd floor T0E 1E0

EVIL DAVE'S GRILL
780/852-3323

THREE DIAMOND New International. Casual Dining. **Address:** 622 Patricia St T0E 1E0

FAMOSO NEAPOLITAN PIZZERIA
780/852-5577

APPROVED Pizza. Casual Dining. **Address:** 607 Patricia St T0E 1E0

FIDDLE RIVER RESTAURANT
780/852-3032

APPROVED Canadian. Casual Dining. **Address:** 620 Connaught Dr T0E 1E0

JASPER BREWING CO
780/852-4111

APPROVED American. Gastropub. **Address:** 624 Connaught Dr T0E 1E0

JASPER PIZZA PLACE 780/852-3225

APPROVED Pizza. Casual Dining. **Address:** 402 Connaught Dr T0E 1E0

KAROUZO'S STEAKHOUSE 780/852-4640

APPROVED Steak. Casual Dining. **Address:** 628 Connaught Dr T0E 1E0

KIMCHI HOUSE 780/852-5022

APPROVED Korean. Casual Dining. **Address:** 407 Patricia St T0E 1E0

L & W FAMILY RESTAURANT 780/852-4114

APPROVED International. Casual Dining. **Address:** 701 Patricia St T0E 1E0

THE MOOSE'S NOOK CHOPHOUSE 780/852-6052

THREE DIAMOND

Steak
Fine Dining
$29-$75

AAA Inspector Notes: This nook of a restaurant is cozy and intimate with an interesting mountain theme design. Great cuts of AAA Alberta beef and bison, as well as regional seafood are found on the tasty menu. You can count on well-prepared and flavorful food as the chef incorporates high-quality ingredients. The service and ambience are upscale without being pretentious and laid-back, yet classy. Check for special openings in the winter season. **Features:** full bar. **Reservations:** suggested. **Address:** 1 Old Lodge Rd T0E 1E0 **Location:** 3 mi (4.8 km) ne via Hwy 16, 2 mi (3.2 km) se off highway via Maligne Rd, follow signs; in Fairmont Jasper Park Lodge. **Parking:** on-site and valet. D CALL

OLIVE BISTRO & LOUNGE 780/852-5222

APPROVED International. Casual Dining. **Address:** 401 Patricia St T0E 1E0

ORSO TRATTORIA 780/852-6052

THREE DIAMOND

New
Italian
Fine Dining
$30-$59

AAA Inspector Notes: This beautiful dining room includes big picture windows that offer lovely views of nearby Mount Edith Cavell and Lac Beauvert. Fresh high-quality ingredients with a focus on organic and sustainable items are crafted into beautifully prepared and tasty dishes with a Northern Italian slant. Almost all the pastas and the delicious desserts are made in house. There is a nice selection of Italian wine by the glass and the friendly servers bring the bottle over so guests can taste before committing. **Features:** full bar, patio dining. **Reservations:** suggested. **Address:** 1 Old Lodge Rd T0E 1E0 **Location:** 3 mi (4.8 km) ne via Hwy 16, 2 mi (3.2 km) se off highway via Maligne Rd, follow signs; in The Fairmont Jasper Park Lodge. **Parking:** on-site and valet. B D CALL

PATRICIA STREET DELI 780/852-4814

APPROVED Deli. Quick Serve. **Address:** 606 Patricia St T0E 1E0

THE RAVEN BISTRO 780/852-5151

APPROVED International. Casual Dining. **Address:** 504 Patricia St T0E 1E0

SUNHOUSE CAFE 780/852-4742

APPROVED Coffee/Tea Sandwiches. Quick Serve. **Address:** 610 Patricia St T0E 1E0

SYRAHS OF JASPER 780/852-4559

THREE DIAMOND International. Casual Dining. **Address:** 606 Patricia St T0E 1E0

WICKED CUP 780/852-1942

APPROVED Coffee/Tea Sandwiches. Quick Serve. **Address:** 912 Connaught Dr T0E 1E0

Hit the Road with Foreign Currency

A treasure trove of artisan masterpieces awaits.

Visit your local AAA office or online at
AAA.com/ForeignCurrency

All products not available at all locations.

KANANASKIS   pop. 249

• Part of Banff National Park area — see map p. 30

KANANASKIS MOUNTAIN LODGE, AUTOGRAPH COLLECTION   403/591-7711

FOUR DIAMOND

Resort Hotel

AUTOGRAPH COLLECTION® HOTELS

AAA Benefit: Members save 5% or more!

Address: 1 Centennial Dr, Kananaskis Village T0L 2H0 **Location:** Trans-Canada Hwy 1, 14.7 mi (23.5 km) s on Hwy 40 (Kananaskis Tr), 1.8 mi (3 km) on Kananaskis Village access road, follow signs. Located in a quiet area. **Facility:** Nestled on a tranquil mountain plateau, this lovely hotel has a striking, modern Canadian Rockies design. Rooms range from appealing standard units to suites and lofts. 247 units. 3 stories, interior corridors. **Parking:** on-site and valet, winter plug-ins. **Terms:** check-in 4 pm. **Amenities:** safes. **Dining:** 4 restaurants. **Pool:** outdoor, heated outdoor, heated indoor. **Activities:** sauna, hot tub, steamroom, tennis, cross country skiing, ice skating, recreation programs, kids club, bicycles, playground, lawn sports, trails, health club, spa. **Guest Services:** valet and coin laundry, area transportation. *(See ad this page.)*

SAVE ECO 🍽 👶 🍸 🏊 🛁 BIZ HS 📶 ✕

🖨 📠 / SOME UNITS 🐾 🍴 🖥

MOUNT KIDD MANOR   403/591-7500

APPROVED   Hotel. **Address:** 2 Terrace Dr T0L 2H0

KANANASKIS COUNTRY   (I-5)

Kananaskis Country is a four-season, multiuse recreation area encompassing more than 4,200 square kilometres (1,622 sq. mi.) of mountains and foothills. West of Calgary, the area contains Bow Valley, Bragg Creek, Canmore Nordic Centre, Peter Lougheed, Sheep River and Spray Valley provincial parks. In addition there are Blue Rock, Bow Valley, Don Getty and Elbow-Sheep wildland parks. There are also numerous provincial recreation areas with campgrounds, day use areas and trails *(see Recreation Areas Chart).*

Year-round recreational activities are offered, including hiking, horseback riding, snowmobiling, kayaking, mountain biking, fishing, snowshoeing and downhill and cross-country skiing. The area begins just south of Hwy. 1 and extends south to the intersection of hwys. 940 and 532. Animals, including elk, deer, bighorn sheep, lynx, moose, mountain goats, bears and porcupines, can be observed in the area.

Three major visitor information centers within Kananaskis Country provide brochures, maps, displays and other travel information. The Barrier Lake Visitor Information Centre is 6.5 kilometres (4 mi.) south of Hwy. 1 on Hwy. 40. Peter Lougheed Provincial Park Visitor Information Centre is 50 kilometres (31 mi.) south off Hwy. 40 on Kananaskis Lakes Trail. Elbow Valley Visitor Information Centre is 5 kilometres (3 mi.) west of Hwy. 22 on Hwy. 66. Phone (403) 678-0760 for information about all three locations. Several campground amphitheaters offer interpretive programs Wednesday through Sunday evenings in July and August. The area is open daily; however, Hwy. 40 is closed December 1 to June 15 between the Kananaskis Lakes Trail and the junction of hwys. 541 and 940.

Kananaskis Country General Inquiries: Provincial Building, 800 Railway Ave., Suite 201, Canmore, AB, Canada T1W 1P1. **Phone:** (403) 678-0760.

🔗 **For complete hotel, dining and attraction listings:**

AAA.com/travelguides

▼ *See AAA listing this page* ▼

#rediscoverkananaskis

At the intersection of Backcountry Beauty And World Class Comfort.

Lodgeatkananaskis.com

POMEROY

KANANASKIS
mountain lodge

AUTOGRAPH COLLECTION®
HOTELS

LAC LA BICHE (C-7) pop. 2,544

South of town, Portage La Biche was discovered in 1798 by renowned geographer and explorer David Thompson of the North West Co. This area encompasses the land between the Churchill and Athabasca-Mackenzie basins. Soon after its discovery the portage became a key link in Canada's main fur trade routes and a passageway to the Pacific Ocean.

The 1853 founding of Lac La Biche Mission played a vital role in the settlement of the area, which quickly developed into a major transportation center of the north.

Lakeland Provincial Park *(see Recreation Areas Chart)*, 13 kilometres (8 mi.) east off Hwy. 663, provides such recreational opportunities as bicycling, bird-watching, camping, cross-country skiing, fishing, hiking and swimming. The park also offers Alberta's only backcountry canoe circuit. Sir Winston Churchill Provincial Park *(see Recreation Areas Chart)*, 11 kilometres (6.8 mi.) northeast off Hwy. 881, is the largest of the 12 islands on Lac La Biche and offers opportunities for camping, hiking and bird-watching.

Lac La Biche and District Chamber of Commerce: 10307 100th St., P.O. Box 804, Lac La Biche, AB, Canada T0A 2C0. **Phone:** (780) 623-2818.

LACOMBE (F-6) pop. 11,707, elev. 846m/2,775'

Lacombe is the site of the Canadian Agriculture Department's experimental farm; visitors can tour the facility. At Gull Lake 17 kilometres (11 mi.) west on Hwy. 12, Aspen Beach Provincial Park is a noteworthy area resort affording such recreational activities as cross-country skiing, ice fishing and water skiing *(see Recreation Areas Chart)*.

ELLIS BIRD FARM, 8 km (5 mi.) e. on Hwy. 12, then 8 km (5 mi.) s. on Prentiss Rd., encourages the conservation of mountain bluebirds, purple martins and other native cavity-nesting birds. A wide variety of garden birds—including a large purple marlin colony and such species as house wrens, owls and warblers—are attracted to the vibrant grounds. A network of trails affords access to butterfly, native wildflower, hummingbird and water gardens. A visitor center featuring interpretive exhibits is on-site, as is a pier where children can try to net aquatic creatures.

Time: Allow 1 hour minimum. **Hours:** Tues.-Sat. and Mon. holidays 11-5, Victoria Day weekend-Labour Day. **Cost:** Admission by donation. Guided tour $3. Reservations are required for guided tours. **Phone:** (403) 885-4477. GT TI ∓

Where Diamonds make the difference:

AAA.com/travelguides/hotels

BEST WESTERN PLUS LACOMBE INN & SUITES
403/782-3535

THREE DIAMOND
Hotel

Best Western PLUS

AAA Benefit: Members save up to 15% and earn bonus points!

Address: 4751 63rd St T4L 1K7 **Location:** Hwy 2 exit 422, 1.5 mi (2.5 km) e. **Facility:** 83 units, some kitchens. 4 stories, interior corridors. **Parking:** winter plug-ins. **Pool:** heated indoor. **Activities:** hot tub, exercise room. **Guest Services:** valet and coin laundry. **Featured Amenity:** full hot breakfast.

SAVE CALL 🛗 🛏 🛁 BIZ HS
📶 ✕ 🐾 🛄 🖥 💬 / SOME UNITS 🎣

WHERE TO EAT

MORRISON HOUSE CAFE   403/789-1234
APPROVED   Sandwiches Desserts. Casual Dining.
Address: 5331 51st Ave T4L 1N5

LAKE LOUISE (H-4)
• **Part of Banff National Park area — see map p. 30**

LAKE LOUISE is 4 km (2.4 mi.) w. of Hwy. 1/93 behind The Fairmont Chateau Lake Louise hotel. Incredibly aqua in summer and glistening with snow and ice in winter, the lake has been the subject of countless photographs. Viewed from the hotel side of the lake, the milky blue water creates a striking foreground framed by steep, densely forested mountains on either side and at the far end, the rocky bulk of Mount Victoria blanketed by a sparkling layer of glacial ice. It's the grinding of this ice against the mountain that creates the fine rock particles that wash down into the lake, giving it the unusual hue.

Benches along the shore near the hotel offer a place to relax and take in the magnificent view, but if you're here in summer, especially in the late morning or early afternoon, you'll have plenty of competition for those seats. It's at this time when RVs and cars cruise the parking lots endlessly, searching for a coveted spot, while one tour bus after another disgorges throngs of tourists. Mid-May through mid-October, overflow parking is available at the Lake Louise Park and Ride, with daily shuttles to and from the lakeshore; fare is $4; $2 (ages 7-17 and 65+) and paid by debit/credit card only.

It's an amazingly beautiful place, but during the high season, not a very peaceful one. To escape the crowds, choose one of the several trails that begin near the hotel and make your escape. The easy Lakeshore Trail follows the northern edge of Lake Louise for about 2 kilometres (1.2 mi.) one way. If you continue another 3.3 kilometres (2 mi.), the trail becomes much more challenging, but eventually you'll reach the Plain of Six Glaciers, a rocky area created by advancing and retreating glaciers. A quaint teahouse sells light lunches and refreshments here (cash only), and the view extends all the way to the other side of the valley. Another way to explore the lake is by canoe, which you can rent at the boathouse on the lake's west shore.

The Lake Louise Visitor Information Centre in nearby Samson Mall has maps and information. Nearby Moraine Lake *(see attraction listing p. 33)* is another spectacular location worth visiting in Banff National Park. **Phone:** (403) 762-8421 for the visitor center.

LAKE LOUISE SUMMER GONDOLA AND WILD-LIFE INTERPRETIVE CENTRE is just n. of Hwy. 1 interchange at Lake Louise Ski Resort, 1 Whitehorn Rd. Fully enclosed gondolas and open-air chairs take 14 minutes to ascend to a height of 2,101 metres (6,893 ft.), offering an impressive aerial view of Lake Louise and the mountains of the Continental Divide. Grizzly bears and other wildlife may be seen.

An interpretive center at the top presents a brief visitor orientation session; interpretive programs, including guided hikes, are available for an additional fee. Ride and dine packages also are offered. A free shuttle provides transportation from the parking lot to Fairmont Chateau Lake Louise and the Samson Mall on a first-come, first-served basis. **Hours:** Daily 9-5, mid-May to mid-Oct. (weather permitting); otherwise varies. Phone ahead to confirm schedule. **Cost:** Gondola $37.95; $16.95 (ages 6-15). Interpretive center free. Guided walk $15.95. **Phone:** (403) 522-3555 or (877) 956-8473. GT 🍴

FAIRMONT CHATEAU LAKE LOUISE   403/522-3511

🔷 **FOUR DIAMOND**

Historic Resort Hotel

Address: 111 Lake Louise Dr T0L 1E0 **Location:** 1.8 mi (3 km) up the hill from the village. **Facility:** This château-style, grande dame hotel sits on a lake—considered by some to be a "Wonder of the World"—surrounded by ruggedly beautiful mountains and glaciers. Lovely rooms range in size and grandeur. 539 units, some two bedrooms. 8 stories, interior corridors. **Parking:** on-site (fee) and valet, winter plug-ins. **Terms:** check-in 4 pm. **Amenities:** safes. **Dining:** 6 restaurants, also, Fairview Bar & Restaurant, see separate listing. **Pool:** heated indoor. **Activities:** hot tub, steamroom, self-propelled boats, boat dock, cross country skiing, ice skating, recreation programs, kids club, bicycles, game room, trails, exercise room, spa. **Guest Services:** valet laundry, rental car service, area transportation.

SAVE ECO 🍴 🛎 🍴 🛄 🎾 📶 ⚓ 🛥 BIZ sHS
📶 ✕ 🎱 🚪 🖥 /SOME UNITS 🐾 🐾

LAKE LOUISE INN   403/522-3791
🔷 **APPROVED**   Hotel. **Address:** 210 Village Rd T0L 1E0

MOUNTAINEER LODGE   403/522-3844
🔷 **APPROVED**   Motel. **Address:** 101 Village Rd T0L 1E0

POST HOTEL & SPA   403/522-3989
🔷 **THREE DIAMOND** Classic Hotel. **Address:** 200 Pipestone Rd T0L 1E0

🔗 **For exclusive AAA member savings and benefits:** AAA.com/hertz

FAIRVIEW BAR & RESTAURANT   403/522-1818

🔷 **FOUR DIAMOND**

New Canadian Fine Dining

$41-$55

AAA Inspector Notes: *Historic.* Oversize windows with commanding views of Lake Louise and the Victoria Glacier are found at this beautiful restaurant. From start to finish, diners can expect professional and knowledgeable service with a tantalizing menu that explores a diverse seasonal selection of cuisine utilizing top-notch ingredients. Afternoon tea is also offered. It is a good idea to check for off-season closures and in high season dining is restricted to in-house guests. **Features:** full bar. **Reservations:** required. **Address:** 111 Lake Louise Dr T0L 1E0 **Location:** 1.8 mi (3 km) up the hill from the village; in Fairmont Chateau Lake Louise. **Parking:** on-site and valet.

D CALL ♿

LAGGAN'S MOUNTAIN BAKERY & DELI   403/522-2017

🔷 **APPROVED**

Deli Quick Serve

$5-$13

AAA Inspector Notes: This popular bakery serves an extensive range of baked goods, freshly-made sandwiches and pizza as well as several soups of the day. Fast food items like chili cheese fries and chicken burgers also are offered. Giant cookies, yummy squares and other goodies satisfy those with a sweet tooth, and delicious Frog Friendly Wild coffee help wash it all down. **Address:** 101 Village Rd T0L 1E0 **Location:** Center; in Samson Mall.

B L D

POST HOTEL DINING ROOM   403/522-3989

🔷 **FOUR DIAMOND**

Continental Fine Dining

$22-$66

AAA Inspector Notes: This restaurant has an exceptional reputation for delicious food which can be enjoyed in a dining room with an elegant, upscale cabin décor. The chef sources excellent quality ingredients, mainly from Alberta, but also from other Canadian regions, to prepare innovative European classics which are wonderfully flavored and colorfully presented. Service is refined and highly professional. A less extensive menu is offered at lunch. You'll feel comfortable in smart casual attire. **Features:** full bar. **Reservations:** suggested, for dinner. **Address:** 200 Pipestone Rd T0L 1E0 **Location:** Just w of main intersection; in Lake Louise village; in Post Hotel & Spa. **Parking:** on-site and valet.

B L D 🍷

THE STATION RESTAURANT   403/522-2600
🔷 **APPROVED**   American. Casual Dining. **Address:** 200 Sentinel Rd T0L 1E0

LEDUC (E-6) pop. 24,279, elev. 764m/2,509'
• Hotels p. 128 • Restaurants p. 128
• Part of Edmonton area — see map p. 84

Just south of Edmonton, Leduc is situated near two large lakes—Saunders Lake and Telford Lake—along with several smaller lakes where residents enjoy water sports. The city has more than 32 kilometres (20 mi.) of multiuse pathways, along with multiple golf courses and a ski hill. The Leduc Recreation Centre, 4330 Black Gold Dr., includes three NHL-size hockey rinks, an aquatic complex, a curling complex and track; it also hosts provincial and national sports tournaments. Phone (780) 980-7177. Leduc's Maclab Centre for the Performing Arts, 4308 50th St., presents a variety of music, theater and dance performances and other events in its 460-seat theater throughout the year; phone (780) 980-1866.

BEST WESTERN PLUS EDMONTON AIRPORT
780/986-6550

THREE DIAMOND
Hotel

AAA Benefit: Members save up to 15% and earn bonus points!

Address: 5705 50th St T9E 6Z8 **Location:** 1.2 mi (2 km) ne of jct Hwy 2 and 39. **Facility:** 116 units. 4 stories, interior corridors. **Parking:** winter plug-ins. **Terms:** check-in 4 pm. **Pool:** heated indoor. **Activities:** hot tub, exercise room. **Guest Services:** valet laundry. **Featured Amenity:** breakfast buffet.

BEST WESTERN PREMIER DENHAM INN & SUITES
780/986-2241

THREE DIAMOND
Hotel

AAA Benefit: Members save up to 15% and earn bonus points!

Address: 5207 50th Ave T9E 6V3 **Location:** Hwy 2 exit Leduc/City Centre, just e. **Facility:** 95 units. 2-5 stories, interior corridors. **Parking:** winter plug-ins. **Terms:** check-in 4 pm. **Amenities:** safes. **Dining:** 2 restaurants. **Activities:** hot tub, exercise room. **Guest Services:** valet and coin laundry.

HAMPTON INN & SUITES BY HILTON EDMONTON INTERNATIONAL AIRPORT
780/980-9775

THREE DIAMOND
Hotel

AAA Benefit: Members save up to 15%!

Address: 3916 84th Ave T9E 7G1 **Location:** Hwy 2 exit Edmonton International Airport, just e. **Facility:** 111 units. 4 stories, interior corridors. **Parking:** winter plug-ins. **Pool:** heated indoor. **Activities:** hot tub, exercise room. **Guest Services:** valet and coin laundry. **Featured Amenity:** full hot breakfast.

HILTON GARDEN INN EDMONTON INTERNATIONAL AIRPORT
780/612-2350

THREE DIAMOND SAVE Hotel. **Address:** 8208 36th St T9E 0H7

AAA Benefit: Members save up to 15%!

PARADISE INN AND SUITES SIGNATURE
780/769-0271

APPROVED Hotel. **Address:** 7118 Sparrow Dr T9E 8A5

RAMADA EDMONTON INTERNATIONAL AIRPORT
780/980-0986

APPROVED Hotel. **Address:** 8340 Sparrow Cres T9E 8B7

SUPER 8-EDMONTON INTERNATIONAL AIRPORT
780/986-8898

APPROVED Hotel. **Address:** 8004 Sparrow Cres T9E 7G1

WINGATE BY WYNDHAM LEDUC EDMONTON AIRPORT
780/769-0079

THREE DIAMOND Hotel. **Address:** 7120 Sparrow Dr T9E 8A5

WYNDHAM GARDEN EDMONTON AIRPORT
780/769-0188

THREE DIAMOND
Contemporary Hotel

Address: 8016 Sparrow Dr T9E 7G3 **Location:** Hwy 2 exit 522, N Sector Leduc, just e. **Facility:** 150 units. 5 stories, interior corridors. **Parking:** winter plug-ins. **Amenities:** safes. **Activities:** hot tub, steamroom, exercise room. **Guest Services:** valet laundry. **Featured Amenity:** breakfast buffet.

WHERE TO EAT

CHEZ CORA 780/986-2672
APPROVED Breakfast. Casual Dining. **Address:** 6108 50th St T9E 6P1

HABANEROS MEXICAN GRILL 780/986-8017
APPROVED Mexican. Casual Dining. **Address:** 5015 48 A St T9E 6Y2

SAWMILL PRIME RIB & STEAK HOUSE 780/739-5616
THREE DIAMOND Steak. Casual Dining. **Address:** 8225 Sparrow Crescent T9E 8P7

LETHBRIDGE (J-7) pop. 83,517, elev. 930m/3,051'
• Restaurants p. 130

Founded in the 1870s, abundant agricultural resources helped Lethbridge to become one of Alberta's major feedlot and grain distribution centers. The region reportedly receives more hours of sunshine annually than any other spot in Canada and therefore requires irrigation to counterbalance the semiarid climate; more than 400,000 hectares (988,000 acres) produce crops of grain and sugar beets. Livestock, oil and gas also support the economic base.

Numerous parks and green spaces complement the city's commercial enterprises. Two popular areas are Lethbridge Nature Preserve in Indian Battle Park at 3rd Avenue S. and Scenic Drive, and Henderson Lake Park at Parkside Drive S. and Mayor Magrath Drive S. The park has a golf course, a 24-hectare (60-acre) lake with tennis courts, a picnic area, playgrounds and a campground. Rose and Japanese gardens, a stadium and an ice-skating center are included. Lethbridge holds Whoop-Up Days in August.

Chinook Country Tourist Association: 2805 Scenic Dr. S., Lethbridge, AB, Canada T1K 5B7. **Phone:** (403) 320-1222 or (800) 661-1222.

Shopping: Park Place Mall (501 1st Ave. S.) has more than 100 stores.

BREWERY GARDENS is just w. off 1st Ave. S. at Brewery Hill on Scenic Dr. Developed by a former brewery, the gardens present eight floral displays

May through the first frost, as well as displays for Easter, Halloween, Remembrance Day and Christmas. The gardens are not walk-through gardens but are a 1-hectare (2.5-acre) plot on the side of a coulee. Visitors view them across the coulee. **Hours:** Daily dawn-dusk. **Cost:** Free. **Phone:** (403) 320-1222, or (800) 661-1222 (Chinook Country Tourist Association).

 NIKKA YUKO JAPANESE GARDEN is on Mayor Magrath Dr. at 9th Ave. Five basic types of traditional Japanese gardens are incorporated into the overall design, which is one of the most authentic of its kind in North America. A pavilion, bridges, a bell tower imported from Japan and cypress wood structures from Taiwan are featured; paths punctuated by footbridges over ponds and streams weave through the gardens.

A variety of ongoing activities are offered, including cultural, historical and horticultural experiences. Visitors can take in art exhibitions or learn pruning and gardening techniques. Guides in traditional Japanese garments conduct tours daily. Special events, which take place regularly, include traditional Japanese art demonstrations of bonsai, flower arranging, origami, sand art and calligraphy. A tea ceremony presentation is offered every Saturday and Sunday.

Time: Allow 1 hour minimum. **Hours:** Mon.-Thurs. 10-6, Fri.-Sun. 10-7, May-Oct. Last Admission 30 minutes before closing. Phone ahead to confirm schedule. **Cost:** $11; $9 (ages 60+ and students with ID); $7 (ages 6-10). **Phone:** (403) 328-3511. GT

SOUTHERN ALBERTA ART GALLERY is at 601 3rd Ave. S. Exhibits showcase works of Canadian and international artists with an emphasis on contemporary art. **Time:** Allow 30 minutes minimum. **Hours:** Tues.-Sat. 10-5 (also Thurs. 5-7), Sun. 1-5. **Cost:** $5; $4 (students with ID and ages 60+); free (ages 0-11, to all on Sun. and on Thurs. from 5-7 p.m.). **Phone:** (403) 327-8770.

BEST WESTERN PLUS SERVICE INN & SUITES
403/329-6844

THREE DIAMOND
Hotel

Best Western PLUS
AAA Benefit: Members save up to 15% and earn bonus points!

Address: 209 41st St S T1J 1Z3 **Location:** Hwy 3 (Crowsnest Tr), just s on 43rd St S. **Facility:** 113 units. 4 stories, interior corridors. **Parking:** winter plug-ins. **Pool:** heated indoor. **Activities:** hot tub, exercise room. **Guest Services:** valet laundry. **Featured Amenity:** breakfast buffet.

🔗 **For complete hotel, dining and attraction listings:** AAA.com/travelguides

COAST LETHBRIDGE HOTEL & CONFERENCE CENTRE
403/327-5701

THREE DIAMOND
Hotel

Address: 526 Mayor Magrath Dr S T1J 3M2 **Location:** Hwy 3 (Crowsnest Tr) exit Mayor Magrath Dr S, just s. **Facility:** 103 units. 3 stories, interior corridors. **Terms:** check-in 4 pm. **Dining:** Firestone Restaurant & Bar, see separate listing. **Pool:** heated indoor. **Activities:** hot tub, exercise room. **Guest Services:** valet laundry.

COMFORT INN
403/320-8874

APPROVED Hotel. **Address:** 3226 Fairway Plaza Rd S T1K 7T5

DAYS INN BY WYNDHAM LETHBRIDGE
403/327-6000

APPROVED Hotel. **Address:** 100 3rd Ave S T1J 4L2

FAIRFIELD INN & SUITES BY MARRIOTT LETHBRIDGE
587/425-0388

THREE DIAMOND SAVE Hotel. **Address:** 4081 2 Ave S T1J 1Z2

AAA Benefit: Members save 5% or more!

HAMPTON INN & SUITES BY HILTON LETHBRIDGE
403/942-2142

THREE DIAMOND SAVE Hotel. **Address:** 4073 2nd Ave S T1J 1Z2

AAA Benefit: Members save up to 15%!

HOLIDAY INN EXPRESS HOTEL & SUITES LETHBRIDGE
403/394-9292

THREE DIAMOND Hotel. **Address:** 120 Stafford Dr S T1J 4W4

HOLIDAY INN HOTEL LETHBRIDGE
403/380-5050

THREE DIAMOND
Hotel

Address: 2375 Mayor Magrath Dr S T1K 7M1 **Location:** Hwy 3 (Crowsnest Tr) exit Mayor Magrath Dr S, 1.8 mi (3 km) s, then just e on 22nd St. **Facility:** 119 units. 4 stories, interior corridors. **Parking:** winter plug-ins. **Pool:** heated indoor. **Activities:** hot tub, exercise room. **Guest Services:** valet and coin laundry.

MOTEL 6 LETHBRIDGE
403/328-4436

APPROVED Motel. **Address:** 1142 Mayor Magrath Dr S T1K 2P8

PREMIER INN & SUITES
403/380-6677

APPROVED
Hotel

Address: 2225 Mayor Magrath Dr S T1K 7M1 **Location:** Hwy 3 (Crowsnest Tr) exit Mayor Magrath Dr S, 1.8 mi (3 km) s, then just e on 22nd St. **Facility:** 50 units. 4 stories, interior corridors. **Parking:** winter plug-ins. **Activities:** hot tub, exercise room. **Guest Services:** coin laundry. **Featured Amenity:** continental breakfast.

QUALITY INN & SUITES BY CHOICE HOTELS   403/331-6440
W/ APPROVED   Hotel. **Address:** 4070 2nd Ave S T1J 3Z2

RAMADA BY WYNDHAM LETHBRIDGE   403/329-0555
W/ APPROVED   Hotel. **Address:** 1303 Mayor Magrath Dr S
T1K 2R1

SANDMAN HOTEL LETHBRIDGE   403/328-1111
W/ APPROVED   Hotel. **Address:** 421 Mayor Magrath Dr S
T1J 3L8

SANDMAN SIGNATURE LETHBRIDGE LODGE   403/328-1123
W/ THREE DIAMOND Hotel. **Address:** 320 Scenic Dr T1J 4B4

WHERE TO EAT

BAADSHAH ROYAL EAST INDIAN CUISINE   403/381-1353
W/ APPROVED   Indian. Casual Dining. **Address:** 310 5th
St S T1J 2B2

COULEE BREW CO.   403/394-2337
W/ APPROVED   American. Brewpub. **Address:** 4085 2nd
Ave T1J 1Z2

EARLS KITCHEN + BAR   403/320-7677
W/ APPROVED   American. Casual Dining. **Address:** 203
13th St S T1J 2V3

EL COMAL   403/380-6836
W/ APPROVED   Mexican. Casual Dining. **Address:** 1020
Mayor Magrath Dr S T1K 2R2

FIRESTONE RESTAURANT & BAR   403/329-3473
W/ THREE DIAMOND American. Casual Dining. **Address:** 532
Mayor Magrath Dr S T1J 3M2

GEORGIO'S DINING   403/328-0676
W/ APPROVED   Mediterranean. Casual Dining. **Address:**
1520 3rd Ave S T1J 0K8

LIGHTHOUSE JAPANESE RESTAURANT   403/328-4828
W/ APPROVED   Japanese   Sushi.   Casual   Dining.
Address: 708 3rd Ave S T1J 0H6

THE MANGO TREE   403/942-0590
W/ APPROVED   Indian. Casual Dining. **Address:** 1264
3rd Ave S T1J 0J9

MIRO BISTRO   403/394-1961
W/ APPROVED   Continental. Casual Dining. **Address:**
212 5th St S T1J 2B3

MOCHA CABANA   403/329-6243
W/ APPROVED   American. Casual Dining. **Address:** 317
4th St S T1J 1Z9

O SHO JAPANESE RESTAURANT   403/327-8382
W/ APPROVED   Japanese. Casual Dining. **Address:** 311
4th St S T1J 1Z9

PENNY COFFEE HOUSE   403/320-5282
W/ APPROVED   Coffee/Tea. Quick Serve. **Address:** 331
5th St S T1J 2B4

PLUM   403/394-1200
W/ THREE DIAMOND New American. Casual Dining. **Address:**
330 6th St S T1J 2C8

STAGECOACH GRILL   403/381-9467
W/ APPROVED   American. Casual Dining. **Address:** 3756
2 Ave S T1J 4Y9

STREATSIDE EATERY   403/328-8085
W/ APPROVED   American. Casual Dining. **Address:** 317
8th St S T1J 2J5

TELEGRAPH TAP HOUSE   403/942-4136
W/ APPROVED   American. Casual Dining. **Address:** 310
6 St S T1J 0H4

TWO GUYS AND A PIZZA PLACE   403/331-2222
W/ APPROVED   Pizza. Casual Dining. **Address:** 316 11th
St S T1J 2N8

LLOYDMINSTER (E-9) pop. 18,032

Lloydminster is the province's only city with one foot planted in Saskatchewan and the other in Alberta. Four 31-metre-tall (100-ft.) border markers—shaped like the survey stakes used during the original survey of the border between the two provinces—represent four themes: oil and gas, agriculture, the Barr Colonists and native North Americans. The downtown monument, erected in 1994, denotes the city's bi-provincial status.

Many nearby lakes, regional parks and campgrounds offer opportunities for fishing, bird-watching and other pursuits. Other recreational opportunities include an 18-hole golf course and an aquatic leisure center with a wave pool and a waterslide.

Summer events include Canada Day celebrations, which are held July 1 in Bud Miller All Seasons Park; Colonial Days, a 4-day fair with a parade, agricultural exhibits and grandstand entertainment held in early July; and racing action at the Canadian Professional Chuckwagon Finals in mid-August.

Lloydminster Tourism: 5420 50th Ave., Lloydminster, AB, Canada T9V 0X1. **Phone:** (780) 875-8881 or (800) 825-6180.

BEST WESTERN PLUS MERIDIAN HOTEL
780/875-8884

W/ THREE DIAMOND
Hotel

 Best Western PLUS. **AAA Benefit:** Members save up to 15% and earn bonus points!

Address: 1402 50th Ave T9V 2K5 **Location:** Hwy 16, just n at 80th Ave. **Facility:** 128 units, some two bedrooms and efficiencies. 4 stories, interior corridors. **Parking:** winter plug-ins. **Terms:** check-in 4 pm. **Pool:** heated indoor. **Activities:** hot tub, exercise room. **Guest Services:** coin laundry. **Featured Amenity:** breakfast buffet.

SAVE ECO [Y|+] CALL [&] [≈] [♿]

[BIZ] [HS] [📶] [✕] [🛏] [🖥] [💻]

DAYS HOTEL & SUITES LLOYDMINSTER   780/875-4404
W/ APPROVED   Hotel. **Address:** 5411 44th St T9V 0A9

🔗 **Get member rates and reservations**

at AAA.com/hertz

HAMPTON INN BY HILTON-LLOYDMINSTER
780/874-1118

 THREE DIAMOND

Hotel

 **AAA Benefit:** Members save up to 15%!

Address: 8288 44 St T9V 2G8 **Location:** Hwy 16 exit 80 Ave, just n. **Facility:** 122 units. 5 stories, interior corridors. **Parking:** winter plug-ins. **Pool:** heated indoor. **Activities:** exercise room. **Guest Services:** valet and coin laundry. **Featured Amenity:** breakfast buffet.

SAVE ▐▌ CALL ♿ ⊃ ✚ BIZ HS 🛜 ✉ 🚪
☐ ▣ / SOME UNITS 🐾

HOLIDAY INN HOTEL & SUITES   780/870-5050
♦ **APPROVED**   Hotel. **Address:** 5612 44th St T9V 0B6

RAMADA BY WYNDHAM LLOYDMINSTER   780/871-6940
♦ **APPROVED**   Hotel. **Address:** 5610 44th St T9V 0B6

ROYAL HOTEL   780/875-6113
♦ **APPROVED**   Hotel. **Address:** 5620 44th St T9V 0B6

WHERE TO EAT

BROWNS SOCIALHOUSE   780/875-0818
♦ **APPROVED**   International. Casual Dining. **Address:** 8120 44th St T9V 3L6

CHEZ CORA   780/872-5294
♦ **APPROVED**   Breakfast. Casual Dining. **Address:** 3708 50th Ave, Unit B T9V 0V7

MR BILL'S FAMILY RESTAURANT   780/875-3388
♦ **APPROVED**   Continental. Casual Dining. **Address:** 5405 44th St T9V 0A9

ORIGINAL JOE'S RESTAURANT & BAR   780/875-3038
♦ **APPROVED**   American. Casual Dining. **Address:** 5027 44th St, Unit 107D St T9V 0A6

ROCK CREEK TAP AND GRILL   780/874-7625
♦ **APPROVED**   American. Casual Dining. **Address:** 8120 44 St T9V 3L6

SPIRO'S   780/875-4241
♦ **APPROVED**   Mediterranean. Casual Dining. **Address:** 1408 50th Ave T9V 0Y1

TASTY K'S   780/872-7713
♦ **APPROVED**   Sandwiches. Quick Serve. **Address:** 5008 39th St T9V 2C3

GET THE APP
Download today.
Connect every day.
AAA.com/mobile
CAA.ca/mobile

LONGVIEW (I-6) pop. 307

BAR U RANCH NATIONAL HISTORIC SITE is 13 km (9 mi.) s. on Hwy. 22. The site focuses on the history of ranching in Canada and the role that occupation played in the country's development. Visitors learn the history of the Bar U Ranch, from the days of open range ranching through its prominence as a breeding center for cattle and Percheron horses to its position as part of a multiple-ranch cattle operation.

The visitor center has exhibits and a video presentation about the site, one of Canada's largest ranching operations 1882-1950. Guests can tour the ranch site on foot or via horse-drawn wagon shuttle. Historic structures include the 1882-83 saddle horse barn, blacksmith shop, stud horse barn, wintering pens, 1910 cook house, storage sheds and ranch office/post office. Ranch activities such as roping, leather working and the making of cowboy coffee also are demonstrated.

Hours: Daily 10-5, mid-May through Sept. 30. **Cost:** $7.80; $6.55 (ages 65+); free (ages 0-16). **Phone:** (403) 395-3044 or (888) 773-8888. ▐▌

MEDICINE HAT (J-9) pop. 60,005, elev. 715m/2,346'
• Hotels p. 132 • Restaurants p. 132

According to popular legend the name Medicine Hat originated because of a battle between Cree and Blackfoot Indians on the banks of a southern Alberta river. The Cree fought bravely until their medicine man deserted them, losing his headdress in midstream. Believing this to be a bad omen, the Cree put down their weapons and were killed by the Blackfoot. This site became known as "Saamis," which translates as "medicine man's hat."

A buried prehistoric river, or aquifer, serves as a source of unlimited cool water. More than 20 billion cubic metres (26 billion cu. yd.) of natural gas reserves inspired Rudyard Kipling in 1907 to describe Medicine Hat as possessing "all hell for a basement."

Outdoor opportunities include swimming and fishing at Echo Dale Regional Park. Circuit cowboys and spectators gather for 3 days in mid-July for the Medicine Hat Exhibition & Stampede.

Tourism Medicine Hat: 330 Gehring Rd. S.W., Medicine Hat, AB, Canada T1B 4W1. **Phone:** (403) 527-6422 or (800) 481-2822.

Shopping: Medicine Hat Mall (3292 Dunmore Rd. S.E.) features Hudson's Bay among its more than 100 stores.

ESPLANADE ARTS & HERITAGE CENTRE, 401 First St. S.E., houses an art gallery featuring works by both local and national artists, a museum with a permanent gallery, two theaters and archives containing more than 1 million documents and photos. The museum presents audiovisual displays detailing the region's cultural heritage as well as a collection encompassing more than 25,000 artifacts. Included are pioneer items and pieces related to the area's petroleum industry.

Time: Allow 1 hour minimum. **Hours:** Galleries and box office Mon.-Fri. 10-5, Sat. noon-5. Closed major holidays. **Cost:** Galleries $6; free (ages 0-5 and to all Thurs.); $19 (family, up to five people). Prices for Esplanade Theatre shows vary; phone ahead. **Phone:** (403) 502-8580. 🍴

MEDALTA is at 713 Medalta Ave. S.E. An innovative industrial museum, contemporary ceramic arts facility and art gallery, Medalta is located within a converted century-old factory and has become a place where modern technologies, historic restoration and archaeology come together. Brick, tile and pottery manufacturing were prominent industries in Medicine Hat starting in the late 19th century due to a supply of clay deposits, natural gas and the availability of railroad transportation. The city once boasted several historic ceramic sites, such as Medalta Potteries, Medicine Hat Potteries (later Hycroft China Ltd.) and Medicine Hat Brick & Tile Factory (Formerly I-XL Industries).

Located in the Historic Clay District, visitors can watch pottery demonstrations, view beehive kilns constructed in the early 1920s and tour the expansive site complete with artifacts, a large collection of Medicine Hat Pottery and production machines. Special events and pottery classes and workshops also take place throughout the year. **Time:** Allow 1 hour minimum. **Hours:** Daily 10-5 (also Thurs. 5-8), Victoria Day-Labour Day; Tues.-Sat. 10-4, rest of year. **Cost:** $12; $10 (ages 6-17 and 60+); $30 (family, two adults and two children). **Phone:** (403) 529-1070. GT

SAAMIS TEEPEE is at jct. Hwy. 1 and South Ridge Dr. Made of steel, the tepee stands about 20 stories high. Storyboards incorporated in the tepee stand 3.6 metres (12 ft.) high and depict First Nations history. Used during the 1988 Olympics in Calgary, the tepee was moved to Medicine Hat where it now stands above the Saamis Archaeological Site—the location of a 16th-century buffalo camp. **Time:** Allow 1 hour minimum. **Hours:** Daily 24 hours. **Cost:** Free. **Phone:** (403) 527-6422 (Tourism Medicine Hat).

BAYMONT BY WYNDHAM MEDICINE HAT   403/548-7070
🛇 APPROVED   Hotel. **Address:** 3216 13th Ave SE T1B 1H8

COMFORT INN & SUITES   403/504-1700
🛇 THREE DIAMOND **Address:** 2317 Trans-Canada Way SE
Hotel T1B 4E9 **Location:** Trans-Canada Hwy 1, just n on Dunmore Rd, just w. Opposite Medicine Hat Mall. **Facility:** 100 units. 3 stories, interior corridors. **Parking:** winter plug-ins. **Terms:** check-in 4 pm. **Pool:** heated indoor. **Activities:** hot tub, exercise room. **Guest Services:** valet and coin laundry. **Featured Amenity:** full hot breakfast.

SAVE ECO 📶 🏊 👥 BIZ HS 🛜 ✕ 🔌 🖨 🖥 / SOME UNITS 🐾

DAYS INN BY WYNDHAM MEDICINE HAT   403/580-3297
🛇 APPROVED   Hotel. **Address:** 24 Strachan Ct SE T1B 4R7

HAMPTON INN & SUITES BY HILTON MEDICINE HAT
403/548-7818
🛇 THREE DIAMOND SAVE Hotel. **Address:** 2510 Box Springs Blvd T1C 0C8

AAA Benefit: Members save up to 15%!

HOLIDAY INN EXPRESS HOTEL & SUITES
403/504-5151
🛇 THREE DIAMOND **Address:** 9 Strachan Bay SE T1B 4Y2
Hotel **Location:** Trans-Canada Hwy 1, just s on Dunmore Rd, just e; east end of city. **Facility:** 96 units, some efficiencies. 4 stories, interior corridors. **Parking:** winter plug-ins. **Amenities:** safes. **Pool:** heated indoor. **Activities:** hot tub, exercise room. **Guest Services:** valet and coin laundry.

SAVE ECO 📶 CALL 👥 🏊 👥
BIZ HS 🛜 ✕ 🔌 🖨 🖥
/ SOME UNITS 🐾

HOME INN EXPRESS MEDICINE HAT   403/527-1749
🛇 APPROVED   Contemporary Hotel. **Address:** 20 Strachan Ct SE T1B 4R7

MEDICINE HAT LODGE RESORT, CASINO & SPA
403/529-2222
🛇 THREE DIAMOND **Address:** 1051 Ross Glen Dr SE T1B
Hotel 3T8 **Location:** Trans-Canada Hwy 1 exit Dunmore Rd, just ne. **Facility:** Many rooms have views of the pool, where a large waterslide will get the kids excited. Units in the south tower offer vanities and some have French doors or multiple shower heads in the bathrooms. 221 units. 4 stories, interior corridors. **Parking:** winter plug-ins. **Terms:** check-in 4 pm. **Amenities:** Some: safes. **Dining:** Redwood Steakhouse & Bar, see separate listing. **Pool:** heated indoor. **Activities:** hot tub, playground, picnic facilities, exercise room, spa. **Guest Services:** coin laundry. **Featured Amenity:** full hot breakfast.

SAVE 🎰 📶 👶 🍽 🏊 👥 🛜 ✕ 🎥 🔌
🖥 / SOME UNITS 🐾 HS 🖨

WHERE TO EAT

EARLS KITCHEN + BAR   403/528-3275
🛇 APPROVED   American. Casual Dining. **Address:** 3215 Dunmore Rd SE T1B 2H2

THE GARAGE PUB AND EATERY   403/580-2588
🛇 APPROVED   American. Casual Dining. **Address:** 710 Gershaw Dr SW T1A 5C8

HAT'S RESTAURANT   403/529-9739
🛇 APPROVED   Chinese. Casual Dining. **Address:** 1701 Dunmore Rd SE T1A 1Z8

REDWOOD STEAKHOUSE & BAR   403/529-2222
🛇 THREE DIAMOND American. Casual Dining. **Address:** 1051 Ross Glen Dr SE T1B 3T8

RUSTIC KITCHEN + BAR   403/525-9938
🛇 APPROVED   New Canadian. Casual Dining. **Address:** 925 7th St SW T1A 7R8

THAI ORCHID ROOM   403/580-8210
♦♦ **APPROVED**   Thai. Casual Dining. **Address:** 3-36 Strachan Ct SE T1B 4R7

THE ZUCCHINI BLOSSOM MARKET AND CAFE   403/526-1630
♦♦ **APPROVED**   Sandwiches Desserts. Quick Serve. **Address:** 50 3rd St NE T1A 5L8

MILK RIVER (K-7) pop. 811

Milk River is on the east side of Milk River Ridge, an area more than 1,200 metres (3,900 ft.) high, 39 kilometres (24 mi.) long and 29 kilometres (18 mi.) wide. Quartzite, granite and gneiss rock formations indicate prehistoric glacial action; meltwater carved the Milk River Valley 10,000 years ago. The river, formed from small streams and springs in southwest Alberta and northern Montana, joins the Missouri and Mississippi rivers to flow to the Gulf of Mexico.

Throughout the area and predominantly in Writing-on-Stone Provincial Park/Áísínai'pi National Historic Site are mushroom-shaped sandstone hoodoos, odd rock formations that once led First Nations people to believe spirits inhabited the valley.

The Alberta Tourism Information Centre: Hwy. 4, Milk River, AB, Canada T0K 1M0. **Phone:** (403) 647-3938.

MORLEY

STONEY NAKODA RESORT & CASINO   403/881-2830
♦♦ **THREE DIAMOND**
Hotel
Address: Jct Trans-Canada Hwy 1 and Hwy 40 T0L 1N0 **Location:** Jct Hwy 40, just s. Located in a rural area. **Facility:** Guests will be intrigued immediately by the striking art and murals in the lobby of this modern hotel. Comfortable, well-appointed guest rooms have soft seating and provide a respite from the casino. 111 units. 4 stories, interior corridors. **Parking:** winter plug-ins. **Terms:** check-in 4 pm. **Amenities:** safes. **Pool:** heated indoor. **Activities:** hot tub, exercise room. **Guest Services:** coin laundry. **Featured Amenity:** breakfast buffet.
⟨SAVE⟩ 🐾 ⟨Tl⟩ 🛎 ⟨Y⟩ ⟨≥⟩ ⟨🔧⟩ ⟨BIZ⟩ ⟨HS⟩ 🔇 ⟨🔌⟩
⟨📺⟩ / SOME UNITS ⟨🔧⟩ ⟨📷⟩

NISKU
• **Part of Edmonton area — see map p. 84**

COMFORT INN & SUITES EDMONTON INTERNATIONAL AIRPORT   780/955-8007
♦♦ **THREE DIAMOND** Hotel. **Address:** 203 19 Ave T9E 8E2

FOUR POINTS BY SHERATON EDMONTON INTERNATIONAL AIRPORT   780/770-9099
♦♦ **THREE DIAMOND** ⟨SAVE⟩ Hotel. **Address:** 403 11th Ave T9E 7N2

> **AAA Benefit:**
> Members save 5% or more!

🔗 **Booth or table?**

AAA.com/travelguides/restaurants

HOLIDAY INN AND SUITES EDMONTON AIRPORT AND CONFERENCE CENTER   780/979-0839
♦♦ **THREE DIAMOND**
Hotel

Address: 1100 4th St T9E 8E2 **Location:** Hwy 2 exit Edmonton International Airport/Nisku Business Park (10th Ave), 0.5 mi (0.9 km) e. **Facility:** 97 units. 5 stories, interior corridors. *Bath:* shower only. **Parking:** winter plug-ins. **Dining:** Eclipse Restaurant & Lounge, see separate listing. **Pool:** heated indoor. **Activities:** hot tub, exercise room. **Guest Services:** valet and coin laundry.
⟨SAVE⟩ ⟨🔧⟩ ⟨Tl⟩ ⟨🛎⟩ ⟨Y⟩ CALL ⟨🖥⟩
⟨≥⟩ ⟨🔧⟩ ⟨BIZ⟩ ⟨HS⟩ 🔇 ⟨✕⟩ ⟨🔌⟩
⟨📺⟩ / SOME UNITS ⟨📷⟩

HOLIDAY INN EXPRESS & SUITES EDMONTON INT'L AIRPORT   780/955-1000
♦♦ **THREE DIAMOND**
Hotel

Address: 1102 4th St T9E 8E2 **Location:** Hwy 2 exit Edmonton International Airport/Nisku Business Park (10th Ave), 0.5 mi (0.9 km) e. **Facility:** 120 units. 4 stories, interior corridors. **Parking:** winter plug-ins. **Pool:** heated indoor. **Activities:** hot tub, exercise room. **Guest Services:** valet and coin laundry. **Featured Amenity:** full hot breakfast.
⟨SAVE⟩ ⟨🔧⟩ ⟨Tl⟩ CALL ⟨🖥⟩ ⟨≥⟩ ⟨🔧⟩
⟨BIZ⟩ ⟨HS⟩ 🔇 ⟨✕⟩ ⟨🔌⟩ ⟨📷⟩ ⟨📺⟩

RENAISSANCE EDMONTON AIRPORT HOTEL   780/488-7159
♦♦ **FOUR DIAMOND** ⟨SAVE⟩
Contemporary Hotel. **Address:** 4236 36th St E/Edmonton International Airport T9E 0A4

> **AAA Benefit:**
> Members save 5% or more!

WHERE TO EAT

ECLIPSE RESTAURANT & LOUNGE   780/770-9131
♦♦ **APPROVED** American. Casual Dining. **Address:** 1100 4th St T9E 8E2

HALO BAR BISTRO   780/890-1420
♦♦ **THREE DIAMOND** International. Casual Dining. **Address:** 4236 36th St E T9E 0V4

OKOTOKS (I-6) pop. 24,511, elev. 1,036m/3,400'
• **Hotels p. 134** • **Restaurants p. 134**
• **Part of Calgary area — see map p. 43**

Incorporated in 1904, Okotoks thrived on brick making, lumber and oil distribution in its early days. Today Okotoks is a commuter community of Calgary. The town gets its name from the Blackfoot name *okatoks,* meaning "rocks." Big Rock, 7 kilometres (4 mi.) west, is the continent's largest known glacial boulder, having been carried here during an ice age.

A popular recreational retreat, Okotoks offers such leisure pursuits as fishing and hiking. Events include Spirit of Okotoks Children's Festival, held in mid-June in conjunction with the Spirit of Okotoks Parade, as well as the Okotoks Pro Rodeo on Labour Day weekend.

Okotoks Visitor Information Centre: 53 N. Railway St., Okotoks, AB, Canada T1S 1K1. **Phone:** (403) 938-3204.

Self-guiding tours: Heritage Walking Tour brochures are available from the visitor information center.

BEST WESTERN PLUS OKOTOKS INN & SUITES
403/995-6262

THREE DIAMOND	Best Western PLUS	**AAA Benefit:** Members save up to 15% and earn bonus points!
Hotel		

Address: 100 Southbank Rd T1S 0N3 **Location:** Hwy 2 exit 209 (Hwy 7), 2.7 mi (4.5 km) w. **Facility:** 82 two-bedroom units, some efficiencies. 4 stories, interior corridors. **Parking:** winter plug-ins. **Amenities:** safes. **Pool:** indoor. **Activities:** hot tub, exercise room. **Guest Services:** valet and coin laundry.

HEARTLAND CAFÉ
403/995-4623
APPROVED   American. Casual Dining. **Address:** 46 McRae St T1S 1B2

OLDS pop. 8,235

BEST WESTERN OF OLDS
403/556-5900

APPROVED	Best Western	**AAA Benefit:** Members save up to 15% and earn bonus points!
Hotel		

Address: 4520 46th St T4H 1P7 **Location:** Hwy 2 exit 340B (Hwy 27), 3 mi (5 km) w. **Facility:** 41 units. 2 stories (no elevator), interior corridors. **Parking:** winter plug-ins. **Pool:** heated indoor. **Activities:** hot tub, exercise room. **Guest Services:** coin laundry. **Featured Amenity:** full hot breakfast.

RAMADA OLDS
403/507-8349
THREE DIAMOND Hotel. **Address:** 500 6700 46th St T4H 0A2

WHERE TO EAT

TASTY THAI
403/556-8850
APPROVED   Thai. Casual Dining. **Address:** 5019 50th Ave T4H 1C8

PATRICIA (I-8) pop. 108

 DINOSAUR PROVINCIAL PARK is 13 km (8 mi.) n.e. via Hwy. 210, following signs. The park, declared a UNESCO World Heritage Site in 1979, covers 81 square kilometres (31 sq. mi.) of badlands and prairie along the Red Deer River. One of the richest Cretaceous Period fossil sites in the world, it contains the remains of 49 species of dinosaurs from 75 million years ago as well as crocodile, fish, flying reptile, small mammal and turtle fossils.

Five self-guiding trails explore three habitats: prairie grassland, badlands and riverside. Each offers opportunities for bird-watching. A variety of interpretive programs, bus tours and guided hikes are offered May to mid-October. Outdoor fossil displays and self-guiding walking trails are available year-round. *See Recreation Areas Chart.*

Time: Allow a full day. **Hours:** Grounds daily 24 hours. Visitor center Sun.-Thurs. 9-5, Fri.-Sat. 9-7, mid-May to early Sept.; Mon.-Fri. 9-4, Sat.-Sun. 10-5, Apr. 1 to mid-May and early Sept.-early Oct.; Mon.-Fri. 9-4, rest of year. **Cost:** Park free. Visitor center exhibit gallery $6; $5 (ages 65+); $3 (ages 7-17); $15 (family). Prices for interpretive programs and other programs vary; phone ahead. **Phone:** (403) 378-4344 for guided hike and tour information, or (877) 537-2757 for camping reservations.

Dinosaur Provincial Park Visitor Centre and Field Station, 13 km (8 mi.) n.e. via Hwy. 210, contains dinosaur skeletons and an 80-seat theater. Interpretive displays depict the park's geological and paleontological resources and cultural history as well as the flora and fauna of the badlands and the prairie environment. **Hours:** Sun.-Thurs. 9-5, Fri.-Sat. 9-7, mid-May to early Sept.; Mon.-Fri. 9-4, Sat.-Sun. 10-5, Apr. 1 to mid-May and early Sept. to mid-Oct.; Mon.-Fri. 9-4, rest of year. Phone ahead to confirm schedule. **Cost:** Exhibit gallery $6; $5 (ages 65+); $3 (ages 7-17); $15 (family). **Phone:** (403) 378-4342.

PEACE RIVER (A-3) pop. 6,744

Formed by the confluence of the Smoky and Heart rivers, the Peace River flows north and east of the town of the same name to Lake Athabasca and to the west into British Columbia. The area was known as "The Forks" by trappers and traders in the 1700s and "Sagitawa" (meeting of the waters) by the Cree Indians. On his historic trek across the northern continent, Alexander Mackenzie explored the region and built a fort and wintered here 1792-93.

A wooden statue honors prospector and local legend Henry Fuller "Twelve-Foot" Davis. The Vermont native, known for his generosity and hospitality, achieved great social stature when he mined $15,000 worth of gold from a 3.5-metre (12-ft.) plot between two gold claims. Davis said on his deathbed that he was not afraid to die because "I never kilt nobody, I never stole from nobody and I kept open house for travelers all my life." His grave overlooks the confluence of the Peace, Heart and Smoky rivers.

Nearby forests, rivers and streams make Peace River a popular center for year-round recreation in northern Alberta. Golfing, swimming, canoeing, downhill skiing and dog sledding are all options.

Peace River and District Chamber of Commerce: 9309 100th St., P.O. Box 6599, Peace River, AB, Canada T8S 1S4. **Phone:** (780) 624-4166.

BEST WESTERN PLUS PEACE RIVER HOTEL & SUITES
780/617-7600

THREE DIAMOND
Hotel

Best Western PLUS

AAA Benefit: Members save up to 15% and earn bonus points!

Address: 8016 99th Ave T8S 1R2 **Location:** Hwy 2 (Queen Elizabeth II), w of town center, just n. **Facility:** 98 units, some two bedrooms and efficiencies. 4 stories, interior corridors. **Parking:** winter plug-ins. **Activities:** sauna, hot tub, exercise room. **Guest Services:** valet and coin laundry. **Featured Amenity: breakfast buffet.**

WHERE TO EAT

MR MIKES STEAKHOUSECASUAL   780/624-8803
APPROVED American. Casual Dining. **Address:** 8006 99 Ave T8S 0A4

PINCHER CREEK (K-6) pop. 3,685

Pincher Creek was established in 1878 by the North West Mounted Police as a horse farm to provide remounts for Fort Macleod *(see place listing p. 112)*. The town was named for a pair of pincers that presumably were left behind by prospectors. After hearing that the area had ample grassland, other settlers soon arrived.

Pincher Creek Visitor Information Centre: 1037 Bev McLachlin Dr., Pincher Creek, AB, Canada T0K 1W0. **Phone:** (403) 627-3684.

HERITAGE INN HOTEL & CONVENTION CENTRE PINCHER CREEK   403/627-5000
APPROVED Hotel. **Address:** 919 Waterton Ave (Hwy 6) T0K 1W0

RAMADA INN & SUITES   403/627-3777
THREE DIAMOND Hotel. **Address:** 1132 Table Mountain St T0K 1W0

WHERE TO EAT

HARVEST COFFEEHOUSE   403/904-4000
APPROVED Coffee/Tea. Quick Serve. **Address:** 766 Main St T0K 1W0

RED DEER (G-6) pop. 90,564, elev. 905m/2,969'
• Restaurants p. 136

Red Deer's name comes from the Cree Indian word *waskasoo,* meaning "elk." Early Scottish settlers mistook the native elk for the red deer of their homeland and the name stuck. A creek and park running through Red Deer still bear the name Waskasoo.

The original settlement was several kilometres upstream on the Red Deer River where the water was shallow and easy to cross. Dr. Leonard Gaetz, a Methodist minister who arrived in 1884, persuaded the Calgary and Edmonton Railway to cross the river on his property by donating half of his land for use as a townsite. The trains came through, and the town took root at its current site. Agriculture and petroleum products are the major local industries.

City Hall Park, 48th Avenue and Ross Street, is a landscaped oasis known for its Christmas light and flower displays. West of town is Sylvan Lake, which accommodates Jarvis Bay and Sylvan Lake provincial parks *(see Recreation Areas Chart)*.

The annual Canadian Finals Rodeo is held late October to early November.

Red Deer Visitor Information Centre: 101-4200 Queen Elizabeth II Hwy. (Hwy. 2), Red Deer, AB, Canada T4N 1E3. **Phone:** (403) 346-0180.

Self-guiding tours: A brochure outlining a walking tour of the historic downtown is available from the Red Deer Museum + Art Gallery and from the visitor information center west of Heritage Ranch in Waskasoo Park *(see attraction listings)*.

Shopping: Bower Place, Gaetz Avenue and Molly Banister Drive, has 115 stores and is anchored by Hudson's Bay. Parkland Mall, 67th Street and Gaetz Avenue, has more than 100 shops.

ALBERTA SPORTS HALL OF FAME & MUSEUM is n. of 32nd St. by Heritage Ranch at 102-4200 Queen Elizabeth II Hwy. (Hwy. 2). Alberta's sports history and heroes are celebrated through the display of 12,000 artifacts, archival material and interactive exhibits. Visitors can play an Alpine ski racer game in the Ice and Snow—the Spirit of Winter gallery or try out five different sports via a virtual computer system. Also on-site are a climbing wall and a putting green.

Time: Allow 1 hour, 30 minutes minimum. **Hours:** Mon.-Fri. 9-5, Sat.-Sun. and Mon. holidays 10-5. Closed Jan. 1, Good Friday, Easter, Christmas and day after Christmas. **Cost:** $5; $3 (ages 4-17); $12 (family, two adults and children). **Phone:** (403) 341-8614.

BAYMONT BY WYNDHAM RED DEER   403/346-8841
APPROVED Hotel. **Address:** 4311 49th Ave T4N 5Y7

BEST WESTERN PLUS RED DEER INN & SUITES
403/346-3555

THREE DIAMOND
Hotel

Best Western PLUS

AAA Benefit: Members save up to 15% and earn bonus points!

Address: 6839 66th St T4P 3T5 **Location:** Hwy 2 exit 401 (67th St), just e. **Facility:** 92 units. 4 stories, interior corridors. **Parking:** winter plug-ins. **Terms:** check-in 4 pm. **Amenities:** *Some:* safes. **Pool:** heated indoor. **Activities:** hot tub, exercise room. **Guest Services:** valet and coin laundry. **Featured Amenity: full hot breakfast.**

CAMBRIDGE RED DEER HOTEL & CONFERENCE CENTRE
403/346-2091

THREE DIAMOND

Hotel

Address: 3310 50th Ave T4N 3X9 **Location:** 1.3 mi (2 km) n on Hwy 2A (Gaetz Ave). **Facility:** 241 units, some two bedrooms. 2-14 stories, interior corridors. **Parking:** winter plug-ins. **Amenities:** *Some:* safes. **Dining:** 2 restaurants, nightclub. **Pool:** indoor. **Activities:** sauna, steamroom, exercise room. **Guest Services:** valet laundry. **Featured Amenity:** continental breakfast.

[SAVE] [icons]

[icons]

/ SOME UNITS [icons]

COMFORT INN & SUITES
403/348-0025
THREE DIAMOND Hotel. **Address:** 6846 66th St T4P 3T5

DAYS INN RED DEER
403/340-3297
APPROVED Hotel. **Address:** 1000 5001 19th St T4R 3R1

HAMPTON INN & SUITES BY HILTON RED DEER
403/346-6688

THREE DIAMOND

Hotel

AAA Benefit: Members save up to 15%!

Address: 128 Leva Ave T4N 5E2 **Location:** Hwy 2 exit 391 (Gasoline Alley), just w. **Facility:** 110 units. 4 stories, interior corridors. **Pool:** heated indoor. **Activities:** hot tub, exercise room. **Guest Services:** valet and coin laundry. **Featured Amenity: continental breakfast.**

[SAVE] [icons] [BIZ] [HS] [icons]

[icons]

HOLIDAY INN EXPRESS RED DEER
403/343-2112
APPROVED Hotel. **Address:** 2803 50th Ave T4R 1H1

HOLIDAY INN EXPRESS RED DEER NORTH
587/457-7829
THREE DIAMOND Contemporary Hotel. **Address:** 6433 Orr Rd T4P 1A6

HOLIDAY INN HOTEL & SUITES RED DEER SOUTH
403/348-8485
THREE DIAMOND Hotel. **Address:** 33 Petrolia Dr T4E 1B3

MICROTEL INN & SUITES BY WYNDHAM RED DEER
403/967-0320
APPROVED Hotel. **Address:** 126 Leva Ave T4E 1B9

MOTEL 6 RED DEER
403/340-1749
APPROVED Hotel. **Address:** 900-5001 19th St T4R 3R1

RADISSON RED DEER
403/342-6567
THREE DIAMOND Hotel. **Address:** 6500 67th St T4P 1A2

RAMADA RED DEER HOTEL & SUITES
403/342-4445

APPROVED

Hotel

Address: 6853 66th St T4P 3T5 **Location:** Hwy 2 exit 401 (67th St), just e. **Facility:** 90 units. 2-4 stories, interior corridors. **Parking:** winter plug-ins. **Pool:** heated indoor. **Activities:** hot tub, exercise room. **Guest Services:** valet and coin laundry. **Featured Amenity: full hot breakfast.**

[SAVE] [icons] [BIZ] [icons]

[icons]

/ SOME UNITS [icons] [HS]

SANDMAN HOTEL RED DEER
403/343-7400
THREE DIAMOND Hotel. **Address:** 2818 Gaetz Ave T4R 1M4

STAYBRIDGE SUITES RED DEER NORTH
587/457-5851
THREE DIAMOND Extended Stay Contemporary Hotel. **Address:** 6329 Orr Dr T4P 3T6

SUPER 8 CITY CENTRE
403/358-7722
APPROVED Hotel. **Address:** 4217 50th Ave T4N 3Z4

TOWNEPLACE SUITES BY MARRIOTT RED DEER
403/341-3589

THREE DIAMOND

Extended Stay Hotel

TOWNEPLACE SUITES MARRIOTT

AAA Benefit: Members save 5% or more!

Address: 6822 66th St T4P 3T5 **Location:** Hwy 2 exit 401 (67th St), just e. **Facility:** 92 units, some two bedrooms, efficiencies and kitchens. 4 stories, interior corridors. **Parking:** winter plug-ins. **Terms:** check-in 4 pm. **Amenities:** safes. **Pool:** heated indoor. **Activities:** hot tub, picnic facilities, exercise room. **Guest Services:** valet and coin laundry. **Featured Amenity: breakfast buffet.**

[SAVE] [icons] CALL [icons] [BIZ] [HS] [icons]

[icons] / SOME UNITS [icons]

WHERE TO EAT

BLUE DRAGON FINE THAI & KHMER CUISINE
403/309-9906
APPROVED Thai. Casual Dining. **Address:** 7611 49th Ave T4P 2J8

BOULEVARD RESTAURANT + LOUNGE
403/314-2583
APPROVED International. Casual Dining. **Address:** 33 Petrolia Dr T4E 1B3

EARLS KITCHEN + BAR
403/342-4055
APPROVED American. Casual Dining. **Address:** 2111 Gaetz Ave T4R 1Z4

FAMOSO NEAPOLITAN PIZZERIA
587/273-3744
APPROVED Pizza. Casual Dining. **Address:** 5016 51 Ave, Bldg B T4N 4H5

Dreaming of s'mores and starry nights?

AAA.com/campgrounds

FUSION CAFE
403/348-5268

 APPROVED   Asian. Casual Dining. **Address:** 6842 50th Ave, Unit 6 T4N 4E3

INDIA FEAST
403/346-9300

APPROVED   Indian. Casual Dining. **Address:** 3235D 50th Ave T4N 3Y1

LA CASA PERGOLA
403/342-2404

APPROVED   Italian. Casual Dining. **Address:** 4909 48th St T4N 1S8

MESSINGER MEATS ARTISAN BUTCHER BISTRO & CAFE
587/273-3838

APPROVED   European. Quick Serve. **Address:** 2067 50th Ave T4R 1Z4

MOXIE'S CLASSIC GRILL
403/340-0111

APPROVED   American. Casual Dining. **Address:** 2828 Gaetz Ave T4R 1M4

MR MIKES STEAKHOUSECASUAL
403/356-0056

APPROVED   American. Casual Dining. **Address:** 6701 Gaetz Ave T4N 4C9

ORIGINAL JOE'S RESTAURANT & BAR
403/343-6793

APPROVED   American. Gastropub. **Address:** 4720 51st St T4N 4H1

QUEEN'S DINER
403/340-3302

APPROVED   Comfort Food. Casual Dining. **Address:** 34 Burnt Basin St T4P 0J2

RED BOAR SMOKERY
403/986-2271

APPROVED   Barbecue. Quick Serve. **Address:** 104-4916 50th St T4N 1X7

SHISO JAPANESE RESTAURANT
403/341-5502

APPROVED   Japanese Sushi. Casual Dining. **Address:** 3731 50th Ave T4N 3Y7

STATE & MAIN
403/343-2047

APPROVED   International. Gastropub. **Address:** 6702 Golden West Ave T4P 1A6

TO THE LOST COCKTAIL LOUNGE
403/986-8080

APPROVED   New American. Casual Dining. **Address:** 4916 50th St T4N 1X7

WESTLAKE GRILL
403/347-4977

THREE DIAMOND Canadian. Casual Dining. **Address:** 6300 Cronquist Dr T4N 7E8

RIMBEY pop. 2,378

BEST WESTERN RIMSTONE RIDGE HOTEL
403/843-2999

THREE DIAMOND

Hotel

Best Western   **AAA Benefit:** Members save up to 15% and earn bonus points!

Address: 5501 50th Ave T0C 2J0 **Location:** Jct Hwy 20 and 20A (50th Ave), 1.2 mi (2 km) w; west end of town. **Facility:** 60 units, some efficiencies. 3 stories, interior corridors. **Parking:** winter plug-ins. **Pool:** heated indoor. **Activities:** hot tub, exercise room. **Guest Services:** coin laundry. **Featured Amenity:** full hot breakfast.

ROCKY MOUNTAIN HOUSE pop. 6,933

BEST WESTERN ROCKY MOUNTAIN HOUSE INN & SUITES
403/844-3100

THREE DIAMOND

Hotel

Best Western   **AAA Benefit:** Members save up to 15% and earn bonus points!

Address: 4407 41st Ave T4T 1A5 **Location:** Hwy 11 and 22, just w on 42nd Ave, just s; east end of town. **Facility:** 81 units. 4 stories, interior corridors. **Parking:** winter plug-ins. **Pool:** heated indoor. **Activities:** hot tub, exercise room. **Guest Services:** valet and coin laundry. **Featured Amenity:** continental breakfast.

CANALTA ROCKY MOUNTAIN HOUSE
403/846-0088

APPROVED   Hotel. **Address:** 4406 41st Ave T4T 1J6

WHERE TO EAT

CUCINA
403/844-2173

APPROVED   International. Casual Dining. **Address:** 5207 48th St T4T 0B1

ROCKY MOUNTAIN HOUSE NATIONAL HISTORIC SITE (G-5)

In west central Alberta about 80 kilometres (50 mi.) west of Red Deer on Hwy. 11 and 6 kilometres (4 mi.) west from the town of Rocky Mountain House via Hwy. 11A, following signs, Rocky Mountain House National Historic Site tells the story of the fur trade era that existed 1799-1875. The site, on the banks of the North Saskatchewan River, protects the remains of four fur-trading posts.

Both the North West Co. and Hudson's Bay Co. were expanding in an attempt to reach the area's native peoples. The two rivals arrived here within a week of each other in 1799, their goal being to stimulate trade with the Kootenai, who were on the western side of the Rocky Mountains. The Blackfoot people blocked the planned trade. Rocky Mountain House traded with eight different aboriginal groups in its 76 years of operation.

Well-known cartographer and fur trader David Thompson used Rocky Mountain House for a time as a base for exploring routes over the mountains. Thompson was the first person of European descent to cross Howse Pass, accomplishing this feat in 1807.

Trade competition remained intense between the two companies until their merger in 1821. The influx of illegal whiskey traders into southern Alberta in 1869 disrupted trade with the aboriginal people, and in 1875 the last of the four posts was abandoned.

Two walking trails along the North Saskatchewan River and through a scenic wooded area connect the remains of the four forts. Eight listening stations and illustrated interpretive panels are spaced along the trail system. A 30-minute walk leads past the two later forts, the reconstructed chimneys at the last fort site, a replica flat-bottom York boat, a Red River cart and a fur press. A longer 90-minute walk travels to the first two forts built at Rocky Mountain House, passing tepees, the 1967 Centennial Canoe Race exhibit and a buffalo viewing area. Visitors often can see deer, coyotes, bluebirds and hawks along the trails.

The visitor center contains exhibits of trade items and aboriginal objects and a theater presenting films. Interpretive programs and special events are offered in summer; phone ahead for current schedule.

The visitor center is open daily 10-5, mid-May to early Sept.; Thurs.-Sun. 10-5, early Sept. to Sept. 30. Admission $3.90; $3.40 (ages 65+); free (ages 0-17)

ST. ALBERT (E-6) pop. 61,466
• Part of Edmonton area — see map p. 84

Alberta's oldest non-fortified community, St. Albert was established in 1861. The city is the site of the first cathedral west of Winnipeg. Its founder—Father Albert Lacombe—devoted 62 years to acting as a peacemaker between the Cree and the Blackfoot and as a negotiator between the Blood Tribe and the Canadian Pacific Railway.

St. Albert lays claim to western Canada's largest outdoor farmers market, which operates every Saturday mid-June to early October, as well as a vibrant arts community. The town also boasts both natural and man-made outdoor features, including Big Lake, just west of Ray Gibbon Drive, and the Woodlands Water Play Park, a small interactive water playground at 165 Sturgeon Rd.

The St. Albert Kinsmen Rainmaker Rodeo & Exhibition takes place the fourth weekend in May. The International Children's Festival—a showcase for performers in theater, music, dance, storytelling and puppetry—is traditionally held the weekend after the rodeo.

St. Albert Visitor Welcome Centre: 71 St. Albert Tr., St. Albert, AB, Canada T8N 6L5. **Phone:** (780) 459-2797.

BEST WESTERN PLUS THE INN AT ST. ALBERT
780/470-3800

THREE DIAMOND
Hotel

AAA Benefit: Members save up to 15% and earn bonus points!

Address: 460 St. Albert Tr T8N 5J9 **Location:** Hwy 2 (St. Albert Tr), just w at Lennox Dr. **Facility:** 90 units. 4 stories, interior corridors. **Parking:** winter plug-ins. **Terms:** check-in 4 pm. **Pool:** heated indoor. **Activities:** hot tub, exercise room. **Guest Services:** valet and coin laundry. **Featured Amenity: full hot breakfast.**

[SAVE] [🍴] [🌊] [💪] [BIZ] [HS] [📶]
[✕] [🐾] [🛏] [📺] [💻] / SOME UNITS [🐾]

WHERE TO EAT

EARLS KITCHEN + BAR   780/459-5200
APPROVED American. Casual Dining. **Address:** 10 McKenney Ave, Unit 300 T8N 5S8

ST. PAUL pop. 5,400

CANALTA HOTEL   780/645-5581
THREE DIAMOND Hotel. **Address:** 5008 43rd St T0A 3A2

SHERWOOD PARK (E-6) pop. 65,475, elev. 764m/2,509'
• Part of Edmonton area — see map p. 84

Sherwood Park is located just outside the eastern boundary of Edmonton. Though designated a hamlet, it is Alberta's seventh-largest municipality. Primarily residential, Sherwood Park offers typical suburban amenities such as restaurants, shops, and fitness and recreation facilities. At the heart of the community is Centre in the Park, a multiuse recreational area featuring a scenic walkway. The path links a central plaza area with Festival Place, a performing arts venue at 100 Festival Way, and Sherwood Park's Heritage Trail System. Phone (780) 449-3378 for the Festival Place box office.

BEST WESTERN PLUS SHERWOOD PARK INN & SUITES
780/416-7800

THREE DIAMOND
Hotel

Best Western PLUS

AAA Benefit: Members save up to 15% and earn bonus points!

Address: 300 Lakeland Dr T8H 0N6 **Location:** Hwy 16 exit 400B westbound; exit 400C (Broadmoor Blvd) eastbound, 0.9 mi (1.5 km) s, then just e. **Facility:** 90 units. 4 stories, interior corridors. **Parking:** winter plug-ins. **Terms:** check-in 4 pm. **Pool:** heated indoor. **Activities:** hot tub, exercise room. **Guest Services:** valet and coin laundry. **Featured Amenity: full hot breakfast.**

[SAVE] [🍴] CALL [🌊] [💪] [BIZ] [HS] [📶] [✕] [🐾]
[🛏] [📺] [💻]

CLARION HOTEL & CONFERENCE CENTRE   780/464-4900
THREE DIAMOND Hotel. **Address:** 2100 Premier Way T8H 2G4

DAYS INN & SUITES SHERWOOD PARK   780/570-8080
THREE DIAMOND Extended Stay Hotel. **Address:** 201 Palisades Way T8H 0N3

HAMPTON INN BY HILTON SHERWOOD PARK   780/449-1609
THREE DIAMOND [SAVE] Hotel. **Address:** 950 Emerald Dr T8H 0W6

AAA Benefit: Members save up to 15%!

HOLIDAY INN EXPRESS & SUITES   780/417-3388
THREE DIAMOND Hotel. **Address:** 11 Portage Ln T8H 2R7

RAMADA-EDMONTON EAST/SHERWOOD PARK
780/467-6727
APPROVED Hotel. **Address:** 30 Broadway Blvd T8H 2A2

SUPER 8 SHERWOOD PARK/EDMONTON AREA
780/464-1000
APPROVED   Hotel. **Address:** 26 Strathmoor Dr T8H 2B6

WHERE TO EAT

CAFE HAVEN   780/417-5523
APPROVED   Coffee/Tea. Quick Serve. **Address:** 9 Sioux Rd T8A 4C7

JOEY RESTAURANTS   780/467-6255
APPROVED   American. Casual Dining. **Address:** 250-222 Baseline Rd T8H 1S8

LA PATRONA   780/570-1200
APPROVED   Mexican. Casual Dining. **Address:** 2 Athabascan Ave T8A 4E3

SUMO SUMO SUSHI BAR & GRILL   780/416-7866
APPROVED   Sushi. Casual Dining. **Address:** 220 Lakeland Dr, #300 T8H 0N6

VICKY'S BISTRO WINE BAR   780/417-1750
APPROVED   International. Casual Dining. **Address:** 100 501 Festival Ave T8A 4X3

SLAVE LAKE (C-5) pop. 6,782

Slave Lake is on the southeast shore of Lesser Slave Lake, the second-largest lake in Alberta. Popular with bird-watchers and recreationalists, the expansive body of water is easily accessible by automobile. Six kilometres (4 mi.) north on Hwy. 88, Lesser Slave Lake Provincial Park *(see Recreation Areas Chart)* hugs the lake's east shore and provides snowshoeing and cross-country skiing opportunities in winter as well as camping and hiking during the summer. The park also is home to the Lesser Slave Lake Bird Observatory and the Boreal Centre for Bird Conservation. Riverboat Daze takes place in early July. Sand sculptors compete during the Sand Blast Competition, held the third weekend in July.

In 2011 a devastating fire that originated in a nearby forest ravaged the Slave Lake community, necessitating the complete evacuation of the town. At the time, the displacement of nearly 7,000 residents was reported to be the largest in Alberta's history. Although about a third of Slave Lake was destroyed in the fire—which gutted the town hall, library and radio station—the community has since made what is considered to be a remarkable recovery and has rebuilt most of what was lost.

HOLIDAY INN EXPRESS & SUITES SLAVE LAKE
780/849-4819
THREE DIAMOND Hotel. **Address:** 1551 Main St SE T0G 2A0

LAKEVIEW INNS & SUITES   780/849-9500
APPROVED Hotel. **Address:** 1550 Holmes Tr SE T0G 2A3

SUPER 8 BY WYNDHAM SLAVE LAKE   780/805-3100
APPROVED   Hotel. **Address:** 101 14th Ave SW T0G 2A0

WHERE TO EAT

MR MIKES STEAKHOUSECASUAL   780/849-6452
APPROVED   American. Casual Dining. **Address:** 1500 Holmes Tr T0G 2A0

SPRUCE GROVE (E-6) pop. 26,171
• Part of Edmonton area — see map p. 84

Olympic gold medalist Jennifer Heil, a freestyle skier, hails from Spruce Grove, as does Carla MacLeod, a retired member of Canada's national women's hockey team. Located just 35 kilometres (22 mi.) west of downtown Edmonton, the city also attracts athletic day-trippers from the provincial capital with such impressive recreational features as the state-of-the-art TransAlta Tri Leisure Centre, the adjacent Bruce and Jeannette Fuhr Sports Park, and Heritage Grove Park, a network of bicycle paths that connects several neighborhoods.

Other local draws include the Horizon Stage Performing Arts Centre, 1001 Calahoo Rd., (780) 962-8995, and the Spruce Grove Grain Elevator Museum, 120 Railway Ave., home to one of the last wood grain elevators in the province. The museum hosts a farmers market on Saturdays from April through December and also contains the Spruce Grove Archives; phone (780) 960-4600.

TRAVELODGE INN & SUITES SPRUCE GROVE   780/962-6050
APPROVED   Hotel. **Address:** 20 Nelson Dr T7X 3X3

STETTLER (G-7) pop. 5,748

Stettler is named after Carl Stettler, a Swiss immigrant who arrived in Alberta in 1903. He helped establish a Swiss community known as Blumenau not far from present-day Stettler. With the arrival of the railroad, the Stettler settlement was established and the residents of Blumenau relocated there.

ALBERTA PRAIRIE RAILWAY EXCURSIONS depart the train station at 4611 47th Ave. Steam- and diesel-powered rail excursions are offered through the Alberta countryside in vintage passenger coaches. Trips last 5 to 6 hours; all include a buffet-style meal at the destination as well as live on-board entertainment and staged train robberies. Theme trips also are scheduled.

Hours: Trains operate Sat.-Sun. and selected weekdays, May-Oct. Departure times vary. **Cost:** Fares $105-$165; $75-$145 (ages 11-17); $45-$140 (ages 4-10). Prices may vary. Reservations are required. **Phone:** (403) 742-2811, or (800) 282-3994 in Canada. GT

RAMADA INN & SUITES   403/742-6555
THREE DIAMOND Hotel. **Address:** 6711 49th Ave T0C 2L1

STONY PLAIN (E-6) pop. 15,051
• Part of Edmonton area — see map p. 84

Plentiful water and abundant fish and game attracted the first settlers to the region in 1881. By 1892 the name of the community itself was changed from Dog Creek to Stony Plain. The Stony Plain of today is an agricultural community.

Murals depicting historical remembrances, events and pioneers prominent in the early settlement of Stony Plain have been painted by local artists on 26 buildings in town. Memories of an early 1900s Christmas from a child's point of view are the basis for one mural, while another shows the multiculturalism of the area's early residents. The Heritage Walk Murals can be seen on a walking tour.

Stony Plain Visitor Information Centre: 4815 44th Ave., Stony Plain, AB, Canada T7Z 1V5. **Phone:** (780) 963-4545.

BEST WESTERN SUNRISE INN & SUITES 780/968-1716
 THREE DIAMOND
Hotel

Best Western. **AAA Benefit:** Members save up to 15% and earn bonus points!

 Address: 3101 43rd Ave T7Z 1L1 **Location:** Hwy 16A (Township Rd 530), just s at S Park Dr, just e. **Facility:** 110 units. 4 stories, interior corridors. **Parking:** winter plug-ins. **Terms:** check-in 4 pm. **Amenities:** safes. **Pool:** heated indoor. **Activities:** hot tub, steamroom, exercise room. **Guest Services:** valet and coin laundry. **Featured Amenity:** continental breakfast.

MOTEL 6 STONY PLAIN   780/968-5123
APPROVED   Hotel. **Address:** 66 Boulder Blvd T7Z 1V7

RAMADA INN & SUITES   780/963-0222
APPROVED   Hotel. **Address:** 3301 43rd Ave T7Z 1L1

WHERE TO EAT

ORIGINAL JOE'S RESTAURANT & BAR   780/963-9373
APPROVED   American. Gastropub. **Address:** 4300 S Park Dr T7Z 2W7

SAWMILL PRIME RIB & STEAK HOUSE   780/968-1130
THREE DIAMOND Steak. Casual Dining. **Address:** 3201 43rd Ave T7Z 1L1

 **For highways, byways and more: AAA.com/maps**

STRATHMORE pop. 12,305
• Part of Calgary area — see map p. 43

BEST WESTERN STRATHMORE INN   403/934-5777
 APPROVED
Hotel

Best Western. **AAA Benefit:** Members save up to 15% and earn bonus points!

Address: 550 Hwy 1 T1P 1M6 **Location:** Jct Trans-Canada Hwy 1 and 817; center. **Facility:** 81 units, some two bedrooms. 3 stories (no elevator), interior corridors. **Parking:** winter plug-ins. **Terms:** check-in 4 pm. **Pool:** heated indoor. **Activities:** hot tub, exercise room. **Guest Services:** coin laundry. **Featured Amenity:** continental breakfast.

DAYS INN & SUITES   403/934-1134
THREE DIAMOND Hotel. **Address:** 400 Ranch Market T1P 0B2

SUPER 8 STRATHMORE   403/934-1808
APPROVED   Hotel. **Address:** 450 Westlake Rd T1P 1H8

TRAVELODGE STRATHMORE   403/901-0000
THREE DIAMOND Hotel. **Address:** 350 Ridge Rd T1P 1B5

WHERE TO EAT

ORIGINAL JOE'S RESTAURANT & BAR   403/934-4715
APPROVED   American. Gastropub. **Address:** 100 Ranch Market T1P 1W2

STRATHMORE STATION RESTAURANT & PUB   403/934-0000
APPROVED   Comfort Food. Casual Dining. **Address:** 380 Ridge Rd T1P 1B5

SUNDRE pop. 2,610

ORIGINAL T'S   403/638-2235
APPROVED   American. Casual Dining. **Address:** 401 Main Ave W T0M 1X0

SYLVAN LAKE pop. 12,327

BEST WESTERN PLUS CHATEAU INN SYLVAN LAKE
403/887-7788
 THREE DIAMOND
Hotel

Best Western PLUS. **AAA Benefit:** Members save up to 15% and earn bonus points!

 Address: 5027 Lakeshore Dr T4S 1R3 **Location:** Jct Hwy 11 and 781 (50th St), 1.9 mi (3.1 km) n, just e. **Facility:** 72 units. 4 stories, interior corridors. **Parking:** winter plug-ins. **Terms:** check-in 4 pm. **Pool:** heated indoor. **Activities:** hot tub, exercise room. **Guest Services:** coin laundry.

WHERE TO EAT

BUKZ   403/858-7789
◆ APPROVED   International. Casual Dining. **Address:** 4903 Lakeshore Dr T4S 1C6

LOKAL KITCHEN   403/864-9996
◆ APPROVED   International. Casual Dining. **Address:** 4923 33rd St T4S 1A7

THREE HILLS   pop. 3,198

BEST WESTERN DIAMOND INN   403/443-7889
◆ APPROVED
Hotel

BW **Best Western.**   **AAA Benefit:** Members save up to 15% and earn bonus points!

Address: 351 7th Ave N T0M 2A0 **Location:** Jct Hwy 21/27 and 583, 1.1 mi (1.9 km) w. **Facility:** 52 units. 3 stories, interior corridors. **Parking:** winter plug-ins. **Activities:** hot tub, exercise room. **Guest Services:** coin laundry.

SAVE ♦♦ ♦♦♦ BIZ HS 🛜 ✕
🞑 🞑 🞑 / SOME UNITS 🐾

WAINWRIGHT   pop. 5,925

BEST WESTERN WAINWRIGHT INN & SUITES   780/845-9934
◆ THREE DIAMOND
Hotel

BW **Best Western.**   **AAA Benefit:** Members save up to 15% and earn bonus points!

Address: 1209 27th St T9W 0A2 **Location:** Jct Hwy 14 and 41, just e. **Facility:** 85 units. 4 stories, interior corridors. **Parking:** winter plug-ins. **Terms:** check-in 4 pm. **Pool:** heated indoor. **Activities:** hot tub, picnic facilities, exercise room. **Guest Services:** coin laundry.

SAVE CALL ♦♦♦ ♦♦♦ BIZ HS
🛜 🞑 🞑 🞑 🞑
/ SOME UNITS 🐾

RAMADA WAINWRIGHT   780/842-5010
◆ THREE DIAMOND   Hotel. **Address:** 1510 27th St T9W 0A4

WHERE TO EAT

THE HONEY POT EATERY & PUB   780/842-4094
◆ APPROVED   American. Casual Dining. **Address:** 823 2nd Ave T9W 1C5

Share the security and savings with those you love

Add drivers in your household as Associate members and give them the same great benefits you trust and enjoy.

Add an Associate membership today:
• Online at AAA.com/membership
• Visit your local club office
• Call 800-Join-AAA (564-6222)

WARNER (K-7) pop. 331, elev. 1,017m/3,336'

DEVIL'S COULEE DINOSAUR & HERITAGE MUSEUM is in the County of Warner Administration Building w. off Hwy. 4, following signs to 300 County Rd. Embryonic fossils in their nests were found on the Milk River Ridge in 1987. The specimens were from a hadrosaur (a duck-billed dinosaur); the location was the first nesting site found in Canada. A 2-hour walking tour allows for first-hand inspection of the dinosaur egg site, where ongoing excavations often yield new scientific discoveries. Museum displays feature a hadrosaur nest, embryo, fossils and models of dinosaurs. Also included are hands-on activities for all ages and an exhibit about early area settlement.

Note: The guided hikes are organized at the museum, but visitors must drive their own private vehicles to the dig site. The nesting site is in a primitive area not suitable for small children or those with mobility or medical problems. Allow 30 minutes minimum for the museum, 3 hours minimum for tour and museum.

Hours: Museum Tues.-Sat. and holiday Mon. 9-5, Victoria Day-Labour Day. Tours of the nesting site are given Tues.-Sat. at 10 and 1, July-Sept.; Fri.-Sat. at 10 and 1, May-June (weather permitting). Phone ahead to confirm schedule. **Cost:** Museum $8; $6 (ages 6-17 and 60+); $25 (family, two adults and three children ages 6-17). Tour of dig site, including museum tour, $20; $18 (ages 6-17 and 60+); $55 (family, two adults and three children ages 6-17). **Phone:** (403) 642-2118. GT

WATERTON LAKES NATIONAL PARK (K-5)

> Elevations in the park range from 1,279 metres (4,200 ft.) in the town of Waterton Park to 2,920 metres (9,580 ft.) at Mount Blakiston. Refer to CAA/AAA maps for additional elevation information.

The most direct approach into the national park from the south is over Chief Mountain International Hwy. (SR 17/Hwy. 6) from Glacier National Park in Montana; the park also is accessible via Hwy. 5 from Cardston or Hwy. 6 from Pincher Creek. Covering 505 square kilometres (195 sq. mi.), Waterton Lakes National Park adjoins Glacier National Park. Together the two parks form Waterton-Glacier International Peace Park. The Chief Mountain border crossing customs office is open daily 7 a.m.-10 p.m., June 1-Sept. 1; 9-6, Victoria Day weekend-May 31 and Sept. 2-30.

Still considered aboriginal territory, the area was home to the Kootenai and Blackfoot aboriginal tribes for thousands of years. In 1858 Lt. Thomas Blakiston became the first European on record to explore the area; he named the lakes for Charles Waterton, an 18th-century English naturalist.

Local rancher Fred Godsal, American journalist and naturalist George Bird Grinnell and others lobbied their respective governments in the late 19th century to set aside parts of this wilderness area for future generations. They succeeded, and Waterton Lakes and Glacier national parks were established in 1895 and 1910, respectively.

Waterton Lake is divided into three parts: Upper, Middle and Lower Waterton lakes. The townsite is on the north shore of Upper Waterton Lake, which juts 4.7 kilometres (3 mi.) into Glacier National Park. The mountains on either side tower up to 1,200 metres (3,937 ft.) above the lake. Mount Crandell rises to the north; Sofa Mountain and Vimy Peak are east across the lake.

Wildlife ranging from squirrels and marmots to deer and bears inhabits the park. A small herd of plains bison can be viewed in a paddock on the northern boundary, 1.6 kilometres (1 mi.) north of the Waterton River Bridge on Hwy. 6. Thousands of waterfowl visit the lakes during spring and fall migrations.

Among the many rare wildflowers that grace prairie and mountain landscapes are bear grass, pygmy poppy and mountain lady-slipper. Evergreens blanket the slopes and peaks below mountain goat country.

General Information and Activities

The park is open all year, though most concessions operate only from Victoria Day weekend through the second Monday in October. Red Rock Canyon, 15 kilometres (11 mi.) up the Red Rock Parkway, offers a .7-kilometre (.4-mi.) loop trail along the canyon and a 1-kilometre (.6-mi.) trail to Blakiston Falls. Riding stables are 2.5 kilometres (1.5 mi.) north of town off the main entrance road; guided trail rides are available.

Just north of the townsite is an 18-hole public golf course that is open daily, Victoria Day weekend through the second Monday in October. A public four-court tennis facility is on Cameron Falls Drive.

The park visitor center, at the junction of the entrance road and Prince of Wales Road, is open daily 8-7, mid-June through Labour Day; 9-5, early May to mid-June and day after Labour Day-second Mon. in Oct. Interpretive display centers at Cameron Lake and the Waterton townsite describe the park's subalpine forest and the history of the International Peace Park. All are open daily 24 hours.

Interpretive talks are given most evenings at 8 at the park's indoor theaters from Canada Day to Labour Day. There also are guided walks and other interpretive programs; phone (403) 859-5133.

Those wishing to camp in Waterton's backcountry campsites must obtain a park use permit ($9.80 per person, per night) at the visitor center. You also can register your outing with the Park Warden Service.

Hunting is prohibited. Anglers need a national park fishing license, which can be obtained along with fishing regulations at the park offices, information center, campgrounds, from park wardens and at the service station in the townsite. Motorboats are permitted on both Upper and Middle Waterton lakes with a boat permit; water skiing, however, is permitted only on Middle Waterton Lake. *See Recreation Areas Chart.*

ADMISSION is $7.80; $6.80 (ages 65+); free (ages 0-16); $15.70 (up to seven people arriving in a single vehicle) per day. An annual pass, valid at all Canadian national parks, is available.

PETS must be leashed at all times while in the park.

ADDRESS inquiries to the Superintendent, Waterton Lakes National Park, P.O. Box 200, Waterton Park, AB, Canada T0K 2M0; phone (403) 859-2224.

WATERTON INTER-NATION SHORELINE CRUISE CO. departs from the Waterton Marina. Narrated sightseeing trips lasting 2.25 hours cross Waterton Lake, which is surrounded by the majestic scenery of the Rocky Mountains. From early June through late September the cruise includes a 30-minute stop at Goat Haunt in Montana; passengers also may stay at Goat Haunt for daylong hiking trips and return on a later boat. Hikes to Crypt Lake also may be enjoyed, with a shuttle picking up and dropping off patrons at Crypt Landing mid-May to early October.

   Note: A passport must be presented by any passenger choosing to disembark at Goat Haunt for the day-long hiking trips. **Hours:** Sightseeing trips landing at Goat Haunt depart daily at 10, 1 and 4, early June-late Sept. (also at 7 p.m., July-Aug.). Non-landing sightseeing trips depart daily at 10 and 1, early May-early June and late Sept.-second Mon. in Oct. Crypt Landing shuttle trips depart daily at 10, mid-May to early Oct. (also at 8:30 and 9, July 1-early Sept.). Phone ahead to confirm schedule. **Cost:** Sightseeing trip $53; $26 (ages 13-17); $18 (ages 1-12); free (under 12 months, but a ticket is required). Crypt Landing shuttle $27; $14 (ages 1-12). **Phone:** (403) 859-2362. GT

RECREATIONAL ACTIVITIES
Horseback Riding
• **Alpine Stables** is in Waterton Lakes National Park, following signs. **Hours:** Daily 9-5. Phone ahead to confirm schedule. **Phone:** (403) 859-2462 May-Sept., or (403) 653-2089 Oct.-Apr. GT

WATERTON PARK (K-6) pop. 88, elev. 1,282m/4,209'

Waterton Park, commonly referred to as Waterton, is a hamlet located just north of the Montana border in southwestern Alberta, within Waterton Lakes National Park *(see place listing p. 142).* The park, which borders Montana's Glacier National Park, is part of the Waterton-Glacier Peace Park, designated by the United Nations Educational, Scientific and Cultural Organization as a World Heritage Site.

BAYSHORE INN RESORT & SPA   403/859-2211
THREE DIAMOND Motel. **Address:** 111 Waterton Ave T0K 2M0

WATERTON GLACIER SUITES   403/859-2004
APPROVED   Hotel. **Address:** 107 Windflower Ave T0K 2M0

WHERE TO EAT

BAYSHORE LAKESIDE CHOPHOUSE   403/859-2211
THREE DIAMOND International. Casual Dining. **Address:** 111 Waterton Ave T0K 2M0

WIENERS OF WATERTON   403/859-0007
APPROVED   Hot Dogs. Quick Serve. **Address:** 301 Windflower Ave T0K 2M0

ZUM'S EATERY & MERCANTILE   403/859-2388
APPROVED   Comfort Food. Casual Dining. **Address:** 116 Waterton Ave T0K 2M0

WESTEROSE

VILLAGE CREEK COUNTRY INN   780/586-0006
APPROVED   Hotel. **Address:** 15 Village Dr, RR 2 T0C 2V0

WHERE TO EAT

DAISY MCBEANS ICE CREAM & COFFEE   780/586-0771
APPROVED   American. Quick Serve. **Address:** 22 Village Dr, RR 2 T0C 2V0

ECOCAFÉ   780/586-2627
APPROVED   International Natural/Organic. Casual Dining. **Address:** 10 Village Dr T0C 2V0

WESTLOCK pop. 4,823

RAMADA INN & SUITES WESTLOCK   780/349-2245
APPROVED   Hotel. **Address:** 11311 100 St T7P 2R8

WHERE TO EAT

APOLLO PIZZA   780/349-3888
APPROVED   International Pizza. Casual Dining. **Address:** 10915 104th Ave T7P 1B4

FIFTH MERIDIAN COFFEE CO LTD   780/349-4559
APPROVED   Coffee/Tea Sandwiches. Quick Serve. **Address:** 10035 106th St T7P 2K3

WETASKIWIN (F-6) pop. 12,525
• Hotels p. 144 • Restaurants p. 144

Wetaskiwin got its name from a Cree phrase meaning "the hills where peace was made." It is believed that a peace agreement between the warring Cree and Blackfoot tribes was made in the area. A stop between the growing outposts of Calgary and Edmonton, Wetaskiwin flourished due to its proximity to the Canadian Pacific Railway; the city was incorporated in 1906. Today Wetaskiwin boasts progressive commercial, agricultural and industrial ties, while a restored downtown area highlights the community's historic roots.

Wetaskiwin Visitor Information Centre: 4910 55A Ave., Wetaskiwin, AB, Canada T9A 2E9. **Phone:** (780) 361-4417.

REYNOLDS-ALBERTA MUSEUM is 2 km (1.2 mi.) w. on Hwy. 13 to 6426 40th Ave. Displays interpret the history of ground and air transportation, agriculture and industry in Alberta. Audiovisual presentations, displays and demonstrations supplement the actual operation of vintage automobiles, bicycles, and farm and industrial machinery. One area features a reproduction of a small drive-in theater, complete with old films, metal speakers and seats shaped like the back end of 1950-era automobiles.

The museum also is home to Canada's Aviation Hall of Fame, situated in a separate exhibit building. Vintage aircraft are displayed. Canadians who have contributed significantly to aviation history are recognized. **Time:** Allow 2 hours minimum. **Hours:** Daily 10-5, Victoria Day-Labour Day; Tues.-Sun. and Mon. holidays 10-5, rest of year. **Cost:** $13; $11 (ages 65+); $9 (ages 7-17); $35 (family, two adults and up to six children under 17). **Phone:** (780) 312-2065. [T]

WETASKIWIN & DISTRICT HERITAGE MUSEUM is at 5007 50th Ave. Housed in a historic building, the museum depicts local history and includes displays about the military, hospitals, early businesses, and Swedish and Chinese immigrants. The Origins Exhibit offers interactive games as well as such archeological finds as dinosaur fossils and Plains Cree artifacts. Women of Aspenland profiles notable women from the community.

A hands-on gallery for children features a one-room schoolhouse, a general store and a pioneer kitchen. **Time:** Allow 30 minutes minimum. **Hours:** Tues.-Sat. 10-5, May-Sept.; Tues.-Fri. 10-5, rest of year. Phone ahead to confirm schedule. **Cost:** Donations. Reservations are required for guided tours. **Phone:** (780) 352-0227. [GT]

BEST WESTERN WAYSIDE INN   780/312-7300

 **THREE DIAMOND**
Hotel

Best Western. **AAA Benefit:** Members save up to 15% and earn bonus points!

 Address: 4103 56th St T9A 1V2 **Location:** On Hwy 2A, just n of jct Hwy 13 W. **Facility:** 28 units. 3 stories, interior corridors. **Parking:** winter plug-ins. **Terms:** check-in 4 pm. **Dining:** 2 restaurants. **Activities:** exercise room.

SUPER 8 WETASKIWIN   780/361-3808
APPROVED Hotel. **Address:** 3820 56th St T9A 2B2

WHERE TO EAT

HUCKLEBERRY'S CAFE   780/352-3111
APPROVED International. Casual Dining. **Address:** 103-3840 56th St T9A 2B2

WHITECOURT (D-4) pop. 9,605, elev. 732m/2,404'

Whitecourt Visitor Information Centre: 3002 33rd St., Whitecourt, AB, Canada T7S 1N6. **Phone:** (780) 778-3433 or (800) 313-7383.

HOLIDAY INN EXPRESS & SUITES WHITECOURT SE
          780/778-2512
THREE DIAMOND Hotel. **Address:** 4721 49th St T7S 1N5

THE KANATA   780/706-3390
THREE DIAMOND Hotel. **Address:** 3315 33rd St T7S 0A2

LAKEVIEW INNS & SUITES   780/706-3349
APPROVED Hotel. **Address:** 3325 Caxton St T7S 1P2

MICROTEL INN & SUITES BY WYNDHAM   780/396-0990
APPROVED
Hotel

 Address: 4915 49th Ave T7S 1N5 **Location:** Hwy 43, just n on 51st St, then just e. **Facility:** 104 units, some two bedrooms and efficiencies. 4 stories, interior corridors. **Parking:** winter plug-ins. **Activities:** sauna, hot tub, exercise room. **Guest Services:** valet and coin laundry.

SUPER 8 BY WYNDHAM WHITECOURT   780/778-8908
APPROVED Hotel. **Address:** 4121 Kepler St T7S 0A3

WHERE TO EAT

KUJIRA SUSHI & GRILL   780/396-8881
APPROVED Japanese. Casual Dining. **Address:** 5006 50th St T7S 2A1

MOUNTAIN PIZZA & STEAK HOUSE   780/778-3600
APPROVED Pizza Steak. Casual Dining. **Address:** 3823 Highway St T7S 1P3

ORIGINAL JOE'S RESTAURANT & BAR   780/778-1981
APPROVED American. Gastropub. **Address:** 5004 Dahl Dr, #100A T7S 1X6

WOOD BUFFALO NATIONAL PARK—
See Northwest Territories and Nunavut p. 393

Get an expert view from AAA inspectors:

AAA.com/travelguides/hotels

Hit the Road with Identity Theft Protection

Identity thieves don't take vacations.
Ensure you're protected before you leave.

Visit your local AAA office or
AAA.com/IDTheft to learn more.

All products not available at all locations.

Over 100 Years in Bloom

The Butchart Gardens

Butchart Gardens

British Columbia

Sailing along Vancouver Island's untamed coast in 1842, James Douglas visited the site of present-day Victoria and reported: "The place itself appears a perfect Eden...one might be pardoned for supposing it had been dropped from the clouds..."

Today, Edenic gardens are the province's forte: From Victoria's renowned, blossom-loaded Butchart Gardens to lush Queen Elizabeth Park atop Vancouver's tallest hill, horticultural delights are everywhere.

And if a single apple was enough to tempt Adam and Eve, they would no doubt have found BC's fertile Okanagan Valley irresistible. Its orchards produce more than a third of Canada's apples, and the valley also lures vacationers with sunny weather, sandy lakefront beaches and picturesque rolling hills striped by orderly rows of grapevines.

If you were searching for the Garden of Eden on Earth, British Columbia wouldn't be a bad place to start.

VanDusen Botanical Garden, Vancouver

Into the Woods

Indeed, a trip here just might recapture a lost youthful expectation of adventure. BC's snowcapped mountains and mist-filled rain forests seem to have sprung from the pages of a novel full of exciting new experiences.

Take a walk among centuries-old Douglas firs in MacMillan Provincial Park's Cathedral Grove; you'll feel child-size by comparison. Look up at the high, dim ceiling of needle-heavy boughs arching overhead and you'll understand how this grove got its name. Stands of old-growth forests continue to thrive in Pacific Rim National Park Reserve and Strathcona Provincial Park.

Another of these sylvan sanctuaries is Vancouver's Stanley Park, an evergreen woodland so extensive that while wandering its paths you might forget you're in the heart of Canada's third largest city.

Especially intriguing are the stylized figures carved into totem poles. A thicket of these cedar columns is at the park's eastern edge, each one communicating its own story—possibly a family history, notable event or age-old myth. More examples carved by the Bella Coola, Haida, Kwakwaka'wakw, Nootka, Salish, Tlingit and Tsimshian peoples rise along the province's mainland coast or offshore islands.

In the Canadian Rockies, Kootenay National Park preserves land that seems equally imbued with magic. At the park's southern end are the Radium Hot Springs, which bubble forth hot, mineral water no matter what time of year.

On the other hand, changing seasons at Victoria's Butchart Gardens make a huge difference. As some plants bloom, others fade, producing a dramatic shift in hues. Meandering paths among blossoming trees and shrubs pass softly splashing fountains and countless flower beds in this floral heaven.

Vancouver's VanDusen Botanical Garden is also endowed. This former golf course is now a showplace of lakes, streams, hedge mazes and whimsical topiaries.

Recreation

The Rocky Mountain and Cascade ranges, a lush valley and rivers, lakes and protected ocean waterways are the hallmarks of British Columbia's natural beauty and the sources of unlimited recreational possibilities.

Extended canoeing trips await you on the Outside Trail, a chain of lakes in the Kootenay region's Champion Lakes Provincial Park, and the coast's Powell Forest Canoe Route, eight lakes connected by portage routes.

The 116-kilometre (72-mi.) canoeing and kayaking circuit (plus portage routes) in Bowron Lake Provincial Park is so popular that reservations are required and daily access is limited to 25 boats. Paddling through this unspoiled wildlife sanctuary could take up to 7 days, depending on the weather or how much time you spend gawking at wildlife or the beautiful Cariboo Mountains.

In addition to spectacular mountain scenery, canoeists will find calm, turquoise glacial lakes nestled in the snowcapped Rockies; two of these, O'Hara and Emerald, are in Yoho National Park.

If rushing water is more your speed, try negotiating the Thompson and Fraser rivers. They converge near Lytton, said to be Canada's white-water rafting capital; outfitters and guides are plentiful.

Hiking trails throughout BC bring you up close with its natural wonders. One of the best coastal hikes is in Pacific Rim National Park Reserve. The Long Beach Unit near Ucluelet offers eight moderately challenging hiking venues ranging from beaches to rain forests. The park's pride and joy, the rugged West Coast Trail, follows the shoreline from Port Renfrew to Bamfield.

But that's just the tip of the iceberg. A National Marine Conservation Area as well as seven national and nearly 650 provincial parks and recreation areas await your discovery.

You can swim, water ski or windsurf at one of Okanagan Lake's seven provincial beach parks or at Osoyoos Lake, the province's warmest; both are in the desertlike Okanagan Valley. The valley's climate and terrain also invite other activities. The Kettle Valley Railway bed, west of Penticton, provides easy mountain biking; tougher trails cross nearby Campbell Mountain and Ellis Ridge.

The skiing amenities at Whistler and Blackcomb mountains north of Vancouver—39 high-speed lifts, 200 trails and 12 alpine bowls—are world renowned and make up one of North America's largest ski resorts. Off the slopes, unlimited après ski options exist in Whistler Village's eclectic mix of pubs, dance clubs and culinary nightspots, shops, spas and art galleries.

The Okanagan Valley's gentle slopes and rolling hills draw snowboarders and cross-country skiers. Resorts and ski areas near Osoyoos, Oliver, Penticton, West Kelowna (Westbank) and Kelowna have quite a following; most offer night skiing, too. Some of western Canada's best cross-country skiing is farther north, from 100 Mile House to Quesnel west of the Cariboo Mountains.

Bridge over Fraser River

Historic Timeline

1750	The Queen Charlotte Islands are occupied by Haida First Nation.
1774	Spanish explorers first sight the coast of Vancouver Island.
1792	George Vancouver, an English explorer, surveys the British Columbian coast.
1820	The powerful Hudson's Bay Co. controls fur trading in the Pacific Northwest.
1849	Vancouver Island becomes a crown colony.
1858	Gold is discovered in the Fraser River Valley.
1871	British Columbia becomes the sixth province of the Dominion of Canada.
1885	A transcontinental railroad links British Columbia with eastern Canada.
1986	Vancouver celebrates its centennial with a world's fair, Expo '86.
1998	The Nisga'a Treaty ends 20 years of negotiations with the Nisga'a nation over land, resources and self-government.
2010	Vancouver and Whistler host the 2010 Olympic Winter Games.

What To Pack

Temperature Averages Maximum/Minimum (Celsius)	JANUARY	FEBRUARY	MARCH	APRIL	MAY	JUNE	JULY	AUGUST	SEPTEMBER	OCTOBER	NOVEMBER	DECEMBER
Fort St. John	-11/-19	-7/-16	-1/-11	8/-2	15/3	19/8	21/10	20/9	14/4	8/-1	-3/-11	-9/-18
Kamloops	-2/-9	3/-5	10/-2	16/2	21/7	25/11	28/13	28/13	22/8	14/3	5/-2	0/-7
Prince George	-6/-14	-1/-11	4/-6	11/-2	16/3	19/6	22/8	21/7	16/3	9/-1	1/-7	-5/-13
Prince Rupert	4/-3	6/-1	7/0	9/1	12/4	14/7	16/9	16/10	15/7	11/4	7/1	4/-2
Vancouver	6/0	8/1	9/2	12/4	16/8	19/11	22/12	22/13	18/10	13/6	9/3	6/1
Victoria	6/0	8/1	10/2	13/3	16/6	19/9	22/11	22/11	19/8	14/5	9/2	7/1

From the records of The Weather Channel Interactive, Inc.

Good Facts To Know

ABOUT THE PROVINCE

POPULATION: 4,400,057.

AREA: 944,735 sq km (364,762 sq mi.); ranks 5th.

CAPITAL: Victoria.

HIGHEST POINT: 4,663 m (15,295 ft.), Mount Fairweather.

LOWEST POINT: Sea level, Pacific Ocean.

TIME ZONE(S): Mountain/Pacific. DST in portions of the province.

GAMBLING

MINIMUM AGE FOR GAMBLING: 19.

REGULATIONS

TEEN DRIVING LAWS: The minimum age for an unrestricted driver's license is 19 (18 years, 6 months with approved driver's ed). No more than one unrelated passenger is permitted unless accompanied by a driver age 25 or older. For more information about British Columbia driver's license regulations, phone (800) 663-3051.

SEAT BELT/CHILD RESTRAINT LAWS: Seat belts are required for driver and all passengers ages 16 and over. Appropriate booster or forward-facing child seats are required for children under age 9 or under 145 cm (57 in.) tall. Infants under 20 pounds must be in a rear-facing seat until they are 12 months old and must not be placed in front of an air bag. AAA recommends the use of seat belts and appropriate child restraints for the driver and all passengers.

CELLPHONE RESTRICTIONS: The use of handheld phones and text messaging while driving are prohibited.

HELMETS FOR MOTORCYCLISTS: Required for all riders.

RADAR DETECTORS: Permitted.

MOVE OVER LAW: Drivers approaching a stopped emergency vehicle displaying flashing lights must slow down and, if traffic permits, move over into the adjacent lane in order to pass by.

FIREARMS LAWS: By federal law, all nonresidents entering Canada with a firearm must declare their weapon in writing and pay a fee of $25 (Canadian). Contact the Canadian Firearms Centre at (800) 731-4000 to receive a declaration form or for additional information.

ALCOHOL CONSUMPTION: Legal age 19.

HOLIDAYS

HOLIDAYS: Jan. 1 ▪ Family Day, Feb. (3rd Mon.) ▪ Good Friday ▪ Easter Monday ▪ Victoria Day, Mon. prior to May 25 ▪ Canada Day, July 1 ▪ British Columbia Day, Aug. (1st Mon.) ▪ Labour Day, Sept. (1st Mon.) ▪ Thanksgiving, Oct. (2nd Mon.) ▪ Remembrance Day, Nov. 11 ▪ Christmas, Dec. 25 ▪ Boxing Day, Dec. 26.

MONEY

TAXES: British Columbia has a 5 percent goods and services tax (GST) and a 7 percent provincial sales tax (PST). Hotel accommodations with more than four rooms are subject to a PST of 8 percent and an additional Municipal and Regional District Tax (MRDT) of up to 3 percent. The PST for alcohol is 10 percent. Restaurants and admission fees are exempt from the 7 percent PST. Automobile rental sales tax is $1.50 per day, or portion of a day, for rentals of more than 8 consecutive hours and up to 28 consecutive days.

VISITOR INFORMATION

INFORMATION CENTERS: British Columbia has more than 138 visitor information centers throughout the province. Of these more than 80 are open all year and can be found in all major cities including Victoria and Vancouver. The smaller community travel information centers are open June through August. For further information phone Hello BC at (800) 435-5622.

ROAD CONDITIONS: DriveBC provides current information about road conditions; phone (800) 550-4997 in British Columbia or anywhere in North America.

FURTHER INFORMATION FOR VISITORS:

HelloBC
Vancouver Visitor Centre
200 Burrard St., Plaza Level
Vancouver, BC V6C 3L6
Canada
(604) 683-2000

FISHING AND HUNTING REGULATIONS:

British Columbia Ministry of Environment
Fish and Wildlife Branch
P.O. Box 9391, Stn. Prov. Gov't.
Victoria, BC V8W 9M8
Canada
(250) 387-9771
(877) 855-3222

RECREATION INFORMATION:

BC Parks
P.O. Box 9398, Stn. Prov. Gov't.
Victoria, BC V8W 9M9
Canada
(800) 689-9025 (camping reservations)

British Columbia Annual Events

Please call ahead to confirm event details.

 Visit AAA.com/travelguides/events to find
AAA-listed events for every day of the year

WINTER

Dec. - WinterFest / Prince
Rupert / 250-624-9118
- Festival of Lights / Vancouver
604-257-8665
- Magic of Christmas / Brentwood
Bay / 250-652-4422

Jan. - Polar Bear Swim / Vancouver
604-665-3424

Feb. - Maple Sugar Festival / Nanaimo
250-729-2776
- BC Home and Garden Show
Vancouver / 905-951-4051
- Vernon Winter Carnival / Vernon
250-545-2236

SPRING

Mar. - CelticFest Vancouver / Vancouver
604-727-3984
- Cowboy Festival / Kamloops
888-763-2224
- Pacific Rim Whale Festival / Ucluelet
250-726-4641

Apr. - Goodbye Chums! / Maple
Ridge / 604-462-8643
- World Ski & Snowboard Festival
Whistler / 604-664-5614
- Okanagan Fest-of-Ale / Penticton
800-663-1900

May - Cloverdale Rodeo and Country Fair
Surrey / 604-576-9461
- North Island Zone Drama Festival
2019 / Qualicum
Beach / 250-752-3522
- Fire & Ice Street Festival / Qualicum
Beach / 250-228-0199
- Victoria Highland Games & Celtic
Festival / Victoria / 250-598-8961

SUMMER

June - Sam Steele Days / Cranbrook
250-426-4161
- Vancouver International Children's
Festival / Vancouver / 604-708-5655
- Seafest / Prince
Rupert / 250-624-9118

July - Bella Coola Music Festival / Bella
Coola / 800-663-5885
- Celebration of Light / Vancouver
604-641-1193
- Billy Barker Days / Quesnel
250-992-1234

Aug. - Abbotsford Airshow / Abbotsford
604-852-8511
- Victoria Dragon Boat Festival
Victoria / 250-472-2628
- Parksville Beach Festival / Parksville
250-248-4819

FALL

Sept. - Vancouver International Fringe
Festival / Vancouver / 604-257-0350
- Coho Festival / West
Vancouver / 604-925-7194

Oct. - Ghostly Walks for Halloween
Victoria / 250-384-6698
- The Mane Event--Equine Education
and Trade Fair / Chilliwack
250-578-7518
- Okanagan Fall Wine Festival
Kelowna / 250-861-6654

Nov. - Heritage Christmas at Burnaby
Village / Burnaby / 604-297-4565
- Kris Kringle Craft Market / Nanaimo
250-758-9750
- Cornucopia--Whistler's Celebration of
Food + Drink / Whistler
604-932-2394

🔗 **Book and save at AAA.com/hertz**

Stanley Park, Vancouver

Yoho National Park

Butchart Gardens,
Brentwood Bay

Mount Robson Provincial Park, Valemount

Victoria Butterfly Gardens, Brentwood Bay

Index: Great Experience for Members

AAA editor's picks of exceptional note

Barkerville Historic
Town

Capilano Suspension
Bridge Park

Mount Robson
Provincial Park

Craigdarroch Castle

See Orientation map on p. 162 for corresponding grid coordinates, if applicable.
*Indicates the GEM is temporarily closed.

Next Best Thing to a
Personal Tour Guide

Purchase at participating AAA/CAA club offices. Selections vary by location.

STAY CONNECTED

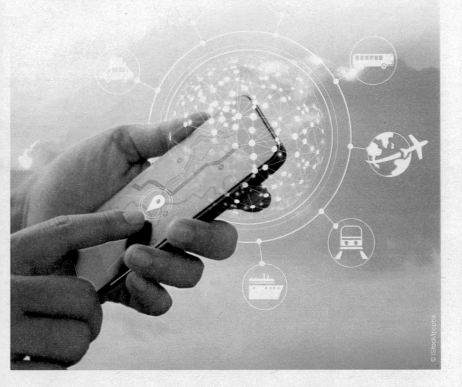

to all the things membership can do for you

- **Member discounts around you**
- **Cheapest gas nearby**
- **Diamond hotels and restaurants**
- **Travel information and reservations**
- **Roadside assistance**

**Download today.
Connect every day.
AAA.com/mobile | CAA.ca/mobile**

British Columbia
Atlas Section

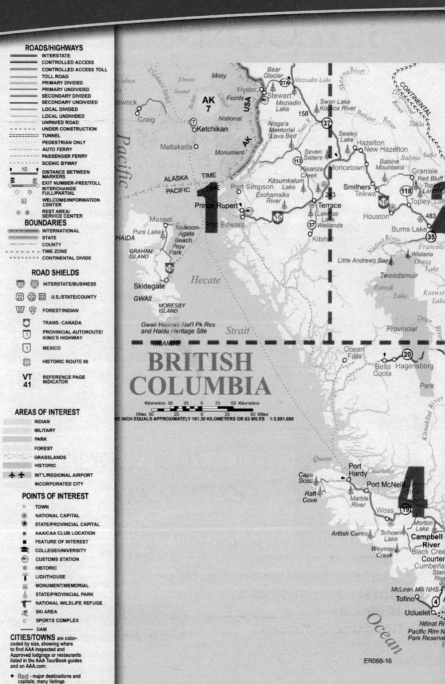

ROADS/HIGHWAYS

INTERSTATE
CONTROLLED ACCESS
CONTROLLED ACCESS TOLL
TOLL ROAD
PRIMARY DIVIDED
PRIMARY UNDIVIDED
SECONDARY DIVIDED
SECONDARY UNDIVIDED
LOCAL DIVIDED
LOCAL UNDIVIDED
UNPAVED ROAD
UNDER CONSTRUCTION
TUNNEL
PEDESTRIAN ONLY
AUTO FERRY
PASSENGER FERRY
SCENIC BYWAY
10   DISTANCE BETWEEN MARKERS
EXIT NUMBER-FREE/TOLL
INTERCHANGE FULL/PARTIAL
WELCOME/INFORMATION CENTER
REST AREA/ SERVICE CENTER

BOUNDARIES

INTERNATIONAL
STATE
COUNTY
TIME ZONE
CONTINENTAL DIVIDE

ROAD SHIELDS

INTERSTATE/BUSINESS

U.S./STATE/COUNTY

FOREST/INDIAN

TRANS- CANADA

PROVINCIAL AUTOROUTE/ KING'S HIGHWAY

MEXICO

HISTORIC ROUTE 66

VT 41   REFERENCE PAGE INDICATOR

AREAS OF INTEREST

INDIAN
MILITARY
PARK
FOREST
GRASSLANDS
HISTORIC
INT'L/REGIONAL AIRPORT
INCORPORATED CITY

POINTS OF INTEREST

TOWN
NATIONAL CAPITAL
STATE/PROVINCIAL CAPITAL
AAA/CAA CLUB LOCATION
FEATURE OF INTEREST
COLLEGE/UNIVERSITY
CUSTOMS STATION
HISTORIC
LIGHTHOUSE
MONUMENT/MEMORIAL
STATE/PROVINCIAL PARK
NATIONAL WILDLIFE REFUGE
SKI AREA
SPORTS COMPLEX
DAM

CITIES/TOWNS are color-coded by size, showing where to find AAA Inspected and Approved lodgings or restaurants listed in the AAA TourBook guides and on AAA.com:

- Red - major destinations and capitals; many listings
- Black - destinations; some listings
- Grey - no listings

BRITISH COLUMBIA

Kilometers 50   25   0   25   50 Kilometers
Miles 50   25   0   25   50 Miles
ONE INCH EQUALS APPROXIMATELY 101.39 KILOMETERS OR 63 MILES   1:3,991,680

Bear Glacier
Misty
97A
Meziadin Lake
Skeena River
CONTINENTAL DIVIDE
Ernest
Hudson
Sound
Hyder
Stewart
Fiords
USA
AK 7
Meziadin Lake
Swan Lake
Kispiox River
Bobine River
Takla
Hawock
Craig
7
Ketchikan
National
Nisga'a Memorial Lava Bed
Nass R.
37
Seeley Lake
Hazelton
New Hazelton
Babine Lake
Metlakatia
Monument
Seven Sisters
113
Kleanza Creek
Moricetown
Babine Mountains
Granisle
Red Bluff
118
Topley Landing
Topley
ALASKA
TIME
Port Simpson
Kitsumkalum Lake
243
Smithers
Telkwa
16
483
Prince Rupert
PACIFIC
TIME
Exchamsiks River
Terrace
Lakelse Lake Wetlands
Houston
Port Edward
37
Kitimat
Burns Lake
35
Little Andrews Bay
Nadina River
Francois Lake
Wistaria
Ootsa Lake
Knewst Lake
Masset
Pure Lake
Naikoon-Agate Beach Prov Park
HAIDA
GRAHAM ISLAND
16
Tweedsmuir
Eutsuk Lake
Hecate
Dean River
Skidegate
GWAII
MORESBY ISLAND
Provincial
Knewst Lake
Gwaii Haanas Nat'l Pk Res and Haida Heritage Site
Strait
ISLANDS
Ocean Falls
Bella Coola
20
Hagensborg
Park
BRITISH COLUMBIA
Klinaklini River
Queen
Charlotte
Port Hardy
Cape Scott
Raft Cove
Port McNeill
Strait
Marble River
Woss
19
Morton Lake
Artlish Caves
Schoen Lake
Weymer Creek
Campbell River
Black Creek
Courtenay
Cumberland
Stan River
McLean Mill NHS
Tofino
Ucluelet
4
Nitinat Ri
Pacific Rim N
Park Reserve
Ocean

ER068-16

Use these detailed driving maps to plan your stops and find your way.
For complete route planning, purchase the latest AAA Road Atlas at
participating AAA/CAA offices, and use the free online TripTik Travel
Planner at AAA.com/maps

AAA
Road
Atlas
2020

UNITED STATES
CANADA
MEXICO

3

5

6

CONTINENTAL

Hudson's
Hope
29
Fort
St John
64
Kiskatinaw
97
Peace River
Moberly Lake
140
Dawson
Creek
49
Moberly
Lake
102
97
Pouce
Coupe
97
Chetwynd
Tomslake
43
52
One
Islands
Lake
52
Gwillim
Lake
29
Tumbler
Ridge
MOUNTAIN
Monkman
PACIFIC
TIME
AB
TIME
Sioux Falls
309
Bear Lake
Crooked
River
James
Site
DIVIDE
Purden
Lake
Carp
Lake
97
McGregor River
Three
Sisters
Lakes
Fraser
Prince
George
97
Morkill R.
Markill Rd.
Jasper
40
Hinton
Hixon
Bowron Lake
Provincial Park
McBride
277
16
79
Jasper
National
Jasper
AB
69
Barkerville
Historic Town
Bowron Lake
Ten Mile
Lake
26
Barkerville
Tête Jaune Cache
103
Mount
Quesnel
234
Cariboo
River
Swift River
Robson
Prov
Pk
93
145
Valemount
5
Park
93
11
Banff
Nazko
Lake
97
Wells
Gray
Columbia River
Nazko Lake
McLeese
Lake
Horsefly
Lake
Blue
River
MOUNTAIN TIME
71
Nat'l
Alexis
Creek
Williams
Lake
Horsefly
Provincial
Caligata
Lake
PACIFIC TIME
CONTINENTAL
Banff
Yoho
Field
Park
169
Nat'l
Lake Louise
Banff
Dead
Man's
Flats
Morley
22
60
Tricana
20
Lac la Hache
108 Mile Ranch
150 Mile House
Lac La Hache
Canim
Lake
326
Park
North Thompson River
Rogers
Pass
Glacier
Nat'l
Golden
95
Park
Parson
Kootenay
131
41
271
258
1
Nunsti
100 Mile House
Moose
Valley
227
Canim
Beach
Silver Beach
Clearwater
Bridge
Lake
205
Spillimacheen
93
Nat'l
118
186
181
248
CALGARY
234
24
70 Mile House
Big Bar
Lake
Green
Lake
Little
Fort
Barriere
Shuswap
Lake
Harald
Revelstoke
Radium Hot Springs
Dry
Gulch
Elk
Lakes
Kananaskis
Turner
Valley
541
23
High
River
156
Gold Bridge
Clinton
Downing
Chasm
McLure
Bridge
Lake
Sun
Peaks
Shelter
Bay
Invermere
Windermere
Fairmont Hot
Springs
22
Birkenhead
Lake
12
Cache
Creek
Kamloops
Sorrento
Salmon Arm
Enderby
23
Nakusp
New
Denver
Canal Flats
Skookumchuck
Fort
Steele
236
Whiteswan
Lake
43
Claresholm
2
Goldpan
Skihist
Savona
Logan Lake
29
106
Monte
610
Silver
Star
Mabel
Lake
6
Silverton
Kaslo
Kimberley
Wasa
182
Crowsnest
Pass
3
Pemberton
Nairn Falls
Provincial
Park
Lytton
Merritt
97C
Monck
Vernon
Lumby
Kalamalka
Lake
Balfour
Cranbrook
Lockhart Cr
Norbury
Mt Fernie
Pincher
Creek
6
Whistler
Garibaldi
176
Boston
Bar
100
Allison
Lk
97
5A
Bear L
Kelowna
87
Okanagan Lake
Big White
Valhalla
Park
6
Nelson
Bos
well
3A
Yahk
73
Elko
Kikomun
Creek
Fernie
53
Mt Fernie
Kiknino
93
Waterton
Park
Squamish
Harrison
Garibaldi
Provincial
Park
Hope
Princeton
Nicolaum Lk
5A
Kickininee
Naramata
Penticton
Okanagan
Falls
33
Castlegar
210
Trail
Salmo
Creston
Erickson
Kikomun
Creek
37
Eureka
MT
AB
New
Westminster
Burnaby
Surrey
121
Abbotsford
211
3
Stem-
winder
Keremeos
Manning Park
Oliver
57
Inkaneep
Grand
Forks
3
127
Salmo
ID
1
Eastport
95
ID
1
57
Glacier
National
Park
White
Rock
Duncan
Ferndale
Lynden
Deming
WA
North
Cascades
Osoyoos
Oroville
20
21
15
25
395
31
ID
20
MT
38
White-
fish
93
Sidney
Abacortes
Burlington
Nat'l Pk
Marblemount
Lake
Chelan
20
WA
62
Winthrop
Twisp
153
Republic
97
Franklin D Roosevelt
Lake
20
Colville
Chewelah
20
Ponderay
Priest
River
34
2
130
Noxon
2
Kalispell
Lakeside
83
Flathead
Victoria
Mt
Vernon
226
5
20
MILES IN U.S.A.
MILES x 1.6 =
KILOMETERS
25
231
395
41
95
Lake
Pend
Oreille
200
28
93

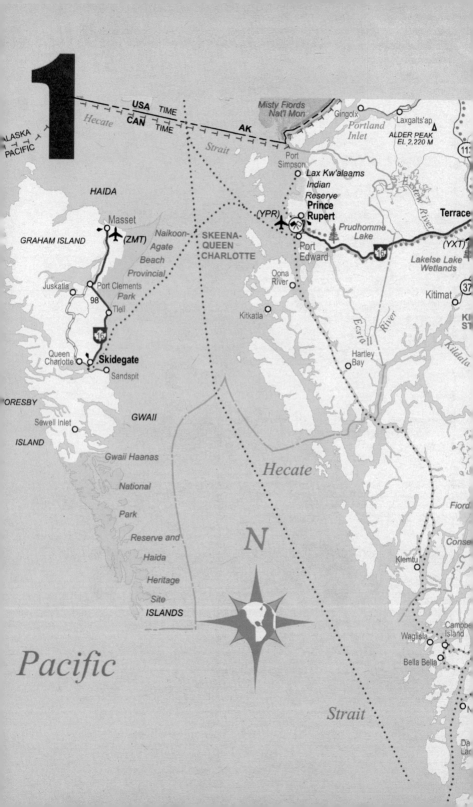

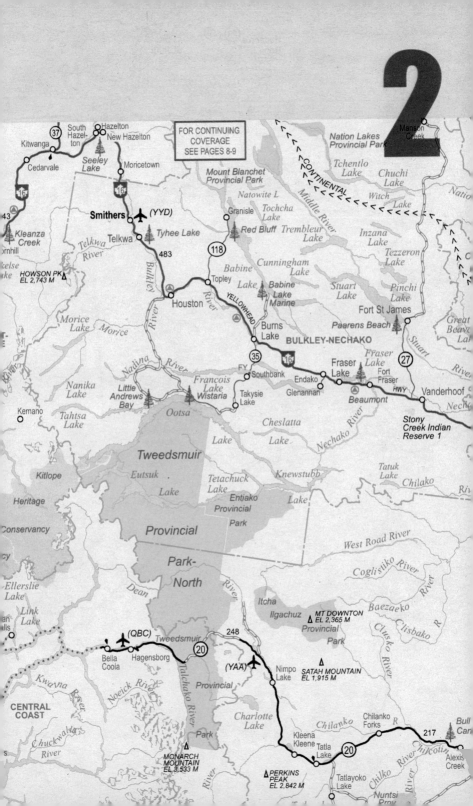

2

FOR CONTINUING
COVERAGE
SEE PAGES 8-9

Manson
Creek

*Nation Lakes
Provincial Park*

37
Kitwanga
South
Hazel-
ton
Hazelton
New Hazelton
Cedarvale
*Seeley
Lake*
Moricetown

*Tchentlo
Lake*
*Chuchi
Lake*

CONTINENTAL

*Mount Blanchet
Provincial Park*
Natowite L
*Tochcha
Lake*

Middle River
*Witch
Lake*

Nation

16
Granisle
Red Bluff
*Trembleur
Lake*

*Inzana
Lake*

*Tezzeron
Lake*

Smithers ✈ *(YYD)*

43
*Kleanza
Creek*
ornhill
Telkwa
Tyhee Lake
*Telkwa
River*
483

*Babine
Lake*
*Cunningham
Lake*

*Stuart
Lake*

*Pinchi
Lake*

*HOWSON PK
EL 2,743 M*

Bulkley River

118
Topley

Houston

YELLOWHEAD

Babine
Lake
Marine

Fort St James
Paarens Beach

*Great
Beave
Lai*

kelse
ake

*Morice
Lake*
Morice

Nadina River

35

FY
Southbank
Glenannan
Endako

Burns
Lake
BULKLEY-NECHAKO

16
Fraser
Lake
Fort
Fraser
*Fraser
Lake*

27

Vanderhoof
Stuart River

*Nanika
Lake*

*Little
Andrews
Bay*

*Francois
Lake
Wistaria*

Takysie
Lake

Beaumont
HWY

Nechi

Kemano
*Tahtsa
Lake*

Ootsa

Cheslatta

Lake

Nechako River

*Stony
Creek Indian
Reserve 1*

Kitlope

Tweedsmuir

Eutsuk

Lake

*Tetachuck
Lake*

Lake

Knewstubb

Lake

*Tatuk
Lake*

Chilako

Ri

Heritage

*Entiako
Provincial
Park*

Provincial

West Road River

Conservancy

cy

Park-

Dean

River

North

Coglistiko River

River

Baezaeko

Clisbako

Ellerslie
Lake

Itcha

Ilgachuz

*MT DOWNTON
EL 2,365 M*

Provincial

Park

Clusko River

an
alls

Link
Lake

248

✈ *(QBC)*
Tweedsmuir

20

Itatchako River

✈ *(YAA)*

Nimpo
Lake

*SATAH MOUNTAIN
EL 1,915 M*

*Bella
Coola*
Hagensborg

**CENTRAL
COAST**

Provincial

*Charlotte
Lake*

Chilanko

Chilanko
Forks

R

217

Bull
Can

*Kwatna
River*

Noeick River

Park

Kleena
Kleene
Tatla
Lake

20

Chilko River
Chilcotin

Alexis
Creek

*Chuckwalla
River*

*MONARCH
MOUNTAIN
EL 3,533 M*

River

*PERKINS
PEAK
EL 2,842 M*

Tatlayoko
Lake

Chilko

*Nuntsi
Prov*

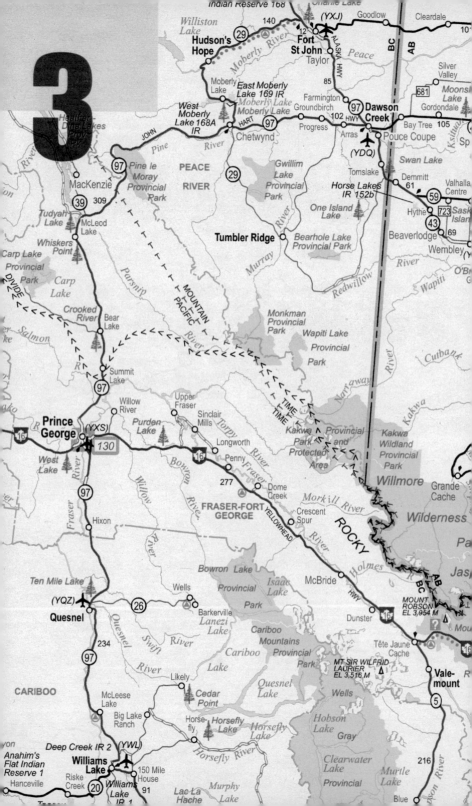

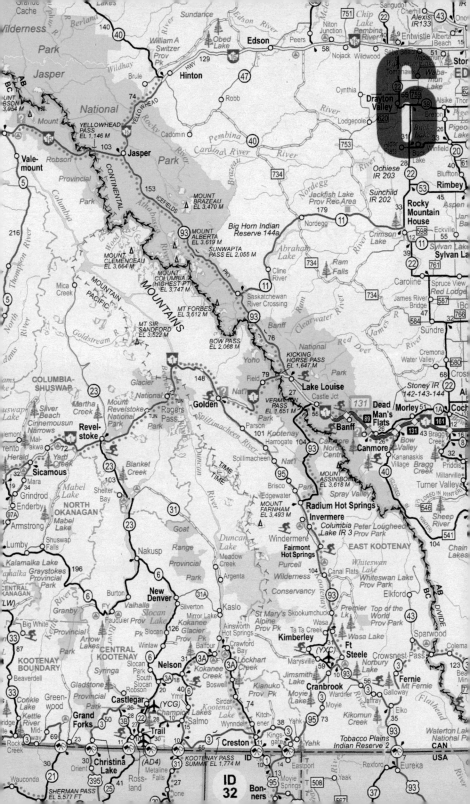

4054-20

© AAA

YUKON
BRITISH COLUMBIA

NORTHWEST TERRITORIES
YUKON

MOUNTAIN TIME
PACIFIC TIME

PACIFIC TIME
ALASKA TIME
CANADA
USA

BRITISH COLUMBIA
ALASKA

ALASKA

British Columbia
Orientation

NOT INTENDED FOR DRIVING.
SEE APPROPRIATE AAA SHEET MAP.

Scale in Kilometers
120   0   120

See p. 6 - Map Legend

ALASKA

ROCKY HWY

37   13   69
88   97
129   Fort Nelson

61   23   Fort St John
29

78   Hudson's Hope   80
Pouce Coupe
93   29   52   131   Dawson Creek
48   99

ALASKA STEWART HWY

37   120   Moricetown
Babine Lake   137
Smithers   144
Prince   154   62   118   112   97   19
Rupert   108   139   5   27
16   Terrace   68   126   41
30   Port Edward   101   155
HAIDA   89   8   160   Prince George
16   27   163
Skidegate   149   109   16
GWAII   70   146   143   12
Ootsa Lake   135   26
Gwaii Haanas   Knewstubb Lake   Quesnel   Barkerville Historic Town
National Park   Eutsuk Lake   97   Valemount
Reserve and   21   Quesnel Lake
Haida Heritage Site   50   85
138   66   5
Queen

Charlotte   20   Williams Lake
16
Sound   COAST   MOUNTAINS

SEE INSET MAP
FOR DETAIL   KAMLOOPS

18   10
Telegraph Cove   99

19
Pacific   119   28   KELOWNA

Tofino   4
VANCOUVER

Pacific Rim   Ucluelet
National Park Reserve   18   BRITISH COLUMBIA
BC   WASHINGTON
Ocean   WA   14   VICTORIA

© 2019 HERE

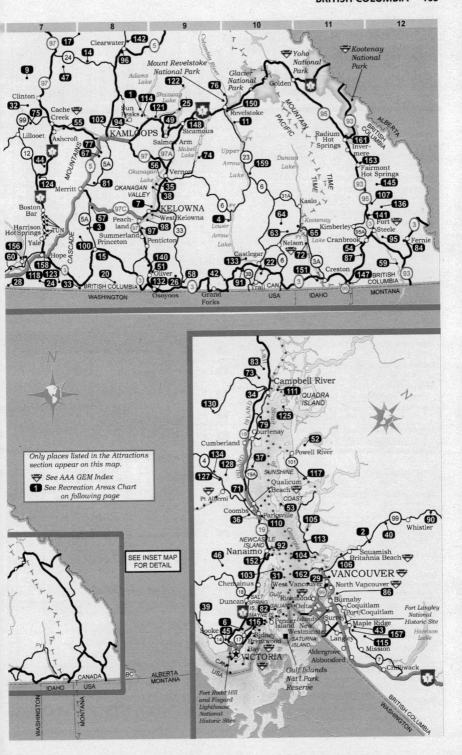

Only places listed in the Attractions section appear on this map.

⬥ See AAA GEM Index

1 See Recreation Areas Chart on following page

SEE INSET MAP FOR DETAIL

Recreation Areas Chart

The map location numerals in column 2 show an area's location on the preceding map.

Find thousands of places to camp at AAA.com/campgrounds

	MAP LOCATION	CAMPING	PICNICKING	HIKING TRAILS	BOATING	BOAT RAMP	BOAT RENTAL	FISHING	SWIMMING	PET FRIENDLY	BICYCLE TRAILS	WINTER SPORTS	VISITOR CENTER	LODGE/CABINS	FOOD SERVICE
NATIONAL PARKS (See place listings.)															
Glacier (A-10) 1,350 square kilometres. Camping, caving, mountaineering.		•	•	•						•	•	•	•	•	•
Gulf Islands (I-10) 33 square kilometres. Golf, kayaking, scuba diving. Recreational activities vary on each island.		•	•	•	•		•	•	•						
Gwaii Haanas (F-1) 1,495 square kilometres. Kayaking.		•		•	•	•		•					•		
Kootenay (A-11) 1,406 square kilometres. Horseback riding, mountain biking, wildlife viewing. Power boats prohibited.		•	•	•				•	•	•		•	•	•	•
Mount Revelstoke (A-9) 260 square kilometres.		•	•	•				•				•	•	•	
Pacific Rim (I-3) 510 square kilometres.		•	•	•	•	•							•		
Yoho (A-11) 1,310 square kilometres. Cross-country skiing; horseback riding. Power boats prohibited.		•	•	•			•	•		•	•	•	•	•	•
PROVINCIAL															
Adams Lake (A-8) 56 hectares 30 km n. of Chase off Hwy. 1. Archeological sites. Canoeing, scuba diving, water skiing, windsurfing; beach.	1	•		•	•	•		•	•	•					
Alice Lake (G-11) 411 hectares 13 km n. of Squamish on Hwy. 99. Canoeing.	2	•	•	•				•	•	•					•
Allison Lake (C-8) 23 hectares 28 km n. of Princeton on Hwy. 5A. Canoeing, water skiing.	3	•	•					•	•	•					
Arrow Lakes (Shelter Bay) (C-9) 93 hectares on Hwy. 23. Canoeing, horseback riding.	4	•	•		•	•		•	•	•					
Babine Lake-Pendleton Bay Marine (E-3) 37 hectares 45 km n. of Burns Lake off Hwy. 16.	5	•			•	•		•							
Bamberton (H-9) 28 hectares 45 km n. of Victoria off Hwy. 1. Canoeing, windsurfing.	6	•	•	•				•	•	•					•
Bear Creek (C-8) 178 hectares 9 km n. off Hwy. 97 w. of Kelowna. Canoeing, water skiing, wildlife viewing; playground.	7	•	•		•	•		•	•	•					
Beaumont (E-4) 178 hectares 134 km w. of Prince George on Hwy. 16. Canoeing, water skiing, wildlife viewing, windsurfing.	8	•	•		•	•		•	•	•					
Big Bar Lake (A-7) 332 hectares 42 km n.w. of Clinton off Hwy. 97. Canoeing.	9	•	•	•	•			•	•	•					
Birkenhead Lake (H-4) 10,439 hectares 54 km n.e. of Pemberton. Canoeing, wildlife viewing, windsurfing.	10	•		•	•			•	•	•					
Blanket Creek (B-10) 318 hectares 25 km s. of Revelstoke on Hwy. 23. Canoeing, cross-country skiing, snowshoeing, wildlife viewing.	11	•	•	•	•			•	•	•		•			
Bowron Lake (F-5) 138,700 hectares 120 km e. of Quesnel via a gravel access road off Hwy. 26. Water circuit of connecting lakes. Canoeing, cross-country skiing.	12	•		•	•	•		•	•	•		•	•		
Boya Lake (B-2) 4,597 hectares 150 km n. of Dease Lake. Canoeing, hunting, kayaking, wildlife viewing.	13	•		•	•	•		•	•	•					
Bridge Lake (A-8) 405 hectares 51 km e. of 100 Mile House off Hwy. 24. Bicycling, canoeing, horseback riding, waterskiing, wildlife viewing.	14	•	•		•	•		•	•	•					
Bromley Rock (C-8) 154 hectares 21 km e. of Princeton on Hwy. 3. Canoeing.	15	•	•					•	•	•		•			
Bull Canyon (G-4) 343 hectares 6 km w. of Alexis Creek off Hwy. 20. Scenic. Bird-watching, wildlife viewing.	16	•	•	•				•		•					
Canim Beach (G-5) 6 hectares on Canim Lake, 43 km n.e. of 100 Mile House off Hwy. 97. Canoeing, kayaking.	17		•	•				•	•	•					
Cape Scott (G-2) 22,294 hectares 64 km w. of Port Hardy. Camping (rustic in winter), canoeing, hunting, kayaking, wildlife viewing.	18	•		•	•	•		•	•				•		
Carp Lake (E-4) 38,149 hectares 32 km s.w. of McLeod Lake off Hwy. 97. Canoeing, hunting, ice fishing, kayaking, skiing, wildlife viewing; playground.	19	•	•	•	•	•		•	•	•	•	•			

Recreation Areas Chart

The map location numerals in column 2 show an area's location on the preceding map.

🔗 **Find thousands of places to camp at AAA.com/campgrounds**

	MAP LOCATION	CAMPING	PICNICKING	HIKING TRAILS	BOATING	BOAT RAMP	BOAT RENTAL	FISHING	SWIMMING	PET FRIENDLY	BICYCLE TRAILS	WINTER SPORTS	VISITOR CENTER	LODGE/CABINS	FOOD SERVICE
Cathedral (D-8) 33,077 hectares 24 km w. of Keremeos off Hwy. 3. Canoeing, climbing, hunting, mountaineering, wildlife viewing.	20	•	•	•	•			•	•					•	
Cedar Point (F-5) 8 hectares 118 km n.e. of Williams Lake off Hwy. 97 on Quesnel Lake. Canoeing, water skiing; mining displays, playground.	21	•	•	•	•	•	•	•	•	•					
Champion Lakes (C-10) 1,452 hectares 10 km s. of Castlegar off Hwy. 3B. Canoeing, cross-country skiing, ice fishing, wildlife viewing, windsurfing; playground. Power boats prohibited.	22	•	•	•	•			•	•	•	•	•	•		
Charlie Lake (D-5) 176 hectares 11 km n. of Fort St. John off Hwy. 97. Playground.	23	•	•	•	•	•		•	•	•					
Chilliwack Lake (D-7) 9,258 hectares 64 km s.e. of Chilliwack via an access road off Hwy. 1. Canoeing, horseback riding, hunting, water skiing, windsurfing; playground. ATVs or unlicensed motorbikes prohibited.	24	•						•	•	•					
Cinnemousun Narrows (A-9) 176 hectares 22.5 km n. of Sicamous via boat. Camping (walk-in only), canoeing, houseboating, scuba diving, water skiing, windsurfing.	25	•		•	•			•	•						
Conkle Lake (D-9) 587 hectares 28 km n.e. of Osoyoos via Hwy. 3, then 26 km to entrance. Canoeing, ice fishing, snowmobiling, windsurfing.	26	•	•	•	•			•	•				•		
Crooked River (E-4) 963 hectares 70 km n. of Prince George on Hwy. 97. Canoeing, cross-country skiing, ice fishing, snowshoeing, wildlife viewing, windsurfing; playground.	27	•	•	•	•			•	•			•	•		
Cultus Lake (D-7) 2,729 hectares 11 km s.w. of Chilliwack off Hwy. 1. Canoeing, horseback riding, water skiing, wildlife viewing, windsurfing; playground.	28	•	•	•	•	•		•	•	•					
Cypress (G-11) 3,012 hectares off Hwy. 1 exit 8 in West Vancouver, then w. following signs. Camping (wilderness only), cross-country and downhill skiing, snowmobiling, wildlife viewing.	29	•	•	•								•	•		
Diana Lake (E-1) 233 hectares 16 km e. of Prince Rupert on Hwy. 16. Canoeing, kayaking and paddling.	30		•	•	•			•	•	•					
Dionisio Point (G-10) 142 hectares on Galiano Island via car ferry. Camping (walk-in only), scuba diving, wildlife viewing.	31	•		•				•	•						
Downing (A-7) 139 hectares 18 km s.w. of Clinton off Hwy. 97. Canoeing.	32	•	•	•		•	•	•							
E.C. Manning (D-7) 70,844 hectares on Hwy. 3 between Hope and Princeton. Scenic. Boating (no motors), canoeing, cross-country and downhill skiing, horseback riding, hunting, kayaking, mountain biking, paddleboarding, snowshoeing, wildlife viewing.	33	•	•	•	•	•	•	•	•	•	•	•	•	•	
Elk Falls (E-10) 1,055 hectares 3 km n.w. of Campbell River off Hwy. 28. Camping (winter), mountain biking (on designated trails), wildlife viewing; playground, waterfall.	34	•	•	•				•	•	•	•				
Ellison (B-9) 200 hectares on Okanagan Lake, 16 km s.w. of Vernon off Hwy. 97. Canoeing, scuba diving, rock climbing.	35			•	•			•	•	•					
Englishman River Falls (G-10) 97 hectares 13 km s.w. of Parksville off Hwy. 4. Wildlife viewing.	36	•	•	•				•	•						
Fillongley (F-10) 26 hectares on Denman Island via ferry from Buckley Bay. Camping (winter), canoeing, kayaking, wildlife viewing.	37	•	•	•											
Fintry (C-9) 357 hectares 34 km n. of Kelowna off Hwy. 97. Canoeing, hunting, scuba diving, water skiing, wildlife viewing, windsurfing; playground.	38	•	•	•	•	•	•	•	•	•					
French Beach (H-9) 55 hectares 20 km w. of Sooke off Hwy. 14. Wildlife viewing, windsurfing; playground.	39	•	•					•	•	•					
Garibaldi (G-12) 194,650 hectares accessible by five trails from Hwy. 99 in Squamish. Camping (backcountry), climbing, cross-country skiing, kayaking. Snowmobiling prohibited.	40	•	•	•				•	•	•		•	•	•	
Giscome Portage Trail (E-4) 160 hectares 40 km n. of Prince George. Historic. Cross-country skiing, hunting, snowshoeing.	41		•	•											

Recreation Areas Chart

The map location numerals in column 2 show an area's location on the preceding map.

Find thousands of places to camp at AAA.com/campgrounds

	MAP LOCATION	CAMPING	PICNICKING	HIKING TRAILS	BOATING	BOAT RAMP	BOAT RENTAL	FISHING	SWIMMING	PET FRIENDLY	BICYCLE TRAILS	WINTER SPORTS	VISITOR CENTER	LODGE/CABINS	FOOD SERVICE
Gladstone (Texas Creek) (D-9) 39,387 hectares 5 km e. of Christina Lake on Hwy. 3. Canoeing, cross-country skiing, horseback riding, hunting, scuba diving, snowshoeing, water skiing.	42	•	•	•	•	•		•	•	•	•	•			
Golden Ears (H-12) 62,540 hectares 11 km n. of Maple Ridge off Hwy. 7. Canoeing, horseback riding, rock climbing, water skiing, windsurfing; playground.	43	•	•	•	•	•	•	•	•	•	•				•
Goldpan (B-7) 5 hectares 10 km s. of Spences Bridge adjacent to Hwy. 1 on the e. bank of the Thompson River. Canoeing, kayaking, wildlife viewing.	44	•	•		•			•	•						
Goldstream (H-9) 477 hectares 16 km n.w. of Victoria via Hwy. 1. Camping (winter), wildlife viewing. Salmon spawning in fall.	45	•	•					•	•	•	•				
Gordon Bay (G-9) 104 hectares 14 km w. of Lake Cowichan off Hwy. 18. Camping (winter), canoeing, scuba diving, water skiing, windsurfing; playground.	46	•	•	•	•	•		•	•	•	•				
Green Lake (A-7) 347 hectares 16 km n.e. of Hwy. 97 at 70 Mile House. Canoeing, horseback riding, water skiing.	47	•	•	•	•	•		•	•	•					
Gwillim Lake (E-5) 32,326 hectares 56 km. s.e. of Chetwynd on Hwy. 29. Canoeing, horseback riding, hunting, kayaking, rock climbing, scuba diving, water skiing, wildlife viewing, windsurfing; playground.	48	•	•		•	•		•	•	•					
Herald (B-9) 79 hectares 14 km e. of Tappen off Hwy. 1. Canoeing, scuba diving, water skiing, windsurfing; playground.	49	•	•		•	•		•	•	•	•				
Horsefly Lake (G-5) 186 hectares 65 km e. of 150 Mile House off Hwy. 97. Canoeing, scuba diving, water skiing, wildlife viewing, windsurfing; playground.	50	•	•	•	•	•	•	•	•	•	•				
Inkaneep (C-9) 16 hectares 6 km n. of Oliver on Hwy. 97. Canoeing, kayaking, wildlife viewing.	51	•						•		•					
Inland Lake (F-11) 2,757 hectares 12 km n. of Powell River on Inland Lake Rd. Canoeing, hunting, kayaking, wildlife viewing; wheelchair accessible trail.	52	•	•	•	•			•	•	•	•				
Jedediah Island Marine (G-10) 603 hectares between Lasqueti and Texada islands in the Sabine Channel of the Strait of Georgia. Accessible only via boat from Lasqueti Island. Camping (wilderness walk-in only), canoeing, kayaking; sandy bays.	53	•		•	•			•	•	•					
Jimsmith Lake (C-11) 14 hectares 5 km e. of Cranbrook off Hwy. 3. Canoeing. Power boats prohibited.	54	•	•	•	•			•	•	•					
Juniper Beach (B-8) 260 hectares 19 km e. of Cache Creek on Hwy. 1. Canoeing.	55	•	•		•	•		•	•	•					
Kalamalka Lake (B-9) 4,209 hectares 8 km s. of Vernon off Hwy. 6. Canoeing, cross-country skiing, fishing, horseback riding, kayaking, snowshoeing, water skiing, wildlife viewing.	56		•	•	•			•	•	•	•	•	•		
Kentucky Alleyne (C-8) 190 hectares 38 km s. of Merritt on Hwy. 5A. Horsepower restriction for boats. Ice fishing.	57	•		•	•			•	•	•					
Kettle River (D-9) 179 hectares 5 km n. of Rock Creek on Hwy. 33. Cross-country skiing, snowshoeing; playground.	58	•	•	•	•			•	•	•					
Kikomun Creek (C-12) 682 hectares 64 km s.e. of Cranbrook via Hwy. 3, then 11 km s. to entrance. Canoeing, hunting; playground.	59	•	•	•	•	•		•	•	•	•				
Kilby (C-7) 3 hectares 2 km e. of Harrison Mills on Hwy. 7. Historic. Water skiing, wildlife viewing.	60	•	•		•	•		•	•						
Kinaskan Lake (C-2) 1,800 hectares on Hwy. 37 100 km s. of Dease Lake. Bicycling, canoeing.	61	•	•		•	•		•	•	•					
Kleanza Creek (E-2) 216 hectares 15 km e. of Terrace on Hwy. 16. Canoeing, snowshoeing, wildlife viewing.	62	•	•							•					
Kokanee Creek (C-10) 260 hectares 19 km e. of Nelson on Hwy. 3A. Canoeing, cross-country skiing, snowshoeing, water skiing, wildlife viewing, windsurfing; playground.	63	•	•	•	•	•		•	•	•			•	•	
Kokanee Glacier (C-10) 32,035 hectares 19 km n.e. of Nelson on Hwy. 3A. Back- and cross-country skiing, snowshoeing. Non-motorized boats and snowmobiles allowed. No pets allowed.	64	•	•	•	•	•		•				•		•	

Recreation Areas Chart

The map location numerals in column 2 show an area's location on the preceding map.

Find thousands of places to camp at AAA.com/campgrounds

	MAP LOCATION	CAMPING	PICNICKING	HIKING TRAILS	BOATING	BOAT RAMP	BOAT RENTAL	FISHING	SWIMMING	PET FRIENDLY	BICYCLE TRAILS	WINTER SPORTS	VISITOR CENTER	LODGE/CABINS	FOOD SERVICE
Kootenay Lake (Davis Creek/Lost Ledge) (C-11) 343 hectares n. of Kaslo on Hwy. 31. Bicycling, camping (wilderness walk-in only), canoeing, kite boarding, water skiing, windsurfing.	65	●	●		●	●		●	●	●					
Lac La Hache (G-5) 24 hectares 13 km n. of Lac la Hache on Hwy. 97. Canoeing, water skiing; playground.	66	●	●	●	●	●	●	●	●	●					
Lac Le Jeune (B-8) 180 hectares 37 km s. of Kamloops off Hwy. 5. Nature programs. Canoeing, cross-country skiing, ice fishing, ice-skating, snowshoeing, wildlife viewing; playground.	67	●	●	●	●	●	●	●	●	●		●	●		
Lakelse Lake (E-2) 354 hectares 20 km s. of Terrace on Hwy. 37. Canoeing, cross-country skiing, ice-skating, snowshoeing, water skiing, wildlife viewing, windsurfing; playground.	68	●	●	●	●	●		●	●	●		●			
Liard River Hot Springs (B-4) 1,082 hectares at Liard River at Km-post 765 on Hwy. 97 (Alaska Hwy.). Camping (winter), wildlife viewing; playground.	69	●	●	●				●	●	●			●		
Little Andrews Bay Marine (E-3) 102 hectares 95 km s. of Houston on Oosta Lake. Canoeing.	70	●	●		●	●		●	●						
Little Qualicum Falls (F-10) 440 hectares 19 km w. of Parksville off Hwy. 4. Canoeing, kayaking, scuba diving, water skiing, windsurfing; playground.	71	●	●	●	●			●	●	●					
Lockhart Beach (C-11) 8 hectares 40 km n. of Creston on Hwy. 3A. Canoeing.	72	●	●		●			●	●	●					
Loveland Bay (E-10) 30 hectares 16 km w. of Campbell River off Hwy. 28. Canoeing, water skiing, windsurfing.	73	●			●	●		●	●						
Mabel Lake (B-9) 193 hectares 60 km n.e. of Vernon via an access road off Hwy. 6. Canoeing, water skiing, wildlife viewing; playground.	74	●	●	●	●	●		●	●	●					
Marble Canyon (B-7) 355 hectares 40 km n.w. of Cache Creek off Hwy. 99. Canoeing, rock climbing, scuba diving, wildlife viewing.	75	●	●	●				●	●	●					
Martha Creek (A-9) 71 hectares 20 km n. of Revelstoke on Hwy. 23. Canoeing, kayaking; playground.	76	●	●	●	●	●		●	●	●			●		
McConnell Lake (B-8) 102 hectares 35 km s. of Kamloops off Hwy. 5. Canoeing, ice fishing, kayaking, snowshoeing.	77		●	●	●	●		●	●	●			●		
Meziadin Lake (D-2) 335 hectares 50 km e. of Stewart off Hwy. 37. Canoeing, wildlife viewing.	78	●	●		●	●		●	●	●					
Miracle Beach (F-10) 137 hectares 22 km n. of Courtenay off Hwy. 19. Camping (wilderness and winter), canoeing, wildlife viewing; playground.	79	●	●	●	●			●	●	●					●
Moberly Lake (D-5) 98 hectares 25 km n.w. of Chetwynd on Hwy. 29. Canoeing, water skiing, windsurfing; playground.	80	●	●	●	●	●		●	●	●					
Monck (B-8) 118 hectares 22 km n. of Merritt off Hwy. 5A. Canoeing, water skiing, wildlife viewing, windsurfing; playground.	81	●	●	●	●	●		●	●	●		●	●		
Montague Harbour Marine (H-10) 97 hectares on Galiano Island via car ferry. Middens. Canoeing.	82	●	●		●	●		●	●				●	●	
Morton Lake (E-10) 74 hectares 27 km n.w. of Campbell River on Hwy. 19. Camping (winter), canoeing.	83	●	●		●	●		●	●	●					
Mount Fernie (C-12) 259 hectares 3 km s. of Fernie on Hwy. 3.	84	●	●	●				●				●	●		
Mount Robson (F-6) 224,866 hectares bordering Jasper National Park on Hwy. 16. Backcountry skiing, camping (winter), canoeing, rock climbing, snowshoeing, spelunking; horse rental, playground.	85	●	●	●	●	●		●	●	●		●	●	●	
Mount Seymour (H-12) 3,508 hectares 24 km n.e. of North Vancouver off Hwy. 1. Camping (backcountry only), cross-country skiing, horseback riding.	86	●	●	●				●				●		●	●
Moyie Lake (C-11) 91 hectares 20 km s. of Cranbrook on Hwy. 3. Canoeing, ice fishing, kayaking, windsurfing; playground.	87	●	●	●	●	●		●	●	●					
Muncho Lake (B-3) 88,420 hectares on Hwy. 97 at Muncho Lake at Km-post 681 of the Alaska Hwy. Camping (walk-in), canoeing, hunting, kayaking, scuba diving, water skiing, wildlife viewing.	88	●	●	●	●	●		●	●	●					

Recreation Areas Chart

The map location numerals in column 2 show an area's location on the preceding map.

🔗 **Find thousands of places to camp at AAA.com/campgrounds**

	MAP LOCATION	CAMPING	PICNICKING	HIKING TRAILS	BOATING	BOAT RAMP	BOAT RENTAL	FISHING	SWIMMING	PET FRIENDLY	BICYCLE TRAILS	WINTER SPORTS	VISITOR CENTER	LODGE/CABINS	FOOD SERVICE
Naikoon (E-1) 69,961 hectares on n. tip of Graham Island in Haida Gwaii. Camping (walk-in), canoeing, hunting.	89	•	•	•	•	•	•	•	•	•	•	•	•		
Nairn Falls (G-12) 170 hectares 32 km n. of Whistler on Hwy. 99. Wildlife viewing.	90	•	•	•				•			•	•	•		
Nancy Greene (D-10) 203 hectares 29 km n.w. of Rossland via Hwy. 3B. Canoeing, cross-country skiing, ice fishing, windsurfing.	91	•	•	•				•	•	•		•			
Newcastle Island Marine (G-10) 363 hectares e. of Nanaimo via foot passenger ferry. Camping (walk-in); playground.	92	•	•	•				•	•	•					•
Nisga'a Memorial Lava Bed (D-2) 17,683 hectares 100 km n. of Terrace on Nisga'a Hwy. (first 70 km is paved). Canoeing, hunting, wildlife viewing.	93	•	•	•	•			•	•	•	•	•	•		
Niskonlith Lake (B-8) 275 hectares 8 km n.w. of Chase off Hwy. 1. Cross-country skiing, ice fishing, scuba diving, snowshoeing, windsurfing, wildlife viewing.	94	•			•	•		•	•						
Norbury Lake (C-12) 97 hectares 16 km s. of jct. hwys. 93 and 95 at Fort Steele. Canoeing.	95	•	•	•	•			•	•	•					
North Thompson River (A-8) 126 hectares 5 km s. of Clearwater off Hwy. 5. Playground.	96	•	•	•				•	•						
Okanagan Lake (C-9) 98 hectares 11 km n. of Summerland off Hwy. 97. Camping (walk-in), canoeing, water skiing, windsurfing, wildlife viewing; playground.	97	•	•	•	•	•		•	•	•			•		•
Okanagan Mountain (C-9) 11,038 hectares 25 km n. of Penticton off Hwy. 97. Camping (walk-in only), canoeing, horseback riding, hunting, kayaking, water skiing, wildlife viewing.	98	•	•	•	•			•	•	•	•	•			
One Island Lake (E-5) 61 hectares 30 km s. of Tupper off Dawson Creek-Tupper Hwy. (Hwy. 2) and Heritage Hwy. (Hwy. 52). Canoeing, kayaking, scuba diving, water skiing, windsurfing; playground.	99	•	•		•	•		•	•						
Otter Lake (C-8) 49 hectares on Otter Lake, 33 km w. of Princeton off Hwy. 5A. Canoeing, ice fishing, water skiing.	100	•	•	•	•	•		•	•	•		•			
Paarens Beach (E-4) 50 hectares 11 km s.w. of Fort St. James off Hwy. 27. Canoeing, water skiing, windsurfing; playground.	101	•	•	•	•	•		•	•	•					
Paul Lake (B-8) 728 hectares 5 km n. of Kamloops off Hwy. 5. Canoeing, cross-country skiing, snowshoeing, wildlife viewing; playground.	102	•	•	•	•	•		•	•	•		•			
Pirates Cove Marine (G-10) 31 hectares 16 km s.e. of Nanaimo on DeCourcy Island via boat. Camping (walk-in only), canoeing, wildlife viewing.	103	•	•	•	•			•	•	•					
Plumper Cove Marine (G-11) 66 hectares on Keats Island. Boat and ferry access only. Camping (winter), canoeing.	104	•	•	•	•			•	•	•					
Porpoise Bay (G-11) 61 hectares 4 km n. of Sechelt off US 101. Canoeing; playground.	105	•	•	•	•			•	•	•					
Porteau Cove (G-11) 56 hectares 38 km n. of Vancouver on Hwy. 99. Camping (walk-in and winter), canoeing, scuba diving, windsurfing, wildlife viewing.	106	•	•	•	•	•		•	•	•	•		•		
Premier Lake (C-12) 837 hectares 12 km s. of Skookumchuck via Hwy. 95. Camping (winter), canoeing, hunting, wildlife viewing; playground.	107	•	•	•	•			•	•	•	•	•			
Prudhomme Lake (E-2) 9 hectares 16 km e. of Prince Rupert on Hwy. 16. Canoeing.	108	•			•			•	•	•					
Purden Lake (F-5) 2,521 hectares 64 km e. of Prince George off Hwy. 16. Canoeing, hunting, water skiing, wildlife viewing, windsurfing; playground.	109	•	•	•	•	•		•	•	•					
Rathtrevor Beach (G-10) 347 hectares 3 km s. of Parksville on Hwy. 19A. Nature programs. Camping (walk-in and winter), canoeing, wildlife viewing, windsurfing; playground.	110	•	•	•	•			•	•	•	•		•		
Rebecca Spit Marine (E-10) 177 hectares on Quadra Island via ferry from Campbell River, then 5 km e. on Heriot Bay Rd. Canoeing, scuba diving, windsurfing.	111		•	•	•	•		•	•	•					

Recreation Areas Chart

The map location numerals in column 2 show an area's location on the preceding map.

Find thousands of places to camp at AAA.com/campgrounds

	MAP LOCATION	CAMPING	PICNICKING	HIKING TRAILS	BOATING	BOAT RAMP	BOAT RENTAL	FISHING	SWIMMING	PET FRIENDLY	BICYCLE TRAILS	WINTER SPORTS	VISITOR CENTER	LODGE/CABINS	FOOD SERVICE
Red Bluff (E-3) 148 hectares 45 km n. of Topley via Hwy. 118. Canoeing, wildlife viewing.	112	•	•	•	•	•		•	•	•					
Roberts Creek (G-11) 40 hectares 9 km s. of Sechelt on Hwy. 101.	113	•	•	•				•	•	•					
Roderick Haig-Brown (A-8) 1,076 hectares 5 km n. of Squilax off Hwy. 1 on both sides of the Adams River. Canoeing, cross-country skiing, snowshoeing, wildlife viewing. Salmon spawning beds. Non-motorized boats only.	114		•	•	•			•	•			•	•	•	
Rolley Lake (H-12) 115 hectares 23 km n.w. of Mission off Hwy. 7. Canoeing, wildlife viewing; playground.	115	•	•	•	•			•	•	•					
Ruckle (H-10) 529 hectares at Beaver Point on Salt Spring Island via ferry from Swartz Bay. Camping (walk-in and winter), kayaking, scuba diving, wildlife viewing, windsurfing.	116	•	•	•	•	•		•	•	•			•		
Saltery Bay (F-11) 69 hectares 1 km n. of Saltery Bay ferry landing on Hwy. 101. Canoeing, kayaking, scuba diving, wildlife viewing.	117	•	•	•	•			•	•	•					
Sasquatch (D-7) 1,217 hectares 6.4 km n. of Harrison Hot Springs via an access road off Hwy. 7. Camping (winter), canoeing, water skiing, windsurfing, wildlife viewing; playground.	118	•	•	•	•	•	•	•	•	•					
Schoen Lake (H-3) 8,775 hectares 45 km s. of Sayward, 12 km off of Hwy. 19 via Davie Road. Backcountry skiing, canoeing, hunting, snowshoeing.	119	•	•	•	•	•		•	•	•					
Seeley Lake (E-3) 24 hectares 10 km w. of Hazelton on Hwy. 16. Electric motors only. Ice-skating, wildlife viewing.	120	•	•	•	•			•	•	•					
Shuswap Lake (A-9) 149 hectares 19 km n. of Squilax. Nature programs. Canoeing, cross-country skiing, kayaking, snorkeling, snowshoeing, water skiing, windsurfing; playground.	121	•	•	•	•	•	•	•	•	•			•		
Silver Beach (A-9) 130 hectares at n. end of Shuswap Lake at Seymour Arm. Canoeing, scuba diving, water skiing, windsurfing.	122	•		•	•	•		•	•	•					
Skagit Valley (D-7) 27,964 hectares 3 km w. of Hope via Hwy. 1, then 37 km s. on entrance portal via Silver Skagit Rd. Interpretive programs. Camping (walk-in wilderness), canoeing, hunting; horse trails, playground.	123	•	•	•	•	•		•	•	•		•	•		
Skihist (B-7) 386 hectares 6 km e. of Lytton on Hwy. 1. Canoeing, wildlife viewing.	124	•	•	•				•		•		•	•		
Smelt Bay (E-10) 20 hectares on s.w. side of Cortes Island via ferry from Campbell River. Canoeing, kayaking.	125	•	•		•			•		•					
Sowchea Bay (E-4) 13 hectares on Stuart Lake, 20 km w. of Fort St. James off Hwy. 27. Canoeing, water skiing, windsurfing.	126	•			•	•		•		•					
Sproat Lake (F-9) 43 hectares 13 km n.w. of Port Alberni on Sproat Lake Rd. Camping (winter), canoeing, scuba diving, water skiing, windsurfing; playground. Prehistoric petroglyphs (K'ak'awin).	127	•	•	•	•	•		•	•	•					
Stamp River (F-10) 327 hectares 14 km w. of Port Alberni on Stamp River Rd. Camping (winter), salmon viewing.	128	•		•				•		•		•			
Stone Mountain (B-4) 25,690 hectares 140 km w. of Fort Nelson on Hwy. 97. Camping (walk-in), canoeing, horseback riding, hunting, kayaking, wildlife viewing.	129	•	•	•	•			•		•		•		•	
Strathcona (E-9) 248,669 hectares 48 km w. of Campbell River via Hwy. 28. Camping (walk-in and winter), canoeing, cross-country skiing, hunting, mountain biking, rock climbing, snowshoeing, water skiing, wildlife viewing, windsurfing; playground. Snowmobiles prohibited.	130	•	•	•	•	•		•	•	•	•	•	•	•	•
Swan Lake (D-5) 82 hectares at Tupper, 35 km s.e. of Dawson Creek via Hwy. 2. Canoeing, kayaking, scuba diving, water skiing, windsurfing; playground.	131	•	•	•	•			•	•	•					
sẃiẃs (Haynes Point) (D-9) 38 hectares 2 km s. of Osoyoos on Hwy. 97. Canoeing, water skiing, wildlife viewing.	132	•	•	•	•	•		•	•	•					

Recreation Areas Chart

The map location numerals in column 2 show an area's location on the preceding map.

🔗 Find thousands of places to camp at AAA.com/campgrounds

	MAP LOCATION	CAMPING	PICNICKING	HIKING TRAILS	BOATING	BOAT RAMP	BOAT RENTAL	FISHING	SWIMMING	PET FRIENDLY	BICYCLE TRAILS	WINTER SPORTS	VISITOR CENTER	LODGE/CABINS	FOOD SERVICE
Syringa (C-10) 4,499 hectares 19 km n.w. of Castlegar off Hwy. 3. Bicycling, canoeing, hunting, kayaking, water skiing, windsurfing; playground.	133	•	•	•	•	•		•	•	•		•			
Taylor Arm (F-9) 71 hectares 23 km n.w. of Port Alberni on Hwy. 4. Canoeing.	134		•	•	•			•	•	•					
Ten Mile Lake (F-4) 343 hectares 12 km n. of Quesnel on Hwy. 97. Canoeing, cross-country skiing, ice fishing, snowshoeing, water skiing; playground.	135	•	•	•	•	•		•	•	•	•	•			
Top of the World (C-12) 8,790 hectares 48 km n.e. of Kimberley off Hwy. 93. Camping (walk-in and winter), cross-country skiing, hunting, mountain biking, snowshoeing; horse trails.	136	•		•				•		•	•	•			
Tudyah Lake (E-4) 56 hectares 9 km n. of McLeod Lake on Hwy. 97. Canoeing, ice fishing, water skiing.	137	•	•		•	•		•							
Tweedsmuir (South and North) (F-3) 989,616 hectares (South) and 446,092 (North) 365 km n.w. of Williams Lake on Hwy. 20. Camping (walk-in), canoeing circuit, cross-country and downhill skiing, horseback riding, hunting, snowmobiling, wildlife viewing.	138	•	•	•	•	•		•	•	•		•			
Tyhee Lake (E-3) 33 hectares 10 km e. of Smithers off Hwy. 16. Canoeing, cross-country skiing, ice-skating, kayaking, snowshoeing, water skiing, wildlife viewing; playground.	139	•	•	•	•	•		•	•	•		•			
Vaseux Lake (C-9) 12 hectares 25 km s. of Penticton on Hwy. 97. Bicycling, camping (winter walk-in), canoeing, ice-skating, kayaking, wildlife viewing.	140	•	•	•	•			•	•	•					
Wasa Lake (C-12) 154 hectares 21 km n. of Fort Steele off Hwy. 93/95. Canoeing, water skiing, windsurfing; playground.	141	•	•	•	•	•		•	•	•	•				
Wells Gray (A-8) 541,516 hectares just n. of Clearwater via an access road off Hwy. 5. Interpretive programs. Camping (walk-in), canoeing, cross-country skiing, horseback riding, hunting, kayaking, snowshoeing, wildlife viewing; playground.	142	•	•	•	•			•	•	•	•	•	•	•	•
West Lake (F-4) 256 hectares 22 km s.w. of Prince George off Hwy. 16. Canoeing, cross-country skiing, snowshoeing, water skiing, wildlife viewing, windsurfing.	143		•	•	•	•		•	•	•		•			
Whiskers Point (E-4) 116 hectares 130 km n. of Prince George off Hwy. 97. Canoeing, kayaking, water skiing, wildlife viewing, windsurfing; nature trail, playground.	144	•	•	•	•	•		•	•	•					
Whiteswan Lake (B-12) 1,994 hectares 22 km s.e. of Canal Flats off Hwy. 93/95. Camping (walk-in and winter), canoeing, hunting.	145	•	•		•	•		•							
Wistaria (E-3) 40 hectares 60 km w. of Hwy. 35, s.w. of Burns Lake on Ootsa Lake.	146		•		•	•		•		•					
Yahk (D-11) 11 hectares on Hwy. 3/93 at Yahk. Canoeing.	147	•	•	•				•		•					
Yard Creek (B-9) 175 hectares 15 km e. of Sicamous on Hwy. 1.	148	•	•	•				•	•	•					
OTHER															
Berman Lake (F-4) 38 hectares 45 km w. of Prince George. Canoeing.	149		•	•	•	•			•	•					
Canyon Hot Springs (A-10) Hot mineral springs 35 km e. of Revelstoke on Hwy. 1.	150	•	•	•				•	•	•				•	•
Creston Valley Wildlife Management Area (D-11) 7,000 hectares 13 km w. of Creston on Hwy. 3. Bird-watching, hunting.	151		•	•				•		•	•	•	•		
Descanso Bay Regional Park (G-10) 16 hectares 1 km e. of Nanaimo on Gabriola Island via ferry. Kayaking.	152	•	•		•	•				•					
Fairmont Hot Springs (B-12) Hot mineral springs on Hwy. 95 in Fairmont Hot Springs. Downhill skiing, fly fishing, ice fishing, rock climbing, snowshoeing, wildlife viewing, winter camping; horse rental.	153	•	•	•				•	•	•		•		•	•
Ferry Island (E-2) 61 hectares 1 km e. of Terrace off Hwy. 16. Cross-country skiing, fly-fishing, snowshoeing.	154	•	•	•				•	•	•	•	•			
Harold Mann (E-4) 13 hectares 50 km n.e. of Prince George via Hwy. 16 E. and Upper Fraser Rd. Canoeing; nature trail.	155		•	•				•	•	•			•		

Recreation Areas Chart

The map location numerals in column 2 show an area's location on the preceding map.

 Find thousands of places to camp at AAA.com/campgrounds

	MAP LOCATION	CAMPING	PICNICKING	HIKING TRAILS	BOATING	BOAT RAMP	BOAT RENTAL	FISHING	SWIMMING	PET FRIENDLY	BICYCLE TRAILS	WINTER SPORTS	VISITOR CENTER	LODGE/CABINS	FOOD SERVICE
Harrison Hot Springs (C-7) Hot mineral springs on Harrison Lake, 5 km n. of Hwy. 7 on Hwy. 9. Canoeing, golf, hunting, rock hunting; horse rental.	156	•	•	•	•	•	•	•	•	•	•		•		•
Kanaka Creek (H-12) 400 hectares 2 km e. of Haney. Canoeing, kayaking; fish hatchery, horse trails.	157		•	•	•			•		•	•				
Kawkawa Lake (C-7) 7 hectares 2.5 km e. of Hope off Hwy. 5. Canoeing, jet skiing, kayaking, tubing. Buggy rentals.	158	•	•	•	•			•	•						
Nakusp Hot Springs (B-10) Hot mineral springs 14 km n. of Nakusp on Nakusp Hot Springs Rd. Cross-country skiing, kayaking, mountain biking, snowmobiling.	159	•	•	•	•			•	•		•	•	•	•	
Ness Lake (E-4) 14 hectares 35 km n.w. of Prince George via Hwy. 97 and Chief Lake Rd. Canoeing, cross-country skiing, ice fishing.	160		•	•				•	•	•					
Radium Hot Springs (B-11) Hot mineral springs near the w. entrance of Kootenay National Park. Hunting, skiing; horse rental.	161	•	•	•	•			•	•	•	•	•	•	•	•
Whytecliff Park (G-11) 16 hectares near Horseshoe Bay off Marine Dr. in West Vancouver. Scuba diving; playground.	162		•	•				•	•	•					•
Wilkins Park (E-4) 57 hectares 15 km w. of Prince George via Otway Rd. Cross-country skiing; nature trail.	163		•	•						•		•			

GET YOUR DRIVE TRIP BACK ON TRACK

When a drive trip takes an unexpected turn, use the mobile app or go online to request roadside service.

 Download on the App Store

 GET IT ON Google play

AAA.com/mobile | CAA.ca/mobile

ABBOTSFORD (H-11) pop. 133,497, elev. 58m/190'

Abbotsford is the regional shopping center as well as the center of trade and industry for the fruit, livestock, poultry and dairy farms of the surrounding Fraser Valley. Several area industries and farms offer tours, including Clayburn Industries Ltd., at Railway and Pine streets, which produces refractory products. Castle Park Golf and Games Amusement Park, 36165 N. Parallel Rd., provides a range of family entertainment.

The city is also the site of the Abbotsford International Air Show, held in early August. In addition to more than 2 dozen planes on display, more than 30 planes, both military and civilian, take to the air.

Tourism Abbotsford Visitor Centre: 34561 Delair Rd., Abbotsford, BC, Canada V2S 2E1. **Phone:** (604) 859-1721 or (888) 332-2229.

BEST WESTERN PLUS REGENCY INN & CONFERENCE CENTRE
604/853-3111

THREE DIAMOND
Hotel

AAA Benefit: Members save up to 15% and earn bonus points!

Address: 32110 Marshall Rd V2T 1A1 **Location:** Trans-Canada Hwy 1 exit 87 (Clearbrook Rd), just e. Located behind an elementary school. **Facility:** 128 units, some efficiencies and kitchens. 2-3 stories, interior corridors. **Terms:** check-in 4 pm. **Pool:** heated indoor. **Activities:** hot tub, exercise room. **Guest Services:** valet and coin laundry. **Featured Amenity: full hot breakfast.**

SUPER 8 BY WYNDHAM ABBOTSFORD
604/853-1141

APPROVED Hotel. **Address:** 1881 Sumas Way V2S 4L5

TRAVELODGE BY WYNDHAM ABBOTSFORD BAKERVIEW
604/859-1341

APPROVED Motel. **Address:** 1821 Sumas Way V2S 4L5

WHERE TO EAT

CACTUS CLUB CAFE
604/852-2582

THREE DIAMOND American. Casual Dining. **Address:** 34650 Delair Rd, Unit B V2S 2C9

MILESTONES GRILL AND BAR
604/381-1222

APPROVED American. Casual Dining. **Address:** 3122 Mount Lehman Rd V4X 2M9

ALDERGROVE (H-11) elev. 61m/200'
• Part of Vancouver area — see map p. 249

A small town on the Lower Fraser Valley's southern side, Aldergrove is near the Fraser River and the Canada-United States border. Dairy, chicken, strawberry and raspberry farms dot the surrounding area. Just northeast of Aldergrove, Bradner grows about 400 varieties of daffodils.

GREATER VANCOUVER ZOO is at 5048 264th St. The 49-hectare (120-acre) zoo is devoted to the preservation of endangered species. More than 600 animals represent 121 species from around the world, including hippopotami, monkeys, giraffes, cougars, coyotes, black bears, elk, reptiles, raptors, bison, tigers and a rescued grizzly bear named Shadow. A narrated miniature train ride takes passengers around the zoo's perimeter; guests can also pedal 2-seater quadra-cycles on a self-guiding tour. Interpretive talks are offered.

Time: Allow 2 hours minimum. **Hours:** Daily 9-7, Apr.-Sept.; 9-4, rest of year. Closed Christmas. **Cost:** $28; $23 (students with ID); $21 (ages 3-17 and 65+). Train ride $5. Quadra-cycle $18 per hour. **Parking:** Parking $6. Rates may vary; phone ahead. **Phone:** (604) 856-6825.

BEST WESTERN PLUS COUNTRY MEADOWS INN
604/856-9880

THREE DIAMOND
Hotel

AAA Benefit: Members save up to 15% and earn bonus points!

Address: 3070 264th St V4W 3E1 **Location:** Trans-Canada Hwy 1 exit 73 (264th St/Aldergrove), 3.1 mi (5 km) s on 264th St (Hwy 13). **Facility:** 77 units, some efficiencies and kitchens. 2 stories, interior corridors. **Terms:** check-in 4 pm. **Pool:** heated indoor. **Activities:** hot tub, exercise room. **Guest Services:** valet and coin laundry.

WHERE TO EAT

FOX & HOUNDS PUB & RESTAURANT
604/856-8111

APPROVED International. Casual Dining. **Address:** 26444 32 Ave V4W 3E8

TOMO SUSHI
604/856-8998

APPROVED Sushi. Casual Dining. **Address:** 26391 Fraser Hwy V4W 2Z7

WHITE SPOT
604/856-0344

APPROVED American. Casual Dining. **Address:** 3070 264th St V4W 3E1

ASHCROFT (B-7) pop. 1,628, elev. 305m/1,000'

Ashcroft Manor, a roadside house on Cariboo Waggon Road, was named for the English home of its settlers, Clement and Henry Cornwall. The Cornwalls established themselves as cattlemen in 1862 and lived the pioneer life in the style of gentlemen, practicing such rituals as afternoon tea and riding to hounds through sagebrush and scrub in pursuit of coyotes. The manor is south of town on Hwy. 1.

For more details, rates and reservations:
AAA.com/travelguides/hotels

BARKERVILLE HISTORIC TOWN
(F-5)

Barkerville is approximately 80 kilometres (50 mi.) east of Quesnel via Hwy. 26. The restored 1870s gold rush town once had the largest population north of San Francisco and west of Chicago. In those days when more than $50 million of gold—at $16 per ounce—had been mined from the area, soap cost $1 a bar and a dance with a hurdy-gurdy girl cost $1 a whirl.

The town was named for Billy Barker, a Cornish miner who first found gold in large quantities in the early 1860s. Barkerville became a virtual ghost town a few years later when the gold ran out.

The Barkerville Hotel, St. Saviours Church, the Mason and Daly General Store and the Wake Up Jake Cafe are just a few of the 169 original or reconstructed buildings in the town; many are manned by attendants in period dress. A replica of Billy Barker's Barker & Co. Discovery Shaft and Shaft House is complete with working windlass and sluice box displays. Board sidewalks and dirt streets help preserve the essence of the original site.

Theatre Royale presents period melodrama, dance and music Victoria Day through September 30. Treasure seekers can pan for gold at Eldorado Mine. A visitor center presents videos and exhibits about the history of Barkerville. Guided town, Chinatown and cemetery tours as well as living-history programs are offered.

Pets are not permitted. The townsite is open daily 8-8. Full visitor services operate daily, mid-May to late Sept. Admission mid-May to late Sept. $16; $13 (ages 13-18 and 65+); $6 (ages 6-12); $40 (family, two adults and four children). Two-day Heritage Package (includes admission, Theatre Royal ticket, stagecoach ride and gold panning) $42; $38 (ages 13-18 and 65+); $26 (ages 6-12); $8 (ages 0-5). Rest of year free. Phone (250) 994-3332 or (888) 994-3332.

BOSTON BAR (C-7) pop. 206,
elev. 309m/1,013'

Boston Bar, which began as a gold mining town, was named for a Dutchman who came from Boston to prospect in the 1860s. Because Boston was the home port to many of the ships bringing prospectors, local First Nations people called the newcomers Boston men. Boston Bar is a logging and trade center, with the Canadian National Railway passing through town. The Canadian Pacific Railway parallels the National on the other side of Fraser River Canyon and passes through the village of North Bend.

Boston Bar is the access point for the Nahatlatch Valley, which features the Nahatlatch River and a chain of lakes. Recreation includes camping, fishing and white-water rafting.

HELL'S GATE AIRTRAM is 11 km (7 mi.) s. on Hwy. 1 to 43111 Trans-Canada Hwy. in Fraser River Canyon. The 25-passenger gondola descends 153 metres (502 ft.) across the river to the narrowest part of Fraser Canyon and across Hell's Gate Fishways, where millions of salmon annually swim upstream to their spawning grounds. Visitors can see eight fishways from the lower observation decks or a suspension bridge.

A film about the life cycle of the salmon is shown at the education center, along with stories about early explorer Simon Fraser and the Fraser River Gold Rush. Panning for gold is available.

Time: Allow 1 hour minimum. **Hours:** Daily 10-5, July-Sept.; 10-4, Apr.-June. Phone ahead to confirm schedule. **Cost:** $24; $22 (ages 65+ and students with ID); $18 (ages 6-18); $84 (family). **Phone:** (604) 867-9277.

BRENTWOOD BAY (H-10)
- Hotels p. 174 • Restaurants p. 174
- Part of Victoria area — see map p. 299

BUTCHART GARDENS is 2 km (1.2 mi.) s. on W. Saanich Rd., then w. to 800 Benvenuto Ave. The magnificent floral displays of Butchart Gardens owe their existence to Jennie Butchart, wife of Robert Pim Butchart, a successful Portland cement pioneer.

When the limestone quarry near their home became depleted in the early 1900s, Jennie lined the empty pit with topsoil and the gardens began to take shape. The Sunken Garden, the site of the former quarry, was soon joined on the 22-hectare (55-acre) site with the Rose Garden, Japanese Garden and Italian Garden as well as the Star Pond and Ross Fountain. The Butcharts named their estate *Benvenuto*, Italian for "welcome."

The spring season brings azaleas, tulips, daffodils and other delicate blossoms. Breathtaking roses, annuals and perennials bloom in summer, while bursts of colorful foliage appear in autumn; subtle colored lighting illuminates the gardens June 15 through Sept. 15.

All summer long, enjoy an electric boat tour departing frequently from our wharf. Explore the local waters surrounding The Gardens during a 45-minute tour while your captain points out historical sites and wildlife of the area including seals, eagles and otters. The Rose Carousel in the Children's Pavilion offers old-fashioned rides on 30 hand-carved animals and two chariots.

July through August, nightly entertainment is offered with fireworks displays Saturday nights. The sparkle of holiday lights and decorations complement the colorful berries on shrubs and trees from Dec. 1 to Jan. 6 during The Magic of Christmas. An outdoor skating rink, with skate rental, also is available in Waterwheel Square.

Time: Allow 2 hours minimum. **Hours:** Gardens open daily at 9 (at 1 on Christmas). Closing times vary depending on the season; phone ahead. Boat tours depart the dock daily every half-hour 11-5, mid-June to mid-Sept.; 11-4, late May to mid-June.

Cost: June 15-Sept. 30, $34.80; $17.90 (ages 13-17); $3 (ages 5-12). Admission in Oct., $29.10; $14.55 (ages 13-17); $2 (ages 5-12). Admission in Nov. $22.65; $11.35 (ages 13-17); $2 (ages 5-12). Admission Dec. 1-Jan. 6, $28.80; $14.40 (ages 13-17); $3 (ages 5-12). Admission Jan. 7-Jan. 14, $19.35; $9.70 (ages 13-17); $2 (ages 5-12). Admission Jan. 15-Mar. 31, $28.85; $12.95 (ages 13-17); $2 (ages 5-12). Admission Apr. 1-June 14, $32.40; $16.20 (ages 13-17); $2 (ages 5-12). Boat tours $20.50; $15.75 (ages 13-17); $12.25 (ages 5-12). Carousel rides $2. Rates may vary; phone ahead. **Phone:** (250) 652-5256 or (866) 652-4422.

🍴 🐾 🎡

SAVE **VICTORIA BUTTERFLY GARDENS** is 2 km (1.2 mi.) s. at jct. Benvenuto Ave. and Keating Cross Rd. at 1461 Benvenuto Ave. This 1,110-square-metre (12,000-sq.-ft.) indoor tropical garden was designed specifically for the housing and breeding of more than 70 exotic butterfly and moth species. Between 600 and 1,200 pupae are imported each week and displayed in the Emerging Window.

Thousands of butterflies—from the 2.5-centimetre-long (1-in.) helicon to the 30.5-centimetre-long (1-ft.) atlas moth—fly free among tropical plants and flowers, including an orchid exhibit and a carnivorous bog. Water falls into a stream that is home to koi fish and tropical ducks. Parrots, flamingos and songbirds also call the gardens home. Other garden residents include poison dart frogs, geckos, chameleons and turtles.

Time: Allow 1 hour minimum. **Hours:** Daily 9:30-6, July-Aug.; 10-5, Mar. 6-Jun. 30, in Sept. and Dec. 16-30; 10-4, Oct. 1-Dec. 15 and Dec. 31-Mar. 5. Last admission 1 hour before closing. Closed Christmas. Phone ahead to confirm schedule. **Cost:** All-day admission $16.50; $12.50 (ages 13-17, ages 65+ and students with ID); $6.50 (ages 5-12). **Phone:** (250) 652-3822 or (877) 722-0272.

🌐 **AAA.com/discounts—**

Your first stop for travel

and shopping savings

BRENTWOOD BAY RESORT & SPA   250/544-2079

💎 **FOUR DIAMOND**

Contemporary Resort Hotel

Address: 849 Verdier Ave V8M 1C5 **Location:** Oceanfront. Jct Brentwood Dr and Verdier Ave. **Facility:** This is a luxury retreat where every room offers a water view, private sun decks, deep soaker tubs, gas fireplaces and soft, fine linens on every bed. The spa offers fine couples' treatments. 36 units, some condominiums. 3 stories, exterior corridors. **Amenities:** safes. **Pool:** heated outdoor. **Activities:** hot tub, self-propelled boats, marina, fishing, exercise room, spa. **Guest Services:** valet and coin laundry.

SAVE ECO 🍴 🖥 🍸 CALL 🦽 🛥 ♿ BIZ HS
📶 ✕ 🚪 💻 / SOME UNITS 🐾 🖨

WHERE TO EAT

ARBUTUS ROOM   250/544-2079
💎 **THREE DIAMOND** Pacific Northwest. Fine Dining. **Address:** 849 Verdier Ave V8M 1C5

CAFE ZANZIBAR   250/652-1228
💎 **APPROVED** Breakfast Sandwiches. Casual Dining. **Address:** 1164 Stelly's Cross Rd V8M 1H3

BRITANNIA BEACH (G-11) pop. 254, elev. 6m/20'

From 1930 to 1935 the Britannia Mine at Britannia Beach was the largest producer of copper in the British Empire. No longer in operation, the mine is now part of the Britannia Mine Museum.

Shopping: At the CRS Trading Post on Hwy. 99 the wood and soapstone carvings, silver jewelry, spirit masks, jade pieces, handcrafted walking sticks, moccasins and other items are created by Coast Salish artists in British Columbia. Look for the rocks displaying hand-painted scenes by well-known local artist Ken Skoda.

GEM **BRITANNIA MINE MUSEUM** is off Hwy. 99/Sea to Sky Hwy., following signs. The Britannia Mine was an important 20th-century copper mining site during its 70-year existence. The company town included libraries, swimming pools and a gym, and social events were held throughout the year.

The towering 20-story 1923 mill building, through which the ore would move as it was crushed and the valuable minerals separated from the rest of the rock, is now a museum. Visitors can explore 17 historic buildings containing mining artifacts which document the history of the site, and other items depicting the social history of mining communities. The Canadian Mining Hall of Fame is in the Beaty Lundin Visitor Centre where interactive displays offer a look into Canadian mining. BOOM is a multi-sensory, live-action show with more than 30 speakers, multiple screens and special effects.

A 45-minute underground mine tunnel tour aboard a mine train is a highlight of the museum, which chronicles mining history through hands-on demonstrations and exhibits. On site is an 800,000 pound super mine truck. Gold panning is included with admission.

Note: The tunnel temperature is a constant 12 C (54 F); warm clothing and comfortable walking shoes are recommended. Hard hats are provided. **Time:** Allow 1 hour, 30 minutes minimum. **Hours:** Tours daily at 10 and every half-hour until 4:30, July 1-Labour Day. Arrive 20 minutes before tour time. Closed Jan. 1 and Christmas. Phone ahead to confirm schedule. **Cost:** $34.95; $31.95 (students with ID and ages 65+); $28.95 (ages 13-17); $19.95 (ages 5-12); $125 (family, two adults and up to three children). **Phone:** (604) 896-2233 or (800) 896-4044. GT

BURNABY (H-11) pop. 223,218, elev. 40m/130'

- Restaurants p. 176
- Hotels & Restaurants map & index p. 276
- Part of Vancouver area — see map p. 249

Burnaby is more than just a suburban, bedroom community of hills, ridges, valleys, plain, and stunning views; it is an urban center which is home to Simon Fraser University and the British Columbia Institute of Technology. It's also home to Playground of the Gods, a stunning collection of 25 non-typical totem poles made by artist Nuburi Toko and his son in the Japanese Ainu animist tradition, in Burnaby Mountain Park, 100 Centennial Way; phone (604) 294-7450.

ACCENT INNS   604/473-5000 13
 APPROVED   Hotel. **Address:** 3777 Henning Dr V5C 6N5

BEST WESTERN PLUS BURNABY HOTEL & CONFERENCE CENTRE   604/438-1383 17

 THREE DIAMOND
Motel

 Best Western PLUS.

AAA Benefit: Members save up to 15% and earn bonus points!

Address: 5411 Kingsway V5H 2G1 **Location:** Trans-Canada Hwy 1 exit 29 (Willingdon Ave), 1.9 mi (3 km) s to Kingsway, then 1.2 mi (2 km) e. Royal Oak, 23. **Facility:** 130 units, some kitchens. 2 stories (no elevator), exterior corridors. **Amenities:** safes. **Pool:** heated outdoor. **Activities:** exercise room. **Guest Services:** valet and coin laundry. **Featured Amenity:** breakfast buffet. (See ad this page.)

DELTA BURNABY HOTEL AND CONFERENCE CENTRE
                                 604/453-0750 14
 THREE DIAMOND   SAVE
Contemporary Hotel. **Address:** 4331 Dominion St V5G 1B2

AAA Benefit: Members save 5% or more!

▼ See AAA listing this page ▼

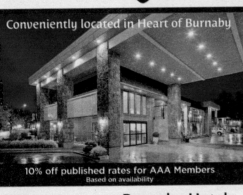

BW Best Western PLUS.

Conveniently located in Heart of Burnaby

- Free Hot Breakfast
- Providing Optic Fabric Wi-Fi & TV
- Parking • Pet Friendly

10% off published rates for AAA Members
Based on availability

 CAA Rewards

Burnaby Hotel
5411 Kingsway • Burnaby, BC V5H 2G1
604-438-1383 | bestwesternburnabyhotel.com

 THREE DIAMOND

Turn dreams into plans using

AAA travel planning tools: AAA.com/maps

(See map & index p. 276.)

ELEMENT VANCOUVER METROTOWN
604/568-3696

THREE DIAMOND
Extended Stay Contemporary Hotel

AAA Benefit: Members save 5% or more!

Address: 5988 Willingdon Ave V5H 2A7 **Location:** Trans-Canada Hwy 1 exit 29 (Willingdon Ave), 2 mi (3.3 km) s. Metrotown, 22. **Facility:** 169 units, some efficiencies. 18 stories, interior corridors. *Bath:* shower only. **Parking:** on-site (fee). **Amenities:** safes. **Dining:** Trattoria, see separate listing. **Pool:** heated indoor. **Activities:** sauna, hot tub, bicycles, picnic facilities, exercise room. **Guest Services:** valet and coin laundry. **Featured Amenity:** breakfast buffet.

EXECUTIVE SUITES HOTELS & CONFERENCE CENTRE BURNABY
604/298-2010

THREE DIAMOND Hotel. **Address:** 4201 Lougheed Hwy V5C 3Y6

HILTON VANCOUVER METROTOWN
604/438-1200

THREE DIAMOND
Hotel

Hilton
HOTELS & RESORTS

AAA Benefit: Members save up to 15%!

Address: 6083 McKay Ave V5H 2W7 **Location:** Trans-Canada Hwy 1 exit 29 (Willingdon Ave), 1.8 mi (3 km) s to Kingsway, then just e. Next to Metropolis at Metrotown Shopping Center. Metrotown, 22. **Facility:** 283 units. 18 stories, interior corridors. **Parking:** on-site (fee) and valet. **Amenities:** safes. **Dining:** Reflect Social Dining + Lounge, see separate listing. **Pool:** heated outdoor. **Activities:** hot tub, exercise room. **Guest Services:** valet laundry.

WHERE TO EAT

CACTUS CLUB CAFE
604/291-6606
THREE DIAMOND New American. Casual Dining. **Address:** 4219B Lougheed Hwy V5C 3Y6

COCKNEY KINGS FISH & CHIPS
604/291-1323
APPROVED Fish & Chips. Casual Dining. **Address:** 6574 E Hastings V5B 1S2

COTTO ENOTECA PIZZERIA
604/299-8002
APPROVED Italian. Casual Dining. **Address:** 6011 Hastings St V5B 1R8

EARLS KITCHEN + BAR
604/205-5025
APPROVED American. Casual Dining. **Address:** 3850 Lougheed Hwy V5C 6N4

HART HOUSE RESTAURANT
604/298-4278
THREE DIAMOND Pacific Northwest. Fine Dining. **Address:** 6664 Deer Lake Ave V5E 4H3

HORIZONS
604/299-1155
THREE DIAMOND Pacific Rim. Fine Dining. **Address:** 100 Centennial Way V5A 2X9

JOEY RESTAURANTS
604/564-5639
APPROVED American. Casual Dining. **Address:** 109-1899 Rosser Ave V5C 6R5

THE PEAR TREE RESTAURANT
604/299-2772
FOUR DIAMOND Regional Canadian. Fine Dining. **Address:** 4120 E Hastings St V5C 2J4

REFLECT SOCIAL DINING + LOUNGE
604/438-1200
APPROVED American. Casual Dining. **Address:** 6083 McKay Ave V5H 2W7

SWISS CHALET
604/299-1761
APPROVED Chicken. Casual Dining. **Address:** 3860 Lougheed Hwy V5C 6N4

TRATTORIA
604/424-8779
THREE DIAMOND Italian. Casual Dining. **Address:** 4501 Kingsway V5H 2A9

CACHE CREEK (B-7) pop. 1,040, elev. 450m/1,500'

HISTORIC HAT CREEK RANCH is 11 km (7 mi.) n. on Hwy. 99 at Hwy. 97 jct. The 130-hectare (320-acre) ranch, on one of the few sections of the Cariboo Waggon Road still accessible to the public, consists of more than 20 historic buildings constructed 1863-1915 when the ranch served as a roadhouse for the horse-drawn stagecoaches and freight wagons of the B.C. Express line (known as the B.X.).

Docents in period costumes conduct guided tours of the 1860s roadhouse, and visitors can explore a heritage apple orchard, a Shuswap native village, a blacksmith shop and a collection of pioneer agricultural machinery. Visitors also can enjoy stagecoach rides and try their hand at gold panning.

Hours: Daily 9-5 (stagecoach and tours 10-4:30), May-Oct. **Cost:** $15; $13 (ages 55+); $9 (ages 6-17); $40 (family, two adults and two children). **Phone:** (250) 457-9722 or (800) 782-0922.

CAMPBELL RIVER (E-10) pop. 31,186, elev. 18m/59'

An important lumber, mining and commercial fishing center, Campbell River is near a noted Vancouver Island timber stand. The Elk Falls Pulp and Paper Mill offers tours in the summer. Campbell River is headquarters of the Tyee Club, whose members must catch a salmon of 14 kilograms (30 lbs.) or more while fishing from a rowboat in the raging waters of Discovery Passage.

Provincial parks preserve the area's natural beauty, typified by waterfalls and mountainous wilderness. At Elk Falls Provincial Park the Campbell River drops 27 metres (90 ft.) into a deep canyon. Strathcona Provincial Park contains Mount Golden Hinde, at 2,200 metres (7,218 ft.) the highest mountain on Vancouver Island, and 440-metre (1,445-ft.) Della Falls, the highest waterfall in Canada. Scuba diving is popular during the winter when the waters are particularly clear. *See Recreation Areas Chart.*

The 183-metre-long (600-ft.) Campbell River Fishing Pier, 655 Island Hwy., is available for fishing, strolling or watching the cruise ships pass through the Strait of Georgia.

Campbell River Visitor Centre: 1235 Shoppers Row, Tyree Plaza, Campbell River, BC, Canada V9W 2C7. **Phone:** (250) 286-6901 or (877) 286-5705.

COMFORT INN & SUITES-CAMPBELL RIVER   250/914-5117
◇◇ THREE DIAMOND Hotel. **Address:** 1351 Shoppers Row V9W 2C9

OCEAN RESORT   250/923-4281
◇◇ APPROVED   Motel. **Address:** 4384 S Island Hwy V9H 1E8

RAMADA BY WYNDHAM CAMPBELL RIVER   250/923-4231
◇◇ APPROVED   Hotel. **Address:** 462 S Island Hwy V9W 1A5

WHERE TO EAT

BAAN THAI RESTAURANT   250/286-4850
◇◇ APPROVED   Thai. Casual Dining. **Address:** 1090B Shoppers Row V9W 2C6

THE DRIFTWOOD RESTAURANT   250/923-5505
◇◇ APPROVED   Chinese. Casual Dining. **Address:** 4329 S Island Hwy V9H 1B7

MOXIE'S CLASSIC GRILL   250/830-1500
◇◇ APPROVED   American. Casual Dining. **Address:** 1360 Island Hwy V9W 8C9

QUAY WEST KITCHEN & CATERING   250/286-9988
◇◇ APPROVED   Pacific Northwest. Casual Dining. **Address:** 921 Island Hwy V9W 2C2

RICKY'S ALL DAY GRILL   250/286-3448
◇◇ APPROVED   American. Casual Dining. **Address:** 811 13th Ave V9W 4G9

SOCAL RESTAURANT AND LOUNGE   250/923-7611
◇◇ APPROVED   Southern California. Casual Dining. **Address:** 2231 S Island Hwy V9W 1C4

CASTLEGAR (C-10) pop. 7,816, elev. 494m/1,620'

At the junction of hwys. 3 and 3A, Castlegar is considered the crossroads of the Kootenays. Just north is the 51-metre-high (167-ft.) Hugh Keenleyside Dam. The upper and lower Arrow Lakes, created by the dam, offer popular summer recreation areas including Arrow Lakes Provincial Park (Shelter Bay) and Syringa Provincial Park *(see Recreation Areas Chart)*.

Castlegar Chamber of Commerce: 1995 Sixth Ave., Castlegar, BC, Canada V1N 4B7. **Phone:** (250) 365-6313.

SUPER 8 BY WYNDHAM-CASTLEGAR   250/365-2700
◇◇ APPROVED   Hotel. **Address:** 651 18th St V1N 2N1

WHERE TO EAT

BLACK ROOSTER CLASSIC BAR & GRILL   250/365-7779
◇◇ APPROVED   American. Casual Dining. **Address:** 651 18th St V1N 2N1

CHASE pop. 2,495

CHASE COUNTRY INN MOTEL   250/679-3333
◇◇ APPROVED   Motel. **Address:** 576 Coburn St V0E 1M0

QUAAOUT LODGE & SPA, TALKING ROCK GOLF
                                      250/679-3090
◇◇ THREE DIAMOND Resort Hotel. **Address:** 1663 Little Shuswap Lake Rd V0E 1M0

WHERE TO EAT

JACK SAM'S RESTAURANT & LOUNGE   250/679-3090
◇◇ APPROVED   Regional Canadian. Casual Dining. **Address:** 1663 Little Shuswap Lake Rd V0E 1M2

CHEMAINUS (H-10) pop. 3,035, elev. 6m/20'
• Restaurants p. 178

A lumber and manufacturing town, Chemainus added tourism to its economy with the creation of murals. More than 40 professional paintings on the walls of buildings portray the history of the Chemainus Valley. Subjects range from First Nations people to dramatic depictions of the logging industry.

Begun by local artists, the series of murals has attracted artists from around the world. Recent additions include interpretations of images created by noted Canadian artist Emily Carr, including a trompe l'oeil mural on the wall of the Chemainus Theatre. Walking tour maps can be bought at the kiosk in the central parking area. Prearranged guided tours and horse-drawn carriage tours also are available for a fee; phone (250) 246-5055 or (250) 246-0063.

The Chemainus Theatre offers dramas, comedies and musical productions; phone (250) 246-9820 or (800) 565-7738.

Chemainus Visitor Centre: 102-9799 Waterwheel Crescent, P.O. Box 575, Chemainus, BC, Canada V0R 1K0. **Phone:** (250) 246-3944.

BEST WESTERN PLUS CHEMAINUS INN   250/246-4181
◇◇ THREE DIAMOND
Hotel

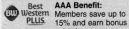
AAA Benefit: Members save up to 15% and earn bonus points!

Address: 9573 Chemainus Rd V0R 1K5 **Location:** Trans-Canada Hwy 1 exit Henry Rd, 0.9 mi (1.4 km) e. **Facility:** 75 units, some two bedrooms and efficiencies. 4 stories, interior corridors. **Terms:** check-in 4 pm. **Amenities:** safes. **Pool:** heated indoor. **Activities:** hot tub, exercise room, massage. **Guest Services:** coin laundry. **Featured Amenity:** full hot breakfast.

WHERE TO EAT

ODIKA CAFE 250/324-3303
APPROVED International. Casual Dining. **Address:** 2976 Mill St V0R 1K0

UTOPIA BAKERY CAFE 250/246-9992
APPROVED Breads/Pastries. Quick Serve. **Address:** A-9780 Willow St V0R 1K0

CHILLIWACK (H-12) pop. 77,936, elev. 10m/33'

In the heart of the upper Fraser River Valley, Chilliwack is the center of a prosperous farming and dairy region. The surrounding lakes, rivers, mountains and nearby provincial parks offer such varied recreation as skiing, hiking, fishing, rock hunting and white-water rafting. Scenic views and picnic facilities are available at Chilliwack Lake Provincial Park, 84 kilometres (54 mi.) southeast off Hwy. 1 *(see Recreation Areas Chart)*, and Cultus Lake Provincial Park, 11 kilometres (7 mi.) southwest off Hwy. 1 *(see Recreation Areas Chart)*.

Tourism Chilliwack Visitor Information Centre: 44150 Luckakuck Way, Chilliwack, BC, Canada V2R 4A7. **Phone:** (604) 858-8121 or (800) 567-9535.

GREAT BLUE HERON NATURE RESERVE is at 5200 Sumas Prairie Rd. This 130-hectare (321-acre) site includes an interpretive center, an observation tower, fish-spawning channels and a self-guiding interpretive walking trail. More than 90 herons build nests here; painted turtles, tailed frogs, beavers, bald eagles and a variety of other birds also dwell at the reserve.

Time: Allow 1 hour minimum. **Hours:** Daily 8-dusk. Interpretive center closed Christmas. **Cost:** Donations. **Phone:** (604) 823-6603.

THE COAST CHILLIWACK HOTEL BY APA 604/792-5552
THREE DIAMOND Hotel. **Address:** 45920 First Ave V2P 7K1

SURESTAY HOTEL BY BEST WESTERN CHILLIWACK 604/795-3828
APPROVED Hotel. **Address:** 43971 Industrial Way V2R 3A4

WHERE TO EAT

BRAVO RESTAURANT & LOUNGE 604/792-7721
THREE DIAMOND Regional Canadian. Fine Dining. **Address:** 46224 Yale Rd V2P 2P5

EARLS KITCHEN + BAR 604/858-3360
APPROVED American. Casual Dining. **Address:** 45585 Luckakuck Way V2R 1A1

MR MIKES STEAKHOUSECASUAL 604/824-0957
APPROVED American. Casual Dining. **Address:** 45200 Luckakuck Way V2R 3C7

RICKY'S ALL DAY GRILL 604/858-5663
APPROVED American. Casual Dining. **Address:** 45389 Luckakuck Way V2R 3C7

SHANDHAR HUT INDIAN CUISINE 604/793-0188
APPROVED Indian. Casual Dining. **Address:** 8835 Young Rd V2P 4P6

VITA BELLA ITALIAN BISTRO 604/846-5001
THREE DIAMOND Italian. Casual Dining. **Address:** 45355 Luckakuck Way V2R 3C7

CHRISTINA LAKE pop. 1,168

NEW HORIZON MOTEL 250/447-9312
APPROVED Motel. **Address:** 2037 Hunter Frontage Rd (Hwy 3) V0H 1E2

CLEARWATER (A-8) pop. 2,331

Clearwater gets its name from the clear waters of the nearby Clearwater River. Opportunities for riding, hiking, canoeing, skiing and fishing abound in the surrounding North Thompson Valley.

Wells Gray Provincial Park, north off Hwy. 5, offers a variety of scenery, particularly with regard to water. Scattered throughout its boundaries are five large lakes, two river systems, many streams and waterways and a multitude of waterfalls. Helmcken Falls, which drops 141 metres (465 ft.), is said to be the fourth highest in Canada. At Bailey's Chute Loop in late summer, visitors can view salmon jumping upstream to spawn. Extinct volcanoes and lava beds recall the region's fiery past. *See Recreation Areas Chart.*

Clearwater & District Chamber of Commerce: 416 Eden Rd., Clearwater, BC, Canada V0E 1N1. **Phone:** (250) 674-3530.

CLINTON (A-7) pop. 636, elev. 274m/898'

During the gold rush of the late 1850s and early 1860s Clinton was the junction of several wagon roads leading to northern goldfields. In 1863 Queen Victoria changed the town's name from Junction to Clinton. Retaining much of its frontier look, Clinton is a supply center for surrounding resorts, fishing camps and ranches. Summer activities include boating, fishing and camping at area lakes, which also attract various wildlife.

The Village of Clinton: 1423 Cariboo Hwy., P.O. Box 309, Clinton, BC, Canada V0K 1K0. **Phone:** (250) 459-2261.

COOMBS (G-10) pop. 1,547

Coombs retains the atmosphere of a quaint village settled around 1910. The Coombs General Store, which has operated continuously since the settlement days, and the Old Country Market, which is unusual for the goats that are kept on the roof in summer, are two landmarks.

The town is on Vancouver Island, midway between Little Qualicum Falls Provincial Park *(see Recreation Areas Chart)* and Englishman River Falls Provincial Park *(see Recreation Areas Chart)*, where there are many recreational opportunities.

COQUITLAM (H-11) pop. 126,456, elev. 137m/449'

- Hotels & Restaurants map & index p. 276
- Part of Vancouver area — see map p. 249

Named for a type of landlocked salmon, Coquitlam borders Pitt Lake and encompasses Burke Mountain. Recreational opportunities, including swimming, canoeing, hiking and fishing, are available throughout the area.

Nearby parks and lakes include Mundy Park, 4 kilometres (2.5 mi.) south off Mariner Way; Belcarra Park, 15 kilometres (9 mi.) northwest off Ioco and Bedwell Bay roads; Buntzen Lake, 12 kilometres (7 mi.) northwest off East and Sunnyside roads; Minnekhada Regional Park, 13 kilometres (8 mi.) northeast off Victoria Drive and Quarry Road; Town Centre Park and Lafarge Lake, on Pinetree Way just north of Lougheed Highway; and Burke Mountain, 11 kilometres (7 mi.) northeast off Coast Meridian and Harper roads.

Coquitlam Tourist/Visitor Info Booth: 2773 Barnett Hwy., Unit 205, Coquitlam, BC, Canada V3B 1C2. **Phone:** (604) 464-2716.

EXECUTIVE PLAZA HOTEL & CONFERENCE CENTRE
604/936-9399 **20**
▼▼ THREE DIAMOND Hotel. **Address:** 405 North Rd V3K 3V9

SURESTAY PLUS HOTEL BY BEST WESTERN COQUITLAM
604/525-7777 **21**
▼▼ APPROVED Hotel. **Address:** 725 Brunette Ave V3K 6A6

WHERE TO EAT

CACTUS CLUB CAFE   604/777-0440 **47**
▼▼ THREE DIAMOND New American. Casual Dining. **Address:** 110-101 Schoolhouse St V3K 4X8

JOEY RESTAURANTS   604/939-3077
▼▼ APPROVED American. Casual Dining. **Address:** 550 Lougheed Hwy V3K 353

JOHN B NEIGHBORHOOD PUB   604/931-5115 **46**
▼▼ APPROVED International. Casual Dining. **Address:** 1000 Austin Ave V3K 3P1

RICKY'S ALL DAY GRILL   604/468-8000
▼▼ APPROVED American. Casual Dining. **Address:** 2929 Barnet Hwy, Unit 2660 V3B 5R5

SUSHI CALIFORNIA   250/931-8284 **45**
▼▼ APPROVED Sushi. Casual Dining. **Address:** 501 North Rd V3J 1N7

COURTENAY (F-10) pop. 24,099, elev. 25m/82'

- Restaurants p. 180

Courtenay was established in the late 1860s when settlers began a major farming community near the Comox Valley. Known for a garden called the Mile of Flowers, the town is now a year-round recreation area with good skiing and sailing nearby.

The 1989 Puntledge River discovery of the fossilized intact skull of a 14-metre-long (46-ft.) elasmosaur, a long-necked Cretaceous marine reptile 80 million years old, brought Courtenay to the attention of the world of paleontology.

Courtenay is the terminus of the Powell River Ferry, which makes round-trip excursions to the mainland.

Vancouver Island Visitor Centre: 101-3607 Small Rd., Cumberland, BC, Canada V9N 3Z8. **Phone:** (250) 400-2882 or (855) 400-2882.

COURTENAY AND DISTRICT MUSEUM AND PALEONTOLOGY CENTRE is at 207 Fourth St., downtown at jct. Fourth St. and Cliffe Ave. Permanent exhibits, enhanced by audiovisuals, focus on native history, exploration, agriculture, logging and pioneer life. A reconstruction of an elasmosaur is displayed along with locally excavated fossil evidence from the age of dinosaurs. The museum has archival material pertaining to the nearby Comox Valley. Guided fossil discovery tours are available.

Time: Allow 1 hour minimum. **Hours:** Mon.-Sat. 10-5, Sun. noon-4, Victoria Day-Labour Day; Tues.-Sat. 10-5, rest of year. Closed Jan. 1, Easter, Victoria Day, Civic Day, Labour Day, Thanksgiving, Christmas Eve, Christmas and day after Christmas. **Cost:** Donations. **Phone:** (250) 334-0686.

KITTY COLEMAN WOODLAND GARDENS is at 6183 Whittaker Rd. The gardens, created by Bryan Zimmerman to share the beauty of the area with others, showcase rhododendrons, with more than 3,000 varieties and sizes planted throughout the landscape. The peak viewing season is mid-April through fall. The gardens host the Kitty Coleman Arts and Bloom Festival over the Victoria Day weekend in mid-May.

Ponds, walking paths lined with granite rocks, a creek, a gazebo, benches and driftwood sculptures add to the beauty of the site. **Hours:** Daily 9-dusk. **Cost:** $7.62; $2.86 (ages 5-12). Cash only. **Phone:** (250) 338-6901. GT ⊞

ANCO INN   250/334-2451
▼▼ APPROVED Motel. **Address:** 1885 Cliffe Ave V9N 2K9

BAYVIEW HOTEL   778/225-0010
▼▼ THREE DIAMOND Hotel. **Address:** 2200 Cliffe Ave V9N 2L4

BEST WESTERN THE WESTERLY HOTEL   250/338-7741
▼▼ THREE DIAMOND
Hotel

BW Best Western. **AAA Benefit:** Members save up to 15% and earn bonus points!

Address: 1590 Cliffe Ave V9N 2K4 **Location:** Corner of Cliffe Ave and Island Hwy 19A N. **Facility:** 66 units. 3-4 stories (no elevator), interior corridors. **Pool:** heated indoor. **Activities:** sauna, hot tub, exercise room. **Guest Services:** valet and coin laundry.

SAVE ECO ⊞ ❙❙ ⬆ ▼
CALL ♿ ⬇ ⬆ BIZ HS 📶
✕ 🗎 🖥 🖨 ▣ / SOME UNITS ⬆

CROWN ISLE RESORT & GOLF COMMUNITY   250/703-5050
THREE DIAMOND Resort Hotel. **Address:** 399 Clubhouse Dr V9N 9G3

KINGFISHER OCEANSIDE RESORT & SPA   250/338-1323
THREE DIAMOND Hotel. **Address:** 4330 S Island Hwy V9N 9R9

TRAVELODGE COURTENAY   250/334-4491
APPROVED Motel. **Address:** 2605 Cliffe Ave V9N 2L8

WHERE TO EAT

ATLAS CAFE   250/338-9838
APPROVED International. Casual Dining. **Address:** 250 6th St V9N 1M1

LOCALS RESTAURANT   250/338-6493
THREE DIAMOND Canadian. Fine Dining. **Address:** 1760 Riverside Ln V9N 8C7

OCEAN 7 RESTAURANT   250/338-1323
THREE DIAMOND Pacific Northwest. Casual Dining. **Address:** 4330 S Island Hwy V9N 9R9

RICKY'S ALL DAY GRILL   250/334-9638
APPROVED American. Casual Dining. **Address:** 795 Ryan Rd V9N 3R6

WHITE WHALE PUBLIC HOUSE   250/338-1468
APPROVED American. Casual Dining. **Address:** 975 Comox Rd V9N 3P7

CRANBROOK (C-11) pop. 19,319, elev. 940m/3,083'

Cranbrook is the key city of the eastern Kootenays *(see Kootenay National Park p. 199)* and the center of many circle tours. Nearby lakes, rivers and mountains provide such recreational opportunities as swimming, fishing, hiking, hunting and skiing. A scenic portion of Hwy. 93 runs north from Cranbrook through Kootenay National Park into Banff National Park to the junction with Hwy. 16 in Jasper National Park. (A valid park pass is required to travel on the Icefields Parkway section of Hwy. 93.)

Cranbrook Chamber of Commerce & Visitor Centre: 2279 Cranbrook St. N. (Hwy. 3/95), P.O. Box 84, Cranbrook, BC, Canada V1C 4H6. **Phone:** (250) 426-5914 or (800) 222-6174.

Self-guiding tours: Information about driving and walking tours is available from the chamber of commerce.

CRANBROOK HISTORY CENTRE is at 57 Van Horne St. S. (Hwy. 3/95). The museum restores and preserves vintage Canadian Pacific Railway passenger train sets, including cars from the luxury Trans-Canada Limited. The lifestyle of rail travel is reflected in trains from 1880 to 1955, including cars of state, business and royalty. On display are a model railway, the Cranbrook Centennial Quilt, the 1864 Broadwood grand piano display room and the train restoration display. Also inside is the Cranbrook Museum, which features exhibits about life in the 1800s and First Nations history as well as 500-million-year-old trilobites.

On the grounds is the original three-story café from the Canadian Pacific Railway's Royal Alexandra Hotel of Winnipeg. Several guided tours, ranging from 15 to 35 minutes in length, are available and can be taken in various combinations. The 90-minute Grand Tour includes 17 railcars.

Time: Allow 1 hour, 30 minutes minimum. **Hours:** Museum Tues.-Sat. 10-5 (also Sun.-Mon. 10-5, mid-May through Aug. 31). Closed Canadian and British Columbia statutory holidays. **Cost:** Museum exhibits by donation. Grand Tour $15.75; $14.50 (ages 65+); $10.50 (students with ID); $4.50 (ages 6-12). **Phone:** (250) 489-3918 to verify tour schedule and rates. **GT**

BEST WESTERN CRANBROOK HOTEL   250/417-4002
THREE DIAMOND
Hotel

Best Western. **AAA Benefit:** Members save up to 15% and earn bonus points!

Address: 1019 Cranbrook St N V1C 3S4 **Location:** Hwy 3 and 95; center. **Facility:** 94 units, some two bedrooms and efficiencies. 4 stories, interior corridors. **Parking:** winter plug-ins. **Pool:** heated indoor. **Activities:** game room, exercise room. **Guest Services:** valet and coin laundry.

DAYS INN BY WYNDHAM CRANBROOK   250/426-6683
APPROVED
Hotel

Address: 600 Cranbrook St N V1C 3R7 **Location:** Corner of 6th St and Cranbrook St N. **Facility:** 89 units, some kitchens. 4 stories, interior corridors. **Parking:** winter plug-ins. **Terms:** check-in 4 pm. **Pool:** heated outdoor. **Activities:** exercise room. **Guest Services:** valet and coin laundry. **Featured Amenity:** full hot breakfast.

PRESTIGE ROCKY MOUNTAIN RESORT & CONVENTION CENTRE   250/417-0444
THREE DIAMOND Hotel. **Address:** 209 Van Horne St S V1C 6R9

ST. EUGENE GOLF RESORT & CASINO   250/420-2000
THREE DIAMOND
Hotel

Address: 7731 Mission Rd V1C 7E5 **Location:** Hwy 3 exit Kimberley/Airport (Hwy 95A) to Mission Rd, 2.8 mi (4.5 km) n. **Facility:** This vine-covered hotel has lovely rooms, but those in the heritage wing are more upscale and feature amenities like robes and wine glasses. The outdoor pool and hot tubs are open year-round. 125 units. 3 stories, interior corridors. **Terms:** check-in 4 pm. **Amenities:** safes. **Dining:** 2 restaurants. **Pool:** heated outdoor. **Activities:** sauna, hot tub, steamroom, regulation golf, trails, exercise room, spa. **Guest Services:** valet laundry.

WHERE TO EAT

ALLEGRA MEDITERRANEAN CUISINE   250/426-8812
THREE DIAMOND Mediterranean. Casual Dining. **Address:** 1225B Cranbrook St N V1C 3S6

MR MIKES STEAKHOUSECASUAL   250/417-2542
APPROVED American. Casual Dining. **Address:** 1028 Cranbrook St N V1C 3S3

CRESTON (D-11) pop. 5,306, elev. 636m/2,086'

The unusual Kutenai canoe, which has a bow and stern that both meet the waterline, was used by First Nations people in the area around Creston in pre-pioneer days. The only other place such a canoe has been found is the Amur River region in southeastern Russia. The canoe's use in this area supports the theory that Asians migrated to North America over a frozen Bering Strait.

In the 1930s about 8,100 hectares (20,000 acres) of land were reclaimed from the Kootenay Delta for agriculture. The Creston Valley floor is now quilted with a variety of seed and root crops, grains and fruit orchards. Other Creston industries include forestry, dairying and brewing.

The Columbia Brewing Co., 1220 Erickson St., offers narrated tours of its facilities Mon.-Fri., mid-May to mid-October, Sat.-Sun., July-Aug. Closed toe shoes are mandatory. Complimentary beer is available at the end of the tour; phone (250) 428-1238. Free guided tours of a candlemaking factory are offered year-round by appointment only at Kootenay Candles, 1511 Northwest Blvd.; phone (250) 428-9785 or (866) 572-9785.

Hikers can trek along the old Dewdney Trail, which carried gold seekers from Hope to the Wild Horse goldfields in the 1860s.

Creston Visitor Centre: 121 Northwest Blvd., Creston, BC, Canada V0B 1G0. **Phone:** (250) 428-4342.

RAMADA BY WYNDHAM CRESTON   250/254-1111
THREE DIAMOND Hotel. **Address:** 1 1809 Hwy 3A V0B 1G8

WHERE TO EAT

A BREAK IN TIME CAFFE   250/428-5619
APPROVED International. Casual Dining. **Address:** 1417 Canyon St V0B 1G0

CHATKA FAMILY RESTAURANT   250/428-7200
APPROVED Polish. Casual Dining. **Address:** 2808 Hwy 3 V0B 1G1

REAL FOOD CAFE   250/428-8882
APPROVED International. Casual Dining. **Address:** 223 10th Ave N V0B 1G4

RICKY'S ALL DAY GRILL   205/428-8826
APPROVED American. Casual Dining. **Address:** 1809 Northwest Blvd V0B 1G8

CUMBERLAND (F-10) pop. 3,398

Cumberland's origins are rooted in the rigors of coal mining. From 1888 until the last of its nine mines closed in 1966, the village produced some 25 million tons of high-grade coal. The lucrative enterprise solidified Cumberland's economy and contributed to its multi-ethnic mix, drawing miners from locations as diverse as England, Scotland, Italy, China and Japan. The village and many of its streets were named for the mining region in England known as Cumbria.

Nestled in the foothills of the Beaufort Mountains and a stone's throw from Comox Lake, Cumberland offers ample snow skiing, hiking, fishing and boating opportunities.

Vancouver Island Visitor Centre: 101-3607 Small Rd., Cumberland, BC, Canada V9N 3Z8. **Phone:** (250) 400-2882 or (855) 400-2882.

DAWSON CREEK (D-6) pop. 11,583, elev. 655m/2,148'

Named for George Mercer Dawson of the Geological Survey of Canada, Dawson Creek was settled in 1912. Growth accelerated during World War II, as this was the southern terminus of the Alaska Highway. The highway was then called the Alcan Military Highway, and it served as a supply road to bases in Alaska. The Mile Zero Cairn, which marks the start of the Alaska Highway, and the Zero Milepost are in the center of town. Alpine skiing, camping, hiking and fishing are popular recreational activities.

Dawson Creek Visitor's Centre: 900 Alaska Ave., Dawson Creek, BC, Canada V1G 4T6. **Phone:** (250) 782-9595 or (866) 645-3022.

DAYS INN BY WYNDHAM DAWSON CREEK
          250/782-8887

APPROVED **Hotel** **Address:** 640 122nd Ave V1G 0A4 **Location:** Hwy 2, just n on 7th St; southeast end of town. Next to Walmart. **Facility:** 85 units. 4 stories, interior corridors. **Parking:** winter plug-ins. **Activities:** exercise room. **Guest Services:** valet and coin laundry. **Featured Amenity: full hot breakfast.**

SUPER 8 BY WYNDHAM DAWSON CREEK   250/782-8899
APPROVED Hotel. **Address:** 1440 Alaska Ave V1G 1Z5

WHERE TO EAT

BAKED CAFE   250/784-0015
APPROVED Coffee/Tea Sandwiches. Quick Serve. **Address:** 937 103rd Ave V1G 2G4

BROWNS SOCIAL HOUSE   250/782-2400
APPROVED International. Gastropub. **Address:** 1100 Alaska Ave, Unit 104 V1G 4V8

MR MIKES STEAKHOUSECASUAL 250/782-1577
APPROVED American. Casual Dining. **Address:** 1501 Alaska Ave V1G 1Z8

NEW TOKYO SUSHI 250/782-4900
APPROVED Japanese. Casual Dining. **Address:** 1325 Alaska Ave V1G 1Z4

SOLA'S BAR & GRILL 250/782-8890
APPROVED American. Casual Dining. **Address:** 1440 Alaska Ave V1G 1Z5

WHITE SPOT 250/782-5442
APPROVED American. Casual Dining. **Address:** 11300 8th St V1G 3R5

DELTA (H-11) pop. 99,863, elev. 10m/33'
- **Hotels & Restaurants map & index p. 276**
- **Part of Vancouver area — see map p. 249**

Delta, composed of the three distinct communities of Ladner, Tsawwassen and North Delta, is an amalgam of commerce, fisheries, industry, farmland, beaches and suburban residences. The warm-water beaches on Boundary Bay and Tsawwassen are popular spots for swimming and sunbathing. Other recreational opportunities in the area include fishing for salmon and boating on the Fraser River and the Strait of Georgia.

Delta Visitor Centre: 6201 60th Ave., Delta, BC, Canada V4K 4E2. **Phone:** (604) 946-4232.

COAST TSAWWASSEN INN 604/943-8221 **48**
APPROVED Hotel. **Address:** 1665 56th St V4L 2B2

WHERE TO EAT

CACTUS CLUB CAFE 604/591-1707 **72**
THREE DIAMOND New American. Casual Dining. **Address:** 7907 120th St V4C 6P6

MARIO'S KITCHEN 604/943-4442 **73**
APPROVED International. Casual Dining. **Address:** 1105 56th St V4L 2A2

RICKY'S ALL DAY GRILL 604/599-1784
APPROVED American. Casual Dining. **Address:** 7135 120th St V4E 2A9

DUNCAN (H-10) pop. 4,932, elev. 15m/49'

Founded in 1887 as Alderlea, Duncan was renamed in 1912 in honor of farmer William Duncan, who gave his land for the original townsite. Settlers were attracted by the promise of copper and coal on nearby Mount Sicker, where abandoned mines and original homesteads still can be seen. The growth of the logging and farming industries brought increasing numbers to Duncan and the Cowichan Valley.

The area around Duncan is known for the hand-spun woolen sweaters produced by the Cowichan people. West on Hwy. 18 is the Cowichan Valley Demonstration Forest with scenic viewpoints and signs describing forest management practices and ecology. More than 80 totem poles dot the town of Duncan.

Duncan-Cowichan Chamber of Commerce: 381 Trans-Canada Hwy., Duncan, BC, Canada V9L 3R5. **Phone:** (250) 746-4636 or (888) 303-3337.

Shopping: Whippletree Junction, a group of shops and boutiques with late 1800s storefronts, is 5 kilometres (3 mi.) south on the Trans-Canada Highway. A Sunday market with local artisans and food producers is open April through October.

PACIFIC NORTHWEST RAPTOR VISITOR CENTRE is 5 km (3 mi.) n. on Trans-Canada Hwy. then 4 km (2 mi.) w. on 1877 Herd Rd. Birds of prey, some captive bred and others non-releasable, can be seen up close at this facility run by The Raptors, a wildlife conservation organization. Those born in captivity are allowed to fly outside their pens during the day, returning home at night. Birds such as hawks, eagles, owls and falcons can be seen in daily flying demonstrations, hands-on encounters and educational talks. Additional fees are charged for the hawk walk, 1-hour encounter and raptor experience.

Note: The center will be closed for renovations Nov. 2017-Dec. 2017 and is scheduled to reopen Mar. 2018. **Time:** Allow 1 hour, 30 minutes minimum. **Hours:** Center open daily 10:30-5, mid-May to early Sept.; daily noon-3, Mar. 1 to mid-May and early Sept. through Oct. 31; Thurs.-Sun. noon-3, Nov.-Dec. Demonstrations are given daily at 11:30 and 1:30, Victoria Day weekend-Labour Day; daily at 1:30, early Mar.-day before Victoria Day weekend and day after Labour Day-Sept. 30. Phone ahead to confirm schedule. **Cost:** $15.24; $13.33 (ages 13-17 and 65+); $7.62 (ages 3-12); $41.90 (family, two adults and two children); $47.62 (family, two adults and three children). **Phone:** (250) 746-0372.

BEST WESTERN COWICHAN VALLEY INN
 250/748-2722

THREE DIAMOND Hotel

Best Western. **AAA Benefit:** Members save up to 15% and earn bonus points!

Address: 6474 Trans-Canada Hwy V9L 6C6 **Location:** 1.8 mi (3 km) n. **Facility:** 64 units. 2 stories, interior corridors. **Terms:** check-in 4 pm. **Pool:** heated outdoor. **Activities:** exercise room. **Guest Services:** valet laundry.

RAMADA DUNCAN COWICHAN VALLEY 250/748-4311
APPROVED Hotel. **Address:** 140 Trans Canada Hwy V9L 3E8

WHERE TO EAT

DOGHOUSE A FAMILY RESTAURANT 250/746-4614
APPROVED American. Casual Dining. **Address:** 271 Trans-Canada Hwy V9L 3R1

ERRINGTON (G-10) pop. 2,678

NORTH ISLAND WILDLIFE RECOVERY ASSOCIATION is at 1240 Leffler Rd. Bald eagles, owls, hawks, swans and black bears are among the animals that can be viewed at this 3-hectare (8-acre) rehabilitation facility. An eagle flight cage houses eagles waiting to be released into the wild. A nature museum, wildlife learning center and public viewing area are on the grounds. Special Event Days are held in July and August.

Time: Allow 30 minutes minimum. **Hours:** Daily 9-5, mid-Mar. through Dec. 19. Raptor presentation Mon, Wed. and Fri. at 1:30, July-Aug. **Cost:** $9.50; $4.75 (ages 3-12). **Phone:** (250) 248-8534.

FAIRMONT HOT SPRINGS (B-11) pop. 476, elev. 810m/2,657'

At the north end of Columbia Lake, Fairmont Hot Springs were discovered about 1840. This popular resort area offers four hot mineral springs with temperatures averaging 35 to 45 C (95 to 113 F). Water sports and alpine and cross-country skiing also are available. *See Recreation Areas Chart.*

FAIRMONT HOT SPRINGS RESORT   250/345-6070

APPROVED
Resort Hotel

Address: 5225 Fairmont Resort Rd V0B 1L1 **Location:** 1 mi (1.6 km) e off Hwy 93 and 95. **Facility:** All the elements are in place for a relaxing stay with the natural hot springs and the appealing rooms equipped with bathrobes and wine glasses. Most bathrooms have an older but pleasant décor. 151 units, some two bedrooms, efficiencies, cabins and cottages. 3 stories (no elevator), interior corridors. **Parking:** winter plug-ins. **Terms:** check-in 4 pm. **Dining:** 3 restaurants. **Pool:** heated outdoor. **Activities:** sauna, hot tub, steamroom, self-propelled boats, fishing, regulation golf, par 3 golf, miniature golf, tennis, downhill & cross country skiing, snowboarding, sledding, ice skating, recreation programs in summer, bicycles, playground, game room, lawn sports, picnic facilities, trails, exercise room, spa. **Guest Services:** coin laundry. **Featured Amenity:** full hot breakfast.

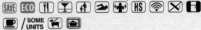

WHERE TO EAT

FROM SCRATCH-A MOUNTAIN KITCHEN   250/345-0008
APPROVED American. Casual Dining. **Address:** 5019 Fairmont Resort Rd, #8 V0B 1L1

FERNIE (C-12) pop. 4,448

At the foot of Trinity Mountain in the British Columbia Rockies, Fernie is a year-round recreation center. The many surrounding lakes and mountains provide opportunities for boating, fishing, hiking, camping and skiing. Mount Fernie Provincial Park is 4.8 kilometres (3 mi.) east *(see Recreation Areas Chart).* Prentice and Rotary parks are downtown.

Fernie Chamber of Commerce: 102 Commerce Rd. (Hwy. 3), Fernie, BC, Canada V0B 1M5. **Phone:** (250) 423-6868.

BEST WESTERN PLUS FERNIE MOUNTAIN LODGE
250/423-5500

THREE DIAMOND
Hotel

Best Western PLUS

AAA Benefit: Members save up to 15% and earn bonus points!

Address: 1622 7th Ave V0B 1M0 **Location:** Jct Hwy 3 and 7th Ave; east end of town. **Facility:** 95 units, some efficiencies. 3 stories, interior corridors. **Parking:** winter plug-ins. **Pool:** heated indoor. **Activities:** hot tub, exercise room, massage. **Guest Services:** coin laundry, area transportation. **Featured Amenity:** full hot breakfast.

CORNERSTONE LODGE   250/423-9211
APPROVED Condominium. **Address:** 5339 Ski Hill Rd V0B 1M6

LIZARD CREEK LODGE AND CONDOMINIUMS AT FERNIE ALPINE RESORT   250/423-2057
THREE DIAMOND Condominium. **Address:** 5346 Highline Dr V0B 1M6

PARK PLACE LODGE   250/423-6871
THREE DIAMOND Hotel. **Address:** 742 Hwy 3 V0B 1M0

WHERE TO EAT

THE BLUE TOQUE DINER   250/423-4637
APPROVED Breakfast. Casual Dining. **Address:** 601 1st Ave V0B 1M0

FERNIE CATTLE CO.   250/423-7498
APPROVED Steak. Casual Dining. **Address:** 561 Hwy 3 V0B 1M0

THE LOAF   250/423-7702
APPROVED American. Casual Dining. **Address:** 641 2nd Ave V0B 1M0

LUNCH BOX FRESH MARKET & SMOOTHIE BAR   250/423-4500
APPROVED American. Quick Serve. **Address:** 561A 2nd Ave V0B 1M0

MUGSHOTS CAFE   250/423-8018
APPROVED Coffee/Tea. Quick Serve. **Address:** 592 3rd Ave V0B 1M0

NEVADOS   250/423-5566
APPROVED New Latin American Small Plates. Casual Dining. **Address:** 531 2nd Ave V0B 1M0

YAMAGOYA RESTAURANT   250/430-0090
APPROVED Japanese Fusion. Casual Dining. **Address:** 741 7th Ave V0B 1M6

FORT LANGLEY NATIONAL HISTORIC SITE (H-11)
• Part of Vancouver area — see map p. 249

Fort Langley National Historic Site is 6.5 kilometres (4 mi.) north of Langley off Hwy. 1 at 23433 Mavis Ave. On the bank of the Fraser River, the 19th-century Hudson's Bay Company trading post was an important supply link in the company's network of fur trading forts west of the Rockies. British

Columbia was proclaimed a colony at the site in 1858.

The site preserves an original 1840 storehouse and reconstructed wooden buildings, including a cooperage and blacksmith's shop and a log palisade. Interpreters in period costumes demonstrate fur-trading activities daily. A visitor center displays contemporary exhibits. Special events are presented throughout the year.

Picnicking is permitted. Allow 1 hour minimum. Daily 10-5. Closed Jan. 1, Christmas and day after Christmas. Admission $7.43; $6.24 (ages 65+); $3.71 (ages 6-16); $18.67 (family, two adults and five children). Prices may vary; phone (604) 513-4777. An annual pass, valid at most Canadian national parks, marine areas and historic sites, is available.

FORT NELSON (B-5) pop. 3,902, elev. 405m/1,350'

Originally a fur-trading post, Fort Nelson thrived with the building of the Alaska Highway during World War II. Nearby mountains, lakes, parks, forests and diverse wildlife populations make Fort Nelson a destination for adventurous tourists, anglers and hunters.

Fort Nelson Visitor Centre: 5500 Alaska Hwy., Fort Nelson, BC, Canada V0C 1R0. **Phone:** (250) 774-6400.

LAKEVIEW INN & SUITES FORT NELSON   250/233-5001
▼ APPROVED   Hotel. **Address:** 4507 50th Ave S V0C 1R0

WOODLANDS INN & SUITES   250/774-6669
▼ APPROVED   Hotel. **Address:** 3995 50th Ave S V0C 1R0

WHERE TO EAT

THE ONE   250/774-6669
▼ APPROVED   American. Casual Dining. **Address:** 3995 50th Ave S V0C 1R0

THE PUB   250/774-3929
▼ APPROVED   American. Casual Dining. **Address:** 4204 50th Ave N V0C 1R0

FORT RODD HILL AND FISGARD LIGHTHOUSE NATIONAL HISTORIC SITES (I-9)
• Part of Victoria area — see map p. 299

Fourteen kilometres (9 mi.) west of Victoria via Hwy. 1A, Fort Rodd Hill was a coastal artillery fort 1895-1956. Of interest are the loophole walls, underground magazines, artillery stores, command posts, barracks and gun and searchlight emplacements. Audio and video presentations, along with period rooms, depict life at the fort. The 1860 Fisgard Lighthouse, restored to its 1873 appearance, was the first built on this part of the coast. Still operational, the lighthouse has two floors of historical exhibits. A nature trail follows the paths formerly used by soldiers. Historical exhibits also are featured. Picnic facilities are available. Pets are not allowed on the grounds.

Allow 1 hour, 30 minutes minimum. Grounds daily 10-5:30, Mar. 1 to mid-Oct.; 10-4:30, rest of year. Exhibits daily 10-5, mid-May to mid-Oct.; Wed.-Sun. 10-5, Mar. 1 to mid-May; Sat.-Sun. 10-4, rest of year. Closed Jan. 1 and Dec. 25-26. Admission $3.90; $3.40 (ages 65+); $1.81 (ages 6-16); $9.80 (family, two adults and five children). An annual pass, valid at most Canadian national parks, marine areas and historic sites, is available. Phone (250) 478-5849.

FORT ST. JAMES (E-4) pop. 1,691, elev. 680m/2,230'

Established in 1806 by Simon Fraser and John Stuart, the fur-trading post of Fort St. James became the capital of New Caledonia in 1821. Furs from outlying New Caledonia posts were brought overland to Fort St. James by dog sled and then shipped south during the spring thaw to the coast by canoe and horse.

During this time George Simpson, governor of the Hudson's Bay Co.'s vast empire, visited the fort. Determined to impress the Carrier First Nation, Simpson organized a flamboyant procession complete with flute, bugle and bagpipe players in Highland dress, accompanied by a dog with a music box around its neck. Thereafter, the awe-struck population reverently referred to Simpson as the "great chief whose dog sings."

A Roman Catholic mission was founded at the fort in 1843. Services continue to be held in Our Lady of Good Hope Church, which was built in 1873 and is one of the oldest churches in British Columbia.

Mining activity supplemented the capital's trapping enterprises after the discovery of gold in the Omineca region in 1869. Interest in mining rekindled during World War II when the Pinchi Mine a few kilometres north yielded more mercury than any other mine in the British Commonwealth.

A lack of highways and railways prompted Fort St. James to pioneer bush flying as a means of transportation; it has served as an air base since the earliest days of charter flight.

The north shore of Stuart Lake, 16 kilometres (10 mi.) west, features some of the earliest signs of habitation in the form of prehistoric rock paintings just above the high-water mark. Although Fort St. James has emerged from relative wilderness, its surrounding evergreen forests continue to be among the best big-game hunting areas in the province. Alpine skiing is available nearby.

Fort St. James Visitor Centre: 115 Douglas Ave., P.O. Box 1164, Fort St. James, BC, Canada V0J 1P0. **Phone:** (250) 996-7023 or (250) 996-8233.

FORT ST. JAMES NATIONAL HISTORIC SITE is 2 blks. w. of Hwy. 27 at 280 Kwah Rd. W. Established on the southern shore of Stuart Lake by the North West Co. in 1806, Fort St. James contains one of the largest groups of original in situ wooden buildings representing Canada's fur trade. A massive fur warehouse is a noted example of Red River framing. The fully restored Hudson's Bay Co. post on the site served as a hub of commerce between fur traders and the indigenous peoples—and as the capital of New Caledonia, now central British Columbia.

The visitor center provides interactive displays, artifacts and an audiovisual presentation. Changing exhibits are offered seasonally. Interpreters in period costume provide living-history demonstrations throughout the day. The site is home to chickens, horses, an ox, ducks, turkeys, goats and rabbits. **Time:** Allow 2 hours minimum. **Hours:** Daily 9-5, June 1-Labour Day; by appointment rest of year. **Cost:** $7.80; $6.55 (ages 65+); free (ages 0-17). An annual pass, valid at most Canadian national parks, marine areas and historic sites, is available. Prices may vary; phone to confirm. **Phone:** (250) 996-7191.

FORT ST. JOHN (D-5) pop. 18,609, elev. 695m/2,280'

One of the oldest European settlements in the province, Fort St. John was established in 1793 as a fur-trading outpost called Rocky Mountain Fort. Residents engage in gas and oil exploration as well as the lumber industry and cattle ranching. There are coalfields to the south and west.

Recreational activities include fishing for Arctic grayling and gray trout in nearby Charlie Lake *(see Recreation Areas Chart)*, canoeing the rapids of the Peace River, skiing, and hunting for mountain caribou, mountain goats and black bears in the Rocky Mountain foothills. Floatplanes operating out of Charlie Lake provide access to the wilderness surrounding Fort St. John, and Hwy. 29 provides scenic driving to Chetwynd.

Fort St. John Visitor Centre: 9324 96th St., Fort St. John, BC, Canada V1J 6V5. **Phone:** (250) 785-3033 or (877) 785-6037.

BEST WESTERN PLUS CHATEAU FORT ST. JOHN
250/787-7555

THREE DIAMOND

Contemporary Hotel

AAA Benefit: Members save up to 15% and earn bonus points!

Address: 8322 86th St V1J 0G7 **Location:** Just s on Hwy 97 (Alaska Hwy) exit 86th St, then just n. **Facility:** 123 units, some two bedrooms and efficiencies. 4 stories, interior corridors. **Parking:** winter plug-ins. **Amenities:** safes. **Activities:** exercise room. **Guest Services:** valet and coin laundry.

HOLIDAY INN EXPRESS FORT ST. JOHN   250/787-7737
THREE DIAMOND Hotel. **Address:** 9504 Alaska Rd V1J 6L5

HOME2 SUITES BY HILTON FORT ST. JOHN   250/785-5356
THREE DIAMOND [SAVE] Extended Stay Contemporary Hotel. **Address:** 9519 111th St V1J 6Y3

AAA Benefit: Members save up to 15%!

MICROTEL INN & SUITES BY WYNDHAM   250/794-3100
APPROVED Hotel. **Address:** 8407 93rd St V1J 6Y3

NORTHERN GRAND HOTEL   250/787-0521
THREE DIAMOND Hotel. **Address:** 9830 100th Ave V1J 1Y5

POMEROY HOTEL & CONFERENCE CENTRE   250/262-3233
THREE DIAMOND Hotel. **Address:** 11308 Alaska Rd V1J 5T5

POMEROY INN & SUITES   250/262-3030
APPROVED Extended Stay Hotel. **Address:** 9320 Alaska Rd V1J 6L5

SUPER 8 BY WYNDHAM FORT ST. JOHN   250/785-7588
APPROVED Hotel. **Address:** 9500 W Alaska Rd V1J 6L5

WHERE TO EAT

BROWNS CRAFTHOUSE   250/785-4464
APPROVED American. Casual Dining. **Address:** 8411 93rd St V1J 6Y3

BROWNS SOCIALHOUSE   250/785-0885
APPROVED International. Casual Dining. **Address:** 9719 100th St V1J 3X9

MASTARO SUSHI   250/261-6595
APPROVED Japanese. Casual Dining. **Address:** 9823 100th St V1J 3Y2

MR MIKES STEAKHOUSECASUAL   250/262-4151
APPROVED American. Casual Dining. **Address:** 9324 Alaska Rd V1J 6L5

NORTH BAR & GRILL   250/787-0521
APPROVED American. Casual Dining. **Address:** 9830 100th Ave V1J 1Y5

SPICY FUSION   250/787-7429
APPROVED Indian. Casual Dining. **Address:** 8111 100th Ave, Suite 201 V1J 1W4

WHOLE WHEAT & HONEY CAFE   250/787-9866
APPROVED American. Quick Serve. **Address:** 10003 100th St V1J 1Y5

FORT STEELE (C-12) elev. 771m/2,529'
• Hotels p. 186

Founded during the 1864 Kootenay gold rush, Fort Steele, then known as Galbraith's Ferry, became the site of the first North West Mounted Police west of the Rockies. In 1888 the settlement's name was changed to honor police superintendent Samuel Steele, who peacefully settled tensions between European settlers and the Ktunaxa people.

As a result of the mining boom of the 1890s the town became a thriving center of trade, transportation, communication and social activity, with a population of more than 2,000. In 1898 the British

Columbia Southern Railroad bypassed Fort Steele in favor of Cranbrook, 16 kilometres (10 mi.) southwest, and the town began its decline. At the end of World War II Fort Steele had fewer than 50 residents.

FORT STEELE HERITAGE TOWN is 3 km (1.9 mi.) s.w. at 9851 Hwy. 93/95. The 11-hectare (27-acre) site preserves an 1890s boomtown. More than 60 restored, reconstructed or original buildings include an operating bakery, restaurant, tinsmith shop, blacksmith shop and newspaper office. Street dramas and demonstrations such as quilting, horse farming and ice cream making help re-create life in the era.

Fort Steele's Clydesdales give wagon rides daily July 1 through Labour Day and perform a six-horse hitch show on July 1. Live entertainment is presented in the Wild Horse Theatre July 1 through Labour Day. Steam train rides are available during this time. A visitor reception center contains exhibits about the town's history.

Hours: Grounds open daily 10-5, July 1-September 1; 10-4, rest of year. Last admission 1 hour before closing. Programs, including street skits depicting daily life of the late 1890s, are presented daily 10-4:30, July 1-September 1. Closed Christmas. **Cost:** Admission July 1-Labour Day $18; $12 (ages 6-17 and 65+). Day after Labour Day to early Oct. $10; $7 (ages 6-17 and 65+). May 1-June 30 $15; $10 (ages 6-17 and 65+). Rest of year by donation. Steam train $15; $10 (ages 6-17 and 65+). Wagon rides $5. Wildhorse Theatre $10; $5 (ages 6-17). **Phone:** (250) 417-6000 or (250) 426-7352.

BULL RIVER GUEST RANCH   250/429-3760
THREE DIAMOND Resort Ranch. **Address:** 2975 Bull River Rd V1C 4H7

GALIANO ISLAND (H-10) pop. 1,138

Named after Spanish explorer Dionisio Alcala Galiano, Galiano Island, part of the Gulf Islands chain *(see place listing p. 188),* is a long narrow island that is a haven for bird watchers and naturalists. Bicycling, horseback riding, kayaking, fishing, sailing, diving, swimming and hiking are popular recreational activities. The efforts of hikers and cyclists are rewarded with grand vistas and viewpoints. Mount Galiano provides climbers with eye-catching views of the southern Gulf Islands and the Olympic Mountains.

Montague Harbour Marine Provincial Park has 3,000-year-old middens; camping facilities are available at the park as well as at Dionisio Point Provincial Park. The Descanso Bay Regional Park offers 30 camping sites. *See Recreation Areas Chart.*

GALIANO OCEANFRONT INN & SPA   250/539-3388
THREE DIAMOND Hotel. **Address:** 134 Madrona Dr V0N 1P0

WHERE TO EAT

ATREVIDA RESTAURANT   250/539-3388
THREE DIAMOND Pacific Northwest. Fine Dining. **Address:** 134 Madrona Dr V0N 1P0

HUMMINGBIRD INN PUB   250/539-5472
APPROVED American. Casual Dining. **Address:** 47 Sturdies Bay Rd V0N 1P0

GLACIER NATIONAL PARK (A-10)

Elevations in the park range from 800 metres (2,625 ft.) at the lower portion of the Beaver River to 3,380 metres (11,089 ft.) at Hasler Peak on Mount Dawson. Refer to CAA/AAA maps for additional elevation information.

West of the Rockies in the southeast interior of British Columbia, Glacier National Park and its smaller counterpart Mount Revelstoke National Park *(see place listing p. 203)* encompass portions of the rugged Columbia Mountains. The park's 1,350 square kilometres (521 sq. mi.) of hard rock terrain present a jagged profile of angular mountains with narrow steep-walled valleys. The steep mountain slopes and enormous snowfall make this region susceptible to avalanches.

Rogers Pass National Historic Site, located in the heart of the park became the scene of a pitched 19th-century battle between the railroad engineers and the surrounding mountains. Sheer walls, numerous slide areas and severe weather proved almost insurmountable obstacles to the completion of Canada's first transcontinental railroad. Some of the largest railroad trestles then known were built to carry the line across raging streams to the summit of this pass.

The tracks crossed to the southern wall of the valley on several loops to avoid the numerous avalanche slopes and reduce the steep downgrade. Despite the ingenuity of its engineers, the new railroad eventually had to be abandoned to the area's devastating winter forces. Avalanches attaining speeds of up to 325 kilometres (202 mi.) per hour tore up sections of the new track and left other sections buried under tons of snow.

Thirty-one snowsheds were built to shield the track, but even this was not enough. In 1910, 58 men were killed by an avalanche as they were clearing snow from an earlier slide. This incident, mounting costs and the dangerous grades of this section convinced the railroad to tunnel under Mount MacDonald.

The Trans-Canada Highway met similar obstacles as it crossed the pass, but the use of mobile howitzers to dislodge potential slides and other methods of controlling avalanches have held the road's position. Evidence of the struggle to build the railroad is visible from the road and the park's various campgrounds.

Several short trails follow the railroad's progress, winding past the ruins of Glacier House, a 19th-century resort hotel, remains of former snow sheds and the stone pillars that once supported the railroad trestles.

History is only part of the park's attractions. Twelve percent of the park is covered perpetually by snow and ice; more than 400 glaciers are scattered throughout the park. The contrast of the deep green forests and meadows with the glacial whites of these crags makes the park especially scenic.

Towering above the richly wooded valleys, the 3,284-metre (10,774-ft.) Mount Sir Donald rises to the east of the campgrounds, with Eagle and Uto peaks to the north. Day-hiking trails lead toward the Illecillewaet and Asulkan glaciers.

General Information and Activities

The park is open all year, although many visitor facilities are closed due to heavy snowfall October through May. In the winter, ski touring enthusiasts take advantage of the park's world-class ski touring opportunities. During the summer months, some of the popular activities include camping, hiking and mountaineering. Camping is offered at three in-park campgrounds: Illecillewaet campground is open June 21-Sept. 30, and Loop Brook and Mount Sir Donald campgrounds are open July 1-Sept. 2.

Parks Canada staff lead a variety of interpretive programs from Illecillewaet campground in July and August.

In addition, an extensive network of challenging day-hiking trails leads to such attractions as the Illecillewaet and Asulkan glaciers; Abbott Ridge; and the Hermit. Grizzly and black bears are common in Glacier National Park; be cautious and make noise frequently as you hike. Climbers and overnight hikers may voluntarily register at the Rogers Pass Discovery Centre before and after every trip. Park entry passes also can be purchased at the Rogers Pass Discovery Centre. *See Recreation Areas Chart.*

ADMISSION to the park $7.43; $6.24 (ages 65+); $3.71 (ages 6-16); $18.67 (all occupants of a private vehicle with up to seven people). An annual pass, valid at most Canadian national parks, marine areas and historic sites, is available.

PETS are permitted in the park provided they are on a leash at all times.

ADDRESS inquiries to the Superintendent, Glacier and Mount Revelstoke National Parks, P.O. Box 350, Revelstoke, BC, Canada V0E 2S0; phone (250) 837-7500.

ROGERS PASS DISCOVERY CENTRE is 1.3 km (.8 mi.) e. of the Rogers Pass summit. Modeled after the snowsheds that once protected the railroad from avalanches, the discovery center includes a theatre, an exhibit hall with railway models and displays about natural history. **Time:** Allow 30 minutes minimum. **Hours:** Daily 7-4. Closed Christmas. Phone ahead to confirm schedule. **Cost:** $7.43;

$6.24 (ages 65+); $3.71 (ages 6-16); $18.67 (all occupants of a private vehicle with up to seven people). **Phone:** (250) 837-7500.

GOLDEN (A-11) pop. 3,701, elev. 785m/2,575'

On the Trans-Canada Highway at the confluence of the Columbia and Kicking Horse rivers, Golden is between Glacier *(see place listing p. 186)* and Yoho national parks *(see place listing p. 330)* and located west of Banff National Park *(see place listing in Alberta p. 30)*. The community also is an outfitting point for sports enthusiasts.

The Golden and District Museum is at 11th Avenue and 13th Street. The museum is housed in a restored one-room schoolhouse and contains local historical items.

Kicking Horse Country Chamber of Commerce: 500 10th Ave. N., P.O. Box 1320, Golden, BC, Canada V0A 1H0. **Phone:** (250) 344-7125 or (800) 622-4653.

BEST WESTERN MOUNTAINVIEW INN   250/344-2333

⬦⬦ **THREE DIAMOND**   **Hotel**

Best Western. **AAA Benefit:** Members save up to 15% and earn bonus points!

Address: 1024 11th St N V0A 1H2 **Location:** Just w of jct Hwy 95 and Trans-Canada Hwy 1; on S Service Rd. **Facility:** 72 units. 3 stories, interior corridors. **Parking:** winter plug-ins. **Pool:** heated indoor. **Activities:** bicycles. **Guest Services:** coin laundry. **Featured Amenity:** breakfast buffet.

[SAVE] [📶] [🚐] [BIZ] [🛜] [✕] [▯]
[🖨] [▯] / [SOME UNITS] [🐾] [HS]

DAYS INN GOLDEN   250/344-2216

⬦ **APPROVED**   Motel. **Address:** 1416 Golden View Rd V0A 1H1

RAMADA LIMITED GOLDEN   250/439-1888

⬦ **APPROVED**   Hotel. **Address:** 1311 12th St N V0A 1H1

WHERE TO EAT

ELEVEN 22 GRILL & LIQUIDS   250/344-2443

⬦⬦ **THREE DIAMOND**   New International. Casual Dining. **Address:** 1122 10th Ave S V0A 1H0

THE ISLAND RESTAURANT   250/344-2400

⬦ **APPROVED**   New Canadian. Casual Dining. **Address:** 101 Gould's Island, 10th Ave V0A 1H0

WHITETOOTH MOUNTAIN BISTRO   250/344-5120

⬦⬦ **THREE DIAMOND**   New Canadian. **Address:** 427 9th Ave N V0A 1H0

THE WOLF'S DEN   250/344-9683

⬦ **APPROVED**   Burgers Steak. Casual Dining. **Address:** 1105 9th St S V0A 1H0

GRAND FORKS (D-9) pop. 3,985

Settlement at the confluence of the Kettle and Granby rivers began in the late 1800s when copper, gold and silver were discovered in the area. After 20 years of prosperity, Grand Forks suffered reverses when the local copper smelter—said to be the largest in the British Empire—closed due to faltering copper prices. The logging industry and seed-growing operations later restored stability to the community.

The downtown Boundary District contains preserved historic homes, stores and civic buildings from the settlement period. It is flanked on the south and east by rivers, on the west by 5th Avenue and on the north by 75th Avenue. A walking tour map is available at the Boundary Museum *(see attraction listing)*.

Chamber of Commerce of the City of Grand Forks: 524 Central Ave., P.O. Box 2140, Grand Forks, BC, Canada V0H 1H0. **Phone:** (250) 442-5835.

BOUNDARY MUSEUM AND INTERPRETIVE CENTRE is at 6145 Reservoir Rd. The museum depicts the area's history from the late 1800s. Artifacts, maps and photographs show the lifestyles of the native peoples as well as the Doukhobor. Other exhibits include a scale model and display of Grand Forks' Chinatown in the 1900s, a wildlife exhibit and a 1929 fire truck.

Hours: Tues.-Fri. 10-4. Guided tours are available by appointment outside of regular hours. Phone ahead to confirm schedule. **Cost:** Donations. **Phone:** (250) 442-3737.

RAMADA LIMITED BY WYNDHAM   250/442-2127
♦ **APPROVED**   Hotel. **Address:** 2729 Central Ave V0H 1H2

WESTERN TRAVELLER MOTEL   250/442-5566
♦ **APPROVED**   **Address:** 1591 Central Ave V0H 1H0
Motel   **Location:** West end of town on Hwy 3. **Facility:** 35 units, some efficiencies and kitchens. 2 stories (no elevator), exterior corridors. **Activities:** picnic facilities, exercise room. **Guest Services:** coin laundry.

WHERE TO EAT

THE WOODEN SPOON BISTRO & BAKE SHOP 250/442-5005
♦ **APPROVED**   Breakfast Sandwiches. Quick Serve.
Address: 211 Market Ave V0H 1H0

GULF ISLANDS

Separated from the San Juan Islands in Washington only by an international boundary, the almost 200 islands of various shapes and sizes that make up the Gulf Islands nestle against the southeast coast of Vancouver Island. Formed by a series of moving land masses beginning about 100 million years ago, today's Gulf Islands are the result of a mass collision of land that produced the long ridges of sandstone, conglomerate and shale that make up the islands' geology.

The area was discovered by Capt. George Vancouver while on a quest to find a northwest passage to the Orient in 1792. Erroneously named Gulf of Georgia by Vancouver, the water separating Vancouver Island from the southwestern portion of British Columbia was later correctly termed the Strait of Georgia. The islands, however, retained the designation Gulf Islands.

The Gulf Islands feature a climate that is sunnier and milder than that found on the nearby mainland. The quiet waters promote a much quieter lifestyle as well, and the islands are a haven from the frantic pace of nearby cities. Each island, though similar in many respects, has its own distinct identity. Easily reached from the mainland, they have become popular weekend retreats offering varying degrees of amenities and activities depending on the destination. Artists and professionals have joined the population of local fishermen and farmers who relish the peaceful lifestyle created by the sparkling waters, cliffs, winding roads and parks. And those on vacation will find plenty of fun things to do and opportunities for relaxation.

The main components of the southern Gulf Islands are Galiano Island, Mayne Island, the Pender Islands (North and South), Quadra Island, Salt Spring Island and Saturna Island *(see place listings)*. The islands can be explored by automobile; cycling is treacherous due to narrow winding and hilly roads. The Islands Trust, a governmental agency, is charged with preserving and protecting the islands and waters in the Strait of Georgia.

If you're wondering how to reach the Gulf Islands, BC Ferries provides year-round service to the main islands from Tsawwassen, south of Vancouver, and Swartz Bay, near Victoria. Reservations are available and recommended for foot passengers traveling to the southern Gulf Islands on the Tsawwassen ferry.

Vehicle reservations are recommended for travel between the mainland and the islands, but are not available for travel between Vancouver Island and the Gulf Islands or for inter-island travel. It is advisable to make reservations as far in advance as possible for summer and holiday travel. For schedule information and reservations phone (250) 386-3431 from the Victoria area and outside British Columbia or (888) 223-3779 from elsewhere in the province. Air service also is available. Contact your AAA travel agency for details about vacation packages and what to do in Gulf Islands, B.C.

GULF ISLANDS NATIONAL PARK RESERVE (I-10)

Elevations in the park range from sea level to 401 metres (1,316 ft.) at Mt. Warburton Pike on Saturna Island. Refer to CAA/AAA maps for additional elevation information.

Gulf Islands National Park Reserve protects an island landscape of rocky headlands, forested hills and shorelines studded with colorful tide pools. The park encompasses areas of lands scattered over fifteen larger islands and includes many smaller islets and reefs. Waters adjacent to park lands, extending 200 metres (650 ft.) seaward, also are under Parks Canada management.

The park shares the larger populated islands of Mayne, Saturna and the Penders with communities that offer a range of tourist amenities. Facilities and services inside the national park reserve include camping, moorage, hiking trails, day use/picnic areas and regularly scheduled interpretation programs from May 15-Sept. 30. The populated larger islands are accessible by vehicle, bicycle and BC Ferries from Vancouver and Victoria. The smaller islands are accessible by only boat or kayak. Water taxis also operate in several areas. In the summer, a passenger ferry takes visitors from the main pier in Sidney to a popular white sand beach and camping area on Sidney Island in Gulf Islands National Park Reserve. Many local tour operators offer such recreational opportunities as cycling, kayaking, scuba diving, whale-watching or hiking. Comfortable, sturdy shoes and water are recommended for all hiking excursions.

The islands are a haven for various wildlife, including such endangered species as the anatum peregrine falcon, the sharp-tailed snake, Townsend's big-eared bat, the olive-sided flycatcher, the western meadowlark and the orcas. The southern Gulf Islands are home to the endangered Garry Oak ecosystem. Various shorebirds, waterfowl, great blue herons, seals and sea lions also inhabit the area. There are two important bird areas in and around the park at Sidney Channel (near Sidney Island) and Active Pass near Mayne Island.

For more information, contact the Gulf Islands National Park Reserve InfoCentre at (250) 654-4000 or (866) 944-1744. For campground reservations, phone (877) 737-3783. See Recreation Areas Chart.

GWAII HAANAS NATIONAL PARK RESERVE AND HAIDA HERITAGE SITE (F-1)

Elevations in the park range from sea level along Kunghit and Moresby islands to 1,123 metres (696 ft.) at Mount de la Touche. Refer to CAA/AAA maps for additional elevation information.

Off the British Columbia coast west of Prince Rupert, Gwaii Haanas National Park Reserve, National Marine Conservation Area Reserve, and Haida Heritage Site is in the southern part of Haida Gwaii, a remote island chain formerly known as the Queen Charlotte Islands (see place listing this page). Haida Gwaii translates to "islands of the people." This protected area is jointly managed by the Government of Canada and the Council of the Haida Nation. In 2010, Gwaii Haanas became the only area in the world protected from mountain top to ocean floor.

The 1,470 square kilometres (912 sq. mi.) of Gwaii Haanas offer a rich and fascinating diversity of flora, sea creatures and wildlife. Whales, bald eagles, nesting seabirds, black bears, sea lions and river otters are commonly seen.

Remnants of Haida village sites on the 138 islands capture the history of the Haida. Haida Gwaii Watchmen basecamps have been established at major sites of cultural significance. Watchmen act as hosts and also provide site security and protection of the cultural features.

Access is challenging: The only way to and around Gwaii Haanas is by air or sea. Solo travel is recommended only for the experienced outdoor traveler. Licensed tour operators provide a variety of excursions. Sea kayaking, sailboat and powerboat charters are the most popular ways to tour Gwaii Haanas. There are no maintained trails or designated campsites, and only limited visitor facilities are provided within the protected area.

Haida Gwaii can be reached by air from Vancouver and Prince Rupert. BC Ferries also provides year-round service between the islands and Prince Rupert. Arrangements for ferry transportation should be made well in advance and reservations are highly recommended; phone (250) 386-3431 from the Victoria area and outside British Columbia or (888) 223-3779 from elsewhere in the province.

Single-day admission $18.67; $15.81 (ages 65+); $9.33 (ages 6-16); $46.67 (all occupants of a private vehicle with up to seven people). Reservations are required to visit the reserve May through September. Regulations allow for no more than 12 people on shore in one place at one time. An annual pass, valid at most Canadian national parks, marine areas and historic sites, is available.

Note: If traveling independently (without a guide), visitors must participate in one 60-minute orientation session offered daily at visitor centers in Sandspit and Queen Charlotte; phone (250) 559-8818 to guarantee a place. For more information, phone (250) 559-8818 or (877) 559-8818. See Recreation Areas Chart.

HAIDA GWAII (E-1)

Haida Gwaii ("islands of the people"), formerly the Queen Charlotte Islands, were occupied by Haida First Nation when Spanish sea captain Juan Pérez sighted the archipelago in 1774. A seafaring and artistic people, the Haida traded sea otter pelts with European traders during the early 1800s. By the late 19th century, however, the Haida had to vacate many of their ancestral villages to escape a devastating smallpox epidemic.

Only a fraction of their original number still inhabit the islands—at Haida, near Masset, and Skidegate, near Queen Charlotte City. Continuing their cultural traditions, they carve elaborate works of art from argillite, a black slatelike stone found only in mountain deposits off the coast.

A group of about 150 islands forming an elongated triangle, Haida Gwaii stretches 250 kilometres (157 mi.) from north to south, 90 kilometres (56 mi.) off the coast of British Columbia. Characterized by fog and low clouds, these islands also are known as the Misty Islands. The towns are small and decidedly rural; the entire population of Haida Gwaii is about 5,000.

The two main islands are Graham and Moresby. The largest and most populated is Graham. In the north on its broad and flat eastern side are most of the archipelago's communities—Masset, Old Masset, Port Clements, Queen Charlotte City, Skidegate, and Tlell—which are linked by a paved road. An airport is at Masset as well as at Sandspit, on the northeastern tip of Moresby Island. A 20-minute ferry ride connects the two islands.

A temperate marine climate supports dense coniferous forests, which, as the basis of the islands' economy, have been logged extensively. The fish and shellfish in the coastal waters supply the islands' important commercial fishing industry.

Visitors are attracted by the pristine wilderness, the hunting and fishing prospects, kayaking and hiking opportunities, and the handicrafts and art of the Haida. In fact the main destination of many travelers to Haida Gwaii is Gwaii Haanas National Park Reserve, National Marine Conservation Area Reserve and Haida Heritage Site (see place listing p. 189), in the southern part of the island chain on Moresby Island.

Wildlife is abundant here; tiny Sitka deer and bald eagles frequent the shores, and seals, sea lions, porpoises and migrating whales often appear in the inlets. Bird-watching, wildlife viewing, hiking, kayaking and freshwater and saltwater fishing are popular activities.

Points of interest include Naikoon Provincial Park (see Recreation Areas Chart) on Graham Island, the remote Haida village sites, the Delkatla Wildlife Sanctuary in Masset, the Haida Heritage Centre at Kaay Llnagaay (see attraction listing p. 239) in Skidegate and the various carving sheds in Skidegate and Old Masset.

Permission to visit Haida unoccupied village sites must be obtained from Band Council offices; phone (250) 559-8225.

The islands' main visitor center in Queen Charlotte City has videos and interactive displays that provide information about life on the islands and in the waters that surround them, including craft galleries and a touch-tank saltwater aquarium. The center is open year-round.

Haida Gwaii can be reached by air from Prince Rupert and Vancouver and by ferry from Prince Rupert. Phone BC Ferries at (250) 386-3431 or (888) 223-3779 for ferry reservations. Kayak rentals, fishing charters and various guided boat and land tours are available.

HARRISON HOT SPRINGS (C-7)
pop. 1,468, elev. 11m/36'

At the foot of Harrison Lake, Harrison Hot Springs (see Recreation Areas Chart) is a well-known health and vacation resort with two mineral springs and a sandy beach on the lakeshore. Strong area winds make this a favorite spot for windsurfing. The surrounding mountains are known as Sasquatch country, where sightings of the legendary apelike creature twice the size of a man have been reported dozens of times.

More likely to be found in the mountains are mutton-fat jades, garnets, agates, fossils and gold; the area is renowned among rock hounds.

Harrison Hot Springs Visitor InfoCentre: 499 Hot Springs Rd., P.O. Box 255, Harrison Hot Springs, BC, Canada V0M 1K0. **Phone:** (604) 796-5581.

HARRISON BEACH HOTEL   604/796-1111
THREE DIAMOND Extended Stay Hotel. **Address:** 160 Esplanade Ave V0M 1K0

WHERE TO EAT

KITAMI JAPANESE RESTAURANT   604/796-2728
APPROVED   Japanese. Casual Dining. **Address:** 318 Hot Springs Rd V0M 1K0

MORGAN'S BISTRO   604/491-1696
THREE DIAMOND Mediterranean. Casual Dining. **Address:** 160 Esplanade Ave V0M 1K0

MUDDY WATERS ESPRESSO BAR & CAFE   604/796-5563
APPROVED   American. Quick Serve. **Address:** 328 Esplanade Ave V0M 1K0

HOPE (C-7) pop. 5,969, elev. 39m/127'

At the entrance to the Fraser River Valley, Hope dates from 1848 when the Hudson's Bay Co. established a fort. The town developed rapidly, especially during the gold rush of 1858. The 1859 Anglican Christ Church is one of the province's oldest churches.

From Hope the Trans-Canada Highway leads north to Fraser Canyon. Kawkawa Lake (see Recreation Areas Chart), Lake of the Woods, Mount Hope, Mount Ogilvie and Skagit Valley (see Recreation Areas Chart) are just some of the nearby places that offer year-round recreational opportunities.

The result of the 1965 Hope Slide is evident about 16 kilometres (10 mi.) east beside Hwy. 3. A plaque at the edge of the present roadway explains the collapse of the side of Johnson Peak, which buried the highway under 45 metres (148 ft.) of rubble.

The Hope Museum, inside the Hope Visitor Info-Centre, portrays the town's history through native artifacts and historical settings; phone (604) 869-2021. Hope was the location of several films, including "Rambo: First Blood," "Shoot to Kill" with Sidney Poitier, and Disney's "Far From Home: The Adventures of Yellow Dog."

The Hope Arts Gallery, 349 Fort St., features the work of more than 20 artists; phone (604) 869-2408. More art can be found scattered throughout downtown Hope. Wood carvings in such shapes as a gold prospector with his horse to a bald eagle holding a salmon in his talons were created from dying trees with a chainsaw; most are on the grounds of Memorial Park. Brochures about the more than two dozen carvings can be picked up at the Hope Visitor InfoCentre.

Hope Visitor Centre and Museum Complex: 919 Water Ave., P.O. Box 370, Hope, BC, Canada V0X 1L0. **Phone:** (604) 869-2021.

HELL'S GATE AIRTRAM—see Boston Bar p. 173.

OTHELLO-QUINTETTE TUNNELS are off Hwy. 3 exit 170 in Coquihalla Canyon Provincial Park; take 6th St. 1 blk. n. to Kawkawa Lake Rd., then 5 km (3 mi.) e. to Tunnels Rd. Five tunnels were built 1911-16 to complete a railroad through Coquihalla Canyon. The Coquihalla River zigzags through the canyon, presenting a challenge to engineer Andrew McCulloch, who used dynamite to blast through the canyon walls to create the narrow tunnels.

The railway ceased operations in 1959; wooden walkways now bridge the river's serpentine course between the tunnels and allow close-up views of the rushing waters.

Note: Wear shoes with good traction, as the gravel path through the tunnels may be wet, slippery and uneven. A flashlight is recommended. **Time:** Allow 1 hour, 30 minutes minimum. **Hours:** Daily dawn-dusk, Apr.-Oct. **Cost:** Free. **Phone:** (604) 986-9371. 🚻

ALPINE MOTEL   604/869-9931
⬧ APPROVED

Motel

Address: 505 Old Hope-Princeton Way V0X 1L0 **Location:** Trans-Canada Hwy 1 exit 173 westbound; exit 170 eastbound, just n from lights. **Facility:** 14 units, some kitchens. 1 story, exterior corridors.

 / SOME UNITS 🐾

WHERE TO EAT

BLUE MOOSE COFFEE HOUSE   604/869-0729
⬧ APPROVED   Coffee/Tea Sandwiches. Quick Serve.
Address: 322 Wallace St V0X 1L0

HUDSON'S HOPE (D-5) pop. 970,
elev. 520m/1,706'
• Hotels p. 192

Hudson's Hope is one of the oldest settlements in the province: Only two communities on Vancouver Island have been continuously occupied from earlier dates. First discovered in 1793 by Alexander Mackenzie, the area was the site of a small fur-trading post built in 1805. In 1900 the post was moved to the present site of Hudson's Hope on the north side of the Peace River, where it flourished as a center of trade for the Hudson's Bay Co.

Hudson's Hope is an important supplier of hydro-electricity; its two dams generate about 38 percent of the hydropower used in British Columbia. The dams also are major recreation centers for the area.

Hudson's Hope Visitor Centre: 9555 Beattie Dr., P.O. Box 330, Hudson's Hope, BC, Canada V0C 1V0. **Phone:** (250) 783-9154 May-Oct., or (250) 783-9901 rest of year.

PEACE CANYON DAM is 4 km (2.5 mi.) s. on Hwy. 29. Completed in 1980, the dam is 50 metres (165 ft.) high and 533 metres (1,750 ft.) long. It reuses water that has generated electricity at the W.A.C. Bennett Dam, 23 kilometres (14 mi.) upstream on the Peace River. Nearby recreational facilities include a campground, picnic facilities and a boat launch to Dinosaur Lake, the dam's reservoir. **Hours:** Daily 8-4, mid-May through Labour Day.

Peace Canyon Dam Visitor Centre is next to the powerhouse. Exhibits reflect the area's natural history, its pioneer past and the Peace Canyon Project. Highlights include a replica of the stern-wheeler SS *Peace River*, a large-scale model of a generating unit, displays about the damming of the Peace River, and mammoth tusks found during excavation. Visitors can view the project's central control system, walk across the dam or visit the observation area on the main floor and a viewing deck.

Guided tours of the visitor center are available. **Hours:** Daily 8-4, mid-May through Labour Day; Mon.-Fri. 8-4, rest of year. Closed Jan. 1, Easter, second Mon. in Oct., Nov. 11, Christmas and day after Christmas. **Cost:** Free. **Phone:** (250) 783-7418 or (888) 333-6667.

W.A.C. BENNETT DAM is 21 km (13 mi.) w. on Canyon Dr. following signs. A major hydroelectric project on the Peace River, the dam was completed in 1967 to produce electrical power for British Columbia. It is 183 metres (600 ft.) high, 2 kilometres (1.2 mi.) long and .8 kilometre (.5 mi.) thick at the base. Backup water from the dam forms 164,600-hectare (406,727-acre) Williston Lake, British Columbia's largest lake. Its shoreline stretches for 1,770 kilometres (1,100 mi.).

W.A.C. Bennett Dam Visitor Centre is about 1 km (.6 mi.) s.e. of the dam. Photographs and artifacts chronicle the history and geology of the region and the construction of the dam and powerhouse. A participatory exhibit demonstrates the generation of electricity and magnetism. Underground bus tours into the powerhouse and manifold chambers are available. A 40-minute multimedia presentation also is offered in the theater.

Note: Cameras, purses and bags are not permitted on the tour, but free lockers are available. **Hours:** Visitor center daily 10-5, mid-May through Labour Day; by appointment rest of year. Underground powerhouse tours are available 10:30-3:30. Phone ahead to confirm times for tours. **Cost:** $8; $7 (ages 6-17 and 55+). Audio tour rental $4. Reservations are required for the tour. **Phone:** (250) 783-5048 or (888) 333-6667. ⏹

SIGMA INN & SUITES   250/783-2300
▼ **APPROVED** Extended Stay Hotel. **Address:** 9006 Clark Ave V0C 1V0

INVERMERE (B-11) pop. 2,955

Nestled in the "Valley of a Thousand Peaks" between the Rocky and Purcell mountain ranges, Invermere's bucolic location on Lake Windermere's north shore makes it the ideal spot for summer recreation, including hiking, camping, fishing, boating and sailboarding. Hang gliders frequently take flight off nearby Mount Swansea.

Birds of a different feather fly freely at Wilmer National Wildlife Area, about 5 kilometres (3 mi.) north of town; bring your binoculars to peep at songbirds, woodpeckers, waterfowl and birds of prey as well as four-legged creatures including deer, elk, muskrats and beavers.

Roam down Main Street in Invermere's downtown, where flowers bloom in abundance and small-town charm pervades the boutiques, antique shops and cafés. Take in a first-run flick at the 1952 Toby Theatre.

Invermere Visitor Centre: 651 Hwy. 93/95 or 1046 7th Ave., P.O. Box 1019, Invermere, BC, Canada V0A 1K0. **Phone:** (250) 342-2844.

COPPERPOINT RESORT   250/341-4000
▼ **THREE DIAMOND** Contemporary Resort Hotel. **Address:** 760 Cooper Rd V0A 1K2

INVERMERE INN & SUITES   250/342-9246
▼ **APPROVED** Hotel. **Address:** 1310 7th Ave V0A 1K0

WHERE TO EAT

BIRCHWOOD RESTAURANT   250/342-0606
▼ **THREE DIAMOND** New International. Casual Dining. **Address:** 722 13th St V0A 1K0

⊘ **Find AAA Inspected & Approved campgrounds at**
AAA.com/campgrounds

BLACK FOREST STEAK & SCHNITZEL HOUSE
                                  250/342-9417
▼ **APPROVED**   **AAA Inspector Notes:** *Classic.* Step into another world at this restaurant with its lovely Bavarian décor. Servers sport matching garb and offer proficient and friendly service. On the menu is a good selection of tasty schnitzels, bratwurst, steak and seafood finely prepared with a respect for tradition. Table d'hotes are offered daily. The aviary on view is a nice spot for birders to enjoy watching the owner's pets while dining. **Features:** full bar, early bird specials. **Reservations:** suggested. **Address:** 540 Hwy 93 & 95 V0A 1K0 **Location:** Hwy 95; just e on Cooper Rd. Ⓓ CALL ♿

Continental Casual Dining
$17-$39

BLUE DOG CAFE   250/342-3814
▼ **APPROVED**   American. Casual Dining. **Address:** 1213 7th Ave V0A 1K0

ELEMENTS GRILL   250/341-4000
▼ **APPROVED**   International. Casual Dining. **Address:** 760 Cooper Rd V0A 1K2

THE INVERMERE BAKERY   250/342-9913
▼ **APPROVED**   Breads/Pastries Coffee/Tea. Quick Serve. **Address:** 1305 7th St V0A 1K0

STRAND'S OLD HOUSE RESTAURANT   250/342-6344
▼ **THREE DIAMOND** Continental. Casual Dining. **Address:** 818 12th St V0A 1K0

KAMLOOPS (H-5) pop. 85,678, elev. 345m/1,131'
• Restaurants p. 194

Founded in 1812 as a North West Co. depot, Kamloops later was a Hudson's Bay Co. post. Developed where the north and south branches of the Thompson River converge to form Kamloops Lake, Kamloops was named after a Secwepemc (Shuswap) word, *Tk'emlúps*, or "the meeting of the waters" or, alternatively, a similar French phrase, *camp des loups*, or "camp of wolves." During the gold rush of the 1860s the Overlanders reached the city by rafting down the North Thompson. A bronze statue at city hall commemorates their arrival and their contributions to the city.

Since the Cariboo's gold supply disappeared in the 1860s, Kamloops has developed as a center of cattle and sheep ranching, forestry and lumber and, in more recent years, tourism.

In summer, Kamloops Heritage Railway, #6-510 Lorne St., operates a sightseeing tour on *The Spirit of Kamloops*, a restored 1912 steam locomotive with hayrack cars, heritage coaches and caboose. The train departs the Canadian National Railway station, passing St. Joseph's Church along the way, and features a train robbery reenactment on the return trip; phone (250) 374-2141.

With an abundance of lakes in the area, Kamloops offers good fishing. In fact, local trout are known to jump a few feet in the air after being hooked. Outdoor enthusiasts also enjoy golfing, nature trails, wildlife viewing, boating, kayaking, canoeing, hiking and mountain biking. Many urban parks also offer recreational activities, including hiking, biking, picnicking and strolling, and skiing can be enjoyed on nearby slopes.

Culturally speaking, Western Canada Theatre and Project X Theatre Productions stage plays virtually year-round; phone (250) 372-3216 and (250) 374-5483 respectively. And the Kamloops Symphony, (250) 372-5000, presents orchestral and chamber music performances September to May.

Kamloops Visitor Centre: 1290 W. Trans-Canada Hwy., Kamloops, BC, Canada V2C 6R3. **Phone:** (250) 374-3377 or (800) 662-1994.

Self-guiding tours: Kamloops is the site of several historical attractions, including the provincial courthouse and several old houses and churches. Self-guiding tour brochures are available from Kamloops Museum and Archives.

ACCENT INNS 250/374-8877
▼▼ APPROVED   Motel. **Address:** 1325 Columbia St W V2C 6P4

BEST WESTERN PLUS KAMLOOPS HOTEL
250/374-7878

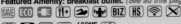

▼▼ THREE DIAMOND   Hotel   BW Best Western PLUS.   **AAA Benefit:** Members save up to 15% and earn bonus points!

Address: 660 Columbia St W V2C 1L1 **Location:** Trans-Canada Hwy 1 exit 369 (Columbia St) eastbound; exit 370 (Summit Dr) westbound to Columbia St via City Centre, 1.1 mi (1.8 km) n. **Facility:** 81 units. 4 stories, interior corridors. **Parking:** winter plug-ins. **Pool:** heated indoor. **Activities:** hot tub, exercise room. **Guest Services:** valet and coin laundry. **Featured Amenity:** breakfast buffet. *(See ad this page.)*

CANADAS BEST VALUE INN AND SUITES 250/374-8100
▼▼ APPROVED   Motel. **Address:** 1200 Rogers Way V1S 1N5

THE COAST KAMLOOPS HOTEL & CONFERENCE CENTRE
250/828-6660
▼▼ THREE DIAMOND   Hotel. **Address:** 1250 Rogers Way V1S 1N5

COMFORT INN & SUITES 250/372-0987
▼▼ APPROVED   Hotel. **Address:** 1810 Rogers Pl V1S 1T7

DELTA HOTELS BY MARRIOTT KAMLOOPS 250/372-2281
▼▼ THREE DIAMOND [SAVE]
Contemporary Hotel. **Address:** 540 Victoria St V2C 2B2   **AAA Benefit:** Members save 5% or more!

DOUBLETREE BY HILTON KAMLOOPS 250/851-0026
▼▼ THREE DIAMOND [SAVE] Hotel. **Address:** 339 St. Paul St V2C 2J5   **AAA Benefit:** Members save up to 15%!

FAIRFIELD INN & SUITES BY MARRIOTT KAMLOOPS
778/471-0902

▼▼ THREE DIAMOND   Hotel   Fairfield   **AAA Benefit:** Members save 5% or more!

Address: 1475 Hugh Allan Dr V1S 1J3 **Location:** Trans-Canada Hwy 1 exit 367 (Pacific Way), just e. **Facility:** 114 units. 5 stories, interior corridors. **Pool:** indoor. **Activities:** hot tub, exercise room. **Guest Services:** valet and coin laundry. **Featured Amenity:** breakfast buffet.

▼ See AAA listing this page ▼

BW Best Western PLUS.

Award-Winning Eco-Friendly Hotel!

Indoor Saltwater Pool & Hot Tub
Pet Friendly rooms available
Earn Best Western Rewards | Free Breakfast

CAA Rewards

Kamloops Hotel
660 Columbia St. West, Kamloops, BC V2C 1L1 CAN
1-877-302-7878 | bestwesternkamloops.com

THREE DIAMOND

FOUR POINTS BY SHERATON KAMLOOPS
250/374-4144

THREE DIAMOND
Hotel

AAA Benefit: Members save 5% or more!

Address: 1175 Rogers Way V1S 1R5 **Location:** Trans-Canada Hwy 1 exit 368 (Hillside Ave), just s. **Facility:** 78 units, some two bedrooms, efficiencies and kitchens. 4 stories, interior corridors. **Parking:** winter plug-ins. **Amenities:** safes. **Dining:** Twisted Olive Steakhouse, see separate listing. **Pool:** heated indoor. **Activities:** sauna, hot tub, exercise room. **Guest Services:** valet and coin laundry.

HAMPTON INN BY HILTON
250/571-7897

THREE DIAMOND
Hotel

Hampton

AAA Benefit: Members save up to 15%!

Address: 1245 Rogers Way V1S 1R9 **Location:** Trans-Canada Hwy 1 exit 368 (Hillside Ave), just s via Hillside Way. **Facility:** 81 units. 3 stories, interior corridors. **Pool:** heated indoor. **Activities:** hot tub, exercise room. **Guest Services:** valet and coin laundry. **Featured Amenity:** breakfast buffet.

HOLIDAY INN & SUITES
250/376-8288

THREE DIAMOND
Hotel

Address: 675 Tranquille Rd V2B 3H7 **Location:** Trans-Canada Hwy 1 exit 374 (Jasper Ave), 2.5 mi (4 km) w on Halston Connector Rd, 1.8 mi (3 km) s on 8th St to Fortune Dr, then just s. **Facility:** 89 units. 4 stories, interior corridors. **Parking:** winter plug-ins. **Pool:** heated indoor. **Activities:** hot tub, exercise room. **Guest Services:** valet and coin laundry.

HOLIDAY INN EXPRESS KAMLOOPS 250/372-3474
THREE DIAMOND Hotel. **Address:** 1550 Versatile Dr V1S 1X4

PACIFIC INN & SUITES 250/372-0952
APPROVED Hotel. **Address:** 1820 Rogers Pl V1S 1T7

QUALITY INN 250/851-0111
APPROVED Hotel. **Address:** 1860 Rogers Pl V1S 1T7

RAMADA KAMLOOPS 250/374-0358
APPROVED Hotel. **Address:** 555 W Columbia St V2C 1K7

RANCHLAND INN 250/828-8787
APPROVED Motel. **Address:** 2357 Trans-Canada Hwy 1 E V2C 4A8

SCOTT'S INN & RESTAURANT
250/372-8221

APPROVED
Motel

Address: 551 11th Ave V2C 3Y1 **Location:** Trans-Canada Hwy 1 exit City Center (from eastern approach), 0.5 mi (0.9 km) w on Battle St, then just s. Located in residential area across from a playground. **Facility:** 51 units, some two bedrooms and kitchens. 2 stories (no elevator), exterior corridors. **Parking:** winter plug-ins. **Pool:** heated indoor. **Activities:** hot tub, picnic facilities. **Guest Services:** coin laundry. **Featured Amenity:** continental breakfast.

SUPER 8 KAMLOOPS 250/374-8688
APPROVED Hotel. **Address:** 1521 Hugh Allan Dr V1S 1P4

THE THOMPSON HOTEL 250/374-1999
APPROVED Hotel. **Address:** 650 Victoria St V2C 2B4

TRAVELODGE KAMLOOPS MOUNTVIEW 250/374-4788
APPROVED Motel. **Address:** 1225 Rogers Way V1S 1R9

WINGATE BY WYNDHAM KAMLOOPS 778/471-7706
THREE DIAMOND Contemporary Hotel. **Address:** 1180 Rogers Way V1S 1N5

WHERE TO EAT

ARIGATO SUSHI 250/314-1185
APPROVED Japanese. Casual Dining. **Address:** 1395 Hillside Dr V2E 2R7

THE ART WE ARE CAFE 250/828-7998
APPROVED Coffee/Tea Sandwiches. Quick Serve. **Address:** 246 Victoria St V2C 2A2

ATLAS STEAK + FISH 250/852-6565
THREE DIAMOND Steak Seafood. Fine Dining. **Address:** 1555 Versatile Dr V1S 1W7

BOLD FIRE INSPIRED PIZZERIA 780/471-2653
APPROVED Pizza. Casual Dining. **Address:** 945 Columbia St W V2C 1M4

BROWNSTONE RESTAURANT 250/851-9939
THREE DIAMOND New Canadian. Fine Dining. **Address:** 118 Victoria St V2C 1Z7

BURGER & CAFE JOY 250/377-0049
APPROVED Japanese Burgers Fusion. Quick Serve. **Address:** 945 Columbia St W, #140 V2C 1L5

CHEZ CORA 778/471-5944
APPROVED Breakfast Sandwiches. Casual Dining. **Address:** 1801 Princeton-Kamloops Hwy V2E 2J7

EARLS KITCHEN + BAR 250/372-3275
APPROVED American. Casual Dining. **Address:** 1210 Summit Dr V2C 6M1

FRICK & FRACK TAPHOUSE 250/851-2030
APPROVED International. Gastropub. **Address:** 577 Victoria St V2C 2B3

GUI KOREAN BBQ 250/377-0771
APPROVED Korean. Casual Dining. **Address:** 1801 Princeton-Kamloops Hwy V2E 2J7

HELLO TOAST 250/372-9322
APPROVED American. Casual Dining. **Address:** 428 Victoria St V2C 2A7

JACOB'S NOODLE & CUTLET 778/471-3597
APPROVED Japanese. Casual Dining. **Address:** 260 4th Ave V2C 2A9

JAMAICA KITCHEN 250/376-1970
APPROVED Jamaican. Casual Dining. **Address:** 451 Tranquille Rd V2B 3H3

MAURYA'S FINE INDIAN CUISINE 250/377-4969
APPROVED Indian. Casual Dining. **Address:** 165 Victoria St V2C 1Z4

MITTZ KITCHEN 778/471-5050
THREE DIAMOND New International. Casual Dining. **Address:** 227 Victoria St V2C 2A1

MR MIKES STEAKHOUSECASUAL 778/471-0722
APPROVED American. Casual Dining. **Address:** 1200 Summit Dr V2C 6L2

THE NOBLE PIG BREWHOUSE 778/471-5999
APPROVED American. Gastropub. **Address:** 650 Victoria St V2C 2B4

ON THE ROCKS PUB & GRILL 250/374-9761
APPROVED International. Sports Bar. **Address:** 1265 Rogers Way V1S 1R9

ORIENTAL GARDENS RESTAURANT 250/372-2344
APPROVED Chinese. Casual Dining. **Address:** 545 Victoria St V2C 2B1

ORIGINAL JOE'S RESTAURANT & BAR 778/471-6116
APPROVED American. Gastropub. **Address:** 1801 Princeton-Kamloops Hwy, #203 V2E 2J7

PASSEKS CLASSICS CAFE & CATERING 250/314-1114
APPROVED Breakfast Sandwiches. Casual Dining. **Address:** 120 3rd Ave V2C 2M3

QUILAS MEXICAN RESTAURANT 778/471-6364
APPROVED Mexican. Casual Dining. **Address:** 330 Victoria St V2C 2A5

ROMEO'S KITCHEN + SPIRITS 250/372-5312
APPROVED International. Casual Dining. **Address:** 1250 Rogers Way V1S 1N5

STORMS ON THE RIVER 250/372-1522
THREE DIAMOND New International. Fine Dining. **Address:** 1502 River St V2C 1Y9

SUSHI VALLEY 250/851-9889
APPROVED Asian. Casual Dining. **Address:** 11-2121 Trans-Canada Hwy E V2C 4A6

TERRA RESTAURANT 250/374-2913
THREE DIAMOND New Canadian. Casual Dining. **Address:** 326 Victoria St V2C 2A5

TWISTED OLIVE STEAKHOUSE 236/425-3001
APPROVED American. Casual Dining. **Address:** 1175 Rogers Way V1S 1R5

WHITE SPOT 778/470-5581
APPROVED American. Casual Dining. **Address:** 675 Tranquille Rd V2B 3H7

KASLO (C-11) pop. 1,026, elev. 588m/1,929'

Kaslo began as a mill site in 1888. Following large silver strikes in 1893 the town quickly expanded to city proportions. A village once again, Kaslo is a distribution center for the Lardeau Valley.

Duncan Dam, 42 kilometres (26 mi.) north, was the first of the three dams constructed by B.C. Hydro in accordance with the Columbia River Treaty, ratified by British Columbia and the United States in 1964. Southwest of the dam is the Kokanee Spawning Channel, built to compensate for the loss of natural spawning areas resulting from the dam's construction. The 3.2-kilometre (2-mi.) channel, one of the longest in the world, is said to be the first constructed for freshwater fish.

KELOWNA (H-6) pop. 117,312, elev. 420m/1,387'

• Hotels p. 196 • Restaurants p. 198
• Hotels & Restaurants map & index p. 216
• Part of Okanagan Valley area — see map p. 212

Kelowna is the center of a fruit and vineyard region around Lake Okanagan, from which one-third of all apples harvested in Canada are shipped. The lake also is known for its legendary monster, the Ogopogo, a Loch Ness type beast reportedly 9 to 21 metres (30-69 ft.) long with a head resembling that of a horse, goat or sheep.

The Kelowna Community Theatre stages productions during fall and winter; phone (250) 763-9018. The Okanagan Symphony Orchestra is another prominent cultural feature; phone (250) 763-7544.

Recreation in the area includes water sports, fishing and golf. City Park on Lake Okanagan is the city's largest park, with a beach, tennis courts and a children's water park.

The fall grape harvest is celebrated for 11 days in early October at the ▽ Okanagan Fall Wine Festival. Wine and food lovers congregate to take in more than 165 events that take place throughout the Okanagan Valley.

Kelowna Visitor Centre: 544 Harvey Ave., Kelowna, BC, Canada V1Y 6C9. **Phone:** (250) 861-1515 or (800) 663-4345.

KELOWNA ART GALLERY is at 1315 Water St. This architecturally striking museum offers changing exhibitions in its four galleries as well as art classes and lectures. **Time:** Allow 1 hour minimum. **Hours:** Tues.-Sat. 10-5 (also Thurs. 5-9), Sun. 1-4. **Cost:** $4.76; $3.81 (ages 65+ and students with ID); $9.52 (family); free (to all Thurs.). **Parking:** Metered street parking and pay lot are nearby. **Phone:** (250) 762-2226.

OKANAGAN MILITARY MUSEUM is at 1424 Ellis St. between Queensway and Doyle Ave. Permanent exhibits focus on the contributions of Okanagan Valley residents in the military. Items from the Boer War, World War I, World War II and others are on display. A reference library holds books on military history, and volunteer veterans are on-site to answer

(See map & index p. 216.)

questions. **Time:** Allow 30 minutes minimum. **Hours:** Tues.-Sat. 10-5. Closed major holidays. **Cost:** Donations. **Phone:** (250) 763-9292.

WINERIES

- **CedarCreek Estate Winery** is 12 km (7 mi.) s. at 5445 Lakeshore Rd., following signs. **Hours:** Tastings daily 10-7, July 1-Sept. 4; 11-6, May-June; 11-5, rest of year. Tours daily at 11, 1 and 3, May 15-Sept. 4. Closed Jan. 1, Christmas and day after Christmas. **Phone:** (778) 738-1020 in Canada. GT

- **Summerhill Pyramid Winery** is at 4870 Chute Lake Rd. **Hours:** Tastings daily 7 a.m.-9 p.m. Tours are given daily at noon, 2, 4 and 6. **Phone:** (250) 764-8000 or (800) 667-3538. GT

 AAA.com/hertz—

When your ideal road trip

includes a comfortable ride

ACCENT INNS   250/862-8888 **16**
 APPROVED   Hotel. **Address:** 1140 Harvey Ave V1Y 6E7

A VISTA VILLA COUPLES RETREAT   250/762-7837 **12**
THREE DIAMOND Bed & Breakfast. **Address:** 962 Ryder Dr V1Y 7T5

BEST WESTERN PLUS KELOWNA HOTEL & SUITES
250/860-1212 **21**

THREE DIAMOND   Best Western PLUS.   **AAA Benefit:** Members save up to 15% and earn bonus points!
Hotel

Address: 2402 Hwy 97 N V1X 4J1 **Location:** 0.6 mi (1 km) s of jct Hwy 97 N (Harvey Ave) and 33; corner of Leckie Rd. **Facility:** 176 units, some two bedrooms, efficiencies and kitchens. 2-8 stories, interior corridors. **Terms:** check-in 4 pm. **Pool:** heated indoor. **Activities:** hot tub, picnic facilities, exercise room, spa. **Guest Services:** valet and coin laundry.
Featured Amenity: breakfast buffet. (See ad this page.)

[SAVE] [ECO] [TI] [🛏] [≖] CALL [⚡] [🛁] [🏋] [BIZ] [HS]
[📶] [✕] [🍳] [🖥] / SOME UNITS [♿] [🐾] [❄]

COMFORT SUITES BY CHOICE HOTELS   250/861-1110 **15**
THREE DIAMOND Hotel. **Address:** 2656 Hwy 97 N V1X 4J4

▼ See AAA listing this page ▼

BW Best Western PLUS.
Kelowna Hotel & Suites

2402 Hwy 97 N, Kelowna, BC
250-860-1212
888-860-1212
Bestwesternkelowna.com

For business or leisure, there's always a little something extra.
- **Free Hot Breakfast Buffet**
- **Garden Courtyard & BBQ Patio**
- **On-site 97 Street Pub**
- **Mineral Water Pool & Hot Tubs**
- **Complimentary Airport & Downtown Shuttle**

Each Best Western® branded hotel is independently owned and operated.

CAA Rewards

(See map & index p. 216.)

DELTA HOTELS BY MARRIOTT GRAND OKANAGAN RESORT
250/763-4500 **11**

THREE DIAMOND

Resort Hotel

DELTA HOTELS **AAA Benefit:** Members save 5% or more!

Address: 1310 Water St V1Y 9P3 **Location:** Waterfront. Hwy 97 (Harvey Ave), 0.6 mi (1 km) w along Water St. **Facility:** Right on the lake, this lovely hotel has a lagoon where boats can dock. Units range from rooms with modern and comfortable décor featuring smart desks with plug-and-play panels to upscale condos. 324 units, some condominiums. 3-10 stories, interior corridors. **Parking:** on-site (fee) and valet. **Terms:** check-in 4 pm. **Pool:** heated outdoor, heated indoor. **Activities:** sauna, hot tub, steamroom, motor boats, self-propelled boats, boat dock, recreation programs in season, bicycles, trails, exercise room, spa. **Guest Services:** valet laundry.

SAVE ECO 🐕 ➡️ 📶 🍽️ 🛗 ▽ CALL 🚹 🏊 🐾 BIZ 📶 ✕ 🎦 🔋 🔲 📺 / SOME UNITS 🐕 HS 🔲

FAIRFIELD INN & SUITES BY MARRIOTT KELOWNA
250/763-2800 **19**

THREE DIAMOND SAVE Hotel. **Address:** 1655 Powick Rd V1X 4L1

AAA Benefit: Members save 5% or more!

FOUR POINTS BY SHERATON KELOWNA AIRPORT
250/807-2000 **10**

THREE DIAMOND

Hotel

FOUR POINTS BY SHERATON

AAA Benefit: Members save 5% or more!

Address: 5505 Airport Way V1V 3C3 **Location:** Hwy 97 (Harvey Ave), just w. **Facility:** 120 units, some efficiencies. 6 stories, interior corridors. **Amenities:** safes. **Pool:** heated indoor. **Activities:** hot tub, exercise room. **Guest Services:** valet and coin laundry, rental car service, area transportation.

SAVE ➡️ 🍽️ 🛗 ▽ CALL 🚹 🏊 🐾 BIZ HS 📶 ✕ 🎦 🔋 🔲 📺 / SOME UNITS 🐕

▼ See AAA listing p. 198 ▼

RAMADA
BY WYNDHAM
HOTEL & CONFERENCE CENTRE, KELOWNA, BC

RAMADA
BY WYNDHAM

Comfortable   *Enjoyable*   *Relaxing*

TF 1.800.665.2518

PH 250.860.9711

ramadalodgehotelkelowna.com

ramadalodge@rpbhotels.com

2170 Harvey Ave (Hwy 97 N)
Kelowna, BC V1Y 6G8

🔗 **What's for dinner?**

AAA.com/travelguides/restaurants

(See map & index p. 216.)

HOLIDAY INN EXPRESS & SUITES KELOWNA - EAST
778/484-2999 **18**
THREE DIAMOND Hotel. **Address:** 1620 Podwick Rd V1X 7G5

HOTEL ELDORADO
250/763-7500 **25**
THREE DIAMOND
Classic Boutique Hotel

Address: 500 Cook Rd V1W 3G9 **Location:** Waterfront. Hwy 97 (Harvey Ave), 2.5 mi (4 km) s on Pandosy St (which becomes Lakeshore Rd). **Facility:** Choose between lovely, cozy Heritage rooms or the more modern Arms suites here. Some have great lake views and verandas. On busy nights, music from the bar can drift to the rooms directly above. 53 units. 3-4 stories, interior corridors. **Terms:** check-in 4 pm. **Amenities:** safes. **Dining:** Lakeside Dining Room & Bar, see separate listing. **Pool:** heated outdoor, heated indoor. **Activities:** hot tub, steamroom, self-propelled boats, marina, bicycles, trails, exercise room. **Guest Services:** valet laundry.

[SAVE] [ECO] [icons] / SOME UNITS [icons]

KANATA KELOWNA HOTEL AND CONFERENCE CENTER
250/763-0500 **20**
THREE DIAMOND
Hotel

Address: 2429 Hwy 97 N V1X 4J2 **Location:** 0.6 mi (1 km) s of jct Hwy 97 N (Harvey Ave) and 33. **Facility:** 190 units. 4-7 stories, interior corridors. **Terms:** check-in 4 pm. **Pool:** heated indoor. **Activities:** hot tub, exercise room. **Guest Services:** valet and coin laundry. **Featured Amenity:** continental breakfast.

[SAVE] [ECO] [icons] CALL [icons]
[BIZ] [icons] / SOME UNITS [icons] [HS]

KELOWNA INN & SUITES
250/762-2533 **14**
APPROVED Motel. **Address:** 1070 Harvey Ave V1Y 8S4

MANTEO RESORT-WATERFRONT HOTEL & VILLAS
250/860-1031 **24**
THREE DIAMOND
Resort Hotel

Address: 3762 Lakeshore Rd V1W 3L4 **Location:** Waterfront. Hwy 97 (Harvey Ave), 2.5 mi (4 km) s on Pandosy St (which becomes Lakeshore Rd). **Facility:** Set on the lake, this resort has spacious, upscale hotel rooms and suites with cozy, plush bedding and either balconies or patios. You could choose to splurge on one of the three-story villas. 102 units, some two bedrooms, three bedrooms and kitchens. 4 stories, interior/exterior corridors. **Terms:** check-in 4 pm. **Amenities:** safes. **Dining:** Smack DAB, see separate listing. **Pool:** heated outdoor, heated indoor. **Activities:** sauna, hot tub, motor boats, self-propelled boats, boat dock, tennis, recreation programs in summer, playground, game room, exercise room. **Guest Services:** valet and coin laundry.

[SAVE] [ECO] [icons] CALL [icons] [BIZ] [icons]
[icons] / SOME UNITS [HS] [icons]

PRESTIGE BEACH HOUSE KELOWNA, BW PREMIER COLLECTION
250/860-7900 **53**
THREE DIAMOND [SAVE] Hotel. **Address:** 1675 Abbott St V1Y 8S3

AAA Benefit: Members save up to 15% and earn bonus points!

RAMADA BY WYNDHAM HOTEL & CONFERENCE CENTRE
250/860-9711 **22**
THREE DIAMOND Hotel. **Address:** 2170 Harvey Ave V1Y 6G8 *(See ad p. 197.)*

THE ROYAL ANNE HOTEL
250/763-2277 **13**
THREE DIAMOND Hotel. **Address:** 348 Bernard Ave V1Y 6N5

SIESTA SUITES
250/763-5013 **23**
APPROVED Motel. **Address:** 3152 Lakeshore Rd V1W 3T1

SUPER 8 BY WYNDHAM KELOWNA
250/762-8222 **17**
APPROVED Motel. **Address:** 2592 Hwy 97 N V1X 4J4

WHERE TO EAT

BAI TONG
250/763-8638 **16**
APPROVED Thai. Casual Dining. **Address:** 275 Bernard Ave V1X 6N2

BLUETAIL SUSHI & BISTRO
778/484-5900 **23**
APPROVED Sushi. Casual Dining. **Address:** 1675 Commerce Ave, #102 V1X 8A9

BOUCHONS BISTRO
250/763-6595 **12**
THREE DIAMOND French. Fine Dining. **Address:** 105-1180 Sunset Dr V1Y 9W6

BREAD CO. FINE BAKED GOODS & EATERY
250/762-3336 **17**
APPROVED Breads/Pastries Sandwiches. Quick Serve. **Address:** 363 Bernard Ave V1Y 6N6

CEDAR CREEK WINERY TERRACE RESTAURANT
778/738-1027 **34**
THREE DIAMOND New Canadian. Casual Dining. **Address:** 5445 Lakeshore Rd V1W 4S5

DAWETT FINE INDIAN CUISINE
250/717-1668 **14**
APPROVED Indian. Casual Dining. **Address:** 1435 Ellis St V1Y 2A3

DUNNENZIES PIZZA CO.
250/763-2420 **19**
APPROVED Pizza. Quick Serve. **Address:** 1559 Ellis St V1Y 2A7

EARLS KITCHEN + BAR
250/763-2777
APPROVED American. Casual Dining. **Address:** 211 Bernard Ave V1Y 6N2

THE FIXX CAFE & PASTA BAR
250/861-3499 **30**
APPROVED International. Casual Dining. **Address:** 3275 Lakeshore Rd, #101 V1W 3S9

THE JAMMERY
250/766-1139 **10**
APPROVED Breakfast Sandwiches. Casual Dining. **Address:** 8038 Hwy 97 N V1X 6A6

JOEY RESTAURANTS
250/860-8999
APPROVED American. Casual Dining. **Address:** 300-2475 Hwy 97 V1X 4J2

LAKESIDE DINING ROOM & BAR
250/763-7500 **32**
THREE DIAMOND Regional Canadian. Fine Dining. **Address:** 500 Cook Rd V1W 3G9

LITTLE HOBO
778/478-0411 **22**
APPROVED Soup Sandwiches. Quick Serve. **Address:** 596 Leon Ave V1Y 6J6

(See map & index p. 216.)

MABUI SUSHI IZAKAYA   250-868-8852 (25)
WWW APPROVED   Japanese Small Plates Sushi. Casual
Dining. Address: 2070 Harvey Ave, #8 V1Y 8P8

MAMMA ROSA RESTAURANT   250-763-4114 (20)
WWW APPROVED   Italian. Casual Dining. Address: 561
Lawrence Ave V1Y 6L8

THE MARMALADE CAT CAFE   250-861-4158 (28)
WWW APPROVED   Sandwiches Desserts. Quick Serve.
Address: 2903 Pandosy St, #103 V1Y 1W1

MOXIE'S CLASSIC GRILL   250-861-6110 (26)
WWW APPROVED   American. Casual Dining. Address: 1730
Cooper Rd V1Y 8V5

OAK + CRU SOCIAL KITCHEN & WINE BAR
                             250-869-3508 (13)
WWW THREE DIAMOND   Regional Canadian. Casual Dining.
Address: 1310 Water St V1Y 9P3

PEARSON'S EUROPEAN DELI   250-762-0800 (27)
WWW APPROVED   European Deli. Quick Serve. Address:
2070 Harvey Ave, Unit 30 V1Y 8P8

RAUDZ REGIONAL TABLE   250-868-8805 (18)
WWW THREE DIAMOND   New Canadian. Casual Dining. Address:
1560 Water St V1Y 1J7

SALT & BRICK   778-484-3234 (15)
WWW APPROVED   Canadian. Casual Dining. Address: 243
Bernard Ave V1Y 6N2

SMACK DAB   250-860-4488 (31)
WWW THREE DIAMOND   American. Gastropub. Address: 3762
Lakeshore Rd V1W 3L4

SUMMERHILL SUNSET ORGANIC BISTRO
                             250-764-8000 (33)
WWW THREE DIAMOND   New Canadian. Casual Dining. Address:
4870 Chute Lake Rd V1W 4M3

VALOROSO FOODS   250-860-3641 (24)
WWW APPROVED   Italian Deli. Quick Serve. Address: 1467
Sutherland Ave V1Y 5Y4

WATERFRONT WINES   250-979-1222 (11)
WWW THREE DIAMOND   New Canadian. Fine Dining. Address:
104-1180 Sunset Dr V1Y 9W6

YAMAS TAVERNA GREEK RESTAURANT 250-763-5823 (21)
WWW APPROVED   Greek. Casual Dining. Address: 1630
Ellis St V1Y 8L1

ZABB THAI RESTAURANT   778-484-3988 (29)
WWW APPROVED   Thai. Casual Dining. Address: 3009
Pandosy St V1Y 1W3

KIMBERLEY (C-11) pop. 6,652

Kimberley is a winter sports center with a Bavarian theme and a pedestrian mall—the Platzl—
complete with wandering minstrels and a huge
cuckoo clock. The Kimberley Community Gardens
present colorful views June through October.

Built on the slopes of Sullivan and North Star hills,
Kimberley is one of Canada's highest cities. It is perhaps best known as the site of the Sullivan Mine, one
of the world's largest underground silver, lead and zinc

mines. The mine closed in 2001 after 92 years of production, yielding more than $20 billion in ore.

In keeping with the Bavarian theme, the city presents the Kimberley Old Time Accordion Championships for a week each year in early July.

Kimberley Visitor Centre: 270 Kimberley Ave.,
Kimberley, BC, Canada V1A 0A3. **Phone:** (778)
481-1891.

KIMBERLEY'S UNDERGROUND MINING RAILWAY
departs the lower train station, 2 blks. n.w. of the
Platzl. The railway offers narrated 1-hour train rides,
transporting passengers through the Mark Creek
Valley on a narrow-gauge mine track. Interactive
mining displays are offered in an underground
tunnel.

Hours: Mine tours daily at 11, 1 and 3, late June-
Labour Day weekend. Resort Express rides Sat.-
Sun. and holiday Mon. at 10, late June-Labour Day
weekend. Phone ahead to confirm schedule. **Cost:**
Mine tours $23.81; $14.24 (ages 13-18); $9.52
(ages 4-12). Resort Express $14.24; $9.52 (ages
4-12); $38.10 (family, two adults and two children, or
one adult and three children). **Phone:** (250)
427-0022 or (250) 427-7365.

MOUNTAIN SPIRIT RESORT   250/432-6000
WWW THREE DIAMOND   Condominium. Address: 400 Stemwinder
Dr V1A 2Y9

TRICKLE CREEK LODGE   250/427-5175
WWW THREE DIAMOND   Extended Stay Hotel. Address: 500 Stemwinder Dr V1A 2Y6

WHERE TO EAT

THE BEAN TREE CAFE   250/427-7889
WWW APPROVED   Coffee/Tea Sandwiches. Quick Serve.
Address: 295 Spokane St V1A 2E6

BEAR'S EATERY   250/427-3412
WWW APPROVED   Comfort Food. Casual Dining. Address:
324 Archibald St V1A 1M9

KOOTENAY NATIONAL PARK (A-11)

Elevations in the park range from 901 metres
(2,956 ft.) at the park's west gate to 3,424
metres (11,235 ft.) at Deltaform Mountain.
Refer to CAA/AAA maps for additional
elevation information.

Straddling the Banff-Windermere Highway (Hwy.
93) from the Continental Divide to the Rocky Mountain Trench, Kootenay National Park encompasses
1,406 square kilometres (543 sq. mi.) of Rocky
Mountain landscape. Following the Vermilion and
Kootenay river valleys, this slender 94-kilometre-
long (63-mi.) park embraces several significant geologic features and is part of the Canadian Rocky
Mountain Parks UNESCO World Heritage Site.

Kootenay's western entrance provides one of the
most dramatic gateways to any of the national parks

in Canada. The highway clings to a sheer cliff before snaking through a narrow gorge and running along an iron-red rock face where bighorn sheep are a frequent sight. Visitors driving this scenic highway will see dramatic landscapes as they travel the Golden Triangle or Hot Springs routes.

Wildfires and prescribed burns in the northern part of the park have left charred trees visible from the road, but nature's renewal is visible through stunning wildflower displays in the burn areas during the summer.

Extensive faults created two of the park's most significant features: the Radium Hot Springs and the Paint Pots. Located in the southern end of the park, Radium Hot Springs is a result of rainwater and runoff being vaporized deep underground. The steam returns to the surface and is condensed in these clear, odorless springs. First used by the indigenous peoples in the area, the hot springs were later popularized by health buffs at the turn of the 20th century.

At the opposite end of the park are the Paint Pots, cold springs with a spiritual significance to the region's inhabitants. These iron-rich mineral springs bubble up into small, emerald green pools before staining the surrounding earth red. The Siksika, Nakoda and Ktunaxa First Nations once used the bright bronze mud called ochre to decorate their homes and draw the rock paintings once visible near Sinclair Canyon.

Good grazing conditions bring herds of bighorn sheep. Bears, deer, mountain goats, mountain goats, elk and countless species of birds are commonly seen throughout the park.

General Information and Activities

The park is open year-round. Parks Canada's facilities, including three frontcountry campgrounds—Redstreak, Marble Canyon and McLeod Meadows—are open during the summer months, with Redstreak staying open the longest. Phone ahead to confirm the schedule.

Kootenay provides a variety of trails ranging from easy hikes to multiday backcountry treks. In July and August, Parks Canada offers guided hikes to the recently discovered Burgess Shale Fossil Beds near Stanley Glacier. Hidden in the mountains near the continental divide, the Burgess Shale fossils continue to help scientists unravel the mystery of life on earth 505 million years ago. Fees range from $27.50-$55 and reservations are required; phone (877) 737-3783.

All backcountry campers must obtain a wilderness pass. Information about trails, park features and facilities can be obtained from the visitor center in the village of Radium Hot Springs from the Victoria Day weekend through Labour Day and at the park's west gate during the remainder of the year.

Nonmotorized watercraft are permitted on all lakes and rivers in the park. *See Recreation Areas Chart.*

ADMISSION to the park $9.80; $8.30 (ages 65+); free (ages 0-17); $19.60 (all occupants of a private vehicle with up to seven people). An annual pass, valid at most Canadian national parks, marine areas and historic sites, is available.

PETS must be leashed at all times. Pets are permitted in the backcountry overnight.

ADDRESS inquiries to the Superintendent, Kootenay National Park, 7556 Main St. E., Box 220, Radium Hot Springs, BC, Canada V0A 1M0; phone (250) 347-9505.

MARBLE CANYON is on Hwy. 93 at the northern end of Kootenay National Park and close to the Alberta border. The walls of marble-like gray limestone make this one of the most beautiful canyons in the Rockies. Tokumm Creek has cut a sheer, narrow cleft to the depth of about 40 metres (130 ft.). A self-guiding trail follows the top edge of the canyon and leads to a waterfall. Interpretive signs describe the power of water in shaping the canyon's features. **Time:** Allow 30 minutes minimum. **Phone:** (250) 347-9505.

 RADIUM HOT SPRINGS is just n. of the w. entrance to Kootenay National Park. Water temperatures range from 37 to 40 C (98 to 104 F). There is a hot pool, a cool pool and a 372-square-metre (4,000-sq.-ft.) day spa. Iron oxide also colors the towering sandstone cliffs, giving a perpetual sunset quality. *See Recreation Areas Chart.*

Hours: Pools open daily 9 a.m.-11 p.m., mid-May to mid-Oct. Hot pools Mon.-Fri. 1-9, Sat.-Sun. 10-9. Cool pools Fri. 6-9 p.m., Sat.-Sun. noon-9, mid-Oct. to mid-May. **Cost:** Day Pass $10.55; $9.55 (ages 65+); $8.10 (ages 3-17); $29.50 (family, two adults and two children; each additional child $4.95). Pool fee $7.30; $6.40 (ages 65+); $4.95 (ages 3-17); $20.20 (family, two adults and two children; each additional child $2.95). **Phone:** (250) 347-9485, (250) 343-6783 in southeastern British Columbia or (888) 347-9331. 🏕️ 🍴 ⊠ 🐾 ⛲

LANGLEY (H-11) pop. 25,081, elev. 10m/33'
- **Hotels & Restaurants map & index p. 276**
- **Part of Vancouver area — see map p. 249**

Langley, the site of a Hudson's Bay Co. fort built in 1840 *(see Fort Langley National Historic Site p. 183)*, is also an important farming and wine-growing region. Orchards, berry farms, horse ranches, vineyards and lavender and heirloom vegetable farms make a patchwork of the countryside.

The city's position on the banks of the Fraser River makes it an easy proposition to enjoy water-based activities. Kayaks and voyageur canoes can be rented and launched at the Fort Langley Marina.

Langley Visitor Centre: 7888 200th St., Unit 2, Langley, BC, Canada V2Y 3J4. **Phone:** (604) 371-1477.

(See map & index p. 276.)

BEST WESTERN PLUS LANGLEY INN

604/530-9311 **64**

THREE DIAMOND
Hotel

Best Western PLUS

AAA Benefit: Members save up to 15% and earn bonus points!

Address: 5978 Glover Rd V3A 4H9 **Location:** Trans-Canada Hwy 1 exit 66 (232nd St), 3.6 mi (6 km) se on Hwy 10, follow signs. **Facility:** 78 units, some two bedrooms, efficiencies and kitchens. 2 stories, interior corridors. **Pool:** heated indoor. **Activities:** hot tub, exercise room. **Guest Services:** valet and coin laundry.

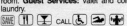

COAST HOTEL & CONVENTION CENTRE 604/530-1500 **65**
THREE DIAMOND Hotel. **Address:** 20393 Fraser Hwy V3A 7N2

DAYS INN & SUITES LANGLEY 604/539-0100 **63**
APPROVED Hotel. **Address:** 20250 Logan Ave V3A 4L6

HOLIDAY INN EXPRESS HOTEL & SUITES LANGLEY

604/882-2000 **62**

THREE DIAMOND
Hotel

Address: 8750 204th St V1M 2Y5 **Location:** Trans-Canada Hwy 1 exit 58 (200th St/Langley City), just e on 88th Ave. **Facility:** 85 units. 4 stories, interior corridors. **Pool:** heated indoor. **Activities:** sauna, hot tub, steamroom, exercise room. **Guest Services:** valet and coin laundry. **Featured Amenity:** full hot breakfast.

WHERE TO EAT

AKANE JAPANESE RESTAURANT 604/882-1134 **83**
APPROVED Japanese. Casual Dining. **Address:** 20349 88th Ave V1M 2K5

AN INDIAN AFFAIR 604/539-8114 **84**
APPROVED Indian. Casual Dining. **Address:** 19653 Willowbrook Dr V2Y 1A5

BAN CHOK DEE THAI CUISINE 778/278-3088 **88**
APPROVED Thai. Casual Dining. **Address:** 20563 Douglas Cres V3A 4B6

CACTUS CLUB CAFE 604/427-2101 **85**
THREE DIAMOND New American. Casual Dining. **Address:** 6070 200th St V3A 1N4

C-LOVERS FISH & CHIPS 604/532-9747 **87**
APPROVED Seafood. Casual Dining. **Address:** 20251 Fraser Hwy V3A 4E7

ESTRELLA'S MONTREAL DELI 604/539-9988 **86**
APPROVED Deli Sandwiches. Quick Serve. **Address:** 5932 200th St V3A 1N3

RICKY'S ALL DAY GRILL
APPROVED American. Casual Dining.
LOCATIONS:
Address: 8720 204th St V1M 2Y5 **Phone:** 604/888-4211
Address: 22314 Fraser Hwy V3A 8M6 **Phone:** 604/530-4317

LILLOOET (B-7) pop. 2,322, elev. 290m/951'

Lillooet, on the Fraser River, marked the first leg of the Cariboo Waggon Road and was therefore sometimes referred to as "Mile 0." The trail reached north to such destinations as 100 Mile House and 150 Mile House, named for their distances from the start of the trail. In 1859, during the Cariboo Gold Rush, the 15,000 inhabitants of Lillooet made it the most populous city north of San Francisco and west of Chicago. The surrounding area now is of particular interest to rock hounds.

MIYAZAKI HOUSE is at 642 Russell Ln., near jct. Main St. and 6th Ave., following signs. Originally owned by prominent citizens Caspar and Cerise Phair, the late 19th-century house is an exceptional example of Victorian architecture. In the late 1940s Dr. Masajiro Miyazaki and his family purchased the house. Visitors will learn about both families and local history through photographs and antiques. The doctor's office also is in the house. Local art, cultural and community events are held here.

Time: Allow 30 minutes minimum. **Hours:** Thurs.-Mon. 10-4, June-Sept. Outdoor concerts are offered Wed. at 7, July-Aug. **Cost:** Donations. **Phone:** (250) 256-6808. **GT**

MAPLE RIDGE (H-11) pop. 76,052, elev. 30m/98'
• Hotels p. 202 • Restaurants p. 202
• Part of Vancouver area — see map p. 249

Maple Ridge lies on the north shore of the Fraser River, with the Coast Mountains to the north and the Stave and Pitt Rivers forming its east and west boundaries. Snow-capped peaks overlook this Fraser Valley community.

The Fraser River Heritage Walk, which starts at Port Haney Wharf, passes many of the town's notable spots. The Haney House at 11612 224th St. was built in 1876 and contains many furnishings and artifacts owned by three generations of the Haney family; phone (604) 463-1377. Displays at Maple Ridge Museum, 22520 116th Ave., reflect the history and geography of the area; phone (604) 463-5311.

Kanaka Creek Regional Park (see Recreation Areas Chart) offers hiking and horseback riding trails as well as canoeing, kayaking, fishing and picnic facilities. A fish hatchery is on the grounds. Phone (604) 530-4983. Maple Ridge also has a large per capita horse population and an extensive riding trail system.

Maple Ridge-Pitt Meadows Chamber of Commerce: 20214 Lougheed Hwy., #6, Maple Ridge, BC, Canada V2X 2P7. **Phone:** (604) 457-4599.

BEST WESTERN MAPLE RIDGE   604/467-1511

Hotel

AAA Benefit: Members save up to 15% and earn bonus points!

Address: 21650 Lougheed Hwy V2X 2S1 **Location:** 1.2 mi (2 km) w on Hwy 7 (Lougheed Hwy). 🚉 Port Haney, 1. **Facility:** 56 units, some efficiencies. 2 stories, interior corridors. **Pool:** heated indoor. **Activities:** sauna, hot tub, exercise room. **Guest Services:** coin laundry.

WHERE TO EAT

BILLY MINER ALEHOUSE CAFE   604/467-6002
✦ APPROVED   Burgers Pizza. Casual Dining. **Address:** 22355 River Rd V2X 2C5

MAYNE ISLAND (H-10) pop. 1,074

Although visited by the Spanish in the 1790s, it was not until the 1850s that British Capt. George Richards surveyed and mapped the area. Capt. Richards named Mayne Island after his lieutenant, Richard Charles Mayne. During the gold rush of the mid-1800s the island, in the Gulf Islands *(see place listing p. 188)* halfway between Victoria and the mouth of the Fraser River, was a stopping point for miners heading for the riches to be found at the gold fields along the river.

The island is known as a haven for artists and artisans. Small and sparsely settled, Mayne offers quiet beaches and hiking trails; wildflowers; a landscape heavy with trees; seals, sea lions, salmon and sole offshore; and a large variety of birds, from tiny hummingbirds to soaring bald eagles.

Mayne Island Community Chamber of Commerce: P.O. Box 2, Mayne Island, BC, Canada V0N 2J0.

MERRITT (C-8) pop. 7,113, elev. 858m/2,814'

Merritt is known for its many lakes. Of particular interest is Nicola Lake, a large warm-water lake 10 kilometres (6 mi.) north of town. For a view of the landmarks, including a giant Canadian flag, hike to the Merritt Lookout from Juniper Drive. Recreational activities in the area include swimming, fishing, sailing, water skiing and windsurfing. Monck Provincial Park, on the west side of the lake, offers camping and picnic facilities.

Merritt Visitor Centre: 2202 Voght St., P.O. Box 1105, Merritt, BC, Canada V1K 1B8. **Phone:** (250) 378-0349.

BEST WESTERN PLUS MERRITT HOTEL   250/378-0700

✦ THREE DIAMOND

Hotel

AAA Benefit: Members save up to 15% and earn bonus points!

Address: 3969 Crawford Ave V1K 0A4 **Location:** Hwy 5 exit 290, just e. **Facility:** 83 units, some two bedrooms, efficiencies and kitchens. 4 stories, interior corridors. **Parking:** winter plug-ins. **Pool:** heated indoor. **Activities:** hot tub, exercise room. **Guest Services:** valet and coin laundry.

QUALITY INN MERRITT   250/378-4253

✦ APPROVED

Motel

Address: 4025 Walters St V1K 1K1 **Location:** Hwy 5 exit 290, 0.6 mi (1 km) w. **Facility:** 56 units. 2 stories (no elevator), exterior corridors. **Parking:** winter plug-ins. **Pool:** heated indoor. **Activities:** hot tub, limited exercise equipment. **Guest Services:** coin laundry. **Featured Amenity:** full hot breakfast.

RAMADA LIMITED   250/378-3567

✦ APPROVED

Motel

Address: 3571 Voght St V1K 1C5 **Location:** Hwy 5 exit 290, just w. **Facility:** 52 units, some two bedrooms and kitchens. 3 stories (no elevator), exterior corridors. **Parking:** winter plug-ins. **Pool:** heated indoor. **Activities:** sauna, hot tub, exercise room. **Guest Services:** coin laundry. **Featured Amenity:** full hot breakfast.

SUPER 8 MERRITT   250/378-9422
✦ APPROVED   Motel. **Address:** 3561 Voght St V1K 1C5

WHERE TO EAT

BRAMBLES BAKERY & CAFE   250/378-6655
✦ APPROVED   Breads/Pastries Sandwiches. Quick Serve. **Address:** 2151 Quilchena Ave V1K 1B8

GAME ON SPORTS BAR AND GRILL   250/315-1022
✦ APPROVED   American. Casual Dining. **Address:** 3701 De Wolf Way V1K 1C4

HOME RESTAURANT   250/378-9112
✦ APPROVED   American. Casual Dining. **Address:** 3561 Voght St V1K 1C5

KEKULI CAFE   250/378-3599
✦ APPROVED   Canadian. Quick Serve. **Address:** 2051 Voght St V1K 1B8

🔗 Love the great outdoors? Find places to camp
at AAA.com/campgrounds

MISSION (H-11) pop. 36,426, elev. 55m/180'
• Part of Vancouver area — see map p. 249

Mission developed from a Roman Catholic mission built in 1861 to serve First Nations tribes. The site became a popular stopping place for trappers, settlers and other river travelers.

The Fraser River provides opportunities for swimming, fishing, boating and water sports; its sandbars are good for rock hounds in search of agates, jades and garnets. Motocross and boat races are held at Mission Raceway from March through October.

Mission Regional Chamber of Commerce: 34033 Lougheed Hwy., Mission, BC, Canada V2V 5X8. **Phone:** (604) 826-6914.

FRASER RIVER SAFARI departs from the harborfront at 33428 Harbour Ave. A 3-hour narrated cruise along the Fraser River in a fully covered jet boat comes complete with scenic mountain views; possible sightings of bears, seals, deer and birds; and entertaining folklore about native legends, fur traders, gold miners and Sasquatch. A stop is made at Kilby Historic Site in Harrison Mills. Eaglewatching tours are available in November and December.

Time: Allow 3 hours, 30 minutes minimum. **Hours:** Trips depart daily at 9:30 and 2, July 15-Dec. 15; at 10, rest of year. Arrive 15 minutes before departure. Closed Christmas. **Cost:** $104.76; $95.24 (ages 60+); $71.43 (ages 5-16); $320 (family, two adults and two children). Reservations are required. **Phone:** (604) 826-7361 or (866) 348-6877.

POWER HOUSE AT STAVE FALLS is 1.3 km (.8 mi.) w. on Ferndale Ave. from jct. Stave Lake St. and Ferndale Ave., then 12.9 km (8 mi.) n.w. on Dewdney Trunk Rd. to 31338 Dewdney Trunk Rd. Through interactive science exhibits and historic displays in Electrica, the facility tells the story of how power helped build British Columbia. Within a 50-seat theater, visitors may start their self-guiding tour with a 9-minute video that gives an overview of the history of Stave Falls and tells why electricity is important in our daily lives. On display in the Generator Hall are generators and turbines within a 1912 generating station. History Hall contains electrical gadgets from yesteryear. There also are outdoor exhibits and walking trails.

Time: Allow 1 hour minimum. **Hours:** Daily 10-4, mid-Sept. to mid-Oct.; Thurs.-Mon. 10-4, Mar. 1 to mid-Sept. Phone ahead to confirm schedule. **Cost:** $5.71; $4.76 (ages 6-17, ages 55+ and students with ID); $14.24 (family, two adults and two children). Guided tour (minimum of 10 people) $3.81; reservations are required. **Phone:** (604) 462-1222.

WESTMINSTER ABBEY is 1.5 km (.9 mi.) e., .7 km (.5 mi.) n. of Hwy. 7 to 34224 Dewdney Trunk Rd. The Seminary of Christ the King is managed by Benedictine monks. Of interest are the view and architecture. Modest dress is required. **Time:** Allow 30

minutes minimum. **Hours:** Mon.-Sat. 1:30-4:30, Sun. 2-4:30. Grounds open daily 6 a.m.-8 p.m. **Cost:** Free. **Phone:** (604) 826-8975.

BEST WESTERN PLUS MISSION CITY LODGE
604/820-5500

 APPROVED
Hotel

AAA Benefit: Members save up to 15% and earn bonus points!

Address: 32281 Lougheed Hwy V2V 1A3 **Location:** Just w of Hwy 11; corner of Lougheed Hwy (Hwy 7) and Hurd St. **Facility:** 80 units, some kitchens. 4 stories, interior corridors. **Pool:** heated indoor. **Activities:** sauna, hot tub, exercise room. **Guest Services:** valet and coin laundry. **Featured Amenity:** full hot breakfast.

MORICETOWN (E-3) elev. 411m/1,348'

Moricetown is a Wet'suwet'en community that still practices the traditional hereditary system of governance. Originally known as Kyah Wiget, it was once the largest village of the Bulkley River Carrier tribe, a settlement built some 4,000 years ago. The town later took the name of Father A.G. Morice, a missionary who lived among the Carrier First Nation in the late 19th century.

MOUNT REVELSTOKE NATIONAL PARK (A-9)

Elevations in the park range from 480 metres (1,575 ft.) at the bottom of Mount Revelstoke to 2,639 metres (8,658 ft.) at the Mount Revelstoke summit at the Inverness Peaks. Refer to CAA/AAA maps for additional elevation information.

On the western edge of the Selkirk Range in southeastern British Columbia, Mount Revelstoke National Park is 260 square kilometres (100 sq. mi.) of sharp peaks, heavily timbered slopes and flowering meadows. The Selkirk Range, flanked on the east by the Purcell Range and on the west by the Monashee Range, are distinguished by their height and geologic complexity.

Erosion by glaciers and the heavy rainfall of the region have carved the rock of the Selkirks into jagged forms. Complementing the park's dense green forests and lush wildflower meadows are glacier-fed streams and lakes as well as the deep snows that blanket the slopes until late June.

Deer inhabit the lower slopes; black and grizzly bears and mountain caribou also may be seen in the park. Most mountain species of birds are represented, including Fox Sparrows, Hermit Thrushes and Northern Hawk Owls.

The Trans-Canada Highway (Hwy. 1) passes through the southeastern portion of the park for 13 kilometres (8 mi.) and parallels its southern boundary for 18 kilometres (11 mi.).

General Information and Activities

Visitor facilities and accommodations are available in the city of Revelstoke at the western park entrance. Park passes are available at the park kiosks at the base of the Meadows in the Sky Parkway and Giant Cedars Boardwalk Trail as well as the Rogers Pass Discovery Centre in Glacier National Park. Phone ahead for schedule.

From Hwy. 1, the Meadows in the Sky Parkway, a 26-kilometre (16-mi.) hard surface road that is open only in summer leads to the summit of Mount Revelstoke and provides an excellent panoramic view. Along its length are 16 switchbacks and several viewpoints. Picnic areas are available at Monashee, the 8-kilometre (5-mi.) viewpoint on this road, and at Balsam Lake, 1 kilometre (.6 mi.) from the summit. Other picnic areas and nature trails are along the Trans-Canada Highway.

Recreation includes subalpine hiking, mountain climbing and catch-and-release fishing. Children can play while enhancing their bicycling skills at the Beaver Lodge Kids Bike Park in the Nels Nelsen area. August is the best time to view wildflowers. A ski-jumping exhibit honors the historic ski jumps located in the park. More than 60 kilometres (37 mi.) of hiking trails lead to such sites as Miller and Jade lakes. Voluntary registration for backcountry travelers is available. Fishing is by permit, available at the park kiosk at the base of the Meadows in the Sky Parkway or the park administrative office in Revelstoke. *See Recreation Areas Chart.*

ADMISSION to the park $7.43; $6.48 (ages 65+); $3.71 (ages 6-16); $18.67 (all occupants of a private vehicle with up to seven people). An annual pass, valid at most Canadian national parks, marine areas and historic sites, is available. Buses and trailers are not permitted on the Meadows in the Sky Parkway. Class A motor homes are not recommended as parking is extremely limited at the summit of the mountain.

PETS are permitted in the park provided they are on leashes at all times.

ADDRESS inquiries to the Superintendent, Mount Revelstoke and Glacier National Parks, P.O. Box 350, Revelstoke, BC, Canada V0E 2S0; phone (250) 837-7500.

NANAIMO (G-10) pop. 83,810, elev. 30m/98'

Some 120 kilometres (75 mi.) north of Victoria, Nanaimo began as a Hudson's Bay Co. outpost called Colvilletown, established for miners brought from England and Scotland to mine coal. A thriving forest and marine products industry replaced coal's influence, and the economy of contemporary Nanaimo is centered on technology, service, manufacturing, tourism and recreation.

Offshore islands and nearby mountains and lakes provide a variety of recreational opportunities including hiking, swimming, camping and picnicking. Charter companies offer wildlife tours year-round to view animals such as the area's bald eagles and sea lions.

For a touch of wilderness in the middle of the city, check out Bowen Park, on the Millstone River just north of downtown. This 36-hectare (89-acre) expanse provides an outlet for a variety of activities. Trails wind through forests of fir, hemlock, cedar and maple, and kids enjoy the 4-H barnyard open July through August. A rhododendron grove, a nature center, duck pond, picnic shelters, swimming pool and sports fields complete the complex. In winter, tobogganers take to the park's big hills.

Exotic trees provide a setting for picnicking at Harmac Arboretum, 11 kilometres (7 mi.) south at Harmac Pulp Mill and Duke Point roads. Newcastle Island (*see Recreation Areas Chart*) is a marine provincial park accessible by a 10-minute ferry ride from Maffeo-Sutton Park on the harborfront. Automobiles are not permitted; the ferry operates daily every 30 minutes on the half hour and hour from spring through mid-October. Return trip fare is $5.

In addition to the ferry, salmon sport fishing, scuba diving, windsurfing and sailing are also available from Nanaimo's natural harbor. An intertidal park with three lighted water curtains and a 4-kilometre (2.5-mi.) walkway along the seawall graces Nanaimo's waterfront. St. Jean's Custom Cannery is one of three factories where fishing enthusiasts can have their catch canned or smoked.

On a landscaped hillside, Vancouver Island University offers views of the city and harbor below and also is the site of Nanaimo Art Gallery (*see attraction listing*). Visitors interested in prehistoric art can see sandstone carvings at Petroglyph Provincial Park, 3.25 kilometres (2 mi.) south on scenic Hwy. 1. Other cultural endeavors can be enjoyed at The Port Theatre, an 800-seat performing arts center at 125 Front St. that hosts local, national and international events; phone (250) 754-8550 for ticket information.

Nanaimo is accessible from the mainland by BC Ferries, which sails from Horseshoe Bay to Departure Bay and from Tsawwassen to Duke Point, 8 kilometres (5 mi.) south of Nanaimo. For more information phone (250) 386-3431 or (888) 223-3779.

Tourism Nanaimo: 2450 Northfield Rd., Nanaimo, BC, Canada V9S 0B2. **Phone:** (250) 756-0106, (250) 751-1556 or (800) 663-7337.

NANAIMO MUSEUM is at 100 Museum Way on the second floor of the Vancouver Island Conference Centre. Nanaimo's history is explored through exhibits depicting life for the city's earliest settlers, its days as a 19th-century mining center and its transition into the 21st century. Visitors can discover stories about the Snuneymuxw First Nation and check out a replica coal mine to feel what it was like to be an underground miner.

Time: Allow 1 hour minimum. **Hours:** Daily 10-5, May-Sept.; Mon.-Sat. 10-5, rest of year. Closed Jan. 1, Nov. 11, Christmas and day after Christmas. Phone ahead to confirm schedule. **Cost:** $1.90; $1.67 (ages 55+ and students with ID); 71c (ages 6-12). **Phone:** (250) 753-1821.

The Bastion is on Front St. across from the Coast Bastion Inn. The small fort was built in 1853 to protect early settlers. A display shows how the bastion was used in the 1860s. A noon ceremonial cannon firing is conducted by staff dressed in period costumes. **Hours:** Daily 10-5, Victoria Day weekend-Labour Day. **Cost:** Donations. **Phone:** (250) 753-1821.

BEST WESTERN DORCHESTER HOTEL 250/754-6835

 THREE DIAMOND

Hotel

Best Western **AAA Benefit:** Members save up to 15% and earn bonus points!

Address: 70 Church St V9R 5H4 **Location:** Hwy 19A (Island Hwy) to Comox Rd; downtown. **Facility:** 71 units. 4 stories, interior corridors. **Amenities:** safes. **Activities:** bicycles, exercise room. **Guest Services:** complimentary and valet laundry.

BEST WESTERN NORTHGATE INN 250/390-2222

 THREE DIAMOND

Hotel

Best Western **AAA Benefit:** Members save up to 15% and earn bonus points!

Address: 6450 Metral Dr V9T 2L8 **Location:** Hwy 19A (Island Hwy), just w on Aulds Rd, just s. **Facility:** 73 units, some efficiencies. 3 stories, interior corridors. **Amenities:** safes. **Activities:** exercise room. **Guest Services:** valet and coin laundry.

BUCCANEER INN 250/753-1246

APPROVED Motel. **Address:** 1577 Stewart Ave V9S 4E3

DAYS INN NANAIMO HARBOURVIEW 250/754-8171

APPROVED Hotel. **Address:** 809 Island Hwy S V9R 5K1

INN ON LONG LAKE 250/758-1144

THREE DIAMOND **Address:** 4700 Island Hwy N V9T 1W6 **Location:** Waterfront. 3.1 mi (5 km) n on Hwy 19A (Island Hwy) from Departure Bay Ferry Terminal. **Facility:** 62 units, some efficiencies and kitchens. 3 stories, exterior corridors. **Activities:** sauna, hot tub, boat dock, fishing, limited exercise equipment. **Guest Services:** valet and coin laundry. **Featured Amenity:** continental breakfast.

Hotel

TRAVELODGE NANAIMO 250/754-6355

APPROVED Hotel. **Address:** 96 Terminal Ave N V9S 4J2

WHERE TO EAT

ASTERAS GREEK TAVERNA 250/716-0451

APPROVED Greek. Casual Dining. **Address:** 347 Wesley St V9R 2T5

CACTUS CLUB CAFE 250/729-0011

THREE DIAMOND New American. Casual Dining. **Address:** 801-5800 Turner Rd V9T 6J4

GINA'S MEXICAN CAFE 250/753-5411

APPROVED Mexican. Casual Dining. **Address:** 47 Skinner St V9R 5K4

LONGWOOD BREWPUB 250/729-8225

APPROVED American. Gastropub. **Address:** 5775 Turner Rd V9T 6L8

POWER HOUSE LIVING FOODS CO. 250/591-7873

APPROVED Raw Foods. Casual Dining. **Address:** 200 Commercial St V9R 5G6

POWER HOUSE LIVING FOODS CO. 250/933-3733

APPROVED Raw Foods. Casual Dining. **Address:** 6560 Metral Dr V9T 2L8

RICKY'S ALL DAY GRILL 250/390-1227

APPROVED American. Casual Dining. **Address:** 6550 Island Hwy N V9V 1K8

SMITTY'S 250/716-8887

APPROVED American. Casual Dining. **Address:** 50 10th St V9R 6L1

ZOUGLA 250/716-3233

APPROVED Mediterranean. Casual Dining. **Address:** 2021 Estevan Rd V9S 3Y9

NARAMATA pop. 1,647

• Hotels & Restaurants map & index p. 216
• Part of Okanagan Valley area — see map p. 212

THE VILLAGE MOTEL 250/496-5535 35

APPROVED Motel. **Address:** 244 Robinson Ave V0H 1N0

WHERE TO EAT

THE PATIO AT LAKE BREEZE 250/496-5659 42

THREE DIAMOND Mediterranean. Casual Dining. **Address:** 930 Sammet Rd V0H 1N0

NELSON (C-10) pop. 10,230, elev. 535m/1,755'

• Hotels p. 206 • Restaurants p. 206

An old iron and silver mining town, Nelson was settled by prospectors in the late 1880s. With the depletion of its mines, the town turned to logging, sawmilling and area trade. However, the legacy of the bonanza days lives on in the more than 350 heritage sites. Most of Nelson's historic commercial buildings are open to the public, but homes are private and closed to visitors. If Fido comes along with you, be sure to follow Nelson's dog ordinance and keep him out of restricted zones.

Nearby parks, lakes, streams and mountains offer all types of summer and winter recreation. Kokanee Creek and Kokanee Glacier provincial parks *(see Recreation Areas Chart)* are 19 kilometres (12 mi.) northeast on Hwy. 3A.

Nelson Chamber of Commerce: 91 Baker St., Nelson, BC, Canada V1L 4G8. **Phone:** (250) 352-3433 or (877) 663-5706.

Self-guiding tours: Maps detailing walking and driving tours are available from the chamber of commerce.

INTERNATIONAL SELKIRK LOOP is a 450 kilometre (280 mi.) scenic byway through southeastern British Columbia and adjoining parts of Washington and Idaho. From Nelson the main route follows Hwy. 6 south to the U.S. border at Nelway. The other leg of the loop heads east on Hwy. 3A to Balfour, where what is said to be the world's longest free ferry service transports vehicles and passengers across Kootenay Lake. Hwy. 3A continues south along the lake's east shore to Creston, where Hwy. 21 connects with the U.S. border at Rykerts.

One 166 kilometre (103 mi.) side route follows Hwys. 3A, 6 and 22 from Nelson to Castlegar and Trail, then Hwy. 3B and 3 from Rossland to Salmo. Another 217 kilometre (135 mi.) side route connects Nelson with Slocan Lake via Hwys. 3A and 6, then continues east from New Denver to Kaslo on Hwy. 31, completing the loop back to Nelson following Hwys. 31 and 3A.

Scenic highlights of the loop include Kootenay Lake, thick coniferous forests, snowcapped peaks and the lush Creston Valley. Museums, historic mining towns, heritage architecture, crafts villages and seasonal produce stands beckon travelers.

Recreational activities abound, including golf, fishing, boating, swimming, hunting, camping, hiking, mountain biking, horseback riding, skiing and snowmobiling. You also can tour a ghost town and soak in a hot spring.

Towns with attraction listings on the loop and its side routes include Ainsworth Hot Springs, Boswell, Castlegar, Creston, Kaslo, Nelson, New Denver, Rossland, Sandon and Trail.

Chambers of commerce and visitor centers on the loop provide maps and more information. Visitors also can write the International Selkirk Loop, P.O. Box 920, Bonners Ferry, ID 83805, United States; or in Canada, P.O. Box 2079, Creston, BC V0B 1G0. **Phone:** (208) 267-0822 or (888) 823-2626.

TOUCHSTONES NELSON: MUSEUM OF ART AND HISTORY is at s.e. corner of jct. Vernon and Ward sts. at 502 Vernon St. This renovated building features permanent visual and interactive exhibitions which examine the area's cultural, developmental and economic history. The Shawn Lamb Archives houses a thorough collection of materials relating to the region's diversified origins. Temporary exhibits and galleries also are available and change monthly.

Hours: Mon.-Sat. 10-5 (also Thurs. 5-8), Sun. 10-4, mid-May to mid-Sept.; Tues.-Sat. 10-5 (also Thurs. 5-8), Sun. 10-4, rest of year. **Cost:** $7.62; $5.71 (ages 60+ and college students with ID); $3.81 (ages 7-18); by donation (Thurs. 5-8); $20.95 (family). **Phone:** (250) 352-9813.

BEST WESTERN PLUS BAKER STREET INN & CONVENTION CENTRE　　250/352-3525

 THREE DIAMOND
Hotel

 **AAA Benefit:** Members save up to 15% and earn bonus points!

Address: 153 Baker St V1L 4H1 **Location:** Jct Hwy 3A and 6. **Facility:** 70 units. 4 stories, interior corridors. **Terms:** check-in 4 pm. **Activities:** hot tub, exercise room. **Guest Services:** coin laundry.

SAVE ECO 🍴 🍸 CALL ♿ 🐾 BIZ HS 📶 ✕ 🛏 📷 🖥 / SOME UNITS 🦌

WHERE TO EAT

ALL SEASONS CAFE　　250/352-0101
THREE DIAMOND American. Casual Dining. **Address:** 620 Herridge Ln V1L 6A7

CANTINA DEL CENTRO　　250/352-3737
APPROVED Mexican. Casual Dining. **Address:** 561 Baker St V1L 4J1

OSO NEGRO COFFEE　　250/352-7661
APPROVED Coffee/Tea. Quick Serve. **Address:** 604 Ward St V1L 7B1

THE OUTER CLOVE　　250/354-1667
APPROVED American. Casual Dining. **Address:** 536 Stanley St V1L 1N2

REL-ISH BISTRO　　250/352-5232
THREE DIAMOND New American. Casual Dining. **Address:** 301 Baker St V1L 4H6

THOR'S PIZZA　　250/352-1212
APPROVED Pizza. Quick Serve. **Address:** 303 Victoria St V1L 4K3

NEW WESTMINSTER (H-11) pop. 65,976, elev. 75m/246'

• Hotels & Restaurants map & index p. 276
• Part of Vancouver area — see map p. 249

The oldest incorporated city in Western Canada, New Westminster—also known as the Royal City—was named by Queen Victoria. Transformed into a boomtown by the lure of gold in 1857, it plunged into a depression when the gold rush subsided in the late 1860s. The city was the provincial capital until 1868.

New Westminster also is known for its architecture. Parts of the city were built by the Royal Engineers,

(See map & index p. 276.)

sent in 1855 to keep order in the new crown colony. Former members of this organization later formed the New Westminster Regiment, whose history is recounted in the Museum of the Royal Westminster Regiment at Sixth Street and Queens Avenue; phone (604) 666-4069.

Other places of interest include old houses in a variety of styles, some of which survived a devastating fire in 1898. The houses can be toured in late May. Tickets must be purchased in advance; for information phone the New Westminster Heritage Preservation Society at (604) 525-4868.

Westminster Quay Public Market, on the waterfront, maintains a tradition started in 1892 when farmers, hunters and settlers came to barter for goods. Fresh meat, baked goods, produce and local crafts can be purchased daily.

Antique Alley, on historic Front Street, is known for its heritage buildings housing stores featuring an array of antiques and collectibles.

Also of interest is *Sampson V* Maritime Museum aboard the stern-wheeler berthed on the Fraser River at 880 Quayside Dr. The stern-wheeler, the last steam-powered paddle wheeler to operate on the Fraser, can be toured; phone (604) 527-4640. The Canadian Lacrosse Hall of Fame, which celebrates Canada's national summer sport, is at 777 Columbia St. in the Anvil Centre; phone (604) 515-3830.

New Westminster Visitor Centre: 777 Columbia St., New Westminster, BC, Canada V3M 1B6. **Phone:** (604) 526-1905 or (604) 551-4974.

IRVING HOUSE, 302 Royal Ave., is an 1865 mansion built with San Francisco Gothic Revival influences for Capt. William Irving, a pioneer of the riverboat trade on the Fraser River. Furnished in period, the 14-room residence is bedecked with Victorian Christmas decor during December. **Hours:** Wed.-Thurs. 3-8, Fri.-Sun. noon-5, May-Sept.; Sat.-Sun. noon-4, rest of year. **Cost:** Donations. **Phone:** (604) 527-4640. 🚇 Columbia, 27

PADDLEWHEELER RIVERBOAT TOURS departs from the boardwalk of the New Westminster Quay Public Market at 788 Quayside Dr. Narrated sightseeing tours of various lengths are offered aboard an authentic paddlewheeler. The MV *Native* is a replica of a late 19th-century riverboat that carried passengers on the historic Gold Rush Trail via the Fraser River. Evening entertainment cruises also are available.

Hours: Cruises depart daily year-round. Phone ahead to confirm schedule. **Cost:** Fare $35-$99.88; $39.95-$69.95 (ages 13-17); $24.95-$59.95 (ages 6-12). Some fares may include meals. Reservations are required. **Phone:** (604) 525-4465 or (800) 825-1302. 🚇 New Westminster, 26

INN AT THE QUAY   604/520-1776 **24**

THREE DIAMOND

Boutique Hotel

Address: 900 Quayside Dr V3M 6G1 **Location:** Waterfront. Along waterfront, follow signs to Westminster Quay. Adjacent to public market. 🚇 New Westminster, 26. **Facility:** Next to the public market, and resting on pillars that stretch out over the Fraser River, this hotel has rooms with wonderful views. They have a delightful design with a modern, blue and violet motif. 126 units. 9 stories, interior corridors. **Parking:** on-site (fee). **Terms:** check-in 4 pm. **Dining:** The Boathouse Restaurant, see separate listing. **Activities:** sauna, hot tub, trails, exercise room. **Guest Services:** valet laundry.

SAVE ECO 🍽 🍸 CALL 🚿 ♿ BIZ 🛜 ✉ 🔌 📺 🚇

WHERE TO EAT

THE BOATHOUSE RESTAURANT   604/525-3474
APPROVED   Seafood. Casual Dining. **Address:** 900 Quayside Dr V3M 6G1

BURGER HEAVEN   604/522-8339 **50**
APPROVED   Burgers Sandwiches. Casual Dining. **Address:** 77 10th St V3M 3X4

NORTH VANCOUVER (H-11) pop. 48,196, elev. 99m/325'

- Hotels p. 210 • Restaurants p. 210
- Hotels & Restaurants map & index p. 276
- Part of Vancouver area — see map p. 249

North Vancouver is a city, and it's also a district. All visitors really need to know, however, is that this North Shore destination is definitely worth checking out.

Lumbering and shipbuilding were important early on, and by the early 20th century the town across Burrard Inlet from Vancouver had incorporated. Today there are no discernible distinctions among the various municipalities that make up the North Shore. The city of North Vancouver does have its own impressive skyline, easily visible from the downtown Vancouver waterfront, while the district of North Vancouver is a bit of a hodgepodge, with pockets of industry and commercial development mixed in with parks and green spaces. It's also the location of Grouse Mountain and the Capilano Suspension Bridge Park *(see attraction listings)*, two of the North Shore's most popular tourist attractions.

From Vancouver, take either the Lions Gate Bridge or the Ironworkers Memorial Second Narrows Crossing (Hwy. 1) to North Vancouver. (The bridge's name honors 27 workers who were killed when several spans collapsed during construction.) But the most scenic approach is aboard TransLink's SeaBus, with terminals on Vancouver's downtown waterfront (near Canada Place) and in North Vancouver next to the Lonsdale Quay Market. These 400-passenger catamaran ferries make the one-way trip across Burrard Inlet in about 12 minutes. Ferries depart from the Vancouver waterfront every 15 minutes Mon.-Fri. 6:16 a.m.-7:46 p.m. (then every 30 minutes until 1:22 a.m.); Sat. every 30 minutes 6:16 a.m.-10:16 a.m. and 6:46 p.m.-1:22 a.m. (every 15

(See map & index p. 276.)

minutes 10:16 a.m.-6:46 p.m.); Sun. every 30 minutes 8:16 a.m.-11:16 p.m. Service from Lonsdale Quay to the Vancouver waterfront follows a similar schedule, with last ferries departing Mon.-Sat. at 1 a.m. and Sun at 11:02 p.m. TransLink's Compass fare system allows passengers to travel freely between buses, the SeaBus and the SkyTrain rapid transit system. For additional schedule and fare information phone (604) 953-3333.

If you arrive via the SeaBus, the first place you must explore is the Lonsdale Quay Market. It's a classic Vancouver fresh market, open daily 9-7, Sun. 9-6 with an abundance of vendors selling fruit, veggies, flowers, seafood and baked goods, plus yummy soups, sauces and other specialty items. You'll be hard pressed to decide on something to go from one of the international food bars—the choices are many and tempting, from noodle stir fries to seafood chowder—but once the decision is made, eat outside on the deck so you can watch the ferry boats come and go with downtown Vancouver as a backdrop. A farmers market sets up on the East Plaza at the Quay Saturdays from 10 to 3, early May-late Oct. Organic farmers, bakers, jam and salsa makers and crafters all peddle their wares.

If peace and quiet are what you're seeking, head to Cates Park. From Vancouver, take the first exit off the Second Narrows bridge, following the signs for Deep Cove; then proceed east on Dollarton Highway about 8 kilometres (5 mi.) to the park entrance (on the right). There are grassy areas, a playground for kids and a pebble-sand beach. Watch the boats heading from Burrard Inlet into Indian Arm, check out the totem pole and indigenous canoe, hike a waterfront trail through stands of Douglas fir and big-leaf maple, or stretch out and take a nap under one of the huge cedar trees near the parking lot.

From Cates Park, get back on Dollarton Highway and continue north a couple of kilometres to the residential community of Deep Cove. The cove in question is a natural indentation of Indian Arm, a fiord-like extension of Burrard Inlet. In the 18th century Northwest tribes traveled up and down Indian Arm hunting and fishing, and lumbering was an important industry in this area in the first half of the 20th century.

What strikes you immediately about Deep Cove is how incredibly picturesque it is. Gallant Avenue is a quaint 2 blocks of eateries (fish and chips followed by a cone from Orca's Favourite Ice Cream makes a nice lunch combo), a shop or three and the Deep Cove Cultural Centre, which includes the Seymour Art Gallery and the Deep Cove Heritage Society, the Deep Cove Shaw Theatre and the First Impressions Theatre Company; phone (604) 929-3200 or (604) 929-9456. The street ends at nicely landscaped Panorama Park, bright with flower beds in the summer. Walk down the stairs to the beach and then out onto the pier.

Sheltered, serene Deep Cove harbor will take your breath away. Trees frame the cove on both sides. Rising beyond the water to the left are the thickly forested slopes of Mount Seymour Provincial Park *(see attraction listing and Recreation Areas Chart)*. The wooded hillsides to the right are speckled with houses that undoubtedly have views to die for. Across Indian Arm loom the Coast Mountains, dark masses in the distance. Sailboats bob on the cove's tranquil surface. Kayakers slice through the water. Canoeists paddle gracefully. It's quite an enchanting vista, one you'll likely end up gazing out on all afternoon.

CAPILANO SUSPENSION BRIDGE PARK is off Hwy. 1 exit 14, then 2 km (1.2 mi.) n. to 3735 Capilano Rd.; a free shuttle is available from several locations in downtown Vancouver. The swinging 137-metre-long (450 ft.) footbridge spans a 70-metre-deep (230 ft.) densely wooded gorge above the Capilano River. George Grant Mackay, a Scottish civil engineer, built the original bridge in 1889 from hemp rope and cedar planks; the fourth structure on the site is reinforced with steel cables and concrete.

The park also features gardens; a totem park; Treetops Adventure, a series of seven suspension bridges high in the treetops; Cliffwalk, a cliffside walkway with a rock-climber's view of the canyon; and a story center that displays artifacts of the bridge. The Living Forest includes interactive displays and naturalist exhibits which guide visitors through a West Coast rain forest. From late November through late January during Canyon Lights, A Winter Lights Festival, the bridge, Treetops Adventure, Cliffwalk and rainforest twinkle with lights, and visitors can view what may be the world's tallest living Christmas tree.

Wheelchairs are not permitted on the attractions. **Time:** Allow 2 hours, 30 minutes minimum. **Hours:** Daily 8:30-8, late May-Labour Day; 9-7, late Apr.-late May; 9-6, mid-Mar. to late Apr. and day after Labour Day to mid-Oct.; 11-9, late Nov.-Jan. 31; 9-5, rest of year. Closed Christmas. Phone ahead to confirm schedule. **Cost:** $53.95; $48.95 (ages 65+); $39.95 (students ages 17+ with ID); $29.95 (ages 13-16); $16.95 (ages 6-12). **Phone:** (604) 985-7474 or (877) 985-7474. *(See ad p. 209.)*

GROUSE MOUNTAIN is at 6400 Nancy Greene Way. Step into The Skyride, an aerial tramway, for a 1.6-kilometre (1 mi.) ride over Grouse Mountain's lofty Douglas firs to the mountaintop where, from a height of 1,100 metres (4,100 ft.), you'll see a breathtaking panorama of downtown Vancouver. On clear nights, gaze at the city's floodlit buildings and twinkling lights reflected in the harbor.

Crowd-pleasing winter activities include skiing, snowshoeing, snowboarding, ice-skating, sleigh rides, a Sliding Zone and Light Walk. In the summer, take in a helicopter tour, paragliding, ziplining and Mountain Ropes and Kids Tree Canopy Adventures; a 45-minute lumberjack show; a Birds in Motion demonstration featuring free-flying birds of prey; and guided or self-guiding interpretive walks that inform about area flora, fauna and geology.

(See map & index p. 276.)

Grouse Mountain also is home to the Refuge for Endangered Wildlife, a 2-hectare (5-acre) habitat also open year-round, is home to two orphaned grizzly bears.

Competitive locals and visitors can do the Grouse Grind (commonly referred to as "Mother Nature's Stairmaster"), a grueling 2.9-kilometre (1.8 mi.) climb up the mountain.

A complimentary summer shuttle service from Canada Place to Grouse Mountain is available with purchase of admission. **Time:** Allow 1 hour, 30 minutes minimum. **Hours:** Grouse Mountain open daily 8:45 a.m.-10 p.m. The Skyride departs every 15 minutes. Shuttle service from Canada Place is offered May-Sept. on a first-come, first-served basis; phone for schedule. Activity hours vary; phone ahead for schedule. **Cost:** Mountain Admission (includes most mountaintop activities) $59; $52 (ages 65+); $32 (ages 5-16); $159 (family, two adults and two children). An additional fee is charged for helicopter tour, paragliding, Mountain Ropes Adventure, Kids Tree Canopy Adventure and ziplining. **Parking:** $8-$10. **Phone:** (604) 980-9311. GT ⊤⊤ ⊠ ⊕

The Eye of the Wind is on top of Grouse Mountain at 6400 Nancy Greene Way. This 65-metre (215 ft.) wind turbine on the mountaintop is reportedly the only one in the world that allows you to stand in a glass "viewPOD" at the top of the tower (just 10 feet from its massive, rotating blades), giving an awe-inspiring 360-degree view of Vancouver, the harbor, the Coastal Mountains and, on a clear day, mounts Baker, Rainier and Garibaldi. The turbine provides about 20 percent of Grouse Mountain's energy requirement.

Time: Allow 1 hour minimum. **Hours:** Grouse Mountain open daily 9:45 a.m.-10 p.m. The Eye of the Wind drop-in visits daily 10:30-8, late May to mid-Oct. The Eye of the Wind guided tours offered rest of year. Phone ahead to confirm schedule. **Cost:** Drop-in visit late May to mid-Oct. $15. Guided tour rest of year $20. Note: Admission does not include mountaintop activities on Grouse Mountain. Fares may vary; phone ahead. Reservations are recommended. **Phone:** (604) 980-9311. ⊤⊤

LYNN CANYON PARK is off Lynn Valley Rd. to the end of Peters Rd., following signs to 3663 Park Rd. The 250-hectare (618-acre) park features natural streams, waterfalls, wading pools and hiking trails through a temperate rainforest. A highlight is the Lynn Canyon Suspension Bridge, a 50-metre-high (166-ft.) bridge spanning the canyon. The Lynn Canyon Ecology Center offers nature displays and children's activities. Food is available seasonally. **Hours:** Park open daily dawn-dusk. Ecology Center open daily 10-5, June-Sept.; Mon.-Fri. 10-5, Sat.-Sun. noon-4, rest of year. Closed Christmas-Jan. 1. **Cost:** Park free. Ecology Center by donation. **Phone:** (604) 990-3755. ⊤⊤ 🐾

PARK & TILFORD GARDENS is at jct. Cotton Rd. and Brooksbank Ave. at 333 Brooksbank Ave. The 2.8-acre botanical site consists of eight interconnected theme gardens. A variety of both native and exotic floral arrangements leads through arboreal displays and to aviaries, where visitors may see parrots and other tropical birds.

An aromatic blend of plant and flower enclosures composes the Rose Garden, home to 24 varieties and more than 250 rose plants. **Time:** Allow 1 hour minimum. **Hours:** Daily 9:30-9:30, in Dec.; 9:30-8, May-Aug.; 9:30-7, in Apr.; 9:30-6:30, in Sept.; 9:30-4:30, rest of year. **Cost:** Free. **Phone:** (604) 984-8200. GT

▼ See AAA listing p. 208 ▼

YOU DIDN'T COME ALL THIS WAY TO GO TO A MALL.

— EXPERIENCE CLIFFWALK —
You came to step beyond a 300 foot cliff face. To be filled with wonder high in a rainforest canopy. To swing high above a deep canyon. You came for this.

Drive, take transit or the free shuttle from Canada Place.
604.985.7474 CAPBRIDGE.COM

🐧 **CAPILANO**
SUSPENSION BRIDGE PARK

(See map & index p. 276.)

ECONO LODGE INN & SUITES NORTH VANCOUVER
604/988-3181 **6**

APPROVED
Motel

Address: 1748 Capilano Rd V7P 3B4 **Location:** Trans-Canada Hwy 1 exit 14 (Capilano Rd). 0.9 mi (1.5 km) s; from north end of Lions Gate Bridge, 0.6 mi (1 km) e on Marine Dr, just n. **Facility:** 95 units, some two bedrooms, efficiencies and kitchens. 2 stories (no elevator), exterior corridors. **Terms:** check-in 4 pm. **Pool:** heated outdoor. **Activities:** hot tub. **Guest Services:** valet and coin laundry. **Featured Amenity:** full hot breakfast.

SAVE ECO 🚹+ CALL ♿ 🛫 BIZ
📶 ✖ 🖥 / SOME UNITS 🅿 🍽

HOLIDAY INN & SUITES NORTH VANCOUVER
604/985-3111 **9**

THREE DIAMOND
Hotel

Address: 700 Old Lillooet Rd V7J 2H5 **Location:** Trans-Canada Hwy 1 exit 22 (Mount Seymour Pkwy), follow signs. **Facility:** 162 units, some efficiencies. 6 stories, interior corridors. **Amenities:** safes. **Pool:** heated indoor. **Activities:** sauna, hot tub, exercise room, spa. **Guest Services:** valet and coin laundry.

SAVE ECO 🚹 🏊 🍽 CALL ♿
🛫 🛬 BIZ HS 📶 ✖ 🎬
🅿 🍽 🖥

PINNACLE HOTEL AT THE PIER
604/986-7437 **8**
THREE DIAMOND Contemporary Hotel. **Address:** 138 Victory Ship Way V7L 0B1

SURESTAY HOTEL BY BEST WESTERN NORTH VANCOUVER
604/987-8185 **7**

APPROVED
Motel

Address: 1634 Capilano Rd V7P 3B4 **Location:** Trans-Canada Hwy 1 exit 14 (Capilano Rd). 0.9 mi (1.5 km) s; from north end of Lions Gate Bridge, 0.6 mi (1 km) e on Marine Dr, just n. **Facility:** 74 units, some two bedrooms and efficiencies. 2 stories (no elevator), interior/exterior corridors. **Pool:** heated outdoor. **Guest Services:** coin laundry.

SAVE 🚹 🛫 BIZ 📶 ✖ 🖥
/ SOME UNITS 🅿 🍽

WHERE TO EAT

ARMS REACH BISTRO   604/929-7442 **31**
THREE DIAMOND Regional Canadian. Casual Dining. **Address:** 4390 Gallant Ave, #107C V7G 1L2

CACTUS CLUB CAFE   604/986-5776 **27**
THREE DIAMOND New American. Casual Dining. **Address:** 1598 Pemberton Ave V7P 2S2

FISHWORKS   778/340-3449 **28**
THREE DIAMOND New Seafood. Casual Dining. **Address:** 91 Lonsdale Ave V7M 2E5

JAGERHOF   604/980-4316 **29**
APPROVED Continental. Casual Dining. **Address:** 71 Lonsdale Ave V7M 2E5

LA CUCINA   604/986-1334 **26**
APPROVED Italian. Casual Dining. **Address:** 1509 Marine Dr V7P 1T8

THE LOBBY RESTAURANT   604/973-8000 **30**
THREE DIAMOND Pacific Northwest. Casual Dining. **Address:** 138 Victory Ship Way V7L 0B1

TOUR DE FEAST   604/980-1811 **32**
APPROVED French. Casual Dining. **Address:** 319 Mountain Hwy V7J 2K7

OAK BAY pop. 18,015
• Hotels & Restaurants map & index p. 311
• Part of Victoria area — see map p. 299

OAK BAY BEACH HOTEL
250/598-4556 **31**

FOUR DIAMOND
Hotel

Address: 1175 Beach Dr V8S 2N4 **Location:** Oceanfront. In Oak Bay district. **Facility:** This outstanding seaside property whisks you back to the days of grand elegant hotels while offering all the modern conveniences of today. Many rooms offer spacious decks or patios. 100 units, some efficiencies and kitchens. 8 stories, interior corridors. **Parking:** on-site and valet. **Terms:** check-in 4 pm, age restrictions may apply. **Amenities:** safes. **Dining:** 4 restaurants. **Pool:** heated outdoor. **Activities:** hot tub, steamroom, regulation golf, recreation programs, bicycles, trails, exercise room, spa. **Guest Services:** valet laundry, boarding pass kiosk, area transportation.

SAVE 🚹 🛁 🍽 🥾 🛫 🛬 BIZ HS 📶 ✖
🅿 🍽 🖥 / SOME UNITS 🐾

WHERE TO EAT

THE MARINA RESTAURANT   250/598-8555 **41**
THREE DIAMOND Pacific Northwest. Fine Dining. **Address:** 1327 Beach Dr V8S 2N4

OTTAVIO ITALIAN BAKERY & DELICATESSEN
250/592-4080 **40**
APPROVED Italian Deli Breads/Pastries. Quick Serve. **Address:** 2272 Oak Bay Ave V8R 1G7

PENNY FARTHING ENGLISH PUB   250/370-9008 **39**
APPROVED Canadian. Gastropub. **Address:** 2228 Oak Bay Ave V8R 1G5

SUNDAY'S CHILD   250/590-2780 **36**
APPROVED New French. Casual Dining. **Address:** 2509 Estevan Ave V8R 2S6

WILLOWS GALLEY   250/598-2711 **38**
APPROVED Fish & Chips. Quick Serve. **Address:** 2559 Estevan Ave V8R 2S8

Explore BC Savings Around the Globe

AAA.com/travel or CAA.ca/travel

LET'S GET SOCIAL

Stay connected with AAA

Visit with us on your favorite social media sites for the latest updates on hot discounts, cool destinations and handy automotive know-how. *Talk with us!*

 AAA.com/Facebook

 AAA.com/Twitter

 Instagram.com/aaa_national

 YouTube.com/AAA

OKANAGAN VALLEY

It's one thing to read about a destination; it's quite another to experience it in person. Evocatively written guides and glossy travel sites can pique the curiosity and whet the appetite of almost any traveler, but when it comes down to it you really need to get out of the armchair and go. This is certainly true of the Okanagan (oh-ka-NOG-an) Valley; in a province almost embarrassingly gifted with scenic riches, it still manages to stand out.

British Columbia—like much of Canada—is notable for its sheer ruggedness: lofty mountains, expansive forests, rushing rivers. The valley, in contrast, is an anomaly; it could almost be Italy or some other sun-kissed land. The sun does indeed shine warmly, and the azure sky is huge. Tawny bluffs rise from the shores of steel-blue lakes. Scraggly pine trees and compact mounds of silvery gray sagebrush cloak hillsides. Parts of the Okanagan are arid enough to meet the meteorological criteria of a desert, but irrigation has transformed it into one of the most productive fruit- and vegetable-growing regions in North America.

A Land Created by Glaciers

This long, narrow valley was shaped over time by glacial movement. Layers of ice more than a mile thick began retreating some 10,000 years ago, scraping the surface of the land and leaving behind deposits of sediment. Flowing mountain rivers caused innumerable cycles of flooding and erosion. All this water action contributed to a slow but steady accumulation of nutrient-rich soils that over time formed fertile deltas, setting the stage for the valley's eventual blossoming as an agricultural powerhouse.

Impressive mountains, with some peaks topping 3,000 metres (9,800 ft.), flank both sides of the Okanagan Valley—the Monashee range to the east, the Cascades to the west. The mountain systems in this part of North America are oriented in a north-south direction paralleling the Pacific coast, and the intervening valleys follow suit. The entire area is part of

This map shows cities in Okanagan Valley where you will find attractions, hotels and restaurants. Cities are listed alphabetically in this book on the following pages.

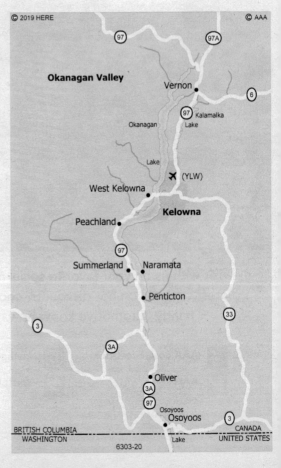

the vast Interior Plateau, an uplifted section of the Earth's crust that covers much of British Columbia's southern interior.

One of the Okanagan Valley's many virtues is its topographical variety—everything from desert to grassland to forest. The northern end is wetter and greener, with a panorama of snowcapped mountains rising off in the distance. As you head south into the heart of the valley the trees become more scattered; ponderosa pines speckling the hills are replaced by shrubs like antelope bush and hardy plants like bunch grass (so named because it grows in individual clumps or tufts rather than forming a uniform carpet), both of which are adapted to a drier climate.

Farther south the Okanagan verges on true desert. In and around Osoyoos the landscape is austere; towering cliffs and bare hillsides flaunt a palette of browns, beiges and grays, and the grasses and other low-growing plants are buffeted by persistent dry winds. The desert plants and animals that inhabit this arid environment are found nowhere else in Canada; the far southern end of the Okanagan Valley lies just above the northernmost reach of the Sonoran Desert, which extends south all the way into Mexico. This also is the country's warmest region, with relatively mild winters, hot summers and abundant sunshine, an ideal combination for irrigation-assisted agriculture.

Between Osoyoos to the east and Princeton to the west is the Similkameen Valley, nestled between steep rocky hills and threaded by the Similkameen River. Although a geographically separate region, it shares the southern Okanagan Valley's dramatic scenery and climatological characteristics. Similkameen country is known for its cattle ranches, horse farms and fruit orchards, and bills itself variously as the "Fruit Stand Capital of Canada" and "BC's Garden of Eden" in an attempt to step out of the better-known Okanagan's shadow.

Hwy. 3, also called the Crowsnest Highway, meanders along the province's southern border from Hope east to the Alberta border. Between Keremeos and Osoyoos the highway traverses an area that climatologists classify as a mid-altitude steppe, although it certainly *looks* like a desert. Away from the sweep of the ever-present irrigation sprinklers, this little portion of extreme southern British Columbia—known as Canada's "pocket desert"—is home to sagebrush, prickly pear cactus, Western rattlesnakes and even the odd scorpion, all of which thrive in these desert-like conditions.

The bracing beauty of the Similkameen countryside is particularly evident in the vicinity of Hedley, a small village about 76 kilometres (47 mi.) west of Osoyoos on Hwy. 3. Here the waters of Hedley Creek rush into the Similkameen River. Stemwinder Mountain looms to the west, Nickel Plate Mountain to the east. Marbled cliffs rise up on both sides of the highway (the Similkameen First Nation named this area Sna-za-ist, meaning "the striped rock place"). Notes of color are supplied by a bright blue sky, the deep green of flourishing fruit trees and (in

season) the gold and purple hues of ripening apricots, peaches, plums and grapes.

About 9 kilometres (5.5 mi.) west of Osoyoos is Spotted Lake, which gets its name from one of the world's highest concentrations of magnesium sulfate, calcium, sodium sulfates and other minerals. In summer much of the lake's water evaporates and the minerals crystallize into circles on the surface that can be white, pale yellow, green or blue, depending on the mineral composition. The lake is on private land, but you can view it from the highway.

The Okanagan Valley's distinguishing feature, in fact, is its chain of long, narrow lakes that stretch from north to south. Created by receding glaciers, they are kept fresh and full by snowmelt and runoff from the mountains that flank both sides of the valley. The largest is Okanagan Lake, which stretches north to south for some 111 kilometres (69 mi.) while averaging just 5 kilometres (3 mi.) wide. Skaha, Vaseux and Osoyoos lakes continue the chain to the south. To the east of Okanagan Lake are Kalamalka and Wood lakes; just north is little Swan Lake.

Cattle, Gold, Fruit and Wine

These valleys were first inhabited by the Okanagan First Nation, an Interior Salish tribe. They hunted wild game, fished salmon runs, foraged for roots and berries and traded with other nations. The first European arrivals were fur traders searching for accessible routes to transport their goods to the Pacific. In the early 19th century they ventured north from Fort Okanogan, a Pacific Fur Co. trading post at the confluence of the Okanagan and Columbia rivers in present-day Washington state. Fur caravans were soon heading in and out of the valley region.

When the Oregon Treaty designated the 49th parallel as the border between the United States and the Canadian territory, Osoyoos became a port of entry, and vast herds of cattle were trailed through customs to supply food for miners who panned for placer gold along the Similkameen River. The bunch grass that grew along the river valley provided abundant forage, and ranches began to be established.

Father Charles Pandosy, an Oblate priest, founded a mission in 1859 on the eastern shore of Okanagan Lake. He and his followers endured a harsh first winter—they were forced to shoot their horses for food—but went on to build other missions in the Okanagan Valley, where Father Pandosy instructed the native people in European agricultural techniques in addition to performing baptisms, marriages and funerals.

The discovery of gold on the Fraser River in 1858 resulted in a full-fledged gold rush. British Columbia's southern interior was further opened up with the building of the Cariboo Road (now Hwy. 97) and the Dewdney Trail (now Hwy. 3). By the late 19th century the Okanagan and Similkameen valleys were buzzing with gold camps and boom towns that began to spring up along the shores of the region's lakes.

The fruit industry that today is a hallmark of the Okanagan began with difficulty. Apple orchards were planted as early as 1892, but it wasn't until the 1920s that fruit crops proved economically successful. The valley's warm temperatures and long growing season—besides providing Canadians with about one-third of their apples—nurtures verdant orchards of apricots, cherries, peaches, pears and plums.

Commercial grape plantings near Kelowna supplied the Okanagan's first wineries. The local wine industry has grown exponentially since the introduction of large-scale irrigation, and almost all British Columbia wine comes from the Okanagan region. The diversity of growing conditions—from the hot, sandy desert soils of the south to the deep topsoil and clay of the cooler north, plus distinct microclimates created by the valley's lakes—help ensure a diversity of wines.

Vineyards at the southern end of the valley produce such vintages as Chardonnay, Merlot, Cabernet Sauvignon, Pinot Gris and Pinot Noir, while vineyards in the central and northern valley specialize in Pinot Blanc, Riesling and Gewürztraminer wines. Some grapes are left to freeze on the vine to produce icewine, a rich, sweet dessert wine. One of the Okanagan's most picturesque things to see is orderly rows of grapevines, often covering a hillside that overlooks a deep blue lake.

Hwy. 97, which runs the length of British Columbia from the U.S. border just south of Osoyoos north to Watson Lake at the Yukon border, is the principal route through the Okanagan Valley. From Osoyoos it travels north to Penticton, then follows the western shore of Okanagan Lake before crossing the lake on a floating bridge (the largest in the country) that is scheduled to be replaced with an overhead bridge.

Okanagan Lake is said to be the home of Ogopogo, the best known of Canada's unexplained lake creatures. Sightings of the mythical beast—most often described as 5 to 6 metres (15 to 20 ft.) long, shaped like a log and with a head resembling that of a horse or goat—date back as far as 1872. Okanagan aboriginals believed that Ogopogo's home was small, barren Rattlesnake Island; they claimed that the island's rocky beaches were sometimes strewn with animal parts, presumably dinner remains, and when crossing the lake during bad weather always took along a small animal that would be thrown overboard in order to appease the monster. Interestingly, there are similarities between Okanagan Lake and Scotland's Loch Ness, home of the famed Loch Ness Monster; both bodies of water are long and narrow, and both lie at about the same latitude.

East of the lake Hwy. 97 winds north to Enderby, the unofficial northern end of the valley, before continuing on toward Sicamous. But whether you proceed from south to north or north to south, this 211-kilometre (131 mi.) journey through the heart of the Okanagan is utterly delightful. One minute the highway is running tantalizingly close to a sparkling lakeshore; the next it's in the shadow of a soaring, sagebrush-dotted bluff or looking down on checkerboard farmland. Each bend and turn reveals a new view, and each one is lovely. The scenery alone would be more than enough to recommend this drive, even if you didn't make a single stop.

Year-Round Fun

But of course you *will* want to stop, because this is Canada's No. 1 year-round recreation destination. Dozens of parks ring Okanagan Lake, offering myriad opportunities for hiking, backpacking, mountain biking, camping and other fun things to do. Bear Creek Provincial Park, about 9 kilometres (6 mi.) west of Kelowna off Hwy. 97, has many hiking trails to explore, all beginning from a common trailhead at the park entrance. Bear Creek runs through the bottom of a tree-walled canyon, and the trails above wind past ponderosa pine, Douglas fir, juniper and prickly pear cactus that frame expansive lake views.

The lakes are, of course, ideal for water recreation, whether it's sailing, paddle boating, water skiing, jet skiing, kayaking, canoeing or freshwater fishing. Okanagan Lake is ringed with sandy beaches and sheltered coves, and numerous marina facilities provide equipment rentals.

For a northern Okanagan getaway head out to Kalamalka Lake Provincial Park, about 8 kilometres (5 mi.) southeast of Vernon off Hwy. 6. Kalamalka is known as a "marl lake," a process that begins when the water warms, forming calcium carbonate and limestone crystals that reflect sunlight. The water's distinctive blue-green color is often shot through with ribbons of deep blue, earning it the nickname "lake of a thousand colors." This largely undeveloped park encompasses rolling grasslands and forested ridges where Douglas fir and lodgepole pine grow; a paved trail leads to secluded beaches. Wildlife ranges from mule deer and minks to bobcats and western painted turtles. Bird-watching is rewarding, and the spring wildflower display is spectacular.

Nearly 40 golf courses are scattered from Vernon south to Osoyoos, with many of them concentrated around Kelowna. Due to the mild climate most courses open as early as March, and golfers frequently play into November. And this being the Okanagan, it's only natural that water and fruit trees figure into course layouts; the grounds of the Kelowna Springs Golf Club include seven spring-fed lakes, while fairways at the Harvest Golf Club are set in the midst of a huge hillside apple orchard and have prime views of Okanagan Lake.

Kelowna is the Okanagan Valley's largest city and a big summer vacation destination. Water sports—sailing, kayaking, windsurfing, fishing—rule the summer calendar, but downtown Kelowna also offers museums, art galleries, pretty lakeside parks, all kinds of restaurants and a lively nightlife. It makes a convenient base for touring the many small wineries in the vicinity.

Breezy Penticton has the best of both worlds; the north end of town fronts the southern tip of Okanagan Lake, while the south end brushes up against the north shore of Skaha Lake. Lakeside beaches give the city a summery feel, and families flock to Penticton's amusement centers, go-cart tracks, miniature golf course and waterslides. Stroll along Front Street, the original business corridor, which is lined with restaurants and funky little shops.

Situated between Swan, Kalamalka and Okanagan lakes, Vernon started out as a camp on the Okanagan Valley trail during the fur trade years; by the turn of the 20th century it was a bustling ranching center. Downtown Vernon truly earns the description "quaint": The tree-lined, flower-filled streets are packed with historic old buildings and specialty stores selling everything from Victorian crafts to homemade jams. Be sure to search out the 27 outdoor murals—some up to 91 metres (300 ft.) long—that depict Okanagan history, folklore and landscapes.

Just a stone's throw from the U.S. border, Osoyoos (oh-SOY-yoos) means, in the local Inkaneep native dialect, "where the water narrows"—a reference to its location spanning a narrow portion of Osoyoos Lake. Vineyards and orchards abound in the surrounding countryside, and the lake is one of Canada's warmest. Stroll along one of the lakeside parks in town while watching windsurfers and parasailing enthusiasts do their thing under sunny summer skies, and it's not that hard to believe you've happened onto some undiscovered Mediterranean resort.

The Okanagan Valley has something to offer regardless of the season. Downhill and cross-country skiers, snowboarders and other winter sports enthusiasts can choose from four ski resorts: Silver Star Mountain Resort, north of Vernon; Big White Ski Resort near Kelowna; Crystal Mountain resort near West Kelowna (Westbank); and Apex Mountain Resort, southwest of Penticton.

Spring and summer are seasons to experience the valley's agricultural bounty. In the spring fruit trees are in full glorious bloom. Spring into early summer also is the time when wildflowers make their appearance in the Okanagan's wilderness parks.

Harvest time for the region's famous fruits and vegetables begins in late June and lasts until mid-October. If you're here in the summer or fall stop at one of the ubiquitous roadside fruit stands, which seem almost as plentiful as the trees themselves. Cherries are first in the fruit parade, ripening from late June through mid-July. Peaches appear from mid-July through September; pears in August and September; plums in September; and apples from August through October.

Practically every town in the valley has a farmers market, and you'll want to check out every single one. In addition to all sorts of fruit, the markets offer tomatoes, pumpkins, squash, asparagus, organic preserves, homemade pies, artisanal cheeses, honey, herbs, flowers—just about everything. Most are open April or May through October.

Grapes are harvested September through mid-October, an ideal time to go winery hopping. Most of the Okanagan's roughly 100 wineries can be visited, many have an intriguing history to share, and practically all of them enjoy a picturesque rural setting. Before hitting the tasting bars, pick up information and maps at any local visitor center.

So when should you plan a trip? Come to think of it, just about *any* time is right.

Destinations in this region listed under their own names are Kelowna, Oliver, Osoyoos, Peachland, Penticton, Summerland, Vernon and West Kelowna (Westbank).

Make the Connction

AAA guidebooks are just the beginning. Open the door to a whole lot more on AAA.com. Get extra travel insight, more information and online booking.

Find this symbol for places to look, book and save on AAA.com.

iStockphoto.com_shapecharge

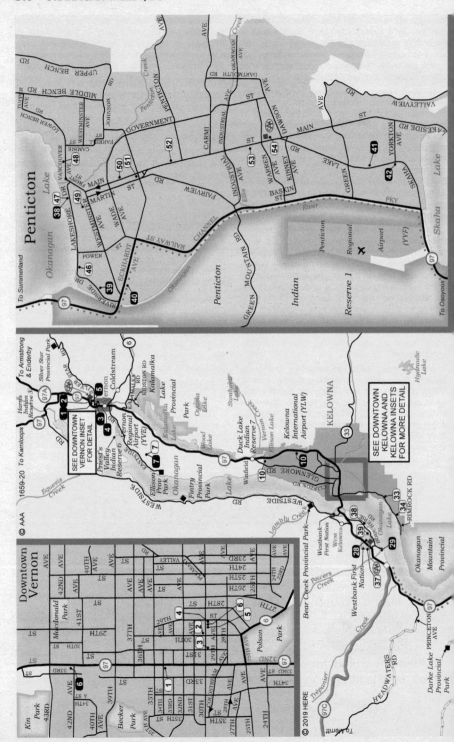

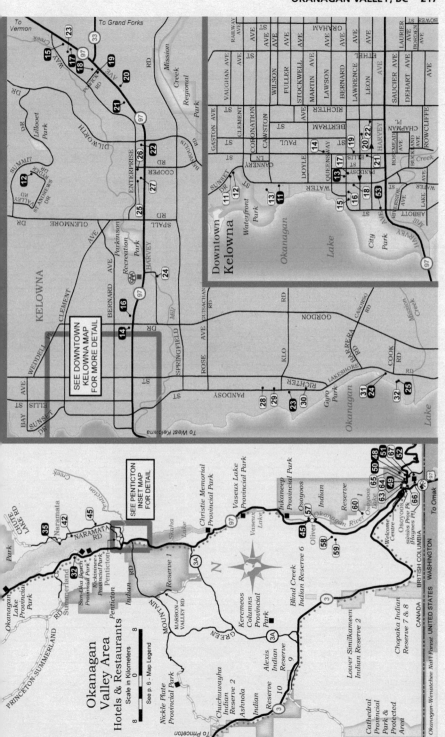

Downtown Kelowna

Okanagan Valley Area
Hotels & Restaurants

Scale in Kilometers

8 ———— 0 ———— 8

See p. 6 - Map Legend

SEE DOWNTOWN KELOWNA MAP FOR MORE DETAIL

SEE PENTICTON INSET MAP FOR DETAIL

Okanagan Valley Area

This index helps you "spot" where hotels and restaurants are located on the corresponding detailed maps. Restaurant price range is a combination of lunch and/or dinner. Turn to the listing page for more information and consult display ads for special promotions.

 For more details, rates and reservations: AAA.com/travelguides/hotels

VERNON

Map Page	Hotels	Designation	Member Savings	Page
① p. 216	Fairfield Inn & Suites by Marriott	THREE DIAMOND	✔	297
② p. 216	Days Inn by Wyndham Vernon	APPROVED		296
③ p. 216	**Best Western Pacific Inn**	THREE DIAMOND	✔	296
④ p. 216	Holiday Inn Express Hotel & Suites Vernon	THREE DIAMOND		297
⑤ p. 216	**Riviera Village Green Hotel**	APPROVED	✔	297
⑥ p. 216	Super 8 by Wyndham Vernon	APPROVED		297
⑦ p. 216	Sparkling Hill Resort	FOUR DIAMOND		297

Map Page	Restaurants	Designation	Cuisine	Price Range	Page
① p. 216	Intermezzo Restaurant	THREE DIAMOND	International	$17-$54	297
② p. 216	Naked Pig	APPROVED	Barbecue	$12-$29	297
③ p. 216	Amarin Thai Restaurant	APPROVED	Thai	$12-$18	297
④ p. 216	Eclectic Med Restaurant Inc	APPROVED	Mediterranean	$12-$38	297
⑤ p. 216	Los Huesos	APPROVED	Mexican	$15-$18	297
⑥ p. 216	The Italian Kitchen Company	APPROVED	Italian	$13-$32	297
⑦ p. 216	PeakFine	THREE DIAMOND	Pacific Northwest	$16-$45	297

KELOWNA

Map Page	Hotels	Designation	Member Savings	Page
⑩ p. 216	**Four Points by Sheraton Kelowna Airport**	THREE DIAMOND	✔	197
⑪ p. 216	**Delta Hotels by Marriott Grand Okanagan Resort**	THREE DIAMOND	✔	197
⑫ p. 216	A Vista Villa Couples Retreat	THREE DIAMOND		196
⑬ p. 216	The Royal Anne Hotel	THREE DIAMOND		198
⑭ p. 216	Kelowna Inn & Suites	APPROVED		198
⑮ p. 216	Comfort Suites by Choice Hotels	THREE DIAMOND		196
⑯ p. 216	Accent Inns	APPROVED		196
⑰ p. 216	Super 8 by Wyndham Kelowna	APPROVED		198
⑱ p. 216	Holiday Inn Express & Suites Kelowna - East	THREE DIAMOND		198
⑲ p. 216	Fairfield Inn & Suites by Marriott Kelowna	THREE DIAMOND	✔	197
⑳ p. 216	**Kanata Kelowna Hotel and Conference Center**	THREE DIAMOND	✔	198
㉑ p. 216	**Best Western Plus Kelowna Hotel & Suites** (See ad p. 196.)	THREE DIAMOND	✔	196
㉒ p. 216	Ramada by Wyndham Hotel & Conference Centre (See ad p. 197.)	THREE DIAMOND		198
㉓ p. 216	Siesta Suites	APPROVED		198
㉔ p. 216	**Manteo Resort-Waterfront Hotel & Villas**	THREE DIAMOND	✔	198
㉕ p. 216	**Hotel Eldorado**	THREE DIAMOND	✔	198
㊾ p. 216	Prestige Beach House Kelowna, BW Premier Collection	THREE DIAMOND	✔	198

Map Page	Restaurants	Designation	Cuisine	Price Range	Page
⑩ p. 216	The Jammery	APPROVED	Breakfast Sandwiches	$12-$17	198
⑪ p. 216	Waterfront Wines	THREE DIAMOND	New Canadian	$26-$36	199
⑫ p. 216	Bouchons Bistro	THREE DIAMOND	French	$26-$44	198
⑬ p. 216	OAK + CRU Social Kitchen & Wine Bar	THREE DIAMOND	Regional Canadian	$14-$40	199
⑭ p. 216	Dawett Fine Indian Cuisine	APPROVED	Indian	$11-$16	198
⑮ p. 216	Salt & Brick	APPROVED	Canadian	$13-$16	199

Map Page	Restaurants (cont'd)	Designation	Cuisine	Price Range	Page
⑯ p. 216	Bai Tong	APPROVED	Thai	$13-$17	198
⑰ p. 216	Bread Co. Fine Baked Goods & Eatery	APPROVED	Breads/Pastries Sandwiches	$8-$10	198
⑱ p. 216	RauDZ Regional Table	THREE DIAMOND	New Canadian	$17-$34	199
⑲ p. 216	DunnEnzies Pizza Co.	APPROVED	Pizza	$11-$25	198
⑳ p. 216	Mamma Rosa Restaurant	APPROVED	Italian	$16-$39	199
㉑ p. 216	Yamas Taverna Greek Restaurant	APPROVED	Greek	$18-$47	199
㉒ p. 216	Little Hobo	APPROVED	Soup Sandwiches	$6-$13	198
㉓ p. 216	Bluetail Sushi & Bistro	APPROVED	Sushi	$10-$23	198
㉔ p. 216	Valoroso Foods	APPROVED	Italian Deli	$8-$15	199
㉕ p. 216	Mabui Sushi Izakaya	APPROVED	Japanese Small Plates Sushi	$9-$25	199
㉖ p. 216	Moxie's Classic Grill	APPROVED	American	$14-$37	199
㉗ p. 216	Pearson's European Deli	APPROVED	European Deli	$7-$15	199
㉘ p. 216	The Marmalade Cat Cafe	APPROVED	Sandwiches Desserts	$7-$12	199
㉙ p. 216	Zabb Thai Restaurant	APPROVED	Thai	$11-$13	199
㉚ p. 216	The Fixx Cafe & Pasta Bar	APPROVED	International	$7-$38	198
㉛ p. 216	Smack DAB	THREE DIAMOND	American	$11-$28	199
㉜ p. 216	Lakeside Dining Room & Bar	THREE DIAMOND	Regional Canadian	$12-$44	198
㉝ p. 216	Summerhill Sunset Organic Bistro	THREE DIAMOND	New Canadian	$17-$42	199
㉞ p. 216	Cedar Creek Winery Terrace Restaurant	THREE DIAMOND	New Canadian	$25-$32	198

WEST KELOWNA

Map Page	Hotels	Designation	Member Savings	Page
㉘ p. 216	**Best Western Plus Wine Country Hotel & Suites.** *(See ad p. 319.)*	THREE DIAMOND	✔	319
㉙ p. 216	The Cove Lakeside Resort	THREE DIAMOND		319

Map Page	Restaurants	Designation	Cuisine	Price Range	Page
㊲ p. 216	Kekuli Cafe	APPROVED	Canadian	$5-$11	319
㊳ p. 216	Old Vines The Restaurant at Quails' Gate	THREE DIAMOND	Regional Canadian	$18-$48	319
㊴ p. 216	The Terrace Restaurant	THREE DIAMOND	New Canadian	$28-$60	320

SUMMERLAND

Map Page	Hotel	Designation	Member Savings	Page
㉜ p. 216	Summerland Motel	APPROVED		241

NARAMATA

Map Page	Hotel	Designation	Member Savings	Page
㉟ p. 216	The Village Motel	APPROVED		205

Map Page	Restaurant	Designation	Cuisine	Price Range	Page
㊷ p. 216	The Patio at Lake Breeze	THREE DIAMOND	Mediterranean	$17-$29	205

PENTICTON

Map Page	Hotels	Designation	Member Savings	Page
㊳ p. 216	**Penticton Lakeside Resort & Conference Centre** *(See ad p. 224.)*	THREE DIAMOND	✔	224
㊴ p. 216	Days Inn & Conference Centre Penticton	APPROVED		224
㊵ p. 216	Ramada by Wyndham Penticton Hotel & Suites	THREE DIAMOND		224
㊶ p. 216	**Best Western Inn at Penticton**	APPROVED	✔	224
㊷ p. 216	Empire Motel	APPROVED		224

Map Page	Restaurants	Designation	Cuisine	Price Range	Page
㊺ p. 216	Hillside Winery Bistro	THREE DIAMOND	New Canadian	$19-$35	225
㊻ p. 216	Salty's Beach House	APPROVED	Caribbean	$13-$24	225

Map Page	Restaurants (cont'd)	Designation	Cuisine	Price Range	Page
⁴⁷ p. 216	Hooded Merganser Bar & Grill (See ad p. 224.)	THREE DIAMOND	Pacific Northwest	$11-$30	225
⁴⁸ p. 216	The Bench Market	APPROVED	Regional Deli Sandwiches	$9-$13	224
⁴⁹ p. 216	Bad Tattoo Brewing Company	APPROVED	Pizza	$22-$29	224
⁵⁰ p. 216	Lachi Fine Indian Cuisine	APPROVED	Indian	$8-$15	225
⁵¹ p. 216	Theo's Restaurant	APPROVED	Greek	$12-$32	225
⁵² p. 216	La Casa Ouzeria	APPROVED	Greek	$14-$40	225
⁵³ p. 216	Shades on Main Family Restaurant	APPROVED	American	$12-$23	225
⁵⁴ p. 216	Buy the Sea	APPROVED	Fish & Chips	$10-$25	225

OLIVER

Map Page	Hotel	Designation	Member Savings	Page
⁴⁵ p. 216	Coast Oliver Hotel	THREE DIAMOND		220

Map Page	Restaurants	Designation	Cuisine	Price Range	Page
⁵⁷ p. 216	Cock & Bull Cappuccino Bar	APPROVED	American	$6-$11	220
⁵⁸ p. 216	Miradoro at Tinhorn Creek	THREE DIAMOND	New Mediterranean	$17-$56	220
⁵⁹ p. 216	Terrafina at Hester Creek	THREE DIAMOND	New Italian	$17-$35	221
⁶⁰ p. 216	The Sonora Room	THREE DIAMOND	Regional Canadian	$18-$42	221

OSOYOOS

Map Page	Hotels	Designation	Member Savings	Page
⁴⁸ p. 216	Spirit Ridge	THREE DIAMOND		221
⁴⁹ p. 216	Watermark Beach Resort	THREE DIAMOND		221
⁵⁰ p. 216	The Coast Osoyoos Beach Hotel	APPROVED	✔	221
⁵¹ p. 216	Best Western Plus Sunrise Inn	THREE DIAMOND	✔	221
⁵² p. 216	Walnut Beach Resort	THREE DIAMOND		221

Map Page	Restaurants	Designation	Cuisine	Price Range	Page
⁶³ p. 216	Wildfire Grill	APPROVED	International	$15-$26	221
⁶⁴ p. 216	Jojo's Cafe	APPROVED	Coffee/Tea Sandwiches	$6-$10	221
⁶⁵ p. 216	Watermark Wine Bar & Patio	THREE DIAMOND	International Small Plates	$20-$35	221
⁶⁶ p. 216	Convivia Bistro Cuisine	APPROVED	Continental	$17-$35	221
⁶⁷ p. 216	Campo Marina	APPROVED	Italian	$16-$28	221

OLIVER (D-8) pop. 4,824, elev. 307m/1,007'
• Hotels & Restaurants map & index p. 216
• Part of Okanagan Valley area — see map p. 212

The northern tip of the American Great Basin Desert, which extends to Mexico, begins at Oliver. Irrigation begun in the 1920s converted the once desertlike valley floor and arid hillsides surrounding the town into productive orchards and vineyards. Abundant sunshine and little rain provide ideal conditions for growing wine grapes.

The area's climate also promotes numerous recreational activities. An 18-kilometre (11-mi.) paved bicycle trail travels through Oliver's rolling hills and along the Okanagan River. The valley lakes and streams offer boating and fishing. Vaseux Lake and Inkaneep provincial parks (see Recreation Areas Chart) are nearby, as are Bear and Madden lakes, known for excellent trout fishing.

The Fairview Townsite, 3 kilometres (1.9 mi.) west on Fairview Road, formerly was the site of an 1880s-eb;normal;j boomtown. The town disappeared along with the gold in 1906; plaques at the site provide historical information.

Oliver Visitor Centre: 6431 Station St., P.O. Box 460, Oliver, BC, Canada V0H 1T0. **Phone:** (778) 439-2363 or (844) 896-3300.

COAST OLIVER HOTEL   250/498-0251 ⁴⁵
THREE DIAMOND Hotel. **Address:** 6273 Station St V0H 1T0

WHERE TO EAT

COCK & BULL CAPPUCCINO BAR   250/498-6261 ⁵⁷
APPROVED American. Quick Serve. **Address:** 6041 Main St V0H 1T0

MIRADORO AT TINHORN CREEK   250/498-3742 ⁵⁸
THREE DIAMOND New Mediterranean. Casual Dining. **Address:** 537 Tinhorn Creek Rd V0H 1T0

(See map & index p. 216.)

THE SONORA ROOM   250/498-0620 60
▼▼ THREE DIAMOND Regional Canadian. Casual Dining.
Address: 500 Burrowing Owl Pl V0H 1T1

TERRAFINA AT HESTER CREEK   250/498-2229 59
▼▼ THREE DIAMOND New Italian. Casual Dining. Address:
877 Rd 8 V0H 1T1

OSOYOOS (D-9) pop. 4,845, elev. 335m/1,099'
- Hotels & Restaurants map & index p. 216
- Part of Okanagan Valley area — see map p. 212

From Osoyoos on the east side of Osoyoos Lake, an area of desert sand extends 48 kilometres (30 mi.) north to Skaha Lake and 24 kilometres (15 mi.) west along the Similkameen River. The area's similarity to Spain in climate and terrain inspired the citizens to adopt an Iberian style in their buildings. Despite its arid surroundings, Osoyoos has 19 kilometres (12 mi.) of sandy beach lining one of Canada's warmest freshwater lakes.

Man-made recreational facilities include Wild Rapids on E. Lakeshore Drive, with three large waterslides, five giant hot tubs and two minislides. Skiing is available nearby.

A heavy concentration of minerals, including evaporated copper, silver, gold and sulfate and Epsom salts, can be found at Spotted Lake, west on Crowsnest Hwy. 3, which provides 446 kilometres (277 mi.) of scenic driving all the way to Hope.

Destination Osoyoos Visitor Services Centre: 8701 Main St., Osoyoos, BC, Canada V0H 1V0. **Phone:** (778) 699-2044.

NK'MIP DESERT CULTURAL CENTRE is at 1000 Rancher Creek Rd. Visitors will experience a desert ecosystem and the traditions of the Okanagan people through interactive exhibits, artifacts, a re-created Okanagan village and self-guiding walking trails. The Village Trail is 1.4 kilometres (.9 mi.) long and has interpretive signs, benches and ramadas; the Loop Trail is 2 kilometres (1.2 mi.) and includes several uphill segments.

Time: Allow 1 hour minimum. **Hours:** Daily 9:30-4:30, Mar.-Oct. Phone ahead for Nov.-Feb. hours and guided tour information. **Cost:** $14; $13 (ages 65+); $10 (ages 5-18); $38 (family, two adults and two or more children). **Phone:** (250) 495-7901 or (888) 495-8555. [GT]

WINERIES
- **Nk'Mip Cellars** is at 1400 Rancher Creek Rd. **Hours:** Tastings daily 9-8, July-Aug.; 9-6, Apr.-June and Sept.-Oct.; 10-5, rest of year. Phone ahead to confirm schedule. **Phone:** (250) 495-2985. [GT]

BEST WESTERN PLUS SUNRISE INN
                                   250/495-4000 51
▼▼ THREE DIAMOND   Best   **AAA Benefit:**
Hotel   Western   Members save up to
              PLUS   15% and earn bonus
                         points!

Address: 5506 Main St V0H 1V0 **Location:** Jct Hwy 97, 1.9 mi (3 km) e on Hwy 3 (Main St). **Facility:** 66 units, some efficiencies and kitchens. 3 stories, interior corridors. **Terms:** check-in 4 pm. **Pool:** heated indoor. **Activities:** hot tub, exercise room. **Guest Services:** coin laundry.

[SAVE] [ECO] [♨] CALL[&] [🛁] [🖥]
[BIZ] [📶] [✕] [📷] [🛗] [💻] /SOME UNITS [🐾] [🚗]

THE COAST OSOYOOS BEACH HOTEL
                                   250/495-6525 50
▼ APPROVED   **Address:** 7702 Main St V0H 1V0 **Loca-**
Hotel   **tion:** Waterfront. Jct Hwy 97, 1.2 mi (2
                km) e. **Facility:** 60 units, some two bed-
                rooms and kitchens. 3 stories (no ele-
                vator), interior/exterior corridors. **Terms:**

check-in 4 pm. **Pool:** heated indoor. **Activities:** hot tub, exercise room. **Guest Services:** coin laundry. **Featured Amenity: continental breakfast.**

[SAVE] [ECO] [♨] [🛁] [🖥] [BIZ] [📶]
[✕] [🛗] [💻] /SOME UNITS [🐾] [🚗]

SPIRIT RIDGE   250/495-5445 48
▼▼ THREE DIAMOND Resort Condominium. **Address:** 1200 Rancher Creek Rd V0H 1V6

WALNUT BEACH RESORT   250/495-5400 52
▼▼ THREE DIAMOND Resort Hotel. **Address:** 4200 Lakeshore Dr V0H 1V6

WATERMARK BEACH RESORT   250/495-5500 49
▼▼ THREE DIAMOND Resort Condominium. **Address:** 15 Park Pl V0H 1V0

WHERE TO EAT

CAMPO MARINA   250/495-7650 67
▼▼ APPROVED Italian. Casual Dining. **Address:** 5907 Main St V0H 1V3

CONVIVIA BISTRO CUISINE   250/495-2223 66
▼▼ APPROVED Continental. Casual Dining. **Address:** 8312 74th Ave V0H 1V0

JOJO'S CAFE   250/495-6652 64
▼▼ APPROVED Coffee/Tea Sandwiches. Quick Serve. **Address:** 8316 Main St V0H 1T0

WATERMARK WINE BAR & PATIO   250/495-5508 65
▼▼ THREE DIAMOND International Small Plates. Casual Dining. **Address:** 15 Park Pl V0H 1V0

WILDFIRE GRILL   250/495-2215 63
▼▼ APPROVED International. Casual Dining. **Address:** 8526 Main St V0H 1V4

PACIFIC RIM NATIONAL PARK RESERVE (I-3)

Elevations in the park range from sea level along the Long Beach area to 140 metres (459 ft.) at Radar Hill. Refer to CAA/AAA maps for additional elevation information.

On the west coast of Vancouver Island, Pacific Rim National Park Reserve consists of three geographically distinct sections with different entry points: the Long Beach unit between Ucluelet and Tofino; the Broken Group Island unit, a cluster of islands in Barkley Sound; and the 75-kilometre-long (47-mi.) West Coast Trail unit between Bamfield and Port Renfrew.

Numerous contrasts exist in the 510-square-kilometre (197-sq.-mi.) reserve, which has sandy beaches, tranquil estuaries and lakes, rugged headlands, dense rain forests and rocky islands. Wildflowers nurtured by the area's moist and temperate climate thrive in an immense old-growth rain forest.

A stopping place for geese and ducks during their yearly migrations, the shoreline zone also accommodates colonies of sea birds and wildlife. Each spring some 20,000 gray whales migrate through the reserve's waters.

General Information and Activities

The reserve is open all year, although many facilities are seasonal. The Long Beach Unit, about 16 kilometres (10 mi.) west of the junction of Hwy. 4 and the Ucluelet highway, has 19 kilometres (12 mi.) of sandy beach and shoreline which are popular year-round with surfers and beachwalkers; wheelchair-accessible trails are available. Pacific Rim Visitor Centre, open mid-March to mid-October, is located at the junction of Hwy. 4 and Pacific Rim Hwy. There are self-guiding nature trails in the surrounding rain forest and other interpretive programs. The Kwisitis Visitor Centre features displays and films chronicling marine life of the Pacific.

The Broken Group Islands, accessible only by boat, offer pristine wilderness spread over a 100-island cluster in the center of Barkley Sound. Eagles and sea lions are abundant, while varied sea life and sunken ships create a diver's paradise. Camping is available in designated areas on eight islands.

The West Coast Trail, which had its beginnings as a telegraph line and then an avenue of rescue for shipwrecked sailors, follows the national park's rugged coastline between Port Renfrew and Bamfield. The trail is recommended to experienced hikers only and offers spectacular coastal scenery along its challenging path. Remnants of former settlements and shipwrecks can be seen along the shoreline.

The West Coast Trail Information and Registration Centres at Pachena Bay near Bamfield and at Port Renfrew are open daily 9-4, May through September. Reservations to hike the trail may be made, beginning mid-March, for June 15 through September 15 dates; phone (877) 737-3783 within Canada and the U.S. *See Recreation Areas Chart.*

ADMISSION to the Long Beach area is $7.80; $6.80 (ages 65+); free (ages 0-17); $15.70 (all occupants of a private vehicle with up to seven people). Camping fee at Long Beach is $27.40-$32.30 per person per night. Camping fee at other designated sites is $9.80 per person per night. West Coast Trail use permit $127.50; reservation fee $24.50 (non-refundable). Ferry fee $15.24. An annual pass, valid at most Canadian national parks, marine areas and historic sites, is available.

PETS are permitted in the Long Beach Unit of the park provided they are on a leash at all times. Pets are not permitted in the Broken Group Islands or the West Coast Trail.

ADDRESS inquiries to the Superintendent, Pacific Rim National Park Reserve, 2040 Pacific Rim Hwy., P.O. Box 280, Ucluelet, BC, Canada V0R 3A0; phone (250) 726-3500, or (250) 726-4212 June 1 to mid-Sept., or (887) 737-3783 for reservations.

PARKSVILLE (G-10) pop. 11,977, elev. 80m/262'

With its 1.6-kilometre-long (1-mi.) sandy beach on the Strait of Georgia, Parksville is a popular summer resort. Nearby Englishman and Little Qualicum rivers and parks, with scenic waterfalls, provide many opportunities for recreation, as do other area lakes, streams, mountains and parks. Rathtrevor Beach Provincial Park offers a beach, camping and picnicking. *See Recreation Areas Chart.*

Artistic endeavors in sand are the main focus of the Parksville Beach Festival. Elaborate sand sculptures compete for prizes in July and August, and attendees can also enjoy fireworks, children's activities and a volleyball tournament.

Parksville & District Chamber of Commerce: 1275 E. Island Hwy., P.O. Box 99, Parksville, BC, Canada V9P 2G3. **Phone:** (250) 248-3613.

ARBUTUS GROVE MOTEL   250/248-6422

APPROVED   Motel. **Address:** 1182 E Island Hwy V9P 1W3

BAYSIDE RESORT, AN ASCEND HOTEL COLLECTION MEMBER   250/248-8333

THREE DIAMOND   Hotel

Address: 240 Dogwood St V9P 1E1 **Location:** Oceanfront. Island Hwy 19 exit 51 (Parksville/Coombs), 1.3 mi (2 km) e, then 0.6 mi (1 km) n on Hwy 19A. **Facility:** 59 units. 3 stories, interior corridors. **Pool:** heated outdoor. **Activities:** hot tub, beach access, exercise room, spa.

SAVE / SOME UNITS

THE BEACH CLUB RESORT   250/248-8999

THREE DIAMOND Contemporary Resort Hotel. **Address:** 181 Beachside Dr V9P 2H5

OCEANSIDE VILLAGE RESORT   250/248-8961
THREE DIAMOND Vacation Rental Cottage. **Address:** 1080
Resort Dr V9P 2E3

SUNRISE RIDGE WATERFRONT RESORT   250/248-4674
THREE DIAMOND Vacation Rental Hotel. **Address:** 1175 Resort Dr V9P 2E3

TIGH-NA-MARA SEASIDE SPA RESORT & CONFERENCE
CENTRE   250/248-2072
APPROVED Resort Hotel. **Address:** 1155 Resort Dr
V9P 2E3

TRAVELODGE PARKSVILLE   250/248-2232
APPROVED Hotel. **Address:** 424 W Island Hwy V9P
1K8

V.I.P. MOTEL   250/248-3244
APPROVED Motel. **Address:** 414 W Island Hwy V9P
1K8

WHERE TO EAT

AMRIKKO'S FINE INDIAN CUISINE   250/951-0682
APPROVED Indian. Casual Dining. **Address:** 487 E
Island Hwy V9P 2H6

BREAD AND HONEY   250/586-1021
APPROVED Pacific Northwest. Casual Dining.
Address: 162 Harrison Ave V9P 1K7

THE CEDARS RESTAURANT   250/248-2333
THREE DIAMOND Pacific Northwest. Casual Dining.
Address: 1155 Resort Dr V9P 2E3

KALVAS RESTAURANT   250/248-6933
APPROVED Steak Seafood. Casual Dining. **Address:**
180 Moilliet St, Island Hwy N V9P 2H4

LEFTY'S FRESH FOOD RESTAURANT   250/954-3886
APPROVED American. Casual Dining. **Address:**
101-280 E Island Hwy V9P 2G3

MEKONG RIVER RESTAURANT   250/586-8000
APPROVED Vietnamese. Casual Dining. **Address:**
625 Island Highway E V9P 1T5

PACIFIC PRIME STEAK AND CHOP RESTAURANT
                                             250/947-2109
THREE DIAMOND Pacific Northwest. Fine Dining. **Address:**
181 Beachside Dr V9P 2H5

REALM FOOD CO.   250/586-1158
APPROVED Natural/Organic. Quick Serve. **Address:**
180 Craig St V9P 2G8

PEACHLAND (C-8) pop. 5,200,
elev. 366m/1,200'
• **Part of Okanagan Valley area — see map p. 212**

Peachland's rolling green countryside is a prosperous fruit-growing, farming, lumber-producing and
mining area. The mining of molybdenum and copper
from the Brenda Mines complex in the hills above
Hwy. 97 spurred significant growth during the 1970s.

Nearby mountains, rivers and lakes, including
Okanagan Lake *(see Recreation Areas Chart)*, offer
abundant opportunities for skiing, hiking, fishing and
water sports.

PENDER ISLANDS (H-10)

Part of the Gulf Islands *(see place listing p. 189)*,
the Penders, consisting of North and South Pender
islands, are connected by a one-lane wooden bridge
that spans the canal linking Bedwell and Browning
harbors. An archeological dig conducted at the time
the bridge was built found evidence of island occupation dating back 4,000 years. The Pender Islands
Museum, set on national park lands at Roseland, offers an overview of area history on Saturday and
Sunday 10-4 in July and August; Saturday and
Sunday 1-4, Easter weekend-Thanksgiving
weekend. Phone (250) 629-6935.

The island's 20 public ocean access points and
many coves allow ample opportunities for swimming
and picnicking. Hiking, boating, fishing, golfing, bicycling, kayaking and scuba diving are other available
recreational activities. Camping is available at Prior
Centennial Campground in Gulf Islands National
Park Reserve from May 15-Sept. 30. Roadside
stands offer locally grown produce. The view from
the summit of Mount Norman, part of Gulf Islands
National Park Reserve, is worth the climb.

POETS COVE RESORT & SPA   250/629-2100
THREE DIAMOND Hotel. **Address:** 9801 Spalding Rd V0N
2M3

PENTICTON (C-8) pop. 32,877,
elev. 345m/1,131'
• **Hotels p. 224 • Restaurants p. 224**
• **Hotels & Restaurants map & index p. 216**
• **Part of Okanagan Valley area — see map p. 212**

The first orchards in Okanagan Valley were
planted by the Oblates at Okanagan Mission
1860-61, and the fruits, especially peaches, became
a staple of the area. Tom Ellis established the first
cattle ranch in 1865 and it was an empire when he
sold it for a hefty sum in 1905; by 1909 orchards had
replaced cattle in the agricultural economy. Today
Penticton's fruit industry combines with tourism and
lumber industries to keep the community strong.

Okanagan and Skaha lakes, at opposite ends of
the city, offer ample expanses of shoreline for recreational pursuits. A popular summer activity is floating
down the 8-kilometre (5-mi.) river channel from the
mouth of Okanagan Lake *(see Recreation Areas
Chart)* to Skaha Lake. The channel has rest and
picnic areas and is paralleled by a bicycle path and
a jogging trail. The *Casabella Princess*, a 48-
passenger paddlewheeler departing from Penticton
Marina, takes passengers on a 1-hour cruise of the
south end of Okanagan Lake or on a 2-hour dinner
cruise (June-Sept.); phone (250) 215-2779.

Penticton & Wine Country Visitor Centre: 553
Vees Dr., Penticton, BC, Canada V2A 8S3. **Phone:**
(250) 276-2170 or (800) 663-5052.

WINERIES
• **Hillside Winery and Bistro** is 3 km (2 mi.) n. of
jct. McMillan Ave. and Naramata Rd. at 1350

(See map & index p. 216.)

Naramata Rd. **Hours:** Tastings and self-guiding tours daily 10-6, Apr.-Oct.; Mon.-Fri. 9-4 in Mar. and Nov.-Dec. **Phone:** (250) 493-6274 or (888) 923-9463. GT

BEST WESTERN INN AT PENTICTON
250/493-0311 **41**

APPROVED

Hotel

AAA Benefit: Members save up to 15% and earn bonus points!

Address: 3180 Skaha Lake Rd V2A 6G4 **Location:** From downtown, 2.5 mi (4 km) s. **Facility:** 64 units, some two bedrooms, efficiencies and kitchens. 2 stories (no elevator), exterior corridors. **Terms:** check-in 4 pm. **Pool:** heated outdoor, heated indoor. **Activities:** hot tub, playground, picnic facilities. **Guest Services:** valet and coin laundry. **Featured Amenity:** continental breakfast.

DAYS INN & CONFERENCE CENTRE PENTICTON
250/493-6616 **39**
APPROVED Hotel. **Address:** 152 Riverside Dr V2A 5Y4

EMPIRE MOTEL
250/493-2323 **42**
APPROVED Motel. **Address:** 3495 Skaha Lake Rd V2A 6G6

PENTICTON LAKESIDE RESORT & CONFERENCE CENTRE
250/493-8221 **38**

THREE DIAMOND

Resort Hotel

Address: 21 Lakeshore Dr W V2A 7M5 **Location:** Waterfront. Main St at Lakeshore Dr W. **Facility:** This superb hotel has nicely appointed guest rooms with balconies. The new building has ultra-modern, spacious suites and king rooms with swanky showers. Amenities include plenty of water sports. 273 units. 6 stories, interior corridors. **Parking:** on-site (fee) and valet. **Terms:** check-in 4 pm. **Amenities:** safes. **Dining:** Hooded Merganser Bar & Grill, see separate listing. **Pool:** heated indoor. **Activities:** hot tub, motor boats, self-propelled boats, boat dock, trails, health club. **Guest Services:** valet laundry. *(See ad this page.)*

RAMADA BY WYNDHAM PENTICTON HOTEL & SUITES
250/492-8926 **40**
THREE DIAMOND Hotel. **Address:** 1050 Eckhardt Ave W V2A 2C3

WHERE TO EAT

BAD TATTOO BREWING COMPANY
250/493-8686 **49**
APPROVED Pizza. Brewpub. **Address:** 169 Estabrook Ave V2A 1G2

THE BENCH MARKET
250/492-2222 **48**
APPROVED Regional Deli Sandwiches. Quick Serve. **Address:** 368 Vancouver Ave V2A 1A5

▼ See AAA listing this page ▼

PENTICTON LAKESIDE RESORT
AND CONFERENCE CENTRE
Experience the heart of the Okanagan

AAA MEMBER?
Save 10% when booking with us!*
Use Promo Code: AAA when booking to redeem offer. Subject to availability.

On-Site Wine Tasting

Three Lakeview Restaurants

Gym, Pool, & Hot Tub Access

www.pentictonlakesideresort.com   1-800-663-9400

(See map & index p. 216.)

| BUY THE SEA | 250/492-3474 | 54 |

APPROVED Fish & Chips. Quick Serve. **Address:** 2100 Main St V2A 5H7

| HILLSIDE WINERY BISTRO | 250/493-6274 | 45 |

THREE DIAMOND New Canadian. Casual Dining. **Address:** 1350 Naramata Rd V2A 8T6

| HOODED MERGANSER BAR & GRILL | 250/487-4663 | 47 |

THREE DIAMOND Pacific Northwest. Casual Dining. **Address:** 21 Lakeshore Dr W V2A 7M5 *(See ad p. 224.)*

| LA CASA OUZERIA | 250/492-9144 | 52 |

APPROVED Greek. Casual Dining. **Address:** 1090 Main St V2A 5E5

| LACHI FINE INDIAN CUISINE | 778/476-5665 | 50 |

APPROVED Indian. Casual Dining. **Address:** 510 Main St V2A 5C7

| SALTY'S BEACH HOUSE | 250/493-5001 | 46 |

APPROVED Caribbean. Casual Dining. **Address:** 1000 Lakeshore Dr W V2A 1C1

| SHADES ON MAIN FAMILY RESTAURANT | 250/493-0465 | 53 |

APPROVED American. Casual Dining. **Address:** 1909 Main St V2A 5H5

| THEO'S RESTAURANT | 250/492-4019 | 51 |

APPROVED Greek. Casual Dining. **Address:** 687 Main St V2A 5C9

PITT MEADOWS pop. 17,736
• Hotels & Restaurants map & index p. 276
• Part of Vancouver area — see map p. 249

BEST WESTERN PLUS PITT MEADOWS INN & SUITES
604/460-9859 **71**

THREE DIAMOND
Hotel

AAA Benefit: Members save up to 15% and earn bonus points!

Address: 19267 Lougheed Hwy V3Y 2J5 **Location:** Jct Lougheed Hwy (Hwy 7) and Harris Rd. Pitt Meadows, 3. **Facility:** 79 units. 3 stories, interior corridors. **Pool:** heated outdoor. **Activities:** hot tub, exercise room. **Guest Services:** coin laundry. **Featured Amenity:** breakfast buffet.

WHERE TO EAT

| KISOJI JAPANESE KITCHEN | 604/457-4567 | 96 |

APPROVED Japanese. Casual Dining. **Address:** 19040 Lougheed Hwy V3Y 2N6

AAA.com/campgrounds—
For overnights under the stars

PORT ALBERNI (F-9) pop. 17,743, elev. 60m/197'
• Hotels p. 226 • Restaurants p. 226

A deepwater port and important fishing and lumber shipping center, Port Alberni was discovered in 1791 by Don Pedro Alberni, a Spanish sea captain. Industry began in 1860 when nine workmen arriving on the schooner *Meg Merrilees* built a sawmill on the harbor's edge.

Port Alberni's harbor remains the city's focal point, enhanced by the Alberni Harbour Quay at the foot of Argyle Street. The facility includes shops, an arts and crafts outlet and the Lady Rose Marine Services office *(see attraction listing)*. From the 1912 CPR Train Station, a logging locomotive takes visitors on a 35-minute journey along the waterfront to McLean Mill National Historic Site *(see attraction listing)*.

Surrounded by mountains, lakes and forests, the city is a good base for naturalists and outdoors enthusiasts. Alpine and cross-country skiing are available nearby. Sproat Lake Provincial Park *(see Recreation Areas Chart)* features First Nations carvings of mythological beasts. There are hundreds of giant Douglas firs, many that date from the late 12th century, at Cathedral Grove in MacMillan Provincial Park, 16 kilometres (10 mi.) east.

The region's natural wonders are protected by the Martin Mars Water Bombers based at Sproat Lake. Designed to combat forest fires, these huge aircraft carry 6,000 imperial gallons (7,206 U.S. gallons) of water.

Port Alberni Visitor Centre: 2533 Port Alberni Hwy., Port Alberni, BC, Canada V9Y 8P2. **Phone:** (250) 724-6535.

ALBERNI VALLEY MUSEUM is at 4255 Wallace St. in the Echo Centre building. The community museum features collections relating to First Nations as well as community and industrial history. Feature exhibits include Nuu chah nulth basketry, folk art and textiles.

Visitors also can see displays about the area's industrial past in logging, fishing, mining and farming. An exhibit about the West Coast Trail tells of its early uses as a telegraph line and a rescue trail for shipwrecked sailors. Changing exhibitions also are offered. **Time:** Allow 30 minutes minimum. **Hours:** Mon.-Sat. 10-5 (also Thurs. 5-8), July-Aug.; Tues.-Sat. 10-5 (also Thurs. 5-8), rest of year. Closed statutory holidays. **Cost:** Donations. **Phone:** (250) 723-2181.

MCLEAN MILL NATIONAL HISTORIC SITE is 6 km (10 mi.) w. on Beaver Creek Rd., then 3 km (1.8 mi.) n. to 5633 Smith Rd., following signs. The 13-hectare (32-acre) site preserves a working 1926 steam sawmill that was operated by the R.B. McLean family until 1965. Thirty structures from the early days of British Columbia's forest industry include the camp where loggers and mill employees lived and worked.

Time: Allow 1 hour, 30 minutes minimum. **Hours:** Grounds open daily 24 hours. Site office open Mon.-Sat. 10-4. Guided tours offered Fri.-Sun. at 11:30, 12:30 and 1:30, July-Aug. Phone ahead to confirm schedule. **Cost:** Guided tours $5; free (ages 1-5). Self-guiding tours by donation. **Phone:** (250) 723-1376 or (855) 866-1376. [image icons]

Alberni Pacific Railway departs from the CPR Station at Argyle and Kingsway sts. Passengers embark upon a 45-minute scenic train ride to McLean Mill National Historic Site. **Hours:** Trips depart Thurs.-Sun. at 11, July-Aug.; Fri.-Sun. at 11, May-June and Sept.-Oct. Phone ahead to confirm schedule. **Cost:** Round-trip fare (includes mill admission) $38.25; $22 (ages 12-18); $98.50 (family, two adults and two children ages 12-18). Rates may vary; phone ahead. **Phone:** (250) 723-2118 or (250) 723-1376.

BEST WESTERN PLUS BARCLAY HOTEL   250/724-7171

THREE DIAMOND

Hotel

Best Western PLUS   **AAA Benefit:** Members save up to 15% and earn bonus points!

Address: 4277 Stamp Ave V9Y 7X8 **Location:** Johnston Rd (Hwy 4), just s on Gertrude St. **Facility:** 84 units. 5 stories, interior corridors. **Pool:** heated outdoor. **Activities:** sauna, hot tub, exercise room. **Guest Services:** valet laundry.

[amenity icons: SAVE, etc., HS, SOME UNITS]

RIVERSIDE MOTEL   250/724-9916

APPROVED   Motel. **Address:** 5065 Roger St V9Y 3Y9

SOMASS MOTEL AND RV   250/724-3236

APPROVED   Motel. **Address:** 5279 River Rd V9Y 6Z3

WHERE TO EAT

BARE BONES FISH & CHIPS   250/720-0900

APPROVED   Fish & Chips. Casual Dining. **Address:** 4824 Johnston Rd V9Y 5M1

THE CLAM BUCKET RESTAURANT   250/723-1315

APPROVED   Seafood. Casual Dining. **Address:** 4479 Victoria Quay V9Y 5G1

LITTLE BAVARIA RESTAURANT   250/724-4242

APPROVED

German
Casual Dining
$12-$25

AAA Inspector Notes: Ask anyone in town about this quaint restaurant with pleasant Bavarian décor, and they'll gladly point the way to this long-established spot serving good old-fashioned German food. Schnitzel, Hungarian goulash, cabbage rolls and fondue are just some of the items you simply must try. Of course, there is house-made black forest cake on the dessert menu. Dinner is served nightly, however lunch is only available on weekdays. **Features:** full bar. **Reservations:** suggested. **Address:** 3035 4th Ave V9Y 2B8 **Location:** Between Argyle and Angus sts. **Parking:** street only.

[L] [D]

SMITTY'S   250/724-5022

APPROVED   American. Casual Dining. **Address:** 3426 3rd Ave V9Y 7M8

PORT COQUITLAM (H-11) pop. 56,342, elev. 10m/33'
• Part of Vancouver area — see map p. 249

Port Coquitlam is bordered by the Pitt and Fraser rivers to the east and south and mountains to the north. The rivers were coveted fishing grounds, and in fact, Coquitlam is derived from the Salish word *kwayhquitlum,* which means "red fish in the river," referring to the annual salmon spawning run. Before the 1800s, the area was occupied by the ancestors of the Kwayhquitlum First Nations tribe. With the arrival of the first European settlers, Port Coquitlam began its growth as a farming and logging community.

Opportunities for recreational activities abound. The 29-kilometre (18-mi.) PoCo Trail passes through wooded areas and runs alongside the Pitt River, providing plenty of opportunities to observe waterfowl and other wildlife; the Pitt Dikes can be seen from the trail. Activities such as hiking, jogging, bicycling and horseback riding also can be enjoyed.

EARLS KITCHEN + BAR   604/941-1733

APPROVED   American. Casual Dining. **Address:** 2850 Shaughnessy St V3C 6K5

PORT EDWARD (E-1) pop. 544

Port Edward, on the Tsimpsean Peninsula, was named after King Edward VI. The town was founded in 1908 and incorporated in 1966.

The river of mists, as the First Nations called the Skeena River, bursts through the Coast Range and empties into the Pacific Ocean near Port Edward. The river provides the community's major commodity, fish, which is processed by local canneries. Salmon and steelhead trout, besides being economic staples, also offer a recreational challenge to anglers. Because of the area's proximity to luxuriant rain forests, mountain ranges and the river, sporting types also will find ample opportunities for canoeing, kayaking, camping, hunting and hiking.

NORTH PACIFIC CANNERY NATIONAL HISTORIC SITE is 10 km (6 mi.) s. of Hwy. 16 at 1889 Skeena Dr. For almost 100 years (1889-1980) this cannery, one of more than 200 such businesses operating along the West Coast at the industry's peak, processed and canned salmon from the Skeena River.

The site consists of 29 buildings and structures representing the factory operations and employee living quarters of a multiethnic workforce in one of the formative industries of British Columbia. The village includes the main cannery, reduction plant, staff housing and mess house. Artifacts of the fishing industry, such as boats, tools and machinery original to the shops as well as some of the workers' personal items are displayed throughout the complex. Guided tours feature a working canning line, stories of cannery life, and a walk along the riverfront boardwalk.

Time: Allow 1 hour minimum. **Hours:** Daily 10-5, July-Aug.; Tues.-Sun. 10-5, May-June and in Sept. Phone ahead to arrange tours. **Cost:** $12; $10 (ages 65+); $8 (ages 6-18); $25 (family of seven, maximum two adults). **Phone:** (250) 628-3538.
GT ⑪

PORT HARDY pop. 4,008

GLEN LYON INN   250/949-7115
APPROVED Hotel. **Address:** 6435 Hardy Bay Rd V0N 2P0

KWA'LILAS HOTEL   250/949-8525
APPROVED Hotel. **Address:** 9040 Granville St V0N 2P0

QUARTERDECK INN & MARINA   250/902-0455
APPROVED Hotel. **Address:** 6555 Hardy Bay Rd V0N 2P0

WHERE TO EAT

HA'ME RESTAURANT   855/949-8884
APPROVED Pacific Northwest. Casual Dining. **Address:** 9040 Granville St V0N 2PO

MARKET STREET CAFE   250/949-8110
APPROVED Breakfast Sandwiches. Quick Serve. **Address:** 7030 Market St V0N 2P0

POUCE COUPE (D-6) pop. 738, elev. 652m/2,139'

The village of Pouce Coupe is referred to as the gateway to Peace Country because it is one of the first communities travelers will see when entering British Columbia from Alberta.

POWELL RIVER (F-10) pop. 13,165, elev. 55m/180'

Rich forests and abundant water brought the founders of the Powell River Company to the area in the early 1900s. The townsite is one of the oldest company-built communities in western Canada.

Separated from the mainland by Jervis Inlet, the area offers year-round recreation including fresh-water and saltwater fishing, scuba diving, boating, kayaking, hiking and bicycling. The Powell Forest Canoe Route connects eight lakes around the Upper Sunshine Coast region with camping areas along the scenic circuit.

A panorama of the Strait of Malaspina unfolds from the Mount Valentine viewpoint, reached by a rock stairway in the heart of town. Bald eagles can be observed at any time of year, especially in late fall when they are attracted by salmon spawning in channels and small streams. Also of interest are Sliammon Fish Hatchery and Powell River Salmon Society Spawning Channel.

Guided 2-hour tours of the Catalyst Paper Mill are offered through the visitor center. Part of the tour is outdoors; appropriate dress and low-heeled, closed footwear are advised. For information and reservations phone (604) 485-4701 or (877) 817-8669.

Powell River Visitor Centre: 4760 Joyce Ave., Powell River, BC, Canada V8A 3B6. **Phone:** (604) 485-4701 or (877) 817-8669.

POWELL RIVER TOWN CENTRE HOTEL   604/485-3000
APPROVED Hotel. **Address:** 4660 Joyce Ave V8A 3B6

WHERE TO EAT

COSTA DEL SOL LATIN CUISINE   604/414-7463
APPROVED Latin American. Casual Dining. **Address:** 4578 Marine Ave V8A 2K6

THE SHINGLEMILL PUB & BISTRO   604/483-2001
APPROVED Canadian. Casual Dining. **Address:** 6233 Powell Pl V8A 4S6

PRINCE GEORGE (E-4) pop. 71,974, elev. 691m/2,267'
• Hotels p. 228 • Restaurants p. 228

At the confluence of the Nechako and Fraser rivers, the area was visited in 1793 by Alexander Mackenzie in his trek down the Fraser to the Pacific. In 1807 it became the site for Simon Fraser's North West Co. fort. Fraser's canoe brigades soon gave way to paddlewheelers and then railroads, which converged on this important northern crossroads. Prince George remains a major transportation and trade center, a role enhanced by a thriving forest industry.

Despite its urban transformation, the city has retained much of its natural heritage in its 116 parks. Of interest are Fort George Park, which contains a replica of Fraser's trading post; Connaught Park's manicured gardens and scenic views; and Cottonwood Island Park, which includes the Prince George Railway & Forestry Museum and its collection of railroad artifacts and cars.

Prince George blends its pastoral features with such cultural centers as Studio 2880 and Vanier Hall. Studio 2880, home to six craft guilds, is the site of craft markets and special events throughout the year. Concerts by the Prince George Symphony and by visiting performers are held in Vanier Hall.

These cultural amenities coexist with the more rugged recreational opportunities available in the wilderness that surrounds the city. Nearby lakes, rivers and mountains present an array of activities ranging from rugged back-country hikes and fishing to skiing and ice-skating.

Prince George Visitor Centre: 1300 First Ave., Suite 201, Prince George, BC, Canada V2L 2Y3. **Phone:** (250) 562-3700 or (800) 668-7646.

[SAVE] **THE EXPLORATION PLACE MUSEUM & SCIENCE CENTRE** is at the end of 20th Ave. at 333 Becott Pl. in Fort George Park. Fort George's history and development are explored through such topics as transportation, lumber and the indigenous culture. The Children's Gallery houses life-size dinosaur sculptures, skeletons and a dig pit. The Explorations Gallery features live animals and interactive computers. A steam locomotive ride is offered on weekends and holidays.

Time: Allow 1 hour minimum. **Hours:** Daily 9-5. Closed Jan. 1, Christmas and day after Christmas. **Cost:** Museum $11; $9 (ages 65+ and students with ID); $8 (ages 3-12); $25 (family, two adults and up to four children ages 0-18). **Phone:** (250) 562-1612 or (866) 562-1612.

HUBLE HOMESTEAD HISTORIC SITE is 38 km (24 mi.) n. on Hwy. 97, then 6 km (4 mi.) e. on Mitchell Rd. The site features several replicas of historic buildings as well as the original home of Al and Annie Huble. Along with his business partner Ed Seebach, Huble was instrumental in establishing a community within the Giscome Portage area. The homestead also offers weekend special events that feature demonstrations, live entertainment, games and contests.

Time: Allow 1 hour minimum. **Hours:** Daily 10-5, Victoria Day-Labour Day; Sat.-Sun. 10-5, day after Labour Day-Thanksgiving. Phone ahead to confirm schedule. **Cost:** $5; $3 (children and ages 65+); $10 (family). **Phone:** (250) 564-7033. GT 🍴 🎁

PRINCE GEORGE RAILWAY & FORESTRY MUSEUM is at 850 River Rd. The museum houses one of the largest collection of railway-related artifacts in British Columbia. Items, circa 1899-1960s, include a wooden snow plow, locomotives, box cars and cabooses.

Time: Allow 1 hour minimum. **Hours:** Daily 10-5, Victoria Day weekend-Labour Day weekend; daily 11-8, Dec. 18-23; 11-6 on Christmas Eve; Wed.-Sun. 11-4, rest of year. Closed Nov. 11. Phone ahead to confirm schedule. **Cost:** $8; $7 (ages 13-17, students with ID and senior citizens); $5 (ages 3-12). **Phone:** (250) 563-7351. 🎁

BON VOYAGE INN   250/964-2333
▼ APPROVED   Motel. **Address:** 4222 Hwy 16 W V2N 5N7

CARMEL INN   250/564-6339
▼ APPROVED   Motel. **Address:** 1502 Hwy 97 S V2L 5L9

COAST PRINCE GEORGE HOTEL BY APA   250/563-0121
▼ THREE DIAMOND   Hotel. **Address:** 770 Brunswick St V2L 2C2

COURTYARD BY MARRIOTT PRINCE GEORGE   250/596-6274
▼ THREE DIAMOND   SAVE
Contemporary Hotel. **Address:** 900
Brunswick St V2L 2C3

AAA Benefit:
Members save 5% or more!

🔗 **Save on travel, shopping and more:**

AAA.com/discounts

FOUR POINTS BY SHERATON PRINCE GEORGE
                                        250/564-7100
▼ THREE DIAMOND   FOUR POINTS BY SHERATON
Hotel

AAA Benefit: Members save 5% or more!

Address: 1790 Hwy 97 S V2L 5L3 **Location:** Hwy 97 exit Spruce northbound; exit City Center southbound via Queensway. **Facility:** 74 units. 3 stories, interior corridors. **Parking:** on-site and valet, winter plug-ins. **Pool:** heated indoor. **Activities:** hot tub, exercise room. **Guest Services:** valet laundry.

SAVE 🍴 🎁 🍷 CALL ♿ 🏊
🛗 BIZ HS 📶 ✕ 🎥 ▯ 💻 /SOME UNITS 📷

POMEROY INN & SUITES PRINCE GEORGE   236/423-4546
▼ THREE DIAMOND   Contemporary Hotel. **Address:** 2700 Recplace Dr V2N 0H4

PRESTIGE TREASURE COVE HOTEL PRINCE GEORGE
                                        250/614-9111
▼ THREE DIAMOND   Hotel. **Address:** 2005 Hwy 97 S V2N 7A3

RAMADA PLAZA BY WYNDHAM PRINCE GEORGE
                                        250/563-0055
▼ THREE DIAMOND   Hotel. **Address:** 444 George St V2L 1R6

SANDMAN SIGNATURE HOTEL & SUITES PRINCE GEORGE
                                        250/645-7263
▼ THREE DIAMOND   Hotel. **Address:** 2990 Recreation Place Dr V2N 0B2

WHERE TO EAT

BETULLA BURNING   250/563-8061
▼ THREE DIAMOND   Italian. Casual Dining. **Address:** 1253 3rd Ave V2L 3E6

THE BLACK CLOVER   250/564-4441
▼ APPROVED   Irish. Casual Dining. **Address:** 1165 5th Ave V2L 3L1

THE CANADIAN BREWHOUSE   778/763-1207
▼ APPROVED   International. Sports Bar. **Address:** 3036 Recplace Dr V2N 0G2

CIMO MEDITERRANEAN GRILL   250/564-7975
▼ APPROVED   Italian. Casual Dining. **Address:** 601 Victoria St V2L 2K3

THE COPPER PIG BBQ HOUSE   250/596-2006
▼ APPROVED   Barbecue. Casual Dining. **Address:** 363 George St V2L 1R4

CROSSROADS BREWING   250/614-2332
▼ APPROVED   Canadian. Brewpub. **Address:** 508 George St V2L 1R7

EARLS KITCHEN + BAR   250/562-1527
▼ APPROVED   American. Casual Dining. **Address:** 1440 E Central St V2M 3C1

MOXIE'S CLASSIC GRILL   250/564-4700
▼ APPROVED   American. Casual Dining. **Address:** 1804 E Central St V2M 3C3

MR MIKES STEAKHOUSECASUAL   250/562-1080
▼ APPROVED   American. Casual Dining. **Address:** 2216 Ferry Ave V2N 0B2

NORTH 54   250/564-5400
THREE DIAMOND American. Fine Dining. **Address:** 1493 3rd Ave V2L 3S1

OHH CHOCOLAT CAFÉ   250/564-2464
APPROVED Sandwiches Desserts. Quick Serve. **Address:** 565 George St V2L 5G4

ORIGINAL JOE'S RESTAURANT & BAR   778/416-5637
APPROVED American. Casual Dining. **Address:** 5224 Domano Blvd V2N 4A1

THE SALTED CRACKER   250/562-1110
APPROVED Soup Sandwiches. Quick Serve. **Address:** 1485 10th Ave V2L 2L2

SUSHI 97   250/563-3997
APPROVED Sushi. Casual Dining. **Address:** 892 Central St E V2M 3B8

THE TWISTED CORK RESTAURANT   250/561-5550
APPROVED International. Casual Dining. **Address:** 1157 5th Ave V2L 3L1

WHITE GOOSE BISTRO   250/561-1002
THREE DIAMOND American. Casual Dining. **Address:** 1205 3rd Ave V2L 1T6

WINSTON'S RESTO-BAR   250/563-0121
THREE DIAMOND International. Fine Dining. **Address:** 770 Brunswick St V2L 2C2

PRINCE RUPERT (E-1) pop. 12,508, elev. 50m/164'

At the turn of the 20th century Prince Rupert existed only in the imagination of Charles Hays, manager of the Grand Trunk Pacific Railway. Hays died with the sinking of the SS *Titanic,* but the Grand Trunk Pacific Railway carried out his intention to build a port to rival Vancouver on this rugged, uninhabited island bordered by a natural harbor. The new site was expected to be successful because it was closer to the Far East than Vancouver and would provide an outlet for the untapped resources of Canada's far north.

Prince Rupert has fulfilled that potential and is now one of Canada's major seaports. It is the southernmost port of the Alaska Ferry System, the northern terminus of the British Columbia Ferry Corp. and the western terminus of the Canadian National Railway. Cruise ships en route to coastal glaciers and fjords also stop at Prince Rupert's harbor, said to be the world's third largest natural ice-free deep-sea harbor.

Before the coming of the railroad the northern coast was home to the Tsimpsean and Haida, cultures whose ancestors inhabited the area for almost 5,000 years. Both are renowned for their stylized artworks, the most familiar of which are totem poles. Many of these graceful monuments are shown in such city parks as Service Park, the colorful terraced Sunken Gardens, and Roosevelt Park with its sweeping views of the Pacific.

On the waterfront, Kwinitsa Railway Station is a relic of the modern era. Restored and moved from its original location, Kwinitsa is one of the last of the Grand Trunk Pacific Railway stations; inside are exhibits about the railroad's history.

Just beyond the city, climate and soil have stunted and twisted lodgepole pines into a natural bonsai garden at Oliver Lake Provincial Park. Another interesting phenomenon is Butze Rapids, a series of reversing rapids between Wainwright and Morse basins that rival the reversing falls at Saint John, New Brunswick. A dramatic view of the rapids occurs during a falling tide and can be seen from a viewing point on Hwy. 16, which offers scenic driving east to Terrace *(see place listing p. 244).*

Guided tours are offered during the summer by Farwest Bus Lines Ltd., 225 Second Ave. W. Trans-Provincial Airlines and Northcoast Air Services offer flight tours of the region.

Prince Rupert Visitor Centre: 200-215 Cowbay Rd. (Atlin Terminal), Prince Rupert, BC, Canada V8J 1A2. **Phone:** (250) 624-5637 or (800) 667-1994.

Self-guiding tours: A walking tour that includes sunken gardens, the harbor, sections of the downtown area and various attractions is detailed on maps and brochures available from the visitor bureau at the Museum of Northern British Columbia *(see attraction listing).*

INN ON THE HARBOUR   250/624-9107
APPROVED Hotel. **Address:** 720 1st Ave W V8J 3V6

WHERE TO EAT

DOLLY'S FISH MARKET   250/624-6090
APPROVED Seafood. Casual Dining. **Address:** 7 Cow Bay Rd V8J 1A4

OPA SUSHI   250/627-4560
APPROVED Japanese Sushi. Casual Dining. **Address:** 34 Cow Bay Rd V8J 1A5

PRINCETON (C-8) pop. 2,724
• Hotels p. 230 • Restaurants p. 230

Named "Vermilion Forks" by fur traders in the early 1800s, Princeton developed as a ranching and mining outpost in the foothills of the Cascade Mountains. In 1860 the town was renamed to honor a visit by the Prince of Wales. Revitalized downtown storefronts boast murals and facades in keeping with Princeton's Western heritage.

Princeton & District Chamber of Commerce: 105 Hwy. 3E, P.O. Box 540, Princeton, BC, Canada V0X 1W0. **Phone:** (250) 295-3103.

Self-guiding tours: Maps detailing walking tours are available from the chamber of commerce.

PRINCETON & DISTRICT MUSEUM AND ARCHIVES is at 167 Vermilion Ave. A tunnel complete with a replica dinosaur fossil welcomes visitors into the museum and provides a thematic preview. The

Pollard Collection of fossils and minerals, considered one of the best in British Columbia, offers eye-catching displays and a glow-in-the-dark section. Additional exhibits include indigenous art and basketry as well as a hand-carved canoe, 1880s cabin and other artifacts from the pioneer era.

Time: Allow 1 hour minimum. **Hours:** Daily 10-6, July-Aug.; by appointment rest of year. Phone ahead to confirm schedule. **Cost:** Donations. Cash only. **Phone:** (250) 295-7588.

CANADAS BEST VALUE PRINCETON INN & SUITES
250/295-3537

APPROVED
Motel

Address: 169 Hwy 3 V0X 1W0 **Location:** Hwy 3, just n on Vermilion Ave. **Facility:** 45 units, some kitchens. 2 stories (no elevator), exterior corridors. **Pool:** heated outdoor. **Activities:** sauna, hot tub.

SAVE [↑↑] CALL 🔥 🏊 BIZ 📶
✕ 🖥 📷 💻 / SOME UNITS 🐾

WHERE TO EAT

COWBOY COFFEE   250/295-3431
 APPROVED   Coffee/Tea Sandwiches. Quick Serve. **Address:** 255 Vermilion Ave V0X 1W0

QUALICUM BEACH (G-10) pop. 8,687, elev. 9m/30'

A popular resort and arts community, Qualicum Beach is known for its white sand beaches. Nearby Little Qualicum Falls *(see Recreation Areas Chart)*, Englishman River Falls *(see Recreation Areas Chart)* and Horne Lake Caves provincial parks also present abundant recreational opportunities. Salmon and trout are raised at fish hatcheries on the Big and Little Qualicum rivers.

Qualicum Beach Visitor Information Centre: 2711 W. Island Hwy., Qualicum Beach, BC, Canada V9K 2C4. **Phone:** (250) 752-9532.

HORNE LAKE CAVES is 15 km (9 mi.) n. on Hwy. 19 to exit 75 (Horne Lake Rd.), then 14 km (9 mi.) w. on a gravel rd., following signs to the parking lot. A part of the Horne Lake Caves Provincial Park, the cave system is considered to be one of the best in Canada. Tours are guided and highlights include crystal formations, ancient fossils and a waterfall.

The 1.5-hour Main Cave Experience teaches about the geology and history of the caves. The interpretive tour starts with a 25-minute walk to the entrance. Once inside the cave, visitors explore the easy passages; no crawling or maneuvering in tight spaces is necessary.

Other 3-, 4-, and 5-hour tours, some of which include climbing and rappeling, are offered. Self-guiding exploration is available in Horne Lake Main and Lower caves year-round. A helmet and two sources of light are required. Helmets may be rented for $5 each during the summer only.

Note: The caves are mostly undeveloped and do not provide lighting. Floors are rocky and uneven; children ages 0-4 are not permitted on the tour and visitors with mobility issues could encounter difficulty walking. Warm clothing and comfortable boots or shoes are highly recommended, as the caves remain cool even in hot weather. Cameras are permitted.

Time: Allow 1 hour, 30 minutes minimum. **Hours:** Tours require a minimum of three people. Main Cave Experience is given on a first-come, first-served basis daily at 10:30, 11:30, 12:30, 2:30 and 5, late June-early Sept.; at 10:30, 12:30, 2:30 and 4:30, May 1-late June; at 10 and 2 in Apr. Schedule and age limits vary for other tours; phone ahead. Closed Jan. 1 and Christmas. **Cost:** Main Cave Experience $29 (ages 5+). Other tours $49-$199 (various age restrictions apply). Phone ahead to confirm rates. **Phone:** (250) 248-7829.

MILNER GARDENS & WOODLAND, 2179 W. Island Hwy., comprises 24 hectares (60 acres) of Douglas fir woodland and 4 hectares (10 acres) of garden surrounding a gabled heritage house. Visitors may view the dining, sitting and drawing rooms as well as the library. Historical photos, artifacts and keepsakes of visits by members of the Royal family also are displayed.

Time: Allow 1 hour minimum. **Hours:** Daily 10-4:30, Apr. 26-Sept. 3; Thurs.-Sun. 10-4:30, Mar. 29-Apr. 22 and Sept. 6-Oct. 7; Sun. 11-3, Feb.-Mar. Phone ahead to confirm schedule. **Cost:** Apr. 26-Sept. 3, $10.48; $6.19 (ages 13-18); free (ages 0-12 with adult). Admission Mar. 29-Apr. 22 and Sept. 6-Oct. 7, $7.86; $4.05 (ages 13-18); free (ages 0-12 with an adult). Admission Feb.-Mar. $5; $3.10 (ages 13-18); free (ages 0-12 with adult). **Phone:** (250) 752-6153. 🍴

QUALICUM BEACH INN   250/752-6914
THREE DIAMOND Hotel. **Address:** 2690 Island Hwy W V9K 1G8

WHERE TO EAT

BISTRO 694   250/752-0301
THREE DIAMOND International. Fine Dining. **Address:** 694 Memorial Ave V9K 1C7

CVIEW   250/752-6914
THREE DIAMOND American. Fine Dining. **Address:** 2690 Island Hwy W V9K 1G8

GARY'S BISTRO   250/752-5800
APPROVED American. Casual Dining. **Address:** 115 W Second Ave V9K 1S7

THE SHADY REST WATERFRONT PUB RESTAURANT
250/752-9111
APPROVED American. Casual Dining. **Address:** 3109 Island Hwy W V9K 2C5

QUESNEL (F-5) pop. 10,007, elev. 545m/1,788'

Discovery of gold in the surrounding area in the 1860s contributed to Quesnel's growth. The city is the center of a popular hunting and fishing region at the junction of the Fraser and Quesnel rivers. Lumber, pulp and plywood manufacturing, tourism, cattle ranching and mining are the city's primary sources of income.

East of the city on Hwy. 26 is a historic remnant of the gold rush days, Barkerville Historic Town (see place listing p. 173), a restored boomtown of that era. Just beyond Barkerville is Bowron Lake Provincial Park (see Recreation Areas Chart), which has a 116-kilometre (72-mi.) canoe circuit of interconnecting lakes. Alpine skiing is available nearby.

Quesnel Visitor Centre: 703 Carson Ave., Quesnel, BC, Canada V2J 2B6. **Phone:** (250) 992-8716 or (800) 992-4922.

QUALITY INN & SUITES   250/992-7247
APPROVED   Hotel. Address: 753 Front St V2J 2L2

TOWER INN & SUITES   250/992-2201
APPROVED   **Address:** 500 Reid St V2J 2M9 **Location:** Hwy 97, just e on Shepherd Ave; downtown. **Facility:** 63 units. 4 stories, interior corridors. **Parking:** winter plug-ins. **Activities:** exercise room. **Guest Services:** valet laundry.

Hotel

SAVE    BIZ HS

TRAVELODGE QUESNEL   250/992-7071
APPROVED   **Address:** 524 Front St V2J 2K6 **Location:** Hwy 97, 0.5 mi (0.8 km) n of Carson Ave. **Facility:** 34 units, some efficiencies and kitchens. 2 stories (no elevator), exterior corridors. **Parking:** winter plug-ins. **Pool:** heated indoor. **Activities:** sauna. **Guest Services:** coin laundry. **Featured Amenity:** continental breakfast.

Motel

SAVE ECO BIZ

/SOME UNITS HS

WHERE TO EAT

BLISS   250/992-7066
APPROVED   Indian. Quick Serve. **Address:** 462B Anderson Dr V2J 1G2

GRANVILLE'S COFFEE   250/992-3667
APPROVED   Breakfast Sandwiches. Quick Serve. **Address:** 383 Reid St V2J 2M5

MR MIKES STEAKHOUSECASUAL   250/992-7742
APPROVED   American. Casual Dining. **Address:** 450 Reid St V2J 2M6

SAVALAS STEAK HOUSE   778/414-9050
APPROVED   International. Casual Dining. **Address:** 240 Reid St V2J 2M2

RADIUM HOT SPRINGS (B-11) pop. 777, elev. 805m/2,641'

Renowned for its mineral hot springs (see Kootenay National Park p. 199 and Recreation Areas Chart), the Village of Radium Hot Springs also is a popular departure point for scenic hikes and white-water river excursions. More than 10 golf courses are in the vicinity.

BIGHORN MEADOWS RESORT   250/347-2323
THREE DIAMOND   Condominium. **Address:** 10 Bighorn Blvd V0A 1M0

CEDAR MOTEL   250/347-9463
APPROVED   Motel. **Address:** 7593 Main St W V0A 1M0

LIDO MOTEL   250/347-9533
APPROVED   Motel. **Address:** 4876 McKay St V0A 1M0

PRESTIGE RADIUM HOT SPRINGS RESORT
250/347-2300

THREE DIAMOND
Hotel

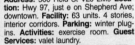
BW Premier COLLECTION by BEST WESTERN   **AAA Benefit:** Members save up to 15% and earn bonus points!

Address: 7493 Main St W V0A 1M0 **Location:** Jct Hwy 93 and 95. **Facility:** 87 units, some efficiencies and kitchens. 3 stories, interior corridors. **Parking:** winter plug-ins. **Dining:** Conrad's Kitchen + Grill and Don Agave Cantina, see separate listing. **Pool:** heated indoor. **Activities:** hot tub, bicycles, exercise room, spa. **Guest Services:** coin laundry. Affiliated with BW Premier Collection.

SAVE  BIZ

/SOME UNITS

WHERE TO EAT

BACK COUNTRY JACKS   250/347-0097
APPROVED   American. Casual Dining. **Address:** 7555 W Main St V0A 1M0

BIG HORN CAFE   403/861-2978
APPROVED   Breads/Pastries Coffee/Tea. Quick Serve. **Address:** 7527 Main St W V0A 1M0

CONRAD'S KITCHEN + GRILL AND DON AGAVE CANTINA
250/347-2340
APPROVED   American. Casual Dining. **Address:** 7493 Main St W V0A 1M0

THE OLD SALZBURG RESTAURANT   250/347-6553
APPROVED

Austrian
Casual Dining
$19-$35

AAA Inspector Notes: This Alpine-style restaurant boasts a warm, mountain-village ambience. With traditional Austrian and European influences, the menu lists hearty portions of schnitzel, spaetzle, pasta, chicken and steak. A few prime window seats have views of the surrounding valley and mountain ranges. It's closed for lunch in the off-season. **Features:** full bar, patio dining. **Reservations:** suggested, in summer. **Address:** 4943 Hwy 93 V0A 1M0 **Location:** Hwy 93 and 95, just w; center.

L D CALL

REVELSTOKE (A-10) pop. 7,139, elev. 440m/1,433'

Revelstoke is located on the Trans-Canada Highway between Rogers and Eagle passes—some of the world's most scenic mountain roads. Downhill skiing is available near the city.

Revelstoke Visitor Centre: 301 Victoria Rd. W., P.O. Box 490, Revelstoke, BC, Canada V0E 2S0. **Phone:** (250) 837-5345 or (800) 487-1493.

REVELSTOKE RAILWAY MUSEUM is at 719 Track St. W. off Victoria Rd. The building of the Canadian Pacific Railway is traced with artifacts, photographs and original equipment. One of the company's largest steam locomotives is displayed beside a restored 1929 solarium car inside the museum, while the yard features such rolling stock as a caboose, a snow plow and a flange car. A diesel cabin simulator allows visitors to experience the feeling of driving a train.

Time: Allow 30 minutes minimum. **Hours:** Daily 9-5, May 1 to mid-Oct.; Wed.-Sat. 11-4, rest of year. Closed Jan. 1, Christmas Eve, Christmas and some winter days. Phone ahead to confirm schedule. **Cost:** $9.52; $7.62 (ages 60+ and students with ID); $4.76 (ages 8-16); $1.90 (ages 4-7); $20.95 (family). **Phone:** (250) 837-6060 or (877) 837-6060.

BEST WESTERN PLUS REVELSTOKE   250/837-2043
THREE DIAMOND
Hotel

AAA Benefit: Members save up to 15% and earn bonus points!

Address: 1925 Laforme Blvd V0E 2S0 **Location:** Trans-Canada Hwy 1, just n. **Facility:** 87 units. 4 stories, interior corridors. **Parking:** winter plug-ins. **Amenities:** safes. **Pool:** heated outdoor. **Activities:** hot tub, bicycles, exercise room, massage. **Guest Services:** complimentary laundry, area transportation. **Featured Amenity:** breakfast buffet.

COAST HILLCREST HOTEL   250/837-3322
THREE DIAMOND
Hotel

Address: 2100 Oak Dr V0E 2S0 **Location:** 2.7 mi (4.3 km) e on Trans-Canada Hwy 1, 0.6 mi (1 km) sw. **Facility:** 75 units. 3 stories, interior corridors. **Amenities:** safes. **Dining:** Begbie Room, see separate listing. **Activities:** sauna, hot tub, steamroom, trails, exercise room, spa. **Guest Services:** valet laundry, area transportation.

RAMADA REVELSTOKE   250/837-4741
THREE DIAMOND Hotel. **Address:** 1750 Trans-Canada Hwy V0E 2S0

SUPER 8 REVELSTOKE   250/837-0888
APPROVED Hotel. **Address:** 1700 Victoria Rd W V0E 2S0

SWISS CHALET MOTEL   250/837-4650
APPROVED Motel. **Address:** 1101 W Victoria Rd V0E 2S0

WHERE TO EAT

BEGBIE ROOM   250/837-3322
THREE DIAMOND American. Casual Dining. **Address:** 2100 Oak Dr V0E 2S0

NOMAD FOOD CO.   250/837-4211
APPROVED Chicken Sandwiches. Quick Serve. **Address:** 1601 Victoria Rd W V0E 3K0

WOOLSEY CREEK BISTRO   250/837-5500
THREE DIAMOND New Canadian. Casual Dining. **Address:** 604 2nd St W V0E 2S0

RICHMOND (H-11) pop. 190,473, elev. 5m/16'
• Hotels p. 234 • Restaurants p. 236
• Hotels & Restaurants map & index p. 276
• Part of Vancouver area — see map p. 249

On an island at the mouth of the Fraser River, Richmond first was settled in 1879. The town grew and prospered with its farming, fishing and waterborne trade industries. Today, Richmond's major industries include aviation, berry farming, high technology and manufacturing.

Golden Village, in central Richmond, affords visitors the opportunity to experience the Asian culture through shopping, dining and festivals.

The Richmond Nature Park, 44 hectares (109 acres) at 11851 Westminster Hwy., has a bird pond, beehive displays, mounted birds, a quaking bog and plants identified by markers. A naturalist conducts hour-long tours of the park on Sunday.

Steveston, tucked away in Richmond's southwest corner, is a bit of a contradiction. It has a historic past, but it's also a residential neighborhood. Commercial fishing was once this area's lifeblood, but today you're just as likely to sample fish that's battered and sharing a plate with a pile of fries at a local restaurant as you are seeing one freshly caught. And while weather-beaten buildings hint at a hardscrabble past, there's also a Starbucks.

Sitting at the confluence of two major bodies of water—the Strait of Georgia and the Fraser River—Steveston's first flush of success was as a salmon canning center. The Fraser's south arm was a fertile fishing ground, and a settlement grew up around this favored coastal location in the 1880s. Salmon turned Steveston into a classic turn-of-the-20th-century boom town: It became one of the busiest fishing ports in the world, with windjammers loading up canned salmon bound for far-flung markets.

The town was boisterous with a capital "B." Saloons and gambling dens thrived, and on Saturday nights crowds of sailors, indigenous peoples and European, Chinese and Japanese immigrants—most of them fishermen and cannery workers—thronged the boardwalks. In the years leading up to World War I eager boosters dubbed Steveston "Salmonopolis," but the boom was not to last. The internment during World War II of Japanese-Canadian

(See map & index p. 276.)

citizens, who made up a large part of the town's population, struck a serious blow. The canning industry slowly declined, finally coming to an end by the early 1990s. You can learn more about this aspect of town history at the Gulf of Georgia Cannery National Historic Site *(see attraction listing).*

Steveston, still an active fishing port that to a large degree has retained its salty character, makes a good day trip. From downtown Vancouver it's about a 30-minute drive. Take Granville Street south to Hwy. 99 (via 70th Avenue W.), then take Hwy. 99 south to exit 32 (Steveston Highway) and turn right (west). Summer, when the weather is usually sunny and a couple of annual festivals are on tap, is the time to go; during the chilly, rainy winter months many restaurants and attractions reduce their hours.

So what do you do? For starters, just explore where your feet take you. Follow the planked wooden boardwalk along the shore of Cannery Channel; interpretive panels provide background about Steveston's fishing and canning past. Have your picture taken sitting on a bench in the garden outside the Prickly Pear Garden Centre (on No. 1 Road, just off Bayview Street). In addition to lovely hanging flower baskets, the large, emerald-green leaves of a banana tree will have you scratching your head and reminding yourself that yes, you are in Canada.

Tramp around Garry Point Park (at the end of Moncton Street). Fronting the Strait of Georgia, it's basically undeveloped and has a wild and windswept look. Sunsets over the water can be showstoppers here, and the flat, open spaces bring out kite flyers. Stop at the Fisherman's Memorial, which takes the shape of a giant net-mending needle and is inscribed with a poem, "Spawning Cycle":

These spring days grow longer

Until the dark comes closing

What tides disclose they again conceal

We're out to fish until again

It's time to be ashore

Because the geese go by

I'll be here with you

'Till it's time to be alone: the way out,

The way back, and all ways this one.

Stroll the boardwalk along bustling Fisherman's Wharf, where seiners, trawlers and other vessels cruise in and out of the harbor. Depending on the season, some of the boats docked along the boardwalk sell fresh catches of salmon, cod, octopus and prawns.

The Steveston Museum, 3811 Moncton St., resembles a one-room country schoolhouse with its red-and-yellow clapboard exterior and steep gabled roof. This former Northern Bank building has a general store layout with displays of late 19th-century furniture and office equipment. It's also a working post office. Phone (604) 271-6868.

For lunch, it really has to be fish and chips. And there's a choice: Dave's Fish & Chips (3460 Moncton St.) or Pajo's (two locations—on the wharf at the corner of Bayview Street and 3rd Avenue, and a takeout stand in the large administrative building at Garry Point Park). Although the menus at both include such non-fishy items as burgers, do the right thing and order fish and chips (aficionados will go for the halibut over cod or salmon). Mushy peas are a veddy British accompaniment.

The big event of the year is the Steveston Salmon Festival, held on July 1 in conjunction with Canada Day. Floats, marching bands, vintage vehicles and local community groups are part of a big parade that begins at 10 a.m. There's a craft fair, an art show, a Japanese cultural show, carnival rides and a midway, martial arts demonstrations and a youth festival. The main attraction, though, is a salmon barbecue; hundreds of fillets are grilled to succulent perfection over open fire pits.

Summer in Steveston can get crowded, especially on nice sunny weekends. But there are several free parking lots in town, plenty of parking at Garry Point Park, and street parking if you're lucky enough to snag a space.

Tourism Richmond: 3811 Moncton St., Richmond, BC, Canada V7E 3A7. **Phone:** (604) 271-8280 or (877) 247-0777.

 **GULF OF GEORGIA CANNERY NATIONAL HISTORIC SITE** is at 12138 Fourth Ave. in Steveston Village. The 1894 salmon cannery on the waterfront of a historic fishing village has been restored to serve as an interpretive center for Canada's West Coast fishing industry. During its heyday, this cannery earned the title of the Monster Cannery, a reference to its size in comparison to about 15 other canneries on Steveston's Cannery Row.

Interactive exhibits of the herring reduction plant and replicated 1930s-50s canning line, a children's activity area, a harbor viewing deck and a 15-minute film about the West Coast fishing industry are offered year-round. The full cannery experience is offered May through October and includes guided tours, salmon tastings and canning machine demonstrations.

Hours: Daily 10-5. Closed Jan. 1, Nov. 11 and Dec. 24-26. **Cost:** $11.70; $10.05 (ages 65+); free (ages 0-17). **Phone:** (604) 664-9009.

STEVESTON SEABREEZE ADVENTURES is at 12551 #1 Rd., Bldg. 43. A narrated whale-watching tour departs from historic Steveston village and transits the Fraser River Delta, Strait of Georgia and Gulf Islands. Hydrophones are used to listen to the whales vocalizing. The scenic trip affords passengers an opportunity to view other marine animals and wildlife.

(See map & index p. 276.)

Time: Allow 3 hours minimum. **Hours:** Departures daily at 9 and 2, mid-June to early Sept.; at noon, early Apr. to mid-June; at 11, early Sept.-late Oct. **Cost:** $130 (includes snack); $105 (ages 65+ and students with ID); $80 (ages 3-12). Reservations are recommended. **Phone:** (604) 272-7200 or (888) 272-7203.

VANCOUVER WHALE WATCH is at 210-12240 Second Ave. Two 40-passenger, semi-covered vessels transports visitors through the Gulf Islands and the San Juan Islands. Led by a wildlife guide, the narrated tour focuses on orcas and humpback whales. Hydrophones are used to listen to the whales communicating. Other wildlife such as porpoises, sea lions, seals and eagles also may be seen. Sightings are guaranteed.

Time: Allow 3 hours minimum. **Hours:** Tours depart daily at 9 and 2, mid-June through Aug. 31; at 11, Apr. 1 to mid-June and Sept.-Oct. **Cost:** $145 (includes water and snack); $125 (students with ID and ages 60+); $85 (ages 4-12). Reservations are recommended. **Phone:** (604) 274-9565 or (844) 474-9565.

ABERCORN INN VANCOUVER AIRPORT　604/270-7576 **34**
APPROVED　Hotel. **Address:** 9260 Bridgeport Rd V6X 1S1

ACCENT INNS　604/273-3311 **37**
APPROVED　Hotel. **Address:** 10551 St Edwards Dr V6X 3L8

THE FAIRMONT VANCOUVER AIRPORT
604/207-5200 **27**

FOUR DIAMOND
Hotel

Address: 3111 Grant McConachie Way V7B 0A6 **Location:** In Vancouver International Airport. YVR Airport, 38. **Facility:** This beautiful airport hotel has lovely rooms featuring sound-insulated windows and high-tech room comfort controls. The jetted lap pool adds extra weight to the high-tech fitness center. 386 units. 14 stories, interior corridors. **Parking:** on-site (fee) and valet. **Amenities:** safes. **Dining:** Globe@YVR Restaurant, see separate listing, entertainment. **Pool:** heated indoor. **Activities:** sauna, hot tub, bicycles, trails, health club, in-room exercise equipment, spa. **Guest Services:** valet laundry, boarding pass kiosk, rental car service, luggage security pick-up.

SAVE ECO ◯ ◯ ◯ CALL ◯ ◯ ◯ BIZ SHS ◯ ◯ ◯ ◯ / SOME UNITS ◯

FOUR POINTS BY SHERATON VANCOUVER AIRPORT
604/214-0888 **39**

THREE DIAMOND
Hotel

FOUR POINTS BY SHERATON

AAA Benefit: Members save 5% or more!

Address: 8368 Alexandra Rd V6X 4A6 **Location:** No. 3 Rd, just e on Alderbridge Way, just n on Hazelbridge Way. Lansdowne, 40. **Facility:** 140 units. 6 stories, interior corridors. **Parking:** on-site (fee). **Amenities:** safes. **Activities:** exercise room. **Guest Services:** valet laundry.

SAVE ECO ◯ ◯ ◯ CALL ◯
◯ BIZ HS ◯ ◯ ◯ ◯ ◯ ◯

HAMPTON INN BY HILTON VANCOUVER AIRPORT
604/232-5505 **31**

APPROVED
Hotel
AAA Benefit: Members save up to 15%!

Address: 8811 Bridgeport Rd V6X 1R9 **Location:** Hwy 99 exit 39 (Bridgeport Rd/Airport) northbound; exit 39A (Richmond/Airport) southbound, just w. Bridgeport, 35. **Facility:** 109 units. 5 stories, interior corridors. **Activities:** exercise room. **Guest Services:** valet laundry. **Featured Amenity:** breakfast buffet.

SAVE ECO ◯ ◯ ◯ ◯ ◯

Hampton by HILTON

2km from Vancouver airport, near Canada line Skytrain and just 15 minutes from downtown Vancouver.

HILTON VANCOUVER AIRPORT　604/273-6336 **40**

THREE DIAMOND
Hotel
Hilton HOTELS & RESORTS
AAA Benefit: Members save up to 15%!

Address: 5911 Minoru Blvd V6X 4C7 **Location:** Corner of Minoru Blvd and Westminster Hwy. Lansdowne, 40. **Facility:** 237 units, some two bedrooms. 15 stories, interior corridors. **Parking:** on-site (fee). **Amenities:** safes. **Dining:** CAVU Kitchen Bar, see separate listing. **Pool:** heated outdoor. **Activities:** hot tub, exercise room. **Guest Services:** valet laundry, rental car service.

SAVE ECO ◯ ◯ ◯ ◯ CALL ◯ ◯ ◯ BIZ
◯ ◯ ◯ ◯ ◯ / SOME UNITS ◯ ◯ ◯

HOLIDAY INN EXPRESS & SUITES RIVERPORT
604/241-1830 **45**
THREE DIAMOND　Hotel. **Address:** 10688 No. 6 Rd V6W 1E7

HOLIDAY INN EXPRESS VANCOUVER-AIRPORT
604/273-8080 **33**
THREE DIAMOND　Hotel. **Address:** 9351 Bridgeport Rd V6X 1S3

HOLIDAY INN VANCOUVER AIRPORT-RICHMOND
604/821-1818 **38**
THREE DIAMOND　Hotel. **Address:** 10720 Cambie Rd V6X 1K8

HOTEL AT RIVER ROCK　604/247-8900 **28**
THREE DIAMOND　Hotel. **Address:** 8811 River Rd V6X 3P8

🔗 **For complete hotel, dining and attraction listings:**

AAA.com/travelguides

(See map & index p. 276.)

PACIFIC GATEWAY HOTEL AT VANCOUVER AIRPORT
604/278-1241 **30**

Hotel

Address: 3500 Cessna Dr V7B 1C7 **Location:** Waterfront. Just s of island airport interchange; at Russ Baker Way. 🚇 Templeton, 36. **Facility:** 388 units. 10 stories, interior corridors. **Parking:** on-site (fee) and valet. **Amenities:** Some: safes. **Pool:** heated outdoor. **Activities:** trails, exercise room. **Guest Services:** valet laundry, boarding pass kiosk.

[SAVE] [ECO] 🛎 ➤ ｜｜ Ⓨ
CALL Ⓗ ➤ 🛗 [BIZ] 📶 ✕
📽 🔲 💻 /SOME UNITS 🍴 🚌

QUALITY HOTEL AIRPORT (SOUTH) 604/244-3051 **42**

APPROVED

Hotel

Address: 7228 Westminster Hwy V6X 1A1 **Location:** Between Gilbert Rd and Alderbridge Way. 🚇 Richmond-Brighouse, 41. **Facility:** 70 units. 4 stories, interior corridors. **Guest Services:** valet laundry. **Featured Amenity: full hot breakfast.**

[SAVE] ➤ ｜｜⁺ CALL Ⓗ [HS] 📶
✕ 🔲 /SOME UNITS 🍴 🚌

RADISSON HOTEL VANCOUVER AIRPORT
604/276-8181 **36**

THREE DIAMOND

Hotel

Address: 8181 Cambie Rd V6X 3X9 **Location:** Corner of No. 3 and Cambie rds. 🚇 Aberdeen, 39. **Facility:** 200 units. 12 stories, interior corridors. **Amenities:** safes. **Pool:** heated indoor. **Activities:** hot tub, exercise room. **Guest Services:** valet laundry, boarding pass kiosk. **Featured Amenity: full hot breakfast.**

[SAVE] [ECO] ➤ ｜｜ 🛗 Ⓨ
CALL Ⓗ ➤ 🛗 [BIZ] 📶 ✕
🔲 💻 /SOME UNITS 🍴 🚌

RAMADA LIMITED VANCOUVER AIRPORT
604/207-9000 **41**

💎 **APPROVED** Hotel. **Address:** 7188 Westminster Hwy V6X 1A1

RIVER ROCK CASINO RESORT 604/247-8900 **29**

FOUR DIAMOND

Resort Hotel

Address: 8811 River Rd V6X 3P8 **Location:** Waterfront. Hwy 99 exit 39 (Bridgeport Rd/Airport) northbound; exit 39A (Richmond/Airport) southbound, just w on Bridgeport Rd, then just n on Great Canadian Way. 🚇 Bridgeport, 35. **Facility:** The beautiful one-bedroom suites with custom made mattresses and luxury bedding include high tech features and amenities. 203 units, some two bedrooms. 9-11 stories, interior corridors. **Parking:** on-site and valet. **Terms:** check-in 4 pm. **Amenities:** safes. **Dining:** 2 restaurants. **Pool:** heated indoor. **Activities:** hot tub, marina, trails, exercise room, spa. **Guest Services:** valet laundry. (See ad this page.)

[SAVE] 🎰 ｜｜ 🛗 Ⓨ CALL Ⓗ ➤ 🛗 [BIZ] [HS]
📶 ✕ 📽 🔲 💻 /SOME UNITS 🍴 🚌

SANDMAN HOTEL VANCOUVER AIRPORT
604/303-8888 **35**

💎 **THREE DIAMOND** Hotel. **Address:** 3233 St Edwards Dr V6X 3K4

SHERATON VANCOUVER AIRPORT HOTEL
604/273-7878 **43**

THREE DIAMOND

Hotel

SHERATON

AAA Benefit: Members save 5% or more!

Address: 7551 Westminster Hwy V6X 1A3 **Location:** Corner of Minoru Blvd and Westminster Hwy. 🚇 Richmond-Brighouse, 41. **Facility:** 390 units. 2-8 stories, interior corridors. **Parking:** on-site (fee) and valet. **Amenities:** safes. **Dining:** Harold's Bistro & Bar, see separate listing. **Pool:** heated outdoor. **Activities:** hot tub, exercise room. **Guest Services:** valet laundry, rental car service.

[SAVE] [ECO] ➤ ｜｜ 🛗 Ⓨ CALL Ⓗ ➤ 🛗 [BIZ]
📶 ✕ 📽 🔲 💻 /SOME UNITS 🍴 📺 🚌

▼ See AAA listing this page ▼

AAA INSPECTOR'S BEST OF HOUSEKEEPING 2019

RiverRock CASINO RESORT

8811 River Road
Richmond, BC V6X 3P8
1.866.748.3718

🔗 **Rest assured: AAA.com/travelguides/hotels**

(See map & index p. 276.)

VANCOUVER AIRPORT MARRIOTT   604/276-2112   44

THREE DIAMOND
Hotel

AAA Benefit: Members save 5% or more!

Address: 7571 Westminster Hwy V6X 1A3 **Location:** Corner of Minoru Blvd and Westminster Hwy. Richmond-Brighouse, 41. **Facility:** 236 units, some two bedrooms. 18 stories, interior corridors. **Parking:** on-site (fee). **Terms:** check-in 4 pm. **Dining:** The American Grille, see separate listing. **Pool:** heated outdoor. **Activities:** hot tub, exercise room. **Guest Services:** valet and coin laundry, boarding pass kiosk.

(SAVE) ✈ 🍴 📶 Ⴤ CALL ⚕ 🛄 🚼 BIZ 🛜
✕ 🔋 🖥 / SOME UNITS 🐾 🖼 🚊

THE WESTIN WALL CENTRE VANCOUVER AIRPORT
604/303-6565   32

THREE DIAMOND
Hotel

WESTIN HOTELS & RESORTS

AAA Benefit: Members save 5% or more!

Address: 3099 Corvette Way V6X 4K3 **Location:** Hwy 99 exit 39 (Bridgeport Rd/Airport) northbound; exit 39A (Richmond/Airport) southbound, just w to No. 3 Rd. Bridgeport, 35. **Facility:** 188 units. 15 stories, interior corridors. **Parking:** on-site (fee) and valet. **Amenities:** safes. **Pool:** heated indoor. **Activities:** hot tub, exercise room. **Guest Services:** valet laundry.

(SAVE) ✈ 🍴 📶 Ⴤ CALL ⚕ 🛄 🚼 BIZ HS
🛜 ✕ 📺 🔋 🖥 / SOME UNITS 🐾 🚊

WHERE TO EAT

THE AMERICAN GRILLE   604/232-2804   64
THREE DIAMOND New American. Casual Dining. **Address:** 7571 Westminster Hwy V6X 1A3

BLUE CANOE WATERFRONT RESTAURANT
604/275-7811   69
THREE DIAMOND Seafood. Casual Dining. **Address:** 3866 Bayview St, Suite 140 V7E 4R7

THE BOATHOUSE RESTAURANT   604/273-7014   54
APPROVED Seafood Steak. Casual Dining. **Address:** 8331 River Rd V6X 1Y1

CACTUS CLUB CAFE   604/244-9969   66
THREE DIAMOND New American. Casual Dining. **Address:** 1666 - 6551 No 3 Rd V6Y 2B6

CAVU KITCHEN BAR   604/232-5001   62
THREE DIAMOND New International. Casual Dining. **Address:** 5911 Minoru Blvd V6X 4C7

EARLS KITCHEN + BAR   604/303-9702
APPROVED American. Casual Dining. **Address:** 5300 No 3 Rd, #304 V6X 2X9

FELICOS RESTAURANT   604/276-8282   60
APPROVED Greek. Casual Dining. **Address:** 8140 Leslie Rd V6X 4A8

FLYING BEAVER BAR & GRILL   604/273-0278   58
APPROVED American. Gastropub. **Address:** 4760 Inglis Dr V7B 1W4

FOGG N' SUDS   604/273-0776   61
APPROVED American. Casual Dining. **Address:** 10720 Cambie Rd V6X 1K8

GLOBE@YVR RESTAURANT   604/207-5200   53
THREE DIAMOND Pacific Northwest. Fine Dining. **Address:** 3111 Grant McConachie Way V7B 1X9

HAROLD'S BISTRO & BAR   604/233-3968   63
APPROVED American. Casual Dining. **Address:** 7551 Westminster Hwy V6X 1A3

ITALIAN TOMATO RESTAURANT   604/247-0040   55
APPROVED Italian. Casual Dining. **Address:** 8380 Bridgeport Rd V6X 3C7

MAN RI SUNG KOREAN RESTAURANT   604/821-9922   59
APPROVED Korean. Casual Dining. **Address:** 4151 Hazelridge Way, #3600 V6X 4J7

MOXIE'S CLASSIC GRILL   604/303-1111   56
APPROVED American. Casual Dining. **Address:** 3233 St Edwards Dr V6X 3K4

PAJO'S   250/204-0767   67
APPROVED Fish & Chips. Quick Serve. **Address:** 12771 7th Ave V7E 6P4

RED STAR SEAFOOD RESTAURANT   604/270-3003   57
APPROVED Chinese. Casual Dining. **Address:** 8181 Cambie Rd, #2200 V6X 3X9

RICKY'S ALL DAY GRILL   604/233-7705
APPROVED American. Casual Dining. **Address:** 9100 Blundell Rd, #490 V6V 1K3

SHANGHAI RIVER RESTAURANT   604/233-8885   65
APPROVED Chinese. Casual Dining. **Address:** 7831 Westminster Hwy V6X 4J4

STEVESTON SEAFOOD HOUSE   604/271-5252   68
THREE DIAMOND Seafood. Casual Dining. **Address:** 3951 Moncton St V7E 3A7

SALMON ARM (B-9) pop. 17,464, elev. 415m/1,364'

R.J. HANEY HERITAGE VILLAGE & MUSEUM is nearly 3 kilometres (2 mi.) e. on Hwy. 1, then just s. on Hwy. 97B. The village grew around the Haney House, built in 1910. Among the buildings in the community, all built in the early 20th century, are Salmon Arm's first gas station, a blacksmith shop, a Methodist church, a fire station and a schoolhouse.

In addition, the Beamish Building contains what is said to be Western Canada's largest collection of records and cylinders. A small museum, which changes displays every 2 years, focuses on local Shuswap history, and a 2-kilometre (1.2 mi.) nature walk, a tea house and a dinner theater also are on the property. Guided tours of the Haney House are available.

Time: Allow 1 hour minimum. **Hours:** Village and office open daily 10-5, July-Aug.; Wed.-Sun. 10-4, mid-May through June 30 and Sept. 1-20; Mon.-Fri. 10-4, rest of year. Dinner theater Wed., Fri. and Sun., July-Aug. Archives and museum Tues.-Thurs.

10-4, year-round. Phone ahead to confirm schedule. **Cost:** Donations. Reservations are required for the dinner theatre. **Phone:** (250) 832-5243.

BEST WESTERN SALMON ARM INN   250/832-9793

 APPROVED
Motel

Best Western. **AAA Benefit:** Members save up to 15% and earn bonus points!

Address: 61 10th St SW V1E 1E4 **Location:** 0.7 mi (1.1 km) w on Trans-Canada Hwy 1. **Facility:** 74 units. 2 stories (no elevator), exterior corridors. **Pool:** heated indoor. **Activities:** hot tub. **Featured Amenity:** breakfast buffet.

COMFORT INN & SUITES   250/832-7711

THREE DIAMOND Hotel. **Address:** 1090 22nd St NE V1E 2V5

PRESTIGE HARBOURFRONT RESORT SALMON ARM, BW PREMIER COLLECTION   250/833-5800

THREE DIAMOND Hotel. **Address:** 251 Harbourfront Dr NE V1E 2W7

AAA Benefit: Members save up to 15% and earn bonus points!

WHERE TO EAT

BARLEY STATION BREWPUB   250/832-0999

APPROVED International. Brewpub. **Address:** 20 Shuswap St N V1E 4H7

SHUSWAP PIE COMPANY   250/832-7992

APPROVED Breads/Pastries. Quick Serve. **Address:** 331 Alexander St NE V1E 4P1

SALT SPRING ISLAND (H-10) pop. 10,322

Originally called Chuan Island, then Admiral Island, Salt Spring Island is the largest of the Gulf Islands *(see place listing p. 189)* and a popular spot for yachting, cycling, fishing and golfing. Bicycle and kayak rentals are available.

Although it is one of the most developed of the islands, it retains a rural feel. Mount Maxwell Park has a scenic drive leading to 610-metre (2,001-ft.) Baynes Peak. Ruckle Provincial Park *(see Recreation Areas Chart)* offers 7 kilometres (4.3 mi.) of shoreline and has walking trails; bicycling, fishing, kayaking and picnicking are permitted.

The island also features popular Saturday farmers markets and arts and crafts, and is home to many fine artists such as Robert Bateman and Carol Evans.

Ganges is the island's largest village and its commercial hub. Much of the seaside community's charm is the result of its status as an artist's colony. Visitors are welcome at many artists' studios, and locally made arts and crafts such as ceramics, jewelry, furniture, stained glass and woodcraft, are sold at many village shops.

A local Ganges landmark is a retired buoy that has been painted with a marine-themed mural. Marine life such as salmon, orcas, cod and octopus seals—all creatures that can be found near Salt Spring Island—join a Coast Guard cutter and kayaks as the mural's focal points.

Ferries operate daily from the island's three ferry terminals—between Swartz Bay and Fulford Harbour, between Crofton and Vesuvius Bay and between Long Harbour (the largest of the terminals) and Tsawwassen. For schedules and information phone BC Ferries, (250) 386-3431 from the Victoria area or outside British Columbia, or (888) 223-3779 from elsewhere in the province.

Salt Spring Island Visitor InfoCentre: 121 Lower Ganges Rd., Salt Spring Island, BC, Canada V8K 2T1. **Phone:** (250) 537-5252 or (866) 216-2936.

Self-guiding tours: Maps describing self-guiding tours to the studios of more than 30 resident artists are available at the island's visitor infocenter as well as at lodgings, the marina and on BC Ferries.

AUNTIE PESTO'S CAFE & DELICATESSEN   250/537-4181

APPROVED Pacific Northwest Sandwiches. Casual Dining. **Address:** 115 Fulford-Ganges Rd V8K 1E2

BARB'S BAKERY & BISTRO   250/537-4491

APPROVED Breads/Pastries. Quick Serve. **Address:** 1-121 McPhillips Ave V8K 2T6

HASTINGS HOUSE DINING ROOM   250/537-2362

FOUR DIAMOND
Pacific Northwest Fine Dining
$110-$180

AAA Inspector Notes: This restaurant offers a truly wonderful dining experience. Dinner guests receive their own personalized menu that features a three-course chef's tasting menu with or without wine pairings. Ingredients are the freshest possible as many are produced on site. Guests are welcome to come earlier for drinks in the lounge. **Features:** full bar. **Reservations:** required. **Address:** 160 Upper Ganges Rd V8K 2S2 **Location:** 0.6 mi (1 km) n on Lower Ganges Rd, just e; towards Long Harbour Ferry Terminal; in Hastings House Country House Hotel. D

RESTAURANT HOUSE PICCOLO   250/537-1844

THREE DIAMOND Scandinavian. Fine Dining. **Address:** 108 Hereford Ave V8K 2V9

SALT SPRING INN RESTAURANT   250/537-5339

APPROVED American. Casual Dining. **Address:** 132 Lower Ganges Rd V8K 2S9

SATURNA ISLAND (H-10) pop. 335

Saturna Island—remote, rugged and sparsely populated—is probably the least visited of the Gulf Islands as well as the southernmost isle. Forty-three percent of the island is protected by Gulf Islands National Park Reserve. Explore via hiking and boating, or hop on a bicycle, but proceed with caution as the narrow winding roads offer no shoulders. Saturna's bays, beaches and tidal pools offer glimpses of many varieties of marine life.

Walk-in or cycle-in camping is offered at Narvaez Bay as part of Gulf Islands National Park Reserve *(see place listing p. 189)*. The seven-site camping area is nestled by a tranquil bay where you can often spot and hear harbour seals. However, the best wildlife viewing is offered at East Point, also in the park reserve; it is the easternmost point of the islands surrounded by active currents where Orcas, sea lions and porpoises can often be spotted. East Point is also one of the best places in the area for land-based whale watching.

SICAMOUS (B-9) pop. 2,441, elev. 352m/1,155'

Flanked by Mara and Shuswap lakes, Sicamous has abundant recreational opportunities, including swimming, fishing, boating and other water sports. Full- and half-day cruises on Shuswap Lake *(see Recreation Areas Chart)* and 2- and 3-hour evening excursions on Mara Lake depart from the public wharf at the foot of Finlayson Street. Houseboats, which can be rented, are a popular way of touring the arms of Shuswap Lake.

At nearby Adams River almost 10 million scarlet sockeye salmon bury their eggs each October; it is one of the largest spawning grounds in the country. Several spawning grounds can be seen at Roderick Haig-Brown Provincial Park, 85 kilometres (53 mi.) northwest off Hwy. 1.

Sicamous Visitor Centre: 11-1133 Eagle Pass Way, Sicamous, BC, Canada V0E 2V0. **Phone:** (250) 836-3313 or (866) 205-4055.

BEST WESTERN SICAMOUS INN   250/836-4117

Motel

 Best Western.

AAA Benefit: Members save up to 15% and earn bonus points!

Address: 806 Trans-Canada Hwy 1 V0E 2V0 **Location:** Jct Trans-Canada Hwy 1 and 97; at east end of town. **Facility:** 65 units. 2 stories (no elevator), interior/exterior corridors. **Pool:** heated indoor. **Activities:** hot tub, lawn sports, picnic facilities. **Guest Services:** coin laundry. **Featured Amenity: full hot breakfast.**

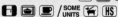

 WHERE TO EAT

BLONDIES CAFE   250/515-2000
 APPROVED Breakfast Sandwiches. Quick Serve. **Address:** 302 Finlayson St V0E 2V0

SIDNEY (H-10) pop. 11,178, elev. 9m/30'
• Part of Victoria area — see map p. 299

People of the Salish First Nation were the earliest known inhabitants of the area now called Sidney. Incorporated into a town in 1967, Sidney is known for its fishing and waterfront activity.

Booktown, the town's nickname, is the result of a dozen book shops concentrated in a five-block area around Beacon Avenue. Picnicking, beachcombing

and camping are popular at Sidney Spit Marine Provincial Park.

Sidney Visitor Centre: 2281 Beacon Ave., Sidney, BC, Canada V8L 1W9. **Phone:** (250) 665-7362.

SHAW CENTRE FOR THE SALISH SEA is at 9811 Seaport Pl. The main concentration of this waterfront aquarium and marine education center is the inland Salish Sea ecosystem. After experiencing the sensation of descending into the ocean in a simulated elevator, visitors reach the Gallery of the Drifters to view plankton, algae and jellyfish.

The Ocean's Heartbeat, a classroomlike environment, has microscopes and live Internet links to undersea sites. The Gallery of the Salish Sea is where you'll find large aquarium habitats that are home to local marine life as well as works by native artists that depict the peoples' relationship with the ocean; an octopus den can be seen overhead.

Touch pools provide an opportunity to get upclose to some of the sea creatures such as sea urchins and sea stars, and docents, called "oceaneers," are available to answer questions. The diverse population of the center's 17 aquariums include wolf eels, rockfish, sea cucumbers and anemones.

Time: Allow 1 hour minimum. **Hours:** Daily 10-5, mid-May to early Sept.; 10-4:30, rest of year. Last admission 30 minutes before closing. Closed Jan. 1, Christmas Eve, Christmas and day after Christmas. Phone ahead to confirm schedule. **Cost:** $17.50; $14 (ages 65+); $12 (ages 13-18); $8 (ages 4-12). **Phone:** (250) 665-7511.

BEACON INN AT SIDNEY   250/655-3288
THREE DIAMOND Bed & Breakfast. **Address:** 9724 3rd St V8L 3A2

BEST WESTERN PLUS EMERALD ISLE   250/656-4441

Hotel

Best Western PLUS.

AAA Benefit: Members save up to 15% and earn bonus points!

Address: 2306 Beacon Ave V8L 1X2 **Location:** Hwy 17 exit 28 (Sidney), just e. **Facility:** 65 units, some kitchens. 2 stories, interior corridors. **Terms:** check-in 4 pm. **Dining:** Smitty's, see separate listing. **Activities:** exercise room. **Guest Services:** valet and coin laundry.

THE CEDARWOOD INN & SUITES   250/656-5551
APPROVED Hotel. **Address:** 9522 Lochside Dr V8L 1N8

THE SIDNEY PIER HOTEL & SPA   250/655-9445
THREE DIAMOND Contemporary Hotel. **Address:** 9805 Seaport Pl V8L 4X3

WHERE TO EAT

DEEP COVE CHALET   250/656-3541
▼▼ THREE DIAMOND   French. Fine Dining. **Address:** 11190 Chalet Rd V8L 4R4

HARO'S RESTAURANT & BAR   250/655-9700
▼▼ THREE DIAMOND   Pacific Northwest. Casual Dining. **Address:** 9805 Seaport Pl V8L 4X3

MARIA'S SOUVLAKI GREEK RESTAURANT   250/656-9944
▼▼ APPROVED   Greek. Quick Serve. **Address:** 9812 Second St V8L 3C6

THE PIER BISTRO   250/655-4995
▼▼ APPROVED   Pacific Northwest. Casual Dining. **Address:** 2550 Beacon Ave V8L 1Y2

SABHAI THAI RESTAURANT   250/655-4085
▼▼ APPROVED   Thai. Casual Dining. **Address:** 2493 Beacon Ave V8L 1X9

SEA GLASS WATERFRONT GRILL   778/351-3663
▼▼ THREE DIAMOND   Northern Pacific Northwest. Casual Dining. **Address:** 2320 Harbour Rd V8L 2P6

SMITTY'S   250/656-2423
▼▼ APPROVED
American Casual Dining   **$8-$18**   **AAA Inspector Notes:** The family-oriented restaurant satisfies patrons with its ever-popular all-day breakfast items, as well as tasty and wholesome soups and salads at lunchtime. A relaxed mood characterizes the dining space. **Features:** full bar. **Address:** 2306 Beacon Ave V8L 1X2 **Location:** Hwy 17 exit 28 (Sidney), just e; in Best Western Plus Emerald Isle. ⬜ B ⬜ L ⬜ CALL ♿

THIRD STREET CAFE   250/656-3035
▼▼ APPROVED   American. Casual Dining. **Address:** 2466 Beacon Ave V8L 1X8

SKIDEGATE (E-1)

◆ GEM   **HAIDA HERITAGE CENTRE AT KAAY LLNAGAAY** is just n. of the BC Ferries terminal on Second Beach Rd. The center, on the site of the old Haida seaside village of Kaay Llnagaay, celebrates the relationship of the Haida people with the land and examines, through audiovisuals and interactive displays, Haida art, history and culture.

Traditional totem poles representing the 14 clans front the facility; three ancient poles are inside. A canoe house, a performing house and a carving shed also may be seen. The Haida Gwaii Museum includes exhibits about plants and wildlife as well as the Haida's belief in the natural and supernatural. A collection of argillite carvings and contemporary art is showcased.

Time: Allow 1 hour minimum. **Hours:** Daily 9-5 (also Thurs. 5-8 p.m.), July-Aug.; Mon.-Sat. 9-5, May-June and in Sept.; Tues.-Sat. 9:30-5, rest of year. Phone ahead to confirm schedule. **Cost:** $16 (includes the heritage center and Haida Gwaii Museum); $12 (ages 65+ and students with ID); $5 (ages 6-12). **Phone:** (250) 559-7885. GT 🍴

JAGS BEANSTALK ROOMS   250/559-8826
▼▼ APPROVED   Motel. **Address:** 100 Hwy 16 V0T 1S1

WHERE TO EAT

JAGS BEANSTALK ESPRESSO & BISTRO   250/559-8826
▼▼ APPROVED   Coffee/Tea Sandwiches. Quick Serve. **Address:** 100 Hwy 16 V0T 1S1

SMITHERS (E-3) pop. 5,404, elev. 520m/1,706'

Named for A.W. Smithers, one-time chairman of the Grand Trunk Pacific Railway, Smithers owes its location to railway construction crews who in 1913 selected the scenic spot at the base of Hudson Bay Mountain. It became a village in 1921 and officially a town in 1967. Today it is a distribution and supply center for local farms, mills and mines. Murals adorn many buildings within its alpine-style Main Street district.

Smithers is popular as a year-round skiing center thanks to 2,652-metre (8,700-ft.) Hudson Bay Mountain. The town also is a convenient starting point for fossil hunting, fishing, mountain climbing and trail riding.

Smithers Visitor Centre: 1411 Court St., P.O. Box 2379, Smithers, BC, Canada V0J 2N0. **Phone:** (250) 847-5072 or (800) 542-6673.

Self-guiding tours: Information about driving and walking tours is available at the chamber of commerce.

SUNSHINE INN   250/847-6668
▼▼ APPROVED   Hotel. **Address:** 3880 Fourth Ave V0J 2N0

WHERE TO EAT

ALPENHORN BISTRO AND BAR   250/847-5366
▼▼ APPROVED   American. Casual Dining. **Address:** 1261 Main St V0J 2N0

BLUE WATER SUSHI   250/847-5341
▼▼ APPROVED   Sushi. Casual Dining. **Address:** 1232 Main St V0J 2N0

SOOKE (H-9) pop. 11,435, elev. 38m/125'

- Hotels p. 240 • Restaurants p. 240
- Part of Victoria area — see map p. 299

A natural harbor off the Juan de Fuca Strait, Sooke was discovered and claimed by the Spanish in 1790. The area, soon traded to the British by treaty, was named after a local First Nation tribe, T'Soke. It is a popular fishing site and the center of a large forest industry. A scenic portion of Hwy. 14 runs 43 kilometres (27 mi.) east from Sooke to Victoria.

Sooke Visitor Centre: 2070 Phillips Rd., Sooke, BC, Canada V9Z 0Y3. **Phone:** (250) 642-6351 or (866) 888-4748.

OCEAN WILDERNESS INN   250/646-2116
◆ APPROVED   Bed & Breakfast. Address: 9171 W Coast Rd V9Z 1G3

PRESTIGE OCEANFRONT RESORT, BW PREMIER COLLECTION   250/642-0805
◆ THREE DIAMOND   (SAVE)
Contemporary Hotel. Address: 6929 W Coast Rd V9Z 0V1

AAA Benefit: Members save up to 15% and earn bonus points!

SOOKE HARBOUR RESORT AND MARINA   250/642-3236
◆ THREE DIAMOND   Condominium. Address: 6971 W Coast Rd V9Z 0V1

WHERE TO EAT

WEST COAST GRILL   778/425-0888
◆ APPROVED   Pacific Northwest. Casual Dining. Address: 6929 W Coast Rd V9Z 0V1

WILD MOUNTAIN FOOD & DRINK   250/642-3596
◆ THREE DIAMOND   Pacific Northwest. Casual Dining. Address: 1831 Maple Ave S V9Z 0N9

SQUAMISH (G-11) pop. 17,158, elev. 5m/16'

Overshadowed by Stawamus Chief Mountain and other snowcapped peaks, Squamish was named for the First Nation's word meaning "mother of the wind." It is a popular stopover for tourists and recreation seekers. Rock climbing and windsurfing are popular activities.

Picnic facilities are available 3 kilometres (1.9 mi.) south at Shannon Falls, and camping facilities are available at Alice Lake Provincial Park (see Recreation Areas Chart) 13 kilometres (8 mi.) to the north.

Squamish Visitor Centre: 38551 Loggers Ln., Squamish, BC, Canada V8B 0H2. **Phone:** (604) 815-4994 or (877) 815-5084.

SEA TO SKY GONDOLA is at 36800 Hwy. 99/Sea to Sky Hwy. Eight-passenger gondolas take 10 minutes to ascend above coastal forests and Howe Sound to a plaza 885 metres (2,904 ft.) above sea level. At the summit are interpretive walking trails with cantilevered viewing platforms, a 100-metre-long suspension bridge, a winter tube park, a lodge and access to trails for hiking and snowshoeing.

Hours: Sun.-Thurs. 10-6, Fri.-Sat. 10-8, mid-May through mid-Sept.; daily 10-5, mid-Sept. through late Oct.; daily 10-4, Dec. 1 through mid-May. Last gondola ride down is 1 hour after closing. Guided walking tours offered daily at 11 and 2, May-Nov.; by appointment, rest of year. Phone ahead to confirm schedule. **Cost:** Round-trip gondola fare $43.95; $39.95 (ages 65+); $25.95 (ages 13-18); $15.95 (ages 6-12); $107.95 (family, two adults and two children or teens). Guided tours free. Snowshoes, crampons, poles and tubes are available for a rental fee. **Phone:** (604) 892-2550 or (855) 732-8675. GT TI

EXECUTIVE SUITES HOTEL & RESORT   604/815-0048
◆ THREE DIAMOND   Extended Stay Hotel. Address: 40900 Tantalus Rd V8B 0R3

MOUNTAIN RETREAT HOTEL & SUITES   604/815-0883
◆ APPROVED   Hotel. Address: 38922 Progress Way V8B 0K5

WHERE TO EAT

PEPE'S CHOPHOUSE + SEAFOOD   604/898-3606
◆ THREE DIAMOND   International. Casual Dining. Address: 40359 Tantalus Way V0N 1T0

SUSHI SEN   604/898-8235
◆ APPROVED   Sushi. Casual Dining. Address: 40382 Tantalus Rd V0N 1T0

TIMBERWOLF RESTAURANT & LOUNGE   604/815-4424
◆ APPROVED   American. Casual Dining. Address: 38922 Progress Way V8B 0K5

SUMMERLAND (C-8) pop. 11,280, elev. 454m/1,489'

- Hotels & Restaurants map & index p. 216
- Part of Okanagan Valley area — see map p. 212

Surrounded by lush orchards and vineyards, Summerland depends on fruit cultivation as its main industry. Overlooking Okanagan Lake (see Recreation Areas Chart), the first commercial orchard in the Okanagan Valley was planted in 1890. Fruit stands are still the best way to sample the region's bountiful produce.

Summerland also was the first town on the lake to employ electricity as an energy source; it was generated by a small hydroelectric plant built on the lakeshore in 1905. These and other historical landmarks are the focus of Summerland Museum at 9521 Wharton St.; phone (250) 494-9395.

Giants Head Park on 910-metre (2,986-ft.) Giants Head Mountain offers picnic facilities and views of Summerland, the valley below and Okanagan Lake.

Many beaches, including Sunoka, Peach Orchard, Powell and Rotary, line the shores of Okanagan Lake. Also of interest is the Freshwater Fisheries Society of BC Trout Hatchery, 13405 Lakeshore Dr. S., where rainbow, brook and kokanee trout are raised; phone (250) 494-0491.

Summerland Visitor Centre: 15600 Hwy. 97, P.O. Box 130, Summerland, BC, Canada V0H 1Z0. **Phone:** (250) 494-2686.

KETTLE VALLEY STEAM RAILWAY is 5 km (3 mi.) w. on Prairie Valley Rd. to 18404 Bathville Rd. Passengers take a 1-hour, 30-minute narrated tour on the only preserved portion of the original Kettle Valley Railway Line, which ran from Midway to Hope.

Hours: The train departs from Prairie Valley Station Thurs.-Mon. at 10:30 and 1:30, late June-early Sept.; Sat.-Mon. at 10:30 and 1:30, mid-May to late June and mid-Sept. to mid-Oct.; at 10:30 and 1:30 on Easter and Mother's Day. **Cost:** $24.50; $22.50

(See map & index p. 216.)

(ages 65+); $19.50 (ages 13-18); $15.50 (ages 3-12). Fares may vary; phone ahead. **Phone:** (250) 494-8422, or (877) 494-8424 in Canada.

NIXDORF CLASSIC CARS, INC. is at 15809 Logie Rd. An inventory of more than 100 restored vehicles dating from 1936 to 1970 is rotated so that no fewer than half reside in the facility at one time. The cars, all of which are two-door hardtops or convertibles, may also be rented for chauffeured wine tours. **Time:** Allow 1 hour minimum. **Hours:** Daily 9-5, May 1 to mid-Oct.; by appointment rest of year. **Cost:** $19; free (ages 0-11 with adult). **Phone:** (250) 494-4111.

WINERIES

- **Sumac Ridge Estate Winery** is 1 km (.6 mi.) n. at 17403 Hwy. 97N. **Hours:** Tastings daily 10-6, July 1-Labour Day; 10-5, Mar.-June and day after Labour Day-Oct. 31; 11-4, rest of year. Tours are given daily at 11 and 2, year-round. Closed Jan. 1-2, Christmas and day after Christmas. **Phone:** (250) 494-0451 or (877) 433-0451. GT

SUMMERLAND MOTEL 250/494-4444 **32**
◆ APPROVED Motel. **Address:** 2107 Tait St V0H 1Z4

SUN PEAKS (B-8)

The resort community of Sun Peaks nestles amid firs and aspen at the base of Tod Mountain and Mount Morrisey in central British Columbia. The core of the village, 31 kilometres (19 mi.) east of Hwy. 5 at Heffley Creek, consists of three- to five-story alpine motif buildings clustered along pedestrian walkways.

With nearly 1,497 hectares (3,700 acres) of terrain, Sun Peaks is reportedly the third largest ski area in Canada, offering both alpine and Nordic skiing as well as a tube park, ice-skating, sleigh rides, snowmobiling and dog sledding. Summer activities include golf, tennis, hiking, mountain biking, kayaking, canoeing, fishing and trail rides.

RECREATIONAL ACTIVITIES
Skiing

- SAVE **Sun Peaks Resort** is 54 km (32 mi.) n. on Hwy. 5 at 1280 Alpine Rd. Other activities are available. **Hours:** Daily 8-4:30, mid-Nov. to mid-Apr. Chairlifts open for summer activities daily 10-7, late June-Sept. 1. Hours may vary; phone ahead to confirm schedule. **Phone:** (250) 578-5474 or (800) 807-3257.

COAST SUNDANCE LODGE 250/578-0200
◆ APPROVED Extended Stay Hotel. **Address:** 3160 Creekside V0E 5N0

HEARTHSTONE LODGE 250/578-6969
◆ APPROVED Extended Stay Hotel. **Address:** 3170 Creekside Way V0E 5N0

THE SUN PEAKS GRAND HOTEL & CONFERENCE CENTER 250/578-6000

◆ **THREE DIAMOND**
Hotel

Address: 3240 Village Way V0E 5N0 **Location:** Just e of Sun Peaks Resort main lodge; then just w on Village Way; center. **Facility:** 262 units, some two bedrooms and kitchens. 4-5 stories, interior corridors. **Parking:** on-site (fee) and valet. **Terms:** check-in 4 pm. **Dining:** Mantles Restaurant, see separate listing. **Pool:** heated outdoor. **Activities:** sauna, hot tub, downhill & cross country skiing, snowboarding, sledding, ice skating, recreation programs in winter, bicycles, game room, trails, exercise room. **Guest Services:** coin laundry.

SAVE ECO 🍴 🍸 CALL 🛗 🛏 🛗 BIZ HS 🛜
✖ 🎞 🔌 💻 / SOME UNITS 🐾 🖼

WHERE TO EAT

BELLA ITALIA RISTORANTE 250/434-0282
◆ **THREE DIAMOND** Italian. Casual Dining. **Address:** 3170 Creekside Way V0E 5N0

MANTLES RESTAURANT 250/578-6060
◆ **THREE DIAMOND** American. Casual Dining. **Address:** 3240 Village Way V0E 5N0

OYA JAPANESE RESTAURANT 250/578-0048
◆ APPROVED Sushi. Casual Dining. **Address:** 3170 Creekside Way V0E 1Z1

SUNSHINE COAST (F-10)

Lining the western edge of the British Columbia mainland, the Sunshine Coast offers a wide variety of marine and land habitats, from coastal rain forests and rocky beaches to an alpine wilderness with peaks reaching 2,500 metres (8,000 ft.).

Powell River *(see place listing p. 227)*, with more than 100 regional dive sites, exceptionally clear water and deep ocean currents, is called the "Dive Capital of Canada." Desolation Sound's warm, sheltered waters also contribute to the destination's popularity with scuba divers and kayakers. Sechelt is known for its rich artisan community, while Gibsons is home to up to 200 bird species throughout the year.

SURREY (H-11) pop. 468,251, elev. 80m/262'
- Hotels p. 242 • Restaurants p. 243
- Hotels & Restaurants map & index p. 276
- Part of Vancouver area — see map p. 249

Surrey's sights are popular with nature buffs. Bear Creek Park features a garden area that includes rhododendrons, azaleas, ornamental grasses and bulb displays. A shoreline walk extends from Crescent Beach to Peace Arch Park. Walkers can observe tide pools, dig for clams or watch the myriad native birds.

Surrey Visitor Centre: 730 176th St., Surrey, BC, Canada V3S 9S6. **Phone:** (604) 531-6646 or (888) 531-6646.

MUSEUM OF SURREY is at 17710-56A Ave. Interactive exhibits and a 42-seat theater portray the history of Surrey. A textile library and weaving studio

(See map & index p. 276.)

are featured on-site. Changing exhibits are offered. On the grounds is the Anderson cabin, the oldest remaining pioneer-era structure in Surrey. The cabin was built in 1872 by Eric Anderson, a Swedish immigrant and one of the first settlers in the area.

Note: The museum is closed for renovations and is scheduled to reopen September 2018; phone ahead for updates. **Time:** Allow 1 hour minimum. **Hours:** Tues.-Fri. 9:30-5:30, Sat. 10-5, early Feb.-late Dec. Closed most major holidays. **Cost:** Donations. **Phone:** (604) 592-6956.

NEWTON WAVE POOL is in the Newton Recreation Centre at 13730 72nd Ave. The indoor aquatic center houses, in addition to the wave pool, two water slides, an interactive water fortress and a three-station water cannon platform. The complex also includes an exercise, a steam and 465-square-metre (5,000-sq.-ft.) weight room as well as a whirlpool.

Hours: Mon.-Sat. 6 a.m.-9 p.m., Sun. 8-8. Phone ahead for leisure swim times. **Cost:** Single drop-in swims $6.17; $4.75 (students with ID and ages 60+); $3.10 (ages 2-18 and adult accompanying child). Prices may vary; phone ahead. **Phone:** (604) 501-5543.

 Get member rates and reservations at AAA.com/hertz

BEST WESTERN KING GEORGE INN & SUITES
604/502-9000   **54**

APPROVED
Hotel

BW Best Western.

AAA Benefit: Members save up to 15% and earn bonus points!

Address: 8033 King George Blvd V3W 5B4 **Location:** Jct Fraser Hwy (Hwy 1A), 2.5 mi (4 km) s to 80th Ave. **Facility:** 71 units, some efficiencies. 3 stories, interior corridors. **Pool:** heated indoor. **Activities:** hot tub, limited exercise equipment. **Guest Services:** valet and coin laundry. **Featured Amenity: breakfast buffet.** *(See ad this page.)*

BEST WESTERN PEACE ARCH INN
604/541-8100   **59**

APPROVED
Hotel

AAA Benefit: Members save up to 15% and earn bonus points!

Address: 2293 King George Blvd V4A 5A4 **Location:** Hwy 99 exit 10 southbound, 2.8 mi (4.5 km) s; exit 2 northbound, 2.1 mi (3.5 km) n. **Facility:** 42 units. 3 stories, interior corridors. **Pool:** indoor. **Activities:** sauna, hot tub, exercise room. **Guest Services:** coin laundry. **Featured Amenity: continental breakfast.**

BW Best Western.

100% Non-Smoking. Free Hot Breakfast, Parking, Wi-Fi, Indoor Pool, Sauna & Fitness Centre!

▼ See AAA listing this page ▼

BW Best Western.

King George Inn & Suites

All rooms include:
Hot Continental
Breakfast
Wifi
Parking

8033 King George Blvd, Surrey, BC V3W 5B4 CAN | 1-866-502-5025 | 604-502-9000
bestwesternsurrey.com

Each Best Western branded hotel is independently owned and operated. Best Western and the Best Western marks are service marks or registered service marks of Best Western International, Inc. ©2014 Best Western International, Inc. All rights reserved. AAA and the AAA marks are service marks or registered service marks of the American Automobile Association.

(See map & index p. 276.)

CIVIC HOTEL, AUTOGRAPH COLLECTION
604/951-3331 **51**

▼ **THREE DIAMOND** [SAVE]
Contemporary Hotel. **Address:** 13475
Central Ave V3T 0L8

AAA Benefit:
Members save 5%
or more!

COMFORT INN & SUITES SURREY   604/576-8888 **55**
▼ **APPROVED**   Hotel. **Address:** 8255 166th St V4N 5R8

FOUR POINTS BY SHERATON SURREY   604/930-4700 **53**
▼ **THREE DIAMOND** [SAVE] Hotel. **Ad-**
dress: 10410 158th St V4N 5C2

AAA Benefit:
Members save 5%
or more!

HAMPTON INN & SUITES LANGLEY/SURREY
604/530-6545 **57**

▼ **THREE DIAMOND**
Hotel

AAA Benefit:
Members save up to
15%!

Address: 19500 Langley Bypass V3S
7R2 **Location:** Trans-Canada Hwy 1
exit 58 (200th St/Langley City), 3.1 mi (5
km) s, then 0.7 mi (1.2 km) w on Hwy
10. **Facility:** 96 units, some efficiencies.
4 stories, interior corridors. **Pool:** heated
indoor. **Activities:** hot tub, exercise
room. **Guest Services:** valet and coin
laundry. **Featured Amenity:** breakfast
buffet.

[SAVE] [❒] [❒] CALL [❒] [❒] [❒] [BIZ] [HS] [❒] [✕]
[❒] [❒] [❒] [❒]

HOLIDAY INN & SUITES   604/576-8862 **56**
▼ **THREE DIAMOND**   **Address:** 17530 64th Ave V3S 1Y9 **Lo-**
Hotel   **cation:** Trans-Canada Hwy 1 exit 53
(176th St/Hwy 15), 4.2 mi (7 km) s, then
just w. Located in Cloverdale area. **Fa-**
cility: 76 units. 4 stories, interior corridors. **Pool:** heated indoor. **Activities:**
exercise room. **Guest Services:** valet
and coin laundry. **Featured Amenity:**
full hot breakfast.

[SAVE] [❒] [❒] [❒] CALL [❒] [❒]
[❒] [BIZ] [HS] [❒] [✕] [❒] [❒]
/ SOME [❒]
UNITS

RAMADA LANGLEY-SURREY   604/576-8388 **58**
▼ **APPROVED**   **Address:** 19225 Hwy 10 (56 Ave)
Hotel   V3S 8V9 **Location:** Trans-Canada
Hwy 1 exit 58 (200th St/Langley City),
3.1 mi (5 km) s on 200th St, then 1.2
mi (2 km) w on Hwy 10 (56th Ave);
corner of 192nd St and Hwy 10. **Fa-**
cility: 83 units, some efficiencies. 3
stories, interior corridors. **Amenities:**
safes. **Pool:** heated indoor. **Activ-**
ities: hot tub, exercise room. **Guest**
Services: valet and coin laundry. **Fea-**
tured Amenity: breakfast buffet.

[SAVE] [❒] CALL [❒] [❒] [❒]

[BIZ] [❒] [✕] [❒] [❒] [❒] / SOME [❒] [HS]
UNITS

🕊
RAMADA

Recipient of an Award of Excellence;
value priced; EV charging stations;
Central location.

SHERATON VANCOUVER GUILDFORD HOTEL
604/582-9288 **52**

AAA Benefit:
Members save 5% or more!

▼ **THREE DIAMOND** [SAVE] Hotel. **Ad-**
dress: 15269 104th Ave V3R 1N5 **(See**
ad p. 289.)

WHERE TO EAT

CRESCENT BEACH BISTRO   604/531-1882 **78**
▼ **APPROVED**   Mediterranean. Casual Dining. **Address:**
12251 Beecher St V4A 3A4

MAGUROGUY   604/560-1424 **79**
▼ **APPROVED**   Japanese. Casual Dining. **Address:** 2670
152nd St, #320 V4P 1M8

MOXIE'S CLASSIC GRILL   604/495-7020 **76**
▼ **APPROVED**   American. Casual Dining. **Address:**
10608 151A St V3R 1J8

RICKY'S ALL DAY GRILL
▼ **APPROVED**   American. Casual Dining.
LOCATIONS:
Address: 8958 152nd St V3R 4E7 **Phone:** 604/581-3212
Address: 1076 Central City V3T 2W1 **Phone:** 604/582-2545

SABAI THAI RESTAURANT   604/588-9819 **77**
▼ **APPROVED**   Thai. Casual Dining. **Address:** 10391
150th St V3R 4B1

THE TURKEY HOUSE & DELI   604/531-6222 **80**
▼ **APPROVED**   Sandwiches Deli. Quick Serve. **Address:**
1433 King George Hwy V4A 4Z5

TELEGRAPH COVE (H-3)
• Hotels p. 244 • Restaurants p. 244

The bay community served as the northern terminus of the telegraph line along the coast of Vancouver Island and later became a logging and
salmon fishing area. Whale watching, fishing and
camping are popular during the summer.

STUBBS ISLAND WHALE WATCHING departs
from the end of the #24 boardwalk. For excursions
on the Johnstone Strait, vessels are equipped with
underwater microphones for listening to whale vo-
calizations. Multiday tours also are available.

Warm clothing is recommended. **Time:** Allow 3
hours, 30 minutes minimum. **Hours:** Daily departures May 1-early Oct. Phone ahead to confirm
schedule. **Cost:** $105; $95 (ages 65+); $90 (ages
1-12). Reservations are required. **Phone:** (250)
928-3185 or (800) 665-3066.

WHALE INTERPRETIVE CENTRE is at the end of
the boardwalk. Interpreters provide hands-on presentations and share information about and promote
awareness of the marine environment. Exhibits include whale skeletons and artifacts. **Time:** Allow 45
minutes minimum. **Hours:** Daily 9:30-5:30, May-
Sept.; by appointment rest of year. Phone ahead to

confirm schedule. **Cost:** $4.76; $2.86 (children). **Phone:** (250) 928-3129, or (250) 928-3187 in the off-season.

TELEGRAPH COVE RESORT   250/928-3131
APPROVED   Resort Hotel. **Address:** 1610 Telegraph Cove Rd V0N 3J0

WHERE TO EAT

KILLER WHALE CAFE   250/928-3131
APPROVED   Pacific Northwest. Casual Dining. **Address:** 1610 Telegraph Cove Rd V0N 3J0

TERRACE (E-2) pop. 11,486, elev. 215m/705'

On the banks of the Skeena River, Terrace and its surrounding area provide excellent recreational opportunities ranging from hiking on a variety of trails to fishing in nearby rivers and creeks. Among the region's wildlife is a rare species of black bear, the white Kermodei. Native to the area, it is the city's symbol.

Among the most popular recreation areas are Lakelse Lake Provincial Park *(see Recreation Areas Chart)*; Lakelse River, a tributary of the Skeena River that harbors record-size salmon; and Williams Creek, which teems with spawning sockeye each August.

Several places of natural interest are nearby. At the eastern entrance to the city is Ferry Island Provincial Park, where you can hike trails and go fishing, swimming and camping *(see Recreation Areas Chart)*. Look closely at the cottonwood trees on the island's trails; more than 50 have faces carved into them by a local artist.

About 20 kilometres (12 mi.) south of Terrace is Mount Layton Hot Springs Resort, which has waterslides and a pool filled with natural hot spring mineral water. Hwy. 16 offers a scenic drive west along the Skeena River to Prince Rupert.

Terrace Visitor Centre: 4511 Keith Ave., Terrace, BC, Canada V8G 1K1. **Phone:** (250) 635-4944 or (877) 635-4944.

BEST WESTERN TERRACE INN   250/635-0083
THREE DIAMOND
Hotel

AAA Benefit: Members save up to 15% and earn bonus points!

Address: 4553 Greig Ave V8G 1M7 **Location:** Hwy 16, just e on Greig Ave, follow City Centre signs. **Facility:** 68 units. 5 stories, interior corridors. **Amenities:** safes. **Activities:** exercise room. **Guest Services:** valet and coin laundry. **Featured Amenity: full hot breakfast.**

COMFORT INN & SUITES   250/635-0788
THREE DIAMOND Hotel. **Address:** 5112 Hwy 16 W V8G 5S6

DAYS INN TERRACE   250-638-8141
APPROVED   Hotel. **Address:** 4620 Lakelse Ave V8G 1R1

WHERE TO EAT

MR MIKES STEAKHOUSECASUAL   250/635-3077
APPROVED   American. Casual Dining. **Address:** 4736 Lakelse Ave V8G 1R6

NORTHERN DHABA HOT HOUSE RESTAURANT
                                                250/615-5800
APPROVED   Indian. Casual Dining. **Address:** 4728 Lazelle Ave V8G 1T2

TOFINO (I-3) pop. 1,876

A fishing and resort village with sandy beaches, Tofino is on the western side of Vancouver Island at the end of Hwy. 4. The area was the site of Fort Defiance, where Boston fur trader Robert Gray and his men spent the winter of 1791. The fort was stripped and abandoned the next spring, and all that remains are scattered bricks and ruins.

Near Clayoquot Sound and the northern end of Pacific Rim National Park Reserve, the town's shoreline and waters are popular with scuba divers and beachcombers. In the spring whales often can be seen migrating along the coast. The Whale Centre and Museum, 411 Campbell St., exhibits scientific and artistic displays, photographs and artifacts depicting past and present whale encounters.

Several companies, including Adventure Tofino Wildlife Tours, (250) 725-2895; Remote Passages Marine Excursions *(see attraction listing)*, (250) 725-3330; and The Whale Centre, (250) 725-2132, offer whale-watching excursions on Clayoquot Sound. Tours lasting up to 3 hours may afford sightings of sea lions, porpoises and eagles. Combination whale-watching and hot springs cruises that last approximately 6.5 hours also are available.

Tofino Visitor Centre: 1426 Pacific Rim Hwy., Tofino, BC, Canada V0R 2Z0. **Phone:** (250) 725-3414 or (888) 720-3414.

REMOTE PASSAGES MARINE EXCURSIONS departs from Tofino harbor off Main St. at 51 Wharf St. Passengers have a choice of an open-air zodiac or a boat with an enclosed cabin and a viewing deck for their 2.5- to 3-hour journey through Clayoquot Sound to spot gray and humpback whales (and occasionally orcas), sea otters, sea lions, seals, porpoises, sea birds and bald eagles. March through May encompasses the gray whale migration, while June through October is when gray and humpback whales linger in the area. Bear-watching tours, daily trips to Hot Springs Cove and sea kayaking trips also are available.

Warm clothing is recommended. **Hours:** Trips are offered daily in zodiacs and an enclosed-cabin boat early Mar.-Oct. 31 (weather permitting). Phone ahead to confirm schedule. **Cost:** Cabin fare $105; $79 (ages 3-12). Zodiac fare $105; $79 (ages 5-12).

A fuel surcharge may apply. Fare may vary; phone ahead. **Phone:** (250) 725-3330 or (800) 666-9833.

TOFINO BOTANICAL GARDENS is at 1080 Pacific Rim Hwy. This site consists of 5 hectares (12 acres) of gardens that include a children's garden, a medicinal herb garden, 1,000-year-old cedar trees, an orchard and a berry patch, and a bird-watching area. An old homestead also is on the grounds. Pets and smoking are not permitted. **Time:** Allow 1 hour minimum. **Hours:** Daily 9-dusk. **Cost:** $11.43; $9.52 (senior citizens); $7.62 (students); free (ages 0-12). **Phone:** (250) 725-1220. [🍴]

BEST WESTERN PLUS TIN WIS RESORT LODGE
250/725-4445

▽▽ THREE DIAMOND
Hotel

 Best Western PLUS

AAA Benefit: Members save up to 15% and earn bonus points!

Address: 1119 Pacific Rim Hwy V0R 2Z0 **Location:** 1.8 mi (3.5 km) s on Hwy 4. **Facility:** 85 units, some efficiencies. 2-3 stories, interior/exterior corridors. **Terms:** check-in 4 pm. **Amenities:** safes. **Activities:** hot tub, limited beach access, recreation programs, exercise room, massage. **Guest Services:** coin laundry, area transportation.

[SAVE] [ECO] [🔌] [🍴] [Y] CALL[♿]

[📶] [BIZ] [HS] [📶] [✕] [🗜] [🔧] [📺] [🖥] / SOME UNITS [🔧] [🦌]

LONG BEACH LODGE RESORT
250/725-2442
▽▽ THREE DIAMOND Contemporary Hotel. **Address:** 1441 Pacific Rim Hwy V0R 2Z0

PACIFIC SANDS BEACH RESORT
250/725-3322
▽▽ THREE DIAMOND Extended Stay Hotel. **Address:** 1421 Pacific Rim Hwy V0R 2Z0

TOFINO MOTEL
250/725-2055
▽▽ APPROVED Motel. **Address:** 542 Campbell St V0R 2Z0

WICKANINNISH INN
250/725-3100
▽▽ FOUR DIAMOND
Contemporary Hotel

Address: 500 Osprey Ln at Chesterman Beach V0R 2Z0 **Location:** 2.7 mi (4.3 km) e on Hwy 4. Located in a quiet area. **Facility:** One of the hotel buildings is built on the rocks overlooking the ocean. Rooms have many extras, ranging from locally made soaps to back packs to beach blankets and an evening glass of port. 75 units, some kitchens. 3 stories, interior corridors. **Parking:** on-site and valet. **Terms:** check-in 4 pm. **Amenities:** safes. **Dining:** The Pointe Restaurant, see separate listing. **Activities:** steamroom, beach access, recreation programs, bicycles, exercise room, spa. **Guest Services:** valet laundry, area transportation.

[SAVE] [ECO] [🔌] [🔌] [🍴] [🔧] [Y] CALL [♿] [🔧] [BIZ]
[HS] [📶] [✕] [🗜] [🔧] [🖥] / SOME UNITS [🔧] [📺]

WHERE TO EAT

1909 KITCHEN
250/726-6122
▽▽ THREE DIAMOND Pacific Northwest. Casual Dining. **Address:** 634 Campbell St V0R 2Z0

KUMA TOFINO
250/725-2215
▽▽ APPROVED Japanese. Casual Dining. **Address:** 101-120 Fourth St V0R 2Z0

THE POINTE RESTAURANT
250/725-3106
▽▽ FOUR DIAMOND

Pacific Northwest Fine Dining
$37-$58

AAA Inspector Notes: Built above the rocks and jutting out into the ocean, this restaurant offers breathtaking scenery. In winter, wild waves crash on the rocks right outside the windows. Since opening in 1996, the restaurant has focused mainly on Canadian West Coast cuisine that reflects the bounty and tastes of Vancouver Island, especially its fresh seafood and amazing selection of B.C. wines. Walk-ins are welcome at breakfast and lunch. **Features:** full bar, Sunday brunch. **Reservations:** required, for dinner. **Address:** 500 Osprey Ln at Chesterman Beach V0R 2Z0 **Location:** 2.7 mi (4.3 km) e on Hwy 4; in Wickaninnish Inn. **Parking:** on-site and valet.

[B] [L] [D] CALL [♿]

RESTAURANT AT LONG BEACH LODGE RESORT
250/725-2442
▽▽ THREE DIAMOND Pacific Northwest. Fine Dining. **Address:** 1441 Pacific Rim Hwy V0R 2Z0

SCHOONER RESTAURANT
250/725-3444
▽▽ THREE DIAMOND Pacific Northwest. Casual Dining. **Address:** 331 Campbell St V0R 2Z0

SHED TOFINO
250/725-7433
▽▽ APPROVED Burgers. Casual Dining. **Address:** 461 Campbell St V0R 2Z0

SHELTER RESTAURANT
250/725-3353
▽▽ APPROVED Pacific Northwest. Casual Dining. **Address:** 601 Campbell St V0R 2Z0

SOBO RESTAURANT
250/725-2341
▽▽ APPROVED Pacific Rim. Casual Dining. **Address:** 311 Neill St V0R 2Z0

WOLF IN THE FOG
250/725-9653
▽▽ THREE DIAMOND Pacific Northwest. Fine Dining. **Address:** 150 Fourth St V0R 2Z0

AAA.com/ **TourBook** Comments

Let Your Voice Be Heard

If your visit to a listed property doesn't meet your expectations, tell us about it.

AAA.com/MemberFeedback

TRAIL (D-10) pop. 7,681, elev. 430m/1,410'

At City Hall a sculptured screen titled "City of Lead and Zinc" illustrates how Trail's mineral and industrial strength steadily developed since the discovery of gold and copper in the area about 1890. Hydroelectric dams along the Kootenay River power extensive mining and smelting operations, dominated by Teck Cominco Ltd. Enjoy free concerts at Gyro Park, 1090 Charles Lakes Dr., on Thursday evenings in July and August.

Trail and District Chamber of Commerce and Visitor Centre: 1199 Bay Ave., Suite 200, Trail, BC, Canada V1R 4A4. **Phone:** (250) 368-3144, or (844) 368-3144 within British Columbia.

Self-guiding tours: Brochures for walking tours are available at the chamber of commerce.

BEST WESTERN PLUS COLUMBIA RIVER HOTEL
250/368-3355

THREE DIAMOND
Hotel

AAA Benefit: Members save up to 15% and earn bonus points!

Address: 1001 Rossland Ave V1R 3N7 **Location:** On Hwy 3B; just n of center. **Facility:** 58 units. 4 stories, interior corridors. **Dining:** Foxy's Fine Food & Drinks, see separate listing. **Activities:** hot tub, exercise room. **Guest Services:** valet laundry. **Featured Amenity: full hot breakfast.**

SAVE 🍴 🍷 ♿ BIZ HS 📶 ✕ 🛗 🖨

CROWN COLUMBIA ALL-SUITE BOUTIQUE HOTEL, BW PREMIER COLLECTION   250/368-3296
THREE DIAMOND SAVE Hotel. **Address:** 1399 Bay Ave V1R 4A7

AAA Benefit: Members save up to 15% and earn bonus points!

WHERE TO EAT

COLANDER RESTAURANT   250/364-1816
APPROVED   Italian. Casual Dining. **Address:** 1475 Cedar Ave V1R 4C5

FOXY'S FINE FOOD & DRINKS   250/368-3355
APPROVED   American. Casual Dining. **Address:** 1001 Rossland Ave V1R 3N7

UCLUELET (I-3) pop. 1,627

On Barkley Sound, Ucluelet was named for a First Nation's word meaning "safe harbor." Charter boats for salmon fishing, whale watching, skin diving and nature excursions are available; phone the chamber of commerce. Lady Rose Marine Services makes round trips between Port Alberni and Ucluelet June through September; phone (250) 723-8313, or (800) 663-7192 Apr.-Sept., for reservations.

He Tin Kis Park allows visitors to experience a Canadian rain forest and follow a boardwalk trail that leads to the ocean. The 5-kilometre (3-mi.) Wild

Pacific Trail passes a lighthouse en route to cliffside ocean views.

Ucluelet Visitor Centre: 2791 Pacific Rim Hwy., Ucluelet, BC, Canada V0R 3A0. **Phone:** (250) 726-4600.

BLACK ROCK OCEANFRONT RESORT   250/726-4800
THREE DIAMOND Contemporary Hotel. **Address:** 596 Marine Dr V0R 3A0

WHERE TO EAT

BARKLEY CAFE   250/726-2999
APPROVED   Coffee/Tea Sandwiches. Quick Serve. **Address:** 1-1636 Peninsula Rd V0R 3A0

FETCH RESTAURANT   250/726-4800
THREE DIAMOND Pacific Northwest. Fine Dining. **Address:** 596 Marine Dr V0R 3A0

VALEMOUNT (F-6) pop. 1,020, elev. 792m/2,600'

Valemount, the valley in the mountains, offers many activities for outdoor enthusiasts. The village, where the Rocky, Cariboo and Monashee mountain ranges meet, is popular for both summer and winter pursuits, including hiking, rafting, skiing and snowmobiling. The area is rich with birds and other wildlife. Off Hwy. 16 is Mount Terry Fox Provincial Park. A viewing area affords vistas of the peak named for the late athlete.

Valemount Visitor Centre: 785 Cranberry Lake Rd., P.O. Box 146, Valemount, BC, Canada V0E 2Z0. **Phone:** (250) 566-9893.

GEORGE HICKS REGIONAL PARK is off Hwy. 5 at 785 Cranberry Lake Rd. The site offers a bird's-eye view of Chinook salmon as they near the end of a 1,280-kilometre (768 mi.) upstream trip from mid-August to mid-September. **Hours:** Daily May 1 to mid-Oct. **Cost:** Donations. **Phone:** (250) 566-9893.

MOUNT ROBSON PROVINCIAL PARK is on Hwy. 16. Mount Robson, at 3,954 metres (12,972 ft.) is the highest peak in the Canadian Rockies. Other park highlights include glacier-fed lakes, valleys, canyons, waterfalls, rivers and streams. More than 180 species of birds reside here along with deer, moose, bears, elk and caribou. Fishing, camping, horseback riding and hiking are just a few of the outdoor activities visitors can enjoy.

Scenic views abound on the many walking and hiking trails. A visitor center is at the Mount Robson viewpoint. *See Recreation Areas Chart.* **Hours:** Park open daily 24 hours. Visitor center open daily 8-7, June 15-Labour Day; 8-5, May 15-June 14; 9-4, day after Labour Day-Thanksgiving. **Cost:** Donations. **Phone:** (250) 566-4038. 🅰 ✕ 🍴 🏕

ROBSON HELIMAGIC INC. tours depart from the Yellowhead Helicopters hangar, 5 km (3 mi.) n. on Hwy. 5 to 3010 Selwyn Rd. Helicopters take passengers on 12-36 minute tours of the Valemount and

Mount Robson areas, providing breathtaking views of glaciers, snow-covered mountains, alpine meadows, valleys, waterfalls, lakes and rivers.

Heli-skiing, heli-snowshoeing and heli-snowboarding also are offered in winter. Summer activities are available. **Hours:** Daily 8-5, June-Aug.; Mon.-Fri. 8-5, rest of year. Phone ahead to confirm schedule. **Cost:** $248.38-$875.06. **Phone:** (250) 566-4401 or (877) 454-4700.

R.W. STARRATT WILDLIFE SANCTUARY is 1 km (.6 mi.) s. on Hwy. 5. The refuge, also known as Cranberry March, is home to more than 140 species of songbirds, waterfowl and other animals. Informational signs line 7 kilometres (4 mi.) of trails and walkways to two viewing platforms. There are 6 kilometres (3.7 mi.) of trails and walkways in the sanctuary, or if you prefer your sightseeing from a boat, you can canoe through.

Time: Allow 30 minutes minimum. **Hours:** Daily 9-9, July-Aug.; 9-8, mid-June through June 30; 10-6, June 1 to mid-June; 9-5, Sept. 1-Labour Day; 10-5, late May-May 31 and day after Labour Day-Sept. 30; 10-4, early May to mid-May. Phone ahead to confirm schedule. **Cost:** Free. **Phone:** (250) 566-4846 or (250) 564-8585.

BEST WESTERN PLUS VALEMOUNT INN & SUITES
250/566-0086

 THREE DIAMOND
Hotel

 Best Western PLUS. **AAA Benefit:** Members save up to 15% and earn bonus points!

Address: 1950 Hwy 5 S V0E 2Z0 **Location:** 0.9 mi (1.5 km) s on Hwy 5 (Yellowhead Hwy). Near a wildlife sanctuary. **Facility:** 78 units. 2 stories (no elevator), interior corridors. **Parking:** winter plug-ins. **Terms:** check-in 5 pm. **Pool:** heated indoor. **Activities:** hot tub, limited exercise equipment. **Guest Services:** coin laundry, area transportation.

WHERE TO EAT

CARIBOU GRILL   250/566-8244
APPROVED   American. Casual Dining. **Address:** 1002 5th Ave V0E 2Z0

THE GATHERING TREE   250/566-0154
APPROVED   Coffee/Tea Sandwiches. Quick Serve. **Address:** 1150 5th Ave V0E 2Z0

Be Vacation Ready
Know Before You Go

Before setting out on your trip, have your car checked out by a dependable AAA/CAA Approved Auto Repair facility.

 Approved Auto Repair

 APPROVED AUTO REPAIR SERVICES CAA

AAA.com/autorepair

Vancouver

Then & Now

You're hiking along a wide, bark-mulched trail through an old-growth forest of towering Western red cedar, Douglas fir and Western hemlock trees. Salmonberry, huckleberry and Alaskan blueberries grow together in luxurious tangles. A raccoon ambles by, giving you an inquisitive look. A goose honks in the distance. You stop and ask, "Wait a minute—am I really in a city?" That question is answered a few minutes later when you emerge from Stanley Park to the hustle and bustle of Georgia Street.

There's no denying the beauty of Vancouver's natural setting. Vistas of green coastal mountains and the shimmering waters of the Strait of Georgia were tailor-made to grace a travel postcard. And downtown is a marvel: skyscrapers, human hubbub and quiet, tree-lined residential streets all coexisting harmoniously in one tightly packed urban cityscape. If that pocket description sounds a bit like San Francisco, it's an apt comparison, but there really is no place like Vancouver.

No doubt the southwestern British Columbia wilderness impressed Capt. George Vancouver. An officer in the British Royal Navy, he sailed into Burrard Inlet on June 13, 1792, while searching for the Northwest Passage, the sea route that connects the Atlantic and Pacific oceans.

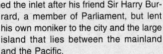
AAA.com/travelguides—
more ways to look, book and save

Vancouver named the inlet after his friend Sir Harry Burrard, a member of Parliament, but lent his own moniker to the city and the large island that lies between the mainland and the Pacific.

Vancouver was incorporated in 1886, quite a young city given its present-day status. A Canadian Pacific Railway passenger train arrived the following year, showering spectators with soot and cinders. By the 1890s transpacific shipping inaugurated the city as a major world port, and the future was looking rosy indeed.

That era produced colorful characters like John Deighton, aka "Gassy Jack," a saloon owner who set up shop in Gastown, the city's oldest section and a popular tourist hangout. The name is a reference to Deighton's reputation for storytelling and tall-tale bluster. A statue of his likeness stands at the circle where Water, Alexander, Powell and Carrall streets converge.

Mandarin and Cantonese are the mother tongues in almost a third of Vancouver's homes; only San Francisco's and New York's Chinatowns are bigger.

Stanley Park

(Continued on p. 250.)

Destination Vancouver

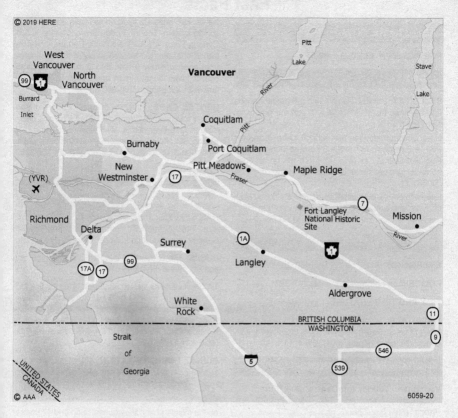

This map shows cities in the Vancouver vicinity where you will find attractions, hotels and restaurants. Cities are listed alphabetically in this book on the following pages.

Fast Facts

ABOUT THE CITY

POP: 603,502 ■ **ELEV:** 3 m/10 ft.

MONEY

SALES TAX: British Columbia has a 5 percent goods and services tax (GST) and a 7 percent provincial sales tax (PST).

Hotel accommodations are subject to an 8 percent PST, a 5 percent GST and a 3 percent Municipal and Regional District Tax (MRDT); there me be an additional 1 percent for a Destination Marketing Fee (DMF).

Expect to pay an additional 3 percent for alcohol. Restaurants and admission fees are exempt from the 7 percent PST. Car rental sales tax is $1.50 per day.

WHOM TO CALL

EMERGENCY: 911

POLICE (non-emergency): (604) 717-3321

TIME AND TEMPERATURE: (604) 664-9010

HOSPITALS: Mount Saint Joseph Hospital, (604) 874-1141 ■ St. Paul's Hospital, (604) 682-2344 ■ Vancouver General Hospital, (604) 875-4111.

VISITOR INFORMATION

Vancouver Tourist InfoCentre: 200 Burrard St., Plaza Level, Vancouver, BC, Canada V6C 3L6. **Phone:** (604) 682-2222.

Maps, lodging reservations and literature about attractions as well as tickets for tours are available at the Vancouver Tourist InfoCentre which is open daily 8:30-6, Victoria Day weekend to mid-Sept.; Mon.-Sat. 8:30-5, rest of year.

TRANSPORTATION

AIR TRAVEL: Vancouver International Airport (YVR), in Richmond, is reached via Granville Street and the Arthur Lang Bridge, then Sea Island Way, which leads into Grant McConachie Way. Check travel sites and with your AAA travel agency for cheap airline flights, cheap plane tickets and the best deals on international flights. Taxi rates are fixed on flat rates according to a zoning system. The trip to downtown/Kitsilano is $31; Canada Place is $35. TransLink's Canada Line rapid transit operates rail service every 7 to 15 minutes, from approximately 5 a.m. to 1 a.m., between Vancouver International Airport and downtown. One-way fare is $4.25; phone (604) 953-3333.

RENTAL CARS: Hertz, with one location at Vancouver International Airport and three locations downtown at 1270 Granville St., 413 Seymour St. and 1150 Station St., offers discounts to AAA members; phone (604) 606-3700 for airport location or (800) 654-3080.

 Book and save at AAA.com/hertz

RAIL SERVICE: The Via Rail passenger train terminal is at 1150 Station St.; phone (888) 842-7245 in Canada or in the United States.

BUSES: The Greyhound bus terminal is at 1150 Station St.; phone (604) 683-8133.

TAXIS: Taxi fares start at $3.20-$3.25 for the first kilometre (.6 mi.), plus $1.84-$1.88 for each additional kilometre. Companies include Black Top & Checker Cabs, (604) 731-1111 ■ MacLure's, (604) 831-1111 ■ Yellow Cab, (604) 681-1111 ■ and Vancouver Taxi, (604) 871-1111.

PUBLIC TRANSPORTATION: TransLink offers bus service as well as SeaBus and SkyTrain service. *See Public Transportation for details.*

BOATS: BC Ferries links Vancouver and other points on the mainland with Vancouver Island and 47 ports of call. Nanaimo and Sunshine Coast ferries leave from Horseshoe Bay, 21 kilometres (13 mi.) west of the city in West Vancouver. From Tsawwassen south of Vancouver automobile/passenger ferries make frequent trips to the southern Gulf Islands, Nanaimo and Swartz Bay, near the town of Sidney north of Victoria. A 1.5-hour ferry ride from Vancouver to Victoria departs daily from Tsawwassen and returns from Swartz Bay; phone (888) 223-3779 for reservations.

For schedules phone the British Columbia Automobile Association (BCAA), (604) 268-5555; BC Ferries Information Centre, (250) 386-3431 outside North America; (888) 223-3779 in North America; or Tourism Vancouver, (604) 682-2000.

(Continued from p. 248.)

The Millennium Gate at Pender and Taylor streets is a symbolic entryway that incorporates both eastern and western symbols. Between 1890 and 1920 Asian immigrants settled on back streets like Shanghai Alley off Pender Street; wall panels tell the story of their lives. Holding out your arms is almost enough to embrace the Sam Kee Building at 8 Pender St., which is only 6 feet wide.

Vancouverites represent a melting pot of nationalities. The original inhabitants of coastal British Columbia were the Northwestern peoples, and their descendants live in urban areas and in reserve communities within ancestral territories. Diversity is the keynote, whether preserved in street names like Barclay and Granville, or in neighborhoods like Little Italy or the East Indian community.

Not bad for a former lumber town, eh?

Must Do: AAA Editor's Picks

- Enjoy fabulous waterside views while strolling, bicycling or in-line skating around the perimeter sea wall of ⬥ **Stanley Park** (main entrance at west end of Georgia St.). Walking the Seawall is one of the most fun things to do with friends and among the best things for couples to do. Or tour the park in a horse-powered trolley provided by **Stanley Park Horse-drawn Tours** (735 Stanley Park Dr.). The 405-hectare (1,000-acre) park also has a pool, a golf course, woodland trails, playgrounds, totem poles, a miniature steam train, beaches and gardens.

- One of the world's great food markets, **Granville Island Public Market** (1689 Johnston St.) is *the* destination for a slice of Vancouver life as well as the freshest fruits, vegetables, cheeses, meats, candy, baked goods and flowers.

- Adorable dolphins steal the show at **Vancouver Aquarium** (845 Avison Way) in Stanley Park; competing for attention are the center's thousands of marine animals including sea lions, sharks and walruses as well as rain forest creatures such as iguanas and crocodiles. Go behind the scenes in close encounters with sea turtles, penguins, Steller sea lions and sea otters.

- Downtown's **Robson Street** (between Burrard and Jervis streets) beckons shoppers with its trendy designer boutiques, shoe stores, jewelry shops and more. When you need a break, grab a seat and a cappuccino at a bistro or coffee shop and watch the world go by.

- On a clear day, you can't beat the scenery at ⬥ **Grouse Mountain** (6400 Nancy Greene Way) in North Vancouver; the Skyride, an aerial cable car, presents a breathtaking view of Vancouver and the harbor on its trip up the mountain. Spend the day here without running out of things to do: Go skiing, zipline above an alpine rain forest, go paragliding or go on a sleigh ride, strap on snowshoes for a wintry hike, watch lumberjacks show off their axe and log-rolling skills, visit grizzly bears and get a 360-degree view of Vancouver from the top of a 20-story-high wind turbine. After you've worked up an appetite, feast on fine cuisine at places to eat like The Observatory or Altitudes Bistro.

- Spot pods of orcas and other sea creatures on a scenic whale-watching cruise. Both **Steveston Seabreeze Adventures** (12551 #1 Rd., Bldg. 43) and **Vancouver Whale Watch** (210-12240 Second Ave.) in Richmond offer the opportunity to hear whales vocalize through hydrophones, see marine animals like sea lions and porpoises and travel through the Fraser River Delta, Strait of Georgia and the Gulf Islands.

- Dine in restaurants that rival New York's; an array of multicultural cuisines is available from local restaurants, but don't leave town without savoring mouth-watering Pacific Northwest and Asian cuisine featuring freshly caught seafood. If you're wondering where to eat, try such favorites as **CinCin** (1154 Robson St.) and **Joe Fortes Seafood & Chop House** (777 Thurlow St.).

- Discover one of Vancouver's trendiest neighborhoods; **Yaletown** (bordered by Homer and Robson streets) has earned comparisons to New York's So'Ho, and rightfully so. Once a warehouse district, the area now attracts the young and hip with its of-the-moment shops, galleries, loft apartments, pubs and outdoor cafés.

- Confront your fear of heights with a walk through the tops of evergreens at ⬥ **Capilano Suspension Bridge Park** (3735 Capilano Rd.) in North Vancouver; the 137-metre (450-foot) bridge sways 70 metres (230 ft.) above the Capilano River Canyon and is a top pick for adventure travel. View the Totem Park and learn about the area's indigenous culture through storytelling, weaving and beadwork demonstrations.

- Take in ⬥ **VanDusen Botanical Garden** (5251 Oak St.), which takes full advantage of the local climate. Wander the meandering paths of the 22-hectare (5-acre) paradise to find 40 themed gardens. A highlight is a hedge maze made of 3,000 pyramidal cedars.

Stanley Park Horse-drawn Tours

Vancouver 1-day Itinerary

AAA editors suggest these activities for a great short vacation experience. Those staying in the area for a longer visit can access a 3-day itinerary at AAA.com/TravelGuides.

Morning

- Kick off your first day of vacation at the **Vancouver Lookout at Harbour Centre Tower** (555 W. Hastings St.). A glass elevator zips to the top of this 168-metre-tall (553-ft.) building, where 360-degree views of the skyline, the North Shore mountains, English Bay, Coal Harbour and Stanley Park will take your breath away. Your admission ticket is valid all day, so plan to return at dusk to see the city twinkling with lights.

- Walk a few blocks toward the waterfront to reach Jack Poole Plaza (outside the Vancouver Convention Centre at 1055 Canada Pl.). Snap a photo of the **Olympic Cauldron**—a memento from the 2010 Winter Olympic Games held in Vancouver—before making your way to the paved waterfront **Seawall**, which affords great views of seaplanes and cruise ships coming and going in Coal Harbour.

- Follow the Seawall west to  **Stanley Park** (main entrance at west end of Georgia Street), your next destination and one of the top things to do in Vancouver. (If you'd rather not walk, you can ride a TransLink bus or rent bicycles from a shop on Denman Street.) Dense forests, beautiful waterfront views, beaches, hiking trails and totem poles are just a few of the things to see within the park's 405 hectares (1,000 acres). Follow the 9-kilometre-long (5.6-mi.) Seawall promenade around the perimeter, or explore the park on a leisurely 1-hour carriage ride offered by **Stanley Park Horse-drawn Tours** (735 Stanley Park Dr.).

- If you're traveling with kids, plan to spend at least an hour or two at the **Vancouver Aquarium** (in Stanley Park at 845 Avison Way), home to penguins, sea lions, otters, sharks and other creatures of the deep.

Afternoon

- When your stomach starts grumbling for lunch, make your way to Granville Island, where the **Granville Island Public Market** (1689 Johnston St.) draws serious foodies. (A pleasant way to get there is by pedestrian-only ferry; Aquabus and False Creek Ferries will whisk you from downtown to Granville Island in less than 10 minutes.) Stalls at the market showcase every type of edible imaginable—all locally sourced or produced, of course—while artists and designers hawk unique gifts and souvenirs.

- If a sit-down lunch is in order, try **The Sandbar Seafood Restaurant** (on Granville Island at 1535 Johnston St.), a lively spot with an outdoor patio and picturesque waterfront views.

- Back on the mainland, spend the afternoon shopping in **Yaletown** (bordered by Homer and

Caption: Spend the afternoon shopping in Yaletown

Robson streets), one of Vancouver's trendiest neighborhoods. Often compared to New York's SoHo, the former warehouse district attracts the young and hip with swank furniture shops, art galleries and clothing boutiques. Another popular shopping district is **Robson Street** (between Burrard and Jervis streets), where you'll find recognizable brands like Banana Republic, Zara and Lululemon Athletica.

Evening

- There's no shortage of outstanding restaurants in Vancouver, so picking a dinner spot may take some time. Enjoy happy hour specials and casual New American cuisine at **Cactus Club Café** (357 Davie St. in Yaletown); go for seafood at **Rodney's Oyster House** (1228 Hamilton St.); or dress up for a romantic dinner amid ivy-covered walls at **Brix & Mortar** (1138 Homer St.).

- On a clear summer evening, watching the sunset from a local beach park is an activity that won't cost you a dime. Head to **English Bay Beach Park** (1700 Beach Ave.) or **Sunset Beach** (1204 Beach Ave.) with an ice cream cone or a coffee in hand. Find a seat on a driftwood log or a bench along the seawall and enjoy the show of vivid oranges and reds streaking across the sky.

- Not ready to call it a night? Dozens of bars, nightclubs and music venues line downtown's **Granville Street**. Or join the locals for microbrews and a billiard game at **Yaletown Brewing Company** (1111 Mainland St.); the doors don't close until 3 a.m. on Friday and Saturday nights.

Top Picks for Kids

Under 13

- **Granville Island** (1689 Johnston St.) lures adults to its markets and shops, but it also has fun things to do and specialty shops that appeal directly to youngsters. Under a rainbow-colored sign, the **Granville Island Kids Market** (1496 Cartwright St.) is a miniature mall that's the perfect destination for little ones. From the moment they step through the diminutive door, kids can eyeball goodies in 23 shops that cater to their every whim, cavort in the arcade and make a splash in the water park (open in summer months).

- What kid doesn't enjoy face painting, storytelling, jugglers, stilt-walkers, puppet shows, dance and music? Find all this and more during May's weeklong **Vancouver International Children's Festival,** also on Granville Island.

- When it's time to quiet growling tummies, longtime favorite **White Spot** is one of the kid-friendly local restaurants; it has several locations throughout the city. Small fries can get a burger, grilled cheese sandwich or spaghetti in a ship-shaped Pirate Pak, complete with a chocolate coin.

Teens

- The flight simulator ride at **FlyOver Canada** (201-999 Canada Pl.) will elicit screams and gasps of delight as it sweeps and soars from east to west over icebergs, Niagara Falls, the Rocky Mountains and other unforgettable landmarks of the Canadian countryside.

Grouse Mountain

- Go on a full-day adventure with **Prince of Whales Whale Watching** (1601 Bayshore Dr.). Your family will have a whale of a time as they gaze in awe at pods of glistening orcas and grey humpbacks leaping out of the Georgia Strait. The trip also includes a stop in Victoria and a visit to Butchart Gardens.

- For adventure and nature lovers (and those who aren't afraid of heights), travel to 🍁 **Grouse Mountain** (6400 Nancy Greene Way) in **North Vancouver.** Ascend to the peak in an enclosed gondola, skimming over treetops on the way up. Brave souls can ride to the top of a wind turbine for views that go on for miles.

- 🍁 **Capilano Suspension Bridge Park** (3735 Capilano Rd.), also in **North Vancouver,** yields more adventure for those in search of adventurous things to do on vacation. Tread slowly along a swaying 137-metre-long (450-ft.) footbridge above the treetops and the Capilano River, which spans 70 metres deep (230 feet). But don't fear, Mom and Dad: The bridge is reinforced with steel cables and concrete, so it's perfectly safe. After you cross the bridge, head for Cliffwalk, a 650-foot cliffside walkway with bridges and viewing platforms suspended from Douglas fir trees with a stunning canyon view.

All Ages

- Combining manicured gardens with West Coast rainforests, beaches, forest trails and surrounded on three sides by water, 🍁 **Stanley Park** (main entrance at west end of Georgia St.) offers amazing views of the mountains, the city and English Bay. Rent a bike and pedal along the 9-kilometre (5.6-mi.) seawall. The park has totem poles, a miniature train, playgrounds, a pool, a water park and other fun places to go.

- Need a break from walking? Hop on a trolley on **Stanley Park Horse-drawn Tours** (735 Stanley Park Dr.) and see the 400-hectare (1,000-acre) park at a leisurely pace.

- Meet the most adorable sea creatures at Stanley Park's **Vancouver Aquarium** (845 Avison Way). Ogle rascally otters, pudgy sea lions and spotted harbor seals are just some of the marine animals that call the aquarium home. Get super close at animal encounters, where you can feed and help train sea lions, otters and penguins.

- From the moment they set eyes on **Science World at TELUS World of Science** (1455 Quebec St.), kids will be psyched; housed in a huge geodesic dome, the science center is even cooler inside. There's something for every age group. Tykes under age 7 can learn about water, color, light and movement in the Kidspace Gallery, and the entire family will enjoy live shows, hands-on exhibits and IMAX films that bring out their inner scientist. Check their calendar for a list of things to do today.

Arriving
By Car

Hwy. 1 (Trans-Canada Highway) and hwys. 1A and 7 are the major east-west routes to Vancouver. To reach downtown on the Trans-Canada Highway, use the First Avenue exit or continue to Hastings Street.

Hwy. 99 to S.W. Marine West becomes the major downtown artery, Granville Street. Before becoming a city street, Hwy. 99 begins its journey as I-5 at the Mexican border and crosses through California and the Pacific Northwest; beyond Vancouver it continues beyond Whistler to meet Hwy. 97, the main north-south route.

Getting Around
Street System

All streets and avenues in downtown Vancouver are named; many are one-way. Outside the business section, east-west avenues are numbered beginning with First Avenue, and north-south streets are named. Addresses begin at Ontario-Carrall streets for all east-west numbering and at Powell-Dundas streets for all north-south numbering.

The downtown peninsula is connected to western Vancouver by the Burrard, Granville and Cambie bridges and to North Vancouver and West Vancouver by the Lions Gate and the Iron Workers Memorial (Second Narrows) bridges.

Rush hours are 6-9:30 a.m. and 3-6:30 p.m. Right turns on red are permitted after a stop, unless otherwise posted; drivers must yield to pedestrians and vehicles in the intersection and to city buses pulling into traffic.

SkyTrain

Some intersections in the metropolitan area have a blinking green light. This is used when there is a stop sign, not a signal, on the cross street and allows pedestrians or bicyclists to turn the main street's light red so they can go through the intersection safely. When driving on a cross street, you must wait for a gap in traffic before you proceed.

Parking

On-street parking, controlled by meter, is restricted on many thoroughfares during rush hours; violators' cars will be towed. When parking at a meter, you can pay by credit card, coins or even by phone if you download the PayByPhone mobile app; phone (604) 909-7275 for information. Off-street parking is available in lots and garages at rates ranging from $1.25 per half-hour to $11 or more per day. Parking in a school zone between 8 and 5 on any school day is strictly prohibited unless otherwise posted.

Public Transportation

TransLink, Metro Vancouver's regional transportation authority, offers an integrated system utilizing bus, rail, SeaBus, cycling paths and roads to points throughout Vancouver and all suburban areas. Conventional buses and electric buses link tourist destinations, transit exchanges and SkyTrain stations; phone (604) 953-3333.

SeaBus is a passenger-only ferry that crosses Burrard Inlet, connecting downtown Vancouver with the North Shore, a destination popular with those in search of adventure travel. The downtown Waterfront terminal connects with buses and the SkyTrain. The Lonsdale Quay terminal connects with an extensive North Shore bus network.

SkyTrain, Vancouver's light-rail rapid transit system, runs from Waterfront Station through downtown Vancouver to the suburbs of Burnaby and New Westminster and across the Fraser River to the suburb of Surrey. SkyTrain is one of the longest and oldest automated, driverless light rapid transit systems in the world and has three lines. The 19-kilometre (12-mi.) Canada Line connects downtown with Richmond and Vancouver International Airport and has 16 stations, including stops at Vancouver City Centre, Olympic Village, Broadway-City Hall, Marine Drive, Vancouver International Airport and four Richmond locations. The train ride from downtown to the airport takes 26 minutes. The Expo Line and Millennium Line connect downtown with the cities of Burnaby, New Westminster and Surrey.

Trains operate every 7 to 15 minutes Mon.-Fri. 5:22 a.m.-1:16 a.m., Sat. 6:50 a.m.-12:30 a.m., Sun. 7:16 a.m.-12:16 p.m. Fares are the same for any TransLink service and a single fare covers travel for up to 90 minutes across Metro Vancouver. A 1-zone fare Monday through Friday until 6:30 p.m. is $3, a 2-zone fare is $4.25 and a 3-zone fare is $5.75; for ages 5-13, students ages 14-19 with a valid GoCard and ages 65+ a 1-zone fare is $1.95, a 2-zone fare is $2.95 and a 3-zone fare is $3.95. The fare for weekdays after 6:30 p.m. and Saturday, Sunday and holidays for all zones is $3; for ages 5-13, students ages 14-19 with a valid GoCard and ages 65+ the fare for all zones is $1.95. A trip from the airport to any destination adds an additional $5.

Every SkyTrain station has information panels. A 1-day pass, available from SkyTrain and SeaBus ticket machines, Safeway food stores and 7-11 stores, costs $10.50 and covers all zones; for ages 5-13, students ages 14-19 with a valid GoCard and ages 65+ the cost is $8.25. If you pay by cash on buses, exact change is required. Phone (604) 953-3333 daily 6:30 a.m.-11:30 p.m. for more information.

The little blue False Creek Ferries provide service from the West End of downtown to Granville Island, with stops at fun places to go like Yaletown, Plaza of Nations, The Village (Science World), Spyglass Place, Stamps Landing, David Lam Park, Granville Island, the Aquatic Centre and the Maritime Museum, departing between every two minutes and every 15 minutes, depending on the route and time of day. Tickets cost $3.50-$11 one-way, $9-$17 round-trip, and $16 for a day pass, with discounts for ages 4-12 and ages 65+.

Aquabus Ltd., (604) 689-5858, provides ferry service with departures every five minutes between Hornby Street, Granville Island, David Lam Park, Stamps Landing, Spyglass Place, Yaletown, Plaza of Nations and The Village daily 7:07 a.m.-9:07 p.m. Times vary according to destination. Fare ranges from $3.50-$6 one-way or $25 for 20 tickets, and $16 for a day pass, with discounts for ages 4-12 and ages 65+. Aquabuses are equipped to carry wheelchairs and bicycles.

Daily bus service between Vancouver International Airport and Whistler is provided by Pacific Coach's YVR Whistler SkyLynx. Passengers can be picked up and dropped off at major Vancouver and Whistler lodgings; reservations are required. Phone (604) 662-7575 or (800) 661-1725 for information or ask your AAA travel agent about vacation packages. To reach the airport from Vancouver by public transit, take Bus 90 B-line from Burrard station to Richmond Centre, then transfer to bus 424 to the airport.

Shopping

Yaletown, reached via Davie Street, is the fashionable downtown residential address for successful young professionals (just look at all those glass-walled condo towers). This former 19th-century rail yard district has morphed into an uber-stylish urban enclave; the industrial brick warehouses of yore are now hip clothing boutiques, designer furniture outlets and local restaurants and bars that draw a crowd.

Art galleries are concentrated along Homer and Mainland streets. Yaletown's many dog owners shop for trendy canine accessories at **barking babies** (1188 Homer St.); phone (604) 647-2275. Keep your head stylishly warm and dry with a fedora, derby or baseball cap from **Goorin Bros.** (1188 Hamilton St.), a cool hat shop that may remind you of your grandfather's living room, complete with Victrola and

Goorin Bros.

leather sofa; phone (604) 683-1895. For a lovely vacation souvenir that doesn't feature a maple leaf, pick up a flowery Royal Albert teapot or some Cristal D'Arques stemware at **The Cross Decor & Design** (1198 Homer St.); phone (604) 689-2900.

Robson Street, however, is downtown's shopping central. Stand at the intersection of Robson and Burrard on any given day and it's a sea of shopping bag-toting humanity. From Burrard up to Jervis Street Robson offers an uninterrupted stretch of window gazing: men's and women's fashions and accessories, shoes, jewelry, eyewear, gifts, chocolates, cosmetics, luggage and travel gear, plus more places to eat than you can shake a stick at. For high-quality clothing and outerwear go to **Roots**, a popular Canadian chain. There are two locations, one for adults (1001 Robson St.), phone (604) 683-4305, and one for kids (1153 Robson St.), phone (604) 684-8801. Founded in Vancouver in 1998, lululemon (970 Robson St.) is now is a global brand selling athletic apparel for yoga, running and dance; phone (604) 681-3118.

Very touristy but always enjoyable **Gastown**, the oldest section of the city, runs for several blocks along Water Street. The atmosphere is turn-of-the-20th-century renovated, with handsome brick buildings and white-globed lamp posts decorated with flowers in hanging baskets. There are lots of art galleries, antique shops, fashion boutiques and souvenir shops. But Gastown isn't all about maple candy or a moose in a can; trendy home furnishings stores sell sleek, contemporary furniture by well-known Canadian and international designers.

Standout shops and fun places to go in Gastown include cutting-edge **John Fluevog Shoes** (65

Water St.) which combines a vintage vibe with Dr Marten-esque cool; phone (604) 688-6228. Stop in at **Kit and Ace** (165 Water St.) and pick up a couple of their affordable, comfy *and* machine-washable cashmere-blend T-shirts; phone (604) 559-8363.

There's a **Coastal Peoples Fine Arts Gallery** here as well (332 Water St.); phone (604) 684-9222. **Gallery Gachet** (9 W. Hastings St.) is a non-profit artist-run center with exhibitions; phone (604) 687-2468. There also are specialty shops like **Button Button** (318 Homer St.); phone (604) 687-0067, with buttons in all shapes and sizes from around the world, and **Jade Mine** (594 176th St. in Surrey), which stocks a big selection of sculptures and jewelry carved from jade mined in northern British Columbia. Phone (604) 538-4525. Pet lovers will want to make the trip to **EZ Dog** (56 Powell St.), packed with goodies for your "best friend"; phone (604) 559-5606.

Note: While exploring the main thoroughfares in Gastown are fun things to do in Vancouver during the day, use big-city common sense regarding any encounters with panhandlers and street people, and avoid wandering around side streets after dark.

Downtown certainly isn't the only place to shop and find things to do. In **Kitsilano**, along the south shore of English Bay, the blocks of West 4th Avenue between Fir and Larch streets are filled with gift shops, wine shops and stores selling fashions, athleisure attire and sports gear from bikes to skis to snowboards.

The 10-block stretch of Granville Street between 6th and 16th avenues—dubbed **South Granville**—is where old-money families do their shopping; think expensive clothing boutiques, upscale furniture retailers and a plethora of home accessories stores. **Urbanity** (2412 Granville St.) sells beautiful knit sweaters, coats and blankets, most bought direct from Scandinavian designers; phone (604) 801-6262.

Much more down to earth is **Commercial Drive**, east of Main Street from Venables Street to East Broadway, one of Vancouver's funkiest shopping experiences. Most of the shops, businesses and nearby restaurants are owner-operated; chains are few, which means that it's really fun to explore. Hit "the Drive" on a Saturday or Sunday afternoon. The heart of Commercial Drive is between Venables Street and 6th Avenue E. Books, CDs, vintage clothing and unusual gifts are all good bets.

If you're looking for things to do this weekend, you could easily spend an entire day doing **Granville Island**, but shoppers and foodies should focus on the **Granville Island Public Market.** The big building is crammed with vendors: produce, meat, seafood, baked goods, coffee and a head-spinning array of specialty foods. Take advantage of fresh BC salmon, artisanal cheeses and ripe, regionally grown fruit. Have lunch here, too; fast food counters offer Asian, Mexican, Indian, sushi, pizza and just about everything else as takeout. Phone (604) 666-6655.

There also are plenty of shops outside the market selling regionally produced art, food, jewelry, clothing, kids' toys and the like. And don't drive—it's much easier to take the False Creek Ferry. It's a 10-minute ride to Granville Island from the Aquatic Centre dock just off Beach Drive in the West End (ferries also depart from the dock at the foot of Davie Street in Yaletown).

Another popular shopping destination is the **Lonsdale Quay Market**, 123 Carrie Cates Ct. at the foot of Lonsdale Avenue in North Vancouver; phone (604) 985-6261. The lower level is a fresh market with vendors selling produce, seafood, baked goods and delicatessen items; specialty boutiques are on the upper level. Get a crab roll, fish and chips or a panini sandwich from one of the numerous stands at the international food bar and enjoy it outside on the dock, which has a great view of downtown and the harbor (don't feed the seagulls; they'll snitch a bite at any opportunity). There's a parkade for market customers—enter your car license plate number at one of the machines (1 hour of free parking, $3 per additional hour, free after 6 p.m. and on weekends), but it often fills up; you also can take the SeaBus, which shuttles between the downtown and North Vancouver terminals every 15 minutes. Conveniently, the SeaBus terminal is just a few minutes' walk from the market.

Malls? Vancouver has several, if that's your shopping thing. Downtown, upscale **Pacific Centre** (corner of Georgia and Howe streets) is anchored by tony Holt Renfrew and Nordstrom's flagship store. The center's 60-plus other stores offer men's

Granville Island

and ladies' wear, casual clothing, fashion accessories, shoes, electronics, sporting goods, handbags and cosmetics; shops include American Eagle Outfitters, Club Monaco, Ermenegildo Zegna, H&M, lululemon, Michael Kors and Ted Baker London; phone (604) 688-7235.

On the North Shore in West Vancouver, the city's second largest mall, **Park Royal** (on either side of Marine Drive, just west of Taylor Way and the Lions Gate Bridge) consists of two enclosed malls with anchor Simons plus more than 200 stores and restaurants as well as **The Village**, specialty shops and cafés in an open-air setting. It is open Mon. 11-7, Tues. 10-7, Wed.-Fri. 10-9, Sat. 9:30-7, Sun and holidays 11-6; phone (604) 922-3211. Park Royal's expanded and modernized south section is now open, while the north section is nearing completion of its renovations; in the south section are such stores as Anthropologie, The Body Shop, Free People, Old Navy, Sephora and Zara, among many others.

McArthurGlen Designer Outlet Mall is next to Vancouver International Airport in Richmond (1000-7899 Templeton Station Rd.) and the Canada Line station; the European-style, open-air mall has more than 70 stores with a focus on designer brands such as Armani, Coach, Cole Haan and Polo Ralph Lauren; hours are Mon.-Sat. 10-9, Sun. and statutory holidays 10-7. The mall also has flight arrival and departure screens for those who are shopping pre-flight. From downtown Vancouver, take the Canada Line to Templeton Station; from there, it's a 3-minute walk. Phone (604) 231-5525.

For a true mega-mall experience, head to **Burnaby** and **Metropolis at Metrotown**, 4700 Kingsway (Hwy. 1A/99A) between Willingdon and Royal Oak avenues; phone (604) 438-4715. It's the province's largest shopping center, with Hudson's Bay (outfitters for the Canadian Olympic team) and more than 350 other stores on three sprawling levels. Expect the usual chains and specialty outlets—everything from American Eagle Outfitters to Zara—plus a food court and the latest box-office biggies at SilverCity. The mall is open Mon.-Sat. 10-9, Sun. and certain holidays 10-7, although a few stores may vary. Parking (plenty of it) is free.

Built in 1959, **Oakridge Centre**, 650 W. 41st Ave. at Cambie Street, is Vancouver's oldest mall, but that doesn't mean it's not packed with popular mall retailers. *Au contraire*, it has about 75 stores, including perennial favorites Apple, Banana Republic, Coach, Crate & Barrel, lululemon, MAC Cosmetics, Michael Kors and Tiffany & Co.; Hudson's Bay is its anchor. The center is open Mon.-Tues. and Sat. 9:30-7, Wed.-Fri. 9:30-9, Sun. 11-6 (holiday hours may vary). Future plans for the mall include a $1.5-billion expansion, part of a massive area redevelopment that will enhance the shopping experience and also include residential and office buildings and green spaces. Phone (604) 261-2511.

Relax over drinks in a quiet, elegant atmosphere.

Nightlife

Hip, cosmopolitan Vancouver has a buzzing nightlife, with plenty of spots where locals and visitors congregate after dark. Several sophisticated hotel lounges offer a space to relax over drinks in a quiet, elegant atmosphere. Downtown is a prime spot for these given its assortment of business-class hotels.

Bacchus Lounge, in The Wedgewood Hotel & Spa (downtown at 845 Hornby St.), is an elegant spot to enjoy a glass of B.C. wine or a martini in surroundings that just ooze luxury—subdued lighting, antique furniture and vases of fresh flowers, with a softly tinkling piano in the background. There's live entertainment here nightly, which makes it an ideal destination if you're looking for things for couples to do. It's recommended to dress to impress. Phone (604) 608-5319.

You'll find a lively vibe at **Shark Club Sports Bar & Grill** in the Sandman Hotel Vancouver City Centre (180 W. Georgia St.). This stylishly renovated sports bar has two massive TVs and a weekday happy hour, and it's just a 5-minute walk from BC Place. If you're wondering where to eat before or after a concert or Canucks game, Shark Club is a safe bet; phone (604) 687-4275.

Opus Bar, in the boutique Opus Hotel (322 Davie St.), is a cool, sleek lounge in trendy **Yaletown**. DJs spin dance music for a fashionably dressed, upwardly mobile crowd on weekends, and there's live music every Wednesday; phone (604) 642-6787.

Another hip spot is **Yaletown Brewing Company** (1111 Mainland St.), where suit-and-ties gather after business hours to shoot some pool and sip on microbrews and burgers; sit by the fireplace or out on the spacious patio, depending on the weather; phone (604) 681-2739.

Granville Street is hopping with nightclubs, all with reasonable cover charges. **The Roxy** (932 Granville St.) draws a young, ready-to-party crowd with house bands pumping out rock and Top 40 and bartenders who put on their own show. If you don't feel like dancing, watch TV or play pool. It's open 8 p.m.-3 a.m. nightly; phone (604) 331-7999.

The **Commodore Ballroom** (868 Granville St.) is an old-time dance hall that is the place to see up-and-coming bands as well as established acts that don't sell out arenas. The dance floor is in front of the stage and table seating is limited; arrive early unless you don't mind standing in the back of the room. Phone (604) 739-4550.

Touristy **Gastown** pulses with nightspots, local restaurants and fun things to do with friends. The **Steamworks Brew Pub** (375 Water St.) is named for the Gastown steam line that runs through the premises. The drink of choice here is beer (brewed nearby in Burnaby, B.C.), from signature Lions Gate lager to such concoctions as an oatmeal stout and a sour IPA. The basement looks like a Bavarian-style drinking hall, while upstairs the atmosphere is clubbier, with leather chairs and windows overlooking the harbor; phone (604) 689-2739.

Energetic live bands tear it up at **The Revel Room** (238 Abbott St.), as they crank out rockabilly, blues, old country, Texas swing, boogie woogie and soul Tues.-Sun. nights beginning at 7 p.m., and there's daily boogie piano during "Sour Hour" (4-6:30 p.m.); phone (604) 687-4088.

You'll literally have to go underground to get to Gastown's **Guilt & Co.** (1 Alexander St.), as it's down a flight of stairs under a restaurant on Gassy Jack Square. This intimate hangout has the feel of a bunker or an unfinished rec room, but reeks of cool and attracts smartly dressed young professionals. The evening's band plays on a small stage backed by a stone wall, a small dance floor sandwiched between it and round tables holding burning candles. Guilt & Co. serves up expertly mixed cocktails with whimsical names like You Can Dance and Like a Virgin; phone (604) 288-1704.

Baby boomers will feel right at home in **The Cascade Room** (2616 Main St.), in the Mount Pleasant neighborhood. This restaurant and bar is a transplanted bit of British pub culture: Lampshades feature Queen Victoria's likeness, and a large glass panel advises patrons to "Keep calm and carry on"—a World War II slogan uttered by stiff-upper-lip Brits. Slide into one of the horseshoe-shaped booths for a cocktail, a beer or a pint of lager; phone (604) 709-8650.

If you're in the Kitsilano area and looking for fun things to do, plan to stop at the **Shameful Tiki Room** (4362 Main St.), a modern-day Trader Vic's. The room is decked out in Polynesian decor from floor to ceiling in painstaking detail, with a thatched ceiling, carved wood Tiki gods, puffer fish lamps, vintage postcards permanently lacquered onto tables and vintage Tiki memorabilia. Sip a mai tai, snack on small plates, or go for the volcano bowl, a potent blend of liquors served in a huge clamshell meant for sharing with three of your closest friends (the drink is accompanied by thunder, lightning and smoke from the bar's erupting volcano). Unlike most clubs, the tunes are played at lower decibels here so you can carry on a conversation, and the overall ambience is relaxing yet fun; phone (604) 999-5684.

If you're into casino games *and* live bands, lucky you! In addition to the usual slot machines and poker tables, the **Hard Rock Casino Vancouver** in nearby Coquitlam has three listening rooms: the intimate Asylum Sound Stage, where performers range from local bands to burlesque to comedy; the 100-seat Unlisted Lounge, with DJ'd jazz and electro-groove music and the occasional live act; and The Molson Canadian Theatre, a 1,000-seat venue hosting tribute bands, up-and-coming performers and 1980s heavy metal bands. Phone (604) 523-6888.

And here's a beautifully simple suggestion for nightlife near downtown Vancouver. On a clear evening, head down to **English Bay Beach** (just off Beach Avenue at the south end of Denman Street). First, stop and get an ice cream cone (or some takeout from one of the many nearby restaurants), then sit on a beach log or a bench along the seawall promenade and watch the sun set over the bay. In addition to the sunset, you'll have a superb view of the mountains rising beyond the North Shore. It's just you and nature—plus the company of similar-minded souls.

The *Georgia Straight*, a news and entertainment weekly that comes out on Thursday, has extensive arts and entertainment listings for things to do in Vancouver.

Big Events

Vancouver is an energetic city with plenty to celebrate, and its citizens know how to start the year off right. On January 1, more than 1,000 fearless swimmers brave the icy waters of **English Bay** in the annual **Polar Bear Swim**. The event includes a 91-metre (100-yd.) race and attracts thousands of spectators, some dressed in wild costumes.

Kung Hay Fat Choy! You'll probably hear this traditional Chinese blessing over and over during Chinese New Year, a Chinese holiday which occurs between late January and mid-February. The ⛩ **Vancouver Chinese New Year Parade** in Chinatown begins with activities at the **Dr. Sun Yat-Sen Classical Chinese Garden**; have your fortune told, learn calligraphy, watch martial artists and listen to storytellers. A parade winds through the streets of Chinatown in the afternoon.

Celebrate the return of spring in April with the **Vancouver Sun Run**, reputedly the second largest 10K run in North America. Cheer on tens of thousands of participants as they sprint or stroll through downtown, enjoying views of English Bay and Stanley Park with live music played along the route. For active travelers, the Sun Run is a great excuse to book a vacation in Vancouver.

In late May and early June, the **Vancouver International Children's Festival** is a weeklong party for kids on **Granville Island**. Entertainers from around the world put on plays and puppet shows as well as dance and musical performances. Fun things to do include face painting, kite flying and playing in clay; jugglers, stilt-walkers, clowns and wandering minstrels create a carnival-like atmosphere.

You'll fall in love with Shakespeare at the **Bard on the Beach Shakespeare Festival** from early June through late September. Watch tragedies and comedies staged in front of the mountains and English Bay in **Vanier Park.** Select performances include a salmon Bard-B-Q during intermission and fireworks after the show. The festival is one of the best things for couples to do in summer.

Cultural entertainment sails into **False Creek** with the **Concord Pacific Dragon Boat Festival** in mid-June. Also held in June is the **Vancouver International Jazz Festival,** which features legendary jazz musicians and vocalists playing at various jazz joints, parks and public places. Past performers include Miles Davis, Wynton Marsalis, Tito Puente and Diana Krall.

Has all that jazz put you in the mood for more music? The **Vancouver Folk Music Festival** at **Jericho Beach Park** draws fans from as far away as Los Angeles for concerts during mid-July. Book your travel packages and vacation packages early or contact your AAA travel agency to plan your trip.

Celebration of Light features 3 nights of fireworks displays and is held at English Bay the last week of July and the first week in August.

In late August, your childhood memories of the county fair will come rushing back at **The Fair at Pacific National Exhibition.** Ride the merry-go-round, root for your favorite swine at a pig race, bite into a crisp candy apple and try your luck on the midway. You'll also find live music, agricultural exhibits, a beer garden, talent contests and much more.

For 11 days in September, step outside of the norm at the **Vancouver International Fringe Festival.** Uncensored theatrical shows by about 100 international groups and performers defy the rules of conventional theater. Most of the shows take place on Granville Island. If you're looking for fun things to do with friends, this is it.

Interested in things to do during the holidays? December brings several holiday-themed events to the city. During the **Carol Ships Parade of Lights,** vessels adorned with Christmas lights and decorations sail in **Vancouver Harbor** almost every night, passing many Vancouver neighborhoods. Landlubbers celebrate with live music, craft workshops, bonfires and hot chocolate.

Bright Nights in Stanley Park, a holiday tradition of more than 30 years, turns the forest and the train into a wonderland with more than 2 million lights and animated displays.

More than a million shimmering lights greet you at ▽ **VanDusen Botanical Garden** during the **Festival of Lights.** Dancing lights on Livingstone Lake twinkle in time to holiday music, and a water terrace is turned into a "magic marsh" complete with fiber-optic lights and whimsical creatures. Choral music and a storytelling Santa add to the magic.

Commemorate the beginning of winter at the **Winter Solstice Lantern Festival,** held on a late-December evening. Join a procession of lantern-holding revelers accompanied by drummers, beginning at either **Science World at TELUS World of Science** or **Strathcona Community Centre** and ending at Dr. Sun Yat-Sen Classical Chinese Garden, where you'll enjoy ethereal music and enchanting lighted gardens.

Sports & Rec

Skiing on Grouse Mountain in the morning, golfing on the banks of the Fraser River in the afternoon, fishing for salmon in Horseshoe Bay at dusk and taking a dip in English Bay, all in one day? It's possible in Vancouver, which offers such a diversity of recreational opportunities that you'll have no trouble finding adventurous things to do and fun places to go while visiting.

Vancouver's park system has tennis courts, swimming pools, putting greens, golf courses, lawn bowling greens, hiking paths and a comprehensive bike route. For information phone the city's Parks and Recreation Department at 311 (within Vancouver).

VanDusen Botanical Garden

Bicyclists will have a field day in Vancouver, which is practically a mecca for two-wheeling types. There are about 400 kilometres (249 mi.) of bike paths in the city. The Stanley Park Seawall, 9 kilometres (6 mi.) long, may be the most well-known bike route in the area, and for good reason. There's no shortage of eye candy and things to see—Burrard Inlet, Coal Harbour, rocky beaches, the North Shore mountains, totem poles, downtown Vancouver—for riders or pedestrians while circling Stanley Park. Want more? The seawall is just one section of the 28-kilometre (17-mi.) Seaside Greenway, which begins at the convention center, runs along Coal Harbour, around Stanley Park to Granville Island and Kitsilano Beach, then west along the Point Grey Road Greenway to Jericho Beach and Spanish Banks Beach Park. Note that bike helmets are required by law.

Head for the hills of the North Shore mountains to practice your **extreme mountain biking** skills. Burnaby Mountain also comes equipped with structures and a 28-kilometre (17-mi.) network of trails where you can practice stunts. For tamer rides, coast flat trails through heavily wooded forests in Pacific Spirit Regional Park. Bicycle rentals (mountain, comfort, cruiser, hybrid and tandem) can be found had at Bayshore Rentals, 745 Denman St.; phone (604) 688-2453. In North Vancouver, rent all-mountain, cross-country, trail and freeride bikes at Endless Biking, 1467 Crown St; phone (604) 985-2519 or (604) 836-2517 after hours.

The North Shore is a good place for **hiking**, too. The 48-km (30-mi.) Baden-Powell Centennial Trail follows a rugged route across the North Shore, stretching from Horseshoe Bay in West Vancouver to Deep Cove on the eastern side of North Vancouver. A nice section of the Baden-Powell Trail for novices and families is accessible from Deep Cove; park near the trailhead at Panorama Park and hike 45 minutes to reach the scenic viewpoint at Quarry Rock. After the hike, you can join the locals for celebratory sweets at Honey Doughnuts & Goodies (4373 Gallant Ave., North Vancouver). More family-friendly hiking trails can be found at Lynn Canyon Park, where there are waterfalls, swimming holes, a suspension bridge and a seasonal café.

Go **swimming** in English Bay, which is bordered by beaches from West Point Grey to Stanley Park, most with lifeguards in summer and various amenities. Beaches are easily accessible from Northwest Marine Drive in West Point Grey, Point Grey Road in Vancouver West and from Beach Avenue downtown. Two of the most popular beaches to visit are Kitsilano Beach (with an outdoor saltwater pool and views of the downtown skyline) and Second Beach in Stanley Park (with another outdoor pool). If you want to avoid the crowds on a sunny day, head to Stanley Park's Third Beach, which has a concession stand, restrooms and its own parking lot. There are additional outdoor pools at Maple Grove and New Brighton.

White-water rafting is available April through September on the nearby Chilliwack River and a little farther afield on the Fraser and Thompson rivers, including the Devil's Gorge. Vancouver rafting companies offering day trips as well as multiday trips include REO Rafting Adventure Resort, (604) 941-9777 or (800) 736-7238, and Kumsheen Rafting Resort, (250) 455-2296 or (800) 663-6667. Lotus Land Tours offers **sea kayaking** trips on Indian Arm, Zodiac tours of Howe Sound and **whale-watching** tours; phone (604) 684-4922 or (800) 528-3531.

Winter visitors in search of **skiing** can head for the hills in North Vancouver to tackle the challenging slopes of Grouse Mountain or Mount Seymour Provincial Park (see attraction listings). East of Vancouver are Hemlock Valley and Manning Park ski resorts, offering both downhill and cross-country treks. Cypress Provincial Park in West Vancouver also has cross-country and downhill skiing (see Recreation Areas Chart). Serious skiers and snowboarders will want to head north of Vancouver to Whistler and Blackcomb mountains.

When the waters sparkle from the summer sun, Vancouver becomes a **boating** paradise. For visitors without a boat, several companies have craft for hourly or daily rental. For **fishing** charters and boat rentals phone Sewell's Marina, (604) 921-3474, at Horseshoe Bay or Granville Island Boat Rentals, (877) 688-2628.

Vancouver residents love spectator sports, especially **football, hockey** and **soccer.** The BC Lions of the Canadian Football League usually play before capacity crowds in BC Place Stadium, 777 Pacific Blvd. Fans of Major League Soccer can watch the Vancouver Whitecaps FC get their kicks at the same stadium. The Canucks of the National Hockey League compete in Rogers Arena, 800 Griffiths Way; phone (604) 899-7440 for the event hotline. The Vancouver Giants, a junior hockey team, play at the Langley Events Centre, 7888 200th St. in Langley; if you can't get tickets for the Canucks, who often sell out, Giants tickets cost less and offer just as many thrills; phone (604) 822-8800. For more football, soccer and hockey ticket information, phone Ticketmaster, (855) 985-5000 or the automated ticket sales line (855) 985-5500.

Baseball is played by the Vancouver Canadians at Scotiabank Field at Nat Bailey Stadium, 4601 Ontario St.; phone (604) 872-5232 for schedule and ticket information. Indoor **lacrosse** can be enjoyed at Bill Copeland Sports Centre, 3676 Kensington Ave. in Burnaby, (604) 297-4521 or the 24-hour info line (604) 298-0533; and at Queens Park Arena at First Street and Third Avenue in New Westminster, (604) 777-5111.

Thoroughbred racing with pari-mutuel betting is held at Hastings Park Race Course on the grounds of the Pacific National Exhibition; phone (604) 254-1631 or (877) 977-7702 (see attraction listing p. 266).

Note: Policies concerning admittance of children to pari-mutuel betting facilities vary. Phone for information.

Performing Arts

The 2,765-seat **Queen Elizabeth Theatre** at the intersection of Hamilton and Georgia streets, (604) 665-3050 or (800) 840-9227, is a top destination for visitors and home to **Ballet British Columbia**, (604) 732-5003, and the **Vancouver Opera**, (604) 683-0222 and also hosts touring shows. The adjacent **Vancouver Playhouse** presents professional theater, dance, recitals, some opera and chamber music; phone (604) 665-3050. The **Vancouver Symphony Orchestra** performs at the **Orpheum Theatre**, Smithe and Granville streets, and is among the fun things to do with friends; phone (604) 665-3050 for ticket information.

Other prominent theaters presenting dramatic productions include the **Arts Club Theatre**, on Johnston Street on **Granville Island**, (604) 687-1644; the **Metro Theatre**, 1370 Marine Dr. S.W., (604) 266-7191; **Langara College's Studio 58**, 100 W. 49th Ave., (604) 323-5227; and **The Cultch**, 1895 Venables St., (604) 251-1363.

During the summer, concerts and musicals are presented in Stanley Park's Malkin Bowl. **Kitsilano Showboat** at **Kitsilano Beach** presents outdoor variety shows and concerts Monday, Wednesday, Friday and Saturday at 7:30 p.m. from early July to late August (weather permitting). For more information phone (604) 734-7332.

Concerts in such genres as classical, country, pop and rock are presented year-round at the 17,500-seat **Pacific Coliseum**, 100 N. Renfrew St. in Hastings Park, (604) 253-2311, and **Rogers Arena**, 800 Griffiths Way, (604) 899-7400.

The daily papers carry listings of cultural events and things to do this weekend, as do weekly and monthly magazines. Ticket outlets include **Tickets Tonight**, 200 Burrard St., inside the Tourism Vancouver Visitor Centre, and **Collector's Den**, a Ticketmaster outlet, in the Metrotown Mall in Burnaby. Plan to make the trip out to one of these outlets, as tickets must be bought in person and sales usually end at 4 p.m.; there's a limit of four tickets per customer.

Check with your AAA travel agent for information about vacation packages, fun places to go and other things to do in Vancouver that are geared toward the performing arts.

INSIDER INFO:
A Stanley Park Jaunt

Stanley Park is the crown jewel in a city uncommonly blessed with scenic attributes. It is not only a paradise for walkers, hikers, cyclists and adventure travel enthusiasts, but also a truly delightful wooded retreat that's all the more special for being only a stone's throw away from downtown Vancouver's skyscrapers. It's frequently at the top of the list of the best things to do in Vancouver, and one of the best ways to experience the park is to walk the seawall promenade around its perimeter, a distance totaling a bit more than 9 kilometres (5.6 mi.) that you can take at a leisurely or vigorous pace. Discover

Lions Gate Bridge at Stanley Park

what to do in Stanley Park and fun places to go with this guide.

A good starting point for a trip into Stanley Park is English Bay Beach in the West End neighborhood; just follow the paved seawall path. (There is a designated lane for walkers and a separate one for cyclists and roller bladers.) One of the best things about this walk is that it offers an uninterrupted series of scenic water views. To your left, keep an eye out for the stacked stone sculptures that people construct when the rocky beach is accessible during low tide; some of them are quite elaborate.

Once past the swimming pool and facilities at Second Beach, you'll leave many of the casual strollers behind. Between Second Beach and Third Beach the waters of English Bay sparkle in the sun as the seawall runs along sandstone cliffs and conifer-covered hillsides. Third Beach is a good destination for beachcombing at low tide, when the receding waters reveal barnacle-encrusted rocks and pieces of driftwood.

Siwash Rock is a distinctive landmark you can't miss. This sea stack—a geologic feature formed when volcanic action caused a portion of rock to break free from the park foundation—is between 15 and 18 metres (50 and 60 ft.) tall. A small Douglas fir stands at its summit. Past Siwash Rock the seawall rounds the northern end of the park. At Prospect Point you'll be treated to outstanding views of the Lions Gate Bridge and mountains rising from the opposite North Shore.

On the other side of Prospect Point the seawall runs along Burrard Inlet. Stands of Douglas fir, western hemlock and western red cedar are in full

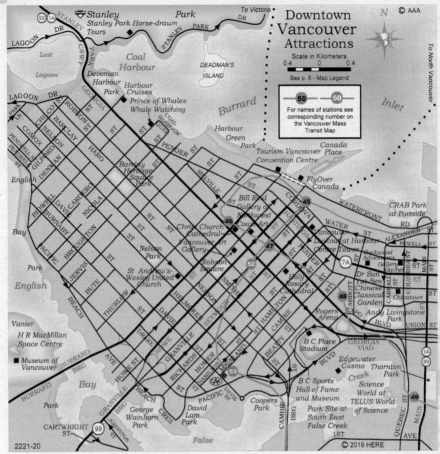

Downtown Vancouver Attractions

Scale in Kilometers
0.4   0   0.4

See p. 6 - Map Legend

For names of stations see corresponding number on the Vancouver Mass Transit Map

© 2019 HERE
2221-20

view on this stretch of the walk. The fierce-looking green dragon arching toward the water is the Empress of Japan Figurehead, a replica of a prow ornament that once graced the RMS *Empress of Japan* ocean liner. Just beyond the dragon is "Girl in Wet Suit," a sculpture of a woman sitting on top of a rock about 9 metres (30 ft.) offshore. Although at first glance you might think she's a mermaid, this girl is wearing flippers and has a scuba mask on her head.

Before reaching Brockton Point you'll see Stanley Park's totem poles standing in a clearing to your right. Interpretive plaques explain the significance of each pole's symbolic figures. Beyond the totems sits the squat Brockton Point Lighthouse. The 9 O'Clock Gun is an old cannon near the tip of Brockton Point; it used to be fired at 6 p.m. to signal the end of the fishing day. Although it goes off electronically these days, the sound is still loud enough to make you jump.

After curving around Brockton Point the seawall runs along the shore of Coal Harbour. There are superb views of the downtown skyline and the yachts and other pleasure craft docked at the harbor. Keep following the paved walkway until you reach the

Georgia Avenue park entrance, which will take you back to the West End. Relaxing at one of the cafes or casual places to eat along Denman Street is a perfect way to end this Stanley Park jaunt. You've earned it.

ATTRACTIONS

For a complete list of attractions, visit AAA.com/travelguides/attractions

BC SPORTS HALL OF FAME AND MUSEUM is at jct. Beatty and Robson sts., Gate A of BC Place Stadium. British Columbia sports history is traced from native traditions to the modern Olympic games. Honorees include amateur and professional teams, athletes, journalists and sports pioneers. Interactive galleries provide opportunities for running, climbing, throwing, riding, rowing and even mini hockey. The All Access Experience includes a behind-the-scenes

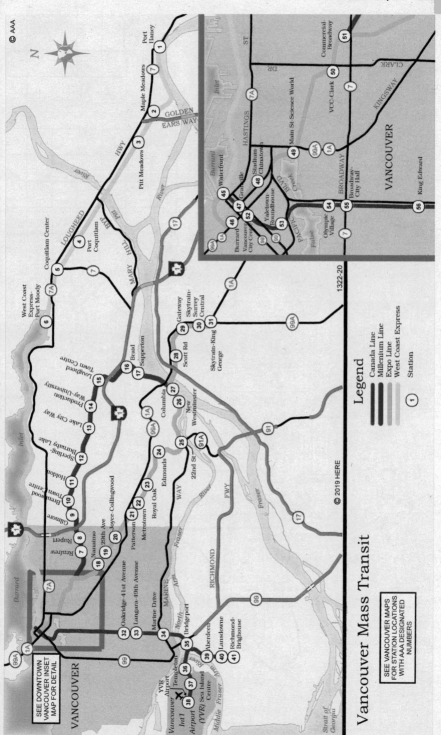

Vancouver Mass Transit

Legend
— Canada Line
— Millenium Line
— Expo Line
— West Coast Express
① Station

SEE VANCOUVER MAPS
FOR STATION LOCATIONS
WITH AAA DESIGNATED
NUMBERS

SEE DOWNTOWN
VANCOUVER INSET
MAP FOR DETAIL

© 2019 HERE

1322-20

© AAA

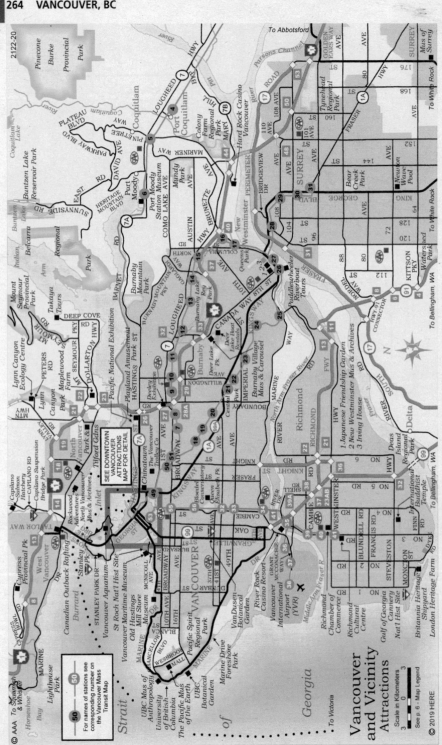

Vancouver
and Vicinity
Attractions

1 Japanese Friendship Garden
2 New Westminster Mus & Archives
3 Irving House

For names of stations see
corresponding number on
the Vancouver Mass
Transit Map

SEE DOWNTOWN
VANCOUVER AREA ON
MAP FOR DETAIL

Scale in Kilometers
See p 6 - Map Legend

© 2019 HERE

tour of areas the public does not normally see, including team locker rooms, the media lounge and the field.

Hours: Daily 10-5. All Access Experience is offered on various days; phone ahead to confirm availability. **Cost:** $18; $12 (ages 6-17, ages 65+ and students with ID); $28 (one adult and one child age 6-17); $48 (family, two adults and two children). All Access Experience $20. **Phone:** (604) 687-5520. ⊞ Stadium-Chinatown, 48

BILL REID GALLERY OF NORTHWEST COAST ART is downtown at 639 Hornby St. between W. Georgia and Dunsmuir sts. The museum is dedicated to Bill Reid, one of Canada's finest artists and a passionate proponent of Northwest Coast art. Reid was a master Haida goldsmith as well as a noted sculptor, carver, broadcaster, writer and spokesman for his native people.

His gold and silver jewelry forms the basis of the museum's permanent collection. Other highlights include his masterpiece, an 8.5-metre (28 ft.) bronze frieze titled "Mythic Messengers," and a massive 6.7-metre (22 ft.) totem pole carved in honor of the artist. Video displays alongside Reid's art allow visitors to watch him at work at different stages of his life. The gallery also hosts changing exhibitions of contemporary indigenous art of the Northwest Coast.

Time: Allow 1 hour minimum. **Hours:** Daily 10-5, late May-late Sept.; Wed.-Sun. 11-5, rest of year. **Cost:** $13; $10 (ages 65+); $8 (students ages 18+ with ID); $6 (ages 13-17); free (ages 0-12); $30 (family, two adults and two children); free (2-5 p.m. first Fri. of the month). Phone ahead to confirm hours and rates. **Phone:** (604) 682-3455. ⊞ Burrard, 46

BLOEDEL CONSERVATORY—see Queen Elizabeth Park p. 266.

DR. SUN YAT-SEN CLASSICAL CHINESE GARDEN is at 578 Carrall St. What this walled garden lacks in size it more than makes up for in serene beauty. Located in the heart of Chinatown, it's a delightful respite from the surrounding hustle and bustle. Modeled after private gardens in the city of Suzhou, the garden embodies the Taoist philosophy of yin and yang, where every element—light, texture, vegetation—is balanced.

The architecture of the pavilions, covered walkways, terraces and viewing platforms evokes Ming Dynasty classical design. Rocks and water are integral elements, while trees and plants—from pine trees and bamboo to graceful weeping willows and winter-flowering plum trees—all have symbolic connotations. The Jade Water Pavilion is graced with beautiful woodwork. Two of the garden's most intriguing elements are the 43 leak windows (each one has a different lattice pattern) and the groupings of Tai Hu rocks, interestingly shaped stones from China's Lake Tai that lend themselves to all sorts of artistic interpretations.

Visitors can walk through the garden on their own, but the guided tour offers historical perspective and encourages you to reflect on the design elements in different ways. Afterward, take a stroll through the adjacent public park, where pathways wind through clumps of bamboo and other plantings.

Art and horticultural exhibits and demonstrations also are offered. Festivals and concerts are featured throughout the year. **Time:** Allow 1 hour minimum. **Hours:** Daily 9:30-7, June 15-Aug. 31; daily 10-6, May 1-June 14 and in Sept.; Tues.-Sun. 10-4:30 (10-2, Dec. 24 and 31), rest of year. **Cost:** $14 (includes guided tour and tea); $11 (ages 65+); $10 (ages 6-17 and students with ID); $28 (family, two adults and up to three children ages 0-17). **Phone:** (604) 662-3207. ⊞ Stadium-Chinatown, 48

FLYOVER CANADA is at 999 Canada Pl. on the Canada Place pier. A 65-foot spherical screen shows a film of Canada while guests sit in moving state-of-the-art seats on an 8-minute whirlwind "flight" soaring across the country. Along with mountainside vistas, urban streetscapes and expansive prairies, visitors will experience sensations such as wind, mist and scents for an all-encompassing and fully immersive journey across Canada.

Note: The ride is not recommended for pregnant women or those with heart conditions, chronic neck or back problems, photosensitive epilepsy or other physical impairments. **Time:** Allow 30 minutes minimum. **Hours:** Daily 10-9. **Cost:** $26-$32; $20-$26 (students with ID ages 13-21 and 65+); $20.75-$26.40 (military with ID); $16-$22 (ages 0-12). Under 12 must be accompanied by a guardian 14+. Under 101.6 centimeters (40 in.) tall are not permitted. **Phone:** (604) 620-8455 or (855) 463-4822. ⊞ Waterfront, 45

GRANVILLE ISLAND PUBLIC MARKET is at 1689 Johnston St. One of the best places in the city to experience a slice of Vancouver life, this popular foodie destination houses more than 50 independent food purveyors and craft stalls in converted industrial buildings. Strawberries, cherries, artisanal cheeses, baked goods, donuts, gelato and locally sourced seafood packed in ready-to-go travel boxes are among the edible highlights. An international food court has fast-food counters with Asian, Mexican, Indian and other cuisines available as takeout. In addition to food items, the market features handmade gifts and crafts from local artists; look for stalls inside the market and in surrounding shops and studios along Johnston, Duranleau, Anderson and Cartwright streets.

The Granville Island Farmers Market sets up outside the market building on Thursdays 10-3, early June-late Sept. Tip: A pleasurable (and easy) way to get to the market from downtown Vancouver is by ferry; Aquabus and False Creek Ferries provide pedestrian-only service across False Creek Inlet to Granville Island. **Hours:** Public market building daily 9-7; closed on Jan. 1, all Mondays in Jan., Christmas and day after Christmas. Most nearby shops are open daily 10-7. **Cost:** Free. **Parking:** $3.50 per hour in designated lots. **Phone:** (604) 666-6655. [🍴] [🚗] [♿] Yaletown-Roundhouse, 53

HOLY ROSARY CATHEDRAL is at 646 Richards St. The church has stained-glass windows and eight bells hung in the rare English ringing style. **Hours:** Cathedral open Mon.-Sat. 7-6, Sun. 7:45 a.m.-9 p.m. Bell ringing Sun. at 10:30 a.m., Tues. at 7:30 p.m. **Cost:** Free. **Phone:** (604) 682-6774.
[♿] Granville, 47

[SAVE] **H.R. MACMILLAN SPACE CENTRE** is at 1100 Chestnut St. in Vanier Park. The center's Planetarium Star Theatre presents full dome tours of astronomy and space exploration. Other features include GroundStation Canada, which uses live science demonstrations to explain the latest discoveries; Cosmic Courtyard, which features interactive exhibits and one of only five touchable moon rocks in the world; an observatory with a 0.5-metre (1.6 ft.) telescope; and hands-on exhibits.

Time: Allow 1 hour, 30 minutes minimum. **Hours:** Daily 10-5, May-Aug.; Mon.-Fri. 10-3, Sat. 10-5, Sun. noon-5, rest of year. Planetarium shows Sat. at 7:30 p.m. and 9 p.m. Observatory open Sat. 7 p.m.-11 p.m. Hours and show times may vary; phone ahead. **Cost:** $19.50; $16.50 (ages 12-18 and 55+); $14 (ages 5-11); $60.50 (family, two adults and up to three children). Evening planetarium shows (includes planetarium and observatory) $14; $11 (ages 12-18 and 55+); $8.50 (ages 5-11); $41 (family, two adults and up to three children). **Phone:** (604) 738-7827.

[SAVE] **MUSEUM OF VANCOUVER,** on the s.w. end of Burrard St. in Vanier Park at 1100 Chestnut St., creates area-focused displays and programs that encourage dynamic conversations about what was, is, and can be Vancouver. Permanent exhibitions present the city's story 1900-1979, and are complemented by contemporary feature exhibits.

Hours: Sun.-Thurs. 10-5 (also Thurs. 5-8), Fri.-Sat. 10-9. **Cost:** $20.50; $17.25 (ages 65+ and students with ID); $13.75 (ages 12-18); $9.75 (ages 5-11); $43 (family, two adults and three children); donations (last Thurs. of the month 5-8). **Phone:** (604) 736-4431.

PACIFIC NATIONAL EXHIBITION is on E. Hastings St. between Renfrew and Cassiar sts. The site occupies 58 hectares (144 acres) and is home to Pacific Coliseum, a tradeshow and entertainment complex, and a skateboard park. Various trade and hobby shows, rock concerts and sporting events are scheduled throughout the year. The annual Fair at the PNE has been an end of summer highlight since it began in 1910.

Hours: Fair daily 11 a.m.-midnight (weather permitting), mid-Aug. through Labour Day. Closed Aug. 21. Last admission 1 hour, 30 minutes before closing. **Cost:** Fair admission $15; $7 (ages 65+); free (up to five children ages 0-13 per paying adult

age 21 and over); $6 (after 9 p.m.). Ride pass $43.75 (over 48 in. tall); $32.75 (under 48 in. tall). Rates may vary; phone ahead. **Phone:** (604) 253-2311. [🍴]

Playland Amusement Park is between Renfrew and Cassiar sts. at 2901 E. Hastings St. The 4-hectare (10-acre) park features games, miniature golf and more than 35 rides, including an internationally-recognized vintage wooden roller coaster, 13 "extreme" rides and 17 family rides.

Hours: Daily 11-6, mid-June to mid-Aug.; otherwise varies early May to mid-June and mid-Aug. through Victoria Day. Phone ahead to confirm schedule. **Cost:** $38 (over 122 centimetres or 48 inches tall); $28 (under 122 centimetres or 48 inches tall); free (ages 0-3). Season pass $99 (over 122 centimetres or 48 inches tall); $61 (under 122 centimetres or 48 inches tall). Rates may vary; phone ahead. **Phone:** (604) 253-2311 or (604) 252-3620.

QUEEN ELIZABETH PARK is off Cambie St. and W. 33rd Ave. On 152-metre (499 ft.) Little Mountain, the highest point in Vancouver, the park offers magnificent views of the city, the harbor and the North Shore mountains. Other highlights include an arboretum; rose, sunken and quarry gardens; dancing fountains; tennis courts; and pitch and putt greens. **Hours:** Daily 24 hours. **Cost:** Free. **Parking:** $3.50 per hour, $13 per day, May-Sept.; $2.50 per hour, $7 per day, rest of year. **Phone:** (604) 873-7000.
[♿] Oakridge-41st Avenue, 32

Bloedel Conservatory is at 4600 Cambie St. Climatically varied species of plants grow in a climate-controlled, illuminated triodetic dome 43 metres (141 ft.) in diameter and 21 metres (70 ft.) high. More than 200 free-flying tropical birds and a fish pond are other highlights. **Time:** Allow 30 minutes minimum. **Hours:** Daily 10-8, May 1-Labour Day; 10-5, rest of year. Phone ahead to confirm schedule. **Cost:** $6.75; $4.55 (ages 13-18 and 65+); $3.50 (ages 5-12). **Phone:** (604) 257-8584.
[♿] King Edward, 56

SCIENCE WORLD AT TELUS WORLD OF SCIENCE, 1455 Quebec St., is housed in a geodesic dome and features hands-on exhibits and demonstrations that explain science and nature. Water, air and motion are some of the physical sciences explored in the Eureka! Gallery. The Wonder Gallery is geared toward young learners ages 0-5. Live, zany science demonstrations with audience participation take place daily in the Peter Brown Family Centre Stage. Watch films in the OMNIMAX Theatre, which projects nature and science films onto a dome screen that's 5 stories high and 27 metres (88 ft.) in diameter; or take a seat in the high-definition Science Theatre, which offers films and live shows.

Human performance and nature are the subjects of additional galleries. Learn about sustainable communities in Our World: BMO Sustainability Gallery, explore human life sciences in BodyWorks and discover the wonders of nature in Search: Sara Stern Gallery. A seasonal outdoor gallery lets visitors plant seeds and gather eggs from chickens.

Time: Allow 2 hours minimum. **Hours:** Daily 10-6 (also Tues. 6-9 p.m.), July 1-Labour Day; Mon.-Fri. 10-5, Sat.-Sun. and Mon. holidays 10-6, day after Labour Day- Jan. 6 and Mar. 12-Dec. 21; Tues.-Fri. 10-5, Sat.-Sun. 10-6, rest of year. Also open 10-6, Dec. 23; 10-3, Dec. 24 and 31; noon-6, Dec. 26 and Jan. 1. Phone ahead to confirm schedule. **Cost:** Exhibits and one OMNIMAX film $33.65; $28.20 (ages 13-18, ages 65+ and students with ID); $24.60 (ages 3-12). Exhibits only $27.15; $21.70 (ages 13-18, ages 65+ and students with ID); $18.10 (ages 3-12). OMNIMAX film only $12.75. **Parking:** $4-$15. Rates may vary; phone ahead. **Phone:** (604) 443-7440.

🍴 🚇 Main St-Science World, 49

STANLEY PARK shares the peninsula where the city's business district is located. Vancouver's first City Council made a momentous decision in 1886, when it petitioned the government to lease 400 hectares (1,000 acres) of largely logged-over land for public and recreation purposes. The result of this wise move was the creation of one of North America's largest urban parks—a cool, lush evergreen oasis right at downtown's doorstep.

Named for Lord Frederick Stanley, Governor General of Canada when the park officially opened in 1888, Stanley Park was once land hunted and foraged by the Musqueam and Squamish First Nations peoples. And a large part of what makes it such a special place is the lush West Coast rain forest growth. One of the park's great pleasures, in fact, is exploring the network of bark-mulched trails that wind through Douglas fir, western hemlock and western red cedar trees. These giants create a hushed environment of subdued light and cool air that is all the more remarkable given the proximity to downtown's hurly-burly.

Such a magnificent setting, of course, offers plenty of inspiring views, and there are more than 27 kilometres (16.7 mi.) of trails. For example, follow Prospect Point Trail, an invigorating uphill trek, to Prospect Point at the northern tip of the peninsula; from this elevated perspective the vista of Burrard Inlet, the Lions Gate Bridge, the North Shore and the mountains beyond is a stunner. For a more relaxed jaunt, amble along the Stanley Park Seawall, a paved path that encircles the peninsula. The route totals about 9 kilometres (5.6 mi.), and you'll be gazing out over water essentially the entire time. There are separate lanes for walkers and cyclists/inline skaters.

There are other ways to enjoy nature. Walk to Beaver Lake, a body of water that is in the process of shrinking as it transitions from lake to bog (and may in time lose its watery aspects completely and become a meadow). Its surface is covered with yellow water lilies in summer. Or take a spin around Lost Lagoon, off the Georgia Street entrance to the park. This man-made body of water (created when the Stanley Park Causeway was built in 1916) provides a nesting ground for ducks, swans and Canada geese. The lagoon is located on the Pacific Flyway, which makes it a favorite haunt of bird watchers as well as one of the park's most popular strolls.

Standing near the Brockton Oval (where you can watch a cricket match), just in from the seawall, are nine totem poles. They make a distinctive photo op, and you can learn about their history by reading the interpretive panels. Another example of First Nations art is the "Raven: Spirit of Transformation" sculpture, created from the stump of a Douglas fir felled by a destructive 2006 windstorm. It stands at the Miniature Railway Plaza. You'll also want to take a ride in a horse-drawn carriage *(see attraction listing)*; breathing in the scent of the cedar trees while listening to the gentle clip-clop of a Clydesdale's hooves is an eminently relaxing way to tour the park.

There are free tennis courts near Lost Lagoon and the Beach Avenue entrance. The Second Beach Pool has English Bay as a backdrop. An 18-hole pitch-and-putt golf course also is located at Second Beach. At low tide, explore the rocky shoreline along Second and Third beaches. For kids there are three playgrounds—including the Variety Kids Water Park (June 1–Sept. 1) at Lumberman's Arch, Second Beach and near the park's Rose Garden—as well as a miniature steam train *(see attraction listing)*.

Shows take place at the open-air Malkin Bowl/Theatre Under the Stars in July and August. A

Stanley Park

park information booth is just inside the Georgia Street entrance, next to the seawall.

Hours: Park open daily 24 hours. Information booth open 9:30-7:30, June 15-Labour Day; hours vary rest of year, phone ahead. **Cost:** Park free. **Parking:** $3.60 per hour; $13 per day, Apr.-Sept.; $2.50 per hour, $7 per day, rest of year. **Phone:** (604) 681-6728. [T] [A]

Miniature Train is near the Georgia St. entrance of Stanley Park off Pipeline Rd. Visitors can take a scenic ride through the park on this miniature train. The trip runs over trestles and through tunnels on its 2-kilometre (1.25 mi.) journey. Special excursions operate during Easter, Halloween and Christmas seasons. **Time:** Allow 1 hour minimum. **Hours:** Daily 10-5, late June-early Sept. 3; Sat.-Sun. 10-5, early Apr.-late June. Phone ahead to confirm holiday excursion schedules. **Cost:** $6.80; $4.86 (ages 13-18 and 65+); $3.40 (ages 3-12); $13.60 (family, two adults and two children ages 3-18). **Phone:** (604) 257-8531. [T] [A]

Stanley Park Horse-drawn Tours depart from beside the information booth at the Coal Harbour parking lot on Park Dr. off the Georgia St. entrance. The narrated, 1-hour tour highlights the park's points of interest. **Hours:** Tours depart daily every 20-30 minutes 9:30-6, July 1-Labour Day; 9:40-5, Apr.-June and day after Labour Day-Sept. 30; 9:40-4, Mar. 15-31 and in Oct. **Cost:** $47.62; $43.81 (ages 13-18, ages 65+ and students with ID); $20.95 (ages 3-12). **Phone:** (604) 681-5115 or (888) 681-5110.

Vancouver Aquarium is at 845 Avison Way. Visitors are greeted by "Chief of the Undersea World," a bronze sculpture by Haida artist Bill Reid. The center is home to more than 50,000 marine animals, with emphasis on such diverse habitats as the Canadian Arctic, the Amazon Rain Forest and the Pacific Northwest. Sharks, moray eels and colorful fish populate the Tropic Zone, while the Strait of Georgia exhibit features divers interacting with marine life.

Interactive multimedia displays in the Canada's Arctic exhibit allow visitors to meet the people of this region and explain the effects and impact of climate change on them and the area's marine life. Programs allowing animal encounters with sea lions, otters and other animals are available for an additional fee. Teck Connections Gallery offers state-of-the-art wraparound screens of digital projections while the Engagement Gallery is available for talks and educational programs.

Walk the BC Hydro Salmon Stream in Stanley Park to learn about a salmon's incredible life journey. Other highlights include daily shark dives and sea otter feedings as well as exhibits that feature sea lions and harbor seals.

Time: Allow 2 hours minimum. **Hours:** Daily 9:30-6 (also Wed. 6-8 p.m.), July-Aug.; 10-5, rest of year. **Cost:** $38; $30 (ages 13-18, ages 65+ and students ages 18+ with ID); $21 (ages 4-12).

Parking: Apr.-Sept. $3.50 per hour, $13 per day; rest of year $2.50 per hour, $7 per day. **Phone:** (604) 659-3400 or (604) 659-3474. [T]

UNIVERSITY OF BRITISH COLUMBIA is on Point Grey. The university, the oldest and largest in the province, has another campus in Kelowna. Encompassing 401.85 hectares (993 acres), the Vancouver campus overlooks the Strait of Georgia and has 11 attractions including museums, gardens, galleries, performing arts venues and historic collections. **Phone:** (604) 822-3313.

Beaty Biodiversity Museum is at 2212 Main Mall on the University of British Columbia campus. This natural history museum exhibits more than 2 million specimens divided among six collections: the Cowan Tetrapod Collection, The Herbarium, the Spencer Entomological Collection, the Fish Collection, the Marine Invertebrate Collection and the Fossil Collection. A highlight is Canada's largest blue whale skeleton, which is suspended in the museum's two-story glass atrium.

Note: Pay parking is available at the Health Sciences Parkade, one block south across East Mall, and near the UBC Bookstore. **Time:** Allow 1 hour, 30 minutes minimum. **Hours:** Tues.-Sun. 10-5 (also third Thurs. of the month 5-8:30). Guided tours are given daily at 3 (also Sat.-Sun. at 11:30). **Cost:** $14; $12 (ages 13-17, ages 65+ and non-UBC students with ID); $10 (ages 5-12); $45 (family, two adults and up to four children under 18); donations (third Thurs. of the month 5-8:30). Combination ticket (UBC Museums Pass) with UBC Museum of Anthropology $25; $20 (ages 13-17, ages 65+ and non-UBC students with ID); $60 (family, two adults and up to four children). **Phone:** (604) 827-4955. [T]

The Pacific Museum of the Earth is just off the West Mall of the university on the main floor of the Earth and Ocean Science Building at 6339 Stores Rd. Highlight of the 30,000-piece mineral and fossil collection is an 80 million-year-old Lambeosaurus dinosaur; a full-sized, 13 meter (42 ft.) long, hanging Elasmosaurus replica; a 2-meter (7 ft.) amethyst tube; an unusual large sedimentary structure; numerous extraordinary mineral, crystal, gold and rock specimens; and the OmniGlobe, a spherical interactive display of Earth with historical and real-time information. **Time:** Allow 30 minutes minimum. **Hours:** Mon.-Fri. 10-5. OmniGlobe and gem gallery Mon.-Fri. 10-4. Closed statutory holidays, Jan. 1-3 and Dec. 20-31. **Cost:** Donations. **Phone:** (604) 822-6992.

UBC Botanical Garden is at 6804 S.W. Marine Dr. More than 30,000 plants from around the world are cultivated on 28 hectares (69 acres). Themed gardens include Asian, alpine, perennial, food, medicinal and native plantings. Within the Asian garden is the Greenheart TreeWalk Ecoadventure, a 308-metre (1,010 ft.) aerial trail through a West Coast forest canopy. This experience takes participants across eight bridges more than 20 metres (65 ft.) above ground level to view plants and animals that live in this environment.

Nitobe Memorial Garden, at 1895 Lower Mall, is one of the most authentic Japanese gardens in North America and features a tea garden and stroll garden with seasonal displays of irises, Japanese maples and flowering cherries.

Pets are not permitted. **Time:** Allow 1 hour minimum. **Hours:** Botanical Garden open daily 10-4:30. Nitobe Memorial Garden daily 10-4:30, Apr.-Oct.; Mon.-Fri. 10-2, rest of year. **Cost:** Botanical Garden $10; $8 (ages 13-17, ages 65+ and non-UBC students with ID); $5 (ages 5-12); $24 (family, two adults and up to four children). Botanical Garden plus Greenheart TreeWalk Ecoadventure $23; $17 (ages 13-17, ages 65+ and students with ID); $10 (ages 5-12); $50 (family, two adults and up to four children). Nitobe Memorial Garden $7; $6 (ages 13-17, ages 65+ and students with ID); $4 (ages 5-12); $18 (family). Botanical Garden plus Nitobe Memorial Garden $15; $13 (ages 13-17, ages 65+ and students with ID); $7 (ages 5-12); $35 (family, two adults and up to four children). **Parking:** Free for 3 hours, then $2 per hour (maximum $6 per day). **Phone:** (604) 822-4208 Botanical Garden, or (604) 822-6038 Nitobe Memorial Garden.

SAVE **UBC Museum of Anthropology** is at 6393 N.W. Marine Dr. on the Point Grey Cliffs. Traditional post-and-beam architecture inspired this concrete and glass building designed by Canadian architect Arthur Erickson. The Great Hall, the main exhibition area, has soaring glass walls that let in natural light and provides a striking setting for a major collection of Northwest Coast First Nations artwork, which includes totem poles, canoes, carved figures, textiles, feast dishes and other objects.

The Bill Reid Rotunda features one of the museum's highlights, "The Raven and the First Men" by Haida artist Bill Reid. Reid, developed an interest in tribal folklore, and this carving—fashioned from a single block of laminated yellow cedar—powerfully depicts a Haida human creation myth. Four accompanying display cases contain more of Reid's works in gold, silver and argillite, a fine-grained sedimentary rock frequently used in Haida carvings.

Stroll the grounds, where monumental totem poles, Haida houses and Musqueam houseboards capture the dramatic beauty of traditional Northwest Coast architecture and design. See historical indigenous artwork through the eyes of contemporary First Nations artists in the innovative Gallery of Northwest Coast Masterworks.

In marked contrast to the often-monumental scale of the indigenous art is the 600-piece collection of 16th- to 19th-century European ceramics comprised of stoneware and tin- and lead-glazed earthenware on display in the Koerner European Ceramics Gallery.

Time: Allow 1 hour minimum. **Hours:** Tues.-Sun. 10-5 (also Thurs. 5-9), mid-May to mid-Oct.; daily 10-5 (also Thurs. 5-9), rest of year. Closed Christmas and day after Christmas. **Cost:** $18; $16 (ages 7-17, ages 65+ and non-UBC students with ID); $10 (Thurs. 5-9); $47 (family, two adults and four children ages 0-17). **Phone:** (604) 822-5087. GT [T]

VANCOUVER AQUARIUM—see Stanley Park p. 268.

SAVE **VANCOUVER ART GALLERY** is downtown at 750 Hornby St.; the museum encompasses a city block bounded by Georgia, Howe, Robson and Hornby sts. One of the largest art museums in Western Canada occupies a turn-of-the-20th-century building that originally was intended to serve as a provincial courthouse. Its stately exterior is a contrast to much of the art inside, which tends to reflect the creative energy and hip, progressive style that the city itself embodies.

While historical masters are given their due, the focus of the gallery's changing thematic exhibitions is on contemporary artists and works from groundbreaking new visionaries that veer toward the cutting edge. The museum's four floors of mixed-media installations contain works by Emily Carr and other well-known Canadian artists.

Time: Allow 1 hour minimum. **Hours:** Daily 10-5 (also Tues. and first Fri. of month 5-9). Guided tours depart Thurs. and Sat. 11-2:30. Closed Jan. 1 and Christmas. **Cost:** $24; $20 (ages 65+); $18 (students with ID); $6.50 (ages 6-12); donations (Tues. 5-9). Rates may vary; phone ahead. **Phone:** (604) 662-4719. [T] [P] Burrard, 46

VANCOUVER LOOKOUT AT HARBOUR CENTRE TOWER is at 555 W. Hastings St. Two glass elevators ascend the outside of this 168-metre (553 ft.) tower, which is crowned with an observation deck that offers a spectacular panoramic view of the city and outlying districts. Hourly guided tours point out the city's landmarks. The complex includes a revolving restaurant and a shopping mall.

Time: Allow 30 minutes minimum. **Hours:** Daily 8:30 a.m.-10:30 p.m., early May-late Sept.; 9-9, rest of year. **Cost:** $18.25; $15.25 (ages 60+); $13.25 (ages 13-18 and students with ID); $9.50 (ages 6-12). Rates may vary; phone ahead. **Phone:** (604) 689-0421. GT [P] Waterfront, 45

GEM **VANDUSEN BOTANICAL GARDEN** is at 5251 Oak St. at W. 37th Ave. One benefit of Vancouver's benevolent maritime climate is that it creates a favorable environment for gardening, and the plant collections at VanDusen Botanical Garden offer spectacular proof. The 22-hectare (55-acre) site, once owned by the Canadian Pacific Railway and logged at the turn of the 20th century, was nurtured into a garden in the early 1970s in order to prevent the land from being developed for housing.

This is a botanical garden, as much scientifically organized and carefully labeled as it is visually pleasing. Trees, shrubs and perennials dominate the plantings, and there's something beautiful to see regardless of the season. Camellias, cherry trees, azaleas, magnolias and rhododendrons bloom from March through May. The Rose Garden begins flowering in June. Late July and August find flowering summer annuals and perennials at their peak. Japanese maples flaunt crimson fall foliage from September into October. And during the winter months, 140 different kinds of hollies along the Holly Trail are bright with berries. The plants represent some 7,500 species of plants from around the world.

Special gardens include the Perennial Garden, the Canadian Heritage Garden (where there is a lovely Korean Pavilion built from red cedar posts), the peaceful retreat that is the Meditation Garden, and the dark-leaved plants in the intriguing Black Garden. Rocks and water are integral elements as well, and the lakes and ponds are lovely spots to stop and reflect. Kids can puzzle their way around the hedges that form the Elizabethan Maze.

Time: Allow 1 hour, 30 minutes minimum. **Hours:** Daily 10-3, Nov.-Feb.; 10-5, Mar. and Oct.; 9-6, Apr. and Sep.; 9-7, May; 9-8, Jun.-Aug. Closed Christmas. **Cost:** Apr.-Sept. $11.25; $8.45 (ages 13-18 and 65+); $5.50 (ages 5-12). Rest of year $8; $5.50 (ages 13-18 and 65+); $4.25 (ages 5-12). **Phone:** (604) 257-8335.

GT ⑪ 🚇 Oakridge-41st Avenue, 32

Sightseeing

Opportunities to sightsee and watch bustling harbor activities are available from several vantage points in Vancouver. Seaplanes, barges, tugboats, cargo ships, ferries and the SeaBus can be observed from Granville Square at the foot of Granville Street; from Canada Place at the foot of Howe St.; from Lonsdale Quay at the foot of Lonsdale Ave.; and from Stanley Park. Breathtaking views of the city, sea and mountains are available at Cypress Bowl, Simon Fraser University atop Burnaby Mountain, Grouse Mountain and Queen Elizabeth Park.

Bus Tours

WESTCOAST Sightseeing Ltd. features a hop-on, hop-off tour of Vancouver as well as narrated sightseeing trips of the city and its surrounding natural areas. Full-day trips to Victoria and Whistler also are available; phone (604) 451-1600 or (877) 451-1777. Contact your local AAA office or travel agency for information about vacation packages and other things to do at this destination.

Gray Line offers guided tours that include travel to Capilano Suspension Bridge Park, Grouse Mountain, downtown Vancouver, Victoria and Whistler; phone (604) 451-1600 or (877) 451-1777.

Plane Tours

Another way to see Vancouver and its surroundings on your vacation is by air. Harbour Air offers flights lasting from 35 minutes to 1.25 hours plus day-long packages, including whale-watching or bus tours; departure is from downtown on Coal Harbour Road, one block west of Canada Place. A trip up in a private plane is one of the most romantic things to do for couples. Fares vary, and reservations are required; phone (604) 274-1277 or (800) 655-0212 for reservations.

Train Tours

Rocky Mountaineer Vacations offers scenic, 2-day, all daylight, narrated rail tours between Vancouver or Whistler, British Columbia, and Banff, Calgary, or Jasper, Alberta. Westbound or eastbound departures are offered mid-April to mid-October, with winter rail trips available in December. Onboard meals and snacks as well as accommodations in Kamloops or Quesnel are included. A 3-hour trip on the Whistler Mountaineer also is available and runs between Vancouver and Whistler May through October. Phone (604) 606-7245 or (877) 460-3200, or (888) 687-7245 for information about Whistler trips.

Walking Tours

ROCKWOOD ADVENTURES departs from downtown hotels. Half- and full-day guided nature walks are offered to area ecological destinations including Lynn Canyon, a rain forest in Capilano River Canyon, a coastal forest at Burrard Inlet and Mount Gardner on Bowen Island. The urban city tour explores such sights as Chinatown, the shopping district, Stanley Park and Gastown. All trips include a snack or lunch and pick-up at downtown hotels.

Hours: Half-day tours offered daily 9-4, Apr. 15-Oct. 15. **Cost:** $115; $90 (students ages 12-25 with ID and ages 65+); $60 (ages 4-11). Rates may vary depending on tour. Reservations are required. **Phone:** (604) 913-1621, or (888) 236-6606 in Canada. 🚇 Stadium-Chinatown, 48

Save time & stay secure year-round

Renew your membership today:
- Online at AAA.com/membership
- Visit your local club office
- Call 800-Join-AAA (564-6222)

For Any Occasion

AAA/CAA Members Save on Hotels
Great Brands/Great Guarantee

VISIT over 1,100 AAA/CAA Offices
CLICK AAA.com/greatrates | **CALL** 1-866-222-7283

AAA Mobile
CAA Mobile

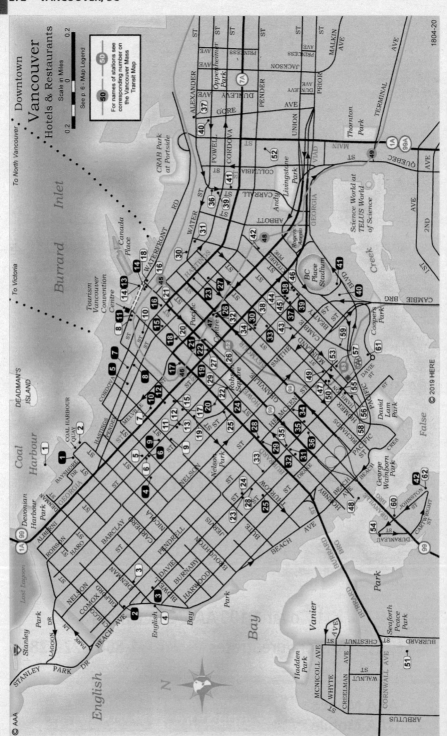

Downtown
Vancouver
Hotels & Restaurants

See p. 6 - Map Legend

Scale in Miles

For names of stations see
corresponding number on
the Vancouver Mass
Transit Map

© AAA

© 2019 HERE

1804-20

Downtown Vancouver

This index helps you "spot" where hotels and restaurants are located on the corresponding detailed maps. Restaurant price range is a combination of lunch and/or dinner. Turn to the listing page for more information and consult display ads for special promotions.

 For more details, rates and reservations: AAA.com/travelguides/hotels

DOWNTOWN VANCOUVER

Map Page	Hotels	Designation	Member Savings	Page
1 p. 272	The Westin Bayshore Vancouver	FOUR DIAMOND	✔	290
2 p. 272	Sylvia Hotel	APPROVED		289
3 p. 272	Best Western Plus Sands *(See ad p. 282.)*	THREE DIAMOND	✔	282
4 p. 272	West End Guest House	THREE DIAMOND		290
5 p. 272	The Coast Coal Harbour Vancouver Hotel by APA	THREE DIAMOND		282
6 p. 272	The Listel Hotel Vancouver	THREE DIAMOND		286
7 p. 272	Pinnacle Vancouver Harbourfront Hotel *(See ad p. 287.)*	THREE DIAMOND	✔	287
8 p. 272	Vancouver Marriott Pinnacle Downtown	FOUR DIAMOND	✔	290
9 p. 272	Blue Horizon Hotel	THREE DIAMOND	✔	282
10 p. 272	Trump International Hotel & Tower Vancouver	FOUR DIAMOND		289
11 p. 272	Fairmont Pacific Rim	FIVE DIAMOND	✔	284
12 p. 272	Shangri-La Hotel Vancouver *(See ad p. 288.)*	FIVE DIAMOND	✔	288
13 p. 272	Pan Pacific Vancouver *(See ad p. 286.)*	FOUR DIAMOND	✔	286
14 p. 272	Fairmont Waterfront	FOUR DIAMOND	✔	284
15 p. 272	Days Inn Vancouver Downtown	APPROVED		282
16 p. 272	Auberge Vancouver Hotel	THREE DIAMOND		282
17 p. 272	Hyatt Regency Vancouver	FOUR DIAMOND	✔	286
18 p. 272	Executive Hotel Le Soleil	FOUR DIAMOND	✔	283
19 p. 272	Fairmont Hotel Vancouver	FOUR DIAMOND	✔	283
20 p. 272	The Sutton Place Hotel	FOUR DIAMOND	✔	289
21 p. 272	Four Seasons Hotel Vancouver	FOUR DIAMOND		284
22 p. 272	Rosewood Hotel Georgia	FOUR DIAMOND		287
23 p. 272	Delta Hotels by Marriott Vancouver Downtown Suites	THREE DIAMOND	✔	282
24 p. 272	The Wedgewood Hotel & Spa	FOUR DIAMOND	✔	290
25 p. 272	Sunset Inn & Suites *(See ad p. 289.)*	THREE DIAMOND	✔	289
26 p. 272	St. Regis Hotel	THREE DIAMOND	✔	287
27 p. 272	Ramada Limited Downtown Vancouver	APPROVED		287
28 p. 272	Sheraton Vancouver Wall Centre Hotel	THREE DIAMOND	✔	288
29 p. 272	The Burrard	APPROVED		282
30 p. 272	L'Hermitage Hotel	FOUR DIAMOND		286
31 p. 272	The Landis Hotel & Suites	THREE DIAMOND	✔	286
32 p. 272	Residence Inn by Marriott Vancouver Downtown	THREE DIAMOND	✔	287
33 p. 272	The Westin Grand, Vancouver	THREE DIAMOND	✔	290
34 p. 272	BW Premier Collection Chateau Granville Hotel & Suites & Conference Centre *(See ad p. 283.)*	THREE DIAMOND	✔	282
35 p. 272	Howard Johnson Hotel Downtown Vancouver	APPROVED		284
36 p. 272	Ramada Vancouver Downtown	APPROVED		287
37 p. 272	Hotel BLU Vancouver	FOUR DIAMOND	✔	284
38 p. 272	Georgian Court Hotel, BW Premier Collection	THREE DIAMOND	✔	284
39 p. 272	Hampton Inn & Suites by Hilton Downtown Vancouver	THREE DIAMOND	✔	284
40 p. 272	the DOUGLAS, Autograph Collection	FOUR DIAMOND	✔	283
41 p. 272	JW Marriott Parq Vancouver	FOUR DIAMOND	✔	286
42 p. 272	Granville Island Hotel *(See ad p. 285.)*	THREE DIAMOND	✔	284

Map Page	Restaurants	Designation	Cuisine	Price Range	Page
① p. 272	LIFT Bar Grill View	THREE DIAMOND	Pacific Northwest	$17-$55	292
② p. 272	Cardero's Restaurant	THREE DIAMOND	Seafood	$14-$46	291
③ p. 272	España	APPROVED	New Spanish Small Plates	$20-$30	291
④ p. 272	Cactus Club Cafe	THREE DIAMOND	New American	$15-$46	291
⑤ p. 272	Ramen Danbo	APPROVED	Japanese Noodles	$10-$15	292
⑥ p. 272	Forage	THREE DIAMOND	New Canadian	$26-$43	291
⑦ p. 272	Mott 32	THREE DIAMOND	Chinese	$25-$58	292
⑧ p. 272	Botanist	FOUR DIAMOND	New Pacific Northwest	$22-$56	291
⑨ p. 272	Breka Bakery & Cafe	APPROVED	Coffee/Tea Breads/Pastries	$8-$10	291
⑩ p. 272	Nightingale	THREE DIAMOND	New Canadian Small Plates	$14-$29	292
⑪ p. 272	CinCin	THREE DIAMOND	New Mediterranean	$29-$42	291
⑫ p. 272	Cactus Club Cafe	THREE DIAMOND	New American	$15-$46	291
⑬ p. 272	Zefferelli's Restaurant	APPROVED	Italian	$14-$32	295
⑭ p. 272	Five Sails Restaurant	FOUR DIAMOND	New European	$38-$45	291
⑮ p. 272	Market by Jean-Georges	FOUR DIAMOND	Pacific Northwest	$16-$36	292
⑯ p. 272	ARC	THREE DIAMOND	Regional Canadian	$22-$50	290
⑰ p. 272	**Joe Fortes Seafood & Chop House**	THREE DIAMOND	Seafood Steak	$17-$55	292
⑱ p. 272	Miku	THREE DIAMOND	Japanese	$19-$38	292
⑲ p. 272	Guu Original	APPROVED	Japanese Small Plates	$8-$13	291
⑳ p. 272	Copper Chimney	THREE DIAMOND	Indian	$15-$32	291
㉑ p. 272	Scoozis Mediterranean Bar & Grill	APPROVED	Mediterranean	$14-$27	292
㉒ p. 272	Boulevard Kitchen & Oyster Bar	FOUR DIAMOND	Seafood	$19-$55	291
㉓ p. 272	Moxie's Classic Grill	APPROVED	American	$14-$45	292
㉔ p. 272	India Bistro	APPROVED	Indian	$12-$24	291
㉕ p. 272	**Le Crocodile**	FOUR DIAMOND	Traditional French	$17-$48	292
㉖ p. 272	YEW Seafood + Bar	THREE DIAMOND	Seafood	$19-$41	295
㉗ p. 272	Hawksworth Restaurant	FOUR DIAMOND	New Pacific Northwest	$23-$58	291
㉘ p. 272	Stepho's Souvlaki Greek Taverna	APPROVED	Greek	$8-$12	292
㉙ p. 272	**Bacchus Restaurant**	FOUR DIAMOND	French	$17-$44	290
㉚ p. 272	Al Porto Ristorante	THREE DIAMOND	Northern Italian	$15-$60	290
㉛ p. 272	Water St. Cafe	THREE DIAMOND	International	$16-$38	292
㉜ p. 272	Gotham Steakhouse & Cocktail Bar	THREE DIAMOND	Steak	$16-$63	291
㉝ p. 272	Banana Leaf Malaysian Cuisine	APPROVED	Asian	$15-$28	290
㉞ p. 272	Kingston Taphouse & Grille	APPROVED	American	$12-$24	292
㉟ p. 272	Breka Bakery & Café	APPROVED	Breads/Pastries Sandwiches	$7-$10	291
㊱ p. 272	**L'Abattoir**	FOUR DIAMOND	New American	$25-$44	292
㊲ p. 272	Ask for Luigi	THREE DIAMOND	Italian	$17-$28	290
㊳ p. 272	Medina Cafe	APPROVED	Mediterranean	$13-$19	292
㊴ p. 272	**Bauhaus Restaurant**	FOUR DIAMOND	New German	$26-$40	291
㊵ p. 272	St Lawrence Restaurant	THREE DIAMOND	French	$38-$39	292
㊶ p. 272	PiDGiN	THREE DIAMOND	Fusion	$17-$38	292
㊷ p. 272	Chambar	FOUR DIAMOND	New Belgian	$15-$36	291
㊸ p. 272	Lupo Restaurant + Vinoteca	THREE DIAMOND	New Italian	$18-$47	292

Map Page	Restaurants (cont'd)	Designation	Cuisine	Price Range	Page
㊹ p. 272	Fanny Bay Oyster Bar & Shellfish Market	APPROVED	Seafood	$16-$28	291
㊺ p. 272	Black Rice Izakaya	APPROVED	Japanese	$13-$27	291
㊻ p. 272	Frankie's Italian Kitchen & Bar	THREE DIAMOND	Italian	$14-$34	291
㊼ p. 272	Brix & Mortar	THREE DIAMOND	Pacific Northwest	$23-$36	291
㊽ p. 272	Ancora Waterfront Dining and Patio	FOUR DIAMOND	New Fusion Seafood	$23-$44	290
㊾ p. 272	Blue Water Cafe + Raw Bar	FOUR DIAMOND	Seafood Sushi	$28-$46	291
㊿ p. 272	**Cioppino's Mediterranean Grill**	FOUR DIAMOND	Italian	$28-$48	291
(51) p. 272	AnnaLena	THREE DIAMOND	New Canadian	$18-$38	290
(52) p. 272	Bao Bei Chinese Brasserie	THREE DIAMOND	New Chinese Small Plates	$20-$35	290
(53) p. 272	Yaletown Brewing Company	APPROVED	International	$15-$39	295
(54) p. 272	Bridges	APPROVED	American	$15-$50	291
(55) p. 272	Cactus Club Cafe	THREE DIAMOND	New American	$15-$46	291
(56) p. 272	Simply Thai	APPROVED	Thai	$10-$19	292
(57) p. 272	Minami	FOUR DIAMOND	New Japanese	$20-$40	292
(58) p. 272	Rodney's Oyster House	APPROVED	Seafood	$14-$30	292
(59) p. 272	La Terrazza	THREE DIAMOND	Northern Italian	$24-$42	292
(60) p. 272	The Sandbar Seafood Restaurant	THREE DIAMOND	Seafood	$15-$46	292
(61) p. 272	Provence Marinaside	THREE DIAMOND	Mediterranean Seafood	$15-$59	292
(62) p. 272	Dockside Restaurant *(See ad p. 285.)*	THREE DIAMOND	New American	$16-$36	291

Hertz AAA

Enjoy AAA membership discounts and benefits wherever you go.*

Up to 20% off the base rate

Free Additional Driver

$6.99 NeverLost® GPS

10% off tank of gas

Click: AAA.com/hertz | Call: 1-800-654-3080 | Visit: Your local AAA branch

*Discount applies to pay later base rate. Taxes and fees excluded. Benefits available at participating Hertz locations in the U.S., Canada and Puerto Rico. Gas savings is only valid when prepaid fuel option is purchased. No charge for additional drivers who are also AAA members, have a credit card in their own name and meet standard rental qualifications. Additional terms apply. © 2019 Hertz System, Inc. All rights reserved.

© AAA

1803-20

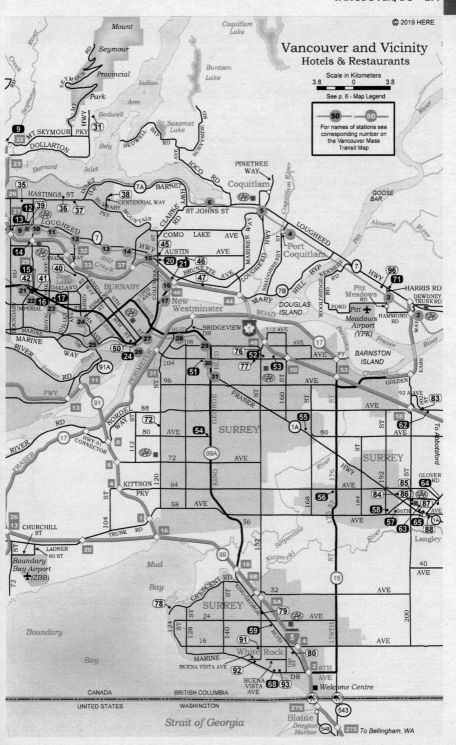

Vancouver and Vicinity
Hotels & Restaurants

© 2019 HERE

Scale in Kilometers

See p. 6 - Map Legend

For names of stations see corresponding number on the Vancouver Mass Transit Map

✈ Airport Hotels

Map Page	VANCOUVER INTERNATIONAL AIRPORT (Maximum driving distance from airport: 4.2 mi (6.8 km))	Designation	Member Savings	Page
34 p. 276	Abercorn Inn Vancouver Airport, 3.1 mi (4.9 km)	APPROVED		234
37 p. 276	Accent Inns, 4.0 mi (6.4 km)	APPROVED		234
27 p. 276	The Fairmont Vancouver Airport, on airport property	FOUR DIAMOND	✔	234
39 p. 276	Four Points by Sheraton Vancouver Airport, 3.7 mi (5.9 km)	THREE DIAMOND	✔	234
31 p. 276	Hampton Inn by Hilton Vancouver Airport, 2.8 mi (4.4 km)	APPROVED	✔	234
40 p. 276	Hilton Vancouver Airport, 4.0 mi (6.4 km)	THREE DIAMOND	✔	234
33 p. 276	Holiday Inn Express Vancouver-Airport, 3.8 mi (6.1 km)	THREE DIAMOND		234
38 p. 276	Holiday Inn Vancouver Airport-Richmond, 4.2 mi (6.8 km)	THREE DIAMOND		234
28 p. 276	Hotel at River Rock, 3.0 mi (4.9 km)	THREE DIAMOND		234
30 p. 276	Pacific Gateway Hotel at Vancouver Airport, 2.2 mi (3.5 km)	THREE DIAMOND	✔	235
42 p. 276	Quality Hotel Airport (South), 4.0 mi (6.4 km)	APPROVED	✔	235
36 p. 276	Radisson Hotel Vancouver Airport, 3.1 mi (5.1 km)	THREE DIAMOND	✔	235
41 p. 276	Ramada Limited Vancouver Airport, 4.0 mi (6.4 km)	APPROVED		235
29 p. 276	River Rock Casino Resort, 3.0 mi (4.9 km)	FOUR DIAMOND	✔	235
35 p. 276	Sandman Hotel Vancouver Airport, 3.6 mi (5.8 km)	THREE DIAMOND		235
43 p. 276	Sheraton Vancouver Airport Hotel, 4.1 mi (6.6 km)	THREE DIAMOND	✔	235
44 p. 276	Vancouver Airport Marriott, 4.1 mi (6.5 km)	THREE DIAMOND	✔	236
32 p. 276	The Westin Wall Centre Vancouver Airport, 2.5 mi (4.1 km)	THREE DIAMOND	✔	236

Vancouver and Vicinity

This index helps you "spot" where hotels and restaurants are located on the corresponding detailed maps. Restaurant price range is a combination of lunch and/or dinner. Turn to the listing page for more information and consult display ads for special promotions.

 For more details, rates and reservations: AAA.com/travelguides/hotels

VANCOUVER

Map Page	Hotels	Designation	Member Savings	Page
1 p. 276	Holiday Inn Vancouver Centre	THREE DIAMOND		295
2 p. 276	Best Western Plus Uptown Hotel (See ad p. 295.)	THREE DIAMOND	✔	295
3 p. 276	Days Inn-Vancouver Metro	APPROVED		295

Map Page	Restaurants	Designation	Cuisine	Price Range	Page
1 p. 276	Teahouse in Stanley Park	THREE DIAMOND	Pacific Northwest	$16-$42	296
2 p. 276	Bishop's	FOUR DIAMOND	Pacific Northwest	$35-$40	295
3 p. 276	Sophie's Cosmic Cafe	APPROVED	American	$9-$20	296
4 p. 276	Las Margaritas Restaurante & Cantina	APPROVED	Mexican	$13-$26	295
5 p. 276	Fable Kitchen	THREE DIAMOND	New Canadian	$12-$34	295
6 p. 276	Maenam	THREE DIAMOND	New Thai	$16-$28	295
7 p. 276	Farmer's Apprentice	THREE DIAMOND	Regional Canadian	$17-$64	295
8 p. 276	Cafe Salade de Fruits	APPROVED	French	$13-$40	295
9 p. 276	Cactus Club Cafe	THREE DIAMOND	New American	$15-$42	295

Map Page	Restaurants (cont'd)	Designation	Cuisine	Price Range	Page
⑩ p. 276	Tojo's Restaurant	THREE DIAMOND	Japanese	$28-$45	296
⑪ p. 276	Salmon n' Bannock	APPROVED	New Canadian	$17-$50	296
⑫ p. 276	West Restaurant	FOUR DIAMOND	Pacific Northwest	$17-$40	296
⑬ p. 276	Bistro Absinthe	THREE DIAMOND	French	$30-$48	295
⑭ p. 276	Cactus Club Cafe	THREE DIAMOND	New American	$15-$46	295
⑮ p. 276	Vij's Restaurant	THREE DIAMOND	New Indian	$19-$36	296
⑯ p. 276	Shaughnessy Restaurant At VanDusen Garden	THREE DIAMOND	Pacific Northwest	$17-$38	296
⑰ p. 276	Seasons in the Park Restaurant	THREE DIAMOND	Pacific Northwest	$16-$59	296
⑱ p. 276	Milltown Bar & Grill	APPROVED	American	$12-$24	296

NORTH VANCOUVER

Map Page	Hotels	Designation	Member Savings	Page
❻ p. 276	**Econo Lodge Inn & Suites North Vancouver**	APPROVED	✔	210
❼ p. 276	**SureStay Hotel by Best Western North Vancouver**	APPROVED	✔	210
❽ p. 276	Pinnacle Hotel at the Pier	THREE DIAMOND		210
❾ p. 276	**Holiday Inn & Suites North Vancouver**	THREE DIAMOND	✔	210

Map Page	Restaurants	Designation	Cuisine	Price Range	Page
㉖ p. 276	La Cucina	APPROVED	Italian	$20-$39	210
㉗ p. 276	Cactus Club Cafe	THREE DIAMOND	New American	$15-$46	210
㉘ p. 276	Fishworks	THREE DIAMOND	New Seafood	$12-$32	210
㉙ p. 276	Jagerhof	APPROVED	Continental	$14-$26	210
㉚ p. 276	The Lobby Restaurant	THREE DIAMOND	Pacific Northwest	$14-$35	210
㉛ p. 276	Arms Reach Bistro	THREE DIAMOND	Regional Canadian	$17-$45	210
㉜ p. 276	Tour de Feast	APPROVED	French	$11-$29	210

BURNABY

Map Page	Hotels	Designation	Member Savings	Page
⓬ p. 276	Executive Suites Hotels & Conference Centre Burnaby	THREE DIAMOND		176
⓭ p. 276	Accent Inns	APPROVED		175
⓮ p. 276	Delta Burnaby Hotel and Conference Centre	THREE DIAMOND	✔	175
⓯ p. 276	**Element Vancouver Metrotown**	THREE DIAMOND	✔	176
⓰ p. 276	**Hilton Vancouver Metrotown**	THREE DIAMOND	✔	176
⓱ p. 276	**Best Western Plus Burnaby Hotel & Conference Centre** (See ad p. 175.)	THREE DIAMOND	✔	175

Map Page	Restaurants	Designation	Cuisine	Price Range	Page
㉟ p. 276	The Pear Tree Restaurant	FOUR DIAMOND	Regional Canadian	$30-$39	176
㊱ p. 276	Cotto Enoteca Pizzeria	APPROVED	Italian	$13-$25	176
㊲ p. 276	Cockney Kings Fish & Chips	APPROVED	Fish & Chips	$9-$21	176
㊳ p. 276	Horizons	THREE DIAMOND	Pacific Rim	$18-$46	176
㊴ p. 276	Cactus Club Cafe	THREE DIAMOND	New American	$15-$49	176
㊵ p. 276	Hart House Restaurant	THREE DIAMOND	Pacific Northwest	$15-$42	176
㊶ p. 276	Trattoria	THREE DIAMOND	Italian	$15-$31	176
㊷ p. 276	Reflect Social Dining + Lounge	APPROVED	American	$16-$32	176

COQUITLAM

Map Page	Hotels	Designation	Member Savings	Page
⓴ p. 276	Executive Plaza Hotel & Conference Centre	THREE DIAMOND		179
㉑ p. 276	SureStay Plus Hotel by Best Western Coquitlam	APPROVED		179

Map Page	Restaurants	Designation	Cuisine	Price Range	Page
㊺ p. 276	Sushi California	APPROVED	Sushi	$9-$20	179

Map Page	Restaurants (cont'd)	Designation	Cuisine	Price Range	Page
46 p. 276	John B Neighborhood Pub	APPROVED	International	$12-$20	179
47 p. 276	Cactus Club Cafe	THREE DIAMOND	New American	$15-$49	179

NEW WESTMINSTER

Map Page	Hotel	Designation	Member Savings	Page
24 p. 276	Inn at the Quay	THREE DIAMOND	✔	207

Map Page	Restaurant	Designation	Cuisine	Price Range	Page
50 p. 276	Burger Heaven	APPROVED	Burgers Sandwiches	$12-$31	207

RICHMOND

Map Page	Hotels	Designation	Member Savings	Page
27 p. 276	The Fairmont Vancouver Airport	FOUR DIAMOND	✔	234
28 p. 276	Hotel at River Rock	THREE DIAMOND		234
29 p. 276	River Rock Casino Resort (See ad p. 235.)	FOUR DIAMOND	✔	235
30 p. 276	Pacific Gateway Hotel at Vancouver Airport	THREE DIAMOND	✔	235
31 p. 276	Hampton Inn by Hilton Vancouver Airport	APPROVED	✔	234
32 p. 276	The Westin Wall Centre Vancouver Airport	THREE DIAMOND	✔	236
33 p. 276	Holiday Inn Express Vancouver-Airport	THREE DIAMOND		234
34 p. 276	Abercorn Inn Vancouver Airport	APPROVED		234
35 p. 276	Sandman Hotel Vancouver Airport	THREE DIAMOND		235
36 p. 276	Radisson Hotel Vancouver Airport	THREE DIAMOND	✔	235
37 p. 276	Accent Inns	APPROVED		234
38 p. 276	Holiday Inn Vancouver Airport-Richmond	THREE DIAMOND		234
39 p. 276	Four Points by Sheraton Vancouver Airport	THREE DIAMOND	✔	234
40 p. 276	Hilton Vancouver Airport	THREE DIAMOND	✔	234
41 p. 276	Ramada Limited Vancouver Airport	APPROVED		235
42 p. 276	Quality Hotel Airport (South)	APPROVED	✔	235
43 p. 276	Sheraton Vancouver Airport Hotel	THREE DIAMOND	✔	235
44 p. 276	Vancouver Airport Marriott	THREE DIAMOND	✔	236
45 p. 276	Holiday Inn Express & Suites Riverport	THREE DIAMOND		234

Map Page	Restaurants	Designation	Cuisine	Price Range	Page
53 p. 276	Globe@YVR Restaurant	THREE DIAMOND	Pacific Northwest	$22-$49	236
54 p. 276	The Boathouse Restaurant	APPROVED	Seafood Steak	$15-$50	236
55 p. 276	Italian Tomato Restaurant	APPROVED	Italian	$14-$33	236
56 p. 276	Moxie's Classic Grill	APPROVED	American	$14-$39	236
57 p. 276	Red Star Seafood Restaurant	APPROVED	Chinese	$15-$30	236
58 p. 276	Flying Beaver Bar & Grill	APPROVED	American	$13-$24	236
59 p. 276	Man Ri Sung Korean Restaurant	APPROVED	Korean	$11-$39	236
60 p. 276	Felicos Restaurant	APPROVED	Greek	$17-$45	236
61 p. 276	Fogg n' Suds	APPROVED	American	$14-$23	236
62 p. 276	CAVU Kitchen Bar	THREE DIAMOND	New International	$14-$36	236
63 p. 276	Harold's Bistro & Bar	APPROVED	American	$14-$33	236
64 p. 276	The American Grille	THREE DIAMOND	New American	$16-$49	236
65 p. 276	Shanghai River Restaurant	APPROVED	Chinese	$12-$50	236
66 p. 276	Cactus Club Cafe	THREE DIAMOND	New American	$15-$49	236
67 p. 276	Pajo's	APPROVED	Fish & Chips	$13-$24	236
68 p. 276	Steveston Seafood House	THREE DIAMOND	Seafood	$14-$37	236
69 p. 276	Blue Canoe Waterfront Restaurant	THREE DIAMOND	Seafood	$15-$38	236

DELTA

Map Page	Hotel	Designation	Member Savings	Page
48 p. 276	Coast Tsawwassen Inn	APPROVED		182

Map Page	Restaurants	Designation	Cuisine	Price Range	Page
72 p. 276	Cactus Club Cafe	THREE DIAMOND	New American	$15-$46	182
73 p. 276	Mario's Kitchen	APPROVED	International	$12-$42	182

SURREY

Map Page	Hotels	Designation	Member Savings	Page
51 p. 276	Civic Hotel, Autograph Collection	THREE DIAMOND	✔	243
52 p. 276	Sheraton Vancouver Guildford Hotel (See ad p. 289.)	THREE DIAMOND	✔	243
53 p. 276	Four Points by Sheraton Surrey	THREE DIAMOND	✔	243
54 p. 276	Best Western King George Inn & Suites (See ad p. 242.)	APPROVED	✔	242
55 p. 276	Comfort Inn & Suites Surrey	APPROVED		243
56 p. 276	Holiday Inn & Suites	THREE DIAMOND	✔	243
57 p. 276	Hampton Inn & Suites Langley/Surrey	THREE DIAMOND	✔	243
58 p. 276	Ramada Langley-Surrey	APPROVED	✔	243
59 p. 276	Best Western Peace Arch Inn	APPROVED	✔	242

Map Page	Restaurants	Designation	Cuisine	Price Range	Page
76 p. 276	Moxie's Classic Grill	APPROVED	American	$14-$45	243
77 p. 276	Sabai Thai Restaurant	APPROVED	Thai	$12-$18	243
78 p. 276	Crescent Beach Bistro	APPROVED	Mediterranean	$12-$35	243
79 p. 276	Maguroguy	APPROVED	Japanese	$10-$25	243
80 p. 276	The Turkey House & Deli	APPROVED	Sandwiches Deli	$10-$14	243

LANGLEY

Map Page	Hotels	Designation	Member Savings	Page
62 p. 276	Holiday Inn Express Hotel & Suites Langley	THREE DIAMOND	✔	201
63 p. 276	Days Inn & Suites Langley	APPROVED		201
64 p. 276	Best Western Plus Langley Inn	THREE DIAMOND	✔	201
65 p. 276	Coast Hotel & Convention Centre	THREE DIAMOND		201

Map Page	Restaurants	Designation	Cuisine	Price Range	Page
83 p. 276	Akane Japanese Restaurant	APPROVED	Japanese	$9-$17	201
84 p. 276	An Indian Affair	APPROVED	Indian	$11-$17	201
85 p. 276	Cactus Club Cafe	THREE DIAMOND	New American	$14-$46	201
86 p. 276	Estrella's Montreal Deli	APPROVED	Deli Sandwiches	$8-$18	201
87 p. 276	C-Lovers Fish & Chips	APPROVED	Seafood	$8-$19	201
88 p. 276	Ban Chok Dee Thai Cuisine	APPROVED	Thai	$14-$22	201

WHITE ROCK

Map Page	Hotel	Designation	Member Savings	Page
68 p. 276	Ocean Promenade Hotel	THREE DIAMOND		328

Map Page	Restaurants	Designation	Cuisine	Price Range	Page
91 p. 276	The Wooden Spoon	APPROVED	Breakfast Comfort Food	$14-$23	328
92 p. 276	Uli's Restaurant	APPROVED	International	$15-$33	328
93 p. 276	La Baia Italian Restaurant	APPROVED	Italian	$15-$27	328

PITT MEADOWS

Map Page	Hotel	Designation	Member Savings	Page
71 p. 276	Best Western Plus Pitt Meadows Inn & Suites	THREE DIAMOND	✔	225

Map Page	Restaurant	Designation	Cuisine	Price Range	Page
96 p. 276	Kisoji Japanese Kitchen	APPROVED	Japanese	$15-$21	225

WEST VANCOUVER

Map Page	Restaurants	Designation	Cuisine	Price Range	Page
21 p. 276	Olive & Anchor	APPROVED	American	$16-$34	321
22 p. 276	Salmon House on the Hill	THREE DIAMOND	Seafood	$32-$48	321
23 p. 276	Cactus Club Cafe	THREE DIAMOND	New American	$15-$46	321

DOWNTOWN VANCOUVER

AUBERGE VANCOUVER HOTEL   604/678-8899
 THREE DIAMOND Hotel. **Address:** 837 W Hastings St V6C 1B6

BEST WESTERN PLUS SANDS   604/682-1831   **3**
 **THREE DIAMOND**

Hotel

 Best Western PLUS. **AAA Benefit:** Members save up to 15% and earn bonus points!

Address: 1755 Davie St V6G 1W5 **Location:** Between Bidwell and Denman sts. Burrard, 46. **Facility:** 121 units. 6 stories, interior corridors. **Parking:** on-site (fee). **Terms:** check-in 4 pm. **Dining:** 2 restaurants. **Activities:** sauna, exercise room. **Guest Services:** valet and coin laundry. *(See ad this page.)*

SAVE ECO ❙❙ 👶 ❤ CALL 🦽

👷 BIZ 📶 ✕ 🔒 🖨 💻 / SOME UNITS 🐾 🚐

BLUE HORIZON HOTEL   604/688-1411   **9**
 THREE DIAMOND

Hotel

Address: 1225 Robson St V6E 1C3 **Location:** Between Jervis and Bute sts. Burrard, 46. **Facility:** 214 units. 31 stories, interior corridors. **Parking:** on-site (fee). **Amenities:** safes. **Pool:** heated indoor. **Activities:** hot tub, steamroom, exercise room. **Guest Services:** valet laundry.

SAVE ECO ❙❙ 🍸 CALL 🦽 🏊

👷 BIZ 📶 ✕ 🔒 💻 🚐

🔗 **Booth or table?**

AAA.com/travelguides/restaurants

THE BURRARD   604/681-2331   **29**
 APPROVED Hotel. **Address:** 1100 Burrard St V6Z 1Y7

BW PREMIER COLLECTION CHATEAU GRANVILLE HOTEL & SUITES & CONFERENCE CENTRE
   604/669-7070   **34**

 **THREE DIAMOND** BW Premier COLLECTION by BEST WESTERN

Hotel

AAA Benefit: Members save up to 15% and earn bonus points!

Address: 1100 Granville St V6Z 2B6 **Location:** Between Davie and Helmcken sts. Yaletown-Roundhouse, 53. **Facility:** 118 units. 15 stories, interior corridors. **Parking:** on-site (fee). **Terms:** check-in 4 pm. **Amenities:** safes. **Activities:** exercise room. **Guest Services:** valet laundry. *(See ad p. 283.)*

SAVE ECO ❙❙ 👶 🍸

CALL 🦽 👷 BIZ HS 📶 ✕ 🐕 🔒 🖨 💻 / SOME UNITS 🐾 🚐

THE COAST COAL HARBOUR VANCOUVER HOTEL BY APA   604/697-0202   **5**
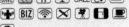 **THREE DIAMOND** Hotel. **Address:** 1180 W Hastings St V6E 4R5

DAYS INN VANCOUVER DOWNTOWN   604/681-4335   **15**
 APPROVED Hotel. **Address:** 921 W Pender St V6C 1M2

DELTA HOTELS BY MARRIOTT VANCOUVER DOWNTOWN SUITES   604/689-8188   **23**
 **THREE DIAMOND**

Hotel

D DELTA HOTELS **AAA Benefit:** Members save 5% or more!

Address: 550 W Hastings St V6B 1L6 **Location:** Between Seymour and Richards sts; entrance in alley way. Waterfront, 45. **Facility:** 225 units. 23 stories, interior corridors. **Parking:** on-site (fee) and valet. **Terms:** check-in 4 pm. **Amenities:** safes. **Activities:** exercise room. **Guest Services:** valet laundry.

SAVE ECO   🍸 CALL 🦽 👷

BIZ HS 📶 ✕ 🔒 💻 / SOME UNITS 🐾 🚐

▼ See AAA listing this page ▼

BW Best Western PLUS. SANDS
1755 Davie Steet
Vancouver, BC
V6G 1W5

You'll find all of the Vancouver's amenities just around the corner along with the beaches, the seawall and beautiful Stanley Park.

Our 3 Diamond full service hotel offers: The Park Restaurant & Pub, The Bayside Lounge, a business centre, a fitness facility & sauna and free high-speed internet access throughout the hotel.

sands@bwsands.com
604-682-1831 or 1-800-661-7887

(See map & index p. 272.)

THE DOUGLAS, AUTOGRAPH COLLECTION

604/676-0889

Boutique Contemporary Hotel

AUTOGRAPH COLLECTION HOTELS

AAA Benefit: Members save 5% or more!

Address: 45 Smithe St V6B 0R3 **Location:** Jct Pacific Blvd. Yaletown-Roundhouse, 53. **Facility:** Guest rooms are handsomely designed, blending natural wood tones with interesting urban elements like textured cement ceilings. Rooms range from smaller upscale units to fantastic suites. 188 units. 27 stories, interior corridors. **Parking:** on-site (fee) and valet. **Terms:** check-in 4 pm. **Amenities:** safes. **Activities:** sauna, hot tub, steamroom, trails, health club, in-room exercise equipment, spa. **Guest Services:** valet laundry, area transportation.

EXECUTIVE HOTEL LE SOLEIL

604/632-3000

Boutique Hotel

Address: 567 Hornby St V6C 2E8 **Location:** Between Dunsmuir and Pender sts. Burrard, 46. **Facility:** As you step into the opulent lobby you'll see the staff is all about pampering guests. In the rooms and suites, every piece of art, furniture and fabric has been hand-picked from European designers. 113 units. 16 stories, interior corridors. **Parking:** valet only. **Terms:** check-in 4 pm. **Amenities:** safes. **Dining:** Copper Chimney, see separate listing. **Activities:** bicycles, limited exercise equipment. **Guest Services:** valet laundry. **Featured Amenity:** full hot breakfast.

FAIRMONT HOTEL VANCOUVER

604/684-3131

Classic Historic Hotel

Address: 900 W Georgia St V6C 2W6 **Location:** Corner of Burrard at W Georgia St; enter from Hornby St. Across from Vancouver Art Gallery. Burrard, 46. **Facility:** Built in 1939, this landmark building was officially opened by the Queen Mother and her husband, King George VI. You'll find smaller upscale rooms up to exceptionally spacious and gorgeous suites. 557 units. 15 stories, interior corridors. **Parking:** on-site (fee) and valet. **Amenities:** safes. **Pool:** heated indoor. **Activities:** sauna, hot tub, bicycles, exercise room, in-room exercise equipment, spa. **Guest Services:** valet laundry.

Mobile Battery Service

1-800-AAA-HELP • 1-800-CAA-HELP
AAA.com/mobile • CAA.ca/mobile

Power You Can Trust!™

▼ See AAA listing p. 282 ▼

BWP PREMIER | BEST WESTERN.

- Recently refurbished hotel located in downtown Vancouver close to Attractions, Shopping and Cruise terminal.
- Featuring 90 spacious suites with a separate living area, balcony and 28 rooms offering a

superior view of downtown Vancouver.
- Free Wi-Fi and Business Centre
- Full-Service Restaurant, Lounge, Tiki Bar and Room Service
- Gated underground parking

10% OR MORE SAVINGS FOR AAA MEMBERS ONLY

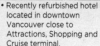 GREEN KEY Eco-Rating Program

 CAA Rewards

 THREE DIAMOND

Chateau Granville Hotel & Suites & Conference Center
1100 Granville St., Vancouver, BC V6Z 2B6 • chateaugranville.com • 800.663.0575

(See map & index p. 272.)

FAIRMONT PACIFIC RIM
604/695-5300 **11**

FIVE DIAMOND

Contemporary Hotel

Address: 1038 Canada Pl V6C 0B9 **Location:** Between Burrard and Thurlow sts. Waterfront, 45. **Facility:** Guests are pampered at this luxury tower, which has a beautiful, innovative design. Gorgeous rooms with super views are rigged with all the latest technological bells and whistles. 367 units. 48 stories, interior corridors. **Parking:** on-site (fee) and valet. **Amenities:** safes. **Dining:** 3 restaurants, entertainment. **Pool:** heated outdoor. **Activities:** sauna, hot tub, steamroom, cabanas, bicycles, health club, in-room exercise equipment, spa. **Guest Services:** valet laundry, boarding pass kiosk, area transportation.

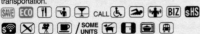

FAIRMONT WATERFRONT
604/691-1991 **14**

FOUR DIAMOND

Hotel

Address: 900 Canada Place Way V6C 3L5 **Location:** Between Howe and Burrard sts. Opposite Canada Place. Waterfront, 45. **Facility:** You will find large TVs with lots of bells and whistles and great views from floor-to-ceiling windows in these lovely rooms. The location is handy to the cruise ship terminal and convention center. 489 units. 23 stories, interior corridors. **Parking:** on-site (fee) and valet. **Amenities:** safes. **Dining:** ARC, see separate listing. **Pool:** heated outdoor. **Activities:** hot tub, steamroom, bicycles, health club, in-room exercise equipment, massage. **Guest Services:** valet laundry.

  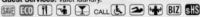

FOUR SEASONS HOTEL VANCOUVER
604/689-9333 **21**

FOUR DIAMOND Hotel. **Address:** 791 W Georgia St V6C 2T4

GEORGIAN COURT HOTEL, BW PREMIER COLLECTION
604/682-5555 **38**

THREE DIAMOND

Boutique Hotel

BW Premier COLLECTION by BEST WESTERN

AAA Benefit: Members save up to 15% and earn bonus points!

Address: 773 Beatty St V6B 2M4 **Location:** Between Georgia and Robson sts. Opposite BC Place Stadium. Stadium-Chinatown, 48. **Facility:** Close to many attractions like Robson Street and Queen Elizabeth Theatre, this lovely property's guest rooms exude charm with extra amenities like robes and slippers, and windows that open. 180 units. 12 stories, interior corridors. **Parking:** on-site (fee). **Amenities:** safes. **Dining:** Frankie's Italian Kitchen & Bar, see separate listing. **Activities:** hot tub, steamroom, bicycles, exercise room. **Guest Services:** valet laundry, area transportation.

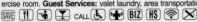

GRANVILLE ISLAND HOTEL
604/683-7373 **42**

THREE DIAMOND

Boutique Hotel

Address: 1253 Johnston St V6H 3R9 **Location:** Granville Island; below the bridge, follow signs. Yaletown-Roundhouse, 53. **Facility:** Rooms are lovely at this distinctive hotel and feature fineries like super soft Italian cotton linens. Just steps from Granville Island Market, there are tons of shopping and entertainment options. 82 units. 3-4 stories, interior corridors. **Parking:** on-site (fee). **Amenities:** safes. **Dining:** Dockside Restaurant, see separate listing. **Activities:** sauna, hot tub, bicycles, trails, exercise room. **Guest Services:** valet laundry. *(See ad p. 285.)*

 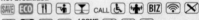

HAMPTON INN & SUITES BY HILTON DOWNTOWN VANCOUVER
604/602-1008 **39**

THREE DIAMOND

Contemporary Hotel

 Hampton by HILTON

AAA Benefit: Members save up to 15%!

Address: 111 Robson St V6B 2A8 **Location:** Between Cambie and Beatty sts. Opposite BC Place Stadium. Stadium-Chinatown, 48. **Facility:** 132 units, some efficiencies. 16 stories, interior corridors. **Parking:** on-site (fee). **Amenities:** safes. **Activities:** sauna, hot tub, bicycles, exercise room. **Guest Services:** valet and coin laundry, area transportation. **Featured Amenity:** full hot breakfast.

HOTEL BLU VANCOUVER
604/620-6200 **37**

FOUR DIAMOND

Boutique Contemporary Hotel

Address: 177 Robson St V6B 0N3 **Location:** Jct Cambie St. Stadium-Chinatown, 48. **Facility:** This upscale hotel has beautiful, bright décor. The comfortable rooms also boast a lovely design, plus many high-tech features like smart TVs and your own in-room, voice-activated concierge. 75 units. 4 stories, interior corridors. **Parking:** on-site (fee) and valet. **Terms:** check-in 4 pm. **Amenities:** safes. **Dining:** 2 restaurants. **Pool:** heated indoor. **Activities:** sauna, hot tub, bicycles, exercise room. **Guest Services:** complimentary and valet laundry, area transportation.

HOWARD JOHNSON HOTEL DOWNTOWN VANCOUVER
604/688-8701 **35**

APPROVED Hotel. **Address:** 1176 Granville St V6Z 1L8

🔗 **For highways, byways and more:**

AAA.com/maps

▼ See AAA listing p. 284 ▼

URBAN RETREAT IN THE HEART OF VANCOUVER

All in a waterfront hotel steps from downtown.

ART ❧ NATURE ❧ RELAXATION

GRANVILLE ISLAND HOTEL
VANCOUVER'S ISLAND OASIS

GRANVILLE ISLAND HOTEL
1253 Johnston Street, Vancouver, BC
1-800-663-1840 or 604-683-7373
www.granvilleislandhotel.com

STAY CONNECTED

GET THE APP
AAA.com/mobile
CAA.ca/mobile

(See map & index p. 272.)

HYATT REGENCY VANCOUVER   604/683-1234   🔟

 FOUR DIAMOND

Hotel

 HYATT REGENCY

AAA Benefit: Members save up to 10%!

Address: 655 Burrard St V6C 2R7 **Location:** Between W Georgia and Melville sts. Connected to shopping center. 🚇 Burrard, 46. **Facility:** In the heart of downtown, there are lots of bright and beautiful areas in which to lounge at this large, convention-oriented hotel. Many of its spacious, modern rooms boast fantastic city views. 644 units. 34 stories, interior corridors. **Parking:** on-site (fee) and valet. **Terms:** check-in 4 pm. **Amenities:** safes. **Dining:** 2 restaurants. **Pool:** heated outdoor. **Activities:** hot tub, exercise room, in-room exercise equipment. **Guest Services:** valet laundry.

JW MARRIOTT PARQ VANCOUVER   604/676-0888   4️⃣1️⃣

FOUR DIAMOND

Contemporary Hotel

JW MARRIOTT

AAA Benefit: Members save 5% or more!

Address: 39 Smithe St V6B 0R3 **Location:** Jct Pacific Blvd. 🚇 Stadium-Chinatown, 48. **Facility:** Part of the Parq Vancouver casino complex, this hotel features upscale rooms with a small sitting area and a large desk. The design includes soothing neutral tones brightened by pastel butterfly art. 329 units. 25 stories, interior corridors. **Parking:** on-site (fee) and valet. **Terms:** check-in 4 pm. **Amenities:** safes. **Dining:** 6 restaurants, entertainment. **Activities:** sauna, hot tub, steamroom, trails, health club, in-room exercise equipment, spa. **Guest Services:** valet laundry, area transportation.

THE LANDIS HOTEL & SUITES   604/681-3555   3️⃣1️⃣

 THREE DIAMOND

Extended Stay Hotel

Address: 1200 Hornby St V6Z 1W2 **Location:** Between Davie and Drake sts. 🚇 Yaletown-Roundhouse, 53. **Facility:** 52 two-bedroom kitchen units. 18 stories, interior corridors. **Parking:** on-site (fee). **Amenities:** safes. **Pool:** heated indoor. **Activities:** hot tub, exercise room. **Guest Services:** valet and coin laundry, area transportation.

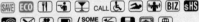

L'HERMITAGE HOTEL   778/327-4100   3️⃣0️⃣

FOUR DIAMOND Boutique Hotel. **Address:** 788 Richards St V6B 3A4

THE LISTEL HOTEL VANCOUVER   604/684-8461   6️⃣

THREE DIAMOND Boutique Contemporary Hotel. **Address:** 1300 Robson St V6E 1C5

PAN PACIFIC VANCOUVER   604/662-8111   1️⃣3️⃣

FOUR DIAMOND

Hotel

Address: 300-999 Canada Pl V6C 3B5 **Location:** Waterfront. Between Howe and Burrard sts. Located at Canada Place. 🚇 Waterfront, 45. **Facility:** This waterfront landmark hotel connects to the convention center, cruise ship terminal, Skytrain and Flyover Canada. Members with advance reservations get complimentary room upgrades on availability. 503 units, some two bedrooms and kitchens. 23 stories, interior corridors. **Parking:** on-site (fee) and valet. **Terms:** check-in 4 pm. **Amenities:** safes. **Dining:** Five Sails Restaurant, see separate listing, entertainment. **Pool:** heated outdoor. **Activities:** sauna, hot tub, trails, health club, in-room exercise equipment, spa. **Guest Services:** valet laundry, boarding pass kiosk. *(See ad this page.)*

▼ *See AAA listing this page* ▼

An experience like no other. Premier luxury in a prime waterfront location.

 PAN PACIFIC VANCOUVER

Toll free Canada: 1.800.663.1515 | USA: 1.800.937.1515
Visit: www.panpacific.com/vancouver

 global hotel alliance

🔗 **Get an expert view from AAA inspectors:**

AAA.com/travelguides/hotels

(See map & index p. 272.)

PINNACLE VANCOUVER HARBOURFRONT HOTEL
604/689-9211 **7**

THREE DIAMOND
Hotel

Address: 1133 W Hastings St V6E 3T3 **Location:** Between Thurlow and Bute sts. Burrard, 46. **Facility:** 442 units. 19 stories, interior corridors. **Parking:** on-site (fee) and valet. **Amenities:** safes. **Pool:** heated indoor. **Activities:** hot tub, bicycles, health club. **Guest Services:** valet laundry.
(See ad this page.)

SAVE ECO

CALL HS

SOME / UNITS

RAMADA LIMITED DOWNTOWN VANCOUVER
604/488-1088 **27**

APPROVED **Hotel. Address:** 435 W Pender St V6B 1V2

RAMADA VANCOUVER DOWNTOWN
604/685-1111 **36**

APPROVED **Hotel. Address:** 1221 Granville St V6Z 1M6

RESIDENCE INN BY MARRIOTT VANCOUVER DOWNTOWN
604/688-1234 **32**

THREE DIAMOND SAVE Extended Stay Contemporary Hotel. **Address:** 1234 Hornby St V6Z 1W2

AAA Benefit:
Members save 5% or more!

ROSEWOOD HOTEL GEORGIA
604/682-5566 **22**

FOUR DIAMOND Historic Boutique Hotel. **Address:** 801 W Georgia St V6C 1P7

ST. REGIS HOTEL
604/681-1135 **26**

THREE DIAMOND
Boutique Hotel

Address: 602 Dunsmuir St V6B 1Y6 **Location:** Corner of Dunsmuir and Seymour sts. Granville, 47. **Facility:** Exceptional and warm hospitality is the norm here with upscale rooms ranging from compact units to suites, all with modern, elegant décor. Guests enjoy extensive off-site fitness facilities. 65 units. 5 stories, interior corridors. **Parking:** valet only. **Amenities:** safes. **Dining:** Gotham Steakhouse & Cocktail Bar, see separate listing. **Activities:** massage. **Guest Services:** valet laundry. **Featured Amenity:** full hot breakfast.

SAVE CALL BIZ HS

SOME / UNITS

🔗 **Book and save**

at AAA.com/hertz

▼ See AAA listing this page ▼

PINNACLE HOTEL
HARBOURFRONT

ROOMS WITH A VIEW.

Located right where you want to be in the heart of downtown Vancouver on Coal Harbour's waterfront.

BEST LOCATION | RESTAURANT & BAR | POOL & FITNESS | FREE WIFI

BOOK NOW

✦ 1 844 337 3118 | PINNACLEHARBOURFRONTHOTEL.COM
1133 WEST HASTINGS STREET | VANCOUVER, BC | V6E 3T3

THREE DIAMOND   CAA/AAA MEMBERS RECEIVE UP TO A 25% DISCOUNT WHEN STAYING TWO NIGHTS OR MORE.

(See map & index p. 272.)

SHANGRI-LA HOTEL VANCOUVER

604/689-1120 **12**

FIVE DIAMOND

**Boutique
Contemporary
Hotel**

Address: 1128 W Georgia St V6E 0A8 **Location:** Between Thurlow and Bute sts. Burrard, 46. **Facility:** The unique underground drive-up entry for this stunning hotel is found along Alberni Street. Luxurious rooms have beautiful African rosewood walls, Italian marble bathrooms and the latest technology. 119 units. 62 stories, interior corridors. **Parking:** on-site (fee) and valet. **Amenities:** safes. **Dining:** Market by Jean-Georges, see separate listing. **Pool:** heated outdoor. **Activities:** sauna, hot tub, steam-room, health club, in-room exercise equipment, spa. **Guest Services:** valet laundry, boarding pass kiosk, area transportation. **Featured Amenity:** full hot breakfast. *(See ad this page.)*

SAVE ECO ❙❙ ♿ ☿ CALL ⚐ ⛵ ♿ BIZ HS ≋ ✕ 🎥 💻 / SOME UNITS 🐾 🚐

SHERATON VANCOUVER WALL CENTRE HOTEL

604/331-1000 **28**

THREE DIAMOND

Hotel

SHERATON

AAA Benefit: Members save 5% or more!

Address: 1088 Burrard St V6Z 2R9 **Location:** Between Helmcken and Nelson sts. Vancouver City Centre, 52. **Facility:** 746 units, some two bedrooms. 27-35 stories, interior corridors. **Parking:** on-site (fee) and valet. **Amenities:** safes. **Pool:** heated indoor. **Activities:** sauna, hot tub, health club. **Guest Services:** valet laundry.

SAVE ECO ❙❙ ☿ ⚐ CALL ♿ ⛵ ♿ BIZ HS ≋ ✕ 🎥 💻 / SOME UNITS 🐾 🚐

▼ See AAA listing this page ▼

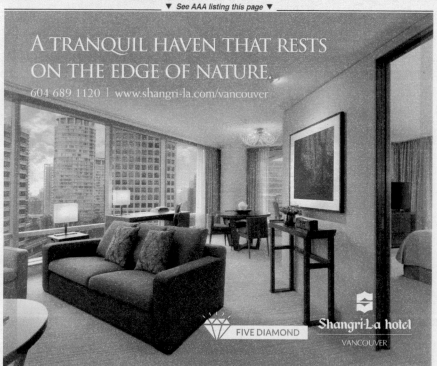

A TRANQUIL HAVEN THAT RESTS ON THE EDGE OF NATURE.

604 689 1120 | www.shangri-la.com/vancouver

FIVE DIAMOND

Shangri-La hotel
VANCOUVER

From simple to spectacular:

AAA.com/travelguides/restaurants

(See map & index p. 272.)

SUNSET INN & SUITES   604/688-2474   **25**

 THREE DIAMOND

Extended Stay Hotel

Address: 1111 Burnaby St V6E 1P4 **Location:** Between Thurlow and Bute sts. Located in a residential neighborhood. [R] Yaletown-Roundhouse, 53. **Facility:** 50 kitchen units. 11 stories, interior corridors. **Terms:** check-in 4 pm. **Amenities:** safes. **Activities:** exercise room. **Guest Services:** coin laundry. **Featured Amenity:** continental breakfast. *(See ad this page.)*

[icons: SAVE, restaurant, accessible, HS, wifi, no-smoking, fitness, lounge, TV, parking]

Get more for less.
Complimentary PARKING,
continental breakfast and much more.
Short walk to beach.

THE SUTTON PLACE HOTEL   604/682-5511   **20**

 FOUR DIAMOND

Hotel

Address: 845 Burrard St V6Z 2K6 **Location:** Between Smithe and Robson sts. [R] Burrard, 46. **Facility:** The lovely lobby has a classic design with antique-style furnishings; the theme spills over to attractive rooms with luxurious bedding. You will find the staff highly attuned to your needs. 397 units. 21 stories, interior corridors. **Parking:** on-site (fee) and valet. **Amenities:** safes. **Dining:** Boulevard Kitchen & Oyster Bar, see separate listing. **Pool:** heated indoor. **Activities:** hot tub, steamroom, health club, spa. **Guest Services:** valet and coin laundry, boarding pass kiosk, area transportation.

[icons: SAVE, ECO, restaurant, accessible, lounge, CALL, accessible, pool, fitness, BIZ, sHS, safe, no-smoking, pet, TV, SOME UNITS, pet, parking]

SYLVIA HOTEL   604/681-9321   **2**

 APPROVED   Historic Hotel. **Address:** 1154 Gilford St V6G 2P6

TRUMP INTERNATIONAL HOTEL & TOWER VANCOUVER   604/979-8888   **10**

 FOUR DIAMOND   Contemporary Hotel. **Address:** 1161 W Georgia St V6E 0C6

▼ See AAA listing p. 243 ▼

Sheraton Vancouver Guildford Hotel

SHERATON
EST. 1937

- Located across from Guildford Town Centre, BC's 2nd largest shopping mall
- Minutes away from the area's top golf courses
- Amenities: Sueno Spa, Outdoor Pool, Fitness Centre, MIXT Lobby Lounge

15269 104th Ave, Surrey BC V3R 1N5

1.888.627.8063

 THREE DIAMOND   (CAA) (AAA)

www.sheratonguildford.com

▼ See AAA listing this page ▼

AAA INSPECTOR'S **BEST OF** HOUSEKEEPING 2019

Sunset Inn & Suites
DOWNTOWN VANCOUVER

1111 Burnaby St.
Vancouver, BC V6E 1P4
604-688-2474

(See map & index p. 272.)

VANCOUVER MARRIOTT PINNACLE DOWNTOWN
604/684-1128

FOUR DIAMOND
Hotel

AAA Benefit: Members save 5% or more!

Address: 1128 W Hastings St V6E 4R5 **Location:** Between Thurlow and Bute sts. Burrard, 46. **Facility:** Just a few blocks from the Convention Centre and in the heart of the downtown business district, the hotel's guest rooms offer breathtaking views of the mountains, water and downtown Vancouver. 438 units. 31 stories, interior corridors. **Parking:** on-site (fee) and valet. **Terms:** check-in 4 pm. **Amenities:** safes. **Pool:** heated indoor. **Activities:** sauna, hot tub, steamroom, exercise room. **Guest Services:** valet laundry.

THE WEDGEWOOD HOTEL & SPA   604/689-7777 ㉔

FOUR DIAMOND
Boutique Hotel

Address: 845 Hornby St V6Z 1V1 **Location:** Between Smithe and Robson sts. Vancouver City Centre, 52. **Facility:** This wonderfully intimate, stylish hotel offers beautiful rooms with gorgeous, classic furnishings. You will also find the service to be warm and highly personalized. 83 units. 13 stories, interior corridors. **Parking:** valet only. **Amenities:** safes. **Dining:** Bacchus Restaurant, see separate listing, entertainment. **Activities:** steamroom, exercise room, spa. **Guest Services:** valet laundry. **Featured Amenity:** continental breakfast.

WEST END GUEST HOUSE   604/681-2889 ❹
THREE DIAMOND Historic Bed & Breakfast. **Address:** 1362 Haro St V6E 1G2

THE WESTIN BAYSHORE VANCOUVER
604/682-3377 ❶

FOUR DIAMOND
Contemporary Hotel

WESTIN
HOTELS & RESORTS

AAA Benefit: Members save 5% or more!

Address: 1601 Bayshore Dr V6G 2V4 **Location:** Waterfront. Jct W Georgia and Cardero sts. Burrard, 46. **Facility:** Enjoy an oasis in the city, where wonderful grounds surround this sprawling hotel. Most of the tasteful rooms and suites offer spectacular harbor, city and mountain views. 499 units. 9-16 stories, interior corridors. **Parking:** on-site (fee) and valet. **Amenities:** safes. **Pool:** heated outdoor, heated indoor. **Activities:** sauna, hot tub, steamroom, marina, trails, exercise room, in-room exercise equipment, spa. **Guest Services:** valet laundry.

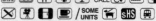

THE WESTIN GRAND, VANCOUVER   604/602-1999 ㉝

THREE DIAMOND
Hotel

WESTIN
HOTELS & RESORTS

AAA Benefit: Members save 5% or more!

Address: 433 Robson St V6B 6L9 **Location:** Between Homer and Richards sts. Vancouver City Centre, 52. **Facility:** 206 units. 26 stories, interior corridors. **Parking:** on-site (fee) and valet. **Amenities:** safes. **Pool:** heated outdoor. **Activities:** sauna, hot tub, steamroom, exercise room, in-room exercise equipment. **Guest Services:** valet laundry.

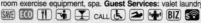

WHERE TO EAT

AL PORTO RISTORANTE   604/683-8376 ㉚
THREE DIAMOND Northern Italian. Fine Dining. **Address:** 321 Water St V6B 1B8

ANCORA WATERFRONT DINING AND PATIO
604/681-1164 ㊽
FOUR DIAMOND New Fusion Seafood. Fine Dining. **Address:** 2-1600 Howe St V6Z 2L9

ANNALENA   778/379-4052 ㈤
THREE DIAMOND New Canadian. Casual Dining. **Address:** 1809 W 1st Ave V6J 5B8

ARC   604/691-1818 ⑯
THREE DIAMOND Regional Canadian. Fine Dining. **Address:** 900 Canada Place Way V6C 3L5

ASK FOR LUIGI   604/428-2544 ㊲
THREE DIAMOND Italian. Casual Dining. **Address:** 305 Alexander St V6A 1C4

BACCHUS RESTAURANT   604/608-5319 ㉙

FOUR DIAMOND
French
Fine Dining
$17-$44

AAA Inspector Notes: *Classic.* Enjoy a fine meal in a luxurious, elegant setting, presided over by a superb likeness of Bacchus himself. The chef has created a wonderful menu, employing locally sourced ingredients and delicious preparations. Menu selections include foie gras, local duck, AAA Alberta beef and fresh caught seafood. The lounge is a beautiful spot to unwind and people-watch when they open the street-side windows in nice weather. **Features:** full bar, Sunday brunch. **Reservations:** suggested. **Address:** 845 Hornby St V6Z 1V1 **Location:** Between Smithe and Robson sts; in The Wedgewood Hotel & Spa. Vancouver City Centre, 52. **Parking:** valet and street only. 🅑 🅛 🅓 CALL

BANANA LEAF MALAYSIAN CUISINE   604/669-3389 ㉝
APPROVED Asian. Casual Dining. **Address:** 1043 Davie St V6E 1M5

BAO BEI CHINESE BRASSERIE   604/688-0876 ㊷
THREE DIAMOND New Chinese Small Plates. Casual Dining. **Address:** 163 Keefer St V6A 1X3

🔗 **For complete hotel, dining and attraction listings: AAA.com/travelguides**

(See map & index p. 272.)

BAUHAUS RESTAURANT   604/974-1147   **39**

FOUR DIAMOND **New German Fine Dining $26-$40** AAA Inspector Notes: This handsome place has a spartan elegance enhanced by original brick walls. The seasonal menu features local ingredients and a variety of dishes with delightful flavors and textures, and presentations that rival works of art. As a nod to the German film director and owner, you will find classics such as Wiener Schnitzel. Competent staff, imaginative cocktails and a thoughtful wine list add to the enjoyment. **Features:** full bar, patio dining. **Reservations:** suggested. **Address:** 1 W Cordova St V6B 2J2 **Location:** Just w of Carrall St. Stadium-Chinatown, 48. **Parking:** street only. D CALL

BLACK RICE IZAKAYA   778/379-0416   **45**

APPROVED Japanese. Casual Dining. **Address:** 782 Cambie St V6B 2R5

BLUE WATER CAFE + RAW BAR   604/688-8078   **49**

FOUR DIAMOND Seafood Sushi. Fine Dining. **Address:** 1095 Hamilton St V6B 5T4

THE BOATHOUSE RESTAURANT   604/669-2225

APPROVED Seafood Steak. Casual Dining. **Address:** 1795 Beach Ave V6G 1Y9

BOTANIST   604/695-5500   **8**

FOUR DIAMOND New Pacific Northwest. Fine Dining. **Address:** 1038 Canada Pl V6C 0B9

BOULEVARD KITCHEN & OYSTER BAR   604/682-5511   **22**

FOUR DIAMOND Seafood. Fine Dining. **Address:** 845 Burrard St V6Z 2K6

BREKA BAKERY & CAFE   604/620-8200   **9**

APPROVED Coffee/Tea Breads/Pastries. Quick Serve. **Address:** 818 Bute St V6E 1Y4

BREKA BAKERY & CAFÉ   604/428-8080   **35**

APPROVED Breads/Pastries Sandwiches. Quick Serve. **Address:** 855 Davie St V6Z 1B7

BRIDGES   604/687-4400   **54**

APPROVED American. Casual Dining. **Address:** 1696 Duranleau St V6H 3S4

BRIX & MORTAR   604/915-9463   **47**

THREE DIAMOND Pacific Northwest. Fine Dining. **Address:** 1138 Homer St V6B 2X6

CACTUS CLUB CAFE

THREE DIAMOND New American. Casual Dining.
LOCATIONS:
Address: 1136 Robson St V6E 1B2 **Phone:** 604/687-3278   **12**
Address: 357 Davie St V6B 1R2 **Phone:** 604/685-8070   **55**
Address: 1790 Beach Ave V6E 1V3 **Phone:** 604/681-2582   **4**

CARDERO'S RESTAURANT   604/669-7666   **2**

THREE DIAMOND Seafood. Casual Dining. **Address:** 1583 Coal Harbour Quay V6G 3E7

CHAMBAR   604/879-7119   **42**

FOUR DIAMOND New Belgian. Casual Dining. **Address:** 568 Beatty St V6B 2L3

CINCIN   604/688-7338   **11**

THREE DIAMOND New Mediterranean. Fine Dining. **Address:** 1154 Robson St V6E 1B5

CIOPPINO'S MEDITERRANEAN GRILL   604/688-7466   **50**

FOUR DIAMOND **Italian Fine Dining $28-$48** AAA Inspector Notes: Chef Pino Posteraro has a real knack for creating flavors with high-quality ingredients. He even has his own trademarked chocolate. The expansive menu may include items such as Digby scallops with black truffle froth, wonderful handmade pasta and wild Alberta boar served two ways. Hospitable servers go out of their way to make sure you have a wonderful evening. The warm and inviting dining room features many wine cabinets showcasing a huge wine collection. **Features:** full bar. **Reservations:** suggested. **Address:** 1133 Hamilton St V6B 5P6 **Location:** Between Helmcken and Davie sts. Yaletown-Roundhouse, 53. **Parking:** on-site (fee) and valet. D CALL

COPPER CHIMNEY   604/689-8862   **20**

THREE DIAMOND Indian. Fine Dining. **Address:** 567 Hornby St V6C 2E8

DOCKSIDE RESTAURANT   604/685-7070   **62**

THREE DIAMOND New American. Casual Dining. **Address:** 1253 Johnston St V6H 3R9 *(See ad p. 285.)*

EARLS KITCHEN + BAR

APPROVED American. Casual Dining.
LOCATIONS:
Address: 1185 Robson St V6E 1B5 **Phone:** 604/669-0020
Address: 905 Hornby St V6Z 1V3 **Phone:** 604/682-6700

ESPAÑA   604/558-4040   **3**

APPROVED New Spanish Small Plates. Casual Dining. **Address:** 1118 Denman St V6G 2M8

FANNY BAY OYSTER BAR & SHELLFISH MARKET   778/379-9510   **44**

APPROVED Seafood. Casual Dining. **Address:** 762 Cambie St V6B 2P2

FIVE SAILS RESTAURANT   604/844-2855   **14**

FOUR DIAMOND New European. Fine Dining. **Address:** 999 Canada Pl, Level R V6C 3E1

FORAGE   604/661-1400   **6**

THREE DIAMOND New Canadian. Casual Dining. **Address:** 1300 Robson St V6E 1C5

FRANKIE'S ITALIAN KITCHEN & BAR   604/688-6368   **46**

THREE DIAMOND Italian. Casual Dining. **Address:** 765 Beatty St V6B 2M4

GOTHAM STEAKHOUSE & COCKTAIL BAR   604/605-8282   **32**

THREE DIAMOND Steak. Fine Dining. **Address:** 615 Seymour St V6B 3K3

GUU ORIGINAL   604/685-8817   **19**

APPROVED Japanese Small Plates. Casual Dining. **Address:** 838 Thurlow St V6E 1W2

HAWKSWORTH RESTAURANT   604/673-7000   **27**

FOUR DIAMOND New Pacific Northwest. Fine Dining. **Address:** 801 W Georgia St V6C 1P7

INDIA BISTRO   604/684-6342   **24**

APPROVED Indian. Casual Dining. **Address:** 1157 Davie St V6E 1N2

(See map & index p. 272.)

JOE FORTES SEAFOOD & CHOP HOUSE
604/669-1940 (17)

THREE DIAMOND

Seafood
Steak
Casual Dining
$17-$55

AAA Inspector Notes: *Classic.* A San Francisco-style seafood grill on trendy Robson Street, this restaurant features delightful rooftop garden dining in season. It also has a popular oyster bar and fireplace lounge. Be sure to ask about the restaurant's namesake, turn-of-the-century legend Joe Fortes. Valet parking is available weekdays and after 6 pm on Saturday and Sunday. **Features:** full bar, Sunday brunch, happy hour. **Reservations:** suggested. **Address:** 777 Thurlow St V6E 3V5 **Location:** Between Robson and Alberni sts. Burrard, 46. **Parking:** valet and street only.

L D CALL

KINGSTON TAPHOUSE & GRILLE
604/681-7011 (34)

APPROVED American. Gastropub. **Address:** 755 Richards St V6B 3A6

L'ABATTOIR
604/568-1701 (36)

FOUR DIAMOND

New
American
Casual Dining
$25-$44

AAA Inspector Notes: The food here is truly inspirational as are the excellent libations from the bar. Capable servers can help you navigate the creative menu; it changes often and examples like veal tartare with smoked yolk or duck breast with whipped foie gras give you an idea of the quality. In a building which housed Vancouver's first jail, space here reflects a chic, industrial design. The vibe is casual and lively with seating either in the upstairs loft area or a glass-enclosed patio at the back. **Features:** full bar, Sunday brunch. **Reservations:** suggested. **Address:** 217 Carrall St V6B 2J2 **Location:** Just s of jct Water, Alexander and Powell sts; in Gastown. Stadium-Chinatown, 48. **Parking:** street only.

D

Creative food; eclectic wine list; unique cocktails

LA TERRAZZA
604/899-4449 (59)

THREE DIAMOND Northern Italian. Fine Dining. **Address:** 1088 Cambie St V6B 6J5

LE CROCODILE
604/669-4298 (25)

FOUR DIAMOND

Traditional
French
Fine Dining
$17-$48

AAA Inspector Notes: *Classic.* This wonderful restaurant has an impressive menu featuring perfectly prepared classic cuisine. Ingredients are of the highest quality and you will find everything from sautéed frog legs to veal with sumptuous sauce and morels. Foie gras and lobster are featured in several dishes and pan-fried Dover sole is filleted tableside. The atmosphere is bustling when the place is full, which is nearly every night, and service is finely tuned. Valet parking is available at dinner only. **Features:** full bar, patio dining. **Reservations:** suggested. **Address:** 909 Burrard St (at Smithe St), Suite 100 V6Z 2N2 **Location:** Jct Smithe and Burrard sts. Burrard, 46. **Parking:** on-site (fee) and valet.

L D CALL

LIFT BAR GRILL VIEW
604/689-5438 (1)

THREE DIAMOND Pacific Northwest. Casual Dining. **Address:** 333 Menchions Mews V6G 3H5

LUPO RESTAURANT + VINOTECA
604/569-2535 (43)

THREE DIAMOND New Italian. Fine Dining. **Address:** 869 Hamilton St V6B 2R7

MARKET BY JEAN-GEORGES
604/695-1115 (15)

FOUR DIAMOND Pacific Northwest. Fine Dining. **Address:** 1115 Alberni St V6E 4T9

MEDINA CAFE
604/879-3114 (38)

APPROVED Mediterranean. Casual Dining. **Address:** 780 Richards V6B 3A4

MIKU
604/568-3900 (18)

THREE DIAMOND Japanese. Casual Dining. **Address:** 200 Granville St, #70 V6C 1S4

MINAMI
604/685-8080 (57)

FOUR DIAMOND New Japanese. Casual Dining. **Address:** 1118 Mainland St V6B 2T9

MOTT 32
604/979-8886 (7)

THREE DIAMOND Chinese. Fine Dining. **Address:** 1161 W Georgia St V6E 0C6

MOXIE'S CLASSIC GRILL
604/678-8043 (23)

APPROVED American. Casual Dining. **Address:** 1160 Davie St V6E 1N1

NIGHTINGALE
604/695-9500 (10)

THREE DIAMOND New Canadian Small Plates. Casual Dining. **Address:** 1017 W Hastings St V6E 0C4

PIDGIN
604/620-9400 (41)

THREE DIAMOND Fusion. Casual Dining. **Address:** 350 Carrall St V6B 2J3

PROVENCE MARINASIDE
604/681-4144 (61)

THREE DIAMOND Mediterranean Seafood. Fine Dining. **Address:** 1177 Marinaside Cres V6Z 2Y3

RAMEN DANBO
604/559-8112 (5)

APPROVED Japanese Noodles. Casual Dining. **Address:** 1333 Robson St V6E 1C6

RICKY'S ALL DAY GRILL
604/602-9233

APPROVED American. Casual Dining. **Address:** 111 Dunsmuir St, #1 V6B 6A3

RODNEY'S OYSTER HOUSE
604/609-0080 (58)

APPROVED Seafood. Casual Dining. **Address:** 1228 Hamilton St V6B 2S8

ST LAWRENCE RESTAURANT
604/620-3800 (40)

THREE DIAMOND French. Casual Dining. **Address:** 269 Powell St V6A 1G3

THE SANDBAR SEAFOOD RESTAURANT
604/669-9030 (60)

THREE DIAMOND Seafood. Casual Dining. **Address:** 1535 Johnston St, Creekhouse #102 V6H 3R9

SCOOZIS MEDITERRANEAN BAR & GRILL
604/684-1009 (21)

APPROVED Mediterranean. Casual Dining. **Address:** 445 Howe St V6C 2X4

SIMPLY THAI
604/642-0123 (56)

APPROVED Thai. Casual Dining. **Address:** 1211 Hamilton St V6B 6K3

STEPHO'S SOUVLAKI GREEK TAVERNA
604/683-2555 (28)

APPROVED Greek. Casual Dining. **Address:** 1124 Davie St V6E 1N1

VERA'S BURGER SHACK
604/893-8372

APPROVED Burgers. Quick Serve. **Address:** 1030 Davie St V6E 1M3

WATER ST. CAFE
604/689-2832 (31)

THREE DIAMOND International. Casual Dining. **Address:** 300 Water St V6B 1B6

WHITE SPOT

APPROVED American. Casual Dining.

LOCATIONS:
Address: 718 Drake St V6Z 2W6 **Phone:** 604/605-0045
Address: 1616 W Georgia St V6G 2V5 **Phone:** 604/681-8034

The **FREEDOM** to Get Where You Want to Go

Take advantage of valuable resources from the leading authority on senior driver safety and mobility.

Before you hit the open road, make the AAA or CAA senior driving site the first stop on your journey.

SeniorDriving.AAA.com
SeniorsDriving.CAA.ca

Red Roof

Pets Stay FREE!*

Sleep Easy. Spend Less.™

Discover why Red Roof is **#1 in online guest reviews** — for 9 years running — with **FREE Wi-Fi, flat-screen TVs** in every room and, for even faster FREE Wi-Fi, we have **Verified Wi-Fi™** coming to more locations every day. It's all the conveniences you'll need for a clean, comfortable and affordable stay.

VERIFIED
WI-FI™

RediRewards™

Earn FREE nights and more.
Choose from FREE nights, discounts, gift cards and merchandise.

10% OFF our already low rates for our AAA guests

Use VP+®/Promo Code 526810 to receive 10% off at any of our locations.
Simply visit redroof.com or call 800.RED.ROOF (800.733.7663) Español 877.733.7244

Restrictions may apply based on availability. Offer cannot be combined with any other discount or offer.
Not valid during special events.

 | Red Roof Plus+ | THE Red COLLECTION® | HOMETOWNE STUDIOS. by Red Roof

**For reservations visit redroof.com or
call 800.RED.ROOF (800.733.7663)**

*Pet accommodations policy may vary at some HomeTowne Studios by Red Roof® locations.

(See map & index p. 272.)

YALETOWN BREWING COMPANY   604/681-2739 53
APPROVED International. Brewpub. **Address:** 1111 Mainland St V6B 2T9

YEW SEAFOOD + BAR   604/692-4939 26
THREE DIAMOND Seafood. Fine Dining. **Address:** 791 W Georgia St V6C 2T4

ZEFFERELLI'S RESTAURANT   604/687-0655 13
APPROVED Italian. Casual Dining. **Address:** 1136 Robson St V6E 1B2

VANCOUVER
• Hotels & Restaurants map & index p. 276

BEST WESTERN PLUS UPTOWN HOTEL
                         604/267-2000 2

THREE DIAMOND   Best Western PLUS   **AAA Benefit:** Members save up to 15% and earn bonus points!
Hotel

Address: 205 Kingsway V5T 3J5 Lo-cation: Corner of E 10th St. Broadway-City Hall, 55. **Facility:** 69 units. 4 stories, interior corridors. **Activities:** exercise room. **Guest Services:** valet laundry. (See ad this page.)

[SAVE] [icons] CALL [icons] / SOME UNITS [icons]

DAYS INN-VANCOUVER METRO   604/876-5531 3
APPROVED Motel. **Address:** 2075 Kingsway V5N 2T2

HOLIDAY INN VANCOUVER CENTRE   604/879-0511 1
THREE DIAMOND Hotel. **Address:** 711 W Broadway V5Z 3Y2

WHERE TO EAT

BISHOP'S   604/738-2025 2
FOUR DIAMOND Pacific Northwest. Fine Dining. **Address:** 2183 W 4th Ave V6K 1N7

BISTRO ABSINTHE   604/566-9053 13
THREE DIAMOND French. Casual Dining. **Address:** 1260 Commercial Dr V5L 3X4

CACTUS CLUB CAFE
THREE DIAMOND New American. Casual Dining.
LOCATIONS:
Address: 575 W Broadway V5Z 1E6 **Phone:** 604/714-6000 14
Address: 1530 W Broadway V6J 5K9 **Phone:** 604/733-0434 9

CAFE SALADE DE FRUITS   604/714-5987 8
APPROVED French. Casual Dining. **Address:** 1555 W 7th Ave V6J 1S1

FABLE KITCHEN   604/732-1322 5
THREE DIAMOND New Canadian. Casual Dining. **Address:** 1944 W 4th Ave V6J 1M5

FARMER'S APPRENTICE   604/620-2070 7
THREE DIAMOND Regional Canadian. Casual Dining. **Address:** 1535 W 6th Ave V6J 1R1

LAS MARGARITAS RESTAURANTE & CANTINA
                         604/734-7117 4
APPROVED Mexican. Casual Dining. **Address:** 1999 W 4th Ave V6J 1M7

MAENAM   604/730-5579 6
THREE DIAMOND New Thai. Casual Dining. **Address:** 1938 W 4th Ave V6J 1M5

MEMPHIS BLUES BARBEQUE HOUSE   604/738-6806
APPROVED Barbecue. Casual Dining. **Address:** 1465 W Broadway V6H 1H6

▼ See AAA listing this page ▼

BW Best Western PLUS

UPTOWN HOTEL

• Restaurant & Lounge on-site
• Free Gated Underground Parking • Fitness Centre
• Close Proximity to Downtown Vancouver

205 Kingsway   888-234-9111
Vancouver, BC V5T 3J5 CAN   604-267-2000

Each Best Western branded hotel is independently owned and operated.
Best Western and the Best Western marks are service marks of Best Western International, Inc. ©2019 Best Western International, Inc. All rights reserved. AAA and the AAA marks are service marks or registered service marks of the American Automobile Association.

CAA AAA   THREE DIAMOND

Bestwesternvancouver.ca

(See map & index p. 276.)

MILESTONES GRILL AND BAR   604/678-8488
▼ **APPROVED**   American. Casual Dining. **Address:** 2425
Cambie St V5Z 4M5

MILLTOWN BAR & GRILL   604/269-2348 (18)
▼ **APPROVED**   American. Gastropub. **Address:** 9191
Bentley St, Suite 101 V6P 6G2

SALMON N' BANNOCK   604/568-8971 (11)
▼ **APPROVED**   New Canadian. Casual Dining. **Address:**
1128 W Broadway V6H 1G5

SEASONS IN THE PARK RESTAURANT   604/874-8008 (17)
▼**THREE DIAMOND** Pacific Northwest. Fine Dining. **Address:**
W 33rd Ave & Cambie St V6G 3E7

SHAUGHNESSY RESTAURANT AT VANDUSEN GARDEN
                                                604/261-0011 (16)
▼**THREE DIAMOND**   Pacific   Northwest.   Casual   Dining.
Address: 5251 Oak St V6M 4H1

SOPHIE'S COSMIC CAFE   604/732-6810 (3)
▼ **APPROVED**   American. Casual Dining. **Address:** 2095
W 4th Ave V6J 1N3

TEAHOUSE IN STANLEY PARK   604/669-3281 (1)
▼**THREE DIAMOND** Pacific Northwest. Fine Dining. **Address:**
7501 Stanley Park Dr V6G 3E2

TOJO'S RESTAURANT   604/872-8050 (10)
▼**THREE DIAMOND** Japanese. Fine Dining. **Address:** 1133 W
Broadway V6H 1G1

VIJ'S RESTAURANT   604/736-6664 (15)
▼**THREE DIAMOND** New Indian. Casual Dining. **Address:**
3106 Cambie St V5Z 2W2

WEST RESTAURANT   604/738-8938 (12)
▼**FOUR DIAMOND** Pacific Northwest. Fine Dining. **Address:**
2881 Granville St V6H 3J4

WHITE SPOT   604/261-2820
▼ **APPROVED**   American. Casual Dining. **Address:**
613A-650 41st Ave V5Z 2M9

VERNON (B-9) pop. 38,150, elev. 383m/1,256'
- Hotels & Restaurants map & index p. 216
- Part of Okanagan Valley area — see map p. 212

At the confluence of five valleys and bounded by
three lakes, Vernon is an important shipping and
trading center for the Okanagan region. The town's
history is portrayed in 26 large murals painted on
downtown buildings. On Hwy. 97 at 25th Avenue,
Polson Park encompasses a Japanese garden, a
Chinese tea house, a floral clock made of 3,500
plants and a children's water park.

Boating, fishing, hiking, mountain biking and golf
are popular in summer; winter activities include
skiing, dogsledding and snowshoeing. Several recreational opportunities are available at nearby El-
lison Provincial Park (see Recreation Areas Chart)
and Kalamalka Lake Provincial Park (see attraction
listing and Recreation Areas Chart).

Silver Star Provincial Park offers mountain biking
tours from late June to mid-September. A chairlift to
the top of Silver Star Mountain operates daily, July 1
to mid-September.

For relaxation, the Kalamalka Lake viewpoint, 5
kilometres (3 mi.) south of 25th Avenue on Hwy. 97,
provides an excellent view of the lake.

Tourism Greater Vernon: 3004 39th Ave., Vernon,
BC, Canada V1T 3C3. **Phone:** (250) 542-1415 or
(800) 665-0795.

ALLAN BROOKS NATURE CENTRE is on a
ridgetop at 250 Allan Brooks Way in the old Vernon
Upper Air Weather Station. The center—named
after naturalist and illustrator Allan Brooks—features
a habitat exhibit about the Northern Okanagan region's ecosystems, the Discovery Room with
hands-on exhibits and an active beehive to view.
The Grassland Trail, Naturescape Gardens and
scenic views can be enjoyed outdoors. To overlook
the countryside and see wildlife, climb the hill for a
quiet spot.

Comfortable walking shoes are recommended.
Time: Allow 1 hour minimum. **Hours:** Mon.-Sat. 9-4.
Closed statutory holidays. **Cost:** $7.62; $5.70 (ages
65+); $4.76 (ages 3-18); $22.80 (family, two adults
and up to four children ages 3-18); donations (viewpoint and grounds only). **Phone:** (250) 260-4227.
GT ☂

HISTORIC O'KEEFE RANCH is at 9380 Hwy 97N.
One of the earliest cattle empires in the Okanagan
Valley, the 1867 O'Keefe homestead includes a dozen
restored structures. Guided tours are offered of the
family's Victorian mansion. Other buildings include a
log house, a church, a general store, a blacksmith
shop, a cowboy bunk house, barns and tool sheds. A
museum depicts the family's history and the ranching
way of life and features a model train display.

Time: Allow 1 hour, 30 minutes minimum. **Hours:**
Daily 10-6, July-Aug.; 10-5, May-June and in Sept.
Cost: $13.50; $12 (ages 60+); $10 (ages 13-18);
$8.50 (ages 6-12); $33 (family, two adults and chil-
dren ages 6-18). Prices may vary; phone ahead.
Phone: (250) 542-7868. ⛽ ☂

BEST WESTERN PACIFIC INN   250/558-1800 (3)
▼**THREE DIAMOND**
Hotel

AAA Benefit: Members save up to 15% and earn bonus points!

Address: 4790 34th St V1T 5Y9 **Location:** Hwy 97 (32nd St); corner of 48th
Ave. **Facility:** 61 units, some kitchens. 4
stories, interior corridors. Bath: shower
only. **Terms:** check-in 4 pm. **Activities:**
exercise room. **Guest Services:** valet
and coin laundry.

DAYS INN BY WYNDHAM VERNON   250/549-2224 (2)
▼ **APPROVED**   Motel. **Address:** 5121 26th St V1T 8G4

(See map & index p. 216.)

FAIRFIELD INN & SUITES BY MARRIOTT   250/260-7829   **1**
THREE DIAMOND SAVE Hotel. Ad-dress: 5300 Anderson Way V1T 9V2

AAA Benefit:
Members save 5% or more!

HOLIDAY INN EXPRESS HOTEL & SUITES VERNON
250/550-7777   **4**
THREE DIAMOND Hotel. Address: 4716 34th St V1T 5Y9

RIVIERA VILLAGE GREEN HOTEL   250/542-3321   **5**
APPROVED   **Address:** 4801 27th St V1T 4Z1 **Location:** Hwy 97 (32nd St), 0.4 mi (0.7 km)
Hotel   e on 48th Ave. **Facility:** 129 units, some kitchens. 2-7 stories, interior corridors. **Pool:** heated indoor. **Activities:** sauna, hot tub, health club. **Featured Amenity:** continental breakfast.

SPARKLING HILL RESORT   250/275-1556   **7**
FOUR DIAMOND Boutique Contemporary Hotel. **Address:** 888 Sparkling Pl V1H 2K7

SUPER 8 BY WYNDHAM VERNON   250/542-4434   **6**
APPROVED Hotel. **Address:** 4204 32nd St V1T 5P4

WHERE TO EAT

AMARIN THAI RESTAURANT   250/542-9300   **3**
APPROVED   Thai. Casual Dining. **Address:** 2903 31st St V1T 5H6

ECLECTIC MED RESTAURANT INC   250/558-4646   **4**
APPROVED   Mediterranean. Casual Dining. **Address:** 2915 30th Ave V1T 2B8

INTERMEZZO RESTAURANT   250/542-3853   **1**
THREE DIAMOND International. Fine Dining. **Address:** 3206 34th Ave V1T 7E2

THE ITALIAN KITCHEN COMPANY   250/558-7899   **6**
APPROVED   Italian. Casual Dining. **Address:** 2916 30th Ave V1T 2B7

LOS HUESOS   250/275-4820   **5**
APPROVED   Mexican. Casual Dining. **Address:** 2918 30th Ave V1T 2B7

NAKED PIG   778/475-5475   **2**
APPROVED Barbecue. Casual Dining. **Address:** 2933 30th Ave V1T 2B8

PEAKFINE   250/275-1556   **7**
THREE DIAMOND Pacific Northwest. Fine Dining. **Address:** 888 Sparkling Pl V1H 2K7

Hit the Road with a Prepaid Card

Stay on budget during travel and use again to save for your next adventure.

Visit your local AAA office or online at
AAA.com/MemberPay

All products not available at all locations.

Victoria

Then & Now

"To realize Victoria," Rudyard Kipling wrote, "you must take all that the eye admires in Bournemouth, Torquay, the Isle of Wight, the Happy Valley at Hong Kong, the Doon, Sorrento, Camp's Bay, add reminiscences of the Thousand Islands and arrange the whole around the Bay of Naples with some Himalayas for the background."

Yet the capital of British Columbia remains quintessentially British. Along with its tearooms, double-decker buses, horse-drawn tallyho carriages and shops that sell china and woolens, Victoria proudly claims another, much older culture. Totem poles can be seen throughout local parks, reflecting the destination's dual heritage.

Regarded as Canada's gentlest city, Victoria has uncluttered streets, gardens that bloom year-round and hotels that have been serving high tea for decades. Sharing a passion for gardening, Victoria residents tend their prim English-style gardens. The city's innumerable flower beds and hanging baskets, nurtured by its mild climate, bloom in bright displays while the rest of Canada shivers.

AAA.com/travelguides—
more ways to look, book and save

The heart of the city curves around the stone-walled Inner Harbour, alive with pleasure craft, fishing boats and coastal shipping vessels. Facing the harbor are the parliament buildings and the block-long, ivy-covered Empress Hotel, a destination for afternoon tea.

Parliament buildings

Emily Carr, a native of Victoria, devoted her artistic career to capturing on canvas the majestic totem poles carved by the vanishing First Nations civilizations of the Pacific coast. Like those she found in deserted tribal villages, the totems in Thunderbird Park evoke the highly developed ancient culture that dominated the area long before Victoria was settled in the mid-19th century.

Fort Victoria was built by Hudson's Bay Co. in 1843. Six years later Vancouver Island became a crown colony, and as British Columbia's only port, it became a passage to the Fraser Canyon goldfields on the mainland in 1858. Thousands of European and Asian miners descended on the city, forming the nucleus of today's diverse citizenry.

Violence around Bastion Square was so commonplace during this rowdy boomtown period that the *Victoria Gazette* reported no deaths "from natural causes in the city during the last 30 days." Local politicians supposedly settled their debates with fist fights.

(Continued on p. 300.)

Destination Victoria

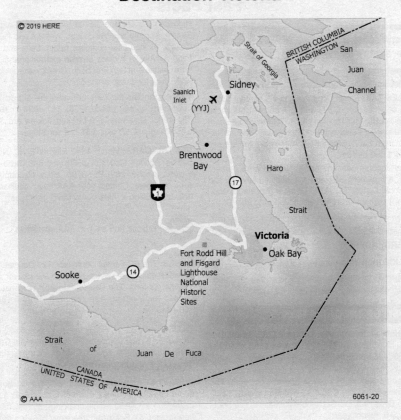

This map shows cities in the Victoria vicinity where you will find attractions, hotels and restaurants. Cities are listed alphabetically in this book on the following pages.

Fast Facts

ABOUT THE CITY

POP: 80,017 ■ **ELEV:** 17m/56 ft.

MONEY

SALES TAX: British Columbia has a 5 percent goods and services tax (GST) and a 7 percent provincial sales tax (PST). Expect to pay an additional 3 percent for alcohol. Restaurants and admission fees are exempt from the 7 percent PST. Automobile rental sales tax is $1.50 per day.

Hotel accommodations are subject to an 8 percent PST, a 5 percent GST and a 3 percent Municipal and Regional District Tax (MRDT); there may be an additional 1 percent for a Destination Marketing Fee (DMF).

WHOM TO CALL

EMERGENCY: 911

POLICE (non-emergency): (250) 995-7654

HOSPITALS: Royal Jubilee Hospital, (250) 370-8000 ■ Victoria General Hospital, (250) 727-4212.

VISITOR INFORMATION

Tourism Victoria Visitor Centre: 812 Wharf St., Victoria, BC, Canada V8W 1T3. **Phone:** (250) 953-2033 or (800) 663-3883.

The center provides maps and brochures outlining various self-guiding walking and driving tours. The center is open daily 8:30-8:30, mid-May to early Sept.; Sun.-Thurs. 9-5, Fri.-Sat. 8:30-8:30, early to late Sept.; daily 9-5, rest of year.

TRANSPORTATION

AIR TRAVEL: Victoria International Airport (YYJ) is 22 kilometres (12 mi.) north on Hwy. 17 (Patricia Bay Highway). Air Canada flies to Victoria from Calgary, Seattle, Toronto and Vancouver. WestJet and Pacific Coastal Airlines offer domestic flights. Delta and Horizon Air/Alaska Airlines provide international flights from Seattle and San Francisco. Check with your local AAA office for cheap airline flights.

YYJ Airport Shuttle runs between the airport and downtown hotels; phone (778) 351-4995 or (855) 351-4995. One-way, pre-booked tickets are $22; $13.50 (ages 4-17) plus a $1 fuel surcharge.

RENTAL CARS: Hertz, 1640 Electra Blvd., North Saanich, phone (250) 657-0380; and 548 David St., Victoria, phone (250) 952-3765, offers discounts to AAA members. Contact your AAA travel advisor for help with adding a rental car to travel packages.

 Book and save at AAA.com/hertz

BUSES: The BC Ferries Connector, 721 Douglas St. provides daily bus service between Vancouver and Victoria via ferry. The vessels transport personal vehicles; reservations are required. Phone (888) 788-8840.

TAXIS: Taxis charge $3.30 minimum plus $1.93 per kilometre (.6 mi.). Companies include Blue Bird Cabs, (250) 382-2222 ■ Yellow Cab of Victoria, (250) 381-2222 ■ and Victoria Taxi, (250) 383-7111.

PUBLIC TRANSPORTATION: BC Transit buses serve Greater Victoria's downtown area 6:30 a.m.-midnight. Fare $2.50 (single boarding); $5 (day pass); free (ages 0-5). Buses run frequently between downtown and the ferry terminal. For route information, phone (250) 382-6161.

BOATS: Several ferry systems make connections with mainland Canada and the U.S. *See Arriving, By Boat.*

(Continued from p. 298.)

After the gold fever broke, Victoria began to assume its characteristic cool reserve. Lured by modest land prices, English settlers developed their queen's namesake city into a thriving government and commercial center. In 1868 Victoria became the capital of the newly joined crown colonies of Vancouver Island and British Columbia and, in 1871 when British Columbia joined the Canadian Confederation, it became the capital of the province.

Since commercial supremacy passed to Vancouver after the completion of the Canadian Pacific Railway, Victoria has adopted a slower pace with few heavy industries. The city is a center for commercial trade as well as the home of Canada's West Coast naval operations.

The city's strong tourism industry is buoyed by the stream of travelers who come by cruise ship or by ferry from Washington and throughout British Columbia. Those travelers come year round, thanks to Victoria's scenic setting and delightful climate. Flowers bloom all year, and the city only occasionally sees snow.

Victoria's climate and proximity to the Pacific Ocean also provide its citizens an opportunity for an active lifestyle. Marine-based activities such as fishing, sailing, kayaking, canoeing and whale watching are popular, as are bicycling, hiking and exploring neighborhoods and parks.

Whether or not Victoria is more British than Britain remains an ongoing debate among Victoria's residents. Few would contest, however, that nature's blessings have endowed the city with ample charm. No one understood this better than its native First Nations people, the Saanich Nation of Coast Salish, whose totems continue to speak the land's wonder.

Must Do: AAA Editor's Picks

- Butchart Gardens (800 Benvenuto Ave., Brentwood Bay) attracts nature lovers from around the world. Thousands of bulbs and flowering trees offer a colorful show from late March to mid-June—but October and November, when the Japanese Garden takes center stage, match spring's glory with a stunning parade of reds, russets and golds.

- Do you know the difference between a head of state and a head of government in Canada? Learn the inner workings of the parliamentary process—and see stunning Renaissance and Romanesque architecture—on a free guided tour of the Legislative Assembly of British Columbia (501 Belleville St.). When the Legislative Assembly is in session, visitors can observe debates and proceedings from a gallery overlooking the Legislative Chamber.

- Victoria's Chinatown isn't as large as Vancouver's, but it is no less authentic, founded by Chinese immigrants in 1858. Wander up and down Fisgard Street, where wall murals depict turn-of-the-20th century Chinese families and the former opium dens, gambling houses and brothels that are now restaurants and businesses. Hunt for souvenirs in the shops along Fan Tan Alley, reputedly Canada's narrowest street.

- Miniature World (649 Humboldt St.) isn't always what you might think—two dollhouses furnished in exquisite detail, as well as a model of the Great Canadian Railway, are among the largest of their kind in the world. But there's also a miniscule, operational sawmill, a tiny circus and scaled-down European castles. What makes this themed fantasyland particularly enthralling—and one of the top things to do for kids—is that it's hands-on; push a button and something, somewhere, will start moving.

- Minutes away from the Inner Harbour, Government Street is packed with stores and art galleries. Do some shopping before settling into a booth at Bard and Banker, a cozy pub housed in an old bank building where you can try beer-battered fish and chips.

- Those who don't feel like walking can ride in style on a horse-drawn carriage tour. Victoria Carriage Tours (Belleville and Menzies sts.) offers a 30-minute narrated tour along the Inner Harbour that includes a peek at the architecturally grand homes in the historic James Bay neighborhood.

- Craigdarroch Castle (1050 Joan Crescent), the home of 19th-century coal mining magnate Robert Dunsmuir, is a must-see. The interior of this massive estate, capped with a distinctive red slate roof, is a feast of oak paneling, stained glass and period room furnishings.

- A pleasant retreat just minutes from downtown, beautifully landscaped Beacon Hill Park (Douglas St. and Dallas Rd.) is named for a pair of masts placed atop a hill that acted as navigational aids for mariners approaching the Inner Harbour. Quiet and tree shaded, it's a stroller's delight right down to the freely roaming peacocks.

- From Kwakwaka'wakw ceremonial masks to Northern sea lions, The Royal BC Museum (675 Belleville St.) explores every facet of British Columbia's natural and human history. Just how vast is this province? The Big Map, an animated audiovisual experience, provides a dramatic answer.

- Ride the Victoria Harbour Ferry water taxi to Fisherman's Wharf (1 Dallas Rd.) to see fishing boats, colorful floating houses and a few resident seals. A handful of food kiosks serve up fish 'n' chips, tacos, sushi and ice cream you can enjoy on the docks.

- The Swiftsure International Yacht Race (Clover Point Park off Dallas Rd.) has been a springtime tradition for more than 80 years. Thousands of people gather along the Dallas Road waterfront to watch fleets of boats navigate the tricky waters of the Strait of Juan de Fuca. The competition is known for exciting starts and nail-biting finishes and is one of the top things to do in Victoria in spring.

Butchart Gardens

Craigdarroch Castle

Victoria 1-day Itinerary

AAA editors suggest these activities for a great short vacation experience.

Morning

- Visit several gardens that serve as reminders of the city's British heritage (we'll get to the horse-drawn carriages and tearooms later in the day). Head to the Oak Bay neighborhood to **Abkhazi Garden** (1964 Fairfield Rd.). Though petite in size, the garden is resplendent in its beauty. Set on a rocky slope, the dramatic landscape is planted in rhododendrons, Japanese maples, azaleas, evergreens and alpine plants.

- Nearby is **Government House and Gardens** (1401 Rockland Ave.), home to the province's lieutenant governor. The formal gardens include spaces devoted to heather, iris and roses and plantings typical of an English country garden.

- A turreted, 39-room, four-story estate is next on your list. ᗒᗕ **Craigdarroch Castle** (1050 Joan Crescent) was built in the 1880s by a Scottish immigrant from a coal mining family who became one of the richest men in British Columbia. The impressive staircase, oak paneling, period furnishings and stained glass reflect 19th-century elegance.

- By this point, you've probably worked up an appetite. Stop at **Bin 4 Burger Lounge** (911 Yates St.) for lipsmacking gourmet burgers made from hormone-free beef, chicken, tofu, bison, lamb, pork or Ahi tuna. Refreshing salads and lettuce wraps are tempting options.

Afternoon

- Spend the rest of the day in the lovely Inner Harbor area. Cultural and natural provincial history is the focus of ᗒᗕ **The Royal BC Museum** (675 Belleville St.), a treasure trove of information about the province's development. Start at the First Peoples Gallery with its ceremonial masks and a full-size chief's house. Hear what a mammoth might have sounded like as well as other sounds from the Ice Age in a gallery devoted to natural history. Step outside to **Thunderbird Park** (Douglas and Belleville streets) to see a collection of Northwest Coast totem poles.

- Practically around the corner in **The Fairmont Empress** (721 Government St.) hotel is ᗒᗕ **Miniature World** (649 Humboldt St.). Incredible attention to detail is obvious in more than 80 dioramas, all intricately created in miniature. The world of the circus is elaborately crafted in teensy elements, as are dollhouses, castles, battle scenes and a 17th-century London cityscape.

- The palatial Fairmont Empress itself is worth a visit. Resembling a castle, the hotel is a Victoria landmark and known for its afternoon teas, a tradition since the hotel opened in 1908. Have a seat in the Tea Lobby and treat yourself to the English ritual (advance reservations are necessary). In addition to tea, sandwiches and pastries (think mango and curried chicken sandwiches and berry tarts) and raisin scones with heavy cream and strawberry preserves are served. Although worth a splurge, other options offer less expensive versions of the afternoon tea experience; try **White Heather Tea Room** (1885 Oak Bay Ave.).

- After the formal tea ceremony, a stroll and shopping on Government Street are in order. Victorian lampposts and colorful hanging baskets add to the city's charm. Browse through the 19th-century shops selling English woolens, fine china and other British imports; chocolates; Northwestern First Nations and Canadian art; clothing; and jewelry.

Evening

- For a very British way to begin the evening, there's a horse-drawn carriage awaiting. Head over to the corner of Belleville and Menzies streets where the carriages queue up.

- If enticing aromas from waterside restaurants beckon, there are many options near the harbor. Depending on your taste and pocketbook, you might want to consider **Pagliacci's** (1011 Broad St.) or **Vista 18** (740 Burdett Ave.).

- After satisfying your appetite, take a romantic walk alongside the stone walls of the Inner Harbor. Enjoy the soothing breezes, the boats bobbing in the marinas and the lights illuminating the classic lines of the **Legislative Assembly of British Columbia** (501 Belleville St.).

Top Picks for Kids

Under 13

- A kid-friendly (and free) alternative to Butchart Gardens, **Beacon Hill Park** (Douglas St. and Dallas Rd.) draws crowds for its waterfront views, winding paths and roaming peacocks. At Beacon Hill Children's Farm, kids will get a kick out of the "Running of the Goats," a stampede that occurs twice daily (at 10:10 a.m. and 4:10 p.m.) when the goats run between the barn and the petting zoo.

- You can touch, hold and observe all sorts of creepy crawlies at **Victoria Bug Zoo** (631 Courtney St.), a miniature indoor zoo near the Inner Harbour. Tour guides introduce visitors to glow-in-the-dark scorpions, giant walking sticks, fuzzy tarantulas and other tropical insects and arachnids from around the world.

- What to do in Victoria on a rainy day? One of the best things to do with kids is **Victoria Butterfly Gardens** (1461 Benvenuto Ave. in Brentwood Bay). The indoor attraction is home to thousands of free-flying butterflies—including 70 exotic species—and educational displays about the butterfly life cycle. You'll also find parrots, flamingos, poison dart frogs, koi fish and other colorful creatures throughout the tropical gardens.

- **Miniature World** (649 Humboldt St.) delights pint-size visitors with more than 80 detailed miniature dioramas depicting the streets of London, fairytale castles, railroads, a frontier settlement and the Swiss Family Robinson treehouse, just to name a few. Kids can push buttons and watch as parts of each display come to life with lights, sound and animation.

Teens

- **The Royal BC Museum** (675 Belleville St.) receives rave reviews even from those who might not consider themselves a fan of museums. Top teen-approved highlights include a full-scale model of a woolly mammoth, a collection of massive First Nations totem carvings and a re-creation of Victoria street scenes from the 1900s.

- Hear about the things that go bump in the night during **Ghostly Walks for Halloween** (560 Johnson St.), a series of special walking tours that take place mid-October through October 31. Talented storytellers combine history and theater to recount the murders, ghosts and spooky happenings around Victoria, often called one of the most haunted cities in the Pacific Northwest.

All Ages

- Pedestrian-friendly **Government Street** offers a multitude of gift stores, clothing boutiques and souvenir shops all housed in Victorian-era buildings. If the shopping bags start to weigh you down, take a break for coffee, fancy tea or a sweet treat at one of the many cafés along the main thoroughfare.

- Hop aboard a water taxi with **Victoria Harbour Ferry** for a sightseeing tour at an affordable price. Knowledgeable skippers narrate the trip around the harbor, and if you disembark at Fisherman's Wharf you'll find some of the city's best options for fish and chips and ice cream cones. Water taxis depart from various locations around the city; the main dock is across from The Fairmont Empress at 721 Government St.

- Family fun is just about guaranteed on a local **whale-watching tour,** where you might spot orcas, humpbacks, porpoises and sea lions from a covered yacht or high-speed, open-air boat. Numerous tour companies operate out of Victoria's Inner Harbour, including **Prince of Whales Whale Watching** (812 Wharf St.) and **SpringTide Whale Watching** (1119 Wharf St.).

- Finding places to eat with kids can be daunting, but cozy burger joint **The Pink Bicycle** (1008 Blanshard St.) is a good option. In addition to the mouthwatering gourmet burgers, you'll want to sample the mac 'n' cheese sticks and poutine made with rosemary gravy and locally sourced cheese curds.

- Young readers can hunt for a new favorite book at **Munro's Books** (1108 Government St.). The beloved independent bookstore is a treat for the mind as well as the eyes— a soaring, coffered ceiling, colorful tapestries and well-stocked shelves create a cozy environment perfect for book lovers. Head straight to the back of the store for the Children's Books section.

Victoria Butterfly Gardens

Arriving
By Car

Victoria is the western terminus of the 7,821-kilometre (4,860-mi.) Trans-Canada Highway. The highway traverses the mainland to Horseshoe Bay in West Vancouver and resumes at the Departure Bay Ferry Terminal (Nanaimo). It then proceeds south along the island's eastern shore to Victoria. Hwy. 17, the other major artery into the city, connects Victoria with the ferry terminals at Swartz Bay and Sidney on the Saanich Peninsula.

By Boat

Several ferry systems connect Vancouver Island and Victoria with mainland Canada and the United States. The most direct route is the Tsawwassen-Swartz Bay automobile/passenger ferry service used by the intercity buses between Vancouver and Victoria; each one-way trip takes about 1 hour, 35 minutes. BC Ferries also connects Nanaimo, 111 kilometres (69 mi.) north of Victoria, to Horseshoe Bay in West Vancouver, and departs from the north end of the island at Port Hardy to travel through the Inside Passage to Prince Rupert, where they connect with the Alaska State Ferry system. Contact British Columbia Ferries for more information; phone (250) 386-3431 outside Canada and the U.S. or (888) 223-3779 within Canada and the U.S.

Ferries linking the southern end of the island and Victoria with the United States include Black Ball Transport Inc., (250) 386-2202 or (888) 993-3779, from Port Angeles, Wash., or (800) 265-6475 for the Victoria terminal; and Washington State Ferries, (206) 464-6400 or (888) 808-7977, from Anacortes, Wash., to Sidney. Reservations are available for the Anacortes, Wash., to Sidney route; phone 1 day in advance to determine estimated waiting time.

For a 2.75-hour trip to Seattle, take the Victoria Clipper, a high-speed passenger ferry; phone (250) 382-8100 for the Victoria terminal, (206) 448-5000 for the Seattle terminal, or (800) 888-2535.

Getting Around
Street System

Most traffic activity is on Wharf, Government and Belleville streets, which embrace the Inner Harbour. Ferries arrive from both Port Angeles and Seattle, Wash. all year. The main east-west streets are Yates, Fort and Johnson. Pandora Avenue, renamed Oak Bay Avenue in midtown, crosses the city from the Inner Harbour to Oak Bay.

Major north-south thoroughfares are Blanshard Street (Hwy. 17) and Douglas Street (Hwy. 1), which begins at Victoria's southern coast along the Juan de Fuca Strait. Dallas Road borders the shore and continues as Beach Drive along Victoria's eastern coast. Many Victoria streets are one-way.

Parking

On-street parking is controlled by meters and posted restrictions daily 9-6; the first hour is free, and rates after that range from $1.50 to $3 per hour (free 6 p.m.–9 a.m. and on holidays). Vehicles parked on specially posted blocks are subject to towing during rush hours. Downtown off-street parking is available in five city parkades, three surface parking lots and shopping center lots. Rates for city-run parking are $2-$3 per hour, charged in 15-minute increments, or $16 per day ($17.50 at Bastion Square Parkade). At city parkades, the first hour is free; parking also is free Mon.-Sat. from 6 p.m.–8 a.m. and on Sundays and holidays. During free parking periods, drivers need their entry ticket to exit the parking facility.

Shopping

Lined with shops carrying English tweeds and fine china, **Government Street** maintains Victoria's heritage as a trading post of the British Empire and offers many fun places to go. Such shops as **Old Morris Tobacconist**, phone (250) 382-4811 or (888) 845-6111, have distinguished Government Street since the 19th century. Established in 1885, **Rogers' Chocolates** is a Victoria institution that counts British royalty in its clientele and is a popular destination for chocolate-lovers. The Rogers' factory, behind the store at 913 Government St., still produces its renowned bittersweet chocolate according to a guarded recipe; phone (250) 384-7021 or (800) 663-2220.

Shoppers determined to bring home something other than a few extra pounds might want to explore the craft and specialty shops in the renovated squares and malls off Government Street. More than 35 quaint stores and local restaurants in revitalized old buildings highlight **Market Square**, bounded by Johnson, Pandora and Store streets; phone (250) 386-2441.

Rogers' Chocolates

Trounce Alley, in the downtown core, is a hideaway of eclectic shops and a few places to eat. Shops of mid-19th-century architecture display modern items in **Bastion Square**, once a hangout for prospectors and drifters. An attractive shopping arcade is in **Centennial Square** off Douglas Street. **Nootka Court** between Courtney and Humboldt streets contains small arts and crafts shops.

Those looking for vacation souvenirs in Victoria will find unique items like handwoven woolens from Ireland and England, hand-knit Cowichan sweaters, Inuit jade sculpture and Northwest First Nations masks and prints. **The Hudson's Bay** department store in The Bay Centre on Douglas Street, sells authentic Cowichan sweaters. Also in Victoria are **Hillside Shopping Centre**, 1644 Hillside Ave.; and **Mayfair Shopping Centre**, 3147 Douglas St.

In keeping with its Victorian image, Victoria has more than 50 antiques shops. Many are found along Government and Fort streets and Oak Bay Avenue and are worth a trip.

Nightlife

Downtown Victoria offers plenty of things to do after dark, whether you're in the mood for live music at a cozy pub, craft cocktails at a hidden gem, a horse-drawn carriage ride around the Inner Harbour or an ice cream cone with a generous side of people watching. Most nightlife options are within a 10-minute walk of Government Street, the main thoroughfare in downtown Victoria, so you should have no trouble getting around and making a night of it. A bonus: Downtown parking is free after 6 p.m.

Two of the best pubs in Victoria, B.C., are located just a block from each other on Government Street. Housed in an 1885 bank building, the **Bard & Banker** (1022 Government St.) is a local favorite for upscale pub grub (breakfast, lunch and dinner), daily happy hour specials and friendly service. Families are welcomed until 9 p.m., and live music is offered seven nights a week with no cover charge (except St. Patrick's Day and New Year's Eve).

Another historic bank building houses the **Irish Times Pub** (1200 Government St.), a sister establishment to Bard & Banker. Beer and whiskey flights pair well with Irish comfort food and nightly live music. On Friday and Saturday afternoons you'll hear traditional Celtic tunes.

You're sure to find a craft beer you like at **The Churchill** (1140 Government St.), where 50 taps showcase brews from British Columbia and beyond. Handcrafted cocktails and hearty pub fare (try the poutine!) round out the menu.

If you're looking for an off-the-beaten-path bar in Victoria, seek out **Little Jumbo** (506 Fort St.) for a drink or two. The intimate venue serves up B.C. wines as well as a rotating menu of specialty cocktails made with exotic ingredients. Little Jumbo opens nightly at 5 p.m.

CANOE Brewpub (450 Swift St.) is the place to go for craft beer and a stunning view. A large outdoor patio overlooking a private marina on Victoria's Inner Harbour draws a crowd at sunset. Sit inside to see their brewing equipment and the beautifully restored interior, complete with crystal chandeliers and soaring timber ceilings. A small indoor stage is the site of live music Thursday through Sunday.

No visit to Victoria is complete without a stroll through The Fairmont Empress, the ivy-covered hotel that has been a landmark on Victoria's harbor since 1908. Dress to impress for drinks at Q Bar (located inside the hotel's restaurant, **Q at the Empress**). It's a good place for signature cocktails, local beers, a fancy dessert and nightly live entertainment.

A few other hotel bars in the city of Victoria are worth a stop. **Clive's Classic Lounge** (in the Chateau Victoria Hotel and Suites at 740 Burdett Ave.) has an extensive whiskey menu as well as handcrafted cocktails and tropical tiki drinks. **Veneto Kitchen and Bar** (in the Hotel Rialto at 1450 Douglas St.) earns rave reviews for its skilled bartending staff and personalized service. **Swans Hotel and Brewpub** (506 Pandora Ave.) is another local hangout where you'll find house-made beers, daily happy hours and a live music scene.

Nightlife in Victoria, B.C., doesn't have to revolve around bars and lounges; there are plenty of family-friendly ways to experience the sights and sounds of the city after dark.

Take a stroll along the stone walls of the Inner Harbour to see boats bobbing in the marina and the lights of the **Legislative Assembly of British Columbia** reflected on the water. If your feet are tired after a long day, opt to see the lights from a horse-drawn carriage ride with **Victoria Carriage Tours**. Private, narrated tours will take you around downtown until 10 p.m. on most summer nights.

And if a decadent, Instagram-worthy dessert sounds right up your alley, don't miss a stop at **Chocolats Favoris** on Government Street. The Quebec-based chocolatier specializes in soft-serve ice cream dipped in any of 12 flavors of real chocolate. The shop stays open year-round until 8 or 9 p.m.

Big Events

In addition to its many cultural and historic landmarks, this destination hosts a number of outstanding festivals, events and fun things to do that may coincide with your vacation.

As a city of traditions, Victoria celebrates many events and festivals each year. The weekend following Victoria Day in May features the classic **Swiftsure International Yacht Race**, which has drawn an armada of more than 185 sailboats from all over the world since 1930. The **Victoria Highland Games & Celtic Festival** takes place in mid-May.

Boating enthusiasts will enjoy the **Victoria Classic Boat Festival at Inner Harbour** over Labour Day weekend. There will be a steamboat cruise, rowing regatta, boat races and lots of nautical fun. Book your travel packages and vacation

Enjoy the Victoria Classic Boat Festival at Inner Harbour

packages early or contact your local AAA travel agency to plan your trip.

Autumn shows off its best colors along the rural **Saanich Peninsula**, where the **Saanich Fair** has been held Labour Day weekend for more than a century and is one of the many family-friendly things to do in Victoria. Fall's lower temperatures provide an energy boost for the mid-October **GoodLife Fitness Victoria Marathon**. During late October, however, guests can experience a chill that has nothing to do with the weather at the **Ghosts Walks for Halloween** guided walking tours.

Wrap up an incredible holiday journey in late November with the "jolly old elf" himself at **Santa's Light Parade** in the streets of Victoria.

Sports & Rec

Victoria still embraces the English spirit, as evidenced by such popular games as **lawn bowling** and **cricket**, both played at various venues throughout the city, including Beacon Hill Park. Any belief, however, that Victoria's sports are too serious is dispelled quickly by a **box lacrosse** game. This offspring of the First Nations game of *baggataway* is a rough-and-tumble version of field lacrosse confined to a smaller, enclosed area. Canada's Parliament designated lacrosse, or boxla, as it also is called, the national sport in 1867 (hockey became the official national winter sport in 1994). Lacrosse is played from April to August at various venues, including The Q Centre, 1767 Island Hwy.

All-star **wrestling** and **ice hockey,** two other spectator sports that hardly could be considered sedate, also are held at the arena.

Water sports have obvious appeal in this island city. The wide variety of game fish around southern Vancouver Island includes rockfish, lingcod, sole and flounder; fishing licenses are required. If you're visiting Victoria on vacation, a 1-day or 8-day angling license is available. Surf **fishing** often yields rewarding catches of salmon and black sea bass. Clamming and oyster harvesting are popular activities on any of the Gulf Islands, which are fun places to go and accessible by ferry from Swartz Bay.

Oak Bay Marina, 1327 Beach Dr., offers fishing charters at an hourly rate. Fishing equipment, a tackle shop and marine store are available; phone (250) 598-3369. Other nearby marinas include Anglers Anchorage Marina, 905 Grilse Ln. in Brentwood Bay, phone (250) 652-3531; North Saanich Marina, 1949 Marina Way in North Saanich, phone (250) 656-5558; and the Westbay Marine Village, 453 Head St., phone (250) 385-1831 or (866) 937-8229.

Boating is enjoyed in the Strait of Georgia and the Saanich Inlet and is a great activity for group travel. Uplands Park on Oak Bay is equipped with boat ramps. Fine beaches border Dallas Road and Beach Drive.

With its scenic coastal location and balmy climate, Victoria offers excellent playing conditions for **golf**. On a peninsula jutting into the Juan de Fuca Strait, Victoria Golf Club, 1110 Beach Dr., is open to members of other clubs.

Other golf clubs include Ardmore Golf Course (nine holes), 930 Ardmore Dr., North Saanich; Cedar Hill Golf Course (18 holes), 1400 Derby Rd., Saanich; Cordova Bay Golf Course (18 holes), 5333 Cordova Bay Rd.; Glen Meadows Golf & Country Club (18 holes), 1050 McTavish Rd., North Saanich; Green Acres Golf Course (nine holes), 3970 Metchosin Rd.; Henderson Park (nine holes), 2291 Cedar Hill Cross Rd.; Mount Douglas Golf Course (nine holes), 4225 Blenkinsop Rd.; and Olympic View Golf Course (18 holes), 643 Latoria Rd.

Many parks are scattered throughout Victoria and its surrounding municipalities of Oak Bay, Saanich and Esquimalt and offer fun things to do this weekend. Some allow **swimming,** such as Elk/Beaver Lake Regional Park, Island View Beach Regional Park, Mount Work Regional Park, Thetis Lake Regional Park and Willows Park.

Hiking, nature and horse trails are found at several parks. For more information contact Victoria Parks, Recreation & Culture; phone (250) 361-0600. Bamberton Provincial Park *(see Recreation Areas Chart)* offers developed recreational facilities, including **camping.**

Swan Lake-Christmas Hill Nature Sanctuary, 6.5 kilometres (4 mi.) north via the Patricia Bay Highway, can be explored by hiking trails and floating walkways weaving through the area. Excellent views of Victoria and the sea are at Mount Douglas, Mount Tolmie and Beacon Hill Park.

Performing Arts

Whether you're in Victoria on vacation or just looking for cultural things to do this weekend, you'll find plenty of options and fun places to go around the city.

McPherson Playhouse in Centennial Square is the center of Vancouver Island's regional and professional theater. The restored 1914 theater regularly presents noontime concerts and musical comedy productions in the evening; phone (250) 386-6121 or (888) 717-6121. The **Pacific Opera Victoria,** (250) 385-0222, performs at the **Royal Theatre.**

The Royal Theatre on Broughton Street is also the home of the **Victoria Symphony Orchestra,** (250) 385-6515, which offers a pop and masterworks series September through May. The **Victoria Conservatory of Music** sometimes offers performances; phone (250) 386-5311.

Contemporary plays, with an emphasis on Canadian works, are staged at the **Belfry,** (250) 385-6815, 1291 Gladstone Ave., while shows at the Royal Theatre, (250) 386-6121 or (888) 717-6121, 805 Broughton, range from touring musicians to classical concerts and ballet. The **University Centre Farquhar Auditorium,** 3800 Finnerty Rd., presents comedy, dance and other cultural events; phone (250) 721-8480. **Butchart Gardens** offers concerts and musical stage shows during the summer that are among the fun things to do with friends. **Kaleidoscope Theatre,** an open-air theater at the Inner Harbour, also offers summer productions.

Top-name entertainers, rock groups and other performers draw large audiences to **Save-on-Foods Memorial Centre,** 1925 Blanshard St.; phone (250) 220-2600. A carillon at the **parliament buildings,** Government and Belleville sts., can be heard daily on the hour. The Royal BC Museum's **IMAX Victoria Theatre** offers big-screen films complementing the museum's natural and human history themes; phone (250) 480-4887 or (877) 480-4887.

Check with your local AAA travel agency for information about vacation packages and other things to do in Victoria that are geared toward the performing arts.

ATTRACTIONS

For a complete list of attractions, visit AAA.com/travelguides/attractions

ABKHAZI GARDEN is e. at 1964 Fairfield Rd. at Shotbolt Rd. This small, residential garden was created and nurtured by an Englishwoman and an exiled Georgian prince. The two met in Paris in the 1920s, spent time in separate World War II internment camps, reunited after the war, married and settled in Victoria.

Prince Nicholas and Princess Peggy Abkhazi built their home and developed this garden along rocky slopes meticulously planted with rhododendrons, Garry oaks and Japanese maples. The Abkhazis' home now houses The Teahouse, open for lunch and late afternoon tea.

Time: Allow 1 hour, 30 minutes minimum. **Hours:** Daily 11-5, Apr.-Sept.; Wed.-Sun. 11-5, rest of year. Last admission 1 hour before closing. Closed Jan. 1, Thanksgiving and Christmas. Phone ahead to confirm schedule. **Cost:** Gardens $10. Tea $22-$50. **Phone:** (778) 265-6466 or (250) 479-8053.

 BUTCHART GARDENS—see Brentwood Bay p. 173.

CHRIST CHURCH CATHEDRAL is at 911 Quadra St., between Burdett and Rockland sts. The Anglican-Episcopal cathedral is reminiscent of the great Gothic churches of the Middle Ages. Originally founded in 1856, the present cathedral is the third church built on this site. Started in the late 1920s and completed in 1986, it is one of Canada's largest cathedrals. The bells are replicas of those at Westminster Abbey in London, England. A labyrinth is on the grounds. **Hours:** Daily 8:30-4:30. **Cost:** Free. **Phone:** (250) 383-2714.

CRAIGDARROCH CASTLE is at 1050 Joan Crescent St. The sandstone mansion was built in the late 1880s for Robert Dunsmuir, a Scottish immigrant who attained wealth and fame through politics and coal mining. Dunsmuir died before the 39-room castle was completed. The building later served as a military hospital, a college and a music conservatory.

Visitors can appreciate the castle's stained-glass windows, intricate woodwork, ceiling murals and Victorian furnishings. There are numerous staircases, but no elevators. A self-guiding tour includes four floors of the castle and an 87-step climb to the tower, which offers stunning views of Victoria, the strait and the Olympic Mountains. An audio tour and an iPad tour also are available.

Time: Allow 1 hour minimum. **Hours:** Daily 9-7, June 15-Sept. 6; 10-4:30, rest of year. **Cost:** $14.60; $13.60 (ages 65+); $9.50 (ages 13-18 and students with ID); $5.10 (ages 6-12). Prices may vary; phone ahead. **Phone:** (250) 592-5323.

THE GARDENS AT HORTICULTURE CENTRE OF THE PACIFIC (HCP) are at 505 Quayle Rd. More than 3 hectares (9 acres) of educational gardens feature more than 10,000 plant varieties and sculptures. Highlights of the site include a bonsai garden, the Takata Japanese Garden and a children's garden. The surrounding 36 hectares (90 acres) include forests, wetlands and a haven for migratory birds.

Time: Allow 1 hour minimum. **Hours:** Daily 9-5, Mar.-Oct.; 10-4, rest of year. Closed Sat. before Christmas-Jan. 2. **Cost:** $12; $9 (ages 60+ and students with ID); free (ages 0-16). **Phone:** (250) 479-6162.

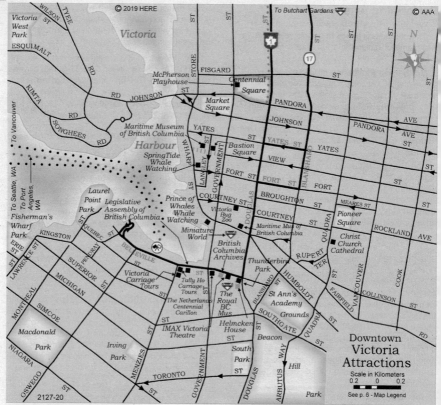

© 2019 HERE

To Butchart Gardens

© AAA

Downtown
Victoria
Attractions

Scale in Kilometers
0.2   0.2

See p. 6 - Map Legend

GOVERNMENT HOUSE AND GARDENS is at 1401 Rockland Ave. Government House is the official residence of the Lieutenant Governor and the ceremonial home of all British Columbians. The grounds embrace 14.5 hectares (36 acres), including formal gardens and a rare Garry oak ecosystem. The Cary Castle Mews Interpretive Centre is a good place to explore the history of this National Historic Site. **Hours:** Gardens daily dawn-dusk. Cary Castle Mews Interpretive Centre and Tea Room Tues.-Sat. 10-4, May-Sept. House tours are scheduled for one Sat. each month at 9:30 and 11, May-Oct.; phone ahead to confirm schedule. **Cost:** Free. **Phone:** (250) 387-2080. GT 🍴 🏕

LEGISLATIVE ASSEMBLY OF BRITISH COLUMBIA overlooks the Inner Harbour. The seat of British Columbia's parliament, the buildings have elaborately carved facades and are surrounded by 5 hectares (12 acres) of lawns, gardens, fountains and statues of dignitaries. The rooms have mosaic tile floors, rotundas, stained-glass windows, woodcarvings and murals.

Guided 30- to 45-minute tours, conducted in several languages, are offered. Self-guiding tours also are available weekdays; a booklet can be picked up at the tour desk. Food and drink are not permitted inside the Legislative Assembly. Visitors must pass through a security screening area with metal detectors. **Hours:** Daily 9-5, mid-May through Labour Day; Mon.-Fri. 8:30-5, rest of year. Phone ahead to confirm schedule. **Cost:** Free. **Phone:** (250) 387-3046. GT

MINIATURE WORLD is in The Fairmont Empress hotel at 649 Humboldt St. Animation, lighting, commentary and sound effects enhance more than 85 highly detailed miniature scenes. Displays include Great Canadian Railway, Frontier Land, Old London Town 1670, Circus World, one of the world's largest dollhouses, a Swiss Family Robinson tree house, a classic car rally, a futuristic space diorama, "Gulliver's Travels" and 11 dioramas depicting the story of King Arthur's Camelot. Scenes illustrate historic battles, fairy tales, nursery rhymes and timeless legends.

Time: Allow 1 hour minimum. **Hours:** Daily 9-9, mid-May through Sept. 30; 9-5, rest of year. **Cost:** $17; $10 (ages 13-17); $8 (ages 5-12). **Phone:** (250) 385-9731.

PRINCE OF WHALES WHALE WATCHING is at 812 Wharf St. Three-hour tours narrated by a marine biologist provide information about marine life. Passengers have a choice of sitting either outside n an open-air deck or inside in a heated cabin aboard the 19-metre (62 ft.) *Ocean Magic* cruiser. High-speed open-boat whale-watching tours in a Zodiac also are available. Hydrophones allow passengers to hear the whales vocalize. Sightseeing tours also are available.

Time: Allow 3 hours minimum. **Hours:** *Ocean Magic* tours depart daily at 9, 12:15 and 3:30, May-Oct.; schedule varies, rest of year. Zodiac tours depart daily every half hour 9-5, year-round. Passengers should arrive 30 minutes prior to departure. **Cost:** Whale-watching $170; $135 (ages 13-17); $110 (ages 2-12). Combination ticket with Butchart Gardens $160; $115 (ages 13-17); $95 (ages 2-12). Phone ahead to confirm tour prices and schedule. Reservations are required. **Phone:** (250) 383-4884 or (888) 383-4884.

THE ROYAL BC MUSEUM is on the Inner Harbour at 675 Belleville St. Two floors of displays reflect the human and natural history of British Columbia. The early 1900s Old Town Gallery has a theater with silent movies, a saloon, shops and a hotel. The Natural History Gallery showcases several different exhibits including a coastal rain forest diorama highlighted by live plants and tidal-pool animals, a life-size replica Woolly Mammoth and a climate change exhibit which explores the province's future climate. The First Peoples Gallery includes a hall of totems, an exhibit focusing on the historic Nisga'a agreement and the present-day Nisga'a community, and Haida argillite carvings.

Adjoining the First Peoples Gallery is "Our Living Languages: First Peoples' Voices in BC," an award-winning feature exhibition. The on-site IMAX Victoria Theatre offers films to complement the natural and human history theme of the museum as well as other exciting IMAX footage. Feature exhibits are presented annually.

Hours: Daily 10-5 (also Fri.-Sat. 5-10, mid-May to early Oct.). **Cost:** Museum 1-day admission $26.95; $18.95 (ages 65+ and students ages 19+ with ID); $16.95 (ages 6-18). Museum two consecutive days $40.43; $28.43 (ages 65+ and students ages 19+ with ID); $25.43 (ages 6-18,). IMAX $11.95; $10.75 (students ages 19+ with ID); $10.25 (ages 6-18 and 65+); $5.40 (ages 3-5). Museum 1-day and IMAX $36.90; $29.70 (students ages 19+ with ID); $27.20 (ages 6-18 and 65+); $5.40 (ages 3-5). Museum two consecutive days and one IMAX ticket $50.38; $39.18 (students ages 19+ with ID); $38.68 (ages 6-18 and 65+); $5.40 (ages 3-5). IMAX 3D add $1 per person. IMAX feature film add $3.25-$4 per person. Admission may increase for feature exhibits. **Phone:** (250) 356-7226 or (888) 447-7977.

British Columbia Archives is at 655 Belleville St. Extensive public and private records are available to those conducting historical, genealogical or other research. Gardens containing native plants surround the building. **Note:** A photo identification is required for registration. **Hours:** The archives are open to the public Mon.-Fri. 10-8 (full services available 10-4), Sat. 1-5 (limited services). **Cost:** Free. **Phone:** (250) 387-1952.

Helmcken House is on the grounds of the Royal BC Museum. One of the oldest houses in British Columbia still on its original site, the 1852 log structure was the home of John Sebastian Helmcken, a surgeon for Hudson's Bay Co. at Fort Victoria and a Father of Confederation. The restored house displays many original furnishings and an impressive collection of period medical instruments.

Time: Allow 30 minutes minimum. **Hours:** Daily noon-4, May 18-Labour Day; by appointment rest of year. Phone ahead to confirm schedule. **Cost:** Donations. **Phone:** (250) 356-7226.

The Netherlands Centennial Carillon is on the grounds of the Royal BC Museum at the corner of Government and Belleville sts. The largest carillon in Canada houses 62 bells donated by British Columbians of Dutch origin in celebration of the 1967 Canadian Confederation Centennial and in recognition of Canada's role in the liberation of the Netherlands during World War II. **Hours:** Carillon chimes ring hourly 10-8, Mar.-Sept.; 10-5, rest of year. Phone ahead to confirm summer Sun. carillon concert schedule. **Cost:** Free. **Phone:** (250) 356-7226.

Thunderbird Park is at the corner of Douglas and Belleville sts. on the grounds of the Royal BC Museum. The park's collection of West Coast totem poles was established in 1941 and recarved via the

Miniature World

Thunderbird Park

Totem Restoration Program 1950-90, when the originals began to decay beyond repair. A new Kwakwaka'wakw Honouring Pole was carved and raised in 1999.

Also showcased is Wawadiła., the ceremonial bighouse built by noted carver and artist Mungo Martin in 1953 that bears the hereditary crests of his family. **Hours:** Park open daily dawn-dusk. **Cost:** Free. **Phone:** (250) 356-7226.

SPRINGTIDE WHALE WATCHING is at 1119 Wharf St. In addition to orcas, visitors also may encounter sea lions; seals; porpoises; humpback, gray and minke whales as well as a variety of birds. Tours are given on a 19-metre (61 ft.) motor yacht as well as on high-speed, open Zodiacs. A harbor tour and sport fishing trips are available year-round.

Time: Allow 3 hours minimum. **Hours:** Whale-watch tours are given daily at 10 and 2, Apr.-Oct. Other times are available; phone for schedule. **Cost:** Whale-watch tour $124; $114 (ages 65+); $104 (ages 13-18 and students with ID); $94 (ages 3-12); A $2 Wildlife Conservation Fee is charged per person. Reservations are recommended. **Phone:** (250) 384-4444 or (800) 470-3474.

Sightseeing

Boat Tours

Sightseers using Victoria as a base for their vacation can explore the Gulf Islands and Vancouver by ferry from Swartz Bay, north of Victoria via Hwy. 17; for schedule and toll phone BC Ferries at (250) 386-3431 or (888) 223-3779.

Opportunities for whale watching are offered by several boating companies, the oldest of which is Orca Spirit, 146 Kingston St.; phone (250) 800-3747 or (877) 815-7255. A whale-watching trip is a great option for group travel and one of the fun things to do with friends in Victoria.

Bus and Carriage Tours

Guided tours of the city in red double-decker buses from London enhance Victoria's British atmosphere. Many of these tour operators are found along Belleville and Menzies streets by the harbor. Gray Line, 4196 Glanford Ave., (250) 385-6553 or (855) 385-6553, conducts bus tours, including a hop-on, hop-off service; tickets can be purchased at a kiosk at 721 Government St.

Narrated horse-drawn carriage tours of the city are offered by several companies, including Tally Ho Carriage Tours, phone (250) 514-9257, and Victoria Carriage Tours, phone (250) 383-2207 or (877) 663-2207. All tours leave from the corner of Belleville and Menzies streets.

Driving Tours

The Visitor Centre has information about things to do and such scenic routes as Marine Drive along the shoreline, a trip to Sooke Harbour on the west coast and the Malahat Drive, which runs along the east coast and reaches an elevation of 381 metres (1,250 ft.). The trip to Butchart Gardens is one of the most popular drives, following Hwy. 17 and Hwy. 17A through the rural communities and pastoral valleys of the Saanich Peninsula.

Walking Tours

Victoria is the perfect size for visitors keen on walking. A favorite thoroughfare of strollers and shoppers is Government Street, graced by banners and five-globe Victorian lampposts supporting baskets of geraniums and petunias. Stop in at the Visitor Centre for details and destination information, or contact your local AAA travel agency for help with vacation packages and travel tips.

COME SEE VICTORIA WALKING TOURS departs from outside the Victoria Visitor Centre at 812 Wharf St. A knowledgeable local guide leads guests on a 2-hour walking tour of landmarks and historic places around the downtown area, including stops along the Inner Harbour, Commercial Row, Bastion Square, Chinatown and Government Street. Additional tours highlight important people and historic figures (the Victorian Characters Walk) and local brew pubs (the Historic Pub Walk).

Time: Allow 2 hours minimum. **Hours:** Tour schedule varies, but History & Architecture Tours are generally offered Sat.-Sun. at 10 a.m. (and on weekdays in summer). Check online schedule to confirm tour times and availability. **Cost:** History & Architecture Tour or Victorian Characters Tour $20; $15 (senior citizens and students); free (ages 0-11); $45 (family). Historic Pub Walk $39. Reservations are required. **Phone:** (778) 676-0142.

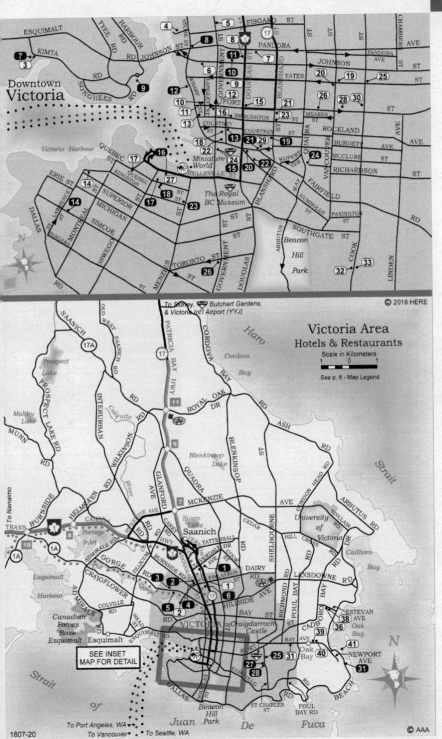

Downtown Victoria

Victoria Area
Hotels & Restaurants

Scale in Kilometers
1   0   1

See p. 6 - Map Legend

© 2019 HERE

© AAA

1807-20

Victoria

This index helps you "spot" where hotels and restaurants are located on the corresponding detailed maps. Restaurant price range is a combination of lunch and/or dinner. Turn to the listing page for more information and consult display ads for special promotions.

 For more details, rates and reservations: AAA.com/travelguides/hotels

VICTORIA

Map Page	Hotels	Designation	Member Savings	Page
1 p. 311	Accent Inns	APPROVED		314
2 p. 311	Mayfair Motel	APPROVED		316
3 p. 311	Robin Hood Inn & Suites	APPROVED		316
4 p. 311	Hotel Zed	APPROVED		316
5 p. 311	**Days Inn Victoria Uptown**	APPROVED	✔	315
6 p. 311	**Comfort Inn & Suites Victoria**	APPROVED	✔	315
7 p. 311	Spinnakers Gastro Brewpub & Guesthouses	THREE DIAMOND		316
8 p. 311	Swans Hotel and Brewpub	APPROVED		316
9 p. 311	**Delta Victoria Ocean Pointe Resort and Spa**	FOUR DIAMOND	✔	315
10 p. 311	**Best Western Plus Carlton Plaza Hotel**	THREE DIAMOND	✔	314
11 p. 311	Hotel Rialto	THREE DIAMOND		316
12 p. 311	**Victoria Regent Waterfront Hotel & Suites**	THREE DIAMOND	✔	317
13 p. 311	**The Magnolia Hotel & Spa**	FOUR DIAMOND	✔	316
14 p. 311	Heathergate House Bed & Breakfast	APPROVED		316
15 p. 311	**The Fairmont Empress**	FOUR DIAMOND	✔	316
16 p. 311	Days Inn by Wyndham Victoria on the Harbour	APPROVED	✔	315
17 p. 311	**Best Western Plus Inner Harbour** *(See ad p. 314.)*	THREE DIAMOND	✔	314
18 p. 311	**Royal Scot Hotel & Suites**	APPROVED	✔	316
19 p. 311	**Quality Inn Downtown Inner Harbour Victoria**	APPROVED	✔	316
20 p. 311	**DoubleTree by Hilton Hotel & Suites Victoria**	THREE DIAMOND	✔	315
21 p. 311	Chateau Victoria Hotel and Suites	THREE DIAMOND		314
22 p. 311	**Victoria Marriott Inner Harbour**	FOUR DIAMOND	✔	316
23 p. 311	Embassy Inn *(See ad p. 315.)*	THREE DIAMOND		315
24 p. 311	Abigail's Hotel	THREE DIAMOND		314
25 p. 311	Villa Marco Polo Inn	FOUR DIAMOND		317
26 p. 311	**James Bay Inn Hotel, Suites & Cottages**	APPROVED	✔	316
27 p. 311	Abbeymoore Manor Bed & Breakfast Inn	THREE DIAMOND		314
28 p. 311	Fairholme Manor	THREE DIAMOND		315

Map Page	Restaurants	Designation	Cuisine	Price Range	Page
1 p. 311	Lot 1 Pasta Bar	APPROVED	Italian	$13-$19	317
2 p. 311	Glo Restaurant & Lounge	THREE DIAMOND	Canadian	$8-$38	317
3 p. 311	Spinnakers Gastro Brewpub & Restaurant	APPROVED	American	$11-$27	318
4 p. 311	CANOE Brewpub	APPROVED	American	$15-$80	317
5 p. 311	Brasserie L'Ecole	THREE DIAMOND	French	$21-$50	317
6 p. 311	Il Terrazzo	THREE DIAMOND	Northern Italian	$15-$44	317
7 p. 311	Nubo Japanese Tapas	THREE DIAMOND	Japanese	$4-$30	317
8 p. 311	Veneto Kitchen and Bar	THREE DIAMOND	Pacific Northwest	$15-$46	318
9 p. 311	The Tapa Bar Restaurant	APPROVED	Spanish Small Plates	$6-$22	318
10 p. 311	Koto Sushi Izakaya	APPROVED	Japanese	$9-$37	317
11 p. 311	Siam Thai Restaurant	APPROVED	Thai	$9-$21	318
12 p. 311	Bard & Banker	THREE DIAMOND	American	$16-$45	317
13 p. 311	Nautical Nellie's Steak & Seafood Restaurant	THREE DIAMOND	Steak Seafood	$17-$70	317

Map Page	Restaurants (cont'd)	Designation	Cuisine	Price Range	Page
⑭ p. 311	IL Covo Trattoria	THREE DIAMOND	Italian	$20-$35	317
⑮ p. 311	Cactus Club Cafe	THREE DIAMOND	New American	$15-$40	317
⑯ p. 311	Pagliacci's	APPROVED	Italian	$14-$38	318
⑰ p. 311	Nourish Kitchen and Cafe	APPROVED	Natural/Organic	$9-$22	317
⑱ p. 311	10 Acres Bistro	APPROVED	Pacific Northwest Natural/Organic	$10-$32	317
⑲ p. 311	Moxie's Classic Grill	APPROVED	American	$18-$45	317
⑳ p. 311	Bin 4 Burger Lounge	APPROVED	Burgers	$12-$18	317
㉑ p. 311	Be Love Pure Nourishment	APPROVED	Natural/Organic	$9-$22	317
㉒ p. 311	10 Acres Kitchen	THREE DIAMOND	Pacific Northwest	$13-$42	317
㉓ p. 311	The Pink Bicycle	APPROVED	Burgers	$11-$16	318
㉔ p. 311	Q at the Empress	THREE DIAMOND	Pacific Northwest	$24-$49	318
㉕ p. 311	Ithaka Greek Restaurant	APPROVED	Greek	$18-$45	317
㉖ p. 311	Cafe Brio	THREE DIAMOND	Pacific Northwest	$13-$34	317
㉗ p. 311	Jonathan's Restaurant	APPROVED	American	$16-$35	317
㉘ p. 311	J & J Wonton Noodle House	APPROVED	Chinese	$15-$20	317
㉙ p. 311	Vista 18	THREE DIAMOND	Regional Canadian	$24-$46	318
㉚ p. 311	Pluto's	APPROVED	American	$9-$18	318
㉛ p. 311	White Heather Tea Room	APPROVED	Desserts Sandwiches	$9-$20	318
㉜ p. 311	Pizzeria Prima Strada	APPROVED	Pizza	$14-$19	318
㉝ p. 311	The Beagle Pub	APPROVED	American	$14-$22	317

OAK BAY

Map Page	Hotel	Designation	Member Savings	Page
㉛ p. 311	**Oak Bay Beach Hotel**	FOUR DIAMOND	✔	210

Map Page	Restaurants	Designation	Cuisine	Price Range	Page
㊱ p. 311	Sunday's Child	APPROVED	New French	$6-$18	210
㊳ p. 311	Willows Galley	APPROVED	Fish & Chips	$7-$24	210
㊴ p. 311	Penny Farthing English Pub	APPROVED	Canadian	$16-$29	210
㊵ p. 311	Ottavio Italian Bakery & Delicatessen	APPROVED	Italian Deli Breads/Pastries	$7-$15	210
㊶ p. 311	The Marina Restaurant	THREE DIAMOND	Pacific Northwest	$19-$48	210

Hit the Road with Identity Theft Protection

Identity thieves don't take vacations. Ensure you're protected before you leave.

Visit your local AAA office or online at **AAA.com/IDTheft**

All products not available at all locations.

VICTORIA

ABBEYMOORE MANOR BED & BREAKFAST INN
250/370-1470 **27**
 THREE DIAMOND Historic Bed & Breakfast. **Address:** 1470 Rockland Ave V8S 1W2

ABIGAIL'S HOTEL
250/388-5363 **24**
THREE DIAMOND Boutique Hotel. **Address:** 906 McClure St V8V 3E7

ACCENT INNS
250/475-7500 **1**
APPROVED Hotel. **Address:** 3233 Maple St V8X 4Y9

BEST WESTERN PLUS CARLTON PLAZA HOTEL
250/388-5513 **10**

THREE DIAMOND
Hotel

 Best Western PLUS. **AAA Benefit:** Members save up to 15% and earn bonus points!

Address: 642 Johnson St V8W 1M6 **Location:** Between Douglas and Broad sts. **Facility:** 103 units, some efficiencies and kitchens. 7 stories, interior corridors. **Parking:** valet only. **Terms:** check-in 4 pm. **Amenities:** safes. **Activities:** exercise room. **Guest Services:** valet and coin laundry.

BEST WESTERN PLUS INNER HARBOUR
250/384-5122 **17**

 THREE DIAMOND Hotel

Best Western PLUS. **AAA Benefit:** Members save up to 15% and earn bonus points!

Address: 412 Quebec St V8V 1W5 **Location:** Between Oswego and Menzies sts. **Facility:** 74 kitchen units. 8 stories, interior corridors. **Parking:** on-site (fee). **Terms:** check-in 4 pm. **Amenities:** safes. **Pool:** heated outdoor. **Activities:** sauna, hot tub, steamroom, exercise room. **Guest Services:** valet and coin laundry. **Featured Amenity:** breakfast buffet. *(See ad this page.)*

CHATEAU VICTORIA HOTEL AND SUITES
250/382-4221 **21**
THREE DIAMOND Hotel. **Address:** 740 Burdett Ave V8W 1B2

Turn dreams into plans using AAA travel planning tools: AAA.com/maps

▼ See AAA listing this page ▼

Winner of the 2019 Best Western Chairman Award & 2019 Best Western Directors Award

A Great Hotel in Victoria's Best Location
• FREE Full Hot Breakfast Buffet
• Easy walk to attractions, shops & dining
• Outdoor pool (seasonal), sauna, steam room, whirlpool & fitness studio

412 Quebec St, Victoria
888.383.2378
VictoriaBestWestern.com

 Best Western PLUS. Inner Harbour

(See map & index p. 311.)

COMFORT INN & SUITES VICTORIA 250/382-4400 **6**

APPROVED

Hotel

Address: 3020 Blanshard St V8T 5C7 **Location:** 1.6 mi (2.6 km) n on Hwy 17 (Blanshard St), just s of Finlayson St. **Facility:** 152 units. 1-5 stories, interior/exterior corridors. **Terms:** check-in 4 pm. **Activities:** exercise room. **Guest Services:** valet and coin laundry. **Featured Amenity:** breakfast buffet.

[SAVE] [ECO] [⏍] [Y] CALL[&] [♿]
[BIZ] [📶] [✕] [🛏] [🖥]
/SOME UNITS [🐾] [HS] [📷]

DAYS INN BY WYNDHAM VICTORIA ON THE HARBOUR 250/386-3451 **16**

APPROVED

Hotel

Address: 427 Belleville St V8V 1X3 **Location:** Between Oswego and Menzies sts. **Facility:** 71 units, some kitchens. 4 stories, interior corridors. **Amenities:** safes. **Pool:** heated outdoor. **Activities:** hot tub. **Guest Services:** valet laundry.

[SAVE] [ECO] [⏍] [Y] [🛫] [BIZ] [📶]
[✕] [🐕] [🛏] [🖥]
/SOME UNITS [🐾] [📷]

DAYS INN VICTORIA UPTOWN 250/388-6611 **5**

APPROVED

Hotel

Address: 229 Gorge Rd E V9A 1L1 **Location:** From Douglas St, 1.2 mi (2 km) w at Washington Ave. **Facility:** 73 units, some efficiencies and kitchens. 3 stories (no elevator), exterior corridors. **Amenities:** safes. **Pool:** heated indoor. **Activities:** sauna, bicycles, exercise room. **Guest Services:** valet and coin laundry.

[SAVE] [ECO] [⏍] [Y] [🛫] [♿] [BIZ]
[📶] [✕] [🛏] [🖥]
/SOME UNITS [🐾] [📷]

🌐 **Find AAA Inspected & Approved campgrounds at AAA.com/campgrounds**

DELTA VICTORIA OCEAN POINTE RESORT AND SPA 250/360-2999 **9**

FOUR DIAMOND

Contemporary Hotel

D DELTA HOTELS — **AAA Benefit:** Members save 5% or more!

Address: 100 Harbour Rd V9A 0G1 **Location:** Waterfront. Just w of Johnson St Bridge; jct Esquimalt and Harbour rds. **Facility:** With its location along the inner harbor, enjoy the waterfront views from the comfort of your room or the many outside patios. A variety of activities such as yoga, ping pong and squash are available. 240 units. 8 stories, interior corridors. **Parking:** on-site (fee) and valet. **Terms:** check-in 4 pm. **Pool:** heated indoor. **Activities:** sauna, hot tub, tennis, recreation programs in summer, health club, spa. **Guest Services:** valet laundry, area transportation.

[SAVE] [ECO] [⏍] [🛏] [Y] CALL[&] [🛫] [♿] [BIZ] [HS]
[📶] [✕] [🛏] [🖥] /SOME UNITS [🐾]

DOUBLETREE BY HILTON HOTEL & SUITES VICTORIA 250/940-3100 **20**

THREE DIAMOND

Hotel

DOUBLETREE by HILTON — **AAA Benefit:** Members save up to 15%!

Address: 777 Douglas St V8W 2B5 **Location:** Between Blanshard (Hwy 17) and Douglas sts; downtown. **Facility:** 181 units, some two bedrooms and efficiencies. 17 stories, interior corridors. **Parking:** valet only. **Terms:** check-in 4 pm. **Amenities:** safes. **Dining:** 2 restaurants. **Activities:** exercise room. **Guest Services:** valet laundry, rental car service.

[SAVE] [⏍] [🛏] [Y] CALL[&] [♿] [BIZ] [HS] [📶] [✕]
[🛏] [🖥] [🖨] /SOME UNITS [🐾]

EMBASSY INN 250/382-8161 **23**

THREE DIAMOND Hotel. **Address:** 520 Menzies St V8V 2H4 *(See ad this page.)*

FAIRHOLME MANOR 250/598-3240 **28**

THREE DIAMOND Bed & Breakfast. **Address:** 638 Rockland Pl V8S 3R2

▼ See AAA listing this page ▼

Memories begin *at...* 𝓔 *The Embassy Inn*

Great Inner Harbour location!
Close to most of Victoria's best attractions!

CAA/AAA members receive 15% off our Best Available Rate *plus...*

FREE • **Breakfast** • **Guest Parking** • **Wi-Fi**

1-800-268-8161 • **www.embassyinn.ca**
520 Menzies Street, Victoria, BC V8V 2H4

(See map & index p. 311.)

THE FAIRMONT EMPRESS
250/384-8111 **15**

FOUR DIAMOND

Classic Historic Hotel

Address: 721 Government St V8W 1W5 **Location:** Between Belleville and Humboldt sts. Located on Inner Harbour. **Facility:** Renowned for its tradition of afternoon tea, this landmark Victorian-style hotel was built in 1908. A variety of rooms with upscale décor is available. Don't miss taking a stroll of the shops. 464 units, some two bedrooms. 8 stories, interior corridors. **Parking:** on-site (fee) and valet. **Terms:** check-in 4 pm. **Amenities:** safes. **Dining:** 2 restaurants, also, Q at the Empress, see separate listing. **Pool:** heated indoor. **Activities:** sauna, hot tub, bicycles, exercise room, spa. **Guest Services:** valet laundry, area transportation.

SAVE ECO ❚❙ ▥ ⛾ CALL ⟨⑆⟩ ⇌ ⦿ BIZ sHS
⟨⟩ ⊠ ❙ 🖥 / SOME UNITS 🐾

HEATHERGATE HOUSE BED & BREAKFAST
250/383-0068 **14**

APPROVED Bed & Breakfast. **Address:** 122 Simcoe St V8V 1K4

HOTEL RIALTO
250/383-4157 **11**

THREE DIAMOND Boutique Contemporary Hotel. **Address:** 653 Pandora Ave V8W 1N8

HOTEL ZED
250/388-4345 **4**

APPROVED Hotel. **Address:** 3110 Douglas St V8Z 3K4

JAMES BAY INN HOTEL, SUITES & COTTAGES
250/384-7151 **26**

APPROVED

Historic Hotel

Address: 270 Government St V8V 2L2 **Location:** Between Toronto and Marifield sts. **Facility:** In the heart of Victoria's heritage residential district, the hotel's lobby and public areas are full of antiques. Due to the building's historic nature, rooms are colorful but some are rather compact. 45 units, some kitchens and cottages. 4 stories (no elevator), interior corridors. **Guest Services:** valet laundry.

SAVE ECO ❚❙ ⛾ BIZ 🛜 ⊠
⟨⟩ / SOME UNITS ❙

THE MAGNOLIA HOTEL & SPA
250/381-0999 **13**

FOUR DIAMOND

Boutique Hotel

Address: 623 Courtney St V8W 1B8 **Location:** Corner of Courtney and Gordon sts. Located on Inner Harbour. **Facility:** This luxury hotel provides a convenient base for those interested in visiting downtown Victoria and its popular attractions. The elegant guest rooms have large bay windows. 64 units. 7 stories, interior corridors. **Parking:** valet only. **Terms:** check-in 4 pm. **Amenities:** safes. **Activities:** sauna, bicycles, exercise room, spa. **Guest Services:** valet laundry. **Featured Amenity:** continental breakfast.

SAVE ECO ❚❙ ⛾ ⛾ CALL ⟨⑆⟩ ⦿ BIZ HS 🛜
⊠ ❙ 🖥 / SOME UNITS 🐾

MAYFAIR MOTEL
250/388-7337 **2**

APPROVED Extended Stay Hotel. **Address:** 650 Speed Ave V8Z 1A4

QUALITY INN DOWNTOWN INNER HARBOUR VICTORIA
250/385-6787 **19**

APPROVED

Hotel

Address: 850 Blanshard St V8W 2H2 **Location:** Between Courtney St and Burdett St. **Facility:** 63 units, some efficiencies. 3 stories, interior corridors. **Parking:** on-site (fee). **Pool:** heated indoor. **Activities:** limited exercise equipment. **Guest Services:** valet and coin laundry.

SAVE ECO ❚❙ ⛾ ⇌ BIZ 🛜
⊠ ⟨⟩ ❙ 🖥 🖥 / SOME UNITS 🐾 HS

ROBIN HOOD INN & SUITES
250/388-4302 **3**

APPROVED Motel. **Address:** 136 Gorge Rd E V9A 1L4

ROYAL SCOT HOTEL & SUITES
250/388-5463 **18**

APPROVED

Hotel

Address: 425 Quebec St V8V 1W7 **Location:** Between Menzies and Oswego sts. **Facility:** 177 units, some two bedrooms and kitchens. 4 stories, interior corridors. **Parking:** on-site (fee). **Terms:** check-in 4 pm. **Amenities:** safes. **Dining:** Jonathan's Restaurant, see separate listing. **Pool:** heated indoor. **Activities:** sauna, hot tub, game room, exercise room. **Guest Services:** valet and coin laundry, area transportation.

SAVE ECO ❚❙ ⛾ ⇌ ⛾
BIZ HS 🛜 ⊠ ⟨⟩ ❙ 🖥
/ SOME UNITS 🐾 🖥

SPINNAKERS GASTRO BREWPUB & GUESTHOUSES
250/386-2739 **7**

THREE DIAMOND Bed & Breakfast. **Address:** 308 Catherine St V9A 3S8

SWANS HOTEL AND BREWPUB
250/361-3310 **8**

APPROVED Boutique Hotel. **Address:** 506 Pandora Ave V8W 1N6

VICTORIA MARRIOTT INNER HARBOUR
250/480-3800 **22**

FOUR DIAMOND

Hotel

MARRIOTT **AAA Benefit:** Members save 5% or more!

Address: 728 Humboldt St V8W 3Z5 **Location:** Between Blanshard (Hwy 17) and Douglas sts. **Facility:** Close to the Inner Harbour and downtown, the full-service hotel offers spacious rooms and lots of attractions within walking distance. For a view, ask for a room on a higher floor. 236 units. 16 stories, interior corridors. **Parking:** on-site (fee) and valet. **Terms:** check-in 4 pm. **Amenities:** safes. **Pool:** heated indoor. **Activities:** hot tub, steamroom, exercise room. **Guest Services:** valet and coin laundry.

SAVE ❚❙ ⛾ ⛾ CALL ⟨⑆⟩ ⇌ ⛾ BIZ HS 🛜
⊠ ❙ 🖥 / SOME UNITS 🐾 🖥

🔗 **AAA.com/hertz**—When your ideal road trip includes a comfortable ride

See map & index p. 311.)

VICTORIA REGENT WATERFRONT HOTEL & SUITES
250/386-2211 **12**

⬦ **THREE DIAMOND** **Address:** 1234 Wharf St V8W 3H9 **Location:** Waterfront. Between Yates and Fort sts. Located on the Inner Harbour. **Facility:** These amazing condo units sit right at the water's edge, where the harbor views are simply spectacular. Modern full kitchens and super large bedrooms are in the many condo units. 39 units, some condominiums. 8 stories, interior corridors. **Terms:** check-in 4 pm. **Amenities:** safes. **Guest Services:** valet and coin laundry. **Featured Amenity:** breakfast buffet.

Vacation Rental Condominium

SAVE ECO ᵀⁱ CALL 🦽 BIZ HS 🛜 ✕ 🍴 💻 / SOME UNITS 🅰 🍽

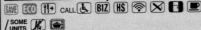

Combine your 10% AAA Member Discount with our free breakfast for great value & exceptional comfort.

VILLA MARCO POLO INN 250/370-1524 **25**
⬦ **FOUR DIAMOND** Historic Bed & Breakfast. **Address:** 1524 Shasta Pl V8S 1X9

WESTIN BEAR MOUNTAIN GOLF RESORT & SPA
250/391-7160
⬦ **THREE DIAMOND** SAVE Hotel. **Address:** 1999 Country Club Way V9B 6R3

AAA Benefit: Members save 5% or more!

WHERE TO EAT

10 ACRES BISTRO 250/220-8008 **18**
⬦ **APPROVED** Pacific Northwest Natural/Organic. Casual Dining. **Address:** 611 Courtney St V8V 4G4

10 ACRES KITCHEN 250/385-4512 **22**
⬦ **THREE DIAMOND** Pacific Northwest. Fine Dining. **Address:** 614 Humboldt St V8W 1A4

BARD & BANKER 604/953-9993 **12**
⬦ **THREE DIAMOND** American. Gastropub. **Address:** 1022 Government St V8W 1X7

THE BEAGLE PUB 250/382-3301 **33**
⬦ **APPROVED** American. Gastropub. **Address:** 301 Cook St V8V 3X5

BE LOVE PURE NOURISHMENT 778/443-7181 **21**
⬦ **APPROVED** Natural/Organic. Casual Dining. **Address:** 1019 Blanchard St V8W 2H4

BIN 4 BURGER LOUNGE 250/590-4154 **20**
⬦ **APPROVED** Burgers. Casual Dining. **Address:** 911 Yates St, #180 V8V 4X3

BRASSERIE L'ECOLE 250/475-6260 **5**
⬦ **THREE DIAMOND** French. Fine Dining. **Address:** 1715 Government St V8W 1Z4

CACTUS CLUB CAFE 250/361-3233 **15**
⬦ **THREE DIAMOND** New American. Casual Dining. **Address:** 1125 Douglas St V8W 3L7

CAFE BRIO 250/383-0009 **26**
⬦ **THREE DIAMOND** Pacific Northwest. Casual Dining. **Address:** 944 Fort St V8V 3K2

CANOE BREWPUB 250/361-1940 **4**
⬦ **APPROVED** American. Gastropub. **Address:** 450 Swift St V8W 1S3

GLO RESTAURANT & LOUNGE 250/385-5643 **2**
⬦ **THREE DIAMOND** Canadian. Casual Dining. **Address:** 104-2940 Jutland Rd V8T 5K6

IL COVO TRATTORIA 250/380-0088 **14**
⬦ **THREE DIAMOND** Italian. Fine Dining. **Address:** 106 Superior St V8V 1T1

IL TERRAZZO 250/361-0028 **6**
⬦ **THREE DIAMOND** Northern Italian. Casual Dining. **Address:** 555 Johnson St V8W 1M2

ITHAKA GREEK RESTAURANT 250/384-6474 **25**
⬦ **APPROVED** Greek. Casual Dining. **Address:** 1102 Yates St V8V 3M8

J & J WONTON NOODLE HOUSE 250/383-0680 **28**
⬦ **APPROVED** Chinese. Casual Dining. **Address:** 1012 Fort St V8V 3Z9

JONATHAN'S RESTAURANT 250/383-5103 **27**
⬦ **APPROVED** American. Casual Dining. **Address:** 425 Quebec St V8V 1W7

KOTO SUSHI IZAKAYA 250/382-1514 **10**
⬦ **APPROVED** Japanese. Casual Dining. **Address:** 510 Fort St V8W 1E6

LOT 1 PASTA BAR 778/265-9311 **1**
⬦ **APPROVED** Italian. Casual Dining. **Address:** 204-815 Cloverdale Ave V8X 2S8

MILESTONES GRILL AND BAR 250/381-2244
⬦ **APPROVED** American. Casual Dining. **Address:** 812 Wharf St V8W 1T3

MOXIE'S CLASSIC GRILL 250/360-1660 **19**
⬦ **APPROVED** American. Casual Dining. **Address:** 1010 Yates St, #1 V8V 3M7

NAUTICAL NELLIE'S STEAK & SEAFOOD RESTAURANT
250/380-2260 **13**
⬦ **THREE DIAMOND** Steak Seafood. Casual Dining. **Address:** 1001 Wharf St V8W 1T6

NOURISH KITCHEN AND CAFE 250/590-3426 **17**
⬦ **APPROVED** Natural/Organic. Casual Dining. **Address:** 225 Quebec St V8V 1W2

NUBO JAPANESE TAPAS 778/265-9909 **7**
⬦ **THREE DIAMOND** Japanese. Casual Dining. **Address:** 739 Pandora Ave V8W 1N9

(See map & index p. 311.)

PAGLIACCI'S 250/386-1662 (16)
💎 **APPROVED** Italian. Casual Dining. **Address:** 1011 Broad St V8W 2A1

THE PINK BICYCLE 250/384-1008 (23)
💎 **APPROVED** Burgers. Casual Dining. **Address:** 1008 Blanshard St V8W 2H5

PIZZERIA PRIMA STRADA 250/590-8595 (32)
💎 **APPROVED** Pizza. Casual Dining. **Address:** 230 Cook St V8V 3X3

PLUTO'S 250/385-4747 (30)
💎 **APPROVED** American. Casual Dining. **Address:** 1150 Cook St V8V 3Z9

Q AT THE EMPRESS 250/384-8111 (24)
💎 **THREE DIAMOND** Pacific Northwest. Fine Dining. **Address:** 721 Government St V8W 1W5

SIAM THAI RESTAURANT 250/383-9911 (11)
💎 **APPROVED** Thai. Casual Dining. **Address:** 512 Fort St V8W 1E6

SPINNAKERS GASTRO BREWPUB & RESTAURANT
250/386-2739 (3)
💎 **APPROVED** American. Gastropub. **Address:** 308 Catherine St V9A 3S8

SWISS CHALET 250/475-0334
💎 **APPROVED** Chicken. Casual Dining. **Address:** 3233 Douglas St V8Z 3K8

THE TAPA BAR RESTAURANT 250/383-0013 (9)
💎 **APPROVED** Spanish Small Plates. Casual Dining. **Address:** 620 Trounce Alley V8W 1K3

VENETO KITCHEN AND BAR 250/383-7310 (8)
💎 **THREE DIAMOND** Pacific Northwest. Fine Dining. **Address:** 1450 Douglas St V8W 2G1

VISTA 18 250/382-4221 (29)
💎 **THREE DIAMOND** Regional Canadian. Fine Dining. **Address:** 740 Burdett Ave V8W 1B2

WHITE HEATHER TEA ROOM 250/595-8020 (31)
💎 **APPROVED** Desserts Sandwiches. Casual Dining. **Address:** 1885 Oak Bay Ave V8R 1C6

STAY CONNECTED

to all the things membership can do for you

- **Member discounts around you**
- **Cheapest gas nearby**
- **Diamond hotels and restaurants**
- **Travel information and reservations**
- **Roadside assistance**

Download today. Connect every day.
AAA.com/mobile | CAA.ca/mobile

WEST KELOWNA (C-8) pop. 30,892, elev. 411m/1,348'

- Hotels & Restaurants map & index p. 216
- Part of Okanagan Valley area — see map p. 212

West Kelowna (Westbank) was a link on the fur-trading route from the north-central part of the province, called New Caledonia, to the Columbia River. In the early 1860s fortune seekers en route to the Cariboo gold fields followed the old trail through the Okanagan Valley.

Ideal climatic conditions in the Okanagan Valley nurture the city's many orchards and vineyards. Vacationers also are drawn by the favorable weather in the valley. Downhill and cross-country skiing in the surrounding countryside are popular in winter.

West Kelowna Visitor Centre: 2376 Dobbin Rd., Suite 4, West Kelowna, BC, Canada V4T 2H9. **Phone:** (250) 768-2712.

WINERIES

- **Mission Hill Family Estate** is 4.5 km (3 mi.) e. off Hwy. 97 via Boucherie Rd. to 1730 Mission Hill Rd. **Hours:** Daily 9:30-7, early July-early Sept.; 10-6, early Sept. to mid-Oct.; 10-5, mid-Oct. through late Oct.; 11-5, late Oct.-Dec. 31. Tours are offered daily; phone for schedule. Reservations are required for some peak season and holiday weekends. Closed Jan. 1, Christmas and day after Christmas. Phone ahead to confirm schedule. **Phone:** (250) 768-6483 or (250) 768-6448. GT

BEST WESTERN PLUS WINE COUNTRY HOTEL & SUITES
250/707-1637 28

 THREE DIAMOND
Hotel

AAA Benefit: Members save up to 15% and earn bonus points!

Address: 3460 Carrington Rd V4T 3C1 **Location:** Hwy 97 (Okanagan Hwy), just e on Elk Rd. **Facility:** 99 units. 4 stories, interior corridors. **Terms:** check-in 4 pm. **Amenities:** safes. **Pool:** heated indoor. **Activities:** hot tub, exercise room. **Guest Services:** valet and coin laundry. *(See ad this page.)*

SAVE ECO 🛏️ CALL 👤 🚗   🛜 🖥️

BIZ HS 🛜 ✕ 🍴 🖥️ 💻

/ SOME UNITS 🦌

THE COVE LAKESIDE RESORT   250/707-1800 29
 THREE DIAMOND Resort Hotel. **Address:** 4205 Gellatly Rd V4T 2K2

WHERE TO EAT

KEKULI CAFE   250/768-3555 37
APPROVED Canadian. Quick Serve. **Address:** 3041 Louie Dr, #505 V4T 3E2

OLD VINES THE RESTAURANT AT QUAILS' GATE
250/769-4451 38
THREE DIAMOND Regional Canadian. Fine Dining. **Address:** 3303 Boucherie Rd V1Z 2H3

▼ See AAA listing this page ▼

IN THE HEART OF THE OKANAGAN VALLEY
Surround yourself in a beautiful landscape and enjoy world-class hospitality.

BW Best Western PLUS

Wine Country Hotel & Suites

THREE DIAMOND

- Pet-friendly
- 24-hour fitness centre
- Waterslide • Free wi-fi
- Indoor pool & jetted hot tub
- Free hot breakfast buffet

3460 Carrington Rd | West Kelowna, BC
V4T 3C1, Canada | 250-707-1637
1-888-348-2227
www.bestwesternwinecountry.com

(See map & index p. 216.)

ORIGINAL JOE'S RESTAURANT & BAR　　　250/768-3835
▼▼ APPROVED　　American. Casual Dining. **Address:** 114-3000 Louie Dr V4T 3E1

THE TERRACE RESTAURANT　　　250/768-6467　㊴
▼▼ THREE DIAMOND　New Canadian. Casual Dining. **Address:** 1730 Mission Hill Rd V4T 2E4

WEST VANCOUVER (H-11) pop. 42,694
- Hotels & Restaurants map & index p. 276
- Part of Vancouver area — see map p. 249

If you're not a Vancouverite—or you're unfamiliar with British Columbia's Lower Mainland—you might think that the North Shore is simply one more spectacularly scenic backdrop to a city already blessed with loads of scenic allure. And you would be wrong. The North Shore is not only uncommonly beautiful; it's also teeming with things to do.

The city and district of North Vancouver are east of the Lions Gate Bridge; the district of West Vancouver spreads along the northern shore of Burrard Inlet from the bridge west to Horseshoe Bay. There's no manufacturing or industry here; "West Van" is primarily residential. It's also affluent, and there are many gorgeous and expensive homes tucked away on winding little streets or perched high on hillsides. West Vancouver is situated on slopes of the Coast Mountains, which means that most of these homes enjoy enviable vistas of water, trees, mountains or all three.

The Lions Gate Bridge, which connects Stanley Park and the North Shore, is the gateway to West Vancouver. This suspension bridge crosses the first narrows of Burrard Inlet, which accounts for its official name, the First Narrows Bridge; "lions gate" is a reference to two mountains known as the Lions.

Construction of the 1,795-metre (5,890-ft.) span began in 1937, and the bridge opened to traffic in 1938. It's similar in appearance to San Francisco's Golden Gate Bridge (although bright green rather than bright orange). Another similarity it shares with Golden Gate is the view from the bridge—it's gorgeous whether you're coming or going. The Guinness family (of beer fame), who for a time owned land on the North Shore, purchased decorative white lights for the bridge in 1986 as a gift to Vancouver, turning it into a distinctive nighttime landmark.

Marine Drive is West Vancouver's main thoroughfare. It runs from the bridge west to Horseshoe Bay, usually within sight of water, passing lovely neighborhoods and commercial blocks packed with shops and restaurants. Ambleside, between 11th and 23rd streets, is one of West Vancouver's oldest neighborhoods. The Centennial Seawalk in Ambleside Park is a breezy waterfront promenade that's a favorite spot for walkers, joggers or anyone who loves to gaze out onto the water and contemplate the awesome views of the bridge and Stanley Park. There's a long, sandy beach and a concession stand where you can grab a cheeseburger or an ice cream cone.

Ambleside also has art galleries and antique shops. The Silk Purse Gallery, 1570 Argyle Ave. (on the waterfront near John Lawson Park), is a comfy old cottage that used to be a haven for honeymooners. It's now home to the West Vancouver Community Arts Council, which presents rotating art exhibits and a series of summer concerts; for ticket information phone (604) 925-7292. Local artists exhibit at the Ferry Building Gallery, a lovingly restored heritage building at 1414 Argyle Ave.; phone (604) 925-7290.

Dundarave is another exceedingly picturesque little seaside community. Stroll along the water once again at Dundarave Park, at the foot of 25th Street, with Cypress Mountain looming in the distance. Old-fashioned lamp posts are installed on Marine Drive between 23rd and 25th streets, flowers cascade from hanging baskets, and the 2 blocks are filled with eateries and specialty shops. It's a nice area to spend an hour or two. Have lunch at the Red Lion Bar & Grill (2427 Marine Dr.), a classic British-style pub—think dark wood walls, stained glass and several fireplaces when the weather's nippy—or stop for coffee and a muffin at Delaney's Coffee House (2424 Marine Dr.).

Marine Drive presses on to Caulfeild (yes, that spelling is correct), an exclusive residential community of narrow, precipitously winding streets and expensive homes shielded by tall privacy hedges. Almost every bend and curve of the road offers a brief, tantalizing water view. Walking the trails in Lighthouse Park *(see attraction listing)*, a protected stand of old-growth coastal forest, is well worth your time.

Past the Lighthouse Park turnoff Marine Drive winds north toward Horseshoe Bay. Side streets lead to tucked-away little green spaces like Kew Park (accessed via Kew Cliff Road and Seaside Place). The multimillion-dollar homes along Kew Cliff Road have stunning views of the Strait of Georgia. A bit farther north Marine Drive winds around Fisherman's Cove, bristling with the masts of pleasure craft moored at the West Vancouver Yacht Club.

Follow the signs to Horseshoe Bay, the North Shore's western bookend. This is where ferries depart for Vancouver Island and the Lower Mainland's "Sunshine Coast." The little community is another North Shore jewel. Take Nelson Avenue off Marine Drive, which leads to the ferry terminal and marina. BC Ferries chug in and out of port while sea gulls wheel overhead. Tree-covered slopes frame Horseshoe Bay, houses perch high above the water and the Coast Mountains loom in the distance. Charming really doesn't begin to describe it.

"Downtown" Horseshoe Bay has just a couple of streets, which makes it perfect for strolling. Browse a few art galleries. Lean against a dock piling and watch the waterfront activity. Get fish and chips or an oyster burger from one of the takeout restaurants on Bay Street and take your feast to Horseshoe Bay Park, where there are picnic tables, a little gravel beach, a playground, two totem poles and a massive cast-bronze propeller that came off a whaling

(See map & index p. 276.)
ship. Listen to the gulls and breathe in the sea air. Now *this* is an afternoon outing.

Backtrack to Marine Drive and turn right instead of left (which will take you back to Hwy. 99). Stay on Marine Drive and you'll reach Whytecliff Park *(see Recreation Areas Chart)*. Designated Canada's first salt water Marine Protected Area (MPA) in 1993, it's located at the entrance to Howe Sound and is known for excellent scuba diving. Seals frolic along this rugged stretch of coastline, and there's a pebbly beach to explore. Or just relax at the park's observation pavilion and—you guessed it—admire the view.

LIGHTHOUSE PARK is off Marine Dr. (watch for the park sign at the turnoff), then a short distance s. via Beacon Ln. to the parking area. Capt. George Vancouver sailed past the rocky peninsula at the entrance to Burrard Inlet in 1792 and named the site Point Atkinson. Today this lush remnant of old growth coastal rainforest encompassing 75 hectares (185 acres) is a peaceful haven and wonderful place to hike. The lofty first-growth Douglas firs and other conifers are up to 500 years old.

Several kilometres of trails crisscross the park; to get to the Point Atkinson Lighthouse take the Beacon Lane Trail south from the parking area. It's about a 15-minute walk to a viewpoint with an expansive vista (on clear days) of the lighthouse (a working one and therefore closed to the public), the inlet and downtown Vancouver on the opposite shore. From the lighthouse viewpoint, short East Beach Trail leads down to the rugged, rocky beach along Starboat Cove.

The group of buildings near the lighthouse were barracks during World War II, when a number of B.C. light stations were used for surveillance purposes. **Time:** Allow 30 minutes minimum. **Hours:** Daily dawn-dusk. **Cost:** Free. **Phone:** (604) 925-7375.

CACTUS CLUB CAFE   604/922-1707 (23)
THREE DIAMOND New American. Casual Dining. **Address:** 855 Main St V7T 2Z3

OLIVE & ANCHOR   604/921-8848 (21)
APPROVED American. Casual Dining. **Address:** 6418 Bay St V7W 2H1

SALMON HOUSE ON THE HILL   604/926-3212 (22)
THREE DIAMOND Seafood. Fine Dining. **Address:** 2229 Folkestone Way V7S 2Y6

WHISTLER (G-12) pop. 9,824, elev. 640m/2,009'
• Hotels p. 325 • Restaurants p. 327
• Hotels & Restaurants map & index p. 324

Whistler would be a special place even without the whole enchilada it offers when it comes to winter sports. It would be special without the superb system of hiking and mountain biking trails that provide outdoor activity when the sun is warm and the snow isn't swirling. And it would be special without the amenities—all sorts of lodgings from basic to luxury, plenty of restaurants (and a few of culinary distinction), a nice selection of specialty shops, evening entertainment from mild to wild—that combine to create this covers-every-base active vacation destination.

The reason why has a lot to do with an old adage: location, location, location. About 2 hours north of Vancouver, Whistler snuggles in a Coast Mountains valley amid a cluster of shimmering small lakes, the reflection of forested slopes etched on their surfaces. Rivers rush through steep-walled canyons. Waterfalls plunge. The stark white of glacier ice contrasts with the black of mountain peaks, framed against a brilliantly blue sky. The wilderness is rugged and unspoiled, the air bracingly fresh. Given such a spectacular setting, it's easy to see why it has become one of Canada's best all-season resorts.

Although the 2010 Olympic Winter Games are now history, Whistler remains a pretty exciting place—and getting there is part of the fun. From Vancouver, the major road link is the Sea-to-Sky Highway (Hwy. 99). The primary road link between Vancouver and Whistler was widened and improved for the games. The 2-hour drive offers a full plate of scenic views as the highway climbs from a coastal rain forest environment in the vicinity of Horseshoe Bay to the rugged mountain landscapes around Whistler. Even so, it's always a good idea to check road conditions before heading to Whistler; for information and traffic updates phone (800) 944-7853.

Between Horseshoe Bay and Squamish the road runs along the eastern edge of Howe Sound, punctuated by a series of fjords. From a distance, islands in the bay look like plump green mounds floating on water that is invitingly blue in sunny weather and a brooding gray on overcast days.

Just south of Squamish water is left behind as the highway veers inland. If you want to take a break or need to make a pit stop before reaching Whistler, there are gas stations and a scattering of fast-food outlets at the intersection of Hwy. 99 and Cleveland Road. Past Squamish, Hwy. 99 twists and turns around tree-covered granite crags and sheer rock faces that rise almost straight up from the side of the road. Be sure to pull off and stop at the designated viewpoints; great views are guaranteed.

Whistler has no grand entrance; there are just two primary access roads off Hwy. 99 (Village Gate Drive and Lorimer Road). Whistler Village may seem small, but it's compact. Sitting at the base of Whistler Mountain's ski runs, this is where lots of hotels, restaurants and shops are concentrated. Blackcomb Way divides Whistler Village from the Upper Village, which lies at the base of Blackcomb Mountain's ski runs. Distinctions are pretty much a moot point, although the Upper Village tends to have more upscale accommodations and Whistler Village a livelier scene after dark.

You can walk between the two villages in about 5 minutes along Fitzsimmons Trail, which crosses burbling Fitzsimmons Creek via a covered bridge. Branching off Fitzsimmons Trail is Bridge Meadows

(See map & index p. 324.)

Trail, a pleasant walk through the woods that follows the creek and ends up near the new Squamish Lil'wat Cultural Centre *(see attraction listing)*. Pick up a copy of the tear-off Whistler walking map at your hotel's front desk, fold it up and stash it in your pocket.

Whistler Mountain and Blackcomb Mountain are Whistler's twin peaks. Each mountain has more than 1,524 metres (5,000 ft.) of vertical rise and more than 100 marked runs that are serviced by multiple lifts; together they offer more than 3,238 hectares (8,000 acres) of ski-worthy terrain. Challenge your thighs on downhill runs, negotiate spectacular alpine bowls or embark on a cross-country trek through deep powder. You can even ski on a glacier. There are lessons and instruction for every skill level, all sorts of equipment rentals and a variety of ski packages to choose from. If skiing doesn't strike your fancy, go snowshoeing, snowboarding, ice-skating or snowmobiling. And if you're not the active sort, sit back and relax under a comfy blanket with a mug of hot chocolate on a Blackcomb Mountain sleigh ride. Even active sorts would enjoy this.

Whistler boasts North America's first gondola connecting two mountain peaks, the Peak 2 Peak Gondola at Whistler-Blackcomb Resort. The gondola's passenger cabins travel the 4.4-kilometre (2.7-mi.) distance between the two towers at the summit of Whistler and Blackcomb mountains in 11 minutes, allowing skiers to take advantage of cruising both mountains in the same day. Each gondola cabin holds up to 28 people, and two of them feature glass floors for a dizzying bird's-eye view of Fitzsimmons Valley 435 metres (1,427 ft.) below. Peak 2 Peak tickets are $32-$63 per person.

But Whistler isn't just about winter sports. Summer is prime time for hiking, mountain biking, windsurfing and canoeing, among other activities. Ski lifts take hikers up the two mountains to explore trails free of snow, but if you'd rather go down a different path, walk to Lost Lake. It takes about 30 minutes to get there from Whistler Village (trail access is off Lorimer Road), a good jaunt if you want to leave the hustle and bustle behind for an afternoon.

This tranquil lake is surrounded by Lost Lake Park's evergreen forests, with lovely views of mountains in the distance. The shallow water makes for good swimming on warm days. Numerous hiking trails crisscross this wooded area. There's no parking at the lake, but free shuttle bus service departs from the Gondola Transit Exchange on Blackcomb Way in July and August.

Walkers, hikers, cyclists and inline skaters all take advantage of the paved Valley Trail, which wends its way for some 30.5 kilometres (19 mi.) around the greater Whistler area, connecting parks, residential neighborhoods and the villages. It's a popular commuter biking route.

Adrenaline junkies head to Whistler Mountain Bike Park, a lift-accessed mountain biking haven. The terrain here covers the bases from gently banked trails through a lush coastal forest environment to single-track trails twisting in a series of tight turns to death-defying descents down the side of steep rock faces (which sounds a bit like skiing on wheels). Access is by lift tickets or park passes; bikes and accessories can be rented. The park is open from mid-May to mid-October.

With four championship courses, Whistler's got some very good golf. The Whistler Golf Club, (604) 932-3280 or (800) 376-1777, is the first course in Canada designed by Arnold Palmer. Robert Trent Jones Jr. was the course architect for the Fairmont Chateau Whistler Golf Club, (604) 938-2092 or (877) 938-2092, at The Fairmont Chateau Whistler. The Golden Bear designed the Nicklaus North Golf Course, (604) 938-9898 or (800) 386-9898. Big Sky Golf and Country Club, (604) 894-6106 or (800) 668-7900, is near Pemberton, about a 25-minute drive north of Whistler. With a Bob Cupp-designed layout along the Green River, you can be assured that water will come into play.

For pure sightseeing fun, take the Whistler Village Gondola up Whistler Mountain. The bird's-eye views of alpine lakes, meadows full of wildflowers (in summertime) and mountain slopes from the enclosed gondola are breathtaking. The ride up takes about 25 minutes. Once at the top, hike back-country trails or have a leisurely lunch at the Roundhouse Lodge, a cool 1,850 metres (6,069 ft.) above sea level, while taking in the scenery all around you. More intrepid souls can continue ascending on the Peak Chair to the 2,182-metre (7,160-ft.) level, where a 360-degree panorama of the Coast Mountains awaits.

And what do you do après skiing or otherwise testing your physical endurance? You stroll around Whistler Village. It's pedestrian-only, it's done in the style of a German mountain village, and it's *cute*. In winter the atmosphere is all woolen caps, puffy ski parkas and oversize mittens; summer brings out the hanging flower baskets and umbrella-shaded tables for outdoor cafe dining. Mogul's Coffee House, next to the drugstore at Village Square, is a funky little place to hang out for a spell.

Four large day-use lots between the two villages offer free parking. Whistler and Valley Express (WAVE) public buses operated by BC Transit provide service to the greater area. Various bus lines serve the resort; shuttle lines 5 and 6 are the most useful if you're staying in or near Whistler Village. The fare is $2.50; free (ages 0-5). Exact change is required. Tickets (ten tickets $22.50; day pass $7) that are good for multiple rides can be purchased at the Whistler Visitor Centre, 4320 Gateway Dr. (as well as at Whistler Village stores and Meadow Park Sports Centre).

Tourism Whistler: 4230 Gateway Dr., Whistler, BC V0N 1B4. **Phone:** (604) 935-3357 or (877) 991-9988.

Shopping: With all kinds of specialty boutiques and eateries, Whistler Village is where it's at. Whistler's

(See map & index p. 324.)

Marketplace (entrance off Lorimer Road) is the main shopping center. It has a ski lodge ambience and retailers like the Escape Route, which carries a full lineup of outdoor recreation wear and accessories—body wear, head wear, hand wear, footwear, snowshoes, backpacks, you name it. Let kids loose in the Great Glass Elevator Candy Shop with its head-turning display of sweets. It just may be enough to drive you to the more adult-oriented Upper Village Market, where you can stock up on gourmet groceries (they'll also deliver to your hotel room).

Also in the Upper Village is Snowflake (in The Fairmont Chateau Whistler), with a selection of Canadian-designed fur and leather jackets, cashmere sweaters, scarves, shawls, boots and accessories for women. Bring lots of money. Back in Whistler Village, New Agers will want to waft into The Oracle at Whistler (on Main Street) and check out the jewelry, candles, incense and gifts. Tarot card and palm readings are given, or you can give in to a relaxing reiki massage.

The Whistler Village Art Gallery exhibits contemporary paintings, sculpture and art and has two locations, in the Four Seasons Whistler and at the Hilton Whistler Resort & Spa's Gallery Row. A popular and long-established showcase for Canadian artists is Adele Campbell Fine Art Gallery in the Westin Resort & Spa. Mountain Galleries at the Fairmont, in The Fairmont Chateau Whistler, exhibits museum-quality work—paintings, glass pieces, bronze sculptures, stone carvings—by respected Canadian artists.

Nightlife: Whistler's a family-oriented kind of place, but that doesn't mean it lacks hotspots for those itching to get down and *party*. Maxx Fish, below the Amsterdam Cafe in Village Square, has plush booths and plasma-screen TVs, plus a light show choreographed to the slammin' beats cooked up by resident and visiting DJs. A similar uninhibited mood and young, good-looking crowd prevails at Tommy Africa's Bar, not far away on Gateway Drive next to the taxi loop.

Garfinkels Night Club, on Main Street in Whistler Village, throws club night bashes on different days of the week; locals and visitors alike flock to "Happy Thursdays," and Saturday is another big party night. The music is DJ dance mixes, augmented by occasional live hip-hop shows. "Garf's" also has VIP hosts and table service, so reservations are a good idea; phone (604) 932-2323. Also in the village is Buffalo Bills Bar and Grill, a high-energy nightspot that packs 'em in with drink specials, a huge dance floor and a mix of mainstream and classic rock.

On the other hand, if crowded clubs and ear-splitting music isn't your cup of tea, you could catch a movie at the Village 8 Cinemas in Whistler Village. Or better yet, pick up a takeout pie at Avalanche Pizza (locals say it's the best in town) and chill out in your room, because you just might want to save your energy for the slopes.

HARBOUR AIR is 3 km (1.9 mi.) n. on Hwy. 99, following signs. The company offers 30-minute to 2-hour carbon-neutral floatplane tours over glaciers, ice caps or alpine lakes. **Hours:** Trips depart daily Apr.-Oct. (weather permitting). **Cost:** $113.05-$346.75; $56.05-$179.55 (ages 2-11); free (ages 0-1 on parent's lap). Schedule and rates may vary; phone ahead. Reservations are required. **Phone:** (604) 932-6615 or (800) 665-0212.

SQUAMISH LIL'WAT CULTURAL CENTRE is at 4584 Blackcomb Way, just s. of Whistler's Upper Village. Conceived as a joint venture between the Squamish and Lil'wat First Nations, this facility is a showcase meant to share and preserve the culture and heritage of these two peoples. The spectacular building, with its rounded contours, was constructed to resemble a traditional Squamish longhouse and a Lil'wat *istken* (an earthen dwelling with a fire pit). Whistler and Blackcomb mountains are on view from the outdoor deck.

Inside, the Great Hall has soaring 22-foot ceilings, cedar wood walls and beautiful polished stone floors inlaid with different patterns. Among the exhibits are two Squamish canoes, traditional clothing and regalia, wall weavings, textiles and baskets. Visitors can watch artists at work and learn how to make a craft. Make sure you see the 15-minute film "Where Rivers, Mountains and People Meet," which provides some fascinating historical and cultural context to what is on display.

Parking is available in Day Lot 4 adjacent to the center. **Time:** Allow 1 hour minimum. **Hours:** Daily 9:30-5; winter and holiday hours are subject to change. **Cost:** $18; $13.50 (ages 65+ and students with ID); $8 (ages 6-12); $49 (family, two adults and two children ages 6-18). **Phone:** (866) 441-7522. 🍴

WHISTLER MUSEUM is at 4333 Main St. behind the public library. Exhibits and videos about Whistler's natural and human history as well as the 2010 Winter Olympics document aspects of mountain life in the area. **Time:** Allow 1 hour minimum. **Hours:** Daily 11-5 (also Thurs. 5-9). Closed Jan. 1 and Christmas. **Cost:** Donations. **Phone:** (604) 932-2019.

🔗 **For exclusive AAA member savings and benefits: AAA.com/hertz**

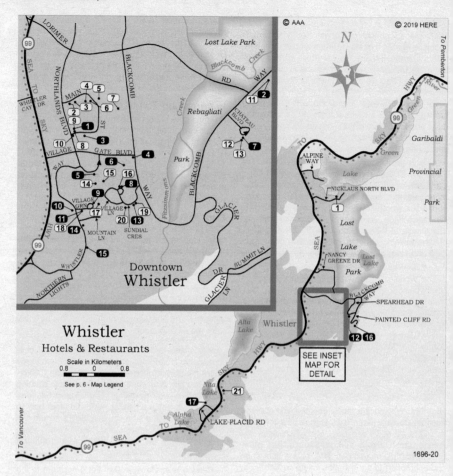

Whistler
Hotels & Restaurants

Scale in Kilometers
0.8   0   0.8

See p. 6 - Map Legend

Whistler

This index helps you "spot" where hotels and restaurants are located on the corresponding detailed maps. Restaurant price range is a combination of lunch and/or dinner. Turn to the listing page for more information and consult display ads for special promotions.

For more details, rates and reservations: AAA.com/travelguides/hotels

WHISTLER

Map Page	Hotels	Designation	Member Savings	Page
1 this page	**Pinnacle Hotel Whistler**	APPROVED	✔	327
2 this page	**Four Seasons Resort and Residences Whistler**	FOUR DIAMOND	✔	326
3 this page	**Delta Whistler Village Suites by Marriott**	THREE DIAMOND	✔	325
4 this page	Pan Pacific Whistler Village Centre	THREE DIAMOND		327
5 this page	Blackcomb Lodge	APPROVED		325
6 this page	Whistler Peak Lodge	APPROVED		327
7 this page	**Fairmont Chateau Whistler** (See ad p. 326.)	FOUR DIAMOND	✔	326
8 this page	Whistler Village Inn & Suites	APPROVED		327
9 this page	Crystal Lodge & Suites	THREE DIAMOND		325
10 this page	Aava Whistler Hotel	APPROVED		325

WHISTLER (cont'd)

Map Page	Hotels (cont'd)	Designation	Member Savings	Page
11 p. 324	The Listel Hotel Whistler	APPROVED		326
12 p. 324	The Aspens On Blackcomb	APPROVED		325
13 p. 324	Pan Pacific Whistler Mountainside	THREE DIAMOND		327
14 p. 324	Hilton Whistler Resort & Spa	THREE DIAMOND	✓	326
15 p. 324	The Westin Resort & Spa, Whistler	FOUR DIAMOND	✓	327
16 p. 324	Blackcomb Spring Suites	THREE DIAMOND		325
17 p. 324	Nita Lake Lodge (See ad p. 327.)	FOUR DIAMOND	✓	327

Map Page	Restaurants	Designation	Cuisine	Price Range	Page
1 p. 324	Table Nineteen Lakeside Eatery	THREE DIAMOND	American	$15-$30	328
2 p. 324	Peaked Pies	APPROVED	Australian Specialty	$6-$10	328
3 p. 324	Splitz Grill	APPROVED	Burgers	$7-$14	328
4 p. 324	Sachi Sushi	APPROVED	Sushi	$7-$35	328
5 p. 324	Purebread	APPROVED	Breads/Pastries	$7-$8	328
6 p. 324	Elements Urban Tapas Lounge	APPROVED	International Small Plates	$9-$30	328
7 p. 324	The Brewhouse	APPROVED	American	$15-$45	328
8 p. 324	Alta Bistro	THREE DIAMOND	New Canadian	$23-$44	327
9 p. 324	Quattro at Whistler	THREE DIAMOND	Italian	$22-$48	328
10 p. 324	Hy's Steakhouse	THREE DIAMOND	Steak	$32-$109	328
11 p. 324	Sidecut	FOUR DIAMOND	Steak Seafood	$27-$59	328
12 p. 324	The Wildflower	THREE DIAMOND	International	$26-$48	328
13 p. 324	The Grill Room	FOUR DIAMOND	Steak	$35-$70	328
14 p. 324	Araxi Restaurant & Oyster Bar	FOUR DIAMOND	Pacific Northwest	$30-$50	327
15 p. 324	Bar Oso	THREE DIAMOND	New Spanish Small Plates	$16-$35	327
16 p. 324	21 Steps Kitchen + Bar	APPROVED	International	$18-$43	327
17 p. 324	Basalt Wine + Salumeria	THREE DIAMOND	Canadian	$28-$38	327
18 p. 324	Bearfoot Bistro	FOUR DIAMOND	New World	$60-$168	328
19 p. 324	Dubh Linn Gate Pub	APPROVED	Irish	$13-$25	328
20 p. 324	Sushi Village Japanese Cuisine	APPROVED	Japanese	$11-$38	328
21 p. 324	Rimrock Cafe	THREE DIAMOND	Continental	$38-$53	328

AAVA WHISTLER HOTEL   604/932-2522 **10**
APPROVED   Hotel. **Address:** 4005 Whistler Way V0N 1B4

THE ASPENS ON BLACKCOMB   604/932-7222 **12**
APPROVED   Condominium. **Address:** 4800 Spearhead Dr V0N 1B4

BLACKCOMB LODGE   604/932-4155 **5**
APPROVED   Hotel. **Address:** 4220 Gateway Dr V0N 1B4

BLACKCOMB SPRING SUITES   604/905-3400 **16**
THREE DIAMOND Condominium. **Address:** 4899 Painted Cliff Rd V0N 1B4

CRYSTAL LODGE & SUITES   604/932-2221 **9**
THREE DIAMOND Hotel. **Address:** 4154 Village Green V0N 1B4

DELTA WHISTLER VILLAGE SUITES BY MARRIOTT
604/905-3987 **3**

THREE DIAMOND

Extended Stay Contemporary Hotel

D DELTA HOTELS **AAA Benefit:** Members save 5% or more!

Address: 4308 Main St V0N 1B4 **Location:** Hwy 99, just e on Village Gate Blvd, just n on Northlands Blvd, then just e. **Facility:** 207 units, some two bedrooms and kitchens. 6 stories, interior corridors. **Parking:** on-site (fee) and valet. **Terms:** check-in 4 pm. **Amenities:** safes. **Dining:** Hy's Steakhouse, see separate listing. **Pool:** heated outdoor. **Activities:** sauna, hot tub, bicycles, exercise room. **Guest Services:** complimentary and valet laundry, area transportation.

▼ See AAA listing this page ▼

WHISTLER'S LANDMARK
SKI-TO-YOUR-DOOR, GOLF
AND SPA RESORT

EXCLUSIVELY FOR AAA/CAA MEMBERS

ENJOY UP TO **20%** SAVINGS & **$50*** CREDIT

FOR DETAILS VISIT
FAIRMONT.COM/WHISTLER
CALL **1 800 606 8244**

CHATEAU WHISTLER

*Subject to seasonal availability and changes.
Minimum night stays apply. Credit must be used
for on-site dining at Fairmont Chateau Whistler.
Please call for complete details.

Let Your
Voice
Be Heard

If your visit to a listed property doesn't
meet your expectations, tell us about it.

AAA.com/MemberFeedback

FAIRMONT CHATEAU WHISTLER   604/938-8000 **7**

FOUR DIAMOND
Resort Hotel

Address: 4599 Chateau Blvd V8E 0Z5 **Location:** Hwy 99, 0.6 mi (1 km) e on Lorimer Rd (Upper Village), just s on Blackcomb Way, then just e. **Facility:** Near the Blackcomb Mountain chairlift, this inspiring château has gorgeous floral arrangements in the impressive lobby and lounge. Upscale rooms, which range in size, feature sumptuous bedding. 528 units, some two bedrooms. 12 stories, interior corridors. **Parking:** on-site (fee) and valet. **Terms:** check-in 4 pm. **Amenities:** safes. **Dining:** 4 restaurants, also, The Grill Room, The Wildflower, see separate listings, entertainment. **Pool:** heated outdoor. **Activities:** sauna, hot tub, steamroom, cabanas, regulation golf, tennis, downhill & cross country skiing, snowboarding, recreation programs, bicycles, lawn sports, trails, health club, in-room exercise equipment, spa. **Guest Services:** valet laundry, area transportation. *(See ad this page.)*

SAVE ECO 🍴 🛎 🍸 CALL 🔊 🏊 📶 BIZ
HS 📶 ✕ 📹 🖥 / SOME UNITS 🐾

FOUR SEASONS RESORT AND RESIDENCES WHISTLER   604/935-3400 **2**

FOUR DIAMOND
Resort Hotel

Address: 4591 Blackcomb Way V0N 1B4 **Location:** Hwy 99, 0.6 mi (1 km) e on Lorimer Rd (Upper Village), just n. **Facility:** Gorgeous public areas feature a unique collection of local art and beautiful wood accents. Spacious suites have a warm and rustic elegance with fireplaces and huge bathrooms. 291 units, some two bedrooms, three bedrooms and kitchens. 6-9 stories, interior corridors. **Parking:** valet only. **Terms:** check-in 4 pm. **Amenities:** safes. **Dining:** Sidecut, see separate listing. **Pool:** heated outdoor. **Activities:** sauna, hot tub, steamroom, tennis, downhill & cross country skiing, snowboarding, recreation programs, bicycles, game room, trails, health club, in-room exercise equipment, spa. **Guest Services:** valet laundry, area transportation.

SAVE 🍴 🛎 🍸 CALL 🔊 🏊 📶 BIZ HS 📶
✕ 📹 🖥 / SOME UNITS 🐾 📋 🍽

HILTON WHISTLER RESORT & SPA   604/932-1982 **14**

THREE DIAMOND
Hotel

Hilton
HOTELS & RESORTS

AAA Benefit:
Members save up to 15%!

Address: 4050 Whistler Way V0N 1B4 **Location:** Hwy 99, just e on Village Gate Blvd, just s. **Facility:** 287 units, some two bedrooms and efficiencies. 5-8 stories, interior corridors. **Parking:** on-site (fee) and valet. **Terms:** check-in 4 pm. **Amenities:** safes. **Dining:** 2 restaurants. **Pool:** heated outdoor. **Activities:** sauna, hot tub, downhill & cross country skiing, snowboarding, trails, exercise room, spa. **Guest Services:** valet and coin laundry, area transportation.

SAVE ECO 🍴 🛎 🍸 CALL 🔊 🏊 📶 BIZ 📶
✕ 📹 📋 🖥 / SOME UNITS 🐾 🍽

THE LISTEL HOTEL WHISTLER   604/932-1133 **11**

APPROVED   Hotel. **Address:** 4121 Village Green V0N 1B4

(See map & index p. 324.)

NITA LAKE LODGE
604/966-5700 **17**

FOUR DIAMOND

Boutique
Contemporary
Hotel

Address: 2131 Lake Placid Rd V0N 1B2 **Location:** 1.8 mi (3 km) s on Hwy 99, just w. **Facility:** This impressive hotel has gorgeous lobby décor and wonderful large, modern suites with upscale comfortable seating and furnishings. Huge bathrooms feature separate showers and soaker tubs. 77 units. 4 stories, interior corridors. **Parking:** on-site (fee) and valet. **Amenities:** safes. **Dining:** 3 restaurants. **Pool:** heated outdoor. **Activities:** hot tub, self-propelled boats, boat dock, fishing, recreation programs in season, bicycles, trails, health club, spa. **Guest Services:** valet and coin laundry, area transportation. (See ad this page.)

[SAVE] [ECO] [🍴] [🍸] [CALL] [👤] [🛫] [♿] [HS] [🛜] [✕] [🍳] [📶] [💳] [📠] / SOME UNITS [🐾]

PAN PACIFIC WHISTLER MOUNTAINSIDE   604/905-2999 **13**
THREE DIAMOND Extended Stay Contemporary Hotel. **Address:** 4320 Sundial Cres V0N 1B4

PAN PACIFIC WHISTLER VILLAGE CENTRE
604/966-5500 **4**
THREE DIAMOND Extended Stay Contemporary Hotel. **Address:** 4299 Blackcomb Way V0N 1B4

PINNACLE HOTEL WHISTLER   604/938-3218 **1**

APPROVED

Extended Stay
Hotel

Address: 4319 Main St V0N 1B4 **Location:** Hwy 99, just e on Village Gate Blvd, just n on Northlands Blvd, then just e. **Facility:** 84 kitchen units. 4 stories, interior corridors. **Parking:** on-site (fee). **Terms:** check-in 4 pm. **Dining:** Alta Bistro, Quattro at Whistler, see separate listings. **Pool:** heated outdoor. **Activities:** hot tub, bicycles, limited exercise equipment. **Guest Services:** coin laundry.

[SAVE] [🍴] [🍸] [CALL] [👤] [🛫] [HS] [🛜] [✕] [📶] [💳] [📠] / SOME UNITS [🐾]

🔗 **For complete hotel, dining and attraction listings: AAA.com/travelguides**

THE WESTIN RESORT & SPA, WHISTLER
604/905-5000 **15**

FOUR DIAMOND

Extended Stay
Hotel

 WESTIN HOTELS & RESORTS

AAA Benefit: Members save 5% or more!

Address: 4090 Whistler Way V0N 1B4 **Location:** Hwy 99, just e on Village Gate Blvd, just s. **Facility:** The gorgeous lobby makes a great first impression as you enter this resort. The units range from moderate size studios to expansive suites. You'll love the convenience of the ski-in, ski-out location. 419 units, some two bedrooms and kitchens. 9-11 stories, interior corridors. **Parking:** on-site (fee) and valet. **Terms:** check-in 4 pm. **Amenities:** safes. **Dining:** 2 restaurants. **Pool:** heated outdoor. **Activities:** sauna, hot tub, steamroom, downhill & cross country skiing, snowboarding, bicycles, trails, health club, spa. **Guest Services:** valet and coin laundry, area transportation.

[SAVE] [ECO] [🍴] [♿] [🍸] [CALL] [👤] [🛫] [♿] [BIZ] [sHS] [🛜] [✕] [📹] [📶] [🍳] [💳] / SOME UNITS [🐾]

WHISTLER PEAK LODGE   604/938-0878 **6**
APPROVED Extended Stay Hotel. **Address:** 4295 Blackcomb Way V0N 1B4

WHISTLER VILLAGE INN & SUITES   604/932-4004 **8**
APPROVED Hotel. **Address:** 4429 Sundial Pl V0N 1B4

WHERE TO EAT

21 STEPS KITCHEN + BAR   604/966-2121 **16**
APPROVED International. Casual Dining. **Address:** 4433 Sundial Pl, RR 4 V0N 1B4

ALTA BISTRO   604/932-2582 **8**
THREE DIAMOND New Canadian. Casual Dining. **Address:** 4319 Main St, #104 V0N 1B4

ARAXI RESTAURANT & OYSTER BAR   604/932-4540 **14**
FOUR DIAMOND Pacific Northwest. Fine Dining. **Address:** 4222 Village Square V0N 1B4

BAR OSO   604/962-4540 **15**
THREE DIAMOND New Spanish Small Plates. Casual Dining. **Address:** 150-4222 Village Sq V0N 1B4

BASALT WINE + SALUMERIA   604/962-9011 **17**
THREE DIAMOND Canadian. Casual Dining. **Address:** 4154 Village Green V0N 1B4

▼ See AAA listing this page ▼

NITA LAKE

exceptional
intimate
authentic

Reservations 1 888 755 6482
2131 Lake Placid Road, Whistler BC
www.nitalakelodge.com

(See map & index p. 324.)

BEARFOOT BISTRO   604/932-3433 **18**
FOUR DIAMOND New World. Fine Dining. **Address:** 4121 Village Green V0N 1B4

THE BREWHOUSE   604/905-2739 **7**
APPROVED American. Brewpub. **Address:** 4355 Blackcomb Way V0N 1B4

DUBH LINN GATE PUB   604/905-4047 **19**
APPROVED Irish. Casual Dining. **Address:** 4320 Sundial Cres V0N 1B4

EARLS KITCHEN + BAR   604/935-3222
APPROVED American. Casual Dining. **Address:** 4295 Blackcomb Way, Unit 220 V0N 1B4

ELEMENTS URBAN TAPAS LOUNGE   604/932-5569 **6**
APPROVED International Small Plates. Casual Dining. **Address:** 102B-4359 Main St V0N 1B4

THE GRILL ROOM   604/938-8000 **13**
FOUR DIAMOND

Steak
Fine Dining
$35-$70

AAA Inspector Notes: From the moment you're seated, you'll feel like a specially invited guest due to the first-rate service and refinement found at this upscale dining room. The menu changes seasonally, offering some perfectly grilled cuts of beef, bison and other meats. Special care is taken to provide sustainable and locally sourced seafood. The appetizers are all enticing, but my first choice is always going to be the mouth-watering tomato and gin soup, which is flambéed at the table. **Features:** full bar. **Reservations:** suggested. **Address:** 4599 Chateau Blvd V0N 1B4 **Location:** Hwy 99, 0.6 mi (1 km) e on Lorimer Rd (Upper Village), just s on Blackcomb Way, then just e; in Fairmont Chateau Whistler. **Parking:** on-site (fee) and valet. **D** CALL

HY'S STEAKHOUSE   604/905-5555 **10**
THREE DIAMOND Steak. Fine Dining. **Address:** 4308 Main St V0N 1B4

PEAKED PIES   604/962-4115 **2**
APPROVED Australian Specialty. Quick Serve. **Address:** 4369 Main St, #105 V0N 1B4

PUREBREAD   604/962-1182 **5**
APPROVED Breads/Pastries. Quick Serve. **Address:** 4338 Main St V0N 1B4

QUATTRO AT WHISTLER   604/905-4844 **9**
THREE DIAMOND Italian. Fine Dining. **Address:** 4319 Main St V0N 1B4

RIMROCK CAFE   604/932-5565 **21**
THREE DIAMOND Continental. Fine Dining. **Address:** 2117 Whistler Rd V0N 1B0

SACHI SUSHI   604/935-5649 **4**
APPROVED Sushi. Casual Dining. **Address:** 4359 Main St V0N 1B4

SIDECUT   604/966-5280 **11**
FOUR DIAMOND Steak Seafood. Fine Dining. **Address:** 4591 Blackcomb Way V0N 1B4

SPLITZ GRILL   604/938-9300 **3**
APPROVED Burgers. Quick Serve. **Address:** 4369 Main St, #104 V0N 1B4

SUSHI VILLAGE JAPANESE CUISINE   604/932-3330 **20**
APPROVED Japanese. Casual Dining. **Address:** 4340 Sundial Crescent V0N 1B4

TABLE NINETEEN LAKESIDE EATERY   604/938-9898 **1**
THREE DIAMOND American. Casual Dining. **Address:** 8080 Nicklaus North Blvd V0N 1B8

THE WILDFLOWER   604/938-8000 **12**
THREE DIAMOND International. Fine Dining. **Address:** 4599 Chateau Blvd V0N 1B4

WHITE ROCK pop. 19,339
- **Hotels & Restaurants map & index p. 276**
- **Part of Vancouver area — see map p. 249**

OCEAN PROMENADE HOTEL   604/542-0102 **68**
THREE DIAMOND Hotel. **Address:** 15611 Marine Dr V4B 1E1

WHERE TO EAT

LA BAIA ITALIAN RESTAURANT   604/531-6261 **93**
APPROVED Italian. Casual Dining. **Address:** 15791 Marine Dr V4B 1E5

ULI'S RESTAURANT   604/538-9373 **92**
APPROVED International. Casual Dining. **Address:** 15021 Marine Dr V4B 1C3

THE WOODEN SPOON   604/560-6018 **91**
APPROVED Breakfast Comfort Food. Casual Dining. **Address:** 15171 Russell Ave V4B 3Z4

WILLIAMS LAKE (G-5) pop. 10,832

The rush for gold brought prospectors to the heart of the Cariboo in the 1860s, but it was the 1920s Canadian Railway push that put Williams Lake on the map. Cattle ranching and timber production now are the economic mainstays. Twenty kilometres (12 mi.) north of Williams Lake, Bull Mountain Trails offers 30 kilometres (19 mi.) of trails for cross-country skiing, hiking and mountain biking.

Williams Lake and District Chamber of Commerce: 1660 S. Broadway, Williams Lake, BC, Canada V2G 2W4. **Phone:** (250) 392-5025 or (877) 967-5253.

BEST WESTERN WILLIAMS LAKE HOTEL
778/412-9000

THREE DIAMOND
Hotel

AAA Benefit: Members save up to 15% and earn bonus points!

Address: 1850 S Broadway Ave V2G 5G8 **Location:** 1.3 mi (2.1 km) s on Hwy 97. **Facility:** 64 units, some kitchens. 3 stories, interior corridors. **Parking:** winter plug-ins. **Pool:** heated indoor. **Activities:** hot tub, exercise room. **Guest Services:** complimentary laundry. **Featured Amenity:** full hot breakfast.

SAVE 11+ 🏊 BIZ HS 🛜
❌ 🛏 🖨 🖵 / SOME UNITS 🐾

DRUMMOND LODGE MOTEL   250/392-5334
APPROVED Motel. **Address:** 1405 Cariboo Hwy V2G 2W3

RAMADA WILLIAMS LAKE   250/392-3321
 APPROVED Hotel. **Address:** 1118 Lakeview Cres V2G 1A3

SUPER 8 WILLIAMS LAKE   250/398-8884
 APPROVED **Address:** 1712 Broadway Ave S V2G 2W4 **Location:** 1.2 mi (2 km) s on Hwy 97. **Facility:** 53 units. 3 stories (no elevator), interior corridors. **Parking:** winter plug-ins. **Guest Services:** coin laundry. **Featured Amenity:** continental breakfast.
Motel

WHERE TO EAT

THE LAUGHING LOON   778/412-6655
 APPROVED American. Gastropub. **Address:** 1730A Broadway Ave S V2G 2W4

MR MIKES STEAKHOUSECASUAL   778/412-9800
 APPROVED American. Casual Dining. **Address:** 299 Oliver St V2G 1M2

SUSHI SAKURA CALIFORNIA   250/305-0035
 APPROVED Japanese. Casual Dining. **Address:** 770 Oliver St V2G 1N1

iStockphoto.com_pixelfit

Love the Great Outdoors?

When getting away means getting off the beaten path,
visit AAA.com/campgrounds or AAA.com/maps for:

△ Thousands of places to camp across the
U.S. and Canada

△ Complete mapping and travel information to
plan your adventure

Look for locations with the
trusted mark of approval.

Inspected & Approved

YALE (C-7) pop. 136

Settled at the southern entrance to Fraser Canyon, Yale was a major steamship port during the gold rush. The town was established in 1848 as a Hudson's Bay Co. fort, taking its name from the commander of Fort Langley. After gold was discovered on Hill's Bar in 1858, Yale's population swelled to 30,000. In later years the number dwindled to 200. Several buildings from the mid-1800s still stand, and a pioneer cemetery contains Victorian monuments to early settlers.

The Alexandra Suspension Bridge, 22 kilometres (14 mi.) north of town, was constructed in 1863 to ferry miners across the Fraser River. From the bridge, which was rebuilt in 1926 with the original foundations, the original wagon road to the Cariboo goldfields is visible and is home to a small 22.25-hectare (55-acre) provincial park. A hiking trail leading to the nearby Spirit Caves offers views of the canyon.

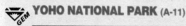

YOHO NATIONAL PARK (A-11)

Elevations in the park range from 1,090 metres (3,576 ft.) at the west boundary to 3,562 metres (11,686 ft.) at the top of Mount Goodsir at the South Tower. Refer to CAA/AAA maps for additional elevation information.

Reached by hwys. 1 and 93, Yoho National Park covers 1,310 square kilometres (507 sq. mi.) and is west of the Great Divide and Banff National Park. In the Cree language, *yoho* is an exclamation of wonder appropriate to the park's spectacular rock walls and towering waterfalls.

At the center of the park's history is Canada's first trans-continental railway. Following the route originally discovered by Sir James Hector, the Canadian Pacific Railway laid tracks through Kicking Horse Pass in 1884. The park was established two years later as a tourist destination for passengers on the newly completed rail line. In 1962, the Trans-Canada Highway opened along this same route.

Takakkaw Falls ("magnificent" in Cree) drops 380 metres (1,265 ft.) in all. Its highest sheer fall is 254 metres (833 ft.), making it one of the highest waterfalls in Canada and a visible landmark along the well-known Iceline trail.

Other highlights in the park include Natural Bridge, Emerald Lake, Wapta Falls and the Canadian Pacific Railway's Spiral Tunnels. Twisting their way under Mount Ogden and Cathedral Mountain, trains can be seen entering and exiting the Spiral Tunnels from the viewpoints on the Yoho Valley Road and the Trans-Canada Highway, 8 kilometres (5 mi.) east of Field.

Nestled high in the mountains are the famous Burgess Shale fossil beds. Discovered in 1909, these exquisitely preserved 505 million-year-old soft-bodied fossils draw visitors to Yoho National Park each year. The park's visitor center, located in Field, hosts an interactive exhibit and display of some of the many fossils found in the park.

General Information and Activities

The park is open all year; Parks Canada operates facilities during the spring, summer and fall. In winter it is popular with ice climbers, and cross-country and backcountry skiers as well as hikers and backpackers in other seasons. During the summer months, canoes and rowboats are available for rent at Emerald Lake.

The park's visitor center, located on Hwy. 1 in Field, is open daily 8:30-7, June-Sept.; 9-5, in May and Oct.-Dec.; 9-4:30, rest of year. Phone (250) 343-6783 for schedule, or (888) 773-8888 rest of year. The adjoining washrooms are open year-round.

The Trans-Canada Highway traverses the park and provides access to most attractions. The 13-kilometre (7.8-mi.) Yoho Valley Road leading to Takakkaw Falls is open mid-June to mid-October, weather permitting.

Access to Burgess Shale fossil beds is restricted to guided hikes July-September. Parks Canada offers two guided hike programs: Walcott Quarry, at 22 kilometers (14 mi.), and Mount Stephen Fossil Beds, at 9 kilometres (6 mi.). Fees range from $52.38-$66.67 and reservations are required (reservation fees $10.48-$12.86); phone (877) 737-3783.

Yoho has four front-country campgrounds with site prices between $15.70-$27.40 per night. Firewood and permits are an additional $8.80. Visitors venturing into the backcountry require a wilderness pass to stay overnight; passes are available from the visitor center for $9.80 per person per night.

Fishing, particularly rewarding to those in search of a variety of trout, requires a $34.30 annual permit or a $9.80 1-day permit from the visitor center. Anglers are allowed to fish in most lakes and rivers in the park. *See Recreation Areas Chart.*

ADMISSION to the park $9.80; $8.30 (ages 65+); free (ages 0-17); $19.60 (all occupants of a private vehicle with up to seven people). An annual pass, valid at most Canadian national parks, marine areas and historic sites, is available.

PETS are permitted in the park provided they are on a leash at all times.

ADDRESS inquiries to the Superintendent, Yoho National Park, P.O. Box 99, Field, BC, Canada V0A 1G0; phone (250) 343-6783.

AAA.com/discounts—Your first stop for travel and shopping savings

Road Trip? We'll be there for you.

AAA/CAA Mobile Battery Service.
Delivered & Installed on the Spot!

 3-year Free Replacement Warranty

Call, Click or Tap to Request Mobile Battery Service
CALL 1-800-AAA-HELP | 1-800-CAA-HELP
AAA.com/mobile | CAA.ca/mobile

Download our apps today

Power You Can Trust!™

Golden seas of wheat

Waves pound a rock-strewn shore at the narrows of Lake Manitoba, producing a noise oddly like a beating drum. To the people of the Cree Nation, this sound was the great spirit Manitou, whose name was given to the lake and, in 1870, the entire province.

From clear water lapping in giant lakes—Winnipeg, Winnipegosis and Manitoba—to the rustling sigh of wind across golden seas of wheat, the great spirit of this province speaks with many voices and conveys many moods.

It echoes in the plaintive cry of migrating geese winging south and the hoarse chuffing of a protective mother polar bear herding her cubs along Hudson Bay's icy shore.

The spirit sings within a chorus of steel wheels as trains carry freight across the prairies. It proclaims itself in the bustling streets of Winnipeg, where sundry languages—French, English, Ukrainian, Chinese and others—blend

Look north into the night sky at the aurora borealis

Manitoba

into a rich, evocative murmur, and laughs amid the joyous din of the city's various celebrations.

Gem of the Prairies

Look north into the night sky. There. See it? A faint glow high above the horizon....

Watch as an arc of yellow light gradually forms. As it drifts upward, shimmering yellow-green streamers rise from it, rippling like a breeze-blown curtain. New arcs appear lined with bright amber streaks that curl like wisps of smoke. Eventually the swirls of color fade and darkness returns, ending your encounter with the aurora borealis.

In Manitoba you won't have to wait long for a repeat performance. This far north you can count on basking in the aurora's eerie luminescence nearly 90 nights a year. Even citizens of Winnipeg, the capital, are often treated to this celestial light show, despite living in the province's extreme south.

Sky-obscuring pollution may be the bane of many cities, but Winnipeg's clean air isn't likely to spoil your auroral view. And while multihued lights dance overhead, visitors to the "Gem of the Prairies" can enjoy an equally colorful cultural spectrum spread out before them. Home to more than half of all Manitobans, Winnipeg is a city of surprising diversity. It's not unusual to find a German butcher shop sandwiched between an Italian clothing store and a Vietnamese restaurant, all within a few steps of a Portuguese café.

In the 18th century, when conflicts escalated between French voyageurs and their English rivals, Fort Rouge—site of modern Winnipeg—was established where the Red and Assiniboine rivers meet. Now known as The Forks, this riverfront park is where you can take a tree-shaded stroll past splashing fountains and vibrantly hued flower beds.

The Great White North

Follow your compass farther north and the chances of seeing Mother Nature's silent fireworks multiply. The northern lights not only occur more frequently in Manitoba's subarctic areas, but are brighter, too.

But the real stars in this small community are its big, furry neighbors: polar bears. Sightings of the great white animals are common in October, when they migrate onto freezing Hudson Bay to fish, and late June, when thawing ice forces a return to shore.

The best way to meet these deceptively cuddly looking carnivores is safely ensconced in a specially designed, balloon-tired tundra vehicle. Climb aboard one for an unforgettable in-the-wild encounter. And when you're ready to thaw out, visit Churchill's Itsanitaq Museum, which is filled with ancient Inuit tools and other artifacts.

Well-acquainted with the aurora's haunting glow, the Inuits crafted stories as elaborate as their carvings to explain what they saw. According to one tale, the lights are torches lit by spirits to guide those who will follow across the narrow bridge to heaven.

But you don't have to study Inuit mythology to appreciate the northern lights' otherworldly beauty; all you really need to know is that the skies are perfect for admiring them.

Recreation

The overwhelming bulk of Manitoba's populace resides in a thin strip just above the U.S. border, which leaves a vast region of unspoiled territory farther north that's prime for exploration.

Colorful sails glide across the surface of Lake Winnipeg as windsurfing enthusiasts take advantage of breezy days. Canoeing down the Grass River, near the junction of hwys. 10 and 39, gives you the opportunity to see the beauty of the northern frontier.

Manitoba's lakes are home to dozens of species of fish, including walleye, northern pike, arctic grayling, sturgeon and channel catfish. Fly-in fishing—at such isolated spots as Aikens and Dogskin lakes, northeast of Bissett in Atikaki Provincial Park; Gods River, Knee Lake, and Island Lake, all in northeast Manitoba; and Big Sand, Egenolf,

and Nueltin lakes in the northwest region—attracts anglers of all skill levels.

When the lakes freeze over, ice fishing and ice-skating are favored pursuits. Smooth blankets of snow—at such places as Assiniboine Park in Winnipeg—are irresistible for snowshoeing and cross-country skiing.

Many adventurers, too, can't resist the snowmobiling trails that crisscross the province. Kick up some powder in Duck Mountain and Turtle Mountain provincial parks.

Although downhill skiing is hard to come by in a province that's known mostly for its lowlands, skiers can take on 25 runs at Asessippi Winter Park ski area.

For tobogganing fun, head for the hills and slides at Kildonan Park and more than a dozen park locations in Winnipeg.

Riding Mountain National Park rises from the flat prairie to provide a wealth of opportunity for activity. Self-guiding hiking trails range from the easy Beach Ridges Trail to the difficult Bald Hill Trail, named for the barren hill towering over scores of lush, green trees. Most memorable is the grueling but beautiful Ochre River Trail, which entices both trekkers and cross-country skiers.

Mountain bikers favor the exhilarating J.E.T. Trail, which rewards risk-takers with great views. The multiuse Central Trail, the longest at 73 kilometres (45 miles), is especially popular for horseback riding.

Canoe in Riding Mountain National Park

Historic Timeline

1612	Capt. Thomas Button winters at Port Nelson on Hudson Bay and claims the land for England.
1690	Henry Kelsey of the Hudson's Bay Co. sets out on a 2-year exploration of the province.
1738	French fur-trader Pierre Gaultier de la Vérendrye arrives at the site now known as Winnipeg.
1812	The Red River Colony, one of Manitoba's earliest settlements, is established with a land grant from the Hudson's Bay Co.
1869	The Métis, native people of mixed ancestry, are led by Louis Riel in the Red River Rebellion.
1870	Manitoba becomes the fifth Canadian province.
1887	The Winnipeg Grain and Produce Exchange is established.
1912	Manitoba's boundary is extended north to Hudson Bay.
1986	The Supreme Court rules that all provincial laws passed since 1870 are invalid because they were written only in English.
1999	The Pan Am Games are held in Winnipeg.
2007	A tornado in Elie is Canada's first officially documented F5 tornado, the highest possible rating on the Fujita scale.

What To Pack

Temperature Averages Maximum/Minimum (Celsius)	JANUARY	FEBRUARY	MARCH	APRIL	MAY	JUNE	JULY	AUGUST	SEPTEMBER	OCTOBER	NOVEMBER	DECEMBER
Churchill	-23 / -32	-22 / -31	-16 / -26	-7 / -17	1 / -6	9 / 1	16 / 7	14 / 7	8 / 2	0 / -6	-10 / -19	-19 / -28
Hecla Island	-14 / -25	-9 / -21	-2 / -13	8 / -3	17 / 3	22 / 9	24 / 12	23 / 10	17 / 5	9 / -1	-2 / -10	-11 / -21
Swan River	-10 / -23	-6 / -19	1 / -12	9 / -5	17 / 2	22 / 7	24 / 10	24 / 8	17 / 3	9 / -2	-2 / -12	-9 / -20
The Pas	-17 / -26	-12 / -23	-4 / -17	6 / -6	15 / 2	21 / 9	23 / 12	22 / 11	14 / 5	7 / -1	-4 / -12	-14 / -22
Thompson	-19 / -31	-14 / -28	-6 / -21	4 / -10	13 / -1	19 / 5	22 / 8	21 / 7	12 / 2	4 / -4	-7 / -17	-17 / -27
Winnipeg	-13 / -23	-10 / -21	-2 / -13	9 / -3	18 / 4	23 / 10	26 / 13	24 / 12	18 / 6	11 / 0	-1 / -9	-10 / -19

From the records of The Weather Channel Interactive, Inc.

Good Facts To Know

ABOUT THE PROVINCE

POPULATION: 1,274,000.

AREA: 552,370 sq km (213,270 sq mi.); ranks 8th

CAPITAL: Winnipeg.

HIGHEST POINT: 831 m (2,727 ft.), Baldy Mountain.

LOWEST POINT: Sea level, Churchill.

TIME ZONE(S): Central. DST.

GAMBLING

MINIMUM AGE FOR GAMBLING: 18.

REGULATIONS

TEEN DRIVING LAWS: Teens may not drive between midnight and 5 a.m. and no more than one passenger is permitted unless a supervising licensed driver is seated in the front passenger seat. When driving with a supervising driver, no more passengers than the number of backseat seat belts are permitted. The minimum age for an unrestricted driver's license is 17 years, 6 months. Phone (204) 985-7000 in Winnipeg or (800) 665-2410 for more information about Manitoba driver's license regulations.

SEAT BELT/CHILD RESTRAINT LAWS: Seat belts are required for the driver and all passengers ages 18 and over. Children ages 5-17 and over 23 kilograms (50 lbs.) are required to be in a child restraint or seat belt; children must remain in a booster seat until age 9 or over 145 centimeters (57 in.) tall or 36 kilograms (80 lbs.); child restraints are required for children under age 5 and under 23 kilograms (50 lbs.). AAA recommends the use of seat belts and appropriate child restraints for the driver and all passengers.

CELLPHONE RESTRICTIONS: The use of handheld cellphones and text messaging while driving are prohibited.

HELMETS FOR MOTORCYCLISTS: Required for all riders.

MOVE OVER LAW: Driver is required to slow down and vacate the lane nearest stopped police, fire or rescue vehicles when those vehicles are using audible or flashing signals. The law also applies to tow trucks or other recovery vehicles.

RADAR DETECTORS: Not permitted.

FIREARMS LAWS: By federal law, all nonresidents entering Canada with a firearm must declare their weapon in writing and pay a fee of $25 (Canadian). Contact the Canadian Firearms Program at (800) 731-4000 to receive a declaration form or for additional information.

ALCOHOL CONSUMPTION: Legal age 18.

SPECIAL REGULATIONS: Dogs and cats transported from the United States must have proof of rabies vaccination. No person may smoke tobacco or have lighted tobacco in a motor vehicle while anyone under 16 is in the vehicle.

HOLIDAYS

HOLIDAYS: Jan. 1 ■ Louis Riel Day (3rd Mon. in Feb.) ■ Good Friday ■ Easter ■ Easter Monday ■ Victoria Day, Mon. prior to May 25 ■ Canada Day, July 1 ■ Civic Holiday, Aug. (1st Mon.) ■ Labour Day, Sept. (1st Mon.) ■ Thanksgiving, Oct. (2nd Mon.) ■ Remembrance Day, Nov. 11 ■ Christmas, Dec. 25 ■ Boxing Day, Dec. 26.

MONEY

TAXES: In addition to Manitoba's provincial sales tax of 7 percent, there is a national 5 percent Goods and Services Tax (GST).

VISITOR INFORMATION

INFORMATION CENTERS: Free travel information is available at these locations: Canada/United States border, Hwy. 75 at Emerson ■ Manitoba/Ontario boundary, Hwy. 1E just east of West Hawk Lake ■ Manitoba/Saskatchewan boundary on Hwy. 1W west of Kirkella ■ Manitoba/Saskatchewan boundary at Hwys. 16W and 83 near Russell ■ and the Travel Manitoba Visitor Information Centre at The Forks National Historic Site in Winnipeg.

FURTHER INFORMATION FOR VISITORS:
The Forks National Historic Site
401-25 Market Rd.
Winnipeg, MB R3C 4S8
Canada
(204) 983-6757
(888) 773-8888 Parks Canada
Travel Manitoba Visitor Information Centre
21 Forks Market Rd.
Winnipeg, MB R3C 4T7
Canada
(204) 927-7800
(800) 665-0040

RECREATION INFORMATION:
Manitoba Conservation and Water Stewardship
200 Saulteaux Crescent
Box 11
Winnipeg, MB R3J 3W3
Canada
(204) 945-6784
(800) 214-6497

Manitoba Annual Events

Please call ahead to confirm event details.

 Visit **AAA.com/travelguides/events** to find
AAA-listed events for every day of the year

WINTER

Dec. - Christmas at the Fort / Dauphin
204-638-6630
- Power Smart Waterfall of Lights
Brandon / 204-729-2257
- Canad Inns Winter Wonderland
Winnipeg / 204-888-6990

Jan. - Westman Multicultural Festival
Brandon / 888-799-1111
- Manitoba AgDays / Brandon
204-534-2010
- Dakota Nation Winterfest / Brandon
204-512-0847

Feb. - Winnipeg's Concert Band Festival
Winnipeg / 204-663-1226
- Master Playwright Festival / Winnipeg
204-956-1340, ext. 415
- Festival du Voyageur / Winnipeg
204-237-7692

SPRING

Mar. - Cluster: New Music + Integrated Arts
Festival / Winnipeg / 204-223-9939
- Aurora Winterfest / Churchill
888-389-2327
- Royal Manitoba Winter Fair
Brandon / 204-726-3590

Apr. - Rodarama Car Show / Winnipeg
204-479-4104
- Winnipeg Comedy Festival
Winnipeg / 204-284-9477
- Brandon Home & Leisure Show
Brandon / 204-727-4837

May - Doors Open Winnipeg / Winnipeg
204-942-2663
- Manito Ahbee Festival / Winnipeg
204-956-1849
- Teddy Bears' Picnic / Winnipeg
204-787-4000

SUMMER

June - Manitoba Summer Fair / Brandon
204-726-3590
- TD Winnipeg International Jazz
Festival / Winnipeg / 204-989-4656
- Red River Exhibition / Winnipeg
204-888-6990

July - Manitoba Stampede and Exhibition
Morris / 204-746-2552
- Winnipeg Fringe Festival / Winnipeg
204-943-7464

Aug. - Winkler Harvest Festival and
Exhibition / Winkler / 204-325-5600

FALL

Sept. - Fall on the Farm / Steinbach
204-326-9661
- ManyFest: All Together Downtown
Winnipeg / 204-958-4640
- Manitoba Mega Train Show
Winnipeg / 204-837-4776

Oct. - Scattered Seeds Craft Market
Winnipeg / 204-222-0111
- Manitoba Ag Ex / Brandon
204-726-3590
- The Russell Beef & Barley Festival
Russell / 204-773-2456

Nov. - All That Glows: Then and Now
Winnipeg / 204-360-7905
- Santa Claus Parade / Winnipeg
204-777-2682
- Signatures Craft Show & Sale
Winnipeg / 888-773-4444

 Save on travel, shopping and more:

AAA.com/discounts

Wind turbines

Hecla/Grindstone Provincial Park, Hecla Island

St. Boniface Basilica

Aurora borealis in Churchill

Riding Mountain National Park

Index: Great Experience for Members

AAA editor's picks of exceptional note

Itsanitaq Museum

Riding Mountain
National Park

Canadian Museum for
Human Rights
(CMHR)

Lower Fort Garry
National Historic Site

See Orientation map on p. 344 for corresponding grid coordinates, if applicable.
* Indicates the GEM is temporarily closed.

Churchill (A-4)
Itsanitaq Museum *(See p. 348.)*

Inglis (F-1)
Inglis Grain Elevators National Historic Site
(See p. 350.)

International Peace Garden (H-1)
International Peace Garden *(See p. 350.)*

Riding Mountain National Park (F-1)
Riding Mountain National Park *(See p. 352.)*

Selkirk (G-5)
Lower Fort Garry National Historic Site
(See p. 353.)

Winnipeg (G-4)
Canadian Museum for Human Rights (CMHR)
(See p. 367.)

The Forks *(See p. 367.)*

FortWhyte Alive *(See p. 368.)*

The Children's Museum *(See p. 368.)*

Manitoba Museum *(See p. 369.)*

Royal Canadian Mint *(See p. 370.)*

AAA DISCOUNTS »REWARDS

DISCOUNTS
WITHOUT LIMITS

AAA.com/discounts

Download on the App Store
GET IT ON Google Play

Hit the Road
with Foreign Currency

A treasure trove of artisan masterpieces awaits.

Visit your local AAA office or
AAA.com/ForeignCurrency
to learn more.

All products not available at all locations.

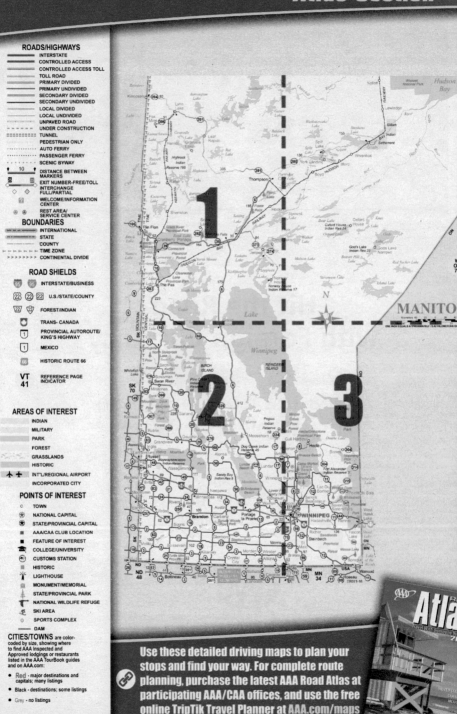

ROADS/HIGHWAYS

- INTERSTATE
- CONTROLLED ACCESS
- CONTROLLED ACCESS TOLL
- TOLL ROAD
- PRIMARY DIVIDED
- PRIMARY UNDIVIDED
- SECONDARY DIVIDED
- SECONDARY UNDIVIDED
- LOCAL DIVIDED
- LOCAL UNDIVIDED
- UNPAVED ROAD
- UNDER CONSTRUCTION
- TUNNEL
- PEDESTRIAN ONLY
- AUTO FERRY
- PASSENGER FERRY
- SCENIC BYWAY
- DISTANCE BETWEEN MARKERS
- EXIT NUMBER-FREE/TOLL
- INTERCHANGE FULL/PARTIAL
- WELCOME/INFORMATION CENTER
- REST AREA/ SERVICE CENTER

BOUNDARIES

- INTERNATIONAL
- STATE
- COUNTY
- TIME ZONE
- CONTINENTAL DIVIDE

ROAD SHIELDS

- INTERSTATE/BUSINESS
- U.S./STATE/COUNTY
- FOREST/INDIAN
- TRANS- CANADA
- PROVINCIAL AUTOROUTE/ KING'S HIGHWAY
- MEXICO
- HISTORIC ROUTE 66
- VT 41 REFERENCE PAGE INDICATOR

AREAS OF INTEREST

- INDIAN
- MILITARY
- PARK
- FOREST
- GRASSLANDS
- HISTORIC
- INT'L/REGIONAL AIRPORT
- INCORPORATED CITY

POINTS OF INTEREST

- TOWN
- NATIONAL CAPITAL
- STATE/PROVINCIAL CAPITAL
- AAA/CAA CLUB LOCATION
- FEATURE OF INTEREST
- COLLEGE/UNIVERSITY
- CUSTOMS STATION
- HISTORIC
- LIGHTHOUSE
- MONUMENT/MEMORIAL
- STATE/PROVINCIAL PARK
- NATIONAL WILDLIFE REFUGE
- SKI AREA
- SPORTS COMPLEX
- DAM

CITIES/TOWNS are color-coded by size, showing where to find AAA Inspected and Approved lodgings or restaurants listed in the AAA TourBook guides and on AAA.com:

- Red - major destinations and capitals; many listings
- Black - destinations; some listings
- Grey - no listings

Use these detailed driving maps to plan your stops and find your way. For complete route planning, purchase the latest AAA Road Atlas at participating AAA/CAA offices, and use the free online TripTik Travel Planner at AAA.com/maps

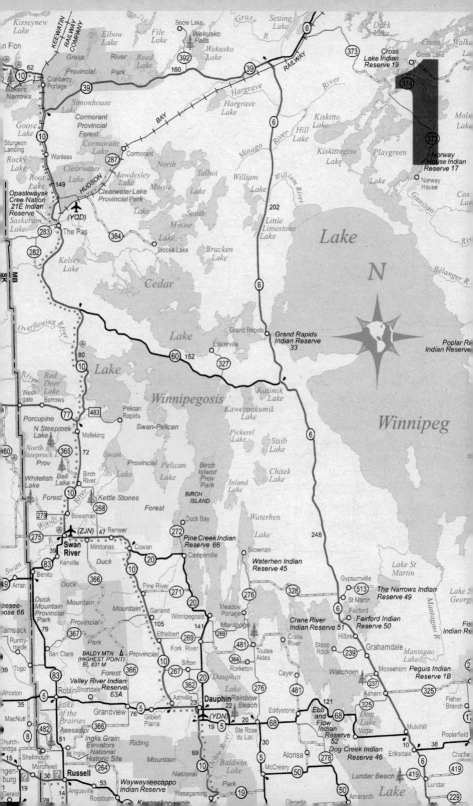

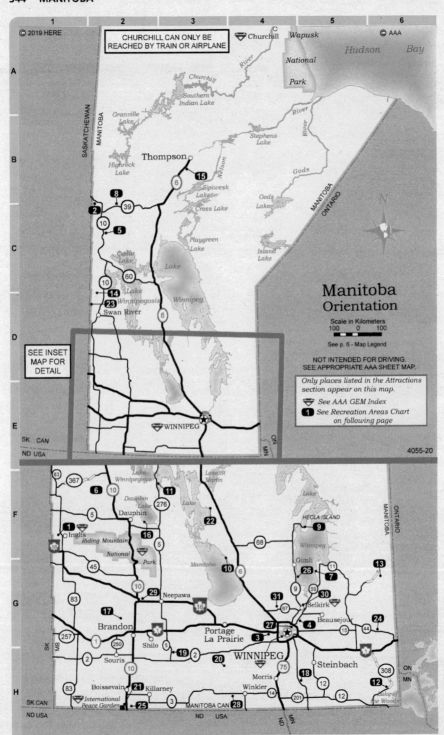

© 2019 HERE

© AAA

CHURCHILL CAN ONLY BE
REACHED BY TRAIN OR AIRPLANE

Churchill *Wapusk*

Hudson *Bay*

Wapusk
National
Park

River

Churchill

Southern
Indian Lake

Granville
Lake

SASKATCHEWAN | MANITOBA

Highrock
Lake

Thompson

15

Nelson

Stephens
Lake

River

Gods

River

8

39

2

10

5

Sipiwesk
Lake

Cross Lake

Gods
Lake

MANITOBA | ONTARIO

Island
Lake

Playgreen
Lake

N

Cedar
Lake

60

Lake
Winnipeg

Manitoba
Orientation

10

14
23
Swan River

Lake
Winnipegosis

6

Scale in Kilometers
100 0 100

See p. 6 - Map Legend

NOT INTENDED FOR DRIVING.
SEE APPROPRIATE AAA SHEET MAP.

SEE INSET
MAP FOR
DETAIL

*Only places listed in the Attractions
section appear on this map.*

⬇ *See AAA GEM Index*
1 *See Recreation Areas Chart
on following page*

WINNIPEG

SK CAN
ND USA

ON
MN

4055-20

83 **367**

Lake
Winnipegosis

Lake St
Martin

6 **10**

Dauphin
Lake

11

276

Lake

Lake

MANITOBA | ONTARIO

5
Dauphin

22

HECLA ISLAND

9

1 ⬇
Inglis

Riding Mountain

16

National

Park

68

Winnipeg

Gimli

26 **11**

13

10

45

5

Manitoba

10 **6**

9 **59**

7

30 ⬇

SK | MB

10

29 Neepawa

17

83

16

31

Selkirk

87

27 ★ **4** Beausejour

15

24

44

Brandon

257

1

250

Shilo

19 **2**

5

20

Portage
La Prairie

3

WINNIPEG ★

Steinbach

75

ON
MN

2

Souris

10

18

12

308

12

83

Boissevain **21** Killarney

International
Peace Garden ⬇

25

3

MANITOBA CAN

28

Morris

Winkler

14

201

12

Lake of
the Woods

SK CAN
ND USA

ND USA

ND | MN

Recreation Areas Chart

The map location numerals in column 2 show an area's location on the preceding map.

Find thousands of places to camp at AAA.com/campgrounds

	MAP LOCATION	CAMPING	PICNICKING	HIKING TRAILS	BOATING	BOAT RAMP	BOAT RENTAL	FISHING	SWIMMING	PET FRIENDLY	BICYCLE TRAILS	WINTER SPORTS	VISITOR CENTER	LODGE/CABINS	FOOD SERVICE
NATIONAL PARKS *(See place listings.)*															
Riding Mountain (F-1) 2,978 square kilometres. Backpacking, cross-country skiing, golf, hiking, horseback riding, scuba diving, tennis, water skiing, wind surfing; boat cruises, paddleboats.		•	•	•	•	•	•	•	•	•	•	•	•	•
PROVINCIAL															
Asessippi (F-1) 2,330 hectares 13 km from Shellmouth Dam on Hwy. 83. Cross-country skiing, fishing, snowmobiling; nature trail.	1	•	•	•	•	•	•	•	•	•		•		•	•
Bakers Narrows (C-2) 145 hectares 27 km s. of Flin Flon on Hwy. 10. Board sailing, canoeing, wildlife viewing; playground.	2	•	•	•	•	•	•	•	•	•		•		•	•
Beaudry (G-4) 939 hectares 10 km w. of Winnipeg on Roblin Blvd./Hwy. 241.	3		•	•				•		•	•	•			
Birds Hill (G-5) 3,550 hectares 24 km n.e. of Winnipeg on Hwy. 59. Interpretive programs. Cross-country skiing, horseback riding, snowmobiling, wildlife viewing; playground.	4	•	•	•				•	•	•	•	•			•
Clearwater Lake (C-2) 59,265 hectares 19 km n. of The Pas on Hwy. 10, then 2.5 km e. on Hwy. 287. Cross-country skiing, snowmobiling; interpretive trail.	5	•	•	•	•	•	•	•	•	•		•		•	•
Duck Mountain (F-2) 142,430 hectares 56 km n. of Roblin off Hwy. 83. Canoeing, cross-country skiing, snowmobiling.	6	•	•	•	•	•	•	•	•	•		•		•	•
Grand Beach (G-5) 2,490 hectares 80 km n.e. of Winnipeg on Hwy. 59, then 6 km w. on Hwy 12. Interpretive programs. Cross-country skiing, sailing, snowmobiling, tennis, windsurfing; sand beaches.	7	•	•	•	•	•	•	•	•	•	•	•		•	•
Grass River (B-2) 228,018 hectares at Cranberry Portage off Hwy. 10. Canoeing; interpretive trail.	8	•	•	•	•	•	•	•	•	•				•	•
Hecla/Grindstone (F-5) 108,440 hectares 165 km n. of Winnipeg via Hwy. 8. Interpretive programs. Cross-country skiing, golf, sailing, snowmobiling, tennis, windsurfing.	9	•	•	•	•	•	•	•	•	•	•	•	•	•	•
Lundar Beach (G-3) 23 hectares 18 km w. of Lundar on Hwy. 419.	10	•	•	•	•			•	•	•					
Manipogo (F-3) 61 hectares 47 km n. of Dauphin on Hwy. 20. Board sailing, wildlife viewing; playground.	11	•	•		•			•	•	•					•
Moose Lake (H-6) 956 hectares 30 km n.e. of Sprague on Hwy. 308. Board sailing, canoeing, snowmobiling, wildlife viewing; playground.	12	•	•		•			•	•	•				•	•
Nopiming (G-6) 142,910 hectares 70 km n.e. of Lac du Bonnet. Canoeing; interpretive trail.	13	•	•	•	•	•		•	•	•				•	•
North Steeprock Lake (D-2) 13 hectares 3 km n. of Birch River on Hwy. 10, then 40 km w. on Hwy. 365.	14	•	•			•	•	•	•	•					
Paint Lake (B-3) 8,848 hectares 32 km s. of Thompson on Hwy. 6. Canoeing, cross-country skiing, ice-skating, snowmobiling, tobogganing, windsurfing.	15	•	•	•	•	•	•	•	•	•		•		•	•
Rainbow Beach (F-2) 52 hectares 17 km e. of Dauphin on Hwy. 20. Board sailing, golf, wildlife viewing; playground.	16	•	•	•				•	•	•	•				
Rivers (G-2) 37 hectares 14 km n. of Brandon on Hwy. 10, then 26 km w. on Hwy. 25. Playground.	17	•	•	•				•	•	•					
St. Malo (H-5) 148 hectares 64 km s. of Winnipeg on Hwy. 59. Motorized boats not allowed.	18	•	•			•		•	•	•		•			•
Spruce Woods (H-3) 26,950 hectares 25 km s.e. of Carberry on Hwy. 5. Interpretive programs. Canoeing, cross-country skiing, ice-skating, snowmobiling, tobogganing; horse trails.	19	•	•	•	•			•	•	•	•	•	•	•	•
Stephenfield (H-3) 94 hectares 10 km w. of Carman on Hwy. 245. Board sailing, golf; playground.	20	•	•	•	•			•	•	•					•
Turtle Mountain (H-2) 18,570 hectares 23 km s. of Boissevain off Hwy. 10. Cross-country skiing, ice-skating, snowmobiling, tobogganing; interpretive trail, horse trails.	21	•	•	•	•	•		•	•	•	•	•			
Watchorn (F-3) 10 hectares 11 km w. of Moosehorn on Hwy. 237. Playground.	22	•	•			•	•	•	•	•					
Whitefish Lake (D-2) 24 hectares 13 km n. of Swan River, then 28 km w. on Hwy. 279. Playground.	23	•	•			•	•	•	•	•					

Recreation Areas Chart

The map location numerals in column 2 show an area's location on the preceding map.

🔗 Find thousands of places to camp at AAA.com/campgrounds

	MAP LOCATION	CAMPING	PICNICKING	HIKING TRAILS	BOATING	BOAT RAMP	BOAT RENTAL	FISHING	SWIMMING	PET FRIENDLY	BICYCLE TRAILS	WINTER SPORTS	VISITOR CENTER	LODGE/CABINS	FOOD SERVICE
Whiteshell (G-6) 272,090 hectares off Hwy. 1 at Falcon Lake, near the Ontario border. Interpretive programs. Cross-country and downhill skiing, golf, horseback riding, sailing, snowmobiling, tennis, tobogganing, windsurfing; museum.	24	•	•	•	•	•	•	•	•	•	•	•	•	•	•
William Lake (H-2) 199 hectares 7 km e. of Horton, then 8 km s. Amphitheater, playground.	25	•	•	•	•	•		•	•	•					
Winnipeg Beach (G-5) 41 hectares 45 km n. of Winnipeg on Hwy. 8, then 5 km e. on PR 229. Soccer, tennis, volleyball, wildlife viewing; playground.	26	•	•	•	•	•	•	•	•	•					•
OTHER															
Kildonan (G-4) 39 hectares at 2015 Main St. in Winnipeg. Cross-country skiing, ice-skating, tobogganing; pool.	27		•	•					•	•		•		•	•
Lake Minnewasta (H-4) 125 hectares 2 km w. of Morden on Hwy. 3, then 1 km s. on Hwy. 434.	28	•	•	•	•			•	•	•		•			
Minnedosa Lake and Beach (G-2) 8 hectares 1.5 km e. of Minnedosa on Beach Dr. (PR 262). Cross-country skiing, ice fishing, ice hockey, snowmobiling; beach, playgrounds. Note: concessions are only offered in summer.	29	•	•	•	•			•	•	•		•			
Selkirk Park (G-5) 81 hectares on the banks of the Red River at Eveline St. in Selkirk. Cross-country skiing, ice fishing; bird sanctuary.	30	•	•	•				•	•				•		
Stonewall Quarry (G-4) 30 hectares 4 blks. n. on Main St. in Stonewall. Nature programs. Cross-country skiing, ice-skating, tobogganing.	31	•	•	•					•	•		•		•	•

Be Vacation Ready
Know Before You Go

Before setting out on your trip, have your car checked out by a dependable AAA/CAA Approved Auto Repair facility.

AAA.com/autorepair

BEAUSEJOUR (G-5) pop. 3,126, elev. 247m/810'

Just 46 kilometres (29 mi.) northeast of Winnipeg, Beausejour is on one of the main roads to Whiteshell Provincial Park. Nature enthusiasts take advantage of the walking, hiking and cross-country ski trails available at Wally Chryplywy Nature Park on First Street.

Town of Beausejour: 639 Park Ave., Beausejour, MB, Canada R0E 0C0. **Phone:** (204) 268-7550.

BOISSEVAIN (H-2) pop. 1,572

Nearby Turtle Mountain Provincial Park *(see Recreation Areas Chart)* is named for the western painted turtle, which lives in the park's many shallow lakes. The park is the year-round home of a large number of waterfowl and of migratory birds in spring and fall. A wildlife center also is available.

As a connection to the park, the town has adopted as its symbol an 8.5-metre-tall (28-ft.) statue known as Tommy Turtle, which can be seen beside the visitor center on Hwy. 10.

An outdoor art gallery throughout the town depicts area history by way of more than 20 colorful wall-size murals, including a large scene painted on a grain elevator in downtown Boissevain. Scenic Hwy. 10 leads south to the North Dakota border and the International Peace Garden *(see place listing p. 350)*.

Boissevain Tourism Information Centre: 298 Mountain St., Boissevain, MB, Canada R0K 0E0. **Phone:** (204) 534-6662 or (800) 497-2393.

Self-guiding tours: Literature for a self-guiding walking tour of the city's historic buildings is available at the Boissevain Tourism Information Centre.

BRANDON (G-2) pop. 46,061, elev. 409m/1,300'
• Restaurants p. 348

An agricultural and industrial center, Brandon is the second largest city in the province after Winnipeg and is known for its small-town warmth and big-city amenities.

The Riverbank Discovery Centre, in addition to providing information about Brandon and the surrounding region, is the starting point for the Assiniboine Riverbank Trail System, 17 kilometres (10.5 mi.) of trails that wind throughout Brandon, linking the downtown area with parks, picnic spots and sports venues.

The Keystone Centre, sitting on some 36.4 hectares (90 acres) and offering 540,000 square feet of multi-use space, plays host to some of Manitoba's larger events, concerts and sports competitions; phone (204) 726-3500. Brandon's Community Sportsplex offers both winter and summer recreational activities. Built for the 1979 Canada Winter Games, the structure houses racquetball courts, an ice arena, swimming pool, indoor water slide and an outdoor running track; phone (204) 729-2470.

The Brandon Hills Wildlife Management Area, just a short drive south of the city on Hwy. 10 and east along Beresford Road, provides a setting for a variety of recreational pursuits such as hiking, mountain bicycling, cross-country skiing and bird-watching.

Regional Tourism Centre/Riverbank Discovery Centre: #1-545 Conservation Dr., Brandon, MB, Canada R7A 7L8. **Phone:** (204) 729-2141 or (888) 799-1111.

Self-guiding tours: A historical walking tour of the residential area between 10th and 18th streets offers interesting architecture and turn-of-the-20th-century homes; a booklet describing the tour is available for $3.50 from the tourism center.

BEST WESTERN PLUS BRANDON INN   204/727-7997

 THREE DIAMOND
Hotel

AAA Benefit: Members save up to 15% and earn bonus points!

Address: 205 Middleton Ave R7A 1A8 **Location:** Jct Trans-Canada Hwy 1 and 10; access via north service road. **Facility:** 79 units, some efficiencies. 3 stories, interior corridors. **Parking:** winter plug-ins. **Terms:** check-in 4 pm. **Amenities:** safes. **Pool:** heated indoor. **Activities:** hot tub, exercise room. **Guest Services:** valet and coin laundry. **Featured Amenity: continental breakfast.**

CANAD INNS DESTINATION CENTRE BRANDON
204/727-1422

 APPROVED
Hotel

Address: 1125 18th St R7A 7C5 **Location:** On Hwy 10 (18th St); jct Brandon Ave. **Facility:** 159 units. 11 stories, interior corridors. **Parking:** winter plug-ins. **Amenities:** *Some:* video games. **Dining:** 3 restaurants, nightclub. **Pool:** heated indoor. **Activities:** hot tub, exercise room. **Guest Services:** valet laundry.

COMFORT INN BRANDON   204/727-6232

 APPROVED
Hotel

Address: 925 Middleton Ave R7C 1A8 **Location:** Trans-Canada Hwy 1; between Hwy 10 (18th St) N and 10 S; on north side of service road. Located in a commercial area. **Facility:** 79 units. 2 stories (no elevator), interior corridors. **Parking:** winter plug-ins. **Activities:** picnic facilities. **Guest Services:** valet laundry. **Featured Amenity: full hot breakfast.**

DAYS INN & SUITES BRANDON   204/727-3600
▽▽ APPROVED   Hotel. **Address:** 2130 Currie Blvd R7B 4E7

LAKEVIEW INNS & SUITES BRANDON   204/728-1880
◆ APPROVED   Hotel. **Address:** 1880 18th St N R7C 1A5

WHERE TO EAT

CLAY POT CAFE   204/726-9467
◆ APPROVED   American. Casual Dining. **Address:** 2604 Victoria Ave R7B 0M8

JOEY'S ONLY SEAFOOD RESTAURANT   204/729-3700
◆ APPROVED   Seafood. Casual Dining. **Address:** 1212 18th St R7A 5C3

LADY OF THE LAKE SHOP, CAFE & PUB   204/726-8785
◆ APPROVED   International. Casual Dining. **Address:** 135-B 17th St N R7A 1G6

MARINO'S PIZZA   204/578-5555
◆ APPROVED   Pizza. Casual Dining. **Address:** 441 10th St R7A 4G3

MUM'S FAMILY RESTAURANT   204/725-0888
◆ APPROVED   American. Casual Dining. **Address:** 505 24th St R7B 1X6

CHURCHILL (A-4) pop. 813, elev. 29m/100'

Churchill, on the shore of Hudson Bay, is Canada's northernmost subarctic seaport. It also is the site of the Hudson's Bay Co.'s Prince of Wales Fort National Historic Site, a partially restored ruin across from Churchill and Cape Merry Battery at the mouth of the Churchill River. Built over a period of 40 years during the 1700s to hold as many as 400 soldiers, the impressive stone fortress housed only 39 untrained men when three French warships mounted a surprise attack in 1782. The fort's governor wisely surrendered without engaging in battle.

After spending 3 unsuccessful days trying to demolish the 12-metre-thick (40-ft.) outer walls, the French abandoned the fort; it was never occupied again. The site is accessible by boat July through August (weather and tides permitting).

The area around Churchill holds an attraction for two giant mammals: the polar bear and the beluga whale. In fact, the Churchill region is said to have the greatest concentration of accessible polar bears in the world. Having spent the winter hunting on the frozen bay, the bears come to shore south of Churchill as the ice melts, scatter along the coast and up to 50 kilometres (31 mi.) inland, and then return to the ice in autumn when the bay refreezes. Beluga whales are often sighted off the coast of Cape Merry during July and August.

Other natural features include flowers, arctic plant life, various wildlife and some 200 species of birds, which nest or pass through Churchill on their annual migrations. An excellent spot for bird-watching is Bird Cove, on the coast 16 kilometres (9 mi.) east of Churchill. The aurora borealis (northern lights) seen from Churchill during the fall and winter months are among the most brilliant in the world.

Churchill can be reached only by train or airplane. Via Rail Canada trains run from Winnipeg and Thompson to Churchill; phone (888) 842-7245.

Calm Air offers flights from Winnipeg to Churchill; phone (800) 839-2256.

The Parks Canada Visitor Reception Centre offers information, interpretive displays and programs, and historical exhibits June through November; by appointment rest of year. Phone (204) 675-8863.

Churchill Chamber of Commerce: 211 Kelsey Blvd., Churchill, MB, Canada R0B 0E0. **Phone:** (204) 675-2022 or (888) 389-2327.

CAPE MERRY NATIONAL HISTORIC SITE, accessible via the Cape Merry Centennial Pkwy., 3 km (1.9 mi.) w. to the e. shore of the Churchill River, is marked by a stone cannon battery built in 1746 to complement the defenses of the Prince of Wales Fort. An original cannon and powder magazine remain. A cairn commemorating Capt. Jens Munk, the first European to enter the Churchill River in 1619, is displayed.

The cape offers views of harbor activity as well as whales, waterfowl and the Prince of Wales Fort. **Time:** Allow 30 minutes minimum. **Hours:** Daily 24 hours. **Cost:** Free. **Phone:** (204) 675-8863.

◆ GEM **ITSANITAQ MUSEUM,** 242 La Verendrye Ave., formerly known as the Eskimo Museum, contains exhibits that depict the history and culture of the northern region of Canada. Founded in 1944 by Roman Catholic missionaries, it pays tribute to the creativity and beliefs of the Canadian Inuits. Highlights of the museum are Inuit carvings in bone, ivory, stone and antler as well as wildlife specimens, artifacts and tools dating from 1700 B.C. **Hours:** Mon. 1-5, Tues.-Sat. 9-noon and 1-5, June-Nov.; Mon.-Sat. 1-4:30, rest of year. **Cost:** Donations. **Phone:** (204) 675-2030.

NORTH STAR TOURS office is at 12 Hearne St. but guests are picked up from their hotel. Guides conduct historical, cultural and wilderness adventure and birding tours of the Churchill area by school bus covering such topics as Fort Churchill, the Hudson's Bay Co., natural history, geology, and polar bears and other wildlife. During summer beluga whale sightings are the highlight, and polar bear season runs October 1 to November. February, March and August are the months for aurora borealis viewing.

Time: Allow 6 hours minimum. **Hours:** Daily 9-5, June-Aug., Oct.-Nov. and Feb.-Mar. (weather permitting). **Cost:** $110-$175; free (ages 1-12). **Phone:** (204) 675-2356 or (800) 665-0690.

PRINCE OF WALES FORT NATIONAL HISTORIC SITE, at the mouth of the Churchill River, is accessible by boat only. A huge stone fortress built 1731-71 by the Hudson's Bay Co., the fort fell to the French without incident in 1782. Independent whale-watching boat tours, including those offered by Sea North Tours Ltd. (see attraction listing), usually include the fort on their itineraries.

Time: Allow 2 hours minimum. **Hours:** Access is possible on the changing tides 6 hours daily, July-Aug. (weather permitting). **Cost:** Boat fare (site admission included) $115; $57.50 (ages 6-12). **Phone:** (204) 675-8863 for Parks Canada historic site information, (204) 675-2195, or (888) 348-7591 for Sea North Tours information.

SEA NORTH TOURS LTD., 153 Kelsey Blvd., offers boat tours to Prince of Wales Fort National Historic Site in craft ranging in size up to the 30-passenger *Sea North II.* This vessel is equipped with stereo hydrophones so that passengers can listen to the sounds made by the beluga whales that swim within feet of the boat. Tours also offer chances of sighting polar bears, ice formations and indigenous birds. Kayak tours and snorkeling also are available.

Time: Allow 3 hours minimum. **Hours:** Daily dawn-dusk (times may vary depending on tides), mid-June to late Aug. **Cost:** $115; $57.50 (ages 6-12). Prices may vary; phone ahead. **Phone:** (204) 675-2195 or (888) 348-7591.

YORK FACTORY NATIONAL HISTORIC SITE is 250 km (150 mi.) s.e. near the mouth of the Hayes River; access to the site is limited to charter plane or boat. The site was established by the Hudson's Bay Co. as part of a series of fur-trading posts. The 1821 depot is the oldest wooden structure still standing on permafrost. Self-guiding tours of the site feature reconstructed buildings containing area artifacts.

Visitors should contact Parks Canada for transportation and safety information. Facilities at the site are limited; camping is permitted in fenced compound. **Time:** Allow 4 hours minimum. **Hours:** Daily 8-5, July 2-Aug. 30 (weather permitting). **Cost:** Free. Guided tours $7.80. **Phone:** (204) 675-8863.

POLAR INN & SUITES   204/675-8878
◇ APPROVED   Hotel. **Address:** 153 Kelsey Blvd R0B 0E0

WHERE TO EAT

THE REEF CAFE & DINING ROOM   204/675-8807
◇ APPROVED   American. Casual Dining. **Address:** 299 Kelsey Blvd R0B 0E0

THE TUNDRA INN PUB & DINING ROOM   204/675-8831
◇ APPROVED   Canadian. Casual Dining. **Address:** 23 Franklin St R0B 0E0

DAUPHIN (F-2) pop. 8,251, elev. 293m/960'

Dauphin (DAW-fin) lies in a fertile farming valley between Duck Mountain Provincial Park *(see Recreation Areas Chart)* and Riding Mountain National Park *(see place listing p. 352).* Lake Dauphin, 15 kilometres (9 mi.) east of Dauphin, is a popular place for watersports and offers camping, fishing and wildlife tours.

Parkland Recreation Complex, 200 1st Ave. S.E., includes two arenas, a playground, a curling rink and an aquatic center with an indoor wave pool; phone (204) 622-3150.

Meet your partner or watch as square dancers from across Manitoba compete in the ◇ Dauphin Friendship Centre Square Dance Competition in late May at the Rotary Arena. If dancing isn't your forte, you can compete in the fiddling competition.

In late June and early July, more than 14,000 country music fans flock to ◇ Dauphin's Countryfest, a 4-day music festival held at Selo Ukraina, a heritage village 12 kilometres (7.5 mi.) south of Dauphin near Riding Mountain National Park.

The nation's rich Ukrainian culture and heritage are celebrated in late July at Selo Ukraina during ◇ Canada's National Ukrainian Festival, a 3-day event featuring Ukrainian music, food and dance.

Dauphin Economic Development & Tourism: 100 Main St. S., Dauphin, MB, Canada R7N 1K3. **Phone:** (204) 622-3216 or (877) 566-5669.

FORT DAUPHIN MUSEUM, 140 Jackson St., is surrounded by a wooden palisade suggestive of an 18th-century fur-trading fort of the North West Co. A trapper's cabin, schoolhouse, church, blacksmith shop, trading post and pioneer house inside the fort are furnished in the style of the early settlers. Archeological, fur trade and pioneer artifacts also are featured.

Time: Allow 1 hour minimum. **Hours:** Mon.-Sat. 9-5, July-Aug.; Mon.-Fri. 9-5, May-June and in Sept.; by appointment rest of year. **Cost:** $4; $3 (students with ID); free (ages 0-12 with adult). **Phone:** (204) 638-6630.

SUPER 8 DAUPHIN   204/638-0800
◇ APPROVED   Hotel. **Address:** 1457 Main St S R7N 3B3

WHERE TO EAT

MR MIKES STEAKHOUSECASUAL   204/701-6453
◇ APPROVED   American. Casual Dining. **Address:** 10 Main St S R7N 1N4

GIMLI (G-4) pop. 5,845, elev. 220m/723'

Established in 1875, Gimli was the site of Canada's first permanent Icelandic settlement, the largest outside Iceland. The town's name, derived from Norse mythology, means "home of the gods." A Viking statue designed by Gissur Eliasson and the oldest Icelandic cemetery in Canada testify to Gimli's Nordic heritage. Gimli is located on the western shore of Lake Winnipeg, one of the largest freshwater lakes in the world.

Lake Winnipeg Visitor Centre: 1 Centre Ave., Gimli, MB, Canada R0C 1B0. Open May-Sept. **Phone:** (204) 642-7974.

[SAVE] **NEW ICELAND HERITAGE MUSEUM** is at 94 1st Ave. Displayed in two buildings are exhibits that focus on the area's Icelandic roots, the fishing industry and Lake Winnipeg's natural history. Multimedia exhibits at the Waterfront Centre examine area history, while displays at the visitor center feature the fishing industry and the lake's natural history. A new permanent exhibit showcases 350 rocks and minerals from Iceland.

Time: Allow 30 minutes minimum. **Hours:** Waterfront Centre daily 10-4, Victoria Day weekend-Labour Day; Mon.-Fri. 10-4, Sat.-Sun. 1-4, rest of year. Visitor center daily 10-6, Victoria Day weekend-Labour Day. **Cost:** $7; $6 (ages 55+ and students with ID); free (ages 0-6); $15 (family). **Phone:** (204) 642-4001. 🍴

HEADINGLEY pop. 3,215
• Hotels & Restaurants map & index p. 374

BEST WESTERN PLUS WINNIPEG WEST
                          204/594-2200

 THREE DIAMOND
Hotel

Best Western PLUS

AAA Benefit: Members save up to 15% and earn bonus points!

Address: 4140 Portage Ave R4H 1C5 **Location:** Jct Trans-Canada Hwy 1 (Portage Ave) and 101, just w; entrance through travel plaza. **Facility:** 110 units, some efficiencies. 4 stories, interior corridors. **Parking:** winter plug-ins. **Pool:** heated indoor. **Activities:** hot tub, exercise room. **Guest Services:** valet and coin laundry. **Featured Amenity:** breakfast buffet.

HECLA ISLAND (F-5) elev. 210m/690'

HECLA/GRINDSTONE PROVINCIAL PARK, 165 km (103 mi.) n. of Winnipeg, or 54 km (34 mi.) n. of Riverton, on Hwy. 8, is comprised of several islands in Lake Winnipeg, the largest of which is Hecla Island. The original settlers were Icelanders displaced from their homeland in 1876, fleeing poverty and Danish rule. Guided walks through the restored buildings of Hecla Village—a church, school, community hall, period house, dockside fish station, a tool display and a partially completed boarding house—are offered. *See Recreation Areas Chart.*

Interpretive programs also are available, as are camping facilities, cabins, hiking trails, snowmobile trails, picnic areas, bicycling, cross-country skiing, fishing and swimming. For further information, contact the Department of Conservation, P.O. Box 70, Riverton, MB, Canada R0C 2R0. **Hours:** Daily 24 hours. **Cost:** One-day pass $5 per private vehicle. Three-day pass $12. An annual pass is available. **Phone:** (204) 279-2056 May-Sept. or (204) 378-2261.

Grassy Narrows Marsh and Wildlife Viewing Tower, at Hecla/Grindstone Provincial Park, offers wildlife viewing from trails and boardwalks along the marsh as well as from towers along the trails. Some trails are designated bicycling trails. The marsh, a

nesting area for Canada geese and other waterfowl, is named after the Narrows, a channel between Hecla Island and the mainland. The tower was built for viewing moose as they feed in the marsh. **Note:** Visitors should bring drinking water and wear comfortable walking shoes. **Hours:** Daily 24 hours. **Cost:** One-day pass $5 per private vehicle. Three-day pass $12. An annual pass is available. **Phone:** (204) 279-2056 May-Sept., or (204) 378-2261 rest of year.

Hecla Fish Station, at Hecla/Grindstone Provincial Park, is in an old icehouse, or "fish station." The site provides a look at the commercial fishing industry of Lake Winnipeg through artifacts, wall plaques and a small museum. During June and September visitors may view fishermen bringing in the day's catch. **Hours:** Daily 11:30-4:30, June 10-Aug. 30. **Cost:** Free. **Phone:** (204) 279-2056 May-Sept. or (204) 378-2261.

Hecla Island Heritage Home Museum, at Hecla/Grindstone Provincial Park, depicts the lifestyle of an Icelandic family from the 1920s to the 1940s. The restored 1928 house is furnished in period with items donated by descendants of the original owners and by other islanders. Walking tours are available. **Hours:** Wed.-Sun. 10-4, June 26-Sept. 2. **Cost:** Donations. **Phone:** (204) 279-2056 May-Sept. or (204) 378-2261.

INGLIS (F-1)

INGLIS GRAIN ELEVATORS NATIONAL HISTORIC SITE is along Railway Ave. These five vintage grain elevators, once a common sight on western Canadian prairies, have been restored and are now the last remaining row of standard wooden grain elevators in Canada. Dating to the 1920s, similar rows of elevators, built by grain companies and agricultural cooperatives, once stood along rail lines in most small Canadian communities.

An interpretive center in the Paterson elevator explains the importance of these structures to the nation's agricultural history. Exhibits and displays complement a video presentation, which shows how the elevators operated, transporting wheat into storage bins. A walking tour of the grounds provides further insights into the development of Canada's grain industry.

Time: Allow 1 hour minimum. **Hours:** Mon.-Sat. 10-6, Sun. noon-6, June 1-early Sept.; otherwise by appointment. **Cost:** $4.76-$9.52; free (ages 0-7). **Phone:** (204) 564-2243, or (204) 773-4231 for appointments. 🍴

INTERNATIONAL PEACE GARDEN (H-1)

On scenic Hwy. 10 and on US 281, the International Peace Garden consists of 1,451 acres (586 hectares) in Manitoba and an adjoining 888 acres (360 hectares) in North Dakota. Set among the lakes and streams of the wooded Turtle Mountains, the botanical garden and park commemorates the friendship between these two countries on the longest unfortified border in the world.

Points of interest include the Peace Chapel, which includes quotations etched in limestone walls; more than 150,000 flowering annuals in the formal gardens that line the boundary; a floral clock; the Carillon Bell Tower, which chimes every 15 minutes; and the 9/11 Memorial, constructed of steel salvaged from the ruins of the World Trade Center, commemorating the tragic events of Sept. 11, 2001.

The Interpretive Centre and Conservatory houses a retail store, a café, small prairie lands library and a conservatory with more than 6,000 cacti, succulents and orchids. The North American Game Warden Museum is dedicated to officers who died in the line of duty.

Facilities include campgrounds, hiking and bicycling trails and picnic areas. Self-guiding walking and driving tours are available. Flowers are in full bloom mid-July to early September (weather permitting).

The International Music Camp Summer School of Fine Arts is held at the garden June through July. The Legion Athletic Camp, held July through August, attracts coaches and athletes from many countries.

After leaving the garden all visitors are required to go through customs (U.S. and Canadian customs stations are a short distance from the entrance gate. Allow 2 hours minimum to visit the site. The garden is open daily 24 hours, and the entrance gate is staffed Mon.-Fri. 9-5, Sat.-Sun. 9-7, late May to mid-Sept. Interpretive Centre daily 10-7. Game Warden Museum Tues.-Sun. 10-4, June 7-early Sept.; daily 11-4, early Sept. to mid-Sept.; Sat.-Sun. 11-4, in May; by appointment rest of year. Daily vehicle permit $20; pedestrian permit $10; season permit $30. Game Warden Museum admission is free. Phone (204) 534-2510 in Canada, (701) 263-4390 in the United States, or (888) 432-6733.

KILLARNEY (H-2) pop. 3,233, elev. 495m/1,625'

The area's resemblance to Ireland's Killarney Lakes prompted John Sidney O'Brien to change the name of the town of Oak Lake to Killarney. Green fire engines and a replica of the Blarney Stone are further evidence of the town's Irish heritage.

MORRIS (H-4) pop. 1,797, elev. 236m/775'

Two rival fur-trading companies—the North West Co. and the Hudson's Bay Co.—set up shop on the Morris River in 1801. Not until 1874 did a permanent settlement take hold; incorporation took place in 1883. Both the town and the river on which it grew were named for Alexander Morris, the second lieutenant governor of Manitoba during the 1870s.

You'll enjoy fair favorites including entertainment, exhibits, fair food and midway rides at the ☗ Manitoba Stampede and Exhibition in mid-July. Highlights include the heart-pounding action of a seven

event pro rodeo, and chuck wagon and chariot racing. Kids can take part in the action at the mutton busting and the pig scramble.

Morris Town Office: 1-380 Stampede Grounds, Box 28, Morris, MB, Canada R0G 1K0. **Phone:** (204) 746-2531.

MORRIS & DISTRICT CENTENNIAL MUSEUM, on Main St. at jct. hwys. 75 and 23, consists of two buildings. The main building is the original Carleton School, which contains pioneer-era displays of farm tools and a laundry and dairy section. The second building contains five rooms featuring furniture and artifacts from the turn of the 20th century. A mural depicts the history of the Red River Valley. **Hours:** Thurs.-Tues. noon-5, Wed. 2-8, June-Aug. (or late Sept., if weather permits). **Cost:** Donations. **Phone:** (204) 746-2169.

NEEPAWA (G-3) pop. 3,629, elev. 400m/1,300'

Neepawa, whose name derives from a native word for plenty, is a service center for the surrounding grain and livestock farms on the fertile plains northwest of Winnipeg. This community of tree-lined streets, well-known as the birthplace of author Margaret Laurence, offers many pleasant diversions for residents and travelers alike, including Riverbend Park, a fitness trail, a camping area, a golf course and opportunities for bird-watching.

The city calls itself the World Lily Capital. This claim is bolstered by the annual ☗ Neepawa Lily Festival held over three days in late July. More than 2,000 varieties of lilies are grown in the Neepawa area, and the community celebrates their beauty with live entertainment, music, street vendors and food kiosks, a quilt show, a parade, tours by bus and horse-drawn vehicles and a photography contest.

Neepawa and District Chamber of Commerce: 282 Hamilton St., Neepawa, MB, Canada R0J 1H0. **Phone:** (204) 476-5292.

BEAUTIFUL PLAINS MUSEUM, 91 Hamilton St., is housed in a former CNR station. The museum features several rooms of historical items. A children's room contains antique toys and books, and a military room has uniforms and pictures of local residents involved in World Wars I and II. Other rooms include items dedicated to nature, stores, Masonic lodges, sports and vintage clothing. An extensive doll collection also is displayed. Railroad artifacts and history displays are housed in an antique railroad car.

Time: Allow 30 minutes minimum. **Hours:** Mon.-Fri. 9-5, Sat.-Sun. 1-5, July-Aug.; Mon.-Fri. 9-5, mid-May through June 30. **Cost:** Donations. **Phone:** (204) 476-3896, or (204) 841-9050 in the off-season.

🔗 **Rest assured:**

AAA.com/travelguides/hotels

PORTAGE LA PRAIRIE (G-3) pop. 12,996, elev. 332m/1,100'

The city's name is derived from the prairie portage between the Red and Assiniboine rivers and Lake Manitoba. In the heart of the city at Crescent Road and Royal Road S. is Island Park. Surrounded by horseshoe-shaped Crescent Lake, this scenic park has a deer sanctuary, a large captive flock of Canada geese and offers opportunities for other bird-watching. Park features include playground areas, exhibition grounds, seasonal harness racing, a golf course, a campground, a water park, a swimming pool, an arboretum, tennis courts, picnic areas, an arena and bicycling and hiking trails.

Portage la Prairie City Hall, built in 1898, was designed by one of Canada's foremost architects, Thomas Fuller.

Portage and District Chamber of Commerce: 20 Saskatchewan Ave. E., Portage la Prairie, MB, Canada R1N 0L2. **Phone:** (204) 857-7778.

FORT LA REINE MUSEUM, PIONEER VILLAGE AND TOURIST BUREAU is at jct. hwys. 26 and 1A E. The central museum includes pioneer household articles and implements, a log fort, school, doctor's office, trading post, furnished homestead and church as well as railway, farming and military displays. Canadian railway official Sir William Van Horne's business car also is displayed. A tourist bureau is available.

Time: Allow 1 hour minimum. **Hours:** Wed.-Sat. 10-5, Sun. 11-6, June 1-Sept. 2 and for occasional special events. **Cost:** $10; $8 (ages 13-18, 60+ and students with ID); $5 (ages 5-12); $25 (family, two adults and three children). **Phone:** (204) 857-3259.

BILL'S STICKY FINGERS 204/857-9999

APPROVED American Casual Dining $16-$27

AAA Inspector Notes: This restaurant offers a wide-ranging menu that includes ribs, chicken, steak, lasagna, gyros and pizza, as well as daily specials. The service is friendly and prompt. Lunch is not served on Saturday and Sunday. **Features:** full bar. **Address:** 210 Saskatchewan Ave E R1N 0K9 **Location:** Just w of Main St. [L] [D] [LATE] CALL

RIDING MOUNTAIN NATIONAL PARK (F-1)

Elevations in the park range from 230 metres (755 ft.) at Henderson Creek in the northeastern area to 756 metres (2,480 ft.) at Bald Hill in the eastern side of the park. Refer to CAA/AAA maps for additional elevation information.

Accessible from the north and south via scenic Hwy. 10, or from the east via Hwy. 19, Riding Mountain National Park lies on the plateau of the Manitoba escarpment, 197 kilometres (123 mi.) north of the U.S. border and 259 kilometres (162 mi.) northwest of Winnipeg. The park also encompasses the historic resort town of Wasagaming on Clear Lake, which offers the amenities of a resort destination. The park's 2,978-square-kilometre (1,150-sq.-mi.) area is blanketed with forests, lakes and meadows. Officially dedicated in 1933, it is home to elk, moose, deer, bears and a wide variety of birds and vegetation. Waterfowl and beavers populate the waterways, and a herd of bison grazes in a large enclosure near Lake Audy. Driving hwys. 10 and 19 as well as Lake Audy Road offer scenic views and opportunities to spot wildlife. Self-guiding bison tour brochures are available at various park facilities.

During the Depression of the 1930s, the Depression Relief Program created jobs for the unemployed, 1,200 of whom were put to work constructing buildings for the park 1934-35. As is the case with much of the architecture found in the country's national parks, the style widely used was a rustic design that incorporated local materials. Perhaps the most eye-catching of their projects here is the East Gate Complex on Hwy. 19, which includes a registration building, two staff buildings and an overhead entrance sign. (Northern and southern complexes had been built but no longer exist.)

Another major international event the following decade further influenced the site's development, when World War II changed the site's focus from recreation to a source of attaining fuelwood. During the war the park was used as a minimum security POW camp, housing German prisoners from North Africa to cut cordwood. When the prisoners were released in late 1945, the function of the park turned once again to recreation.

General Information and Activities

Although the park is open year-round, complete facilities are available only from mid-May to mid-October. Recreational activities available within the park include bicycling, boating, camping, tennis, golfing, lawn bowling, swimming, hiking, fishing, canoeing, sailing, horseback riding, swimming, skateboarding, ice-skating, cross-country skiing and snowshoeing. Snowmobiling is permitted on Clear Lake and around the park's perimeter. Clear Lake has a beach and boat launches, and scuba diving is possible; divers must register with the park. More than 400 kilometres (250 mi.) of hiking, bicycling and horseback trails lead to lakes, meadows and evergreen forests. Bicycle and boat rentals are available. The park has more than a dozen picnic sites.

Note: Except for in Wasagaming, water must be boiled for all uses. Swimming areas are unsupervised; lifeguards are not available. Due to the presence of a parasite in most of the bodies of water in the park, developing swimmer's itch is a concern; take proper precautions. Camping permits and fishing licenses are required.

Several forms of recreation can be pursued nearby. Guides and outfitters offer horseback riding and wagon excursions along with other wilderness activities. See Recreation Areas Chart.

ADMISSION is $7.43; $6.24 (ages 65+); $3.71 (ages 6-16); free (ages 0-5); $18.67 (family, up to seven people). An annual pass is available.

PETS are allowed in the park. Dogs must be leashed at all times.

ADDRESS inquiries to Visitor Information, Riding Mountain National Park, Wasagaming, MB, Canada R0J 2H0; phone (204) 848-7275 or (204) 848-7272.

VISITOR INFORMATION CENTRE OF WASAGAMING is on the s. shore of Clear Lake. The center maintains exhibits and displays about the natural and human history of the area. Interpretive programs include nature walks, campfires, theater programs and guided hikes. **Hours:** Daily 9:30-8, June 29-early Sept.; 9:30-5:30, mid-May to June 28 and early Sept. to mid-Oct. **Cost:** Free. **Phone:** (204) 848-7275 or (204) 848-7272. ▲

RUSSELL pop. 1,669

THE RUSSELL INN HOTEL & CONFERENCE CENTRE
204/773-2186
◈ APPROVED   Hotel. **Address:** Hwy 16 R0J 1W0

WHERE TO EAT

RUSSELL INN DINING ROOM   204/773-7507
◈ APPROVED   American. Casual Dining. **Address:** Hwy 16 R0J 1W0

SCANTERBURY

SOUTH BEACH CASINO & RESORT   204/766-2100
◈ THREE DIAMOND   Hotel

Address: One Ocean Dr R0E 1W0 **Location:** On Rt 59, just s of town. **Facility:** Near the shores of Lake Winnipeg, this Art Deco-style hotel has attractive rooms with triple-sheet bedding. Standard units are compact, but you can upgrade to spacious suites with sitting areas. 95 units. 6 stories, interior corridors. **Parking:** winter plug-ins. **Pool:** heated indoor.
SAVE ECO 🚗 ⑪ 🍸 Ⓨ CALL 🄳 🏊 BIZ HS 🛜 🎥 🔒 🖥 / SOME UNITS 🖨

SELKIRK (G-5) pop. 9,834, elev. 231m/800'

Selkirk's name honors Lord Selkirk, the Scottish philanthropist whose 1812 settlement in the Red River Valley to the south laid the foundation for Winnipeg. During the late 19th- and early 20th centuries, Selkirk's position on the Red River made it a base for commerce and communication with communities on Lake Winnipeg. The Manitoba Marine Museum, at the entrance to Selkirk Park, harbours five of the original lake boats.

Chuck the Channel Catfish, a 9-metre (30-ft.) fiberglass statue, greets visitors on Main Street. The oversize catfish is an apt representation of the live version: Catfish weighing more than 9 kilograms (20 lbs.) abound in the Red River between Selkirk and Lockport.

St. Peter's Dynevor Church, 6.5 kilometres (4 mi.) northeast off Hwy. 59, was built in 1853. The original church, erected in 1836, was the center for Anglican missionary work among the Saulteaux First Nation.

Selkirk Biz : 200 Eaton Ave., Selkirk, MB, Canada R1A 0W6. **Phone:** (204) 482-7176.

◣GEM **LOWER FORT GARRY NATIONAL HISTORIC SITE,** 5 km (3 mi.) s. on Hwy. 9, is purportedly the oldest intact stone fur-trading post in North America. Farm produce constituted the majority of trade that went on between the locals and the Hudson's Bay Co. The 19th-century buildings have been restored and are furnished as they might have been in their early days. Costumed staff members perform tasks and reenact events that recreate the early 1850s atmosphere of the fort in its heyday. Guests can engage in hands-on historic experiences such as candlestick making and bannock baking. In the 1870s the site served other purposes, including serving as a training base for the North-West Mounted Police.

The grounds contain an impressive collection of early stone buildings; an exhibit showcases the historic architectural styles. The Visitor Reception Centre offers exhibits about the fort's history. Special events are held occasionally throughout the season.

Time: Allow 2 hours minimum. **Hours:** Daily 9:30-5, early May-Labour Day (limited services on weekends early May-June 30). **Cost:** $7.80; $6.55 (ages 65+). **Phone:** (204) 785-6050 or (888) 773-8888. GT ⑪ 🐾 🍽

AAA.com/ TourBook Comments

Let Your Voice Be Heard

If your visit to a listed property doesn't meet your expectations, tell us about it.

AAA.com/MemberFeedback

SHILO (G-2)

THE ROYAL REGIMENT OF CANADIAN ARTILLERY MUSEUM is on the Canadian Forces Base Shilo via Hwy. 340. One of the largest military museums in Canada, this indoor-outdoor museum exhibits more than 10,000 articles of dress, technical instruments, ammunition, small arms, guns and vehicles dating from World War II to the present. Among the more than 150 pieces of major military equipment dating to 1796 are German, Russian and French guns. The outdoor Gun Park features more than 30 exhibits and a picnic area.

Time: Allow 1 hour minimum. **Hours:** Daily 10-4, Victoria Day-Labour Day; Mon.-Fri. 10-4, rest of year. **Cost:** $6; $4 (veterans, including RCMP, ages 6-18 and 65+); free (ages 0-5). Guided tour $25. Cash only. **Phone:** (204) 765-3000, ext. 3570 or 3331 for information; ext. 4563 for tour reservations. 🕂

SOURIS (H-2) pop. 1,837, elev. 396m/1,300'

The free-swinging 177-metre (581-ft.) footbridge built in 1904 over the Souris (SIR-iss) River is considered the second longest free-suspension footbridge in Canada. The bridge was reconstructed after being destroyed by a flood in 1976. Victoria Park has more than 6 kilometres (4 mi.) of walking trails, a viewing tower and a bird sanctuary; phone (204) 483-5200.

Rockhounding in nearby agate pits yields agate, dendrite, jasper, petrified wood and epidote; the area offers one of the largest varieties of semi-precious stones found in North America. Permits are required and cost $21.52 per private vehicle. Contact the Rock Shop, 8 First St. S., Souris, MB, Canada R0K 2C0; phone (204) 483-2561.

STEINBACH (H-5) pop. 13,524, elev. 261m/900'

SAVE **MENNONITE HERITAGE VILLAGE,** 3 km (1.9 mi.) n. on Hwy. 12, centers on a replica of a Mennonite village with more than 20 completely furnished buildings that were moved to the site. On the 16-hectare (40-acre) grounds are a fruit garden, stock pens, a steam engine, gas tractors and other machinery. The village windmill is said to be one of only two of its kind in Canada. A museum displays antiques and manuscripts.

Time: Allow 2 hours minimum. **Hours:** Mon.-Sat. 9-6, Sun. 11:30-6, July-Aug.; Mon.-Sat. 9-5, Sun. 11:30-5, May-June and in Sept.; Tues.-Sat. 9-5, rest of year. **Cost:** $12; $10 (ages 13-22 and 65+); $6 (ages 6-12). **Phone:** (204) 326-9661 or (866) 280-8741.

DAYS INN   204/320-9200
🔷 APPROVED   Hotel. **Address:** 75 Hwy 12 N R5G 1T3

STONEWALL (G-4) pop. 4,536

Nobody knows for sure if Stonewall was named after founding father S.J. "Stonewall" Jackson or the limestone ridge on which the town is built. The name fits well, though, since limestone quarrying sustained the area's economy from the early 1880s until 1967. Stonewall's past is captured through the old stone buildings dotting its streets.

Town of Stonewall: 293 Main St., Box 250, Stonewall, MB, Canada R0C 2Z0. **Phone:** (204) 467-7979.

SWAN RIVER (D-2) pop. 3,907, elev. 340m/1,116'

During the last 13 years of the 18th century, control of the Swan River Valley was sought by both the North West Co. and the Hudson's Bay Co. Each company built fur-trading posts in the area, but by 1800 the concentrated trapping generated by the rivalry had depleted the number of fur-bearing animals. The Hudson's Bay Co. abandoned the area until the two companies joined in 1821.

The Swan River Valley, nestled between the Duck and Porcupine mountains, offers fishing, hunting, boating, camping, swimming and picnicking. Scenic Hwy. 10 passes just east of town.

Swan Valley Chamber of Commerce: 1500 Main St., Swan River, MB, Canada R0L 1Z0. **Phone:** (204) 734-3102.

SWAN VALLEY SUPER 8   204/734-7888
🔷 APPROVED   Hotel. **Address:** 115 Kelsey Tr R0L 1Z0

THOMPSON (B-3) pop. 12,829, elev. 206m/675'

Thompson sprang up after the discovery of one of the world's largest nickel deposits and is a major mining, communications, transportation, medical and retailing center. The King Miner statue sits atop underground mines and honors men and women miners at the southern entrance to town, 2.5 kilometres (1.5 mi.) south on Hwy. 6.

Lakes and rivers abound in this rugged, picturesque area. Paint Lake Provincial Recreation Park (see Recreation Areas Chart) is 32 kilometres (20 mi.) south on Hwy. 6.

Also south of Thompson on Hwy. 6 is the starting point for a 10 kilometre (6-mi.) hiking trail that will take you over a bridge to Kwasitchewan Falls, the highest waterfall in the province. Between Wabowden and Thompson, within Pisew Falls Provincial Park, is Pisew Falls, the second-highest waterfall in Manitoba accessible by road. A 1.3-kilometre (.8-mi.) trail leads from the highway through the dense foliage to a platform overlooking the 12.8-metre (42-ft.) falls. Twelve site plaques describe the flora and fauna of this boreal forest. Picnic facilities are available.

Thompson Spirit Way is a combination gravel and pavement path that offers 16 points of interest. Designed for bicycling or walking, the route starts at the Heritage North Museum and ends at Miles Hart

Bridge. Though hiking boots are not required, it is essential to wear comfortable walking shoes. The route stretches for 2 kilometres (1 mi.) and highlights include an 86-foot-tall wolf mural that is said to be the largest lighted mural in the world as well as a restored Norseman floatplane and a tribute to firefighters. Display panels share information about the sites and vantage points present scenic views. Official Spirit Way guidebooks may be purchased from the museum or the chamber of commerce.

Thompson Chamber of Commerce: #103 - 55 Selkirk Dr., Thompson, MB, Canada R8N 0M5. **Phone:** (204) 677-4155 or (888) 307-0103.

BEST WESTERN THOMPSON HOTEL & SUITES
204/778-8887

 THREE DIAMOND
Hotel

Best Western **AAA Benefit:** Members save up to 15% and earn bonus points!

Address: 205 Mystery Lake Rd R8N 1Z8 **Location:** Hwy 6 exit Mystery Lake Rd. **Facility:** 80 units, some efficiencies. 4 stories, interior corridors. **Parking:** winter plug-ins. **Amenities:** safes. **Activities:** sauna, exercise room. **Guest Services:** valet and coin laundry. **Featured Amenity:** breakfast buffet.

[SAVE] [↑] CALL [&] [↓↑] [BIZ] [HS]
[wifi] [X] [♣] [❚] [▭] [▱]

DAYS INN & SUITES   204/778-6000
APPROVED   Hotel. **Address:** 21 Thompson Dr N R8N 2B5

WAPUSK NATIONAL PARK (A-4)

Elevations in the park range from sea level along the Hudson Bay coastal areas to 94 metres (308 ft.) at Silcox Creek. Refer to CAA/AAA maps for additional elevation information.

South and east of Churchill on the shore of Hudson Bay, Wapusk (pronounced to rhyme with tusk) was established in 1996. The park consists of 11,475 square kilometres (7,119 sq. mi.). Translated from the Cree language, Wapusk means "white

bear," a fitting name for a park that has an area where polar bears den and produce offspring.

Much of the national park, part of the Hudson Bay and James Bay lowlands, is a flat plain covered by an extensive layer of peat; a layer of permafrost lies underneath. The treeless tundra consists mainly of wetlands—lakes, streams, bogs and rivers.

Polar bears congregate in the northern part of the park near Churchill around October, as they wait for freezing weather and the time when they can return to the ice in search of seals, their main food. The females dig their dens, and their young are born in late November and in December. The area around Churchill *(see place listing p. 348)* is one of the world's best places for viewing polar bears in their native habitat. Specialized tundra vehicles take visitors for close-up encounters.

The park, along a migratory flyway, also is a popular spring and fall feeding spot for waterfowl and shorebirds, including such rare species as the king eider, Ross' gull and gyrfalcon. Many build their nests here on the coast of Hudson Bay during the summer.

Churchill, in a somewhat remote location in northern Manitoba, can be reached by air and rail from Winnipeg. Since Wapusk is a wilderness park, it has no roads or trails. In order to visit the park, it is necessary to be part of an organized tour group, and several commercial operators provide tours into the park by plane or helicopter. The park office can provide a list. Park admission is free. For additional information contact Wapusk National Park, P.O. Box 127, Churchill, MB, Canada R0B 0E0; phone (204) 675-8863 or (888) 773-8888.

WINKLER (H-4) pop. 10,670, elev. 271m/890'

PEMBINA THRESHERMEN'S MUSEUM, 5 km (3 mi.) w. on Hwy. 3, features guided tours through displays of agricultural machinery, tools and household items as well as a steam threshing unit, a working sawmill and a seed elevator. **Time:** Allow 1 hour minimum. **Hours:** Mon.-Fri. 10-5, Sat.-Sun. and holidays 1-5, mid-May through Sept. 30. **Cost:** $10; $5 (ages 9-15 and 65+); free (ages 0-8). Prices may vary for special events. **Phone:** (204) 325-7497.

Hands-Free
IS NOT Risk-Free

Use hands-free systems cautiously and keep your focus on the road when driving.

AAA.com/**Distraction**

Winnipeg

Then & Now

The real estate agent's cry of "Location, location, location!" could have been invented in Winnipeg; the position of Manitoba's capital has determined the city's past and present. Archeological evidence shows that Winnipeg has been an important place of settlement for more than 6,000 years.

The confluence of the Red River, which flows south to north, and the Assiniboine River, whose eastward flowing waters were a main route of Western exploration, led to the founding of fur-trading posts in the early 18th century near Winnipeg's present site. The fertile lands created by the rivers later drew farmers and other settlers.

Still later, the area's position south of the rocks and peaks of the Canadian Shield meant that roads and railroads were forced to meet at Winnipeg, making it the point through which the eastbound raw materials of the West and the westbound manufactured goods of the East passed. Profiting by the hydroelectric power generated from its rivers, the city emerged in the 20th century as a manufacturing center.

French Canadian explorer and trader Pierre Gaultier de la Vérendrye founded Fort Rouge at the confluence of the rivers in 1738. This fur-trading post was succeeded by Fort Gibraltar, built by the North West Co. in 1804, and Fort Garry, founded by the Hudson's Bay Co. in 1821. In the same year, Lord Selkirk brought a party of Scottish settlers to these lands, a move that greatly disturbed the trappers and voyageurs who feared the destruction of their livelihoods.

AAA.com/travelguides—
more ways to look, book and save

The settlement managed to survive, shifting from trapping and hunting to agriculture. Because of aggressive Canadian advertising campaigns in Europe and a homestead policy similar to that being used to settle the plains of the United States, large numbers of immigrants began to move into the area in the 1860s.

In 1873 the village was incorporated and named for the Cree Nation words *win* ("muddy") and *nipee* ("water"). The railroad helped Winnipeg's growth still further: In 1876 the city began to ship wheat east, and when the Canadian Pacific Railway connected the coasts in 1885, freight and passengers began to flow through the city in both directions.

Winnipeg's diversity mirrors the many nationalities of its settlers, drawn by agriculture, the railroad or industry. From countries throughout Great Britain and Europe they came, creating a cultural mix reflected in the city's skyline, which includes the neoclassical splendor of the Manitoba Legislative Building, the century-old buildings of the Exchange

Manitoba Legislative Building

(Continued on p. 357.)

Fast Facts

ABOUT THE CITY

POP: 663,617 ▪ **ELEV:** 229 m/763 ft.

MONEY

SALES TAX: Manitoba's provincial sales tax is 8 percent. A 5 percent Goods and Services Tax (GST) is levied in Canada on most sales and services. There is a 5 percent accommodations tax on hotel/motel rooms where there are four or more letting rooms.

WHOM TO CALL

EMERGENCY: 911

POLICE (non-emergency): (204) 986-6222

TEMPERATURE: (204) 983-2050

HOSPITALS: Concordia Hospital, (204) 667-1560 ▪ Grace Hospital, (204) 837-0111 ▪ Health Sciences Centre, (204) 787-3661 ▪ St. Boniface Hospital, (204) 233-8563 ▪ Seven Oaks General Hospital, (204) 632-7133 ▪ Victoria General Hospital, (204) 269-3570.

VISITOR INFORMATION

Tourism Winnipeg: Suite 810, One Lombard Pl., Winnipeg, MB, Canada R3B 0X3. **Phone:** (204) 943-1970 or (855) 734-2489.

Tourism Winnipeg is open Mon.-Fri. 8:30-4:30.

Travel Manitoba Visitor Information Centre at The Forks: 21 Forks Market Rd., Winnipeg, MB, Canada R3C 4T7. **Phone:** (204) 927-7838 or (800) 665-0040. Travel Manitoba is staffed with on-site travel counselors daily 9-6. The telephones are manned daily 8:30-4:30. The 24-hour Forks Hot Line, (204) 957-7618, also provides information. The center features dioramas depicting the various regions of the province.

TRANSPORTATION

AIR TRAVEL: Cheap airline flights can be found from cities all over the country as well as internationally.

Winnipeg James Armstrong Richardson International Airport (YWG) is about 8 kilometres (5 mi.) northwest of downtown off Metro Rte. 90. Daily bus service between the airport and downtown is provided by Winnipeg Transit routes 15 and 20 between 5:50 a.m. and 12:49 a.m. The one-way fare is $2.95; $2.45 (ages 6-16 and 65+); passengers must have exact change—bills and pennies are not accepted. Phone 311 or (877) 311-4974 for information. Taxis to downtown cost around $20 and a sedan costs around $32. Major hotels offer limousine service for travel to and from the airport.

RENTAL CARS: Hertz, (800) 654-3080, offers discounts to AAA members. Winnipeg locations are at Winnipeg James Armstrong Richardson International Airport, phone (204) 925-6625, and 1577 Erin St., phone (204) 925-6629. Contact your AAA travel agent to add rental car reservations to your vacation packages.

 Book and save at **AAA.com/hertz**

RAIL SERVICE: The VIA Rail Canada depot is downtown at Union Station, 123 Main St.; phone (888) 842-7245.

TAXIS: Cab companies include Duffy's, (204) 925-0101 ▪ and Unicity, (204) 925-3131. Winnipeg rates start at $3.50 plus an average rate of $1.71 per kilometre or $2.02 per mile.

PUBLIC TRANSPORTATION: Winnipeg Transit, the public bus system, serves downtown Winnipeg and its suburbs. Route maps and route information are available by phoning 311 (within Winnipeg) or visiting the Winnipeg Transit website. Bus fare is $2.95, $2.45 (ages 6-16, ages 65+ and students with ID); riders must have exact change. More than 500 of the buses have accessibility features including low floors, electric ramps and priority accessible seating.

(Continued from p. 356.)
District and the rounded spires of the Ukrainian Orthodox Cathedral.

Archeological digs have uncovered evidence that The Forks' current site was a seasonal meeting place for aboriginal peoples more than 6,000 years ago. Tools, bones, footprints and pottery have been unearthed at the site located at the confluence of the Red and Assiniboine rivers. Still a meeting place, The Forks now has amenities like a food hall, a playground, entertainment venues, a skate park and a hotel. The Manitoba Children's Museum, the Canadian Museum for Human Rights and the Assiniboine Riverwalk are three highlights.

The Golden Boy, sculpted by Georges Gardet of Paris, is a 5.25-metre-tall (17.2-ft.) statue sheathed in 24 karat gold leaf atop the dome of the Manitoba Legislative Building. The statue was diverted on its journey from a French foundry during World War I, while the vessel carrying it transported troops for 2 years. After crossing the Atlantic many times, the golden immigrant was finally placed where he stands today, one hand holding aloft the torch of progress, the other cradling a symbolic sheaf of wheat.

Must Do: AAA Editor's Picks

- Roam 7 kilometres of mulch and limestone trails and explore floating wetland boardwalks at **FortWhyte Alive** (1961 McCreary Rd.), a nature park where you can get up close with wildlife and spot all sorts of critters—from bison and prairie dogs to deer and Canadian geese—in their natural habitat.

- Salute the province's beloved "Golden Boy" statue at the **Manitoba Legislative Building** (450 Broadway). The 5.25-metre-tall statue, gilded with 23.75-karat gold, stands atop the building's dome. A torch in one hand represents economic development and a sheaf of wheat in the other symbolizes agriculture. Visitors can tour the building on their own or with the help of a guide and see the remarkable architecture inside.

- Contemplate sculptures made of caribou antlers and dozens of handmade Inuit stone carvings at the **Winnipeg Art Gallery** (300 Memorial Blvd.), a strikingly designed Modernist building with European and Canadian pieces as well as one of the world's largest collections of contemporary Inuit art.

- Go on a behind-the-scenes tour of the production facilities at the **Royal Canadian Mint** (520 Lagimodiere Blvd.), where billions of Canadian circulation coins roll off the assembly line each year. Touring the mint is one of the many educational and fun things to do in Winnipeg.

- Survey the city skyline and the spot where the Red and Assiniboine rivers meet from a six-story-high viewing platform atop **The Forks Market** (1 Forks Market Rd.) at **The Forks,** one of the city's most popular gathering places. Inside the market are dozens of food stalls and mini restaurants where you can sample the best of Winnipeg cuisine. The Forks is also home to the **Canadian Museum for Human Rights (CMHR)** (85 Israel Asper Way), where powerful exhibits encourage visitors to discuss and take action to promote human rights. A glass spire at the top of the museum offers panoramic views of downtown.

- Hunt for treasures in the **Exchange District** (just north of Portage and Main), a historic neighborhood with early-20th-century architecture and independent shops and places to eat. If you're interested in an indoor shopping destination, you'll find more souvenir stores and local goodies at **The Forks Market** and in **Johnston Terminal** (25 Forks Market Rd.).

- Chant "GO Jets GO" like a true Jets fan at **Bell MTS Place** (300 Portage Ave.), where you can cheer on the Peg City's home team during a fast-paced hockey game. Just don't forget to wear your blue and white.

- Stroll on winding paths around flower beds in the English Gardens at **Assiniboine Park** (2355 Corydon Ave.), then explore the **Leo Mol Sculpture Garden,** where bronze statues and a water feature are highlights. If wildlife viewing is among your top things to do, visit **Assiniboine Park Zoo** for a peek at lions, tigers and bison. Snap a selfie with the statue of Winnie the Bear and his owner located by the Nature Playground; the lovable bear cub was the inspiration for A.A. Milne's character Winnie-the-Pooh. The 10-acre Arctic species exhibit, Journey to Churchill, includes polar bears, musk ox, wolves, ringed seals and harbor seals.

- Pack a picnic basket and head to **Kildonan Park** (2015 Main St.) for a bit of R & R and a stroll along the Red River on a tree-shaded path. Catch a Broadway-caliber musical on summer nights at the park's outdoor theater, Rainbow Stage, and don't miss the Witch's Hut (think "Hansel and Gretel") at the park's northern end.

- Cross the Esplanade Riel footbridge and step into **St. Boniface,** the French-speaking district filled with some of Winnipeg's oldest buildings. Visit **Le Musée de Saint-Boniface Museum** (494 Taché Ave.) for a lesson on Louis Riel and other early settlers, then stop by Riel's gravesite marked by a red granite tombstone in the churchyard of the **St. Boniface Cathedral** (180 Avenue de la Cathedrale).

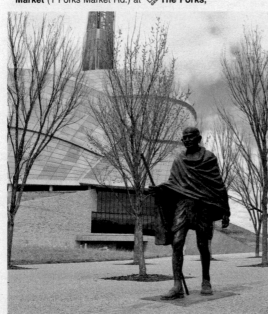

Canadian Museum for Human Rights

Winnipeg 1-day Itinerary

AAA editors suggest these activities for a great short vacation experience.

Morning

- Kick off your tour of the Peg City with an early start at **Stella's Café** (166 Osborne St.) just across the Assiniboine River in Osborne Village. This casual-yet-trendy eatery serves up yummy homemade breakfast foods all day, with options like heart-shaped waffles, baked eggs and fluffy banana pancakes topped with wild blueberries. Put in a takeout order for grilled cinnamon buns.

- After breakfast, a walking tour of vibrant and artsy **Osborne Village** is a must. Hunt for chic shoes, vintage threads or secondhand records in the stores along Osborne Street. The Village is a charming mix of old and new, with modern high-rises standing alongside turn-of-the-20th-century stone buildings.

- One of the best ways to get acquainted with Winnipeg in summer is by boat aboard **Splash Dash Guided River Tours.** Relax as your guide shares entertaining stories about city history on a 30-minute sightseeing cruise of the Red and Assiniboine rivers. Tours depart every 15 minutes from the dock at The Forks, but a water taxi can pick you up from any of seven city docks, including one at Osborne Street Bridge at the north end of Osborne Village.

Afternoon

- A great place to disembark is ▽ **The Forks,** the popular outdoor gathering spot where the Red and Assiniboine rivers meet. Make your way to **The Forks Market** (1 Forks Market Rd.) and **Johnston Terminal** (25 Forks Market Rd.), where you'll find coffee bars, souvenir shops and food stalls housed in renovated buildings from the railway era. For a casual alfresco lunch, **Smith** (the restaurant at **Inn at the Forks,** 75 Forks Market Rd.) is a sure bet.

- Follow the river walk north along the Red River to the Provencher Bridge. Look for the strikingly designed Esplanade Riel footbridge and cross the river to **St. Boniface,** Winnipeg's historic French district. At Tache and Cathedral avenues next to St. Boniface Cathedral is the grave of Louis Riel, the Métis leader celebrated as Manitoba's founder. Constructed in 1908 and severely damaged by fire in 1968, the beautiful stone façade of the cathedral is a magnificent photo spot. A stop at **Le Musée de Saint-Boniface Museum** (494 Taché Ave.) can provide a good overview of local history.

- Back in downtown Winnipeg, spend the rest of the afternoon at ▽ **Manitoba Museum** (190 Rupert Ave.). Climb aboard a full-size replica of the "Nonsuch," the British ship whose 1668 voyage to Hudson Bay opened western Canada to commerce. In the Urban Gallery, walk the streets of Winnipeg circa the 1920s in a recreated streetscape, complete with wooden boardwalks and boomtown-era storefronts.

The Forks Market

Evening

- Treat yourself to a fancy meal at a local restaurant. **Hy's Steakhouse & Cocktail Bar** (1 Lombard Pl.) offers perfectly prepared steaks in an upscale atmosphere. Seemingly made for special occasions is **529 Wellington** (at 529 Wellington Crescent), where you'll find an excellent selection of Canadian Prime beef and Manitoba wines served in a restored mansion. You can dine in a converted 1913 train station—complete with an attached rail car—at **Resto Gare** (630 Des Meurons St.), known for its French-Canadian cuisine.

- Looking for fun nightlife options? When the sun goes down, head to the **Exchange District** (just north of Portage and Main). The 20-block historic area gets its name from the Winnipeg Grain & Produce Exchange that formed here in the late 1800s. Today the district is chock-full of shops, bars and a few breweries known to attract a nighttime crowd. Find a bench in **Old Market Square** (Bannatyne Avenue and King Street) for prime people-watching or, if you're lucky, watch an outdoor performance on the stage during summer months.

- If indoor performances are more your style, take in a show at the **Royal Manitoba Theatre Centre (MTC) Mainstage** (174 Market Ave.). The theater presents classics, comedies and modern dramas October through May. Or, reserve seats at **Centennial Concert Hall** (555 Main St.) to see the **Canada's Royal Winnipeg Ballet.** For information and tickets, phone (204) 942-6537 for the MTC Mainstage or (204) 956-2792 for the Royal Winnipeg Ballet.

Top Picks for Kids

Under 13

- Little ones can burn off excess energy at **Assiniboine Park** (2355 Corydon Ave.), where the Nature Playground gets rave reviews. Colorful rubber "mountains" encourage running up and down between slides, swings, net ladders, a crow's nest and other creative play areas. See if you can find the statue of Winnie the Bear and his owner near the playground; the black bear cub was the inspiration for A.A. Milne's character Winnie-the-Pooh.

- Visiting the Nature Playground is just one of the many fun things to do at Assiniboine Park. Stroll around the duck pond, grab lunch at the café or take a ride on the miniature steam train. Another kid-friendly spot is the **Assiniboine Park Zoo** (2595 Roblin Blvd.), where you can check out polar bears, wolves, tigers and shaggy-coated musk oxen, among other species.

- Looking for family-friendly activities in June? The **Winnipeg International Children's Festival** (1 Forks Market Rd.), aka "Kidsfest," boasts a full schedule of interactive and fun activities for kids including storytelling, theater, live music performances, puppetry, acrobatic acts and dance. A one-time admission fee covers all events during this 4-day festival.

- Reward good behavior with a sweet treat from **Sargent Sundae** (2053 Portage Ave.), a popular spot for ice cream near Assiniboine Park. There's almost always a line out the door at this local favorite, especially on hot summer days.

Sweet treat from Sargent Sundae

Two points to note: it's cash only, and it's open seasonally, March through November.

Teens

- Snap an Instagram-worthy photo at the **Royal Aviation Museum of Western Canada** (958 Ferry Rd.). Housed in an aircraft hangar, the museum showcases restored bush planes, military aircraft and commercial airliners. You can even get a peek inside a 1970s Air Canada jet in near-perfect condition. (Note: The museum is temporarily closed until 2021 as it relocates to a new facility.)

- Ditch the mall and head to **The Exchange District** (near Portage Avenue and Main Street), a 20-square-block area with early-20th-century buildings housing specialty shops, clothing boutiques, vintage stores and cafés. It's easy to hop from one store to the next and browse all sorts of goods in search of the perfect souvenir to remember your trip to Winnipeg.

- Part natural history museum, part science gallery and part planetarium, **Manitoba Museum** (190 Rupert Ave.) is a good spot to spend a day if you're wondering what to do with kids and teens. Walk-through galleries and detailed dioramas introduce visitors to Manitoba history, while planetarium shows offer a high-tech look at the solar system.

All Ages

- Celebrate the start of summer at one of the top family events in Winnipeg—the **Red River Exhibition** (3977 Portage Ave. W.). The 10-day fair boasts what is said to be the world's largest traveling midway, with about 50 rides and coasters to entertain kids both big and small. Other highlights include dog agility shows, a petting zoo, nightly concerts and plenty of deep-fried fair foods.

- A gathering place for visitors and Winnipeggers alike, **The Forks** (1 Forks Market Rd.) is the spot for shopping, dining, entertainment and outdoor recreation. Kids will make a beeline for the imaginative Variety Heritage Adventure Park playground and splash pad, while older teens will want to browse the shops and food stalls in Johnston Terminal and **The Forks Market.**

- Root for the home team at a **Winnipeg Goldeyes** baseball game. The minor league team plays ball at **Shaw Park** (1 Portage Ave.) from May to late August. Hot dogs for the kiddos, craft beer for the parents and crowd-pleasing entertainment for all guarantees a day that is memorable for the whole family.

- Finding places to eat with kids can be a challenge, but **Stella's Café** (166 Osborne St.) makes it easy. A local favorite for kid-friendly dining, Stella's has a casual atmosphere and simple, fresh dishes that are sure to please picky eaters. Order off the all-day breakfast menu or choose from lunch items like grass-fed burgers, pasta bowls or chili.

Arriving
By Car

Forming a circle around Winnipeg is a perimeter highway. To the north of the Trans-Canada Highway, the major approach from the east and west, this perimeter road is designated Hwy. 101. To the south of the Trans-Canada Highway it is numbered Hwy. 100.

There are three major approaches to the perimeter highway: the Trans-Canada Highway, which approaches from both the east and west, and Hwy. 75, which approaches from the south. To the west of the city the Trans-Canada Highway is posted Hwy. 1W; from the east, Hwy. 1E.

Within the perimeter highway all three major approaches change designation: Hwy. 1W becomes Metro Rte. 85, Hwy. 1E becomes Metro Rte. 135, and Hwy. 75 becomes Metro Rte. 42.

Getting Around

Generally, rush hour in Winnipeg is from 7:30 to 9 a.m. and 3:30 to 5:30 p.m. and should be avoided if possible. If driving during these times, be careful and be patient; the city's speed limit is 50 kilometres per hour (30 mph) unless otherwise posted.

Note the pedestrian crosswalks marked by pavement stripes and illuminated overhead signs. All vehicles must stop if the crosswalk is occupied by a pedestrian or if a pedestrian on the curb indicates an intention to cross. No vehicle may pass another that is stopped or slowing to yield to a pedestrian. Right turns on red are permitted after a stop, unless otherwise posted.

Street System

Winnipeg's streets are laid out in a number of grids, but each is oriented to a different compass direction. Visitors will find it easiest to orient themselves to the major thoroughfares, which have signs carrying the word "Route" and a number. Routes ending in even numbers designate north-south thoroughfares, and those ending in odd numbers designate major east-west arteries.

The primary north-south routes that cross the downtown area are 42, 52 and 62. The major east-west highways include 105, 115, 57 and 85. A good street map will help drivers to see how the various grids of named streets connect with the main numbered routes.

Parking

It is recommended for visitors to park in a commercial lot, where rates average $1–$5 per hour. Daily rates are about $10. Parking meters downtown cost $2.50–$3.50 per hour (8 a.m. to 5:30 p.m.), but most carry a 2-hour limit. Free 2-hour parking in designated metered areas downtown is offered on Saturday while parking is free all day on Sunday.

Parking is strictly controlled along major downtown streets. Cars parked between signs reading "No Parking Between" from 7 to 9 a.m. and 3:30 to 5:30 p.m. will be towed. Once a vehicle has been parked at a meter for the maximum time for which a

Johnston Terminal

fee can be paid, it must be moved through an intersection before parking at a different meter. Remetering (putting additional money into the meter after time has expired) is not allowed.

Shopping

Winnipeg's malls, local boutiques and farmers' markets offer all sorts of unique gifts and souvenirs. Check out our picks for the best places to shop in Winnipeg.

For local goods and one-of-a-kind souvenirs, you'll want to check out the shops in downtown Winnipeg. ⧩ The Forks (1 Forks Market Rd.) is a fun place to explore; it is home to The Forks Market *(see attraction listing p. 368)*, a two-story building with numerous food stalls and souvenir stores, and Johnston Terminal, which has additional specialty boutiques and a basement-level antique mall.

Overwhelmed by the shopping options at The Forks? Two highlights you shouldn't miss are Forks Trading Company (upstairs at The Forks Market) and WAG@The Forks, an outpost of the Winnipeg Art Gallery (on the ground floor of Johnston Terminal).

Another good place to browse for Winnipeg-themed gifts is the boutique inside the ⧩ Canadian Museum for Human Rights (CMHR), adjacent to The Forks. The shop is free to enter and remains open 30 minutes after the museum closes.

The historic Exchange District (just north of the intersection of Portage and Main streets) has the best selection of Winnipeg clothing boutiques, vintage shops and art galleries. A few standouts: Toad

Hall Toys (54 Arthur St.) has games, books and vintage toys; **Tiny Feast** (217 McDermot Ave.) is a stationary shop with artsy gifts; **Lennard Taylor** (246 McDermot Ave.) stocks high-end women's fashions; and **Tara Davis Studio Boutique** (246 McDermot Ave.) is the place to go for handmade goods from locals.

If you prefer your shopping experience to be climate-controlled and under one roof, several Winnipeg malls may be of interest. Downtown malls include **cityplace**, 333 St. Mary Ave. at Hargrave Street, which is connected to Bell MTS Place and the RBC Convention Centre via a system of elevated skywalks, and **Portage Place** at 393 Portage Ave. Both shopping centers have food courts popular with downtown office workers.

For shopping on a larger scale, head west of downtown to **CF Polo Park**, 1485 Portage Ave. Said to be the largest shopping center in Manitoba, it counts Hudson's Bay among its more than 200 stores.

Relatively new to the Winnipeg shopping scene is **Outlet Collection Winnipeg**, 555 Sterling Lyon Pkwy., with close to 100 stores perfect for bargain hunters, including Banana Republic Factory Store, Nike Factory Store, Saks Fifth Avenue Off 5th, Samsonite Factory Outlet and Winners. An IKEA store is nearby at 500 Sterling Lyon Pkwy.

About 15 minutes south of downtown is **St. Vital Centre**, 86-1225 St. Mary's Rd., where you'll find Hudson's Bay, Chapters and more than 100 other stores. **Kildonan Place**, 1555 Regent Ave. W., is 15 minutes east of downtown Winnipeg and counts H&M, HomeSense, Marshalls and Urban Planet among its stores.

If you're hunting for deals, a few additional factory outlet stores might be worth a stop. **Canada West Boots**, 1250 Fife St., has a large selection of Western wear, boots and hats. **Winnipeg Outfitters Inc.** is near the Winnipeg airport at 250 McPhillips St. and offers discounted outerwear and cold weather accessories.

Browse locally made goods and gifts at the **Downtown Winnipeg Farmers' Market**, held on Thursdays 10-2:30 in two locations: Manitoba Hydro Place Plaza (360 Portage Ave.) and True North Square Plaza (242 Hargrave St.). Another popular shopping event is the **Downtown Winnipeg Night Market**, which takes place the last Friday of the month (4-11) in June, July and August at Manitoba Hydro Place Plaza and along Kennedy Street between Portage and Graham avenues.

Looking for things to do this weekend? Pay a visit to Winnipeg's largest and most popular farmers' market, the **St. Norbert Farmers' Market**. The market sets up on Saturdays 8-3 (mid-May to mid-October) and also on Wednesdays 11-3 (early June to early September) at 3514 Pembina Hwy., 16 kilometres (10 mi.) south of downtown. You'll find baked goods, fresh produce, flowers, furniture, jewelry and other items from more than 50 local vendors.

Nightlife

Winnipeg offers plenty of things to do after dark. Whether you're in the mood for cocktails and local beers or a night out at a Winnipeg Jets hockey game, here are some of your best options for Winnipeg nightlife. (Note: The legal drinking age in Winnipeg, Manitoba, is 18 years of age.)

Chat with artists and browse pop-up shops during **First Fridays in the Exchange,** a free event held on the first Friday evening of the month in the Exchange District. Participating art galleries, boutiques and Winnipeg bars in the Exchange District (a 20-block area centered at 133 Albert St.) cater to the after-dark crowd with special events and deals from 5 to 9 p.m.

Coffee shop and restaurant by day, bar and event space by night, hipster-friendly **Forth** (171 McDermot Ave.) promises a night out like a true Winnipeg local. Head down to the basement level for specialty cocktails, live music and various events in a candlelit room (just not on Mondays when the bar is closed), or ascend to the rooftop patio (open Tues.-Sat. weather permitting) for drinks with a view. Check their website to see what's on.

If you speak the language of hops and IBUs, you'll be happy to know that Winnipeg's craft beer scene is booming thanks to recent changes to Manitoba liquor laws. Two Winnipeg brewpubs are worth a stop: **Nonsuch Brewing Company** (125 Pacific Ave.) pours Belgian-style ales in a cozy, Instagram-worthy taproom, while **Little Brown Jug** (336 William Ave.) serves their signature pale ale in an industrial building that once served as the livery stables for City Hall. (Note: Many Winnipeg breweries are closed on Sundays and Mondays.)

Gather 'round long communal tables and sip on Canadian craft beers and international wines at **The Common,** located inside **The Forks Market** food hall (1 Forks Market Rd.). If you'd rather wander than sit, you can take your drinks with you as you browse the market's food stalls and kiosks on the ground floor. Expect a great selection of libations, as The Common's beer and wine lists are carefully curated by one of the top sommeliers in the world.

Linger over handcrafted cocktails, desserts, digestifs and non-alcoholic cocktails at **SMITH**, the AAA Three Diamond restaurant inside **Inn at the Forks** (75 Forks Market Rd.). The lounge is a popular place to congregate on Friday and Saturday evenings for live music, and an outdoor patio draws a crowd in summer.

Another Winnipeg hotel bar near The Forks has a good nightlife scene: **The Palm Lounge** at **The Fort Garry Hotel Spa & Conference Centre** (222 Broadway). A soaring domed ceiling and nightly live music will make for a memorable evening whether you're looking for a romantic night out or a nightcap after a long day of sightseeing.

While many bars in Winnipeg are closed on Sundays, the **Times Change(d) High & Lonesome Club** (234 Main St.) throws its doors wide open on

Sunday evenings for its long-running blues jam, a favorite among Winnipeggers. You can count on live music a few other nights of the week at this gritty-yet-friendly honky-tonk; check the online calendar for the current schedule.

Music performers, face painters, vendor booths and a family-friendly beer and wine garden are among the big draws at the **Downtown Winnipeg Night Market,** held on the last Friday of the month in June, July and August. Vendors set up shop at Manitoba Hydro Place Plaza (360 Portage Ave.) and along Kennedy Street between Portage and Graham avenues from 4 to 11 p.m.

Hockey is big in the 'Peg, and cheering on the National Hockey League's **Winnipeg Jets** at a home game is one of the fun things to do with kids in Winnipeg after dark. Home games take place at Bell MTS Place (300 Portage Ave.), said to be one of the loudest arenas in the league. The Jets' regular season runs October through April.

Big Events

Winnipeg's calendar of events, with more than 170 days of festivals, reflects more than 43 nationalities that have made the city home. The *joie de vivre* spirit of the French voyageurs is revived each February during ▽ **Festival du Voyageur,** a 10-day-long celebration that includes winter sports, ice-sculpting contests, music and food. With the 18th-century fur trade as its theme, the event takes place in St. Boniface, Winnipeg's French quarter.

In early May, crowds yuk it up at the **Winnipeg Comedy Festival** featuring humor-industry headliners. In May, **Manito Ahbee** celebrates Indigenous music, art and culture. The name, which means "where the creator sits," honors a sacred site in Whiteshell Provincial Park where Indigenous people gathered for hundreds of years to teach and share wisdom. Events and fun things to do include music awards, a marketplace and an international powwow.

A festival at The Forks and a parade through the streets of downtown are part of the festivities that take place during the **Pride Winnipeg Festival,** held in late May or early June. The city plays host to the 4-day **Winnipeg International Children's Festival** at **The Forks** in early June. Music, theater, dance and comedy performances are offered as well as hands-on workshops and evening shows that are fun activities to add to your family vacation.

The **Winnipeg International Jazz Festival** in mid-June features jazz performers on an outdoor stage in Old Market Square as well as at indoor venues across the city. The ▽ **Red River Exhibition,** known locally as "The Ex" is held during mid- and late June. The Ex's many rides, midway activities and games of chance as well as nightly concerts take place at **Red River Exhibition Park** off Perimeter Highway behind Assiniboia Downs. The event also includes a petting zoo and agricultural displays.

Early July brings the 4-day ▽ **Winnipeg Folk Festival** to nearby **Birds Hill Provincial Park,** where more than 200 concerts, children's activities, music workshops and food are highlights. Consider adding this event to your vacation packages. In mid- and late July is the **Winnipeg Fringe Festival,** with various independent theater performances in the Exchange District and other locations throughout the city.

Early August brings the 2-week ▽ **Folklorama** multicultural celebration, Winnipeg's largest event and reputedly the largest and longest-running multicultural festival of its kind. The costumes, dances and food of more than 40 cultures are showcased. It's one of the many fun things to do with friends.

Celebrate the holidays from early December through early January in Red River Exhibition Park at **Canad Inns Winter Wonderland,** one of Manitoba's largest drive-through light displays. Illuminated by more than 1 million lights, the 2.25-kilometre route features 26 themed areas and a 75-foot-tall Christmas tree. Ice-skating and sleigh rides are offered on the weekends; the outdoor activities are among the romantic things for couples to do in winter.

Sports & Rec

Devotees of organized sports will find many opportunities to cheer on the local teams in Winnipeg. Canadians love **hockey,** and those who fancy flying sticks and flashing skates will find the National Hockey League's **Winnipeg Jets** facing off against their opponents downtown at **Bell MTS Place** (formerly MTS Centre, 300 Portage Ave.), September through April. Also at this venue is the **Manitoba**

Attend the Winnipeg International Jazz Festival

Play racquetball at athletic clubs

Moose of the American Hockey League, who play October through April; phone (204) 987-7825.

Football fans can watch the Canadian Football League's **Winnipeg Blue Bombers** play at **IG Field** at the University of Manitoba from June to November; phone (204) 784-2583 for office. The American Association of Independent Professional **Baseball**'s **Winnipeg Goldeyes** play at **Shaw Park** (near The Forks at 1 Portage Ave. E.) from May to late August; phone (204) 982-2273 for tickets.

Sports car racing enthusiasts converge at the **Red River Co-op Speedway,** (204) 582-0527, on Cartier Road, Ste. Adolphe, off Hwy. 75, 8 kilometres (5 mi.) south of St. Norbert, from May through October (weather permitting).

Assiniboia Downs, 3975 Portage Ave. at the Perimeter Highway, offers **Thoroughbred racing** early May to late September. Simulcast races are offered year-round; phone (204) 885-3330.

Note: Policies concerning admittance of children to pari-mutuel betting facilities vary. Phone for information.

Other spectator sports and things to see in Winnipeg include minor league hockey, **curling** and **ringette** games, held at municipal skating rinks, and **cricket** played in Assiniboine Park. Ringette, similar to hockey, is a popular women's sport developed in Canada.

There are 27 **golf** courses in the Winnipeg area. Nine-hole public courses include **Crescent Drive,** 781 Crescent Dr., (204) 986-5911; **Harbour View,** 1867 Springfield Rd., (204) 222-2751; **The Players Course,** 2695 Inkster Blvd., (204) 697-4976; and **Winnipeg Canoe Club,** 50 Dunkirk Dr., (204)

233-1105. Among the 18-hole public courses are **Kildonan Park,** 2021 Main St., (204) 986-5679; **Tuxedo,** 400 Shaftesbury Blvd., (204) 888-2867; **Meadows at East St. Paul,** 2511 McGregor Farm Rd. N. (adjacent to Hwy. 59), (204) 667-4653; **Shooters Family Golf Centre,** 2731 Main St., (204) 339-2326; and **Windsor Park,** 10 Des Meurons St., (204) 986-3006. **John Blumberg,** 4540 Portage Ave., (204) 986-3490, offers both nine- and 18-hole layouts.

Winnipeg has 115 **tennis** courts, some lighted for night matches. Many courts are at community centers. Championship matches are held during the summer at various locations throughout the city. **Squash, handball** and **racquetball** players can find courts at a number of athletic clubs and local universities. For information contact Sport Manitoba; phone (204) 925-5600.

Fans of **bicycling** and **in-line skating** take to the marked paths in Winnipeg's city parks. Bicycle trails along less-traveled side streets in and around Winnipeg also have been established. A multi-use path along the Red River connects the Exchange District with Osborne Village and offers great views of the waterfront; the stretch through Stephen Juba Park is particularly scenic.

In winter, The Forks offers **ice-skating** on the Red River Mutual Trail, said to be the world's longest naturally frozen skating trail. Warming huts are stationed along the trail, and rental skates are available in season (typically January through March).

Cross-country skiing, tobogganing and ice-skating facilities are available at Assiniboine, Kildonan and St. Vital parks; facilities for ice-skating also are found at numerous schools and community clubs. **Downhill skiing** is available at **Springhill Winter Park Ski Area,** (204) 224-3051, near **Birds Hill Provincial Park** at the junction of Hwy. 59N at the Floodway; and **Stony Mountain Ski Area,** (204) 344-5977, 11 kilometres (6 mi.) north of the Perimeter Highway on Hwy. 7. Birds Hill Provincial Park, (204) 654-6730, also is a site for **snowmobiling** and cross-country skiing.

Swimming can be pursued all year in Winnipeg, where numerous indoor pools include those at four YM-YWCAs; phone (204) 947-3044. The **Pan Am Pool,** 25 Poseidon Bay, is one of the largest indoor bodies of water in Canada and is open all year; phone (877) 311-4974.

Many recreational activities and fun things to do are available at the **Harbour View Recreation Complex** in the northeastern section of Winnipeg in **Kilcona Park,** 1867 Springfield Rd. At this 162-hectare (400-acre) park are facilities for **miniature golf, lawn bowling, shuffleboard** and **horseshoes** as well as tennis courts, a 27-hole golf course and a driving range during the summer. Golf and tennis lessons are available April to October. Ice-skating, tobogganing and cross-country skiing are available during the winter. Phone (204) 222-2751.

Performing Arts

If you're looking for cultural things to do in Winnipeg, you're in luck, as there are many venues that celebrate the performing arts around the city. Canada's **Royal Winnipeg Ballet**, Winnipeg Symphony Orchestra and Manitoba Opera perform in Centennial Concert Hall, 555 Main St., opposite City Hall. The oldest company in Canada and the second oldest in North America, Canada's Royal Winnipeg Ballet is known for its versatile style and performs an eclectic mix of classical and contemporary ballets. At-home performances are from October through May. For ticket information phone (204) 949-3999.

The **Winnipeg Symphony Orchestra** performs mid-September to May and offers classical, contemporary and popular orchestral music; for concert information phone (204) 949-3999. The **Manitoba Opera** performs October through May; phone (204) 942-7479, or (204) 944-8824 for tickets.

Modern dance is presented by **Winnipeg's Contemporary Dancers** from October through April at the **Rachel Browne Theatre**, 211 Bannatyne Ave.; for information phone (204) 452-0229.

Theater lovers and those looking for things for couples to do can enjoy performances of the classics, comedies and modern dramas at the **Royal Manitoba Theatre Centre (Royal MTC) John Hirsch Mainstage**, 174 Market St., from October to May; for general information or tickets phone (204) 942-6537. The **Royal MTC Tom Hendry Warehouse Theatre**, 140 Rupert Ave., (204) 942-6537, is a good destination for alternative theater performances from November to April. **The Lyric Theatre**, 55 Pavilion Crescent, just east of the Pavilion in Assiniboine Park, (204) 927-6000, is an outdoor theater showcasing performances by the Winnipeg Pops Orchestra, the Winnipeg Symphony Orchestra and other musical groups.

For adults and young people interested in fun things to do with friends, the **Prairie Theatre Exchange**, at Portage Place, 393 Portage Ave., (204) 942-5483 for ticket information, presents a season of modern Canadian plays from October to April. **Rainbow Stage** in Kildonan Park offers musicals in a covered outdoor theater from June through August; phone (204) 989-0888 or (888) 989-0888. **Celebrations Dinner Theatre**, 1824 Pembina Hwy. in the Canad Inns Destination Centre Fort Garry, combines an original, three-act musical comedy with a four-course dinner for a one-stop evening out; phone (204) 982-8282.

A variety of theatrical productions for children of all ages is presented at the **Manitoba Theatre for Young People** in The Forks; for information phone (204) 942-8898.

The **Burton Cummings Theatre for the Performing Arts** (The Burt), 364 Smith St., was constructed in 1906-07. Originally named Walker Theatre, it was designed to host ballets, Broadway shows and operas. The Burt now offers touring shows and concerts by top-name performers; phone (204) 987-7825.

The French Canadian heritage of St. Boniface, in the heart of the French district, is remembered through the support of the **Centre Culturel Franco-Manitobain** at 340 Provencher Blvd.; phone (204) 233-8972. The center is the home of such cultural groups as **Le Cercle Molière** theater company (North America's longest running theater company), phone (204) 233-8053; the dance group **L'Ensemble Folklorique de la Rivière Rouge**, phone (204) 233-8972; and the choral groups **L'Alliance Chorale Manitoba** and **La Chorale des Intrépides**; phone (204) 233-7423 for more information.

ATTRACTIONS

 For a complete list of attractions, visit AAA.com/travelguides/attractions

ASSINIBOINE PARK is at jct. Park Blvd. and Corydon Ave.; it also may be accessed from Portage Ave. via a footbridge over the Assiniboine River. The 153-hectare (378-acre) park has an English garden, a sculpture garden, a duck pond, a miniature steam train, a children's playground, a small art gallery (the Pavilion Gallery Museum), a zoo and an outdoor theater where concerts are held in summer. Large grassy areas and walking and biking paths provide recreational opportunities; tobogganing, cross-country skiing and ice-skating are available in the winter. Winnipeg's only cricket tournaments are played in the park.

Assiniboine Forest, south of the park off Grant Avenue, is one of the largest urban nature parks in Canada. The 283-hectare (700-acre) forest of aspen and oak is home to more than 39 species of mammals, including deer and foxes, and more than 80 species of birds. The 1-kilometre (.6-mi.) Saginay Trail leads hikers to Eve Werier Pond, where a variety of waterfowl can be seen. **Hours:** The park is open daily 24 hours. Playground daily 8-dusk. Pavilion Gallery Museum daily 9-5, mid-Mar. to mid-Oct.; 9-4, rest of year. **Cost:** Free. **Phone:** (204) 927-6000 or (877) 927-6006.

Assiniboine Park Zoo, in Assiniboine Park at 2595 Roblin Blvd., has more than 1,500 animals representing some 200 different species in naturalistic settings. The zoo specializes in animals found in cooler climates from around the world as well as native North American species. Siberian tigers, snow leopards, two Asian lions, Stellar sea eagles, lynxes, bison, and many other hardy species can be seen outside throughout the year. The Journey to Churchill exhibit features polar bears and other northern species. Large indoor facilities provide warm-weather viewing of many tropical animals. A butterfly

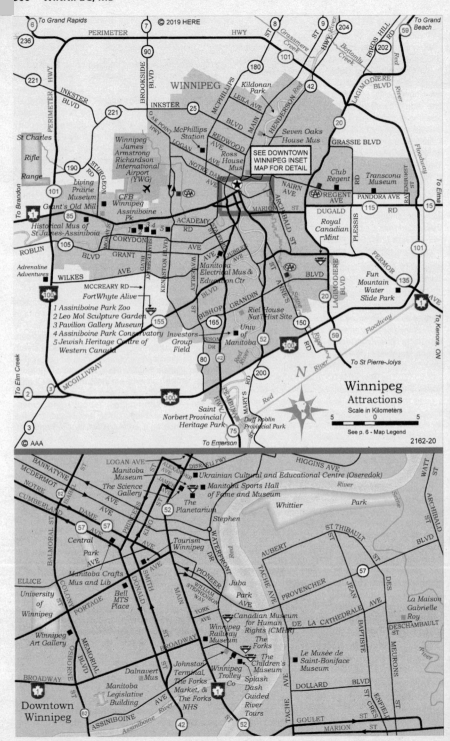

To Grand Rapids

© 2019 HERE

To Grand Beach

PERIMETER   HWY

WINNIPEG

SEE DOWNTOWN
WINNIPEG INSET
MAP FOR DETAIL

1 Assiniboine Park Zoo
2 Leo Mol Sculpture Garden
3 Pavilion Gallery Museum
4 Assiniboine Park Conservatory
5 Jewish Heritage Centre of
   Western Canada

Winnipeg
Attractions
Scale in Kilometers

See p. 6 - Map Legend

© AAA

2162-20

Downtown
Winnipeg

garden is open in the summer months. A 360-degree theater also is on site.

Hours: Daily 9-5, mid-Mar. to mid-Oct.; 9-4, rest of year. Phone ahead for schedule on Nov. 11, Christmas Eve and Dec. 31. Closed Christmas. **Cost:** $20.50; $17.75 (ages 13-17 and 60+); $11.25 (ages 3-12). **Phone:** (204) 927-6000 or (877) 927-6006. 🍴 🎨

Leo Mol Sculpture Garden, in Assiniboine Park at 2355 Corydon Ave., is said to be the first sculpture garden in North America dedicated to the works of a single artist. The garden and gallery feature bronze sculptures, porcelains, paintings and sketches by the Winnipeg artist. The gardens also are home to the Leo Mol Schoolhouse Studio. A reflecting pool and fountain are located in front of the gallery. **Hours:** Grounds open daily 9-dusk, mid-Mar. to mid-Oct. **Cost:** Donations. **Phone:** (204) 927-6000.

Pavilion Gallery Museum is in Assiniboine Park at 55 Pavilion Crescent. Housed on the second and third floors of a restored 1930 pavilion, the museum contains a permanent collection featuring the work of prominent Manitoba artists Ivan Eyre, Walter J. Phillips, Leo Mol and Clarence Tillenius. The Pooh Gallery tells the story of Winnie-the-Pooh and his connection to Winnipeg. **Time:** Allow 30 minutes minimum. **Hours:** Daily 9-5, mid-Mar. to mid-Oct.; daily 9-4, rest of year. **Cost:** Free. **Phone:** (204) 927-6000.

DALNAVERT MUSEUM, .5 blk. s. of Broadway at 61 Carlton St., is the former home of Sir Hugh John Macdonald, prominent lawyer and politician and son of John A. Macdonald, the first prime minister of Canada. Built in 1895, it was one of the first houses in Winnipeg to have hot-water heating, electric lighting and indoor plumbing.

Named after the Scottish birthplace of Macdonald's grandmother, the red brick Queen Anne Revival-style house features stained-glass windows and a wraparound verandah. The restored house, which was saved from demolition in 1969, is opulently furnished with Victorian antiques. Tours include a guided tour of the house and a self-guiding audio tour providing a glimpse into the lifestyles of early 20th-century Winnipeg society and the Macdonald family.

The visitor center at the rear of museum has been designed as a "green" building, incorporating reclaimed and recycled materials during its construction and utilizing geothermal energy to heat and cool the building.

Time: Allow 1 hour minimum. **Hours:** Wed.-Sat. 12-4. Hours may vary; phone ahead to confirm schedule. Closed major holidays. **Cost:** $6; $5 (ages 65+); $4 (ages 4-17). Rates may vary during special events. **Phone:** (204) 943-2835.

THE FORKS, at the confluence of the Red and Assiniboine rivers at 1 Forks Market Rd. at jct. Waterfront Dr., has been a meeting place for more than 6,000 years, beginning with the aboriginal peoples. By virtue of location the 23-hectare (56-acre) site evolved into the center of the European fur trade in the 1730s. Métis, natives and eventually European settlers created a community along the rivers.

Now Winnipeg's main gathering spot, The Forks is a favorite place for shopping, dining, entertainment and outdoor fun. Attractions include the Canadian Museum for Human Rights, The Forks Market food hall, The Forks National Historic Site, The Children's Museum, a playground and a skateboarding park. Also on the grounds are sculptures, walking paths, restored railcars and a public amphitheater. Johnston Terminal, 25 Forks Market Rd., is a renovated railway cold storage warehouse that now houses shops and an antique mall; phone (204) 947-1250.

The Riverwalk, open in summer depending on water levels, follows the water's edge from The Forks to the Manitoba Legislature Building through downtown Winnipeg. Canoes can be rented seasonally at The Forks Historic Port. Concerts and special events take place at The Forks throughout the year (see Big Events p. 363). The Travel Manitoba Visitor Information Centre at The Forks provides information about events and attractions around the province. **Hours:** Grounds daily 24 hours. The Forks Market daily 7 a.m.-11 p.m. Johnston Terminal daily 10-6 (also Fri. 6-9). Hours vary for the museums. **Cost:** Free. Admission is charged at the Canadian Museum for Human Rights and The Children's Museum. **Phone:** (204) 947-9236. 🍴

Canadian Museum for Human Rights (CMHR) is at The Forks, 85 Israel Asper Way. On a self-guiding audio tour you can leisurely stroll up the glowing ramps from floor to floor to view 11 galleries housing art, artifacts, film, photography and interactive digital exhibits that encourage visitors to discuss and take action to promote human rights. A highlight of the museum is a circular theater in which you can view a 360-degree film featuring four generations of indigenous people sharing stories about responsibilities and rights.

The eight-story building features four main parts: the Roots, the Mountain, the Cloud and the Tower of Hope. The journey of discovery begins at the Roots, where you will find temporary gallery and the Great Hall. The Mountain galleries display the museum's core exhibits, and the three-story glass Cloud wraps around an interior Garden of Contemplation, a space with basalt rock and pools of water. The Cloud is made up of 1,300 panes of glass. The glass-spire Tower of Hope provides panoramic views of Winnipeg and surrounding areas. Guided and self-guiding tours are available. **Time:** Allow 2 hours minimum. **Hours:** Daily 10-5 (also Wed. 5-9), Victoria Day-Labour Day; Tues.-Sun. and Mon. holidays 10-5 (also Wed. 5-9), rest of year. Architectural and gallery tours are offered; phone for schedule. Closed Christmas and one week in mid-Jan. Phone ahead to confirm schedule. **Cost:** $18; $14 (ages

65+ and students with ID); $8 (ages 7-17); $47 (family, two adults and four children); $5 (Wed. 5-9 p.m.); free (first Wed. 5-9 p.m.). **Phone:** (204) 289-2000 or (877) 877-6037. GT 🍴

The Children's Museum, at The Forks, 45 Forks Market Rd., occupies Manitoba's oldest train repair facility. The museum houses a dozen colorful galleries offering a wide variety of educational and fun hands-on activities. Junction 9161 and the Engine House galleries immerse visitors in train history with a 1910 Pullman passenger coach and a 1952 diesel locomotive. A walk through the Illusion Tunnel will test perceptions. Tot Spot caters to little ones. Other areas include Splash Lab, Pop m'Art, Story Line, Tumble Zone, Lasagna Lookout and Milk Machine.

During the holiday season (mid-November to mid-January), visitors can reminisce with a trip to Eaton's Fairytale Vignettes, the original holiday display from downtown's Eaton's department store. The setup features 15 scenes from various fairytales. Special events, public programs and workshops are offered throughout the year.

Time: Allow 1 hour minimum. **Hours:** Daily 9:30-6, July 1-Labour Day; Sun.-Thurs. and holidays 9:30-4:30, Fri.-Sat. 9:30-6, rest of year. Closed Tues.-Fri. following Labour Day, Christmas Eve and Christmas. **Cost:** $11. Children must be accompanied by an adult. **Phone:** (204) 924-4000. 🅰️

The Forks Market, is at The Forks, 1 Forks Market Rd., jct. Israel Asper Way. Housed in refurbished stable buildings, the market contains dozens of

Canadian Museum for Human Rights

vendors offering specialty and ethnic foods as well as sweet treats, coffee and grab-and-go items. A central food court has communal seating and a beer and wine bar called The Common; the second floor includes a bookstore and a few shops with souvenirs, art and gifts. A six-story glass tower, accessible by stairs or elevator, affords a view of the rivers and the downtown area. **Hours:** Daily 7 a.m.-11 p.m. Hours may vary for some vendors inside the market. **Cost:** Free. **Phone:** (204) 957-9236. 🍴

The Forks National Historic Site, at The Forks, on Forks Market Rd., is a 3.5-hectare (9-acre) park that offers walking paths with views of the Red River, a children's playground with a seasonal splash pad and a Riverwalk open in summer months (water levels permitting). Interpretive programs and festivals are held Victoria Day through Labour Day. A variety of guided tours and theatrical presentations are available July through August.

In winter months, Arctic Glacier Winter Park provides cold-weather fun with horse-drawn wagon rides, lighted pathways, a toboggan hill, ice-skating trails and a skating rink. The Parks Canada information desk is located in the Travel Manitoba Visitor Information Centre at The Forks. **Hours:** Daily 24 hours. Splash pad daily 11-5, June 29-Labour Day. **Cost:** Free. **Phone:** (204) 983-6757, (204) 984-1762 (Parks Canada information desk) or (888) 773-8888. 🐾 🅰️

FORTWHYTE ALIVE is at 1961 McCreary Rd. Visitors can immerse themselves in the wilderness without even leaving the city at this urban nature oasis where a bison herd, deer, foxes, prairie dogs, waterfowl and songbirds can be seen. The 259-hectare (640-acre) protected green space includes 7 kilometres (4.35 mi.) of mulched trails plus floating boardwalks over marshland, bird-feeding stations in a forest, a herd of bison visible from a viewing mound, a tree house, teepees, a sod house and an interpretive center with a taxidermy touch museum and an aquarium.

Seasonal gear rentals are available and include binoculars, cruiser bikes, fishing equipment, wagons, family adventure bags, walking poles, canoes and snowshoes. **Time:** Allow 1 hour, 45 minutes minimum. **Hours:** Daily 9-5 (also Mon.-Thurs. 5-8). Schedule may vary; phone ahead. Evening hours are extended Sept.-Oct. for viewing migrating Canada geese. Closed Christmas. **Cost:** $10; $9 (ages 65+); $8 (ages 3-17 and students with ID). **Phone:** (204) 989-8355. 🍴 🅰️

FUN MOUNTAIN WATER SLIDE PARK, off Hwy. 1E on Murdock Rd., offers 10 waterslides, a swimming area, a hot tub, bumper boats, miniature golf, ziplining and locker and changing facilities. **Hours:** Wed.-Sun. 11-6 (also Wed. and Sun. 6-10 p.m. for ages 18+), Mon.-Tues. noon-6, mid-June to late Aug. (weather permitting). **Cost:** $25; $22 (under 48 inches tall). All-inclusive ticket (includes boat tour, bumper boats, miniature golf and unlimited sliding)

$30 (all heights); $27 (under 48 inches tall). All-inclusive Plus ticket (includes the all-inclusive features plus hot dog or burger) $35 (all heights). Fast Pass VIP (to bypass lines at slides; 200 per day available) $50 (all heights). Ziplining $14.29. **Phone:** (204) 255-3910. ⌐T⌐

HISTORICAL MUSEUM OF ST. JAMES-ASSINIBOIA, 3180 Portage Ave., houses a collection of artifacts relating to the history of the St. James-Assiniboia area and a display building of pioneer activities. Guided interpretive tours through the mid-19th-century William Brown Red River Log House offer a glimpse of the pioneer lifestyle. **Time:** Allow 1 hour minimum. **Hours:** Daily 10-5, mid-May through Labour Day; Mon.-Fri. 10-5, rest of year. **Cost:** Donations. **Phone:** (204) 888-8706.

JEWISH HERITAGE CENTRE OF WESTERN CANADA, 123 Doncaster St., site of the Fort Osborne Barracks, shares the history, experiences, achievements and culture of Jewish people in Western Canada. The Corridor Museum exhibit depicts the settlement of Jews in Western Canada through artifacts, photographs and archival material. The Holocaust Education Centre features items from the Holocaust and stories and artifacts from local survivors.

Time: Allow 30 minutes minimum. **Hours:** Mon.-Fri. 8:30-4:30. Closed major Jewish holidays; phone ahead to confirm. **Cost:** Donations. **Phone:** (204) 477-7460 for tours or appointments.

SAVE **LE MUSÉE DE SAINT-BONIFACE MUSEUM,** s.e. on Main St. (Hwy. 1), then n. to 494 Taché Ave., was built 1846-51 as the first convent and hospital in western Canada. Displays depict the Red River Settlement and early French and Métis Manitoba; an exhibit is dedicated to Louis Riel, founder of Manitoba. Visitors also can view the nearby ruins of the cathedral as well as the cemetery where Riel is buried.

Time: Allow 30 minutes minimum. **Hours:** Mon.-Fri. 10-4, Sat. noon-4. Additional hours may vary; phone ahead. Closed major holidays. **Cost:** $7; free (ages 0-11); $20 (family, two adults and all children). Reservations are required for tours. **Phone:** (204) 237-4500, ext. 400. GT

LIVING PRAIRIE MUSEUM is at 2795 Ness Ave. This 12-hectare (30-acre) unplowed tract of tall grass is a remnant of the prairie that once covered much of North America. Hike the trails to see more than 160 species of plants and native wildlife. An interpretive center features prairie displays and an observation deck. Nature talks and guided hikes are offered, and a self-guiding trail brochure is available. The annual Monarch Butterfly Festival is held in mid-July and includes workshops, family-friendly crafts, a butterfly release and free milkweed. **Time:** Allow 1 hour minimum. **Hours:** Trail open daily dawn-dusk. Interpretive center daily 10-5, July-Aug.; Sun. 10-5, May-June and in Sept.; by appointment rest of year. **Cost:** Free. **Phone:** (204) 832-0167.

MANITOBA ELECTRICAL MUSEUM & EDUCATION CENTRE is 1 blk. w. of jct. Pembina Hwy. and Stafford St. at 680 Harrow St. The museum's six galleries tell the story of hydroelectric development in the province beginning in the 1870s. The lower-level discovery area features interactive electrical and natural gas safety exhibits and films, seasonal exhibits and a Van de Graaff static electricity generator.

Themed areas such as The Light Goes On 1882-1900, Energizing Manitoba 1900-1960 and Powering up the Farm 1942-1960 provide an idea of the museum's offerings. A yellow turbine runner from one of the oldest hydroelectric stations in Manitoba is outside the 1931 building. **Time:** Allow 1 hour minimum. **Hours:** Tues.-Sat. 1-4, or by appointment. Closed major holidays. **Cost:** $3; free (ages 0-5). **Phone:** (204) 360-7905. GT

MANITOBA LEGISLATIVE BUILDING, bordered by Broadway Ave., Kennedy and Osborne sts. and the Assiniboine River, reflects neoclassical design in native Tyndall limestone. The building houses the Legislative Assembly as well as the offices of government officials.

The interior can be explored via guided or self-guiding tours, which allow visitors to see the Grand Staircase, made of Italian marble and guarded at its base by two life-size bronze bison, the emblems of Manitoba; a rotunda surrounded by Corinthian columns; the Speakers' Gallery with portraits of Manitoba's former speakers; and the Legislative Reading Room with views of the Assiniboine River. When the Assembly is in session, visitors may watch the proceedings from a public gallery.

Atop the building's dome is the Golden Boy statue by Parisian sculptor Georges Gardet. The torch, in the right hand, points to economic development and progress in the north; the sheaf of wheat in the left arm represents agriculture. This 5.25-metre-tall (17.2-ft.) statue weighs 1,650 kilograms (3,638 lbs.) and is sheathed in 24 karat gold leaf. The landscaped grounds include statues of such noteworthy figures as Queen Victoria, Queen Elizabeth II and Louis Riel. **Hours:** Guided tours are conducted daily on the hour 9-4, July 1-Labour Day; by appointment rest of year. Self-guiding tours are available daily 8-8, year-round. **Cost:** Free. **Phone:** (204) 945-5813. GT

GEM **MANITOBA MUSEUM,** 190 Rupert Ave. at jct. Main St., illustrates the relationship of people and their environment in Manitoba's history through nine permanent galleries. The Earth History Gallery displays rare fossils, the Arctic/Sub-Arctic Gallery explores Inuit culture and northern Manitoba, and the Boreal Forest Gallery features a diorama of a granite cliff, waterfall, marsh, a Cree family, and wildlife, including moose. A bat cave, snake pit and a Ukrainian rye farm can be seen at the Parklands/Mixed Woods Gallery.

Visitors can see a replica of the ketch *Nonsuch;* the ship's 1668 voyage to Hudson Bay opened western Canada to commerce and European settlement. The Hudson's Bay Company Gallery highlights fur trading

Royal Canadian Mint

and early exploration. A teepee and a log house are part of the Grasslands Gallery, and the Urban Gallery shows a 1920s boomtown Winnipeg.

The museum also houses a planetarium and science gallery. **Time:** Allow 3 hours minimum. **Hours:** Daily 10-5 (also Thurs. 5-9), Victoria Day-Labour Day; Tues.-Fri. 10-4, Sat.-Sun. and holidays 11-5, rest of year (Remembrance Day 1-5, Christmas Eve 10-1). Closed Christmas. **Cost:** Admission to one area (museum galleries, science gallery or planetarium) $19.50; $17.50 (ages 65+); $16.50 (students ages 13-17 or with ID); $11.50 (ages 3-12). Two areas $27.90; $24.50 (ages 65+); $22.80 (students ages 13-17 or with ID); $16.40 (ages 3-12). Three areas $32.70; $28.50 (ages 65+); $26.40 (students ages 13-17 or with ID); $19.20 (ages 3-12). **Phone:** (204) 956-2830 or (204) 943-3139.

The Planetarium, on the lower level of Manitoba Museum at 190 Rupert Ave., presents interactive and multimedia shows about space, science and the universe. **Time:** Allow 1 hour minimum. **Hours:** Shows are presented several times per day. Show times vary; phone ahead to confirm schedule. **Note:** Latecomers cannot be admitted after the show has begun. **Cost:** Admission to one area (museum galleries, science gallery or planetarium) $19.50; $17.50 (ages 65+); $16.50 (students ages 13-17 or with ID); $11.50 (ages 3-12). Two areas $27.90; $24.50 (ages 65+); $22.80 (students ages 13-17 or with ID); $16.40 (ages 3-12). Three areas $32.70; $28.50 (ages 65+); $26.40 (students ages 13-17 or with ID); $19.20 (ages 3-12). **Phone:** (204) 956-2830, or (204) 943-3139 for show times.

The Science Gallery, on the lower level of Manitoba Museum at 190 Rupert Ave., features 100 hands-on exhibits for the kid in everyone. **Time:** Allow 1 hour minimum. **Hours:** Daily 10-5, Victoria Day weekend-Labour Day weekend; Tues.-Fri. 10-4, Sat.-Sun. and most holidays 11-5, rest of year (Remembrance Day 1-5, Christmas Eve 10-1). Closed Christmas. **Cost:** Admission to one area (museum galleries, science gallery or planetarium) $19.50; $17.50 (ages 65+); $16.50 (students ages 13-17 or with ID); $11.50 (ages 3-12). Two areas $27.90; $24.50 (ages 65+); $22.80 (students ages 13-17 or with ID); $16.40 (ages 3-12). Three areas $32.70; $28.50 (ages 65+); $26.40 (students ages 13-17 or with ID); $19.20 (ages 3-12). **Phone:** (204) 956-2830 or (204) 943-3139.

RIEL HOUSE NATIONAL HISTORIC SITE, 330 River Rd., was the home of the mother of Louis Riel. Although this leader of the Métis and founder of the provisional government of Manitoba never lived in the house, his body lay in state for several days after his execution in 1885. Interpretive panels near the walkway to the house explain the history of the Métis and of the Riel family. **Time:** Allow 30 minutes minimum. **Hours:** Fri.-Wed. 10-5, Thurs. 1-8, July-Aug. **Cost:** Entry and self-discovery program $3.90; $3.40 (ages 65+); free (ages 0-16). **Phone:** (204) 983-6757.

ROYAL AVIATION MUSEUM OF WESTERN CANADA, in an aircraft hangar off Ellice Ave. at 958 Ferry Rd., displays numerous vintage aircraft. All aspects of aviation are exhibited, from bush planes to commercial airliners to military planes and home-made aircraft. Children can explore the interactive Skyways exhibit. A research library and archives can be seen by appointment.

CLOSURE INFORMATION: The museum is currently closed while it moves to a new location; reopening is scheduled for 2021. **Phone:** (204) 786-5503.

ROYAL CANADIAN MINT is at 520 Lagimodière Blvd. at jct. Trans-Canada Hwy. and Hwy. 59. This high-tech, high-volume manufacturing facility is considered one of the world's most modern mints; its high-speed coining presses can each strike 750 coins per minute. The Winnipeg mint produces all circulation coinage for Canada as well as coinage for more than 75 foreign countries.

Guided tours explain the coin manufacturing process and allow access to the second floor, where large windows offer a peek down into various production rooms where coins are pressed, sorted and packaged. The ground floor is open to the public and includes a landscaped interior courtyard, a gift shop, windows that look into the packaging room and an exhibit which lets visitors pull a lever to lift a gold bar worth more than $600,000.

Hours: Daily 9-5, mid-May through early Sept.; Tues.-Sat. 9-5, rest of year. Tour schedule varies; phone ahead. **Cost:** Ground floor free. Guided tour with access to second floor windows (Mon.-Fri.) $8;

$7 (ages 65+); $4.50 (ages 5-17); $20 (family, two adults and two children). Guided tour (Sat.-Sun.) $6; $5.25 (ages 65+); $3.50 (ages 5-17); $18 (family, two adults and two children). Reservations are recommended. **Phone:** (204) 984-1144 or (877) 974-6468. GT

TRANSCONA MUSEUM is at 141 Regent Ave. W. In a 1925 bank building, the museum explores the origins of Transcona, a railroad town amalgamated into Winnipeg, and the accomplishments of its residents. Exhibits rotate yearly, showcasing the museum's collection and the history and community spirit of Transcona.

Time: Allow 30 minutes minimum. **Hours:** Mon.-Sat. 9-4, June-Aug.; Mon.-Fri. 11-4, Sat. noon-4, rest of year; closed holiday weekends. Hours may vary; phone ahead. **Cost:** Donations. **Phone:** (204) 222-0423.

WINNIPEG ART GALLERY is at 300 Memorial Blvd. Nine galleries contain contemporary and historical works by Manitoba, Canadian and international artists, from the gallery's collection of almost 24,000 works of art. The Inuit art collection is reputed to be the largest public collection of contemporary Inuit art in the world; a small portion of the collection is always on display. Guided tours are offered; phone for scheduled tours and talks.

Time: Allow 1 hour minimum. **Hours:** Tues.-Sun. 11-5 (also Fri. 5-9 or 5-11 on first Fri. of the month). Closed Good Friday, Easter Monday, Thanksgiving and Christmas. **Cost:** $12; $10 (ages 60+ and students with ID); free (ages 0-5); $28 (family, two adults and up to four children). **Phone:** (204) 786-6641 or (204) 789-1760. [¶]

Sightseeing

Boat Tours

SPLASH DASH GUIDED RIVER TOURS departs from the bottom of the river walk at The Forks. The boats provide 30-minute guided historical tours of a section of the Red and Assiniboine rivers. Points of interest are noted along the way. **Time:** Allow 30 minutes minimum. **Hours:** Departures daily every 15 minutes 10 a.m.-dusk, mid-May through Aug. 31; noon-dusk, Sept. 1-Oct. 15 (weather permitting). **Cost:** $11.50; $9.50 (ages 4-18 and 65+). **Phone:** (204) 783-6633.

Bus and Trolley Tours

WINNIPEG TROLLEY COMPANY departs from The Forks Market, 1 Forks Market Rd. Guides aboard the orange and cream trolleys share stories including why the River City was once called the wickedest city in Canada, how the local hockey team became history's first Olympic champions in 1920 and how Winnipeg is connected to the famous spy James Bond.

More than 90 sites along the Heart of a Nation City Tour include the Exchange District National

Historic Site, where you'll learn about corruption and heroes and see the largest intact collection of turn-of-the-century commercial architecture in North America; The Forks, a gathering place for more than 6,000 years and a great place for shopping, dining and entertainment; and St. Boniface, Winnipeg's historic French district and the final resting place of Louis Riel, the Métis leader and founder of Manitoba.

Time: Allow 2 hours, 30 minutes minimum. **Hours:** Tours depart Tues.-Thurs. at 10 and 1, Fri.-Sat at 10 and Sun. at 1 and 4, June 23-Sept. 1; Tues., Thurs. and Sun. at 1, Sat. at 10, May 25-June 22. **Cost:** $28.50; $25.50 (students with ID); $14.50 (ages 6-12). Reservations are recommended. **Phone:** (204) 226-8687.

Train Tours

Antique rail cars pulled by a vintage locomotive take passengers on 3-hour trips departing from Inkster Junction Station, 3 kilometres (1.9 mi.) west of Hwy. 90 off Inkster Boulevard. The Prairie Dog Central Railway makes a stop at a country market destination in Grosse Isle. The scenic ride operates weekends and holidays, May through September; phone (204) 832-5259.

Walking Tours

Looking for fun things to do with friends or ideas for group travel? Take a self-guiding tour of the city's urban areas that begins and ends at The Forks Market. Maps highlighting more than 50 cultural, historical and modern points of interest in downtown Winnipeg and Old St. Boniface are available at visitor centers at [◆] The Forks, Tourisme Riel (219 Provencher Blvd.), Downtown Winnipeg BIZ (426 Portage Ave.), The Exchange District BIZ (492 Main St.) and on the Tourism Winnipeg website. Other themed travel tours and vacation packages are available; phone (204) 958-4640 or check with your local AAA travel agency.

Guided walking tours of the 20-block Exchange District near Portage Avenue and Main Street are available June through Labour Day weekend. Departing from Old Market Square at the corner of King St. and Bannatyne Ave., these tours visit many of Manitoba's finest historical buildings; for schedule information phone (204) 942-6716.

Although now part of Winnipeg, the historical district of St. Boniface (across the Esplanade Riel footbridge) has retained its French Canadian identity. A monument honoring the explorer Pierre Gaultier de la Vérendrye is on Taché Avenue opposite St. Boniface Hospital. Also in St. Boniface is the grave of Louis Riel, leader of the Métis and of the provisional government 1869-70. The grave is at Taché and Cathedral avenues in the churchyard of the St. Boniface Cathedral. Guided walking tours of the St. Boniface area are available Victoria Day through Labour Day or by request; phone (204) 233-8343 or (866) 808-8338 for information and reservations.

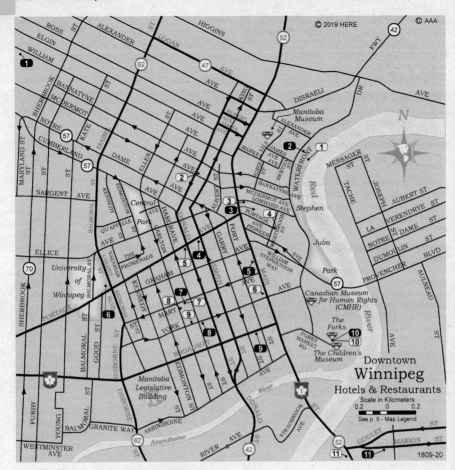

Downtown Winnipeg

This index helps you "spot" where hotels and restaurants are located on the corresponding detailed maps. Restaurant price range is a combination of lunch and/or dinner. Turn to the listing page for more information and consult display ads for special promotions.

 For more details, rates and reservations: AAA.com/travelguides/hotels

DOWNTOWN WINNIPEG

Map Page	Hotels	Designation	Member Savings	Page
1 this page	**Canad Inns Destination Centre Health Sciences Centre**	THREE DIAMOND	✔	377
2 this page	Mere Hotel	THREE DIAMOND		377
3 this page	**Fairmont Winnipeg**	THREE DIAMOND	✔	377
4 this page	**Radisson Hotel Winnipeg Downtown**	THREE DIAMOND	✔	377
5 this page	Humphry Inn & Suites	APPROVED		377
6 this page	**Holiday Inn & Suites Winnipeg Downtown**	THREE DIAMOND	✔	377
7 this page	**Delta Hotels by Marriott Winnipeg**	THREE DIAMOND	✔	377
8 this page	**Best Western Plus Downtown Winnipeg**	APPROVED	✔	377
9 this page	The Fort Garry Hotel Spa & Conference Centre	THREE DIAMOND		377
10 this page	**Inn at the Forks**	THREE DIAMOND	✔	377

DOWNTOWN WINNIPEG (cont'd)

Map Page	Hotels (cont'd)		Designation	Member Savings	Page
11 p. 372	Norwood Hotel		◈ APPROVED		377

Map Page	Restaurants	Designation	Cuisine	Price Range	Page
① p. 372	Cibo Waterfront Cafe	◈ APPROVED	Mediterranean	$17-$32	377
② p. 372	deer + almond	◈ THREE DIAMOND	New World Small Plates	$12-$38	377
③ p. 372	Hy's Steakhouse & Cocktail Bar	◈ THREE DIAMOND	Steak	$17-$109	378
④ p. 372	Clay Oven East Indian/Hakka Restaurant	◈ APPROVED	Indian	$16-$28	377
⑤ p. 372	Moxie's Classic Grill	◈ APPROVED	American	$14-$30	378
⑥ p. 372	Ivory Restaurant & Bar	◈ APPROVED	Indian	$14-$25	378
⑦ p. 372	Blaze Restaurant & Lounge	◈ THREE DIAMOND	Regional Canadian	$9-$35	377
⑧ p. 372	Ichiban Japanese Steak House	◈ APPROVED	Japanese	$29-$47	378
⑨ p. 372	East India Company Pub & Eatery	◈ APPROVED	Indian	$15-$18	378
⑩ p. 372	SMITH	◈ THREE DIAMOND	Canadian	$11-$37	378
⑪ p. 372	Santa Lucia Pizza	◈ APPROVED	Italian	$10-$24	378

EXPLORE
BIG
SAVINGS
AAA.com/travel or CAA.ca/travel

Plan it, book it and save at
AAA.com/travel or CAA.ca/travel

Circle the globe! Enjoy up to 20% savings with our exclusive offers on hotels, up to 20% on car rentals, and out-of-this-world deals on complete vacation packages. With a website that's easy to navigate and customer support you can trust, expect something more when you travel with AAA and CAA.

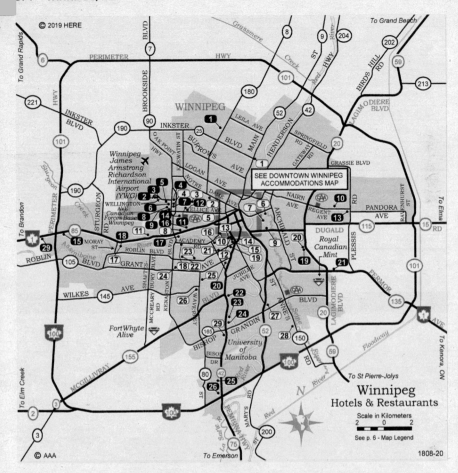

Winnipeg
Hotels & Restaurants

Scale in Kilometers

See p. 6 - Map Legend

© AAA   To Emerson   1808-20

✈ Airport Hotels

Map Page	WINNIPEG JAMES ARMSTRONG RICHARDSON INTERNATIONAL AIRPORT (Maximum driving distance from airport: 1.8 mi (2.9 km))	Designation	Member Savings	Page
4 this page	**Best Western Plus Winnipeg Airport Hotel, 1.8 mi (2.9 km)**	THREE DIAMOND	✔	378
3 this page	Courtyard by Marriott Winnipeg Airport, 0.9 mi (1.5 km)	THREE DIAMOND	✔	379
8 this page	Days Inn & Suites Winnipeg Airport, 1.2 mi (1.9 km)	THREE DIAMOND		379
2 this page	Four Points by Sheraton Hotel Winnipeg Airport, on airport property	THREE DIAMOND	✔	379
6 this page	Hampton Inn by Hilton Winnipeg Airport/Polo Park, 1.2 mi (1.9 km)	THREE DIAMOND	✔	380
5 this page	**Hilton Winnipeg Airport Suites, 1.1 mi (1.7 km)**	THREE DIAMOND	✔	380
9 this page	MainStay Suites Winnipeg, 1.4 mi (2.2 km)	THREE DIAMOND		380
7 this page	Sandman Hotel & Suites Winnipeg Airport, 1.4 mi (2.3 km)	THREE DIAMOND		380

Winnipeg

This index helps you "spot" where hotels and restaurants are located on the corresponding detailed maps. Restaurant price range is a combination of lunch and/or dinner. Turn to the listing page for more information and consult display ads for special promotions.

 For more details, rates and reservations: AAA.com/travelguides/hotels

WINNIPEG

Map Page	Hotels	Designation	Member Savings	Page
1 p. 374	**Canad Inns Destination Centre Garden City**	APPROVED	✔	379
2 p. 374	Four Points by Sheraton Hotel Winnipeg Airport	THREE DIAMOND	✔	379
3 p. 374	Courtyard by Marriott Winnipeg Airport	THREE DIAMOND	✔	379
4 p. 374	**Best Western Plus Winnipeg Airport Hotel**	THREE DIAMOND	✔	378
5 p. 374	**Hilton Winnipeg Airport Suites**	THREE DIAMOND	✔	380
6 p. 374	Hampton Inn by Hilton Winnipeg Airport/Polo Park	THREE DIAMOND	✔	380
7 p. 374	Sandman Hotel & Suites Winnipeg Airport	THREE DIAMOND		380
8 p. 374	Days Inn & Suites Winnipeg Airport	THREE DIAMOND		379
9 p. 374	MainStay Suites Winnipeg	THREE DIAMOND		380
10 p. 374	**Canad Inns Destination Centre Club Regent Casino Hotel**	APPROVED	✔	379
11 p. 374	Homewood Suites by Hilton Winnipeg Airport-Polo Park	THREE DIAMOND	✔	380
12 p. 374	Fairfield Inn & Suites by Marriott Winnipeg	THREE DIAMOND	✔	379
13 p. 374	**Canad Inns Destination Centre Transcona**	APPROVED	✔	379
14 p. 374	**Canad Inns Destination Centre Polo Park**	APPROVED	✔	379
15 p. 374	Howard Johnson Express Inn	APPROVED		380
16 p. 374	Clarion Hotel & Suites	THREE DIAMOND		379
17 p. 374	Viscount Gort Hotel *(See ad p. 380.)*	APPROVED		380
18 p. 374	**Holiday Inn Winnipeg Airport West**	THREE DIAMOND	✔	380
19 p. 374	**Canad Inns Destination Centre Windsor Park**	APPROVED	✔	379
20 p. 374	Quality Inn & Suites	APPROVED		380
21 p. 374	Super 8 Winnipeg East	APPROVED		380
22 p. 374	Holiday Inn Winnipeg South	THREE DIAMOND		380
23 p. 374	**Best Western Plus Pembina Inn & Suites** *(See ad p. 378.)*	THREE DIAMOND	✔	378
24 p. 374	**Canad Inns Destination Centre Fort Garry**	APPROVED	✔	379
25 p. 374	**Four Points by Sheraton Winnipeg South**	THREE DIAMOND	✔	379
26 p. 374	**Comfort Inn Winnipeg South**	APPROVED	✔	379

Map Page	Restaurants	Designation	Cuisine	Price Range	Page
1 p. 374	Santa Lucia Pizza	APPROVED	Italian	$10-$24	381
2 p. 374	Ducky's Fish & Chips	APPROVED	Fish & Chips	$8-$19	381
3 p. 374	Cafe Dario	THREE DIAMOND	Latin American Fusion	$14-$44	381
4 p. 374	Chop Steakhouse & Bar	THREE DIAMOND	Steak Seafood	$14-$48	381
5 p. 374	India Palace Restaurant	APPROVED	Indian	$10-$24	381
6 p. 374	Resto Gare	THREE DIAMOND	French	$15-$34	381
7 p. 374	Beaujena's French Table	THREE DIAMOND	French	$39-$59	381
8 p. 374	Moxie's Classic Grill	APPROVED	American	$14-$30	381
9 p. 374	Inferno's Bistro	THREE DIAMOND	Canadian	$13-$32	381
10 p. 374	Bistro Dansk Restaurant	APPROVED	European	$12-$24	381
11 p. 374	Joe Black Coffee Bar	APPROVED	Coffee/Tea	$7-$16	381
12 p. 374	Buccacino's Fresca Italiana	APPROVED	Italian	$14-$45	381

Map Page	Restaurants (cont'd)	Designation	Cuisine	Price Range	Page
⑬ p. 374	Segovia Tapas Bar & Restaurant	THREE DIAMOND	New Spanish Small Plates	$10-$28	381
⑭ p. 374	Naru Sushi Japanese Restaurant	APPROVED	Japanese Sushi	$14-$28	381
⑮ p. 374	Baked Expectations	APPROVED	Breads/Pastries Breakfast	$12	381
⑯ p. 374	529 Wellington	THREE DIAMOND	Steak Seafood	$14-$69	381
⑰ p. 374	Bellbottoms Restaurant	APPROVED	American	$10-$26	381
⑱ p. 374	Fusion Grill	THREE DIAMOND	Canadian Wild Game	$14-$47	381
⑲ p. 374	Confusion Corner Bar & Grill	THREE DIAMOND	International	$13-$27	381
⑳ p. 374	Aaltos	APPROVED	American	$8-$22	381
㉑ p. 374	Santa Lucia Pizza	APPROVED	Italian	$10-$24	381
㉒ p. 374	Mona Lisa Ristorante Italiano	THREE DIAMOND	Northern Italian	$5-$37	381
㉓ p. 374	Bonfire Bistro	APPROVED	Mediterranean	$14-$36	381
㉔ p. 374	Stella's Cafe	APPROVED	Breakfast	$9-$16	381
㉕ p. 374	Wasabi Sabi	THREE DIAMOND	New Sushi	$16-$125	381
㉖ p. 374	Bellissimo Restaurant & Lounge	THREE DIAMOND	Italian	$12-$28	381
㉗ p. 374	Maxime's Restaurant & Lounge	APPROVED	Mediterranean	$15-$27	381
㉘ p. 374	La Fiesta Cafecito	APPROVED	Salvadoran	$9-$22	381
㉙ p. 374	Nicolino's Restaurant	APPROVED	Italian	$19-$30	381

HEADINGLEY

Map Page	Hotel	Designation	Member Savings	Page
㉙ p. 374	**Best Western Plus Winnipeg West**	THREE DIAMOND	✔	350

Save time and stay secure year-round

Continue receiving the benefits you know and love. Renew your AAA membership or inquire about auto renewal.

Renew your membership today:
- Online at AAA.com/membership
- Visit your local club office
- Call 800-Join-AAA (564-6222)

DOWNTOWN WINNIPEG
• Hotels & Restaurants map & index p. 372

BEST WESTERN PLUS DOWNTOWN WINNIPEG
204/942-0101 **8**

APPROVED

Hotel

AAA Benefit: Members save up to 15% and earn bonus points!

Address: 330 York Ave R3C 0N9 **Location:** Between Hargrave and Donald sts. Located in business district. **Facility:** 87 units. 5 stories, interior corridors. **Parking:** on-site (fee), winter plug-ins. **Dining:** 2 restaurants. **Activities:** exercise room. **Guest Services:** valet and coin laundry, area transportation.

SAVE ECO 🚗 🍽 📶 🍸 CALL 👤 👥 BIZ HS 📶 🖅

🎮 📱 🖨 💻

CANAD INNS DESTINATION CENTRE HEALTH SCIENCES CENTRE
204/594-9472 **1**

THREE DIAMOND

Hotel

Address: 720 William Ave R3E 3J7 **Location:** Between Sherbrook and Tecumseh sts. Attached to Health Sciences Centre. **Facility:** 191 units. 16 stories, interior corridors. **Parking:** on-site (fee), winter plug-ins. **Amenities:** *Some:* safes. **Dining:** 2 restaurants. **Activities:** exercise room. **Guest Services:** valet laundry.

SAVE 🚗 🍽 📶 🍸 CALL 👤 👥 HS 📶 🖅 📱 🖨 💻

DELTA HOTELS BY MARRIOTT WINNIPEG
204/942-0551 **7**

THREE DIAMOND

Contemporary Hotel

D DELTA HOTELS **AAA Benefit:** Members save 5% or more!

Address: 350 St. Mary Ave R3C 3J2 **Location:** Jct Hargrave St. Adjacent to convention center. **Facility:** 393 units, some two bedrooms. 18 stories, interior corridors. **Parking:** on-site (fee) and valet. **Terms:** check-in 4 pm. **Dining:** Blaze Restaurant & Lounge, see separate listing. **Pool:** heated outdoor, heated indoor. **Activities:** hot tub, bicycles, exercise room. **Guest Services:** complimentary and valet laundry, area transportation.

SAVE ECO 🍽 📶 🍸 CALL 👤 🏊 👥 BIZ HS 📶 🖅 💻 / SOME UNITS 🐾 📱

FAIRMONT WINNIPEG
204/957-1350 **3**

THREE DIAMOND

Hotel

Address: 2 Lombard Pl R3B 0Y3 **Location:** Just e of Portage Ave and Main St. Located in a commercial area. **Facility:** 340 units. 21 stories, interior corridors. **Parking:** on-site (fee) and valet, winter plug-ins. **Amenities:** safes. **Pool:** heated indoor. **Activities:** sauna, hot tub, bicycles, exercise room, massage. **Guest Services:** valet laundry.

SAVE ECO 🍽 📶 🍸 CALL 👤 🏊 👥 BIZ sHS 📶 🖅 🎮 💻 / SOME UNITS 🐾

THE FORT GARRY HOTEL SPA & CONFERENCE CENTRE
204/942-8251 **9**

THREE DIAMOND Historic Hotel. **Address:** 222 Broadway R3C 0R3

HOLIDAY INN & SUITES WINNIPEG DOWNTOWN
204/786-7011 **6**

THREE DIAMOND

Hotel

Address: 360 Colony St R3B 2P3 **Location:** Corner of Portage Ave. **Facility:** 140 units. 11 stories, interior corridors. **Parking:** on-site (fee), winter plug-ins. **Amenities:** video games. **Pool:** heated indoor. **Activities:** hot tub, exercise room. **Guest Services:** valet and coin laundry.

SAVE 🍽 📶 🍸 CALL 👤 🏊 👥 BIZ HS 📶 🖅 🎮 📱 💻 / SOME UNITS 🖨

HUMPHRY INN & SUITES
204/942-4222 **5**

APPROVED Hotel. **Address:** 260 Main St R3C 1A9

INN AT THE FORKS
204/942-6555 **10**

THREE DIAMOND

Hotel

Address: 75 Forks Market Rd R3C 0A2 **Location:** At The Forks. Located in a park and entertainment area. **Facility:** 117 units. 5 stories, interior corridors. **Parking:** on-site (fee) and valet, winter plug-ins. **Amenities:** safes. **Dining:** SMITH, see separate listing. **Activities:** exercise room, spa. **Guest Services:** valet laundry, area transportation.

SAVE ECO 🍽 📶 🍸 CALL 👤 👥 BIZ 📶 🖅 🎮 📱 💻

MERE HOTEL
204/594-0333 **2**

THREE DIAMOND Boutique Contemporary Hotel. **Address:** 333 Waterfront Dr R3C 0A2

NORWOOD HOTEL
204/233-4475 **11**

APPROVED Hotel. **Address:** 112 Marion St R2H 0T1

RADISSON HOTEL WINNIPEG DOWNTOWN
204/956-0410 **4**

THREE DIAMOND

Hotel

Address: 288 Portage Ave R3C 0B8 **Location:** At Smith St. Located in a commercial area. **Facility:** 263 units. 29 stories, interior corridors. **Parking:** on-site (fee) and valet, winter plug-ins. **Amenities:** *Some:* safes. **Activities:** steamroom, exercise room. **Guest Services:** valet and coin laundry, area transportation.

SAVE ECO 🚗 🍽 📶 🍸 👥 BIZ HS 📶 🖅 📱 💻 / SOME UNITS 🐾 🖨

WHERE TO EAT

BLAZE RESTAURANT & LOUNGE
204/944-7259 **7**

THREE DIAMOND Regional Canadian. Casual Dining. **Address:** 350 St. Mary Ave R3C 3J2

CIBO WATERFRONT CAFE
204/594-0339 **1**

APPROVED Mediterranean. Casual Dining. **Address:** 339 Waterfront Dr R3B 0V1

CLAY OVEN EAST INDIAN/HAKKA RESTAURANT
204/982-7426 **4**

APPROVED Indian. Casual Dining. **Address:** 1 Portage Ave R3B 3N3

DEER + ALMOND
204/504-8562 **2**

THREE DIAMOND New World Small Plates. Casual Dining. **Address:** 85 Princess St R3B 1K6

(See map & index p. 372.)

EAST INDIA COMPANY PUB & EATERY   204/947-3097 9
▼ APPROVED Indian. Casual Dining. **Address:** 349 York Ave R3C 3S9

HY'S STEAKHOUSE & COCKTAIL BAR   204/942-1000 3
▼ THREE DIAMOND Steak. Fine Dining. **Address:** 1 Lombard Pl R3B 0X3

ICHIBAN JAPANESE STEAK HOUSE   204/925-7400 8
▼ APPROVED Japanese. Casual Dining. **Address:** 189 Carlton St R3C 3H7

IVORY RESTAURANT & BAR   204/944-1600 6
▼ APPROVED Indian. Casual Dining. **Address:** 200 Main St R3C 4V9

MOXIE'S CLASSIC GRILL   204/926-5757 5
▼ APPROVED American. Casual Dining. **Address:** 300 Portage Ave R3C 5S4

SANTA LUCIA PIZZA   204/237-4134 11
▼ APPROVED Italian. Casual Dining. **Address:** 4 St. Mary's Rd R2H 1H1

SMITH   204/944-2445 10
▼ THREE DIAMOND Canadian. Casual Dining. **Address:** 75 Forks Market Rd R3C 0A2

🔗 **Where Diamonds make the difference:**

AAA.com/travelguides/hotels

WINNIPEG
- Restaurants p. 381
- Hotels & Restaurants map & index p. 374

BEST WESTERN PLUS PEMBINA INN & SUITES
204/269-8888 23

▼ THREE DIAMOND Hotel   Best Western PLUS

AAA Benefit: Members save up to 15% and earn bonus points!

Address: 1714 Pembina Hwy R3T 2G2 **Location:** 0.6 mi (1 km) n of jct Bishop Grandin Blvd. Located in a commercial area. **Facility:** 104 units. 4 stories, interior corridors. **Parking:** winter plug-ins. **Amenities:** safes. **Pool:** heated indoor. **Activities:** hot tub, exercise room. **Guest Services:** valet and coin laundry. **Featured Amenity:** full hot breakfast. *(See ad this page.)*

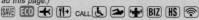
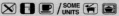

BEST WESTERN PLUS WINNIPEG AIRPORT HOTEL
204/775-9889 4

▼ THREE DIAMOND Hotel   Best Western PLUS

AAA Benefit: Members save up to 15% and earn bonus points!

Address: 1715 Wellington Ave R3H 0G1 **Location:** Jct Century St. Located in a commercial area. **Facility:** 213 units. 6 stories, interior corridors. **Parking:** winter plug-ins. **Pool:** heated indoor. **Activities:** hot tub, exercise room. **Guest Services:** valet and coin laundry.

▼ See AAA listing this page ▼

BW **Best Western PLUS**

Comfort. Value. Extras.
- Indoor saltwater pool with water-slide & hot tub
- Complimentary Hot Breakfast
- Pet Friendly

Pembina Inn & Suites
1714 Pembina Hwy. Winnipeg, MB R3T 2G2 CAN
204-269-8888 | 1-877-269-8811 | bestwestern.com/aaa

THREE DIAMOND   CAA Rewards

Each Best Western® branded hotel is independently owned and operated. Best Western and the Best Western marks are service marks or registered service marks of Best Western International, Inc. ©2018 Best Western International, Inc. All rights reserved. AAA and the AAA marks are service marks or registered service marks of the American Automobile Association.

(See map & index p. 374.)

CANAD INNS DESTINATION CENTRE CLUB REGENT CASINO HOTEL
204/667-5560 **10**

APPROVED
Hotel

Address: 1415 Regent Ave W R2C 3B2 **Location:** 1.3 mi (2.1 km) e of Lagimodiere Blvd (Hwy 20); between Plessis Rd and Lagimodiere Blvd (Hwy 20). **Facility:** With direct access to an adjacent casino, this hotel offers pleasant rooms with comfortable seating. The bathrooms are on the basic side. 146 units. 6 stories, interior corridors. **Parking:** winter plug-ins. **Dining:** 2 restaurants. **Activities:** exercise room. **Guest Services:** valet laundry.

SAVE ECO ⏱ 🍽 👶 🍸

CALL ♿ 🐕 BIZ HS 🛜 ✕ 🍴 🖥 🖨

CANAD INNS DESTINATION CENTRE FORT GARRY
204/261-7450 **24**

APPROVED
Hotel

Address: 1824 Pembina Hwy R3T 2G2 **Location:** Just n of Bishop Grandin Blvd. **Facility:** 106 units, some two bedrooms. 2 stories, interior corridors. **Parking:** winter plug-ins. **Dining:** 3 restaurants. **Pool:** heated indoor. **Activities:** hot tub, exercise room. **Guest Services:** valet laundry.

SAVE ECO ✈ 🍽 👶 🍸

CALL ♿ 🐕 HS 🛜 ✕

🍴 🖥 🖨 / SOME UNITS 🐾

CANAD INNS DESTINATION CENTRE GARDEN CITY
204/633-0024 **1**

APPROVED
Hotel

Address: 2100 McPhillips St R2V 3T9 **Location:** At Jefferson Ave. Located in a commercial area. **Facility:** 72 units, some two bedrooms. 3 stories, interior corridors. **Parking:** winter plug-ins. **Dining:** 2 restaurants. **Pool:** heated indoor. **Activities:** hot tub.

SAVE ECO 🍽 👶 🍸 🐕 🛜

✕ 🍴 🖥 🖨

CANAD INNS DESTINATION CENTRE POLO PARK
204/775-8791 **14**

APPROVED
Hotel

Address: 1405 St. Matthews Ave R3G 0K5 **Location:** Just e of St James St. **Facility:** 107 units. 6 stories, interior corridors. **Parking:** winter plug-ins. **Dining:** 3 restaurants. **Pool:** heated indoor. **Activities:** hot tub, exercise room. **Guest Services:** valet and coin laundry.

SAVE ECO ✈ 🍽 👶 🍸

CALL ♿ 🐕 BIZ HS 🛜

✕ 🍴 🖥 🖨 / SOME UNITS 🐾

CANAD INNS DESTINATION CENTRE TRANSCONA
204/224-1681 **13**

APPROVED
Hotel

Address: 826 Regent Ave W R2C 3A8 **Location:** 1.9 mi (3 km) e of Lagimodiere Blvd (Hwy 20); between Plessis Rd and Lagimodiere Blvd (Hwy 20). **Facility:** 100 units, some two bedrooms. 2 stories, interior corridors. **Parking:** winter plug-ins. **Dining:** 3 restaurants. **Pool:** heated indoor. **Activities:** hot tub. **Guest Services:** valet laundry.

SAVE ECO 🍽 👶 🍸 CALL ♿

🐕 🛜 ✕ 🍴 🖥 🖨

CANAD INNS DESTINATION CENTRE WINDSOR PARK
204/253-2641 **19**

APPROVED
Hotel

Address: 1034 Elizabeth Rd R2J 1B3 **Location:** Just s of Maginot St and w of Lagimodiere Blvd (Hwy 20). Located in a residential/commercial area. **Facility:** 52 units, some two bedrooms. 2 stories (no elevator), interior corridors. **Parking:** winter plug-ins. **Dining:** Aaltos, see separate listing, nightclub. **Pool:** heated indoor. **Activities:** hot tub. **Guest Services:** valet laundry.

SAVE ECO 🍽 👶 🍸 CALL ♿

🐕 🛜 ✕ 🍴 🖥 🖨

CLARION HOTEL & SUITES
204/774-5110 **16**

THREE DIAMOND Hotel. **Address:** 1445 Portage Ave R3G 3P4

COMFORT INN WINNIPEG SOUTH
204/269-7390 **26**

APPROVED
Hotel

Address: 3109 Pembina Hwy R3T 4R6 **Location:** Just n of jct Perimeter Hwy 100 and 75. Located in a residential/commercial area. **Facility:** 83 units. 2 stories (no elevator), interior corridors. **Parking:** winter plug-ins. **Guest Services:** valet and coin laundry. **Featured Amenity:** full hot breakfast.

SAVE ECO CALL ♿ BIZ 🛜 ✕

🍴 🖥 🖨 / SOME UNITS 🐾

COURTYARD BY MARRIOTT WINNIPEG AIRPORT
204/505-8600 **3**

THREE DIAMOND SAVE
Contemporary Hotel. **Address:** 780 Powerhouse Rd R3H 1C7

AAA Benefit: Members save 5% or more!

DAYS INN & SUITES WINNIPEG AIRPORT
204/505-1500 **8**

THREE DIAMOND Hotel. **Address:** 695 Berry St R3H 0S4

FAIRFIELD INN & SUITES BY MARRIOTT WINNIPEG
204/783-7900 **12**

THREE DIAMOND SAVE Hotel. **Address:** 1301 Ellice Ave R3G 0N5

AAA Benefit: Members save 5% or more!

FOUR POINTS BY SHERATON HOTEL WINNIPEG AIRPORT
204/775-5222 **2**

THREE DIAMOND SAVE Hotel. **Address:** 1999 Wellington Ave R3H 1H5

AAA Benefit: Members save 5% or more!

FOUR POINTS BY SHERATON WINNIPEG SOUTH
204/275-7711 **25**

THREE DIAMOND
Hotel

FOUR POINTS BY SHERATON **AAA Benefit:** Members save 5% or more!

Address: 2935 Pembina Hwy R3T 2H5 **Location:** Jct Perimeter Hwy 100 and 75, 0.7 mi (1.1 km) n. **Facility:** 76 units. 5 stories, interior corridors. **Parking:** winter plug-ins. **Pool:** heated indoor. **Activities:** hot tub, exercise room. **Guest Services:** valet laundry, area transportation.

SAVE 🍽 👶 🍸 🐕 👶 BIZ

HS 🛜 ✕ 📷 🍴 🖨

/ SOME UNITS 🐾

(See map & index p. 374.)

HAMPTON INN BY HILTON WINNIPEG AIRPORT/POLO PARK
204/772-3000 **6**

  THREE DIAMOND [SAVE] Hotel. **Ad-dress:** 730 Berry St R3H 0S6

AAA Benefit:
Members save up to 15%!

HILTON WINNIPEG AIRPORT SUITES
204/783-1700 **5**

 THREE DIAMOND
Hotel

 Hilton
HOTELS & RESORTS

AAA Benefit:
Members save up to 15%!

Address: 1800 Wellington Ave R3H 1B2 **Location:** At Berry St. Located in a commercial area. **Facility:** 159 units. 6 stories, interior corridors. **Parking:** on-site (fee), winter plug-ins. **Amenities:** *Some:* safes. **Pool:** heated indoor. **Activities:** sauna, hot tub, bicycles, exercise room. **Guest Services:** valet laundry, area transportation.

[SAVE] [ECO] [⊞] [✈] [¶] [🏊] [Y]

CALL [♿] [🏊] [✟] [BIZ] [📶] [✗] [🎾] [🖥] [🛎] [☕]
/ SOME UNITS [🦌]

HOLIDAY INN WINNIPEG AIRPORT WEST
204/885-4478 **18**

THREE DIAMOND
Hotel

Address: 2520 Portage Ave R3J 3T6 **Location:** Just e of Moray St. Located in a residential/commercial area. **Facility:** 228 units, some two bedrooms and efficiencies. 15 stories, interior corridors. **Parking:** winter plug-ins. **Dining:** Bell-bottoms Restaurant, see separate listing. **Pool:** heated indoor. **Activities:** hot tub, playground, exercise room. **Guest Services:** valet and coin laundry, area transportation.

[SAVE] [✈] [¶] [🏊] [Y] [🏊] [✟]
[BIZ] [📶] [✗] [🖥] [🛎] [☕]

HOLIDAY INN WINNIPEG SOUTH   204/452-4747 **22**
THREE DIAMOND Hotel. **Address:** 1330 Pembina Hwy R3T 2B4

HOMEWOOD SUITES BY HILTON WINNIPEG AIRPORT-POLO PARK   204/515-1941 **11**
THREE DIAMOND [SAVE] Extended Stay Hotel. **Address:** 1295 Ellice Ave R3G 0N5

AAA Benefit:
Members save up to 15%!

HOWARD JOHNSON EXPRESS INN   204/837-5831 **15**
APPROVED Motel. **Address:** 3740 Portage Ave R3K 0Z9

MAINSTAY SUITES WINNIPEG   204/594-0500 **9**
THREE DIAMOND Extended Stay Hotel. **Address:** 670 King Edward St R3H 0P2

QUALITY INN & SUITES   204/453-8247 **20**
APPROVED Hotel. **Address:** 635 Pembina Hwy R3M 2L4

SANDMAN HOTEL & SUITES WINNIPEG AIRPORT
204/775-7263 **7**
THREE DIAMOND Hotel. **Address:** 1750 Sargent Ave R3H 0C7

SUPER 8 WINNIPEG EAST   204/253-1935 **21**
APPROVED Hotel. **Address:** 1485 Niakwa Rd E R2J 3T3

VISCOUNT GORT HOTEL   204/775-0451 **17**

APPROVED Hotel. **Address:** 1670 Portage Ave R3J 0C9 *(See ad this page.)*

▼ See AAA listing this page ▼

We have you covered

- 10 Min from CF Polo Park
- 15 Min from the Bell MTS Place
- 15 Min from Outlet Collection Winnipeg
- Newly Renovated Rooms
- Free WI-FI
- Free Airport Shuttle
- Pet Friendly Rooms
- Microwave, Coffee Maker, Refrigerator
- Hot Tub, Fitness Room and Water Slide

$**116**⁹⁹
Single or Double
Sunday - Thursday

VISCOUNT GORT HOTEL
Banquets & Conferences

1670 Portage Ave • Winnipeg, MB R3J 0C9
Tel: (204)775-0451 • Fax: (204)772-2161
reservations@viscount-gort.com
www.viscount-gort.com

TOLL- FREE
1-800-665-1122

(See map & index p. 374.)

WHERE TO EAT

529 WELLINGTON 204/487-8325 16
THREE DIAMOND Steak Seafood. Fine Dining. **Address:**
529 Wellington Cres R3M 0A5

AALTOS 204/958-5012 20
APPROVED American. Casual Dining. **Address:** 1034
Elizabeth Rd R2J 1B3

BAKED EXPECTATIONS 204/452-5176 15
APPROVED Breads/Pastries Breakfast. Casual Dining.
Address: 161 Osborne St R3H 1B2

BEAUJENA'S FRENCH TABLE 204/233-4841 7
THREE DIAMOND French. Fine Dining. **Address:** 302
Hamel Ave R2H 0K9

BELLBOTTOMS RESTAURANT 204/885-4478 17
APPROVED American. Casual Dining. **Address:** 2520
Portage Ave R3J 3T6

BELLISSIMO RESTAURANT & LOUNGE 204/489-0495 26
THREE DIAMOND Italian. Casual Dining. **Address:** 877
Waverly St, #1 R3T 5V3

BISTRO DANSK RESTAURANT 204/775-5662 10
APPROVED European. Casual Dining. **Address:** 63
Sherbrook St R3C 2B2

BONFIRE BISTRO 204/487-4440 23
APPROVED Mediterranean. Casual Dining. **Address:**
1433 Corydon Ave R3N 0J2

BUCCACINO'S FRESCA ITALIANA 204/452-8251 12
APPROVED Italian. Casual Dining. **Address:** 155
Osborne St R3L 1Y7

CAFE DARIO 204/783-2813 3
THREE DIAMOND Latin American Fusion. Casual Dining.
Address: 1390 Erin St R3L 1Y7

CHEZ CORA 204/415-7730
APPROVED Breakfast Sandwiches. Casual Dining.
Address: 101C-1440 Jack Blick Ave R3G 0L4

CHOP STEAKHOUSE & BAR 204/788-2015 4
THREE DIAMOND Steak Seafood. Casual Dining. **Address:**
1750 Sargent Ave R3H 0C7

CONFUSION CORNER BAR & GRILL 204/284-6666 19
THREE DIAMOND International. Casual Dining. **Address:**
500 Corydon Ave R3L 0P1

DUCKY'S FISH & CHIPS 204/772-5600 2
APPROVED Fish & Chips. Casual Dining. **Address:**
884 Notre Dame Ave R3E 0M7

EARLS KITCHEN + BAR 204/975-1845
APPROVED American. Casual Dining. **Address:** 1455
Portage Ave R3G 0W4

FUSION GRILL 204/489-6963 18
THREE DIAMOND Canadian Wild Game. Casual Dining.
Address: 550 Academy Rd R3N 0E3

INDIA PALACE RESTAURANT 204/774-6061 5
APPROVED Indian. Casual Dining. **Address:** 770
Ellice Ave R3G 0B8

INFERNO'S BISTRO 204/262-7400 9
THREE DIAMOND Canadian. Casual Dining. **Address:** 312
rue Des Meurons St R2H 2N5

JOE BLACK COFFEE BAR 204/415-1660 11
APPROVED Coffee/Tea. Quick Serve. **Address:** 2037
Portage Ave R3K 0K6

JOEY RESTAURANTS
APPROVED American. Casual Dining.
LOCATIONS:
Address: 1550 Kenaston Blvd R3P 0Y4 **Phone:** 204/477-5639
Address: 635 St. James St R3G 3R4 **Phone:** 204/339-5639

LA FIESTA CAFECITO 204/257-7108 28
APPROVED Salvadoran. Casual Dining. **Address:**
730 St. Anne's Rd, Unit M R2N 0A2

MAXIME'S RESTAURANT & LOUNGE 204/257-1526 27
APPROVED Mediterranean. Casual Dining. **Address:**
1131 St. Mary's Rd R2M 3T9

MONA LISA RISTORANTE ITALIANO 204/488-3687 22
THREE DIAMOND Northern Italian. Casual Dining. **Address:**
1697 Corydon Ave R3N 0J9

MOXIE'S CLASSIC GRILL 204/783-1840 8
APPROVED American. Casual Dining. **Address:** 1485
Portage Ave, 234B R3G 0W4

NARU SUSHI JAPANESE RESTAURANT 204/888-0028 14
APPROVED Japanese Sushi. Casual Dining.
Address: 159 Osborne St R3L 1Y7

NICOLINO'S RESTAURANT 204/269-5004 29
APPROVED Italian. Casual Dining. **Address:** 4-2077
Pembina Hwy R3T 5J9

RESTO GARE 204/237-7072 6
THREE DIAMOND French. Casual Dining. **Address:** 630
Des Meurons St R2H 2P9

SANTA LUCIA PIZZA 204/488-8090 21
APPROVED Italian. Casual Dining. **Address:** 905
Corydon Ave R3M 0W8

SANTA LUCIA PIZZA 204/586-8171 1
APPROVED Italian. Casual Dining. **Address:** 1473
Main St R2W 3V9

SEGOVIA TAPAS BAR & RESTAURANT 204/477-6500 13
THREE DIAMOND New Spanish Small Plates. Casual
Dining. **Address:** 484 Stradbrook Ave R3L 0J9

STELLA'S CAFE 204/453-8562 24
APPROVED Breakfast. Casual Dining. **Address:** 166
Osborne St R3L 1Y8

WASABI SABI 204/415-7878 25
THREE DIAMOND New Sushi. Casual Dining. **Address:**
1360 Taylor Ave, #3 R3M 3Z1

Get member rates and reservations at AAA.com/hertz

Frozen lake in Nunavut

Take a journey into northern Canada and you may be surprised at your options for enjoyment.

Residents joke that the four seasons in the Northwest Territories and Nunavut—June, July, August and winter—are a bit unlike seasons in the rest of the world. The absence of a "real" spring or fall leaves busy summers and extra-long winters.

Arrive in June, July or August and you can dip your toes in the Arctic Ocean and marvel at the wildflower-dotted tundra under a midnight sun.

Or visit during the 6 months of winter and you can choose from activities involving snow and ice: snowmobiling, building an igloo, ice fishing, riding on a paw-powered sled or driving on an "ice highway," made of hard-packed snow piled on frozen lakes.

Celebrate the end of a long, dark winter by living it up at Inuvik's Sunrise Festival—held in January in honor of the sun's appearance after months of hiding.

Yellow buttercups

Northwest Territories and Nunavut

Canada's Newest Territory

On April Fools' Day, 1999, in the eastern Northwest Territories, Inuit people celebrated the birth of Nunavut, Canada's newest territory.

Twenty-four years after a separation was proposed, Nunavut (meaning "our land" in the Inuktitut language) officially seceded from the Northwest Territories to form its own territory. A new line on the Canadian map allows its approximately 29,474 residents—85 percent of whom are Inuit—the chance to govern their homeland.

Nunavut is a giant chunk of arctic earth stretching so far northeast it almost tickles the shores of Greenland, and yet it contains only one road within its nearly 2 million square kilometres (772,204 sq. mi.). Above the tree line it's a place where animals outnumber humans; where brightly colored rhododendron, yellow buttercups and mountain avens sprinkle treeless tundra; and where it may be easier to hook a trout for dinner than pick up a burger at a drive-thru.

Despite the recent division of Nunavut and Northwest Territories, the two still share similar features. During summer above the Arctic Circle, days have no end. A shining sun never dips below the horizon, and the sky is illuminated 24 hours a day. In winter the opposite occurs as days and nights melt together under a cold, dark sky.

Picture a black sky pin-pricked with stars surrounding a full, glowing moon, its light sprawling across wide, snow-covered tundra and frozen lakes. On such a clear winter night the flat, stark-white landscape glistens.

Bright Lights, Small Cities

The northern lights, or "aurora borealis," painting the winter sky are no less impressive. A faint glow slightly above the horizon serves as the show's opening act. When the lights rise, they resemble curtains in shades of red, lavender and green. Feather-shaped and stretching across the night sky, the lights ripple to form watercolor waves.

In the Northwest Territories you'll have a good chance to catch this dazzling display October through March. A spot void of city lights is best; try giant Great Slave Lake near Yellowknife. Frozen in winter, this fifth largest freshwater lake in North America provides a fine view of the vivid night sky.

Then visit Yellowknife, on the lake's north arm. Once glittering with gold, this former 1930s mining camp now flaunts its colorful past in Old Town, where shops and quaint neighborhoods nestle against the shore.

West of the city is Nahanni National Park Reserve, where Virginia Falls plummets 90 metres (295 ft.) into South Nahanni River. The falls, arguably more spectacular than Niagara, form a pool of eddies and perilous rapids surrounded by cliffs taller than Toronto's CN Tower.

Recreation

Welcome to the top of the world. The vast Northwest Territories and Nunavut boast an area filled with wild rivers, icy seas, lofty mountains and Arctic tundra. Summer days, typically June through August, are long and surprisingly mild. Hikers can check out a variety of topography, from steep mountain trails to frozen tundra. The Canol Heritage Trail, en route to the Yukon, offers some challenging terrain.

Snowmobiling, snowshoeing, dog sledding and cross-country skiing are a way of life that can extend into May—the warmer air and long days make this the perfect time for such outdoor pursuits. Many outfitters offer snowmobile tours or flights to remote areas to observe the spectacular northern lights. Hint: The best time for viewing this brilliant display is October through March.

Travel anywhere in the territories can include aircraft, boat, automobile, snowmobile, Inuit qomatiq (sled) and even dogsled. Of

the Northwest Territories' five national parks, only Wood Buffalo can be reached by road. Nahanni's rugged beauty is accessible solely by air. One of the newest parks, Tuktut Nogait, is a hiker's paradise where float planes begin landing on the Homaday River in mid-June.

Water challenges come in varying degrees of difficulty. Arctic rivers can offer the ultimate thrill if explored cautiously. Sea kayakers can flow beside towering icebergs, while the many rivers stemming off the Mackenzie are a canoeist's dream. Paddlers will be dazzled by the breathtaking scenery on the Nahanni. Hoist your sails on Great Slave Lake, or if you are brave enough, scuba dive in the frigid waters.

Cold northern waters yield excellent fishing. Plenty of spots are full of prize catches, from the feisty arctic char to the fierce northern pike. Some of the area's waters are ranked the best in the world for angling, including Great Slave, Great Bear and Murky lakes and the Stark and Snowdrift rivers.

The land's beauty, combined with unspoiled wilderness and vast game selections, makes hunting a rewarding experience. And for those who like to shoot with a camera, wildlife viewing also is rewarding. Bird-watchers flock to the Mackenzie River delta, one of the world's biggest nesting grounds.

Snowshoeing is way of life that can extend into May

Historic Timeline

1576	Sir Martin Frobisher, searching for the Northwest Passage to the Orient, arrives.
1763	The Treaty of Paris grants Canada to the British.
1771	Hudson's Bay Co. explorer-trader Samuel Hearne arrives at Great Slave Lake.
1789	Alexander Mackenzie leads an expedition along a westward-flowing river, unearthing another route to the Arctic Ocean.
1850	Capt. Robert John Le Mesurier McClure discovers the Northwest Passage.
1870	Hudson's Bay Co. cedes the region to Canada.
1920	Oil is discovered at Norman Wells.
1934	Gold is discovered at Yellowknife on Great Slave Lake.
1978	A Soviet nuclear-powered satellite crashes into the Great Slave Lake area; debris is spread over 124,000 square kilometres.
1993	The Nunavut Land Claims Agreement, under which the Inuit gain the power to govern their own territory, is passed.
1999	Northwest Territories divides into two territories; the eastern, Inuit-governed territory becomes Nunavut.

What To Pack

Temperature Averages Maximum/Minimum (Celsius)	JANUARY	FEBRUARY	MARCH	APRIL	MAY	JUNE	JULY	AUGUST	SEPTEMBER	OCTOBER	NOVEMBER	DECEMBER
Fort Liard	-20 / -28	-8 / -19	-2 / -15	9 / -4	15 / 2	21 / 8	23 / 11	21 / 9	15 / 3	3 / -4	-8 / -15	-15 / -23
Fort Smith	-19 / -28	-14 / -25	-5 / -19	6 / -6	15 / 1	20 / 7	22 / 10	20 / 8	13 / 2	4 / -3	-7 / -15	-16 / -25
Iqaluit, Nunavut	-22 / -30	-22 / -31	-18 / -28	-10 / -19	-1 / -8	6 / 0	11 / 3	10 / 3	4 / -1	-2 / -8	-9 / -17	-16 / -26
Inuvik	-24 / -33	-23 / -33	-18 / -30	-8 / -20	4 / -6	16 / 4	19 / 8	16 / 5	7 / -1	-5 / -12	-17 / -26	-21 / -31
Tulita	-24 / -30	-21 / -27	-13 / -24	0 / -10	11 / -1	20 / 7	22 / 10	19 / 11	11 / 4	-1 / -2	-15 / -15	-21 / -24
Yellowknife	-24 / -32	-19 / -29	-13 / -24	-1 / -12	10 / -1	18 / 8	21 / 12	18 / 10	10 / 3	1 / -4	-11 / -19	-20 / -28

From the records of The Weather Channel Interactive, Inc.

Good Facts To Know

ABOUT THE TERRITORIES

POPULATION: Northwest Territories 41,462. Nunavut 31,906.

AREA: Northwest Territories 140,835 sq km (440,479 sq mi.); ranks 3rd. Nunavut 1,932,255 sq km (746,048 sq mi.); ranks 1st.

CAPITAL: Yellowknife, Northwest Territories; Iqaluit, Nunavut.

HIGHEST POINT: 2,762 m (9,062 ft.), Cirque of the Unclimbables Mountain in Nahanni National Park Reserve.

LOWEST POINT: Sea level, Beaufort Sea.

TIME ZONE(S): Mountain/Central/Eastern/Atlantic. DST.

REGULATIONS

TEEN DRIVING LAWS: Minimum age for an unrestricted driver's license is 17. Phone (867) 873-7406 for more information about Northwest Territories driver's license regulations.

SEAT BELT/CHILD RESTRAINT LAWS: Seat belts are required for driver and all passengers; children under 18 kilograms (40 lbs.) are required to be in a child restraint; children less than 9 kilograms (20 lbs.) must be in a rear-facing seat. AAA recommends the use of seat belts and appropriate child restraints for the driver and all passengers.

CELLPHONE RESTRICTIONS: Text messaging and handheld cellphone use while driving is prohibited in Northwest Territories.

HELMETS FOR MOTORCYCLISTS: Required for all riders.

RADAR DETECTORS: Not permitted, even if unplugged.

MOVE OVER LAW: In the Northwest Territories, drivers must reduce their speed to a safe speed that does not exceed one-half of the posted limit, and must vacate the lane closest to a stopped emergency or law enforcement vehicle with lights flashing. In Nunavut there is no requirement to slow down or move to an adjacent lane when passing stopped emergency vehicles.

FIREARMS LAWS: By federal law, all nonresidents entering Canada with a firearm must declare their weapon in writing and pay a fee of $25 (Canadian). Contact the Canadian Firearms Centre at (800) 731-4000 to receive a declaration form or for additional information.

ALCOHOL CONSUMPTION: Legal age 19.

HOLIDAYS

HOLIDAYS: Jan. 1 ▪ Good Friday ▪ Easter Monday ▪ Victoria Day, May 24 (if a Mon.) or the closest prior Mon. ▪ Aboriginal Day, June 21 ▪ Canada Day, July 1 ▪ Nunavut Day, July 9 ▪ Civic Holiday, Aug. (1st Mon.) ▪ Labour Day, Sept. (1st Mon.) ▪ Thanksgiving, Oct. (2nd Mon.) ▪ Remembrance Day, Nov. 11 ▪ Christmas, Dec. 25 ▪ Boxing Day, Dec. 26.

MONEY

TAXES: The Northwest Territories and Nunavut have no territorial sales tax. However, a 5 percent Goods and Service Tax (GST) is levied.

VISITOR INFORMATION

INFORMATION CENTERS: Territorial welcome centers in the Northwest Territories include an office on Hwy. 1 at the Alberta border (on the 60th parallel) near Enterprise ▪ Dempster/Delta Visitor Information Centre at Km-post 77 on Hwy. 8 near Fort McPherson ▪ the Western Arctic Regional Visitor Information Centre at the termination of the Dempster Hwy. in Inuvik ▪ the Northern Frontier Visitor Centre in Yellowknife.

In Nunavut the Unikkaarvik Visitor Centre is in Iqaluit.

FURTHER INFORMATION FOR VISITORS:
Northwest Territories Tourism
P.O. Box 610
Yellowknife, NT X1A 2N5
Canada
(867) 873-5007
(800) 661-0788

Travel Nunavut
P.O. Box 1450
Iqaluit, Nunavut, NU X0A 0H0
Canada
(866) 686-2888

FISHING AND HUNTING REGULATIONS:
Northwest Territories Environment and Natural Resources
7 Forestry Dr.
Norman Wells, NT X0E 0V0
Canada
(867) 587-3500

FERRY AND ROAD INFORMATION:
Northwest Territories Department of Transportation
New Government Building, 4th Floor
5015 49th St.
Yellowknife, NT X1A 2L9
Canada
(867) 767-908231042

Northwest Territories and Nunavut Annual Events

Please call ahead to confirm event details.

 Visit **AAA.com/travelguides/events** to find
AAA-listed events for every day of the year

WINTER

Dec. - New Year's Eve Fireworks
Yellowknife / 867-920-5676
Jan. - Children's Festival of Silliness
Yellowknife / 867-766-6101
- World Snow Day / Yellowknife
867-669-9754
Feb. - NWT Ski Day / Yellowknife
867-669-9754
- Yellowknife Heritage Days
Yellowknife / 867-920-5693
- Great Northern Music Conference
Yellowknife / 867-445-8458

SPRING

Mar. - Snowking Winter Festival
Yellowknife / 867-669-1571
- Long John Jamboree / Yellowknife
867-920-0770
Apr. - Yellowknife Gold Loppet / Yellowknife
867-669-9754
- Jayman BUILT MS Walk / Yellowknife
867-444-0338
May - Ptarmigan Ptheatrics Spring Musical
Yellowknife / 867-766-6101
- Skills Canada NWT Territorial Skills
Competition / Yellowknife
867-873-8743
- Yellowknife Music Festival
Yellowknife / 867-873-4950

SUMMER

June - Yellowknife Solstice Festival
Yellowknife / 867-873-6762
- Aboriginal Day / Yellowknife
867-446-1060
- NorthWords Writers Festival
Yellowknife / 867-445-6800
July - Folk on the Rocks Music Festival
Yellowknife / 867-920-7806
Aug. - Yellowknife Overlander Marathon
Yellowknife / 867-446-6721

FALL

Sept. - Dirt Digger Duathlon / Yellowknife
867-669-9724
- Yellowknife Golf Club Glow Ball
Tournament / Yellowknife
867-873-4326
Oct. - Halloween Skate / Yellowknife
867-920-5676
- Yellowknife Watercolour Society
Annual Show / Yellowknife
867-873-6291
- Yellowknife International Film Festival
Yellowknife / 867-766-2586
Nov. - Geoscience Forum / Yellowknife
867-873-5281
- Santa Claus Parade / Yellowknife
867-920-5676

Mobile Battery Service

Delivered & Installed on the Spot!

1-800-AAA-HELP · 1-800-CAA-HELP
AAA.com/mobile · CAA.ca/mobile

Power You Can Trust!™

Northern lights in
Yellowknife

Baffin Island, Nunavut

Nahanni National Park Reserve

Bison, Wood Buffalo National Park

Ingraham Trail, Yellowknife

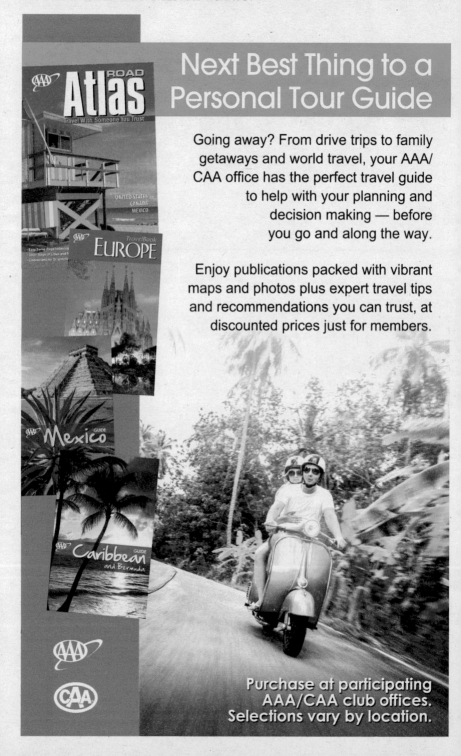

Next Best Thing to a Personal Tour Guide

Going away? From drive trips to family getaways and world travel, your AAA/CAA office has the perfect travel guide to help with your planning and decision making — before you go and along the way.

Enjoy publications packed with vibrant maps and photos plus expert travel tips and recommendations you can trust, at discounted prices just for members.

Purchase at participating AAA/CAA club offices. Selections vary by location.

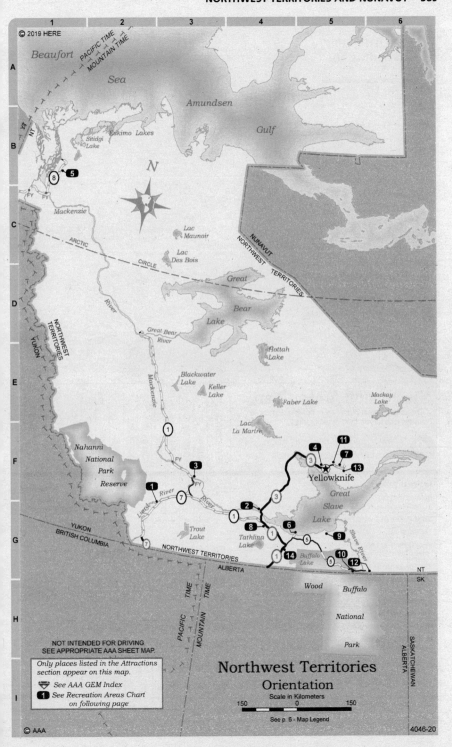

© 2019 HERE

Northwest Territories
Orientation

Scale in Kilometers
150 | 150

NOT INTENDED FOR DRIVING.
SEE APPROPRIATE AAA SHEET MAP.

Only places listed in the Attractions
section appear on this map.

See AAA GEM Index

See Recreation Areas Chart
on following page

See p. 6 - Map Legend

© AAA

4046-20

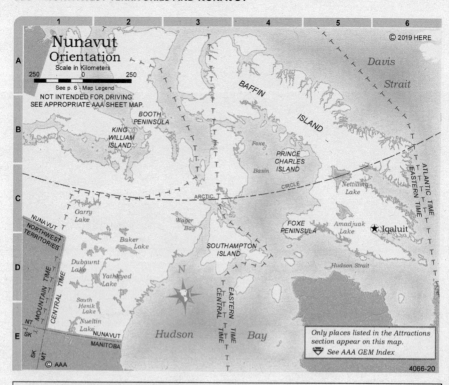

Recreation Areas Chart

The map location numerals in column 2 show an area's location on the preceding map.

🔗 Find thousands of places to camp at AAA.com/campgrounds

	MAP LOCATION	CAMPING	PICNICKING	HIKING TRAILS	BOATING	BOAT RAMP	BOAT RENTAL	FISHING	SWIMMING	PET FRIENDLY	BICYCLE TRAILS	WINTER SPORTS	VISITOR CENTER	LODGE/CABINS	FOOD SERVICE
NATIONAL PARKS *(See place listings.)*															
Nahanni (F-1) 30,000 square kilometres 145 km w. of Fort Simpson. The park is not accessible by road; no motor boats allowed.		•	•	•	•			•	•						
Wood Buffalo (H-5) 44,807 square kilometres on Hwy. 5.		•	•	•	•			•	•	•			•	•	
TERRITORIAL															
Blackstone (F-2) 1,430 hectares 166 km s. of Fort Simpson. on Hwy. 7 or 115 km n. of Fort Liard on Hwy. 7.	❶	•	•	•	•			•		•			•		
Fort Providence (G-4) 10 hectares at Fort Providence on Hwy. 3.	❷	•	•	•	•			•		•			•		
Fort Simpson (F-3) 18 hectares in Fort Simpson on Hwy. 1.	❸	•	•	•	•			•		•			•		
Fred Henne (F-5) 500 hectares on Hwy. 3 across from Yellowknife airport. Sailing.	❹	•	•	•	•			•	•	•	•		•		
Gwich'in Reserve (B-1) 8,800 hectares s. of Inuvik on Hwy. 8.	❺	•	•		•			•		•					
Hay River (G-4) 11 hectares on Vale Island in Hay River.	❻	•	•		•			•	•	•					
Hidden Lake (F-5) 3,000 hectares 45 km e. of Yellowknife along Hwy. 4. Scenic. Canoeing; golf; interpretive displays.	❼	•	•	•	•			•		•					
Lady Evelyn Falls (G-4) 5 hectares 6.5 km off Hwy. 1 near Kakisa.	❽	•	•	•				•		•			•		
Little Buffalo River Crossing (G-5) 33 hectares off Hwy. 6, 30 km w. of Fort Resolution.	❾	•	•		•			•		•					
Little Buffalo River Falls (G-5) 33 hectares off Hwy. 5, 50 km n.w. of Fort Smith.	❿	•	•	•	•			•		•					
Prelude Lake (F-5) 95 hectares 29 km w. of Yellowknife on Hwy. 4.	⓫	•	•	•	•	•		•	•	•			•		

Recreation Areas Chart

The map location numerals in column 2 show an area's location on the preceding map.

 Find thousands of places to camp at AAA.com/campgrounds

	MAP LOCATION	CAMPING	PICNICKING	HIKING TRAILS	BOATING	BOAT RAMP	BOAT RENTAL	FISHING	SWIMMING	PET FRIENDLY	BICYCLE TRAILS	WINTER SPORTS	VISITOR CENTER	LODGE/CABINS	FOOD SERVICE
Queen Elizabeth (G-5) 38 hectares off Hwy. 5 in Fort Smith.	12	•	•	•				•		•	•		•		
Reid Lake (F-5) 68 hectares 60 km e. of Yellowknife on Hwy. 4.	13	•	•	•	•	•		•	•	•					
Twin Falls Gorge (G-4) 673 hectares at Km-post 75 on Hwy. 1.	14	•	•	•	•					•			•		

Make the Connction

AAA guidebooks are just the beginning. Open the door to a whole lot more on AAA.com. Get extra travel insight, more information and online booking.

 Find this symbol for places to look, book and save on AAA.com.

iStockphoto.com_shapecharge

BAFFIN ISLAND, NUNAVUT (A-4)

High in Nunavut's Eastern Arctic is Baffin Island, the homeland of the Inuit. It is a land of majestic fiords, icebergs, bountiful wildlife and the midnight sun, which shines until 3 a.m. from March to June. Although Baffin Island is not accessible by car, Iqaluit, Nunavut's capital city, is served by two airlines.

Qaummaarviit Territorial Park, 12 kilometres (7 mi.) west of Iqaluit, can be reached by boat in summer or by dogsled and snowmobile in spring. An easy-to-follow trail links the island's ruins with signs depicting aspects of prehistoric life and culture.

Auyuittuq National Park, 28 kilometres (17 mi.) from Pangnirtung, is accessible by dogsled, snowmobile or boat. The park is notable for its fiords and glaciated valleys and mountains and for being the first national park established above the Arctic Circle. Polar bears, arctic foxes, caribou, seals, walruses, whales and narwhals inhabit the region.

Included in the approximately 40 bird species spotted in the park are the rare gyrfalcon and whistling swan. Remains of the 1,000-year-old Thule Eskimo culture have been found in Cumberland Sound. Hikers and mountain campers traversing Auyuittuq's Akshayuk Pass—commonly known as the "Pang Pass"—will find challenging trails, abundant wildlife and spectacular scenery.

Quttinirpaaq National Park (formerly known as Ellesmere Island National Park Reserve) is the most northerly land mass in Canada and contains 2,604-metre (8,544-ft.) Mount Barbeau, the highest mountain in eastern North America, and Lake Hazen, one of the largest lakes north of the Arctic Circle. The reserve is primarily a polar desert encompassing 39,500 square kilometres (15,250 sq. mi.) of mountain ranges, glaciers, ice shelves and fiords. Remains of buildings from European expeditions can be found on the rocky terrain. Outfitters in Grise Fiord, Iqaluit and Resolute Bay can arrange trips into the park.

Katannilik Territorial Park, between Kimmirut and Iqaluit, is rich with wildlife and unique flora. River tours, hiking and northern survival challenge even the hardiest adventurers. Information can be obtained from Nunavut Tourism, (866) 686-2888, or from the park's visitor center, (867) 939-2416.

In spring and summer licensed guides from Angmarlik Visitor Centre lead expeditions into Kekerten Territorial Park, 50 kilometres (32 mi.) south of Pangnirtung; phone (867) 939-2416. Visitors can see remains of whale lookouts, blubber vats, whalers' houses and Inuit homes. A self-guiding trail connects dozens of ruins.

In the northeasternmost part of Baffin Island is Sirmilik National Park, approximately 22,200 square kilometres (8,572 sq. mi.) of rugged mountains, glaciers, ice fields, ocean fiords and coastal lowlands. In fact Sirmilik translates to "the place of glaciers." Pond Inlet, the closest community to the park, is 25 kilometres (16 mi.) south. Travel to the park—by boat, dogsled or snowmobile (depending on the season)—can be arranged through outfitters in Pond Inlet or Arctic Bay.

The park is accessible year-round, except in October and November when the ice freezes up and in July during ice break up. Popular with mountain climbers, Sirmilik is also a haven for bird-watchers. Colonies of seabirds, including thick-billed murres, black-legged kittiwakes and greater snow geese, inhabit Bylot Island. For additional information contact the park office in Pond Inlet; phone (867) 899-8092.

NAHANNI NATIONAL PARK RESERVE (F-1)

Elevations in the park range from 1,853 metres (6,079 ft.) at the South Nahanni River to 2,762 metres (9,062 ft.) in the Cirque of the Unclimbables in the park's northwest corner. Refer to CAA/AAA maps for additional elevation information.

About 145 kilometres (90 mi.) west of Fort Simpson and accessible only by air, the park uses Fort Liard and Fort Simpson in the Territories, Muncho Lake in British Columbia, and Watson Lake and Whitehorse in the Yukon as its major supply and jumping-off points. Steeped in myth, mystery and adventure, Nahanni National Park Reserve covers more than 30,000 square kilometres (11,583 sq. mi.) of wilderness in the South Nahanni country.

Liard Highway, linking Fort Nelson and Fort Simpson, passes Blackstone Territorial Park, east of Nahanni National Park Reserve, providing access to Liard River and Nahanni Butte, 30 kilometres (19 mi.) upriver.

A land of rivers, ragged peaks, more than 30 species of mammals and a waterfall twice the height of Niagara Falls, Nahanni National Park Reserve was created in 1972. It was placed on the UNESCO (United Nations Educational, Scientific and Cultural Organization) World Heritage list 6 years later and cited as an "exceptional natural site forming part of the heritage of mankind."

In the early 1900s the area received a reputation for myth and adventure. Gold prospectors, drawn by rumors of placer deposits, began to arrive. When the decapitated bodies of the two MacLeod brothers were found, stories of huge mountain men proliferated.

Although no real mountain men ever were seen, the park remains a place of rugged beauty with little development, including few accommodations for visitors. Those who come to raft and canoe on the rivers and hike the forests, alpine tundra and canyons of Nahanni will find it a bracing experience. Travel by water is an excellent way to enjoy the park; however, it can be dangerous and should be attempted only by those experienced in canoeing and rafting. Reservations are required for river trips. Due to the trips' popularity, reservations should be made well in advance; phone the park office for information.

Less experienced river travelers should hire a licensed outfitter for guided river trips down the South Nahanni River. Tours pass Virginia Falls, where the South Nahanni River plunges more than 90 metres (295 ft.); the Gate, a 90-degree river bend below 213-metre (700-ft.) vertical cliffs; and hot springs such as those at First Canyon and Rabbitkettle. Visitors to Rabbitkettle **must** register at the warden's cabin and have park staff accompany them to the springs. Daytime air trips to Virginia Falls should be prearranged through an air charter company in Fort Simpson, Fort Liard, Watson Lake, Whitehorse or Muncho Lake.

Fishing for arctic grayling, lake and bull trout and northern pike is permitted with a national park fishing license (annual pass $34.30), which can be obtained at the Fort Simpson Administration Office or at the warden's cabin at Rabbitkettle Lake. All national park regulations apply. Firearms are not permitted.

Wildlife species include moose, beavers, woodland caribou, Dall sheep, grizzly and black bears, white-tailed deer and mountain goats. Visitors should take particular care when traveling in areas where they are likely to encounter bears.

The park is open year-round. The park administration office at Fort Simpson is open daily 8:30-noon and 1-5, July-Aug.; Mon.-Fri. 8:30-noon and 1-5, rest of year. Overnight visitors and those planning river rafting or canoe trips must register before entering the park and upon leaving.

One-day admission to the park is $24.50 per person. For route information, park regulations, weather conditions and park activities contact the Superintendent, Nahanni National Park Reserve, P.O. Box 348, Fort Simpson, NT, Canada X0E 0N0; phone (867) 695-7750. *See Recreation Areas Chart.*

Bordering Nahanni National Park Reserve to the northeast, Náàts'ihch'oh National Park Reserve was established in 2012 as Canada's 44th national park. Combined with Nahanni, Náàts'ihch'oh (pronounced naats-each-choh) protects 86 percent of the South Nahanni River watershed including land that is culturally and spiritually important to aboriginal peoples. Trumpeter swans, caribou, mountain goats and grizzly bears live within the park's boundaries.

WOOD BUFFALO NATIONAL PARK (H-5)

Elevations in the park range from 183 metres (600 ft.) at the Little Buffalo River to 945 metres (3,100 ft.) in the Caribou Mountains. Refer to CAA/AAA maps for additional elevation information.

Accessible by Hwy. 5, which connects with Mackenzie Hwy. at Hay River, Wood Buffalo National Park is the second largest park in the world. Covering about the same area as the states of Maryland and New Jersey combined, the national park straddles the border between the Northwest Territories and Alberta.

This vast subarctic wilderness contains such remarkable geological features as the Salt Plains, Alberta Plateau, the deltas and lowlands of the Peace River and Athabasca River, and extensive gypsum karst formations. The park was established in 1922 to protect one of the world's largest free-roaming herds of wood bison; approximately 5,000 of these animals now live there. Moose, caribou, muskrats, beavers and black bears are among other park residents.

The Peace Athabasca Delta is an important stopover for North America's four major waterfowl flyways. A large variety of waterfowl as well as hawks, eagles and pelicans, are present for part of the year. The northeastern corner of the park is one of the last nesting grounds in the world for the endangered whooping crane. Some of the park's lakes and rivers contain pike, pickerel, trout, whitefish and goldeye. Wildflowers and berries abound in the rolling meadows.

The 508-kilometre (316-mi.) Fort Chipewyan Winter Road is open mid-December to mid-March (weather permitting). The road runs from Fort McMurray, Alberta, to Fort Smith; part of the road is formed by ice. To check road conditions between Fort Chipewyan and Fort Smith, phone the park office or (867) 872-7962 for recorded information. To check road conditions between Fort Chipewyan and Fort McMurray, phone the Regional Municipality of Wood Buffalo at (780) 697-3600.

STAY CONNECTED

GET THE APP

AAA.com/mobile
CAA.ca/mobile

Visitors can see such magnificent snow-covered scenery as boreal forest, lakes and wide-open meadows. Before departure travelers should contact the park office for a list of driving regulations and recommended travel supplies.

Boating, picnicking and camping are permitted at Pine Lake. The park has hiking trails, which can be used for snowshoeing and cross-country skiing in winter. Contact the park for information about guided nature hikes and other interpretive events.

The park is open year-round; however, campgrounds and facilities are open Victoria Day weekend through Labour Day. The Fort Smith Visitor Reception Centre at 149 McDougal Rd. is open daily 9-6, June 1 through Labour Day; Mon.-Fri. 9-noon and 1-5, rest of year. Phone (867) 872-7960, or TTY (867) 872-7961. The Fort Chipewyan Visitor Reception Centre on MacKenzie Avenue is open Mon.-Fri. 9-noon and 1-5, year-round. Hours may vary; phone ahead. Phone (780) 697-3662.

Admission to the park is free. For route information, road conditions or details about park activities contact the Superintendent, Wood Buffalo National Park, P.O. Box 750, Fort Smith, NT, Canada X0E 0P0; phone (867) 872-7960. *See Recreation Areas Chart.*

YELLOWKNIFE (F-5) pop. 19,234

Although the Dene hunted the Yellowknife region for thousands of years and Europeans explored it in 1771, a permanent settlement was not established until the discovery of gold in 1934. Taking the name of the copper knives carried by the Chipewyan Indians, the town is now the capital of the Northwest Territories and the site of a gold mine and a booming diamond industry.

In 1967 Yellowknife replaced Ottawa as the seat of government for the Northwest Territories. Tours of the Legislative Assembly are available Mon.-Fri. at 10:30, 1:30 and 3:30, Sun. at 1:30, June-Aug.; Mon.-Fri. at 10:30, rest of year. Phone (867) 669-2200. On the northern shore of Great Slave Lake, this "metropolis" of the north lies less than 500 kilometres (311 mi.) from the Arctic Circle and is an excellent place to shop for Northern arts.

The city's historic Old Town retains the gold rush excitement of the 1930s with quaint restaurants, art galleries, shops, and boat, kayak, canoe and yacht rentals. Planes are available for sightseeing and fishing trips. The visitor center on 49th Street can provide information about rentals and excursions.

Best viewed October through March, the aurora borealis, or northern lights, is produced when atomic particles from outside the atmosphere strike and excite atoms within the upper atmosphere. The lights sweep mysteriously across the clear night sky as luminescent curtains of red, green, pink and purple light in patterns called rayed bands. Guided viewing trips are available.

The scenic 71-kilometre (44-mi.) Ingraham Trail (Hwy. 4) to Tibbitt Lake allows year-round access to several chains of lakes and streams. Seven boat launches and two campgrounds lie along the road. Prelude Nature Trail runs 3 kilometres (1.8 mi.) from Prelude Lake Territorial Park *(see Recreation Areas Chart)* through the wilderness to several lookout points, while another trail leads to Cameron Falls.

Prospector's Trail is in Fred Henne Territorial Park *(see Recreation Areas Chart)*, west near Long Lake. The 4-kilometre (2.5-mi.) loop points out the region's varied geological features and is of interest to rock hounds; sturdy footwear and insect repellent are necessary. Other hiking trails lead from Ingraham Trail; information and brochures are available at the visitor center.

Easily accessible area lakes include Prosperous Lake, Pontoon Lake, Prelude Lake, Reid Lake and Tibbitt Lake. Walsh Lake has good trout fishing, but is accessible only by going through Reid Lake.

The scenic portion of Hwy. 3 runs north from Mackenzie Bison Sanctuary to Edzo, then parallels the northern shore of Great Slave Lake. Driving anywhere in the area, or throughout the Northwest Territories, demands that a vehicle be in top mechanical condition.

Yellowknife Visitors' Centre (Extraordinary Yellowknife): 4807 52nd St., Yellowknife, NT, Canada X1A 2P4. **Phone:** (867) 920-8687.

Self-guiding tours: The visitor center provides brochures for a walking tour of Old Town and New Town.

DAYS INN & SUITES YELLOWKNIFE   867/873-9700
APPROVED   Hotel. **Address:** 4401 50th Ave X1A 2N2

THE EXPLORER HOTEL   867/873-3531
THREE DIAMOND Hotel. **Address:** 4825 49th Ave X1A 2R3

SUPER 8 YELLOWKNIFE   867/669-8888
APPROVED   Hotel. **Address:** 308 Old Airport Rd X1A 3G3

WHERE TO EAT

THE BLACK KNIGHT PUB   867/920-4041
APPROVED   International. Gastropub. **Address:** 4910 49th St X1A 2N8

BULLOCK'S BISTRO   867/873-3474
APPROVED   Regional Canadian. Casual Dining. **Address:** 3534 Weaver Dr X1A 2J6

RED APPLE RESTAURANT   867/766-3388
APPROVED   Chinese. Casual Dining. **Address:** 4701 50 Ave X1A 2N6

TRADER'S GRILL   867/873-3531
THREE DIAMOND Canadian. Casual Dining. **Address:** 4825 49th Ave X1A 2R2

A Few Good Reasons to Know When Help Will Arrive

When a road trip stalls and you request AAA/CAA assistance, opt to receive text updates.

Messages:

- Confirm receipt of your service request
- Alert you when a service vehicle is en route
- Provide the service vehicle's estimated arrival time

Opt in and stay informed.

AAA.com/mobile | CAA.ca/mobile

Wheat crop in Saskatchewan

A visit to Saskatchewan is a perfect escape from the hustle and bustle.

Named after the Plains Cree term *kisiskatchewan,* meaning "the river that flows swiftly," Saskatchewan boasts more than just a great river with an unusual name.

Along country roads, you'll encounter prairies, mountains, grasslands and even sand dunes. While about half the province is covered in pine, white spruce and other trees, a good portion is blanketed with fields of wheat.

Look for signs marked with a barn symbol; they designate bed and breakfast inns and vacation farms, where you can take part in milking cows and enjoy homemade berry preserves or baked goods.

Take a dip into one of more than 100,000 freshwater lakes, including those nestled among resorts and golf courses with rolling fairways in the Qu'Appelle Valley.

Legislative Building

Saskatchewan

For history, head to towns that preserve the origin of the Mounted Police, the heritage of Métis culture or the rough-and-tumble cowboy lifestyle.

Or visit the Beaver Lodge Cabin on Ajawaan Lake in Prince Albert National Park, residence of naturalist author Grey Owl, who coined the popular belief that "you belong to nature, not it to you."

Colors of the Province

The hues of Saskatchewan's palette were determined both with and without man's help. Painted by nature and the history of the plains, vibrant gold, green and red figure prominently in the province's scheme.

Shimmering fields of grain glint gold in the sunlight. The plains stretch to the horizon in a never-ending series of undulating waves, interrupted only by an occasional silo. More than 50 percent of Canada's wheat crop comes from this land. Proof of the grain's economic importance to the province is the three golden wheat sheaves on its coat of arms. Saskatchewan's flag provides further evidence; its lower half, a solid band of gold, represents the grain fields dominating the province's southern portion.

Color Regina green—the city has more than 350,000 trees. A particularly verdant section of town is Wascana Centre, a 930-hectare urban park that's the heart of Saskatchewan's capital. Lining the rambling shoreline of Wascana Lake, the center is home to cultural and educational institutions and the architecturally impressive Legislative Building, the seat of provincial government.

Prince Albert National Park contributes to the emerald color scheme with nearly 1 million acres of spruce, evergreens and grassland.

The Royal Canadian Mounted Police are immediately recognizable by their scarlet tunics. In fact, the route they took in 1874 to establish law and order in western Canada is retraced along Hwy. 13, the Red Coat Trail.

Regina is home to the RCMP Heritage Centre, the RCMP's only training academy. Watch the cadets drill at the Sergeant Major's Parade, usually held Monday, Wednesday and Friday at 12:45 p.m. In July and early August, the province's colors are displayed in the Sunset Retreat Ceremony. The golden glow cast by the setting sun seems especially fitting while you watch crimson-clad cadets proudly march in formation against the backdrop of lush greenery that borders the parade grounds.

Recreation

Contrary to popular belief, Saskatchewan is not all prairie. Even in the southern half, where farming is predominant, lakes and parks overflow with recreational options.

Choose from more than 100,000 lakes, rivers and streams for freshwater fishing. While northern pike, rainbow trout and walleye will take your bait throughout the province, head for northern waters to land trophy-size lake trout, Arctic grayling and other sport fish.

Lake Diefenbaker, south of Outlook, is a favorite destination for walleye or northern pike. The Canadian Shield, in the northern third of the province, is a safe bet for anglers; almost 40 percent of its area consists of H_2O. Try Lac la Ronge for trout. Outfitters will fly you to more remote northern fishing lakes.

Tumbling east to west across the province north of the 55th parallel, the Churchill River provides some of North America's best white-water canoeing. Experience white-water rafting on the Clearwater River.

If the rush of white-water action is too intense, paddle your boat along calmer waters. The Bagwa Canoe Route, in Prince Albert National Park, travels through several pristine lakes. Dip your oars in late May through September, when the lakes are warmest.

For the ultimate in calm, head to Little Manitou Lake, near the resort community of Manitou Beach. The lake is believed to have curative powers; its high concentration of minerals makes sinking impossible.

When winter makes its appearance, go cross-country skiing on groomed and marked trails. Prince Albert National Park has about 150 kilometres (93 mi.) of trails. Moose Mountain Provincial Park, north of Carlyle, adds another 50 kilometres (30 mi.). Thousands of kilometres of groomed trails link towns and parks along Canada's version of Route 66, a cross-country snowmobile route. Put-in points include Nipawin, North Battleford and Yorkton. Snowmobile registration is mandatory; phone Tourism Saskatchewan, (877) 237-2273, for a provincial snowmobile trail map.

When warm weather finally returns, Saskatchewanians and visitors alike head to Prince Albert National Park. Three loop trails—Boundary Bog, Mud Creek and Treebeard—traverse fairly level terrain and put you in touch with some of Mother Nature's creations—a black spruce and tamarack bog; sightings of beavers and great blue herons; and forests of aspens and balsam firs.

Another popular summer playground is the Qu'Appelle Valley, a broad swath of land in southern Saskatchewan bordered by rolling hills. A chain of lakes and three provincial parks are the setting for resort villages where guests enjoy boating, water skiing and swimming.

Royal Canadian Mounted Police

Historic Timeline

1690	Henry Kelsey, an English fur trader, explores Saskatchewan.
1774	The Hudson's Bay Company builds Saskatchewan's first permanent settlement.
1870	Canada acquires present-day Saskatchewan as part of the Northwest Territories.
1873	The massacre of a band of Assiniboine First Nations by U.S. wolf hunters prompts the creation of the Mounted Police.
1885	Louis Riel leads the Métis tribe's battle for land rights in the Northwest Rebellion.
1905	Saskatchewan becomes a province.
1962	Saskatchewan establishes the first public health insurance program in North America.
1979	John Diefenbaker, Canada's 13th prime minister, is buried at the University of Saskatchewan.
1994	An almost complete Tyrannosaurus rex skeleton is unearthed near Eastend.
2001	Prince Charles makes his first royal visit to Saskatchewan.
2017	Canada marks its 150th birthday with celebrations across the province.

What To Pack

Temperature Averages Maximum/Minimum (Celsius)	JANUARY	FEBRUARY	MARCH	APRIL	MAY	JUNE	JULY	AUGUST	SEPTEMBER	OCTOBER	NOVEMBER	DECEMBER
Maple Creek	-2/-14	1/-12	7/-6	14/0	20/5	25/9	29/12	28/11	22/5	14/-1	5/-7	0/-13
Meadow Lake	-10/-19	-7/-17	-1/-10	10/-2	17/4	21/8	23/11	22/9	16/4	9/-2	-2/-11	-8/-17
Prince Albert	-14/-26	-9/-22	-3/-16	9/-4	18/3	22/8	24/11	23/9	16/3	9/-3	-3/-13	-12/-22
Regina	-11/-22	-8/-18	-1/-12	10/-3	18/4	23/9	26/12	26/11	18/4	12/-2	0/-11	-9/-19
Saskatoon	-13/-23	-9/-19	-2/-13	10/-2	18/4	23/9	25/12	24/10	17/4	11/-2	-2/-11	-10/-19
Yorkton	-13/-23	-9/-21	-3/-14	8/-3	17/3	22/9	24/11	24/9	17/4	10/-2	-2/-11	-11/-20

From the records of The Weather Channel Interactive, Inc.

Good Facts To Know

ABOUT THE PROVINCE

POPULATION: 1,033,381.

AREA: 651,036 sq km (251,365 sq mi.); ranks 7th.

CAPITAL: Regina.

HIGHEST POINT: 1,392 m (4,566 ft.), Cypress Hills.

LOWEST POINT: 65 m/213 ft., Lake Athabasca.

TIME ZONE(S): Central and Mountain.

GAMBLING

MINIMUM AGE FOR GAMBLING: 19.

REGULATIONS

TEEN DRIVING LAWS: Teens who have had a license less than 6 months may transport no more than one non-family member. Other passengers must be family members, all of whom must have a seat belt. The minimum age for an unrestricted license is 17 years, 6 months. Phone (844) 855-2744 for more information about Saskatchewan's driver's license regulations.

SEAT BELT/CHILD RESTRAINT LAWS: Seat belts are required for the driver and all passengers ages 16 and over. Children under age 16 and weighing more than 18 kilograms (40 lbs.) are required to wear a child restraint or seat belt; those under 7 and weighing less than 36 kilograms (79 lbs) and less than 145 cm (4 feet, 9 inches) in height are required to be placed in a booster seat. Child restraints are required for children weighing less than 18 kilograms.

CELLPHONE RESTRICTIONS: All drivers are prohibited from holding, viewing or manipulating a cellphone or text messaging while driving. Drivers in the graduated driver's licensing program also are prohibited from any type of use.

HELMETS FOR MOTORCYCLISTS: Required for all riders.

RADAR DETECTORS: Permitted.

MOVE OVER LAW: Motorists may not drive greater than 60 kph (37 mph) while passing highway workers or equipment, stopped emergency vehicles with flashing emergency lights, and stopped tow trucks with flashing amber lights.

FIREARMS LAWS: By federal law, all nonresidents entering Canada with a firearm must declare their weapon in writing and pay a fee of $25 (Canadian). Contact the Canadian Firearms Centre at (800) 731-4000 for additional information or to receive a declaration form.

ALCOHOL CONSUMPTION: Legal age 19.

HOLIDAYS

HOLIDAYS: Jan. 1 ■ Family Day, Feb. (3rd Mon.) ■ Good Friday ■ Victoria Day, May 24 (if a Mon.) or the closest prior Mon. ■ Canada Day, July 1 ■ Saskatchewan Day, Aug. (1st Mon.) ■ Labour Day, Sept. (1st Mon.) ■ Thanksgiving, Oct. (2nd Mon.) ■ Remembrance Day, Nov. 11 ■ Christmas, Dec. 25 ■ Boxing Day, Dec. 26.

MONEY

TAXES: The federal Goods and Services Tax (GST) is 5 percent. Saskatchewan's provincial sales tax also is 5 percent.

ATTRACTION ADMISSIONS: Quoted attraction admission rates do not include applicable provincial taxes. Admission rates paid in cash are rounded up or down to the nearest 5 cents; rates paid with a credit or debit card are not rounded.

VISITOR INFORMATION

INFORMATION CENTERS: Provincial welcome centers are along Hwy. 1 east of Fleming ■ at 1922 Park St. in Regina ■ and Maple Creek on Hwy. 1 ■ Hwy. 16 at Langenburg and Lloydminster ■ and Hwy. 39 at North Portal. Provincial welcome centers are open Mon.-Fri. 8-5, year-round.

FURTHER INFORMATION FOR VISITORS:
Tourism Saskatchewan
189-1621 Albert St.
Regina, SK S4P 2S5
Canada
(306) 787-9600
(877) 237-2273

FISHING AND HUNTING REGULATIONS:
Ministry of Environment
3211 Albert St.
4th Floor
Regina, SK S4S 5W6
Canada
(306) 787-2314
(800) 567-4224 (in Canada)

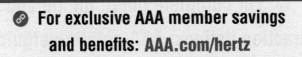

For exclusive AAA member savings and benefits: AAA.com/hertz

Saskatchewan Annual Events

Please call ahead to confirm event details.

 Visit **AAA.com/travelguides/events** to find
AAA-listed events for every day of the year

WINTER	SPRING
Dec. - Sundog Arts and Entertainment Faire Saskatoon / 306-384-7364 　　 - Enchanted Forest Holiday Light Tour Saskatoon / 306-975-3382 **Jan.** - Western Canadian Crop Production Show / Saskatoon / 306-931-7149 　　 - Lieutenant Governor's New Year's Day Levee / Regina / 306-787-4070 　　 - Knights of Columbus Saskatchewan Indoor Games / Saskatoon 306-955-4818 **Feb.** - Saskatoon Blues Festival / Saskatoon 306-345-9587 　　 - Canadian Challenge Sled Dog Race Prince Albert / 306-278-7724 　　 - Prince Albert Winter Festival / Prince Albert / 306-764-7595	**Mar.** - Antiques and Collectibles Swap Meet Moose Jaw / 306-693-7315 　　 - Spring Home Show / Regina 306-546-5223 　　 - Thunder Creek Model Railroad Club Model Train Show / Moose Jaw / 306-693-5989 **Apr.** - GlassArt / Saskatoon / 306-343-7450 　　 - First Nations Spring Celebration Pow Wow / Regina / 306-790-5950 　　 - Yorkton Spring Expo / Yorkton 306-783-4800 **May** - Saskatchewan Highland Gathering and Celtic Festival / Regina 306-789-6516 　　 - Cathedral Village Arts Festival Regina / 306-569-8744 　　 - Vesna Festival / Saskatoon 306-652-7717

SUMMER	FALL
June - Summer Sizzler / Humboldt 306-682-3444 　　 - Mosaic: A Festival of Cultures Regina / 306-757-5990 　　 - SaskTel Saskatchewan Jazz Festival Saskatoon / 306-652-4700 **July** - Shakespeare on the Saskatchewan Saskatoon / 306-653-2300 　　 - Lloydminster Colonial Days Fair Lloydminster / 306-825-5571 　　 - Saskatchewan Festival of Words Moose Jaw / 306-691-0557 **Aug.** - Saskatoon Folkfest / Saskatoon 306-931-0100 　　 - Queen City Ex / Regina 306-781-9200 　　 - The Saskatoon EX / Saskatoon 888-931-9333	**Sept.** - Goose Festival / Kindersley 306-463-6620 　　 - Tapestrama / Prince Albert / 306-763-4438 　　 - Maple Creek Cowboy Poetry Gathering and Western Art and Gear Show / Maple Creek / 306-671-7338 **Oct.** - Reflections of Nature Art Show Saskatoon / 306-931-7149 　　 - Haunted Museum / Moose Jaw / 306-630-5727 　　 - Thanksgiving Pow Wow / Prince Albert / 306-764-4751 **Nov.** - Canadian Western Agribition / Regina 306-565-0565 　　 - Lloydminster Stockade Roundup Lloydminster / 306-825-5571 　　 - Yorkton Grain Miller's Harvest Showdown / Yorkton / 306-783-4800

For complete hotel, dining and attraction listings: AAA.com/travelguides

Sunflowers, Outlook

Saskatoon and the South
Saskatchewan River

Canola field and red barn

Grasslands National Park

Lake Diefenbaker, Elbow

Index: Great Experience for Members

AAA editor's picks of exceptional note

Prince Albert National Park

RCMP Heritage Centre

Royal Saskatchewan Museum

Wanuskewin Heritage Park

See Orientation map on p. 408 for corresponding grid coordinates, if applicable.
*Indicates the GEM is temporarily closed.

Prince Albert National Park (B-3)
Prince Albert National Park *(See p. 417.)*

Regina (E-4)
Government House Museum and Interpretive Centre *(See p. 418.)*

RCMP Heritage Centre *(See p. 419.)*
Royal Saskatchewan Museum *(See p. 419.)*

Saskatoon (D-3)
Wanuskewin Heritage Park *(See p. 426.)*

LET'S GET SOCIAL

Connect with AAA for the latest updates.

 AAA.com/Facebook

AAA.com/Twitter

 Instagram.com/aaa_national

 YouTube.com/AAA

Saskatchewan
Atlas Section

ROADS/HIGHWAYS
- INTERSTATE
- CONTROLLED ACCESS
- CONTROLLED ACCESS TOLL
- TOLL ROAD
- PRIMARY DIVIDED
- PRIMARY UNDIVIDED
- SECONDARY DIVIDED
- SECONDARY UNDIVIDED
- LOCAL DIVIDED
- LOCAL UNDIVIDED
- UNPAVED ROAD
- UNDER CONSTRUCTION
- TUNNEL
- PEDESTRIAN ONLY
- AUTO FERRY
- PASSENGER FERRY
- SCENIC BYWAY
- DISTANCES BETWEEN MARKERS
- EXIT NUMBER–FREE/TOLL
- INTERCHANGE FULL/PARTIAL
- WELCOME/INFORMATION CENTER
- REST AREA/ SERVICE CENTER

ROAD SHIELDS
- INTERSTATE/BUSINESS
- U.S./STATE/COUNTY
- FOREST/INDIAN
- TRANS-CANADA
- PROVINCIAL AUTOROUTE/ KING'S HIGHWAY
- MEXICO
- HISTORIC ROUTE 66
- VT 41 REFERENCE PAGE INDICATOR

BOUNDARIES
- INTERNATIONAL
- STATE
- COUNTY
- TIME ZONE
- CONTINENTAL DIVIDE

POINTS OF INTEREST
- TOWN
- NATIONAL CAPITAL
- STATE/PROVINCIAL CAPITAL
- AAA/CAA CLUB LOCATION
- FEATURE OF INTEREST
- COLLEGE/UNIVERSITY
- CUSTOMS STATION
- HISTORIC
- LIGHTHOUSE
- MONUMENT/MEMORIAL
- NATIONAL WILDLIFE REFUGE
- STATE/PROVINCIAL PARK
- SKI AREA
- SPORTS COMPLEX
- DAM

AREAS OF INTEREST
- INDIAN
- MILITARY
- PARK
- FOREST
- GRASSLANDS
- HISTORIC
- INT'L/REGIONAL AIRPORT
- INCORPORATED CITY

CITIES/TOWNS are color-coded by size, showing where to find AAA Inspected and Approved lodgings or restaurants listed in the AAA TourBook guides and on AAA.com:
- Red - major destinations and capitals; many listings
- Black - destinations; some listings
- Grey - no listings

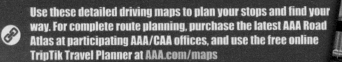

Use these detailed driving maps to plan your stops and find your way. For complete route planning, purchase the latest AAA Road Atlas at participating AAA/CAA offices, and use the free online TripTik Travel Planner at AAA.com/maps

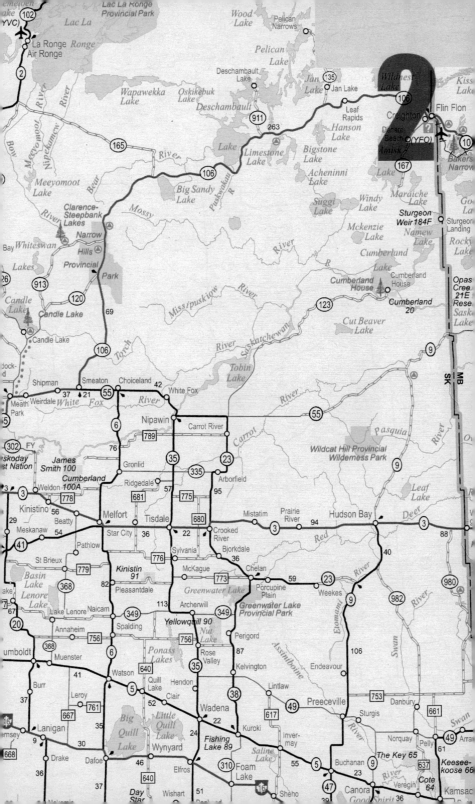

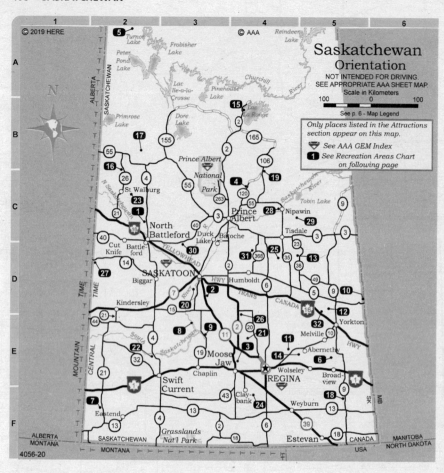

Recreation Areas Chart

The map location numerals in column 2 show an area's location on the preceding map.

🔗 Find thousands of places to camp at AAA.com/campgrounds

	MAP LOCATION	CAMPING	PICNICKING	HIKING TRAILS	BOATING	BOAT RAMP	BOAT RENTAL	FISHING	SWIMMING	PET FRIENDLY	BICYCLE TRAILS	WINTER SPORTS	VISITOR CENTER	LODGE/CABINS	FOOD SERVICE
NATIONAL PARKS *(See place listings.)*															
Grasslands (F-3) 906 square kilometres.		•	•	•						•			•		
Prince Albert (B-3) 3,875 square kilometres. Horse rental.		•	•	•	•	•	•	•	•	•			•		
PROVINCIAL															
The Battlefords (C-2) 600 hectares 4.75 km n. of Cochin off Hwy. 4. Cross-country skiing; golf.	**1**	•	•	•	•	•	•	•	•	•	•	•	•	•	•
Blackstrap (D-3) 530 hectares 8 km e. of Dundurn via Hwy. 211. Cross-country and downhill skiing; sailboard and water bike rental.	**2**	•	•	•	•	•	•	•	•	•		•	•	•	•
Buffalo Pound (E-4) 1,930 hectares 19 km n. of Moose Jaw on Hwy. 2, then 13 km e. on Hwy. 202. Cross-country and downhill skiing; tennis; pool.	**3**	•	•	•	•	•		•	•	•		•	•		
Candle Lake (C-4) 1,270 hectares 60 km n.e. of Prince Albert on hwys. 55 and 120. Cross-country skiing.	**4**	•	•	•	•	•	•	•	•	•	•	•	•	•	•

Recreation Areas Chart

The map location numerals in column 2 show an area's location on the preceding map.

Find thousands of places to camp at AAA.com/campgrounds

	MAP LOCATION	CAMPING	PICNICKING	HIKING TRAILS	BOATING	BOAT RAMP	BOAT RENTAL	FISHING	SWIMMING	PET FRIENDLY	BICYCLE TRAILS	WINTER SPORTS	VISITOR CENTER	LODGE/CABINS	FOOD SERVICE
Clearwater River (A-2) 224,040 hectares 50 km n.e. of La Loche on Hwy. 955 (north of area shown on map). Canoeing (experienced only).	5	•	•	•				•							
Crooked Lake (E-5) 190 hectares 30 km n. of Broadview on Hwy. 605. Golf.	6	•	•	•	•	•	•	•	•	•			•	•	•
Cypress Hills Interprovincial (F-2) 20,451 hectares 30 km s. of Maple Creek on Hwy. 21. Historic. Interpretive programs. Canoeing, cross-country skiing, golf, horseback riding, kayaking, sailing, windsurfing; amphitheater.	7	•	•	•	•	•	•	•	•	•	•	•	•	•	•
Danielson (E-3) 2,910 hectares on n. end of Lake Diefenbaker via hwys. 44, 45 or 219. Geocaching, ice fishing.	8	•	•		•	•	•	•					•		•
Douglas (E-3) 4,430 hectares 11 km s.e. of Elbow on Hwy. 19. Cross-country skiing, houseboat rental.	9	•	•	•	•	•	•	•	•				•	•	•
Duck Mountain (D-5) 26,160 hectares 25 km e. of Kamsack on Hwy. 57. Cross-country and downhill skiing, golf, tennis; horse rental.	10	•	•	•	•	•	•	•	•	•	•	•	•	•	•
Echo Valley (E-4) 640 hectares 8 km w. of Fort Qu'Appelle off Hwy. 10. Cross-country skiing (ski trails can be used by bicyclists in summer); horse rental.	11	•	•	•	•	•		•	•	•		•	•	•	•
Good Spirit Lake (D-5) 1,900 hectares 24 km n.e. of Springside via Hwy. 47. Cross-country skiing, tennis.	12	•	•	•	•	•	•	•	•	•		•	•	•	•
Greenwater Lake (D-5) 20,720 hectares 38 km n. of Kelvington on Hwy. 38. Cross-country skiing, ice-skating, golf, tennis.	13	•	•	•	•	•	•	•	•	•	•	•	•	•	•
Katepwa Point (E-4) 8 hectares 10 km s.e. of Lebret on Hwy. 56.	14		•		•	•		•	•						•
Lac La Ronge (B-4) 344,470 hectares 48.25 km n. of La Ronge on Hwy. 102. Cross-country skiing; houseboat rental.	15	•	•	•	•	•	•	•	•	•		•	•	•	•
Makwa Lake (B-2) 2,560 hectares n.w. of Loon Lake off Hwy. 26. Cross-country skiing, golf; horse rental.	16	•	•	•	•	•	•	•	•	•		•	•	•	•
Meadow Lake (B-2) 156,970 hectares 5 km n. of Goodsoil via Hwy. 26. Cross-country skiing, tennis; horse rental, sailboat rental.	17	•	•	•	•	•	•	•	•	•		•	•	•	•
Moose Mountain (F-5) 40,060 hectares 22.5 km n. of Carlyle on Hwy. 9. Cross-country skiing, golf (18 holes), horseback riding, tennis.	18	•	•	•	•	•	•	•	•	•	•	•	•	•	•
Narrow Hills (C-4) 53,610 hectares 64.25 km n. of Smeaton on Hwy. 106. Canoeing, cross-country skiing, snowmobiling; ATV trails, playground.	19	•	•	•	•	•	•	•	•	•		•	•	•	•
Pike Lake (D-3) 500 hectares 30.5 km s. of Saskatoon on Hwy. 60. Golf, tennis; pool. Ten horsepower limit for boats.	20	•	•	•	•	•	•	•	•	•		•	•		•
Rowan's Ravine (E-4) 270 hectares 22.5 km w. of Bulyea on Hwy. 220.	21	•	•	•	•	•	•	•	•	•			•	•	•
Saskatchewan Landing (E-2) 5,600 hectares 45 km n. of Swift Current via Hwy. 4. Bicycling (park roads only), golf (18 holes), geocaching. Horse rental, windsurfing rental.	22	•	•	•	•	•	•	•	•	•			•	•	•
OTHER															
Brightsand Lake (C-2) 648 hectares 27 km e. of St. Walburg off Hwy. 26 on a gravel road. Bird-watching, canoeing, cross-country skiing, golf (nine holes), miniature golf, mountain biking, snowmobiling; beach, canoe rental, nature trails with interpretive signs, playground.	23	•	•	•	•	•	•	•	•	•	•	•	•	•	•
Dunnet (F-4) 50 hectares 7 km s. of Avonlea on Hwy. 334. Cross-country skiing, ice fishing, snowmobiling.	24	•	•	•				•	•	•		•	•		•
Kipabiskau (D-4) 16 hectares 35 km s.w. of Tisdale off Hwy. 3 or Hwy. 35. Cross-country skiing, ice fishing, snowmobiling; beach, canoe and kayak rental, nature trails, playground.	25	•	•	•	•	•	•	•	•	•		•	•	•	•
Last Mountain Lake National Wildlife Area (E-4) 65 hectares 20 km n.w. of Govan off Hwy. 20 on a gravel road. Bird-watching, ice fishing; pool.	26	•	•	•				•	•	•		•	•		•
Macklin Lake (D-2) 154 hectares .4 km s. of Macklin on Hwy. 31. Golf (nine holes); beach, playground, wildlife preserve.	27	•	•	•	•	•	•		•	•	•				•

Recreation Areas Chart

The map location numerals in column 2 show an area's location on the preceding map.

Find thousands of places to camp at AAA.com/campgrounds

	MAP LOCATION	CAMPING	PICNICKING	HIKING TRAILS	BOATING	BOAT RAMP	BOAT RENTAL	FISHING	SWIMMING	PET FRIENDLY	BICYCLE TRAILS	WINTER SPORTS	VISITOR CENTER	LODGE/CABINS	FOOD SERVICE
Nipawin and District (C-4) 121 hectares 3 km n.w. of Nipawin on Hwy. 55. Cross-country skiing, golf (18 holes), snowmobiling; petting zoo, playground, spray pool.	28	•	•	•	•	•	•		•	•	•	•	•	•	•
Pasquia (C-5) 65 hectares 12 km n. of Arborfield on Hwy. 23. Cross-country and downhill skiing, golf (nine holes), river canoeing; playground, pool. Road access to Pasquia paleontological site (inquire at the visitor center).	29	•	•	•					•	•	•	•			•
Redberry Lake (D-3) 5,600 hectares 12.8 km e. of Hafford on Hwy. 40. Cross-country skiing, golf (nine holes), playgrounds.	30	•	•	•	•	•		•	•	•	•	•	•	•	•
St. Brieux (D-4) 65 hectares 1 km w. of St. Brieux on Hwy. 368. Historic. Cross-country skiing, golf (nine holes), miniature golf; beach, playground.	31	•	•	•	•	•	•	•	•	•	•	•	•		•
Whitesand (E-5) 49 hectares 9 km n.e. of Theodore off Hwy. 16. Golf, miniature golf (nine holes); playground.	32	•	•	•	•	•		•		•	•				•

Exciting Itineraries | Engaging Experiences | Exclusive Values

AAA Vacations

DESIGNED FOR AAA MEMBERS

AAA Vacations® offers vacation options and experiences all over the world. In addition to our 24/7 Member Care and Best Price Guarantee*, we deliver value with every itinerary.

These exclusive values may include:

- Savings or spending credits
- Pre-night hotel stay
- Priority check-in
- *And more!*
- Complimentary excursions
- Complimentary specialty dining
- Pre-paid gratuities

Call your AAA Travel Agent or visit AAA.com/AAAVacations

* If you book a qualifying *AAA Vacations*® cruise or tour package and find a valid better rate for the exact itinerary within 24 hours of your booking, AAA will match the lower rate and send you a $50 *AAA Vacations*® future travel credit certificate. Certain restrictions apply. Visit AAA.com/AAAVacations for full details.

ABERNETHY (E-5) pop. 196

In 1882, about 2 decades before he began his distinguished career in Canadian politics, William Richard Motherwell arrived in southeastern Saskatchewan from his Ontario birthplace and acquired a 64-hectare (160-acre) homestead grant near Abernethy. He farmed the land using several techniques of scientific agriculture then considered revolutionary.

Motherwell was later instrumental in launching the Territorial Grain Growers Association. His knowledge of the land groomed him for later roles as Saskatchewan's minister of agriculture 1905-18 and federal minister of agriculture during the 1920s.

MOTHERWELL HOMESTEAD NATIONAL HISTORIC SITE is 9 km (5 mi.) s. of jct. hwys. 10 and 22. The site commemorates William Richard Motherwell and his contributions to Canadian agriculture. Motherwell's farmstead, including 3 hectares (8 acres) of landscaped grounds, Ontarian-style barn and six-bedroom fieldstone house, have been restored to the pre-World War I era. **Time:** Allow 1 hour minimum. **Hours:** Mon.-Fri. 10-4, late May-June 30 (also Sat.-Sun., July 1-early Sept.). Phone ahead to confirm schedule. **Cost:** $3.90; $3.40 (ages 65+); free (ages 0-17). **Phone:** (306) 333-2116.

BATOCHE (C-3)

The Métis—a people of mixed First Nations and French heritage—migrated to the area around Batoche, in the valley of the South Saskatchewan River, around 1870. They built a settlement along the riverbank, but conflict arose with a Canadian government that was determined to settle the country's western reaches. Although the Métis petitioned for rights to the land, their requests were ignored. Batoche National Historic Site chronicles the history behind the events that led to armed conflict in 1885.

BATOCHE NATIONAL HISTORIC SITE is w. on Hwy. 225. The decisive battle of the Northwest Rebellion/Métis Resistance of 1885 was fought at this site, which covers 1,080 hectares (1,650 acres). Features include the ruins of a Batoche village, the St. Antoine de Padoue church and a rectory. The Visitor Reception Centre has an audiovisual presentation and exhibits about the culture and traditions of Métis descendants. Interpretive signs are at key locations throughout the park, and costumed interpreters are on hand to answer questions.

Hours: Daily 9-5, July 1-early Sept.; Mon.-Fri. 9-5, late May-June 30 and early Sept.-early Oct. **Cost:** $7.80; $6.55 (ages 65+); free (ages 0-17). **Phone:** (306) 423-6227.

BATTLEFORD (C-2) pop. 4,065

Once capital of the Northwest Territories, Battleford is one of Saskatchewan's oldest communities. As soon as the Canadian Pacific Railway began construction, citizens made plans for their town to become a western metropolis. But the railroad took a more southerly route, and in 1883 the capital was moved to Regina.

Battleford's hopes revived in 1905 when the Canadian Northern Railway proposed a westward route, but the line was built north of town on the other side of the Saskatchewan River, leading to the establishment of sister city North Battleford (see place listing p. 416).

FORT BATTLEFORD NATIONAL HISTORIC SITE is 2 km (1.2 mi.) off Hwy. 4. The North West Mounted Police district headquarters was established here in 1876 to enforce law and order. The fort became the site of armed confrontations between the First Nations and federal troops in 1885. Five buildings have been preserved; various illustrative exhibits are featured. Costumed staff members provide interpretive information. Historic weapons demonstrations are given, and historic trails also are on site.

Time: Allow 1 hour, 30 minutes minimum. **Hours:** Daily 10-4, July 1-Sept. 5; Mon.-Fri. 10-4, late May-June 30. Phone ahead to confirm schedule. **Cost:** $3.90; $3.40 (ages 65+); free (ages 0-17). **Phone:** (306) 937-2621. 🎟

FRED LIGHT MUSEUM is at jct. hwys. 4 and 40, just e. on 22nd St., then just s. to 11 20th St. E. Housed in the 1914 St. Vital School, the museum contains a general store, turn-of-the-20th-century furniture, a re-created schoolroom, and displays of farm tools and uniforms from the 1885 Rebellion and World Wars I and II. A firearm collection has more than 250 rifles and pistols dating from 1645. A replica of the Battleford Fire Hall, in operation from 1905-1912 before being destroyed by fire, is also on site. **Time:** Allow 1 hour minimum. **Hours:** Daily 9-8, Victoria Day weekend-Aug. 21; 9-6, Aug. 22-Sept. 1; 9-4, Sept. 2-Oct. 1; by appointment rest of year. **Cost:** Donations. Cash only. **Phone:** (306) 937-7111. 🎟

BIGGAR (D-2) pop. 2,161

Named in honor of W.H. Biggar, General Counsel for the Grand Trunk Pacific Railroad, Biggar is the birthplace of three-time world curling champion and 1998 Olympic curling gold medalist Sandra Schmirler. Sandra Schmirler Olympic Gold Park, at the corner of 8th Avenue E. and King Street, features a wall of fame outlining the athlete's accomplishments. The park also has an interpretive walking trail, picnic areas and a playground.

BROADVIEW (E-5) pop. 574

Broadview began as a division point on the Canadian Pacific Railway. A marker in a park on the west side of town designates the location of the original tracks, laid in 1882.

CHAPLIN (E-3) pop. 218, elev. 674m/2,214'

CHAPLIN NATURE CENTRE is at the western approach to town via Hwy. 1. The center is in the midst of the Chaplin Lake area, which encompasses some 6,000 hectares (15,000 acres) of inland saline water. More than 30 species of shorebirds, some endangered, either rest and refuel here during migratory journeys or nest and raise their young in the summer, feasting on brine shrimp that teem in the salty, shallow water.

Guided van tours are available; binoculars are provided. **Time:** Allow 1 hour, 30 minutes minimum. **Hours:** Daily 9-5, Victoria Day weekend-Aug. 31. **Cost:** Center displays by donation. Guided 30-minute tour $10 per person ($20 minimum); 2-hour tour $20 per person ($40 minimum). Reservations are recommended. **Phone:** (306) 395-2770.

CLAYBANK (F-4) pop. 25

CLAYBANK BRICK PLANT NATIONAL HISTORIC SITE is 1 km (.6 mi.) e. on Hwy. 339. In operation from 1914 to 1989, it is considered to be North America's most intact early 20th-century brick factory complex. The large site, which comprises more than 20 structures, can be seen on a self-guiding tour, and visitors can also hike through the adjacent Massold Clay Canyons. The brick-making process can be observed on special event days.

Time: Allow 1 hour minimum. **Hours:** Daily 10:30-4:30, July-Aug.; Mon.-Thurs. 10:30-4:30, late May-June 30 (also on Heritage Day Sunday); by appointment rest of year. **Cost:** $10; $6 (ages 65+); $5 (ages 6-16); $25 (family, up to seven people arriving in a single vehicle with a maximum of two adults). **Phone:** (306) 868-4474. 🍴 🎢

CUT KNIFE (C-2) pop. 517

In 1885 Cut Knife was the site of several First Nations uprisings that were inspired by the Métis rebellion *(see Batoche p. 411)*. The Battle of Cut Knife Hill, between the Cree tribe led by Chief Poundmaker and the North West Mounted Police under Col. W.D. Otter, ended in the retreat of the Mounties to Battleford.

Poundmaker, who stopped his warriors from pursuing and ambushing Otter's troops, later surrendered to the authorities to help restore peace between the First Nations and settlers. A national historic plaque and a framework of tepee poles mark the chief's grave at the Poundmaker Reserve.

A massive tomahawk, constructed in 1971, stands in Tomahawk Park, on the southwest side of town off Hwy. 40. The handle, 17 metres (57 ft.) long and weighing 3,928 kilograms (8,660 lbs.), pierces the top of a 30-foot-tall concrete teepee.

DUCK LAKE (C-3) pop. 577

The town of Duck Lake lies between the North Saskatchewan and South Saskatchewan rivers. The actual lake is a few kilometres west of town. A nearby cairn marks the site of the Battle of Duck Lake, in which the Métis First Nations defeated the North West Mounted Police on Mar. 26, 1885.

EASTEND (F-2) pop. 527

T.REX DISCOVERY CENTRE is at 1 T-rex Dr. In partnership with the Royal Saskatchewan Museum, the center houses fossils and replicas of dinosaurs, a 98-seat theater and interpretive displays. Educational activities also are offered. A nearly complete T. rex skeleton was discovered in the area in 1991.

Time: Allow 1 hour minimum. **Hours:** Daily 10-6, mid-May through Labour Day. **Cost:** Donations. **Phone:** (306) 295-4009. GT

ESTEVAN (F-5) pop. 11,054, elev. 570m/1,870'

Estevan is a major center for coal and oil production. Based on records for average annual hours of sunshine, it's also one of the sunniest spots in Canada.

On Hwy. 39 at 118 4th St. is the Estevan Art Gallery & Museum. The museum provides information about local events, presents changing exhibitions and also offers occasional interpretive programs and tours. Museum and gallery open Mon.-Fri. 10-6 (also Thurs. 6-9 p.m.), May-Aug. The museum is also open Sat. 1-4; phone (306) 634-7644.

Adjacent to the museum is the Wood End Building, a former barracks for the North West Mounted Police. It contains artifacts relating to that organization's early days. Nearby Heritage Park contains an oil field display.

Tours to Shand Power Station and Prairie Mines and Royalty can be arranged from June through August at the Estevan Tourism Booth; phone (306) 634-6044.

Southeast of town off Hwy. 39 is Roche Percée, a group of strangely eroded rock formations that were once venerated by local First Nations peoples. Although most of the animals and initials carved on the rocks are no longer discernible, legend maintains that the rocks are visited by spirits whose murmurs can be heard when the wind blows.

Tourism Estevan: 1102 4th St., Estevan, SK, Canada S4A 0W7. **Phone:** (306) 634-1892.

🔗 **Save on travel, shopping and more: AAA.com/discounts**

BEST WESTERN PLUS ESTEVAN INN & SUITES

306/634-7447

 THREE DIAMOND
Hotel

 Best Western PLUS

AAA Benefit: Members save up to 15% and earn bonus points!

Address: 92 King St S4A 2T5 **Location:** Hwy 39, 1 mi (1.6 km) n at Kensington Ave. **Facility:** 94 units, some efficiencies and kitchens. 4 stories, interior corridors. **Parking:** winter plug-ins. **Pool:** heated indoor. **Activities:** hot tub, exercise room. **Guest Services:** valet and coin laundry.

/ SOME UNITS 🐾

MICROTEL INN & SUITES BY WYNDHAM ESTEVAN

306/634-7474

▽ **APPROVED**   Hotel. **Address:** 120 King St S4A 2T5

SUPER 8 BY WYNDHAM

306/634-8585

▽ **APPROVED**   Hotel. **Address:** 134 2nd Ave S4A 2W6

WHERE TO EAT

EDDIE WEBSTER'S NEIGHBOURHOOD GRILL & BAR

306/634-5656

▽ **APPROVED**   International. Casual Dining. **Address:** 122 4th St S4A 0T4

MR MIKES STEAKHOUSECASUAL

306/634-6453

▽ **APPROVED**   American. Casual Dining. **Address:** 415 Kensington Ave S4A 2A5

GRASSLANDS NATIONAL PARK (F-3)

Elevations in the park range from 747 metres (2,450 ft.) at the Frenchman River to 998 metres (3,275 ft.) at Horse Creek. Refer to CAA/AAA maps for additional elevation information.

Grasslands National Park encompasses the grasslands in two separate blocks between Val Marie and Killdeer in the southern part of the province. When completed, the park will preserve 900 square kilometres (350 sq. mi.) of Saskatchewan's original mixed-grass prairie, including such topographic features as buttes, badlands and coulees. Among the wildlife species found in the park are black-tailed prairie dogs, golden eagles, rattlesnakes, short-horned lizards, pronghorn antelopes, mule deer and more recently, reintroduced plains bison and black-footed ferrets.

These grasslands also have a rich history. The first recorded discovery of dinosaur remains in western Canada was made in the badlands in 1875. Proof of early habitation includes remnants of tepee rings, ranch buildings, corrals and old homestead shacks.

Ranching operations exist in the area, and some of the proposed parkland is still under private ownership. Before entering the park, contact or stop at the visitor center located in Val Marie to obtain information, maps and permits. The center also conducts interpretive programs, guided hikes and special events.

Park open year-round. Visitor center open daily 9-5 (also Fri. 5-7), July-Aug.; Thurs.-Mon. 9-5, Victoria Day weekend-June 30 and Sept. 1-Thanksgiving. Admission is free. Write Grasslands National Park, P.O. Box 150, Val Marie, SK, Canada S0N 2T0; phone (877) 345-2257 (West Block Visitor Centre) or (306) 476-2018 (East Block Visitor Centre). *See Recreation Areas Chart.*

HUMBOLDT (D-4) pop. 5,678

Humboldt is on Hwy. 5 about 111 kilometres (69 mi.) east of Saskatoon; the drive takes about 90 minutes. Named for German author, explorer and scientist Baron Friedrich Heinrich Alexander von Humboldt, Humboldt's ethnic heritage is on display in seven downtown wall murals, and a number of buildings exhibit the German half-timber architectural style. Folk art, utilitarian as well as decorative, is a cottage industry.

Annual events include the Summer Sizzler, held the last weekend in June.

KINDERSLEY (D-2) pop. 4,678

Kindersley is a popular destination for birdwatchers; the surrounding region is a haven for thousands of migrating geese, more than 10 species of ducks, and occasional whistling swans and whooping cranes. The Kindersley Goose Festival, a community event featuring a parade, a goose-plucking competition, a horse pull, barbecues and family entertainment, is celebrated in late September.

Kindersley Chamber of Commerce: 903 11th Ave. East, Box 1537, Kindersley, SK, Canada S0L 1S0. **Phone:** (306) 463-2320.

BEST WESTERN PLUS KINDERSLEY HOTEL

306/463-3600

 THREE DIAMOND
Hotel

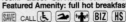 Best Western PLUS

AAA Benefit: Members save up to 15% and earn bonus points!

Address: 501 13th Ave E S0L 1S0 **Location:** Jct Hwy 21 and 7, 0.7 mi (1.1 km) e, then just n. **Facility:** 114 efficiencies. 4 stories, interior corridors. **Parking:** winter plug-ins. **Pool:** heated indoor. **Activities:** hot tub, exercise room. **Guest Services:** coin laundry. **Featured Amenity:** full hot breakfast.

/ SOME UNITS 🐾

SUPER 8 BY WYNDHAM - KINDERSLEY

306/463-8218

▽ **APPROVED**   Hotel. **Address:** 508 12th Ave E S0L 1S0

LLOYDMINSTER pop. 9,772
See also Alberta p. 130

MICROTEL INN & SUITES BY WYNDHAM   306/825-3820
APPROVED   Hotel. **Address:** 4257 44th St S9V 2H1

SUPER 8 LLOYDMINSTER   306/825-7988
APPROVED   Hotel. **Address:** 4351 41st Ave S9V 2H1

WHERE TO EAT

SAWMILL PRIME RIB & STEAK HOUSE   306/825-0811
APPROVED   Steak. Casual Dining. **Address:** 3902 44 St S9V 2B7

MAPLE CREEK (F-2) pop. 2,176

Canadian Pacific Railway workers who spent the winter of 1882 on the banks of Maple Creek named this town, located in Saskatchewan's southwestern corner. The Maple Creek Golf Club's 18-hole layout offers views of the Cypress Hills from every fairway. The course is at 705 Herbert St.; to book a tee time phone (306) 662-2886.

South of town via Hwy. 21 is Cypress Hills Interprovincial Park *(see Recreation Areas Chart)*. This region of lofty hills, forest-covered buttes, plateaus and ridges is also marked by large tracts of ranchland.

The Great Sand Hills region is located about 70 kilometres (44 mi.) north of Maple Creek via Hwy. 21. Covering approximately 190,000 hectares (469,500 acres), it is characterized by fragile native grasslands interspersed with sand dunes up to 25 metres (82 ft.) high, fringed with small clumps of aspen, birch and willow trees, sagebrush and choke cherry. Strong winds blowing from the northwest shift the dunes east at a rate of almost 4 metres (13 ft.) annually.

Maple Creek Visitor Centre: 114 Jasper St., P.O. Box 428, Maple Creek, SK, Canada S0N 1N0. **Phone:** (306) 662-4005.

FORT WALSH NATIONAL HISTORIC SITE is 55 km (34 mi.) s.w. on Hwy. 271. A preserved, early North West Mounted Police fort features reconstructed period buildings housing exhibits of original post artifacts. Guided tours include excursions to the fort and the site of the 1873 Cypress Hills massacre. Visitor activities include bird-watching, walking a self-guiding nature trail and geocaching. A bus trip around the park includes an interpretive commentary.

Time: Allow 2 hours minimum. **Hours:** Daily 9:30-5, Canada Day-Labour Day; Tues.-Sat. 10-5, rest of year. Phone ahead to confirm schedule. **Cost:** $9.80; $8.30 (ages 65+); free (ages 0-17). **Phone:** (306) 662-3590.

THE JASPER CULTURAL AND HISTORICAL CENTRE is at 311 Jasper St. Several rooms of historical displays and art are housed in a two-story brick school building built in 1913. In addition to school memorabilia, there are exhibits pertaining to ranching, rodeos and the railroad. **Time:** Allow 30 minutes minimum. **Hours:** Mon.-Fri. 9:30-5:30, Sat.-Sun. and holidays 1-5, June-Sept.; Mon.-Fri. 1-5, rest of year. **Cost:** $6; $4 (ages 6-17 and 65+); $20 (family, two adults and children under age 18). **Phone:** (306) 662-2434.

MELVILLE (E-5) pop. 4,517, elev. 555m/1,820'

Located on the east-west main line of the Canadian National Railway as well as on a major north-south line of that company, Melville is—appropriately—known as "The Rail Centre." The railway is still the city's largest employer, its presence essential in marketing agricultural products as well as potash from nearby Esterhazy.

Melville & District Chamber of Commerce: 430 Main St., Melville, SK, Canada S0A 2P0. **Phone:** (306) 728-4177.

MOOSE JAW (E-4) pop. 33,274, elev. 542m/1,778'

Moose Jaw's intriguing name is likely a reference to Moose Jaw Creek. The First Nations called this waterway *moosichappishannissippi*, or "the creek that bends like a moose's jaw." Local legend also attributes it to an early traveler who repaired his cart wheel with a moose's jawbone. Today's visitors are greeted by "Mac," a 9-metre-tall (30 ft.) moose statue said to be the world's largest.

During U.S. Prohibition Moose Jaw was home to an industrious band of bootleggers and American gangsters, earning the town the nickname "Little Chicago of the Prairies." Today Moose Jaw is an industrial center as well as a producer of hard spring wheat. The Canadian Forces base just south of the city is home to one of Canada's busiest airports and headquarters of the Snowbirds, the Canadian armed forces aerobatic team.

Downtown's seasonal roaming "ambassadors" provide visitors with information and brochures. The Murals of Moose Jaw, painted on several downtown buildings, are a collection of more than 50 scenes depicting the town's history. The Moose Jaw Trolley Company provides a tour of the murals and heritage buildings. The Yvette Moore Gallery, downtown at 76 Fairford St. W., exhibits this local artist's work; her paintings are also displayed in Moose Jaw hotels. Phone (306) 693-7600 or (866) 693-7600.

Wakamow Valley is a recreational complex that includes Plaxton's Lake, North River Park, Kiwanis River Park, Kinsmen Wellesley Park, Connor Park, McCaig Gardens, the Ecological Zone and the Devonian Trail, a pedestrian and bicycle trail system. Visitors can picnic, camp, bird-watch, hike, jog and bicycle. For more information phone (306) 692-2717 Mon.-Fri.

Hwy. 2 heading south from the city was once part of the Powder River Trail, which provided access to Denver before the advent of the railroad. About 42 kilometres (26 mi.) north on Hwy. 2 is Buffalo Pound Provincial Park (see Recreation Areas Chart), where 350 hectares (865 acres) are set aside as grazing land for a herd of buffaloes.

Moose Jaw Chamber of Commerce: 88 Saskatchewan St. E., Box 1359, Moose Jaw, SK, Canada S6H 0V4. **Phone:** (306) 692-6414.

Self-guiding tours: Brochures outlining a self-guiding tour of downtown Moose Jaw's historic sites are available at the Moose Jaw Art Museum and National Exhibits in Crescent Park.

SUKANEN SHIP, PIONEER VILLAGE AND MUSEUM is 13 km (8 mi.) s. on Hwy. 2. The large, unfinished ship was built by Tom Sukanen, a Finnish settler who had planned to sail the boat home to his native country by way of the South Saskatchewan River, Hudson Bay, Greenland and Iceland. The village consists of an old post office, blacksmith shop, school, church, railroad station, a general store, drug store and the Diefenbaker homestead. Also on site is a collection of antique tractors, trucks and cars.

Hours: Mon.-Sat. 9-5, Sun. noon-6, mid-May to mid-Sept. **Cost:** $8; $7 (students with ID and ages 60+); $5 (ages 6-15). **Phone:** (306) 693-7315.

TUNNELS OF MOOSE JAW is at 18 N. Main St. Two themed, 50-minute tours take visitors beneath the streets of Moose Jaw. Miss Fanny and Gus are the guides for the Chicago Connection tour, which explores gangster Al Capone's bootlegging operation and the tunnels he is said to have used to escape American authorities. The Passage to Fortune tour depicts the story of early Chinese immigrants who came to build the Canadian Pacific Railway and their footsteps through adversity and persecution to eventual success.

Hours: Tours depart daily 10-7 (also Fri.-Sat. 7-8 p.m.), July-Aug.; Mon.-Fri. 10-4:30, Sat. 10-5:30, Sun. noon-4:30, Sept.-Oct.; Mon.-Fri. noon-4:30, Sat. 10-5:30, rest of year. Departure times may vary; phone ahead to confirm schedule. Closed Christmas. **Cost:** Individual tour fee $15; $12 (ages 65+); $11.50 (ages 13-18); $8.50 (ages 6-12). Both tours $25; $21 (ages 65+); $20 (ages 13-18); $14 (ages 6-12). Reservations are recommended. **Phone:** (306) 693-5261.

BEST WESTERN PLUS MOOSE JAW   306/972-3334

 THREE DIAMOND
Hotel

 Best Western PLUS. **AAA Benefit:** Members save up to 15% and earn bonus points!

Address: 350 Diefenbaker Dr S6J 1N2 **Location:** Trans-Canada Hwy 1; just w on Thatcher Dr. Adjacent to Welcome & Information Center. **Facility:** 88 units, some efficiencies. 4 stories, interior corridors. **Parking:** winter plug-ins. **Terms:** check-in 4 pm. **Pool:** heated indoor. **Activities:** hot tub, exercise room. **Guest Services:** valet and coin laundry. **Featured Amenity:** full hot breakfast.

COMFORT INN BY CHOICE HOTELS   306/692-2100
 APPROVED   Hotel. **Address:** 155 Thatcher Dr W S6J 1M1

HERITAGE INN HOTEL & CONVENTION CENTRE MOOSE JAW   306/693-7550
APPROVED   Hotel. **Address:** 1590 Main St N S6J 1L3

RAMADA MOOSE JAW   306/693-3050
APPROVED   Hotel. **Address:** 379 Diefenbaker Dr S6J 0C1

SUPER 8 BY WYNDHAM-MOOSE JAW   306/692-8888
APPROVED   Hotel. **Address:** 1706 Main St N S6J 1L4

WHERE TO EAT

DÈJA VU CAFÈ   306/692-6066
APPROVED   Chicken Sandwiches. Casual Dining. **Address:** 23 High St E S6H 0B7

HARWOOD'S   306/693-7778
APPROVED   Continental. Casual Dining. **Address:** 24 Fairford St E S6H 0C7

HOUSTON PIZZA   306/693-3934
APPROVED   American. Casual Dining. **Address:** 117 Main St N S6H 0V9

ROCK CREEK TAP AND GRILL   306/693-3300
APPROVED   American. Casual Dining. **Address:** 857 Thatcher Dr S6J 0A9

MOOSOMIN pop. 2,485

BEST WESTERN PLUS MOOSOMIN HOTEL   306/435-4700

 THREE DIAMOND
Hotel

Best Western PLUS. **AAA Benefit:** Members save up to 15% and earn bonus points!

Address: 405 Moose St S0G 3N0 **Location:** Jct Trans-Canada Hwy 1 and Main St, just s. **Facility:** 79 efficiencies. 3 stories, interior corridors. **Parking:** winter plug-ins. **Pool:** heated indoor. **Activities:** hot tub, exercise room. **Guest Services:** coin laundry. **Featured Amenity:** full hot breakfast.

AAA DISCOUNTS >>> REWARDS
DISCOUNTS WITHOUT LIMITS
AAA.com/discounts

NIPAWIN (C-4) pop. 4,265

The Nipawin Hydroelectric Station, about 5 km (3 mi.) south of town via Hwy. 35, following signs, uses water impounded in Codette Lake by the Francois-Finlay Dam to generate 1.1 billion kilowatt hours of electricity annually. Vista Viewpoint, on a plateau overlooking the dam, offers a spectacular view of the river gorge below.

Nipawin & District Chamber of Commerce: 308 Nipawin Rd. E., Box 177, Nipawin, SK, Canada S0E 1E0. **Phone:** (306) 862-5252.

NORTH BATTLEFORD (C-2) pop. 13,888

On the bank of the North Saskatchewan River, North Battleford is the gateway to the province's vast northwestern wilderness. Agriculture is the backbone of the area's economy; farms produce crops of cereal grains, oil seeds and hay as well as cattle, hogs, poultry and bison. Forestry, manufacturing and heavy crude oil development also are important industries.

The Battlefords Provincial Park *(see Recreation Areas Chart)* is approximately 42 kilometres (26 mi.) north off Hwy. 4 and offers summer fishing, water skiing, boating and hiking. Cross-country skiing and ice fishing are popular winter activities.

Destination Battlefords: 801 River Valley Dr., P.O. Box 1715, North Battleford, SK, Canada S9A 3W2. **Phone:** (306) 445-2000 or (800) 243-0394.

ALLEN SAPP GALLERY is at 1 Railway Ave. This award-winning public gallery features powerful and sensitive images of the Northern Plains Cree by renowned Cree artist Allen Sapp (1928-2015). Sapp's works capture the life and history of the Cree at the turn of the 20th century. Other exhibits include large-screen videos and historical artifacts.

Hours: Daily 11-5, June-Sept.; Wed.-Sun. noon-4, rest of year. **Cost:** Donations. **Phone:** (306) 445-1760.

WESTERN DEVELOPMENT MUSEUM'S HERITAGE FARM AND VILLAGE is at jct. hwys. 16 and 40. A preserved 1920s pioneer village features the exhibit Winning the Prairie Gamble. Also part of the complex is a working farm where visitors can see demonstrations of early agricultural techniques utilizing vintage equipment.

Time: Allow 2 hours minimum. **Hours:** Daily 9-5, Apr.-Dec.; Tues.-Sun. 9-5, rest of year. Closed provincial holidays Oct.-Apr. Outdoor village closed mid-Oct. through Apr. 30. Hours and admission rates are subject to change; phone to confirm. **Cost:** (good for 2 consecutive days) $10; $9 (ages 65+); $7 (students with ID); $4 (ages 6-12); $25 (family, parents or guardians and dependent children under age 18). **Phone:** (306) 445-8033.

COMFORT INN & SUITES BY CHOICE HOTELS 306/445-3678
THREE DIAMOND Hotel. **Address:** 610 Carlton Tr S9A 3W3

GOLD EAGLE LODGE 306/446-8877
THREE DIAMOND
Hotel

Address: 12004 Railway Ave E S9A 3W3 **Location:** Jct Hwy 4 and 16 (Yellowhead Hwy), just w. **Facility:** 112 units, some two bedrooms and kitchens. 4 stories, interior corridors. **Parking:** winter plug-ins. **Terms:** check-in 4 pm. **Pool:** heated indoor. **Activities:** sauna, hot tub, steamroom, picnic facilities, exercise room. **Guest Services:** valet and coin laundry. **Featured Amenity:** full hot breakfast.

WHERE TO EAT

KIHIW RESTAURANT 306/486-3833
APPROVED American. Casual Dining. **Address:** 11902 Railway Ave S9A 3K7

PORTA BELLA RESTAURANT 306/937-3785
APPROVED Canadian. Casual Dining. **Address:** 2491 99th St S9A 3W8

PRINCE ALBERT (C-3) pop. 35,129

Prince Albert is one of the province's oldest communities. Trapper Peter Pond built a trading post on the north side of the North Saskatchewan River in 1776. The Rev. James Nesbit, credited with founding the town, settled on the south shore in 1866.

The log Presbyterian church that Nisbet built that year stands in Kinsmen Park, on the west side of Central Avenue between 22nd and 28th streets W. A blockhouse next to the church dates from the Northwest Rebellion/Métis Resistance of 1885. The Historical Museum occupies the site of the church built by Nisbet.

Prince Albert Tourism: 3700 2nd Ave. W., Prince Albert, SK, Canada S6W 1A2. **Phone:** (306) 953-4385.

HISTORICAL MUSEUM is at 10 River St. E. at Central Ave. The museum, housed in an old fire hall overlooking the North Saskatchewan River, displays the first fire engine pumper used in the Saskatchewan territory. Other exhibits include First Nations, fur trade and pioneer artifacts as well as a table and benches carved by the Rev. James Nisbet. A tearoom provides a view of the river. **Time:** Allow 1 hour minimum. **Hours:** Daily 9-5, Victoria Day-Sept. 2. **Cost:** $4; $2 (ages 6-12); $10 (family, up to six people). **Phone:** (306) 764-2992.

For complete hotel, dining and attraction listings:

AAA.com/travelguides

BEST WESTERN MARQUIS INN & SUITES
306-922-9595

Hotel

AAA Benefit:
Members save up to
15% and earn bonus
points!

Address: 602 Marquis Rd E S6V 7P2 **Location:** Jct Hwy 3 (6th Ave E). **Facility:** 77 units. 2 stories, interior corridors. **Parking:** winter plug-ins. **Terms:** check-in 4 pm. **Amenities:** safes. **Activities:** exercise room.

🆂🅰🆅🅴 🍴 ♿ 🛎 CALL ♿ ✈

BIZ HS 📶 ✕ 🔋 🖨 💻
/ SOME UNITS 🐾

HOLIDAY INN EXPRESS HOTEL & SUITES   306-922-6988
⬥ APPROVED   Hotel. **Address:** 3580 2nd Ave W S6V 5G2

SUPER 8 BY WYNDHAM - PRINCE ALBERT   306-953-0088
⬥ APPROVED   Hotel. **Address:** 4444 2nd Ave W S6V 5R7

WHERE TO EAT

AMY'S ON SECOND   306/763-1515
⬥ APPROVED   American. Casual Dining. **Address:** 2990 2nd Ave W S6V 7E9

MR MIKES STEAKHOUSECASUAL   306/763-6453
⬥ APPROVED   American. Casual Dining. **Address:** 801 15 St E S6V 0C7

SHANANIGAN'S COFFEE & DESSERT BAR   306/764-2647
⬥ APPROVED   Coffee/Tea Desserts. Quick Serve. **Address:** 2144 6th Ave W S6V 5K6

SMITTY'S   306/764-5627
⬥ APPROVED   American. Casual Dining. **Address:** 2995 2nd Ave W, #20 S6V 5V5

THE SPICE TRAIL   306/970-9443
⬥ APPROVED   Indian. Casual Dining. **Address:** 2901 2nd St W S6V 7R2

SPICY PEPPERCORN   306/763-7755
⬥ APPROVED   Chinese. Casual Dining. **Address:** 3590 6th Ave E S6V 7S5

VENICE HOUSE FAMILY RESTAURANT   306/764-6555
⬥ APPROVED   Italian. Casual Dining. **Address:** 1498 Central Ave S6V 4W5

◬GEM PRINCE ALBERT NATIONAL PARK (B-3)

Elevations in the park range from 488 metres (1,600 ft.) on the western side of the park to 724 metres (2,375 ft.) on the southern side of the park. Refer to CAA/AAA maps for additional elevation information.

The main entrance to Prince Albert National Park is 81 kilometres (50 mi.) north of the city of Prince Albert via hwys. 2 and 264.

The park covers 3,875 square kilometres (1,496 sq. mi.) of wilderness in central Saskatchewan. Its lakes, ponds, streams, bogs and rolling hills are a legacy of the glacial epoch. Notable are Sandy, Waskesiu, Kingsmere, Namekus, Crean and the Hanging Heart lakes. There also are several hundred smaller lakes and ponds and many sand beaches.

Heavy growths of conifers and several species of hardwoods surround the lakes, along with numerous shrubs and wildflowers. Fall foliage is especially colorful. Such wild animals as elk, deer, moose and bears are plentiful. A herd of bison roams the southwest corner of the park.

Early morning and evening provide the best chances of seeing wildlife along park roads, especially the Narrows and Kingsmere roads along Waskesiu Lake. Although some animals may seem tame, they are wild and should be observed only from a safe distance.

The park also preserves the legacy of Grey Owl. Born Archibald Stansfeld Belaney, this controversial Englishman arrived in Canada in 1905. Adopted by the Ojibwa First Nations and later married into the tribe, Grey Owl turned his love of nature to the re-establishment of the region's beaver population, which had been decimated by hunters and trappers. For 7 years he lived at Beaver Lodge on Ajawaan Lake, where he continued his restoration and conservation efforts.

General Information and Activities

Although the park is open throughout the year, complete facilities are provided Victoria Day-Labour Day only. Information is available from the information bureau in the Waskesiu Lake Visitor Services Centre, 8 kilometres (5 mi.) from the park's main gate on Hwy. 264.

Roads provide access to Waskesiu, Namekus, Sandy and the Hanging Heart lakes and to the Kingsmere River. Although no roads lead directly to Kingsmere and Crean lakes, access is possible by boat. A light railway with handcars assists in portaging around the unnavigable stretch of the Kingsmere River.

More than 100 kilometres (60 mi.) of hiking trails traverse the park. Some are suitable for day walks, while others require an overnight stop. Pamphlets outlining self-guiding tours are available for the Mud Creek and Boundary Bog nature trails. From the boat dock on the north shore of Kingsmere Lake a 3-kilometre (1.9-mi.) trail leads to the home and grave of Grey Owl.

Park facilities include boat launching and berthing areas at the Hanging Heart Lakes, the Narrows and the main marina on Waskesiu Lake. Boats, canoes and outboard motors can be rented at all three marinas; paddle-wheeler tours are offered daily in summer. There are bicycle rentals, tennis and volleyball courts and bowling greens at the Waskesiu Lake Visitor Services Centre.

Waskesiu Lake's 18-hole layout ranks among Canada's finest golf courses. A 150-kilometre (93-mi.) network of groomed cross-country ski trails is open in winter. Snowshoeing and ice fishing also are permitted. Fishing licenses are required and can be obtained at the park information center, park entrances and campground offices.

Park naturalists offer a free summer interpretive program that includes car caravans on park roadways and special daily events. Interpretive programs are regularly presented in the Nature Center theater on Lakeview Drive, and at the outdoor theaters at the Narrows and Beaver Glen campgrounds.

Within the Waskesiu Lake Visitor Services Centre is the Park Nature Centre, which has natural history exhibits, a bookstore and a theater; it is open in July and August. *See Recreation Areas Chart.*

ADMISSION to the park is $7.80; $6.80 (ages 65+); free (ages 0-17); $15.70 (up to seven people arriving in a single vehicle).

PETS (dogs and cats) are permitted in the park as long as they are on leashes.

ADDRESS inquiries to the Superintendent, Prince Albert National Park, 969 Lakeview Dr., P.O. Box 100, Waskesiu Lake, SK, Canada S0J 2Y0; phone (306) 663-4522.

REGINA (E-4) pop. 193,100, elev. 578m/1,896'
• Hotels p. 423 • Restaurants p. 424
• Hotels & Restaurants map & index p. 421

First Nations people once used the banks of Wascana Creek for drying buffalo meat and cleaning and stretching the hides. Thus the area became known as *Oscana,* a Cree word meaning "pile of bones." In 1882 the Canadian Pacific Railway completed its track across the plains, and the settlement of Pile-O-Bones sprang up at the rail terminal on Wascana Creek.

The seat of government of the Northwest Territories and the headquarters of the North West Mounted Police were established the same year. A few years later Princess Louise, the wife of Canada's governor-general, renamed the city Regina (Latin for queen) to honor her mother, Queen Victoria. In 1905 Saskatchewan became a province, with Regina as its capital.

In the heart of downtown is City Centre, the site of such buildings as the municipal government offices and the public library. The Prairie History Room, which documents local history, and the Dunlop Art Gallery, which displays works by regional artists, are both housed in the library.

The Globe Theatre in the old City Hall is the home of Regina's professional acting company. Another restored building is Union Station, a transportation hub in the early years of rail travel that is now occupied by Casino Regina. Guided historical tours explore parts of a tunnel system that once stretched beneath downtown streets and also offer a behind-the-scenes look at casino operations. Under 19 are not permitted on the tours; for ticket and schedule information phone the casino at (800) 555-3189.

The Regina Floral Conservatory, 1450B 4th Ave., is a small greenhouse where seasonal floral displays have the backdrop of a waterfall and luxuriant foliage; phone (306) 781-4769.

Following Wascana Creek for about 8 kilometres (5 mi.) is the Devonian Pathway, a paved bicycle trail that passes through six city parks and is used for jogging and walking as well as other activities; in winter it is groomed and lighted for cross-country skiing. The grassland and marsh habitats at the Condie Nature Refuge, just north of the city off Hwy. 11, are crisscrossed by nature trails.

Regina's No. 1 spectator sport is summer football. The Canadian Football League's Saskatchewan Roughriders play at the new Mosaic Stadium, 1734 Elphinstone St. (near the intersection with Saskatchewan Drive). For ticket information phone (888) 474-3377.

Regina Regional Opportunities Commission and Tourism Regina: 1925 Rose St., Regina, SK, Canada S4P 3H1. **Phone:** (306) 789-5099 or (800) 661-5099.

Shopping: Regina's major shopping mall is Cornwall Centre, 2101 11th Ave. The specialty shops and eateries of Scarth Street Mall, downtown between 11th and 12th avenues, line a pedestrian-only street. The Cathedral Village shopping district, another downtown cluster of shops, is centered around 13th Avenue from Albert to Argyle streets and from Saskatchewan Drive to College Avenue.

GOVERNMENT HOUSE MUSEUM AND INTERPRETIVE CENTRE is at 4607 Dewdney Ave. This Italianate-style mansion was the home of the lieutenant governors of the Northwest Territories from 1891 to 1905 and the lieutenant governors of Saskatchewan from 1905 to 1945. From 1945 to the mid-1970s the house served as a rest home for World War II veterans as well as an adult education center.

Flanked by 2.5 hectares (6 acres) of gardens and orchards, the official residence is restored to reflect its original Victorian elegance. Docents dressed in period garb conduct guided house tours. An interpretive center chronicles provincial history and features hands-on exhibits.

Time: Allow 1 hour minimum. **Hours:** Daily 9-5, Victoria Day weekend-Labour Day weekend; Tues.-Sun. 9-4, rest of year. Guided tours offered at 11, 1 and 3. Closed Jan. 10-13, Nov. 14-17, Christmas and day after Christmas. **Cost:** $6; $5 (ages 65+ and ages 12-18); $3 (ages 0-17); $15 (family). **Phone:** (306) 787-5773. GT 🅰

HOLY ROSARY CATHEDRAL is at 3125 13th Ave., just w. of jct. Cameron St. This Cruciform/Romanesque structure, built in 1912, features 43 stained-glass windows installed in 1951 by French artisan Andre Rault, who designed windows for more than 50 other Canadian churches. Their

(See map & index p. 421.)

artistry is best appreciated on a sunny day. A Casavant pipe organ, known for its exceptional sound quality, plays during Sunday services.

Guided tours are available; reservations are required 2 weeks in advance. **Time:** Allow 30 minutes minimum. **Hours:** Tues.-Fri. 9-1. The cathedral is kept locked for security purposes. Phone ahead to confirm schedule. **Cost:** Donations. **Phone:** (306) 565-0909.

RCMP HERITAGE CENTRE is on Dewdney Ave. at the entrance to the RCMP Academy, "Depot" Division. The center tells the story of the Royal Canadian Mounted Police (RCMP), created by an act of Parliament in 1873 to maintain law and order on the Canadian frontier and pave the way for westward settlement. Stretching the length of the main exhibition hall, the sculptural procession "March of the Mounties" anchors the core exhibit areas; graphics trace Canada's geography from west to east and depict the historical evolution of the RCMP from its inception to the present day.

The interactive educational exhibit Maintaining Law and Order in the West chronicles the force's late 19th-century efforts to suppress the whiskey trade, establish amicable relations with Native tribes and ensure the safety of settlers and rail workers. Serving All of Canada is an overview of the RCMP's 20th-century evolution, while Cracking the Case is a hands-on look at the high-tech side of contemporary policing. The 22-minute multimedia presentation "Courage in Red" is shown in the center's SGI Canada Theatre.

Time: Allow 2 hours minimum. **Hours:** Daily 10-5, Canada Day-Labour Day; 11-5, rest of year. A colorful Sergeant Major's Parade is held Mon.-Fri. at 12:45 p.m.; register at the center by noon. Sunset Retreat Ceremonies are held Tues. at 6:30 p.m., Canada Day to mid-Aug. Closed Jan. 1, Good Friday and Christmas. **Cost:** $10; $8 (ages 60+ and students with ID); $6 (ages 6-17); $30 (family, two adults and up to five children); free (military veterans and law enforcement). **Phone:** (306) 719-3000 or (866) 567-7267.

WASCANA CENTRE surrounds Wascana Lake. This 930-hectare (2,300-acre) park complex is the city's recreational and cultural center and includes the Conexus Arts Centre, a performing arts venue. Wascana Place has information about attractions and event listings; on the building's fourth floor is the Joe Moran Gallery, which exhibits photographs from 1882 to the present.

Points of interest include Speakers' Corner, a circular plaza located in the park's southwest corner. Ten vintage gas lamps surround the plaza, which was dedicated in 1966 as a tribute to free speech and the people's right to assemble. Waterfowl display ponds are a haven for geese and ducks. Ferry boats transport visitors to Willow Island, a picnic area. **Hours:** Grounds daily dawn-dusk. Wascana Place Mon.-Fri. 8-4:30. Phone ahead to confirm schedule. **Cost:** Grounds free. **Phone:** (306) 522-3661.

Legislative Building (Capitol) is off Albert St. in Wascana Centre. Surrounded by 67 hectares (165 acres) of landscaped grounds, this imposing landmark, topped by a gleaming new copper dome unveiled in May 2016, is the seat of provincial government. Completed in 1912, it is modeled on the architectural style of the English Renaissance and Louis XIV of France.

The building houses several art galleries, including the Cumberland Gallery, a showcase for works of the Native Heritage Foundation of Canada. Green marble columns are among the many handsome decorative accents. The flower gardens just north of the building are at their loveliest in the summer months. On the building's east side is the Trafalgar Fountain, which stood in London's Trafalgar Square from 1845 to 1939.

Guided tours of the building are offered. Tours in French are available. **Time:** Allow 30 minutes minimum. **Hours:** Daily 8 a.m.-5 p.m., Victoria Day-Labour Day; 8-noon and 1-4, rest of year. Guided tours are given daily on the half-hour, Victoria Day-Labour Day; on the hour, rest of year. Last tour departs 30 minutes before closing. Closed Jan. 1, Good Friday and Christmas. **Cost:** Free. **Phone:** (306) 787-5358 or (306) 787-5416.

MacKenzie Art Gallery is in the T.C. Douglas Building at Albert St. and 23rd Ave., in the s.w. corner of Wascana Centre. This major exhibition center features permanent and changing exhibits by Canadian and international artists. **Time:** Allow 1 hour minimum. **Hours:** Mon. and Wed.-Sat. 10-5:30, Sun. and holidays noon-5:30. **Cost:** Free; donations accepted. **Phone:** (306) 584-4250. GT

Royal Saskatchewan Museum is at College Ave. and Albert St. in Wascana Centre. The Earth Sciences Gallery focuses on Saskatchewan's geological and paleontological evolution and includes Canada's only resident robotic dinosaur, while the Paleo Pit features hands-on exhibits. Artwork and artifacts in the First Nations Gallery explore the culture and heritage of the province's aboriginal population.

Saskatchewan's natural history is surveyed in the Life Sciences Gallery, which also covers present-day environmental issues. Exhibits depict life in a beaver pond and a Costa Rican rain forest, and address human actions that are affecting global ecosystems. **Time:** Allow 1 hour minimum. **Hours:** Daily 9:30-5 (closes at 3 on Dec. 24 and 31); noon-5, Jan. 1 and day after Christmas. Closed Christmas. **Cost:** Donations. Cash only for suggested donation amounts under $10. **Phone:** (306) 787-2815.

Saskatchewan Science Centre is at 2903 Powerhouse Dr. in Wascana Centre, on the n. side of Wascana Lake. The Powerhouse of Discovery houses

(See map & index p. 421.)

more than 100 permanent hands-on science exhibits and features live stage shows and demonstrations. Visitors who want to test their physical skills can tackle one of the tallest climbing walls in Canada. The 165-seat Kramer IMAX Theatre presents science and nature films on a five-story screen enhanced by a digital sound system, as well as selected classic movies at the monthly After Dark Film Series event.

Time: Allow 2 hours minimum. **Hours:** Mon.-Fri. 9-6; Sat.-Sun. and statutory holidays 10-6, Victoria Day-Labour Day; Tues.-Fri. 9-5, Sat.-Sun. and statutory holidays noon-6, rest of year. Kramer IMAX Theater Tues.-Fri. 9-5, Sat.-Sun. noon-6; show times vary. Phone ahead to confirm schedule. **Cost:** Science center $12; $11 (ages 13-17); $10 (ages 3-12 and 60+). IMAX film showing $10; $9 (ages 13-17); $8 (ages 3-12 and 60+). Combination science center and IMAX theater ticket (or IMAX double feature) $20; $18 (ages 13-17); $16 (ages 3-12 and 60+). IMAX feature-length film $17; $16 (ages 13-17); $15 (ages 3-12 and 60+). **Phone:** (306) 791-7900, or (306) 522-4629 for the IMAX box office. 🍴

Expert Travel Insight

iStockphoto.com_LeoPatrizi

Make a good trip great with insight from AAA's travel experts. Use their recommended picks and itineraries to find best places to go, stay, dine and play.

Photo source iStockphoto.com

 Get AAA travel information at club offices and on AAA.com for experiences you'll remember for a lifetime.

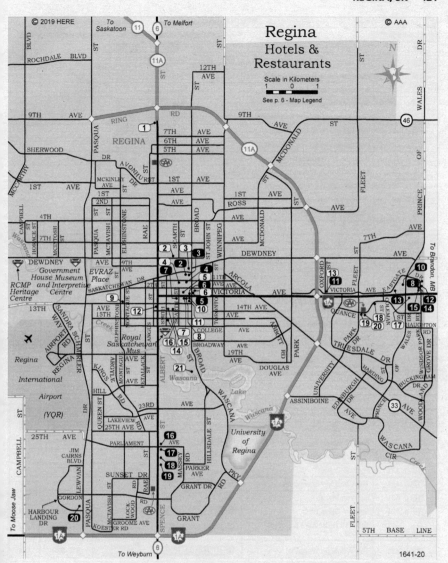

Regina

This index helps you "spot" where hotels and restaurants are located on the corresponding detailed maps. Restaurant price range is a combination of lunch and/or dinner. Turn to the listing page for more information and consult display ads for special promotions.

For more details, rates and reservations: AAA.com/travelguides/hotels

REGINA

Map Page	Hotels	Designation	Member Savings	Page
2 this page	**Delta by Marriott Regina**	⬦⬦ THREE DIAMOND	✔	423
3 this page	**Wingate by Wyndham Regina**	⬦⬦ THREE DIAMOND		424
4 this page	Holiday Inn Express Hotel & Suites Regina	⬦⬦ THREE DIAMOND		423
5 this page	**DoubleTree by Hilton Hotel & Conference Centre Regina**	⬦⬦ THREE DIAMOND	✔	423

REGINA (cont'd)

Map Page	Hotels (cont'd)	Designation	Member Savings	Page
6 p. 421	Ramada Plaza by Wyndham	APPROVED		423
7 p. 421	The Hotel Saskatchewan, Autograph Collection	FOUR DIAMOND	✔	423
8 p. 421	Hampton Inn & Suites by Hilton	THREE DIAMOND	✔	423
10 p. 421	Holiday Inn Hotel & Suites	THREE DIAMOND		423
11 p. 421	Sandman Hotel Suites & Spa Regina	THREE DIAMOND		424
12 p. 421	Best Western Plus Eastgate Inn & Suites	THREE DIAMOND	✔	423
13 p. 421	Comfort Inn by Choice Hotels	APPROVED		423
14 p. 421	HomeSuites Hotel Regina East	THREE DIAMOND		423
15 p. 421	Days Inn by Wyndham - Regina	APPROVED		423
16 p. 421	Fairfield Inn & Suites by Marriott Regina	THREE DIAMOND	✔	423
17 p. 421	Executive Royal Hotel Regina	THREE DIAMOND		423
18 p. 421	Travelodge Hotel & Conference Centre Regina	THREE DIAMOND		424
19 p. 421	Holiday Inn Express & Suites	THREE DIAMOND		423
20 p. 421	Days Inn-Regina Airport West	THREE DIAMOND		423

Map Page	Restaurants	Designation	Cuisine	Price Range	Page
① p. 421	Luiggi's Pasta House	APPROVED	Italian	$14-$30	424
② p. 421	Bushwakker Brewpub	APPROVED	American	$14-$21	424
③ p. 421	The Last Spike	APPROVED	American	$8-$23	424
④ p. 421	Beer Bros. Gastropub & Deli	APPROVED	American	$12-$25	424
⑤ p. 421	Siam Authentic Thai Restaurant	APPROVED	Thai	$9-$18	424
⑥ p. 421	Wild Sage Kitchen & Bar	APPROVED	International	$13-$30	424
⑦ p. 421	Golf's Steak House	THREE DIAMOND	Steak	$14-$71	424
⑧ p. 421	Crave Kitchen + Wine Bar	APPROVED	International Small Plates	$15-$35	424
⑨ p. 421	The Creek In Cathedral Bistro	THREE DIAMOND	American	$13-$31	424
⑩ p. 421	The Rooftop Bar + Grill	APPROVED	American	$12-$37	424
⑪ p. 421	The Diplomat Steakhouse	APPROVED	Steak	$14-$70	424
⑫ p. 421	Slow Brew Pub & Sports Bar	APPROVED	American	$6-$14	424
⑬ p. 421	Moxie's Classic Grill	APPROVED	American	$12-$33	424
⑭ p. 421	Henry's Cafe	APPROVED	American	$8-$13	424
⑮ p. 421	Tangerine the food bar	APPROVED	American	$9-$14	424
⑯ p. 421	Fireside Bistro	THREE DIAMOND	American	$14-$42	424
⑰ p. 421	The Canadian Brewhouse	APPROVED	American	$12-$24	424
⑱ p. 421	Houston Pizza	APPROVED	American	$10-$40	424
⑲ p. 421	Smokin' Okies BBQ	APPROVED	Barbecue	$6-$32	424
⑳ p. 421	Table 10 Restaurant & Cocktail Lounge	THREE DIAMOND	American	$15-$34	424
㉑ p. 421	The Willow on Wascana	THREE DIAMOND	Regional Canadian	$12-$39	424

Safe Travels -
We've Got You Covered

Insurance

Stop by your local AAA office or visit us online.
AAA.com/Insurance

(See map & index p. 421.)

BEST WESTERN PLUS EASTGATE INN & SUITES
306/352-7587 **12**

 THREE DIAMOND
Hotel

 Best Western PLUS

AAA Benefit: Members save up to 15% and earn bonus points!

Address: 3840 Eastgate Dr S4Z 1A5 **Location:** Trans-Canada Hwy 1, 1.5 mi (2.4 km) e of Ring Rd, just n. **Facility:** 100 units, some efficiencies. 4 stories, interior corridors. **Parking:** winter plug-ins. **Terms:** check-in 4 pm. **Pool:** heated indoor. **Activities:** hot tub, exercise room. **Guest Services:** valet and coin laundry. **Featured Amenity:** full hot breakfast.

SAVE 🍴 CALL ♿ 🏊 🛁 BIZ HS 🛜 ✕ 🖥 🖨 💻 / SOME UNITS 🐾

COMFORT INN BY CHOICE HOTELS
306/789-5522 **13**

APPROVED Hotel. **Address:** 3221 E Eastgate Dr S4Z 1A4

COMFORT SUITES BY CHOICE HOTELS REGINA
306/949-4000

THREE DIAMOND Hotel. **Address:** 4300 Diefenbaker Dr S4X 0M2

DAYS INN BY WYNDHAM - REGINA
306/522-3297 **15**

APPROVED Hotel. **Address:** 3875 Eastgate Dr E S4Z 1A4

DAYS INN-REGINA AIRPORT WEST
306/584-3297 **20**

THREE DIAMOND Hotel. **Address:** 4899 Harbour Landing Dr S4N 0B7

DELTA BY MARRIOTT REGINA
306/525-5255 **2**

THREE DIAMOND
Hotel

DELTA HOTELS

AAA Benefit: Members save 5% or more!

Address: 1919 Saskatchewan Dr S4P 4H2 **Location:** At Rose St; center. Across from Casino Regina. **Facility:** 274 units. 10-25 stories, interior corridors. **Parking:** on-site (fee), winter plug-ins. **Amenities:** safes. **Pool:** heated indoor. **Activities:** hot tub, exercise room, spa. **Guest Services:** valet laundry.

SAVE ECO 🍴 🏊 🛁 🖥 🖨 💻 / SOME UNITS 🐾

CALL ♿ 🏊 🛁 BIZ 🛜 ✕ 🖥 💻 / SOME UNITS 🐾

DOUBLETREE BY HILTON HOTEL & CONFERENCE CENTRE REGINA
306/525-6767 **5**

THREE DIAMOND
Hotel

DOUBLETREE

AAA Benefit: Members save up to 15%!

Address: 1975 Broad St S4P 1Y2 **Location:** Jct Victoria Ave; center. **Facility:** 235 units. 15 stories, interior corridors. **Parking:** on-site (fee) and street, winter plug-ins. **Terms:** check-in 4 pm. **Amenities:** safes. **Dining:** Wild Sage Kitchen & Bar, see separate listing. **Activities:** exercise room. **Guest Services:** valet laundry.

SAVE ECO 🍴 🏊 🛁 🖥 BIZ

HS 🛜 ✕ 🖥 💻 / SOME UNITS 🐾

EXECUTIVE ROYAL HOTEL REGINA
306/586-6755 **17**

THREE DIAMOND Hotel. **Address:** 4025 Albert St S S4S 3R6

FAIRFIELD INN & SUITES BY MARRIOTT REGINA
306/545-9777 **16**

 THREE DIAMOND
Hotel

Fairfield

AAA Benefit: Members save 5% or more!

Address: 3915 Albert St S4S 3R4 **Location:** 1.1 mi (1.7 km) n of jct Trans-Canada Hwy 1. **Facility:** 123 units. 2 stories, interior corridors. **Parking:** winter plug-ins. **Terms:** off-site registration. **Pool:** indoor. **Activities:** hot tub, exercise room. **Guest Services:** valet and coin laundry. **Featured Amenity:** full hot breakfast.

SAVE 🍴 🏊 🛁 CALL ♿ 🏊

🛁 BIZ 🛜 ✕ 🖥 🖨 💻

HAMPTON INN & SUITES BY HILTON
306/721-6000 **8**

THREE DIAMOND SAVE Hotel. **Address:** 3830 East Gate Dr S4Z 1A5

AAA Benefit: Members save up to 15%!

HOLIDAY INN EXPRESS & SUITES
306/789-5888 **19**

THREE DIAMOND Hotel. **Address:** 4255 Albert St S4S 3R6

HOLIDAY INN EXPRESS HOTEL & SUITES REGINA
306/569-4600 **4**

THREE DIAMOND Hotel. **Address:** 1907 11th Ave S4P 0J2

HOLIDAY INN HOTEL & SUITES
306/789-3883 **10**

THREE DIAMOND Hotel. **Address:** 1800 Prince of Wales Dr S4Z 1A4

HOMESUITES HOTEL REGINA EAST
306/522-4434 **14**

THREE DIAMOND Extended Stay Hotel. **Address:** 3841 Eastgate Dr E S4Z 1A5

THE HOTEL SASKATCHEWAN, AUTOGRAPH COLLECTION
306/522-7691 **7**

FOUR DIAMOND
Historic Hotel

AUTOGRAPH COLLECTION HOTELS

AAA Benefit: Members save 5% or more!

Address: 2125 Victoria Ave S4P 0S3 **Location:** At Scarth St; center. Opposite Victoria Park. **Facility:** This 1927 beauty has an ornate, richly decorated lobby with stunning architectural features. Recently updated rooms have a sophisticated and elegant design. For more space ask about the larger suites. 227 units, some two bedrooms. 10 stories, interior corridors. **Parking:** on-site (fee) and valet, winter plug-ins. **Amenities:** *Some:* safes. **Activities:** hot tub, steamroom, health club, spa. **Guest Services:** valet laundry.

SAVE ECO 🍴 🛁 🏊 🛁 BIZ HS 🛜 ✕ 🖥

💻 / SOME UNITS 🐾

RAMADA PLAZA BY WYNDHAM
306/569-1666 **6**

APPROVED Hotel. **Address:** 1818 Victoria Ave S4P 0R1

🔵 **Where Diamonds make the difference:**

AAA.com/travelguides/hotels

(See map & index p. 421.)

SANDMAN HOTEL SUITES & SPA REGINA
306/757-2444 **11**
THREE DIAMOND Hotel. **Address:** 1800 Victoria Ave E S4N 7K3

TRAVELODGE HOTEL & CONFERENCE CENTRE REGINA
306/586-3443 **18**
THREE DIAMOND Hotel. **Address:** 4177 Albert St S S4S 3R6

WINGATE BY WYNDHAM REGINA   306/584-7400 **3**
THREE DIAMOND Hotel. **Address:** 1700 Broad St S4P 1X4

WHERE TO EAT

BEER BROS. GASTROPUB & DELI   306/586-2337 **4**
APPROVED American. Gastropub. **Address:** 1821 Scarth St S4P 2G9

BUSHWAKKER BREWPUB   306/359-7276 **2**
APPROVED American. Brewpub. **Address:** 2206 Dewdney Ave S4R 1H2

THE CANADIAN BREWHOUSE   306/522-1613 **17**
APPROVED American. Sports Bar. **Address:** 2005 Prince of Wales Dr S4V 3A3

CRAVE KITCHEN + WINE BAR   306/525-8777 **8**
APPROVED International Small Plates. Casual Dining. **Address:** 1925 Victoria Ave S4P 0R3

THE CREEK IN CATHEDRAL BISTRO   306/352-4448 **9**
THREE DIAMOND American. Casual Dining. **Address:** 3414 13th Ave S4T 1P7

THE DIPLOMAT STEAKHOUSE   306/359-3366 **11**
APPROVED Steak. Fine Dining. **Address:** 2032 Broad St S4P 1Y3

EARLS KITCHEN + BAR
APPROVED American. Casual Dining.
LOCATIONS:
Address: 2606 28th Ave S4S 6P3 **Phone:** 306/584-7733
Address: 1875 Victoria Ave E S4N 6E6 **Phone:** 306/949-4955

FIRESIDE BISTRO   306/761-2305 **16**
THREE DIAMOND American. Casual Dining. **Address:** 2305 Smith St S4P 2P7

GOLF'S STEAK HOUSE   306/525-5808 **7**
THREE DIAMOND Steak. Fine Dining. **Address:** 1945 Victoria Ave S4P 0R3

HENRY'S CAFE   306/791-7889 **14**
APPROVED American. Casual Dining. **Address:** 2320 14th Ave S4P 0Y1

HOUSTON PIZZA   306/585-6888 **18**
APPROVED American. Casual Dining. **Address:** 2815 Quance St S4V 3B7

THE LAST SPIKE   306/781-7000 **3**
APPROVED American. Casual Dining. **Address:** 1880 Saskatchewan Dr S4P 0A8

LUIGGI'S PASTA HOUSE   306/949-7427 **1**
APPROVED Italian. Casual Dining. **Address:** 470 Albert St N S4R 3C1

MOXIE'S CLASSIC GRILL   306/781-5655 **13**
APPROVED American. Casual Dining. **Address:** 1800A Victoria Ave S4N 7K3

RICKY'S ALL DAY GRILL   306/775-3000
APPROVED American. Casual Dining. **Address:** 777 Albert St S4R 2P6

THE ROOFTOP BAR + GRILL   306/359-7663 **10**
APPROVED American. Casual Dining. **Address:** 1845 Victoria Ave S4P 1Y2

SIAM AUTHENTIC THAI RESTAURANT   306/352-8424 **5**
APPROVED Thai. Casual Dining. **Address:** 1946 Hamilton St S4P 2C4

SLOW BREW PUB & SPORTS BAR   306/751-0000 **12**
APPROVED American. Gastropub. **Address:** 2124 Albert St S4P 2T9

SMOKIN' OKIES BBQ   306/347-2800 **19**
APPROVED Barbecue. Quick Serve. **Address:** 2547 Quance St E S4V 2X7

TABLE 10 RESTAURANT & COCKTAIL LOUNGE
306/543-8836 **20**
THREE DIAMOND American. Casual Dining. **Address:** 2589 Quance St S4V 2X7

TANGERINE THE FOOD BAR   306/522-3500 **15**
APPROVED American. Quick Serve. **Address:** 2234 14th Ave S4P 0X8

WILD SAGE KITCHEN & BAR   306/525-6767 **6**
APPROVED International. Casual Dining. **Address:** 1975 Broad St S4P 1Y2

THE WILLOW ON WASCANA   306/585-3663 **21**
THREE DIAMOND Regional Canadian. Casual Dining. **Address:** 3000 Wascana Dr S4P 3B2

Sit. Stay. Play.

Discover thousands of pet-friendly places to stay, play and dine. And enter your favorite photo in the next **AAA Pet Travel Photo Contest***.

Visit AAA.com/PetTravel

*Contest entry open to U.S. residents only.

ST. WALBURG (C-2) pop. 716, elev. 634m/2,083'

IMHOFF GALLERY is 2.5 mi. (4 km) s. on Hwy. 26 to the jct. with a gravel road (the turnoff is signed "RGE RD 3224"), then 4 km w. on the gravel road to the farmstead turnoff on the right (TWP RD 532). Born in Germany, religious artist Berthold Von Imhoff moved to St. Walburg in 1913, residing there until his death in 1939. Imhoff's works adorn more than 100 churches throughout Canada and the United States; he was knighted by the pope in 1937.

The artist's original working studio holds many original large canvases and photos. Two rooms in the original homestead are filled with antiques, including a sculpture of Custer, and several mounted game heads attest to Imhoff's prowess as a hunter. Visitors also can watch a 20-minute video about his life.

Time: Allow 1 hour minimum. **Hours:** Daily 10-5, July 1-Labour Day; Mon.-Sat. 10-5, in June. **Cost:** $8; $5 (students ages 6-18 with ID). **Phone:** (306) 248-3812. GT

SASKATOON (D-3) pop. 222,189, elev. 487m/1,598'
• Hotels p. 426 • Restaurants p. 428

Saskatoon was founded in 1882 as a temperance colony under leader John Lake. According to legend, a member of the Cree tribe brought Lake a handful of the purple berries that grew in abundance alongside the river. Lake was so taken with the fruit that he named his settlement Saskatoon, after *misaskquatoomina,* the First Nations name for the wild berries. A slice of pie made with Saskatoon berries (known as serviceberries in the U.S.) is a traditional, fruity treat.

Straddling the South Saskatchewan River, Saskatoon is known as "The City of Bridges" because of the seven spans connecting its banks. It also is home to the University of Saskatchewan, which is building a reputation for research and development in science, medicine and agriculture. The Diefenbaker Canada Centre on campus showcases memorabilia pertaining to Canada's 13th prime minister.

The Local History Room on the second floor of the Frances Morrison Library, 311-23rd St. E., serves as a research facility for information that focuses on prairie history relating to Saskatoon in particular and western Canada in general. Collections include more than 60,000 historic photographs and thousands of books, pamphlets, maps, artifacts and periodicals. An art gallery is adjacent to the room. Phone (306) 975-7558.

The Saskatchewan Railway Museum, 6 kilometres (4 mi.) west on Hwy. 7, then 2 kilometres (1.2 mi.) south on Hwy. 60, is operated by the Saskatchewan Railroad Historical Association. Displays include old railroad buildings and artifacts, including locomotives, cabooses and streetcars; phone (306) 382-9855 May through September.

TCU Place—Saskatoon's Art & Convention Centre, 35 22nd St., is home to the Saskatoon Symphony and the site of concerts and events throughout the year; phone (306) 975-7777. Rock concerts, trade shows, hockey games and other sporting events take place at the SaskTel Centre, on the city's north side next to hwys. 2 and 16; phone (306) 938-7800.

The Meewasin Valley Trail, following the South Saskatchewan River through the heart of the city, has bicycle and jogging trails, picnic areas and playgrounds; winter activities include cross-country skiing and ice-skating. More recreational opportunities are available at nearby Pike Lake and Blackstrap provincial parks *(see Recreation Areas Chart)*.

Racing fans can enjoy horse racing at Marquis Downs, 503 Ruth St., from late May to early September. Races are held Fri.-Sat. 7-10 p.m.; phone (306) 242-6100. Drag racing heats up the Saskatchewan International Raceway, 13 kilometres (8 mi.) s. on Hwy. 11, from early May to mid-September; phone (306) 955-3724. Stock car racing takes place at the Wyant Group Raceway, north on Hwy. 12, from May through September; phone (306) 651-3278.

Note: Policies concerning admittance of children to pari-mutuel betting facilities vary. Phone for information.

Tourism Saskatoon: 101-202 4th Ave. N., Saskatoon, SK, Canada S7K 0K1. **Phone:** (306) 242-1206 or (800) 567-2444.

Shopping: Midtown Plaza, downtown at 1st Avenue and 21st Street, is a two-level mall with more than 130 shops, including anchor store Hudson's Bay. The Centre, at Circle Drive and 8th Street, has more than 90 stores and services in "East" and "West" sections connected by an underground walkway.

DIEFENBAKER CANADA CENTRE is at 101 Diefenbaker Pl. on the University of Saskatchewan campus. The archives and personal belongings of Prime Minister John Diefenbaker are housed at the only Prime Ministerial center in Canada; his grave site is on the grounds. The museum also offers changing national and international exhibits about Canadian history, citizenship, leadership, art, politics, science, culture, current affairs and Canada's role in the international community.

Hours: Mon.-Thurs. 9:30-8, Fri. 9:30-4:30, Sat.-Sun. and holidays noon-4:30. Reservations are recommended for guided tours. Closed Family Day (third Mon. in Feb.), Good Friday, Labour Day, Thanksgiving, Nov. 11 and mid-Dec. to early Jan. Phone ahead to confirm schedule. **Cost:** Donations. **Phone:** (306) 966-8384. GT

MUSEUM OF ANTIQUITIES is on the University of Saskatchewan campus at 107 Administration Pl., Room 106 in the Peter MacKinnon Building. Exhibits include original antiquities and pieces of art; a collection of original Greek, Roman and medieval coins; and replicas of Greek, Roman, Egyptian and Near Eastern sculptures. **Hours:** Mon.-Fri. 9-4, Sat. noon-4:30. Guided tours are available by appointment. Closed late Dec.-early Jan. **Cost:** Free; donations accepted. **Phone:** (306) 966-7818.

 WANUSKEWIN HERITAGE PARK is 5 km (3.1 mi.) n. on Hwy. 11, 3 km (1.9 mi.) s. on Warman Rd., then 2 km (1.2 mi.) e. on Penner Rd., following signs. This First Nations park traces more than 6,000 years of area history. The park's interpretive center contains a DVD theater and features state-of-the-art exhibits and art pertaining to Northern Plains culture. Cultural offerings include storytelling, children's activities and traditional dance performances.

Self-guiding trails take visitors through the 360-acre (146-hectare) park's prairie landscape, with interpretive signs explaining past uses of the land. Trails lead to 19 sites representing the Northern Plains peoples, including summer and winter campsites, archeological sites, four bison kill sites, a tipi ring site and a boulder alignment known as a medicine wheel.

Time: Allow 2 hours minimum. **Hours:** Daily 9-4:30 (11-4 on statutory holidays), Victoria Day-Labour Day; Mon.-Fri. 9-4:30, Sat. 11-3 (closed statutory holidays), rest of year. Dance performances take place daily at 2, May-Aug. **Cost:** $8.50; $7.50 (ages 65+); $6.50 (students with ID); $5 (ages 6-12); $25 (family, parents and children). **Phone:** (306) 931-6767 or (877) 547-6546. [GT] [¶]

WESTERN DEVELOPMENT MUSEUM'S 1910 BOOMTOWN is at 2610 Lorne Ave. This indoor representation of a typical prairie town features more than 30 buildings. Displays include transportation artifacts and vintage agricultural equipment. **Time:** Allow 2 hours minimum. **Hours:** Daily 9-5, Apr.-Dec. (closes at 3 on Dec. 24 and 31); Tues.-Sun. 9-5, rest of year. Closed Jan. 1, Family Day (third Mon. in Feb.), Thanksgiving (second Mon. in Oct.), Nov. 11, Nov. 20, Christmas and day after Christmas. **Cost:** $12; $10 (ages 65+); $8 (students with ID); $5 (ages 6-12); $27 (family, parents or guardians and dependent children under age 18). **Phone:** (306) 931-1910. [¶]

BEST WESTERN BLAIRMORE   306/242-2299

THREE DIAMOND
Hotel

Best Western
AAA Benefit: Members save up to 15% and earn bonus points!

Address: 306 Shillington Crescent S7M 1L2 **Location:** Jct Hwy 7 and 14. **Facility:** 100 units. 4 stories, interior corridors. **Parking:** winter plug-ins. **Terms:** check-in 4 pm. **Amenities:** *Some:* safes. **Pool:** heated indoor. **Activities:** hot tub, exercise room. **Guest Services:** valet and coin laundry. **Featured Amenity:** full hot breakfast.

[SAVE] [¶+] CALL [&] [⊕] [⊕] [BIZ]
[HS] [⊛] [✕] [❚] [⊟] [⊡] / SOME UNITS [🐾]

BEST WESTERN PLUS AIRPORT INN & SUITES
306-1514

THREE DIAMOND
Extended Stay Hotel

Best Western PLUS
AAA Benefit: Members save up to 15% and earn bonus points!

Address: 317 Aerogreen Cres S7L 1S4 **Location:** From Hwy 16 (Circle Dr), just n on Airport Dr. **Facility:** 100 efficiencies. 4 stories, interior corridors. **Parking:** winter plug-ins. **Pool:** heated indoor. **Activities:** hot tub, exercise room. **Guest Services:** valet and coin laundry.

[SAVE] [✦] [¶+] [⊡] CALL [&] [⊕]
[⊕] [BIZ] [HS] [⊛] [✕] [❚] [⊟]
[⊡] / SOME UNITS [🐾]

BEST WESTERN PLUS EAST SIDE   306/986-2400

THREE DIAMOND
Hotel

Best Western PLUS
AAA Benefit: Members save up to 15% and earn bonus points!

Address: 3331 8th St E S7H 4K1 **Location:** Hwy 16 exit 8th St E, just e. **Facility:** 101 units. 4 stories, interior corridors. **Parking:** winter plug-ins. **Terms:** check-in 4 pm. **Amenities:** safes. **Pool:** heated indoor. **Activities:** hot tub, exercise room. **Guest Services:** valet and coin laundry.

[SAVE] CALL [&] [⊕] [⊕] [BIZ] [HS]
[⊛] [✕] [❚] [⊟] [⊡] / SOME UNITS [🐾]

COLONIAL SQUARE INN & SUITES   306/343-1676

APPROVED
Hotel

Address: 1301 8th St E S7H 0S7 **Location:** 1.5 mi (2.4 km) e of jct Hwy 11 (Idylwyld Dr S); 1.4 mi (2.3 km) w of jct Circle Dr. Opposite Cumberland Park. **Facility:** 76 units. 2 stories (no elevator), interior/exterior corridors. **Parking:** winter plug-ins. **Dining:** 3 restaurants. **Activities:** exercise room. **Guest Services:** coin laundry.

[SAVE] [¶] [✦] [⊡] [⊕] [BIZ] [⊛]
[✕] [❚] [⊡] / SOME UNITS [🐾]

COMFORT INN BY CHOICE HOTELS   306/934-1122

APPROVED
Motel

Address: 2155 Northridge Dr S7L 6X6 **Location:** Just ne of jct Hwy 11 (Idylwyld Dr N) and Circle Dr. **Facility:** 78 units. 2 stories (no elevator), interior corridors. **Parking:** winter plug-ins. **Guest Services:** valet laundry. **Featured Amenity:** full hot breakfast.

[SAVE] [ECO] [¶+] [BIZ] [HS] [⊛] [✕]
[❚] [⊟] [⊡] / SOME UNITS [🐾]

COMFORT SUITES SASKATOON   306/955-6565

THREE DIAMOND Hotel. **Address:** 203 Bill Hunter Ave S7R 1E3

COURTYARD BY MARRIOTT SASKATOON AIRPORT
306/986-4993

THREE DIAMOND [SAVE] Hotel. **Address:** 333 Aerogreen Crescent S7L 1S4

AAA Benefit: Members save 5% or more!

DAYS INN BY WYNDHAM-SASKATOON
306/242-3297

APPROVED
Hotel

Address: 2000 Idylwyld Dr N S7L 7M7 **Location:** Just nw of jct Circle Dr. **Facility:** 101 units. 4 stories, interior corridors. **Parking:** winter plug-ins. **Amenities:** *Some:* safes. **Pool:** heated indoor. **Activities:** hot tub, exercise room. **Guest Services:** valet and coin laundry. **Featured Amenity:** continental breakfast.

DELTA HOTELS BY MARRIOTT BESSBOROUGH
306/244-5521

FOUR DIAMOND
Historic Hotel

DELTA HOTELS
AAA Benefit: Members save 5% or more!

Address: 601 Spadina Crescent E S7K 3G8 **Location:** Jct 21st St E; center. **Facility:** A local landmark since the 1930s, this lovely castle on the river features a variety of lovely rooms with modern, elegant décor, sweeping draperies and huge desks. 225 units. 6 stories, interior corridors. **Parking:** onsite (fee) and valet, winter plug-ins. **Dining:** Samurai Japanese Restaurant, see separate listing. **Pool:** heated indoor. **Activities:** sauna, hot tub, steamroom, health club, spa. **Guest Services:** valet laundry.

DELTA HOTELS BY MARRIOTT SASKATOON DOWNTOWN
306/665-3322

THREE DIAMOND
Hotel

DELTA HOTELS
AAA Benefit: Members save 5% or more!

Address: 405 20th St E S7K 6X6 **Location:** At 4th Ave S; center. **Facility:** 291 units. 19 stories, interior corridors. **Parking:** on-site (fee) and street, winter plug-ins. **Amenities:** *Some:* safes. **Dining:** AROMA Resto Bar, see separate listing. **Pool:** heated indoor. **Activities:** hot tub, exercise room. **Guest Services:** valet laundry.

FOUR POINTS BY SHERATON SASKATOON
306/933-9889

THREE DIAMOND
Hotel

FOUR POINTS BY SHERATON
AAA Benefit: Members save 5% or more!

Address: 503 Cope Way S7T 0G3 **Location:** Hwy 11 (Louis Riel Tr) exit Clarence Ave S, just s, then just e. **Facility:** 119 units. 4 stories, interior corridors. **Parking:** winter plug-ins. **Amenities:** safes. **Pool:** heated indoor. **Activities:** hot tub, exercise room. **Guest Services:** valet and coin laundry.

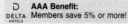

HAMPTON INN & SUITES BY HILTON SASKATOON AIRPORT
306/933-1010

THREE DIAMOND
Hotel

AAA Benefit: Members save up to 15%!

Address: 110 Gateway Blvd S7L 1S4 **Location:** From Hwy 16 (Circle Dr), just n on Airport Dr. **Facility:** 137 units. 7 stories, interior corridors. **Parking:** winter plug-ins. **Pool:** heated indoor. **Activities:** hot tub, exercise room. **Guest Services:** valet and coin laundry.

HAMPTON INN BY HILTON - SASKATOON SOUTH
306/665-9898

THREE DIAMOND
Hotel

AAA Benefit: Members save up to 15%!

Address: 105 Stonebridge Blvd S7T 0G3 **Location:** Hwy 11 (Louis Riel Tr) exit Clarence Ave S, just s, then just e. **Facility:** 100 units. 4 stories, interior corridors. **Parking:** winter plug-ins. **Pool:** heated indoor. **Activities:** exercise room. **Guest Services:** valet and coin laundry. **Featured Amenity:** breakfast buffet.

HILTON GARDEN INN SASKATOON DOWNTOWN
306/244-2311

THREE DIAMOND [SAVE] Hotel. **Address:** 90 22nd St E S7K 3X6

AAA Benefit: Members save up to 15%!

HOLIDAY INN EXPRESS & SUITES SASKATOON EAST - UNIVERSITY
306/954-1250

THREE DIAMOND Hotel. **Address:** 1838 College Dr S7N 2Z8

HOLIDAY INN EXPRESS HOTEL & SUITES SASKATOON CENTRE
306/384-8844

THREE DIAMOND Hotel. **Address:** 315 Idylwyld Dr N S7L 0Z1

HOLIDAY INN SASKATOON DOWNTOWN   306/986-5000

THREE DIAMOND Hotel. **Address:** 101 Pacific Ave S7K 1N8

HOME INN & SUITES - SASKATOON SOUTH   306/657-4663

THREE DIAMOND Hotel. **Address:** 253 Willis Cres S7T 0V2

MOTEL 6 SASKATOON   306/665-6688

APPROVED Hotel. **Address:** 231 Marquis Dr S7R 1B7

RAMADA HOTEL BY WYNDHAM-SASKATOON
306/665-6500

APPROVED
Hotel

Address: 806 Idylwyld Dr N S7L 0Z6 **Location:** On Hwy 11 (Idylwyld Dr), 2.5 mi (4 km) s of jct Circle Dr. **Facility:** 148 units. 6 stories, interior corridors. **Parking:** winter plug-ins. **Pool:** heated indoor. **Activities:** hot tub, miniature golf, exercise room. **Guest Services:** complimentary laundry.

SANDMAN HOTEL SASKATOON   306/477-4844
 APPROVED ▐ Hotel. **Address:** 310 Circle Dr W S7L 2Y5

SHERATON CAVALIER SASKATOON HOTEL
                                                306/652-6770

▐ **THREE DIAMOND**
Hotel

SHERATON

AAA Benefit:
Members save 5% or
more!

Address: 612 Spadina Crescent E S7K
3G9 **Location:** Jct 21st St E; center. **Facility:** 237 units. 8 stories, interior corridors. **Parking:** on-site (fee), winter plug-ins. **Amenities:** safes. **Dining:** Carver's Steakhouse, see separate listing. **Pool:** heated indoor. **Activities:** hot tub, bicycles, exercise room. **Guest Services:** valet laundry.

🆂🅰🆅🅴 ECO 🍴 🍸 CALL 🦽 🛥
✈ BIZ HS 📶 ✖ 📹 🛏 🖥 / SOME UNITS 🦌

STAYBRIDGE SUITES SASKATOON - UNIVERSITY
                                                306/952-4888
▐ **THREE DIAMOND** Extended Stay Hotel. **Address:** 1838 College Dr S7N 2Z8

SUPER 8 BY WYNDHAM EAST-SASKATOON   306/384-8989
▐ **APPROVED** Hotel. **Address:** 706 Circle Dr E S7K 3T7

TOWNEPLACE SUITES BY MARRIOTT-SASKATOON
                                                306/952-0400
▐ **THREE DIAMOND** 🆂🅰🆅🅴 Extended
Stay Hotel. **Address:** 247 Willis Cres
S7T 0V2

AAA Benefit:
Members save 5%
or more!

WHERE TO EAT

2ND AVE GRILL   306/244-9899
▐ **APPROVED** ▐ International. Casual Dining. **Address:** 123 2nd Ave S S7K 7E6

ALEXANDER'S RESTAURANT & BAR   306/956-7777
▐ **APPROVED** ▐ International. Casual Dining. **Address:** 414 Cumberland Ave N S7N 1M6

AMIGOS CANTINA   306/652-4912
▐ **APPROVED** ▐ Tex-Mex. Casual Dining. **Address:** 806 Dufferin Ave S7H 2B8

AROMA RESTO BAR   306/667-2358
▐ **APPROVED** ▐ Canadian. Casual Dining. **Address:** 405 20th St E S7K 6X6

CALORIES BAKERY & RESTAURANT   306/665-7991
▐ **APPROVED** ▐ French. Casual Dining. **Address:** 721 Broadway Ave S7N 1B3

CARVER'S STEAKHOUSE   306/652-8292
▐ **THREE DIAMOND** Steak. Fine Dining. **Address:** 612 Spadina Cres E S7K 3G9

CHIANTI   306/665-8466
▐ **APPROVED** ▐ Italian. Casual Dining. **Address:** 102 Idylwyld Dr N S7L 0Y7

CHRISTIES IL SECONDO BAKERY PIZZERIA   306/384-0506
▐ **APPROVED** ▐ Breads/Pastries Pizza. Quick Serve. **Address:** 802C Broadway Ave S7N 1B6

EARLS KITCHEN + BAR   306/664-4060
▐ **APPROVED** ▐ American. Casual Dining. **Address:** 610 2nd Ave N S7K 2C8

GENESIS FAMILY RESTAURANT   306/244-5516
▐ **APPROVED** ▐ Chinese. Casual Dining. **Address:** 901 22nd St W S7M 0R9

KEO'S KITCHEN   306/652-2533
▐ **APPROVED** ▐ Thai. Casual Dining. **Address:** 1808 Broadway Ave S7N 1C1

LAS PALAPAS RESORT GRILL   306/244-5556
▐ **APPROVED** ▐ Mexican. Casual Dining. **Address:** 910 Victoria Ave S7N 0Z6

MANO'S RESTAURANT & LOUNGE   306/955-5555
▐ **APPROVED** ▐ International. Casual Dining. **Address:** 1820 8th St E S7H 0T6

MI CASA RESTAURANTE   306/979-4700
▐ **APPROVED** ▐ Mexican. Casual Dining. **Address:** 618 Circle Dr E S7K 0T9

MOXIE'S CLASSIC GRILL   306/374-9800
▐ **APPROVED** ▐ American. Casual Dining. **Address:** 3134 8th St E S7H 0W2

MR MIKES STEAKHOUSECASUAL   306/242-3775
▐ **APPROVED** ▐ American. Casual Dining. **Address:** 2105 8th St E S7H 0T8

ODD COUPLE   306/668-8889
▐ **THREE DIAMOND** New Asian. Casual Dining. **Address:** 228 20th St W S7M 0W9

RICKY'S ALL DAY GRILL   306/652-3222
▐ **APPROVED** ▐ American. Casual Dining. **Address:** 1715 Idylwyld Dr N S7L 1B4

ROCK CREEK TAP AND GRILL   306/954-4220
▐ **APPROVED** ▐ American. Casual Dining. **Address:** 3020 Preston Ave S, #210 S7T 0G3

ST. TROPEZ BISTRO   306/652-1250
▐ **THREE DIAMOND** Canadian. Casual Dining. **Address:** 238 2nd Ave S S7K 1K9

SAMURAI JAPANESE RESTAURANT   306/683-6926
▐ **APPROVED** ▐ Japanese. Casual Dining. **Address:** 601 Spadina Crescent E S7K 3G8

🔗 **AAA.com/hertz**—When your ideal
road trip includes a comfortable ride

SWIFT CURRENT (E-3) pop. 15,503

Swift Current's beginnings date to the establishment of a North West Mounted Police encampment on Swift Current Creek in 1874. Soon after, the Canadian Pacific Railway built a depot, and the settlement became the freight terminus for western Canada. Beyond this point goods were hauled by wagon on overland trails; deep ruts still exist along the old North Battleford Trail north of the city.

Turn-of-the-20th-century farmers and ranchers bolstered the local economy. Oil was discovered in 1952, and in the succeeding decades Swift Current became a business hub for the oil, gas and agricultural industries as well as the major health care center for southwestern Saskatchewan.

Swift Current Creek runs through town, and two nearby lakes offer recreational facilities. At Saskatchewan Landing Provincial Park *(see Recreation Areas Chart)*, a plaque marks the spot where pioneers once forded the South Saskatchewan River on their way into the wilds of the northern province. In the park's hills are several First Nations grave sites and tepee rings.

Doc's Town Heritage Village, 17th Avenue S.E. and S. Railway Street in Kinetic Park, has a collection of buildings typical of early 20th-century prairie towns, including a blacksmith shop, church and school. Costumed staff are on hand to answer questions. It's open Fri.-Sun. 1-5, Father's Day-Labour Day; phone (306) 773-2944.

Tourism Swift Current: 44 Robert St. W., Swift Current, SK, Canada S9H 4M9. **Phone:** (306) 778-9174.

Self-guiding tours: A brochure with details about a walking tour of historic buildings in downtown Swift Current is available at the Swift Current Museum and from downtown merchants.

ART GALLERY OF SWIFT CURRENT is at 411 Herbert St. E. This public gallery offers exhibitions spotlighting local, provincial and national artists. Cultural events and festivals are scheduled throughout the year. Guided tours are given upon request. **Hours:** Open Mon.-Thurs. 1-5 and 7-9 p.m., Fri.-Sun. 1-5, Sept.-May; Mon.-Thurs. 1-5 and 7-9 p.m., Fri.-Sat. 1-5, rest of year. Closed major holidays and during exhibition changes. Phone ahead to confirm schedule. **Cost:** Free. **Phone:** (306) 778-2736.

COAST SWIFT CURRENT HOTEL   306/773-4643
APPROVED   Hotel. **Address:** 905 N Service Rd E S9H 3V1

DAYS INN BY WYNDHAM SWIFT CURRENT   306/773-4660
APPROVED   Hotel. **Address:** 105 George St W S9H 0K4

HOLIDAY INN EXPRESS & SUITES   306/773-8288
THREE DIAMOND Hotel. **Address:** 1301 N Service Rd E S9H 3X6

MOTEL 6 SWIFT CURRENT   306/778-6060
APPROVED   Hotel. **Address:** 1185 5th Ave NE S9H 5N7

WHERE TO EAT

AKROPOL FAMILY RESTAURANT   306/773-5454
APPROVED   International. Casual Dining. **Address:** 133 Central Ave N S9H 0K9

HORIZONS RESTAURANT   306/778-5759
APPROVED   American. Casual Dining. **Address:** 1401 N Service Rd E S9H 3X6

MISO HOUSE   306/778-4411
APPROVED

Japanese
Casual Dining
$9-$24

AAA Inspector Notes: This restaurant offers a good selection of reasonably priced entrées. Most dishes include miso soup, rice and kimchi. Favorites include bento boxes, nigiri sushi and beef, chicken or salmon teriyaki. Tempura dishes include vegetable, prawn, fish and chips, and gyoza. **Features:** beer & wine. **Address:** 285 N Service Rd W S9H 3S8 **Location:** Trans-Canada Hwy 1, 0.4 mi (0.6 km) w of Hwy 4 (Central Ave). L D

ORIGINAL JOE'S RESTAURANT & BAR   306/971-0121
APPROVED   American. Gastropub. **Address:** 935 Central Ave N S9H 3V3

SPRINGS GARDEN   306/773-2021
APPROVED   Comfort Food. Casual Dining. **Address:** 1 Springs Dr, Suite 323 S9H 3X6

WONG'S KITCHEN   306/773-4636
APPROVED   Chinese. Casual Dining. **Address:** 320 S Service Rd E S9H 3T6

TISDALE (C-4) pop. 3,180

This rural community in northeastern Saskatchewan provides easy access to several provincial parks offering recreational activities from fishing and boating in summer to skiing in winter. A roadside attraction, allegedly the world's largest honeybee, stands on the south side of Hwy. 3 in town.

Greville Jones Wildlife Sanctuary is reached by a gravel access road about 6.4 kilometres (4 mi.) southwest of Tisdale off Hwy. 3, following signs. The site of an old farmstead, it's a pleasant spot for a summer picnic or a hike along one of several nature trails.

Another scenic route is the Doghide River Trail, a system of walking, cycling and skiing trails that run along several sections of the riverbank. The trail can be accessed from Kinsmen McKay Park; from the junction of Hwys. 3 and 35, proceed east .8 kilometre (.5 mi.), then north .5 kilometre (.3 mi.) and turn right into the park.

🔗 **What's for dinner?**

AAA.com/travelguides/restaurants

WEYBURN (F-4) pop. 10,484

Weyburn's name was coined in 1893 by Scottish railroad workers, who called the surrounding marshy area at the headwaters of the Souris River "wee burn." Weyburn is the southeastern terminus of scenic Hwy. 39, which continues to Moose Jaw.

W.O. Mitchell, author of the popular novel "Who Has Seen the Wind," was born and raised in Weyburn. His works often dealt with life on the Canadian prairie, and in them he immortalized the town as "Crocus, Saskatchewan." Local history is depicted on the "Wheel of Progress" at the Weyburn Public Library, 45 Bison St. Between the spokes of this brass-rimmed mahogany wheel, which weighs 909 kilograms (2,000 lbs.) and has a diameter of 3.9 metres (13 ft.), are 10 mosaic panels showing past city highlights.

Weyburn Chamber of Commerce: 11 3rd St. N.E., Weyburn, SK, Canada S4H 0W1. **Phone:** (306) 842-4738.

SOO LINE HISTORICAL MUSEUM is e. on Hwy. 39 at 411 Industrial Ln. In addition to pioneer and Native artifacts, there is a collection of more than 5,000 pieces of silver—everything from opera glasses to a full tea service—dating from 1750 to 1970. The collection was willed to the museum by local resident Charles Wilson, who spent a lifetime attending auction sales in order to amass his treasures. The museum also houses the Weyburn Visitor Centre. **Time:** Allow 30 minutes minimum. **Hours:** Daily 10-6, Victoria Day weekend-Aug. 31; Sat. 1-5, rest of year. Guided tours are available by appointment. **Cost:** $4.76; $2.86 (ages 13-17 and 65+); $1.90 (ages 6-12). Tours include an audio handset. **Phone:** (306) 842-2922.

MICROTEL INN & SUITES BY WYNDHAM WEYBURN
306/842-5700
💠 APPROVED   Hotel. **Address:** 88 Grace St S4H 3N9

TRAVELODGE HOTEL BY WYNDHAM WEYBURN
306/842-1411
💠 APPROVED   Motel. **Address:** 53 Government Rd S S4H 2A2

WHERE TO EAT

DALLAS PIZZA   306/842-2933
💠 APPROVED   International. Casual Dining. **Address:** 72 3rd St NE S4H 0V9

YORKTON (E-5) pop. 15,669

In 1882 some 200 settlers from Ontario bought land in the Northwest Territories in what is now southeastern Saskatchewan. They called the community around their trading post York City. In 1890 the railroad arrived; York City settlers relocated to be near the railroad line and chose the name Yorkton. A plaque marks the site of York City; millstones from the original settlement's gristmill can still be seen.

Good Spirit Lake Provincial Park offers summer recreation. The park, a Hudson's Bay Co. post in the 1880s, is noted for miles of sandy beaches and dunes. *See Recreation Areas Chart.*

Tourism Yorkton Visitor Information Centre: Hwys. 9 and 16, Box 460, Yorkton, SK, Canada S3N 2W4. **Phone:** (306) 783-8707.

Self-guiding tours: The Yorkton Historical Walking Tour route includes gardens and historic buildings. The City Cemetery Walking Tour features the grave sites of many early pioneers, while the Art Walk highlights public art installations, monuments and murals. A nature trail winds through the Ravine Ecological Reserve. Tour brochures are available at the information center.

WESTERN DEVELOPMENT MUSEUM – YORKTON is .4 km (.25 mi.) w. on Hwy. 16A. Exhibits focus on the cultural roots of western Canadian settlers. **Time:** Allow 1 hour minimum. **Hours:** Daily 9-5, mid-June to mid-Aug.; Mon.-Fri. 9-5, Sat.-Sun. noon-5, Apr. 1 to mid-June and mid-Aug. through Dec. 30; Tues.-Fri. 9-5, Sat.-Sun. noon-5, rest of year (closes at 3 on Dec. 24 and 31). Closed national holidays and Saskatchewan Family Day. Phone ahead to confirm schedule. **Cost:** $10; $9 (ages 65+); $7 (students with ID); $4 (ages 6-12); $25 (family, parents or guardians and dependent children under age 18). **Phone:** (306) 783-8361. 🎟

DAYS INN & SUITES YORKTON   306/782-3112
💠 THREE DIAMOND Hotel. **Address:** 1-275 Broadway St E S3N 0N5

QUALITY INN & SUITES YORKTON   306/783-3297
💠 APPROVED   Hotel. **Address:** 2 Kelsey Bay S3N 3Z4

WHERE TO EAT

MR MIKES STEAKHOUSECASUAL   306/783-6453
💠 APPROVED   American. Casual Dining. **Address:** 275 Broadway St E S3N 3G7

STAY CONNECTED

GET THE APP

AAA.com/mobile
CAA.ca/mobile

Hertz

Enjoy AAA membership discounts
and benefits wherever you go.*

Up to 20% off the base rate	Free Additional Driver	$6.99 NeverLost® GPS	10% off tank of gas

Click: AAA.com/hertz I Call: 1-800-654-3080 I Visit: Your local AAA branch

*The up to 20% off discount will vary depending on location, date, length of rental, car class and other factors. Discount applies to pay later base rate. Taxes and fees excluded. AAA Club Discount Code (CDP#) must be provided at time of reservation for full-offer discounts. Benefits available at participating Hertz locations in the U.S., Canada and Puerto Rico. Age, driver, credit and qualifying rate restrictions for the renting location apply. Gas savings is only valid when prepaid fuel option is purchased. At the time of rental, present your AAA membership card or Hertz/AAA discount card for identification. No charge for additional drivers who are also AAA members, have a credit card in their own name and meet standard rental qualifications. Additional terms apply. © 2019 Hertz System, Inc. All rights reserved. CS 319038

Bennett Lake

Yukon

To find gleaming gifts of topaz in out-croppings of rock. To wander trails once trodden by miners and trappers. To cry "Mush!" behind a stalwart team of sturdy Alaskan huskies.

To do any of these is to begin to understand the allure of the endless Yukon.

The roughly triangular territory is a place of majesty and adventure; a lonely wilderness; a rugged, pristine land of splendor and beauty.

Klondike or Bust

"Thick between the flaky slabs, like cheese sandwiches"—this was how prospector George Washington Carmack described the gold he saw glimmering between rocks in Bonanza Creek near Dawson City in 1896.

In 1897 the steamship *Excelsior* arrived in San Francisco carrying a treasure worth more than $500,000; a few days later the *Portland* docked in Seattle with a ton of gold piled on its deck. News of these recently discovered riches spread like wildfire.

Miles Canyon

That winter 100,000 prospectors hopeful of getting rich quick began a long, arduous journey to the Yukon to seek their fortunes. While the rush only lasted about 5 years, history was left in its trampled tracks.

If stampeders survived the trek through Chilkoot Pass—a climb over frozen mountains with heavy backpacks full of supplies—they crossed the border into the Yukon Territory at Bennett Lake.

The lake, surrounded by mighty peaks and woodlands, links to the Yukon River. Most fortune seekers waited out the harsh winter in a crowded tent city. Transients built boats, temporary shelter and a little log church out of timber hewn from the forest. When the lake's ice broke, 7,000 handmade vessels headed across its waters.

Today, those miners' cabins still line Bennett Lake at Carcross, a town full of gold rush history. The 1898 Caribou Hotel, built to welcome gold rushers, is downtown, and graves of early pioneers dot the cemetery.

From Carcross the gold route followed the Yukon River to Miles Canyon, south of Whitehorse. Dangerous currents here caused hundreds of boats to capsize, and licensed guides were a must for piloting would-be miners with smaller vessels through the rocks and whirlpools.

Cheechakos (newcomers) relied upon their own floating devices until stern-wheelers became a popular means of travel. Though boats were specifically designed for the river, many still ran aground or were smashed by rapids or rocks.

The River to Riches

After stopping to relax and dry out in Whitehorse, miners pressed on, traversing Lake Laberge to a stretch of the Yukon called Thirty Mile. Due to swift currents and rocks, it was perhaps the route's most dangerous portion. Historical sites along Thirty Mile include abandoned Northwest Mounted Police posts, grave markers, woodcutters' cabins, telegraph stations, old log buildings and remains of beached paddlewheelers.

More dangerous eddies remained at Five Finger Rapids, outside Carmacks, before exhausted voyagers reached Dawson City.

Downtown Dawson City looks much as it did when prospectors arrived, since codes require that fronts of new buildings be reminiscent of the gold rush era. And old buildings have been restored: Cancan dancing takes place at Diamond Tooth Gertie's Casino and author Jack London's and poet Robert Service's log cabins remain as examples of gold rush housing.

Recreation

Hiking the Chilkoot Trail, Yukon's original inroad, is the best way to understand the challenges faced by gold-rush stampeders. Beginning in Dyea, Alaska, the trail is a 53-kilometre (33-mi.), one-way walk through history that can take 3 to 5 days.

Preparation—proper gear, provisions, permits and registration—is key to this demanding trip through boreal forests, alpine tundra and snow-patched mountains. You must reserve a campsite for each night on the trail through the Trail Centre in Skagway, Alaska. The center offers maps, safety tips and a few words about bears; phone Parks Canada year-round at (800) 661-0486.

Camping in summer (June to mid-September) is a true wilderness experience. Firewood is free, but you'll have to pump your own water. Government campgrounds are spread throughout the Yukon roughly 81-121 kilometres (50-75 mi.) apart, many beside lakes, rivers or streams where you might hook Arctic graylings for dinner. Of the 10 campgrounds along the Alaska Highway (Hwy. 1), Watson Lake is one of the first as you enter Yukon from British Columbia. Farther west is Congdon Creek, one of Yukon's largest. You can fish, swim and hike at both.

Take scenic Dempster Highway (Hwy. 5) from Dawson City to Rock River Campground, the northernmost public facility. Congratulate yourself: You've crossed the Continental Divide—twice—and the Arctic Circle! There's no well water, so get supplies in Dawson City or Eagle Plains (your last chance).

The Klondike Highway (Hwy. 2), open all year, has roadside respites for camping and picnicking. You also can camp just off the Robert Campbell and Silver Trail highways (Hwys. 4 and 11). Travelers can get daily road condition reports from the Department of Highways and Public Works hotline, (877) 456-7623 within the Yukon or (867) 456-7623 outside the Yukon. Watch for wildlife, especially near viewing areas identified with a sign picturing binoculars.

With almost 7 months of winter (October through April), snow skiing is a way of life. Near Whitehorse a chalet and night lighting draw cross-country skiers to Mount McIntyre's trails, while Mount Sima, one of Yukon's largest ski areas, appeals to downhill skiers. Snowboarding is a favorite at Mount Sima as well as on groomed trails around Whitehorse, or over more rugged terrain out of Dawson City, Yukon's snowmobiling capital.

Whitehorse offers kayaking or white-water rafting on the Tatshenshini's Class III and IV rapids, or through Kluane National Park and Reserve on the Alsek, a designated heritage river. Many sections of the Yukon River are easily navigated by canoe.

Go Kayaking in Whitehorse

Historic Timeline

1800	The Hudson's Bay Co. sets up trading posts in the Yukon.
1895	Yukon Territory becomes a provisional district of the Northwest Territories.
1898	More than $100 million in gold is mined in the region over a 6-year span beginning just before the turn of the 20th century.
1942	The Alaska Highway is constructed, creating a new overland transportation route.
1953	Yukon's capital is moved from Dawson City to Whitehorse.
1959	At a cost of $1 million, a large fish ladder is built at the Whitehorse Rapids for migrating chinook salmon.
1979	Kluane National Park is declared a Natural World Heritage Site.
1993	The Council for Yukon Indians and the Canadian and Yukon governments agree on final territorial land claim settlements.
1999	Yukon's accord with the Vuntut Gwitchin marks the territory's first recognition of a First Nation tribe as a valid government.
2003	The name of the Yukon Territory is officially changed to Yukon.
2015	Yukon to spend an additional $1.4 million on mining exploration.

What To Pack

Temperature Averages Maximum/Minimum (Celsius)	JANUARY	FEBRUARY	MARCH	APRIL	MAY	JUNE	JULY	AUGUST	SEPTEMBER	OCTOBER	NOVEMBER	DECEMBER
Burwash Landing	-16/-29	-11/-26	-3/-19	4/-9	12/-2	17/3	19/6	17/4	11/-2	2/-9	-9/-21	-14/-26
Dawson City	-21/-30	-16/-27	-3/-20	8/-8	15/1	21/6	23/8	20/5	11/-1	-1/-10	-14/-22	-20/-29
Faro	0/-5	1/-5	5/-2	11/1	14/5	18/9	19/11	18/10	14/6	9/3	3/-3	0/-6
Mayo	-22/-32	-13/-26	-3/-18	6/-6	14/1	20/7	22/8	19/6	12/1	2/-7	-13/-21	-18/-28
Watson Lake	-19/-30	-12/-25	-3/-18	6/-7	13/0	19/6	21/8	19/7	13/2	4/-5	-11/-20	-18/-28
Whitehorse	-14/-23	-8/-18	-2/-13	6/-6	12/0	18/5	20/7	18/6	12/2	4/-3	7/-14	-12/-20

From the records of The Weather Channel Interactive, Inc.

Good Facts To Know

ABOUT THE TERRITORY

POPULATION: 33,897.

AREA: 482,443 sq km (186,271 sq mi.); ranks 9th.

CAPITAL: Whitehorse.

HIGHEST POINT: 5,959 m (19,545 ft.), Mount Logan.

LOWEST POINT: Sea level, Beaufort Sea.

TIME ZONE(S): Pacific.

GAMBLING

MINIMUM AGE FOR GAMBLING: 19.

REGULATIONS

TEEN DRIVING LAWS: Driving is not permitted midnight-5 a.m. unless with a qualified co-driver or if a teen has been granted a work exception. Minimum age for an unrestricted driver's license is 17 years, 6 months. For more information about Yukon driver's license regulations, phone (867) 667-5315.

SEAT BELT/CHILD RESTRAINT LAWS: Seat belts are required for driver and all passengers. An Infant must be secured in a rear-facing seat until they are at least 10 kilograms (22 lbs.) and walking unassisted, then a front-facing 5-point harness child restraint system may be used until the child weighs 22 kilograms (48 lbs.). A booster seat must be used until a child weighs 45 kilograms (100 lbs.) or 145 centimeters tall (4 feet 9 inches) whichever comes first. AAA recommends the use of seat belts and appropriate child restraints for the driver and all passengers.

CELLPHONE RESTRICTIONS: Drivers may not use a hand-held device to talk, text or send emails while driving.

HELMETS FOR MOTORCYCLISTS: Required for all riders.

RADAR DETECTORS: Not permitted.

FIREARMS LAWS: By federal law, all nonresidents entering Canada with a firearm must declare their weapon in writing and pay a fee of $25 (Canadian). Contact the Canadian Firearms Centre at (800) 731-4000 to receive a declaration form or for additional information.

ALCOHOL CONSUMPTION: Legal age 19.

HOLIDAYS

HOLIDAYS: Jan. 1 ▪ Heritage Day, Feb. 27 ▪ Good Friday ▪ Easter Monday ▪ Victoria Day, May 24 or the closest prior Mon. ▪ Canada Day, July 1 ▪ Discovery Day, Aug. (3rd Mon.) ▪ Labour Day, Sept. (1st Mon.) ▪ Thanksgiving, Oct. (2nd Mon.) ▪ Remembrance Day, Nov. 11 ▪ Christmas, Dec. 25 ▪ Boxing Day, Dec. 26.

MONEY

TAXES: Yukon has no territorial sales tax. The federal Goods and Services Tax (GST) is 5 percent.

VISITOR INFORMATION

INFORMATION CENTERS: Territorial information centers in Beaver Creek ▪ Carcross ▪ Dawson City ▪ Haines Junction ▪ Watson Lake ▪ and Whitehorse are open 12 hours a day, mid-May to mid-Sept., with reduced hours early to mid-May and mid- to late Sept. The Whitehorse Visitor Information Centre also is open daily 8-8, May 5-Sept. 20 ▪ Mon.-Fri. 8:30-5, Sat. 10-2, rest of year

ROAD CONDITIONS: Through its Yukon Network the Canadian Broadcasting Corporation reports road conditions on the Alaska Highway and all other Yukon highways. Major participating stations, with their frequencies in kilohertz (kHz), are listed from south to north: Watson Lake, 990; Swift River, 970; Teslin, 940; Whitehorse, 570; Haines Junction, 860; Destruction Bay, 940; Beaver Creek, 690; Carmacks, 990; Mayo, 1230; Elsa, 560; Dawson City, 560; Faro, 105.1 FM; and Ross River, 990.

ROAD CONDITIONS: For changes in Yukon road conditions, phone (867) 456-7623, (877) 456-7623 or 511 within Yukon.

FERRY SCHEDULES AND INFORMATION: The Department of Highways runs ferries along Dempster Highway and at Dawson City; phone (867) 667-3710.

FURTHER INFORMATION FOR VISITORS:
Department of Tourism & Culture
100 Hanson St.
Whitehorse, YT Y1A 2C6
Canada
(867) 667-5036
(800) 661-0494

FISHING AND HUNTING REGULATIONS:
Environment Yukon
10 Burns Rd.
Whitehorse, YT Y1A 2C6
Canada
(867) 667-5652
(800) 661-0408ext. 5652 in Canada

Yukon Annual Events

Please call ahead to confirm event details.

 Visit **AAA.com/travelguides/events** to find AAA-listed events for every day of the year

WINTER

Dec. - TH (Tr'ondek Hwech'in) Last Minute Christmas Bazaar / Dawson City / 867-993-7100
- Snowmobile Drags, Enduro and Sno Cross Races / Whitehorse 867-633-4967
- Christmas Lights Tour / Whitehorse 867-668-8394

Jan. - Women's and Men's Curling Championship / Whitehorse 867-667-2875
- Pivot Theatre Festival / Whitehorse 867-393-6040

Feb. - Yukon Sourdough Rendezvous Whitehorse / 867-393-4467
- Kiki Karnival / Watson Lake / 867-536-7469
- Yukon Quest International Sled Dog Race / Whitehorse / 907-452-7954

SPRING

Mar. - Burning Away the Winter Blues Whitehorse / 867-633-4844
- Percy DeWolfe Memorial Mail Race Dawson City / 867-993-5320
- Thaw-Di-Gras Spring Carnival Dawson City / 867-993-5575

Apr. - Rotary Music Festival / Whitehorse 867-633-3755
- Dawson City International Short Film Festival / Dawson City / 867-993-5005
- A Celebration of Swans / Whitehorse 867-667-8291

May - Dawson City International Gold Show Dawson City / 867-993-5274
- Sounds of Spring / Whitehorse 867-667-8044

SUMMER

June - Aboriginal Day Celebrations Dawson City / 867-993-5385
- Solstice and Saint-Jean-Baptiste Celebrations / Whitehorse 867-668-2663, ext. 232
- Yukon River Quest Canoe and Kayak Race / Whitehorse / 867-333-5628

July - Yukon Gold Panning Championships Dawson City / 867-993-5575
- Canada Day Festivities / Watson Lake / 867-536-2246

Aug. - Yukon River Trail Marathon Whitehorse / 867-668-7592
- Discovery Days Festival / Dawson City / 867-993-2353
- Discovery Days / Watson Lake / 867-536-8020

FALL

Sept. - Labour Day Slo-Pitch Classic Dawson City / 867-993-5575
- Terry Fox Run / Watson Lake / 867-536-8020
- Klondike Trail of '98 International Road Relay / Whitehorse 867-393-8330

Oct. - Halloween Bonfire and Fireworks Watson Lake / 867-536-8022
- Halloween Dance / Watson Lake / 867-536-8022
- Halloween Spooktacular / Whitehorse 867-668-8677

Nov. - Spruce Bog Christmas Craft Sale Whitehorse / 867-633-2416
- Cranberry Fair / Whitehorse 867-393-2389
- Onde de Choc / Whitehorse 867-668-2663, ext. 560

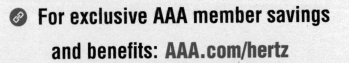

For exclusive AAA member savings and benefits: AAA.com/hertz

Sign Post Forest, Watson Lake

Red fox

Autumn foliage

White Pass & Yukon Route, Skagway

Miles Canyon, Whitehorse

Index: Great Experience for Members

AAA editor's picks of exceptional note

The SS *Klondike*
National Historic Site

Yukon Beringia
Interpretive Centre

See Orientation map on this page for corresponding grid coordinates, if applicable.

*Indicates the GEM is temporarily closed.

Whitehorse (D-2)
The SS *Klondike* National Historic Site
(See p. 443.)

Yukon Beringia Interpretive Centre
(See p. 444.)

CARCROSS (D-2) pop. 289

Carcross, 74 kilometres (46 mi.) from Whitehorse on the S. Klondike Highway, originally was called Caribou Crossing. The town's current name is a combination of the first syllable of each word. From this settlement George Carmack's party set out on the prospecting trip that began the gold rush of 1898. On July 29, 1900, the railroad's final spike was driven, marking the completion of the White Pass & Yukon Route, which linked Alaska and the Yukon Territory by rail.

Today the White Pass & Yukon Route *(see attraction listing in Alaska p. 513)* transports passengers between Carcross and Bennett, British Columbia; phone (907) 983-2217 or (800) 343-7373 for schedule and reservations.

Near the town's train depot is the "Duchess," a tiny locomotive that ran the 6.4-kilometre (4-mi.) line from Taku Arm on Tagish Lake to Atlin Lake in the early 1900s. It supposedly was the shortest and most expensive rail trip in the world—one-way fare was $2—and passengers had to sit on their baggage in the cramped compartment.

Recalling the feverish gold rush days is the Caribou Hotel. Regarded as the Yukon's oldest operating hotel, the historic building, which opened in 1898 to accommodate gold seekers heading north, is a Yukon Historic Site. **Note:** Hotel renovations are ongoing; phone (867) 393-4551.

The Carcross Visitor Information Centre is at the Carcross Pavilion, adjacent to the historic White Pass & Yukon Route train depot. The center provides extensive information about Carcross, one of the Yukon's most picturesque areas; phone (867) 821-4431.

Just north of town along the Klondike Highway lies the Carcross Desert, considered the smallest desert in the world. The 260-hectare (650-acre) area was created by retreating glaciers that left a sandy lake bottom; today winds from Lake Bennett constantly shift the sand, limiting vegetation to such plants as kinnikinnick and lodgepole pine.

DAWSON CITY (C-1) pop. 1,319
• Hotels p. 441 • Restaurants p. 441

Dawson City was the center of the excitement caused by one of the world's most fabulous gold strikes. On Aug. 16, 1896, George Washington Carmack and his companions Skookum Jim and Tagish Charlie made the first strike on Bonanza Creek, a tributary of the Klondike River.

In the summer of 1897 miners from Dawson City arrived in Seattle and San Francisco with nearly $2 million as they carried word of the discovery to the United States, then in the midst of a depression. By the next spring more than 60,000 men and women had passed through Seattle and Alaska's Chilkoot and White passes on their way to the Klondike.

The Dawson settlement, which sprang up at the confluence of the Yukon and Klondike rivers, became a thriving city with some 30,000 inhabitants by the summer of 1898, making it the largest city west of Winnipeg and north of San Francisco.

All the creeks in the area had been staked by the spring of 1899. Hillside and bench claims were made, some yielding rich gold finds in the White Channel gravels. Between 1896 and 1904 Klondike creeks brought in more than $100 million in gold.

This period of Dawson City's history has been preserved by Rex Beach, Jack London, Robert W. Service and others who wrote colorful tales of personal experiences.

It was in Dawson City that London became acquainted with a large dog that he named Buck, a cross between a St. Bernard and a German shepherd that became the prototype for the dog in "Call of the Wild." Daily readings from the works of Jack London are given at a replica of his cabin on Eighth Avenue at Firth Street, part of the Jack London Museum.

A fire destroyed the town center after residents' 1897 Thanksgiving Day celebrations. The Dawson City Firefighters Museum, across from the ferry landing, displays artifacts, early fire extinguishers, gear, and historic vehicles in order to preserve Dawson City's firefighting heritage; a gallery showcases pictures and art created for the museum. Phone (867) 993-7407 or (867) 993-7400 for more information.

However, many historic buildings—some still in use—do survive from the days when Dawson City was the gold capital of the world. The Downtown and Eldorado hotels conjure memories of a lively past.

Harrington's Store, Princess Street and Third Avenue, has a free photographic exhibit titled "Dawson as They Saw It," open June through September. The post office and other restored buildings can be seen as part of various Parks Canada tours. Tickets for the tours are available at the visitor information center at Front and King streets.

The summit of Midnight Dome, 7 kilometres (4 mi.) southeast via Front Street, offers a panorama of Dawson City, the Yukon and Klondike rivers and the gold fields. Many Dawson City pioneers are buried in cemeteries on the hillsides flanking the dome.

The *Klondike Spirit* runs daily paddlewheeler trips up and down the Yukon River; phone (867) 993-5323 for schedule and information.

South on Bonanza Creek Road is the Discovery Claim National Historic Site, the place of the gold discovery that started the great rush. Panning for gold is possible at several locations along the Klondike Highway: Claim 33, Free Claim #6 and Gold Bottom Mine Tours.

The Dawson City Visitor Information Centre features exhibits about Klondike history and is open daily 8-8, May-Sept.

The town celebrates its gold mining heritage during 🔺 Discovery Days Weekend, a weeklong event held at various locations in mid-August.

Dawson City Visitor Information Centre: Front and King streets, Dawson City, YT, Canada Y0B 1G0. **Phone:** (867) 993-5566.

Self-guiding tours: A brochure describing walking tours of historic sites is available at the visitor information center.

INSIDER INFO:
Sourdoughs and Cheechakos

To distinguish between the fortune seekers who entered the Yukon Territory during the 1897-98 Klondike Gold Rush, veterans of the '49 California Rush labeled the seasoned arrivals "Sourdoughs" and the greenhorns "Cheechakos" (CHE-cha-kos). Named after the staple bread of the frontier, Sourdoughs were prospectors who had survived a Yukon winter. The term Cheechako came from the Chinook Indian word for "new to come."

Once off the steamer at Skagway, Alaska, these newcomers had to transport thousands of pounds of survival gear—the Northwest Mounted Police wisely required each prospector to bring a year's supply of food—over the precipitous Chilkoot Pass. After that they had to float their unwieldy cargo over the treacherous rapids of the Yukon River.

More obstacles awaited the greenhorns at the gold sites. By the time the Cheechakos arrived, much of the gold field already was depleted or staked. To make things worse, Cheechakos were often directed to the hills by unscrupulous Sourdoughs who knew the gold nuggets tended to settle in creek beds. Nonetheless, some did tap into a channel of an ancient gold-bearing stream on Cheechako Hill.

Those who had survived to see the ice melt were dubbed Sourdoughs; the graveyards of those who had not succeeded dotted the route all the way back to Skagway. As one cynical Sourdough put it: "We were SOUR on the Yukon and didn't have enough DOUGH to get out."

DANOJA ZHO CULTURAL CENTRE is at 1131 Front St., across from the Dawson City Visitor Information Centre. Guided tours, exhibits, video presentations, dance performances and hands-on activities give visitors an interesting perspective into the culture of the Tr'ondek Hwech'in First Nations peoples. Displays include archeological artifacts, traditional costumes and reproduction tools. Special events also are featured. **Time:** Allow 30 minutes minimum. **Hours:** Mon.-Sat. 10-5, June-Sept. **Cost:** $6; $2.50 (ages 12-18); free (ages 0-11). **Phone:** (867) 993-7100.

DAWSON CITY'S _KLONDIKE SPIRIT_ CRUISE departs at Front Street Dock. During 90-minute tours downriver from Dawson City, passengers aboard the paddlewheeler-style _Klondike Spirit_ have a choice of barrier-free views from the observation deck or main deck. A 2-hour evening outing with an option for dinner takes in a few areas north of the city, including the Stern-wheeler Graveyard with its decaying watercrafts, Mooseheide Village and a cave occupied by one of the local characters before the tour heads south for a scenic segment.

Inquire about weather policies. **Time:** Allow 2 hours minimum. **Hours:** Dawson City's _Klondike Spirit_ departs daily at 6:45, late May-early Sept. Dinner cruise departures require a minimum of 15 people. Phone ahead to confirm schedule. **Cost:** $68.25; free (ages 0-12). Fare with dinner $110.25; $10.50 (ages 0-12). Reservations are required for dinner cruise. **Phone:** (867) 993-5323, or (800) 764-3555 in Canada. GT ⍥

DAWSON HISTORICAL COMPLEX NATIONAL HISTORIC SITE comprises more than a dozen restored buildings scattered throughout Dawson City. The structures evoke the time and place of the Klondike Gold Rush of the 1890s. Visitors may explore the richly appointed Palace Grand Theatre where the interactive presentation, Greatest Klondiker Contest, is offered Sunday through Thursday; the Commissioner's Residence mansion and gardens where themed talks take place along with such activities as flower-pressing and croquet; the Robert Service Cabin, where the Bard of the Yukon lived and wrote many of his ballads and poems 1909-12; and Harrington's Store, which displays photographs and letters from the gold rush.

Self-guiding audio tours and guided tours led by costumed site interpreters are available. A hike with the Poetry of Robert Service is offered daily. Tour tickets are available at the visitor information center. **Hours:** Programs offered daily 9:30-8, Victoria Day-Labour Day. Tour departure times vary. Palace Grand Theatre tours offered daily. Commissioner's Residence tours open daily; hours vary. Robert Service Cabin program offered daily in the afternoon. Phone for additional tours and departure times. **Cost:** All programs $6.30 each; free (children). **Phone:** (867) 993-7200.

TOMBSTONE TERRITORIAL PARK is 71 km (44 mi.) n. of jct. Dempster and Klondike hwys. This park spans an area of more than 2,164 square kilometres (836 sq. mi.) and features a diversity of wildlife and bird species as well as a variety of vegetation. This is a remote park with few established hiking trails, but there are accessible portions off the highway that offer short hikes and challenging backpacking and ridge walking excursions. The park's arctic tundra environment creates a landscape with spectacular views. The interpretive center offers campfire programs, guided walks and hikes and special events.

Note: When traveling to the park have enough gas and spare tires since there are no roadside services available until Eagle Plains, which is 369 kilometres (229 mi.) north of the Klondike Highway.

Once in the park, be aware that it is an isolated and potentially hazardous environment. Rough terrain, drastic weather changes and encounters with wildlife are factors to consider. Use leave-no-trace etiquette when hiking and travel lightly on this sensitive environment. **Time:** Allow 3 hours minimum. **Hours:** Park is open daily 24 hours. Interpretive center open daily 9-5, mid-May to mid-Sept. Phone ahead to confirm schedule. **Cost:** Free. **Phone:** (867) 667-5648.

THE ELDORADO HOTEL 867/993-5451
▽ APPROVED Hotel. **Address:** 902 3rd Ave Y0B 1G0

KLONDIKE KATE'S CABINS 867/993-6527
▽ APPROVED Cabin. **Address:** 331 King St Y0B 1G0

WESTMARK INN DAWSON CITY 867/993-5542
▽ APPROVED Hotel. **Address:** 813 5th Ave Y0B 1G0

YUKON HOTEL 867/993-5451
▽ APPROVED Extended Stay Hotel. **Address:** 702 Front St Y0B 1G0

WHERE TO EAT

ALCHEMY CAFE 867/993-3831
▽ APPROVED Natural/Organic Vegetarian. Casual Dining. **Address:** 878 3rd Ave Y0B 1G0

BONANZA DINING ROOM & SLUICE BOX LOUNGE
867/993-5451
▽ APPROVED American. Casual Dining. **Address:** 903 3rd Ave Y0B 1G0

THE DRUNKEN GOAT TAVERNA 867/993-5868
▽ APPROVED Traditional Greek. Casual Dining. **Address:** 952 2nd Ave Y0B 1G0

KLONDIKE KATE'S RESTAURANT 867/993-6527
▽ APPROVED
Canadian
Casual Dining
$15-$29
AAA Inspector Notes: *Historic.* Get a sense of Dawson City's history and the gold rush era at this restaurant located across the street from the theater. The menu features a good variety of appetizers and enticing fish and meat entrées. Rather than dining inside, opt for a seat on the covered, heated patio in the summer. Off-season hours and meal openings can vary, so it is a good idea to check with the restaurant. **Features:** full bar, patio dining, Sunday brunch, happy hour. **Reservations:** suggested. **Address:** 1102 3rd Ave Y0B 1G0 **Location:** Corner of 3rd Ave and King St; center; in Klondike Kate's Cabins. D CALL

RIVER WEST BISTRO 867/993-6339
▽ APPROVED American. Quick Serve. **Address:** 958 Front St Y0B 1G0

SOURDOUGH JOE'S RESTAURANT 867/993-6590
▽ APPROVED Seafood. Casual Dining. **Address:** 902 Front St Y0B 1G0

IVVAVIK NATIONAL PARK (A-1)

Ivvavik National Park is in the extreme northwestern corner of the Yukon. Virtually untouched by humans, the Arctic wilderness is of great geologic interest; it is one of the few regions in Canada that contains areas never covered by glaciers.

Every spring it becomes the calving grounds of Porcupine caribous that arrive after a long, difficult migration from the south and west. From mid-June to early July the park offers 5-day, catered base camp trips led by Parks Canada staff and Inuvialuit cultural hosts. The only access to the park is by air. Phone (867) 777-8800.

Make the Conn🔗ction

AAA guidebooks are just the beginning. Open the door to a whole lot more on AAA.com. Get extra travel insight, more information and online booking.

Find this symbol for places to look, book and save on AAA.com.

iStockphoto.com_shapecharge

KLUANE NATIONAL PARK AND RESERVE (D-1)

Elevations in the park range from 400 metres (1,300 ft.) in the Alsek River to 5,959 m (19,545 ft.) at Mount Logan. Refer to CAA/AAA maps for additional elevation information.

Kluane (kloo-AH-nee) National Park and Reserve is bounded by the Haines (Hwy. 3) and Alaska (Hwy. 1) highways along its northeastern border. The park covers 21,980 square kilometres (8,487 sq. mi.) of wilderness.

The land has drawn a number of people, including the indigenous Southern Tutchone, who have lived in the area for generations. Near the park's southeastern boundary was the Dalton Trail, a route used during the Klondike Rush of 1898. In 1904 a North West Mounted Police post was established on the south shore of Kluane Lake, and in 1942 the lake became a meeting place for crews building the Alaska Highway.

During the building of the highway the wilderness area was preserved as the Kluane Game Sanctuary. In 1979 Kluane was declared a World Heritage Site for its impressive topographical features and its massive nonpolar ice fields. Today the Kluane First Nation and Champagne and Aishihik First Nations peoples cooperatively manage the park with Parks Canada.

The park is dominated by the Saint Elias Mountains, which run through the park in a southeasterly direction. Mount Logan, Canada's highest peak at 5,959 m (19,545 ft.), and Mount St. Elias at 5,489 metres (18,008 ft.) dominate the range. The Saint Elias Mountains hold extensive ice fields that date from the last ice age and constitute the largest nonpolar glacier systems in the world.

An extensive network of glaciers, together with the ice fields, covers more than half of the park's area throughout the year. Notable are the Steele Glacier, which moves sporadically at a relatively rapid rate, and the Kaskawulsh and Lowell glaciers, which are flanked by moraines—accumulations of earth and stones carried and deposited by the glaciers. The movement and debris of the glaciers contribute to such park features as sand dunes and dust storms.

The park has a variety of flora. Such coniferous species as white spruce characterize the boreal forest of the river valleys. Lichens, dwarf birch trees and low shrubs distinguish the tundra uplands in the northern section, and colorful Arctic flowers cling to the crevices and ledges of the mountains. In the southeastern section, where the Pacific Ocean's moderating influence is felt in the climate, the vegetation is more luxuriant.

Arctic grayling, lake trout, northern pike and kokanee salmon are found in lakes and streams. Other park species include golden eagles, ptarmigans, Dall sheep, mountain goats, caribou, moose and wolves. Kluane has one of the largest populations of grizzly bears and subspecies of moose in the world.

General Information and Activities

The park is open all year, but access may be limited in the winter, depending on weather conditions. The Kluane National Park and Reserve Visitor Centre, at Km-post 1635 in Haines Junction, is open daily 9-7, early June to early September; 9-5 mid-May to early June and early September to late September. The Tachäl Dhäl (Sheep Mountain) Visitor Centre at Km-post 1707 is open daily 9-4 mid-May to early September.

The park primarily is a wilderness area, so there are no roads except on the eastern and northern perimeters, traversed by Hwy. 3 and Hwy. 1, respectively. Hiking is the most popular activity in the park, with approximately 250 kilometres (155 mi.) of hiking trails. Hiking is possible along a few old mining roads, creekside paths and marked trails. Some trails are self-guiding. All overnight hikers must register at one of the information centers before and after hikes.

Mountain climbing should be done only by well-trained climbers, who must obtain a climbing permit and register before and after climbs.

Other recreational pursuits include fishing, backpacking, boating, cross-country skiing and ice fishing. All anglers within the park must obtain a national park fishing license, available at the park visitor centers and from area stores and lodges. Camping, fishing and picnic facilities are available at Kathleen Lake, 27 kilometres (17 mi.) south of Haines Junction.

During the summer the park sponsors interpretive activities including campfire talks and guided walks. A relief map, interactive computer touch screens and a video are available. Information about recreational opportunities, sightseeing by small aircraft and other guided tours is available.

ADMISSION to the park is free.

PETS are permitted in the park if kept on a leash.

ADDRESS inquiries about the park to Kluane National Park and Reserve, P.O. Box 5495, Haines Junction, YT, Canada Y0B 1L0; phone (867) 634-7207.

TESLIN (D-2) pop. 122

The Nisutlin Bay Bridge, the longest water span on the Alaska Highway, crosses an arm of Teslin Lake at Teslin. The highway parallels the 116-kilometre (72-mi.) lake for about 55 kilometres (34 mi.), providing a scenic drive bordered on both sides by mountains. The area is noted for abundant game, and the fjord-like lake provides excellent fishing. The economy of the community depends heavily on hunting, fishing and trapping.

Teslin has one of the largest indigenous populations in the Yukon, with many of its residents descended from the coastal Tlingit tribe. The original settlement is reached by a loop road. In the old village are Catholic and Anglican missions as well as a Royal Canadian Mounted Police station.

TESLIN TLINGIT HERITAGE CENTRE is 4 km (2.5 mi.) w. on Hwy. 1. Totem poles, hand-carved masks, crafts, artifacts and photographs provide insight into the life and culture of the Teslin Tlingit people. **Time:** Allow 30 minutes minimum. **Hours:** Daily 9-5, June-Aug. **Cost:** $5; $4 (ages 55+); free (ages 0-5); $15 (family). **Phone:** (867) 390-2532 ext. 335. ⛱

WATSON LAKE (D-3) pop. 802

At Km-post 1016.8 on the Alaska Highway, Watson Lake is an important transportation, distribution and communication center for the southern Yukon. The town was named for Frank Watson, a trapper from England who settled there in 1898.

Watson Lake is known as the Sign Post Forest for its signpost collection that was begun by a homesick soldier during construction of the Alaska Highway in 1942. Over the years, tourists have continued adding signs showing the names of their hometowns, and now the collection includes more than 70,000 signs.

From Watson Lake the historic Robert Campbell Highway loops north and west through the wilderness of southeastern Yukon.

WHITEHORSE (D-2) pop. 23,276, elev. 689m/2,260'
• Hotels p. 444 • Restaurants p. 444

Whitehorse began during the Klondike gold rush when thousands of prospectors journeyed by ship to Skagway, Alaska, then climbed the rugged mountain passes to the headwaters of the Yukon River. They constructed nearly anything floatable for the more than 900-kilometre (559-mi.) trip to Dawson City via Whitehorse. Above Whitehorse many prospectors died in the dangerous Whitehorse Rapids.

When stern-wheeler service to Dawson became available, the trip from Whitehorse took 2.5 days; the return trip against the current took 5 days. The first rails of the White Pass & Yukon Route were laid at Skagway in May 1898, and the line to Whitehorse opened in July 1900.

During World War II Canadian and United States Army personnel building the Alaska Highway moved to Whitehorse, which became the capital of the Yukon Territory in 1953.

Evolving into the transportation, communication and distribution center of the Yukon, Whitehorse also became the territorial headquarters of the Royal Canadian Mounted Police as well as the heart of the territorial government and federal departments.

Attractions on a much larger scale include Lake Laberge, the setting for Robert W. Service's "The Cremation of Sam McGee," and the Robert Lowe Suspension Bridge across Miles Canyon.

The Whitehorse Power Dam features one of the world's longest wooden fish ladders; the salmon,

running in late July or early August, can be seen from viewing windows. Lake Schwatka, impounded by the power dam, was named after Frederick Schwatka, the first U.S. army lieutenant to navigate the entire length of the Yukon River.

Visible from the Alaska Highway, 24 kilometres (15 mi.) south of Whitehorse, is Marsh Lake Lock, the northernmost lock in the Western Hemisphere. It is used by small craft navigating the upper Yukon River.

Guided tours of the town and surrounding area are available through Whitehorse City Tour. A few companies provide Yukon River cruises, guided hikes, and canoe, boat and raft trips on area rivers. The Yukon Conservation Society gives guided nature walks in the summer. For a self-guided walk, there's the City of Whitehorse Millennium Trail, a 5-kilometre (3.1-mi.) paved path along the Yukon River.

The Swan Haven Interpretive Centre, on the shores of M'Clintock Bay, affords bird enthusiasts the opportunity to learn about migratory birds, in particular trumpeter swans. The center is open Mon.-Fri. 5-9 p.m., Sat.-Sun. noon-7, in April. Phone (867) 667-8291.

Yukon Visitor Information Centre, 100 Hanson St., features exhibits and audiovisual presentations about the Yukon. The center is open daily 8-8, early May-Sept. 30; Mon.-Fri. 8:30-noon and 1-5, Sat. 10-2, rest of year. Phone (867) 667-3084.

Whitehorse is the terminus for the 1,000-mile 🐾 Yukon Quest International Sled Dog Race, which starts in Fairbanks, Alaska, and takes place over a 2-week period from early to mid-February.

Yukon Visitor Information Centre: 100 Hanson St., Whitehorse, YT, Canada Y1A 1E7. **Phone:** (867) 667-3084.

Self-guiding tours: Guidebooks are available from the Yukon Historical and Museums Association, 3126 Third Ave., P.O. Box 4357, Whitehorse, YT, Canada Y1A 1E7; phone (867) 667-4704. Self-guiding audio walking tour podcasts can be downloaded from the association's website.

THE SS *KLONDIKE* NATIONAL HISTORIC SITE is next to the river at Second Ave. and Robert Campbell Bridge. One of the largest stern-wheelers on the Yukon River, the *Klondike* ran its route 1937-55. The original *Klondike* struck a gravel bar in 1936; a replacement was built the same year. The video, "In the Days of the Riverboats," is presented continuously. Both guided and self-guiding tours are available. **Time:** Allow 30 minutes minimum. **Hours:** Daily 9:30-5, late May-Labour Day. **Cost:** Free. $3 for self-guiding brochure. Guided tours $6.05; $1.90 (ages 6-17). **Phone:** (867) 667-4511.

WATERFRONT TROLLEY departs northbound from Rotary Peace Park and southbound from Spook Creek Station. Visitors may ride a restored narrow-gauge 1925 trolley originally from Portugal. The bright yellow car seats 24 passengers and travels along the waterfront in downtown Whitehorse, making stops along the way at Rotary Peace Park, the visitor center, White Pass Train Depot, the Roundhouse, Jarvis Street, Black Street, Shipyards Park, Kishwoot Island and Spook Creek. The conductor provides narration about the waterfront and the development of Whitehorse.

Hours: Trips depart daily on the hour 10-5 from Rotary Peace Park and on the half-hour 10:30-5:30 p.m. from Spook Creek Station, mid-May to mid-Sept. **Cost:** Fare $1; free (ages 0-5). **Phone:** (867) 667-6355.

YUKON BERINGIA INTERPRETIVE CENTRE is 2 km (1.2 mi.) e. on the Alaska Hwy. to Km-post 1473 (mi. 886) by Whitehorse Airport. An area of the Yukon, Alaska and Siberia never covered by glaciers during the ice age, Beringia is believed to be the route traveled by the first peoples who entered the Americas from Asia.

Fossils, life-size animal and first peoples exhibits, interactive computer kiosks, and murals and dioramas of Beringia's landscape illustrate the area's history, geographical events and culture, from the ice age to the present. Highlights include fossils of woolly mammoths, scimitar cats, giant beavers, short-faced bears and steppe bison. A diorama depicts the Bluefish Caves, an important North American archeological site.

Hours: Daily 9-6, mid-May through Sept. 30; Sun.-Mon. noon-5, rest of year. Guided tours offered daily at 11:15 and 2:45, mid-May through Sept. 30. Phone ahead to confirm schedule. **Cost:** $6; $5 (ages 55+); $4 (ages 6-12 and students with ID); $25 (family, yearly pass). Combination pass with Yukon Transportation Museum $12. **Phone:** (867) 667-8855. [GT]

MIDNIGHT SUN INN BED & BREAKFAST   867/667-2255
[APPROVED] Bed & Breakfast. **Address:** 6188 6th Ave Y1A 1N8

SKKY HOTEL   867/456-2400
[APPROVED] Contemporary Hotel. **Address:** 91622 Alaska Hwy Y1A 3E4

WESTMARK WHITEHORSE HOTEL & CONFERENCE CENTER
867/393-9700
[APPROVED] Hotel. **Address:** 201 Wood St Y1A 2E4

WHERE TO EAT

ALPINE ORGANIC BAKERY   867/668-6871
[APPROVED]
Natural/Organic
Soup
Quick Serve
$8-$15
AAA Inspector Notes: *Classic.* A short walk from the downtown core, this organic bakery/café is housed in its own two-story log building and features a hand-crafted, authentic masonry oven. A wide variety of wholesome breads, pastries, pizza, soup and raw foods—all organic and vegetarian—are offered. Homemade, fair-trade dark chocolates speckled with wild, Yukon cranberries are a specialty. A sunny deck with an organic herb and edible flower garden is out back. Repeat customers should pre-order favorite breads. **Features:** patio dining. **Address:** 411 Alexander St Y1A 2L8 **Location:** Jct 4th Ave and Alexander St. **Parking:** on-site and street.
[B] [L] [Ⅸ]

ANTOINETTE'S   867/668-3505
[APPROVED] New International. Casual Dining. **Address:** 4121 4th Ave Y1A 1H7

BAKED CAFE & BAKERY   867/633-6291
[APPROVED] American. Quick Serve. **Address:** 108-100 Main St Y1A 2A8

BURNT TOAST CAFE   867/667-2605
[APPROVED] American. Casual Dining. **Address:** 2112 2nd Ave Y1A 1B9

THE CLAIM CAFE   867/667-2202
[APPROVED] American. Quick Serve. **Address:** 305 Strickland St Y1A 2J9

THE DELI   867/667-7583
[APPROVED] Deli. Quick Serve. **Address:** 203 Hanson St Y1A 1Y3

G & P STEAKHOUSE ON MAIN   867/668-4708
[THREE DIAMOND] Steak Seafood. Fine Dining. **Address:** 209 Main St Y1A 2B2

GIORGIO'S CUCCINA   867/668-4050
[APPROVED] Italian. Casual Dining. **Address:** 206 Jarvis St Y1A 2H1

KLONDIKE RIB & SALMON BBQ   867/667-7554
[APPROVED] Seafood. Casual Dining. **Address:** 2116 2nd Ave Y1A 2B9

SANCHEZ CANTINA   867/668-5858
[APPROVED] Mexican. Casual Dining. **Address:** 211 Hanson St Y1A 1Y3

BEST WESTERN GOLD RUSH INN   867/668-4500
[THREE DIAMOND]
Hotel

[Best Western] **AAA Benefit:** Members save up to 15% and earn bonus points!

Address: 411 Main St Y1A 2B6 **Location:** Between 4th and 6th aves; downtown. **Facility:** 99 units, some two bedrooms and kitchens. 4 stories, interior corridors. **Parking:** winter plug-ins. **Activities:** exercise room. **Guest Services:** coin laundry.
[SAVE] [ECO] [icons] [BIZ] [icon]
[icons]
/SOME UNITS [icons]

COAST HIGH COUNTRY INN   867/667-4471
[APPROVED]
Hotel
Address: 4051 4th Ave Y1A 1H1 **Location:** 0.4 mi (0.6 km) e of Main St. **Facility:** 82 units, some efficiencies. 4 stories, interior corridors. **Parking:** winter plug-ins. **Activities:** exercise room. **Guest Services:** coin laundry.
[SAVE] [ECO] [icons] CALL [icon]
[icons]
/SOME UNITS [icons]

Get INVOLVED and Keep Teens Safe

Exploring the countryside or visiting nearby cities can be perfect opportunities to teach your teens good habits and rules of the road — before and after they learn to drive.

TeenDriving.AAA.com
DriveRight.CAA.ca

Plane in Denali

Alaska

Natives didn't call this state *Alyeska*—the Great Land—for nothing. There are approximately 3 million lakes, 3,000 rivers, 1,800 islands and 100,000 glaciers in Alaska's 586,000 square miles of untamed wilderness. And if that isn't enough, nine national parks and preserves and two expansive national forests total about 66 million acres of undisturbed land.

Alaska's diversity is illustrated through its distinct natural features. The state is home to towering Denali—so high that it's cloaked in clouds most of the time. Long, bright days are typical during the summer solstice, when the sun never completely disappears.

Options for excitement in The Land of the Midnight Sun seem endless. Walk on an ice field and feel the crunch of ice under your boots; peer over chunky glaciers and sweeping mountain ranges from a helicopter; gaze at a sky painted with brilliant northern lights; ride on a boat navigating through blue-green

Totem poles in Saxman Village

waters packed with bobbing icebergs; marvel at 25-foot-tall sand dunes; or board a bush plane to catch a glimpse of steam from an active volcano.

Tribe members, ingenious at adapting to their variable and sometimes hostile surroundings, made the most of the state's natural offerings, which includes the creatures portrayed in their art. Salmon and orcas are just a couple of animals that appear on totem poles. Used for sustenance, they were often depicted in oral tales; today animals remain the focus of many pictures and the subjects of travelogues. Visitors relish the opportunity to snap a photograph of a moose cow nibbling grass alongside her twins or grizzly cubs wrestling under the protective watch of mama bear.

For many residents Alaska's riches are liquid: The creation of the Trans-Alaska Pipeline made it possible to transport crude oil almost 800 miles from Prudhoe Bay south to Valdez. The pipeline, an amazing engineering feat crossing three mountain ranges and three fault lines, can withstand an earthquake measuring up to 8.5 on the Richter scale as well as temperatures as low as minus 80 F.

Oil isn't Alaska's only rich resource. Discoveries of gold in Fairbanks, Fort Yukon, Juneau, Nome, Skagway and Wrangell lured prospectors from the "Lower 48" to seek their fortune. Visit abandoned gold dredges, camps and mines and imagine the fervor that once pervaded these sites. And there was more money to be made; Russian trappers came in search of valuable sea otter pelts.

But Alaska's native tribes have left the most enduring impact. Traditions of the Aleut, Alutiiq, Athabascan, Cup'ik, Haida, Inupiaq, Tlingit, Tsimpshian and Yup'ik tribes can be appreciated through the acts of proud dancers and storytellers who keep family legacies alive. Artisans create soapstone and whalebone carvings, clothing adorned with intricate beading and baskets made from white birch bark.

And totem poles, Alaska's silent, symbolic sentries, are just one reminder of what makes this land truly great.

Recreation

In the Land of the Midnight Sun, chances for wildlife viewing are as plentiful as snowflakes during winter.

Alaska has one of the largest bald eagle populations in the world. They aren't difficult to spot at the Chilkat Bald Eagle Preserve near Haines; more than 3,500 visit the area to feed from October to February.

Many wildlife cruises headed for the Inside Passage depart from Juneau. Arm yourself with some good binoculars, a camera and a journal to record your sightings. Entries might include descriptions of huge, barking Steller sea lions lounging on top of each other; Dall's porpoises frolicking in a boat's wake; or Sitka black- or white-tailed deer sipping from a stream.

Black bears fish for salmon in Anan Creek near Wrangell Island, and the west coast of Prince of Wales Island (near Ketchikan) is a great spot for watching tufted puffins. It's no "fluke" to see a whale tail; humpbacks often make appearances in Prince William Sound, and wherever there's an iceberg, you can find harbor seals resting upon floating ice chunks.

Day cruises depart from Seward and Whittier to explore Prince William Sound and Kenai Fjords National Park, home to sea mammals galore. Along the Kenai Peninsula, both humpback and beluga whales perform aquatic acrobatics near the Turnagain Arm. Nearby, Dall sheep can be seen grazing atop steep cliffs that grace Cook Inlet.

Looking for bears? The Kodiak National Wildlife Refuge is home to some 3,000 Kodiak bears, and Brooks Camp in Katmai National Park and Preserve safeguards one of the world's largest brown bear populations.

Grizzlies as well as caribou and moose roam the desertlike tundra of Denali National Park and Preserve; take a narrated bus tour to catch a glimpse. Near the park entrance, forest rangers give a demonstration of sled dogs at work. Even better, hang on tight for a sled ride pulled by Iditarod huskies in Seward.

Many activities in Alaska include a magnificent view: Try rafting in Denali on the Nenana River Gorge or canoeing near Admiralty Island National Monument. Kayakers also enjoy the Sarkar Lake Canoe Route in Tongass National Forest. Winter options include cross-country skiing, dog sledding or snowmobiling on the Twin Ridge or Upper Twin ski trails in Tongass National Forest, or downhill skiing at Mount Alyeska in Girdwood.

Want to stand on a glacier? Hikers in Kenai Fjords National Park follow rangers on nature walks to a nearby ice field. Floatplane or helicopter sightseeing is an excellent way to see glaciers, ice fields, mountain ranges, waterfalls, lakes or stark tundra. Nearly every city has flightseeing tour operators.

A fishing charter from one of various harbors is a good way to hook steelhead, grayling or rainbow trout. Sport fishing yields red snapper or cod—and Resurrection Bay (near Seward), Sitka and Wrangell are home to world-class halibut and salmon.

Bald eagle at the Chilkat Bald Eagle Preserve

Historic Timeline

1741	Russian explorer Vitus Bering, sent by Peter the Great to explore the North Pacific, is the first European to set foot on Alaskan soil.
1867	In a deal known as "Seward's Folly," Secretary of State William Seward buys Alaska from Russia for 2 cents per acre.
1880	"Seward's Folly" becomes a gold mine as vast deposits of precious metals are discovered in Juneau and other cities.
1903	A submarine cable links Seattle to Sitka and Sitka to Valdez, increasing communication between Alaska and the world.
1942	Japan attacks Dutch Harbor and consequently occupies the Aleutian Islands for nearly a year during World War II.
1964	A Good Friday earthquake severely damages Anchorage, Valdez, the Northwest Panhandle and Cook Inlet.
1968	Oil is discovered on Prudhoe Bay, spurring the construction of an 800-mile pipeline to transport the oil to Valdez.
1989	The *Exxon Valdez* spills some 11 million gallons of crude oil into Prince William Sound.
2004	Mitch Seavey of Seward wins the Iditarod Trail Sled Dog Race on his 11th attempt.
2008	Gov. Sarah Palin is the first woman to be on a Republican presidential ticket after Sen. John McCain names her his running mate.
2015	President Barack Obama announces Mount McKinley will be renamed Denali—what it originally was called in the Athabascan Native language.

What To Pack

Temperature Averages Maximum/Minimum (Fahrenheit)	JANUARY	FEBRUARY	MARCH	APRIL	MAY	JUNE	JULY	AUGUST	SEPTEMBER	OCTOBER	NOVEMBER	DECEMBER
Anchorage	22/9	26/12	34/18	44/29	55/39	62/47	65/52	63/49	55/41	40/28	28/16	24/11
Utqiaġvik	-8/-20	-10/-22	-7/-20	6/-7	25/15	40/30	47/34	44/34	35/28	19/10	5/-6	-5/-16
Fairbanks	2/-13	10/-10	26/1	44/19	61/35	71/47	73/50	67/45	55/34	32/16	12/-2	5/-9
Juneau	31/21	34/24	39/28	48/33	56/40	62/46	64/49	63/48	56/44	47/38	38/29	33/24
Kotzebue	4/-9	3/-10	7/-8	20/3	38/25	51/39	60/49	57/47	46/37	28/19	13/3	6/-6
Nome	13/-2	14/-2	18/1	27/12	43/31	54/41	59/47	56/45	49/37	34/23	23/11	16/1

From the records of The Weather Channel Interactive, Inc.

Good Facts To Know

ABOUT THE STATE

POPULATION: 626,932.

AREA: 665,384 square miles; ranks 1st.

CAPITAL: Juneau.

HIGHEST POINT: 20,310 ft., Denali.

LOWEST POINT: Sea level, Pacific Ocean.

TIME ZONE(S): Alaska for most of the state; Hawaii-Aleutian for the extreme western portion of the Aleutian Islands. DST.

REGULATIONS

TEEN DRIVING LAWS: Driving is not permitted midnight-6 a.m. No passengers under age 21, with the exception of family members, are permitted for the first 6 months. The minimum age for an unrestricted driver's license is 17. Phone (907) 269-5551 for more information about Alaska driver's license regulations.

SEAT BELT/CHILD RESTRAINT LAWS: Seat belts are required for driver and all passengers 16 and over. Children under age 1 or under 20 pounds must be in rear-facing child restraints. Children ages 8-15 are required to be in a child restraint or seat belt; appropriate child restraints are required for children under age 8 unless they are at least 4 feet, 9 inches tall or weigh more than 65 pounds. AAA recommends the use of seat belts and appropriate child restraints for the driver and all passengers.

CELLPHONE RESTRICTIONS: All drivers are prohibited from text messaging while driving.

HELMETS FOR MOTORCYCLES: Required for all passengers, operators under 18 years old and those with instructional permits.

RADAR DETECTORS: Permitted. Prohibited for use by commercial vehicles.

MOVE OVER LAW: State law requires drivers approaching stationary emergency vehicles that are displaying flashing flights, including tow trucks, traveling in the same direction, to vacate the lane closest if safe and possible to do so, or to slow to a speed reasonable and prudent for traffic, road and weather conditions. Also included in the law are road maintenance and animal control vehicles.

FIREARMS LAWS: Vary by state and/or county. Contact the Alaska Dept. of Public Safety, Permits and Licensing Unit, 5700 E. Tudor Rd., Anchorage, AK 99507; phone (907) 269-0393.

HOLIDAYS

HOLIDAYS: Jan. 1 ■ Martin Luther King Jr. Day, Jan. (3rd Mon.) ■ Washington's Birthday/Presidents Day, Feb. (3rd Mon.) ■ Seward's Day, Mar. (last Mon.) ■ Memorial Day, May (last Mon.) ■ July 4 ■ Labor Day, Sept. (1st Mon.) ■ Columbus Day, Oct. (2nd Mon.) ■ Alaska Day, Oct. 18 ■ Veterans Day, Nov. 11 ■ Thanksgiving ■ Christmas, Dec. 25.

MONEY

TAXES: Alaska does not have a statewide sales tax, but cities and boroughs may levy a sales tax of up to 7 percent, plus special taxes on goods and services. A 10 percent tax is levied on rental cars; 3 percent for rental recreational vehicles.

VISITOR INFORMATION

INFORMATION CENTERS: Tourist literature and reports on highway and weather conditions are available at the Log Cabin Visitor Information Center, jct. F St. and 4th Ave. in Anchorage ■ the Fairbanks Visitor Information Center, 101 Dunkel St. in Fairbanks ■ the Southeast Alaska Discovery Center, 50 Main St. in Ketchikan ■ and the Tok Information Center, jct. SR 2 (Alaska Hwy.) and SR 1 in Tok.

ROAD CONDITIONS: Information about road conditions or construction can be obtained from the Alaska Department of Transportation & Public Facilities; phone 511 or, outside of the state, (866) 282-7577.

FURTHER INFORMATION FOR VISITORS:
Alaska Travel Industry Association
610 E. 5th Ave., Suite 200
Anchorage, AK 99501
(907) 929-2842

NATIONAL FOREST INFORMATION:
U.S. Forest Service
8510 Mendenhall Loop Rd.
Juneau, AK 99801
(907) 586-8806
(877) 444-6777 (reservations)
TTY (907) 790-7444 (TTY)

NATIONAL PARK INFORMATION:
Alaska Public Lands Information Center
101 Dunkel St., Suite 110
Fairbanks, AK 99701
(907) 459-3730

FISHING & HUNTING REGULATIONS:
Alaska Department of Fish and Game
1255 W. 8th St.
Juneau, AK 99811
(907) 465-4180 (Division of Sport Fishing)
(907) 465-4190 (Division of Wildlife Conservation)

ALASKA FERRY INFORMATION:
Alaska Marine Highway
6858 Glacier Hwy.
Juneau, AK 99811-2505
(907) 465-3941
(800) 642-0066

Alaska Annual Events

Please call ahead to confirm event details.

 Visit **AAA.com/travelguides/events** to find AAA-listed events for every day of the year

WINTER

Dec. - Anchorage International Film Festival Anchorage / 907-338-3690
- New Year's Eve Torchlight Parade and Fireworks / Anchorage 907-754-2111

Jan. - Anchorage Folk Festival / Anchorage 907-276-4118
- Polar Bear Festival / Seward 907-422-7763
- Alcan 200 Road Rally / Haines 907-766-2051

Feb. - World Ice Art Championships Fairbanks / 907-451-8250
- Homer Winter Carnival / Homer 907-235-7740
- Valdez Ice Climbing Festival / Valdez 907-835-5182

SPRING

Mar. - Fur Rendezvous (Rondy) Winter Festival / Anchorage / 907-274-1177
- Iditarod Trail Sled Dog Race Anchorage / 907-376-5155

Apr. - NYO Games / Anchorage 907-793-3267
- Alaska Hummingbird Festival Ketchikan / 907-228-6220

May - Juneau Jazz & Classics / Juneau 907-463-3378
- Kodiak Crab Festival / Kodiak 907-486-5557

SUMMER

June - Nome River Raft Race / Nome 907-443-6624
- Sitka Summer Music Festival / Sitka 907-277-4852

July - Golden Days / Fairbanks 907-452-1105
- Southeast Alaska State Fair / Haines 907-766-2476

Aug. - Seward Silver Salmon Derby Seward / 907-224-8051
- Tanana Valley State Fair / Fairbanks 907-452-3750

FALL

Sept. - Kodiak Rodeo and State Fair Kodiak / 907-487-4440
- Kachemak Bay Wooden Boat Festival Homer / 907-235-2628
- Seward Music and Arts Festival Seward / 907-362-1131

Oct. - Alaska Day Festival / Sitka 907-747-5124
- Make It Alaskan Festival / Anchorage 907-279-0618
- Alaska Native Arts and Crafts Fair Anchorage / 907-274-3611

Nov. - Holiday Tree Lighting / Anchorage 907-279-5650
- Crafted in Alaska and ReadAlaska Book Fair / Anchorage 907-929-9200
- Sitka WhaleFest / Sitka 907-747-5940

AAA.com/maps—Dream, plan, go

with AAA travel planning tools

Denali State Park

Moose calf

Totem pole, Juneau

Alaska Raptor Center, Sitka

Kenai Fjords National Park

Index: Great Experience for Members

AAA editor's picks of exceptional note

Denali National Park
and Preserve

Alaska Raptor Center

Mendenhall Glacier

Sitka National
Historical Park

See Orientation map on p. 464 for corresponding grid coordinates, if applicable.
* Indicates the GEM is temporarily closed.

iStockphoto.com_pixelfit

Love the Great Outdoors?

When getting away means getting off the beaten path, visit AAA.com/campgrounds or AAA.com/maps for:

Look for locations with the trusted mark of approval.

⚠ Thousands of places to camp across the U.S. and Canada

⚠ Complete mapping and travel information to plan your adventure

Inspected & Approved

Safe Travels
We've Got You Covered

AAA Insurance

INSURANCE POLICY

From vacations to recreation, downtime should be
worry free. Trust your knowledgeable AAA insurance
representative to help you get the right
coverage for every phase of life.
Enjoy quality products at competitive rates.

Stop by your local AAA office
or visit us online.
AAA.com/Insurance

Auto • Home • Life & Other Insurance Products

Product availability may vary by AAA club.

Alaska, Yukon and

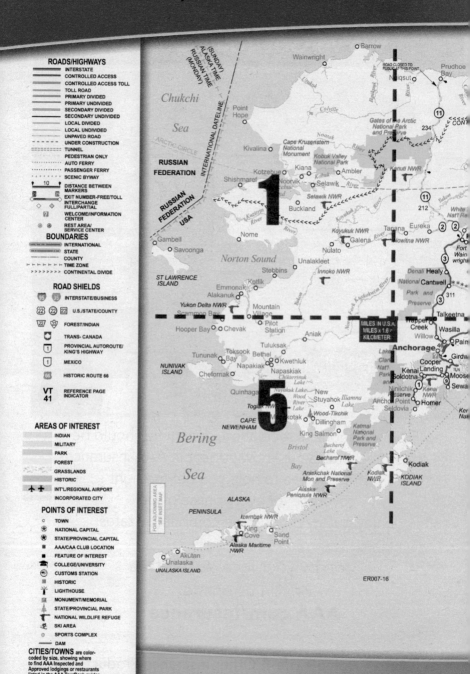

ROADS/HIGHWAYS

- INTERSTATE
- CONTROLLED ACCESS
- CONTROLLED ACCESS TOLL
- TOLL ROAD
- PRIMARY DIVIDED
- PRIMARY UNDIVIDED
- SECONDARY DIVIDED
- SECONDARY UNDIVIDED
- LOCAL DIVIDED
- LOCAL UNDIVIDED
- UNPAVED ROAD
- UNDER CONSTRUCTION
- TUNNEL
- PEDESTRIAN ONLY
- AUTO FERRY
- PASSENGER FERRY
- SCENIC BYWAY
- 10 DISTANCE BETWEEN MARKERS
- EXIT NUMBER-FREE/TOLL
- INTERCHANGE FULL/PARTIAL
- WELCOME/INFORMATION CENTER
- REST AREA/ SERVICE CENTER

BOUNDARIES

- INTERNATIONAL
- STATE
- COUNTY
- TIME ZONE
- CONTINENTAL DIVIDE

ROAD SHIELDS

- 95 / 95 INTERSTATE/BUSINESS
- 22 / 22 / 22 U.S./STATE/COUNTY
- 127 / 127 FOREST/INDIAN
- TRANS- CANADA
- 1 PROVINCIAL AUTOROUTE/ KING'S HIGHWAY
- 1 MEXICO
- 66 HISTORIC ROUTE 66
- VT 41 REFERENCE PAGE INDICATOR

AREAS OF INTEREST

- INDIAN
- MILITARY
- PARK
- FOREST
- GRASSLANDS
- HISTORIC
- INT'L/REGIONAL AIRPORT
- INCORPORATED CITY

POINTS OF INTEREST

- ○ TOWN
- ✳ NATIONAL CAPITAL
- ✳ STATE/PROVINCIAL CAPITAL
- ■ AAA/CAA CLUB LOCATION
- ■ FEATURE OF INTEREST
- ♠ COLLEGE/UNIVERSITY
- ☺ CUSTOMS STATION
- ■ HISTORIC
- ♀ LIGHTHOUSE
- ▥ MONUMENT/MEMORIAL
- ♣ STATE/PROVINCIAL PARK
- ♣ NATIONAL WILDLIFE REFUGE
- ⛷ SKI AREA
- ◎ SPORTS COMPLEX
- — DAM

CITIES/TOWNS are color-coded by size, showing where to find AAA Inspected and Approved lodgings or restaurants listed in the AAA TourBook guides and on AAA.com:

- ● Red - major destinations and capitals; many listings
- ● Black - destinations; some listings
- ● Grey - no listings

ER007-16

Northwest Territories

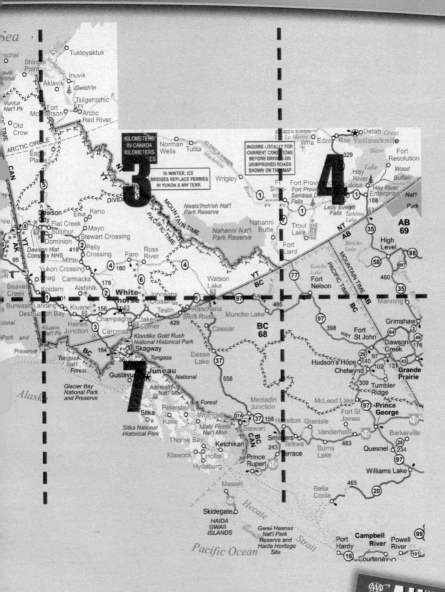

3

KILOMETERS
IN CANADA
KILOMETERS
ES

IN WINTER, ICE
BRIDGES REPLACE FERRIES
IN YUKON & NW TERR.

INQUIRE LOCALLY FOR
CURRENT CONDITIONS
BEFORE DRIVING ON
UNIMPROVED ROADS
SHOWN ON THE MAP

4

Sea

Tuktoyaktuk
Shingle Point
Inuvik
Aklavik
Gwich'in
Tsiigehtchic
Fort McPherson
Arctic Red River
Old Crow
Eagle Plains
ARCTIC CIRCLE
CAN
Vuntut Nat'l Pk

Norman Wells
Tulita
Wrigley

Wha
Lu Marthe
Edzo
Rae
Detah
Yellowknife
Great Slave
Fort Resolution
Wood Buffalo Nat'l Park
329

Naats'ihch'oh Nat'l Park Reserve
MOUNTAIN TIME
Nahanni Nat'l Park Reserve
Nahanni Butte

Fort Simpson
Fort Providence
Sambaa Deh Falls
Lady Evelyn Falls
Kakisa
Hay River
Hay River Enterprise
188
Kakisa

Dawson City
Flat Creek
Sulphur
Dominion
419
Elsa
Keno
Mayo
Stewart Crossing
Pelly Crossing
Minto
Yukon Crossing
Stewart Crossing
Ross River
Faro
160

AK
95
Snag
Carmacks
Koidern
Aishihik
178
Watson Lake
YT
BC

Trout Lake
Fort Liard
77
Kotcho Lake
Fort Nelson
460

High Level
AB
69
Bistcho Lake
58
88
697
35

Beaver Creek
Burwash Landing
Destruction Bay
Kluane Nat'l Pk
Haines Junction
Champagne
Carcross
Whitehorse
Johnsons Crossing
Teslin
Rancheria
Swift River
Muncho Lake
485
329
Jakes Corner
Tagish
164
Kluane Nat'l Pk
Preserve
Park and Preserve
301
156
3
Kluane
429
Cassiar
BC
68
398
Fort St John
140
29
102
131
309
Tumbler Ridge
Dawson Creek
Grande Prairie
Grimshaw
64
49
176
43
26

Skagway
Juneau
Gustavus
Glacier Bay National Park and Preserve
Tongass Nat'l Forest
Klondike Gold Rush National Historical Park
38
Tongass
Dease Lake
37
558
Hudson's Hope
Chetwynd
McLeod Lake
97
Prince George
16

Sitka
Sitka National Historical Park
Petersburg
Kake
Thorne Bay
Wrangell
Misty Fiords Nat'l Mon
Ketchikan
Klawock
Hollis
Hydaburg
97A
Stewart
BC
CAN
Meziadin Junction
Forest
37
Hazelton
158
Granisle
Smithers
Telkwa
243
Terrace
Burns Lake
483
Vanderhoof
Fort St James
Barkerville
Quesnel
234
Williams Lake
97
16

Alaska
Admiralty Nat'l Mon
National

Masset
HAIDA GWAII ISLANDS
Skidegate
Gwaii Haanas Nat'l Park Reserve and Haida Heritage Site
Hecate Strait
Prince Rupert
15
Bella Coola
465
20

Pacific Ocean
Port Hardy
19
Courtenay
Campbell River
Powell River
99
101

AAA
Atlas
ROAD
Travel With Someone You Trust
2020
UNITED STATES CANADA MEXICO

Use these detailed driving maps to plan your stops and find your way.
For complete route planning, purchase the latest AAA Road Atlas at
participating AAA/CAA offices, and use the free online TripTik Travel
Planner at AAA.com/maps

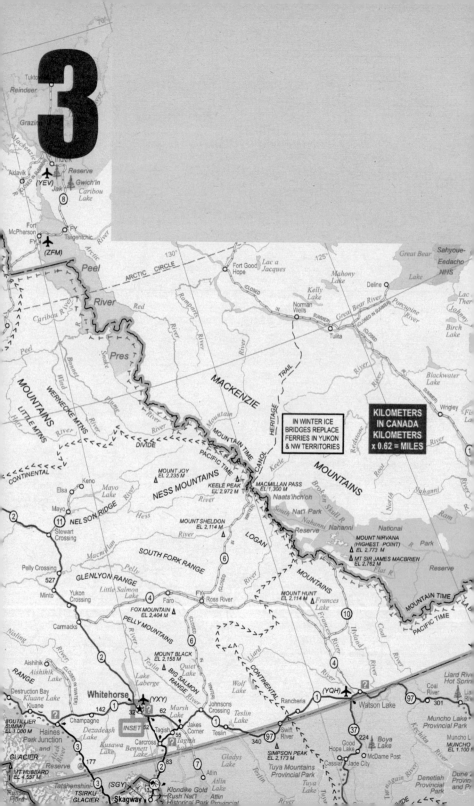

ALASKA & Northwestern CANADA

1:6,019,200
Scale in Miles
Scale in Kilometers

MILES IN U.S.A.
MILES x 1.6 = KILOMETERS

INQUIRE LOCALLY FOR CURRENT
CONDITIONS BEFORE DRIVING
ON UNIMPROVED ROADS
SHOWN ON THIS MAP

BC 128

Hit the Road
with Financial Services

Providing peace-of-mind benefits
exclusively for members—
at home or abroad.

- Credit Cards
- Prepaid Cards
- Gift Cards
- Deposit Accounts
- Foreign Currency
- Loans
- Identity Theft Protection

Visit your local AAA office or online
to learn more. **AAA.com/Financial**

All products not available at all locations.

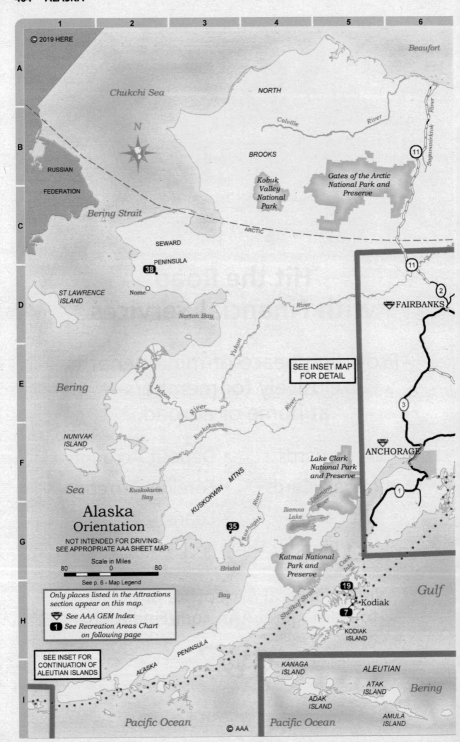

© 2019 HERE

Beaufort

Chukchi Sea

NORTH

N

Colville River

Sagavanirktok River

RUSSIAN

FEDERATION

BROOKS

Kobuk Valley National Park

Gates of the Arctic National Park and Preserve

11

Bering Strait

ARCTIC

SEWARD

38

PENINSULA

Nome

ST LAWRENCE ISLAND

Norton Bay

Yukon River

SEE INSET MAP FOR DETAIL

11

2

FAIRBANKS

Bering

Yukon River

3

ANCHORAGE

NUNIVAK ISLAND

Kuskokwim River

Lake Clark National Park and Preserve

1

Sea

Kuskokwim Bay

KUSKOKWIN MTNS

35

Nushagak River

Iliamna Lake

Tazimina River

Alaska
Orientation

NOT INTENDED FOR DRIVING. SEE APPROPRIATE AAA SHEET MAP.

Scale in Miles

80   0   80

See p. 6 - Map Legend

Bristol

Katmai National Park and Preserve

Cook Inlet

Gulf

19

Kodiak

7

Only places listed in the Attractions section appear on this map.

⬦ See AAA GEM Index

1 See Recreation Areas Chart on following page

Bay

Shelikof Strait

KODIAK ISLAND

SEE INSET FOR CONTINUATION OF ALEUTIAN ISLANDS

ALASKA   PENINSULA

KANAGA ISLAND

ALEUTIAN

Bering

ATAK ISLAND

ADAK ISLAND

AMULA ISLAND

Pacific Ocean

© AAA

Pacific Ocean

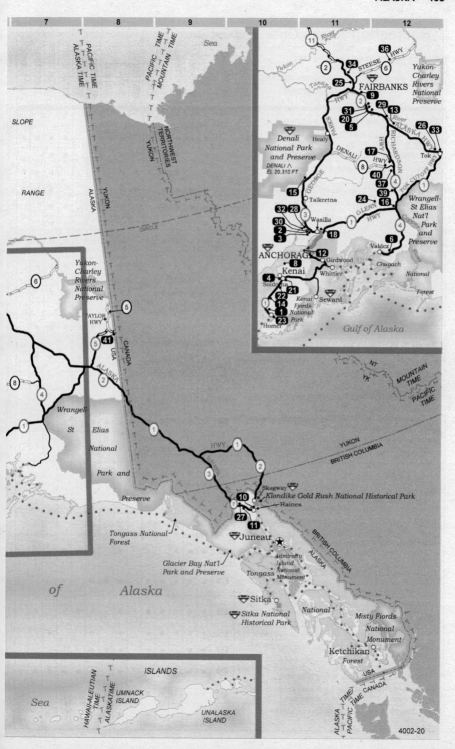

7 8 9 10 11 12

Sea

SLOPE

PACIFIC TIME
ALASKA TIME

PACIFIC TIME
MOUNTAIN TIME

NORTHWEST
TERRITORIES

YUKON

RANGE

ALASKA

YUKON

CIRCLE

Yukon-
Charley
Rivers
National
Preserve

6

TAYLOR
HWY

5

5 41

USA

CANADA

ALASKA

2

Wrangell-
St Elias

National

Park and

Preserve

8

4

1

HWY

1

3

2

Skagway
Klondike Gold Rush National Historical Park
Haines

7 10

27

11

Juneau

YUKON

BRITISH COLUMBIA

BRITISH COLUMBIA

ALASKA

NT

YK

MOUNTAIN
TIME

PACIFIC
TIME

Tongass National
Forest

Glacier Bay Nat'l
Park and Preserve

Tongass

Admiralty
Island
National
Monument

of Alaska

Sitka

Sitka National
Historical Park

National

Misty Fiords

National
Monument

Ketchikan

Forest

USA

ALASKA TIME
PACIFIC TIME CANADA

ISLANDS

HAWAII-ALEUTIAN
TIME
ALASKA TIME

UMNACK
ISLAND

UNALASKA
ISLAND

Sea

11

2

34

25

STEESE HWY

36

6

FAIRBANKS

9

Yukon-
Charley
Rivers
National
Preserve

Yukon

Tanana

River

PARKS

HWY

2

31

20

5

29

13

26 33

ALASKA HWY

Tok

Denali
National Park
and Preserve

DENALI EL 20,310 FT

Healy

17

8

HWY

DENALI

GEORGE

15

Talkeetna

3

32 28

30

2

3

Wasilla

18

40

37

24

39

16

RICHARDSON HWY

4

1

TOK CUTOFF HWY

Wrangell-
St Elias
Nat'l
Park
and
Preserve

GLENN HWY

1

4

Valdez

6

ANCHORAGE

12

8

Kenai

Girdwood

Whittier

Chugach

National

Forest

4

Soldotna

22 21

14

1

1

23

Homer

Kenai
Fjords
National
Park

Seward

Gulf of Alaska

4002-20

Recreation Areas Chart

The map location numerals in column 2 show an area's location on the preceding map.

Find thousands of places to camp at AAA.com/campgrounds

	MAP LOCATION	CAMPING	PICNICKING	HIKING TRAILS	BOATING	BOAT RAMP	BOAT RENTAL	FISHING	SWIMMING	PET FRIENDLY	BICYCLE TRAILS	WINTER SPORTS	VISITOR CENTER	LODGE/CABINS	FOOD SERVICE
NATIONAL PARKS AND PRESERVES *(See place listings.)*															
Denali (B-10) 6,028,203 acres. Cross-country skiing, dog mushing, snowmobiling, snowshoeing.		•	•	•				•		•		•	•	•	•
Gates of the Arctic (B-5) 8,500,000 acres. Bird-watching.		•		•	•			•					•	•	
Glacier Bay (G-9) 3,283,168 acres. Bird-watching, hunting, kayaking, rafting.		•		•	•	•	•	•					•	•	•
Katmai (G-4) 4,159,097 acres. Canoeing, hunting, kayaking.		•	•	•	•			•						•	
Kenai Fjords (D-11) 600,000 acres. Cross-country skiing, kayaking, snowmobiling.		•						•		•			•	•	
Kobuk Valley (C-4) 1,710,000 acres. Sand dunes.		•						•					•		
Lake Clark (F-5) 4,000,000 acres. Bird-watching, hunting, kayaking, rafting.		•						•		•				•	
Wrangell-St. Elias (C-12, F-8) 3,000,000 acres. Cross-country skiing, hunting, sea kayaking, snowmobiling, snowshoeing; all-terrain vehicle trails.		•		•				•		•		•	•	•	
Yukon-Charley Rivers (A-12, D-7) 500,000 acres. Historic. Hunting.		•			•			•							
NATIONAL FORESTS *(See place listings.)*															
Chugach (D-12) 5,500,000 acres in south-central Alaska. Cross-country skiing, hunting, snowboarding, snowmobiling.		•	•	•	•			•		•	•	•	•	•	
Tongass (G-10) 17,000,000 acres in southeastern Alaska. Backpacking, bird-watching, canoeing, crabbing, cross-country and downhill skiing, hunting, ice skating, kayaking, snowboarding, snowmobiling.		•	•	•	•			•	•	•	•	•	•	•	•
STATE															
Anchor River (D-10) 264 acres near Anchor Point on Sterling Hwy., Milepost 157.	**1**	•	•	•	•	•		•		•					
Big Lake (North) (C-10) 19 acres 10 mi. w. of Wasilla on Parks Hwy., then 6 mi. s.w. on Big Lake Rd.	**2**	•	•		•	•		•	•	•		•			
Big Lake (South) (C-10) 16 acres 10 mi. w. of Wasilla on Parks Hwy., then 4 mi. s.w. on Big Lake Rd. and 2 mi. s. Jet skiing, water skiing.	**3**	•	•		•	•		•	•	•					
Bings Landing (D-10) 126 acres e. of Soldotna on Sterling Hwy., Milepost 79.	**4**	•	•	•	•	•		•							
Birch Lake (B-11) 191 acres n.e. of Delta Junction on Richardson Hwy., Milepost 305.5. Ice fishing, jet skiing, snowmobiling, water skiing; ice fishing huts.	**5**	•	•		•	•		•	•	•		•			
Blueberry Lake (C-12) 192 acres e. of Valdez on Richardson Hwy., Milepost 23. Berry picking.	**6**	•	•					•	•						
Buskin River (H-5) 168 acres 4 mi. s.e. on Base-Town Rd. in Kodiak. Historic. Beachcombing, berry picking, cross-country skiing.	**7**	•	•	•				•		•		•			
Captain Cook (C-10) 3,460 acres 24 mi. n. of Kenai on N. Kenai Rd., Milepost 36. Beachcombing, berry picking (in season), bird-watching, canoeing, hunting, ice fishing.	**8**	•	•	•	•	•		•	•	•			•		
Chena River (A-12) 254,000 acres 27 mi. e. of Fairbanks at 3530 Geraghty Ave. Canoeing, cross-country skiing, kayaking, rock climbing, snowmobiling.	**9**	•	•	•	•	•		•		•		•		•	
Chilkat (F-10) 9,837 acres 7 mi. s. of Haines on Haines Hwy.	**10**	•	•	•				•		•			•		
Chilkoot Lake (G-10) 80 acres 11 mi. n. of Haines on Lutak Rd., Milepost 10.	**11**	•	•		•	•		•	•						
Chugach (C-11) 495,204 acres just e. of Eagle River on Glenn Hwy. Numerous access points. Rafting; horse rental.	**12**	•	•	•				•		•	•	•	•		
Clearwater (B-12) 27 acres 11 mi. s.e. of Delta Junction on Alaska Hwy., Milepost 1415, then 8 mi. n.e. on side road.	**13**	•	•		•	•		•							
Deep Creek (D-10) 155 acres near Ninilchik on Sterling Hwy., Milepost 137.3. Bird-watching.	**14**	•	•		•	•		•		•					

Recreation Areas Chart

The map location numerals in column 2 show an area's location on the preceding map.

🔗 **Find thousands of places to camp at AAA.com/campgrounds**

	MAP LOCATION	CAMPING	PICNICKING	HIKING TRAILS	BOATING	BOAT RAMP	BOAT RENTAL	FISHING	SWIMMING	PET FRIENDLY	BICYCLE TRAILS	WINTER SPORTS	VISITOR CENTER	LODGE/CABINS	FOOD SERVICE
Denali (C-10) 325,240 acres n. of Talkeetna on Parks Hwy., Milepost 135-164.	15	•	•	•	•	•	•	•	•	•		•		•	
Dry Creek (C-12) 360 acres n. of Glennallen on Richardson Hwy., Milepost 117.5. Open mid-May to mid-Sept.	16	•	•	•				•		•					
Fielding Lake (B-12) 300 acres s. of Delta Junction on Richardson Hwy., Milepost 201.	17	•			•	•		•		•					
Finger Lake (C-11) 69 acres 4 mi. w. of Palmer on Palmer-Wasilla Rd., then 1 mi. n. and .5 mi. w.	18	•	•	•	•	•		•	•	•		•			
Fort Abercrombie (H-5) 182 acres 4.5 mi. s.e. of Kodiak on Miller Point. Historic.	19	•	•	•				•		•			•		
Harding Lake (B-11) 169 acres .5 mi. n.e. from Milepost 321 on the Richardson Hwy. Canoeing, jet skiing.	20	•	•	•	•	•		•	•	•		•			
Izaak Walton (D-10) 8 acres e. of Soldotna off Glenn Hwy.	21	•	•			•	•	•		•					
Johnson Lake (D-10) 332 acres 16 mi. s. of Soldotna on Glenn Hwy. Canoeing.	22	•	•		•	•		•		•					
Kachemak Bay (D-10) 400,000 acres near Seldovia, at the end of Sterling Hwy., then by boat or plane across Kachemak Bay. Bird-watching, kayaking.	23	•	•	•	•			•		•				•	
Lake Louise (C-11) 511 acres n.w. of Glennallen on Glenn Hwy., Milepost 160.	24	•	•		•	•		•	•	•					
Lower Chatanika River (A-11) 400 acres w. of Fairbanks off Elliott Hwy. (SR 2), Milepost 10.5. Cross-country skiing, ice fishing, snowmobiling.	25	•	•		•	•		•		•		•			
Moon Lake (B-12) 22 acres 18 mi. w. of Tok on Alaska Hwy., near Milepost 1332. Water skiing.	26	•	•		•	•		•	•	•					
Mosquito Lake (G-10) 10 acres 27.5 mi. w. of Haines on Haines Hwy., then 2.5 mi. on Mosquito Lake Rd.	27	•	•		•			•		•					
Nancy Lake (C-10) 22,685 acres 3.5 mi. s. of Willow on Parks Hwy., then 7 mi. w. on side road. Cross-country skiing, snowmobiling.	28	•	•	•	•			•		•		•		•	
Quartz Lake (A-12) 600 acres 2 mi. n.w. of Delta Junction on Alaska Hwy.	29	•	•	•	•	•		•	•	•		•			•
Rocky Lake (C-10) 49 acres 28 mi. w. of Palmer via Wasilla off Parks Hwy. at Milepost 3.5 of Big Lake Rd.	30	•	•		•			•		•					
Salcha River (B-11) 61 acres s.e. of North Pole on Alaska Hwy., Milepost 323.3. Canoeing.	31	•	•		•	•		•		•			•		
South Rolly Lake (C-10) 200 acres just w. of Wasilla off Parks Hwy. at Milepost 6.5 of Nancy Lake Pkwy.	32	•	•	•	•		•	•	•	•		•			
Tok River (B-12) 9 acres 5 mi. e. of Tok Junction on Alaska Hwy., Milepost 1309. Beach.	33	•	•	•	•	•		•	•	•					
Upper Chatanika River (A-11) 73 acres n.e. of Fairbanks off Steese Hwy., Milepost 39. Canoeing, rafting.	34	•	•		•			•		•					
Wood-Tikchik (G-3) 1,600,000 acres n. of Dillingham.	35	•			•			•						•	
OTHER															
Cripple Creek (A-12) 5 acres 50 mi. n.e. of Fairbanks on Steese Hwy., Milepost 60.	36	•	•	•				•		•					
Paxson Lake (B-12) 80 acres 10 mi. s. of Paxson on Richardson Hwy., Milepost 175.	37	•	•		•	•		•		•					
Salmon Lake (D-2) 20 acres 40 mi. n. of Nome. Beach.	38	•	•		•	•		•		•					
Sourdough Creek (C-12) 140 acres 35 mi. n. of Glennallen on the Richardson Hwy. (SR 4), Milepost 148.	39	•	•		•			•		•					
Tangle Lakes (B-12) 100 acres 22 mi. w. of Paxson on Denali Hwy., Milepost 22.	40	•	•		•	•		•		•					
Walker Fork (D-8) 10 acres 80 mi. n.e. of Tok on Taylor Hwy., Milepost 82.	41	•	•	•				•		•					

ADMIRALTY ISLAND NATIONAL MONUMENT (G-10)

Accessible by floatplane from Juneau and Sitka or via ferries of the Alaska Marine Highway to Angoon, Admiralty Island is part of Tongass National Forest (see place listing p. 516). Between the rocky beaches and high mountain peaks lie a million acres of coastal rain forests, freshwater lakes and streams, alpine meadows and dense thickets of wild currants and other berries.

Alaskan brown bears outnumber human beings, and the greatest concentration of bald eagles in North America nests along the coast. Beavers, martens, minks, river otters, Sitka black-tailed deer and weasels share the island with Vancouver Canada geese and trumpeter and whistling swans. Offshore are harbor seals, sea lions and whales.

Motorboating and sea kayaking are popular in protected saltwater bays, and a canoe portage trail connects nine interior lakes to bays on the east and west shores. Rustic cabins can be reserved, and campsites and open shelters are available on a first-come, first-served basis. Most of the island is a wilderness area; be prepared for rain and follow no-trace camping practices.

For more information contact the U.S. Forest Service at (907) 586-8806, TTY (907) 790-7444 or (877) 444-6777 (reservations).

ANCHORAGE (F-6) pop. 291,826, elev. 118'
• Hotels p. 478 • Restaurants p. 482
• Hotels & Restaurants map & index p. 475

Anchorage, on a high bluff enfolded by the two branches of Cook Inlet, lies as far west as the Hawaiian Islands and as far north as Helsinki, Finland. The tides in the inlet rise from 30 to 33 feet, and the surrounding mountains loom several thousand feet overhead. The protective mountain barrier and the proximity of the ocean afford Anchorage a surprisingly moderate climate, relative to most of Alaska.

Anchorage is Alaska's largest city and is home to almost half of the state's residents. While not a dazzling metropolis, each summer the city is beautifully decorated with almost 100,000 hanging flower baskets brimming with brightly colored blooms.

Established in 1915 as the construction headquarters for the Alaska Railroad (see attraction listing), it is the transportation and business center of south-central Alaska and a major winter recreation area. Anchorage's heritage as a road town is recalled by a number of historic buildings, notably the Pioneer Schoolhouse in Ben Crawford Memorial Park and two nearby one-room log cabins.

Reminders of Native American and even Russian influences can be found. In downtown, several landmarks denote Alaska Native heritage. For Russian heritage with a distinct Dena'ina Athabascan influence, Eklutna Historical Park—30 miles from

▼ *See AAA listing p. 472* ▼

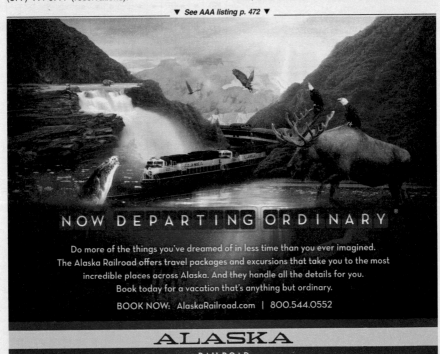

NOW DEPARTING ORDINARY®

Do more of the things you've dreamed of in less time than you ever imagined. The Alaska Railroad offers travel packages and excursions that take you to the most incredible places across Alaska. And they handle all the details for you. Book today for a vacation that's anything but ordinary.

BOOK NOW: AlaskaRailroad.com | 800.544.0552

ALASKA
RAILROAD

AS BIG AS YOUR IMAGINATION

ALASKA

With over 20 years of experience we're ready to help you find the Alaska you have always dreamed about. From Denali National Park to glacier cruises and a domed car ride on the Alaska Railroad we create custom tour packages for all interests.

Alaska
TOUR & TRAVEL

TOURS • LODGING • TRANSPORTATION   AlaskaTravel.com   1.800.208.0200

Request Your Free Tour Planner and Map

(See map & index p. 475.)

downtown—is a good bet mid-May to mid-September; phone (907) 688-6026 for more information.

Anchorage suffered from the effects of the 1964 Good Friday earthquake, one of the strongest in history, which destroyed much of downtown. Earthquake Park, at the west end of Northern Lights Boulevard, has a walking trail and interpretive signs that provide information about the massive temblor. The 134-acre park also provides a stunning vista of Cook Inlet.

The dramatic beauty of the nearby mountains, inlets and glaciers offers an easily accessible sampling of Alaska's natural splendors. Two roads affording beautiful views link to Anchorage; scenic SR 1/9 (Seward Highway) extends south to Seward, and SR 1 (Glenn Highway) extends north to Glennallen.

From Anchorage visitors also can take various sightseeing tours of the area, including the Kenai Peninsula and places of interest inaccessible by road. Among the more novel sightseeing trips are dog sled tours, which leave from the Alyeska Resort and Ski Area *(see Girdwood p. 495)* December through March. Trolley tours given by Anchorage City Trolley Tours depart daily May through September from the Log Cabin Visitor Information Center at Fourth Avenue and F Street; phone (907) 276-5603 or (888) 917-8687.

The Park Connection offers twice-daily shuttle service from Anchorage to Denali National Park and Preserve and Seward mid-May to mid-September; phone (907) 344-8775 or (800) 266-8625.

Float trips on the Matanuska River depart by van from Anchorage to the launch point. Panning for gold is available an hour from downtown. For a different perspective, try flightseeing—operators can be found at the airport and Lake Hood.

Gray Line of Alaska, (907) 264-7983 or (888) 425-1737, and Princess Rail Tours, (800) 426-0500, offer a float adventure on Eagle River; tours to Utqiaġvik (Barrow), Juneau, Kodiak Island, Kotzebue, Matanuska Valley, Nome, Portage Glacier and Prudhoe Bay; fishing on the Kenai River; cruises on Prince William Sound to Columbia Glacier; and a city tour of Anchorage. There's also Alaska Tour & Travel *(See ad p. 469, p. 487.)* , which offers transportation and tours across Alaska, including Fairbanks, Whittier and various national parks; phone (800) 208-0200.

Most agencies offer 2-, 3- and 4-day round trips between Anchorage and Denali National Park and Preserve. The trips include travel in railway cars equipped with glass ceiling panels. Many of these companies also offer longer excursions to the interior and cruises up the Inside Passage.

Then there are places to explore independently. Ship Creek, with multiple access points along East Ship Creek Drive, is a popular sport salmon fishery and salmon viewing area. King salmon run in June

and silver salmon from mid-July to late September. During these months, fishermen line the banks from the mouth of Ship Creek upstream to the Chugach Power Plant Dam. Several viewing platforms span the creek between Whitney Road and the Ship Creek walking trail. The Bait Shack, 212 W. Whitney Rd., sells fishing licenses and rents tackle and fishing gear; phone (907) 522-3474. The William Jack Hernandez Sport Fish Hatchery is 2 miles upstream from the mouth of the creek at the corner of Reeve Boulevard and Post Road. The hatchery's visitor corridor is open 8 a.m. to 4 p.m.; phone (907) 269-2000 for more information.

Bring the outdoors inside: The Alaska Center for the Performing Arts Sydney Laurence Theatre, at 621 W. 6th Ave., presents a 40-minute, large-screen slide show called "AurorA" that displays a series of stunning images of the aurora borealis synchronized to classical music. Shows are offered daily late May through August; tickets are available at the door. Phone (907) 263-2993 to confirm schedule information

Anchorage serves as the starting line for the 1,049-mile 🐾 Iditarod Trail Sled Dog Race, which begins the first Saturday in March. The actual mileage of the 2018 race is 1,112 miles; however, 1,049 is often used as a symbolic figure because the distance is always more than 1,000 miles, and 49 was added to symbolize Alaska's place as the 49th state to enter the Union. Dogs and mushers travel over the Alaska Range and across frozen Norton Bay, arriving in Nome nearly 2 weeks later.

The Bear & Raven Adventure Theater, 315 E St., offers "The Amazing Trail," a 30-minute multimedia presentation relating the history of the Iditarod race as well as interactive sledding, ballooning and fishing exhibits. The theater is open mid-May to mid-September and during the Iditarod; phone (907) 277-4545.

Visit Anchorage: 524 W. Fourth Ave., Anchorage, AK 99501-2212. **Phone:** (907) 276-4118, or (800) 446-5352 to request a visitor guide. *(See ad p. 471, p. 492.)*

Self-guiding tours: A guide outlining a walking tour and driving tours north and south of the city is available at Log Cabin Visitor Information Center, Fourth Avenue and F Street; phone (907) 257-2363.

26 GLACIER CRUISE BY PHILLIPS CRUISES— see Whittier p. 519.

ALASKA BOTANICAL GARDEN is 3 mi. e. of New Seward Hwy. on Tudor Rd., then just s. to 4601 Campbell Airstrip Rd. Northern latitude horticulture is showcased in a 110-acre birch and spruce woodland replete with more than 1,100 varieties of perennials, 150 species of native Alaskan plants as well as herb and alpine rock gardens. The garden includes a wildflower walk, a 1-mile nature trail and a creek where salmon spawn in the summer. The peak blooming season commences in late May and

THE BEST OF ALASKA
ALL IN ONE PLACE

Look for Dall sheep, beluga whales and experience amazing trails along Turnagain Arm — loved by locals and recognized as one of the most scenic spots in Alaska.

Learn more at VisitAnchorage.net

VISIT
anchorage
ALASKA

Anchorage Attractions

Scale in Miles

0.5   0   0.5

See p. 6 - Map Legend

Joint   Base   Creek

Elmendorf-Richardson

Cook

ANCHORAGE

Anchorage Trail System
The Alaska Railroad
Anchorage Museum at Rasmuson Center
Alaska Public Lands Information Center
Welcome Center

To Fairbanks & Alaska Native Heritage Center

Inlet

Merrill   Field

Russian Jack Springs

Airport (MRI)

Westchester

Lagoon

Sitka Street Park

Woodside Park

Creek Park

Eastchester Park

Chester Greenbelt

Anchor Park

Goose Lake Park

Alaska Pacific University

Alaska Heritage Museum at Wells Fargo

Alaska Jewish Museum

University of Alaska-Anchorage

University Lake

University Lake Park

To Ted Stevens International Airport (ANC)

To Seward

© 2019 HERE   © AAA   2100-20

(See map & index p. 475.)

culminates in mid-September, occasionally lasting into October.

Note: Enter the garden through a pedestrian gate in the tall moose fence. Though the garden is open in winter, it is often snow-covered. **Time:** Allow 1 hour, 30 minutes minimum. **Hours:** Daily dawn-dusk. **Cost:** Admission May-Sept. $12; $10 (ages 5-18, senior citizens and students and military with ID). Admission rest of year $7; $5 (ages 5-18). **Phone:** (907) 770-3692. GT

ALASKA NATIVE HERITAGE CENTER is about 3 mi. e. on Glenn Hwy. to N. Muldoon Rd. exit, then 1 mi. e. on Heritage Center Dr. Situated on 26 wooded acres, the center presents information about the regional, Alaska Native groups that inhabit Alaska: the Aleut and Alutiiq; Athabascan; Eyak, Tlingit, Haida and Tsimshian; Inupiaq and St. Lawrence Island Yup'ik; and Yup'ik and Cup'ik cultures.

The main building offers the Gathering Place for storytelling, Alaska Natives dance and games and musical performances as well as a theater for cultural films. The Hall of Cultures exhibit is divided into five areas with changing multimedia displays about the ways of life of Alaska Natives cultures. Artisans create and display their crafts in adjacent studios.

Outside, five village sites surround Lake Tiulana, and guided village site tours are available to explain each dwelling, aspects of daily life and customs. **Time:** Allow 2 hours minimum. **Hours:** Daily 9-5, mid-May to mid-Sept.; select Sat. 10-5, rest of year. Phone ahead to confirm schedule. **Cost:** $24.95; $21.15 (ages 62+ and military with ID); $16.95 (ages 7-16); $71.50 (family, two adults and two children). Combination ticket with Anchorage Museum at Rasmuson Center also is available. **Phone:** (907) 330-8000 or (800) 315-6608. GT 🍴

THE ALASKA RAILROAD departs from 411 W. First Ave. Narrated sightseeing tours on the Denali Star Train are offered northward between Anchorage and Fairbanks with stops at Wasilla, Talkeetna and Denali National Park and Preserve. The Glacier Discovery Train travels south from Anchorage to Whittier following the Turnagain Arm of Cook Inlet. Stops include Girdwood, Portage, Spencer Glacier—a whistle stop where passengers can take a 1.5-mile ranger-guided hike to see the glacier—and Grandview. The Coastal Classic Train runs from Anchorage to Seward and offers a glimpse of wildlife and glaciers.

(See map & index p. 475.)

Domed cars with glass-covered viewing platforms allow for 180-degree views. Special winter routes as well as excursions and connections to air, rail and boat tours are available. **Hours:** Trips depart daily, mid-May to mid-Sept.; trains depart Sat.-Sun., rest of year. Phone ahead to confirm schedule. **Cost:** One-way fares $63-$239; $32-$120 (ages 2-11). An extra fee applies for first-class seating. Reservations are required. **Phone:** (907) 265-2494, (800) 544-0552 or TTY (907) 265-2620. *(See ad p. 468.)* GT

ALASKA ZOO is 7.5 mi. s. on SR 1 (Seward Hwy.), then 2 mi. e. to 4731 O'Malley Rd.; a shuttle provides transportation from the Log Cabin Visitor Information Center mid-May to mid-Sept. The grounds encompass a 25-acre wooded home to arctic, subarctic and Alaskan native animals, including Amur (Siberian) tigers, seals, snow leopards, Tibetan yaks, wolves and black, brown and polar bears. Visitors may interact with selected animals during the 2-hour Discovery Tour.

Time: Allow 1 hour, 30 minutes minimum. **Hours:** Daily 9-9, June-Aug.; 9-6, May and Sept.; 10-5, Mar.-Apr. and in Oct.; 10-4, rest of year (weather permitting). Discovery Tour departs daily at 12:15, late May to mid-Sept. Closed Thanksgiving and Christmas. Phone ahead to confirm schedule. **Cost:** $15; $10 (ages 65+ and military with ID); $7 (ages 3-17). Discovery Tour $28; $20 (ages 3-17). **Phone:** (907) 346-2133. GT 🍴 ⚟

ANCHORAGE MUSEUM AT RASMUSON CENTER, 625 C St., has exhibits focusing on the art, history, science and cultures of Alaska and the Circumpolar North. The state-of-the-art Smithsonian Arctic Studies Center

has multimedia exhibits and displays more than 600 Alaska Native artifacts. Contemporary Alaska Native artists blend traditional and contemporary techniques to examine what it means to be an Alaska Native today.

The interactive Discovery Center offers exhibits that explore nature, science and technology, including a marine wildlife area, reptile exhibits and a bubble lab. Spark!Lab Smithsonian allows kids and families to create, innovate, collaborate and problem-solve.

The Alaska exhibit reflects essential aspects of the state's history organized in 15 themed areas. Housed in the Rasmuson Wing, the Art of the North explores life in the region through paintings, sculpture, photography, video and other media. Other highlights include the Thomas Planetarium and traveling exhibitions.

Time: Allow 1 hour minimum. **Hours:** Daily 9-6, May-Sept.; Tues.-Sat. 10-6, Sun. noon-6, rest of year. Guided tours daily at 11, noon and 1, Memorial Day-Labor Day. Closed Jan. 1, Thanksgiving and Christmas. **Cost:** $20; $15 (ages 65+ and military and students with ID); $10 (ages 6-12). Combination ticket with Alaska Native Heritage Center also is available. **Phone:** (907) 929-9200. 🍴

CHUGACH STATE PARK is e. on Seward Hwy. Wildlife populations flourish within the park's 773 square miles of mountains, rivers, lakes and glaciers, home to a variety of wildlife including large mammals like black and brown bears, Dall sheep, moose and mountain goats, and small mammals such as beaver, lynx, wolverines and wolves as well as spawning salmon and numerous birds. Major areas are Eklutna Lake, Eagle River, Anchorage

▼ *See AAA listing p. 519* ▼

CALM WATERS   WILD SIGHTS   PRINCE WILLIAM SOUND

26 Glacier Cruise In One Day!

GLACIERS

Phillips CRUISES & TOURS

NO SEASICKNESS GUARANTEED!   INDUSTRY EXCLUSIVE

U.S. Forest Service Ranger Narration

• Smooth cruising on stable catamarans
• See bird rookeries, otters, sea lions, whales
• Hot meal, full-service bar, reserved seating

907-276-8023 • 800-544-0529 www.26glaciers.com 100 West Camp Rd, Whittier AK

(See map & index p. 475.)

Hillside and Turnagain Arm. A number of recreational activities are available. The park's headquarters is in the historic Potter Section House, at Milepost 115 of the Seward Highway. *See Recreation Areas Chart.*

Hours: Headquarters open Mon.-Fri. 10-noon and 1-4:30. **Cost:** Free. **Parking:** $5 at many trailheads. **Phone:** (907) 345-5014.

MAJOR MARINE TOURS—see Seward p. 509.

PORTAGE GLACIER RECREATION AREA—see Chugach National Forest p. 484.

RUST'S FLYING SERVICE departs from the south shore of Lake Hood off International Airport Rd. at Anchorage International Airport. The service provides narrated sightseeing tours that vary from 30 minutes to 12 hours by seaplane, wheeled planes and ski planes. Tours include flights to Denali National Park and Preserve, Knik Glacier, Prince William Sound and Chugach Mountains. Bear-viewing tours include flights to Katmai and Lake Clark National Parks as well as Redoubt Bay. Glacier landings and one-day to three-night fishing trips also are available.

Note: A 3 percent transportation fee is added to the cost of each trip. Departures require a minimum of 2 people. Singles are accommodated on a space-available basis. **Time:** Allow 1 hour, 30 minutes minimum. **Hours:** Daily 7 a.m.-8 p.m., mid-May to mid-Sept.; Mon.-Fri. 9-5, Sat.-Sun. by appointment, rest of year. Closed Jan. 1, Thanksgiving and Christmas. **Cost:** Fare $110-$895. Reservations are recommended. **Phone:** (907) 243-1595, or (800) 544-2299 (not available from Anchorage landlines). *(See ad this page.)* GT

TRANS ARCTIC CIRCLE TREKS—see Fairbanks p. 492.

▼ *See AAA listing this page* ▼

Tours from Anchorage... Flightseeing | Bear Viewing | Fly-in Fishing | Denali

See Alaska from Our View!

flyrusts.com | 907.243.1595 | Located in Anchorage RUST'S FLYING SERVICE

AAA/CAA Members Save on Hotels - For Any Occasion

ASSURED STAY

BW | Best Western Hotels & Resorts

Hilton

HYATT

Marriott INTERNATIONAL

MGM RESORTS INTERNATIONAL

VISIT over 1,100 AAA/CAA Offices | CLICK AAA.com/greatrates | CALL 1-866-222-7283

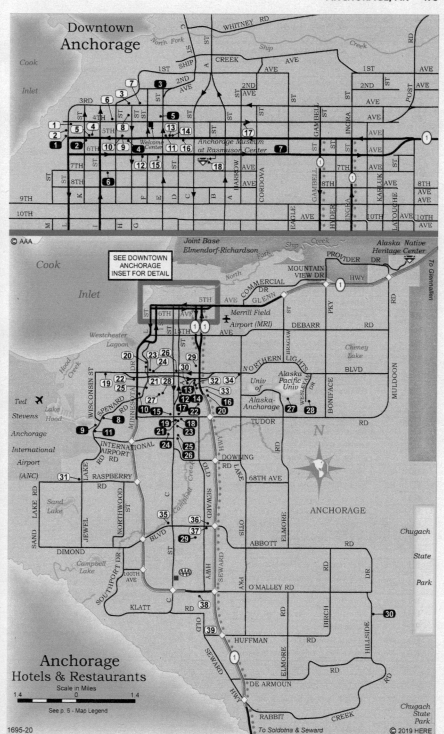

Downtown
Anchorage

Anchorage
Hotels & Restaurants

Scale in Miles

See p. 6 - Map Legend

1695-20

© 2019 HERE

✈ Airport Hotels

Map Page	ANCHORAGE INTERNATIONAL (Maximum driving distance from airport: 2.2 mi)	Designation	Member Savings	Page
11 p. 475	Courtyard by Marriott Anchorage-Airport, 1.7 mi	⬦⬦⬦ THREE DIAMOND	✔	479
8 p. 475	Holiday Inn Express Anchorage-Airport, 2.1 mi	⬦⬦⬦ THREE DIAMOND	✔	481
9 p. 475	The Lakefront Anchorage Hotel, 2.2 mi	⬦⬦⬦ THREE DIAMOND		481

Anchorage

This index helps you "spot" where hotels and restaurants are located on the corresponding detailed maps. Restaurant price range is a combination of lunch and/or dinner. Turn to the listing page for more information and consult display ads for special promotions.

 For more details, rates and reservations: AAA.com/travelguides/hotels

ANCHORAGE

Map Page	Hotels	Designation	Member Savings	Page
1 p. 475	**Copper Whale Inn Downtown** *(See ad p. 479.)*	⬦ APPROVED	✔	479
2 p. 475	**The Voyager Inn**	⬦ APPROVED	✔	482
3 p. 475	Anchorage Grand Hotel	⬦ APPROVED		478
4 p. 475	Westmark Anchorage Hotel	⬦ APPROVED		482
5 p. 475	**Historic Anchorage Hotel**	⬦ APPROVED	✔	480
6 p. 475	Anchorage Marriott Downtown	⬦⬦⬦ THREE DIAMOND	✔	478
7 p. 475	**Sheraton Anchorage Hotel & Spa**	⬦⬦⬦ THREE DIAMOND	✔	481
8 p. 475	**Holiday Inn Express Anchorage-Airport**	⬦⬦⬦ THREE DIAMOND	✔	481
9 p. 475	The Lakefront Anchorage Hotel	⬦⬦⬦ THREE DIAMOND		481
10 p. 475	La Quinta Inn & Suites by Wyndham Anchorage-Airport	⬦⬦⬦ THREE DIAMOND		481
11 p. 475	**Courtyard by Marriott Anchorage-Airport**	⬦⬦⬦ THREE DIAMOND	✔	479
12 p. 475	**SpringHill Suites by Marriott-Midtown**	⬦⬦⬦ THREE DIAMOND	✔	481
13 p. 475	Embassy Suites by Hilton Anchorage	⬦⬦⬦ THREE DIAMOND	✔	479
14 p. 475	TownePlace Suites by Marriott Anchorage-Midtown	⬦⬦⬦ THREE DIAMOND	✔	482
15 p. 475	Hampton Inn by Hilton Anchorage-Midtown	⬦⬦⬦ THREE DIAMOND	✔	479
16 p. 475	**Residence Inn by Marriott Anchorage-Midtown**	⬦⬦⬦ THREE DIAMOND	✔	481
17 p. 475	**Hyatt Place Anchorage-Midtown**	⬦⬦⬦ THREE DIAMOND	✔	481
18 p. 475	Aspen Suites Hotel Anchorage-Midtown	⬦ APPROVED	✔	478
19 p. 475	Home2 Suites by Hilton Anchorage-Midtown	⬦⬦⬦ THREE DIAMOND	✔	481
20 p. 475	**Best Western Golden Lion Hotel**	⬦ APPROVED	✔	478
21 p. 475	Hilton Garden Inn Anchorage-Midtown	⬦⬦⬦ THREE DIAMOND	✔	480
22 p. 475	My Place Hotel - Anchorage	⬦ APPROVED		481
23 p. 475	Homewood Suites by Hilton Anchorage-Midtown	⬦⬦⬦ THREE DIAMOND	✔	481
24 p. 475	**Hyatt House Anchorage-Midtown**	⬦⬦⬦ THREE DIAMOND	✔	481
25 p. 475	**Fairfield Inn & Suites by Marriott Anchorage-Midtown**	⬦ APPROVED	✔	479
26 p. 475	**Crowne Plaza Anchorage-Midtown**	⬦⬦⬦ THREE DIAMOND	✔	479
27 p. 475	**SpringHill Suites by Marriott - University Lake**	⬦⬦⬦ THREE DIAMOND	✔	482
28 p. 475	Camai Bed and Breakfast	⬦⬦⬦ THREE DIAMOND		478
29 p. 475	**Dimond Center Hotel**	⬦⬦⬦ THREE DIAMOND	✔	479
30 p. 475	Highland Glen Lodge Bed & Breakfast	⬦⬦⬦ THREE DIAMOND		480

Map Page	Restaurants	Designation	Cuisine	Price Range	Page
1 p. 475	Snow City Cafe	⬦ APPROVED	American	$10-$17	483
2 p. 475	Simon & Seafort's Saloon & Grill	⬦⬦⬦ THREE DIAMOND	Regional American	$18-$47	483
3 p. 475	49th State Brewing Company	⬦ APPROVED	American	$12-$28	482
4 p. 475	**Crow's Nest Restaurant**	⬦⬦⬦⬦ FOUR DIAMOND	New American	$36-$58	482

Map Page	Restaurants (cont'd)	Designation	Cuisine	Price Range	Page
⑤ p. 475	Bangkok Cafe	APPROVED	Thai	$10-$15	482
⑥ p. 475	Haute Quarter Grill	THREE DIAMOND	American	$20-$50	482
⑦ p. 475	**Marx Bros. Café**	FOUR DIAMOND	New American	$35-$40	482
⑧ p. 475	Crush Wine Bistro & Cellar	APPROVED	Small Plates	$12-$34	482
⑨ p. 475	ORSO Restaurant	THREE DIAMOND	Seafood	$19-$40	483
⑩ p. 475	Glacier Brewhouse	APPROVED	American	$9-$34	482
⑪ p. 475	Fat Ptarmigan Wood Fired Pizza	APPROVED	Italian	$11-$21	482
⑫ p. 475	Humpy's Great Alaskan Ale House	APPROVED	American	$10-$45	482
⑬ p. 475	Ginger	APPROVED	Pacific Northwest	$9-$40	482
⑭ p. 475	Club Paris	APPROVED	Steak Seafood	$13-$43	482
⑮ p. 475	Pangea Restaurant & Lounge	THREE DIAMOND	International	$12-$33	483
⑯ p. 475	Sullivan's Steakhouse	THREE DIAMOND	Steak	$14-$65	483
⑰ p. 475	La Cabana Mexican Restaurant	APPROVED	Mexican	$9-$22	482
⑱ p. 475	Muse	APPROVED	Regional Pacific Northwest	$15-$26	483
⑲ p. 475	Rustic Goat	APPROVED	American	$12-$42	483
⑳ p. 475	Ray's Place Vietnamese Restaurant	APPROVED	Vietnamese	$9-$21	483
㉑ p. 475	Organic Oasis Restaurant & Juice Bar	APPROVED	Vegan Vegetarian	$10-$25	483
㉒ p. 475	City Diner	APPROVED	American	$6-$20	482
㉓ p. 475	Spenard Roadhouse	THREE DIAMOND	American	$10-$32	483
㉔ p. 475	Sweet Basil Cafe	APPROVED	American	$7-$15	483
㉕ p. 475	Yak and Yeti Himalayan Restaurant	APPROVED	Indian	$8-$18	483
㉖ p. 475	Alaska Bagel Restaurant	APPROVED	Breakfast Sandwiches	$9-$17	482
㉗ p. 475	Jens' Restaurant	THREE DIAMOND	Pacific Northwest	$13-$45	482
㉘ p. 475	Campobello Bistro	APPROVED	Italian	$14-$38	482
㉙ p. 475	Sorrento's Restaurant	APPROVED	Italian	$17-$29	483
㉚ p. 475	Table 6 Grill & Restaurant	APPROVED	American	$13-$27	483
㉛ p. 475	Kincaid Grill	THREE DIAMOND	Regional Alaskan	$28-$36	482
㉜ p. 475	Kinley's Restaurant & Bar	THREE DIAMOND	Fusion	$12-$36	482
㉝ p. 475	Moose's Tooth Pub & Pizzeria	APPROVED	American	$11-$22	482
㉞ p. 475	Turkish Delight	APPROVED	Turkish	$10-$21	483
㉟ p. 475	Las Margaritas	APPROVED	Mexican	$9-$20	482
㊱ p. 475	Sushi Ya Japanese Restaurant	APPROVED	Japanese	$10-$24	483
㊲ p. 475	Suite 100 Restaurant, Bar & Lounge	APPROVED	Seafood Steak	$15-$46	483
㊳ p. 475	South Cafe & Coffee House	APPROVED	Breakfast Sandwiches	$12-$18	483
㊴ p. 475	Southside Bistro	THREE DIAMOND	New American	$9-$34	483

AAA DISCOUNTS »»» REWARDS

DISCOUNTS
WITHOUT LIMITS
AAA.com/discounts

(See map & index p. 475.)

ANCHORAGE GRAND HOTEL   907/929-8888 **3**
 APPROVED   Extended Stay Hotel. **Address:** 505 W 2nd Ave 99501

ANCHORAGE MARRIOTT DOWNTOWN   907/279-8000 **6**
 THREE DIAMOND SAVE Hotel. **Address:** 820 W 7th Ave 99501

> **AAA Benefit:** Members save 5% or more!

ASPEN SUITES HOTEL ANCHORAGE-MIDTOWN
907/770-3400 **18**
 APPROVED
Extended Stay Hotel

Address: 100 E Tudor Rd 99503 **Location:** SR 1 (Seward Hwy) exit Tudor Rd, 0.6 mi w. **Facility:** 92 efficiencies. 4 stories, interior corridors. **Parking:** winter plug-ins. **Activities:** exercise room. **Guest Services:** valet and coin laundry.

BEST WESTERN GOLDEN LION HOTEL
907/561-1522 **20**
 APPROVED
Hotel

 Best Western

AAA Benefit: Members save up to 15% and earn bonus points!

Address: 1000 E 36th Ave 99508 **Location:** SR 1 (Seward Hwy) and 36th Ave. **Facility:** 83 units. 3 stories, interior corridors. **Activities:** exercise room. **Guest Services:** valet and coin laundry.

CAMAI BED AND BREAKFAST   907/333-2219 **28**
 THREE DIAMOND Bed & Breakfast. **Address:** 3838 Westminster Way 99508

STAY CONNECTED

to all the things membership can do for you

- **Member discounts around you**
- **Cheapest gas nearby**
- **Diamond hotels and restaurants**
- **Travel information and reservations**
- **Roadside assistance**

Download today. Connect every day.
AAA.com/mobile | CAA.ca/mobile

▼ See AAA listing p. 518 ▼

BW **Best Western.**   Lake Lucille Inn   THREE DIAMOND

ONLY 45 MILES NORTH OF ANCHORAGE!

1300 W. Lake Lucille Dr.
Wasilla, AK 99654
Tel: (907)373-1776
Fax: (907)376-6199

On the way to Denali National Park | Superb location on beautiful Lake Lucille | Premier Hotel with Breathtaking views on the Chugach Mountains Free Hot Breakfast Buffet | Free Wi-Fi | Fitness Room

www.BestWestern.com/LakeLucilleInn | 1-800-897-1776

(See map & index p. 475.)

COPPER WHALE INN DOWNTOWN   907/258-7999   ①

APPROVED
Boutique Hotel

Address: 440 L St 99501 **Location:** 5th Ave and L St. **Facility:** Close to dining and an 11-mile coastal trail, the main house of this cozy inn dates back to 1939. Multiple waterfalls surround the property. All guest rooms feature a fan and upscale bedding. 15 units, some kitchens. 2-3 stories (no elevator), interior corridors. *Bath:* some shared. **Parking:** street only. **Activities:** bicycles. **Guest Services:** coin laundry. *(See ad this page.)*

SAVE 🍴 BIZ 🛜 ✕ 🐾 ▣

COURTYARD BY MARRIOTT ANCHORAGE-AIRPORT
907/245-0322   ⑪

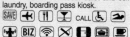

THREE DIAMOND
Contemporary Hotel

COURTYARD   **AAA Benefit:** Members save 5% or more!

Address: 4901 Spenard Rd 99517 **Location:** Just ne of Jewel Lake and International Airport rds. **Facility:** 154 units. 3 stories, interior corridors. **Pool:** heated indoor. **Activities:** hot tub, exercise room. **Guest Services:** valet and coin laundry, boarding pass kiosk.

SAVE ✈ 🍴 🛜 ☎ CALL ♿ 🏊
🚐 BIZ 🛜 ✕ 🔌 📺 ▣
/ SOME UNITS HS

CROWNE PLAZA ANCHORAGE-MIDTOWN
907/433-4100   ㉖

THREE DIAMOND
Hotel

Address: 109 W International Airport Rd 99518 **Location:** Jct C St, just n on A St. **Facility:** 165 units. 6 stories, interior corridors. **Parking:** winter plug-ins. **Terms:** check-in 4 pm. **Pool:** heated indoor. **Activities:** hot tub, exercise room. **Guest Services:** valet and coin laundry.

SAVE ✈ 🍴 🛎 ☎ CALL ♿
🚐 🔌 BIZ 🛜 ✕ 🔌 📺
▣

DIMOND CENTER HOTEL   907/770-5000   ㉙

THREE DIAMOND
Hotel

Address: 700 E Dimond Blvd 99515 **Location:** SR 1 (Seward Hwy) exit Dimond Blvd, just w, then s on Dimond Center Dr. Adjacent to Dimond Center. **Facility:** 109 units. 3 stories, interior corridors. **Activities:** exercise room. **Guest Services:** valet and coin laundry. **Featured Amenity:** full hot breakfast.

SAVE ✈ 🍴 ☎ CALL ♿ 🚐
🛜 ✕ 🔌 📺 ▣

EMBASSY SUITES BY HILTON ANCHORAGE
907/332-7000   ⑬

THREE DIAMOND SAVE Hotel. **Address:** 600 E Benson Blvd 99503

AAA Benefit: Members save up to 15%!

FAIRFIELD INN & SUITES BY MARRIOTT ANCHORAGE-MIDTOWN   907/222-9000   ㉕

APPROVED
Hotel

Fairfield   **AAA Benefit:** Members save 5% or more!

Address: 5060 A St 99503 **Location:** Jct C St, just e on International Airport Rd, then just n. **Facility:** 106 units. 4 stories, interior corridors. **Pool:** heated indoor. **Activities:** hot tub, picnic facilities, exercise room. **Guest Services:** valet and coin laundry. **Featured Amenity:** breakfast buffet.

SAVE ✈ 🍴 CALL ♿ 🚐 🔌
BIZ 🛜 ✕ 🔌 📺 ▣

HAMPTON INN BY HILTON ANCHORAGE-MIDTOWN
907/550-7000   ⑮

THREE DIAMOND   SAVE
Contemporary Hotel. **Address:** 4301 Credit Union Dr 99503

AAA Benefit: Members save up to 15%!

▼ See AAA listing this page ▼

INSPECTOR'S **BEST OF** HOUSEKEEPING 2019

Copper Whale Inn
THE GEM OF DOWNTOWN ANCHORAGE!

440 L Street
Anchorage, AK 99501
907-258-7999

🔗 **Turn dreams into plans using**
AAA travel planning tools: AAA.com/maps

(See map & index p. 475.)

HIGHLAND GLEN LODGE BED & BREAKFAST
907/336-2312 **30**
THREE DIAMOND Bed & Breakfast. **Address:** 11651 Hillside Dr 99507

HILTON GARDEN INN ANCHORAGE-MIDTOWN
907/729-7000 **21**
THREE DIAMOND SAVE
Contemporary Hotel. **Address:** 4555 Union Square Dr 99503

AAA Benefit: Members save up to 15%!

HISTORIC ANCHORAGE HOTEL   907/272-4553 **5**

APPROVED
Historic Boutique Hotel

Address: 330 E St 99501 **Location:** On E St, between 3rd and 4th aves; downtown. **Facility:** Established in 1916, this hotel retains its Old World charm, but with modern amenities. The standard rooms are meant for one or two people while suites are more spacious. 26 units. 3 stories, interior corridors. **Parking:** on-site (fee). **Activities:** exercise room. **Guest Services:** valet laundry. **Featured Amenity:** full hot breakfast.

▼ See AAA listing p. 495 ▼

DINE
WITH A VIEW

Credit to Ralph Kristopher

Seven Glaciers, Alyeska Resort's Award-Winning Mountain-Top Restaurant is Accessible Via Scenic Aerial Tram.

Surrounded by spectacular Alaskan wilderness and located only 40 miles from Anchorage, Alyeska Resort is your year-round adventure base camp. Stay at the luxurious Hotel Alyeska and catch a scenic ride on the aerial tram.

SEVEN GLACIERS
THE HOTEL ALYESKA
ALYESKA RESORT • ALASKA

EXCELLENCE FOR OVER 20 YEARS

FOUR DIAMOND

Wine Spectator
BEST OF AWARD OF EXCELLENCE
2019

800-880-3880
ALYESKARESORT.COM

(See map & index p. 475.)

HOLIDAY INN EXPRESS ANCHORAGE-AIRPORT
907/248-8848   **8**

THREE DIAMOND
Hotel

Address: 4411 Spenard Rd 99517 **Location:** 0.5 mi ne of Jewel Lake and International Airport rds. **Facility:** 129 units. 3 stories, interior corridors. **Pool:** heated indoor. **Activities:** hot tub, exercise room. **Guest Services:** valet and coin laundry. **Featured Amenity:** breakfast buffet.

SAVE ✈ CALL ♿ 🏊 👶 BIZ
HS 📶 ✕ 🔌 📧 🖥

HOME2 SUITES BY HILTON ANCHORAGE-MIDTOWN
907/561-5618   **19**

THREE DIAMOND SAVE Extended Stay Contemporary Hotel. **Address:** 4700 Union Square Dr 99503

AAA Benefit: Members save up to 15%!

HOMEWOOD SUITES BY HILTON ANCHORAGE-MIDTOWN
907/762-7000   **23**

THREE DIAMOND SAVE Extended Stay Hotel. **Address:** 101 W 48th Ave 99503

AAA Benefit: Members save up to 15%!

HYATT HOUSE ANCHORAGE-MIDTOWN
907/992-2200   **24**

THREE DIAMOND

HYATT house™

AAA Benefit: Members save up to 10%!

Extended Stay Contemporary Hotel

Address: 5141 Business Park Blvd 99503 **Location:** Jct W International Airport Rd and C St, just nw. **Facility:** 144 units, some two bedrooms and efficiencies. 6 stories, interior corridors. **Pool:** heated indoor. **Activities:** picnic facilities, exercise room. **Guest Services:** valet and coin laundry, area transportation. **Featured Amenity:** breakfast buffet.

SAVE ✈ 🍴 🍽 CALL ♿ 🏊 👶 BIZ 📶 ✕
🔌 📧 🖥 /SOME UNITS 🐾

HYATT PLACE ANCHORAGE-MIDTOWN
907/562-1235   **17**

THREE DIAMOND

HYATT PLACE®

AAA Benefit: Members save up to 10%!

Contemporary Hotel

Address: 101 E Tudor Rd 99503 **Location:** SR 1 (Seward Hwy) exit Tudor Rd, 0.5 mi w. **Facility:** 150 units. 4 stories, interior corridors. **Parking:** winter plug-ins. **Pool:** heated indoor. **Activities:** hot tub, exercise room. **Guest Services:** valet and coin laundry, area transportation.

SAVE ✈ 🍴 🍽 CALL ♿ 🏊
👶 BIZ 📶 ✕ 🔌 🖥
/SOME UNITS 🐾

THE LAKEFRONT ANCHORAGE HOTEL   907/243-2300   **9**
THREE DIAMOND Hotel. **Address:** 4800 Spenard Rd 99517

LA QUINTA INN & SUITES BY WYNDHAM ANCHORAGE-AIRPORT
907/276-8884   **10**
THREE DIAMOND Contemporary Hotel. **Address:** 3501 Minnesota Dr 99503

MY PLACE HOTEL - ANCHORAGE
907/929-3500   **22**
💎 **APPROVED** Extended Stay Hotel. **Address:** 729 E 40th Ave 99503

RESIDENCE INN BY MARRIOTT ANCHORAGE-MIDTOWN
907/563-9844   **16**

THREE DIAMOND
Extended Stay Contemporary Hotel

 Residence INN.

AAA Benefit: Members save 5% or more!

Address: 1025 E 35th Ave 99508 **Location:** Jct SR 1 (Seward Hwy) and 36th Ave. **Facility:** 148 units, some two bedrooms, efficiencies and kitchens. 3 stories, interior corridors. **Pool:** heated indoor. **Activities:** hot tub, picnic facilities, exercise room. **Guest Services:** valet and coin laundry. **Featured Amenity:** breakfast buffet.

SAVE ✈ 🍴 CALL ♿ 🏊 👶 BIZ HS 📶 ✕
🔌 📧 🖥 /SOME UNITS 🐾

SHERATON ANCHORAGE HOTEL & SPA
907/276-8700   **7**

THREE DIAMOND
Contemporary Hotel

 SHERATON

AAA Benefit: Members save 5% or more!

Address: 401 E 6th Ave 99501 **Location:** Jct 6th Ave and Denali St. **Facility:** 370 units. 16 stories, interior corridors. **Parking:** on-site (fee). **Terms:** check-in 4 pm. **Amenities:** safes. **Dining:** 2 restaurants. **Activities:** exercise room, spa. **Guest Services:** valet and coin laundry.

SAVE 🍴 👶 🍽 CALL ♿ 👶
📶 ✕ 🎥 🔌 🖥 /SOME UNITS 🐾

SPRINGHILL SUITES BY MARRIOTT-MIDTOWN
907/562-3247   **12**

THREE DIAMOND SPRINGHILL SUITES MARRIOTT

AAA Benefit: Members save 5% or more!

Contemporary Hotel

Address: 3401 A St 99503 **Location:** Jct W 36th Ave and A St. **Facility:** 101 units. 3 stories, interior corridors. **Pool:** heated indoor. **Activities:** hot tub, exercise room. **Guest Services:** valet and coin laundry, boarding pass kiosk, area transportation. **Featured Amenity:** breakfast buffet.

SAVE ✈ 🍴 CALL ♿ 🏊 👶
BIZ 📶 ✕ 🔌 📧 🖥 /SOME UNITS HS

GET THE APP
Download today.
Connect every day.
AAA.com/mobile
CAA.ca/mobile

(See map & index p. 475.)

SPRINGHILL SUITES BY MARRIOTT - UNIVERSITY LAKE
907/751-6300 **27**

 THREE DIAMOND

Contemporary Hotel

SPRINGHILL SUITES MARRIOTT

AAA Benefit: Members save 5% or more!

Address: 4050 University Lake Dr 99508 **Location:** SR 1 (Seward Hwy), 2 mi e on E 36th Ave and Providence Dr, just s on University Dr, then just e. **Facility:** 159 units. 3 stories, interior corridors. **Pool:** heated indoor. **Activities:** hot tub, trails, exercise room. **Guest Services:** valet and coin laundry, boarding pass kiosk, area transportation. **Featured Amenity:** breakfast buffet.

TOWNEPLACE SUITES BY MARRIOTT ANCHORAGE-MIDTOWN
907/334-8000 **14**

THREE DIAMOND [SAVE] Extended Stay Contemporary Hotel. **Address:** 600 E 32nd Ave 99503

AAA Benefit: Members save 5% or more!

THE VOYAGER INN
907/277-9501 **2**

APPROVED

Boutique Hotel

Address: 501 K St 99501 **Location:** 5th Ave and K St; downtown. **Facility:** The lobby is stylish and the decor offers a hint of elegance. Room highlights include upscale bedding, lovely drapery, robes, USB ports, upgraded coffee machines and thoughtful amenities. 40 units. 4 stories, interior corridors. **Parking:** on-site (fee). **Amenities:** safes. **Guest Services:** valet laundry, boarding pass kiosk. **Featured Amenity:** full hot breakfast.

WESTMARK ANCHORAGE HOTEL
907/276-7676 **4**

APPROVED   Hotel. **Address:** 720 W 5th Ave 99501

WHERE TO EAT

49TH STATE BREWING COMPANY   907/277-7727 **3**
APPROVED   American. Brewpub. **Address:** 717 W 3rd Ave 99501

ALASKA BAGEL RESTAURANT   907/276-3900 **26**
APPROVED   Breakfast Sandwiches. Casual Dining. **Address:** 113 W Northern Lights Blvd 99503

BANGKOK CAFE   907/274-2233 **5**
APPROVED   Thai. Casual Dining. **Address:** 930 W 5th Ave 99501

CAMPOBELLO BISTRO   907/563-2040 **28**
APPROVED   Italian. Casual Dining. **Address:** 601 W 36th Ave 99503

CITY DINER   907/277-2489 **22**
APPROVED   American. Casual Dining. **Address:** 3000 Minnesota Dr 99503

CLUB PARIS   907/277-6332 **14**
APPROVED   Steak Seafood. Casual Dining. **Address:** 417 W 5th Ave 99501

CROW'S NEST RESTAURANT
907/276-6000 **4**

FOUR DIAMOND

New American Fine Dining

$36-$58

AAA Inspector Notes: A visit to this restaurant and lounge is a must while in Anchorage. Perched high on the 20th floor of The Hotel Captain Cook, the eatery affords one of the best panoramic views of mountains and Cook Inlet, especially on long summer days. The menu features fresh seafood and beef dishes served in an old world dining room with lots of wood accent walls. **Features:** full bar. **Reservations:** suggested. **Address:** 939 W 5th Ave 99501 **Location:** Between I and K sts; downtown; in The Hotel Captain Cook. **Parking:** on-site and valet. [D] CALL

CRUSH WINE BISTRO & CELLAR   907/865-9198 **8**
APPROVED   Small Plates. Casual Dining. **Address:** 328 G St 99501

FAT PTARMIGAN WOOD FIRED PIZZA   907/777-7710 **11**
APPROVED   Italian. Casual Dining. **Address:** 441 W 5th Ave, #100 99501

GINGER   907/929-3680 **13**
APPROVED   Pacific Northwest. Fine Dining. **Address:** 425 W 5th Ave 99501

GLACIER BREWHOUSE   907/274-2739 **10**
APPROVED   American. Gastropub. **Address:** 737 W 5th Ave, Suite 110 99501

HAUTE QUARTER GRILL   907/622-4745 **6**
THREE DIAMOND   American. Casual Dining. **Address:** 525 W 4th Ave 99501

HUMPY'S GREAT ALASKAN ALE HOUSE   907/276-2337 **12**
APPROVED   American. Casual Dining. **Address:** 610 W 6th Ave 99501

JENS' RESTAURANT   907/561-5367 **27**
THREE DIAMOND   Pacific Northwest. Fine Dining. **Address:** 701 W 36th Ave 99503

KINCAID GRILL   907/243-0507 **31**
THREE DIAMOND   Regional Alaskan. Fine Dining. **Address:** 6700 Jewel Lake Rd 99502

KINLEY'S RESTAURANT & BAR   907/644-8953 **32**
THREE DIAMOND   Fusion. Casual Dining. **Address:** 3230 Seward Hwy 99503

LA CABANA MEXICAN RESTAURANT   907/272-0135 **17**
APPROVED   Mexican. Casual Dining. **Address:** 312 E 4th Ave 99501

LAS MARGARITAS   907/349-4922 **35**
APPROVED   Mexican. Casual Dining. **Address:** 541 W Dimond Blvd 99515

MARX BROS. CAFÉ
907/278-2133 **7**

FOUR DIAMOND

New American Fine Dining

$35-$40

AAA Inspector Notes: *Historic.* For a truly exquisite meal, look no further than the dining rooms of this renovated 1916 home. Innovative and artistic selections of Alaskan seafood highlight the menu, and the locally renowned Caesar salad is prepared tableside. Choices include not only a wide selection of seafood, such as oysters, salmon and halibut, but also lamb, elk and other meats. Save room for one of the divine desserts. The atmosphere is delightful, and the service is friendly and genuine. **Features:** beer & wine. **Reservations:** suggested. **Address:** 627 W 3rd Ave 99501 **Location:** Between F and G sts; downtown. **Parking:** street only. [D] [AC]

MOOSE'S TOOTH PUB & PIZZERIA   907/258-2537 **33**
APPROVED   American. Casual Dining. **Address:** 3300 Old Seward Hwy 99503

(See map & index p. 475.)

MUSE   907/929-9210 (18)
APPROVED Regional Pacific Northwest. Casual Dining. **Address:** 625 C St 99501

ORGANIC OASIS RESTAURANT & JUICE BAR
                                    907/227-7882 (21)
APPROVED Vegan Vegetarian. Quick Serve. **Address:** 2610 Spenard Rd, Suite B 99503

ORSO RESTAURANT   907/222-3232 (9)
THREE DIAMOND Seafood. Fine Dining. **Address:** 737 W 5th Ave 99501

PANGEA RESTAURANT & LOUNGE   907/222-3949 (15)
THREE DIAMOND International. Casual Dining. **Address:** 508 W 6th Ave 99501

RAY'S PLACE VIETNAMESE RESTAURANT
                                    907/279-2932 (20)
APPROVED Vietnamese. Casual Dining. **Address:** 2412 Spenard Rd 99503

RUSTIC GOAT   907/334-8100 (19)
APPROVED American. Gastropub. **Address:** 2800 Turnagain St 99517

SIMON & SEAFORT'S SALOON & GRILL   907/274-3502 (2)
THREE DIAMOND Regional American. Casual Dining. **Address:** 420 L St 99501

SNOW CITY CAFE   907/272-2489 (1)
APPROVED American. Casual Dining. **Address:** 1034 W 4th Ave 99501

SORRENTO'S RESTAURANT   907/278-3439 (29)
APPROVED Italian. Casual Dining. **Address:** 610 Fireweed Ln 99503

SOUTH CAFE & COFFEE HOUSE   907/770-9201 (38)
APPROVED Breakfast Sandwiches. Quick Serve. **Address:** 11124 Old Seward Hwy 99515

SOUTHSIDE BISTRO   907/348-0088 (39)
THREE DIAMOND New American. Casual Dining. **Address:** 1320 Huffman Park Dr 99515

SPENARD ROADHOUSE   907/770-7623 (23)
THREE DIAMOND American. Casual Dining. **Address:** 1049 W Northern Lights Blvd 99503

SUITE 100 RESTAURANT, BAR & LOUNGE
                                    907/341-1000 (37)
APPROVED Seafood Steak. Casual Dining. **Address:** 1000 E Dimond Blvd 99515

SULLIVAN'S STEAKHOUSE   907/258-2882 (16)
THREE DIAMOND Steak. Fine Dining. **Address:** 320 W 5th Ave, Suite 100 99501

SUSHI YA JAPANESE RESTAURANT   907/522-2244 (36)
APPROVED Japanese. Casual Dining. **Address:** 1111 E Dimond Blvd 99515

SWEET BASIL CAFE   907/274-0070 (24)
APPROVED American. Casual Dining. **Address:** 1021 W Northern Lights Blvd 99503

TABLE 6 GRILL & RESTAURANT   907/562-6000 (30)
APPROVED American. Casual Dining. **Address:** 3210 Denali St 99503

TURKISH DELIGHT   907/258-3434 (34)
APPROVED Turkish. Casual Dining. **Address:** 2210 E Northern Lights Blvd, #110 99508

YAK AND YETI HIMALAYAN RESTAURANT
                                    907/743-8078 (25)
APPROVED Indian. Casual Dining. **Address:** 3301 Spenard Rd 99503

CANTWELL pop. 219

BACKWOODS LODGE   907/987-0960
APPROVED Motel. **Address:** 133.7 Denali Hwy 99729

CHUGACH NATIONAL FOREST (D-12)

Elevations in the forest range from sea level at the Pacific Ocean at Prince William Sound to 13,176 ft. at Mount Marcus Baker. Refer to AAA maps for additional elevation information.

Extending along the Gulf of Alaska from Cape Suckling to Seward, Chugach (CHEW-gatch) National Forest covers 5,500,000 acres, roughly as large as New Hampshire. It is second in size only to the Tongass National Forest *(see place listing p. 516)* and includes many of the islands and much of the land bordering Prince William Sound and the northeastern portion of the Kenai Peninsula.

Within the 700,000-acre Copper River Delta Wildlife Management Area just east of Cordova is one of the largest concentrations of trumpeter swans in North America. Also in abundance are dusky Canada geese, short-billed dowitchers, red-throated loons and green-winged teal. Prince William Sound has spectacular scenic opportunities with its 3,500 miles of coastline as well as dramatic tidewater glaciers and marine life that includes many species of whales.

Both saltwater and freshwater fishing are available in abundance in the forest. Halibut, red snapper, salmon and crabs are plentiful along the more than 3,500 miles of saltwater shoreline. Popular spots are Resurrection Bay at Seward and in Prince William Sound around Valdez and Cordova. Freshwater lakes and streams provide red salmon, Dolly Varden char and rainbow trout. A sportfishing license is required for all types of fishing within the forest.

For photographers and sport hunters, the forest offers a variety of big game, including black and brown bears, moose and Dall sheep. Hunting is subject to Alaska's fish and game management laws, seasons and bag limits.

Seward Highway offers 127 miles of scenic driving along saltwater bays, ice-blue glaciers and valleys dotted with native wildlife. The highway connects the cities of Anchorage and Seward. Bordering the forest on the northwest is SR 4; its scenic portion extends from Valdez to the junction of SR 10 west of Chitina. Portions of one of the most famous trails, The Historic Iditarod Trail, can be hiked, skied, dog sledded or explored on snowmobile.

In addition to 14 road-accessible campgrounds and 200 miles of hiking trails, the Forest Service operates 42 cabins in remote areas near lakes, bays and streams. Accessible by trail, boat or floatplane, the cabins are equipped with bunks, tables, chairs, wood or oil stoves and outdoor sanitary facilities, but not electricity.

The fee is $40-$85 per night per party. Reservations are required and can be made up to six months in advance. Further information also can be obtained from the Chugach National Forest, 161 E. 1st Ave., #8, Anchorage, AK 99501; phone (907) 743-9500. The U.S. Forest Service (8510 Menden Hall Loop Rd., Juneau, AK 99802) also can provide information; phone (907) 586-8806, (877) 444-6777 for reservations or TTY (907) 790-7444. *See Recreation Areas Chart.*

ALASKA WILDLIFE CONSERVATION CENTER, Seward Hwy. Milepost 79, is a 200-acre, drive-through wildlife refuge. Musk oxen, red foxes, lynx, wood bison, Sitka black-tailed deer, caribou, eagles, moose, reindeer, elk and bears may be seen on the 1.5-mile loop. A self-guiding walking tour, Behind the Scene guided tour and moose encounter also are available. **Time:** Allow 30 minutes minimum. **Hours:** Daily 8-8, mid-May to mid-Sept.; daily 10-6, mid-Feb. to mid-May; daily 10-5, mid-Sept. through Nov. 30; daily 10-4 in Dec.; Sat.-Sun. 10-5, rest of year. Last admission is 1 hour before closing. Phone ahead to confirm schedule. **Cost:** $15; $12 (ages 65+ and active military with ID); $10 (ages 7-17). Behind the Scene tour $100; children 0-9 are not permitted. Moose encounter $10. **Phone:** (907) 783-2025. GT

PORTAGE GLACIER CRUISES depart 1.5 mi. s. of the Begich-Boggs Visitor Center in the Portage Glacier Recreation Area *(see attraction listing).* A 1-hour narrated cruise aboard the MV *Ptarmigan* takes passengers to the face of Portage Glacier. Sections of the glacier "calving" or breaking away into the lake below often can be seen. The 144-passenger ship has a climate-controlled cabin with oversize windows and an open-air observation deck. Shuttle and tour packages from Anchorage also are available.

Inquire about weather policies. **Time:** Allow 1 hour, 30 minutes minimum. **Hours:** Cruises depart daily at 10:30, noon, 1:30, 3 and 4:30, mid-May to mid-Sept. **Cost:** Fare $39; $19 (ages 2-12). **Phone:** (907) 277-5581 or (800) 544-2206. GT

PORTAGE GLACIER RECREATION AREA is 5.5 mi. e. from Milepost 79 of the Seward-Anchorage Hwy. Large icebergs calve off the face of the glacier into 650-foot-deep Portage Lake. An observation platform and a wayside exhibit are at the entrance to Williwaw Campground. Wayside exhibits also are available at Explorer Glacier. Iceworm safaris—hikes centered on spotting the elusive worms living in the glacier ice—are offered. **Hours:** The road to and within the area is open all year. Iceworm safaris depart the Byron Glacier trailhead Tues. and Sat. at

3, May-Sept. **Phone:** (907) 783-2326 (May-Sept.), or (907) 783-3242 (rest of year). GT ❚❙ ⌖

Begich-Boggs Visitor Center, off the Seward-Anchorage Hwy. on Portage Valley Rd., contains an observatory, orientation area, exhibit hall and learning center. A 20-minute film titled "Voices from the Ice" is shown every half hour. **Hours:** Daily 9-6, Memorial Day weekend to mid-Sept.; hours vary rest of year. Phone ahead to confirm schedule. **Cost:** Visitor center and film $5; free (ages 0-15). **Phone:** (907) 783-2326 (May-Sept.), or (907) 783-3242 (rest of year).

▽ DENALI NATIONAL PARK AND PRESERVE (B-10)
• Hotels p. 488 • Restaurants p. 488

Elevations in the park and preserve range from 626 ft. at the northwest corner of the park at Chilcukabena Lake to the 20,310 ft. Denali. Refer to AAA maps for additional elevation information.

In the interior of Alaska, primitive and wild Denali National Park and Preserve covers 9,419 square miles and offers spectacular views of quiet lakes, snowcapped peaks and varicolored tundra. In addition to 20,310-foot Denali, the highest peak in North America, the park encompasses 17,400-foot Mount Foraker, 13,220-foot Silverthrone and 11,670-foot Mount Russell.

Denali, "the high one" in the Athabascan Indian language, was known for a time as Mount McKinley. It has two peaks: South Peak, the true summit, and 2 miles away, 19,470-foot North Peak. Most of the mountain is covered by ice and snow all year. Excellent views of the mountain are possible along the park road (weather permitting); clouds hide the summit about 75 percent of the time in summer and 60 percent the rest of the year.

The park's many glaciers originate on the slopes of the Alaska Range. Muldrow Glacier, the largest northward-flowing glacier in Alaska, stretches from between Denali's twin peaks to within a few miles of the park road; it can be seen from several vantage points.

More than 167 species of birds and 39 kinds of mammals inhabit the park; grizzly bears, moose, Dall sheep, wolves and caribou are some of the larger mammals. Equally varied is the vegetation. The chief conifers are black and white spruce, while dwarf birch grow in thickets on the lower slopes and along the intermountain valleys. Low, boggy meadows are the habitat of stunted, twisted black spruce.

Above the river valleys, forests give way to vast stretches of wet tundra supporting shrubby plants and often underlain by permafrost. Dry alpine tundra blankets the slopes and ridges at the higher elevations.

General Information and Activities

From Anchorage and Fairbanks, the George Parks Highway (SR 3) provides access to the park all year, and SR 8 from Paxson is usually open from early June to mid-October. The park also is accessible from Anchorage or Fairbanks via the Alaska Railroad; there is daily service from late May to mid-September. Trains run northbound to Fairbanks on Saturday and southbound to Anchorage on Sunday the rest of the year. Charter flights are available from principal airports. Visitors often stay in the year-round community of Healy *(see place listing p. 497),* which is 11 miles from the park entrance.

Denali Park Road, beginning at SR 3 at the park's eastern boundary, runs about 90 miles westward through the park, terminating at a partly abandoned mining town, Kantishna. Only the first 14.8 miles to Savage River are paved, and most of the road is narrow with many sharp curves. It is usually open from early June to mid-September. The George Parks Highway (SR 3) runs along the eastern border of the park and offers sweeping views of the park's alpine scenery from Willow to Nenana.

Private vehicles may be used only on the first 14.8 miles of Denali Park Road unless you have a registered campsite at Teklanika River Campground. Transportation beyond Savage River or to Sanctuary Creek, Igloo Creek and Wonder Lake campgrounds is provided by shuttle buses that operate to Toklat, Wonder Lake and other points in the park.

Fare for the shuttle varies with destination. Fare to Kantishna $64; free (ages 0-15). Fare to Wonder Lake $58.75; free (ages 0-15). Fare to Toklat River $33.50; free (ages 0-15). Fare to Eielson Visitor Center $42.75; free (ages 0-15). Three- and 6-day trip passes are available; prices vary by destination. These fares do not include the park admission fees.

More than half of the shuttle seats can be reserved by telephone and Internet; phone (907) 272-7275 or (800) 622-7275 in advance. The rest of the spaces can be reserved only in person within 2 days of departure; phone (907) 683-9274 for more information. Buses depart approximately every half-hour beginning at 5:15 a.m. from the Wilderness Access Center near the entrance at Milepost 0.5 on Denali Park Road. The bus stops to view wildlife when conditions are safe. Shuttle buses also drop off and pick up passengers along the park road on a space-available basis. The center houses a small theater.

The Denali Visitor Center, Milepost 1.5 on Denali Park Road, has an information desk, exhibits, a 20-minute film, a bookstore and interpretive programs. It is open daily 8-6, mid-May to mid-September. Only accessible by shuttle bus, the Eielson Visitor Center, Milepost 66 on Denali Park Road, houses a small art gallery and offers ranger-led programs. The center is open daily 9-5:30, June 1 to mid-September.

The Murie Science and Learning Center, at Milepost 1.4 on Denali Park Road, is dedicated to research and education about America's eight northernmost national parks and offers field seminars and educational programs. It is open daily 9:30-5; closed major winter holidays. Phone (907) 683-6432.

The Walker Harper Talkeetna Ranger Station, Milepost 100 on George Parks Highway (SR 3), also offers interpretive programs and is open daily 8-5:30, mid-April through Labor Day; Mon.-Fri. 10-4, rest of year. Phone (907) 733-2231.

To camp outside the established campgrounds, stop at the Wilderness Access Center for a back-country permit. Reservations for all campgrounds may be made here.

Sled dog demonstrations are given by rangers at the park kennels, Milepost 3 on Denali Park Road. The 30-minute presentations are offered daily at 10, 2 and 4, June through August; phone ahead for availability. Ranger-naturalists also present various lectures, hikes and other activities daily at various campgrounds. Information about activities is available at the park Visitor Center and ranger stations, or pick up a copy of the park's informational newspaper, *Denali Alpenglow.*

Guided and self-guiding hikes are available along several nature trails with trailheads along the paved portion of the park road. Throughout the rest of the park, hiking is generally cross-country. The Spruce Forest Trail loop takes about 15 minutes, while the Morino Trail takes 30 minutes to complete. Backcountry permits are available from the Backcountry Information Center, adjacent to the Wilderness Access Center. The park offers several ranger-guided hikes. The hikes are free; however, hikers must purchase shuttle bus tickets to reach the various trails that do not originate at the Denali Visitor Center.

Do not feed or disturb wildlife. Grizzly bears in particular can be dangerous; inquire at the Visitor Center about how to avoid close encounters with grizzlies. Firearms must be declared and made inoperative when you enter the park; hunting and shooting are forbidden.

Most fishing is poor in the park; only streams that are free of glacial silt are good fishing spots. No license is required within the national park; the daily creel limit is 10 fish, only two of which may be lake trout. An Alaska fishing license is required in the national preserve areas. Check at a ranger station for further information.

Temperatures during the park season can vary from 40 to 80 degrees Fahrenheit, with an average of 50 to 54 degrees June through August. Daylight generally lasts for more than 18 hours during the summer months.

Morino Grill, a cafeteria-style restaurant, is next to the Denali Visitor Center. A store near the park entrance contains supplies, but no gas is available; the store is open approximately 7 a.m.-9 p.m. during peak season, shorter hours at other times. A gas station north of the park entrance on George Parks Highway (SR 3) is open in the summer. Food and supplies also are available at Riley Creek Campground just inside the park boundaries. *See Recreation Areas Chart.*

ADMISSION , valid for 7 days, is $15 per person; free (ages 0-15).

PETS are permitted in the park only if they are leashed or otherwise physically restrained; they are not allowed on trails, shuttle buses or in the backcountry.

ADDRESS inquiries to the Superintendent, Denali National Park and Preserve, P.O. Box 9, Denali Park, AK 99755; phone (907) 683-9532 or (800) 622-7275 for reservations.

ALASKA CABIN NITE DINNER THEATER is 1.7 mi. n. of the park entrance on George Parks Hwy. (SR 3) at Milepost 239. The theater presents a 1915-style dinner show that highlights Alaska's gold-mining history. A pre-show dinner is served family-style. **Time:** Allow 2 hours minimum. **Hours:** Shows Mon.-Fri. at 5:30 and 7:30 p.m., mid-May to mid-Sept. Phone ahead to confirm schedule. **Cost:** $75; $37.50 (ages 3-15); free (ages 0-2 on adult lap). Reservations are required. **Phone:** (907) 683-8200, or (800) 276-7234 for reservations. [1]

DENALI AIR is 10 mi. s. on George Parks Hwy. (SR 3) at Milepost 229.5. Commentary about history, scenery and topography complements both the 60-70-minute Denali Peak Experience Flight and the 45-minute Denali Express Flight along the Alaska Range and around Denali. **Hours:** Denali Peak Experience Flights depart every even hour daily 8-8 (weather permitting), mid-May to mid-Sept. Denali Express Flights depart daily at noon and 2, mid-May to mid-Sept. **Cost:** Fare $315-$399; $193-$205 (ages 2-12). Reservations are recommended. **Phone:** (907) 683-2261. [GT]

DENALI BACKCOUNTRY ADVENTURE departs from Denali Cabins, Milepost 229, George Parks Hwy. (SR 3), 9 mi. s. of park entrance or from the Alaska Railroad Depot. This narrated bus tour travels along the 95-mile Denali Park Road to Denali Backcountry Lodge in Kantishna. Along the route, the guide points out wildlife such as moose and caribou, and makes stops at various times for photography. The complete trip lasts 13 hours and includes either gold panning or a guided nature walk to Fannie Quigley's historic pioneer cabin. Lunch and snacks are provided.

Allow a full day. **Hours:** Tours depart daily at 6 a.m., early June to mid-Sept. **Cost:** Fee $194 (plus $15 per person park entrance fee). **Phone:** (907) 376-1992 or (877) 376-1992. [GT] [1]

DENALI NATURAL HISTORY TOUR, departing from the Wilderness Access Center, takes visitors on a bus tour across sections of the park where they can enjoy views of the Alaska Range from Denali to Mount Deborah. Driver-guides explain the region's natural history, unusual geological formations and local flora and fauna. A stop at the Wilderness Access Center allows time to view the film "Across Time and Tundra."

Time: Allow 4 hours, 45 minutes minimum. **Hours:** Trips depart daily 5:30-7:30 a.m. and 1:30-3:30, mid-May to mid-Sept. Phone ahead to confirm schedule. **Cost:** Fare (includes park admission and a snack) $100.50; $42.75 (ages 0-15). **Phone:** (907) 272-7275 or (800) 276-7234. [GT]

DENALI SUMMIT FLIGHTS—see Healy p. 497.

DENALI WILDERNESS SAFARIS, at Milepost 216 on George Parks Hwy. (SR 3), offers 3-hour heated jet boat rides or 3-hour sled dog-pulled cart rides to a camp in the Alaskan "bush" country, where locals share their methods of hunting, prospecting and trapping. Gold panning opportunities are presented. Free transportation is provided from all area hotels. **Hours:** Wilderness boat trips and dog sled rides depart daily at 8, 2:30 and 6, mid-May to mid-Sept. **Cost:** Boat fare $129.95; $89.95 (ages 5-12); free (active military with ID). Ages 0-4 are not permitted on jet boat tours. Dog sled $99; $69 (ages 0-12); free (active military with ID). Fees include a snack. Reservations are recommended. **Phone:** (907) 768-2550. [GT]

FLY DENALI departs from the entrance of Denali National Park and Preserve, 224 George Parks Hwy., for scenic flightseeing tours. Complimentary shuttle service is available to and from Healy River Airport. The tour features a 2.5-hour trip around Denali, including a 20-30 minute landing on the Great Gorge of the Ruth Glacier at the Don Sheldon Amphitheatre.

Note: Inquire about weather policies and total weight capacity. **Time:** Allow 3 hours minimum. **Hours:** Tours depart daily at 8:30, noon, 3:15 and 6:15, early May to mid-Sept. **Cost:** Denali Glacier Landing $549; $412 (ages 0-9 weighing less than 100 pounds). Reservations are required. **Phone:** (907) 683-2359, or (877) 770-2359 Sales. [GT]

KANTISHNA EXPERIENCE TOUR departs from local hotels. This bus tour takes visitors along the Gold Rush trails once traveled by pioneer Fannie Quigley to Kantishna. An interpretive park ranger explains in detail the region's geology, flora and fauna as well as the history of Kantishna on the 11- to 12-hour tours. The trip is 92 miles each way. Guests may bring binoculars for a better view of such wildlife as moose, caribou and bears.

Note: Guests are advised to dress in layers. The tour is not recommended for the physically impaired. **Time:** Allow 12 hours minimum. **Hours:** Trips depart daily 6:15-7:15 a.m. from area hotels, early June to mid-Sept. Phone ahead to confirm schedule. **Cost:** Fare (includes park admission, lunch, beverages and snacks) $237.25; $111 (ages 0-15). Reservations are required. **Phone:** (907) 272-7275 or (800) 276-7234. [GT] [1]

TUNDRA WILDERNESS TOURS depart the Wilderness Access Center. Buses travel 63 miles to Stony Hill Overlook, making frequent stops en route for photography. Driver-guides explain in detail the region's geology, flora and fauna on the 7- to 8-hour tour. Binoculars are recommended for spotting moose, caribous, bears and other wildlife. A 52-mile, 4.5-hour Toklat Shoulder Season Tour to Toklat River is available mid- to late May; phone for information.

Inquire about weather policies. **Hours:** Trips depart daily at 7:10 and 1:40, June 1 to mid-Sept. Phone ahead to confirm schedule. **Cost:** Fare (includes park admission and a box lunch) $160.25; $72.75 (ages 0-15). Reservations are recommended. **Phone:** (907) 272-7275 or (800) 276-7234. GT 🍴

RECREATIONAL ACTIVITIES
White-water Rafting

- **Denali Raft Adventures, Inc.,** .5 mi. n. of the park entrance at Milepost 238.6 on George Parks Hwy. (SR 3), offers 2-hour to full-day excursions. **Hours:** Trips depart daily mid-May to mid-Sept.; check-in times vary depending on trip. **Phone:** (907) 683-2234 or (888) 683-2234. GT

- **Explore Denali Rafting** departs from the McKinley Chalet at Milepost 238 on George Parks Hwy. (SR 3) for excursions on the Nenana River. **Hours:** Trips depart daily at 7:30, 1:30 and 6, late May-late Aug.; daily 7:30, 1:30 and 5:30, late Aug. to mid-Sept. **Phone:** (907) 276-7234 or (800) 276-7234. GT

▼ See AAA listing p. 470 ▼

ADVENTURE AWAITS
ALASKA

Alaska is like no other place, epic in scale and experience. From its natural wonders to its rich cultural influences, it will always inspire.

We're here to help you discover your Alaska.

Alaska TOUR & TRAVEL

Request Your Free Tour Planner and Map

TOURS • LODGING • TRANSPORTATION   AlaskaTravel.com   1.800.208.0200

Make the Connection

Find this symbol for places to look, book and save on AAA.com.

DENALI BLUFFS HOTEL   907/683-7000
▼ APPROVED   Hotel. **Address:** Milepost 238.4 Parks Hwy 99755

DENALI CABINS   907/683-2643
▼ APPROVED   Cabin. **Address:** Milepost 229 Parks Hwy 99755

DENALI PRINCESS WILDERNESS LODGE   907/683-2282
▼ THREE DIAMOND   Hotel. **Address:** Milepost 238.5 Parks Hwy 99755

GRANDE DENALI LODGE   907/683-5100
▼ APPROVED   Hotel. **Address:** Milepost 238.2 Parks Hwy 99755

MCKINLEY CHALET RESORT   907/683-6450
▼ APPROVED   Hotel. **Address:** Milepost 238.9 Parks Hwy 99755

MCKINLEY CREEKSIDE CABINS & CAFE   907/683-2277
▼ APPROVED
Cabin

Address: Milepost 224 Parks Hwy 99755 **Location:** Waterfront. 13 mi s; Milepost 224, on SR 3 (Parks Hwy). **Facility:** 48 units, some houses and cabins. 2 stories (no elevator), exterior corridors. **Terms:** check-in 4 pm. **Dining:** Creekside Cafe, see separate listing. **Activities:** lawn sports, picnic facilities.

SAVE 🍴 CALL 🔌 🛜 ✕ 🚫
🔲 📠 💻 / SOME UNITS W ✉

WHERE TO EAT

CANYON STEAKHOUSE   907/683-6460
▼ THREE DIAMOND   American. Casual Dining. **Address:** Milepost 238.9 Parks Hwy 99755

CREEKSIDE CAFE   907/683-2277
▼ APPROVED   American. Casual Dining. **Address:** Milepost 224 Parks Hwy 99755

KING SALMON   907/683-2282
▼ THREE DIAMOND   American. Casual Dining. **Address:** Milepost 238.5 Parks Hwy 99755

MORINO GRILL   907/683-9225
▼ APPROVED   American. Quick Serve. **Address:** Denali Visitor Center 99755

THE PERCH RESTAURANT & BAR   907/683-2523
▼ APPROVED   Regional American. Casual Dining. **Address:** Milepost 224 Parks Hwy 99755

PREY PUB & EATERY AT DENALI CABINS   907/683-2611
▼ APPROVED   American. Casual Dining. **Address:** 229 Parks Hwy 99755

PROSPECTORS PIZZERIA & ALEHOUSE   907/683-7437
▼ APPROVED   American. Casual Dining. **Address:** Milepost 238.9 Parks Hwy 99755

DENALI STATE PARK

MT. MCKINLEY PRINCESS WILDERNESS LODGE
                                                 907/733-2900
▼ THREE DIAMOND   Resort Hotel. **Address:** Milepost 133.1 Parks Hwy 99683

Sit. Stay. Play.

Discover thousands of pet-friendly places to stay, play and dine.
Get insight to guide your decisions. And enter your favorite
photo in the next **AAA Pet Travel Photo Contest***.

Visit AAA.com/PetTravel

Contest entry open to U.S. residents only.

FAIRBANKS (D-6) pop. 31,535, elev. 432'
• Hotels p. 493 • Restaurants p. 494

Fairbanks, near the geographical center of Alaska, is a major visitor center and the northern terminus of the Alaska Railroad. The military, transportation and market nucleus of the Alaskan interior, Fairbanks is a supply point for arctic oil operations and a departure point for airlines statewide.

In 1901 Capt. E.T. Barnette founded a trading post where Fairbanks now stands—a riverboat captain refused to ferry him any farther up the Chena River due to the low water level. Gold was discovered nearby a year later, and the first wave of prospectors flooded up the river. The settlement was named for Charles Warren Fairbanks of Indiana, a U.S. senator who later became vice president to Theodore Roosevelt.

The construction of the Alaska Highway and the influx of the military into Fairbanks heralded a second boom. And in 1968 the discovery of oil in Prudhoe Bay, 390 miles north, triggered a third wave of development.

Fairbanks offers a variety of winter sports and other activities, including aurora viewing, cross-country and downhill skiing, curling, ice hockey and dog mushing. The city's geographical location allows the semiprofessional Alaska Goldpanners team to play its 🔻 Midnight Sun Baseball Game at 10:30 p.m. on June 21 at Growden Memorial Park without using artificial lighting.

The Robert G. White Large Animal Research Station, 2220 Yankovich Rd., is a 134-acre facility offering .25-mile narrated walking tours of its grounds, allowing visitors to observe caribou, musk oxen and reindeer. Tours are conducted Wednesday through Sunday at 10, noon and 2, June-Aug. Phone (907) 474-5724.

Local sightseeing tours to Alaska's arctic zone and other remote places are available from Fairbanks. Using railway cars with skylights, Gray Line of Alaska and Princess Rail Tours offer trips between Anchorage and Fairbanks via Denali National Park and Preserve; phone (907) 479-9660 or (888) 425-1737 for Gray Line Alaska and (800) 426-0500 for Princess Rail Tours. Canoes for trips on the Chena River can be rented from several outfitters.

Interesting drives include visits to Chena Hot Springs and the town of Ester. Abandoned gold dredges can be seen outside of Fairbanks along the roads to Chatanika and Ester. The Alaska Public Lands Information Center, at the Morris Thompson

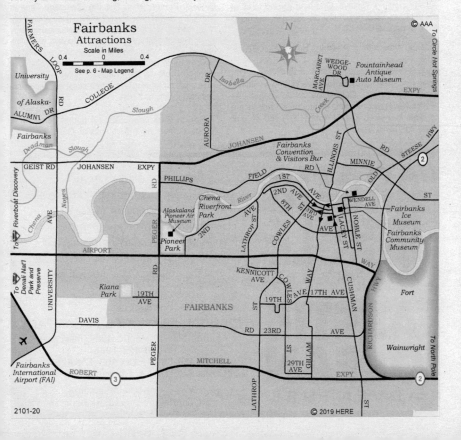

© 2019 HERE

2101-20

Cultural and Visitors Center at 101 Dunkel St., has museum exhibits, shows free movies and offers information about public lands and parks; phone (907) 459-3730 or (866) 869-6887.

Explore Fairbanks: 101 Dunkel St., Suite 111, Fairbanks, AK 99701. **Phone:** (907) 456-5774 or (800) 327-5774. *(See ad p. 491.)*

Self-guiding tours: Information about a historical walking tour is available from the Alaska Public Lands Information Center, at the Morris Thompson Cultural and Visitors Center, 101 Dunkel St.

FOUNTAINHEAD ANTIQUE AUTO MUSEUM is off Johansen Expwy. exit 4 (College Rd.), just w. on College Rd., then .2 mi. n. on Margaret Ave.; the museum is at 212 Wedgewood Dr. on the grounds of the Wedgewood Resort. The museum's collection of more than 85 pristine working condition automobiles, which date from the turn of the 20th century to the late 1930s, includes the only surviving 1920 Argonne; a 1917 Owen-Magnetic M-25 Touring, a gas hybrid; and series of early and rare examples that explain the expanding technical changes.

Other exhibits include historical photographs and vintage clothing displays. One-hour guided tours of the vehicles, 55 of which are displayed at any given time, are offered.

Time: Allow 1 hour minimum. **Hours:** Sun.-Thurs. 10-8, Fri.-Sat. 11-6, mid-May to mid-Sept.; Sun. noon-6, rest of year. **Cost:** $10; $5 (ages 6-12 and Fountainhead Hotel guests). Guided tour prices vary; phone ahead. Reservations and a minimum of 2 people are required for guided tours. **Phone:** (907) 450-2100 or (800) 528-4916. GT

NORTHERN ALASKA TOUR COMPANY departs from the e. ramp of the Fairbanks International Airport. Tours highlight the natural and cultural aspects of Alaska's arctic region. Excursions, which last a full day to multiple days, explore the arctic circle by plane, or bus along the Dalton Highway. Other trips visit the Anaktuvuk Pass, Beaver Village, Brooks Range, Utqiaġvik (Barrow) and the Arctic Ocean. Guides offer insight along the route. **Time:** Allow 1 hour minimum. **Hours:** Tours depart daily, mid-May to mid-Sept.; Mon.-Sat., rest of year. Hours vary by trip. **Cost:** Fare $229-$1,899. Reservations are required. **Phone:** (907) 474-8600 or (800) 474-1986. *(See ad this page.)* GT

PIONEER PARK is at 2300 Airport Way. The pioneer theme park offers four museums; the Kitty Hensley and Wickersham houses, two restored early 20th-century dwellings; the renovated *S.S. Nenana*, one of the largest wooden stern-wheelers ever constructed; Roela's Carousel; and a train that travels and offers unique views of the park. The Mining Valley showcases early mining equipment. The Tanana Valley Railroad Museum operates train rides, houses exhibits including Fairbanks' first steam locomotive and has an area where visitors can see historic locomotives being repaired (Open daily noon-8, Memorial Day-Labor Day). At Pioneer Hall, The Big Stampede Theater highlights paintings by Rusty Heurlin. The Palace Theatre presents Golden Heart Revue, a musical comedy show. Rental bicycles, canoes and kayaks are available. Such activities as miniature golf are provided; bocce courts as well as horseshoe and volleyball areas also are on the premises. Bring a blanket or lawn chair for seating at the free summer concert series held nightly at 7 p.m.

Hours: Park open daily 24 hours, year-round. Vendors open noon-8, Memorial Day-Labor Day.

▼ *See AAA listing this page* ▼

ARCTIC CIRCLE
ADVENTURE®

ARCTIC OCEAN
ADVENTURE®

Experience Alaska's Arctic!

Northern Alaska Tour Company, the pioneers of Arctic Circle touring on Alaska's Dalton Highway, invites you to experience for yourself the legendary hospitality and authentic interpretation of our one-day and overnight Arctic Circle Adventures.

NORTHERN ALASKA TOUR COMPANY
Sharing Alaska's Arctic With The World
1-800-474-1986
907-474-8600 • Fax 907-474-4767
PO Box 82991-AAA, Fairbanks, AK 99708

www.northernalaska.com
adventure@northernalaska.com

Train trips depart every 15 minutes noon-4 and 5-7:45, Memorial Day-Labor Day. Palace Theater show nightly at 8:15. Big Stampede shows are presented daily at 11:30, 1, 2:30 and 4. Big Stampede show is not recommended for children under 13. **Cost:** Park free. Palace Theater show $22; $11 (ages 4-13). Big Stampede show $4; $2 (ages 6-16). Carousel $3. Train ride $2; $1 (ages 0-12 and 65+). A small fee is applicable at several of the attractions and museums. **Phone:** (907) 459-1087, (907) 452-7274 for Palace Theatre, or (907) 456-8579 for Big Stampede Show. GT 🍴 ✂ 🌲

Alaskaland Pioneer Air Museum, in Pioneer Park at 2300 Airport Way, is housed in a gold-domed building and offers an aeronautical collection consisting of 14 intact aircraft, including a Stinson SR-5 Junior and a UH-1 Iroquois "Huey" helicopter, as well as a variety of recovered plane wrecks. A large assortment of flight records, newspaper articles, pilot manuscripts and some 500 photographs details the history of solo aviators, early flight and selected airlines. Such items as engines, propellers, model aircraft and memorabilia also are displayed.

▼ See AAA listing p. 490 ▼

Be inspired by the light of the Aurora Borealis.
Renew your energy under the Midnight Sun.
Experience the warmth of Fairbanks—Alaska's Golden
Heart—and the gateway to Denali, Interior and Arctic
Alaska. Make the Morris Thompson Cultural and Visitors
Center your first stop to planning your Alaskan adventure.

explore
FAIRBANKS
ALASKA

Morris Thompson Cultural and Visitors Center
101 Dunkel Street • Downtown Fairbanks
8am – 9pm Summer • 8am – 5pm Winter

www.explorefairbanks.com
(907) 456-5774
info@explorefairbanks.com

Time: Allow 1 hour minimum. **Hours:** Daily noon-8, mid-May to mid-Sept. **Cost:** $4; free (ages 0-12); $8 (four adults). **Phone:** (907) 451-0037. GT

RIVERBOAT DISCOVERY, departing from a pier on Discovery Rd. off Airport Way, provides 3.5-hour trips on the Chena and Tanana rivers aboard the stern-wheeler *Discovery III*. Guides discuss area wildlife, history, anthropology, geology and customs. Views vary from wilderness to elegant houses, and the trip includes a guided walking tour of the Chena Indian village. **Hours:** Trips depart daily at 9 and 2, mid-May to late Sept. Phone ahead to confirm schedule. **Cost:** Fare $69.95; $42.95 (ages 3-12). Reservations are required. **Phone:**

(907) 479-6673 or (866) 479-6673. *(See ad this page.)* GT

TRANS ARCTIC CIRCLE TREKS is at 3820 University Ave. This tour company offers a variety of guided excursions including day trips to the Arctic Circle and multiday trips to the Arctic Ocean, Brooks Range, Prudhoe Bay and Point Barrow. Visitors on the 1-day tour can enjoy mountain scenery, a walk through alpine tundra and a hands-on Trans-Alaska Pipeline demonstration. Add-on land and air excursions are available.

Hours: One-day tour departs daily June-Aug.; departs 3-5 days per week in May and Sept. Other

▼ *See AAA listing this page* ▼

COME TO FAIRBANKS, ALASKA FOR

adventure

Everyone finds gold, guaranteed.

Cruise the great rivers
of The Last Frontier on
a Sternwheeler

&fortune

Taste the thrill of discovery that drew
thousands of pioneers to Alaska

• Experience pioneer living and
Native culture

• See an Alaskan
bush pilot in action

• Open and closed
decks with restrooms onboard

• Trans Alaska Pipeline viewing

• Gold panning

• Fresh baked cookies
& coffee

• Daily Tours

Reservations and questions

866-479-6673
RiverboatDiscovery.com

866-479-6673
GoldDredge8.com

Gold Dredge 8
FAIRBANKS • ALASKA

▼ *See AAA listing p. 470* ▼

THE BEST OF ALASKA
ALL IN ONE PLACE

VISIT
anchorage
ALASKA

📍 Portage Glacier

tours depart throughout the year. Phone ahead to confirm schedule. **Cost:** Fare for 1-day tour $229. Rates vary according to tour; phone ahead. Reservations are required. **Phone:** (907) 479-5451 or (800) 336-8735. GT

A TASTE OF ALASKA LODGE　907/488-7855
APPROVED　Bed & Breakfast. **Address:** 551 Eberhardt Rd 99712

AURORA BOREALIS LODGE　907/389-2812
APPROVED　Condominium. **Address:** 1906 Ridge Run Rd 99707

BEST WESTERN PLUS CHENA RIVER LODGE FAIRBANKS　907/328-3500
THREE DIAMOND
Hotel

AAA Benefit: Members save up to 15% and earn bonus points!

Address: 1255 Tvsa Way 99709 **Location:** Jct Airport and Sportsman ways, just w on Boat St. **Facility:** 67 units. 3 stories, interior corridors. **Parking:** winter plug-ins. **Terms:** check-in 4 pm. **Activities:** exercise room. **Guest Services:** coin laundry, area transportation.

BEST WESTERN PLUS PIONEER PARK INN　907/479-8080
APPROVED
Hotel

AAA Benefit: Members save up to 15% and earn bonus points!

Address: 1908 Chena Landings Loop Rd 99701 **Location:** From airport, exit Peger Rd, 1 mi n, just e on Phillips Field Rd, then just s. **Facility:** 74 units. 3 stories, interior corridors. **Parking:** winter plug-ins. **Pool:** heated indoor. **Activities:** picnic facilities, exercise room. **Guest Services:** coin laundry, area transportation.

BRIDGEWATER HOTEL DOWNTOWN　907/452-6661
APPROVED
Boutique Contemporary Hotel

Address: 723 1st Ave 99701 **Location:** Just w of Cushman St; downtown. **Facility:** Open year round, this stylish hotel is across from the Chena River and a walking path. A few highlights include a gift shop, smart flat-panel TV and USB ports. Some rooms are compact. 93 units. 5 stories, interior corridors. **Parking:** winter plug-ins. **Terms:** check-in 4 pm. **Guest Services:** coin laundry, area transportation.

Newly renovated boutique hotel in downtown Fairbanks. Walking distance to many points of interest.

CANDLEWOOD SUITES FAIRBANKS　907/328-3200
APPROVED　Extended Stay Hotel. **Address:** 551 Harold Bentley Ave 99701

CHENA HOT SPRINGS RESORT　907/451-8104
APPROVED　Resort Motel. **Address:** MM 56.5 Chena Hot Springs Rd 99711

FAIRBANKS PRINCESS RIVERSIDE LODGE　907/455-4477
THREE DIAMOND　Hotel. **Address:** 4477 Pikes Landing Rd 99709

HAMPTON INN & SUITES BY HILTON FAIRBANKS　907/451-1502
THREE DIAMOND SAVE Hotel. **Address:** 433 Harold Bentley Ave 99701

AAA Benefit: Members save up to 15%!

HOLIDAY INN EXPRESS FAIRBANKS　907/328-1100
THREE DIAMOND
Hotel

Address: 400 Merhar Ave 99701 **Location:** Jct SR 2 (Steese Hwy) and Johansen Expwy, 0.6 mi w, just s at Hunter St. **Facility:** 114 units. 4 stories, interior corridors. **Parking:** winter plug-ins. **Pool:** heated indoor. **Activities:** hot tub, exercise room. **Guest Services:** coin laundry, area transportation. **Featured Amenity:** breakfast buffet.

LA QUINTA INN & SUITES BY WYNDHAM - FAIRBANKS AIRPORT　907/328-6300
THREE DIAMOND Hotel. **Address:** 4920 Dale Rd 99709

MINNIE STREET INN　907/456-1802
APPROVED　Hotel. **Address:** 345 Minnie St 99701

PIKE'S WATERFRONT LODGE　907/456-4500
THREE DIAMOND
Hotel

Address: 1850 Hoselton Rd 99709 **Location:** Waterfront. Jct Airport Way and Hoselton Rd. **Facility:** 208 units, some cabins. 3 stories, interior/exterior corridors. **Parking:** winter plug-ins. **Amenities:** safes. **Dining:** Pike's Landing Restaurant, see separate listing. **Activities:** steamroom, boat dock, miniature golf, lawn sports, trails, exercise room. **Guest Services:** coin laundry, boarding pass kiosk, area transportation. **Featured Amenity:** continental breakfast.

Love the Great Outdoors?
Visit AAA.com/campgrounds

RIVER'S EDGE RESORT
907/474-0286

APPROVED

Cottage

Address: 4200 Boat St 99709 **Location:** Waterfront. Airport Way, just n on Sportsman Way, 0.5 mi w. **Facility:** 94 units, some cottages. 1-2 stories (no elevator), interior/exterior corridors. **Dining:** Chena's Alaskan Grill, see separate listing. **Activities:** trails. **Guest Services:** coin laundry.

RIVER'S EDGE RESORT

Experience authentic Alaska on the banks of the Chena River. First class services and amenities.

SOPHIE STATION SUITES
907/479-3650

APPROVED Extended Stay Hotel. **Address:** 1717 University Ave S 99709

SPRINGHILL SUITES BY MARRIOTT FAIRBANKS
907/451-6552

THREE DIAMOND

Hotel

SPRINGHILL SUITES MARRIOTT

AAA Benefit: Members save 5% or more!

Address: 575 1st Ave 99701 **Location:** Waterfront. Corner of Cushman St and 1st Ave; downtown. Next to the Chena River. **Facility:** 140 units. 6 stories, interior corridors. **Parking:** winter plug-ins. **Dining:** Lavelle's Bistro, see separate listing. **Pool:** heated indoor. **Activities:** hot tub, trails, exercise room. **Guest Services:** valet and coin laundry, boarding pass kiosk, area transportation. **Featured Amenity:** breakfast buffet.

WEDGEWOOD RESORT
907/452-1442

APPROVED Extended Stay Hotel. **Address:** 212 Wedgewood Dr 99701

WESTMARK FAIRBANKS HOTEL & CONFERENCE CENTER
907/456-7722

APPROVED Hotel. **Address:** 813 Noble St 99701

WHERE TO EAT

ALASKA COFFEE ROASTING CO
907/457-5282

APPROVED Coffee/Tea Desserts. Quick Serve. **Address:** 4001 Geist Rd 99709

ALASKA SALMON BAKE
907/452-7274

APPROVED Seafood. Casual Dining. **Address:** 2300 Airport Way 99701

BLUE ROOF BISTRO
907/799-5913

APPROVED American. Quick Serve. **Address:** 13 Timberland Dr 99701

BOBBY'S DOWNTOWN
907/456-3222

APPROVED Greek. Casual Dining. **Address:** 609 2nd Ave 99701

CHENA'S ALASKAN GRILL
907/474-3644

APPROVED Alaskan. Casual Dining. **Address:** 4200 Boat St 99709

THE COOKIE JAR RESTAURANT
907/479-8319

APPROVED American. Casual Dining. **Address:** 1006 Cadillac Ct 99701

EDGEWATER DINING ROOM
907/455-4477

THREE DIAMOND American. Casual Dining. **Address:** 4477 Pikes Landing Rd 99709

GERALDO'S ITALIAN RESTAURANT
907/452-2299

APPROVED Italian. Casual Dining. **Address:** 701 College Rd 99701

HOT LICKS
907/479-7813

APPROVED Desserts. Quick Serve. **Address:** 3453 College Rd 99709

JAZZ BISTRO ON 4TH
907/328-3663

APPROVED Cuban. Casual Dining. **Address:** 527 4th Ave 99701

LAVELLE'S BISTRO
907/450-0555

THREE DIAMOND Regional American. Casual Dining. **Address:** 575 1st Ave 99701

LEMONGRASS THAI RESTAURANT
907/456-2200

APPROVED Thai. Casual Dining. **Address:** 388 Chena Pump Rd, Suite K 99709

LULU'S BREAD & BAGELS
907/374-3804

APPROVED Breads/Pastries. Quick Serve. **Address:** 388 Chena Pump Rd, Suite A 99709

PIKE'S LANDING RESTAURANT
907/479-6500

APPROVED American. Casual Dining. **Address:** 4438 Airport Way 99709

THE PUMP HOUSE RESTAURANT & SALOON
907/479-8452

APPROVED

American Casual Dining $14-$48

AAA Inspector Notes: *Historic.* An authentic former tin pump house used in gold-mining operations, this restaurant is listed on the National Register of Historic Places. The décor exudes a warm Victorian mining era charm. The large deck and glassed-in dining area afford great views of the Chena River. Fresh oysters feature on the menu, as do a variety of Alaskan seafood, steaks and other game meats. It's closed on Mondays during the winter. **Features:** full bar, patio dining, Sunday brunch. **Reservations:** suggested. **Address:** 796 Chena Pump Rd 99708 **Location:** Jct Parks Hwy and Geist Rd, just e to Chena Pump Rd, 1.3 mi s.

THAI HOUSE RESTAURANT
907/452-6123

APPROVED Thai. Casual Dining. **Address:** 412 5th Ave 99701

THE TURTLE CLUB
907/457-3883

APPROVED American. Casual Dining. **Address:** 2098 Old Steese Hwy 99712

WOLF RUN RESTAURANT
907/458-0636

APPROVED American. Casual Dining. **Address:** 3360 Wolf Run 99709

🔗 **AAA.com/maps—**

Dream, plan, go with

AAA travel planning tools

GATES OF THE ARCTIC NATIONAL PARK AND PRESERVE (B-5)

Elevations in the park and preserve range from 300 ft. along the Kobuk River to 8,510 ft. at Mount Igikpak. Refer to AAA maps for additional elevation information.

Lying north of the Arctic Circle, Gates of the Arctic National Park and Preserve's 8.5 million acres features a raw, austere landscape of sparse vegetation and jagged spires. The rocky spine of the Brooks Range forms the park's backbone, and a boreal forest, or taiga, of spruce, birch and poplar meets the almost treeless tundra that rolls uninterrupted to the Arctic Ocean.

Despite being four times the size of Yellowstone National Park, Gates of the Arctic is a meager larder for the caribou, moose, wolves and bears that roam the park in search of food. Fortunately much of their arctic range is protected, as Gates of the Arctic is joined on either side by Noatak National Preserve and nearby Arctic National Wildlife Refuge.

It was a forester on leave, Bob Marshall, who, in exploring this uncharted region in the late 1930s, christened this land Gates of the Arctic. The term both describes and evokes the grandeur of this wilderness—the soaring immensity of sky and mountains, the burst of wildflowers in summer and the cyclical abundance of wildlife.

But as Marshall remarked, the greatest pleasure is its undeveloped and wild character, which gives the visitor the sense of being the first to visit the tundra foothills or one of the park's nameless peaks. Today a good way to enjoy the park is to follow Marshall's example and hike the park's rugged terrain, which offers challenging backpacking. A popular alternative is to canoe or raft the network of rivers and lakes.

Most visitors use various air charter services from Fairbanks and Bettles Field to reach the park's interior. The Dalton Highway skirts the park's eastern edge and is the only road that approaches the park. Because of Gates of the Arctic's fragile ecology, there are no park facilities, trails or campgrounds within the park.

Bettles Ranger Station and Visitor Center open daily 8-5, mid-June through Sept. 30; Mon.-Fri. 1-5, rest of year. For trip planning assistance and a list of outfitters, guides and air taxi operators, write Gates of the Arctic National Park and Preserve, P.O. Box 30, Bettles, AK 99726; phone (907) 692-5494. *See Recreation Areas Chart.*

GIRDWOOD (C-11) elev. 23'

Initially called Glacier City, Girdwood was established at the turn of the 20th century as a gold mining town. The community prospered until mine closures in the 1930s reduced it to a virtual ghost town. Misfortune struck again when the 1964 Good Friday earthquake caused massive destruction along the coast, forcing residents to move the town

2.5 miles inland to its present location. Today Girdwood thrives as a year-round recreation destination.

Girdwood is on Turnagain Arm, a fjord carved by glaciers and known for its dramatic bore tides, which can be 6 feet high and travel at speeds of up to 15 miles an hour. The town also is located at the base of 3,939-foot Mount Alyeska; a 60-passenger tramway ascends to the 2,300-foot level and offers a panorama of the valley and Turnagain Arm.

RECREATIONAL ACTIVITIES

Skiing

* **Alyeska Resort and Ski Area** is on SR 1 (Seward Hwy.). Other activities are offered. **Hours:** Mid-Nov. to mid-Apr., weather permitting. **Phone:** (907) 754-2111.

THE HOTEL ALYESKA   907/754-1111

 THREE DIAMOND   **Address:** 1000 Arlberg Ave 99587
Resort Hotel   **Location:** SR 1 (Seward Hwy), 3 mi n on Alyeska Blvd, 1 mi e. Located in a quiet area. **Facility:** Enjoy a stunning mountain setting as this hotel sits at the base of Mt. Alyeska surrounded by seven glaciers. Throughout the year, this resort offers more recreational activities than you can imagine. 303 units. 8 stories, interior corridors. **Parking:** on-site and valet. **Terms:** check-in 4 pm. **Amenities:** safes. **Dining:** 7 restaurants, also, Sakura Asian Bistro, Seven Glaciers Restaurant, see separate listings. **Pool:** heated indoor. **Activities:** sauna, hot tub, downhill & cross country skiing, snowboarding, ice skating, recreation programs, bicycles, trails, exercise room, spa. **Guest Services:** valet laundry, boarding pass kiosk, area transportation. *(See ad p. 480.)*

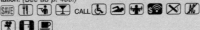

WHERE TO EAT

DOUBLE MUSKY INN   907/783-2822

 APPROVED   Regional Cajun. Casual Dining. **Address:** Milepost 0.3 (Crow Creek Rd) 99587

GIRDWOOD PICNIC CLUB   907/754-3161

 APPROVED   Sandwiches Breakfast. Casual Dining. **Address:** 194 Hightower Rd 99587

SAKURA ASIAN BISTRO   907/754-1111

 THREE DIAMOND   **AAA Inspector Notes:** This restaurant
Asian   makes the most of its cozy space with
Casual Dining   seating at the sushi bar and family-style
$12-$39   at long granite tables. The temptations are endless—fresh white king salmon, black cod, eel, octopus or king crab presented as sushi, sashimi, nigiri or maki. Bento box meals also are available. For those who may want their fish cooked, the chef expertly grills your choice for a mouthwatering meal. **Features:** full bar. **Address:** 1000 Arlberg Ave 99587 **Location:** SR 1 (Seward Hwy), 3 mi n on Alyeska Blvd, 1 mi e; in The Hotel Alyeska. **Parking:** on-site and valet. D CALL

🔗 **Save on travel, shopping and more: AAA.com/discounts**

SEVEN GLACIERS RESTAURANT 907/754-2237

FOUR DIAMOND

Regional American Fine Dining $29-$75

AAA Inspector Notes: This phenomenal mountaintop eatery is accessible by an aerial tram from the hotel. The menu centers on creative Alaskan and West Coast preparations such as seafood, beef, dry-aged pork chops, exotic game and a nightly chef's tasting menu. The crab cakes and scallop bisque are extraordinary. The wow factor begins the moment the elevator doors open to the Northern Lights display on the reception desk and continues while you dine surrounded by the spectacular, panoramic view of the seven glaciers. Features: full bar. Reservations: suggested. Address: 1000 Arlberg Ave 99587 Location: SR 1 (Seward Hwy), 3 mi n on Alyeska Blvd, 1 mi e; in The Hotel Alyeska. Parking: on-site and valet. *(See ad p. 480.)*

D CALL

GLACIER BAY NATIONAL PARK AND PRESERVE (G-9)

Elevations in the park and preserve range from sea level at Glacier Bay to 15,320 ft. at Mount Fairweather. Refer to AAA maps for additional elevation information.

Stretching northward from Cross Sound to the Canadian border, Glacier Bay National Park is one of the most scenic spots in Alaska. In this 3,283,168-acre park, blue-white glaciers flow from the snow-clad peaks of the Fairweather Range to fiord-like inlets.

The park features 15,320-foot Mount Fairweather and Glacier Bay. The bay, about 65 miles long and 2.5 to 10 miles wide, was filled with ice 5,000 feet thick as recently as 200 years ago. The park contains some of the world's most impressive tidewater glaciers. Icebergs that crack off, or calve, from the nearly vertical ice cliffs dot the waters of the upper bay. Boaters are likely to encounter numerous harbor seals and an occasional whale.

This spectacular region is accessible only by plane, boat or cruise ship. Alaska Airlines offers flights from Juneau daily late May through early September. A 10-mile road connects the park headquarters with the small community of Gustavus, where charter vessels and air and boat service to Juneau are available.

An 8-hour boat tour of the bay departs at 7:30 a.m. from Glacier Bay Lodge May 23-Sept. 7 (weather permitting). Phone ahead for schedule and rates. Reservations are strongly recommended; phone (888) 229-8687. Free guided walks are offered daily at 1:30 (also Fri. at 10:30), late May through early September.

Due to concern for the endangered humpback whale, permits are required from June through August for private vessels to enter Glacier Bay. An Alaska fishing license is required for fishing. Boaters should contact the National Park Service for current regulations; phone (907) 697-2627. A visitor center for boaters and campers, at head of the public-use dock in Bartlett Cove, open daily 7-7, June-Aug.; daily 8-5, in May and Sept. Phone (907) 697-2627.

Glacier Bay National Park Visitor Center, in Glacier Bay Lodge, open daily 11-8, late May-early Sept. Phone (907) 697-2661.

For further information about the park contact the Superintendent, Glacier Bay National Park and Preserve, P.O. Box 140, Gustavus, AK 99826; phone (907) 697-2230. *See Recreation Areas Chart.*

GUSTAVUS pop. 442

ANNIE MAE LODGE AT GLACIER BAY 907/697-2346
APPROVED Country Inn. Address: 2 Grandpa's Farm Rd 99826

GLACIER BAY LODGE 907/697-4000
APPROVED Motel. Address: 179 Bartlett Cove Rd 99826

GLACIER BAY'S BEAR TRACK INN 907/697-3017
THREE DIAMOND Country Inn. Address: 5021 Rink Creek Rd 99826

WHERE TO EAT

FAIRWEATHER DINING ROOM 907/697-4000
APPROVED American. Casual Dining. Address: 179 Bartlett Cove 99826

HAINES (G-10) pop. 1,713, elev. 66'

Haines lies in a spectacular setting on the Chilkat Peninsula near the northern end of Lynn Canal between the waters of the Inside Passage and the Chilkat River. The Alaska Marine Highway links Haines with Prince Rupert, British Columbia, and Bellingham, Wash., and enables visitors to connect with the Alaska Highway at Haines Junction, Milepost 1016, via SRs 7 and 4. For information about the Alaska Marine Highway phone (907) 465-3941 or (800) 642-0066.

The 40-acre Kroschel Wildlife Center, 27 miles north on scenic Haines Highway, is home to reindeer, wolverines, bears, falcons and other native species. Reservations are required for tours; phone (907) 767-5464.

Nearby, from late October through February the 48,000-acre Chilkat Bald Eagle Preserve, between Mileposts 9 and 31 on Haines Highway, harbors one of the largest congregations of bald eagles in the world. More than 3,500 of the birds gather to feed on the salmon in the Chilkat River; sometimes as many as 30 eagles roost in a tree during this time. Use roadside pull-offs for viewing; stopping on the road is prohibited. Tour information is available at Haines Convention & Visitors Bureau.

Other interesting drives near Haines include Lutak Road, leading to Chilkoot Lake, and Mud Bay Road, which passes Pyramid Harbor and an old cannery with its salmon boats before approaching Chilkat State Park *(see Recreation Areas Chart)*. Davidson and Rainbow glaciers also are visible from this route.

Buildings that once comprised Fort William H. Seward, the site of the first permanent Army post in Alaska, have been restored and contain several inns, private residences and galleries. A historic area at the south end of Haines Highway, the fort also contains a replica of a tribal house. The old hospital houses carvers who use traditional Tlingit Indian methods. Phone (907) 766-2234 for fort information.

Fjord Express, (800) 320-0146, and Haines-Skagway Fast Ferry, (907) 766-2100 or (888) 766-2103, provide efficient transportation between Haines, Skagway and Juneau.

Haines Convention & Visitors Bureau: 122 Second Ave., P.O. Box 530, Haines, AK 99827. **Phone:** (907) 766-2234 or (800) 458-3579.

Self-guiding tours: Brochures featuring walking tours of Haines and Fort William H. Seward are available from Haines Convention & Visitors Bureau and Hotel Halsingland.

ASPEN SUITES HOTEL - HAINES 907/766-2211
▼ APPROVED Extended Stay Contemporary Hotel. **Address:** 409 Main St 99827

CAPTAIN'S CHOICE MOTEL 907/766-3111
▼ APPROVED Motel. **Address:** 108 2nd Ave N 99827

WHERE TO EAT

CHILKAT RESTAURANT & BAKERY 907/766-3653
▼ APPROVED American. Casual Dining. **Address:** 25 5th Ave 99827

LIGHTHOUSE RESTAURANT 907/766-2442
▼ APPROVED
American Casual Dining $8-$34
AAA Inspector Notes: Overlooking the boat harbor marina, guests can dine in a casual setting and watch the ferry and cruise ships come in. Fresh seafood is available in season. The rest of the year diners can enjoy great burgers and sandwiches. **Features:** full bar. **Address:** 101 N Front St 99827 **Location:** Waterfront; next to marina. L D X

RUSTY COMPASS COFFEEHOUSE 907/766-2770
▼ APPROVED Sandwiches Soup. Quick Serve. **Address:** 116 Main St, Suite 928 99827

HEALY (B-11) pop. 1,021

This small community in the interior of Alaska originated from what was once a mining and hunting camp circa 1904. Many of the current residents still work in the nearby Usibelli Coal Mine. Recreational opportunities range from hiking in summer to dog sledding in winter.

Denali Chamber of Commerce: Mile .4 Healy Spur Rd., P.O Box 437, Healy, AK 99743. **Phone:** (907) 683-4636.

DENALI SUMMIT FLIGHTS depart from Healy River Airport near Denali National Park and Preserve. Passengers are treated to views of Denali National Park and Preserve, and the flights are oxygen-equipped to aim for the 21,000-foot summit of Denali. Flights from Fairbanks to Denali National Park and Preserve are available in winter. **Time:**

Allow 2 hours minimum. **Hours:** Daily 6 a.m.-midnight, mid-May to mid-Sept.; 9-5, rest of year (weather permitting). **Cost:** Fare $429; other tours are available. **Phone:** (907) 474-8600 or (800) 474-1986. GT

RECREATIONAL ACTIVITIES
Dog Sledding
- **Dog Sledding Tours at EarthSong Lodge** is on Mile Post 4.0 Stampede Rd. Other activities are offered. **Hours:** Nov.-Mar., weather permitting. Phone ahead to confirm schedule. **Phone:** (907) 683-2863. GT

DENALI DOME HOME BED & BREAKFAST 907/683-1239
▼ THREE DIAMOND Bed & Breakfast. **Address:** 137 Healy Spur Rd 99743

DENALI LAKEVIEW INN 907/683-4035
▼ APPROVED Bed & Breakfast. **Address:** Milepost 1.2 Otto Lake Rd 99743

HEALY HEIGHTS FAMILY CABINS 907/683-2639
▼ APPROVED Cabin. **Address:** Hill Top Rd 99743

WHERE TO EAT

BLACK DIAMOND GRILL 907/683-4653
▼ APPROVED American. Casual Dining. **Address:** Otto Lake Rd 99743

HOMER (D-10) pop. 5,003, elev. 67'
• Hotels p. 498 • Restaurants p. 498

Homer Pennock landed a party of gold and coal prospectors in the schooner *Excelsior* in 1896 and established Homer. Gold was not found, but an abundance of coal was and the settlement remained.

Healthy fishing and tourism industries support Homer's economy. Kachemak Bay, a 30-mile arm of lower Cook Inlet, provides a usually ice-free deep-water harbor for Homer. A small boat harbor has launching facilities and charter boats. Charter planes are available in town for hunting, fishing, wildlife viewing and sightseeing expeditions. Cross-country skiing is popular in winter. The city is linked by daily air service with Anchorage and once a month in the summer with Juneau, and by the Alaska Marine Highway with Kodiak and Seldovia.

Skyline Drive, accessible from West and East Hill roads, follows the rim of the plateau behind the town and offers access to ski slopes and views of the bay, Homer Spit and the Kenai Mountains. Chartered bush flights afford panoramas of the bay, open coal seams and Harding Icefield to the southeast.

Homer Chamber of Commerce: 201 Sterling Hwy., Homer, AK 99603. **Phone:** (907) 235-7740.

ALASKA ISLANDS & OCEAN VISITOR CENTER is at 95 Sterling Hwy. The center presents an overview of the area through interpretive exhibits about Kachemak Bay; local estuaries; research ships; and the seabird and marine inhabitants of the Alaska Maritime National Wildlife Refuge. An outdoor nature trail links the 60-acre site with Bishop's Beach Park on Kachemak Bay. Naturalist-led tours are offered, and a short movie about the Aleutian Islands is shown.

Time: Allow 2 hours minimum. **Hours:** Daily 9-5, Memorial Day-Labor Day; Tues.-Sat. noon-5, rest of year. Closed major holidays. **Cost:** Free. **Phone:** (907) 235-6961. **GT**

SMOKEY BAY AIR is at 2100 Kachemak Dr. This 5-hour excursion will take you to Katmai National Park or Lake Clark National Park, depending on bear activity and weather restrictions. En route to the bear-viewing beach, you can see glaciers, active volcanoes and wilderness. **Note:** Passengers should dress in warm clothing layers and bring gloves, hats, rain gear and snacks to eat during the flight. Passengers should be able to walk unassisted up to 5 miles on uneven, moderate terrain. **Time:** Allow 5 hours minimum. **Hours:** Bear viewing tours depart twice daily (departure times vary), late May to mid-September (weather permitting). The schedule is tide dependent for beach landing. Additional glacier and volcano flightseeing tours are available. Phone ahead to confirm schedule. **Cost:** Bear viewing experience $625 (2-person minimum). Children ages 0-6 are not permitted on the tour. **Phone:** (907) 235-1511 or (888) 482-1511.

RECREATIONAL ACTIVITIES
Fishing
- **Homer Ocean Charters** is at Cannery Row boardwalk on Homer Spit Rd. Kayak and hiking trips also are available. **Hours:** Trips depart daily by appointment, May-Sept. **Phone:** (907) 235-6212 or (800) 426-6212. **GT**

ASPEN SUITES HOTEL HOMER   907/235-2351
APPROVED Extended Stay Contemporary Hotel. **Address:** 91 Sterling Hwy 99603

BEST WESTERN BIDARKA INN   907/235-8148
APPROVED
Hotel

Best Western. **AAA Benefit:** Members save up to 15% and earn bonus points!

Address: 575 Sterling Hwy 99603 **Location:** Just n of Pioneer Ave on SR 1 (Sterling Hwy). **Facility:** 74 units. 2 stories (no elevator), interior/exterior corridors. **Parking:** winter plug-ins. **Terms:** check-in 4 pm. **Activities:** exercise room. **Guest Services:** coin laundry, area transportation. **Featured Amenity:** breakfast buffet.

LAND'S END RESORT   907/235-0400
APPROVED Hotel. **Address:** 4786 Homer Spit Rd 99603

PIONEER INN   907/235-5670
APPROVED Motel. **Address:** 244 W Pioneer Ave 99603

THE BAGEL SHOP   907/299-2099
APPROVED Sandwiches Coffee/Tea. Quick Serve. **Address:** 3745 E End Rd 99603

CAFE CUPS   907/235-8330
THREE DIAMOND American. Fine Dining. **Address:** 162 W Pioneer Ave 99603

CAPTAIN PATTIE'S FISH HOUSE   907/235-5135
APPROVED Seafood. Casual Dining. **Address:** 4241 Homer Spit Rd 99603

THE CHART ROOM RESTAURANT & LOUNGE   970/235-0406
APPROVED American. Casual Dining. **Address:** 4786 Homer Spit Rd 99603

COSMIC KITCHEN   907/235-6355
APPROVED Mexican. Quick Serve. **Address:** 510 E Pioneer Ave 99603

DON JOSE'S MEXICAN RESTAURANT & CANTINA
          907/235-7963
APPROVED Mexican. Casual Dining. **Address:** 127 W Pioneer Ave 99603

DUNCAN HOUSE DINER   907/235-5344
APPROVED Breakfast Sandwiches. Casual Dining. **Address:** 125 E Pioneer Ave 99603

FAT OLIVES RESTAURANT   907/235-8488
APPROVED Pizza Sandwiches. Casual Dining. **Address:** 276 Ohlson Ln 99603

FRESH SOURDOUGH EXPRESS BAKERY & CAFE
          907/235-7571
APPROVED Natural/Organic Sandwiches. Casual Dining. **Address:** 1316 Ocean Dr 99603

LA BALEINE CAFE   907/299-6672
APPROVED Sandwiches Soup. Casual Dining. **Address:** 4460 Homer Spit Rd, Suite A 99603

LITTLE MERMAID BISTRO   907/399-9900
APPROVED American. Casual Dining. **Address:** 4246 Homer Spit Rd 99603

TWO SISTERS BAKERY   907/235-2280
APPROVED American. Casual Dining. **Address:** 233 E Bunnell Ave 99603

JUNEAU (G-10) pop. 31,275, elev. 12'
• Hotels p. 502 • Restaurants p. 502

Juneau, Alaska's capital city, lies along the beautiful Gastineau Channel at the foot of snowcapped mounts Roberts and Juneau. The borough of Juneau covers 3,108 square miles of towering mountains, islands, saltwater bays, forested valleys and residential flatlands. Its road system extends from Thane, 6 miles southeast of downtown, northwest to Echo Cove at Milepost 40.2 on the Glacier Highway. The city is accessible by air or by sea.

When Joe Juneau and Richard Harris discovered gold in 1880, they started the first rush in American Alaska. At one time the Alaska-Juneau and

Treadwell mines were producing about 20,000 tons of ore daily. Not until 1944, when the low price of gold and the high cost of extraction rendered it impractical, did mining operations cease.

The Alaska State Capitol offers free 30-minute guided tours mid-May to mid-September; the immense building lies between 4th and 5th streets and Main and Seward streets. The State Office Building, one block west of the capitol at 333 Willoughby Ave., contains a century-old totem pole and a Kimball Theatre pipe organ equipped with such accessories as a glockenspiel, sleigh bells and bird whistles. Free concerts are held Friday at noon May through September in the eighth-floor atrium. Also on the eighth floor, a terrace affords panoramas of the harbor and the surrounding mountains.

Impromptu, informal tours of one of the oldest churches in southeastern Alaska are available in summer. Built in 1894, St. Nicholas Russian Orthodox Church is at Fifth and Gold streets; inquire at the church gift shop, or phone (907) 586-1023. The Shrine of St. Thérèse, near Milepost 23 on the Glacier Highway, is a stone chapel on an island connected to shore by a gravel causeway; phone (907) 586-2227.

There are many ways to tour Juneau. Nearby hiking trails, which vary in length and difficulty, lead to fishing spots, scenic mountain areas, old mine ruins and points near Mendenhall Glacier. Bus tours circle points of interest in Juneau and visit Mendenhall Glacier and the log Chapel-by-the-Lake at Auke Lake. Tours depart from the cruise ship docks during the summer. Visitors also can charter boats for sightseeing or fishing.

A good way to see the ice field is to take a charter flight. Companies that offer flightseeing tours from Juneau are Alaska Fly 'n' Fish Charters, (907) 790-2120; Alaska Seaplane Service, (907) 789-3331; Ward Air, (907) 789-9150; and Wings of Alaska, (907) 789-0790. Helicopter tours, float trips, gold-panning excursions and several tours of nearby and more distant points of interest are available through Gray Line of Alaska, (907) 364-7234 or (888) 425-1737; and Princess Rail Tours, (800) 426-0500.

Travel Juneau: 800 Glacier Ave., Suite 201, Juneau, AK 99801. **Phone:** (907) 586-2201 or (888) 586-2201.

Self-guiding tours: Free walking tour maps of the historical and governmental districts are available at the Travel Juneau office.

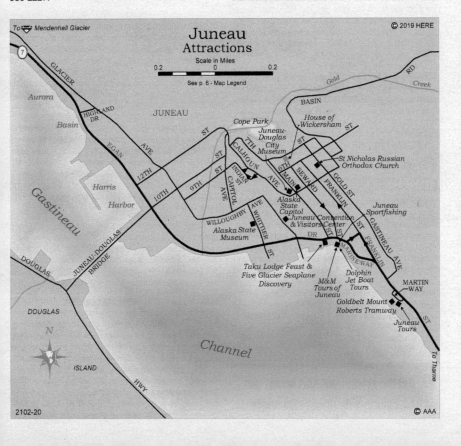

ALASKA STATE MUSEUM, w. of Egan Dr. at 395 Whittier St., chronicles the state's history and preserves and exhibits Tlingit and Athabascan Indian, Eskimo and Aleut culture. There are wildlife, timber, maritime and mining displays; Russian-American historical exhibits; and fine art.

Time: Allow 1 hour minimum. **Hours:** Daily 9-5 (also first Fri. 5-7 p.m.), mid-May to late Sept.; Tues.-Sat. 10-4, rest of year. Closed major holidays. **Cost:** Mid-May to late Sept. $12; $11 (ages 65+); free (ages 0-18 and active military with ID). Rest of year $7; $6 (ages 65+); free (ages 0-18, active military with ID and to all first Fri. of the month 5-7). Admission and schedule may vary; phone ahead. **Phone:** (907) 465-2901. ⊺⊺

DOLPHIN JET BOAT TOURS provides pick-up downtown at the tram parking area. Two-hour tours on a jet boat offer the opportunity to view humpback and orcas, porpoises, sea lions, seals and eagles. Other tours are available. **Hours:** Tours depart daily at various times, May-Sept. **Cost:** Fare (includes beverages and snacks) $95-$140. Phone ahead to confirm fare and schedule. Reservations are recommended. **Phone:** (907) 463-3422 or (800) 719-3422. GT

ERA HELICOPTERS FLIGHTSEEING TOURS depart from the North Douglas Heliport. Narrated, 1-hour tours (with 30 minutes of flight time) offer views of the capital city, the pristine Alaskan backcountry and four glaciers in the Juneau Icefield. Highlights include a 25-minute glacier landing to explore the blue ice. A 95-minute tour (with 30 minutes in the air) visits a dog sled camp on the Norris Glacier where passengers learn hands-on how to mush a team of dogs across a snow-capped glacier. **Note:** Weight restrictions apply. **Time:** Allow 2 hours minimum. **Hours:** Daily 8-5, May-Sept. **Cost:** Fare $350-$750. Flights require a minimum of four passengers. **Phone:** (907) 586-2030 or (800) 843-1947. GT

GLACIER GARDENS RAINFOREST ADVENTURE is at 7600 Glacier Hwy. A motorized shuttle takes passengers on a guided tour up Thunder Mountain through temperate botanical gardens nestled in a lush Alaskan rain forest. Guests travel past streams, ponds, waterfalls and such flora as rhododendrons, Japanese maples, ferns, and upside-down Flower Tower planters, which are inverted Sitka spruce and Western hemlock trees with various flowers planted in the root ball of the trees. A scenic overlook, 600 feet above sea level offers a spectacular view of downtown Juneau, the Taku Inlet, Douglas Island, Chilkat Mountains, the Mendenhall Valley and Mendenhall State Game refuge. **Time:** Allow 1 hour minimum. **Hours:** Daily 9-6, May-Sept. **Cost:** $26.95; $17.95 (ages 6-12). **Phone:** (907) 790-3377. GT

⊘ **Get the scoop from AAA inspectors:**

AAA.com/travelguides/restaurants

GOLDBELT MOUNT ROBERTS TRAMWAY, 490 S. Franklin St. on the cruise ship dock, offers a 5-minute ride to the 1,800-foot level of Mount Roberts. At the top, visitors can stop at the nature center, view native and historical artwork, see a live bald eagle displayed by the Juneau Raptor Center, take wildlife or nature walks in a rainforest and alpine meadow and view the spectacular scenery, including the Chilkat Mountains and Gastineau Channel. Common wildlife sightings from the outlooks include marmots, ravens, eagles, deer, mountain goats, black bear and a variety of songbirds.

"Seeing Daylight," a movie about Alaska's native Tlingit, is presented in the Chilkat Theater. Entertainment and demonstrations are offered. **Time:** Allow 1 hour, 30 minutes minimum. **Hours:** Tues.-Sun. 8 a.m.-9 p.m., Mon. 11-9, May-Sept. Phone ahead to confirm schedule. **Cost:** Fare $35; $18 (ages 3-12). **Phone:** (907) 463-3412 or (888) 461-8726. **(See ad p. 501.)** ⊺⊺

JUNEAU TOURS depart from the parking lot adjacent to the Mt. Roberts Tramway at 490 S. Franklin St.; other tours depart from the downtown cruise ship docking area (transportation is provided). On whale-watching tours, you may spot humpback whales and other wildlife including sea lions, black bears and bald eagles. The fully narrated 1.75-hour City Trolley and Hatchery Tour begins in historic downtown Juneau, passes the state capitol and governor's mansion, then travels to Douglas Island and Red Dog Saloon. A 45-minute narrated trolley tour of downtown Juneau is available. The company also offers a shuttle to and from Mendenhall Glacier; 3-, 4.5-, 5- and 6.5-hour whale-watching tours; 2.5- and 3.5-hour airboat and helicopter tours; 2.5-hour motor coach tours; 1- and 3-hour seaplane tours; and 1.5-hour dog sled tours.

Time: Allow 45 minutes minimum. **Hours:** Tours depart daily late-Apr. to Sept. Phone ahead to confirm schedule. **Cost:** Motor coach and trolley tours $30-$60; $25-$55 (ages 3-12); whale-watching tours $115-$169; $100-$159 (ages 3-12). Additional tours are available. **Phone:** (907) 523-6095.

MACAULAY SALMON HATCHERY is at 2697 Channel Dr. During 15- to 20-minute presentations, tour guides explain hatchery processes, beginning with the imprinting of young salmon to ensure a return at the end of their lifespan and concluding with egg retrieval. In May-June, visitors may observe the juvenile salmon pre-release; from mid-June through October, the returning salmon may be seen in their outdoor holding tanks where they are separated and prepared for egg harvesting. Indoor aquariums contain more than 100 species of southeast Alaska sea life, including anemones, crabs and octopi. Visitors may feel such animals as starfish in touch tanks.

Time: Allow 30 minutes minimum. **Hours:** Mon.-Fri. 10-6, Sat.-Sun. 10-5, May-Sept.; by appointment rest of year. **Cost:** $5; $3 (ages 2-12). **Phone:** (907) 463-4810. GT

MENDENHALL GLACIER, 13 mi. n.w. via SR 7 and Mendenhall Loop Rd., is an impressive river of blue ice, 13 miles long and 1.5 miles wide at its widest point. The glacier is fed by the 1,500-square-mile Juneau Icefield, part of the Tongass National Forest *(see place listing p. 516)*.

Trails on either side of the glacial valley afford scenic views. To the east are Mendenhall Lake and Nugget Creek Falls; the west trail ascends above the glacier. Camping and picnic facilities are available at Mendenhall Lake. An easily traversable .5-mile nature trail begins near the visitor center; brochures are available.

The Steep Creek viewing platform near the visitor center parking lot is a good vantage point from which to see spawning sockeye salmon mid-July through mid-September. The salmon run attracts bald eagles and black bears mid-September through November. **Hours:** Trails open daily 6 a.m.-midnight.

Mendenhall Glacier Visitor Center, at the end of Glacial Spur Rd., contains a model depicting glacier dynamics, dioramas and display cases that interpret five evolving ecosystems at the glacier and a naturalistic salmon-filled stream that tumbles over rocks. A film is shown three times every hour during the summer, otherwise by request. Interpretive talks and nature hikes also are offered. **Hours:** Daily 8-7:30, May-Sept.; Fri.-Sun. 10-4, Oct.-Mar. Closed winter holidays. **Cost:** $5 (May-Sept.); free (ages 0-15 and Oct.-Mar.). **Phone:** (907) 789-0097 or (907) 789-6640. GT

TAKU LODGE FEAST & FIVE GLACIER SEA-PLANE DISCOVERY departs from the wharf near the cruise ship docks. A Wings Airways floatplane takes passengers to a 1923 fishing and hunting lodge in the Taku River Valley for a salmon feast. Aerial views include mountains, Taku Inlet, waterfalls and five glaciers. Walking trails explore the area surrounding the historic lodge, which is across the river from the Hole-in-the-Wall Glacier. **Time:** Allow 3 hours minimum. **Hours:** Trips depart daily, May 1-late Sept. Phone ahead to confirm schedule. **Cost:** Fare $320; $275 (ages 2-11); free (ages 0-1 on lap). Reservations are recommended. **Phone:** (907) 586-6275. GT

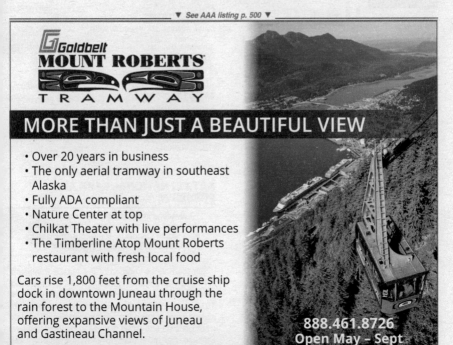

ASPEN SUITES HOTEL JUNEAU   907/500-7700

THREE DIAMOND

Extended Stay Contemporary Hotel

Address: 8400 Airport Blvd 99801 **Location:** Just e on Yandukin Dr, just n on Crest St, just e. **Facility:** 78 efficiencies. 3 stories, interior corridors. **Parking:** winter plug-ins. **Activities:** exercise room. **Guest Services:** coin laundry.

BARANOF HOTEL, BW SIGNATURE COLLECTION
907/586-2660

APPROVED SAVE Hotel. **Address:** 127 N Franklin St 99801

AAA Benefit: Members save up to 15% and earn bonus points!

BEST WESTERN COUNTRY LANE INN   907/789-5005

APPROVED

Motel

Best Western. **AAA Benefit:** Members save up to 15% and earn bonus points!

Address: 9300 Glacier Hwy 99801 **Location:** Just e off Egan Dr. **Facility:** 55 units. 2 stories (no elevator), exterior corridors. **Parking:** winter plug-ins. **Guest Services:** valet and coin laundry, area transportation. **Featured Amenity:** full hot breakfast.

BEST WESTERN GRANDMA'S FEATHER BED
907/789-5567

THREE DIAMOND

Country Inn

Best Western. **AAA Benefit:** Members save up to 15% and earn bonus points!

Address: 2358 Mendenhall Loop Rd 99801 **Location:** Just e off Egan Dr. **Facility:** What used to be a restaurant has been converted into this country inn. The historic charms carries over to the guest rooms which feature modern amenities. Outdoor activities and shopping are close by. 14 units. 2 stories (no elevator), interior corridors. **Guest Services:** valet laundry, area transportation.

FOUR POINTS BY SHERATON JUNEAU   907/586-6900

THREE DIAMOND SAVE Contemporary Hotel. **Address:** 51 Egan Dr 99801

AAA Benefit: Members save 5% or more!

🔗 **For complete hotel, dining and attraction listings:**

AAA.com/travelguides

PEARSON'S POND LUXURY INN AND ADVENTURE SPA
907/789-3772

FOUR DIAMOND

Bed & Breakfast

Address: 4541 Sawa Cir 99801 **Location:** From Egan Dr, 3.5 mi n on Mendenhall Loop Rd. Located in a quiet residential area. **Facility:** A tranquil pond beautifies the lovely grounds, which feature gazebos and sitting areas where you can view the Mendenhall Glacier or soak in an outdoor hot tub. Every whim is taken care of. 5 efficiencies. 2 stories (no elevator), interior/exterior corridors. **Terms:** check-in 4 pm. **Activities:** sauna, hot tub, boat dock, bicycles, exercise room, massage. **Guest Services:** complimentary laundry. **Featured Amenity:** full hot breakfast.

WHERE TO EAT

GRANDMA'S FEATHER BED RESTAURANT   907/789-5568
APPROVED American. Casual Dining. **Address:** 2359 Mendenhall Loop Rd 99801

THE HANGAR ON THE WHARF   907/586-5018
APPROVED Regional American. Casual Dining. **Address:** 2 Marine Way, Suite 106 99801

MI CASA RESTAURANT   907/789-3636
APPROVED Mexican. Casual Dining. **Address:** 9200 Glacier Hwy 99801

THE ROOKERY CAFE   907/463-3013
APPROVED Breads/Pastries Coffee/Tea. Casual Dining. **Address:** 111 Seward St 99801

SALT   907/780-2221
THREE DIAMOND New Alaskan Small Plates. Casual Dining. **Address:** 200 Seward St 99801

SUWANNA THAI CAFE   907/789-1250
APPROVED Thai. Quick Serve. **Address:** 8800 Glacier Hwy 99801

TIMBERLINE BAR & GRILL   907/463-1338
APPROVED American. Casual Dining. **Address:** 490 S Franklin St 99801

TWISTED FISH COMPANY ALASKAN GRILL   907/463-5033
APPROVED Seafood. Casual Dining. **Address:** 550 S Franklin St 99801

KATMAI NATIONAL PARK AND PRESERVE (G-4)

Elevations in the park and preserve range from sea level at the Shelikof Strait to 7,606 ft. at Mount Dennison. Refer to AAA maps for additional elevation information.

On the northern portion of the Alaska Peninsula, 4.1-million-acre Katmai National Park and Preserve displays an outstanding example of volcanism. In 1912 one of the greatest volcanic explosions in recorded history turned a nameless green valley into what became known as the Valley of Ten Thousand Smokes. For more than 45 years the eruption was attributed to Mount Katmai, but recent studies indicate that the source was a new volcanic vent called Novarupta, some 6 miles distant.

During or shortly after the eruption, the peak of Mount Katmai collapsed, forming a caldera that subsequently filled with water. Molten material released from Novarupta and surrounding vents flowed down the valley, and thousands of holes from which smoke and gases arose formed as gases and vaporized surface water percolated through the volcanic deposits. These fumaroles, which gave the valley its name, lasted only about 20 years.

Although nearly all of the "smokes" have died out, steam columns from nearby volcanoes sometimes can be seen. By air it is possible to see the jade-green lake in the crater of Mount Katmai and to circle over still-active mounts Trident, Mageik and Martin.

In addition to its superlative scenery—large lakes, rivers, glaciers and active volcanoes—the park is noted for its abundant wildlife. The most prominent mammal is the Alaskan brown bear, the world's largest carnivore, averaging 500 pounds with some reaching 1,200 pounds. It is recommended that visitors maintain at least 50 yards from individual bears and 100 yards from sows with young. Visitors also should make noises while walking or hiking.

Katmai National Park can be reached only by boat or plane. A boat ramp is at Lake Camp, 10 miles by dirt road from King Salmon. Commercial airlines serve King Salmon, 35 miles from Brooks Camp. Amphibious aircraft make daily scheduled flights between King Salmon and Brooks Camp. Bush planes can be chartered.

Daily 7-hour bus and hiking tours to the Valley of Ten Thousand Smokes begin at Brooks Lodge at 9 a.m., early June to mid-Sept. Fare $96 (with bag lunch); $88 (no lunch); $51 (one way). Departures require a minimum of 2 people. The free ranger-led Cultural Walk departs the Brooks Camp Visitor Center daily at 2, early June to mid-Sept. Other tours are available; for more information phone Katmailand, Inc., (907) 243-5448 or (877) 708-1391. For further information about the park contact the Superintendent, Katmai National Park and Preserve, P.O. Box 7, King Salmon, AK 99613; phone (907) 246-3305. *See Recreation Areas Chart.*

KENAI pop. 7,100, elev. 86'

Established as Fort St. Nicholas by Russian fur traders in 1791, Kenai (KEEN-eye) is one of the oldest permanent settlements in Alaska. Until 1953 the town grew under a squatters' rights policy. Kenai is the closest settlement to the south-central region's most promising oil-development fields and is the site of major petrochemical plants.

Kenai's Russian Orthodox Church, established in 1894, contains religious and art objects brought from Russia in 1841; phone (907) 283-4122.

A popular, colorful pastime during the summer months in Kenai is berry picking. Such berries as Alaska blueberries (a smaller version of its common cousin), nagoonberries (reddish purple in color), cloudberries and salmonberries (both peach in color), crowberries (black in color), northern red currants, wild raspberries and cranberries grow on the peninsula.

Kenai Chamber of Commerce and Visitors Center: 11471 Kenai Spur Hwy., Kenai, AK 99611. **Phone:** (907) 283-1991.

KENAI NATIONAL WILDLIFE REFUGE—see Soldotna p. 513.

ASPEN SUITES HOTEL KENAI   907/283-2272

APPROVED

Extended Stay Hotel

Address: 10431 Kenai Spur Hwy 99611 **Location:** 0.8 mi e of center; jct Kenai Spur Hwy and Walker Ln. Located in a commercial area. **Facility:** 78 efficiencies. 3 stories, interior corridors. **Parking:** winter plug-ins. **Activities:** picnic facilities, exercise room. **Guest Services:** valet and coin laundry.

SAVE ﹖➕ CALL ⬥ ﹖ BIZ 🛜 ✕ 🅟 📠 📋

WHERE TO EAT

CHARLOTTE'S CAFE   907/283-2777

APPROVED   Sandwiches Soup. Casual Dining. **Address:** 115 S Willow Cir, Suite 102 99611

FLATS BISTRO   907/335-1010

THREE DIAMOND   American. Casual Dining. **Address:** 39847 Kalifornsky Beach Rd 99611

VERONICA'S CAFE   907/283-2725

APPROVED   Sandwiches Soup. Quick Serve. **Address:** 602 Petersen Way 99611

KENAI FJORDS NATIONAL PARK (D-11)

Elevations in the park range from sea level at Nuka Bay to 6,400 ft. at a peak on the Harding Icefield. Refer to AAA maps for additional elevation information.

On the southeastern side of the Kenai Peninsula, Kenai Fjords National Park covers more than 600,000 acres. Access to the park is by private vehicle, plane or boat from Seward. Air charters also are available from other communities on the Kenai Peninsula. Scheduled bus service is available between Seward and Anchorage. Several tour companies offer trips to Exit Glacier and boat trips to the fjords.

The park encompasses a coastal mountain range that includes most of Harding Icefield, one of the four largest ice fields in the United States. A remnant of the ice age, it blankets all but the top of the Kenai Mountains. Along the coast is the rugged shoreline of the glacier-carved Kenai Fjords. Seals, porpoises, whales and sea otters are some of the 23 marine mammal species that inhabit the coastal waters.

Exit Glacier is the most accessible of the glaciers that flow from Harding Icefield. Three miles north of Seward via the Seward Highway and Exit Glacier Road, the glacier is reached by a .7-mile trail that begins at the Exit Glacier parking area; guided tours depart daily at 10, 2 and 4, mid-May to mid-September. A strenuous 8.2-mile round-trip journey from the base of Exit Glacier to Harding Icefield departs from the Exit Glacier Nature Center on Saturdays at 9, July through August. Bald eagles, bears, moose, mountain goats and Steller sea lions inhabit the area.

Picnicking and backcountry camping are permitted; a 12-site walk-in tent campground and three rustic cabins are available. Winter activities at Exit Glacier include skiing, snowmobiling, snowshoeing and dog sledding. Boat and air charters provide access to the coast during the summer.

Both park headquarters and a visitor center are in Seward. Park headquarters is at 500 Adams St., Suite 103, and the visitor center is at 1212 4th Ave. next to the harbormaster's office. The Exit Glacier Nature Center is inside the park at the Exit Glacier parking area. Slide shows, exhibits and information about ranger-conducted activities are available.

The visitor center in Seward is open daily 9-7, Memorial Day-Labor Day; Sat.-Sun. 9-5, mid- to late May. The Exit Glacier Nature Center is open daily 9-7, Memorial Day-Labor Day; 9-5, day after Labor Day to mid-Sept.; 9-4:30, mid- to late May. Admission to Exit Glacier is free. For information write the Superintendent, Kenai Fjords National Park, P.O. Box 1727, Seward, AK 99664; phone (907) 422-0535 or (907) 422-0573 for recorded information. *See Recreation Areas Chart.*

KETCHIKAN (H-12) pop. 8,050

Alaska's southernmost city sits on stilts at the base of the Tongass National Forest *(see place listing p. 516)*. On Revillagigedo Island, separated from the mainland by Behm Canal, Ketchikan claims to be the salmon capital of the world. An average annual rainfall of 156 to 162 inches makes it the wettest community in North America. The city's economic base relies on fishing, canning, mineral exploration, tourism and logging and cold-storage operations.

The town is populated with native culture and contains the largest concentration of Tlingit (KLINK-it), Haida (HY-dah), and Tsimshian (SIMP-shee-ane) people in Alaska. This heritage can be seen in the many totem poles that populate the area. Totem poles—tall cedar logs carved with eagles, ravens, wolves, bears, whales and other figures—depict stories or designate clans or lineage, and Ketchikan is reputed to contain the most in the world.

Creek Street is a relic of Ketchikan's rough-and-tumble past. Built on stilts over Ketchikan Creek, the street was once the site of a thriving red-light district. Highlights include art galleries, shops and a museum. The creek is a spawning ground for salmon.

Gray Line of Alaska, (907) 225-2404 or (888) 425-1737, and Princess Rail Tours, (800) 426-0500, are among the companies that offer tours of the city. Ketchikan Visitors Bureau, 50 Front St., can provide a more complete list; phone (907) 225-6166 or (800) 770-3300. Information about charter aircraft, boats, rental cars, buses and taxis is available at the Visitors Bureau, the airport and the ferry terminal.

Southeast Alaska Discovery Center: 50 Main St., Ketchikan, AK 99901. **Phone:** (907) 228-6220 or TTY (907) 228-6237.

Self-guiding tours: Information about a 2-hour walking tour of downtown is provided at the Ketchikan Visitors Bureau, 50 Front St., Ketchikan, AK 99901; phone (907) 225-6166 or (800) 770-3300.

Shopping: The Creek Street boardwalk area in downtown contains a number of specialty shops and boutiques.

ALASKA AMPHIBIOUS TOURS is inside the Ketchikan Visitor Center on the cruise ship dock, booth # 10, 131 Front St. Take a 90-minute historic tour through downtown Ketchikan, passing by Ketchikan Creek and then splashing into the Tongass Narrows waterway, where you can see fishing boats and sea planes in the harbor as well as nearby canneries where bald eagles are known to visit. Passengers ride on an amphibious vehicle which is driven on dry land and becomes a boat in the water. **Time:** Allow 1 hour, 30 minutes minimum. **Hours:** Tours depart daily 7:30-3, May-Sept. Phone ahead to confirm schedule. **Cost:** $49; $29 (ages 3-12). Duck whistle $3. **Phone:** (907) 225-9899 or (866) 341-3825. GT

BERING SEA CRAB FISHERMEN'S TOUR departs from the Tender Float at the main downtown dock. This 3-hour excursion on the waters of the Metlakatla Indian Reservation is conducted aboard the *Aleutian Ballad* — a vessel featured on season two of the TV show "Deadliest Catch" — and offers passengers a firsthand look at the king crab fishing industry. As the tour proceeds, passengers are regaled with tales of life at sea and educated about the state's fishing history and the variety of fishing vessels used. A heated and sheltered amphitheater allows passengers to observe the ship's crew as they unload 700-pound crab pots.

Often seen among the ship's catch are such sea creatures as octopus, prawns, sharks and wolf eels; many animals are placed in an on-deck tank for observation and photo opportunities prior to release back into the sea. Such local wildlife as bald eagles, sea lions, seals and humpback whales may be seen during the tour.

Note: Prior to boarding, potential passengers should locate a tour representative on the dock at least 30 minutes before the scheduled departure time. Passengers should dress in comfortable and warm layers of clothing. Each passenger should be of sufficient age (minimum age 5) and capacity to remain in the ship's passenger-designated zones and outside its working areas as well as be able to navigate the ship's aisles and stairs. Limited storage space is available.

Time: Allow 3 hours, 15 minutes minimum. **Hours:** Tours depart once or twice daily (departure times vary), May to Sept. The schedule is designed to accommodate cruise ship passengers; phone ahead to verify departure times. **Cost:** Fare $179; $115 (ages 5-12). Children ages 0-4 are not permitted on the tour. Reservations are recommended. **Phone:** (907) 821-2722 or (888) 239-3816. GT

TOTEM BIGHT STATE HISTORICAL PARK, 10 mi. n. on N. Tongass Hwy., displays 14 poles by Haida and Tlingit clans and a model of a Tlingit clan house. The site is reached by a short trail through a forest from the parking area. A brochure describes typical totem characters and gives insight to the art of totem carving. More totem poles are in Saxman Native Village, 2.5 miles south on S. Tongass Highway. **Time:** Allow 30 minutes minimum. **Hours:** Daily 6 a.m.-10 p.m., May-Sept.; Mon.-Fri. 10-4, rest of year. **Cost:** Free. **Phone:** (907) 247-8574.

CAPE FOX LODGE   907-225-8001
THREE DIAMOND
Hotel

Address: 800 Venetia Way 99901 **Location:** Above Creek St (tramway from Creek St). **Facility:** 72 units. 3 stories (no elevator), interior/exterior corridors. **Dining:** Cape Fox Lodge Dining Room & Lodge, see separate listing. **Activities:** trails, exercise room. **Guest Services:** valet and coin laundry, boarding pass kiosk, area transportation.

THE LANDING HOTEL   907-225-5166
THREE DIAMOND
Hotel

Address: 3434 Tongass Ave 99901 **Location:** Across from marina and near ferry terminal. **Facility:** 107 units. 2-4 stories, interior/exterior corridors. **Parking:** winter plug-ins. **Amenities:** safes. **Dining:** The Landing, see separate listing. **Activities:** exercise room. **Guest Services:** coin laundry, area transportation. **Featured Amenity:** continental breakfast.

MY PLACE HOTEL KETCHIKAN   907/220-9201
APPROVED Extended Stay Hotel. **Address:** 3612 Tongass Ave 99901

ANNABELLE'S FAMOUS KEG & CHOWDER HOUSE
                                  907/225-6009
APPROVED Regional Seafood. Casual Dining. **Address:** 326 Front St 99901

BAR HARBOR RESTAURANT   907/225-2813
APPROVED Alaskan. Casual Dining. **Address:** 2813 Tongass Ave 99901

CAPE FOX LODGE DINING ROOM & LODGE   907/225-8001
APPROVED American. Casual Dining. **Address:** 800 Venetia Way 99901

THE EDGEWATER INN RESTAURANT & MARINA
                                  907/247-2600
APPROVED American. Casual Dining. **Address:** 4871 N Tongass Hwy 99901

THE LANDING   907/225-5166
APPROVED American. Casual Dining. **Address:** 3434 Tongass Ave 99901

THE TIMBERS AT SALMON FALLS RESORT   907/225-2752
APPROVED Regional American. Casual Dining. **Address:** 16707 N Tongass Hwy 99901

KLONDIKE GOLD RUSH NATIONAL HISTORICAL PARK—
See Skagway p. 412

See Skagway p. 412

KOBUK VALLEY NATIONAL PARK (B-4)

Elevations in the park range from 100 ft. at the point where the Kobuk River flows out of the southwest corner of the park to 4,700 ft. in the Brooks Range, which forms the park's northern border. Refer to AAA maps for additional elevation information.

Some 25 miles north of the Arctic Circle, Kobuk Valley National Park covers 1,710,000 acres in the heart of the arctic wildlands, where the boreal forest gives way to the frozen tundra. The broad Kobuk Valley is enclosed almost completely by the Baird Mountains to the north and the Waring Mountains to the south. Traversing the valley from east to west, the wide and placid Kobuk River offers good fishing and idyllic float trips. The swifter Salmon River, a designated Wild and Scenic River, flows south from the Baird Mountains.

Preserved within the park are the 25-square-mile Great Kobuk Sand Dunes, the largest active dunes in the Arctic. Created by the grinding action of ancient glaciers, the sand was carried by wind and water to a wide area south of the Kobuk River. The 100-foot dunes are accessible by a difficult hike from the river along Kavet Creek.

Home to seminomadic tribes for more than 12,500 years, the region still supports the native Inupiats; they are granted by law the right to continue subsistence hunting, trapping and other practices. Important to their survival is North America's largest caribou herd, numbering some 500,000. Many can be seen crossing the Kobuk River in September during their migration southward.

Other wildlife common to the region include moose, grizzly and black bears, wolves, red foxes, lynxes, wolverines and martens. Golden eagles can be seen in the northern latitudes; other birds include sandhill cranes, arctic loons, American golden plovers and arctic terns.

The park attracts experienced backpackers, campers and river travelers. Though the park is open year-round, the elements limit most visits to June through September. Fishing is good when the rivers are clear of silt; catches include salmon, pike, arctic char, whitefish and grayling. An Alaska fishing license is required. Hunting is not permitted, but it is legal to carry a firearm for protection from bears.

Access to the region is by daily commercial flights from Anchorage and Fairbanks to Kotzebue, where connections to the villages of Kiana and Ambler can be made. Air taxi service into the park is available from Kotzebue, Kiana and Ambler. There are no facilities, services, trails or campgrounds in the park. Park headquarters is at the Northwest Arctic Heritage Center in Kotzebue and is open Mon.-Fri. 9-6:30, Sat. 10-6:30, June-Aug.; Mon.-Fri. 9-noon and 1-6:30, rest of year. The visitor center has museum exhibits and can provide information about the park; phone (907) 442-3890.

Due to its location, the area is subject to harsh weather and high winds. It is advisable to carry protection against hypothermia, mosquitoes and biting flies.

For trip planning assistance and a list of authorized outfitters, guides and air taxi operators, write the Superintendent, Western Arctic National Parklands, P.O. Box 1029, Kotzebue, AK 99752; phone (907) 442-3890. *See Recreation Areas Chart.*

KODIAK   (H-5) pop. 6,130

One of the oldest towns in Alaska, Kodiak is on the northeastern tip of Kodiak Island and is home to the Kodiak brown bear. A Russian explorer-trader's quest for sea otter pelts led to the European settlement of the island in 1784. The community was established about 1792 when Alexander Baranov moved his headquarters from the original 1784 settlement at Three Saints Bay, making Kodiak the first capital of Russian America.

Kodiak was nearly destroyed twice; in June 1912, an eruption from Mount Novarupta covered the town with ash. On Good Friday in 1964 an earthquake in south central Alaska created tsunamis that enveloped the islands. Citizens found refuge on nearby Pillar Mountain and returned with the task of rebuilding the city.

Kodiak is a leading commercial fishing port. Several cruise lines dock at the Port of Kodiak for shore excursions. On days when cruise ships are in port, visitors can enjoy performances by the Kodiak Alutiiq Dancers at 11 a.m. at the Kodiak Tribal Council building, 312 W. Marine Way; phone (907) 486-4449. The blue, onion-shaped domes of the Holy Resurrection Russian Orthodox Church recall the days when the Russian Empire in the North Pacific was administered from Kodiak; phone (907) 486-5532.

Kodiak can be reached by air service from Anchorage or by the Alaska Marine Highway, a passenger/vehicle ferry, from Homer and Seward. Reservations are required well in advance for the ferry; write Alaska Marine Highway, P.O. Box 703, Kodiak, AK 99615, or phone (907) 486-3800 or (800) 642-0066.

Discover Kodiak: 100 Marine Way, Suite 200, Kodiak, AK 99615. **Phone:** (907) 486-4782 or (800) 789-4782.

ALUTIIQ MUSEUM is at 215 Mission Rd. in the Alutiiq Center building across from Holy Resurrection Russian Orthodox Church. Permanent exhibits tell the 7,500-year history, lifestyle and cultural traditions of the Alutiiq people through archeological artifacts, photographs, petroglyph rubbings, oral histories, videos and contemporary art. Learn about the Alutiiq through hands-on activities and a children's play corner. **Time:** Allow 1 hour minimum. **Hours:** Tues.-Fri. 10-4, Sat. noon-4, Mon. by appointment. Closed major holidays. **Cost:** $7; free (ages 0-16). **Phone:** (844) 425-8844. GT

FORT ABERCROMBIE STATE HISTORICAL PARK, 4 mi. n.e. on Rezinof Dr., is a National Historic Landmark due to World War II fortification. The 182-acre park offers a view of the rocky coastline and nearby islands. Interpretive displays and a self-guiding walking tour highlight the remnants and remaining bunkers of the coastal defense system, reflecting Alaska's participation in World War II. Scheduled interpretive tide pool and historical programs are given, and approximately 7 miles of hiking trails are available. There are generally abundant views of birds, wildlife and marine mammals in the area. *See Recreation Areas Chart.*

Hours: Park open daily 24 hours. Visitor center daily 8-4, May-Sept. **Cost:** Free. $5 (day use). **Phone:** (907) 486-6339. GT ◼ ◼ ◼ ◼

KODIAK LABORATORY AQUARIUM & TOUCH TANK is at the Kodiak Fisheries Research Center at 301 Research Ct. The 3,500-gallon aquarium displays specimens collected from Kodiak Island's waters, including crabs, mollusks and other invertebrates as well as such echinoderms as urchins, sea cucumbers and starfish. A giant Pacific octopus also can be seen while a touch tank allows visitors to interact with selected intertidal organisms.

Time: Allow 30 minutes minimum. **Hours:** Mon.-Sat. 8-4:30, in summer; Mon.-Fri. 8-4:30, rest of year. Closed major holidays. **Cost:** Free. **Phone:** (907) 481-1800.

BEST WESTERN KODIAK INN & CONVENTION CENTER
907/486-5712

◇ APPROVED   Hotel

🅱 Best Western. **AAA Benefit:** Members save up to 15% and earn bonus points!

Address: 236 W Rezanof Dr 99615 **Location:** Just w of ferry terminal; downtown. Across from St. Paul's Harbor. **Facility:** 82 units. 3 stories (no elevator); interior/exterior corridors. **Parking:** on-site and street. **Dining:** Chart Room Restaurant, see separate listing. **Activities:** hot tub, exercise room. **Guest Services:** coin laundry, area transportation. **Featured Amenity:** full hot breakfast.

SAVE 🔌 🍽 🍷 CALL 🛗 📶 BIZ 🛜 ✕ 🞬
🔲 🖨 🖥 / SOME UNITS 🐾 HS

KODIAK COMPASS SUITES   907/486-1086
THREE DIAMOND Contemporary Hotel. **Address:** 203 Alder
Ln 99615

WHERE TO EAT

CHART ROOM RESTAURANT   907/486-5712
APPROVED Regional American. Casual Dining.
Address: 236 W Rezanof Dr 99615

HENRY'S GREAT ALASKAN RESTAURANT   907/486-8844
APPROVED American. Casual Dining. **Address:** 512
Marine Way 99615

KODIAK HANA RESTAURANT   907/481-1088
APPROVED Sushi Seafood. Casual Dining. **Address:**
516 E Marine Way 99615

MONK'S ROCK COFFEEHOUSE   907/486-0905
APPROVED Deli Breads/Pastries. Quick Serve.
Address: 202 E Rezanof Dr 99615

OLDS RIVER INN RESTAURANT   907/486-6040
APPROVED American. Casual Dining. **Address:**
32233 Pasagshak Rd 99615

LAKE CLARK NATIONAL PARK AND PRESERVE (F-5)

Elevations in the park and preserve range
from sea level along Cook Inlet to 10,197 ft.
at Mount Redoubt. Refer to AAA maps for
additional elevation information.

West of Cook Inlet, Lake Clark National Park and
Preserve is an almost 4-million-acre mountainous
crossroads where ice and fire meet. The Pacific
crust grinds beneath the North American plate, creating the Chigmit Mountains, a jagged array of
spires and two steaming volcanoes, Mount Redoubt
and Mount Iliamna. Mount Redoubt, the more active, last erupted in March 2009; it continues to emit
steam.

Covered by massive ice fields, the seemingly im-
penetrable Chigmit Mountains are formed by the
linkage of two great ranges, the Alaska and the
Aleutian. Together the ranges divide the park into
distinct areas: the eastern flank's coastal plain bordering Cook Inlet and the lake and tundra region on
the western flank. Lake Clark, 50 miles long, juts in
from the southwest.

Moisture abounds along the park's coastal area,
which is characterized by rocky cliffs along its
southern portion, giving way to tidal marshes and
grasslands in the north. In contrast to the luxuriant
alder thickets and Sitka spruce along Cook Inlet,
lakes, boreal forests and rolling tundra highlands
distinguish the park's western landscape.

Numerous glacier-fed rivers and creeks are chan-
neled through Lake Clark, creating one of the richest
sockeye salmon spawning grounds in the world. The
park was created primarily to protect this fruitful
breeding area.

Although the park is open all year, most people
visit during the peak of the summer season, late
June through August. Even in summer months,
weather conditions vary in the interior; it is advisable
to bring protection against insects as well as
clothing for sunny, wet or freezing weather. Visitors
should outfit themselves in Kenai, Homer or Anchorage, as the communities closer to the park have
limited supplies.

For anglers the rivers and lakes on the park's
western side provide a variety of trophy-size fish, including salmon, arctic grayling and trout. A 2- to
3-mile trail to Tanalian Falls and Kontrashibuna Lake
is accessible from Port Alsworth, near Lake Clark.
The open foothills are ideal for backpacking. River-
running also is popular on the Mulchatna, Tlikakila
and Chilikadrotna rivers, all federally designated
wild and scenic rivers.

As there are no roads in the park, access is almost exclusively by air. Most travelers charter aircraft; the closest airport is south of the park in
Iliamna. A 1- to 2-hour flight from Anchorage, Homer
or Kenai will provide access to most points within
the park and preserve.

The National Park Service facility is at Port Alsworth
and contains a visitor center with displays regarding
natural history topics; phone (907) 781-2117. The
center is open daily 9-5:30, Memorial Day-Labor Day;
Mon.-Fri. 9-5, day after Labor Day-Sept. 30. While
there are minimal National Park facilities—staffed pa-
trol cabins at Telaquana Lake, Twin Lakes, Crescent
Lake and Chinitna Bay—there are a number of private
lodges and cabins in the park.

For information about accommodations as well as
a list of outfitters and maps, write the Superintendent, Lake Clark National Park and Preserve,
240 W. 5th Ave., Suite 236, Anchorage, AK 99501;
phone (907) 781-2218. *See Recreation Areas Chart.*

MISTY FIORDS NATIONAL MONUMENT (H-11)

East of Ketchikan and within the Tongass National Forest *(see place listing p. 516)*, Misty Fiords
National Monument covers about 3,580 square
miles of wilderness. The area is accessible by floatplane from Ketchikan and other communities near
the national forest. An information center and
cruises to the monument are available in Ketchikan
(see place listing p. 504).

Behm Canal, a deep inlet of the Pacific Ocean,
leads to the interior of the monument, where rock
walls that rise 3,000 feet surround Walker Cove and
Rudyerd Bay. Geological features include mineral
springs, 237-foot-tall New Eddystone Rock, 3,150-
foot-tall Punchbowl Face, lava flows, five major
rivers and hundreds of small streams. The region receives more than 120 inches of precipitation each
year. Bald eagles, brown and black bears, wolves
and mountain goats inhabit the area; whales, porpoises, seals and sea lions can be sighted in Behm
Canal or in the ocean nearby.

Recreational activities include backpacking, picnicking, bird-watching, hunting, fishing and crabbing. Thirteen rustic cabins are available for $25-$45 per day; reservations may be made by calling Reserve America, (877) 444-6777. Four free Adirondack-type shelters are available on a first-come, first-served basis. For further information contact the Southeast Alaska Discovery Center, 50 Main St., Ketchikan, AK 99901; phone (907) 228-6220, or TTY (907) 228-6237.

NOME (D-2) pop. 3,598, elev. 13'

Placer gold washed from the hillsides to the beaches at Nome lured thousands to the remote shores of the Bering Sea in 1898. At the height of the gold rush, 20,000 people lived in Nome, once the largest settlement in Alaska.

On the Seward Peninsula, Nome is the judicial and commercial center of northwestern Alaska and the main supply point for nearby mining districts and Eskimo villages. The city is accessible daily by plane from Anchorage. Regularly scheduled and charter flights are available to various Eskimo villages.

Cruise ships serve Nome during the summer, and rental cars provide visitors with opportunities for self-guiding trips to nearby villages.

When a diphtheria epidemic threatened the town in 1925, the necessary serum was delivered by dog team. The annual ☙ Iditarod Trail Sled Dog Race commemorates this emergency mission. The race, which begins in Anchorage *(see place listing p. 468)* the first Saturday in March, encompasses treacherous climbs, river passages and bone-chilling blizzards. Mushers cross the finish line in Nome after traveling roughly 1,112 miles, exhausted but invigorated by cheers from supporters lining the chute on Front Street.

One of the activities during the final week of the race is the Bering Sea Ice Classic, a six-hole golf tournament played on frozen Norton Sound. The golf balls are green; the tees are miniature, inverted liquor bottles; the holes are coffee cans in the ice and one is usually found in "Nome National Forest," a forest of dead Christmas trees stuck into the ice; and there's a three-stroke penalty for hitting a polar bear.

The Midnight Sun Folk Fest celebrates the summer solstice, the longest day of the year with almost 24 hours of sunlight. The mid-June festival lasts several days and includes a parade, live music and The Nome River Raft Race.

Nome Convention and Visitors Bureau: 301 Front St., Nome, AK 99762. **Phone:** (907) 443-6555.

INSIDER INFO:
The Last Great Race

To commemorate the 1925 event in which 20 mushers relayed serum to Nome to save children who contracted diphtheria, the first Iditarod Trail Sled Dog Race took place on Mar. 3, 1973.

Beginning in Anchorage and culminating in Nome, the race trail covers some 1,112 miles of rugged terrain, takes between 9-17 days to complete and can reach temperatures of minus 60 F.

In preparation for the great race, the trail is broken and marked with reflector tape, and checkpoints are chosen where teams stop to eat and rest. Since it's not feasible for mushers to carry all of their provisions in their sleds, the bulk of food and supplies is shipped to the checkpoints prior to the race.

To aid in endurance, dogs ingest 5,000 calories or more each day, gobbling such delicacies as moose, caribou or even seal meat. Concern for the dogs' health is strong: Booties are worn for paw protection, and about 25 veterinarians man the checkpoints to examine each dog.

While teams may begin the race with as many as 16 dogs, some drop from the race. "Dropped dogs"—dogs that do not finish the race due to dehydration, flu or fatigue—are carried to the nearest checkpoint and flown back to Anchorage. A musher must finish the race with at least five dogs.

Teams travel at night as well as during the day, and dogs rest about 10-12 hours per 24-hour period. But mushers don't enjoy that luxury: Responsible for feeding and caring for the dogs (including changing their booties every 100 miles), they rarely sleep more than 2 hours per night.

The goal? Nome's Burled Arch on Front Street. At this finish line, teams are greeted by cheering crowds and the sounding of the city's fire siren.

SEWARD (D-11) pop. 2,693, elev. 70'
• Hotels p. 510 • Restaurants p. 510

Named for William H. Seward, who negotiated the purchase of Alaska, Seward is an ice-free port in a setting of great beauty. At the northeast end of a bay named Resurrection by Russians who arrived in its waters on Easter, the city is surrounded by lush, tall mountains and ice fields.

Charter boats and planes can be hired for fishing, hunting and sightseeing trips. Seward is the southern terminus of the Seward Highway, a national scenic byway extending north to Anchorage through an alpine terrain of glaciers and lakes. Seward also is the main access point to Kenai Fjords National Park *(see place listing p. 503)*, which includes Exit Glacier, one of the few accessible glaciers.

Seward Chamber of Commerce: 2001 Seward Hwy., Seward, AK 99664. **Phone:** (907) 224-8051.

Self-guiding tours: Information about a walking tour is available at the chamber of commerce's visitor information center, 2001 Seward Hwy.; phone (907) 224-8051 for details.

[SAVE] **ALASKA SEALIFE CENTER,** on Seward Hwy. (SR 9) at Milepost 0, generates and shares scientific knowledge to promote understanding and stewardship of Alaska's marine ecosystems. Highlights include Steller sea lions, harbor seals, Giant Pacific octopus and a sea bird habitat that allows visitors to get up close to puffins, red-legged kittiwakes and other Alaskan avian wonders.

Exhibits also include a jellyfish display, the hands-on Discovery touch pool and the Lifecycles of Pacific Salmon, which examines the life stages of all five species of Pacific salmon. More than 300 of the fish may be observed in 2,200- to 6,000-gallon tanks. Guided behind-the-scenes tours are available in addition to marine mammal, octopus and puffin encounters.

Time: Allow 1 hour, 30 minutes minimum. **Hours:** Mon.-Thurs. 9-5, Fri.-Sun. 8 a.m.-5 p.m., mid-Aug. to early Sept.; otherwise varies, rest of year. Behind-the-scenes tours depart daily at 10, 1:30 and 4:30, Memorial Day-Labor Day; otherwise varies, rest of year (under age 12 not permitted). Marine mammal encounters depart daily at 3, Memorial Day–Labor Day; otherwise varies, rest of year (under age 10 not permitted). Puffin encounters depart daily at 11 and 2, Memorial Day-Labor Day; otherwise varies, rest of year (under age 10 not permitted). Octopus encounter tours depart daily at 1, Memorial Day–Labor Day; otherwise varies, rest of the year (under age 6 not permitted). Sea otter tours depart daily at 12:30 and 7. Closed Thanksgiving and Christmas. **Cost:** $29.95; $25.95 (ages 65+); $17.95 (ages 4-12). Behind-the-scenes tours $14.95. Marine mammal, puffin or octopus encounters $74.95. Sea otter tour $24.95; $19.95 (ages 2-12). Reservations for tours and encounters are recommended. **Phone:** (907) 224-6300, (888) 378-2525 for reservations or (800) 224-2525. GT ⑪

KENAI FJORDS TOURS depart from the Seward Small Boat Harbor. The company offers glacier and wildlife cruises into the waters of Kenai Fjords National Park. Cruises also explore Resurrection Bay and the Northwestern Fjords, where active tidewater glaciers are a highlight. A variety of marine mammals can be seen; humpback whales and orcas often are spotted on whale-watching tours. Six- and 8.5-hour Kenai Fjords National Park tours; 9-hour Northwestern Fjords tours; and 5-hour Resurrection Bay wildlife cruises with a wild Alaska salmon bake and prime rib buffet at Fox Island, are available.

Inquire about weather policies. **Hours:** Tours depart daily, mid-May to mid-Sept. Kenai Fjords National Park 6-hour tours depart at 8 and 11:30; 8.5-hour tour departs at 10. Northwestern Fjord tour departs at 8:30. Resurrection Bay wildlife cruises depart at noon. Phone ahead to confirm schedule. **Cost:** National Park tour $199; $99.50 (ages 2-11). Northwestern Fjord tour $199; free (ages 0-1). Bay tour $112; $56 (ages 2-11). Reservations are recommended. **Phone:** (907) 224-8068 or (877) 777-4051. GT

MAJOR MARINE TOURS depart from Harbor 360 Hotel at 1412 4th Ave., 1 blk. e. of Seward Hwy. A park ranger narrates full- and half-day glacier and wildlife sightseeing cruises in Kenai Fjords National Park. Passengers may spot bald eagles, otters, porpoises, puffins, sea lions and whales.

Inquire about weather policies. Full-day cruise not recommended for infants and toddlers. **Hours:** Cruises depart daily, early Mar. to mid-October. Half-day cruises depart at 9, noon and 1:30; full-day cruises depart at 9, 10 and 11:30. **Cost:** Half-day fare $79-$84; $39.50-$42 (ages 2-11). Full-day fare $159-$224; $79.50-$89.50 (ages 2-11). Reservations are recommended. **Phone:** (907) 274-7300 or (800) 764-7300. *(See ad this page.)* GT ⑪

▼ *See AAA listing this page* ▼

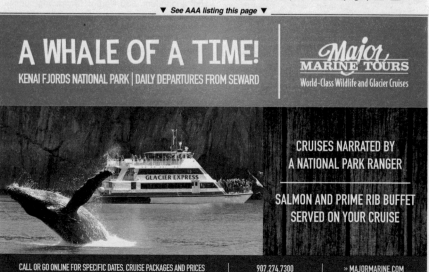

A WHALE OF A TIME!
KENAI FJORDS NATIONAL PARK | DAILY DEPARTURES FROM SEWARD

Major MARINE TOURS
World-Class Wildlife and Glacier Cruises

GLACIER EXPRESS

CRUISES NARRATED BY A NATIONAL PARK RANGER

SALMON AND PRIME RIB BUFFET SERVED ON YOUR CRUISE

CALL OR GO ONLINE FOR SPECIFIC DATES, CRUISE PACKAGES AND PRICES | 907.274.7300 | » MAJORMARINE.COM

SCENIC MOUNTAIN AIR (FLIGHTSEEING) operates wheeled planes from Seward Airport to Anchorage and float flightseeing planes from Trail Lake in Moose Pass. Sights on the varied tours include Harding Icefield, Kenai Fjords and wildlife. Fly-in fishing tours also are available. **Hours:** Flights depart daily 8 a.m.-7 p.m., early May to mid-Sept. (weather permitting). **Cost:** Fares $50-$1,650, depending on length of tour. Reservations are recommended. **Phone:** (907) 288-3646 or (800) 478-1449. GT

BEST WESTERN PLUS EDGEWATER HOTEL
907/224-2700

APPROVED
Hotel

AAA Benefit: Members save up to 15% and earn bonus points!

Address: 202 5th Ave 99664 **Location:** Waterfront. Downtown; just e of Alaska SeaLife Center. Across from Resurrection Bay. **Facility:** 76 units. 3 stories, interior corridors. **Parking:** on-site and street. **Terms:** check-in 4 pm. **Guest Services:** coin laundry, area transportation.

BOX CANYON CABINS   907/224-5046
APPROVED   Cabin. **Address:** 31515 Lois Way 99664

HARBOR 360 HOTEL   907/865-6224
APPROVED   Hotel. **Address:** 1412 4th Ave 99664

HARBORVIEW INN   907/224-3217
APPROVED   Motel. **Address:** 804 3rd Ave 99664

HOTEL SEWARD   907/224-8001
APPROVED
Hotel

Address: 221 5th Ave 99664 **Location:** Downtown; just n of Alaska SeaLife Center. **Facility:** 62 units. 3 stories (no elevator), interior corridors. **Parking:** on-site and street. **Terms:** check-in 4 pm. **Dining:** Ms. Gene's Place, see separate listing. **Activities:** fishing, recreation programs in summer. **Guest Services:** coin laundry, area transportation.

SEWARD WINDSONG LODGE   907/224-7116
APPROVED   Hotel. **Address:** 31772 Herman Leirer Rd 99664

WHERE TO EAT

CHINOOKS WATERFRONT RESTAURANT   907/224-2207
APPROVED   Alaskan. Casual Dining. **Address:** 1404 4th Ave 99664

THE COOKERY & OYSTER BAR   907/422-7459
THREE DIAMOND   Seafood Small Plates. Casual Dining. **Address:** 209 5th Ave 99664

MS. GENE'S PLACE   907/224-8001
APPROVED   American. Casual Dining. **Address:** 221 5th Ave 99664

RESURRECTION ROADHOUSE RESTAURANT   907/224-7116
THREE DIAMOND   Regional American. Fine Dining. **Address:** 31772 Herman Leirer Rd 99664

SALMON BAKE RESTAURANT   907/224-2204
APPROVED   American. Casual Dining. **Address:** 31832 Herman Leirer Rd 99664

SEWARD BREWING COMPANY   907/422-0337
APPROVED   American. Gastropub. **Address:** 139 4th Ave 99664

WOODY'S THAI KITCHEN   907/422-0338
APPROVED   Thai. Casual Dining. **Address:** 800 4th Ave 99664

ZUDY'S CAFE   907/224-4710
APPROVED   Sandwiches Soup. Quick Serve. **Address:** 501 Railway Ave 99664

SITKA (H-10) pop. 8,881

Surrounded by high peaks and small wooded islands, historic Sitka is accessible by air or the Alaska Marine Highway.

In 1804 Russians led by Alexander Baranov established a settlement on the site of an ancient Tlingit (KLINK-it) village; that settlement became the capital of Russian America. Originally named New Archangel, it was a thriving port of nearly 3,000 when San Francisco was just a mission village. Castle Hill marks the site of Baranov's headquarters and commemorates the 1867 ceremony that transferred ownership of Alaska from Russia to the United States. St. Michael's Cathedral, a restored Russian church with an onion-shaped dome, contains a collection of religious icons and artwork; phone (907) 747-8120.

The colorfully costumed New Archangel Dancers perform Russian dances in the Harrigan Centennial Hall auditorium, 330 Harbor Dr., during summer when large ships are in port; phone (907) 747-5516. Performances by the Sheet'ka Kwaán Naa Kahidi Native Dancers are given at the Tribal Community House on Katlian Street; phone (907) 747-7290.

For cruise ship and ferry passengers, Sitka Tribal Tours offers a short bus tour of Sitka, which includes guide service and round-trip transportation from the port; its native Alaskan guides all live in the Sitka community. The company also offers performances by native dancers as well as walking tours of the town and Sitka National Historical Park; phone (907) 747-0110.

Visit Sitka: 104 Lake St., Sitka, AK 99835. **Phone:** (907) 747-8604 or (800) 557-4852.

ALASKA RAPTOR CENTER, .8 mi. e. of Lake St. at 1000 Raptor Way, is home to more than 20 "raptors in residence," including bald and golden eagles, hawks, falcons and owls. The 17-acre rehabilitation center, surrounded by muskeg, mountains and the Indian River, provides medical treatment to more than 100 eagles and other birds of prey each year. A stage presentation, a video, live demonstrations of birds in flight training and a .25-mile nature trail are available.

Raptors unable to be released into the wild help educate visitors and travel to schools nationwide to raise awareness of wild birds and their habitats. Feathers, bones, photographs and a national map indicating where birds have been released are displayed. Visitors can view raptors in their natural habitats outside the center as well as in the clinic's treatment room and recuperation areas.

Time: Allow 1 hour, 30 minutes minimum. **Hours:** Viewing and tours daily 8-4, May-Sept.; viewing only Mon.-Fri. 10-3, rest of year. **Cost:** $13; $6 (ages 6-12). **Phone:** (907) 747-8662 or (800) 643-9425. GT

ASPEN SUITES HOTEL SITKA   907/747-3477
▼ APPROVED Extended Stay Contemporary Hotel. **Address:** 210 Lake St 99835

SUPER 8 SITKA   907/747-8804
▼ APPROVED Hotel. **Address:** 404 Sawmill Creek Rd 99835

WESTMARK SITKA   907/747-6241
▼ APPROVED Hotel. **Address:** 330 Seward St 99835

WILD STRAWBERRY LODGE FISHING RESORT
                                        907/747-3232
▼ APPROVED Resort Motel. **Address:** 724 Siginaka Way 99835

WHERE TO EAT

ASIAN PALACE   907/966-4600
▼ APPROVED Asian. Casual Dining. **Address:** 327 Seward St 99835

CHANNEL CLUB   907/747-7440
▼ THREE DIAMOND Regional American. Fine Dining. **Address:** 2906 Halibut Point Rd 99835

LITTLE TOKYO   907/747-5699
▼ APPROVED Sushi. Quick Serve. **Address:** 315 Lincoln St 99835

LUDVIG'S BISTRO   907/966-3663
▼ THREE DIAMOND Mediterranean. Casual Dining. **Address:** 256 Katlian St 99835

RAVEN DINING ROOM   907/747-6241
▼ APPROVED American. Casual Dining. **Address:** 330 Seward St 99835

SITKA NATIONAL HISTORICAL PARK (H-10)

Near downtown Sitka on Lincoln Street, this urban park commemorates the Battle of Sitka, fought in 1804 between the Kiksadi Tlingit Indians and the fur hunters and Aleut natives of the Russian-American Co. The battle marked the last major armed resistance by Alaska Natives to European domination. The 113-acre park preserves the Tlingit fort site, the battlefield and the 1842 Russian Bishop's House.

A fine collection of Tlingit (KLINK-it) and Haida (HY-dah) totem poles, some more than a century old, is displayed along a 1-mile trail through the park's temperate rain forest and coastal intertidal area. During August and September visitors may view salmon spawning in the Indian River. Ranger-lead programs and walking tours are offered Memorial Day weekend through Labor Day.

The visitor center contains exhibits and audiovisual presentations about the area's Tlingit Indian heritage as well as its Russian legacy. A 12-minute video, "Voices of Sitka," also is available. Within the visitor center skilled Alaska Natives artisans demonstrate traditional crafts at the Cultural Center, which is open most weekdays.

Trails open daily 6 a.m.-10 p.m., May-Sept.; 7 a.m.-8 p.m., rest of year. Visitor center open daily 8-5, May-Sept.; Tues.-Sat. 9-3, rest of year. Visitor center closed Thanksgiving and Christmas. Park and visitor center free. Address inquiries to the Superintendent, Sitka National Historical Park, 103 Monastery St., Sitka, AK 99835; phone (907) 747-0110.

THE RUSSIAN BISHOP'S HOUSE, 501 Lincoln St. across from Crescent Harbor, is a two-story log structure completed in 1842. It is one of the last surviving colonial Russian buildings in North America. Restored to its 1853 appearance, the building reflects the influence of the Russian Orthodox Church and the traders of the Russian-American Co., who made Sitka the economic center of colonial Russian America.

Time: Allow 30 minutes minimum. **Hours:** Guided tours depart daily on the half-hour 9-5, mid-May to late Sept.; by appointment rest of year. Last tour begins 30 minutes before closing. **Cost:** Free. **Phone:** (907) 747-0110. GT

SKAGWAY (F-10) pop. 920, elev. 2'
• Hotels p. 513 • Restaurants p. 513

During the icy winter of 1897-98 hordes of enthusiastic would-be prospectors who had heard of the Klondike gold strike swarmed ashore at Dyea. They assembled their gear and began the trek over treacherous mountains and down raging rivers to the Klondike. Within 3 months of the first gold strike, the settlement at Skagway grew from one cabin into a thriving city of more than 20,000 people. But the gold rush ended suddenly, and those who had come to Skagway moved on.

The notorious outlaw Jefferson R. "Soapy" Smith and Frank Reid, who represented the outraged citizenry, shot it out in a battle that cost both men their lives. Gold Rush Cemetery, 1.5 miles from town, contains the graves of both "Soapy" Smith and Frank Reid.

A stop on many summer cruises along the Inside Passage, Skagway is the northern terminus of the Alaska Marine Highway. Sightseeing opportunities include visits to Reid Falls and flower gardens; tours of the city and the harbor; flightseeing tours to Glacier Bay, gold rush trails and the Juneau Ice Cap; bus excursions to Dyea and Carcross, Yukon; and hiking trips to AB Mountain and the Dewey Lakes.

Gray Line of Alaska offers historical points-of-interest tours daily mid-May to mid-September; phone (907) 983-6088 or (888) 425-1737.

Skagway Convention & Visitors Bureau: 245 Broadway, P.O. Box 1029, Skagway, AK 99840. **Phone:** (907) 983-2854 or (888) 762-1898.

JEWELL GARDENS & GLASSWORKS is 1.5 mi. n. on Klondike Hwy. Once the site of a late 19th-century vegetable farm known best for its rhubarb, the gardens feature such spectacular flowers as begonias, delphiniums, lilacs, nasturtiums and poppies. The mountains along the Lynn Canal serve as a backdrop to the site, which also is home to organic herb and vegetable gardens and a greenhouse. At the glassblowing theater, visitors may observe daily demonstrations. Guided tours feature hands-on glassblowing demonstrations.

Time: Allow 3 hours minimum. **Hours:** Daily 9-5, early May-late Sept. **Cost:** $12.50; $6 (ages 0-12). Guided tour $39-$98. **Phone:** (907) 983-2111.

GT TI A

KLONDIKE GOLD RUSH NATIONAL HISTORICAL PARK includes the Skagway Historic District and Chilkoot and White Pass trails, over which each prospector was required to haul nearly a ton of supplies during the gold rush of 1897-98. It was during this stampede that Skagway's population boomed from 5 to more than 10,000.

The park visitor center at Broadway and Second Avenue is in the original White Pass and Yukon Route Railroad Depot, one of Alaska's oldest. Highlights include the 25-minute film "Gold Fever: Race for the Klondike." The Jeff. Smiths Parlor Museum contains exhibits and interpretive programs about the era. The Moore House belonged to Skagway's first homesteading family. The Junior Ranger Activity Center, in the Pantheon Saloon at 4th and Broadway streets, features animal furs, Victorian dress-up clothes, coloring sheets, historic artifacts and other activities for kids to enjoy. Walking tours led by a park ranger explore the Skagway Historic District, where many restored buildings represent a colorful history. The Chilkoot Trail Center provides information about day hikes and backpacking on the Chilkoot Trail.

Hours: Visitor center and museum daily 8:30-5:30. Film is shown on the hour at 9 and 11-5. Moore House daily 10-5. Junior Ranger Activity Center Mon.-Fri. 10-noon and 1-3. Walking tours depart the visitor center Mon.-Fri. on the hour 9-11 and 2-3, Sat.-Sun. at 10 and 2, early May-late Sept. Trail center daily 8-5, June-Labor Day weekend. Phone

▼ *See AAA listing p. 513* ▼

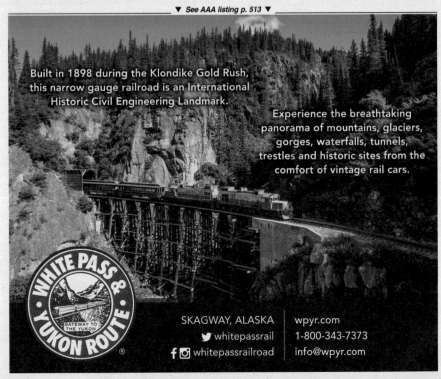

Built in 1898 during the Klondike Gold Rush, this narrow gauge railroad is an International Historic Civil Engineering Landmark.

Experience the breathtaking panorama of mountains, glaciers, gorges, waterfalls, tunnels, trestles and historic sites from the comfort of vintage rail cars.

WHITE PASS & YUKON ROUTE
GATEWAY TO THE YUKON

SKAGWAY, ALASKA | wpyr.com
🐦 whitepassrail | 1-800-343-7373
f 🅾 whitepassrailroad | info@wpyr.com

ahead to confirm schedule. **Cost:** Visitor center (including exhibits), Moore House, Junior Ranger Activity Center, walking tours and trail center free. Jeff. Smiths Parlor Museum $1 per on-line reservation fee. Fees apply, and reservations are recommended for Chilkoot Trail backpacking. **Phone:** (907) 983-9223 for the visitor center, (907) 983-9234 for trail information June-Aug., or (800) 661-0486 for trail information rest of year. GT

WHITE PASS & YUKON ROUTE is at Second Ave. and Spring St. A vintage train chugs across mountain rivers and chasms during fully narrated narrow-gauge rides. The rail line was built in 1898 to carry people and supplies to the Klondike gold rush. Passengers travel round-trip in a period parlor car to the summit of White Pass or Fraser Meadows, past granite gulches, cascading waterfalls and spectacular scenery. A narrator tells the story of the stampede north into the gold fields through some of the most rugged terrain in the United States and Canada.

The 3-hour White Pass Summit Excursion rises from tidewater elevations to 2,888 feet in 20 miles. The 4-hour steam excursion to Fraser Meadows rises from tidewater elevation to 3,000 feet in 27 miles. One-way and round-trip excursions to Lake Bennett and Fraser, British Columbia, as well as to Carcross, Yukon, also are available.

Hours: Ticket office open daily 7:30-4:30, May-Sept. White Pass Summit Excursion departs daily at 8:15 and 12:45 (also Tues.-Wed. at 4:30, late May-late Aug.), early May-late Sept. Fraser Meadows Steam Excursion departs Thurs.-Fri. at noon, Mon. at 8 or noon, mid-July to early Sept. Phone ahead to confirm schedule. **Cost:** White Pass Summit Excursion fare $129; $64.50 (ages 3-12). Fraser Meadows Steam Excursion fare $170; $85 (ages 3-12). Reservations are required. **Phone:** (800) 343-7373. *(See ad p. 512.)* GT

WESTMARK INN SKAGWAY   907/983-6000
APPROVED Contemporary Hotel. **Address:** 3rd Ave & Spring St 99840

WHERE TO EAT

BONANZA BAR & GRILL   907/983-6214
APPROVED American. Casual Dining. **Address:** 3rd Ave & Spring St 99840

GLACIAL SMOOTHIES & ESPRESSO   907/983-3223
APPROVED Vegetarian Sandwiches. Quick Serve. **Address:** 363 3rd Ave 99840

STARFIRE THAI FOOD   907/983-3663
APPROVED Thai. Casual Dining. **Address:** 230 4th St 99840

SWEET TOOTH CAFE   907/983-2405
APPROVED American. Casual Dining. **Address:** 315 Broadway St 99840

SOLDOTNA (D-10) pop. 4,163
• **Restaurants p. 514**

Soldotna's location on the Kenai Peninsula at the junction of Sterling and Kenai Spur highways has ensured its steady growth since homesteading began in 1947. World War II veterans were among the first homesteaders; they were given a 90-day preference right in choosing and filing for land.

The area is rich with opportunities for year-round recreation—hiking, fishing, camping, canoeing and ice fishing are favored activities. Nearby Kenai River yields record catches of salmon and rainbow trout.

Soldotna Chamber of Commerce and Visitor Information Center: 44790 Sterling Hwy., Soldotna, AK 99669. **Phone:** (907) 262-9814.

KENAI NATIONAL WILDLIFE REFUGE, with its headquarters in Soldotna, 1 mi. s.e. of the Kenai River Bridge to 1 Ski Kill Rd., covers about 1,920,000 acres. The refuge was established in 1941 by President Franklin D. Roosevelt to preserve the area's large moose population. Other wildlife include Dall sheep, coyotes, black bears and bald eagles. Fishing and hunting are subject to state and federal regulations. Boat ramps, camping and hiking trails from one-quarter mile to more than 2 miles are available. **Hours:** The refuge is open all year, except when roads are impassable. Headquarters open Mon.-Fri. 9-5. **Phone:** (907) 262-7021 or TTY (907) 260-2803.

Visitor Center, 1 mi. s.e. of the Kenai River Bridge on Ski Hill Rd., exhibits wildlife dioramas and presents films. **Hours:** Mon.-Fri. 8-4:30, Sat. 9-5, June 1-Labor Day; Mon.-Fri. 8-4:30, Sat. 10-5, rest of year. Phone ahead to confirm schedule. **Cost:** Free.

ASPEN HOTEL SOLDOTNA   907/260-7736
APPROVED
Hotel

Address: 326 Binkley Cir 99669 **Location:** Jct Sterling Hwy (SR 1) and Binkley Cir, 0.6 mi w of Kenai Spur Hwy. **Facility:** 63 units, some efficiencies. 2 stories, interior corridors. **Parking:** winter plug-ins. **Pool:** heated indoor. **Activities:** hot tub, fishing, trails, exercise room. **Guest Services:** coin laundry. **Featured Amenity:** continental breakfast.

BEST WESTERN KING SALMON MOTEL   907/262-5857
APPROVED
Best Western.
Motel

AAA Benefit: Members save up to 15% and earn bonus points!

Address: 35540A Kenai Spur Hwy 99669 **Location:** Jct Sterling Hwy (SR 1), 1 mi n. **Facility:** 47 units. 2 stories (no elevator), exterior corridors. **Parking:** winter plug-ins. **Terms:** check-in 4 pm. **Activities:** exercise room. **Guest Services:** coin laundry.

ORCA LODGE ON THE KENAI RIVER   907/262-5649
APPROVED   Cabin. **Address:** 44240 Oehler Rd 99669

WHERE TO EAT

BUCKETS SPORTS GRILL   907/262-7220
APPROVED   American. Casual Dining. **Address:** 43960 Sterling Hwy (SR 1) 99669

EVERYTHING BAGELS   907/252-8135
APPROVED   Sandwiches Coffee/Tea. Quick Serve. **Address:** 35251 Kenai Spur Hwy 99669

FINE THYME CAFE   907/262-6620
APPROVED   Sandwiches Desserts. Casual Dining. **Address:** 43965 Sterling Hwy 99669

FROSO'S FAMILY DINING   907/262-7797
APPROVED   American. Casual Dining. **Address:** 35433 Kenai Spur Hwy 99669

ST. ELIAS BREWING COMPANY   907/260-7837
APPROVED   Pizza Sandwiches. Casual Dining. **Address:** 434 Sharkathmal Ave 99669

SENOR PANCHO'S MEXICAN RESTAURANT   907/260-7777
APPROVED   Mexican. Quick Serve. **Address:** 44096 Sterling Hwy 99669

TALKEETNA (C-11) pop. 876, elev. 355'

Situated at the confluence of the Talkeetna, Susitna and Chulitna rivers, Talkeetna takes its name from the Tanaina Indian word for "river of plenty." The village was an important supply station for gold prospectors from the late 1800s to 1940, but is now a popular staging area for outdoors enthusiasts.

Self-guiding tours: A map of a downtown walking tour is available at Talkeetna Historical Society Museum *(see attraction listing)* and the visitor center next to Village Park on Main Street.

K2 AVIATION is at Talkeetna State Airport off Talkeetna Spur Rd. Flightseeing tours of varying types and lengths include the 1-hour Denali Experience, which offers views of Denali (formerly called Mount McKinley) and Ruth Glacier; the 60-minute Denali Climber & Summit Tour to the mountain's summit; the Denali Flyer Tour, which lasts 75 minutes and offers views of the mountain range's south side; and the 90-minute Denali Grand Tour, which encircles the mountain and offers views of Kahiltna and Ruth glaciers. Glacier landings are available for an additional fee.

Note: A 5.5 percent transportation fee is added to the cost of each trip. **Hours:** Daily 7 a.m.-9 p.m., mid-May to late-Sept.; Mon.-Fri. 8:30-4, rest of year (weather permitting). Closed Jan. 1, Thanksgiving and Christmas. **Cost:** Denali Climber & Summit Tour fare $345; $460 (with glacier landing). Denali Grand Tour fare $335; $425 (with glacier landing). Denali Flyer Tour fare $285; $375 (with glacier landing). Denali Experience fare $220; $310 (with glacier landing). Reservations are recommended. **Phone:** (907) 733-2291 or (800) 764-2291. *(See ad this page.)* GT

MAHAY'S JET BOAT ADVENTURES departs from 22333 Talkeetna Spur Rd. The company offers three excursions: a 2-hour, 20-mile Wilderness Jetboat Adventure; a 3.5-hour, 50-mile three-river tour on the Chulitna, Susitna and Talkeetna rivers; a 4-hour River, Rail & Trail tour that includes a jet boat ride, an excursion aboard the Hurricane Turn Train and a guided walk through Curry; and a 5-hour Devil's Canyon tour. Tours offer a leisurely .25-mile nature walk to a Dena'ina Indian encampment and a view into the lives of turn-of-the-century trappers.

▼ See AAA listing this page ▼

Let the Adventure Begin... Denali Flight Tours | Glacier Landings | Day Hikes

Make it an Awesome Day!

K2 aviation flyk2.com | 907.733.2291 | Located in Talkeetna, AK

Time: Allow 2 hours minimum. **Hours:** Office open daily 7:30 a.m.-9 p.m., mid-May to mid-Sept. Wilderness Jetboat Adventure departs daily at 8:45, noon, 2:30 and 6:30, mid-May to mid-Sept. Three-river tour departs daily at 3:30, mid-May to mid-Sept. Devil's Canyon tour departs daily at 9:30, mid-May to mid-Sept. River, Rail & Trail tour departs Thurs.-Mon. at 1, mid-May to mid-Sept. **Cost:** Wilderness Jetboat Adventure $75; $57 (ages 0-12). Three-river tour $130; $98 (ages 0-12). Devil's Canyon tour $175; $132 (ages 0-12). River, Rail & Trail tour $165; $124 (ages 0-12). **Phone:** (907) 733-2223 or (800) 736-2210. GT

TALKEETNA AIR TAXI, at Talkeetna State Airport off Talkeetna Spur Rd., offers flightseeing tours: a 1-hour South Face McKinley Tour, with views of Ruth Gorge; a 75-minute McKinley Base Camp Tour, which circles over Kahiltna Glacier; a 90-minute Grand Denali Tour, which offers views of active gold mines, Kahiltna base camp and Wickersham Wall; and a 2-hour Summit Flight Tour, which takes in the summits of Denali, Foraker and Hunter, and includes a glacier landing. Other activities such as mountain climbing, glacier landing, support and wilderness touring, and scenic helicopter touring also are offered. **Note:** Full mobility is required for the 2-hour Summit Flight Tour.

Hours: Daily 7 a.m.-8 p.m., May-Sept.; 9-4, Mar.-Apr. and in Oct.; 9-3, rest of year (weather permitting). Phone ahead to confirm schedule. **Cost:** South Face McKinley Tour fare May-Sept. $210; $147 (ages 0-10 and under 100 lbs.); with glacier landing $305; $213.50 (ages 0-10 and under 100 lbs.). McKinley Base Camp Tour fare May-Sept. $275; $192.50 (ages 0-10 and under 100 lbs.); with glacier landing $370; $259 (ages 0-10 and under 100 lbs.). Grand Denali Tour fare May-Sept. $325; $227.50 (ages 0-10 and under 100 lbs.); with glacier landing $420; $294 (ages 0-10 and under 100 lbs.). Summit Flight Tour fare with glacier landing May-Sept. $450 (ages 12+). Phone ahead for helicopter fares and winter rates. Reservations are recommended. **Phone:** (907) 733-2218 or (800) 533-2219. GT

TALKEETNA HISTORICAL SOCIETY MUSEUM, in five buildings at the corner of First Alley and D Street, displays a wealth of local history memorabilia within two historic log cabins, a one-room schoolhouse, a railroad depot and section house. Of interest is a large-scale model of Denali (formerly called Mount McKinley) and the surrounding area. **Time:** Allow 30 minutes minimum. **Hours:** Daily 10-6, May 1-Sept. 20; Sat.-Sun. 11-4, rest of year. Phone ahead to confirm schedule. **Cost:** $5; $4 (ages 65+ and military with ID); free (ages 0-10); $15 (family). **Phone:** (907) 733-2487.

TALKEETNA ALASKAN LODGE   907/733-9500
▼⧸ THREE DIAMOND Hotel. **Address:** 23601 S Talkeetna Spur Rd 99676

WHERE TO EAT

FORAKER DINING ROOM   907/733-9500
▼⧸ THREE DIAMOND Continental. Casual Dining. **Address:** 23601 S Talkeetna Spur Rd 99676

TALKEETNA ROADHOUSE   907/733-1351
▼⧸ APPROVED Breakfast Breads/Pastries. Casual Dining. **Address:** 13550 E Main St 99676

WILDFLOWER CAFE   907/733-2695
▼⧸ APPROVED American. Casual Dining. **Address:** 13578 E Main St 99676

TOK (B-12) pop. 1,258

• Hotels p. 516 • Restaurants p. 516

On the Alaska Highway 93 miles from the Canadian border, Tok is a trade center for nearby Athabascan villages. Some claim that Tok's name derives from the native word meaning "peace crossing"; others say Tok was the name of a survey crew's dog.

A center for dog breeding, training and mushing, Tok claims the title "Dog Capital of Alaska."

Tok Chamber of Commerce: P.O. Box 389, Tok, AK 99780. **Phone:** (907) 883-5775.

TETLIN NATIONAL WILDLIFE REFUGE is in e. central Alaska, directly s. of the Alaska Hwy. and n. of Wrangell-St. Elias National Park and Preserve; the visitor center is at Milepost 1229 on Alaska Hwy. The gateway to Alaska, the refuge occupies 682,604 acres along a major bird migration corridor. At least 115 of the 186 bird species stay to nest in the vast wetlands. Abundant waterfowl such as ducks, geese, swans and loons can be seen on the many streams and lakes. Black and grizzly bears, moose, wolves and caribou are year-round residents.

A visitor center—built in a log trapper's cabin style with a sod roof—contains an observation deck with telescopes overlooking the vast valley as well as Alaska Native cultural exhibit and demonstrations. Ranger-led interpretive programs are offered in the visitor center and evening programs are presented at Deadman Campground at 7 p.m. Recreational activities include bird-watching, canoeing, fishing, hiking, photography and hunting.

The refuge operates two seasonal, public campgrounds: Deadman Campground, at Milepost 1249.5 on Alaska Hwy., and Lakeview Campground, at Milepost 1256.6 on Alaska Hwy. Both are located on a lake with a boat ramp and are fee-free with only nine spots available. Larger rigs are limited as the road is narrow. Nine pullouts along the highway offer interpretive signs. Historic Seaton Roadhouse has a small pond, wildlife viewing and 4 miles of short-loop hiking trails available. **Hours:** Refuge open daily 24 hours. Visitor center open daily 8-4:30, May 15-Sept. 15. Schedule may vary; phone ahead to confirm. **Cost:** Free. **Phone:** (907) 883-5312 or (907) 883-9404. GT ⌂ ⌧

CLEFT OF THE ROCK BED & BREAKFAST   907/883-4219
◇ **APPROVED** Bed & Breakfast. **Address:** 0.5 Sun Dog Tr 99780

WHERE TO EAT

FAST EDDY'S PIZZA & RESTAURANT   907/883-4411
◇ **APPROVED** American. Casual Dining. **Address:** 1313 Alaska Hwy 99780

TONGASS NATIONAL FOREST (G-10)

Elevations in the forest range from sea level at the Pacific Ocean to 10,290 ft. at Mount Ratz. Refer to AAA maps for additional elevation information.

In southeastern Alaska, Tongass National Forest covers about 17 million acres, making it the largest national forest. In 1907 Teddy Roosevelt created the forest, taking the name from the "Tongass" clan of Tlingit Indians that lived along the southern edge of the forest's present-day boundaries. It boasts more than 5 million acres of preserved wilderness, including Misty Fiords National Monument *(see place listing p. 507)* and Admiralty Island National Monument *(see place listing p. 468)*.

Consisting mostly of islands, the forest also includes a mountainous mainland strip deeply cleft by rock-walled fiords, bays, inlets and channels with glaciers, ice fields and waterfalls. The abundant wildlife includes trumpeter swans, bald eagles and Alaskan brown (grizzly) and black bears. Licenses are required for hunting and fishing.

The largest island within the National Forest and one of the largest islands in the United States is Prince of Wales Island. Long inlets and deep bays mark its 1,000-mile coastline, while U-shaped valleys and low mountains rising up to 3,800 feet distinguish its interior. Thanks to a moist climate, a dense forest of spruce and hemlock blankets the landscape.

One of the most interesting features of the island is its caves, including El Capitan, a large limestone cave system with 11,000 feet of mapped passages. Grizzly bear bones more than 12,000 years old have been found inside. The Forest Service provides free 2-hour tours of El Capitan from mid-May to early September; reservations are required. Access to the cave entrance is via a steep 1,100-foot-long trail and visitors need to bring their own equipment for the tour, including flashlights and sturdy footgear. The underground temperature is a constant 40 degrees Fahrenheit. Phone (907) 828-3304 for information and reservations.

The Forest Service provides cabins at several locations within Tongass National Forest. Many rental cabins are near lakes and streams or high in alpine meadows. Although a few can be reached by boat or trail, most are accessible only by charter plane from Craig, Hoonah, Juneau, Ketchikan, Petersburg, Sitka, Wrangell and Yakutat. Charter planes seating two to five people cost about $325-$550 an hour.

A $25-$45 per-party, per-night fee is charged for cabins. There is a 7-night limit May through September; a 10-night limit the rest of the year. Cabin permits are necessary and can be requested up to 180 days prior to use; full payment is required at the time the reservation is made. Forest information centers with exhibits, films and cabin reservation information are in Juneau *(see place listing p. 498)*, Ketchikan *(see place listing p. 504)* and Petersburg.

For further information write Southeast Alaska Discovery Center, 50 Main St., Ketchikan, AK 99901; phone (907) 228-6220, TTY (907) 228-6237, or (877) 444-6777 for camping and cabin reservations. *See Recreation Areas Chart.*

◆ **MENDENHALL GLACIER**—see Juneau p. 501.

VALDEZ (C-12) pop. 3,976, elev. 15'

Called the "Switzerland of Alaska," Valdez (val-DEEZ) is ringed by snowcapped mountains. As the northernmost ice-free port, the town was established in 1898 as an outfitting point for miners taking the hazardous pack trail over Valdez Glacier to the northern gold fields.

In addition to the gold rush, Valdez's rich history includes the 5-minute, 9.2-magnitude Good Friday earthquake in 1964; construction of the Trans-Alaska Pipeline and Marine Terminal in the 1970s; and the 1989 *Exxon Valdez* oil spill and cleanup.

Access into Valdez is by scheduled air service, ferry or via the scenic Richardson Highway. Near Milepost 16 are Bridal Veil and Horsetail falls and the Historic 1899 Trans-Alaska Military Trail & Wagon Road. Thompson Pass, Milepost 26, offers a spectacular view of the Chugach Mountains, valley rivers and historic Keystone Canyon. At Milepost 28.7 is Worthington Glacier State Recreation Site, which has picnic tables and walking trails.

Nearby glaciers in Prince William Sound include Mears, Shoup and Columbia, the second largest tidewater glacier in North America.

Valdez Convention and Visitors Bureau: 309 Fairbanks Dr., Valdez, AK 99686. **Phone:** (907) 835-2984.

MAXINE & JESSE WHITNEY MUSEUM is on the grounds of Prince William Sound College at 303 Lowe St. The museum's collection of Alaskan native art, artifacts, beadwork, dolls and furs comprises one of the largest of its kind. Its pieces were collected over more than 50 years of travel to Alaskan villages by Jesse Whitney and wife Maxine after the couple moved to Alaska in 1947. The Paul Kulik History of Transportation Collection features to-scale vehicle models made of Eskimo ivory and that interpret the state's aviation history.

Time: Allow 30 minutes minimum. **Hours:** Daily 9-7, Memorial Day-Labor Day; by appointment rest of year. Closed major holidays. **Cost:** Donations. **Phone:** (907) 834-1690.

STAN STEPHENS GLACIER & WILDLIFE CRUISES departs from 112 N. Harbor Dr., 3 blks. e. of jct. Richardson Hwy. and Meals St. The outfit offers 6- and 8.5-hour narrated sightseeing cruises on Prince William Sound to Columbia or Meares glaciers. Along the way, guests might glimpse bald eagles, Dall's porpoises, black bears, sea otters, Steller sea lions, puffins, mountain goats and humpback, minke and orcas. A narrator details area history and information about the Trans-Alaska Pipeline. A light meal is included.

Hours: Columbia Glacier trips depart daily at 11, mid-May to mid-Sept. Meares Glacier trips depart daily at 10, early June-Aug. 31. Meares Glacier trips are not available on some days. Phone ahead to confirm schedule. **Cost:** Fare $132-$165; $66-$82 (ages 3-12). Reservations are recommended. **Phone:** (907) 835-4731 or (866) 867-1297. *(See ad this page.)* GT

BEST WESTERN VALDEZ HARBOR INN   907/835-3434

APPROVED
Hotel

BW Best Western

AAA Benefit: Members save up to 15% and earn bonus points!

Address: 100 N Harbor Dr 99686 **Location:** Waterfront. Just s at Meals Ave. Located at Small Boat Harbor. **Facility:** 88 units. 2 stories (no elevator), interior corridors. **Terms:** check-in 4 pm. **Activities:** exercise room. **Guest Services:** coin laundry, area transportation.

TOTEM HOTEL & SUITES   907/835-4443
THREE DIAMOND   Contemporary Hotel. **Address:** 144 E Egan Dr 99686

WHERE TO EAT

FU KUNG CHINESE & SUSHI RESTAURANT   907/835-5255
APPROVED   Chinese Sushi. Casual Dining. **Address:** 207 Kobuk St (Box 263) 99686

MIKE'S PALACE   907/835-2365
APPROVED   Regional International. Casual Dining. **Address:** 210 N Harbor Dr 99686

ROGUE'S GARDEN   907/835-5880
APPROVED   Natural/Organic Sandwiches. Quick Serve. **Address:** 354 Fairbanks Dr 99686

AAA.com/
TourBook
Comments

Let Your Voice Be Heard

If your visit to a listed property doesn't meet your expectations, tell us about it.

AAA.com/MemberFeedback

▼ See AAA listing this page ▼

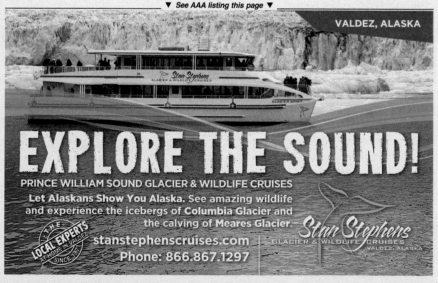

VALDEZ, ALASKA

EXPLORE THE SOUND!

PRINCE WILLIAM SOUND GLACIER & WILDLIFE CRUISES

Let Alaskans Show You Alaska. See amazing wildlife and experience the icebergs of **Columbia Glacier** and the calving of **Meares Glacier.**

Stan Stephens
GLACIER & WILDLIFE CRUISES
VALDEZ, ALASKA

THE LOCAL EXPERTS AT HOME IN VALDEZ SINCE 19

stanstephenscruises.com
Phone: 866.867.1297

WASILLA (C-11) pop. 7,831

Founded in 1917 with the construction of the Alaska Railroad, the community of Wasilla is contiguous to the junction of SRs 1 and 3, both of which are scenic highways, and rests in the Matanuska-Susitna Valley. The area's name originates from that of a respected Native American chief and has varying interpretations; some believe the word is defined as "breath of air" in the Dena'ina Athabascan Indian dialect, while others attribute it to a variation of the Russian word for the name William, "Vasili."

Gold miners from nearby Knik and Willow Creek flocked to Wasilla in the early 1900s due to its proximity to the gold fields and newly constructed railroad. With the advent of Anchorage in 1915 and Wasilla's founding two years later, Knik and other neighboring communities were rapidly abandoned. Mining in Wasilla played an integral role through much of World War II and the mid-20th century; a handful of the area's mines, which once numbered more than 50, remain active to this day.

The Dorothy G. Page Museum, 323 N. Main St., contains historical artifacts and relates the heritage of Wasilla, Knik and Willow Creek. The museum is open Tuesday through Friday, year-round; phone (907) 373-9071. Adjoining the museum is the Old Wasilla Town Site, which preserves Wasilla's first school, two log cabins, a post office, a smithy and the town's first public bath.

In August 2008, former Alaska Gov. Sarah Palin, who served two terms as mayor of Wasilla 1996-2002, was chosen by Arizona Sen. John McCain as his running mate in the November presidential election. Her GOP nomination set several precedents as Palin became the first Alaskan and only the second woman—and the first woman as a Republican—to appear on a major party's presidential ticket.

Greater Wasilla Chamber of Commerce: 415 E. Railroad Ave., Wasilla, AK 99654. **Phone:** (907) 376-1299.

AGATE INN   907/373-2290
◆ APPROVED   Hotel. **Address:** 4725 Begich Cir 99654

BEST WESTERN LAKE LUCILLE INN   907/373-1776

THREE DIAMOND   BW Best Western.   **AAA Benefit:** Members save up to 15% and earn bonus points!
Hotel

Address: 1300 W Lake Lucille Dr 99654 **Location:** Waterfront. SR 3 (George Parks Hwy), just w on Hallea Ln. Located on Lake Lucille. **Facility:** 54 units. 2 stories (no elevator), interior corridors. **Activities:** boat dock, exercise room. **Guest Services:** coin laundry. (See ad p. 478.)

MAT-SU RESORT ON WASILLA LAKE   907/357-5000
◆ APPROVED   Hotel. **Address:** 1850 E Bogard Rd 99654

WHERE TO EAT

EVANGELO'S RESTAURANT   907/376-1212
◆ APPROVED   Italian. Casual Dining. **Address:** 2530 E Parks Hwy 99654

EVERETT'S ON WASILLA LAKE   907/357-5000
THREE DIAMOND   American. Fine Dining. **Address:** 1850 E Bogard Rd 99654

KRAZY MOOSE SUBS   907/357-8774
◆ APPROVED   Sandwiches Soup. Quick Serve. **Address:** 405 E Herning Ave 99654

Hands-Free
IS NOT Risk-Free

Not all voice-activated technologies are equal. Complicated interactions can take your attention away from the road.

Use hands-free systems cautiously and keep your focus on the road when driving.

AAA.com/**Distraction**

WHITTIER (D-11) pop. 220

Nearly surrounded by mountains and perched at the edge of beautiful Prince William Sound, Whittier remained relatively isolated until June 2000 when a 2.5-mile railroad tunnel was converted to accommodate automobile traffic. The unusual Anton Anderson Memorial Tunnel is a single-lane combination highway and railway that enables cars and trains to take turns passing through the tunnel. Because the tunnel has only one lane, the direction of traffic alternates, ceasing altogether while trains travel through.

Phone (877) 611-2586 for the tunnel's traffic schedule. Tunnel information also is broadcast by radio on 530 AM in Whittier and 1610 AM in Portage and Bear Valley. A toll of $13 per car is charged at the tunnel's western entrance; toll increases with size of vehicle.

26 GLACIER CRUISE BY PHILLIPS CRUISES & TOURS, LLC departs from the port of Whittier. High-speed catamarans provide a comfortable, smooth cruise to get an up-close view of massive tidewater glaciers and a variety of wildlife that may include bald eagles, harbor seals, porpoises, sea lions, sea otters or whales. Explore the pristine wilderness of Prince William Sound on the 5-hour 26 Glacier Cruise or 3.75-hour Glacier Quest Cruise. All cruises are narrated by a Chugach National Forest Service Ranger.

Hours: 26 Glacier Cruise departs daily at 12:30, early May-early Oct. Glacier Quest Cruise departs daily at 1, May-Sept. **Cost:** 26 Glacier Cruise (includes onboard hot meal) $159; $99 (ages 2-11). Glacier Quest Cruise (includes onboard hot meal) $109; $69 (ages 2-11). Bus or rail service is offered from Anchorage, Girdwood or Whittier at an additional cost. Reservations are recommended. **Phone:** (907) 276-8023 or (800) 544-0529. *(See ad p. 473, this page.)* GT ⑪

RECREATIONAL ACTIVITIES
Kayaking
- **Alaska Sea Kayakers** depart from the Whittier Boat Harbor. **Hours:** Daily 8-7, May-Sept. **Phone:** (907) 472-2534 or (877) 472-2534. GT

WRANGELL-ST. ELIAS NATIONAL PARK AND PRESERVE (C-12, E-7)

Elevations in the park and preserve range from sea level at the Gulf of Alaska to 18,008 ft. at Mount St. Elias. Refer to AAA maps for additional elevation information.

In southeast Alaska bordering Canada's Yukon, Wrangell-St. Elias National Park and Preserve is the country's largest national park. It is a place of overpowering dimensions, embracing an area larger than Massachusetts, Rhode Island and Connecticut combined; glaciers five times the size of Manhattan; and nine of the 16 highest peaks in North America.

In this 13-million-acre park, the collision of two continental plates has produced some of the world's highest coastal ranges. Forming a barrier along the Gulf of Alaska are the Chugach Mountains, and paralleling them to the north are the Wrangell Mountains.

Between these two ranges are the St. Elias Mountains, extending like the stem of the letter "Y" into Canada's Kluane National Park. Atop these towering peaks are ice fields so immense that they act as a natural cooling system, affecting areas as far south as Chicago and the Central Plains.

As imposing as its ice fields are, it was another commodity traded by the Ahtna Dene or "people of the Copper River" that caught the world's attention. These and other tribes forged tools of locally mined copper. The first person of European descent to verify the source of the copper trading was Lt. Henry Allen, who in 1885 explored much of Alaska's interior.

▼ *See AAA listing this page* ▼

CALM WATERS   WILD SIGHTS   PRINCE WILLIAM SOUND

GLACIERS

26 Glacier Cruise In One Day!

Phillips CRUISES & TOURS
- Smooth cruising on stable catamarans
- See bird rookeries, otters, sea lions, whales
907-276-8023 • 800-544-0529
www.26glaciers.com 100 West Camp Rd. Whittier AK

INDUSTRY EXCLUSIVE NO SEASICKNESS GUARANTEED!

U.S. Forest Service Ranger Narration

🔗 **For complete hotel, dining and attraction listings: AAA.com/travelguides**

Fifteen years later two miners discovered the malachite cliffs above the Kennicott Glacier, which became one of the world's richest sources of copper. The subsequent founding of the Kennicott Mine became one of the most significant events in Alaska's history: The great wealth and development it spawned affected not only Alaska but the entire nation. Currently the ruined mine, a 14-story mill building and a few historic structures are all that remain of this immense enterprise, preserved as the Kennecott Mines National Historic Landmark. St. Elias Alpine Guides offers two-hour guided tours of the mill building daily at 9:30, 1:30 and 3:30 (also at 11:30, early July to mid-Aug.), late May to mid-Sept.; the cost is $28, $14 (ages 0-17). The Kennecott Visitor Center is open daily 9:30-6:30, Memorial Day-Labor Day; phone (907) 554-1105 for ranger-guided program information. Phone (907) 554-4445 for mill building tour information, or inquire in person at the visitor center.

Legacies of the Kennecott Mine and the Yukon gold fields are some of the area's roads, which provide limited access to the park. One of Alaska's oldest roadways is the Richardson Highway, which was completed in 1919 and was the first all-Alaska route to the Yukon gold fields. Both the Richardson and Glenn highways follow the curve of the park's western boundary and offer several spectacular views of 12,011-foot Mount Drum, 14,163-foot Mount Wrangell and 16,237-foot Mount Sanford.

Two other roads penetrate the park's interior—the Chitina-McCarthy and the Nabesna. Both of these gravel roads offer good views of the mountains and are convenient jumping-off places for hiking and river-running. The 60-mile McCarthy Road follows an abandoned railroad bed. Visitors should allow a minimum of 3 hours to drive between Chitina and McCarthy. Before using either of these routes, check with the ranger stations in Slana and Chitina.

The park's headquarters and visitor center, 3 miles north of Copper Center on Richardson Highway at Milepost 106.8, provides trip-planning assistance and information about park activities. Fishing, hiking, rafting and wildlife- viewing, especially of the park's large population of Dall sheep, are just some of the activities pursued in the park; phone (907) 822-7250.

On the southeastern edge of the park and accessible only by sea is Hubbard Glacier on Disenchantment Bay. In 1986 this vast, active tidewater glacier advanced so quickly that for several months it blocked the entrance to Russell Fjord behind a dam of ice, briefly turning it into a lake.

For more information write the Superintendent, Wrangell-St. Elias National Park and Preserve, P.O. Box 439, Copper Center, AK 99573; phone (907) 822-5234. *See Recreation Areas Chart.*

YUKON-CHARLEY RIVERS NATIONAL PRESERVE (A-12, D-7)

Elevations in the preserve range from 600 ft. on the Yukon River where it leaves the preserve near Circle to 6,435 ft. in the Cirque Lakes area on the Charley River drainage. Refer to AAA maps for additional elevation information.

Near the Canadian border in east central Alaska, more than 140 miles of the Yukon River and the entire watershed of the Charley River are encompassed within the 2.5 million acres of the Yukon-Charley Rivers National Preserve. John McPhee remarked in his book "Coming into the Country" that New Jersey could easily fit into this vast emptiness between Eagle and Circle.

Although only 10 year-round residents now live within the preserve's boundaries, it was not always so sparsely populated. During the gold rush, the Yukon—a summer waterway and winter highway—was thronged with people who briefly transformed such communities as Circle and Dawson City, Canada into the "Paris of the North." This rough-and-tumble gold rush region was the grist of Robert Service's poetry and Jack London's stories.

Now quiet has returned, and where riverboats once departed from Eagle, river runners make the 5- to 7-day float down the river to Circle. One of the pleasures of this trip is the opportunity to see Peregrine falcons, a threatened species that makes its home in the bluffs along the river. Hikers can catch a glimpse of caribous and Dall sheep in the preserve's upland regions and moose in the lowlands.

The Taylor and Steese highways are the primary summer access routes to the national preserve, terminating respectively in Eagle and Circle just outside the preserve's boundaries. The scenic portion of the Taylor Highway from Chicken to Eagle runs through mountains, rolling tundra and river valleys. Most people, however, reach the park by boat or float on the Yukon River and its tributaries.

The preserve has no roads and no established trails or maintained public airstrips. Seven public-use cabins are available on a first-come, first-served basis. Food service, basic supplies, lodgings and charter boat and air service are available during the summer months in nearby Eagle and Circle. A list of authorized guides can be obtained from the preserve headquarters and visitor center in Eagle.

In addition, the Bureau of Land Management administers Fort Egbert and a campground in Eagle. The park visitor center is open daily 8-5, mid-May through Labor Day; Mon.-Fri. 8-5, rest of year. The center can be contacted at P.O. Box 167, Eagle, AK 99738; phone (907) 547-2233 (June-Sept.) or (907) 459-3730 (rest of year). For more information write the Superintendent, Yukon-Charley Rivers National Preserve, 4175 Geist Rd., Fairbanks, AK 99709. *See Recreation Areas Chart.*

 *Offices*

Main office listings are shown in **BOLD TYPE** and toll-free member service numbers appear in *ITALIC TYPE*.
All are closed Saturdays, Sundays and holidays unless otherwise indicated.
The addresses, phone numbers and hours for any AAA/CAA office are subject to change.
The type of service provided is designated below the name of the city where the office is located:

✛ Auto travel services, including books and maps, and on-demand TripTik® routings.
● Auto travel services, including selected books and maps, and on-demand TripTik® routings.
■ Books/maps only, no marked maps or on-demand TripTik® routings.
▲ Travel Agency Services, cruise, tour, air, car and rail reservations; domestic and international hotel reservations; passport photo services; international and domestic travel guides and maps; travel money products; and International Driving Permits. In addition, assistance with travel related insurance products including trip cancellation, travel accident, lost luggage, trip delay and assistance products.
✪ Insurance services provided. If only this icon appears, only insurance services are provided at that office.
◖ Car Care Plus Facility provides car care services.
▥ Electric vehicle charging station on premises.

AAA NATIONAL OFFICE: 1000 AAA DRIVE, HEATHROW, FLORIDA 32746-5063, (407) 444-7000

ALASKA

ANCHORAGE—AAA MOUNTAINWEST, 317 W 104TH AVE STE 400, 99515. WEEKDAYS (M-F) 8:00-5:00. (907) 344-4310, *(888) 460-4222.* ● ▲ ✪

ALBERTA

CALGARY—ALBERTA MOTOR ASSOCIATION, #600 85 SHAWVILLE BLVD SE, T2Y 3W5. WEEKDAYS (M-F) 9:00-6:00, SAT 9:00-5:00. (403) 254-6776, *(800) 642-3810.* ● ▲ ✪

CALGARY—ALBERTA MOTOR ASSOCIATION, 220 CROWFOOT CRES NW, T3G 3N5. WEEKDAYS (M-F) 9:00-6:00, SAT 9:00-5:00. (403) 239-9200, *(800) 642-3810.* ● ▲ ✪

CALGARY—ALBERTA MOTOR ASSOCIATION, 3650 20 AVE NE, T1Y 6E8. WEEKDAYS (M-F) 9:00-6:00, SAT 9:00-5:00. (403) 590-0009, *(800) 642-3810.* ● ▲ ✪

CALGARY—ALBERTA MOTOR ASSOCIATION, 4700 17TH AVE SW, T3E 0E3. WEEKDAYS (M-F) 9:00-6:00, SAT 9:00-5:00. (403) 240-5300, *(800) 642-3810.* ● ▲ ✪

CALGARY—ALBERTA MOTOR ASSOCIATION, 524-10816 MACLEOD TRL SE, T2J 5N8. WEEKDAYS (M-F) 9:00-6:00, SAT 9:00-5:00. (403) 278-4840, *(800) 642-3810.* ● ▲ ✪

CAMROSE—ALBERTA MOTOR ASSOCIATION, 6702 48 AVE, T4V 4S3. WEEKDAYS (M-F) 9:00-5:30, SAT 9:00-2:00. (780) 689-5092, *(800) 642-3810.* ● ▲ ✪

EDMONTON—**ALBERTA MOTOR ASSOCIATION,** 10310 GA MACDONALD AVE NW, T6J 6R7. WEEKDAYS (M-F) 9:00-6:00, SAT 9:00-5:00. (780) 430-5468 ● ▲ ✪

EDMONTON—ALBERTA MOTOR ASSOCIATION, 11220 109 ST NW, T5G 2T6. WEEKDAYS (M-F) 9:00-6:00, SAT 9:00-5:00. (780) 474-8700, *(800) 642-3810.* ● ▲ ✪

EDMONTON—ALBERTA MOTOR ASSOCIATION, 5040 MANNING DR NW, T5A 5B4. WEEKDAYS (M-F) 9:00-6:00, SAT 9:00-5:00. (780) 473-3123, *(800) 642-3810.* ● ▲ ✪

EDMONTON—ALBERTA MOTOR ASSOCIATION, 9938 170 ST, T5T 6G7. WEEKDAYS (M-F) 9:00-6:00, SAT 9:00-5:00. (780) 484-1221, *(800) 642-3810.* ● ▲ ✪

FORT MCMURRAY—ALBERTA MOTOR ASSOCIATION, 4 HOSPITAL ST, T9H 5E4. WEEKDAYS (M-F) 9:00-5:30. (780) 743-2433, *(800) 642-3810.* ● ▲ ✪

GRANDE PRAIRIE—ALBERTA MOTOR ASSOCIATION, 11401 99 ST, T8V 2H6. WEEKDAYS (M-F) 9:00-5:30, SAT 9:00-2:00. (780) 538-1152, *(800) 642-3810.* ● ▲ ✪

LETHBRIDGE—ALBERTA MOTOR ASSOCIATION, 120 SCENIC DR S, T1J 4R4. WEEKDAYS (M-F) 9:00-5:30, SAT 9:00-2:00. (403) 328-7921, *(800) 642-3810.* ● ▲ ✪

MEDICINE HAT—ALBERTA MOTOR ASSOCIATION, 2710 13 AVE SE, T1A 3P8. WEEKDAYS (M-F) 9:00-5:30, SAT 9:00-2:00. (403) 527-1166, *(800) 642-3810.* ● ▲ ✪

RED DEER—ALBERTA MOTOR ASSOCIATION, 141 2004 50TH AVE, T4R 3A2. WEEKDAYS (M-F) 9:00-5:30, SAT 9:00-5:00. (403) 342-6633, *(800) 642-3810.* ● ▲ ✪

SHERWOOD PARK—ALBERTA MOTOR ASSOCIATION, #19 101 BREMNER DR, T8H 0M5. WEEKDAYS (M-F) 9:00-6:00, SAT 9:00-5:00. (780) 467-8074, *(800) 642-3810.* ● ▲ ✪

ST. ALBERT—ALBERTA MOTOR ASSOCIATION, 200 665 ST ALBERT TRL, T8N 3L3. WEEKDAYS (M-F) 9:00-6:00, SAT 9:00-5:00. (780) 418-8944, *(800) 642-3810.* ● ▲ ✪

BRITISH COLUMBIA

ABBOTSFORD—CAA BRITISH COLUMBIA, 120-32650 FRASER WAY, V2T 4W2. WEEKDAYS (M-F) 9:00-5:30, SAT 9:00-5:00. (604) 870-3850, *(888) 268-2222.* ✛ ✪

BURNABY—CAA BRITISH COLUMBIA, 4480 LOUGHEED HWY, V5C 3Z3. WEEKDAYS (M-F) 9:00-6:00, SAT 9:00-5:00. (604) 268-4060, *(888) 268-2222.* ✛ ✪ ▥

BURNABY—CAA BRITISH COLUMBIA, 4567 CANADA WAY, V5G 4T1. WEEKDAYS (M-F) 9:00-5:30, SAT 9:00-5:00. (604) 268-5500, *(888) 268-2222.* ✛ ✪ ▥

CHILLIWACK—CAA BRITISH COLUMBIA, #1-45609 LUCKAKUCK WAY, V2R 1A3. WEEKDAYS (M-F) 9:00-6:00, SAT 9:00-5:00. (604) 824-2720, *(888) 268-2222.* ✛ ✪

COQUITLAM—CAA BRITISH COLUMBIA, 50-2773 BARNET HWY, V3B 1C2. WEEKDAYS (M-F) 9:00-6:00, SAT 9:00-5:00. (604) 268-5750, *(888) 268-2222.* ✛ ✪

COURTENAY—CAA BRITISH COLUMBIA, UNIT 17-1599 CLIFFE AVE, V9N 2K6. WEEKDAYS (M-F) 8:30-5:30, SAT 9:00-5:00. (250) 703-2328, *(888) 268-2222.* ✛ ✪

DELTA—CAA BRITISH COLUMBIA, 7343 120TH ST, V4C 6P5. WEEKDAYS (M-F) 9:00-6:00, SAT 9:00-5:00. (604) 268-5900, *(888) 268-2222.* ✛ ✪

KAMLOOPS—CAA BRITISH COLUMBIA, 400-500 NOTRE DAME DR, V2C 6T6. WEEKDAYS (M-F) 9:00-6:00, SAT 9:00-5:00. (250) 852-4600, *(888) 268-2222.* ✛ ✪

KELOWNA—CAA BRITISH COLUMBIA, #18-1470 HARVEY AVE, V1Y 9K8. WEEKDAYS (M-F) 9:00-6:00, SAT 9:00-5:00. (250) 870-4900, *(888) 268-2222.* ✛ ✪

KELOWNA—CAA BRITISH COLUMBIA, 1545 KEEHN RD, V1X 5T3. WEEKDAYS (M-F) 7:30-6:00, SAT 8:30-5:00. (250) 979-4950, *(888) 268-2222.* ◖

LANGLEY—CAA BRITISH COLUMBIA, #10 -20190 LANGLEY BYPASS, V3A 9J9. WEEKDAYS (M-F) 9:00-6:00, SAT 9:00-5:00. (604) 268-5950, *(888) 268-2222.* ✛ ✪

MAPLE RIDGE—CAA BRITISH COLUMBIA, #500 20395 LOUGHEED HWY, V2X 2P9. WEEKDAYS (M-F) 9:00-6:00, SAT 9:00-5:00. (604) 205-1200, *(888) 268-2222.* ✚ ✿

NANAIMO—CAA BRITISH COLUMBIA, #400 6581 AULDS RD, V9T 6J6. WEEKDAYS (M-F) 9:00-6:00, SAT 9:00-5:00. (250) 390-7700, *(888) 268-2222.* ✚ ✿

NANAIMO—CAA BRITISH COLUMBIA, #600-6581 AULDS RD, V9T 6J6. WEEKDAYS (M-F) 7:30-6:00, SAT 8:30-5:00. (250) 390-7380, *(888) 268-2222.* ◖

NELSON—CAA BRITISH COLUMBIA, 596 BAKER ST, V1L 4H9. WEEKDAYS (M-F) 9:00-5:00, SAT 9:00-5:00. (250) 505-1720, *(888) 268-2222.* ✚ ✿

NEW WESTMINSTER—CAA BRITISH COLUMBIA, 501 SIXTH ST, V3L 3B9. WEEKDAYS (M-F) 9:00-6:00, SAT 9:00-5:00. (604) 268-5700, *(888) 268-2222.* ✚ ✿

NORTH VANCOUVER—CAA BRITISH COLUMBIA, 1527 LONSDALE AVE, V7M 2J2. WEEKDAYS (M-F) 9:00-6:00, SAT 9:00-5:00. (604) 205-1050, *(888) 268-2222.* ✚ ✿

PENTICTON—CAA BRITISH COLUMBIA, #162-2111 MAIN ST, V2A 1A3. WEEKDAYS (M-F) 7:30-6:00, SAT 8:30-5:00. (250) 487-2430 ◖

PENTICTON—CAA BRITISH COLUMBIA, 100-2100 MAIN ST, V2A 5H7. WEEKDAYS (M-F) 9:00-6:00, SAT 9:00-5:00. (250) 487-2450, *(888) 268-2222.* ✚ ✿

PRINCE GEORGE—CAA BRITISH COLUMBIA, 100 - 2324 FERRY AVE, V2N 0B1. WEEKDAYS (M-F) 9:00-6:00, SAT 9:00-5:00. (250) 649-2399, *(888) 268-2222.* ✚ ✿

RICHMOND—CAA BRITISH COLUMBIA, #618-5300 NO 3 RD, V6X 2X9. WEEKDAYS (M-F) 9:00-6:00, SAT 9:00-5:00. (604) 268-5850, *(888) 268-2222.* ✚ ✿

SURREY—CAA BRITISH COLUMBIA, #D1-15251 101 AVE, V3R 9V8. WEEKDAYS (M-F) 9:00-6:00, SAT 9:00-5:00. (604) 205-1000, *(888) 268-2222.* ✚ ✿

SURREY—CAA BRITISH COLUMBIA, 16140 24TH AVENUE, V3Z 0R5. WEEKDAYS (M-F) 7:30-6:00, SAT 9:00-5:00. (604) 205-1150, *(888) 268-2222.* ✚ ✿ ◖ ▭

VANCOUVER—CAA BRITISH COLUMBIA, 2301 CAMBIE ST, V5Z 2T9. WEEKDAYS (M-F) 9:00-6:00, SAT 9:00-5:00. (604) 268-5600, *(888) 268-2222.* ✚ ✿

VANCOUVER—CAA BRITISH COLUMBIA, 2347 W 41ST AVE, V6M 2A3. WEEKDAYS (M-F) 9:00-6:00, SAT 9:00-5:00. (604) 268-5800, *(888) 268-2222.* ✚ ✿

VANCOUVER—CAA BRITISH COLUMBIA, 289 DAVIE ST, V6B 0H8. WEEKDAYS (M-F) 9:00-6:00, SAT 9:00-5:00. (604) 801-7130, *(888) 268-2222.* ✚ ✿

VANCOUVER—CAA BRITISH COLUMBIA, 428 SW MARINE DR, V5X 0C4. WEEKDAYS (M-F) 9:00-6:00, SAT 9:00-5:00. (604) 268-4000 ✚ ✿ ▭

VERNON—CAA BRITISH COLUMBIA, #103-5710 24TH ST, V1T 9T3. WEEKDAYS (M-F) 9:00-6:00, SAT 9:00-5:00. (250) 550-2400, *(888) 268-2222.* ✚ ✿

VERNON—CAA BRITISH COLUMBIA, 5460 ANDERSON WAY, V1T 9W2. WEEKDAYS (M-F) 7:30-6:00, SAT 8:30-5:00. (250) 558-2340, *(888) 268-2222.* ◖

VICTORIA—CAA BRITISH COLUMBIA, #170-777 ROYAL OAK DR, V8X 4V1. WEEKDAYS (M-F) 8:30-6:00, SAT 9:00-5:00. (250) 704-1750, *(888) 268-2222.* ✚ ✿

VICTORIA—CAA BRITISH COLUMBIA, 712 BAY STREET, V8T 1R2. WEEKDAYS (M-F) 8:00-6:00, SAT 9:00-5:00. (250) 360-3670, *(888) 268-2222.* ◖

VICTORIA—CAA BRITISH COLUMBIA, UNIT 115 1644 HILLSIDE AV, V8T 2C5. WEEKDAYS (M-F) 9:30-5:30, SAT 9:30-5:30, SUN 11:00-5:30. (250) 414-8320, *(800) 663-1956.* ✚ ✿

WEST VANCOUVER—CAA BRITISH COLUMBIA, 710 MAIN ST PARK ROYAL S, V7T 0A5. WEEKDAYS (M-F) 9:00-6:00, SAT 9:00-5:00, SUN 11:00-5:00. (604) 268-5650, *(888) 268-2222.* ✚ ✿

WESTBANK—CAA BRITISH COLUMBIA, 301 3550 CARRINGTON RD, V4T 2Z1. WEEKDAYS (M-F) 9:00-6:00, SAT 9:00-5:00. (250) 707-4800, *(888) 268-2222.* ✚ ✿

MANITOBA

ALTONA—CAA MANITOBA, 61 2ND AVE NE, R0G 0B0. WEEKDAYS (M-F) 9:00-5:00, SAT 10:00-1:00. (204) 324-8474 ✚ ▲ ✿

BRANDON—CAA MANITOBA, 305 - 18TH ST N, R7A 6Z2. WEEKDAYS (M-F) 9:00-5:00, THU 9:00-8:00, SAT 9:00-4:00. (204) 571-4111, *(800) 222-4357.* ✚ ▲ ✿

WINNIPEG—CAA MANITOBA, 1555 REGENT AVE W, R2C 4J2. WEEKDAYS (M-F) 9:00-6:00, THU 9:00-8:00, SAT 9:00-4:00. (204) 262-6000, *(800) 222-4357.* ✚ ▲ ✿

WINNIPEG—CAA MANITOBA, 501 ST ANNES RD, R2M 3E5. WEEKDAYS (M-F) 9:00-6:00, THU 9:00-8:00, SAT 9:00-4:00. (204) 262-6000, *(800) 222-4357.* ✚ ▲ ✿

WINNIPEG—CAA MANITOBA, 870 EMPRESS ST, R3G 3H3. WEEKDAYS (M-F) 9:00-6:00, THU 9:00-8:00, SAT 9:00-4:00. (204) 262-6000, *(800) 222-4357.* ✚ ▲ ✿

SASKATCHEWAN

ESTEVAN—CAA SASKATCHEWAN, 1208 4TH ST, S4A 0W9. WEEKDAYS (M-F) 9:00-5:30. (306) 637-2185, *(800) 564-6222.* ✚ ▲ ✿

MOOSE JAW—CAA SASKATCHEWAN, 80 CARIBOU ST W, S6H 2J6. WEEKDAYS (M-F) 9:00-5:30, SAT 9:00-5:30. (306) 693-5195, *(800) 564-6222.* ✚ ▲ ✿

NORTH BATTLEFORD—CAA SASKATCHEWAN, 2002-100TH ST, S9A 0X5. WEEKDAYS (M-F) 9:00-5:30, SAT 9:00-5:30. (306) 445-9451, *(800) 564-6222.* ✚ ▲ ✿

PRINCE ALBERT—CAA SASKATCHEWAN, #29 2995 2ND AVE W, S6V 5V5. WEEKDAYS (M-F) 9:00-5:30, SAT 9:00-5:30. (306) 764-6818, *(800) 564-6222.* ✚ ▲ ✿

REGINA—CAA SASKATCHEWAN, 200 ALBERT ST, S4R 2N4. WEEKDAYS (M-F) 9:00-5:30, SAT 9:00-5:30. (306) 791-4337, *(800) 564-6222.* ✚ ▲ ✿

REGINA—CAA SASKATCHEWAN, 200 ALBERT ST N, S4R 5E2. WEEKDAYS (M-F) 8:30-5:00. (306) 779-6635, *(800) 564-6222.*

REGINA—CAA SASKATCHEWAN, 2510 E QUANCE ST, S4V 2X5. WEEKDAYS (M-F) 9:00-5:30, SAT 9:00-5:30. (306) 791-4323, *(800) 564-6222.* ✚ ▲ ✿

REGINA—CAA SASKATCHEWAN, 4528 ALBERT ST, S4S 6B4. WEEKDAYS (M-F) 9:00-5:30, SAT 9:00-5:30. (306) 791-4322, *(800) 564-6222.* ✚ ▲ ✿

REGINA—CAA SASKATCHEWAN, 980 DEWDNEY AVE, S4N 0G8. WEEKDAYS (M-F) 7:30-5:00. (306) 791-9500 ◖

SASKATOON—CAA SASKATCHEWAN, 150 - 1ST AVE S, S7K 1K2. WEEKDAYS (M-F) 9:00-5:30, SAT 9:00-5:30. (306) 668-3737, *(800) 564-6222.* ✚ ▲ ✿

SASKATOON—CAA SASKATCHEWAN, 3110 8TH ST E #1, S7H 0W2. WEEKDAYS (M-F) 9:00-5:30, SAT 9:00-5:30. (306) 668-3770, *(800) 564-6222.* ✚ ▲ ✿

SWIFT CURRENT—CAA SASKATCHEWAN, 15 DUFFERIN ST W, S9H 5A1. WEEKDAYS (M-F) 9:00-5:30, SAT 9:00-5:30. (306) 773-3193, *(800) 564-6222.* ✚ ▲ ✿

WEYBURN—CAA SASKATCHEWAN, 110 SOURIS AVE, S4H 2Z8. WEEKDAYS (M-F) 9:00-5:30, SAT 9:00-5:30. (306) 842-6651, *(800) 564-6222.* ✚ ▲ ✿

YORKTON—CAA SASKATCHEWAN, 159 BROADWAY ST E, S3N 3K6. WEEKDAYS (M-F) 9:00-5:30, SAT 9:00-5:30. (306) 783-6536, *(800) 564-6222.* ✚ ▲ ✿

Border Information

U.S. Residents Traveling to Canada

Border crossing requirements: Travelers are required to present proper travel documents in order to enter Canada and return to the U.S.

Air travel: A U.S. passport is required.

Land or sea travel: Proof of citizenship and proof of identity are required. Approved documents include a passport or passport card, Enhanced Driver's License or NEXUS trusted traveler program card. Visit the U.S. Department of State website travel.state.gov for the most current information on these requirements. Canadian citizens should refer to the Canada Border Services Agency website www.cbsa-asfc.gc.ca.

U.S. resident aliens: An Alien Registration Receipt Card (Green Card) as well as a passport from the country of citizenship is required.

Children: All children must provide their own travel documents. In lieu of a U.S. passport or passport card, children under 16 traveling to Canada by land or sea may present an original or copy of their birth certificate, a Report of Birth Abroad obtained from a U.S. Consulate or a Naturalization Certificate. Minors must be accompanied by both parents; if one parent is absent, a notarized

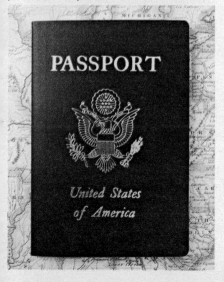

letter of consent from the absent parent giving permission to go on the trip is required.

Legal Issues: Persons with felony convictions, DUI convictions or other offenses may be denied entry into Canada.

Firearms: Canada has strict laws regarding the importing, exporting, possession, use, storage, display and transportation of firearms. These are federal laws that apply across the country. Firearms are divided into classes: non-restricted (most ordinary rifles and shotguns); restricted (mainly handguns) and prohibited (full and converted automatics and certain handguns, among others).

To bring a non-restricted or restricted firearm into Canada you must:
- Be 18 years of age or older
- Declare firearm(s) in writing at the first point of entry
- Obtain an Authorization to Transport (ATT) from a provincial or territorial Chief Firearms Officer prior to arrival at the point of entry; contact the Canadian Firearms Centre at (800) 731-4000 for additional details.

Hunters may bring in, duty-free, 200 rounds of ammunition; a valid license or declaration to purchase ammunition is required. Those planning to hunt in multiple provinces or territories must obtain a hunting license from each one.

Firearms are forbidden in many of Canada's national and provincial parks, game reserves and adjacent areas. For additional information regarding the temporary importation and use of firearms consult the Canada Border Services Agency website.

Personal items: Clothing, personal items, sports and recreational equipment, automobiles, snowmobiles, cameras, personal computers and food products appropriate for the purpose and duration of the visit may be brought into Canada duty and tax-free. Customs may require a refundable security deposit at the time of entry.

Tobacco products: Those meeting age requirements (18 years in Alberta, Manitoba, Northwest Territories, Nunavut, Saskatchewan, Quebec and Yukon; 19 years in other provinces) may bring in up to 50 cigars, 200 cigarettes, 200 grams of tobacco and 200 tobacco sticks.

Alcohol: Those meeting age requirements (18 years in Alberta, Manitoba and Quebec; 19 years in other provinces and territories) may bring in limited alcoholic beverages: 40 fluid ounces (1.14 litres) of liquor, 53 fluid ounces (1.5 litres) of wine (about two 750-ml bottles) or 287 fluid ounces (8.5 litres) of beer or ale (the equivalent of 24 12-ounce bottles or cans).

- Amounts exceeding the allowable quantities are subject to federal duty and taxes, and provincial/territorial liquor fees.
- Provincial fees are paid at customs at the time of entry in all provinces and Yukon.
- It is illegal to bring more than the allowable alcohol quantity into the Northwest Territories or Nunavut.

Purchases: Articles purchased at Canadian duty-free shops are subject to U.S. Customs exemptions and restrictions; those purchased at U.S. duty-free shops before entering Canada are subject to duty if brought back into the United States.

Prescription drugs: Persons requiring medication while visiting Canada are permitted to bring it for their own use. Medication should be in the original packaging with a label listing the drug and its intended use. Bring a copy of the prescription and the prescribing doctor's phone number.

Gifts: Items not exceeding $60 (CAN) in value (excluding tobacco, alcoholic beverages and advertising matter) taken into or mailed to Canada are allowed free entry. Gifts valued at more than $60 are subject to regular duty and taxes on the excess amount.

Pets: You must have a certificate for a dog or cat 3 months and older. It must clearly describe the animal, declare that the animal is currently vaccinated against rabies and include a licensed veterinarian signature.

- Collar tags are not sufficient proof of immunization.
- Be sure the vaccination does not expire while traveling in Canada.
- The certificate is also required to bring the animal back into the U.S.

Exemptions: Service animals; healthy puppies and kittens under 3 months old with a health certificate signed by a licensed

veterinarian indicating that the animal is too young to vaccinate.

Vehicles

- Vehicles entering Canada for leisure travel, including trailers not exceeding 8 feet 6 inches (2.6 m) in width, are generally subject to quick and routine entry procedures.
- To temporarily leave or store a car, trailer or other goods in Canada if you must leave the country, you must pay an import duty and taxes or present a valid permit. Canadian Customs officials issue vehicle permits at the point of entry.
- You are required to carry your vehicle registration document when traveling in Canada.
- If driving a car other than your own, you must have written permission from the owner.
- If driving a rented car, you must provide a copy of the rental contract.
- A valid U.S. driver's license is valid in Canada.
- In all Canadian provinces and territories except Alberta, British Columbia and Saskatchewan, it is illegal to use radar detectors, even if unplugged.
- Seat belt use is required for the driver and all passengers.

Financial Responsibility Laws in Canada: When an accident involves death, injury or property damage, Canadian provinces and territories require evidence of financial responsibility.

U.S. motorists should check with their insurance company regarding whether they are required to obtain and carry a yellow Non-Resident Inter-Province Motor Vehicle Liability Insurance Card (accepted as evidence of financial responsibility throughout Canada). Those not carrying proper proof may be subject to a substantial fine. If renting a vehicle, check with the rental car company.

U.S. Residents Returning to the U.S.

U.S. citizens returning to the U.S. from Canada by air must have a valid passport. Those returning by land or sea are required to present the appropriate travel documents outlined above.

Every individual seeking entry into the United States—foreign visitors, U.S. citizens or lawful permanent residents—must be inspected at the point of entry and each family (persons living in the same household related by blood, marriage, domestic partnership or adoption) must complete a declarations form. Random searches may be conducted by U.S. Customs and Border Protection agents.

U.S. Exemptions for a Stay in Canada of 48 Hours or More

- Each individual may bring back tax- and duty-free articles not exceeding $800 in retail value.
- Any amount over the $800 exemption is subject to duty.
- The exemption is allowed once every 31 days.
- A family may combine purchases to avoid exceeding individual exemption limits.
- Exemptions are based on fair retail value (keep receipts of all purchases as proof).
- Exemptions apply to articles acquired only for personal or household use or as gifts and not intended for sale.
- The exemption may include 100 cigars, 200 cigarettes and 1 litre (33.8 fluid ounces) of liquor per person over age 21. Customs enforces state liquor laws.
- All articles must accompany you on your return.

U.S. Exemptions for a Stay in Canada Less Than 48 Hours

- Each individual may bring back tax- and duty-free articles not exceeding $200 in retail value.
- The exemption may include no more than 10 cigars, 50 cigarettes, 150 millilitres (5 fluid ounces) of alcohol or 150 millilitres of perfume containing alcohol.
- A family may not combine purchases.
- If purchases exceed the $200 exemption, you forfeit the exemption and all purchases become subject to duty.
- All articles must be declared and accompany you upon return.

Gifts

- Gifts up to $100 fair retail value may be sent to friends or relatives in the United States provided no recipient receives more than one gift per day (gifts do not have to be included in the $800 exemption).
- Gifts of tobacco products, alcoholic beverages or perfume containing alcohol valued at more than $5 retail are excluded from this provision.

- Mark the contents, retail value and "Unsolicited Gift" on the outside of the package.

Prohibited: Narcotics and dangerous drugs, drug paraphernalia, obscene articles and publications, seditious or treasonable matter, lottery tickets, hazardous items (fireworks, dangerous toys, toxic or poisonous substances) citrus products and switchblade knives. Also prohibited are any goods originating in embargoed countries.

Canadian Residents Traveling to the U.S.

Canadian citizens entering the U.S. by air must have a valid passport. Canadian citizens entering the U.S. by land or sea are required to present the appropriate travel documents; refer to the Canada Border Services Agency website www.cbsa-asfc.gc.ca or travel.state.gov for the most current information on these requirements.

If traveling to the United States with a minor 15 years or younger, carry documentation proving your custodial rights. A person under age 18 traveling to the United States alone or with only one parent or another adult must carry certified documentation proving that the trip is permitted by both parents.

U.S. Customs permits Canadian residents to bring—duty-free for personal use and not intended for sale—the following: clothing, personal items and equipment appropriate to

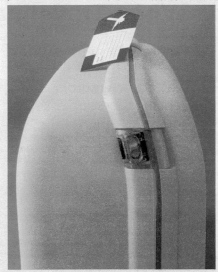

the trip, up to 200 cigarettes, 50 cigars or 2 kilograms of tobacco, and 1 litre of liquor.

Canadian Residents Returning to Canada

There are no exemptions for same-day cross-border shoppers.

Canadian residents may claim a $200 (CAN) exemption on goods, excluding alcoholic beverages and tobacco products, if returning after less than 48 hours and not using any other exemption. This exemption may apply any number of times in a year. No tobacco or alcohol may be brought back if returning from a visit of less than 48 hours.

For each absence of 48 hours or more (but fewer than seven days), residents may bring back, free of duty and taxes, goods valued up to $800 (CAN) any number of times a year, provided the visit to the United States is 48 hours or more and all goods accompany the purchaser (a written declaration may be required).

If returning after 7 days or more (not counting the departure day from Canada) you may claim up to a $800 (CAN) exemption, but goods other than alcohol and tobacco products need not accompany you (a written declaration may be required).

Permitted within the $200 and $800 exemptions: up to 50 cigars, 200 cigarettes, 200 tobacco sticks and 200 grams of tobacco; and up to 1.14 litres (40 fluid ounces) of liquor, 1.5 litres (53 fluid ounces) of wine (about two 750-ml bottles) or 8.5 litres (287 fluid ounces) of beer or ale (the equivalent of 24 12-ounce bottles or cans). You must meet the minimum age requirement of the province or territory entered to claim alcohol or tobacco products.

While AAA makes every effort to provide accurate and complete information, AAA makes no warranty, express or implied, and assumes no legal liability or responsibility for the accuracy or completeness of any information contained herein.

KNOW the Local Driving Laws When Traveling

Wherever you travel, know the local laws that govern motor vehicle operation and registration.

DrivingLaws.AAA.com

Photo Credits

Page numbers are in bold type. Picture credit abbreviations are as follows:
- (i) numeric sequence from top to bottom, left to right ▪ (AAA) AAA Travel library.

- **(Cover)** Canadian Pacific Railway, Canada / © iStockphoto.com / ferrantraite
- **8** (i) Courtesy of Sky 360
- **8** (ii) © AAA / Frank Swanson
- **9** © AAA / Katie McPhee
- **10** (i) Courtesy of Wikimedia Commons / CC0
- **10** (ii) © Resolute / Wikimedia Commons / CC BY SA
- **13** (i) © iStockphoto.com / Jesse_Martineau
- **13** (ii) © iStockphoto.com / MartinM303
- **13** (iii) © iStockphoto.com / jeu
- **13** (iv) © iStockphoto.com / AutumnSkyPhotography
- **13** (v) © iStockphoto.com / IngerEriksen
- **14** (i) © AAA / Katie McPhee
- **14** (ii) © AAA / Katie McPhee
- **14** (iii) © Banff & Lake Louise Tourism / Paul Zizka Photography
- **14** (iv) © AAA / Katie McPhee
- **42** © AAA / Katie McPhee
- **45** © AAA / Katie McPhee
- **46** © AAA / Katie McPhee
- **47** © AAA / Katie McPhee
- **48** © AAA / Katie McPhee
- **49** © AAA / Katie McPhee
- **50** © AAA / Katie McPhee
- **83** © iStockphoto.com / Jacek_Sopotnicki
- **86** © AAA / Katie McPhee
- **87** © AAA / Katie McPhee
- **88** © Bzuk / Wikimedia Commons / CC0
- **89** © AAA / Katie McPhee
- **90** © AAA / Katie McPhee
- **92** © AAA / Katie McPhee
- **94** © AAA / Katie McPhee
- **146** (i) © AAA / Katie McPhee
- **146** (ii) © AAA / Diana Beyer
- **147** © iStockphoto.com / Siegfried Schnepf

- **148** (i) Courtesy of Wikimedia Commons / CC0
- **148** (ii) © Murray Foubister / flickr / CC BY
- **151** (i) © iStockphoto.com / GlowingEarth
- **151** (ii) © iStockphoto.com / wholden
- **151** (iii) © iStockphoto.com / anouchka
- **151** (iv) © iStockphoto.com / GlowingEarth
- **151** (v) © iStockphoto.com / ValaGrenier
- **152** (i) © iStockphoto.com / x1mask2013
- **152** (ii) © iStockphoto.com / powerofforever
- **152** (iii) © iStockphoto.com / powerofforever
- **152** (iv) © iStockphoto.com / gregobagel
- **248** © AAA / Diana Beyer
- **251** © AAA / Diana Beyer
- **252** © AAA / Patricia Miller
- **253** © AAA / Patricia Miller
- **254** © AAA / Diana Beyer
- **255** © AAA / Patricia Miller
- **256** © AAA / Diana Beyer
- **257** © iStockphoto.com / portostock
- **259** © AAA / Diana Beyer
- **261** © AAA / Diana Beyer
- **267** © iStockphoto.com / anouchka
- **298** © AAA / Katie McPhee
- **301** © AAA / Katie McPhee
- **302** © AAA / Inspector 66
- **303** © AAA / Katie McPhee
- **304** © AAA / Katie McPhee
- **306** © iStockphoto.com / SMJoness
- **309** © AAA / Katie McPhee
- **310** © iStockphoto.com / digidreamgrafix
- **332** (i) © iStockphoto.com / OlgaRadzikh
- **332** (ii) © iStockphoto.com / AndreAnita
- **333** © iStockphoto.com / mysticenergy
- **334** (i) Courtesy of Wikimedia Commons / CC0
- **334** (ii) John Todd / Alamy Stock Photo

(cont'd)

- **337** (i) © iStockphoto.com / mysticenergy
- **337** (ii) © iStockphoto.com / castaveron
- **337** (iii) © iStockphoto.com / ImagineGolf
- **337** (iv) © iStockphoto.com / 2686832
- **337** (v) © iStockphoto.com / creighton359
- **338** (i) Stuart Forster / Alamy Stock Photo
- **338** (ii) © iStockphoto.com / creighton359
- **338** (iii) All Canada Photos / Alamy Stock Photo
- **338** (iv) © iStockphoto.com / Paula Jones
- **356** © AAA / Katie McPhee
- **358** © AAA / Katie McPhee
- **359** © AAA / katie McPhee
- **360** © iStockphoto.com / Greenseas
- **361** © AAA / katie McPhee
- **363** © iStockphoto.com / Furtseff
- **364** © iStockphoto.com / revelpix
- **368** © AAA / Katie McPhee
- **370** © AAA / Katie McPhee
- **382** (i) © iStockphoto.com / HeartSurgeon
- **382** (ii) © iStockphoto.com / FrankvandenBergh
- **383** © iStockphoto.com / Onfokus
- **384** (i) © National Gallery of Canada / Wikimedia Commons / CC BY SA
- **384** (ii) © Ansgar Walk / Wikimedia Commons / CC BY SA
- **387** (i) © iStockphoto.com / HeatherECampbell
- **387** (ii) © iStockphoto.com / RyersonClark
- **387** (iii) © iStockphoto.com / vadimgouida
- **387** (iv) © iStockphoto.com / RyersonClark
- **387** (v) © iStockphoto.com / Lisay
- **396** (i) © iStockphoto.com / IanChrisGraham
- **396** (ii) © iStockphoto.com / skyscapes
- **397** © iStockphoto.com / Carnegie42
- **398** (i) © H. C. Barley / Wikimedia Commons / CC0
- **398** (ii) © iStockphoto.com / jzabloski
- **401** (i) © iStockphoto.com / Dougall_Photography
- **401** (ii) © iStockphoto.com / wwing
- **401** (iii) © iStockphoto.com / Gligatron
- **401** (iv) © iStockphoto.com / IanChrisGraham
- **401** (v) © iStockphoto.com / Yails
- **402** (i) © iStockphoto.com / Dougall_Photography
- **402** (ii) Finnbarr Webster / Alamy Stock Photo
- **402** (iii) © AAA / Inspector 76
- **402** (iv) © iStockphoto.com / Yails
- **432** (i) © iStockphoto.com / Orchidpoet
- **432** (ii) © iStockphoto.com / cnicbc
- **433** © iStockphoto.com / edb3_16
- **434** (i) Courtesy of Wikimedia Commons / CC0
- **434** (ii) © Wikibunt / Wikimedia Commons / CC BY SA
- **437** (i) © Adam Jones / flickr / CC BY SA
- **437** (ii) © iStockphoto.com / brytta
- **437** (iii) © iStockphoto.com / Tashka
- **437** (iv) © iStockphoto.com / katyenka
- **437** (v) © iStockphoto.com / benedek
- **438** (i) © iStockphoto.com / Orchidpoet
- **438** (ii) © Mark Newman / age fotostock
- **446** (i) © iStockphoto.com / 1111IESPDJ
- **446** (ii) © iStockphoto.com / CREATISTA
- **447** © iStockphoto.com / John Morrison
- **448** (i) Courtesy of Wikimedia Commons / CC0
- **448** (ii) © Frank Kovalchek / Wikimedia Commons / CC BY
- **451** (i) © iStockphoto.com / studiodr
- **451** (ii) © iStockphoto.com / arnoaltix
- **451** (iii) © iStockphoto.com / bilbot
- **451** (iv) © iStockphoto.com / matabum
- **451** (v) © iStockphoto.com / HarryKolenbrander
- **452** (i) © iStockphoto.com / Cappan
- **452** (ii) © iStockphoto.com / BraunS
- **452** (iii) © iStockphoto.com / chaolik
- **452** (iv) © iStockphoto.com / woolzian
- **523** Garry Gay / Alamy Stock Photo
- **525** © image100 / age fotostock